ENCYCLOPEDIA OF WORLD BIOGRAPHY

SUPPLEMENT

18

ENCYCLOPEDIA OF
WORLD BIOGRAPHY

SUPPLEMENT

 **18**

GALE

DETROIT • LONDON

Staff

Project Editor: Terrie M. Rooney
Senior Editor: Paula K. Byers

Editorial Staff: Suzanne M. Bourgoin, Luann Brennan, Leah Burton, Frank V. Castronova, Karen E. Lemerand, Bruce A. MacDonald, Jennifer Mossman, Maria L. Munoz, Katherine H. Nemeh, and Neil E. Walker

Indexer: Susan Carroll

Permissions Manager: Susan M. Trosky
Permissions Specialist: Maria L. Franklin
Permissions Associates: Edna M. Hedblad and Michele M. Lonoconus
Image Cataloger: Mary K. Grimes

Production Director: Mary Beth Trimper
Production Manager: Evi Seoud
Production Associates: Shanna Heilveil and Carolyn Fischer
Product Design Manager: Cynthia Baldwin
Senior Art Director: Mary Claire Krzewinski

Research Manager: Victoria B. Cariappa
Research Specialist: Barbara McNeil
Administrative Assistant: Phyllis P. Blackman

Graphic Services Supervisor: Barbara Yarrow
Image Database Supervisor: Randy Bassett
Imaging Specialist: Mike Logusz

Manager of Technology Support Services: Theresa A. Rocklin
Programmers/Analysts: Mira Bossowska and Jeffrey Muhr

ISBN 0-7876-2945-6
ISSN 1099-7326

Printed in the United States of America
10 9 8 7 6 5 4 3

CONTENTS

INTRODUCTION

The study of biography has always held an important, if not explicitly stated, place in school curricula. The absence in schools of a class specifically devoted to studying the lives of the giants of human history belies the focus most courses have always had on people. From ancient times to the present, the world has been shaped by the decisions, philosophies, inventions, discoveries, artistic creations, medical breakthroughs, and written works of its myriad personalities. Librarians, teachers, and students alike recognize that our lives are immensely enriched when we learn about those individuals who have made their mark on the world we live in today.

Encyclopedia of World Biography Supplement, Volume 18, provides biographical information on nearly 200 individuals not covered in the 17-volume *Encyclopedia of World Biography* (*EWB*). Like the second edition of *EWB,* the *Supplement* represents a unique, comprehensive source for biographical information on those people who, for their contributions to human culture and society, have reputations that stand the test of time. Consisting of original articles, each ending with a bibliographic section, there is also an index to names and subjects in which the names are a cumulation of all persons appearing in both *EWB,* second edition, and this *Supplement*—nearly 7,200 people!

Articles. Arranged alphabetically following the letter-by-letter convention (spaces and hyphens have been ignored), the articles begin with the full name of the person profiled in large, bold type. Next is a boldfaced, descriptive paragraph that includes birth and death years in parentheses and provides a capsule identification and a statement of the person's significance. The long essay that follows is an average of 800 words and is a substantial treatment of the person's life. Some of the essays proceed chronologically while others confine biographical data to a paragraph or two and move on to a

consideration and evaluation of the subject's work. Where very few biographical facts are known, the article is necessarily devoted to analysis of the subject's contribution.

Following the essay is a Further Reading section. Bibliographic citations contain both books and periodicals as well as Internet addresses for World Wide Web pages, where current information can be found.

Portraits accompany many of the articles and provide either an authentic likeness, contemporaneous with the subject, or a later representation of artistic merit. For artists, occasionally self-portraits have been included. Of the ancient figures, there are depictions from coins, engravings, and sculptures; of the moderns, there are many portrait photographs.

Index. The *EWB Supplement* Index is a useful key to the encyclopedia. Persons, places, battles, treaties, institutions, buildings, inventions, books, works of art, ideas, philosophies, styles, movements—all are indexed for quick reference just as in a general encyclopedia. The Index entry for a person includes a brief identification with birth and death dates *and* is cumulative so that any person for whom an article was written who appears in volumes 1 through 16 as well as volume 18 can be located. The subject terms within the Index, however, apply only to volume 18. Every Index reference includes the title of the article to which the reader is being directed as well as the volume and page numbers.

Because *EWB Supplement,* Volume 18, is an encyclopedia of biography, its Index differs in important ways from the indexes to other encyclopedias. Basically, this is an Index about people, and that fact has several interesting consequences. First, the information to which the Index refers the reader on a particular topic is always about people associated with that topic. Thus the entry "Quantum theory (physics)" lists articles on people associated with quantum theory. Each article may discuss a person's contribution to quantum theory, but no single article or group of articles is intended to provide a comprehensive treatment of quantum theory as such. Second, the Index is rich in classified entries. All persons who are subjects of articles in the encyclopedia, for example, are listed in one or more classifications in the index—abolitionists, astronomers, engineers, philosophers, zoologists, etc.

The Index, together with the biographical articles, make *EWB Supplement* an enduring and valuable source for biographical information. As the world moves forward and school course work changes to reflect advances in technology and further revelations about the universe, the life stories of the people who have risen above the ordinary and earned a place in the annals of human history will continue to fascinate students of all ages.

We Welcome Your Suggestions. Mail your comments and suggestions for enhancing and improving the *Encyclopedia of World Biography Supplement* to:

The Editors
Encyclopedia of World Biography Supplement
Gale Research
27500 Drake Road
Farmington Hills, MI 48331-3535
Phone: (800) 347-4253

ADVISORY BOARD

ACKNOWLEDGMENTS

Photographs and illustrations in the *Encyclopedia of World Biography Supplement,* Volume 18, have been used with the permission of the following sources:

American Automobile Manufacturers Association: Horace Dodge, John Dodge, Ransom Olds

AP/Wide World Photos, Inc.: Rafael Alberti, Alan Ayckbourn, Ella Baker, Tony Blair, David Bowie, Helen Caldicott, Clive Callender, Fernando Henrique Cardoso, Ben Carson, Eric Clapton, Arthur C. Clarke, William Cohen, Sean Connery, Aleister Crowley, Dorothy Dandridge, Nora Ephron, Carlos Flores, Hiram Leong Fong, Anna Freud, Millard Fuller, Roberto C. Goizueta, Thomas Gold, Ekaterina Gordeeva, Pamela Gordon, Cathy Guisewite, Suzan Shown Harjo, Edith Head, John A. Howard, L. Ron Hubbard, Dolores Huerta, Lynn Johnston, Alexander Lebed, Trent Lott, Vilma S. Martinez, Constance Baker Motley, Audie Murphy, Ogden Nash, Antonia Novello, Sir Arthur Pinero, Beatrix Potter, Robert Redford, Betty Schiess, Muriel F. Siebert, Neil Simon, William Joseph Slim, Dean Smith, Barbra Streisand, C. DeLores Tucker, Preston Tucker, Faye Wattleton, J.C. Watts, Annie D. Wauneka, Tiger Woods, Franco Zeffirelli, Paul Zindel

Archive Photos, Inc.: Max Abramowitz, Joy Adamson, Aleksei Ivanovich Adzhubei, Bertie Ahern, Walter Bedell Smith, Ben & Jerry (Ben Cohen and Jerry Greenfield), Milton Berle, Paul Biya, Hassanal Bolkiah, Sonny Bono, Brian Boru, Pierre Cardin, Catherine of Aragon, Jacqueline Cochran, Francis Ford Coppola, Arthur da Costa e Silva, Eve Curie, Erasmus Darwin, Bette Davis, Andrea Doria, Daphne Du Maurier, Edsel Ford, John Galt, James Galway, Andrew Grove, Veronica Guerin, Uta Hagen, David Halberstam, Pamela Harriman, Anthony Hopkins, Alfred Jodl, Elton John, Laurent Kabila,

Wilhelm Keitel, Viktor Klima, C. Everett Koop, Stanley Kubrick, Milan Kucan, Jonathan Larson, Bruce Lee, Vivian Leigh, Sophia Loren, Yuri Luzhkov, Henry Mancini, Duong Van Minh, Jim Morrison, Lord Louis Mountbatten, Paul Newman, Odemegwu Ojukwu, Ytzak Perlman, Rainier III, Christopher Reeve, Cal Ripken Jr., Alice Rivlin, Susan Sarandon, Oskar Schindler, Selena, Dawn Steel, Jimmy Stewart, Josef Tosovsky, Sebastien de Vauban, Wei Jingsheng

Jerry Bauer: Marion Zimmer Bradley, Robertson Davies, Umberto Eco, Dario Fo, Erica Jong, Thomas Keneally, Maxine Hong Kingston

Corbis Images: Howard Baker, Anne Boleyn, Boudicca, Frances Eliza Hodgson Burnett, Shelby Foote, LaDonna Harris, Fred Hoyle, Ursula K. Le Guin, Wangari Maathai, Masayuki Matsunaga, Joseph Murray, Dith Pran, Dave Thomas

EPD Photos: Lady Mary Wortley Montagu

Family Communications, Inc.: Fred Rogers, Helen Zia

The Granger Collection Ltd.: Jacques Piccard

The Kobal Collection: Richard Attenborough, Ruth Prawer Jhabvala, Louis Malle

The Library of Congress: Maria Callas, Henry Stuart Foote, Gregory XII, Percy Lavon Julian, Little Wolf, Peyton Randolph, Frederic Remington, Carl Van Vechten, Maurice Hugh Frederick Wilkins

Doris Langley Moore: Ada Byron Lovelace

The National Portrait Gallery: Abigail Adams

Public Domain: Frances Ellen Watkins Harper

Thomas Victor: Madeleine L'Engle, Michael Ondaatje

ENCYCLOPEDIA OF WORLD BIOGRAPHY, SECOND EDITION, OBITUARIES

The following people, appearing in volumes 1-17 of the *Encyclopedia of World Biography*, have died since the publication of the second edition. Each entry lists the volume where the full biography can be found.

ASHMORE, HARRY SCOTT (born 1916), American journalist and former executive editor of *The Arkansas Gazette* who won a Pulitzer Prize for his editorials against segregation at the start of the Civil Rights Movement, suffered a stroke and died a few weeks later in Santa Barbara, California, January 20, 1998 (Vol. 1).

BANDA, HASTINGS KAMUZU (born 1905), former president of Malawi in southern Africa who ruled for three decades and earned a reputation for both his conservative government and human rights abuses, died of respiratory failure in Johannesburg, South Africa, November 23, 1997 (Vol. 1).

BERLIN, ISAIAH (born 1909), British philosopher and respected intellectual, author of the influential *Two Concepts of Liberty* (1959), and the first president of Wolfson College in Oxford, England, died November 6, 1997 (Vol. 2).

CALDERÓN, ALBERTO P. (born 1920), Hispanic American mathematician known for his work in the field of mathematical analysis who founded what came to be considered the Chicago school of analysis with his mentor, Antoni Zygmund, died at Northwestern Memorial Hospital in Chicago, Illinois, April 16, 1998 (Vol. 3).

CALVIN, MELVIN (born 1911), American chemist and Nobel Prize winner who investigated the "dark," or light independent, stages of photosynthesis, died at Alta Bates Hospital in Berkeley, California, January 8, 1997 (Vol. 3).

CHATICHAI CHOONHAVAN (born 1922), former prime minister of Thailand who was originally elected to Parliament in 1975 and re-elected 8 times before serving in his country's highest office, died of liver cancer in London, England, May 5, 1998 (Vol. 3).

CLEAVER, LEROY ELDRIDGE (born 1935), American writer and former Black Panther leader who exchanged the revolutionary ideals of his youth for a more conservative outlook and a concern for the environment by the time of his death at Pomona Valley Hospital Medical Center in California, May 1, 1998 (Vol. 4).

COMMAGER, HENRY STEELE (born 1902), American historian, essayist, and textbook author (considered to be one of the leading historians in the United States) who opposed in print both McCarthyism and U.S. involvement in Vietnam, died in Amherst, Massachusetts, March 2, 1998 (Vol. 4).

GOLDSMITH, JAMES MICHAEL (born 1933), British-French industrialist and financier known both for his charisma and the controversy that surrounded him and who founded the Referendum Party in Great Britain, died of cancer, July 19, 1997 (Vol. 6).

GOLDWATER, BARRY (born 1909), conservative Republican U.S. senator from Arizona known for his candid manner of speaking and political campaign for U.S. president in 1964, died in Paradise Valley, Arizona, May 29, 1998 (Vol. 6).

JÜNGER, ERNST (born 1895), controversial yet highly regarded German author who was known for his accounts of war, especially his book *Storm of Steel*, died in Wilflingen, Germany, February 17, 1998 (Vol. 8).

KARAMANLIS, CONSTANTINE (born 1907), Greek politician who served his country as a member of parliament, prime minister, and later president and who was instrumental in restoring democracy to Greece after a period of military rule and improving economic conditions in the country, died April 23, 1998 (Vol. 8).

KENDREW, JOHN C. (born 1917), English biochemist, winner of the Nobel Prize for Chemistry, and founder and editor-in-chief of the *Journal of Molecular Biology*, died in Cambridge, England, August 23, 1997 (Vol. 8).

KNOWLES, MALCOLM SHEPHERD (born 1913), American professor of education and author known as the father of adult education, died in Fayetteville, Arkansas, November 27, 1997 (Vol. 9).

LINH, NGUYEN VAN (born 1915), Vietcong military leader responsible for the Tet offensive in 1968 and former secretary-general of the Vietnamese Communist Party who reformed Vietnam's economy in the late 1980s, died in Ho Chi Minh City, Vietnam, April 27, 1998 (Vol. 9).

PAZ, OCTAVIO (born 1914), Mexican poet, critic, editor, translator, essayist, and diplomat who was awarded the Nobel Prize in Literature in 1990, died in Mexico City, April 19, 1998 (Vol. 12).

POL POT (born 1928), leader of the revolutionary Khmer Rouge and communist dictator of Democratic Kampuchéa (Cambodia) who had a reputation as one of the twentieth century's most brutal leaders, died of heart failure, April 15, 1998 (Vol. 12).

REID, WILLIAM RONALD (born 1920), Canadian artist known for sculptures based on his Native American heritage and who worked to preserve the art of the Haida (Native Americans of the northwest Pacific coast), died in Vancouver, British Columbia, March 13, 1998 (Vol. 13).

RUDOLPH, PAUL MARVIN (born 1918), American architect known for his modernist structures, such as Yale University's Art and Architecture Building, died of asbestos cancer in New York, New York, August 8, 1997 (Vol. 13).

SHANKER, ALBERT (born 1928), American education leader and president of the American Federation of Teachers who lead the fight for national education standards, died February 22, 1997 (Vol. 14).

SINATRA, FRANCIS ALBERT (born 1915), award-winning American singer and actor, informally known as "Ol' Blue Eyes," who won an Academy Award for his performance in *From Here to Eternity,* died of a heart attack in Los Angeles, California, May 14, 1998 (Vol. 14).

SPOCK, BENJAMIN McLANE (born 1903), American pediatrician and child care author who published the popular reference book, *Baby and Child Care,* died in his home in San Diego, California, March 15, 1998 (Vol. 14).

TIPPETT, MICHAEL KEMP, SIR (born 1905), English composer and conductor considered to be one of the leading figures in twentieth-century British music, died in London, England, January 8, 1998 (Vol. 15).

ULANOVA, GALINA (born 1910), Russian ballerina, regarded as one of the greatest dancers of the twentieth century, who danced with the internationally acclaimed Bolshoi Ballet for 16 years, died in Moscow, Russia, March 21, 1998 (Vol. 15).

VASARELY, VICTOR (born 1908), Hungarian-French artist and graphic designer known as a leader of the Op Art movement in the 1960s and founder of his own personal art empire that included the Vasarely Museum, the Vasarely Foundation, and the Vasarely Center, died in Paris, France, March 15, 1997 (Vol. 15).

WEAVER, ROBERT C. (born 1907), first African American U.S. cabinet officer (served as secretary of the Department of Housing and Urban Development during the Johnson administration) and former national chair of the National Association for the Advancement of Colored People (NAACP), died in New York, New York, July 17, 1997 (Vol. 16).

YOUNG, COLEMAN ALEXANDER (born 1918), one of the first African Americans to become mayor of a major city—Detroit, Michigan—where he served in the post for 20 years, died of respiratory failure in Detroit, November 29, 1997 (Vol. 16).

ENCYCLOPEDIA OF
WORLD BIOGRAPHY
SUPPLEMENT

18

Max Abramovitz

The neoclassical building designs of Max Abramovitz (born 1908) figure prominently into the architectural history of the mid-twentieth century.

Architect Abramovitz helped to define the shape of the twentieth century skyline during the years following World War II. Abramovitz, together with his partner, Wallace K. Harrison, were remembered for his innovative contributions in the design of many of New York City's finest buildings. The Secretariat tower of the United Nations complex and Avery Fisher Hall at the Lincoln Center for the Performing Arts are among his most impressive accomplishments.

Abramovitz was born in Chicago, Illinois, on May 23, 1908, the son of Benjamin and Sophia (Maimon) Abramovitz. He received a Bachelor of Science degree from the University of Illinois at Champagne-Urbana, in 1929.

The Great Depression

After college, he moved to New York City where he attended Columbia University, and earned a Master of Science degree, in 1931. It was during this time that he first began to work in the architectural office of Harrison, as part of an apprentice team from the university. It was an excellent opportunity for Abramovitz, because Harrison had recently made a name for himself as a key architect in the design of Rockefeller Plaza.

In 1932, Abramovitz took second place in the Prix de Paris design competition. He received a fellowship from Columbia University to study at the world famous École des Beaux Arts in Paris for the next two years.

When Abramovitz returned from France, he rejoined Harrison, who had just opened a new architectural office at Rockefeller Plaza. The field of architecture at the time was in a depression, along with the rest of America, but the members of Harrison's firm used ingenuity to stay busy. They spent some of their time entering competitions, and even came up with a scheme to redesign Central Park in New York. It was around this time that Harrison became partners with the French architect, André Fouilhoux. The three architects—Harrison, Fouilhoux, and Abramovitz—would soon form a partnership, which would significantly influence twentieth century architecture.

First Assignments

In 1936, Abramovitz was assigned to develop the final drawings of the elegant art deco designs of the Rockefeller Apartments at 17 West Fifty-fourth Street, in Manhattan. In November of that same year, the firm of Harrison & Fouilhoux won a contract to design the Theme Center for the upcoming 1939 New York World's Fair. Abramovitz was assigned to the project.

He worked intensively as part of a design team which included Harrison. The architects came up with a futuristic exhibit consisting of a 610-foot vertical spike, called the Trylon, and a 180-foot diameter globe, called the Perisphere. The Perisphere housed the exhibit, where visitors entered by means of "the world's longest escalator," and exited down a 950-foot ramp, called the Helicline. In *Wallace K. Harrison, Architect,* publisher and architectural historian Victoria Newhouse compared the impact of the Trylon and Perisphere structures to the Eiffel Tower in Paris, and declared the exhibit, "One of the most popular architectural symbols of our time."

On September 4, 1937, Abramovitz married Anne Marie Causey. They had two children: Michael and Katherine. The couple divorced in 1964, and Abramovitz married Anita Zeltner Brooks, on February 29, 1964.

Partnership with Harrison and Fouilhoux

Abramovitz became partners with Harrison and Fouilhoux, in 1941. The partnership continued until Fouilhoux's death, in 1945, after which Abramovitz and Harrison remained partners until 1976. Newhouse commented of the alliance between Harrison and Abramovitz, "[It] became a major force in the torrent of architectural activity after the Second World War."

Between 1939 and 1942, the partners, Abramovitz and Harrison, were both employed as associate professors at Yale University. The two men were credited with revitalizing the study of architecture by introducing "new academism," a modernist approach, in place of the classical École des Beaux Arts school of thought, that permeated architectural schools in the United States, at the time.

In 1941, with the outbreak of World War II, Abramovitz enlisted in the U.S. Army. He served as a colonel and designed military installations, in China. He served the government until 1952, at which time, he was made a special assistant to the Assistant Secretary of the Air Force.

Back in New York, the partnership of Abramovitz and Harrison survived the war, and the country moved into a post-war business boom. The Harrison & Abramovitz architectural firm was already renowned for its neoclassical designs and for its ability to manage expansive buildings and large projects.

Post-war Contributions to Architecture

It came as no surprise that the two architects were asked to oversee the project to build the United Nations (UN) headquarters in New York City, from 1947-52. Abramovitz was named deputy director of the UN Headquarters Planning Office. The international design team included Oscar Niemeyer of Brazil, Le Corbusier from Switzerland, plus noted professionals from China, France, Russia, and England. Sir Banister Fletcher critiqued the completed complex, writing in *A History of Architecture on the Comparative Method,* "Sited by the East River . . . dominated by the towering slab block of the Secretariat Building . . . its narrow end walls rising like sheer white cliffs and its longer sides clad in glass curtain walling, [it] has had considerable influence on subsequent high buildings throughout the world."

In 1953, shortly after the completion of the UN complex, the firm was contracted to design the Alcoa Building in Pittsburgh, Pennsylvania. The architects were instructed to do something that had never before been done: to design the huge building entirely of aluminum, except for the structural steel. The 30-story building, made of pre-fabricated, pressed aluminum panels, was the first aluminum skyscraper.

In 1955, Abramovitz contracted to design three chapels at Brandeis University. This was the same year that an Exploratory Committee was assembled to develop Lincoln Square, in New York. In 1958, Abramovitz was officially designated to design the Philharmonic Hall for what would be the new Lincoln Center in New York. Abramovitz's Philharmonic Hall, which was renamed as the Avery Fisher Music Hall in 1973, was perhaps Abramovitz's most recognizable design.

Along with Abramovitz, the Lincoln Center project team involved many of the most respected architects of the twentieth century: Ralph Bunshaft, Ludwig Mies van der Rohe, and Philip Johnson. The public mood altered dramatically between the conception of the center and its completion in 1966, and this affected the final design. Although the Philharmonic Hall was completed in 1962, Abramovitz admitted to Newhouse, in retrospect, "Lincoln Center was to be the biggest and best of its kind in America. . . . [S]uch an undertaking created a feeling of unlimited possibilities. The staff . . . threw in every technical and design innovation they could think of. The sky was the limit. Then realistic estimates came in."

According to Trewin Copplestone, editor of *World Architecture: an Illustrated History,* the Lincoln Center design was praised as, "The monumental side of the growing Neo-academicism . . . transforming and reshaping the innovations of the twentieth century . . . a New-academic idiom of colonnades and arcades, in unexpected shapes and proportions, to mask the complexity of interior services and functions."

The year 1963 saw the opening of another of Abramovitz's unique designs, the Assembly Hall of the University of Illinois at Champaign-Urbana. The building featured one of the largest edge-supported domes in the world (400 feet in diameter, 128 feet above ground).

The End of an Era

In the late 1950's, New York Governor Nelson Rockefeller began planting the seeds for a massive complex of administrative offices for the state to be constructed in Albany. The mall, which was known as the Nelson A. Rockefeller Empire State Plaza, was eventually completed after eighteen years and nearly one billion dollars had been expended. The project did not go forward until the 1970's, when the firm of Harrison & Abramovitz was contracted to design the mall.

It was not clear what happened, but the Albany Mall project somehow signaled the end of the 35-year partnership between Abramovitz and Harrison. Abramovitz spent much of his time working independently, away from New York for the duration of the mall project. Then, in 1976, Harrison, quietly moved his belongings and equipment to a private office, and the grand partnership ended.

Abramovitz reorganized his business interests into the firm of Abramovitz-Harris-Kingsland, of New York City. The firm turned over once more in 1985, and became Abramovitz-Kingsland-Schiff.

Abramovitz was a fellow of the American Institute of Architects, and a member of the American Society of Civil Engineers. He was chairman of the board of the Regional Planning Association, from 1966-68, and assumed a directorship of that association, in 1968. Additionally he was a member of the Architectural League of New York, and a member of the Century Association of New York City. He was governor of the New York Building Congress, from 1957-64, and was a trustee at Mount Sinai Medical Center in New York City.

He was the author of two books and a number of articles. He was honored each year by his alma mater, the University of Illinois Champaign-Urbana campus, with an annual lecture series given in his name.

Further Reading

Contemporary Architects, Third Edition, St. James Press, 1994.
Copplestone, Trewin, editor, *World Architecture: an Illustrated History,* McGraw-Hill, 1963.
Fletcher, Sir Banister, *A History of Architecture on the Comparative Method,* Athlone Press, 1961.
Lampugnani, Vittorio Magnago (general editor) *Encyclopedia of 20th-century Architecture,* Harry N. Abrams, 1986 (English translation).
Newhouse, Victoria, *Wallace K. Harrison, Architect,* Rizzoli, 1989.

Abigail Adams

American First Lady Abigail Adams (1744-1818), an early proponent of humane treatment and equal education for women, is considered a remarkable

woman for her times. Perhaps best known for her prolific letter writing, she is credited with having a notable influence on her husband, John Adams, second President of the United States.

Abigail Smith Adams was born in a parsonage at Weymouth, Massachusetts, on November 11, 1744. Her mother, Elizabeth Quincy Smith, was related to the Bay Colony's Puritan leadership. Her well-educated father, Reverend William Smith, was minister of the North Parish Congregational Church of Weymouth. Despite the fact that many of Adams' relatives were well-to-do merchants and ship captains, Adams was raised in a simple, rural setting. In accordance with the times, she was educated at home. She learned domestic skills, such as sewing, fine needlework, and cooking, along with reading and writing. She took advantage of her father's extensive library to broaden her knowledge. Her lack of a formal education became a life-long regret and, as an adult, she favored equal education for women. She once argued that educated mothers raised intelligent children.

On October 25, 1764, Adams married John Adams, a struggling, Harvard-educated, country lawyer nine years her senior. Although John Adams was not from a prominent social family and his chosen profession lacked high regard, the couple was well matched intellectually and the marriage was a happy one. During their years together, Abigail Adams successfully managed the family farm, raised her

children, travelled with her husband on diplomatic missions to Europe, and carried on a voluminous correspondence with many of the well-known political figures of that time. Her character was forged by the events of her life, including the United Colonies' separation from England, the formation of the United States, her husband's political career and subsequent years of separation from him, the deaths of three of her children, and personal illness.

Early Political Years

During the first few years of their marriage, John Adams lived mostly in Boston, Massachusetts, building his law career and becoming more and more involved with the fomenting political unrest. Abigail Adams, however, remained at the family farm in Braintree (later renamed Quincy), Massachusetts. Her successful management of the farm was a feat uncommon for a woman of that era. The profits from this venture, combined with John Adams' legal practice, helped support the family. When John Adams declined to stand for re-election as selectman in Braintree, he rented a house in Boston and the family was reunited in their new urban home.

This was a time of great political upheaval. The Colonists wished to affirm their loyalty to their Sovereign while at the same time refusing to submit to taxation without representation. Rumors circulated that British troops were en route to Boston. The situation was explosive. Leaders like John Adams believed that armed opposition would isolate Boston from the rest of the Colonies. When John Adams was offered the post of advocate general of the Court of Admiralty, a high tribute to his ability as a lawyer and politician, he refused, claiming the position would be incompatible with his principles.

During the next few unsettling months, Abigail Adams suffered from migraines and chronic insomnia, as well as a difficult pregnancy. The Adams' third child, Susanna, was born towards the end of 1768, but the baby girl only lived for a year. Four months after Susanna's death, Abigail Adams gave birth to their son Charles. Despite her own bouts with illness, Abigail Adams gave birth to four children in just over five years.

The Start of the Revolution

During the next two years, hostilities between the Tories (those settlers who supported the English king) and the Patriots increased. John Adams, who had successfully defended British soldiers in two major trials, keenly felt the negative reaction of the Patriots. Then, in 1771, concerned with Abigail Adams' continuing poor health, John Adams returned his family to their home in Braintree. Sixteen months later, after Abigail Adams gave birth to their third son, Thomas, John Adams returned to Boston, leaving the family behind.

After being chosen as a delegate to the Continental Congress in Philadelphia, John Adams relentlessly travelled the law circuit, earning as much as he could so that he could leave Abigail Adams with a bit of cash reserve until he would be able to return. Riding the circuit, though, gave him time to mull over the problems faced by the Colonies and by

himself. His consolation was to write long letters to Abigail Adams, sometimes several a day, expressing his hopes and fears. Abigail Adams, in turn, wrote to her husband of her own loneliness, doubts, and fears.

During this time, John Adams relied strongly on his wife. She was his political sounding board as well as the caretaker and manager of their home and farm. In one letter, he instructed her to encourage the Braintree militia to exercise as much as possible, but to avoid a war if they could. As the Continental Congress drew to a close, Abigail Adams' letters to her husband encouraged his return home.

The War Begins

When word of the Battle of Lexington reached the Adams family in Braintree, there was a sense of relief because the wait and preparation for war were over. John Adams travelled to Lexington to see and hear for himself the accounts of the battle. Upon returning to Braintree, he gave Abigail Adams an accounting of what he'd learned, then took ill. The Continental Congress was reassembling in Philadelphia, and John Adams was determined to attend. Nursed back to health by his wife, John set-out for Philadelphia two days after the other delegates had left. Correspondence to her friends reveals that Abigail Adams sent her husband off with a cake from her mother, a mare from her father, and a young man, John Bass, to take care of him. She wrote that she tried to be "very sensible and heroic" as he left, but her heart "felt like a heart of lead."

Braintree, while in no danger from the British, nonetheless felt the impact of war. Militiamen stopped at the Adams' home at almost any hour of the day or night, seeking a meal, a drink of water, a cup of cider or rum, a place to spend the night. Refugees from the city found temporary shelter there. Although meat was plentiful, many other goods were in short supply; in one letter, Abigail Adams wrote that she especially needed pins—she would gladly give ten dollars for a thousand!

In the fall of 1775, an epidemic of dysentery hit Braintree and neighboring towns. The illness hit the youngest and oldest most hard; it was not unusual for three and four people in a family to die within days of each other. Abigail Adams and her son, Thomas, took ill, but slowly recovered. Even though she was ill herself, Abigail Adams travelled from Braintree to Weymouth to nurse her mother. Despite Abigail Adams' attentive nursing care, her mother died. During the next six weeks, five more members of her family succumbed to the illness. She wrote to her husband, "I cannot overcome my too selfish sorrow. . . ."

The Battle Reaches Boston

Meanwhile, in cities like Boston and Philadelphia, the move for a declaration of independence grew stronger, stirred by Thomas Paine's pamphlet, *Common Sense*. As the fighting drew closer to Boston in 1776, the militia of Braintree mustered on the North Commons, and marched off to the city, taking rations for three days. Abigail Adams, seated at the top of Penn's Hill, watched the cannon fire between the British and Americans. She later wrote to John Adams, "The sound is one of the grandest in nature, and is of the true species with the sublime! 'Tis now an incessant roar; but oh! the fatal ideas which are connected with the sound! How many of our dear countrymen must fall?!''

Within a week, the militia was once more ordered to be prepared to march at a moment's notice. British ships were in the harbor and it was reported that troops were plundering the city. But it was a British withdrawal—Boston's siege was over. On July 8th, 1776, the Declaration of Independence was published. Unfortunately, the war still raged and the Congress had to write a constitution for the new government. Though John Adams wished to return home, his work was far from over. His wife's letters held him steady; it was the intellectual as well as emotional bond that supported him.

In her letter of March 13, 1776, Abigail Adams suggested to her husband that women be taken into consideration: "[I]n the new code of laws which I suppose it will be necessary for you to make, I desire you would remember the ladies and be more generous and favorable to them than your ancestors. Do not put such unlimited power into the hands of the husbands. Remember, all men would be tyrants if they could. If particular care and attention is not paid to the ladies, we are determined to foment a rebellion, and will not hold ourselves bound by any laws in which we have no voice or representation."'

During their many years of separation, Abigail Adams continued her successful management of the household and family finances. Although women of that time period did not normally conduct affairs of business, and married women were prevented by law from owning land in their own name, it was Abigail Adams who traded stock, hired help, coped with tenants, bought land, oversaw construction, and supervised the planting and harvesting. "I hope in time to have the reputation of being as good a Farmess as my partner has of being a good Statesman," she once wrote. In his autobiography, their grandson, Charles Francis Adams, credited Abigail Adams' sound management skills with saving the family from the financial ruin that affected so many of those who held public office during those first years of the new government.

John Adams Is Sent to France

With the war still being fought, John Adams was asked to replace the Paris commissioner. On a leave of absence from the Continental Congress to visit the family shortly after the request was made, John Adams was asked to handle a difficult legal case in Portsmouth. In his absence, dispatches arrived at the Braintree farm from Congress. Upon reading the dispatches, Abigail Adams was dismayed to learn of her husband's appointment as French minister. She wrote to General Roberdeau, thanking him for his hospitality to her husband, and added, "I have made use of his absence to prepare my mind for what I apprehend must take place lest I should unnecessarily embarrass him." Although John Adams left the decision up to Abigail Adams as to whether he would accept or decline the appointment, she knew what the choice must be. In her letter to her good friend, Mercy Warren, Abigail Adams wrote that she "found his honor and reputation much dearer to me than my own

present pleasure and happiness. . . ." It was decided that their 10-year-old son, John Quincy, would accompany his father to France. John Adams and his son left Braintree in early February, 1778.

This separation from her husband was seemingly harder for Abigail Adams to endure than all the years John Adams had spent in Congress. Letters took weeks to travel across the ocean. John Adams, fearing that his letters would be intercepted by the British and published, wrote very little. Nonetheless, Abigail Adams implored him to write more frequently. "Let me entreat you to write me more letters. . . . They are my food by day and my rest by night. . . . Cheerfulness and tranquility took the place of grief and anxiety [upon receipt of a packet of three letters]." Abigail Adams also wrote of daily life at the farm. With the war continuing, luxury items became scarce in the colonies. Abigail Adams wrote to her husband to send her goods from France, so that she could sell them at a profit in Massachusetts. During this time, she also speculated in currency.

After eighteen long months, John Adams' homecoming was a time of celebration. But soon after his arrival, Congress voted to send him to France again, as minister plenipotentiary, to negotiate a peace treaty between the United States and several European countries, particularly Great Britain. This time, John Adams took along two of his sons, John Quincy, and his younger brother, Charles. In September, 1783, a treaty between England, France, Spain, Holland, and the United States was signed.

Shortly after, John Adams received notice of another appointment. He, along with Benjamin Franklin and John Jay, were to negotiate a treaty of commerce with Great Britain. Abigail Adams joined her husband and sons in Europe at this point, bringing her daughter, Nabby, with her. After a long ocean voyage, Abigail Adams arrived in London, only to learn her husband had to make a political trip to Holland. She and her daughter waited almost a month for John Adams to return. When the couple finally reunited, it had been five years since they had last seen each other. Although pleased to be together, neither John nor Abigail Adams enjoyed their time in England. In April, 1788, five years after Abigail Adams' arrival, the family set sail for home. During those years in Europe, Abigail Adams had served as hostess for both political and social gatherings and as political advisor to her husband.

John Adams Becomes Vice-President

When the Electoral College tallied votes in March of 1789, George Washington was the clear Presidential winner. John Adams, with 34 votes, placed second and became Vice-President. Although Abigail Adams had been upset by her husband's earlier political assignments, when he had to be away from home for years at a time, she fully supported his decision to accept the vice-presidency.

Once more, the Adams family relocated. This time, their destination was a newly-built home in Philadelphia. Once in the city, Abigail Adams was faced with mass confusion. Boxes and furniture were scattered everywhere, the house was damp and cold, and beds had to be set-up before nightfall. Within days of their arrival, though, her son,

Thomas, and the two maids had taken ill. Even while she nursed the invalids, Abigail Adams had to assume the role of hostess and welcome visitors to the Adams' home. With spring's arrival, and her oldest children off in their own directions, Abigail Adams decided to return to Braintree with Thomas, in hopes that fresh country air would hasten his recovery.

With John Adams in Philadelphia, and Abigail Adams in Quincy, the couple once more began their correspondence. Their letters now openly discussed political situations; both were concerned with the antagonistic political atmosphere in Philadelphia. When a Federalist friend of John Adams proposed making Abigail Adams the Autocratix of the United States, Abigail Adams wasted no time in sending her reply. "Tell [him] I do not know what he means by abusing me so. I was always for equality as my husband can witness."

John Adams Becomes President

When John Adams learned that Washington planned to retire in 1797, he promptly sought Abigail Adams' advice. If he ran for the office and didn't win enough electoral votes to become President, he would be obliged to accept the Vice-Presidency under the winner, whom they expected to be Thomas Jefferson. John Adams, although hoping to win the Presidency, most definitely did not want to serve as second-in-command underneath Jefferson; their political positions were too far apart. Abigail Adams' response was filled with reservations, but once again, she knew that turning away from the Presidency would not be in her husband's nature. After winning the election, John Adams asked his wife to join him in the capital city.

Abigail Adams arrived in Philadelphia in early May. The house was shortly put in order, and Abigail Adams quickly held a reception as First Lady. John Adams discussed nearly every important problem with her, and most often followed her advice. Abigail Adams also continued to write many letters to friends, and those who knew the strength of her influence with her husband took pains to enlist her support. She even continued managing the Quincy (formerly Braintree) farm through correspondence with her sister, Mary Cranch, and with Dr. Cotton Tufts.

As was to be expected, John Adams' years as President were filled with political challenges. Abigail Adams fretted about her husband's health, but admitted he had never been in finer spirits. Abigail Adams, on the other hand, was not well. When Congress convened for the summer, the couple set forth for their Quincy farm. By the time the entourage reached Quincy, Abigail Adams was exhausted and ill with fever, diarrhea, and diabetes. When John Adams returned to Philadelphia in November, he had to leave his wife behind.

It wasn't until after the next summer recess that Abigail Adams was able to return with her husband to Philadelphia, where she remained for the term. This time, on her route back to Quincy, Abigail Adams stopped in New York to call on her daughter, Nabby, and her son Charles. Nabby's husband, Colonel Smith, was a wastrel and had spent his family's money. Charles, though glad to see his mother, was

in even worse straits than his sister. Charles was an alcoholic, and his health was rapidly deteriorating.

Although John Adams moved into the new Presidential mansion on the Potomac River, his stay was not to be for long. He lost the next election. Before leaving to join her husband in Washington, D.C., Abigail Adams wrote to her son, Thomas, "My journey is a mountain before me, but I must climb it." Once again she stopped in New York to visit her son and daughter. Charles did not have long to live, and it was with great sadness that Abigail Adams bade him farewell. John Adams received news of his election defeat at the same time he learned of the death of his son, Charles.

Retirement to Quincy

After his political retirement, John Adams slowly adjusted to life on the farm, and once again began corresponding with friends. Abigail Adams, concerned about finances, continued to keep herself busy with the day-to-day details of running her home. Throughout the next year, the family remained plagued with illness. Both Mary Cranch, Abigail Adams' sister, and Mary's husband, died within days of each other. Nabby, John and Abigail's daughter, had been diagnosed with cancer. She brought her two daughters to the farm and underwent surgery. John Adams stumbled over a stake in the ground, tore the skin off his leg, and was forced to sit in his chair for several weeks. Once again, Abigail Adams and her two maids nursed the sick. Despite the surgery, Nabby's cancer returned by the summer of 1814. Knowing she would die soon, Nabby made the agonizing journey back to the Quincy farm and died three weeks after arriving. Abigail Adams nursed her daughter until the end.

In October of 1818, Abigail Adams suffered a stroke. She died quietly on October 28th, 1818, surrounded by her family. Her husband, John Adams lived several more years, passing away quietly on July 4th, 1826. Abigail Adams has the distinction of being the only woman in the United States who was the wife of one president (John Adams) and the mother of another (John Quincy Adams).

Although Abigail Adams may be viewed as an early advocate for women's rights, she never saw herself as such. While her management abilities and financial aptitude kept the family solvent, she saw her main role in life as wife and mother and used her talents to maintain the family. Her marriage was a successful and loving partnership, and she considered herself equal to her husband. She freely advised John Adams on a number of topics, and her advice was respected and often followed. She also suggested that the law be amended to protect women from male tyranny; however, she never took an active role in securing change. As a woman of the eighteenth century, she witnessed a great deal of political turmoil, war, and the birth of a new nation. Abigail Adams' voluminous correspondence with her husband, family, and friends provides a historical record of the times as well as showing her as an intelligent and capable woman.

Further Reading

Adams, Abigail, and John Adams, *The Book of Abigail and John: Selected Letters of the Adams Family, 1762-1784,* edited by L.H. Butterfield, Harvard University Press, 1975.

Adams, Abigail, and John Adams, *Familiar Letters of John Adams and His Wife Abigail Adams, During the Revolution,* Hurd and Houghton, 1876.

Adams, Charles Francis, and John Quincy Adams, *The Life of John Adams,* [1871], reprinted, Haskell House, 1968.

Akers, Charles W., *Abigail Adams: An American Woman,* Little, Brown, 1980.

Butterfield, L.H., editor, *Diary and Autobiography of John Adams,* Belknap Press, 1962.

Ferling, John, *John Adams, A Life,* University of Tennessee Press, 1992.

Gelles, Edith B., *Portia: The World of Abigail Adams,* Indiana University Press, 1992.

Levin, Phyllis Lee, *Abigail Adams: A Biography,* St. Martin's Press, 1987.

Smith, Page, *John Adams,* Volume I: *1735-1784,* Doubleday, 1962.

Joy Adamson

Joy Adamson (1910-1980) is best known for the books and films depicting her work in Africa with "Elsa the Lioness," introduced in her book *Born Free.* Together with husband George Adamson, she raised the orphaned Elsa from a cub and trained the lioness to fend for herself in the wild. Adamson spent almost 40 years living on game reserves in Kenya, and became heavily involved in wildlife preservation activities.

Noted naturalist and wildlife preservationist Joy Adamson was born Friederike Victoria Gessner, in 1910, to a wealthy Austrian family; her birthplace in the Silesian region of Austria is now part of Slovakia. In her autobiography, *The Searching Spirit,* Adamson tells of a childhood game that foretold her future: "Was it a portent that as children our favorite game was a lion hunt and that because of my blond hair and reputation for being a quick runner, I was always assigned the role of the lioness?" Hunting was a favorite sport on her family's estate but, after she shot a deer with the estate's gamekeeper while a teenager, Adamson vowed never to kill for sport again.

Married Three Times

Creative since a young child, Adamson dreamed of becoming a concert pianist, but her hands were too small. So she turned to such varied fields as psychoanalysis, archaeology, and painting. After studying medicine but never taking her final exam, Adamson married Victor von Klarwill in 1935. Her new husband, a Jew, decided that the couple should move to Kenya to escape the rising Nazi movement in Austria, and sent his young wife ahead to Africa. Unfortunately, on the voyage there, she met Peter Bally, a botanist,

and when her husband arrived in Kenya, Adamson announced her intention to divorce him. She married Bally shortly afterward, in 1938.

Bally travelled through Kenya, studying its plant life, and his wife accompanied him. She began to paint their findings, and eventually completed 700 paintings that were published in several books; the paintings themselves are now housed at the National Museum in Nairobi, Kenya. However, within only a few years, there was a second divorce, closely followed in 1943 by a third and final marriage for Adamson. She had met and fell in love with George Adamson, a game warden in an outlying area of Kenya, and the couple, while often living apart in later years, spent the rest of their lives traveling through the Kenyan wilderness. Early in her marriage to Adamson, Joy once again used her talents as an artist, painting the 600 portraits of Kenyan tribal members that were later published in her book *The Peoples of Kenya.*

Began Working with Lions

George Adamson, as a game warden, often encountered lions and other wildlife during his travels. In 1956 he was forced to kill a lioness that attacked him; it was later discovered that she was apparently trying to protect her three cubs. Two of the cubs were sturdy enough to be sent to a zoo, but the Adamsons kept the third cub, a small female that they named Elsa. In her book *Born Free,* Adamson tells the story of how she and her husband raised the cub, and then had to train her to fend for herself and return to the wilderness. After a great deal of work with Elsa, the

Adamsons knew for certain that they had been successful when they left Elsa in the wild for a week and returned to find that she had killed a waterbuck. Elsa's story in *Born Free* ended with the news that the lioness had three cubs of her own.

In Adamson's two sequels to *Born Free*—*Living Free* and *Forever Free*—she tells the further stories of Elsa's cubs: Jespah, Gopa, and Little Elsa. The Kenyan government was not altogether pleased with the Adamsons' project, and asked them to move the lions to an outlying area of the Serengeti Plain. While the search for a new home was going on in early 1961, Elsa became ill and died. There is a marker on her grave in the Meru Game Reserve in Kenya. The Adamsons then had to train her cubs, who were still too young to be released in the wild, how to become hunters. Eventually they too were released, but were never sighted again.

Elsa an Inspiration to Many

Although Elsa was gentle with those she trusted, she nevertheless was a wild creature, and biographical works about Adamson tell of the deep scratches, cuts, and bites that Elsa inflicted on Joy and others. Nevertheless, Adamson long mourned the loss of Elsa, saying in her autobiography, "My relationship with Elsa had not only widened my understanding of animal behavior and psychology but also had introduced me to a world denied to most human beings. With Elsa's death a vital part of myself died also."

All three of the "Elsa" books were extremely well received, and films were made of all of them, 1966's *Born Free* being the most popular. This book also was made into a television series. The stars of the film series, Virginia McKenna and her husband Bill Travers, were so moved by the Adamsons' work that they later founded the Born Free Foundation in England to support wildlife conservation. It is estimated that the "Elsa" series and other Adamson books have been translated into at least 35 languages. According to Adamson biographer, Adrian House, in his *The Great Safari: The Lives of George and Joy Adamson, Born Free* served as inspiration for Iain Douglas Hamilton, a major activist working to protect the African elephant from extinction, to become a zoologist. House also notes that anthropologist Desmond Morris credits *Born Free* with affecting an entire generation's attitude toward animals.

After Elsa's death and the release of her cubs, Adamson adopted a young cheetah, Pippa, who had been the house pet of a British army officer. For several years, Pippa also was trained to survive in the wild. Her story is told in Adamson's *The Spotted Sphinx*. Pippa is buried in the Meru Game Reserve, near Elsa. Adamson also studied and worked with a variety of other animals, including baby elephants, buffaloes, and colobus monkeys. Not all of the Adamsons' work with wildlife was successful. One lion that had been returned to the wilderness was destroyed after it returned to areas inhabited by humans, attacked a child, and killed one of the Adamsons' servants.

Focused Later Life on Wildlife Preservation

As is still the case today, preservation of African wildlife was a serious problem in the 1960s and 1970s. The Kenyan government did not place a particularly high priority on saving wildlife, and even in protected reserves poaching was a common event. Adamson went on an international tour to speak about wildlife preservation in 1962, and became a founder of the World Wildlife Fund and the Elsa Wild Animal Appeal. The royalties from her books about Elsa were used to set up animal reserves and to fund numerous preservation organizations. Adamson also was an early activist in the movement to boycott clothing made from animal fur.

While publicly Adamson remain steadfast in her dedication to wildlife-related causes, her domestic life was not altogether tranquil during her third marriage. At least twice during the marriage one of the partners filed for divorce. During the last 15 years of Adamson's life, she and her husband often traveled through Kenya separately, although they maintained a permanent home near Nairobi.

Mysteriously Murdered in the Wilderness

On January 3, 1980, the world heard the shocking news that Adamson had been killed in the Shaba Game Reserve in northern Kenya, where she had been observing leopard behavior. Even more shocking was the original explanation for Adamson's death, as reported by her chief assistant, Pieter Mawson: that she had been mauled by a lion. George Adamson was at a remote area elsewhere in Kenya at the time of the murder and was unable to return for an entire day. But even from that distance he refused to believe that a lion had killed his wife. It quickly became apparent to the authorities as well that human forces were responsible. Adamson's body had been found on a road near her camp by Mawson, but her injuries were caused by stabs from a swordlike weapon and head injuries, not by a lion's fangs and claws. Her tent also had been opened, and the contents of a trunk had been scattered.

Because Mawson had been so quick to blame a lion for Adamson's death when the injuries were obviously not caused by a lion, he was at first considered a suspect in the case. But the police then arrested Paul Ekai, a young Kenyan who had been fired by Adamson and claimed that she owed him money. After Ekai was interrogated and confessed, he was convicted of murder. Because of his youth, he was sentenced to an undetermined prison sentence instead of death. However, Ekai insisted during his trial that the Kenyan police had tortured him into confessing. Shortly afterward, Mawson was killed in an automobile accident, and so the full truth about Adamson's death will probably never be known.

A quiet funeral ceremony for Adamson was held near Nairobi. Her second husband, Peter Bally, attended, as well as their current friends working in the wildlife preservation movement. However, as George Adamson would be quoted as saying in *The Great Safari*, "None of Joy's oldest and closest friends was there that day for they were either dead or in Europe." Adamson had specified in her will that her body be cremated, and her ashes be buried in Elsa and Pippa's graves. Her husband and several colleagues took her ashes, divided them in half, and placed them in the graves of Adamson's two dear friends in the Meru Game Reserve.

George Adamson carried on his work alone after his wife's murder. On August 20, 1989, the elderly Adamson also was killed in the Kenyan wilderness, along with two co-workers. The murders were blamed on several *shifta*, or bandit-poachers, who were roaming the area. Nevertheless, the work of Joy and George Adamson lives on, through the books that Adamson wrote and the organizations she founded.

Further Reading

Adamson, Joy, *Born Free: A Lioness of Two Worlds*, Pantheon, 1960.
Adamson, Joy, *Forever Free*, Harcourt, 1963.
Adamson, Joy, *Living Free: The Story of Elsa and Her Cubs*, Harcourt, 1961.
Adamson, Joy, *The Peoples of Kenya*, Collins & Harvill, 1967.
Adamson, Joy, *The Searching Spirit*, Harcourt, 1979.
Adamson, Joy, *The Spotted Sphinx*, Harcourt, 1969.
Cass, Caroline, *Joy Adamson: Behind the Mask*, Weidenfeld & Nicolson, 1992.
House, Adrian, *The Great Safari: The Lives of George and Joy Adamson*, Morrow, 1993.
Born Free Foundation Home Page, http://web.ukonline.co.uk/bornfree/bornfree.htm (March 4, 1998).

Gambled in Reno

While still busy with his graduate-level journalism courses, Adzhubei began working for *Komsomolskaya Pravda*, the official newspaper of the Communist youth organization, Komsomol. It was the third national newspaper in the Soviet Union, behind *Pravda* ("Truth," the organ of Communist Party), and *Izvestia* ("Information," the official government newspaper). From 1951 on, Adzhubei wrote for the paper and sat on its editorial board. While serving as its foreign correspondent in 1955, he traveled to the United States as part of a delegation of Soviet journalists, where he visited the gambling mecca of Reno, Nevada, and played blackjack.

Adzhubei also served as *Komsomolskaya Pravda*'s arts and literature editor before being promoted to editor in 1957. His two-year tenure there saw marked changes in the paper. Circulation nearly doubled after he introduced numerous editorial changes, including photographs, feature stories, and first-person tales from average Soviet citizens. He also sent *Komsomolskaya Pravda* reporters onto the street and encouraged them to meet the people about whom they wrote; it was a practice almost unheard of at the time in the socialist press.

The Thaw

Ultimately, it was the political career of Adzhubei's father-in-law, Khrushchev, that his own trajectory would mirror. Adzhubei had married Rada Khrushchev in the early 1950s, and the two had three sons. With the death of

Aleksei Ivanovich Adzhubei

Aleksei I. Adzhubei (1924-1993) was a prominent Soviet journalist during the Cold War era, and was married to the daughter of Nikita Khrushchev. When his father-in-law emerged as leader of the Soviet Union in the mid-1950s, Adzhubei became part of a group of political insiders close to the premier who served as advisors and speechwriters. He also served as editor of the Soviet Union's second leading newspaper, *Izvestia*.

Aleksei Ivanovich Adzhubei was born in 1924 in the historic city of Samarkand, located in Soviet Central Asia (now Uzbekistan). His surname was the Russification of a common Tatar surname, Hadji Bey. Though his father died when he was a child, Adzhubei was fortunate enough to grow up in Moscow, where food, educational opportunities, and cultural offerings were in relative abundance. During World War II, from 1943 to 1945, he served in the Russian Army. After the war's end, he began his studies at Moscow University, and it was in the late 1940s that he began dating Rada Khrushcheva, whose father Nikita was then First Secretary of the Kiev Community Party organization.

longtime Soviet leader Josef Stalin, a notorious communist hardliner and fear-inducing tyrant, a political vacuum was created, and Khrushchev—then secretary of the Central Committee and first secretary of the Moscow Communist Party—surprised many when he emerged as part of a new troika of leaders. Over the next few years, Khrushchev consolidated his power and launched a series of reforms that ushered in a new, far less totalitarian era for the Soviet Union.

Newspapers such as *Izvestia* and *Pravda* gave the first hints of this relaxation. They, for the first time, began to print letters from citizens complaining of consumer inconveniences, and shortages of goods. Next, a February 1956 speech by Khrushchev at the 20th Party Congress inaugurated a period in Soviet Communism referred to as "The Thaw." In it, Khrushchev denounced the massive human-rights violations of Stalin's rule. That summer, millions of political prisoners were freed, and sweeping changes were made in the judicial system.

In 1959, Adzhubei was elected as Supreme Soviet deputy representing the Krasnodar Territory, the same year he took over as editor of *Izvestia*. Again, Adzhubei initiated a series of changes at the paper whose moribund style had become legendary. *Izvestia* introduced first-person stories, photojournalism, and cut the long-winded speeches by government officials that had usually been reprinted in full. Under his leadership, *Izvestia*'s circulation rose significantly.

Khrushchev and Disneyland

The year 1959 also marked the first visit by a Soviet premier to the United States when Khrushchev arrived in September. Back in Moscow, Adzhubei and *Izvestia* chronicled the historic trip in detail. Adzhubei wrote about his father-in-law's attitudes toward the security measures he was subject to, which made him feel almost as if he were under arrest. In another incident of nearly farcical proportions, Khrushchev was unable to visit the Southern California amusement park, Disneyland. "Adzhubei suggested that the real reason Mr. Khrushchev was not allowed to go to Disneyland was that it was a Saturday, a day on which tens of thousands of ordinary people and their children filled the park, people whom the authorities did not want to meet the Soviet Premier," reported the *New York Times* on September 22, 1959. After the visit, Adzhubei wrote a 700-page book about Khrushchev's trip titled *Litsom k litsu s Amerikoi* ("Face to Face with America").

With the election of John F. Kennedy to the White House in 1960, a new period of reapprochement between the United States and Soviet Union developed, and Adzhubei came to play an increasingly important role. Neither Khrushchev nor Kennedy trusted their foreign ministers completely, and often used close advisors and friends to carry private messages across borders. This climate helped land Adzhubei an exclusive interview with Kennedy in November of 1961. It was a first for a Soviet journalist, and heralded a new era for both U.S.-Soviet openness and for Soviet journalism. The two-hour interview took place at the Kennedy family home in Hyannis Port, Massachusetts.

Interview Broke New Ground

When he emerged from the momentous conversation, Adzhubei answered questions for reporters at a press conference. "He is a young President of a great country," the *New York Times* reported Adzhubei as saying. "All of you should be proud of that." The *Izvestia* editor also displayed a similar sense of humor as his father-in-law—who once took off his shoe and banged it on a table at a United Nations session. Giving reporters a short biography of himself, Adzhubei finished by joking, "then according to the American doctrine, I met a pretty daughter of a future Premier and that's how my career got started."

Yet discussion between Adzhubei and Kennedy was anything but lightweight. Adzhubei asked Kennedy about the divided German city of Berlin with its newly-erected Wall. When the full transcript of the interview was published three days later in *Izvestia*, it made the front page of the *New York Times* as well. "President Kennedy told the Soviet people today that they could live in peace and plenty if their government halted its efforts to promote conspiratorial communism throughout the world," wrote the *New York Times'* s Max Frankel in his lead sentence.

Adzhubei also questioned the American leader about the chance of a ban on nuclear testing and of the possibility of West Germany possessing nuclear weapons. More significantly, the *New York Times* noted that Kennedy cast all blame for U.S.-Soviet tensions on the U.S.S.R., and those "words were faithfully reproduced in today's edition of the Soviet government's official newspaper, *Izvestia*." Two months later Adzhubei returned to the United States and lunched at the White House with his wife. The pair also attended a White House press conference at which Kennedy introduced the editor, and joked that Adzhubei "combines two hazardous professions of politics and journalism," according to the *New York Times*.

West German Trip Irked Others

Over the next few years, Khrushchev grew increasingly reliant on Adzhubei to serve in an unofficial diplomatic capacity. He toured Latin America in 1962, and early the next year helped improve relations between the Vatican and the Soviet Union when he became the first Communist dignitary to be officially received by the pontiff. Yet Khrushchev's sweeping changes also earned him numerous secret enemies. Not just his reforms but his very personality incited disapproval—he was an unusual leader for the Soviet Union, possessing an ebullient personality, and was anything but dour and imposing.

In the summer of 1964 Khrushchev sent Adzhubei to the West German capital of Bonn, ostensibly to smooth the way for an official meeting between Khrushchev and the West German chancellor at a later date. Adzhubei, who had no real diplomatic credentials, was considered an unlikely choice for such a mission, given the fact that the two countries had still not resolved some key issues lingering from World War II. Adzhubei, according to William J. Tompson in *Khrushchev: A Political Life,* "was reported to have promised the West Germans that the Berlin Wall would disappear after Khrushchev visited [West Germany]. This triggered a crisis for the East German leadership, which still harboured fears of being sold out by Moscow."

Back in Moscow, Adzhubei denied having made such a statement, but his brother-in-law Sergei Khrushchev later wrote in his book *Khrushchev on Khrushchev: An Inside Account of the Man and His Era* that his father and other Soviet leaders were informed that intelligence sources had Adzhubei's remark on tape; Sergei Khrushchev did concede that the tape may have been fabricated.

Vanished into Obscurity

Three months later Khrushchev was ousted from power by a coalition of Politburo hardliners headed by Leonid Brezhnev and Aleksei Kosygin. According to *Khrushchev: A Political Life,* when Soviet Foreign Minister Andrei Gromyko was queried about the event, he said, "'Why was Khrushchev removed? Because he sent Adzhubei to Bonn, that's why.'" The inside coup was announced by radio shortly after one October midnight in 1964. The *New York Times* reported that day that "unofficial but reliable sources" claimed that Adzhubei had lost his job as editor of *Izvestia.* He was given the editor post at the illustrated monthly, *Sovetsky Soyuz* (Soviet Union), but lost his seat on Central Committee for "mistakes in his work."

By some accounts, Adzhubei was harassed by the KGB after Khrushchev's memoirs were smuggled into the West for publication—an extremely illegal act in the Soviet Union at the time. "They called him in and 'suggested' he leave Moscow for a job with a publisher in the Soviet Far East," wrote Sergei Khrushchev in *Khrushchev on Khrushchev: An Inside Account of the Man and His Era.* "Aleksei . . . was frightened, and he sounded all the alarms. He refused to relocate and declared that he was going to write an official complaint immediately to the secretary general of the United Nations. Surprisingly, his threat worked and he wasn't bothered again."

Khrushchev died in 1971. One week before his death, the former premier visited his daughter and Adzhubei, and told his once-prominent son-in-law, "Never regret that you lived in stormy times and worked with me in the Central Committee. We will yet be remembered!" In his own later years, the once-robust journalist would be plagued by health problems. During the glasnost era, Adzhubei's account of the Khrushchev ouster was published in the Russian journal *Ogonek.* His own memoirs were published in 1991, but have not appeared in English translation. He died in March of 1993 at the age of 68.

Further Reading

Khrushchev, Sergei, *Khrushchev on Khrushchev: An Inside Account of the Man and His Era,* edited and translated by William Taubman, Little, Brown, 1990.

Tompson, William J., *Khrushchev: A Political Life,* St. Martin's Press, 1995.

New York Times, May 9, 1959, p. 2; September 15, 1959; September 22, 1959, p. 21; December 31, 1959; November 26, 1961, pp. 1, 3; November 29, 1961, pp. 1, 18-19; February 1, 1962, p. 1; October 16, 1964, pp. 1, 14; October 30, 1964, p. 13; November 24, 1964; March 21, 1993.

Bertie Ahern

In June 1997, Bertie Ahern (born 1951) was elected as the Prime Minister (Taoiseach) of the Republic of Ireland. He became the youngest person to have ever occupied the post up to that time. Ahern was one of the major engineers of the so-called "Irish Miracle" that, over the span of a decade, helped to shift the focus and balance of trade on the island from an emphasis on mostly agrarian and cottage industries to that of a noted industrial and technological exporter.

Ahern was born Bartholomew Ahern on September 12, 1951, in Dublin, Ireland. His parents, Julia and Cornelius Ahern, raised their son in one of the working-class neighborhoods on the north side of the city. Ahern's father was a farmer who had joined the Irish Republican Army (IRA) in the early 1920s when Ireland was fighting for its independence from England. Ahern's parents were staunch supporters of the republican political party of Ireland (Fianna Fail).

At the age of 17, Ahern joined Fianna Fail. He attended the Rathmines College of Commerce and the University College Dublin, from which he received a degree in accounting. In 1975, he married his wife, Miriam Kelly. They had two daughters. Ahern was elected to the lower house of the Irish Parliament (Dail Eireann) in 1977. He was representing a constituency in the Finglas area of Dublin's north side.

Moving on Up

Throughout much of the early 1980s, Ahern held a number of junior and senior level posts both within his party and in the Irish government. In 1980, he became Fianna Fail's Assistant Whip. Ahern held this position for one year, during which time he was also named party spokesperson on youth affairs. The following year Ahern became Assistant Chief Whip and Leader of the House for Fianna Fail. Along with assuming the role of the leader of the opposition party in the Dail Eireann, Ahern was named as a Minister of State at the departments of the Taoiseach and Defence and the government Chief Whip in 1982.

Ahern assumed the vice-presidency of Fianna Fail in 1983. He continued to hold this position for over ten years. A few years into his rather lengthy tenure as the vice-president of Fianna Fail, Ahern was elected as the Lord Mayor of Dublin. As a result of being named Lord Mayor in 1986, his visibility and name recognition in Ireland started to dramatically increase along with his appointments both within his political party and in the government.

The "Irish Economic Miracle"

After a one-year tenure as Lord Mayor of Dublin, Ahern relinquished his position so that he could devote all of his time and energy to his newest appointment. In 1987, he

received his first appointment to a position in the Taoiseach's cabinet. Ahern was named the Minister for Labour. He was re-nominated to serve as the Minister for Labour in 1989 and held that position for the next two years. During this time, Ahern was also named the director of the 1990 Irish presidential election. Also that same year, he was elected President of the European Union (EU) Council of Ministers for Social Affairs.

In 1991 Ahern was named the Minister of Finance for the first time in his career. It was a post he would continuously be re-nominated to for the next three years. His post as Minister of Finance was to become his most successful and highly influential role in the government of Ireland up to that time. Ahern was responsible for helping to creatively design the economic policies that would foster what is known as the "Irish Economic Miracle."

Throughout the history of modern Ireland, the nation had been known as a rural society that was more than content to focus its energies and resources on agricultural products and cottage industry goods to be traded on the world market. All of this was to change when Ahern took over as Minister of Finance in the early 1990s.

Ireland had been receiving subsidies from the EU throughout much of the 1980s and 1990s. Unlike many of the other European nations which had also received such financial grants-in-aide and incentives, Ireland rather wisely decided to invest its money from the EU into developing and strengthening the infrastructure of the nation, including building new roads, training the work force in the use of new technologies, and delving into telecommunications. This not only helped to greatly improve the state of the nation internally; it also served to show to potential foreign investors that Ireland was willing and able to compete as a rather credible player in the world marketplace. The major technological developments in Ireland also enticed potential investors to establish operations in Ireland because of the nation's newfound commitment to progress and the future as the gateway to Europe's Common Market.

According to *Forbes'* s Dyan Machan, "in 1987, the Irish economy was on the brink of collapse. Scrapping 40 years of semi-socialistic policies, Ahern, as Finance Minister, cut the government work force by 20 percent, axed spending across the board, and maintained a ten percent tax rate for most corporations." These rather drastic changes in the economic policies of Ireland managed to finally entice numerous American corporations to invest there, which was something Irish governments had been struggling to accomplish for many generations. After Ahern's radical re-working of the economic climate in Ireland, the nation managed to get investments from nearly 500 American companies and corporations eager to start trading with the European Common Market. The majority of the new foreign investments came from such booming fields as pharmaceuticals and high technology.

Determined to keep attracting new investors to come to Ireland and to maintain the ones who were already there, Ahern would later promise to slash in half the capital gains tax and to top off the personal income tax. These changes in the Irish economy were further enhanced by a local work force that was highly educated and highly skilled. Commenting on the so-called "Irish Economic Miracle," Ahern said to Machan, "it's a very good time for the Irish economy."

"The Bertie Factor"

In 1994, a scandal erupted in the government of Ireland. The scandal forced the Taoiseach, Albert Reynolds, who was the president of Fianna Fail, to resign. With the resignation of Reynolds as president of Fianna Fail and as the Taoiseach, Ahern, who was vice-president of Fianna Fail, was all set to become the next Taoiseach of the Republic of Ireland. Unfortunately for Ahern, this was not to come to pass. The leader of the Labour Party, Dick Spring, who was a member of the coalition that helped Fianna Fail come to power and form the current government, withdrew his support from the coalition and subsequently from Fianna Fail. Spring then placed the support of his Labour Party behind Fianna Fail's opposition party, Fine Gael. The leader of Fine Gael then assumed the position of the Taoiseach of Ireland. Ahern, however, resigned his position as the vice-president of Fianna Fail and assumed the position as Fianna Fail's new president.

Ahern, as president of Fianna Fail, became the leader of the opposition. He held this post until the summer of 1997 when a new general election in Ireland was called. At that time, Ahern faced quite a daunting task. He had to convince the electorate that they should not return to office a government that had spurred growth in the economy, increased foreign investments, and had presided over low inflation. Ahern focused his campaign on the ever escalating problem with violent crime, the dwindling hope for a peaceful resolution to the problems in the north of Ireland, and the relatively high unemployment rates.

There was another, somewhat subliminal factor at play in Ahern's election campaign in 1997. It was dubbed "The Bertie Factor," as Nina Rossing explained in a web site that dealt with the Irish General Election Campaign in 1997. According to Rossing, "it didn't hurt that the Fianna Fail policy program seemed sensible either; but undoubtedly it was the personal charisma of the relatively young new leader and his honest, upright down-to-earth level of communication with the people that made the difference. He certainly did not fake a popular image, and by introducing parts of the same popular appearance to the other Fianna Fail candidates, Bertie gave people a reason to vote for his party in other constituencies than his own."

On June 6, 1997, Fianna Fail won 77 seats in the Dail Eireann. Even with the seats won by their coalition partner, the Progressive Democrats, Fianna Fail's total number of seats in the Dail Eireann rose by only four seats. It would take the Fianna Fail/Progressive Democrats coalition nearly a month before they were able to sway enough "unaffiliated" members of the Dail Eireann to come over to their side in order for Fianna Fail to declare a victory for the party and the coalition. On June 26, 1997, Ahern, as president of Fianna Fail, the majority party in the new coalition government, was named as next Taoiseach of the Republic of Ireland. When he assumed the position of Taoiseach in 1997, Ahern became the youngest person to have ever held that post in the history of Ireland.

Ahern was determined to keep on supporting the "Irish Economic Miracle" by offering tax breaks to both corporations and private individuals. He also espoused a "zero tolerance" stance on crime, especially of the drug-related variety. Ahern quipped that there can be no acceptable level of crime in the Republic of Ireland. He was also very determined to work with the Prime Minister of England, Tony Blair, and the various representatives of both the unionist and nationalist communities in Northern Ireland to seek a peaceable compromise to try to end the violence in Northern Ireland. In a momentous settlement reached on Good Friday, April 10, 1998, Ahern, Blair and other political leaders of Britain and Ireland agreed to establish a new form of government in Northern Ireland. At the time Ahern commented, "We have seized the initiative from the men of violence. . . . Let's not relinquish it, now or ever."

Yet Ahern remained a man of the people who preferred a pint with his mates in the local pub over a posh dinner affair. He was quoted by Suzanne Barrett in an article on the Irish Mining Company's web site as saying that, "I am very conscious of the support I received in every constituency throughout the country."

Further Reading

Current Leaders of Nations, Gale, 1998.
Forbes, March 9, 1998, p. 86.
Newsweek, April 20, 1998, p. 34.

"Bertie Ahern," http://goireland.guide@miningco.com (March 6, 1998).
"Talks a Chance to Renew Relations," http://www.irish-times.com/irish-times/paper/1997/0906/hom1.html (April 6, 1998).
"Bertie Ahern," http://www.irlgov.ie/taoiseach/biogs/frmain.html (March 23, 1998).
"Irish General Election '97: 'The Bertie Factor,'" http://www.stud.ntnu.no/studorg/jsestin/issues/97-3/civilisation.html (April 6, 1998).

Rafael Alberti

A member of the group of Spanish poets known as the "Generation of 1927," Rafael Alberti (born 1902) was forced to leave his home at the conclusion of the Spanish Civil War. During his nearly 40 years in exile he established a reputation as one of the most prolific and diverse poets of his generation.

Rafael Alberti is regarded today as one of the greatest of modern Spanish poets. A member of the "Generation of 1927," a group of Spanish poets known for revitalizing the art to a quality not seen since the sixteenth century, Alberti gradually turned away from the lyric traditions of his homeland, embracing communism and a more utilitarian style. After the Spanish Civil War, he fled the country and lived in exile, first in Argentina, then in Rome, before finally returning to Spain in 1977, after the death of Franco.

Early Life

Alberti was born December 16, 1902 in the Andalusian town of Puerto de Santa María, which sits on Spain's Atlantic coast, overlooking the Bay of Cádiz. He attended a Jesuit school there until he reached the age of 15, when he was expelled due to a romantic interest which the Jesuit teachers did not approve of. At this point he moved with his family to Madrid, and his Andalusian youth was fixed forever in his memory as an image of Lost Paradise, an image which appears often in his poetry.

In Madrid, he developed an interest in painting. In 1920, a friend convinced him to put on a show of his work. He did, and it was met with anger and mockery from the public. That same year, his father died of tuberculosis. Alberti persisted with his painting for a while longer after this traumatic period, until 1922, when he was struck himself with the early stages of tuberculosis. There is no clear evidence that the events are related, but it was shortly after this that he gave up painting and concentrated solely on his poetry. He would not return to painting until much later in life.

Poetic Career Begins

His very first collection of poetry, *Marinero en tierra,* was a tremendous success. Influenced by the Andalusian folksong of his youth, the work won him the National Prize

for Literature in 1925 and catapulted him to national fame. That such a young and untested poet could produce writing of such natural power was a matter of great amazement to critics. According to Ben Belitt, who would translate much of Alberti's poetry later, "It would appear that, with his very first book, Alberti was already a craftsman in total command of his medium, writing with effortless grace and impeccable versification, in brilliant and controlled imagery: a poet at the peak of his form."

He was immediately accepted into the elite circles of Spanish poetry, the group now known as the "Generation of 1927." This band, including such poets as Vicente Aleixandre, Luis Cernuda, Frederico García Lorca, Jorge Guillén, and Pedro Salinas, was widely regarded as the fullest flowering of Spanish verse since the sixteenth century. Alberti seemed to enjoy the public attention, as well as the company of these fine writers.

In 1927, on the 300th anniversary of the death of the great Spanish poet Góngora, Alberti again amazed readers with his skillful and seamless appropriation of Góngora's tradition. He was no simple mimic, however. He was equally capable of writing with the exquisite formality of Góngora or with sardonic absurdity, or even of combining the two, as in his "Madrigal on A Tram Ticket." His command of Spanish traditional elements was always focused toward creating his own expressions, as were his departures from that tradition. Subsequently, as his views on Spain began to change from love and remembrance of his Andalusian youth into something more deeply bound with the nation's future, his departures from tradition became more

frequent and more severe. This too surprised his readers. Such was the case with his 1929 volume, *Sobre los ángeles.*

Political Involvement

The change that occurs in *Sobre los ángeles* was not an idle one, calculated to achieve some superficial effect. The year 1929 marked the beginning of a radical transformation for Alberti. He found himself faced with a great spiritual crisis. The book reflects this in its sharp, restless language, asking at the very outset, "Where is that Paradise, / shadow, lately your home? / Ask it in stillness." This was not an unusual situation for a poet in this decade—his colleagues Pablo Neruda, Frederico García Lorca, César Vallejo, T.S. Elliot and many other artists of all sorts experienced similar breakdowns at some point in the 1920s, as though the period after the First World War were somehow laced with a premonition of the Second. In Alberti, the crisis is particularly notable, given the marked contrast with the lyric zest of his earlier poetry.

The difficulty of this period was offset somewhat by his marriage to María Teresa León, a novelist, in 1929. However, it was his involvement in politics that increasingly soothed his conscience. Prior to 1931, Alberti had avoided politics altogether. In April of that year, the Spanish Republic was declared, and a wave of grassroots socialism swept through the country. Alberti reflected the change. In 1933 he said of the difference in his poetry, "Since 1931 my life and my work have been placed at the service of the Spanish revolution and the international proletariat." He became a member of the Communist Party in Spain, and with his wife, he began publishing the revolutionary journal, *Octubre,* in 1934. That same year, he began an extended tour of the Americas, a trip that would ultimately stretch over two years. Only when the political situation in Spain reached a climax did he finally return.

Alberti's Exile

In 1936, the Spanish Civil War began, with the Nationalist forces of General Francisco Franco pitted against the Loyalists—those who supported the Republic. Alberti rallied the Loyalist cause in his journal and other writings, and even served in the Air Force, though not as a flier. The war was devastating, with the Nazis and the Soviets weighing in either side. His friend Lorca was executed by Franco's forces in 1936, but Alberti and his wife remained in Spain until the very end. Shortly before the fall of Madrid on March 27, 1939, they were evacuated.

Alberti spent a brief period in France before moving to Argentina. His writing slowed slightly, but he returned to painting, and began to ponder ways in which graphics and poetry might be mixed. Though he regretted his exile, he was reasonably happy during this time, mainly due to the birth of his daughter Aitana in 1941. In 1944, his work began to make inroads on the English speaking world with his publication in *New Directions Poet of the Month.* The following year he was added to Eleanor Turnbull's anthology.

Though he never had quite the international appeal as Lorca, with whom he is often associated, he began to be sufficiently recognized as to allow for the extensive touring he undertook between 1944 and 1959. This period included two trips to China and the Soviet Union, as well as trips to Poland, Czechoslovakia, Rumania, Germany, France, and Italy. Nine volumes of poetry were published during Alberti's stay in Argentina, and for his sixtieth birthday, Losada published his complete works up to that time.

As in his younger days, Alberti moved in the most elite circles. Among his friends were many other expatriates, including Pablo Picasso, César Vallejo, Miguel Angel Asturias, Alejo Carpentier, Boris Pasternak, Louis Aragon, Sergei Eisenstein, Sergei Prokofiev, and André Malraux. One might almost assume that he enjoyed his status as an exile, were it not for the longing which always moved through his poetry, a nostalgia for his long-lost Andalusia. In 1964, he relocated to Rome, where he was taken in warmly by the Italian people, who considered him their very own favorite expatriate. By this time, he was devoted primarily to painting and graphics, though he still wrote occasionally. In 1965, he was awarded the Lenin Prize for Peace, and at the end of his seventh decade, he produced his last great collection, *Les ocho nombres de Picasso,* a pictorial/poetic attempt to capture various facets of the great painter's work.

Back to Spain

On April 27, 1977, after nearly forty years of exile, Alberti was able to return to Spain, following the death of Franco. He was heartily welcomed by the Spanish people, especially by Spanish communists, who even elected him for a short term to the Cortes—the Spanish legislature. His plays were staged in Barcelona and Madrid, and interest in his poetry was revived. He was awarded the Cervantes Prize, a prestigious literature prize, in 1983. His wife passed away in 1989 and he remarried in 1990. A book of poetry *To Painting* was published in 1997.

Alberti's work is frequently said to span the entire development of modern Spanish poetry, and he is considered to have been one of the greatest influences on that course. According to the critic Ricardo Gullón, to read the works of Alberti from 1924 to 1962 is to study the evolution of contemporary poetry in full. Nor did he limit himself to poetry. Among his works are books in prose, an autobiography, and several plays. In short, he has been, over his entire career, one of the most prolific and diverse writers of his generation.

Many believe that he has not received the recognition he deserves. Another writer on Alberti's poetry noted in 1978 that relatively little has been written about him, particularly by comparison to his Andalusian friend and rival, Lorca. His return to Spain has done much to change this, but the pendulum is still swinging, and much is left to be done to increase the international awareness of this 20th century Spanish genius.

Further Reading

Alberti, Rafael, *Concerning the Angels,* City Lights Books, 1995.
Alberti, *The Eight Names of Picasso,* Gas Station Editions, 1992.
Alberti, *The Lost Grove,* University of California Press, 1976.
Alberti, *Marinero en tierra,* Castalia, 1992.
Belitt, Ben, *Rafael Alberti: Selected Poems,* University of California Press, 1966.
Jimenez-Fajardo, Salvador, *Multiple Spaces: The Poetry of Rafael Alberti,* Tamesis Books, 1985.
Manteiga, Robert C., *The Poetry of Rafael Alberti,* Tamesis Books, 1978.
Nantell, Judith, *Rafael Alberti's Poetry of the Thirties,* University of Georgia Press, 1986.
Popkin, Louise B., *The Theatre of Rafael Alberti,* Tamesis Books, 1975.
Wesseling, Pieter, *Revolution and Tradition: The Poetry of Rafael Alberti,* Albatros Hispanofila, 1981.

Dr. Edwin Eugene Aldrin Jr.

Edwin Eugene "Buzz" Aldrin (born 1930) and fellow American astronauts Neil Armstrong and Michael Collins received world-wide recognition for their *Apollo 11* lunar spaceflight in July of 1969. Aldrin, who followed Armstrong from the lunar landing module *Eagle,* became the second person to ever walk on the moon.

Edwin Eugene "Buzz" Aldrin was born on January 20, 1930, in Montclair, New Jersey. Nicknamed "Buzz" by his sister, Aldrin's upbringing contributed greatly to his later career choices. His mother, Marion Moon, was the daughter of an army chaplain. His father, Air Force Colonel Edwin Eugene Aldrin, Sr., was a former student of rocket scientist Robert Goddard, and an aviation pioneer in his own right.

Aldrin graduated from the United States Military Academy at West Point in 1951, ranking third in his graduating class. After graduation, Aldrin was as an officer in the Air Force. A year later, he was sent to Korea as a fighter pilot. He completed 66 fighter missions during the Korean War, and was awarded the Distinguished Flying Cross. He then served as an Air Force instructor in Nevada before being assigned to the Air Force Academy as an aide and later a flight instructor. In 1956, he became a flight commander for a squadron in West Germany (now Germany).

In 1959, Aldrin decided he needed a new career challenge and became interested in the developing U.S. space program. He enrolled in an engineering program at the Massachusetts Institute of Technology (MIT). He graduated in 1963 with a Doctor of Science degree in Orbital Mechanics; his thesis dealt with the piloting and rendezvous of two spacecraft in orbit.

Training as an Astronaut

In the formative years of the Space Program, in order to participate in the National Aeronautics & Space Administration's (NASA) astronaut program, candidates were required to have attended test-pilot school. Aldrin passed the age limit to enter test-pilot school while he was at MIT, but believed this requirement would soon eliminated. He was right. After he completed a series of strenuous mental and physical fitness tests, Aldrin was selected to be in NASA's third group of astronauts in October of 1963. There were 14 pilots chosen for this group—seven Air Force pilots, including Aldrin, four Navy pilots, one Marine pilot, and two civilian pilots. Aldrin was the first astronaut to hold a doctoral degree and the only astronaut who was not a test pilot.

This new group of astronauts, selected for the *Gemini* and *Apollo* space missions, spent eighteen months undergoing intensive basic training in the general duties required of an astronaut. During this time Aldrin and the other trainees also had to participate in strenuous physical training exercises, attend classes, and maintain their flying skills by participating in flight exercises. To prepare for his first space mission as Command Pilot for *Gemini 12,* Aldrin had to complete another 2,000 hours of specialized training. During these months, Aldrin pioneered the use of underwater training to simulate spacewalking.

Aldrin's first space mission was *Gemini 12,* which was with Jim Lovell, Jr. in November of 1966. During this flight, Aldrin established a new record for extra vehicular activity. In other words, his spacewalk proved that astronauts could work outside an orbiting vehicle to make repairs—a necessary ability if lunar flight was to become reality.

Training for the *Apollo 11* Mission

Following completion of the *Gemini* missions, the race was on between the United States and Russia to see who would reach the moon first. Aldrin completed many more hours of training to prepare for his role in different *Apollo* spaceflights. Intensive static and dynamic training classes were key components of the study program. (Static training simulates space flight conditions. Dynamic training prepares astronauts for the physical stresses of spaceflight.) However, his studies also included geology. Field trips to Hawaii, Idaho, Oregon, and Iceland gave him an opportunity to study rock formations similar to those expected to be found on the moon.

During his months in training, Aldrin created ways to improve various operational techniques, such as those used with navigational star displays. It was a combination of his temperament and skill that led to his being named Back-up Command Module pilot for *Apollo 8* (December 21, 1968), the United States' first attempt to orbit a manned lunar spacecraft. Then, in 1969, Neil Armstrong, Michael Collins and Aldrin were chosen as the *Apollo 11* crew. The United States was ready to launch a lunar landing flight.

Personal Experiences of the *Apollo 11* Space Crew

In "Apollo Expeditions to the Moon," edited by Edgar M. Cortright, the three astronauts related their personal reactions to the lunar mission. Aldrin's reflections, made on that momentous morning, give a sense of the tension and drama surrounding the launch. He shared, "While Mike and Neil were going through the complicated business of being strapped in and connected to the spacecraft's life-support system, I waited near the elevator on the floor below. I waited alone for fifteen minutes in a sort of serene limbo. . . . I could see the massiveness of the Saturn V rocket

below and the magnificent precision of Apollo above. I savored the wait and marked the minutes in my mind as something I would always want to remember." At 9:32 a.m., July 16, 1969, *Apollo 11* lifted-off the launch pad.

Three hours later, it was time to separate the command module, *Columbia* from the Saturn rocket's third stage, then turn around and connect with the lunar module, *Eagle.* This was the next critical step in the *Apollo* mission. If anything went wrong during the separation and docking, the astronauts were to return to earth. Aldrin commented to Cortright that he felt "no apprehension about it (the maneuver) and the entire separation and docking proceeded perfectly to completion."

By July 20th, the pressures were building. In Collins' own words, "Day 4 has a decidedly different feel to it. . . . Despite our concentrated effort to conserve our energy on the way to the Moon, the pressure is overtaking us, and I feel that all of us are aware that the honeymoon is over and we are about to lay our little pink bodies on the line. Our first shock comes as we stop our spinning motion and swing ourselves around so as to bring the Moon into view. We have not been able to see the Moon for nearly a day now, and the change is electrifying. . . . It is huge, completely filling our window."

During the next few minutes, precision was critical. The *Columbia* had to move into a closer circular orbit of the Moon, one where the *Eagle* could separate and continue onward. An overburn (firing of the rocket engines) of even two seconds would send the *Columbia* on an impact course with the far side of the Moon.

As the *Eagle* moved towards the lunar surface, a yellow caution light came-on. Aldrin continued his narration, "Back in Houston, not to mention on board the *Eagle,* hearts shot up into throats while we waited to learn what would happen. We had received two of the caution lights when Steve Bales, the flight controller responsible for the LM (lunar module) computer activity, tells us to proceed. We receive three or four more warnings but kept on going." When the astronauts received their Medals of Freedom from President Nixon, Bales also received one. "He certainly deserved it," said Aldrin, "because without him we might not have landed."

Then, on July 20th, 1969, at 4:17 p.m., the *Eagle* landed on the Moon. "Houston, Tranquility Base here. The *Eagle* has landed." Aldrin radioed. He continued, "We opened the hatch and Neil, with me as his navigator, began backing out of the tiny opening. It seemed like a small eternity before I heard Neil say, 'That's one small step for man . . . one giant leap for mankind.' In less than fifteen minutes I was backing awkwardly out of the hatch and onto the surface to join Neil, who, in the tradition of all tourists, had his camera ready to photograph my arrival. I felt buoyant and full of goose pimples when I stepped down on the surface."

Neither Armstrong nor Aldrin slept much during their one night sleepover on the moon. They were elated, but cold. After staying on the Moon for twenty-one hours, raising the American flag, testing equipment, and gathering Moon rocks, the two astronauts lifted-off in the LM for its return trip to the *Columbia*. Collins' excitement bubbles over when his two teammates reentered the Command Module: "The first one through is Buzz, with a big smile on his face. I grab his head, a hand on each temple, and am about to give him a smooch on the forehead, as a parent might greet an errant child; but then, embarrassed, I think better of it and grab his hand, and then Neil's. We cavort about a little bit, all smiles and giggles over our success, and then it's back to work as usual."

On July 24th, eight days after launch, *Columbia* reenters the earth's atmosphere, and the journey of *Apollo 11* ends with splashdown. After being recovered from the ocean, the astronauts, the equipment, and the lunar rocks were placed in isolation for 17 days. This was done to make certain no harmful material had been brought back with the space voyagers.

After the Moon Landing

After the successful moon landing, the astronauts reluctantly embarked on a good will tour for NASA. Parades were given in their honor. They were awarded Presidential Medals of Freedom and were asked to speak to Congress about their experiences. They were also asked to write a book about their experiences. The result was *First on the Moon*, published in 1970. The Air Force also promoted Aldrin to Commander of the Test Pilot School at Edwards Air Force Base.

Unhappy with his new assignments, Aldrin resigned from NASA in 1971. Shortly afterwards, having undergone treatment for depression, he retired from the Air Force. Aldrin was one of the few celebrities of that time period who publicly acknowledged that he was a recovering alcoholic. He later chaired the National Association of Mental Health and made appearances across the country discussing his battle with depression. He also appeared at a news conference sponsored by the National Council on Alcoholism and openly discussed how his alcoholism and depression were intertwined.

Into the Future

In 1972, Aldrin founded his own company, now known as Starcraft Enterprises. He sees his commercial relationships as an important link in the promotion of space tourism and the colonization of Mars. In an interview with Stephen Ring, journalist for The *Coast Star*, he stated, "We need another great goal, another great endeavor, that will once again inspire us to bring out our best." During an interview with *USA Weekend*, Aldrin expressed his belief that low-Earth orbiting tourism is "going to be what allows NASA to get funding for vehicles for exploration."

According to Ring of The *Coast Star*, Aldrin has designed and patented several spacecraft, including the *Star Booster*, the *Stargrazer*, and the *Cycler*. The *Star Booster*, a cylindrically-shaped, all-aluminum aircraft, with an internal Zenit rocket, would launch a *Stargrazer* into a suborbital path around Earth. The *Star Booster* would then return to Earth and be readied for its next flight. In the meantime, the *Stargrazer* would continue in its suborbital path around the Earth, taking passengers on a space cruise, much the way cruise ships take passengers on ocean tours. As discussed in an interview with *USA Weekend, Cyclers* would use the gravitational pull of the planets to perpetually cycle themselves between Earth and Mars. Smaller ships, stored inside the *Cycler* space station, would ferry people and supplies between the Cycler and Mars.

In 1974, Aldrin wrote his autobiography, *Return to Earth*. In 1989, he and Malcolm McConnell co-authored *Men From Earth* which describes Aldrin's trip to the Moon. In 1996, Aldrin and John Barnes co-authored a science fiction novel, *Encounter with Tiber*. He has also served as chairman of the National Space Society's Board of Directors, and has been awarded 50 distinguished medals and citations from nations all over the world, including the United States' Presidential Medal of Freedom.

Further Reading

Aldrin, Buzz and Malcolm McConnell, *Men from Earth*, 1989.
Aldrin, Edwin E., *Return to Earth*, 1974.
Ad Astra, September-October 1996.
Independent, July 11, 1996.
Life, July 4, 1969; July 17, 1970.
Omni, January 1993.
People, July 25, 1994.
Popular Science, July 1993.
Space News, July 18, 1994.
"Buzz Aldrin Comes to Town," *Coast Star*, (Manasquan, New Jersey, June 19, 1997) http://www.thecoaststar.com/6.19.97/Aldrin.html (March 31, 1998).
"Buzz Aldrin's Official Website," *The National Space Society*, http://www.buzzaldrin.com/excerpt.html (March 31, 1998).
Cortright, Edgar M., ed. "Apollo Expeditions to the Moon, NASA/Kennedy Space Society," *Space Flight Archives, Project Apollo*, http://www.ksc.nasa.gov/history/apollo/apollo-11/apollo-11.html (March, 31 1998).
"From Moonwalker to Professional Hawker: The Selling of Buzz Aldrin," *FLORIDA TODAY Space Online*, (May 10, 1997) http://www.flatoday.com/space/explore/stories/1997/051097a.htm (March 31, 1998).
"Q & A with Buzz Aldrin — The Next Giant Leap: Mars?" *USA Weekend*, (June 29, 1997) http://www.usaweekend.com/97_issues/970629/970629resp_aldrin_mars.html (March 31, 1998).

Tadao Ando

Tadao Ando (born 1941) is one of the most renowned contemporary Japanese architects. His designs are often compared to those of Louis Kahn and Le Corbusier and obviously take some inspiration from their work. Characteristics of his work include large expanses of unadorned walls combined with wooden or slate floors and large windows. Active natural elements, like sun, rain, and wind are a distinctive inclusion to his contemporary style.

Tadao Ando was born a few minutes before his twin brother in Osaka, Japan, in 1941. When he reached the age of two, his family decided that he would be raised by his grandmother while his brother would remain with their parents. Ando's childhood neighborhood contained the workshops of many artisans, including a woodworking shop where he learned the techniques of that craft. As an adult, his earliest design attempts were of small wooden houses and furniture.

Ando told Watanabe Hiroshi, in a 1993 article for *Japan Quarterly,* that his grandmother "wasn't very strict with regard to school.... But she was strict about me keeping my word." He was a mediocre student, so rather than pursuing an education, Ando followed in the footsteps of his brother to become a professional boxer at the age of 17. A series of boxing matches soon took him to Bangkok, Thailand. While there, he visited Buddhist temples in his spare time and became fascinated by their design. He then spent several years traveling in Japan, Europe, and the United States, observing building design.

Ando abandoned his boxing career to apprentice himself to a carpenter and might have started a career as a builder instead of an architect except that he kept encouraging his clients to accept his unconventional design ideas. He had no formal architectural training. Using a list of the books architecture students were assigned to read in four years, he trained himself within one year. He did not apprentice to another architect because every time he tried, he has explained in interviews, he was fired for "stubbornness and temper."

Ando further demonstrated his independence by refusing to establish an office in Tokyo, which is generally thought to be essential for architectural success in Japan. He opened his practice, in 1969, at the age of 28, in his native Osaka. His firm, which is managed by his wife, Yumikio Ando, is still based in Osaka. Consequently, the great majority of his buildings are in or around Osaka, including several projects in nearby Kobe.

Ando first achieved recognition with the *Azuma House* which received the Architectural Institute of Japan's annual award in 1979. Completed in 1976, and also known as the *Rowhouse in Sumiyoshi,* this small house in a working-class section of Osaka introduced all the elements of his later work: smooth concrete walls, large expanses of glass, uncluttered interiors, and an emphasis on bringing nature into contact with the residents. Only two stories high and just over three meters wide, its windowless front wall is made entirely of reinforced concrete with a single recessed area that shelters the entrance. The home is composed of three cubic components. The first cube contains the living room on the ground floor, and the master bedroom above. The third segment contains the kitchen, dining area, and bathroom on the lower floor, and the children's bedroom on the upper floor. The second section, between the other two, is a central courtyard.

The courtyard that lies between the two bedrooms is walled but completely open to the sky above. A bridge spans the courtyard and joins with a side staircase that descends to the courtyard. With the exception of the kitchen/ dining/bath grouping, one must go outside to pass between rooms even during the winter and rainy seasons. Ando believes the inconvenience and discomfort are not without recompense. His buildings force an awareness onto their inhabitants of their place in the world. Moreover, the introspective design of the home insulates its occupants from the sound and sights of the city and offers a tranquil space which is still open to the sun, wind, and clouds.

One of Ando's larger well-known housing projects is his *Rokko Housing Complex.* The complex, which was built in three stages on the sixty degree slope of the Rokko mountains, contains open public spaces and insular private apartments. Each apartment features a terrace with a spectacular view of the port of Kobe and the Bay of Osaka. Ando's *Church on the Water,* in Hokkaido, is a Christian church which features an artificial lake which comes to the very edge of the building. The cubic concrete chapel has one entirely glass wall that slides completely away in good weather. The pews in the chapel face the lake and overlook a large steel cross standing in the middle of the water. *Church of Light,* in Osaka, which is recognized as another masterful work, is a rectangular concrete box, intersected at a 15 degree angle by a freestanding wall which defines the entrance. Behind the altar, a clear glass cross-shaped opening in the concrete wall floods the interior with light. *Water Temple,* in Hyogo, is a Buddhist temple built under a lotus pond. The entrance to the temple is a stairwell which bisects the pond and leads to the temple below.

Ando's four-story *Japan Pavilion* was considered the most impressive work of architecture at Expo '92 in Seville, Spain. One of the largest wooden buildings in the world, the pavilion measures 60 meters wide, 40 meters deep, and 25 meters high at its tallest point. Unpainted wood, one of the most traditional construction materials in Japan, was juxtaposed with such modern elements as a translucent Teflon-coated screen roof. Though conceptually different from his concrete and glass constructions, the pavilion still exhibits his style by not having front openings save a single breezeway that allows the sun and wind free passage between the two wings. The focus remains internally oriented with an emphasis on tangible natural participation within the defined space.

Ando has lectured widely and has taught architecture at such American universities as Yale, Columbia, and Harvard. According to Herbert Muschamp in an interview for the *New York Times* in 1995, Ando considers Japan "boring. He prefers the United States because Americans are encouraged to have their own dreams and to pursue them. In Japan, he says, people do not let themselves dream." His building debut in the United States was the design of a gallery for the Art Institute of Chicago as part of the 1992 addition to house their collection of Japanese, Chinese, and Korean art. More recently, he won the 1997 commission to design the new building for the Modern Art Museum of Fort Worth, Texas.

Style

Ando's use of concrete draws on work by Le Corbusier and Louis Kahn, with whom he is often compared. Ando adds a mastery of nature, light, and space which become as important and tangible as the walls. In an interview with Philip Jodidio, for the book, *Tadao Ando,* Ando says, "I am interested in a dialogue with the architecture of the past but it must be filtered through my own vision and my own experience. I am indebted to Le Corbusier or to Mies van der Rohe, but in the same way, I take what they did and interpret it in my own fashion." His fashion includes a very high quality concrete with a flawlessly lustrous finish achieved by casting in watertight formwork. Generally there is little or no ornamentation on his walls except for precise and ever-changing washes of sunlight and shadow which constantly emphasize the passage of time. Many of his homes and public buildings utilize large amounts of natural light and often contain open courtyards. These walled havens give his buildings an internal orientation which effectively closes out urban chaos. The open-aired isolation enables the inhabitants of his buildings the opportunity to reflect and observe their relationship to natural rhythms.

Ando is also known for his fusion of Eastern and Western architecture. He designs buildings that seem universal in their balance of introspection and assertiveness. His massive concrete walls define carefully assembled geometric compositions of squares, circles, and angles in endlessly fresh and unpredictable patterns. He is often touted for simple serene buildings that are reminiscent of ancient Zen gardens but which have been realized in the vernacular of modern architecture. They are traditionally Japanese in their air of reserve, but they are fully committed to modernity.

Ando's inclusion of nature in his designs has been described as domesticating, abstracting, or stylizing nature. His courtyards are generally paved, and vegetation is at a minimum, if there are plants at all. He prefers atmospheric elements. His buildings incorporate light, wind, temperature, and precipitation to make the inhabitants conscious of their interaction with the space. This introspective awareness is offered as an antidote to the uniformity of contemporary urban life. Electric lighting and climate-controlled environments desensitize people to natural rhythms and even to their own existence as being separate from and reactive to their environment. Awareness of the cold, hard concrete helps lead to the remembrance that humans are soft and warm. Having to grab an umbrella to go to the bathroom reminds one of being part of the natural world. Seeing shadows slowly cross the wall visually tracks the passing of time.

In his wing of the Art Institute of Chicago, Ando constructed a grouping of freestanding columns that obscure parts of the displays as seen from the room's entrance. This leads the viewer to pay close attention to small areas of the art before the room opens up to reveal the display in its entirety. Likewise, when working with such natural settings as a view of the ocean or wooded landscapes, Ando often uses architectural elements to establish a contrasting frame. This evokes a Japanese tradition of blocking panoramic views and leaving a little opening which forces viewers to focus on a smaller area. This encourages people to see that small part of the universe more clearly.

Further Reading

Co, Francesco Dal, *Tadao Ando,* Phaidon Press Limited, 1995.
Contemporary Architects, 3rd ed., St. James Press, 1994.
Frampton, Kenneth, ed., *Tadao Ando: Buildings, Projects, Writings,* Rizzoli International Publications, Inc., 1984.
Furuyama, Masao, *Tadao Ando,* 3rd ed., Birkhäuser—Verlag Für Architektur, 1996.
Jodidio, Philip, *Tadao Ando,* Benedikt Taschen Verlag GmbH, 1997.
Architectural Record, September, 1992, p. 90; November, 1995, p. 74.
Architecture: The AIA Journal, May, 1995, p. 23.
Art in America, April 1, 1990, p. 220.
Christian Science Monitor, April 17, 1995, p. 14.
House Beautiful, July, 1995, p. 33.
Japan Quarterly, October, 1993, p. 426.
New York Times, April 17, 1995, p. C13; April 23, 1995, sec. 2, p. 38; September 21, 1995, p. C1; May 18, 1997, sec. 2, p. 1.
Wall Street Journal, July 23, 1997, p. A16.
Washington Post, April 17, 1995, p. C1.

Kofi Annan

International diplomat Kofi Annan (born 1938) of Ghana is the seventh secretary-general of the United Nations and the first black African to head that organization.

Noted for his cautious, serene style of diplomacy, United Nations (UN) Secretary-General Kofi Annan is sometimes criticized for his soft-spokenness, which some say may be mistaken for weakness. But Annan abides by a lesson he learned back in his college days. Unused to the frigid winters of St. Paul, Minnesota, where he studied economics at Macalester College, he took one look at the local students and decided they looked ridiculous in their huge earmuffs. Then he took a walk around campus. When his ears froze, he went out and bought earmuffs. He said of that experience, as noted in *U.S. News & World Report,* "I learned an important lesson. You never walk into a situation and believe that you know better than the natives. You have to listen and look around. Otherwise you can make some very serious mistakes." As the head peacekeeping officer of the world's chief peacekeeping organization, mistakes are just what Annan wants to avoid.

Early Career

Kofi Atta Annan was born in Kumasi, in central Ghana, on April 8, 1938. Located between the Ivory Coast and Togo on the southern coast of west Africa, Ghana has been a republic within the British Commonwealth since 1960. Named for an African empire along the Niger River, it was ruled by Great Britain for 113 years as the Gold Coast. Annan is descended from tribal chiefs on both sides of his family. His father was an educated man, and Annan became accustomed to both traditional and modern ways of life. He has described himself as being "atribal in a tribal world."

After receiving his early education at a leading boarding school in Ghana, Annan attended the College of Science and Technology in the provincial capital of Kumasi. At the age of 20, he won a Ford Foundation scholarship for undergraduate studies at Macalester College in St. Paul, Minnesota, where he learned about economics and earmuffs. Even then he was showing signs of becoming a diplomat. As communications professor Roger Mosvick commented in *U.S. News & World Report,* "I don't think anyone on this planet has heard Kofi raise his voice in anger." Annan received his bachelor's degree in economics in 1961.

Shortly after completing his studies at Macalester College, Annan headed for Geneva where he attended the Institut Universitaire des Hautes Etudes Internationales for graduate classes in economics. A decade later, he became the Alfred P. Sloan fellow at the Massachusetts Institute of Technology (MIT). At the end of his fellowship in 1972, he was awarded a master of science degree in management.

Following his graduate studies in Geneva, Annan joined the staff of the World Health Organization (WHO), a branch of the United Nations. He served as an administrative officer and as budget officer in Geneva. Later UN posts took him to Addis Ababa, Ethiopia, and New York City, New York. Annan had always assumed that he would return to his native land after college, although he was disturbed by the unrest and numerous overturns of government that occurred there during the 1970s. Rather than return to Ghana during this period, he accepted a position with UN headquarters in New York City. In 1974, he moved to Cairo, Egypt, as chief civilian personnel officer in the UN Emergency Force. Annan briefly changed careers in 1974 when he left the UN to serve as managing director of the Ghana Tourist Development Company.

Annan returned to international diplomacy and the UN in 1976, leaving the private sector permanently. For the next seven years, he was associated with the Office of the United Nations High Commissioner for Refugees in Geneva. He returned to the UN headquarters in New York City in 1983 as director of the budget in the financial services office. Later in the 1980s, he filled the post of assistant secretary-general in the Office of Human Resources Management and served as security coordinator for the United Nations. In 1990, he became assistant secretary-general for another department at the UN, the Office of Program Planning, Budget, and Finance. In fulfilling his duties to the United Nations, Annan has spent most of his adult life in the United States, specifically UN headquarters in New York.

Annan has filled a number of roles at the UN, ranging from peacekeeping to managerial, and the 1990s were no different. In 1990, he negotiated the release of hostages in Iraq following the invasion of Kuwait. Five years later, he oversaw the transition of the United Nations Protection Force (UNPROFOR) to the multinational Implementation Force (IFOR). In this transfer of responsibility, operations in the former Yugoslavia were turned over to the North Atlantic Treaty Organization (NATO). Annan had been associated with the Office of Peace-keeping Operations since 1992. In 1993, he had been promoted to under-secretary-general of this office. In recognition of his abilities, Annan

was appointed Secretary-General of the United Nations by the General Assembly in December of 1996. He began serving his four-year term of office on January 1, 1997.

Joining him in this new post was his second wife, former attorney Nane Lagergren. The secretary-general has been married twice, first to a woman from Nigeria, with whom he has two children. His second wife, Nane Lagergren, is from Sweden. She is the niece of the diplomat Raoul Wallenberg, who saved thousands of European Jews from the Nazis during World War II. Annan and Lagergren were married in 1985. The couple has one child.

Heading the UN

The post of Secretary-General of the United Nations has been called one of the world's "oddest jobs." According to the United Nations website, "Equal parts diplomat and activist, conciliator and provocateur, the Secretary-General stands before the world community as the very emblem of the United Nations. The task demands great vigour, sensitivity and imagination, to which the Secretary-General must add a tenacious sense of optimism—a belief that the ideals expressed in the Charter can be made a reality." The Secretary-General is the boss of 10,000 international civil servants and the chief administrator of a huge international parliamentary system.

In this post, Annan is expected to coordinate, although he does not control, the activities of such groups as the World Health Organization (WHO) and the United Nations Educational, Scientific, and Cultural Organization (UNESCO). He is also obliged to practice "preventive diplomacy," meaning he and his staff must try to prevent, contain, or defuse international disputes. Above all, Annan must try to maintain world peace. In an address to the National Press Club, Annan declared: "If war is the failure of diplomacy, then . . . diplomacy, both bilateral and multilateral, is our first line of defence. The world today spends billions preparing for war; shouldn't we spend a billion or two preparing for peace?"

Almost immediately after Annan's election came the question: Is this man just too nice a person for the job? His reputation for "soft-spokenness," according to *U.S. News & World Report,* could be mistaken for weakness. *National Review* contributor Stefan Halper, however, called Annan a "subtle and capable presence" with "an extraordinary feel for the [United Nations]. . . . [H]is influence on world opinion, and hence his power, is striking." Another factor that made people question Annan's toughness was his involvement in the UN efforts at peacekeeping in Bosnia from 1992 to 1996. Despite the UN's presence, Bosnia remained the site of an ethnic war where thousands died. Sir Marrack Goulding, head of peace-keeping, once commented that Annan never expressed his doubts about the UN policy in a forceful manner. Annan disagreed, saying that he always pressed the involved countries—the United States, Britain, France, and Russia—to rethink their limited mandate on sending soldiers to the peace-keeping force. Not one to raise his voice in anger, Annan favored diplomacy. In a press conference in Baghdad in 1998, Annan noted: "You can do a lot with diplomacy, but of course you can do a lot more with diplomacy backed up by fairness and force.''

All eyes turned to Annan and his handling of the touchy situation with Iraq in 1998. Early in that year, threats of war seemed all too real. Saddam Hussein, President of Iraq, was once again a threatening presence, refusing to let UN observers into certain areas of his country, as previously agreed upon, to check for illegal possession of chemical warfare items and the like. President Bill Clinton of the United States hinted strongly at the use of force to make Saddam comply. In his role as Secretary-General, Annan went to Iraq in February of 1998 to meet with the Iraqi leader. After talking with Annan, Saddam agreed to what he had refused before—unlimited UN access to the eight sites that he had previously called completely off-limits. Due to Annan's intervention, war was averted. ''There were millions of people around the world rooting for a peaceful solution and praying for us—this is why in Baghdad I said you should never underestimate the power of prayer,'' declared Annan upon returning to UN headquarters that month, as noted on the UN website.

Annan's code of soft-spoken diplomacy was given a boost by the outcome of his talks with Saddam Hussein in 1998. United Nations observers wait to see how additional crises will be handled by the gentle but determined man from Ghana. As a long-time acquaintance of Annan commented to *People,* ''He has in mind a goal: world peace.''

Further Reading

Christian Century, April 1, 1998.
Maclean's, March 9, 1998.
Nation, March 16, 1998.
National Review, April 20, 1998.
New Republic, January 6, 1997.
Newsweek, March 9, 1998, pp. 28-32.
New York Times Magazine, March 29, 1998.
U.S. News & World Report, March 9, 1998, pp. 36-37; March 23, 1998.
''Kofi Annan,'' Newsmaker Profiles, CNN Interactive, http://www.cnn.com (May 14, 1998).
United Nations website, http://www.un.org (March 2, 1998).
Annan's address to the National Press Club, Washington, D.C., January 24, 1997.
Annan's joint press conference with Deputy Minister of Iraq Tariq Aziz, Baghdad, February 23, 1998.

Richard Samuel Attenborough

After spending several decades working as a character actor, Richard Attenborough (born 1923) gained worldwide recognition when he won an Oscar as best director for the motion picture *Gandhi,* which he also produced. In all, this labor of love, detailing the life of India's great spiritual leader, won eight Academy Awards, including best picture and best actor.

Attenborough's career in the arts dates back to the early 1940s when—after winning a scholarship to the Royal Academy of Dramatic Art—he appeared in productions of Eugene O'Neill's *Ah, Wilderness!* and Noel Coward's wartime drama *In Which We Serve.* After parting from the academy in 1942, Attenborough played in a broad range of West End productions and acted in several films before embarking on his acclaimed profession as a director.

From Cambridge to the Theater

Richard Samuel Attenborough, the oldest of three sons, was born August 29, 1923, to Frederick Levi and Mary Clegg Attenborough. He was raised in a family atmosphere of egalitarian ethics and common sense values. This was reflected in the actions of Attenborough's parents, who, in 1939, adopted two young Jewish girls who were refugees from Germany. His parents' actions made a strong impact on Attenborough, who subsequently led a life that emphasized goodwill to others in his art and everyday life.

Barely in his teens, Attenborough announced his desire to become an actor. He did some acting while a pupil at Wyggeston Grammar School for Boys in Leicester, as well as at the Leicester Little Theatre. In 1940, he was admitted to the Royal Academy of Dramatic Art in London on a competitive scholarship. Two years later, he won the school's Bancroft Medal for fine acting. By then he had made his first stage and screen appearances, in *Ah, Wilderness!* and *In Which We Serve,* respectively.

As it did for many young men, World War II interrupted Attenborough's budding career. After making his stage debut in London's West End in Clifford Odets' *Awake and Sing* and appearing in several other roles, he joined the Royal Air Force in 1943 and flew film reconnaissance missions over Germany. In 1945 he married actress Sheila Sim (they have three children, Jane, Charlotte, and Michael). After Attenborough's discharge from the RAF in 1946, he signed a contract with the motion picture team of John and Ray Boulting. Although Attenborough appeared in a number of films, his career in that medium seemed limited. He did, however, have some success on the stage, especially in *The Mousetrap,* Agatha Christie's perpetually running murder mystery in London.

Actor Turns Director

Determined to bring himself better film roles by developing his own productions, Attenborough teamed with screenwriter and director Bryan Forbes to form Beaver Films in 1959. The next year the duo completed *The Angry Silence,* a grim drama featuring Attenborough as an industrial laborer who refused to cooperate when his coworkers strike. With its somber, unflinching depiction of British working-class life, *The Angry Silence* won acclaim as one of the year's better pictures, and it earned Attenborough renewed consideration as a proficient screen performer.

After expanding their partnership to form Allied Film Makers, Attenborough went on to distinguish himself in a range of productions, from comedy to drama, thrillers to wartime sagas. Considered to be among his best roles of the 1960s is that of a beleaguered husband in the unsettling thriller *Seance on a Wet Afternoon.* For his performance in this 1964 film, he won a British Academy Award for best actor. He also made a distinct impression in a pair of ambitious Hollywood productions: director Robert Aldrich's *Flight of the Phoenix,* which featured Attenborough as the alcoholic navigator of a military aircraft downed in the Sahara; and director Robert Wise's *The Sand Pebbles,* a somber epic in which Attenborough won a Golden Globe Award for his portrayal of a sailor whose interracial love affair ends tragically in 1920s China.

In 1969 Attenborough made his directorial debut with the ambitious *Oh! What a Lovely War,* a fantastical series of vignettes related to World War I. This film, adapted from Joan Littlewood's stage musical, featured a vast array of notable British performers—including Laurence Olivier, John Gielgud, Susannah York, Ralph Richardson, Vanessa Redgrave, Michael Redgrave, and Dirk Bogarde. It was roundly hailed as an impressive first effort and subsequently won the Golden Globe for best English-language foreign film of that year.

Attenborough next directed *Young Winston,* a lengthy account of former British prime minister Winston Churchill's life from his schooldays to his first election to Parliament. Especially impressive in this film is Attenborough's handling of battle sequences, which were generally considered by critics to be exhilarating and breathtaking. Notable, too, were the performances executed by Anne Bancroft,

Robert Shaw, Ian Holm, Anthony Hopkins, Jane Seymour, and—as Churchill—Simon Ward.

With his first two works as director Attenborough had proved himself capable of handling both the logistics of epic storytelling and the coordination of sizeable, star-studded casts. In his following film, *A Bridge Too Far,* he again attempted a narrative of considerable scope—recounting the disastrous Allied assault at Arnheim, Holland, a German stronghold during World War II. Some reviewers lamented that the film was greater in its parts than in its entirety, and some found it dull and contrived. But *Newsweek'* s Jack Kroll contended that the film had "its own power and impact." Lauding Attenborough as "a fine director," Kroll declared: "In only his third directorial effort, Attenborough . . . has done an excellent job of weaving a strong, clear and often moving tapestry of a thousand details. He deserves great credit for the intelligence and integrity of this film."

Attenborough's next venture was the horror story *Magic,* featuring Anthony Hopkins as a deranged ventriloquist committing murder at the imagined behest of his profane dummy. Among the film's many detractors was *New Yorker'* s Pauline Kael, who complained that William Goldman's script lacked polish and Attenborough's direction lacked complexity. "The director . . . grinds along so seriously that there's no suspense, no ambiguity," she wrote.

The *Gandhi* Obsession

Next, Attenborough turned his attention to a project with which he had been obsessed since 1962—bringing the life of Indian leader Mahatma Mohandas K. Gandhi to the screen. That year Attenborough had received a copy of Louis Fischer's biography of the famous Indian nationalist and spiritual leader and aspired to film the story. The idea of making a film about the pacifist leader proved easier than the actual task. Attenborough went through years of meeting with Indian government officials, attempting to iron out the logistic and legal matters needed for the production's commencement. Along the way he took numerous acting and directing jobs, all to fund the Gandhi film. And, Attenborough's involvement with both *A Bridge Too Far* and *Magic* were predicated on the agreement that, for directing those films, he would get a green light for *Gandhi* from producer Joe Levine who owned the rights to the material. Levine eventually reneged on the agreement, and Attenborough was forced to buy the rights from the producer. Finally, after years of struggle and numerous script attempts, Attenborough was ready to begin filming in the late 1970s.

Gandhi became the film that defined Attenborough's career, nearly eclipsing his work as an actor. The epic traces the Indian nationalist's life from his early activism in 1890s South Africa through his ascent to power in India and his assassination five decades later. Memorable sequences included the 1919 Amritsar massacre, in which innocent Indians were fired upon by British troops; Gandhi's calm exposition of nonviolent resistance before a group of reactionary Indians; his two-hundred-mile protest march to the sea; and his starvation protest against British occupation in India. In the scene depicting Gandhi's funeral procession,

Attenborough utilized some three hundred thousand extras to line the streets. In a moment of unplanned synchronicity, the crew shot the funeral scene on January 31, 1981, exactly thirty-three years to the day of Gandhi's actual funeral.

Upon release in 1982, *Gandhi* won acclaim as a powerful inspiring film. Among its many supporters was *Newsweek'* s Kroll, who hailed its "mixture of high intelligence and immediate emotional impact." Kroll accorded special recognition to John Briley's screenplay and to Ben Kingsley's performance as Gandhi. But he reserved greatest praise for Attenborough's skillful direction and for his twenty-year perseverance on the project. "It's hard to decide what is more miraculous," Kroll wrote, "the fact that [Attenborough] actually made the film or the fact that it's turned out so fresh, so electric, so moving." Citing the film's production values as "impeccable," *New Statesman* reviewer John Coleman cited *Gandhi* as an example of "sterling craftsmanship."

In 1985 Attenborough directed *A Chorus Line,* the film version of Michael Bennett's hugely popular behind-the-scenes musical constructed as a series of auditions. He also published a book on the making of the film. Ralph Novak, writing in *People,* called Attenborough's book, *Richard Attenborough's Chorus Line,* "far more to the point than the movie it comes from." Although reviewers found the film well cast and technically impressive, they generally agreed that it failed to match the energy and intensity of the stage version.

Attenbourough next directed *Cry Freedom,* an account, by *Gandhi* screenwriter John Briley, of prize-winning reporter Donald Woods' observations and experiences in South Africa's system of apartheid. Apartheid was a network of laws set up by the white ruling minority of South Africa to effectively separate blacks and whites, but the majority of blacks saw the laws as thinly veiled slavery and outright discrimination in an economic, racial, and humane sense. The film begins by depicting the growing friendship between Woods, a white liberal journalist, and Steven Biko, a charismatic community leader and anti-apartheid activist. Through their relationship, Woods learns of the true ravages that apartheid forces upon the black community. When Biko is taken prisoner by South African security forces, he is brutally beaten and dies in prison. Woods sees his friend's battered body and realizes that the government's claims that Biko died from a hunger strike are lies. The film follows his efforts to publicize Biko's untimely demise. For his involvement with the anti-apartheid activist, Woods is banned from publishing in South Africa and he eventually flees the country. *New Statesman* reviewer Judith Williamson, while acknowledging that *Cry Freedom* is imperfect, affirmed that it is "a powerful film; far more political than it needed to be," and she deemed it "an impressive example both of the strengths of a liberal mainstream cinema, and of its limitations—and of the strange way in which these are bound together." David Denby, writing in *New York,* averred, "In many ways, *Cry Freedom* is a major event in the history of liberal agitation."

Since *Cry Freedom* Attenbourough has directed *Chaplin* (1992), *Shadowlands* (1993) and *In Love and War*

(1996). He also played John Harmond in *Jurassic Park* (1993) and its sequel *Lost World* and Kris Kringle in *Miracle on 34th Street* (1994).

In accordance with the values he learned from his parents, Attenborough also sought to extend himself in terms beyond the artistic. He has won substantial recognition for his lifelong humanitarian concerns. He has long been involved in a range of charities and has worked in an administrative capacity for various institutions and organizations. In addition, he has donated his personal services to numerous philanthropic enterprises, and he has long been a force in Britain's charitable fundraising endeavors. For such work, he has received many honors, including the Martin Luther King Jr. Peace Prize and India's Padma Bhushan.

Attenborough's work as an actor, and particularly as a director, is considered by many to be invaluable to modern cinema. Observers view his foray into production, to secure better roles for himself, as influential to many contemporary actors such as Jane Fonda, Robert Redford, and Goldie Hawn. Attenborough's success as an actor is seen as paving the way for his work as an important director. His understanding of acting techniques allows him to relate to his actors and thus draw exemplary performances from them. He is also credited with bringing a level of social consciousness on subjects such as war, pacifism, and apartheid to a large audience. In describing his impetus to bring the story of Mahatma Gandhi to the masses, Attenborough told an interviewer from the *New York Daily News:* "Not being able to cope very happily with many of the formalities and constraints of organized religion that in many instances result in the most monstrous examples of man's inhumanity to man, I found it an enormous relief to come across someone who said, 'I am a Hindu and a Christian and a Muslim and a Jew and so are all of you'—meaning that if God is truth, then that is what we are seeking and the manner in which we find truth is to some degree an irrelevancy."

Further Reading

Attenborough, Richard, *In Search of Gandhi,* New Century, 1982.
Film Encyclopedia, Harper, 1990.
Entertainment Weekly, September 6, 1996.
New Statesman, December 3, 1982; December 4, 1987.
Newsweek, June 20, 1977; November 13, 1978; December 13, 1982; December 30, 1985.
New York, December 11, 1978; September 21, 1987; November 16, 1987.
New York Daily News, December 4, 1982.
New Yorker, June 20, 1977; November 30, 1987.
People, March 10, 1986.

Alan Ayckbourn

Alan Ayckbourn (born 1939), a prolific author of comedy plays about middle-class life in England, is considered one of the world's pre-eminent dramatists.

nglish playwright Alan Ayckbourn is a master satirist of middle-class manners who has often been compared to Noel Coward and Harold Pinter. He draws upon his own upbringing to paint scathing portraits of people leading dull, mechanical lives. Often his works straddle the line between comedy and farce. His plays have been translated into more than 25 foreign languages and have been performed all over the world. Harold Clurman, writing in the *Nation,* called Ayckbourn "a master hand at turning the bitter apathy, the stale absurdity which most English playwrights now find characteristic of Britain's lower-middle-class existence into hilarious comedy."

Unhappy Childhood

Alan Ayckbourn was born in Hampstead, London, England, on April 12, 1939. His father, Horace Ayckbourn, was an accomplished musician who served as deputy leader of the London Symphony Orchestra. His mother, Irene (Worley) Ayckbourn, was a journalist who wrote for popular women's magazines. When Ayckbourn was five, his parents divorced. He remained with his mother, who married a bank manager and moved to rural Sussex. The new marriage was troubled as well, however, and Ayckbourn endured a very unhappy childhood. "I was surrounded by relationships that weren't altogether stable, the air was often blue, and things were sometimes flying across the kitchen," he told the *New York Times.*

Ayckbourn spent much of his childhood in various boarding schools. At the age of 12, he received a scholarship to attend Haileybury, a respected public school. There

he took an interest in drama under the influence of his teacher, Edgar Matthews. By the time he was 17, he had decided to pursue a career as an actor. He started out with small repertory theater companies, often working as a stage manager in addition to performing.

From Actor to Playwright

In 1957, Ayckbourn took a position with the Stephen Joseph Company in Scarborough. This experimental theater-in-the-round troupe specialized in so-called "underground" dramatic techniques. Originally, Ayckbourn was hired as a bit player and assistant stage manager. Like a lot of young actors, however, he began to lobby for bigger and better parts. Stephen Joseph, the leader of the company, thought Ayckbourn had more potential as a writer than an actor. He appealed to the actor's vanity. "If you want a better part, you'd better write one for yourself," Joseph told Ayckbourn, according to *Drama* magazine. Ayckbourn accepted the challenge, and in 1959 produced his first two plays, *The Square Cat* and *Love After All.* He refused to put his own name on these works and no longer allows them to be staged. Other plays Ayckbourn crafted during his time at Scarborough were *Dad's Tale* and *Standing Room Only.*

In 1959, Ayckbourn married Christine Roland. Their union produced two children, Steven Paul and Philip Nicholas. In 1961, Ayckbourn left Scarborough to found his own company, the Victoria Theatre Company in Stoke-on-Trent. From 1965 to 1970, he also worked for the British Broadcasting Company (BBC) as a producer of radio dramas. Meanwhile, he continued to write occasional plays for the Scarborough company.

First Taste of Success

In 1967, Ayckbourn enjoyed his first major London success with the play *Relatively Speaking.* Originally titled *Meet My Father,* it depicts the farcical complications that ensue when a young suitor visits the home of his girlfriend's former lover, believing it to be the home of her parents. The play introduces what would become one of Ayckbourn's stock devices, the interaction of major characters with incompatible characters, settings, and situations. Writing in *The New British Drama: Fourteen Playwrights Since Osborne and Pinter,* critic Oleg Kerensky observed that the play established Ayckbourn "as a writer of ingenious farcical comedy, with an ear for dialogue and with a penchant for complex situations . . . and ingenious plots."

In 1969, *How the Other Half Loves,* starring Robert Morley, was produced in the West End. The play features an ambitious set design in which the two halves of the set represent rooms in two different houses connected by one adulterous love affair. Comical complications result when a third couple becomes involved in the attendant cover-up. Like many of Ayckbourn's works, this one relies on a strange situation that grows increasingly absurd as its characters get tangled up in lies and misunderstandings. "How Mr. Ayckbourn contrives to get his people into such states and persuade us to believe that they are reasonable is a secret of his comic flair," wrote critic Walter Goodman in the *New York Times.*

Experiments with Staging

In 1970, Ayckbourn returned to the Scarborough Company on a full-time basis, in the post of artistic director. He used the company as a laboratory for his new comedies, which he then revised and handed over to a different director for production in London's West End. The fruits of this arrangement include some of his best comedies to date. *Absurd Person Singular* (1972) was a black comedy centered around a girl's attempt at suicide. Like *How the Other Half Loves,* the play relies on some experimental staging. The action takes place in a kitchen while a party goes on simultaneously in the nearby living room—outside the view of the audience. Only bits of dialogue can be heard from the living room scenes as the kitchen door opens. In fact, some important characters are talked about but never actually seen on stage.

Even more daring was *The Norman Conquests* (1973), a trilogy of plays, each featuring the same characters and dealing with the same events in the same time frame. The three parts cover an afternoon in the life of an unsavory character named Norman. ("Norman Conquest" refers to both the conquest of Britain by the French in 1066 and Norman's romantic conquests.) Each installment contains action that occurs offstage in the other installments. The first play, *Table Manners,* is set in a dining room; the second, *Living Together,* in a living room; and the third, *Round and Round the Garden,* outside in a garden. Characters drift in and out of each play, only to appear at that moment in one of the others. In order to understand the work in its entirety, it is necessary to see or read all three "pieces." But *The Norman Conquests* was more than a gimmick. Its complex plot was tied together by the unseen "presence" of Norman's cantankerous, bedridden mother. The various characters, most of them Norman's relatives or romantic partners, were archly drawn, and as Richard Christiansen noted in the *Chicago Tribune,* the three plays "fit together like Chinese boxes." Observed Guido Almansi in *Encounter:* "As we view the second and then the third play of the trilogy, our awareness of what is going on in the rest of the house and likewise the satisfaction of our curiosity grow concurrently ... I dare surmise that this innovation will count in the future development of theatrical technique."

Prolific Playwright

The Norman Conquest won the *London Evening Standard'* s best play award for 1974, a prize Ayckbourn would claim several more times over the course of his career. He was soon recognized as one of Britain's leading playwrights, with some critics likening him to his American counterpart Neil Simon. In 1974, he produced two successful new works, *Absent Friends* and *Confusions.* The former featured a female protagonist driven to distraction by her uncaring husband, a common theme in Ayckbourn's work. Some critics related it to his own unhappy upbringing as the child of divorce. For these and his previous efforts, Ayckbourn was named 1974's "playwright of the year" by the Variety Club of Great Britain.

Ayckbourn wrote prolifically throughout the 1970s and 1980s, producing at least one new play every year. Some of his most important works during this period included *Bedroom Farce, Way Upstream,* and *A Chorus of Disapproval,* which was adapted as a feature film in 1989. Ayckbourn continued writing at a breakneck pace well into the 1990s. All of his works were first produced at Scarborough, then debuted in revised form on the West End in London. A series of omnibus volumes collecting all of Ayckbourn's plays was launched by Faber Publishing in 1985.

In 1997, Alan Ayckbourn was knighted by Queen Elizabeth II for his contributions to British theatre. As Sir Alan Ayckbourn, he continued to write and produce his own plays, including *Things We Do For Love* in 1997. With each new work, he enhances his reputation as one of the leading lights in contemporary drama.

Further Reading

Kerensky, Oleg, *The New British Drama: Fourteen Playwrights Since Osborne and Pinter,* Hamish Hamilton, 1977.
Chicago Tribune, July 17, 1982; July 15, 1983; August 2, 1987.
Drama, autumn, 1974; spring, 1979; summer, 1979; January, 1980; October, 1980; first quarter, 1981; second quarter, 1981; autumn, 1981; spring, 1982; summer, 1982; Volume 162, 1986.
Encounter, December, 1974; April, 1978.
Nation, March 8, 1975; December 27, 1975; April 21, 1979; April 8, 1991; June 8, 1992.
New York Times, October 20, 1974; February 16, 1977; April 4, 1977; March 25, 1979; March 30, 1979; March 31, 1979; May 1, 1979; October 16, 1981; May 29, 1986; June 15, 1986; June 25, 1986; October 3, 1986; October 29, 1986; November 26, 1986; July 20, 1987; April 15, 1988; June 5, 1988.

B

Ella Josephine Baker

American activist Ella Baker (1903-1986) was the consummate organizer and unsung brains behind many of the most effective African American civil rights and political organizations in the twentieth century.

Ella Baker's democratic vision and grass-roots activism left an indelible imprint on African American civil rights and political movements in the twentieth-century. She was regarded as a brilliant strategist, a radical intellectual, and superb organizer. Her political legacy forever linked criticisms of racism and gender-based discrimination to criticisms of capitalism and social imperialism. She combined liberation rhetoric with direct activism, and developed strong internal structures that made organizational growth and progress possible. Baker was a proponent of the "under class," and believed "ordinary" people could become political leaders. An article in *Black Scholar* attributed her low profile in the civil rights movement to her preference of taking political directives from the poor and working class, rather than civil rights elites, some of whom marginalized her and the importance of her contributions. Baker considered herself a facilitator, rather than a leader and she believed in the strength and power of the common man to help themselves.

Political activism began shaping her life in Harlem during the Great Depression. She helped found and eventually became coordinator, and then director of the Young Negroes Cooperative League (YNCL), which organized stores and buying clubs to achieve economic self-sufficiency among the African American community. This expe-

rience, along with that of writing about New York City's African American domestics, deepened her understanding of the relationship between politics and economic exploitation of people according to gender, race, and class. She went on to establish a grass-roots field network for the National Association for the Advancement of Colored People (NAACP), becoming a national leader in the 1940s. She became the first director of the Southern Christian Leadership Conference (SCLC) in the 1950s and was a founder of and adviser to the Student Nonviolent Coordinating Committee (SNCC) in the 1960s. She worked well into her 70s with numerous political organizations to further social and racial justice. Baker was always striving to form a bridge among different socio-economic groups to foster communication and cooperation.

A Heritage of Strength

Born in Norfolk, Virginia, and raised in Littleton, North Carolina, Ella Josephine Baker was the middle child of educated parents who were active participants in community life. *Black Scholar* describes her early years as somewhat protected and privileged. She was part of a close-knit racially proud family, whose ancestors had been community leaders with a southern African American tradition of cooperating with and helping one another that was carried on by her family. They were not wealthy, but were able to send her to Shaw boarding school in Raleigh for high school—there was no secondary school in Littleton. She excelled academically, and continued her education at Shaw University, a conservative institution with a "classical" curriculum of literature, philosophy, foreign languages, and mathematics. Her sense of social justice began to form while she was a student; she led several protests against strict rules, such as not being allowed to wear silk

stockings on campus. She majored in sociology, and graduated as valedictorian of the class of 1927.

A Time of Testing

Full of energy, idealism, and possibilities, she rejected an offer to teach school realizing that mostly white school boards would control her future. Instead, on the eve of the Great Depression, she moved to New York City—worlds apart from the confines of university life. She was appalled by the suffering, poverty, and hunger, as well as the sense of desperation that hung over the streets of Harlem. Her first job was as a waitress. Rather than succumb to exploitation, she started organizing with others for jobs and helped found The Young Negroes Cooperative League (YNCL) as a means to help people save money and gain economic power by buying collectively. As a group organizer, she learned firsthand the devastation caused by the Depression. Elected to be the YNCL's first national director, she viewed the organization as a proving ground for communalism and interdependency. Such groups were branded as radical because they embraced socialism and some forms of communism; in fact, the YNCL resembled Baker's memory of the cooperative community environment in which she grew up. The YNCL was based on democratic principles, for men and women alike, and its leaders were drawn from the membership.

Throughout the 1930s Baker was involved in numerous organizations, but a few were particularly influential in her development as a social activist. One was the Workers Education Project, which was part of the Works Progress Administration (WPA). There, in addition to teaching subjects that enabled people to re-enter the workforce, she came in contact with left-wing activists and the growing union movement. Others, such as the Women's Day Workers and Industrial League, a union for domestic workers; the Harlem Housewives Cooperative; and the Harlem Young Women's Christian Association (YWCA), brought her in touch with her identity as an African American woman. She began to consider how social, political, and government structures exploited race, and refused to be classified as anything other than a "person." Even in marriage she did not assume her husband's last name, an act that was considered highly unusual in the 1930s. She commented, "I began to see that there were certain social forces over which the individual had very little control. It wasn't an easy lesson for me to learn, but I was able to learn it. It was out of that context that I began to explore; more in the area of ideology and the theory of social change.... I began to confront poverty, to identify to some extent with the unemployed. . ."

Oppression on the Block

Baker had the opportunity to see people's lives from many different venues, including that of a reporter. In 1935 she co-authored with Marvel Cooke an exposé on the precarious situations of African-American domestic workers. Entitled "The Bronx Slave Market," the sexual and racial exploitation unique to African American women was described. Both writers posed as domestics looking for jobs in the "slave marts," auction blocks where day workers negotiated wages, as part of their research. With 15 million Americans without jobs and savings, the Depression intensified the poverty conditions tying African Americans to domestic service. Wages ranged from 15 to 30 cents an hour. In desperation, African Americans turned to the federal government for assistance, which although it provided a safety net for some, failed to include domestic work in most legislation—and did nothing to establish a basic wage. The dehumanizing experience of facing derision from "respectable" wage earners, as well as fraudulent employment agencies that bilked workers' wages, lead Baker to conclude that economic justice should be the primary objective in political struggles. According to *Black Scholar*, her labor activism placed "work" central to critiques of racism, classism, and sexism; and made the struggles against racism and sexism indispensable to dismantling economic oppression.

Into the Mainstream

In 1940, Baker started working with the NAACP as a field secretary and from 1943-1946 as director of branches criss-crossing the south and establishing a vast network of contacts. Baker disagreed with the NAACP's reliance on legal approaches to combat discrimination, advocating instead a strategy that would involve the entire membership. Also impatient with the organization's bureaucracy, she resigned, but volunteered as president of the New York branch.

In the 1950s, her interests turned to the growing southern civil rights movement. Along with two friends, she founded In Friendship, an organization that raised money to help organizations, such as the Montgomery Improvement Association, which coordinated the bus boycott, as well as needy individuals who lost property in retribution for their participation. The advent of the Southern Christian Leadership Conference (SCLC), which was formed to maximize the momentum generated by the Montgomery boycott, rendered the smaller organization unnecessary. Baker joined the SCLC as its first director working along side Dr. Martin Luther King, Jr., even though they had differences of opinion on leadership issues. For two years she coordinated the SCLC's voter rights campaign, called Crusade for Citizenship, expanded grass-roots participation, and ran the office. Eventually, however, she resigned due to her strong belief that the organization was relying too heavily on King's persona to mobilize people.

Coincidentally, about the same time, students in Greensboro, North Carolina, led a successful desegregation sit-in. Baker immediately shifted her attention to maximizing this new activism among African-American students, and took a job with the local YWCA in order to be nearby and involved. Under her direction, a new independent youth organization, the Student Nonviolent Coordinating Committee (SNCC), was formed as an alternative to more politically moderate organizations. Egalitarian in structure, it was based on grass-roots democracy managed on a local level, which gave women, young people, and the poor a chance to become leaders. This organization epitomized Baker's philosophy of sharing knowledge and skills with others, which PBS later captured in a documentary, *Fundi: The Story of Ella Baker*. *Fundi* is a Swahili word meaning "one who hands down a craft from one generation to another."

Black Scholar noted that the SNCC distinguished itself by using mass direct-action tactics and by going into rural areas of the Deep South, where racism and violence were worst. The SNCC lead a wave of sit-in demonstrations throughout the South and became one of the most effective student movements in US history. It remained an independent organization, declining to become affiliated with the SCLC, a decision supported by Baker that reinforced her split with the SCLC.

Baker taught people not to be ashamed of their race, made them believe in themselves, and understand the power of unity. Behind the scenes and out of the limelight, she nurtured generations of African Americans to keep the spirit of freedom going. While she was content to work in supportive roles, she urged African American women to take up their struggle for equality. She explained the social environment of the 1950s and 1960s: "The movement . . . was carried largely by women, since it came out of church groups. It was sort of second nature to women to play a supportive role. . . . [I]t's true that the number of women who carried the movement is much larger than that of men. Black women have had to carry this role, and I think the younger women are insisting on an equal footing." Always

a pioneer, Baker anticipated and encouraged the next wave of social activism in the 1970s and 1980s.

Baker's later years were spent advising countless organizations. She was an organizer who identified with all people, and who sought to create change by empowering people to act on their own behalf. Ella Baker died in New York, New York in 1986 and left behind a legacy that lived well beyond her eighty-three years.

Further Reading

Black Women in America, edited by Darlene Clark Hine, Carlson Publishing, 1993.
Notable Black American Women, Gale, 1992.
Papers of the Southern Christian Leadership Conference, 1954-1970, University Publications of America, 1995.
Black Scholar, Fall, 1994.
Journal of Black Studies, May, 1996. □

Howard Henry Baker Jr.

Howard H. Baker, Jr. (born 1925) served four terms in the United States Senate, including four years as minority leader and four years as majority leader. He was appointed the White House Chief of Staff by President Ronald Reagan.

Howard Henry Baker, Jr., served in the United States Senate for 18 years. He won the respect of his colleagues for his non-extremist views and his willingness to compromise. He distinguished himself as the Republican leader of the Senate for eight consecutive years: as minority leader for four years, (1977-81) and as majority leader for the next four years (1981-85). He retired from the Senate in 1985 and served as White House Chief of Staff under President Ronald Reagan in 1987 and 1988.

Born to Politics

Baker was born on November 15, 1925, in Huntsville, Tennessee. The Bakers were a politically active family. Baker's father, Howard Baker, Sr., served in the United States House of Representatives as a Republican from Tennessee from 1951-64. Baker's stepmother was also a Republican congresswoman, and Baker's grandfather was a judge.

Baker eventually married Joy Dirksen, the daughter of former Senate Minority leader Everett Dirksen. Baker was widowed in 1993 when Joy Baker died of cancer. In December of 1996 he married Nancy Kassebaum, a retired Republican Senator from Burdick, Kansas. The extended family of Baker and Kassebaum combined includes six children and 12 grandchildren.

Baker attended the University of the South (in Sewanee) and Tulane University. He enlisted in the United States Naval Reserve and was discharged as a Lieutenant, junior grade, after serving in World War II. He studied law at the University of Tennessee and earned an LL.B. in 1949.

Early Political Career

For 15 years Baker practiced law in Knoxville, Tennessee, and held other business and financial interests as well. He first ran for the United States Senate in 1964, on a conservative Republican platform, but he lost to a moderate Democratic opponent. He learned a lesson from the defeat and revised his stance to a more moderate platform before making his second attempt at the Senate in 1966.

This strategy worked. He won the 1966 senatorial election in Tennessee. He was the first Republican to be elected from that state since the Civil War. Additionally he earned the distinction as the first Republican Senator elected by popular vote in Tennessee.

Observers sometimes criticized his moderate political philosophies and suggested that he lacked decisiveness. In retrospect it is clear that despite Baker's moderate approach to politics, he demonstrated a consistent platform on each specific issue, and he upheld these policies throughout his career.

Baker's conservative views were evident in matters of the courts, and he strongly endorsed military spending and initiatives to strengthen the national defense.

On other issues he took a liberal standpoint. For example, he was known to back almost every civil rights legislation to come before the Senate, and he took a significant interest in environmental issues. As a member of the Senate Public Works Committee he was instrumental in developing clean air and water legislation in 1970 and again in 1972. The committee also championed the highway bill, a legisla-

tive initiative to foster mass transit. In keeping with his middle-of-the-road philosophy, and as a concession to industry, Baker supported the building of a natural gas pipeline between Alaska and the continental U.S. in the 1970s.

Baker disliked "big government." He was always a staunch supporter of any revenue sharing initiative that would force the federal government to allocate revenues to the states on a regular basis. He worked most diligently for revenue sharing until the passage of the Revenue Sharing Act of 1972.

In foreign affairs Baker threw his support behind Presidents Nixon and Ford during the 1970s. Baker was a member of the Senate Foreign Relations Committee. He favored the development of anti-ballistic missiles (ABM), and the Trident missile program. While he opposed the withdrawal of troops from southeast Asia during the late 1960s and early 1970s, he sternly opposed the bombing of Cambodia and Laos in 1973.

Watergate

Baker gained national recognition in 1973 as the co-chairman of the Senate Select Committee on Presidential Activities. The committee was formed to investigate the notorious Watergate scandal that ultimately led to the resignation of President Richard Nixon, under threat of impeachment. The Watergate investigation involved the discovery of numerous cover-ups by Nixon's White House aides during the campaign to re-elect President Nixon in 1972. President Nixon's closest advisers and confidants were indicted for involvement in the conspiracy. Some were convicted, and they spent time in prison.

Baker was a close ally of Nixon and was actively involved in Nixon's first successful campaign for the presidential candidacy in the late 1960s, yet Baker remained impartial during the investigation. In doing so he garnered approval from Democrats and Republicans alike. They praised him for his handling of the politically charged probe. Baker was not only impartial but thorough in delving into the mysteries of the Watergate affair. Given the conspiracy nature of the charges, the close relationship that once flourished between Baker and Nixon, and the powerful position that Baker held as chairman of the committee, it was exceptional to think that Baker refused to abet the cover-up and searched for the truth instead.

Not all of Washington approved of Baker's impeccable honesty and investigative skill, however. Conservative Republican factions in Washington were dismayed when Baker, on a separate occasion, served on a similar panel to investigate the Central Intelligence Agency (CIA). Baker's role in the CIA probe, combined with his non-partisan scrutiny of the Watergate affair, did not sit well with some of his colleagues.

New Political Challenges

In 1969 and again in 1971, Baker failed in his first two bids to be elected to the minority leadership of the Senate. He ran successfully in 1977, however, after the Republican debacle over the Watergate scandal: President Nixon had since resigned under threat of impeachment, and the Republicans lost the presidential election of 1976. The party needed an unspoiled image to help the public to forget the unpleasant days of the Watergate hearings. Baker provided that image. His tenure as minority leader lasted four years, from 1977 until 1981.

In 1979 Baker made a bid for the 1980 Republican presidential nomination. As a perennial opponent of big government, he ran on a platform of limited government controls. He promoted a four-year plan to cut income taxes, and he staunchly opposed wage and price controls for industry. He favored cutbacks in federal spending and the imposition of spending limits for the federal government, and he supported a "windfall profits" tax for oil companies to pay on excessive profits.

By March of 1980 it was clear that former actor and California Governor Ronald Reagan would win the Republican nomination, but Baker was under consideration as a vice-presidential candidate on the Reagan ticket. He never did receive the vice-presidential nomination, but a landslide victory by Ronald Reagan in the election of 1980 brought with it the added benefit of a Republican majority in the Senate. Baker won reelection as the Republican Party leader, to become the Senate Majority Leader in 1981. Two years later he was elected once again. He served as Majority Leader of the Senate until he retired from the legislature in 1985.

The Reagan Years

With Reagan in the White House, Baker proved to be a political asset to the President on more than one occasion. He came to Reagan's defense in support of cutbacks in defense spending, an issue which antagonized the conservative Republican members of the legislature. With a bigger issue at stake (the need to balance the federal budget), Baker publicly criticized Reagan's opponents and accused them [of] "voting with their money . . . voting the wrong way . . . playing a dangerous game," according to a report by Peter McGrath, Rich Thomas, and Henry Hubbard of *Newsweek.*

Baker retired from the legislature in 1985. In the wake of an 18-year senatorial career, he never left Washington, D.C., altogether. In 1987 Reagan appointed Baker as White House Chief of Staff to replace the ousted Donald Regan. Baker held the position until 1988, and his talent for compromise proved invaluable during that time. He helped to quell public furor over the Iran-Contra scandal that erupted during the Reagan Administration. Iran-Contra was a notorious affair that implicated the United States government in a scheme to procure arms from Central American rebels and then re-sell the weapons to hostile governments in the middle east.

The incident was aggravated because President Reagan insisted that he could not remember whether or not he had authorized any part of the deal. Howard Baker's calm disposition and professional demeanor, combined with his affinity for compromise, proved invaluable in calming Democratic demands for an impeachment investigation. In *The Acting President,* Bob Schieffer and Gary Paul Gates observed, "Baker's forte was the art of conciliation."

Personal Notes

Baker lives with his wife in Tennessee. He maintains an office in Washington, D.C., where he is involved with the tobacco lobby. He is an accomplished photographer in his own right. His book, *Big South Fork Country,* (1993) is a pictorial essay on the Big South Fork National River on the Tennessee-Kentucky Border. The river is nicknamed the "Yosemite of the East."

There are many stories about Baker's good nature and his sense of humor. One report in *People,* quoted the invitations he sent for his wedding rehearsal in 1966. The invitations read like the U.S. Constitution, "In order to form a more perfect union."

Another story surfaced in 1984. It was rumored in *50 Plus* that the *New York Times* reported that Baker was listed among the "10 best dressed men" in a list compiled by a dubious trade organization called the Tailors Council of America. Baker knew it was a joke, and he admitted candidly, "I am a slob. I want to say that I have absolutely no taste in clothes."

Baker's personal and political style was summed up by his stepmother, who was quoted by Schieffer and Gates, "Howard is like the Tennessee River. He flows right down the middle."

Further Reading

Cannon, Lou, *Reagan,* G.P. Putnam's Sons, 1982.
Schieffer, Bob, and Gary Paul Gates, *The Acting President,* G.P. Putnam's Sons, 1982.
Schoenebaum, Eleanora W., Ph.D. (editor), *Political Profiles: Nixon/Ford years,* Facts on File, 1979.
World Almanac Biographical Dictionary, World Almanac, 1990.
50 Plus, March 1984, p. 11.
Fortune, January 24, 1983, p. 35(2).
Newsweek, September 31, 1961, pp. 26-28.
People, December 23, 1996, p. 88.
U.S. News & World Report, February 11, 1980; January 31, 1983, p. 18(2).

Walter Bedell Smith

General Walter Bedell Smith (1895-1961) distinguished himself during World War II as chief of staff to General Dwight D. Eisenhower. Immediately after the war, he was the ambassador to the Soviet Union and, from 1950-53, he directed the Central Intelligence Agency.

Bedell Smith's military career began in 1911 when he joined the Indiana National Guard and ended almost 40 years later when he retired as a four-star general in the U.S. Army. Initially, he envisioned himself fighting battles on the front lines but because of his impressive organizational skills, he ended up working for General George C. Marshall, the chairman of the joint chiefs of staff and the head of America's military forces after the president.

By 1942, Bedell Smith was sent to Europe to be the chief of staff to General Eisenhower. As the allies fought in North Africa, Italy, France, and Germany, Bedell Smith was known by top military and political leaders as an effective and efficient manager. After the war, however, he was comparatively less successful as ambassador to the Soviet Union, director of the Central Intelligence Agency, and, briefly, undersecretary of state. Finally, Bedell Smith left the military to make a fortune working with corporations that manufactured and supplied war materiel.

Middle-Class Upbringing

Walter Bedell Smith was born in Indianapolis of a family Bedell Smith himself described as "normal, substantial middle class." His childhood consisted mostly of household chores and outside activities such as fishing, baseball, and roller skating, while his father worked as a silk buyer for a dry goods company. He did not show much interest in studying, however, and, since his grades were not high, he was unable to attend the nearby Catholic high school. Instead, he went to the Emmerich Manual Training High School—a vocational school where he learned to be a machinist. He found employment at a local automobile manufacturer. He also worked as a soda jerk and a mechanic for a company that supplied equipment to the railroads.

Yet young Bedell Smith's dream was to become a soldier. A member of his family had served in every American war going back to the Revolution. Therefore, when he turned 16 years old, Bedell Smith joined the Indiana National Guard. The monthly mustering of his unit became the

center of his life. Bedell Smith was first called away from home when his National Guard unit was needed in the spring of 1913 to help during a time of serious flooding. A few months later, his unit was needed again to restore order when the streetcar operators went on strike. Bedell Smith's exemplary service during this time came to the attention of his commanding officers, and he was promoted to corporal and, shortly afterwards, company sergeant. A few years later, military trouble in Mexico spilled over into the United States, forcing President Woodrow Wilson to federalize National Guard units and use them to secure the American-Mexican border. But Bedell Smith was now the primary supporter of his family, due to his father's ill health, and he had to stay behind in Indiana while his unit went south. However, back in Indiana, he gained his first experience doing military staff work.

When the United States entered World War I in 1917, Bedell Smith was recommended by his company commander to attend officer training school. At the end of training school, he was a lieutenant in the U.S. Army and, just before Christmas of 1917, was sent to Camp Greene, NC, to become part of the Fourth Infantry. Approximately four months later, Bedell Smith was on a ship headed for France. After quick training by British and French forces, he saw action when his unit became part of a combined Franco-American counteroffensive against German positions. Bedell Smith was wounded during the fighting and after recovering from his wounds, he was assigned to the reorganized and expanded War Department General Staff in Washington, D.C., based primarily on the staff work he had done for the Indiana National Guard. He became part of the new Bureau of Military Intelligence and, when World War I ended, he was selected to remain on active duty.

Between the Wars

During the 1920s and 1930s, Bedell Smith's promotion through the military ranks seemed frustratingly slow. He served in various staff positions nationwide, as well as in the Philippine Islands. Army officials eventually decided that he was best suited as a teacher and assigned him to be a student instructor at a succession of military schools. He also attended the Leavenworth Command and General Staff Schools and the Army War College in Washington, D.C. By 1939, Bedell Smith was a major. Old military institutions and old officers had given way to the new reorganized military preparing for another possible war with Germany. Bedell Smith was promoted to the headquarters of Army Chief of Staff George C. Marshall in Washington, D.C. His work there earned him promotions to the rank of colonel and a position as secretary of the general staff. In this role, he helped formulate allied strategy and was considered part of Marshall's inner circle.

Shortly before World War II, Bedell Smith was known as a capable, efficient organizer. After the attack on Pearl Harbor and America's entry into the war, Bedell Smith put in long hours in support of Marshall. His staff work came to the attention of General Dwight D. Eisenhower, who was to become the supreme commander of the allied forces. He wanted Bedell Smith as his chief of staff in Europe. Eisenhower valued Bedell Smith's abilities and the relationship Bedell Smith had developed with Marshall. Reluctantly, Marshall let Bedell Smith go to Europe in September 1942.

Eisenhower's Manager

During World War II, Bedell Smith was promoted to a brigadier-general in February of 1942, major-general in December of 1942, and lieutenant-general in January of 1943. He gained a reputation as quick-tempered, harsh, and arbitrary, but no one questioned his genius as Eisenhower's chief of staff. He became Eisenhower's gatekeeper. He decided who would see Eisenhower. He handled Eisenhower's diplomatic duties and frequently represented Eisenhower at meetings.

In addition, he was closely involved in the plans for allied forces to wrest control of North Africa and Sicily from Nazi Germany. He was also involved in the decisions leading up to the Normandy invasion and the subsequent operations in Europe. Allied military leaders and political leaders, including President Franklin D. Roosevelt and British Prime Minister Winston Churchill, knew of Bedell Smith and admired his clear grasp of military strategy. His operation of Eisenhower's staff is believed to have contributed to allied successes in the war. Eisenhower himself recognized his chief of staff's contributions and asked him to arrange the surrender with Germany and sign the German surrender documents with German General Alfred Jodl at Eisenhower's headquarters in Belgium on May 7, 1945.

Assignments After the War

Bedell Smith was at the peak of his military career when the war ended. But the subsequent time of peace led to disappointment for him. He was passed over to assume command of American forces in Europe. As relations with Russia worsened, President Harry Truman desired an ambassador in Moscow whom the Soviets would not push around. He chose Bedell Smith. Although he retained his military rank as a major-general, Bedell Smith thus began his career as a diplomat. His first job was to attend the Paris Peace Conference in 1946 as part of the American delegation. During his three years as ambassador, he carried out his duties in a soldierlike manner. Unfortunately, this did not allay Soviet fears of American intentions. Soviet-American relations continued to deteriorate. Bedell Smith later wrote a book, entitled *My Three Years in Moscow,* in which he stated that the differences between the Soviets and Americans were irreconcilable. "We [the United States] are [being] forced into a continued struggle for a free way of life that might extend over a period of many years," he wrote.

In March 1949, Bedell Smith turned down an offer to serve as Truman's undersecretary of state for European affairs, hoping to advance his military career further. Instead, he was assigned command of the First Army on Governor's Island, NY. Although he attained the rank of a four-star general with the assignment, he considered this a dead-end job for officers on the verge of retirement. Three times, however, he was offered the position as director of the Central Intelligence Agency (CIA), based on his experiences as ambassador in Moscow. He turned down the offer twice

but told Eisenhower that since the intelligence organization had not foreseen the problems that had developed with the Communists in Korea, he could not refuse the third time.

The performance of the CIA shortly after World War II had been poor and did not improve with Bedell Smith as director. Bedell Smith had earned a reputation as an expert on Communist activities, but he endorsed the view that the Chinese would never intervene in the Korean War, based on intelligence he received from the military. When they did, United Nations forces in Korea were unprepared. Neither did the CIA accurately characterize problems in Iran, a revolution in Egypt, and coups in Latin America.

His problems in the CIA were made worse by his loathing of Communism. He hated the Soviets, and this made him intolerant of anyone seeming to accommodate the Communists. He told a Senate committee that the State Department and the CIA had been infiltrated by Communists. His statements gave critics of Truman the ability to label his administration as soft on Communism.

When Eisenhower became president, he asked Bedell Smith to be the undersecretary of state. Bedell Smith accepted out of loyalty to Eisenhower. The president, however, was aware of Bedell Smith's liabilities during peacetime and distanced himself from his former chief of staff. In addition, secretary of state John Foster Dulles saw Bedell Smith as a threat. Consequently, Bedell Smith was never promoted within the Eisenhower administration. With his health deteriorating, he resigned on October 1, 1954.

Military-Industrial Leader

Once retired from politics, Bedell Smith decided to use his connections to make money. By the end of October 1954, he was the director of a fruit company that he had given preferential treatment to as undersecretary of state while managing a Guatemalan coup that, once resolved, increased the company's profits. By 1958, in another instance of seeming conflict of interest, Bedell Smith was appointed special advisor to the secretary of state on disarmament while serving as president and chairman of the board of two weapon-manufacturing companies with Pentagon contracts. He was also vice-chairman of the American Machine and Foundry Company and director of RCA and Corning Glass. As a result, Bedell Smith became one of the first major military-industrial leaders during the Cold War.

On August 6, 1961, Bedell Smith died of a heart attack in Washington, D.C. He had amassed $2.5 million. After a simple funeral, with military honors, his body was taken to Arlington National Cemetery where he was buried.

Further Reading

Ancell, R. Manning and Miller, Christine M., *Biographical Dictionary of World War II Generals and Flag Officers: U.S. Armed Forces,* Greenwood Press, 1996.
Crosswell, D.R.K., *Chief of Staff: Military Career of General Walter Bedell Smith,* Greenwood Press, 1991.
Leckie, Robert, *Story of World War II,* Random House, 1964.
Mason, David, *Who's Who in World War II,* Weidenfeld and Nicolson, 1978.

Oxford Companion to World War II, edited by I.C.B. Dear, Oxford University Press, 1995.

Who Was Who in World War II, Arms & Armour Press, 1990.

"Walter Bedell Smith," *Office of the Director of Central Intelligence,* http://www.odci.gov/cia/publications/dci/dcis/smith.html (March 13, 1998).

Aphra Behn

English poet, novelist, and playwright Aphra Behn (c. 1640-1689) was the first of her gender to earn a living as a writer in the English language.

Aphra Behn was a successful author at a time when few writers, especially if they were women, could support themselves solely through their writing. For the flourishing London stage she penned numerous plays, and found success as a novelist and poet as well—and through much of her work ran a decidedly feminist strain that challenged society's restrictions upon women of her day. For this she was scorned, and she endured criticism and even arrest at times. Another similarly free-thinking female novelist of a more recent era, Virginia Woolf, declared that "all women together ought to let flowers fall upon the tomb of Aphra Behn," according to Carol Howard's essay on Behn in the *Dictionary of Literary Biography,* ". . .for it was she who earned them the right to speak their minds."

A Childhood in Kent

It is likely that Behn was the infant girl Eaffry Johnson, born in late 1640 according to baptismal records from the church of St. Michael's in Harbledown, a small village near Canterbury, England. This region of England, Kent, was a conservative, insular county during Behn's youth, but the English realm itself was anything but calm during her era; Behn's fortunes and alliances would be tied to the series of political crises that occurred during the seventeenth century, and her literary output drew from and even satirized the vying factions. First came a Civil War that pitted Puritans against King Charles I; the monarchy was abolished with the king's beheading in 1649. Until 1658 England was ruled by Puritan revolt leader Oliver Cromwell, and upon his death in 1658 the monarchy was restored; hence the term for the era in which Behn wrote, Restoration England.

Behn was likely the daughter of a barber and a wet-nurse, and through her mother's care for the children of local landed gentry, the Colepeppers, Behn probably had access to some educational opportunities. Literary scholars agree that Behn most likely left England as a young woman with her family in 1663 when her father was appointed to a military post in Surinam, on the northeast coast of South America. It was an arduous journey, and some evidence suggests that Behn's father did not survive the trip. In any event, Behn, her mother, and sister stayed on at the English settlement for a time until a return trip home was possible,

and the experience provided the basis for her most famous literary work, *Oroonoko; or, The Royal Slave.*

Oroonoko in the Annals of English Literature

This novel, published only near the end of Behn's career in 1688, chronicles the tale of a cultivated, intelligent West African prince who speaks several European languages. He falls in love with a West Indian woman named Imoinda, who is also the lover of his grandfather, the king. Imoinda is sold into slavery, and Oroonoko is kidnapped by the English and brought to Surinam as a slave. Imoinda is also in Surinam and becomes pregnant by him. Oroonoko then leads a slave rebellion—an actual event from the era—but is captured, and falsely promised freedom for Imoinda and her unborn child. When this is rescinded, he kills her so she and his child will not fall into enemy hands, and dies by rather barbarous means in English hands at the conclusion. Some of the villains and heroes were actual names from the period, English men who held posts in Surinam before it became a Dutch colony.

Literary historians trace the development of realism in the novel back this 1688 volume. Realism is a literary style that uses real life as the basis for fiction, without idealizing it or imbuing it with a romantic bias, and it became prevalent in the nineteenth century. Behn's *Oroonoko* has also been termed groundbreaking for its depiction of the institution of slavery as cruel and inhumane, making it one of literary history's first abolitionist proclamations. Behn has been praised for her characterization of Oroonoko, a just and decent man who encounters some very cruel traits among his white enemies; critics point to him as European literature's first portrayal of the "noble savage."

Astrea the Spy

England's troubles with Holland played a decisive part in Behn's fortunes as a young woman. Following her return to England in 1664, she met and married a Dutch merchant by the name of Hans Behn. Though it has been hinted that her brief marriage may have been her own fiction—widows were more socially respectable than single women during her era—other sources indicate the unfortunate Hans Behn died in an outbreak of the bubonic plague that swept through London in 1665. Later, many of Behn's works satirized Dutch merchants, the cultural icons of the era when Holland was growing rich from trade and giving birth to the first class of savvy capitalists. Behn may have been well-off herself for a time, and became a favorite at the Court of Charles II for her ebullient personality and witty repartee.

But then Behn's fortunes took a turn for the worse. It appears that she suddenly became destitute—perhaps after her husband died—and in 1666 was summoned into the service of the King as an agent in the war against Holland. She went to Antwerp to renew contact with a former lover, William Scot, who was a spy in the city; Scot was an Englishman who was involved in an expatriate group who once again wanted to abolish the monarchy. Behn's mission was to get him to switch sides, and to send reports on behalf of Charles II back to England in invisible ink using the code name "Astrea." During her work as an infiltrator Behn learned of plans to annihilate the English fleet in the Thames and, in June of 1667, Dutch naval forces did so. Yet her English spymasters left her virtually abandoned in a foreign enemy nation with no money—for a woman in the seventeenth century, this necessitated a very distressing and extreme crisis. She probably borrowed a sum, managed to return to England, and still was unremunerated by Charles II. Her numerous pleading letters, which still survive, were met with silence. She landed in debtor's prison in 1668, but at this point someone paid her debt and she was released.

Writing as a Profession

It was at this juncture that Behn resolved to support herself. She moved to London, and took up writing in earnest—not a revolutionary act at the time for a woman, but to expect to make a living at it certainly was. In Behn's day, a woman possessed no assets, could not enter into contracts herself, and was essentially powerless. Financial support came from a woman's father, and then her husband. Some well-born women escaped such strictures by becoming mistresses; others did so by entering a convent. The Restoration was a somewhat debauched period in English history, however, and its libertine ways were well-documented. Behn's ambitions coincided with the revival of the London stage; the Civil War had darkened the city's already-famed theaters in the 1640s and the London plague further shuttered them, but as England regained stability Charles II re-instituted the two main companies. Behn began writing for one of them, Duke's Company at Dorset Garden, and her first play was produced in September of 1670. *The Forc'd Marriage; or, The Jealous Bridegroom* ran for six nights, a successful run, since playwrights usually went unpaid until the third evening's box-office take. The plot concerned a romantic comedy of errors, which was standard fare for the day.

Behn would pen a number of works for the stage over the next dozen years. Most were lighthearted tales of thwarted love and cavalier seduction. These included *The Amorous Prince; or, The Curious Husband* (1671); *The Dutch Lover* (1673), with its vicious caricature of a Dutch merchant; *Abdelazer; or, The Moor's Revenge* (1676); and her most successful play, *The Rover; or, the Banish'd Cavaliers.* This 1677 work is centered around an English regiment living in exile in Italy during the Cromwell era; one of its officers, Willmore, is the "rover" of the title, a libidinous sort for whom Behn seemed to have modeled on the similarly randy Charles II.

Found Fodder in Restoration Foibles

One of her final plays, *The Roundheads; or, The Good Old Cause,* was produced in 1682 and achieved notoriety for the way in which Behn's pen ridiculed a faction of republican parliamentarians. But Behn's strong opinions landed her in trouble that same year when she was arrested for writing a polemic on the Duke of Monmouth, Charles II's illegitimate son and claimant to the throne. This also coincided with a merging of London's two main theaters and a subsequent decline of the medium. Behn then turned to writing novels. One of her best-known works was published in three volumes between 1684 and 1687, and was based on an actual scandal of the time. *Love-Letters Between a Nobleman and His Sister* was a thinly-disguised fictional treatment of the antics of one Lord Grey, who in 1682 eloped with his wife's sister; Grey was a Whig, or anti-monarchist, and would go on to play a real-life role in other political machinations between the throne and Parliament.

Behn's other novels include *The Lucky Chance; or, An Alderman's Bargain* (1686); a 1688 tale of a clever and remorseless woman serving as a spy in Holland, *The Fair Jilt; or, The History of Prince Tarquin and Miranda;* and *The History of the Nun; or, The Fair Vow-Breaker* from the same year. This last work was Behn's fictional saga of Isabella, who breaks her vow of chastity, marries two men, and in the end slays them both. In the twilight years of her brief career, Behn earned a living from Latin and French translations, and also penned versions of *Aesop's Fables* and poetry—some of which was quite racy. Yet she still struggled financially, and historians surmise that her lack of funds forced her to submit to substandard medical care when her health began to decline, which only worsened the situation. During the winter of 1683-1684, she was involved in a carriage accident, and also may have been plagued by arthritic joints; from some of her letters it can be inferred that she was also suffering from some sort of serious illness that may have been syphilis.

Behn died on April 16, 1689. She was buried in the cloisters at Westminster Abbey, and her admirers paid for a tombstone with an epitaph that read: "Here lies a proof that wit can never be/Defence enough against mortality," which she probably penned herself. Behn's literary reputation then sunk into obscurity for the next few centuries, and in England's Victorian era she was vilified. In 1871 a collection of her works, *Plays, Histories, and Novels of the Ingenious Mrs. Aphra Behn,* appeared in print, and the *Saturday Review,* a leading London periodical of the time, condemned it as a sordid assemblage. The reviewer noted that any person curious about the forgotten Behn and her infamous works will "find it all here, as rank and feculent as when first produced." It was not until well into the twentieth century that literary scholarship restored Behn's contribution to English letters. "Aphra Behn is worth reading," wrote her 1968 biographer Frederick M. Link, "not because she ends or begins an era, or contributes significantly to the development of a literary genre or to the progress of an idea, but because she is an entertaining craftsman whose life and work reflect nearly every facet of a brilliant period in English literary history."

Further Reading

Dictionary of Literary Biography, Volume 39: *British Novelists, 1660-1800,* Gale, 1985.

Duffy, Maureen, *The Passionate Shepherdess: Aphra Behn, 1640-89,* Jonathan Cape, 1977.

Link, Frederick M., *Aphra Behn,* Twayne, 1968.

Literature Criticism from 1400 to 1800, Volume 1, Gale, 1984.

Todd, Janet, *The Secret Life of Aphra Behn,* Rutgers University Press, 1996.

Saturday Review, January 27, 1872.

Ben & Jerry

Both born in Brooklyn, New York, Bennett Cohen (born 1951) and Jerry Greenfield (born 1951) were lifelong friends who would go on to establish one of the most successful American ice cream brands of all time—Ben & Jerry's Homemade.

Ben Cohen (left) and Jerry Greenfield (right)

Bennett Cohen and Jerry Greenfield established Ben & Jerry's Homemade, a popular American ice cream brand. Yet Ben & Jerry's Homemade evolved into more than just a company producing such premium offerings as Holy Cannoli! and New York Super Fudge Chunk—its founders who had inadvertently become business moguls realized they were indeed swimming in shark-infested waters. Cohen and Greenfield's struggle to adapt their own Sixties-era personal values—the ideas of tolerance, of giving back to the community, and respect for the individual—has not been an easy one at times for the reluctant executives, but one that has consistently landed their company on lists of the most employee-friendly workplaces in the United States.

The Ben & Jerry's Homemade ice cream empire that gained a national cult following during the 1980s had its origins in a suburban New York junior high school. The families of Bennett Cohen and Jerry Greenfield were each refugees from Brooklyn. The boys met in the gym class at their Merrick, Long Island, school in the early 1960s. It was a friendship, both would later joke, based on their mutual status as misfits—the overweight kids who were forced to run track. They remained friends though high school and both graduated from Merrick's Calhoun High in the late 1960s.

Cohen then enrolled in Colgate University, but uninspired by college life, he dropped out in his sophomore year. However, during his high school years, Cohen had driven an ice-cream truck in the suburban idylls of Long Island, and it was a mission he now happily returned to since he needed work. He began taking unusual college courses that reflected his interests—pottery and jewelry-making, for instance, and over the next few years held a series of equally unusual jobs. These included a stint in the emergency room of New York City's notorious Bellevue Hospital and another as a Pinkerton guard at the Saratoga Raceway.

Greenfield had spent his college years in Ohio, and the pair lost contact for a while. A National Merit Scholar in high school, Greenfield had hoped to become a doctor. He studied pre-med at Oberlin College but was rejected when he applied to medical school. He moved back to New York City and took a job as a lab technician, grinding up cow hearts inside test tubes in a research facility. At that time, he shared an apartment with Cohen on East 10th Street. Greenfield again applied to medical school but was rejected again. From 1974 to 1976 he lived in North Carolina with his future wife, Elizabeth, and upon his return found Ben in Saratoga Springs, New York, where he worked as an art

therapist at a center for emotionally disturbed children. Reviving an old dream of beginning their own food enterprise together, the duo signed up for a correspondence course in ice-cream-making from Pennsylvania State University.

Ben and Jerry received "A"s in the $5 course (it was an open-book exam), and forged ahead with their plan to open their own ice-cream parlor. Since Saratoga Springs already had one, they packed up and moved to an old gas station in Burlington, Vermont, a college town they both liked. They used their savings—a combined $8,000—and borrowed another $4,000 to open "Ben & Jerry's Scoop Shop" in May of 1978. It was an immediate success and soon a favorite spot in Burlington. Greenfield made most of the ice cream, while Cohen handled all the other aspects of the operation. From the start, they began developing their own wild flavors—inspired by the ice cream, cookie, and candy concoctions Cohen used to mix up as a kid—and gained a cult following that soon began to spread outside Burlington.

Ben and Jerry's ice-cream enterprise became known for its instigation of fun, community-oriented projects. A free outdoor movie night was one such event, along with giving away free cones on the anniversary of their store's opening. Though their civic spirit was in the right place, Cohen and Greenfield did not quite grasp the profit-and-loss part of running a business. They eventually hired a successful Burlington nightclub entrepreneur, Fred "Chico" Lager, to take control of the books, deal with suppliers, and forge ahead with expansion plans.

By 1980, Cohen and Greenfield had found an old spool and bobbin mill to rent as a home for their larger-scale ice cream production and packing operations. A distributorship route was set up to deliver to grocery and small family-owned specialty stores in the region. Cohen became the designated delivery person and carted the frozen goods in the back of his Volkswagen station wagon. In 1981, the cult following surrounding their exquisitely rich, addictive flavors—such as Heath Bar Crunch and Dastardly Mash—achieved mainstream approval when Time began a cover story on ice cream with an opening sentence stating that Ben & Jerry's was the best in the world.

Over the next few years, the Ben & Jerry's Homemade company began opening franchises elsewhere in New England, and gained a wider distribution in stores. But the pressures of running what had become an extremely profitable, ever-expanding ice-cream empire were taking their toll on the founders, who were anything but profit-oriented, executive types. For a time, Greenfield left the day-to-day business, moving to Arizona with Elizabeth as she pursued a graduate degree. He returned in 1985, not long after Cohen had put the company on the market—he was also uncomfortable with the changes that running a successful business had forced upon his beliefs—but then changed his mind and decided to keep it.

That year marked a turning point for Cohen and Greenfield. With a new sense of mission, they vowed to adapt their business to suit their philosophies—rather than letting their business concerns dictate their ideology. This was partially accomplished by the establishment of the Ben & Jerry Foundation, which received 7.5 percent of the ice cream company's pre-tax profits and then donated them to the community through various charitable organizations. Long known as friendly, concerned bosses, the duo tried to enshrine such attitudes into company policy. To work at a Ben & Jerry's outlet or plant was to become part of a team, where each individual was valued. Respect for employees took a far greater precedence than any corporate or profit-oriented concerns.

Such a liberal spirit, combined with the overwhelming success of the actual Ben & Jerry product, earned the company an enemy—food giant Pillsbury, which owned the Haagen-Dazs premium ice cream brand. Haagen-Dazs had achieved success in many markets, but its primary competition was the Ben & Jerry brand. Pillsbury attempted, via legal channels, to stop Ben & Jerry ice cream outlets from opening near theirs, and also forced Ben & Jerry's to file suit against them when Pillsbury put pressure on outside suppliers who sold to both companies. Reflecting upon their own anti-corporate spirit, Ben & Jerry's launched a media offensive centered around the slogan, "What's the Doughboy Afraid Of?," in reference to the Pillsbury's cuddly emblem.

By 1986, Cohen and Greenfield's business was reporting sales of $20 million annually. New flavors attracted more Ben & Jerry devotees every year, and some of the additions to the roster were suggestions sent in to the company. Cherry Garcia, for example, was a fruity homage to

the Grateful Dead lead singer Jerry Garcia that had come from two followers of the band; New York Super Fudge Chunk had been the idea of a chocaholic New York writer. Meanwhile, the founders continued to concentrate much of their energies on setting an example of giving back to the community—in this case, the global community. For some ingredients—cashews from Brazil, blueberries from Maine—the company began a policy of purchasing from indigenous peoples and paying a fair rate. Closer to home, a "Partnershop" with a Harlem shelter for homeless men opened in 1992; the ice cream shop is staffed by residents and the shelter receives 75 percent of the store's profits.

Another example of such commitment to their ideals was the Ben & Jerry Foundation's "1 percent for Peace" drive. This was a non-profit organization that actively worked to redirect one percent of the United States military budget to life-improving—not life-taking—goals. Their Peace Pops, introduced that same year, served as a marketing tool for the foundation, providing information on the 1 percent for Peace campaign and directing the interested toward action. A voter registration drive and taking on the sponsorship for the failing counterculture staple, Rhode Island's Newport Jazz Festival, were other typical Ben & Jerry corporate activities during this era.

In 1988, Cohen and Greenfield received the Corporate Giving Award from the Council on Economic Priorities for their Ben & Jerry Foundation. That same year, the iconoclastic pair was named Small Business Leaders of the Year by President Ronald Reagan and attended an award ceremony at the White House. Over the next few years, as their business suffered the ups and downs of market demand—a diet-conscious public had begun to eschew premium ice cream for lowfat versions or frozen yogurt—Ben & Jerry's Homemade continued to back their philosophies with concrete actions. In one 1991 episode derided by the mainstream business periodical Fortune, they paid above-market prices to their local milk suppliers after cutbacks in a federal dairy-subsidy program caused market prices to drop severely. This had brought some hardship to many small dairy farmers—Vermont's among them—but instead of profiting from the decline, Ben & Jerry's Homemade made a decision to show explicit support for small, people-oriented businesses like their own.

In 1992 Ben & Jerry's Homemade was awarded the Optimas "Quality of Life" Award from Personnel Journal for growing into a company that had created an unusually nurturing workplace. High wages and excellent benefits consistently landed the company on lists of the best companies in America at which to work. At the production plant and offices, workers are subject to an unusual corporate entity initiated by Greenfield known as the "Joy Gang." This group is made up of employees whose mission is to inject a bit of zaniness into the workday on a random basis through such actions as prizes or a surprise party for the late shift at the plant.

Ben & Jerry's 700 employees also enjoy on-site daycare, a health club, and a generous profit-sharing plan. Since 1989, the company also offers benefits to domestic partners and management is encouraged to dress as casual as plant employees. On one occasion, a slowdown dictated a three-month hiatus for one shift at the plant; instead of laying off the workers, Ben & Jerry's kept them on the payroll to do odd jobs, as well as community service ventures such as painting the town's fire hydrants and winterizing the homes of senior citizens. It is also policy to allow employees paid time off to do volunteer work, and perhaps best of all, each is allowed to take home three free pints a day of the company product.

Cohen and Greenfield's innovations in what they call "values-led" capitalism has also earned them praise for their early efforts at recycling at their facilities, a mission also encouraged on their packaging. Their idea of "caring capitalism," Greenfield explained in an interview with *USA Today*'s Ellen Neuborne, means a plan "where you consider effects on the community alongside products and profits." The pair has penned a book on this theme—*Ben & Jerry's Double Dip: Lead with Your Values and Make Money, Too,* published in 1997.

Cohen resigned as chief executive officer (CEO) in June of 1994, but remains chair of the board and invents new ice cream flavors. To replace him, Ben & Jerry's launched a well-publicized campaign called "Yo! I Want to be CEO!" The interested were invited to send a postcard telling why they would make an ideal executive leader of Ben & Jerry's Homemade. They eventually settled on a rather traditional corporate chief discovered through an executive-search firm.

Greenfield remains vice-chair of the board and director of mobile promotions. He and Cohen own 42 percent of the Ben & Jerry voting stock and devote much of their time to an organization called Businesses for Social Responsibility, of which Cohen is a founding member. "It's ironic that when we started, [naysayers] said all our social concerns would be our undoing," Greenfield told in *USA Today*'s Neuborne. "Now everyone agrees it works, and we made the business work. Now they say it's just a way to hype ice cream. It's a journey."

Further Reading

Cohen, Ben, and Jerry Greenfield, *Ben & Jerry's Double Dip: Lead with Your Values and Make Money, Too,* Simon and Schuster, 1997.
Lager, Fred, *Ben & Jerry's, the Inside Scoop: How Two Real Guys Built a Business with Social Conscience and a Sense of Humor,* Crown, 1994.
Newsmakers, 1991 Cumulation, Gale, 1991.
Business Week, July 15, 1996, pp. 70-71.
Fortune, June 3, 1991, pp. 247-248.
Personnel Journal, November 1992.
USA Today, April 30, 1996, p. 4B.
http://www.benjerry.com □

Milton Berle

American comedian Milton Berle (born 1908), known as "Mr. Television," has given the world a rich entertainment legacy stretching from the days of vaudeville to radio and television.

Few actors and entertainers have contributed as much to as many facets—or entire eras—of show business as Milton Berle. In a life that has filled most of the twentieth century and a career that has spanned over 80 years, Berle applied his enormous energy and talent to every area of show business except burlesque. Never afraid of change, he took professional risks that other stars avoided. Acknowledging his accomplishments is to chronicle the evolution of entertainment, particularly comedy in twentieth century America. His career began as a child actor in silent movies and plays on the stage, and proceeded to vaudeville and night clubs where he developed an original style that made his name in comedy. Known as "Mr. Television," Berle is credited for bringing entertainment into the living rooms of America, and doing more than any other single person to make television the medium of choice. By the 1930s his star status was well established, but the advent of television and his launch of *Texaco Star Theater* in 1948, TV's first hit show, catapulted him into show business history and onto the covers of *Time* and *Newsweek* magazines. By 1949, Berle was embedded into the minds of several generations, and well on his way to becoming a household name as "Uncle Miltie." He received one of the first Emmy Awards ever given for starring in NBC's *Texaco Star Theater* (1948), was the first person to be inducted to the Television Hall of Fame (1984), the first inductee into the Comedy Hall

of Fame (1992), and the first to receive a Lifetime Achievement Award from the New York Television Academy (1996).

Mama's Boy

Even as a young child, Berle was a natural entertainer. Moses and Sarah Berlinger welcomed their fourth child on July 12, 1908, and by the age of six he was winning Charlie Chaplin contests. The talent that didn't come naturally was cultivated by his mother, who became his most ardent supporter. Thanks to her efforts, he had had bit parts in over 50 silent films before he was eight, appearing with many stars of the time including Mary Pickford, Douglas Fairbanks, and Charlie Chaplin.

When the movie business moved west, Berle's mother found work for him in vaudeville kiddie acts—partly out of necessity, and partly to encourage him. Health problems kept his father from working full time in the painting business, and Berle contributed to the family's finances. Berle remembered those early years in a 1996 interview with *Broadcasting & Cable* magazine: "She was the backbone of my career. She forged me and worked on me like a son of a gun. Every place I ever appeared—whether it was vaudeville, theaters, nightclubs or TV—she was in the audience being a one-woman flack for me." In fact, her loud laugh and applause at strategic points in the act became part of the act itself.

At the age of 12, Berle made his debut on the legitimate stage in *Floradora,* and by 16 he was a veteran of vaudeville. According to an interview with John Hughes for the *Orange County Register,* he also had an eye for the good life, and smoked his first cigar in 1920 at the tender age of 12. It wasn't long before he started his own vaudeville group and became master of ceremonies. By his own admission, he was "a smart ass kid, insulting audiences with one liners, such as 'I never liked you and I always will.'" However flip he was on stage, there was never a question about his dedication to perfecting the art of comedy. While other boys his age were collecting baseball cards and thinking about girls, Berle was collecting joke books and honing his craft. But he also pirated other comedians' material so shamelessly that he was called the "Thief of Badgags," according to *Mr. Showbiz.*

Celebrity

Berle worked tirelessly at becoming a master of timing. Some called him a scholar of comedy. He was known as a brash young comic, with a very physical style of humor that included dressing in drag—a trademark "shtick" that stayed with him throughout his career.

In a 1994 documentary produced by the Arts & Entertainment network, Berle talked about patterning himself after one of the great comics of his day, Ted Healy. "He was flattered that I imitated him, and took me aside and said, 'There's no such thing as an old joke. If you haven't heard it before, it's new.'" Thus, Berle felt justified in using other comedians' material, believing that all jokes are public domain.

The mother-son duo was a hit on the vaudeville circuit, with Berle on stage and mom in the audience prompting laughter when she felt a lull. Success followed him wherever he plied his craft: on Broadway as a popular master of ceremonies introducing variety acts, in night clubs around the country with stand up routines, in starring roles with the Ziegfeld Follies, and in Hollywood motion pictures in the 1930s and 1940s. Radio was the least successful of all his ventures. Although he performed on radio, he never enjoyed the same success there. His style was too visual—the raised eyebrow, turned head, a wink, a tap of the ever-present cigar ("cigaahhhhh" as Berle would say)—to be conveyed entirely through voice and innuendo.

Berle's career came first, and his personal life suffered as a result. His first marriage to a show girl, Joyce Matthews was stormy. They married in 1941, divorced, remarried, and divorced again in 1947. Berle was obsessed with getting bigger audiences, and compared himself to other comedians who were attracting big audiences on radio. Apparently, money was not enough, as it was widely known that Berle was one of the most highly paid comedians in the business. He was always ready to try something new, and in 1948 went to Chicago to do one of the first experimental television programs.

The King of Television

With the advent of television, the entertainment world underwent a seismic change, which presented a great opportunity for those willing to take a chance. Berle, along with a few other comedians, took turns hosting the *Texaco Star Theater* during its debut. This show was fast, funny, visual, and live—the perfect showcase for Berle's style of comedy. According to *Variety,* "The fifties is known as the Golden Age of Television in large part because of the variety shows which dominated the early part of the decade. . . . They were just vaudeville on TV." Berle became television's first big star, leading NBC to dub him "Mr. Television."

He got into every aspect of the show, writing, producing, and directing. He could be a tough taskmaster, but his perfectionist tendencies paid off—ratings of *Texaco Star Theater* and *Kraft Music Hall* soared so high that NBC signed him to a 30-year "lifetime" contract in 1951, which paid $100,000 a year, whether he worked or not. Many in the industry credited Berle with television's success because he was able to attract major sponsors. Some even felt he was responsible for selling television sets. Within one season the number of sets in the country increased from 500,000 to one million.

Berle had the country's attention—young and old alike—which is how he inadvertently acquired another nickname, "Uncle Miltie." In an interview with *Hollywood Online,* he explained how he acquired the dubious title: "I received a lot of complaints from parents who wrote and told me that their kids wouldn't go to sleep until our show was over. So I went on the air and told all the children watching to 'listen to their Uncle Miltie and go to bed right after the show.' The next day I was in a parade in Boston and a couple of workmen in hard hats yelled, 'Hi, Uncle Miltie.' I had no idea when I first used it that the name would stick."

Over the years Berle was romantically linked to several of Hollywood's leading ladies, including Lucille Ball and Veronica Lake. The love of his life, however, was Hollywood publicist Ruth Cosgrove, whom he married in 1953. They were devoted to each other for almost 40 years, until she died of cancer.

Berle was the first star to take a risk on TV, but his success led to strong competition. By the mid-fifties, the public's tastes had changed, preferring musical comedies and westerns to variety shows. As television audiences grew, Berle's ratings began to decline, and in 1956 the show was canceled. Berle then concentrated on dramatic acting, appearing in scores of films and made for TV movies, including *It's a Mad Mad Mad Mad World* (1963); *The Oscar* (1965); *Where Angels Go, Trouble Follows* (1968); and *Seven in Darkness* (1970).

In an interview for *Hollywood Online,* Berle described what it takes to succeed as a performer, especially as a comedian: "You have to be a good actor. There's a difference between being a comic and a comedian. A comic is a guy who says funny things and a comedian is a guy who says things funny, and he has a style and point of view that will last much longer."

Berle's acting career continued well into the 1990s. He remarried; and, with his third wife, Lorna Adams, launched a magazine named *Milton.* A tribute to indulgence, the magazine's motto is: "We Drink. We Smoke. We Gamble," and includes articles such as "How to Play Craps Without Looking Like a Dork."

Comedy's Elder Statesman

Often called a living legend, Berle's career has spanned most of the twentieth century. Along the way he has collected over six million jokes and has been loved by several generations. He has also repaid his mother's gift of mentoring by coaching and helping others get started in the business.

Further Reading

Broadcasting & Cable, October 28, 1996.
Folio, March 4, 1998.
Media Week, May 12, 1997.
Orange County Register, January, 23, 1997.
People Weekly, October 27, 1997.
Hollywood Online, http://chat.hollywood.com (February 19, 1998).
"Milton Berle," *Mr. Showbiz,* http://www.mrshowbiz.com (February 19, 1998).
Variety: The Golden Age of Television, http://www.fiftiesweb.com (February 19, 1998).
"Milton Berle," *Arts & Entertainment* (documentary), September 4, 1997.
The History of Showbiz, PBS, January 18, 1998.

Bernardo Bertolucci

Bernardo Bertolucci (born 1940), director of *Last Tango in Paris* and *The Last Emperor,* is considered

one of the modern masters of international filmmaking.

The grandchild of a revolutionary who grew up loving the fine arts and literature, Bernardo Bertolucci revolutionized the art of cinema with his frank films about politics and sexuality. The Italian director has made some of the landmark films of the modern era, earning international recognition and industry accolades along the way. He has worked with some of the finest actors in the world, including Marlon Brando, Gerard Depardieu, and Robert De Niro. Bertolucci's films have ranged from the exquisitely personal to the grand epic, but he has always kept his political and philosophical concerns front and center in his work. His resume of achievements includes multiple Academy Award nominations and a Best Director statuette for his 1987 masterpiece *The Last Emperor.*

Life of Leisure

Bertolucci was born on March 16, 1940 in Parma, Italy. His lineage was one of intellectual curiosity and radical politics. His maternal grandfather was an Italian revolutionary forced into exile in Australia. His mother, Ninetta, worked as a teacher. His father, Attilio Bertolucci, wrote poetry and taught art history. Bertolucci also had a younger brother, Giuseppe. The family lived in a large house filled with books and staffed by dedicated servants. Bertolucci enjoyed a very privileged upbringing that allowed him to pursue his artistic and intellectual interests.

At an early age, Bertolucci developed an interest in cinema. His father wrote a film column for a prominent newspaper. On many days Bertolucci would accompany him to see the latest releases. Since these trips often involved traveling to the big city, Bertolucci began to associate movies with the strangeness and wonder of urban life. Later on in his childhood, the family moved to Rome.

Begins Making Movies

When Bertolucci graduated from high school, he received a 16-millimeter camera for a present. He used it to make his first short films, using his brother and cousins as actors. He enrolled at the university in Rome and began studying modern literature. Besides filmmaking, his major passion during this period was writing poetry. In 1962, his first collection of poems, *In Search of Mystery* was awarded the Viareggio Prize. Encouraging Bertolucci in both his poetry and filmmaking was Pier Paolo Pasolini, a famous Italian director who also wrote poetry. Pasolini became a mentor to the young Bertolucci. He gave him the position of assistant director on his film *Accattone* (1961). Working with the great director convinced Bertolucci that filmmaking could be a kind of poetry in itself. He soon left Rome University to concentrate on a filmmaking career. "I had to find my own language," he told *Time.* "That language was cinema."

In 1962, Bertolucci directed his first feature, *La commare secca (The Grim Reaper).* The dark murder story was filmed on location with a cast of amateurs. It received mixed reviews, though many critics saw potential in the young director. Bertolucci's next effort came two years later. *Prima della rivoluzione (Before the Revolution)* (1964) was a love story set against political developments in contemporary Parma. Reviewers likened it to the works of great directors like Orson Welles, Jean-Luc Godard, and Luigi Visconti. It was given the young critics' award and the Prix Max Ophuls at the 1964 Cannes Film Festival.

Artistic and Political Growth

Critical acclaim did not make it any easier for Bertolucci to get the financial backing to make his films. During the mid-1960s, he worked for the Shell Oil Company making documentaries about the petroleum industry. He contributed to other people's films and wrote scripts in this period as well. It took until 1968 for him to direct another full-length feature. *Partner* concerns a man with an evil twin, and is based on the works of Edgar Allen Poe and Fyodor Dostoyevsky. That same year, Bertolucci joined the Communist Party. He went through a period of soul-searching that included psychoanalysis.

Now committed to the Marxist ideology, Bertolucci made his most political film yet, *Il conformista (The Conformist)*. The movie concerns a decadent intellectual who is lured into the Fascist movement during the 1930s. Bertolucci's script received an Academy award nomination for Best Adapted Screenplay, and he was widely hailed as a filmmaker of international importance.

Cinematic Master

Bertolucci's next feature, *Ultimo tango a Parigi (Last Tango in Paris)* (1972) cemented his reputation as an international master. The controversial picture starred Marlon Brando as a lonely man grieving for his late wife who has a passionate affair with a young Parisian woman, played by Maria Schneider. The movie's sex scenes were quite graphic for the time, and it was dismissed as obscene by some. But most critics found it riveting and honest in its depiction of contemporary relationships. It became on of the most talked-about films of the year and earned Bertolucci an Academy Award nomination for Best Director.

In the wake of the success of *Last Tango in Paris,* Bertolucci made a very different film. The 1977 release, *1900,* was a sweeping epic that spanned over 40 years of Italian history. It came in at over five hours and featured an international cast that included Robert DeNiro and Gerard Depardieu. The film was cut by over an hour when it was released in America, however, which enraged Bertolucci to no end. In 1991, the "restored" original version was finally released to American theaters.

In 1978, Bertolucci married Clare Peploe, an English woman whom he had been seeing since 1973. She collaborated with him on the script for his next film, *La Luna* (1979), which starred Jill Clayburgh as a woman who has an incestuous relationship with her son. The movie received mostly poor reviews and failed at the box office. Returning to Italian subjects, Bertolucci next made *La tragedia di un uomo ridiculo (The Tragedy of a Ridiculous Man)* (1981). A "small" movie about the kidnapping of a cheesemaker's

son, it got a mixed critical reception and was largely ignored by audiences.

Gains Academy Recognition

Bertolucci scored a major hit by returning to the grand scale with *The Last Emperor* (1987), the epic story of Pu Yi, the last emperor of China. In the film, based on Pu Yi's autobiography, the child ruler survives court intrigues, Japanese invasion, and Communist revolution to end up a gardener in Peking. The film was shot on location in the People's Republic of China and immediately restored Bertolucci's international reputation. When it was nominated for multiple Academy Awards, Bertolucci could barely contain his excitement. "I got colitis, my heart began beating fast, I even started smoking again," he told *Time.*

The Last Emperor won the Academy Award for Best Picture, as well as eight others, with Bertolucci taking the prize for Best Director. In accepting his prize, Bertolucci tweaked Hollywood by referring to it as "the big nipple." "I wanted to say that I was overwhelmed by this gratification," he later explained to *Time,* "which poured forth like milk."

Films in the 1990s

Bertolucci moved into a new decade with his next release, *The Sheltering Sky,* about the collision between western and non-western cultures. The film was well cast and boasted some beautiful desert scenery, but critics found it a poor adaptation of Paul Bowles' novel. His 1994 feature *Little Buddha* starred teen heart throb Keanu Reeves as an ancient prince on a quest for meaning. *Stealing Beauty* (1996) was a more intimate film, about a 19-year-old American, played by Liv Tyler, who undergoes her rite of passage into adulthood at the Tuscany, Italy home of her dead mother's friends.

In 1988, Bertolucci told *Time* that he remains true to his radical convictions. He still votes Communist, he reported, and remains leery of the "Hollywood" lifestyle despite the freedom his success has given him. "Nothing has really changed," he remarked. "My movies are too risky. But it gives me a feeling of being more secure."

Further Reading

International Dictionary of Film and Film Makers, Volume 2 - Directors, St. James Press, 1991.
American Film, October 1986; November 1987.
People, May 9, 1988.
Premiere, May 1994.
Time, April 25, 1988.
Vogue, March 1994.
Stealing Beauty, http://www.cecchigori.com/cinema/stealing/ (April 28, 1998). □

Paul Biya

Considered to be a worldly and educated man, Paul Biya (born 1933) served Cameroon in many positions as a career bureaucrat. When he became presi-

dent of his west Africa nation in 1982, he acted to create a more efficient government. Over time however, many critics believe Biya's rule has become repressive and ineffective.

Paul Biya was born in 1933 in the southern Cameroonian village of Mvomeka'a. His parents were not wealthy, but his small village was a surprising springboard for his accomplishments. At age 7 his parents sent him to the Catholic mission at Ndem, approximately 30 miles from his home. One of Biya's French tutors there found his work excellent, and determined that Biya should become a priest. At age fourteen he was admitted to Edea and Akono Junior Seminaries, run by the Saint Esprit fathers. His future was brightened further when he gained admission to the Lycee General Leclerc in Yaounde, Cameroon's capital; Lycee Leclerc is French Cameroon's most prestigious high school. At the Lycee, Biya studied Latin, Greek, and philosophy.

Biya's excellent work in secondary school allowed him to study at the University of Paris, where he focused on law and political science. He received his law degree in 1960. After graduation, Biya lived in France and studied public law at the Institute of Overseas Studies. In 1962, when Biya returned to Cameroon, he did so at a historic point in his nation's history. That turning point for Cameroon would provide opportunities and difficulties for Biya in the coming years.

Division Between North and South

To understand the challenges facing Cameroon, it is important to know its history. The Republic of Cameroon was once a German protectorate. In 1916, France and the United Kingdom (U.K.) came to rule over it. The colonial rule continued even after the creation of the League of Nations, a precursor to the United Nations: In 1922, the League allowed France and the U.K. to rule the segments of Cameroon that were then under their control.

Thus it happened that the nation was divided, north from south, French from British. Although those nations no longer rule over the country, the division is still a real one in a country split by language—French and British—and by religion—Muslim and Christian.

On January 1, 1960, the French part of the country achieved independence from French rule. Named as its first president was Ahmadou Ahidjo, a Muslim from the north. The English section also gained independence on October 1, 1961; part of the British zone voted to join neighboring Nigeria, and part voted to join the former French zone. The reconfigured nation had become the Federal Republic of Cameroon.

This was the nation to which Biya returned in 1962. He was put in charge of the Department of Foreign Development Aid. That position reported directly to President Ahidjo, and also gave the young Biya experience in money matters on an international scale.

Worked Closely by President's Side

Biya's relationship with the president was a fascinating one, and would define much about Biya's future. Over time, Ahidjo became Biya's political mentor, and the men became very close. Their backgrounds, and even their personalities, were very different, however. Ahidjo had worked as a telephone operator before becoming president, and he had only an elementary school education. Although Biya came from humble beginnings, he was highly educated and enjoyed classical music and tennis. Despite these differences, Biya became a loyal follower of the president.

Under Ahidjo, Biya held a number of positions. He worked as chief of the cabinet, secretary general of the presidency, and minister of state, Cameroon's highest-ranking minister. In 1975, Ahidjo chose him as prime minister, a position Biya held until 1982. According to the Cameroonian constitution, this made Biya Ahidjo's legal successor.

At that time, Cameroon had a single-party government. Biya also achieved success in the party, the Cameroon National Union (CNU). His skill at party politics would prove invaluable to him later, as he jockeyed for position with Ahidjo, who served as head of the party as well as president.

Assumed Presidency

The events of November 6, 1982, are still debated by historians. On that day, President Ahidjo, citing health concerns, resigned as president. As was required by the constitution, he handed over the presidency to Biya. The action stunned the nation; Biya was largely unknown to the populace, and he was untried as a head of state.

It appears that Ahidjo expected that he would remain firmly in control of the country after his resignation. He, like many, believed the party head position to be superior to that of president. The CNU, as the only party, set policy for all government actions; the president was expected merely to carry out the directives.

Biya's initial actions as president confirmed this view. Soon, however, the historic rivalry and tension between north and south caused him to shift gears. When he discovered that the bureaucrats from the north would not follow his lead and his orders, he began to replace some of Ahidjo's ministers and closest aides—many of whom were northerners—with men loyal to him, often southerners.

Strengthened His Power

Two coup attempts also strengthened Biya's control. In August 1983 a coup attempt was seen as an effort by Ahidjo to regain power and influence. This failed coup resulted in Ahidjo's forced resignation from the party chairmanship and his exile to France. The more deadly coup occurred in April 1984, when members of the presidential guard loyal to Ahidjo tried to capture the palace. After three days of fighting the rebels were defeated. Ahidjo, living in France, was again officially accused of plotting the attack.

While these plots were hatched and coming undone, Biya's star was rising. In September 1983, he was elected president of the CNU; he abolished that party and established the Cameroon People's Democratic Movement, or CPDM. And on January 14, 1984, he was reelected to be Cameroon's president. Flush with success, he made the puzzling promise that there would from then on be more democracy within the party, but that no opposition could be admitted. However, repression, not democracy, has been the hallmark of his administration.

Despite the contradiction, hopes were high after Biya's election. The economy was booming, and his focus on appointments based on merit rather than on cronyism suggested a turning point for the country. As Howard French wrote in the *New York Times,* "Western investors briefly considered Cameroon, rich in natural resources, to be Central Africa's promised land."

Biya's rule had some successes. Later elections showed that he allowed more choice of candidates within the one party. In 1986, Cameroon resumed diplomatic relations with Israel, relations that had broken down after the 1973 Middle East war; Cameroon was only the fourth black African state to do so. And in 1987, a visit to Cameroon by the Nigerian president improved relations with that neighboring country, historically soured by border clashes.

Biya's rule has been dogged by a number of problems. One was a severe economic crisis that began in 1984 and that continued for years. When the price of oil on the world market collapsed, the prices for Cameroon's main crops— cocoa, cotton, coffee, and palm oil— also dropped. Oil is Cameroon's main export, and accounted for about 35% of the budget. Beginning in 1987, Cameroon's economy

shrunk for nine consecutive years; some modest growth was evident in 1996.

Also problematic was a large and ineffectual government work force. Biya reduced the budget, throwing many employees out of work. In 1988, Biya agreed to accept loans from the International Monetary Fund. Although the infusion of cash aided the economy, its austerity demands were severe for the poor population.

Ruled Through Repression and Human Rights Violations

Perhaps most characteristic of Biya's presidency is its repressive nature. This was nowhere more evident than in the first multiparty elections to be held in Cameroon. In the late 1980s, a movement was sweeping Africa to allow candidates from more than just the official government parties. Biya resisted the movement, but finally allowed multiparty elections by mid-1990. The presidential election of 1992, however, was a shambles as an exercise in democracy. Most historians believe that Biya was defeated in that election by opposition leader John Fru Ndi. However, Biya had himself declared the winner.

Following the election, Biya declared a state of emergency to combat demonstrations. Large-scale arrests of opposition supporters occurred. Amnesty International recorded numerous instances of illegal arrests, torture, and death at the hands of Cameroonian police. In September of 1997, Amnesty International commented, "Fundamental human rights are persistently violated in Cameroon."

Oddly, it appears that the multiparty elections, which Biya initially opposed, have the power to revive his sagging presidency. Writing for *Africa Report,* Mark Huband noted the ironic phenomenon: "Biya and other repressive African leaders are becoming rejuvenated with their claimed electoral successes. With enormous confidence, the dictators are bouncing back."

Biya's ability to manipulate public information continued throughout the 1997 presidential election. As the election approached, Biya's government refused to allow the creation of an independent body to organize and monitor the elections. As a result, the three main opposition leaders, including Fru Ndi, opted to boycott the vote, "rather than participate in what they and many Cameroonians considered a charade," according to Howard French in the *New York Times.*

The ultimate result of Biya's repressive regime cannot be predicted, but popular unrest is growing. A reporter for *The Economist* wrote "Anti-government feeling, spurred by corruption, extortion and brutality, is widespread." By apparently manipulating the electoral process fraudulently, Biya's administration has blocked the only avenue to peaceful political change. One Cameroonian told the *New York Times* that Biya has built his power base exclusively around his own ethnic group, and that he has mismanaged the economy: "All of the ingredients are now in place for a civil war," said the citizen.

Certainly, the authoritarian political structures in Cameroon were inherited by Biya; they were not entirely created by him. Historian Mark DeLancey has noted that the author-itarianism Biya inherited was so strong that Cameroonians, while dismayed with Biya's slow pace toward open democ-racy, also criticize him for his inability to take charge and face opposition. The heritage of repression has been a diffi-cult one to overcome, both for Cameroon and for its leader.

Biya had one child with his first wife, the former Jeanne Atyam. After his wife died, he remarried. The material bene-fits of authoritarianism have been great for Biya. The *New York Times* in 1997 reported estimates of Biya's private fortune as $75 million. This amount reportedly is in addition to two presidential Boeing 747s, two massive homes in Cameroon, and other homes in France and Switzerland.

Further Reading

DeLancey, Mark W., *Cameroon: Dependence and Independence,* Westview Press, 1989.

DeLancey, Mark W. & Mokeba, H. Mbella, *Historical Dictionary of the Republic of Cameroon,* Scarecrow Press, Inc., 1990.

Njeuma, Martin, editor, *Introduction to the History of Cameroon in the Nineteenth and Twentieth Centuries,* St. Martin's Press, 1989.

Africa Report, January-February 1993, p. 41.

The Economist, January 22, 1994, p. 45.

New York Times, October 14, 1997, p. 3.

"Country Report: Cameroon—Blatant Disregard for Human Rights," September 16, 1997, *Amnesty International,* http://www.amnesty.org/ailib/aipub/1997/AFR/11701697.htm (March 18, 1998).

"Many people stay away as Cameroon votes for president," Oc-tober 13, 1997, *Minnesota Daily Online,* http://www.daily.umn.edu/daily/1997/10/13/world_nation/wn2.ap/ (March 18, 1998).

Elizabeth Helen Blackburn

American molecular biologist Dr. Elizabeth H. Blackburn (born 1948) is credited with the discovery of telomerase, an enzyme critical to the reproduc-tive process of gene cells.

D r. Elizabeth H. Blackburn is renowned for her discovery of the genetic enzyme "telomerase." Blackburn isolated and precisely described telo-meres in 1978, thus enhancing the understanding of deoxy-ribonucleic acid (DNA) on the part of molecular biologists around the world. The subsequent discovery of telomerase in 1985 brought new insight into the complex functions of gene cells and the mysteries of their replication. Impor-tantly, the discovery has given new hope to cancer re-searchers and opened new vistas for the science of gerontology.

Tasmanian Roots

Blackburn was born in Hobart, on the island of Tasma-nia (in Australia), on November 26, 1948. Her parents, Drs. Harold and Marcia (Jack) Blackburn, were physicians, and their only child quickly developed a love of science.

Higher Education

Blackburn started college at the University of Mel-bourne on the Australian mainland. There she completed her undergraduate studies, earning a bachelor of science degree in 1970. She continued at Melbourne and received her master of science degree in 1971. She went on to Cambridge University in England, where she earned a Ph.D. in molecular biology in 1975. She developed her doctoral thesis on sequencing of nuclear acids.

From England she moved to the United States, to Yale University in New Haven, Connecticut. At Yale, from 1975 until 1977, she studied chromosomes—their structures and replication—on a research fellowship. It was during those years that she first began to explore the phenomenon of telomeres, the tiny structures that cap the ends of chromo-somes and which contribute to the stability of the gene cells.

In 1977 Blackburn moved to California, to the San Francisco Bay Area, to continue her research into the nature of the telomere projections of chromosomes. She worked, once again as a research fellow, at the University of Califor-nia in San Francisco (UCSF). By that time she had traveled halfway around the world in pursuit of her educational goals. In 1978 she accepted her first position, as an assistant professor at the University of California in Berkeley.

The Discovery of Telomerase

As an assistant professor at Berkeley, Blackburn contin-ued her research on the behavior of telomeres. Eventually she noticed a relationship between telomere size and the ability of a chromosome to divide and duplicate.

In 1985, she and her graduate assistant, Carol W. Greider, successfully isolated "telomerase." Telomerase is the enzyme that synthesizes new telomeres in DNA and controls the length of the telomeres. The discovery was a breakthrough for biologists everywhere. It enabled re-searchers to create artificial telomeres to control the dupli-cation of gene cells. The discovery was a great stimulant to genetic research.

The historical discovery, isolation of the telomerase enzyme, brought international acclaim to Blackburn. In 1988, in recognition of her scientific accomplishment, she received the Eli Lilly Award for Microbiology. She was also elected a foreign associate of the National Academy of Science in 1993, having in 1990 received that academy's Molecular Biology Award. Yale University, home of her first postdoctoral research and her early studies of telomeres, bestowed her with an Honorary Doctor of Science degree in 1991. She was elected a Fellow of the Royal Society of London in 1992.

A Professor and a Writer

Blackburn was promoted to a full professorship at Berkeley in 1986, where she taught and managed a labora-tory until 1990. She then transferred to the San Francisco campus of the University of California as a professor in the Department of Microbiology and Immunology and of Bio-chemistry and Biophysics.

In 1992, Blackburn was a contributing writer to the *Harvey Lectures: 1990-91,* an annual reference publication by prominent scientists. *Harvey Lectures* features information on biomedical research. The 1990-91 edition spotlights Elizabeth Blackburn, together with David Beach, and Francis S. Collins.

One year later, in 1993, Blackburn was named Chairwoman of the Department of Microbiology and Immunology at UCSF. That assignment further distinguished Blackburn: she was the first woman in the history of the university to hold the post.

In 1995 she published *Telomeres (Monograph 29),* a collection of essays on telomeres, which she edited along with Carol W. Greider. The book was well received, and, according to *Science* editor Carolyn Price, the publication, "is both timely and much needed. The literature [on telomeres] has become increasingly diverse and voluminous, making it difficult for the newcomer to the field. . . . *Telomeres* provides an excellent, easy-to-read introduction for such readers. . . . A major strength of the book lies in the breadth of its coverage and the way it links diverse topics. . . ."

In 1990, with her students Guo-Liang Yu, John Bradley, and Laura Attardo, Blackburn published an article wherein they described the detrimental effect on genetic reproduction of the inability to make proper telomeric sequences. They found that telomeres cannot function properly when telomerase is defective. The telomeres eventually shrink, so that the genes cannot reproduce themselves properly, and the genes eventually die. This effect is significant to cancer research, because cancer cells are known to have excessive telomere length. Gerontologists (scientists who study the aging process) are also studying the effect of telomerase on telomeres, because the telomeres in human cells are known to shrink in connection with the aging process.

In addition to her research duties and her professorship at the University of California, Blackburn gives lectures and seminars on telomeres and cancer. She was among the presenters of the Dean's Research Seminar Series on Telomeres and Cancer in January of 1997. The Conference was transmitted via video relay to major San Francisco Hospitals.

Blackburn's scientific research is supported in part by the National Institute of General Medical Sciences (NIGMS). This work overall falls under the category of "basic biomedical research," or undirected research. This means that she is exploring to learn whatever can be known about cells. She is not looking for something in particular. The American Cancer Society also supports her work by providing postdoctoral fellowship assistance for her activities, and the National Science Foundation (NFS) supports predoctoral fellowship assistance for research by her students.

Personal Highlights

In all, Elizabeth Blackburn is a scientist, a teacher, a wife, and a mother. She met her husband, John Sedat, in England. Their mutual interest in molecular biology brought them together as students at Cambridge. They were married

in 1975, after Blackburn moved to the United States. Sedat is a scientist in his own right, and is a professor of biochemistry and biophysics at UCSF. The couple has one son, Benjamin, born in 1986. Blackburn takes motherhood very seriously, and publicly attests to the importance of time spent with her family. In her on-line article, "Balancing Family and Career: One Way That Worked," she spoke out on several topics, including the importance of devoting the appropriate time to parenting.

In the article she upheld the right of every woman to choose a career without fear of discrimination for embracing motherhood. Blackburn commented, "It makes no sense that career avenues be closed to a woman because of a temporary situation [the responsibilities of mothering young children]. . . . [The woman who chooses to be a mother] has been educated and trained for years in her . . . work . . . a huge investment of her life. . . . [T]he culture . . . needs to change so that when a woman says she has family needs, she won't feel this forever damns her as a serious scientist."

Blackburn further discussed (in her article) the most memorable week of her life, which occurred at age 37 when she received her full professorship at UCSF and discovered in the same week that she was about to become a mother.

Professional Memberships

Blackburn was elected to the American Association for the Advancement of Science (AAAS) in 1991. She has been a foreign associate of the National Academy of Science since 1993, and a Fellow of the Royal Society of London since 1992. She served as president of the American Society for Cell Biology (ASCB) in 1998, and represented the ASCB to the Joint Steering Committee for Public Policy and Bioethical Research Advocacy.

Blackburn's discovery of telomerase brings new promise of the eradication of fungal infections such as those in "immunocompromised" patients, and hopes that new cures will be found for many cancers. Further research on telomerase one day might even provide a means to significantly slow the aging process that afflicts every human being.

Further Reading

Beach, David, Elizabeth H. Blackburn, and Francis S. Collins, *The Harvey Lectures: 1990-1991* (Harvey Lecture Series, 86), Wiley-Liss, 1992.
Blackburn, Elizabeth H., and Carol W. Greider, *Telomeres (Monograph 29),* Cold Spring Harbor Laboratory Press, 1995.
Kipling, David, *The Telomere,* Oxford University Press, 1995.
Science, July 21, 1995, p. 396(5); January 26, 1996, p. 455(2).
"Balancing Family and Career: One Way That Worked," *Next Wave,* http://www.nextwave.org/pastfor/blackbur.htm (March 18, 1998).

Tony Blair

British politician and Prime Minister Tony Blair (born 1953) ushered a new generation into parlia-

ment, and refashioned the Labour Party along the way.

Great Britain's youngest prime minister of the twentieth century, Tony Blair, is leading the charge into the next century. He changed the Labour Party from a backward-looking leftist, socialist, labor-union based political party to a forward-thinking, centrist, free enterprise-friendly organization. He rebranded—a favorite word of "New Labour"—the old Labour Party and, under his leadership, Great Britain is getting a makeover as well. The government tourist agency now touts "Cool Britannia" instead of "Rule Britannia"—a place which is young, arty, technologically advanced, and fun.

Born in Edinburgh, Scotland, on May 6, 1953, Anthony Charles Lynton Blair learned early on about politics and responsibility. His father, Leo, a successful lawyer and law lecturer, chose to run for parliament as a Tory (conservative) in 1963. He suffered a stroke just before the election, leaving him unable to speak for three years. The three children, Bill the oldest, Tony, and Sarah, the youngest, had to learn to become self-reliant, to be able to cope with the family's financial and emotional stress. His father subsequently transferred his political ambition to his children; and, as Blair said in an interview with Martin Jacques for the London Sunday *Times* magazine, "It imposed a certain discipline. I felt I couldn't let him down."

But there was another part of the family tree whose genes influenced the young Blair. His natural grandparents (his father was adopted) had been actors and dancers, and Blair followed in their footsteps during his student days. He got rave reviews for his performances at Fettes College, organized gigs for rock groups, and later as a student at St. John's College at Oxford University, he was the lead singer for Ugly Rumors, a rock band playing the music of such groups as Fleetwood Mac, the Rolling Stones, and the Doobie Brothers.

In time, however, he followed his father's, not his grandfather's career, and studied law. Upon leaving Oxford, he got an internship with Queen's Counsel (QC) Alexander Irvine. His fellow intern was Cherie Booth, a top graduate of the London School of Economics, a laborite and daughter of actor Tony Booth. Although they were competitors professionally, personal attraction won, and they were married on March 29, 1980. They have three children: Euan, Nicholas, and Kathryn.

Irvine remembered Blair in the *New Yorker* as being able to absorb difficult issues: "One of his principal skills was absorbing enormously complicated material. Make your best points on the issues—he was very good at that." Blair successfully worked on employment law and commercial cases. This talent to communicate well proved very useful as Blair became involved in local politics.

A Quick Rise Up the Ranks

While Blair's father had been a Tory, Blair joined the Labour Party. In the university days he had read Karl Marx and Leon Trotsky, and even then was exploring how to change the Labour Party. An article in *New York Review of Books* also claimed, "it is inconceivable that Blair was left untouched" by witnessing the power of the local miners where he grew up. (The Blair family had moved to the industrial city of Durham in northern England after spending several years in Australia.) Nationally, the miners were the main strength of the Labour Party, and the Durham miners were an important political force. In fact, Durham City and County Durham voted labour; only the cathedral, castle and university were Tory.

In 1983 Blair was elected to parliament along with 208 other Labour M.P.s (Members of Parliament), the smallest number since 1935. The Labour Party was in crisis. The crippling public-sector strikes by several unions in the winter of 1978 had contributed to the widespread Tory victory in 1979 because the general populace saw the Labour Party as being controlled by the unions. Prime Minister Margaret Thatcher's re-election in 1983 was seen as a resounding defeat for the left wing of the Labour Party, and so in October of 1983, Neil Kinnock became the new leader of the party.

Kinnock promoted Blair to opposition spokesperson on treasury and economic affairs (1984-1987), and opposition spokesperson on trade and industry (1987). Blair was then appointed deputy to Bryan Gould, the shadow trade and industry secretary, where he investigated the causes of the October, 1987, stock market crash. In 1988 he made it to the shadow cabinet itself, first as shadow energy secretary, then as shadow employment secretary (1989-1991). After the 1992 election, which brought the Tory John Major to power, Kinnock had to resign, and John Smith, another moderate succeeded him. He appointed Blair shadow home secretary. After Smith's death in 1994, Blair was elected as leader of the Labour Party.

Government and Individual Responsibility

If Labour was going to win the 1997 election, it was going to have to refashion its message. Blair combined the traditional emphasis of Labour on the responsibility of the community with the Conservative's emphasis on the individual. As he said during an interview in January of 1993 on BBC Radio 4's *The World This Weekend,* a Labour government would be "tough on crime and tough on the causes of crime." Blair also called for a nation "where people succeed on the basis of what they give to their country," as noted in Knight-Ridder/Tribune News Service.

This philosophy had evolved during his early years. During university he was confirmed in the Church of England and had become committed to social change using Christian values. Family and community values were to be reintroduced into liberal rhetoric, and it was government's job to create the condition in which families could prosper. There was to be social accountability for the community and government as well as the individual. Blair also saw the disintegration of the Soviet Union and knew that the Labour Party could not hope to appeal to voters just using the old ideas of the welfare state with its emphasis on nationalized industry, union privileges, and social entitlements.

Blair was able to push through his ideas because the Labour Party had changed how it elected its leaders. In the past, officials had been elected by a system of block votes, which were divided among special interest groups and leaders—trade unions and M.P.s, for example—rather than by one vote per person. Blair had tried to institute "one person, one vote" at his local party branch in 1980, but failed. However, the system had just been changed with a compromise version of one vote per person when Blair ran for the party leadership in 1994. This worked to his advantage because the new voting method used his skills. According to biographer John Rentoul's *Tony Blair,* "Blair is a mass politician rather than a club operator. His straightforward, clear-speaking style, combined with his openness to the media, are qualities now needed for both kinds of contest."

A New Party Platform

In another move to reform British politics, Blair succeeded in persuading members to have the party's charter rewritten. He specifically targeted the 1918 Clause Four which called for the redistribution of wealth—a "communist equality"—through "common ownership of the means of distribution, production, and exchange." This section was rewritten to reflect modern social democratic aims. A major stumbling block had now been removed as the party could no longer be labeled just the party of the working class. Blair also eliminated planks on full employment, the welfare state, and unilateral nuclear disarmament.

New Labour supported European integration and free enterprise while downsizing budget deficits and resisting inflation. It worked. Blair, with no union roots, won the national election in May of 1997, with Labour winning a majority of 179 seats out of 659 in the House of Commons, Labour's biggest majority ever.

That summer, Blair's popularity stood at 82 per cent. "His youthful enthusiasm and energy add to his popularity," noted Barry Hillenbrand in *Time.* Britons liked his style, and as Adam Gopnik put it in his July 7, 1997, article for the *New Yorker,* they liked New Labour's "desire to end the deference culture." No more looking towards the upper classes, the past, or the nation's history; this was the new generation. As reported in the *New Yorker,* Blair told the October 1994 Labour Party conference, "I want us to be a young country again. Not resting on past glories. Not fighting old battles. . . . Not saying, 'This was a great country.' But 'Britain can and will be a great country again.'" Blair, with his focus on the future, was able to "make optimism fashionable," according to Gopnik.

"Modernization is the young Prime Minister's mantra," noted Hillenbrand. Blair's proposed reforms to welfare spending and programs were generally well-received. "Blair thinks the government does have a role to play in helping people and assuring social justice," declared Hillenbrand. Blair's $4.33 billion training program for young welfare recipients provided education to expand employment opportunities. He also ended steps to privatize the British National Health Service, thus ensuring that all British citizens had access to health care. One of his more unpopular proposals—decreasing benefits to single parents on welfare—still passed by a large majority in the House of Commons. While Blair has made no move to change the previous administration's anti-union laws, he has managed to lessen the class divisions that separate the nation. If, as some argued, Blair had taken the "labour" out of the party, no one was listening.

Blair has also taken a high profile position on British-Irish relations. In the 30-year war in Northern Ireland between the Catholic minority and the Protestant, British-favoring majority, he has broken with the previous administration's position that all sides must lay down arms before sitting down to talk. Instead, "parallel decommissioning" calls for both sides to gradually lay down arms while talking. Although not handicapped as were his predecessors by a reliance on Northern Ireland's Protestant voters, Blair has been aware of trying to look even handed. In a series of peace talks between the warring factions, Blair has supported a peaceful Northern Ireland. He continually negotiated to keep all the political parties at the table, even those with paramilitary links. In April of 1998, the leaders in Northern Ireland reached agreement, ending three decades of warfare. According to the terms of the agreement, a new Northern Ireland Assembly would be created, giving the Irish Republic (the Southern portion of the island) a say in the affairs of the North. In return, the Irish Republic would cease efforts to reclaim the North. A British-Irish Council would also be created to link Northern Ireland with Wales,

Scotland, and England. Blair has received much credit for his diplomatic skills in seeing this peace achieved.

A Euro-star

In Europe, Blair has taken a more traditional stand. While his popularity has crossed borders and he has become a well-known and respected politician, he is definitely aware of the resistance to integration at home. While portraying Britain as "a leading player" in Europe, the country is still keeping its right to "opt-out." In his first major meeting with European leaders, he voted to block an enhanced defense role for the European Union, keep passport controls at the borders, and sided with Germany when France's socialist government tried to ease the economic rigor agreed upon to establish a single currency.

Whether or not Great Britain eventually joins the European Union, Blair hopes to turn the country into a leading force. His efforts to modernize both his political party and his country have not gone unnoticed. Hillenbrand noted that contemporary European politicians are imitating his policies, from Gerhard Schroeder in Germany to Dutch Prime Minister Wim Kok. As Blair declared in his address to the October 1994 Labour Party conference: "I didn't come into politics to change the Labour Party. I came into politics to change the country."

Further Reading

Rentoul, John, *Tony Blair,* Warner Books, 1996.
Economist, May 31, 1979, p. 47-48; June 14, 1997, p. 16; June 21, 1997.
Knight-Ridder/Tribune News Service, September 1, 1994; October 7, 1995.
New Statesman, June 20, 1997; June 27, 1997, p. 15.
Newsweek, April 20, 1998, p. 34.
New Yorker, August 22, 1994, p. 66; February 5, 1996, p. 39; July 7, 1997.
New York Review of Books, June 12, 1997, p. 10-11.
Time, May 18, 1998, pp. 60-62.
U.S. News & World Report, May 12, 1997, p. 39.
Village Voice, June 3, 1997, p. 26.
Tony Blair interview with Nick Clarke, *The World This Weekend,* BBC Radio 4, January 10, 1993.

Anne Boleyn

Although she was Queen of England for just under three years, Anne Boleyn (ca. 1504-1536), second wife of King Henry VIII, was the center of scandal when she was executed. She was a central reason for the split between England and the Roman Catholic Church. She was also the mother of Elizabeth I, who is considered one of the greatest English rulers.

No accurate record of the birth of Anne Boleyn exists. Various scholarly and academic research has pinpointed her birth between 1499 and 1504, but other sources say as late as between 1507 and 1509.

Exact details about her birth and early life are also sketchy. Her father, Sir Thomas Boleyn, had his daughter educated, something of a rarity in those times.

She was known for her striking beauty—slight build, long slender neck (popular legends state she had an extra cervical vertebra), black silky hair, and dark eyes. In contrast to the fine features, Anne had two deformities: a mole the size of a strawberry on her neck and the start of a sixth finger on her right hand.

Anne Boleyn and her sisters were attendants to various members of royalty, and in 1523 she was placed as a lady in waiting in the court of Catherine of Aragon, wife of Henry VIII. At court, she caught the king's eye; however, she also caught the eye of a lesser noble, Harry Percy. Cardinal Thomas Wolsey rebuked the boy, but that didn't work, so Wolsey called for the Earl of Northumberland (Harry Percy's father) to come to court. Soon after the earl's arrival, an announcement of a betrothal was made. Harry Percy risked being disinherited if he did not marry; so he did, and Anne left the court, vowing revenge on Cardinal Wolsey.

A King's Infatuation

Henry's infatuation with Anne grew. He visited her at her father's estate, Hever Castle, though Sir Thomas kept his daughter at bay. She toyed with the emotions of Henry VIII for four years—teasing him, nagging him, refusing to be his mistress as her sister had—and all the time demanding that he be divorced before she would allow him into her bed.

Because she wanted to be his queen and not his mistress, she eventually gained that recognition.

Henry VIII tried to earn Anne Boleyn's favor through her father, making him Sir Thomas the Viscount Rochford. He tried to woo her through poetry and songs, writing and performing declarations of his love. Nothing worked. Henry was desperate to have Anne as his Queen and to have a son, as his only living heir was a daughter with Catherine. Henry concocted a mock court which called into question the validity of his marriage to Catherine, as she was his brother's widow. He cited a bible passage as proof that God did not view their marriage favorably (and that was why he had no sons). This led to messages and meetings with the Pope and his ambassadors, all the while Anne Boleyn and Henry VIII were getting more and more impatient.

Waiting to be Married

Public opinion in England, however, was not on the side of Henry and Anne. For the most part, the commoners viewed Catherine as the noble queen and Anne as a not so noble outsider. As Henry's infatuation with Anne grew, so did his impatience with Cardinal Wolsey and the Pope. Henry VIII wanted his marriage annulled so he could marry Anne. He brought her back not only to London but to his court. Although Catherine was officially his wife and queen, Anne acted as if she were.

About this time, Henry VIII replaced Wolsey with Sir Thomas More as Chancellor of England. More was a lawyer not a priest, and this change, or reformation, is often blamed on Anne. This act marked the beginning of the split between the Roman Catholic Church and England.

After years of waiting—waiting for the Pope, waiting for Catherine—Henry VIII finally banished Catherine, but to his dismay (and to the dismay of Anne), royal subjects filled the streets of England as Catherine rode away. In 1532 in an attempt to appease Anne as they awaited news of his annulment, Henry granted her a title that no other female had ever carried—Marquis of Pembroke. Through all of this, Catherine remained graceful and full of dignity, even chiding one of her attendants who cursed Anne with the remark, "Curse her not, rather pity her."

Becoming Queen

In January of 1533 Anne was pregnant with Henry's child, having finally allowed him into her bed. Since, of course, they couldn't be publically married, they married in secret. At this time Henry VIII nominated Thomas Cranmer as Archbishop of Canterbury. Cranmer favored granting Henry's notion that his union with Catherine was really a "non-marriage" and through an Act of Parliament, Cranmer received all spiritual power in England, and Catherine was reduced in name to Dowager Princess of Wales (meaning she was the widow of Henry's brother and not Henry's wife). The marriage between Henry VIII and Anne Boleyn was then made public.

Besides public opinion in England being against the marriage, in July the Pope declared the union of Henry and Anne as null and void and threatened Henry with excommunication if Catherine wasn't taken back as Queen by

September. Henry VIII was in a bind at this time. Not only was he in a political battle with the Roman Catholic Church, Anne was expecting a child, his heir to the throne, and he also had a new mistress.

On September 7, 1533, Elizabeth was born. Henry VIII was disappointed that she wasn't a male heir, and didn't attend her christening. He was however at least encouraged that Anne had given birth to a healthy child, as Catherine had suffered six miscarriages. Not willing to back down from the Pope, in the next year Henry had Parliament pass the Act of Supremacy, effectively naming the monarch as leader of the Church of England, thus finalizing the split between England and the Roman Catholic Church.

The Beginning of the End

Anne was pregnant again the next year, but suffered a miscarriage. Scholars suggest that, because of the sores on the legs of Henry VIII and the fact that his wives suffered so many miscarriages, he suffered from syphilis. Early in 1536, Catherine died, and Anne thought she had no more problems as to who was truly considered the Queen of England. However a few weeks later, after learning that Henry had been seriously injured during a jousting match, Anne gave birth to a stillborn boy. Her fate sealed, as Henry VIII had no desire to remain with her. He now had a fancy for one of her ladies-in-waiting, Jane Seymour. About this time, talk that Anne was really a witch and ascended to the throne via witchcraft circulated throughout England. Henry wanted Anne gone, and Thomas Cromwell conspired with Henry VIII to get rid of her.

Cromwell decided he needed to prove that Anne had committed adultery. For the Queen to commit such an offense was treason, and she'd be put to death. Cromwell and his cronies tortured court musician Mark Smeaton into confessing an affair, and in his confession, he named four other men—Sir Henry Norris, Sir Francis Weston, William Brereton, and Lord Rochford (Anne's brother). The insinuation of incest was as bad as the accusation of adultery.

Anne and the others accused all denied the charges, but all were held in the Tower of London until tried. Sir Henry Norris defended Anne Boleyn's reputation to his own death, and the others also protested. All were executed. The trumped-up charges also changed public opinion about Anne, who was now pitied.

Although there wasn't any evidence, Anne was found guilty and sentenced to death. Until the end, though, she continued to cause problems for Henry VIII. If Anne died, Elizabeth could still potentially be an heir to the throne (if he didn't get a male heir from Jane Seymour).

Thomas Cranmer met with Anne Boleyn privately before her death. Although the specifics of their conversation will never be known, Anne did receive a more merciful death sentence (beheading rather than burning at the stake). Also, Cranmer declared the marriage between Henry VIII and Anne Boleyn invalid. This, ironically, should have spared Anne's life—only the Queen's adultery could be considered treasonable, but Henry wasn't taking any chances, and nobody spoke up for her.

Henry did show a bit of mercy at the end, as he called for a skilled headsman from France, who used a sword (a quick form of decapitation when compared to an axe) to execute Anne on May 19, 1536. Eleven days later Henry VIII married Jane Seymour. Although she didn't live to see the day, Anne's daughter Elizabeth did eventually ascend to the throne, ruling England for forty-five years.

Further Reading

Bruce, Marie Louise, *Anne Boleyn: A Biography,* Coward, McCann & Geoghegan, Inc., 1972.
Erickson, Carolly, *Mistress Anne,* Summit Books, 1984.
Fraser, Antonia, *The Wives of Henry VIII,* Knopf, 1993.
Ives, Eric W., *Anne Boleyn,* Basil Blackwell, 1986.
Lofts, Norah, *Anne Boleyn,* Coward, McCann & Geoghegan, Inc., 1979.
Anne Boleyn—The Six Wives of Henry VIII, (videocassette series) BBC TV, New York: Time-Life Media, 1976.

Hassanal Bolkiah, Sultan of Brunei

One of the last remaining absolute monarchs, Sultan Hassanal Bolkiah (born 1946) has used enormous income from vast reserves of oil and natural gas to make his tiny sultanate one of the world's most economically prosperous and socially secure societies. As one of the world's wealthiest individuals, his own lifestyle has become famous for its extravagance and record-setting excesses.

The sultan of Brunei, whose official title is Sultan Hassanal Bolkiah Mu'izzaddin Waddaulah, first came to worldwide attention in the 1980's when the financial press revealed that this ruler of a traditional Islamic monarchy on the northwest coast of Borneo controlled a fortune in excess of $25 billion. For a time, he was regarded as the world's richest man, but in the late 1990's he may have lost that title to an American businessman. The sultan's current holdings, which officially belong to the country, are believed to be at least $40 billion. If his assets continue to grow at present rates, the Sultan's eldest son will almost certainly become the world's first trillionaire.

Hassanal is the 29th sultan in a dynasty that is believed to be one of the oldest in the world. Once a powerful trading nation, Brunei fell under British influence in 1846 and became a protectorate in 1888. Except for a brief period of Japanese occupation, Brunei continued to be closely tied to Britain until 1959, when a constitution transferred virtually all internal governing power to Hassanal's father, Sir Omar Ali Saifuddin. In an experiment with democratic elections urged by the British in 1962, all legislative seats were captured by the Brunei People's Party, which opposed involvement with the British and ultimately joined other revolutionaries in launching a revolt against the sultan. With the aid of British troops, the brief rebellion was crushed, and

Omar declared a state of emergency and assumed almost unlimited powers of absolute leadership that persist to this day.

Hassanal was educated by tutors and attended schools in Brunei and Kuala Lumpur until 1961, when he was installed as the crown prince. In 1965 he married a cousin, Pengiran Anak Saleha, in an arranged marriage. As a cadet at Britain's Sandhurst Military Academy, he was recalled to Brunei when his father voluntarily abdicated the throne in a last desperate move to resist both communism and pressure from the British to permit greater democracy. The young sultan reluctantly was installed as the new ruler on October 5, 1967, and was coronated on August 1, 1968. His devoutly Muslim father continued to rule behind the scenes, however, in an increasingly tense power struggle over policy differences and his son's playboy image. In 1981, Hassanal displeased his father further by marrying his second wife, a former airline hostess and commoner named Mariam Bell. Father and son waged a public dispute over Radio Television Brunei, but in the end the police and the army declared allegiance to Hassanal.

Although oil was discovered in Brunei in the 1920's, it did not generate significant wealth until the oil crisis of the 1970's, when natural gas production also began. Profits, royalties, and taxes from hydrocarbon production and shipping were controlled from the beginning by the royal family in partnership with divisions of the Shell Oil company, and other international business interests were expected to include the sultan's family in their profits as well. The boundary between family and national assets is vague, but it is known that Hassanal's real estate holdings alone include an unknown number of luxury hotels and other properties in the United States, Great Britain, and southeast Asia as well as cattle stations in Australia that are larger than his entire country.

Like his father, Hassanal is an anglophile who wanted to preserve the British protectorate, but the British insisted on giving up their quasi-colonial relationship. Full independence came on January 1, 1984, when the State of Brunei became Brunei Negara Darussalam ("Country of Brunei, the Abode of Peace") in a celebration whose pageantry was staggering in its extravagance. To mark the occasion, a new palace was built which *Forbes* called "a gold-filigreed fanciful cross between an airport terminal and a Las Vegas casino." The Istana Nurul Iman, which houses government ministries as well as the royal family, has 1,788 rooms, gold-leafed domes, an 800-car garage, and dozens of record-setting interior features. Its cost has been estimated at between $300 million and $600 million, and it is the largest occupied palace in the world.

Upon independence, Hassanal became prime minister and minister of defense and installed various family members in high cabinet positions. In 1984 he also brought Brunei into the United Nations. In the early years of his rule, Hassanal showed little interest in affairs of state, preferring instead to indulge his taste for gambling, polo, race cars, and the company of international jet-setters such as arms dealer Adnan Khashoggi, from whom he acquired the world's largest yacht. In the 1980's, however, he began increasing Brunei's role in regional affairs and in 1985 joined ASEAN, the Association of Southeast Asian Nations. He also began investing in international real estate while continuing to spend astonishing sums on hundreds of cars, polo ponies, works of art, jewels, custom airliners, and innumerable other items.

In the 1980's, Hassanal also became involved in several embarrassing financial transactions. He was alleged to be the funding source for Mohamed Al-Fayed's controversial attempt to take over the House of Fraser and other business interests in Great Britain. He also may have unknowingly provided capital for fraudulent deals made by another foreign advisor, Khoo Teck Puat. In 1986, he was secretly approached by Elliott Abrams, a senior official in the U.S. Department of Defense, who requested money for Contra "freedom fighters" battling against the government of Nicaragua. Months later, as the Iran-Contra scandal began to break, the donation was returned to Hassanal after it was learned that it had been deposited to the wrong Swiss bank account.

After independence, Hassanal did not, however, encourage the development of democratic institutions or delegate his power. He serves as king, prime minister, finance minister, and commander of the armed forces as well as head of the Royal Brunei Police, the Petroleum Unit, the Broadcasting and Information Services, and Supreme Head of Islam for Brunei. He allowed formation of The Brunei National Democratic Party in 1985, but it was dissolved in 1988 after calling for the Sultan to resign as head of state. There are no immediate plans to introduce elections or

party politics, although in a rare interview with the *New Yorker* in 1991, Hassanal affirmed that he did have a plan for political reform, but he did not intend to reveal it in the interview. There is no free press in Brunei, however limited freedom of expression has recently been permitted in the *Borneo Bulletin*, which the royal family owns. Hassanal is believed to acknowledge that his absolute power can not last forever and to favor a gradual introduction of limited democracy.

Hassanal's immediate concerns are for maintaining Brunei's stability while reducing its dependence on oil. Beginning in 1990, Hassanal began trying to strengthen the role of Islam through the concept of Melayu Islam Beraja (or Malay Islamic Monarchy), which links Malay identity, Islam, and the role of the monarchy as an official ideology. He has warned against Islamic fundamentalism, however, and declared that he would not permit extreme religious forces to influence his people. Even though Brunei has a long tradition of popular support for monarchy as a stabilizing institution, he is said to be concerned about external influences eroding his support as he tries to attract foreign investment and diversify the economy. Some problems of a wealthy welfare state are emerging, including drug use, crime, and limited job opportunities for the young.

In 1997, Hassanal was again exposed to world scrutiny when an American former beauty queen, Shannon Marketic, alleged sexual abuse by Hassanal's brother, Prince Jefri. At the same time, Hassanal replaced Jefri as finance minister, most likely because of problems involving Jefri's business interests. Marketic brought suit against the royal family in the United States, but a U.S. judge later ruled that Hassanal had sovereign immunity. Prince Jefri's indulgent personal life was further publicized in a 1998 British court case involving property deals he had failed to honor.

During the Asian currency crisis of 1997-98, Hassanal took an aggressive and highly visible role in supporting fellow ASEAN member nations by increasing investments in Malaysia and offering significant aid to Indonesia and Thailand. With government incentives to attract new industries, particularly tourism, Brunei's absolute monarch will be increasingly faced with the dilemma of how to cooperate on a global scale, guarantee future security, and open his country to outside influences without sacrificing its traditional values.

Further Reading

Bartholomew, James, *The Richest Man in the World: The Sultan of Brunei,* Viking, 1989.
Leake, David, *Brunei: The Modern Southeast-Asian Islamic Sultanate,* McFarland, 1989.
Asian Survey, February 1997.
Cosmopolitan, June 1995.
Far Eastern Economic Review, April 29, 1993.
Forbes, July 14, 1989.
Los Angeles Times, February 8, 1998.
Newsweek, October 21, 1985.
New Yorker, October 7, 1991.
New York Times, July 14, 1988.
People, June 1, 1987; June 23, 1997.
"Richest of the Rich," *Asia Inc. Online,* http://www.asia-inc.com (April 2, 1998).

"Fun Brunei?," *Asia Week,* http://www.pathfinder.com (March 27, 1998).

"Settlement for Record Civil Case," *BBC News,* http://news. bbc.co.uk (April 4, 1998).

"Monarch Who Really Cares," *Brunei Home Page,* http:// www.jtb.brunet.bn (April 2, 1998).

"Background," *Brunei Web Page,* http://www.asean.or.id (March 24, 1998).

"Brunei Sultan Plans to Help Asian Crisis," *Excite News,* http:// my.excite.com (April 1, 1998).

"Affair of State or Family Dispute?," *Newsmap: Brunei,* http:// www.pathfinder.com (March 24, 1998).

Hermann Bondi

English astrophysicist Hermann Bondi (born 1919) made his career out of studying the universe and its origins. Although his "steady state" theory was eventually discarded in favor of the "big bang" theory of creation, Bondi opposed what he called the "arrogance of certainty" that discouraged scientists and others from questioning current theories of the universe's origins.

Born in Vienna, Austria, on November 1, 1919, Bondi grew up with Jewish parents who disagreed about the importance of religious observances. "My father didn't believe, but liked the religious observances and rituals as social cement. My mother was a nonbeliever who didn't like the forms," he said in an interview in *Free Inquiry.* He credited his attraction to humanism to this division between his parents.

By 1933, social strife in Austria was peaking; Nazi leader Adolf Hitler had come to power, and Bondi's country struggled to remain independent. The increasing prominence of the Nazi party in Austria led to two civil wars within six months. In his autobiography, Bondi recalled, "It was against this background that I threw myself into my mathematical physics and dreamt of going to live elsewhere." By 1936, Bondi realized that his academic potential could never be realized while still living in Austria, and he began to work toward acceptance at Cambridge University, in England. He moved to England to attend Trinity College, Cambridge, in 1937 and considered it his home ever since.

Despite his allegiance to England, anti-German and anti-Nazi fervor during World War II put all immigrants and foreigners under suspicion, and Bondi, despite his Jewish heritage, was not an exception. In May of 1940, he was interned along with most other foreigners in Britain, remaining confined on the Isle of Man. He was later transferred to Canada and while there he attempted to immigrate to the United States, where his family had moved to escape Nazi persecution. Because he had arrived in Canada as an internee, very nearly a prisoner of the British government, the United States refused to permit his immigration. He returned to the Isle of Man, still under internment, and was not released until August 1941.

Advanced the Steady-State Theory

Upon returning to Cambridge, Bondi worked with other astro-physicists who would be influential in his career: Thomas Gold and Fred Hoyle. In the *Bulletin of the Institute of Mathematics and its Applications,* Hoyle claimed that he persuaded both Bondi and Gold to become interested in astronomy. "Hermann was the most confident manipulator of equations I had ever seen," Hoyle recalled. Hoyle reported that Bondi had a very theoretical mind, which "led him at times of course to lose contact with physical reality."

In 1948, Gold and Bondi worked together to develop the steady-state theory of the creation of the universe, which held that the universe is ever-expanding, without a beginning and without an end. They supported the theory by appealing to the perfect cosmological principle, according to which the universe is the same at all points; their colleague Hoyle advanced the same theory according to physical laws. The theory addressed a crucial problem of astrophysics: How do the stars continually recede without disappearing altogether? Dr. Edwin Hubble had already demonstrated that the stars actually do recede, but no one had yet explained why their recession did not leave a void in the universe.

As Bondi explained in his book *Cosmology,* "Since the universe must be expanding, new matter must be continually created in order to keep the density constant." Cosmologists had previously believed that the expansion of the universe marked the beginning of time, and that as it expanded outward it was approaching the end of its existence. These views were based on the belief that there was a moment when everything was suddenly created together in a dense mass. According to Bondi and Gold's steady-state theory, creation was continuous: it did not occur suddenly, and it was still occurring. The spontaneous creation of matter, they maintained, was brought about by the interchangeability of matter and energy, as demonstrated by Albert Einstein.

While Bondi accepted that the steady-state theory was as yet only an unproven hypothesis, he argued that the theory would create more possibilities for scientific discovery than the belief that creation was an event in the past: "The hypothetical character of continual creation has been pointed out, but why is it more of a hypothesis to say that creation is taking place now than that it took place in the past? On the contrary, the hypothesis of continual creation is more fertile in that it answers more questions and yields more results, and results that are, at least in principle, observable. To push the entire question of creation into the past is to restrict science to a discussion of what happened after creation while forbidding it to examine creation itself. This is a counsel of despair to be taken only if everything else fails."

Failed Theory Led to Applied Science

Bondi later worked with R.A. Lyttleton of Imperial College, London. In 1959, the two proposed that the outward movement of planets and stars was the result of electrical "leaks" in space. The theory was founded on the assumption that galaxies have electrical charges on the surface, producing a force of repulsion that surpassed the force of gravitational attraction. As the *New York Times* reported, one of the strengths of the theories was its potential to explain the origin of cosmic rays. The equipment to test their theory, however, was not available, although physicists were not able to find a flaw in their logic.

A strong believer in scientists' responsibility to explain their work to society, Bondi began writing books for students and laypeople and appearing on BBC educational programs in Britain. Chief among his efforts was his attempt to explain the theory of relativity and the works of Isaac Newton and Albert Einstein. As John Durston explained in the preface to Bondi's book *Relativity and Common Sense: A New Approach to Einstein,* "Where previous writers have tried to develop relativity in opposition to the ideas of Isaac Newton, Professor Bondi derives relativity from Newtonian ideas. He pictures relativity as being neither revolutionary nor destructive of classical dynamics but rather as being an organic growth." Bondi felt strongly that all scientific advancement came from, as Newton had said, "standing on the shoulders of giants."

As Bondi was reflecting on the inevitable evolution of scientific theories, he saw his own steady-state theory threatened with obsolescence. In 1965, Arno Penzias and Robert Wilson discovered a radiation background in microwaves. This radiation, it was hypothesized, was background noise from the "big bang." Although the "big bang" theory has roots as early as 1922, the discovery of this radiation brought it back into prominence. Cambridge radio astronomer Martin Ryle told *Newsweek,* "I think after this few students will go into the steady-state theory in detail."

While Bondi's colleague, Hoyle, began revising the steady-state theory to take into account the new data, Bondi moved on to problems in applied science. In 1967, Bondi was appointed director of the European Space Research Organization. One of his main achievements while in office was the development of plans for phone and air-traffic satellites for Western Europe. These satellites would enable international phone connections that had previously required several hours to complete. Perhaps more important, they would increase air-traffic controllers knowledge of a plane's location, particularly as it began to "disappear" over the horizon of the Atlantic Ocean. In 1971, he became chief scientific advisor to Britain's Ministry of Defence, a post he maintained through 1977, when he became chief scientist for the Department of Energy. Bondi also served as chairman and chief executive of the Natural Environment Research Council (NERC), for which he traveled widely, attempting to generate interest and income for scientific research.

Returned to Cambridge

Throughout this time, Bondi continued his scholarly pursuits, publishing several papers and serving twice as president of the Institute of Mathematics and its Application. Staying active in his academic discipline enabled him to return to Cambridge when he retired from government service in 1980. He took the position of Master of Churchill College, Cambridge, from 1983-1990, and continued as a fellow there from 1990 onward.

Bondi was also an active advocate for humanism, signing in 1973 the "Humanist Manifesto II," in which 120 religious leaders, philosophers, scientists, and other thinkers declared, "Reason and intelligence are the most effective instruments that humankind possesses. There is no substitute: neither faith nor passion suffices in itself. The controlled use of scientific methods, which have transformed the nature and social sciences since the Renaissance, must be extended further in the solution of human problems. But reason must be tempered by humility, since no group has a monopoly on wisdom or virtue."

In 1992 Bondi became president of the British Humanist Association, through which he lobbied for tolerance of differing viewpoints and appreciation for the life-enhancing benefits of science. In particular, he stressed the importance of continuing to question the origins of life and of the universe. "I don't think answers to these question are the business of us humans," he said in *Free Inquiry,* "Trying to get there—asking questions, investigating, discussing, sharing views, sharing arguments—that is the important thing. The continuing quest is what we humans must work for, not achieving the final answer."

Further Reading

Bondi, Hermann, *Cosmology,* Cambridge University Press, 1952.
Bondi, Hermann, *Relativity and Common Sense: A New Approach to Einstein,* Heinemann, 1965.
Bondi, Hermann, *Science, Churchill and Me: The Autobiography of Hermann Bondi,* Pergamon, 1990.
Bulletin of the Institute of Mathematics and its Applications, December, 1989.
Free Inquiry, Spring 1992.
Newsweek, October 25, 1965.
New York Times, May 24, 1952; May 24, 1959; October 13, 1970; August 26, 1973.

Gertrude Simmons Bonnin

Native American activist and writer of the Sioux tribe Gertrude Simmons Bonnin (1876-1938) was prominent in the Pan-Indian movement of the 1920s and 1930s. She devoted her life to lobbying for the rights of Native Americans.

One of the most outspoken voices raised on behalf of Native Americans during the early twentieth century was that of Gertrude Simmons Bonnin, a granddaughter of the famous Sioux chief Sitting Bull. As a writer, she produced a number of essays and short stories that established her as a significant figure in Native American literature. Her enduring legacy, however, is that of a reformer and activist devoted to improving the lives of Native Americans both on and off the reservation. Calling upon her skills as an orator, Bonnin made numerous appearances before government officials in Washington and ordinary citizens throughout the nation to draw attention to the plight of Native Americans trapped in poverty and despair.

Bonnin was born to a Native American mother and a white father at the Yankton Sioux Agency in South Dakota on February 22, 1876. She spent her early childhood on the reservation, immersed in traditional Sioux ways. But when she was about eight, she left to attend a Quaker missionary school for Indians located in Wabash, Indiana. After a difficult and unhappy adjustment period, young Gertrude finally settled in and completed a three-year term, then returned home for four years before going back for another three-year course of study. Following her graduation in 1895, she went on to Earlham College in Richmond, Indiana, earning recognition as the winner of a state-wide oratory contest.

After leaving college in 1897, Gertrude Simmons, as she was then known, secured a teaching position at Pennsylvania's Carlisle Indian School. While the time she spent there was not pleasant, she did manage to make some contacts in the eastern literary establishment that enabled her to begin publishing some of her work (under her Sioux name, Zitkala-Sa, or Red Bird) in such well-known magazines as *Harper's* and *Atlantic Monthly*. In 1899, she resigned from the Carlisle faculty and enrolled at the New England Conservatory of Music in Boston to study violin. Free to pursue her writing and her music in a cultural milieu she enjoyed, she was happier than she had been in many years. In 1901, she published her first full-length book, *Old Indian Legends,* a collection of Native American stories. But she still felt somewhat torn between two worlds, and she very much wanted to do something for those she had left behind on the reservation.

Returning to South Dakota around 1902, she met and married a fellow Yankton Sioux, Raymond Talesfase Bonnin, who worked for the Indian Service. They soon moved to the Uintah and Ouray Reservation in Utah, where Gertrude Simmons Bonnin worked as a clerk and a teacher. During this same period, she also became involved with the Society of American Indians, a Native American reform organization founded in 1911 at Ohio State University. The first group of its kind to be established and managed solely by Native Americans, it operated on the principle that assimilation was ultimately the best course for the country's Native American population. To that end, the Society focused its efforts not only on government reforms but on activities such as increasing Native American employment in the Indian Service (the federal agency charged with managing Indian affairs), codifying laws pertaining to Native Americans, achieving Native American citizenship, opening the courts to all just claims regarding land settlements between Native Americans and the government, and preserving Native American history.

In 1916, Bonnin was elected secretary of the Society of American Indians, and not long after, she and her husband moved to Washington, D.C. From her new base in the nation's capital, which she would call home for the rest of her life, she continued to serve as secretary of the Society (until 1919) and editor of its major publication, *American Indian Magazine.* She also joined forces with a number of other organizations spearheading Native American rights and reform, including the American Indian Defense Association and the Indian Rights Association. In addition, she began lecturing extensively from coast to coast, speaking to women's clubs and other groups on Indian affairs and lobbying for Indian citizenship. Her work on behalf of the latter met with success in 1924 with the passage of the Indian Citizenship Bill.

Both Bonnin and her husband devoted a great deal of their time to meeting with officials of the federal government on behalf of individual Native Americans and tribes. They also testified before various congressional committees on a wide variety of issues. Many of their findings were the result of their own investigations and travels throughout the country visiting reservations and noting the need for improvements in areas such as health care, education, conservation of natural resources, and preserving Native American cultural traditions.

In 1926, following the disbanding of the Society of American Indians, the Bonnins formed the National Council of American Indians (NCAI). Like the Society, the NCAI was made up exclusively of Native Americans; Gertrude Bonnin served as its president. Its focus was also on reform, and to that end, Bonnin directed her energies toward lobbying for Native American legislation in Congress and calling attention to the deficiencies of the Indian Service.

The spirit that motivated these efforts finally prompted some government officials to take a closer look at the Indian Service. In 1928, U.S. Secretary of the Interior Hubert Work commissioned a group of scholars to study living conditions among Native Americans, focusing in particular on economic activity, education, health, and the federal government's administrative policies and practices. Under the direction of Dr. Lewis Meriam, the Institute for Government Research conducted an exhaustive survey and published the results in a landmark report entitled *The Problem of Indian Administration,* more commonly known as the Meriam Report. Its description of the "deplorable" state of life on the reservations—the high death rate among all age groups, the failure of the educational system, the widespread poverty and malnutrition—focused national attention on the plight of Native Americans and increased pressure on the government to take immediate action.

In mid-December of 1928, Bonnin voiced her thoughts on the findings of the Meriam Report at a meeting of the Indian Rights Association in Atlantic City, New Jersey. According to the text of the speech, as furnished by the Harold B. Lee Library at Brigham Young University, which houses the Gertrude Simmons Bonnin Collection, Bonnin declared: "As an Indian, speaking earnestly for the very life of my race, I must say that this report by the Institute for Government Research, *The Problem of Indian Administration,* is all too true, although I do not always concur in their conclusions, which tend to minimize the responsibility of the Bureau [of Indian Affairs]." Bonnin described the conditions on most reservations as below poverty level, with food being scarce and very few educational and employment opportunities. In the speech, Bonnin detailed provisions available in reservation schools: "The subcommittee of the Senate Indian Affairs Committee is holding hearings right now, and sworn testimony reveals horrible conditions— rotten meat, full of maggots, and spoiled flour which mice and cats had defiled, are fed to children in government schools. Sworn statements amply show that the report of the Institute for Government Research could all be transformed into the superlative degree and not begin to tell the whole story of Indian exploitation."

Bonnin also commented on the quality of education available to young Native Americans in her address: "The Indian race is starving—not only physically, but mentally and morally. It is a dire tragedy. The government Indian schools are not on a par with the American schools of today. The so-called 'Indian Graduates from Government Schools' cannot show any credentials that would be accepted by any business house. They are unable to pass the Civil Service examinations. The proviso in Indian treaties that educated Indians, wherever qualified, be given preference in Indian Service employment is rendered meaningless. Indians are kept ignorant and 'incompetent' to cope with the world's trained workers, because they are not sufficiently educated in the government schools."

While it did not bring about major improvements, the Meriam Report did exert some influence on government policies regarding Native Americans during the administrations of Herbert Hoover (1928-33) and his successor, Franklin D. Roosevelt (1933-45). Hoover, for example, appointed two leading members of the Indian Rights Association as commissioner and assistant commissioner of the Bureau of Indian Affairs. As part of his Depression-era reforms, Roosevelt pushed for the Indian Reorganization Act of 1934 and its promised "Indian New Deal," which granted Indians more self-government and the right to keep observing their own cultural ceremonies and other events.

As for Bonnin, she remained active in the reform movement throughout the 1930s. She continued lobbying Congress, particularly on behalf of the Sioux and the Utes, and frequently lectured across the United States, often appearing in native dress to dramatize her message. While she devoted less time to her writing, she renewed her interest in music and even composed an Indian opera entitled *Sun Dance*. After her death in 1938 at the age of only sixty-one, Bonnin was buried in Arlington National Cemetery.

Further Reading

Bonnin, Gertrude Simmons, *Old Indian Legends* (reprint of original 1901 edition), University of Nebraska Press, 1985.
Bonnin, Gertrude Simmons, *American Indian Stories* (reprint of original 1921 edition), University of Nebraska Press, 1985.
Gridley, Marion E., *American Indian Women,* Hawthorn Books, 1974.
Jones, Louis Thomas, *Aboriginal American Oratory: The Tradition of Eloquence Among the Indians of the United States,* Southwest Museum (Los Angeles), 1965.
American Indian Quarterly, winter, 1988, pp. 27-40.
Journal of the West, July, 1984, pp. 3-6.
New York Times, January 27, 1938, p. 21. □

Gertrude Simmons Bonnin Collection, Harold B. Lee Library, Brigham Young University.

Sonny Bono

Elected to the U.S. House of Representatives in 1994, Sonny Bono (1935-1998) made a career out of reinventing himself. He played the straight man to his then-wife Cher, on the *Sonny and Cher Comedy Hour* in the 1970s and later served as mayor of Palm Springs, California. On Capitol Hill, he quickly established himself as a hard worker and a popular fundraiser for the Republican party.

Even though he was a dedicated congressman, a popular mayor, and a successful restauranteur, pop icon Sonny Bono will probably first and foremost be remembered, as the "shorter" half of "Sonny and Cher." From 1971 until mid-1974, this husband and wife team was one of the hottest acts on television. The *Sonny and Cher Comedy Hour* presented elaborate song numbers, comedy skits, and lots of banter between the two stars. Sonny usually got the short end of the deal, with Cher making comments about his height, his Italian ancestry, or his limited singing voice. Through it all, he suffered the putdowns with good-natured, bumbling grace, and the audience loved it. No matter how many barbs and off-color remarks the couple exchanged, the act always ended on a happy note as they sang their signature song, "I Got You, Babe."

Canny Showman

Salvatore Phillip Bono was born in Detroit, Michigan, on February 16, 1935, to Santo and Jean Bono, poor immigrants from Sicily. The family moved to Los Angeles when he was seven years old, and his parents later divorced. Although he was dedicated to writing songs, Bono did not have the same interest in school. He dropped out and tried to sell his tunes to recording companies. He did not have much luck with that either, although his song "Koko Joe" was somewhat successful for the Righteous Brothers. Between jobs as a waiter, butcher's assistant and truck driver, Bono occasionally worked with Little Richard and Sam Cooke, then was hired by Philles Records, where he worked with Phil Spector and got a complete education in the television and music business. For a time, he sang background for groups such as the Ronettes and Crystals.

Love and a brand new career came into Bono's life when he met an exotic-looking, dark-haired teenager named Cherilyn LaPiere Sarkisian, known as Cher, in 1963. By this time, Bono was breaking up with his first wife, Donna Rankin, with whom he has a daughter, Christy. Cher, born in El Centro, California in 1946, was trying to get into show business. Bono thought that her voice and his songs could make them stars. They were married in Mexico in 1964 and had a daughter, Chastity, in 1969.

Sonny and Cher became the entertainment world's "odd couple." According to the *Detroit Free Press,* "Bono was well-known for his droopy moustache, bell bottoms and playing the fall guy to his much taller and sharp-tongued wife." Their public personas were those of two kooky flower children in the advanced stage of puppy love. They dressed in outlandish outfits and sang Bono's songs in a way that delighted audiences. But underneath the affable, bumbling exterior, Bono was growing an uncanny showman with drive, talent, and ambition. He knew he could make them into top stars.

In June of 1965, Sonny and Cher hit it big with the recording of "I Got You, Babe." This was followed by "Laugh at Me," "All I Really Want to Do," and then the rock classic, Bono's most recorded song, "The Beat Goes On." At one point, they had five songs in the Top 20 at the same time. The only others ever to do that were Elvis Presley and the Beatles. After a 1967 movie, *Good Times,* in which the couple more or less played themselves, their popularity was on the downswing. In 1969, Bono mortgaged his house to put every cent he could into a film about a runaway girl, starring Cher, called *Chastity.* It was a flop, but Bono promised they'd be back on top. It took three years, but he was right.

To the Top and Back to the Bottom

Bono developed a nightclub act that featured Cher as the bored, generally superior wife who always gets the best of her husband who is a clown. Throwing in old and new tunes, many of them his, they exuded a kind of charm that intrigued audiences and led them to the weekly *Sonny and Cher Comedy Hour* on CBS. It lasted from 1971 until mid-1974 and propelled them into the hottest couple on television. Together, they were a hit. While critics debated the merits of the show, it consistently drew high ratings.

The show was still going strong when in 1974, Cher announced she was leaving her husband. In a blaze of headlines over their divorce, they charged each other with extramarital affairs and the parting was bitter. Claiming surprise at his ex-wife's unhappiness, Bono dropped out of show business, with the exception of a few guest appearances on television shows. He also married his third wife, model Susie Coelho, in 1982. They were divorced in 1984.

Show Biz Loss, Political Gain

Never one to be idle, Bono sought a new career. In 1983, he opened a restaurant called "Bono" in West Hollywood. There he met a recent University of Southern California graduate, Mary Whitaker, about 25 years his junior. They were married in 1986 and had two children, Chesare and Chianna. After moving to Palm Springs, Bono decided to open another restaurant. According to the *New York Times,* when he encountered frustrating red tape over his attempt to change the sign on the building, the consummate showman decided on another new career— politics.

As unlikely as it seemed to the world outside Palm Springs, a desert resort city of about 40,000, Bono ran for and won the mayor's election. His well-known face and affable manner may have gotten him the job, but many residents began to think he was good for the town. He donated his mayor's salary one year—$15,000—to an anti-drug campaign, banned skimpy bikinis, and started an international film festival. Although his time in office was not without controversy, he helped erase the city's $2.5 million dollar deficit and successfully promoted tourism.

However, there were many raised eyebrows when Bono decided to run for a seat in the U.S. Senate in 1992. He lost the Republican primary, and the seat was eventually won by Democrat Dianne Feinstein. But in 1994, swept in on a Republican tide, Bono won a seat in the U.S. House of Representatives. He beat his Democratic opponent by winning 56 percent of the vote. According to the *New York Times,* Bono arrived in Washington D.C. "with the image of a well-heeled but lightweight show-business celebrity. He quickly proved engaging and shrewd, a fairly dutiful legislator and an engaging speaker."

Bono had always taken pride in never having been taken too seriously, and according to the *New York Times,* he was almost proud of his lack of qualifications. He settled down to work, showed interest in protecting the environment and was according to the *New York Times,* "the second most popular fundraiser behind House Speaker Newt Gingrich." He was well-liked by his colleagues as a member of the Judiciary and National Security committees. He was re-elected in 1996.

The Accident

Life was looking good for Congressman Bono, now age 62. He had a happy marriage, a job he liked, and the respect of his colleagues. His relationship with ex-wife, Cher had become friendlier, and he was closer to their daughter, Chastity, a gay rights activist, than he had ever been. He was happy with what he had.

Bono, his wife, and their two children, ages nine and seven, went to South Lake Tahoe on the California-Nevada line. In the early afternoon of January 5, 1998, Bono left them to ski alone. When he failed to appear after several hours, his wife called the ski patrol. He was found later that evening, having been killed in a skiing accident. He was mourned by political colleagues, family and fans. A few months after his death, Mary Bono won his congressional seat in a special election. In May of 1998, "Sonny & Cher" received a "star" on the Hollywood Walk of Fame. CBS also aired a special presentation hosted by Cher entitled "Sonny & Me—Cher Remembers," which provided a nostalgic look at Bono's career.

Shortly after he was elected to Congress in 1994, Bono was asked how he'd like to be remembered. The *New York Times* shared that Bono, although a little overwhelmed that he was actually there in Washington, D.C., replied, "As someone who is his own man, a maverick and really a person of substance like other people. Not necessarily the brilliant person, but recognize that there is substance there."

Further Reading

Bono, Sonny, *And the Beat Goes On,* Pocket Books, 1992.
Chicago Tribune, January 7, 1998.
Detroit Free Press, January 6, 1998; January 7, 1998.
New York Times, December 14, 1988; January 7, 1998.
New York Times Magazine, March 29, 1989.
People, March 21, 1988; October 2, 1989; January 19, 1998; May 11, 1998.
Rolling Stone, February 19, 1998.
Time, January 19, 1998.
U.S. News & World Report, December 12, 1994.
"Sonny Bono—Pop Song & Politics," *A & E Biography Television Network,* 1998. (Rebroadcast, May 22, 1998). □

Boudicca

Iceni Queen Boudicca (died 61) ruled over a small tribe of Celts who challenged the colonization plans of the Roman Empire in England. The insurrection she lead almost succeeded in turning back the Roman colonizers.

V ery little historical evidence survives about the queen named Boudicca, ruler of a small tribe of Celtic peoples known as the Iceni during the first century C.E. The Iceni made their home near what is now Norfolk, England, and it is known that Boudicca inherited her crown upon the death of her husband. Not long afterward, she was integral in forming a pan-tribal alliance of Celtic warriors who carried through a decisive, bloody, and very nearly successful uprising against their despised Ro-

man colonizers in C.E. 61. The revolt that bears Boudicca's name would be remembered in history as one of the most significant insurrections against the mighty Roman Empire during Europe's classical era.

The Iceni and Pre-Roman Britain

Boudicca, whose name is sometimes spelled Boadicea, may or may not have been of direct Icenian heritage; it is only known that she was married to the Iceni king, Prasutagus, and among royal Celtic houses marital alliances with other tribes were not unusual. Knowledge of Boudicca survives from the writings of two historians of the Roman empire, Tacitus and Cassius Dio. The latter penned his impression of the Iceni queen: Boudicca, wrote Dio as quoted in *The Rebellion of Boudicca,* "was huge of frame, terrifying of aspect, and with a harsh voice. A great mass of bright red hair fell to her knees: she wore a great twisted golden necklace, and a tunic of many colours, over which was a thick mantle, fastened by a brooch."

The Iceni held the territory in what is present-day Norfolk, England, and historians assume they migrated at one point in the late Bronze Age from the European continent. In England they established a farming economy, were weavers of cloth and also made pottery. Their stability was threatened by the arrival of the Belgae from Gaul (France). The Belgae had earned the enmity of the Roman emperor Caesar for providing help to their brethren back in Gaul who were resisting Caesar and Roman rule there. For this, Caesar began attacking Britain around 55 B.C.E.

Matters were further complicated by the superiority of the Belgae over their Celtic neighbors, such as the Iceni. The Belgae were skilled ironsmiths, more adept at farming, and most importantly, possessed a well-organized military force. They soon began taking over other tribes in the area. The Iceni built forts against them, but when the Romans launched a massive military invasion of the British Isles in C.E. 43, the Belgae capitulated. In total, eleven kings of varying Celtic tribes surrendered in a formal signing. The Arch of Claudius in Rome commemorates this historic surrender. Two kings, however, had engineered agreements with the Romans early on in exchange for retaining some power over their tribes. These rulers were Cogidubnus of the Regni tribe and Prasutagus, Boudicca's husband.

The Roman Empire in Britain

Over the next few years, Romans established a strong military presence in Britain, as they did elsewhere in Europe, North Africa, and the Middle East. Roman colonization meant financial hardship for the conquered peoples. Their economy was immediately forced to gear itself toward the production of food for the massive legions of Roman soldiers stationed in their lands. Also, Roman officials imposed heavy taxes for an array of services and goods, and Roman moneylenders arrived in Britain to take advantage of the situation by making loans. Britain's Rome-appointed governor, Suetonius Paulinus, was also dedicated to eradicating Druidism, the native Celt religion. Its priests retained a great deal of influence over both common Celts and royal lines.

The origins of Boudicca's revolt began when the despised Procurator Catus Decianus rescinded the terms of a financial agreement between the Emperor Claudius and Prasutagus. It had been called a grant, but then was renamed a loan. In response, Prasutagus left a stipend of half his kingdom in his will to Nero, Claudius's successor, to satisfy the debt. Roman officials under Catus Decianus arrived in Iceni lands and instead took the whole. Boudicca, who had inherited the kingdom since she and Prasutagus had no male heirs, was arrested and beaten, and her two daughters raped. The estates of wealthy Iceni were liquidated, and lesser relatives of the royal house sold into Roman slavery.

Boudicca's Revenge

During the summer months of C.E. 61, after nearly two decades of Roman rule and at a time when Suetonius was leading an attack on the Celts in Wales, a revolt against Roman rule was planned. Such insurrections were not new to the Romans, despite their famously peremptory conquests of nearly all of Western and Southern Europe. Gaul resisted Caesar a hundred years before in the Gallic Wars, and a Germanic prince, Arminius, almost stalled Roman entry into Germany with his C.E. 9 victory at the Teutoburg Forest. Tacitus wrote that the Britons' knowledge of Arminius's victory fueled their resistance.

The uprising began with a secret meeting of Boudicca, her Iceni, and several other tribes—among them the Trinovantes, who were resentful of Roman imposition at their lands near Camulodunum (now Colchester), a tribe from the west known as the Cornovii, and the Celts of Dorset known as the Durotiges. The historian Cassius Dio claims that this well-planned and unnoticed conference may have numbered as high as 120,000. A propaganda campaign was launched in Camulodunum, then the center of Roman rule in Britain. Designed to worry the Romans, it included such actions as turning the river red and toppling the Roman victory statue erected in the center.

In the summer of C.E. 61, Boudicca's legions of united Briton tribes attacked Camulodunum in chariots. The uprising was launched there because the negligent Romans had erected little in the way of walls or forts for the city's defense. Celtic soldiers painted themselves blue to frighten the enemy; women also played a decisive role by remaining at the rear of the battles with the wagons and draught-oxen. Sometimes the wives appeared near the battlefront in black robes carrying torches, as did Druid priests who shouted curses meant to frighten Romans. Just as Suetonius achieved victory in Wales with nearly two-thirds of the total Roman forces in Britain with him, he received word about the uprising in the East. He hurried back, but by then Catus Decianus had fled by ship, along with other top Roman officials.

Subdued London

Over the next three weeks, Boudicca's army—estimated by historians to be around 100,000 warriors—launched two other successful attacks on Roman strongholds. The second victory came at Londinium (London). Suetonius had no time to evacuate Roman citizens from what was then Britain's largest city (25,000), and the Britons slaughtered them mercilessly. Horrific atrocities were inflicted on its women, and the heads of Romans were offered up by Druid priests in ceremonies honoring the goddess of victory. Next, Boudicca and the Britons took Verulamium (St. Albans) a few days later. This was the capital of the Catuvellauni tribe and had won official status as Roman Britain's first *municipium,* the all-important "city" designation; for this its Briton inhabitants were seen as collaborators with the Romans, and they too were treated without mercy.

By this point, Boudicca's rebellion had devastated the three main cities in Roman Britain, and the number of dead Romans and collaborating Britons was estimated at 70,000. Yet the Britons had not tended to their spring harvest, since they assumed they would be able to easily plunder Roman stores—which Suetonius ordered burned—and the troops soon faced famine. Moreover, Boudicca had difficulty in controlling such a large, non-homogenous army, which possessed little military discipline in comparison to the Roman troops. The last tactical error came in her army's failure to capture Roman military installations: these were well-defended, and housed Roman troops and supplies, including food, that Suetonius could use to his advantage.

A huge final battle marked the end of Boudicca's uprising against the Roman colonization of Britain. It is not known when or where exactly this battle took place, but probably occurred near the end of summer in C.E. 61 at some place between Towchester and Wall. According to later accounts, Suetonius and the Romans had amassed on a rocky landscape that offered good protection, and Briton troops then charged uphill. When they were out of breath and tactically vulnerable, the Romans attacked. Boudicca's army was soundly defeated. She herself fled back to the Norfolk area, and in anticipation of a terrible end at Roman hands, ingested a deadly poison. She was the last ruler of the Iceni royal line, and was allegedly buried with all its treasure in a grave that remained a well-kept secret to both her Roman foes and modern archaeologists.

Boudicca's Legacy and Legend

Boudicca's rebellion was a crucial moment in early British history, especially in light of the Roman occupation that radically altered its course over the next four centuries. Her confederacy of Briton tribes had taken the placid Roman occupiers literally by surprise; they had assumed that the Celtic "barbarians" were far too disorganized to mount any insurrection. As a result, the Romans made certain that their installations were secure and that the Briton population never more posed such a threat. Roman officials also instituted reforms that meant a lessening of some of the onerous demands of their colonial rule, including a fairer system of taxation. England's occupiers departed only when the Roman Empire itself fell into disintegration in the fifth century C.E.

Boudicca remained nearly lost to historical record after her death. Much of what was later written about Britain's Roman era failed to mention her. It was only when the Italian writer Giovanni Boccaccio (*The Decameron*) visited a little-known monastery in 1360 and found Tacitus's manuscript that historical scholarship became aware of her role in history. Boudicca's reputation grew to great proportions during the reign of Queen Elizabeth I, as historians and writers trumpeted the legacy of strong female leaders in the British Isles' past—especially ones who attempted to battle mighty foreign powers. The first official biography of Boudicca came in 1591 from an Italian living in England, Petruccio Ubaldini, *The Lives of the Noble Ladies of the Kingdom of England and Scotland*. In 1610 John Fletcher's play, *Bonduca*, a variant of the name Boudicca, debuted on the London stage; it and other works of the era celebrated her as a "virago," or a woman with masculine traits. John Milton wrote of her in his *History of Britain*, published in 1670.

The significance of Boudicca's heroic exploits endured well into the twentieth century—Winston Churchill wrote of her in his *History of the English-Speaking Peoples*. The former prime minister of England during World War II declared that her revolt was "probably the most horrible episode which our Island has known. We see the crude and corrupt beginning of a higher civilization blotted out by the ferocious uprising of the native tribes. Still, it is the primary right of men to die and kill for the land they live in, and to punish with exceptional severity all members of their own race who have warmed their hands at the invader's earth."

Further Reading

Churchill, Winston, *A History of the English-Speaking Peoples,* Dodd, Mead, 1956-58.
Dudley, Donald R. and Graham Webster, *The Rebellion of Boudicca,* Barnes & Noble, 1962.
Dudley, Donald R. and Graham Webster, *The Roman Conquest of Britain, A.D. 453-57,* B. T. Batsford, 1965.
Durant, G. M., *Britain: Rome's Most Northerly Province,* St. Martin's, 1972.

David Bowie

English singer David Bowie (born 1947) has been called a cultural chameleon throughout his long and colorful career. From music and film to art and the Internet, Bowie has challenged the perceptions of fans and critics alike with his many malleable personas which seemed to mirror the cutting edge trends of the day. In 1996, Bowie became the first artist of his stature to release a single, "Telling Lies," exclusively via the Internet.

Born January 8, 1947, and raised in Brixton, a poor section of London, Bowie claims to have mapped out his destiny at an early age. The son of Hayward Jones, a publicist, and Margaret Mary (Burns) Jones, a movie theater usher, Bowie turned to music as the way to change his life. After having heard a single by Little Richard, the nine-year-old Bowie decided he wanted to be one of Little Richard's saxophone players. A short time later, he got his first saxophone and began working as a butcher's delivery boy in order to pay it off. Upon learning that jazz player Ronnie Ross lived in the neighborhood, Bowie persuaded Ross to give him some lessons. After ten or so lessons, Bowie quit going to see Ross because he felt that he was ready to become a rock star.

Bowie immersed himself in music because of the lack of communication between his parents and himself. He told Hanif Kureishi of *Interview* that "I could never, ever talk to my father. I really loved him, but we couldn't talk about anything together. There was this really British thing that being even remotely emotional was absolutely verboten." Putting it down to the "classic case of British reserve," Bowie consoled himself by withdrawing to his room where he was alone with his books and music and thoughts.

While a teenager, Bowie plied his trade with numerous London area bands including the Kon-Rads, King Bees, Mannish Boys, and the Lower Third. During this time he flirted with a number of the musical styles and genres popular in Britain in the early- to mid-1960s, most notably folk and mod. Bowie also studied commercial art, worked briefly at an advertising agency, painted, and acted in some small stage roles.

The worldwide success of the made-for-television American pop band The Monkees forced Bowie to change

his name in the late 1960s. The Monkees' lead singer was named Davey Jones and Bowie did not want to be confused with him, so he adopted the surname Bowie. Bowie started his solo career in 1966 and released his first singles about the same time. The singles were mostly unmemorable and easily forgettable until 1969. In that year, Bowie released his first classic signature song "Space Oddity," which eventually peaked at number five on the British pop singles chart. Two years later, his album, *The Man Who Sold the World*, was released. It has been claimed that the birth of the glam rock movement occurred when this album was released. Also that year, Bowie went on his first promotional tour of America and in the summer, his wife Angela Barnet gave birth to a son, Zowie, now known as Joey.

The year 1972 was a rather eventful one for Bowie. He went on another promotional tour of America, although this time it was to cement relations with his new label RCA. *Hunky Dory*, was culled from tracks on the demo that got Bowie his new recording contract. It contained the singles "Life on Mars" and "Changes". The follow-up to *Hunky Dory* established Bowie as a star. *The Rise and Fall of Ziggy Stardust and the Spiders from Mars* gave Bowie not only the abbreviated title track but it also gave him his first and perhaps most beloved persona—Ziggy Stardust. On his chameleon-like character changes, Bowie told Kureishi of *Interview* that "I know now for a fact that so much of my ambition and drive came from wanting to escape from myself and from feelings of inadequacy and vulnerability and not feeling I was loved by anybody, particularly. I would drive those feelings out by throwing myself not only

into work, but eventually into characters." The tour to support the album was a rock spectacle full of theatrics and innovations.

During this time, Bowie produced Lou Reed's *Transformer* album and Mott the Hoople's *All the Young Dudes*. He also discussed his bisexuality in an interview with the British music magazine *Melody Maker*. The resulting controversy lingered on for years. Later Bowie told Kurt Loder in *Rolling Stone:* "The biggest mistake I ever made . . . was telling that . . . writer that I was bisexual. Christ, I was so *young* then. I was *experimenting.*"

Aladdin Sane was released in the spring of 1973, while the world was still enchanted by Ziggy Stardust. In June of that year, Bowie gave up the Ziggy Stardust persona which started a trend that would continue throughout his career. The shock of this announcement was heightened by the fact that it was made on the last date of the Ziggy Stardust tour and not even members of Bowie's band had known about it ahead of time.

Bowie then went to France and started to work on his next album *Pin Ups*, which was released in the fall of 1973. It was in homage to the artists who had influenced him when he was starting out in the music industry. Six months later saw the release of *Diamond Dogs,* which was a reaction to the disco music that was slowly starting to inundate society. The success of Bowie's biggest American tour to date was chronicled on *David Live,* a recording of the Philadelphia concert.

Bowie's fascination with America manifested itself on his 1975 release *Young Americans.* It gave Bowie his first American number one single, "Fame," which was a collaboration with John Lennon that barely made the album. Shortly after the release of the album, Bowie moved to Los Angles and began his film career with a role in the 1976 movie *The Man Who Fell to Earth.* Also that year, Bowie released *Station to Station* and RCA released his first greatest hits album *Changesonebowie.*

Not long after this, Bowie moved to Berlin and began collaborations with avante garde experimentalists Brian Eno and Robert Fripp. According to Bowie's official web site, the vibe of the Berlin recording sessions with Fripp and Eno featured "surrealism and experimentation [as] the themes of the day. The incorporation of cut and paste techniques into unique instrumentation birthed what are now heralded as luminary ambient soundscapes." *Low,* which was released in 1977, perplexed both RCA and Bowie's fans although the single "Sound & Vision" made it to number two on the British pop charts. During this time, Bowie also produced and collaborated on *The Idiot* by his friend Iggy Pop.

Stage was released in the fall of 1978 and featured material culled from Bowie's Berlin period and material from his most recent American concert tour. He then relocated to Switzerland before setting off on expeditions to the continents of Asia and Africa. His next album *Lodger* was recorded in France and released in the spring of 1979. In September of the following year, Bowie made his debut on a Broadway stage in the role of the Elephant Man. He received numerous positive reviews for his performance.

Around the same time as his Broadway debut, Bowie divorced his wife, Angela Barnet.

Bowie chose to drop out of the music scene for awhile, in order to concentrate on acting. His first film role during his self-imposed sabbatical was in *The Hunger,* which was released in 1982. This was followed very closely by *Merry Christmas Mr. Lawrence.* RCA released his second greatest hits package *Changestwobowie* in that year as well.

With the 1983 signing of Bowie to EMI came the release of yet another of his signature albums *Let's Dance.* Jay Cocks of *Time* called it a "record of shrewd and unsentimental dynamism." It introduced the former Thin White Duke and Ziggy Stardust to a whole new generation of fans through videos on MTV. *Let's Dance* included the hit singles "Let's Dance," "Modern Love," and "China Girl," which was a collaboration between Bowie and Pop from their time spent in Berlin. His next album, *Tonite,* was released in 1984. Three years later saw the release of *Never Let Me Down.*

In 1988, Bowie announced the formation of his new band Tin Machine. This was notable for two reasons. It was the first time Bowie would be part of a group as opposed to a solo singer with a backing band. Also, as Bowie was quick to point out, this was to be a collaborative effort, not a Bowie side project. Virgin released Tin Machine's self titled debut album in 1989. Tin Machine signed to Victory and released *Tin Machine II* in 1991. The following year, the live album *Oy Vey Baby* was released. In 1992, Tin Machine was put on indefinite hold as Bowie decided to revive his solo career.

Bowie toured the world in support of the Rykodisc box set *Sound + Vision.* This tour served as the long awaited and much anticipated greatest hits tour. On April 24, 1992, not far from his home in Switzerland, Bowie wed his second wife, the Somalian model, Iman. The following year brought the Virgin release *Black Tie White Noise,* which was informally called the wedding album in honor of his nuptials from the previous year. It marked the first solo Bowie record since 1987. Two years later, Bowie was once again collaborating with Eno, this time on *Outside.*

In 1995, Bowie toured the United States with the group Nine Inch Nails, and featured his songs from *Outside.* In 1996, he was inducted into the Rock and Roll Hall of Fame, starred in the film *Basquiat,* and released the Internet-only single "Telling Lies." One of the challenges Bowie faced in 1997 was the marketing and selling of the "Bowie Bonds." The sale of the bonds enabled him to obtain royalty money up front as opposed to waiting for it. The bonds were backed by the future royalties from his albums which were released prior to 1990. He also released *Earthling* in 1997.

Bowie has developed a solid reputation in the art world as an artist and writer. According to the Virgin Records website, during 1996 and 1997 Bowie had art exhibitions in Switzerland, Italy, and England. He also sold art exclusively through his "Bowieart" website, and his interview with the late pop artist Roy Lichtenstein was published in the January 1998 issue of *Interview.* In May of 1997, Bowie and three colleagues founded *21 Publishing* in Great Britain. According to the "Bowieart" website, "*21* aims to address the cultural issues of the 21st century and will create a platform for new words, new images and new ideas."

Nicholas Roeg, who directed Bowie in *The Man Who Fell to Earth,* summed up the Bowie mystique to Cocks of *Time* as "David's a real living Renaissance figure. That's what makes him spectacular. He goes away and re-emerges bigger than before. He doesn't have a fashion, he's just constantly expanding. It's the world that has to stop occasionally and say 'My God, he's still going on.'"

Further Reading

Buckley, David, *David Bowie,* Omnibus, 1996.
Thompson, Dave, and Dave Thomson, *David Bowie: Moonage Daydream,* Plexus Pub, 1994.
Tremlett, George, *David Bowie: Living on the Brink,* Carroll & Graf, 1997.
Amusement Business, October 30, 1995, p. 8.
Billboard , August 2, 1997, p. 6.
CFO, April 1997, p. 20.
Entertainment Weekly, April 4, 1997, p. 26; November 14, 1997, p. 89.
Fortune, April 28, 1997, p. 50.
Interview, May 1993, pp. 92-97; February 1997, pp. 46-50.
People, May 18, 1992, p. 72.
Rolling Stone, May 12, 1983; October 25, 1984; April 23, 1987.
Time, July 18, 1983, pp. 54-60; February 17, 1997, p. 70.
"Bowieart," http://www.bowieart.com (March 9, 1998).
"David Bowie," *Celeb site,* http://www.celebsite.com/people/davidbowie/ (March 9, 1998).
"David Bowie," http://www.davidbowie.com/2.0/history/biography (February 13, 1998).
"David Bowie," http://www.virginrecords.com/artists (February 13, 1998).

Marion Zimmer Bradley

Popular fantasy writer Marion Zimmer Bradley (born 1930) is considered a pioneer in the field of woman-based science fiction, creating strong, independent female protagonists in her many popular novels and short stories.

B eginning her career in the 1950s, author Marion Zimmer Bradley has built almost a cult following on the heels of her popular "Darkover" books. While largely ignored by mainstream reviewers, Bradley's fiction has been embraced by her fans as what *Feminist Writers* essayist Nancy Jesser calls "one of the early manifestations of proto-feminist science fiction." In her writing, the prolific Bradley has worked in several genres, including Gothic novels, teleplays, children's books, lesbian novels, and bibliographies of gay and lesbian fiction. She addresses such issues as gender, technology, alienation, the evolution of society, culture, and human relationships by placing her characters in highly imaginary worlds, many with a Celtic flavor.

Began Professional Writing Career
at Age 17

Bradley, who was born in Albany, New York, on June 3, 1930, knew from an early age that she wanted to be a writer. Fascinated by the science-fiction writing of the era, she started her own amateur science-fiction magazine before she was even out of high school. However, Bradley was too practical to think that a young woman could make writing her life's work; after graduating from high school she enrolled at New York State College with the intention of becoming a teacher. But her marriage to Robert Alden Bradley in 1949 would put a halt to these career plans, and the birth of a son would occupy much of her time during the 1950s. It was not until 1964 that the industrious Bradley completed her education, graduating from Abilene, Texas's Hardin-Simmons University with a triple bachelor's degree in English, Spanish, and psychology. She then attended graduate school at the University of California, Berkeley for another three years. Meanwhile, she continued to write, composing short stories and experimenting with longer works containing science-fiction and fantasy elements.

In 1949, the same year she got married, Bradley sold her first story to a sci-fi publication. Three years later she began what she considers her "professional" writing career, with the sale of yet another story to the magazine *Vortex Science Fiction.* Throughout the remainder of the 1950s she managed to juggle the demands of motherhood—at the time moms were expected to stay at home—with her desire to write. Bradley would not publish her first full-length book

until 1961, when the sci-fi novel *The Door through Space* was released. This novel seemed to open a floodgate for Bradley; in 1962 alone her byline would appear on five different volumes: three novels under her own name and two other works under various pseudonyms. While readers might marvel at how Bradley could be so prolific, at least one of the novels published in 1962—*The Planet Savers*—had actually made its first appearance serialized in the pages of *Amazing Science Fiction Stories* three years earlier. Now in book form, *The Planet Savers* would become the first of Bradley's "Darkover" novels.

The World of Darkover

The 20 novels that comprise the bulk of the "Darkover" series are among Bradley's most popular works of fiction. The series is named after a lost colony wherein social habits and technology develop independently of the earthlings who established it because it was overlooked for many generations. In addition to developing psychic abilities, Darkoverians have divided along gender lines: a patriarchal society exists apart from a woman-centered society of "Free Amazons." In Bradley's futuristic world, nothing is gained without sacrifice. According to Susan M. Shwartz in *The Feminine Eye: Science Fiction and the Women Who Write It,* "For every gain, there is a risk; choice involves a testing of will and courage . . . on Darkover any attempt at change of progress carries with it the need for pain-filled choice." Clearly, to survive within such a world Bradley's protagonists—particularly the female characters her readers most closely identify with—must be strong, intelligent, and determined.

Among the most popular Darkover novels are 1965's *Star of Danger,* 1976's *The Shattered Chain,* and *Heirs of Hammerfell,* a more recent work published in 1989. *The Shattered Chain* is agreed upon by most critics as among the best of the series. It is the story of a quest, a traditional story form in which the main character must surmount a series of obstacles on her way to achieving her goals. In Bradley's version, Lady Rohana, a member of the privileged ruling class, attempts to free a friend from a tribe of men who chain women up to demonstrate their power over them. To accomplish her task, Rohana gains the help of the Free Amazons, but only at the cost of reassessing her own life and values.

The Darkover novels occupied much of Bradley's time during the 1960s and 1970s, although she also managed to find the time to publish a collection of short fiction, *The Dark Intruder and Other Stories,* as well as several volumes of literary criticism. Bradley's personal life was undergoing transition during this period as well; she divorced her first husband in 1964, and married for a second time shortly thereafter. She and her second husband, Walter Henry Breen, would raise three children (Bradley's son from her first marriage, plus a son and daughter of their own) before divorcing in 1990. The demands of parenthood on her limited time may have multiplied, but they did little to staunch Bradley's enthusiasm for writing—or her published output. Perhaps these demands are at the root of her efforts to find, through the dilemmas of her fictional female protagonists, that ideal balance between a woman's duty to self and her obligations to others. She published over 30 books between 1965 and 1980, and in 1984 undertook a long-term project: editing a series of short-story collections for New York-based DAW publishers under the *Sword and Sorceress* title.

A Sci-Fi Writer in King Arthur's Court

Hailed by several critics as Bradley's most notable novel, *The Mists of Avalon* was published in 1983 and remained on the *New York Times* best-seller list for 16 weeks. Taking place in Arthurian Britain, called Britannia, the novel features such well-known female characters as Morgan Le Fay and the Lady of the Lake, given heightened strength of will under Bradley's pen as they perform their parts in the tragic legend of King Arthur. Although published afterward, the novels *The Forest House* and *Lady of Avalon* serve as precursors to *The Mists of Avalon,* detailing the chain of events leading up to the events surrounding Bradley's version of the King Arthur legend. *The Forest House* tells of the relationship between the priestess Eilan and Gaius Marcellius, an officer in the Roman occupation army with whom she conceives a son, Gawan. *Lady of Avalon* finds Britannia now firmly ruled by the Romans, with Christian priests working to gain strides with the population against the ancient Druidic religions. In *The Mists of Avalon*—a lengthy volume of over 850 pages—the Arthurian legends are retold from the perspective of the enchantress Morgaine, a follower of the ways of wicca and a priestess of the ancient Goddess religion. Despite her powers, Morgaine is unable to defend the ancient goddesses against the inexorable crush of Christianity, and her failure embitters her. She must watch as womankind reverts from a respected sex to a berated one, condemned as the source of original sin by the patriarchal Christian teachings.

Fantasy as a Means to Discover a Different Truth

Women of another quasi-mythic period of history fall under Bradley's scrutiny in *The Firebrand,* which she published in 1987. Taking the written history surrounding the Trojan War as her starting point, Bradley weaves a tale of heroism as Kassandra, daughter of the King of Troy and an Amazon, attempts to save her kingdom from patriarchal Dorian invaders. In this novel, as in much of her work, Bradley constructs an alternative to the male-dominated "reality" passed down through traditional written histories. She admitted in an interview with Lisa See of *Publishers Weekly* that the transition from the bronze to the iron age did indeed cause the destruction of such Cretan cities as Mycenae, the home of the legendary ruler Agamemnon. But Bradley believes that in viewing this period of history objectively—"as though no one had ever written about [it] before"—another history is revealed. "Here were two cultures that should have been ruled by female twins—Helen and Klytemnestra," she stated to See. "And what do you know? When they married Menelaus and Agamemnon, the men took over their cities." This interest in viewing the past through a different perspective—a perspective that might ultimately reveal hidden truths—is at the heart of Bradley's intent as a writer.

In response to her many fans, Bradley began the *Marion Zimmer Bradley's Fantasy Magazine* in 1988. While she has remained active as an editor, working on her magazine as well as editing the annual *Sword and Sorcery* anthology for DAW, her output as a novelist has decreased in recent years due to health issues. Still, imaginative fictions such as 1995's *Ghostlight* and its sequel, *Witchlight,* continue to issue from Bradley's pen on occasion, to the pleasure of her many fans. Interestingly, from her home in Berkeley, California, Bradley has also managed to extend the Darkover saga beyond her own novels by inviting others to create their own vision of her mythic world. Under her editorship, anthologies such as *Domains of Darkover* and *Towers of Darkover* allow other writers to navigate Bradley's fantastic worlds, taking new paths, creating characters with fresh viewpoints, and entertaining readers with alternative renditions of Bradley's sci-fi saga.

Further Reading

Arbur, Rosemarie,*Leigh Brackett, Marion Zimmer Bradley, Anne McCaffrey: A Primary and Secondary Bibliography,* Hall, 1982.
Feminist Writers, St. James Press, 1996, pp. 60-63.
Spivak, Charlotte, *Merlin's Daughters: Contemporary Women Writers of Fantasy,* Greenwood Press, 1987.
Staicar, Tom, editor,*The Feminine Eye: Science Fiction and the Women Who Write It,* F. Ungar, 1982.
Wise, S., *The Darkover Dilemma: Problems of the Darkover Series,* T-K Graphics, 1976.
Extrapolation, summer 1993.
Journal of Popular Culture, summer 1993, pp. 67- 80.
Los Angeles Times Book Review, February 3, 1983.
Publishers Weekly, October 30, 1987.
Science Fiction Review, summer, 1983.
New York Times Book Review, January 30, 1983.
West Coast Review of Books, number 5, 1986.
Marion Zimmer Bradley Homepage, http://www.mzb.fm.com (March 15, 1998). ☐

Brian Boru

Celtic military leader Brian Boru (c. 940-1014) was the first king of a united Ireland.

Through shrewd military acumen Brian Boru became the first king of a united Ireland, in an era when the isle was little more than a verdant home to Celtic peoples whose society still reflected much of the traditions of the late Iron Age. During his reign, domestic political stability invigorated Ireland, and religious and cultural life was able to flourish. "Brian Boru was remarkable in the Ireland of his time," wrote Máire and Liam de Paor in *Early Christian Ireland,* "because he seems to have thought in terms of the feudal organization which had already developed in Europe rather than in terms of the primitive and unstable kingship-system of Ireland." His achievement has earned him comparisons with another great uniter of warring lands, the Holy Roman Emperor Charlemagne.

Ireland Before Brian

The Irish were a Celtic people, a population that dominated central Europe after the fifth century B.C.E. Known as fierce warriors, they migrated to the British Isles and retained many aspects of their past there for centuries after Celtic culture in Europe was supplanted by Roman and other civilizations. In Ireland, they organized into groups of related families called *tuaths*, fought other *tuaths* viciously on horseback, and possessed a social hierarchy that was dominated by Druid priests and chief-like kings called *ri*. Christianity was introduced in the fifth century C.E. by Ireland's legendary St. Patrick, but it was a religion imposed on an unsettled, agrarian land with few urban centers. Instead, Ireland's repositories of culture were its monasteries, which dotted the countryside. There, monks lived austere, simple lives but wrote treatises on religious topics and transcribed Celtic mythology in Latin.

Sea-faring Vikings from various parts of Scandinavia started to plunder Ireland beginning in 795. Like other settlements near coastal waters in northern Europe, the Irish feared the sudden onslaught of Viking ships and the ruthlessness of their men, who quickly sacked towns and loaded livestock and anything else of value onto their ships. In their own lands, some of these Scandinavians had been subdued by Frankish conquerors in the name of Charlemagne and Christianity, and it made them determined foes of any Chris-

tian people. The Scandinavians found much of Ireland's artistic treasures—ceremonial metalwork and a wealth of other precious-metal handicrafts in a unique, curvilinear style—in its monasteries and plundered them as well; many of these ornamental swords or belts were later excavated from graves in Norway. Over the next few decades, these Vikings also began to winter over in Ireland instead of returning home; they built walled towns such as Dubl-Linnhe (Dublin), whose origins date to 840. Both Dublin and other coastal towns became hubs of commercial activity as the Vikings set up lucrative trade monopolies. Organized Irish military resistance to Viking rule was successful only in the north. In the south, warring *tuaths* and provinces could not muster the same unity of forces to do battle.

By 940 C.E., roughly the time of Brian's birth, Ireland was segregated into five provinces of connected *tuaths* known as the Five Fifths. These were Ulster, Connacht, Meath, Munster, and Leinster. Since the fifth century C.E., varying kings of the first three provinces dominated the northern lands, and sometimes claimed all of Ireland in name; in reality, however, the *ard ri,* or high king, held true power only in the north, leaving Munster and Leinster quite sovereign. The north's royal seat was at Tara. In the south, a *ri* of the Eogannacht *tuath* reigned at Cashel in Munster, near present-day Tipperary.

Brian Boru and the Dal Chais

Brian Boru was, with his brother Mahon, prince of a tribe in Munster called the Dal Chais. Their home ground was an area known as Thomond at the mouth of the River Shannon, in what is now County Clare. The tribe and the brothers gained a reputation as astute, fierce mercenaries, and in 964 Mahon decided to battle the Eogannacht family for the throne of Cashel. This center of power in the south of Ireland was located between Viking settlements at Limerick and the seaside city of Waterford. Mahon emerged victorious and took the Eogannacht crown for himself, but a Viking settlement at Limerick effectively sundered him at Cashel from the Dal Chais lands at Thomond.

At Brian's urging, plans were made to oust the Vikings from Limerick, beginning with raids on the outer settlements. The first serious battle came at Sulcoit and the settlement was sacked. Brian, at the age of 26, then stormed Limerick on his brother's behalf. Typical of the skirmishes of the time and place, men on each side were clad in mail and did battle on horseback with swords, spears, and axes. The Irish were known to behead their enemies, and they also rounded up Scandinavians and immediately slaughtered anyone who was fit to fight.

The beginning of Brian's eventual vanquish of Viking power came with this victory at Limerick in 968. When Mahon was murdered, Brian became king of Munster, and over the next few years consolidated his power in the rest of the south. He constructed a fleet of ships and kept them anchored on the River Shannon, and sent out plundering raids to the north. He overwhelmed the Vikings in Waterford and rid them from the surrounding islands as well. He then set his sights on attacking the Viking king in Dublin. To do so he allied with Meath's ruler, his onetime rival

Malachy, to do battle with the King of Leinster, who was allied with Dublin. After a decisive and bloody fight, Brian entered Dublin victorious in 1000 C.E. The Vikings were allowed to stay, but hefty tribute was levied from them.

Now Brian firmly controlled Munster and Leinster, and set his sights farther north. He assembled an army of Irish and Danes and rode to Tara, where the high king of Ireland, the Ui Neill *ri,* sat. By this point Brian's reputation was so widespread that the north capitulated with almost no resistance. Brian further consolidated power by marrying Gormflaith, the sister of the King of Leinster. However, Gormflaith was also mother of Sitric, the former Viking leader in Dublin; to complicate matters, Sitric then married Brian's sister.

"Imperator Scottorum"

In 1002 Brian deposed Malachy and thus became true *ard ri* of all Ireland. Historical corroboration of this comes from his signature, written for him by his scribe in 1004, in the *Book of Armagh.* The manuscript, which also contained the *Confessio,* or autobiographical writing of St. Patrick, was the treasure of Armagh, the seat of the Christian Church in Ireland at the time. Brian paid 20 ounces of gold to the church fathers there in exchange for being allowed to sign, "Brian, Imperator Scottorum" (meaning "king of the Scots," from the Latin writings of the day that named the Celts of the British Isles *Scoti*), in the sacred manuscript.

Brian's reign as king of Ireland lasted twelve years, and the country prospered during his rule. Monasteries and schools that had previously been sacked and closed as a result of continuous warfare were reopened, or rebuilt. He decreed the construction of roads and bridges, and built many churches along the Shannon, a symbolic statement since the river had once been the main highway for the Vikings and their plundering inland raids. Bronze artistry, which had fallen into decline, also experienced a revival. Trade increased, and emissaries were even sent across the sea to Scotland and Wales to extract tribute.

The Battle of Clontarf

The end of Brian's rule and his own demise had its origins in a quarrel between the King of Leinster and Brian's son Murrough over a chess game in 1013. When the King stormed out of Brian's Kincora castle, his sister Gormflaith went with him. She then rallied her son Sitric along with some Vikings from the Isle of Man and Hebrides, and assembled a fleet at mouth of the Liffey. The Vikings also sent out word back home for reinforcements, and Scandinavian mercenaries arrived in huge numbers. The actual battle took place at Clontarf, near Dublin, on Good Friday, 1014. It lasted from dawn to sunset. Brian was now 74, and since it was a holy day he remained in a tent near the rear of the battle site and prayed. The Irish were victorious: Brian's army slew 7,000 Vikings, while only 4,000 Irish lost their lives. Both Brian's son and grandson died on the field, however. As the Vikings fled to the sea, the flanks guarding Brian's encampment scattered, and he was surprised by a Viking king, Brodar of the Isle of Man. Brodar was able to ride into the tent, and Brian reacted by cutting Brodar's leg off below the knee; Brodar then split Brian's skull, killing him with the blow.

Brian's body was carried to Armagh in a solemn cortege. Yet his 1014 victory at Clontarf remains a momentous date in Irish history, the year that marked the end of Viking aggression in Ireland. Though Ireland lapsed back into disunion for some time afterward, it would not be invaded for another 150 years until Anglo-Saxons from England set their sights on its green hills. Most of the Vikings that remained in Ireland converted to Christianity and intermarried; they would never dominate the Irish again. Brian's descendants are the O'Brien clan. One of them later married a Norman noble, and an offspring of this union was Elizabeth de Burgh. She later married the Duke of Clarence, who was the son of English king Edward III, and from their union came the York kings and the mother of Henry VIII.

Further Reading

de Paor, Máire and Liam, *Early Christian Ireland,* Thames and Hudson, 1958.
Edwards-Rees, Désirée, *Ireland's Story,* Barnes & Noble, 1967.
Newark, Tim, *Celtic Warriors: 400 B.C.–1600 A.D.,* Blandford Press, 1986.

Frances Hodgson Burnett

English-born American author Frances Hodgson Burnett (1849-1924) had a long and productive writing career, during which she penned 55 titles, 5 of which became best-sellers and 13 of which were adapted for the stage. Although remembered primarily for her children's books, such as *Little Lord Fauntleroy, A Little Princess,* and *The Secret Garden,* Burnett also wrote for adults, including the well-received novel *That Lass o' Lowrie's.*

B urnett was born Frances Eliza Hodgson in Manchester, England, on November 24, 1849, to Edwin and Eliza (Boond) Hodgson. She was the middle of five children. When her father died in 1865, his hardware wholesaling business collapsed, leaving the family with few financial resources. A short while later, Burnett immigrated with her siblings and her mother to rural Tennessee, where they lived with her mother's brother. Burnett was about 16 years old at the time. The only education she had received was in a dame school in England, but she had spent vast amounts of time reading and educating herself on her own. The family had little money, and Burnett's first attempt at earning an income involved running a private school, which was unsuccessful. She then decided to try to sell a story to a magazine. She had been reading stories in ladies' periodicals since she was seven years old and had learned the formula quite well. She was so good, in fact, that the editor of *Godey's Lady's Book,* the magazine to which she submitted the tale, questioned whether it was original. It did

not seem likely that a young girl from Tennessee could write such a good story for a British women's magazine. Burnett wrote a second tale to prove her authenticity, and eventually both stories were accepted for publication. "Hearts and Diamonds" appeared in the summer of 1868, and "Miss Carruther's Engagement" was published the following year.

In 1870, Burnett and her family moved to Knoxville, Tennessee, to a house called "Vagabondia." Soon after, Burnett's mother died. At age 20, Burnett found herself in charge of the family, and she continued to write for women's magazines in order to earn an income. She published numerous stories over the next few years, as many as five or six a month. Her first long work, *Vagabondia,* was serialized as *Dolly* in *Peterson's Magazine* in 1873.

Wife, Mother, and Developing Writer

Burnett married Dr. Swan Moses Burnett, an ear and eye specialist, in 1873. Almost exactly one year later, they had their first son, Lionel. In 1875, the Burnetts moved to Paris, where their second son, Vivian, was born in 1876. During this time, Burnett continued to write and provide financial support for the family. In 1876 she published her first novel, *That Lass o' Lowrie's,* which had first appeared as a serial in *Scribner's Monthly.* The novel, a story of an independent woman in an English mining town, was well received and published in England only a few weeks after its release in America. One reviewer in the *New York Herald* stated that "there is no living writer (man or woman) who has Mrs. Burnett's dramatic power in telling a story. . . . The publication of *That Lass o' Lowrie's* is a red letter day in the world of literature." With the publication of *That Lass o' Lowrie's,* Burnett's popularity as a writer in both the United States and England grew quickly.

In 1877 the Burnetts moved to Washington, D.C., and the next five years became Burnett's most productive time as a writer. During this period she published many works, including *Surly Tim and Other Stories* (1877), which was a collection of early tales; *Haworth's* (1879), about Lancashire industrial life; *Louisiana* (1880), a portrayal of a farmer's daughter; *A Fair Barbarian* (1881), about a young American woman in rural England; and *Through One Administration* (1881), which was based on Burnett's observations while living in Washington. Her novels continued to be received with critical acclaim.

The strains of maintaining a household, raising two children, participating in Washington society, and writing so much during these years took their toll on Burnett. She was often ill and depressed, and referred to herself at this time as a "pen-driving machine." Her marriage was also troubled; she and her husband became estranged. Beginning in 1884, the couple spent more and more time living apart, with the children alternating between their father and mother. Burnett and her husband divorced in 1898.

Little Lord Fauntleroy

Even though Burnett's married life was not without flaw, she found she could still maintain the ideal through her fiction. She often stated, "The one perfect thing in my life was the childhood of my boys," and with the writing of *Little Lord Fauntleroy,* Burnett immortalized her statement. Basing the main character on her son Vivian, Burnett wrote a story about a disinherited American boy who wins back his noble title and fortune without corrupting his own innocence or debasing aristocratic values. The tale was published first as a serial in *St. Nicholas,* a magazine for children, in 1885, then as a book in 1886. The volume was a phenomenal success. *Little Lord Fauntleroy* became a best-seller, was translated into more than a dozen languages, and was produced for the stage in England and France. In addition, a variety of products were created based on the book, including toys, playing cards, writing paper, chocolate, and of course the dark velvet suits with lace collars that characterized Little Lord Fauntleroy in the book's illustrations. Much later, in 1921, Hollywood actress Mary Pickford starred in the first film version.

Because of the success of *Little Lord Fauntleroy,* Burnett and her sons were soon enjoying an expensive, international life-style, including trips to such places as London, Rome, and the French Riviera. The volume also changed the course of Burnett's writing career. From 1886 until 1896, she wrote mainly for children. She also continued to write for the theater, although her plays were not as popular as her novels. One of Burnett's works written during this time was her memoirs, *The One I Knew Best of All: A Memory in the Mind of a Child,* which was written in third person and published in 1893.

Trouble with the Critics

Phyllis Bixler Koppes noted in *American Women Writers* that Burnett's "life and writing were characterized by tensions between the serious artist and the popular writer, the independent woman and the self-sacrificing wife and mother." As Burnett's career advanced, these tensions were discussed by critics. Some claimed that she had given up serious writing in return for artificial, crowd-pleasing manuscripts that sold well. Other reviewers claimed she had a superficial personality. Details of her life were also critiqued, including her divorce and, later, her unconventional second marriage to her business and stage manager, Stephen Townesend, who was ten years her junior. When Burnett and Townesend separated permanently in 1902, just two years after their nuptials, the reviewers again focused on Burnett's personal life. In more recent times, a contributor to *A Reader's Guide to Twentieth-Century Authors* referred to Burnett as "the image of the popular Victorian lady novelist," who wore wigs, dressed in frilly clothing, and went by the nickname "Fluffy."

Not all critics were so harsh, and many praised Burnett's writing, especially her juvenile fiction. A contributor to the *New York Times* commented, "Many authors can write delightful books for children; a few can write entertaining books about children for adults; but it is only the exceptional author who can write a book about children with sufficient skill, charm, simplicity, and significance to make it acceptable to both young and old. Mrs. Burnett is one of the few thus gifted. . . ." Another reviewer, *Bookman* contributor Katharine Tynan, had similar sentiments, declaring that "[i]t is a privilege when such a writer as Mrs. Burnett gives her fresh and living art to writing stories for children." In *Children's Literature in Education*, Rosemary Threadgold compared Burnett's adult fiction to her children's tales, noting that Burnett's adult novels tended to follow "the formula that had brought her so much success." In writing for children, however, Threadgold judged Burnett to be "something of a leader. Her attention to detail, her gifts as a storyteller, and her interest in children all stand her in good stead."

"The knowledge that she had never lost an appreciative audience for her adult and children's books, however, probably helped Burnett overlook the frequent condescension of the critics," declared Phyllis Bixler in the *Dictionary of Literary Biography*. Burnett responded to the critics' demands for more serious writing by publishing *A Lady of Quality* in 1896. The heroine of the novel is a strong-willed girl raised as a boy, who later accidentally kills her former boyfriend, hides his body, and lives happily without punishment or regrets. To many reviewers, this book was a sign that Burnett was no longer interested in being taken seriously. Her popularity with the reading public, however, continued to grow.

Burnett published two more very successful children's books after *Little Lord Fauntleroy*. *A Little Princess*, released in 1905, was adapted for the stage and performed in London and New York. The book was also made into a feature film in 1939 that starred child-actress Shirley Temple. In 1911, *The Secret Garden* was published and has since become a children's classic. The novel tells the tale of an orphan who befriends her sickly cousin (based on Burnett's son Lionel who died of consumption at age 15) and finds an enclosed garden. *The Secret Garden* has been adapted into several films, a number of television programs, and a musical produced in 1993. "*The Secret Garden* will charm every one from the children to the grown-ups," declared a reviewer in a September, 1911, issue of *Literary Digest*.

Burnett also continued to be popular with adults, and several of her novels made the best-seller list. Some of her better known works of this period are tales of fashionable American and British life, such as *The Shuttle* (1907) and its sequel *T. Tembarom* (1913). In 1922, she published *The Head of the House of Coombe,* about social life in London before World War I. During these years, she had moved from her country estate in Kent, England, called Maytham Hall, to a cottage named Plandome on Long Island in New York.

Remembered as a Children's Author

"Burnett's reputation as a superior children's author remains secure," according to Phyllis Bixler, who further noted that Burnett's best children's books "can entertain a child and often an adult reader almost a century after they were written, an unusual longevity for children's fiction." Fittingly, Burnett's last public appearance was at the opening of the film of *Little Lord Fauntleroy*. She died on October 29, 1924, in Plandome, New York. Burnett once commented to her son Vivian, "With the best that I have in me, I have tried to write more happiness into the world."

Further Reading

Bixler, Phyllis, *Frances Hodgson Burnett*, Twayne, 1984.
Carpenter, Angelica Shirley, and Jean Shirley, *Frances Hodgson Burnett: Beyond the Secret Garden*, Lerner, 1990.
Dictionary of Literary Biography, Volume 42: *American Writers for Children before 1900*, Gale, 1985.
Greene, Carol, *Frances Hodgson Burnett: Author of the Secret Garden*, Children's Press, 1995.
Mainiero, Lina, editor, *American Women Writers*, Frederick Ungar, 1979.
McGillis, Roderick, *A Little Princess: Gender and Empire*, Twayne, 1996.
Thwaite, Ann, *Waiting for the Party: The Life of Frances Hodgson Burnett,* Faber and Faber, 1974.
Ward, Martha, et al., editors, *Authors of Books for Young People,* Scarecrow, 1990.
Bookman, December, 1911.
Children's Literature in Education, fall, 1988.
Literary Digest, September 2, 1911.
New York Herald, 1877.
New York Times, September 3, 1911.

Edgar Rice Burroughs

Edgar Rice Burroughs (1875-1950) was an American adventure writer whose Tarzan stories created a folk hero known around the world. His novels sold more than 100 million copies in 56 languages, making him

one of the most widely read authors of the twentieth century.

Edgar Rice Burroughs was born September 1, 1875, in Chicago, Illinois, to George Tyler and Mary Evaline (Zeiger) Burroughs. His father was successful in business, and worked as a distiller and a battery manufacturer. Burroughs was educated at private schools in Chicago and in the state of Michigan. After his graduation from the Michigan Military Academy, he joined the U.S. Cavalry for a tour of duty in Arizona in 1896. He was not suited to this life and, thanks to his father's wealth and position, he left the military the following year. He briefly owned a stationary store in Idaho before moving back to Chicago and a position with the American Battery Company. Burroughs married Emma Centennia Hulbert on January 1, 1900; the couple would have three children: Joan, Hulbert, and John Coleman. A few years after the marriage, Burroughs again tried to seek his fortune in the West, holding various jobs in Idaho and Utah. By 1906, he was back in Chicago and working for Sears, Roebuck and Company. After several attempts to start his own business, Burroughs turned to writing as a career.

Many reviewers and biographers have often described Burroughs as a failed pencil-sharpener salesman who just wanted to support his wife and children when he began writing. Others note that it was the company that had failed, not Burroughs, and that he had succeeded in numerous jobs. In any case, Burroughs began his writing career with a Martian tale, best known by its hardback title: *A Princess of Mars*. The story was written in 1911, and published under the pseudonym Normal Bean (to let readers know he was not crazy and had a "normal bean") in *All-Story* magazine in 1912. The tale was not published in hardback until 1917. Astronomer Percival Lowell's theories of the canals of Mars were at the height of their popularity in 1911, and fired Burroughs' imagination. There were eleven books in the Mars series, the last of which, *John Carter of Mars*, was published fourteen years after the author's death.

The main character of the Mars series is John Carter, a gentleman from Virginia. In the first story, he falls into a cave only to wake up on the planet Mars—a sort of death that brings him to a new life. An adventurous man throughout the series, he saves women from villains, rescues the planet, and shows the various colored Martians that they need each other to survive. One year after the publication of *A Princess of Mars* in book form, Burroughs released *The Gods of Mars*. Additional installments of the John Carter saga appeared on a regular basis, including *The Warlords of Mars* (1919), *Thuvia, Maid of Mars* (1920), *The Chessmen of Mars* (1922), *The Master Mind of Mars* (1928), and *A Fighting Man of Mars* (1931). John Hollow, writing in the *Dictionary of Literary Biography*, praised the first three novels of the series as "a particularly fine instance of science fiction's attempt to cope with what Burroughs himself called 'the stern and unalterable cosmic laws,' the certainty that both individuals and whole races grow old and die."

Best Known for His Tarzan Books

The appearance of Burroughs' second published story, *Tarzan of the Apes*, in *All-Story* magazine in 1912, and the publication of the novel in hardcover form in 1914, made him a best-selling author. Thereafter, he devoted himself exclusively to writing. Although Burroughs wrote almost all types of popular fiction, he is perhaps most famous for the Tarzan series. The lead character, Tarzan, is the son of an English noble who is adopted by a female ape in the African jungle. He learns English, grows into manhood, meets and falls in love with Jane, the daughter of an American scientist, and recovers his title—all in the first two of 26 stories.

Tarzan of the Apes captured the public's imagination and the series proved to be a success. Only a few fictional heroes, such as Robin Hood and Superman, are as famous as Tarzan. People might not remember the author, but most everyone, including small children, recognize the name of the main character, often responding with a Tarzan-like yell. The Tarzan stories have been translated into more than 56 languages, and reportedly more than 25,000,000 copies of the Tarzan books have been sold worldwide. Burroughs' novels were so financially rewarding that he was able to open his own publishing house, named after himself and called Burroughs. Beginning with the 1931 release, *Tarzan the Invincible*, he published his own works.

The character of Tarzan has been the subject of comic strips, radio serials, three television series, and at least 40 movies, including a Disney animated film and a 1998 spoof, *George of the Jungle*. *Tarzan of the Apes* was first made into a silent film in 1918, with Elmo Lincoln as Tarzan. More than a dozen actors have since starred in the role, the most popular having been Johnny Weissmuller, a former Olympic swimming champion. Most of the actors in Tarzan films were in fine physical shape, but they still faced risks. In the 1920 serial, *The Son of Tarzan*, Hawaiian actor Kamuela Searle was seriously injured by an elephant and a stand-in had to be used to complete the film; Searle later died of his injuries.

Not Without Controversy

Burroughs and his Tarzan character have not been without controversy. Burroughs, who himself has been accused of racism in his portrayal of Africa, disliked how films usually made Tarzan a grunting savage. He portrayed Tarzan in his novels as an erudite and wealthy heir to the House of Greystoke, equally at home in the jungle or polite society. Novels such as *The Return of Tarzan* (1915), *The Beasts of Tarzan* (1916), *Tarzan and the Jewels of Opar* (1918), and *Tarzan and the Golden Lion* (1923) continued this tradition. The last volume in the series, *Tarzan and the Castaways*, was released in 1965. As George P. Elliott noted in the *Hudson Review*, Burroughs' "prejudices are so gross that no one bothers to analyze them out or to attack them. . . . They were clear-eyed, well-thewed prejudices arrayed only in a loin cloth; you can take them or leave them, unless *your* big prejudice happens to be anti-prejudice. What matters is the story, which tastes good."

Burroughs' Tarzan series received other criticism. Although a favorite with readers, the Tarzan books have been dismissed by literary critics as cheap pulp fiction. Brian Attebury, writing in *The Fantasy Tradition in American Literature: From Irving to Le Guin,* commented: "Burroughs was neither more nor less than a good storyteller, with as much power—and finesse—as a bulldozer." Details of the Tarzan books have come under scrutiny, and even anthropologists have taken Burroughs to task, insisting that he was wrong in writing that great apes raised Tarzan. They insisted that the young Tarzan could not possibly have learned to swing through the trees so gracefully with a chimpanzee as his tutor. For him to have achieved such agility his instructor must have been an orangutan. Burroughs fans argue, however, that the apes in the Tarzan series were neither chimpanzees nor orangutans but a man-like invention of the author. Burroughs himself claimed that he never tried to do more than entertain his readers, and was honest about his need for money. "I had a wife and two babies," he once explained.

Burroughs envisioned his Tarzan stories as wholesome family entertainment. Not all portrayals of Tarzan have had the family in mind, however, and Burroughs' descendants, who still run the company bearing his name from Tarzana, California (an estate near Hollywood, California, Burroughs bought in 1919 and later named), have found it necessary to go to court. In 1996, for example, the family filed a law suit against the makers of "Jungle Heat," alleging that the interactive CD-ROM was "the antithesis to the good, wholesome and attractive images of Tarzan," as noted in the *Los Angeles Times.* There have been countless imitations of Tarzan, such as a jungle man called Tongo on the television series *Gilligan's Island,* and a Listerine commercial in which a Tarzan-like character swings on a vine barefoot while in a tuxedo. But many of these imitations are either protected by the legal safeguards for satire, or use material in the public domain—fair game after the expiration of copyright protection, which is limited in time. But Burroughs not only copyrighted the books, he covered the character of Tarzan with a trademark—which does not expire. In 1923, the author founded the family corporation, establishing the trademark to forever control products that used the name or likeness of Tarzan, from movies to comic books and T-shirts.

Later Career and Other Novels

Later in his career, Burroughs began corresponding with scientists to learn all that was known about the planet Venus. Provided with these ideas, he started a new series. Beginning with the publication of *Pirates of Venus* in 1934, Burroughs published four more volumes in this set, including *Lost on Venus* (1935), *Carson of Venus* (1939), and *Escape from Venus* (1946). His last book in the series, *The Wizard of Venus,* was released in 1970. As the first book in the Venus series was getting published, Burroughs divorced his wife of 34 years; he married his second wife, Florence Dearholt, in 1935.

Burroughs also wrote four western adventure stories, all carefully researched and based on his experience as a cowboy on his older brothers' ranch in Idaho as a young man and as a cavalry soldier in Arizona. Some critics consider these the best of his writing, particularly the sympathetic treatment of Geronimo and his renegade Apaches. Among the novels written in this genre include *Apache Devil* (1933) and *The Deputy Sheriff of Comanche County* (1940).

Burroughs continued to write novels for the rest of his life, ultimately publishing some 68 titles in all. During World War II, he served as a journalist with the United Press and, at age 66, was the oldest war correspondent covering the South Pacific theater. Burroughs died of a heart attack on March 19, 1950. A number of his novels were published posthumously. Even after his death, Burroughs remained a popular author, and he sold millions of books in paperback.

The University of Louisville Library owns the largest institutional archive of Burroughs' works. The collection contains more than 67,000 items ranging in scope from the author's earliest school books to promotional materials from the 1990s. The library's collection of Tarzan memorabilia includes film stills and posters featuring 19 Tarzan actors. It also includes the best and most celebrated book artists, including J. Allen St. John, who illustrated a total of 33 first editions of Burroughs. Other artists featured in the collection include Frank Frazetta, whose works adorned the first paperback Burroughs books of the 1960s, and John Coleman Burroughs, the author's son, who illustrated eleven first editions of his father's stories. The collection also includes items from Burroughs' personal life and affairs, samples of his books, pulp editions, letters, merchandising goods and many photographs taken over the last 100 years.

Further Reading

Attebury, Brian, *The Fantasy Tradition in American Literature: From Irving to Le Guin,* Indiana University Press, 1980.
Contemporary Authors, Volume 132, Gale, 1991.
Dictionary of Literary Biography, Volume 8: *Twentieth Century American Science Fiction Writers,* Gale, 1981.
Twentieth-Century American Science-Fiction Writers, Part 1: A-L, Gale, 1991.
Economist, July 22, 1995, p. 76.
Hudson Review, autumn 1959.
Los Angeles Times, August 9, 1996, Home Edition, p. 1; August 24, 1996, Valley Edition, p. B1; March 9, 1997, Valley Edition, Metro, p. 3.
Time, May 26, 1997, p. 105.
"Tarzan: The Legacy of Edgar Rice Burroughs," http://www.eb.com:180/cgi-bin/g?DocF=micro/583/20.html (March 8, 1998).
"Tarzan films do a poor job of teaching African history," http://www.sunspot.net/colmnists/data/kane/061497kane.html (March 30, 1998).
"Tarzan of the Comics: Usually Better Than the Movies," http://www.netuser.com/~erp/Tarzan.html (March 30, 1998).
"Tarzan Meets the 21st Century: An exhibition from the Edgar Rice Burroughs Collection," http://www.louisville.edu/groups/library-www/ekstrom/special/tarzan/tarz_exh.html (March 30, 1998).

C

Antoine de Lamothe Cadillac

Some historical controversy clouds the achievements of Antoine Laumet de Lamothe Cadillac (1658-1730), a French adventurer who in 1701 founded the first significant European post west of the Allegheny Mountains and named it Detroit. The letters that Cadillac left behind give evidence of a spirited, determined, and ambitious man, and those written about him during his era reveal that these same qualities earned him an abundance of enemies.

The very name "Cadillac" was mired in debate for many years, but historians now believe that the explorer was not of noble French birth as he claimed, but simply adopted the "Lamothe Cadillac" surname when he arrived in North America. Instead he was born Antoine Laumet in 1658 in the village of St. Nicolas-de-la-Grave in southern central France, and hailed from relatively prosperous local families on each side of his parentage; his father was a local magistrate. It is thought that Cadillac was educated at the Doctrinal College at Moissac, or perhaps at an institution in Toulouse called L'Esquile.

Abandoned Europe

There is some mystery concerning Cadillac's military service as a young man that allegedly began around 1677—he claimed to have been in regiments of Dampierre-Lorraine and Clairambault, but some historians surmise he may have earned a criminal record instead during this period of

his life, and hence the name change. In any case, Cadillac yearned to leave Europe and its seemingly stifling social, economic, and religious constraints behind, and looked toward the new lands across the Atlantic to which England and France were then staking claim. Fur traders, Jesuit priests, and ordinary adventurers were settling the regions of what is now New England, Canada's Maritime Provinces, and Quebec. In Cadillac's day, the exploits of the men who had first claimed these lands were legendary—such as Samuel de Champlain's founding of Quebec in 1608—and perhaps he saw for himself similar glory as a conqueror of the unfamiliar territories.

Cadillac probably first set foot on North American shores when he landed at Port Royal, Acadia (now Annapolis Royal, Nova Scotia) in 1683. During his residency there, he explored the coastline, made maps, and sent informative reports back to the French government. By 1687 he was involved in business dealings with a Quebec transplant named Guyon, and married the trader's daughter, Marie-Therese, in June of 1687. His marriage record contains the first official appearance of the name "Lamothe Cadillac." He even appropriated another noble family's coat of arms, but historians point out that such name-changes were not unusual among the French both in Europe and the new settlements.

Trusted Attaché in New World

In 1688 Cadillac was granted land in Acadia, was made a notary and court clerk at Port Royal, and began a family. Over the next few years, Cadillac traveled frequently back to France to give official reports at Court, and won the confidence of officials in the Ministry of Marine. For many years he lobbied for an increased naval presence along the interior waters in New France, from the St. Lawrence River to the Great Lakes.

The French government named Cadillac a captain in the Marines and naval ensign in April of 1694. He was sent to command the fort at Michilimackinac, located at what is now Mackinac City, Michigan. The settlement had a Jesuit mission, villages of Ottawa and Huron Indians, and some French families. Cadillac relished the time spent there, learning much about the indigenous culture of the region. His reports back to France were translated into English in 1947, and in them he wrote detailed accounts of the tribes. "It is always healthy at Michilimackinac; this may be attributed to the good air or to the good food, but it is better to attribute it to both," Cadillac observed in an excerpt reprinted in *Michigan, A State Anthology: Writings about the Great Lakes State, 1641-1981*. "A certain proof of the excellence of the climate is to see the old men there, whose grandsons are growing gray; and it would seem as if death had no power to carry off these specters."

Cadillac and the Jesuits

Though as commander of Fort Michilimackinac Cadillac strengthened ties with the Huron and other nations already there, he also came into conflict with another influential New World presence—the Jesuit missionaries, there to convert indigenous nations to Catholicism. It is thought that Cadillac may have received some of his early schooling from teachers belonging to this order, who were known as strict disciplinarians and devout friars, and a marked hostility to the order would brand his career in North America. One point of contention was the Jesuits' desire to keep the Native American nations free from a dependency on alcohol, and they had enjoined the French king to issue royal decrees barring its trade. Yet white traders sometimes exchanged brandy for beaver pelts, and Cadillac was accused of doing so in 1695. The Jesuit posted nearby complained to Count de Frontenac, the governor-general of New France, but Cadillac was exonerated.

France still considered the savvy, intrepid Cadillac a valuable asset, and the king and royal advisors finally heeded his arguments that France should establish a trading center on the Great Lakes to compete with New York and thwart English ties with Native American nations to the West. In December of 1698 he successfully convinced Louis XIV and his Minister of Marine, Count Pontchartrain, to decree the establishment of a fort on the Detroit River. This had been planned before, but the explorer Duluth instead founded a settlement some sixty miles north near what is now Port Huron, Michigan. There was only a handful of small Indian settlements in the region, since tribes of the powerful Iroquois nation controlled territory to the south, and their enemies maintained lands near the St. Clair River.

Founded Oldest City in Midwest

With royal approval and funding, Cadillac departed Montreal on June 5, 1701, with a flotilla of 25 canoes and a contingent of one hundred French. Accompanying them were canoes plied by Native Americans, who served as guides. They traveled down the St. Lawrence River into Georgian Bay and Lake Huron, and then down the St. Clair River and through Lake St. Clair. On July 24, 1701, they disembarked at the narrowest point in the Detroit River where 40-foot bluffs abutted the land near what is present-day downtown Detroit; he claimed it formally in the name of the King of France. Immediately a fortification was started, which Cadillac named after his ally at Court, Count Pontchartrain. The name "Detroit" has its origins in Cadillac's naming of the "ville de troit" or "city of the straits."

As commander, Cadillac immediately established cordial relations with nearby Ottawa, Huron, Potawatomi, Miami, and Wyandotte tribes, and encouraged them to group together in villages near the fort for mutual protection against both Iroquois and English enemies. There were only a few dozen soldiers stationed at Fort Pontchartrain in its early years, and Cadillac lobbied unsuccessfully for "christianized" Indian women from Michilimackinac to be brought to Detroit as brides for the men, a plan the Jesuits opposed. Cadillac's own wife arrived in 1702, after leaving two of their daughters behind at a convent in Quebec. Madame Cadillac, along with the wife of his second-in-command, Alphonse de Tonty, made an arduous trek of almost a thousand miles in open canoe to become the first European women settlers in Detroit. Madame Cadillac also brought along their seven-year-old son Jacques.

Contentious Times

The contentious Cadillac again earned enemies in his new post—for instance, he punished some clerks at the fort for illegal trading in 1703. When they brought countercharges, he was summoned to Quebec to answer to them. That same year he suspected Tonty of allying with the Jesuits to establish a trading post at Port Huron. Despite these and other conflicts, the Detroit settlement grew over the next few years and began to thrive economically. The area's first officially recorded birth came with his daughter, Marie-Therese, in 1704. At least four other Cadillac offspring were born there, but three died before the age of five.

Hostilities between indigenous nations increased around 1705, threatening the stability of the Fort. Reports reached Count Pontchartrain that same year that Cadillac was defying royal decree and trading the Indians brandy for pelts. A commissioner, Francois Clairambault d'Aigremont, was dispatched to investigate. Arriving in 1707, he found Cadillac guilty of several charges, including falsification of the number of permanent households. Clairambault also reported that Cadillac possessed the only horse in Detroit and rented it out. As a result, in a 1709 issuance from King Louis XIV, Cadillac was praised for his success in establishing the fort, but the troops that held it were officially recalled back to Montreal. So was Cadillac, who was arrested there on the charges of extortion and abuse of power.

Again, Cadillac managed to outwit his detractors and instead was named governor of the territory of Louisiana in November 1710. This huge territory, centered around what is now the southeastern United States, held little interest for Cadillac, and he dallied for over two years before arriving near what is now Mobile, Alabama, in June of 1713. His governorship of the area was less than noteworthy; he had managed to interest a financier in the trade possibilities of the area, but came into conflict with him and the officials already there. Spanish settlements, hostile Native Americans, and the oppressive tropical climate added further to Cadillac's dissatisfaction with his posting. He was finally recalled to France in 1716 after many requests on his part. Not long after he and his son arrived in Paris in September of 1717, they were incarcerated at the infamous Bastille prison.

Half a Year in the Bastille

Though they were officially charged with the suspicion of speaking treasonous words, historians surmise that Cadillac's son was jailed because he and his father had made an expedition to Illinois lands to the north in 1715 and reported to the king that they had discovered vast mineral deposits. Both father and son spent six months in the Bastille, and after his release in early 1718 Cadillac reestablished ties with his allies in the Ministry of Marine. He petitioned the court for compensation for a large swath of land he claimed to have cleared in Detroit, and returned with his family to St. Nicolas-de-la-Grave.

In 1722, Cadillac was awarded a pension, rights to some of the Detroit holdings, monetary restitution, and the Cross of Saint-Louis for three decades of service to the crown in New France. That same year he sold his Detroit real estate, and with the money purchased a commission from the Crown that gave him the governorship of the nearby town of Castelsarrasin. He was inducted as mayor of the town as well, but was removed from the post by the king not long afterward. Cadillac died in Castelsarrasin in October of 1730. Though he and Marie-Therese had a total of 13 children, only three survived their father. He was buried in the cemetery of a Carmelite church, and the whereabouts of the single portrait of him remain undiscovered.

Further Reading

Brown, Henry D., Henri Negrie, Frank R. Place, Rene Toujas, Leonard N. Simons, Solan Weeks, and others. *Cadillac and the Founding of Detroit,* Wayne State University Press, 1976.
Catlin, George, *The Story of Detroit,* Detroit News, 1926.
Michigan, A State Anthology: Writings about the Great Lakes State, 1641-1981, edited by David D. Anderson, Gale, 1981.

Helen Broinowski Caldicott M.D.

Although Helen Caldicott (born 1938) started her career as a physician, she is perhaps best known for her anti-nuclear activism and for authoring several books which dealt with the issues around nuclear energy and broader environmental concerns.

Helen Caldicott has always maintained that the United States needed to set an example for the rest of the world in carrying out sound environmental practices. Much of her life was devoted to activism; in earlier years she focused on educating people about the dangers of nuclear energy. In the late 1980s and beyond when the threat of nuclear war had lessened, Caldicott focused on broader environmental issues. She decried the population explosion and corporate practices which harmed the environment. She insisted that the responsibility for sound ethical policy lay with political leaders; and that the media had a role in educating the public about the true extent of the earth's environmental problems. Her activist work was melded with her medical background; she had a scientific and clinical interest in the effects of nuclear energy and advocated knowledgeably on the harm that nuclear energy could cause to humans and other life on earth.

Formative Years

Caldicott was born Helen Broinowski in Melbourne, Australia on August 7, 1938. She was later to state that she was lucky to live as long as she had, given the environmental toxins she was exposed to as a child. Her father died of cancer at age 51 after a lifetime of constructing houses with asbestos; she often assisted him by handing him the asbestos material. Her mother died at 58 and beat Caldicott severely as a child, even though Caldicott once commented that her mother was "the most fascinating person I ever knew, the most intelligent, and really my best friend when I grew up."

She attended college at the University of Adelaide Medical School and graduated in 1961 with the Australian equivalent of a Doctor of Medicine. She went on to work in pediatrics and general practice; later she founded and ran a cystic fibrosis clinic at a hospital in Adelaide. During this time, she met and married a fellow physician, William Caldicott, in 1962. They went on to have three children.

Roots of Early Activism

Caldicott's interest in activism began to surface publicly when in 1971, she warned the Australian public about the French government's plans to conduct atmospheric testing of nuclear weapons in the South Pacific. In her own words, her first speech as an activist was to five little old ladies at the YWCA in Adelaide. Caldicott backed her arguments against nuclear energy by pointing out the extent to which nuclear fallout was already present in food and water. Caldicott was able to build successful coalitions with the public, other scientists, and the media in opposing the French testing; the results of her activism included boycotts of French products and demonstrations.

In another victory for Caldicott and Australian antinuclear activists, the Labor Party was elected into office in 1972 with opposition to testing as part of their platform. Caldicott also pushed for an Australian ban on the export of uranium, a substance used in the process to create nuclear energy. The suggested ban was initially opposed by mining and government interests but in 1975 she succeeded in getting the Australian Council of Trade Unions to ban the mining, transport, and sale of uranium. The ban remained in place until 1982.

Caldicott continued her medical career when in 1975, she and her family relocated to Boston, Massachusetts, so that her husband could pursue a research appointment at Harvard. Initially working at Children's Hospital Medical Center in Boston, she also served as a pediatric instructor at Harvard Medical School between 1977-1980.

Stint as Author

She published her first book in 1978, *Nuclear Madness: What Can You Do!* The book, which she co-authored with Nancy Herrington and Nahum Stiskin, explained for the layperson the issues and the consequences of nuclear technology. After the book was published, Caldicott made numerous appearances on television and the lecture circuit to promote the book's message. By 1981, the emphasis in her life was activism rather than medicine. In an article in *Newsday,* she explained that "I felt that nuclear war was so imminent, I couldn't in conscience keep treating children with cystic fibrosis when the whole world was threatened. I practice global preventive medicine."

Led Activist Organizations

Caldicott's antinuclear activism did not remain limited to authoring books. In 1978 she took charge of and revived a pre-existing organization called Physicians for Social Responsibility. Redirecting the organization's vision to focus on the health risks of nuclear fallout, Caldicott increased membership in the organization to 30,000 by 1982, particu-

larly after the Three Mile Island incident in Pennsylvania during 1979.

In 1980, she took her organizational skills further and founded a lobbying group, Women's Action for Nuclear Disarmament. Organizational leadership was not without growing pains, however; Caldicott stepped down as president of Physicians for Social Responsibility in 1983, claiming that her vision and the vision of the membership had diverged too widely. The organization had become increasingly bureaucratic and some members found her either overpowering or lacking in ability to lobby and lead. One climax of her activist role may have occurred in 1982, when she and others spoke to a crowd of one million at a peace rally in New York City's Central Park.

Documentary Film and Foray into Politics

Caldicott's views on the nuclear industry were represented in a 1982 Academy Award documentary film *If You Love This Planet.* Although the film was produced in Canada, the U.S. government controlled its distribution and labeled it political propaganda. Caldicott generally lacked trust in most political leaders, although she was a great admirer of Mikhail Gorbachev of the Soviet Union and personally thanked him for ending the Cold War. She had less respect for then-president Ronald Reagan, whom she met in 1983 and who astounded her with what she called his ignorance on nuclear issues. According to Caldicott, Reagan told her that anyone who supported the nuclear freeze movement was either a "KGB dupe or a Soviet agent." Caldicott also differed with the Pope regarding population control, although she admired the social justice tradition of the Catholic Church.

In an attempt to make further impact in U.S. politics, Caldicott lent her name and efforts to the Mondale presidential campaign in 1984, even though he largely ignored her ideas. Caldicott was stunned when his running mate, Geraldine Ferraro, pledged to pushed the nuclear button if necessary. Mondale's defeat served to crush Caldicott's psyche even further. However, Caldicott's contributions to the world and humanity were publicly recognized when she was nominated for a Nobel Peace Prize in 1985. She was also the recipient of other humanitarian awards.

Hiatus and Return

In 1987, Caldicott suffered another blow in her life when her husband of 25 years decided to leave their marriage. She retreated from the public eye until 1991, living in seclusion in Australia. That was the amount of time she needed, she claimed, to work through her grief. She emerged ready to speak again, not only on nuclear issues but on broader environmental issues which seemed relevant at the time. Her focus remained on the health impacts which stemmed from environmental problems and she believed that the U.S. needed to serve as a model for the rest of the world in taking appropriate action. Caldicott felt that in particular, corporations needed to be more concerned with the health of people and less concerned with the bottom line at the expense of the environment. Additionally, she stated that the media needed to be doing a better job of educating people on global environmental issues.

Caldicott continued to publish books that addressed nuclear energy; *Missile Envy: The Arms Race and Nuclear War* was published in 1984. She also published *If You Love This Planet: A Plan to Heal the Earth* in 1992, the book went beyond nuclear energy and addressed a range of environmental issues. In 1996, she published her autobiography, *A Desperate Passion*. In the book she credits the power of women, who she believes could make an effective activist force because they are "much more open with their feelings and the truth, and they're one of the golden keys to the salvation of this planet." Caldicott advocated for an increase of women in political positions, stating that even though women made up 53 percent of the American population, they comprised only two percent of the congressional delegation.

In the late 1990s, Caldicott remained a vocal opponent of nuclear energy when she spoke out against a U.S. proposal to sell nuclear reactors to China; a deal that was mentioned when Chinese Premier Jiang Zemin visited the U.S. in late 1997 to discuss human rights in China. She criticized the fact that the deal was being offered as a solution to global warming, claiming that tremendous amounts of fossil fuel were utilized in the construction of the reactors and of the storage rods for spent nuclear fuel. She also remarked on the irony of the human rights issue, claiming that nuclear reactors in China would violate human rights and would impact human life, either by death, genetic destruction, or disease. She continued to maintain that the United States needed to set an example for the rest of the world in abstaining from the use of nuclear power. She also continued to discuss her views in the media by hosting a New York radio show called "Fair Dinkum."

Further Reading

Caldicott, Helen Broinowski, *A Desperate Passion: An Autobiography,* W.W. Norton & Company, 1996.

Caldicott, *If You Love This Planet: A Plan to Heal the Earth,* revised edition, W.W. Norton & Company, 1992.

Caldicott, Helen Broinowski, Nancy Herrington, and Nahum Stiskin, *Nuclear Madness: What You Can Do,* W.W. Norton & Company, 1994.

E Magazine, January 11, 1997.

Independent on Sunday, April 27, 1997.

Los Angeles Times, October 3, 1997; November 30, 1997.

Newsday, May 21, 1996.

The Progressive, September 1, 1996.

Maria Callas

Maria Callas (1923-1977) was one of the great coloratura sopranos of the twentieth century.

Maria Callas was one of the greatest operatic voices of the 20th century. She revitalized opera and increased its appeal because of her dramatic skill. The extensive range of her singing voice (nearly three octaves) and her ability to emote enabled her to sing many operas that were rarely performed otherwise. Callas biographer Ariana Stassinopoulos said of the singer's dramatic flair, "She brought 'finish' back to the music: each phrase, each word was meticulously weighed . . . she never allowed it to become meaningless embroidery." And Michael Mark of *American Record Guide* noted of the American soprano, "Her strange, haunting, beautiful . . . voice was complemented by an unerring dramatic sense."

Childhood in America

By most accounts Maria Callas was born Maria Kalogeropoulos in New York City, on December 3, 1923, just four months after her parents, George and Evangelia (Litza) Kalogeropoulos, arrived in New York harbor after emigrating from Greece. Callas was formally baptized Cecilia Sophia Anna Maria. It was around the time of her birth that her father shortened the family name to Callas, and Maria Kalogeropoulos was known as Maria Callas by the time she started school.

Callas and her sister, Jackie, grew up enmeshed in bitter sibling rivalries. Jackie, the elder by five years, was tall and slim—everyone's favorite. Maria was not short, but she was not as tall as Jackie, and so appeared more plump in comparison. When Callas was only five years old, she suffered a concussion and was hospitalized for over three weeks, after being dragged unconscious by an automobile. She quickly learned to appreciate the attention she received from concerned family and friends during her recuperation.

At age seven Callas began her musical studies by taking piano lessons. She loved opera music even as a youngster, and she had a beautiful voice. She especially loved to sing *La Paloma.* She took great comfort in listening to the many opera records in her family's collection. Young Callas soon discovered that she had a natural talent and a flair for the dramatic. She won several amateur talent contests while she was in elementary school, and was a popular performer on children's radio shows.

Adolescence in Greece

When Callas graduated from the eighth grade in 1937, her mother decided to return to Greece in order for Callas to receive voice training in the classical tradition. Once in Greece, Callas never resumed her academic studies. Instead she studied with popular voice coaches. First with Maria Trivella at the National Conservatory in Athens, and then with Elvira de Hidalgo at the Odeon Athenos. Callas also studied French and drama. She was a dedicated pupil, driven by a spirit of excellence. At times she observed even David, her pet canary, and attempted to learn from his warble. Her other bird, Elmina, was known to faint and fall off her perch from the intensity and pitch of Callas's high notes. It was all fun to Callas, who seemed happy only when she was singing. Callas's teachers, and later her directors and producers, were continually amazed at her exceptional memory. She easily learned music and lyrics in a matter of days, where others would require weeks or months.

As Callas matured, she developed a close relationship with her music coach, Elvira de Hidalgo, and it was de Hidalgo who arranged for Callas's first professional performance at the National Lyric Theater in Athens in November of 1940. While her performance would be a success, life in Athens soon changed; the outbreak of World War II and the Nazi occupation of Greece had a profound effect on everyone in the country, including the young soprano. Stories are told that during the occupation Callas sometimes performed for enemy soldiers in return for food and security for herself, her mother, and her sister. Her career, meanwhile, was stifled.

Finds Success in Italy

After the occupation, de Hidalgo encouraged Callas to move to Italy to establish her career. However, against all advice, Callas returned to the United States in 1945, determined that she could make a name for herself on her own terms. Although she remained in America for the next two years, it was at the Arena in Verona, Italy where she finally got her start.

After rejection and failure in the United States she finally went to Verona, on a contract. Her Italian debut, held on August 3, 1947, was a performance of *La Gioconda* at the Verona Arena. She went on to perform *Tristan and Isolde* and *Turandot* in Venice in 1948. She sang the title role in Bellini's *Norma,* her most popular role, for the first time in Florence in 1948.

Initially Callas received minimal acclaim, although audiences in Italy were receptive to her talent. It was a quirk of fate in 1949 that finally brought her to prominence. When

another diva fell ill during a run of *I Puritani,* Callas agreed to sing the part of Elvira on one week's notice. Callas, who was performing as Brunhilde in *Die Walkure* at the time, managed to perform both operas, alternating between the two works from one night to the next. The public was duly impressed at her versatility. Critics took note, and her career began to soar.

Marriage and International Acclaim

Almost immediately upon her arrival in Verona in 1947 she met Giovanni Battista Meneghini, a wealthy Veronian industrialist. He was 30 years her senior, and his family did not approve of Callas or her profession, yet the two fell in love. They married on April 21, 1949. The couple lived mostly in Verona. Meneghini withdrew from his business interests to manage Callas's promising career and generally devoted his life to fulfilling her every need.

During the late 1940s and 1950s, Callas toured Argentina, Mexico, and Brazil. She worked with famed Maestro Tullio Serafin, and noted directors Franco Zefferelli, Francesco Siciliani, and Luchino Visconti.

Highly professional, Callas performed 47 roles during her brief career. Her greatest role was that of Norma, which she performed 90 times. Callas developed a strong identity with the Druid priestess of the operatic tale, and once confided to Serafin, "It, *Norma,* will never be as good as it is now in my mind unsung." Whenever Callas performed in *Norma,* she reportedly became exhausted and drained from the physical intensity of her emotion.

Callas's first performance at La Scala in Milan was in *Aida,* in April of 1950, as a stand-in, a replacement for famed soprano Renata Tibaldi. On December 7, 1951, she made her official debut at the noted Italian opera house as Elena in *I Vespri Siciliani.* She went on to perform there for ten years, a total of nearly 200 performances. She interpreted nearly two dozen roles, including her most famous, Norma.

Finds Fame in America

Callas's U.S. debut was at the Lyric Opera of Chicago in 1954. On October 19, 1956 she debuted at the New York Metropolitan Opera where she performed in *Norma.* Coinciding with her Metropolitan Opera debut, Callas was featured on the cover of *Time,* on the issue dated October 27, 1956.

During the peak of her career Callas easily fit the stereotype of a portly and highly emotional diva, but in 1952 she experienced a dramatic weight loss. By 1954 she was 65 pounds lighter. She continued to perform, and her career exploded into greatness. She added new operas to her repertoire, including *Madame Butterfly,* which she had previously avoided because she felt awkward and ungraceful.

New Image Expands Opportunities

After the mid-1950s Callas successfully resurrected the macabre operas, including Cherubini's *Medea,* Verdi's *Macbeth,* and Donizetti's *Anna Bolena,* each of which required exceptional vocal range and acting talent. Will

Crutchfield commented of her unique ability in *New Yorker,* "Callas presented to the . . . public a phenomenon of sheer capacity, . . . she revived a repertory based on capacity. High notes and low, power in full cry and delicacy in pianissimo, fast passagework and sustained legato had not been completely present in one soprano in generations."

The list of Callas's performances is lengthy: *Tosca, La Traviata, Abduction from the Seraglio, Parsifal, Aida, Nabucco, Il Trovatore,* and many more. In 1951 she performed the world premiere of Hayden's *Orfeo ed Euridice.* Surviving tapes and recordings of Callas include her 1952 *La Gioconda,* the complete opera, with Fedora Barbieri. Miscellaneous tapes also remain from a series of master classes she gave at the Juilliard School of Music in New York, where Callas taught briefly before her death.

The Years of Decline

During the late 1950s the vocalist's personal life began to deteriorate, and this tragically affected her career. She became increasingly linked socially with the "international jet set," those people of wealth and power known as the "idle rich." Through her new-found friends she became acquainted with shipping magnate Aristotle Onassis, and the couple's friendship soon developed into an extramarital affair. This was not the first time that Callas's name was associated with illicit liaisons, and she and her husband separated in 1959, divorcing finally in 1971. Onassis eventually divorced his wife, Tina, and married Jacqueline Kennedy, widow of the late President John F. Kennedy, but he also remained involved with Callas.

The intrigues of Callas's personal life soon overshadowed her professional life. The stresses of jet set living, as well as the strain she had put on her voice throughout her career began to take their toll. Callas cancelled a performance at the Edinburgh Festival in 1957. In 1958 she answered to breach of contract charges from the American Guild of Musical Artists. A downward spiral was in motion. Her former manager, Richard Bagarozy, sued her for back commissions. She cancelled a performance in Rome after the first act. She was dismissed from the Metropolitan Opera. Although she returned briefly to perform at the Met between 1964 and 1965, she never resurfaced as the great talent of her youth.

The Callas Persona

As an actress, Callas was known for her timing and spontaneity, as well as for her incredible vocal range. She attributed her extraordinary stage presence to myopia: She was rarely nervous, she claimed, because she could not see the audience. In fact, Callas insisted she could barely see the conductor, and was free therefore to lose herself in the composer's work to the exclusion of all else.

Callas's timing and spontaneity even extended to curtain calls. After one memorable performance, she was showered with flowers. She took one and handed it to famed conductor Arturo Toscanini who had attended the performance. The audience was ecstatic. Even during the years of her decline, when some of the audience threw vegetables instead of flowers, to express their annoyance, Callas retained her composure. She kept the flowers for herself and tossed the vegetables down to the orchestra.

Callas died unexpectedly in Paris on September 16, 1977, shortly before her 55th birthday. Just as no record exists of Callas's birth, her death also remains shrouded in mystery, the cause of her death never fully explained. (Her body was cremated without an autopsy.) Such facts serve to intensify the mystique of the soprano's life. Duncan Scott of *Knight-Ridder/Tribune News Service* said of Callas: "As in the case of . . . other icons, Callas's real accomplishments were swallowed up by the power of her own myth."

Further Reading

Meneghini, Giovanni Battista, *My Wife Maria Callas,* translated by Henry Wisneski, Farrar Straus, 1982.
Stassinopoulos, Arianna, *Maria Callas, The Woman behind the Legend,* Simon & Schuster, New York, 1981.
American Record Guide, November-December 1993, p. 272.
Atlantic Monthly, October 1997, p. 102.
Knight-Ridder/Tribune News Service, September 15, 1997, p. 915K0226.
New Yorker, November 13, 1995, pp. 94-102.
Opera News, April 16, 1994, p. 12.
Time, October 27, 1956.

Clive Orville Callender

Clive Callender (born 1936) is one of the foremost specialists in organ transplant medicine in the United States. The Howard University Hospital surgeon has focused much of his career on transplant medicine among minority segments of the population, along with the unique health and social issues relevant to them as potential donors.

Callender was born in New York City on November 16, 1936. As a child, he dreamed of becoming a missionary doctor as a result of one sermon he witnessed at Ebenezer Gospel Tabernacle: "I was listening to the minister who spoke about the two greatest occupations in the world: ministering to the souls of mankind and to the bodies of mankind," he told *Black Enterprise* in 1988. Callender enrolled in New York City's Hunter College, and had earned degrees in chemistry and physiology by 1959. From there, he entered Nashville's Meharry Medical College, a prestigious school that had long been an important training ground for African-American doctors and medical professionals. Callender graduated first in his class there in 1963.

Originally intending to practice internal medicine, Callender's first internship was at the University of Cincinnati. Yet he realized how little opportunity there was for him as an internist to actually heal patients, and so switched to surgery as his area of interest. From 1964 to 1965 he was a resident at Harlem Hospital, and then was awarded an American Cancer Society fellowship for the following aca-

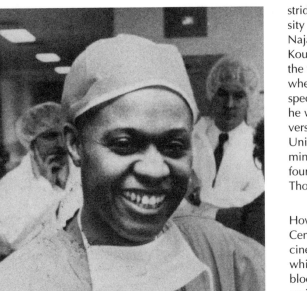

demic year. That was also Callender's first year at Howard University and Freedmen's Hospital, where he was an assistant resident. Another residency at Memorial Hospital for Cancer and Allied Disease was completed, and then Callender returned to Howard University Hospital to become chief resident in 1968. He became an instructor there the following year.

Biafran Civil War

Callender spent part of 1970 and 1971 at D.C. General Hospital as a medical officer, and then was invited to Nigeria's Port Harcourt General Hospital just as the Biafran Civil War was ending in the country; this helped Callender fulfill his childhood goal to work in an altruistic capacity. Biafra was an independent state that seceded from Nigeria in 1967, and the internal strife brought suffering, starvation, and death to the region. After his return to the United States in 1971, the young physician grew increasingly interested in transplant surgery as a specialty; only four years before, South African surgeon Dr. Christiaan Barnard shocked the world with his first successful human heart transplant surgery. Medical professionals were growing increasingly proficient in transplanting kidneys and livers successfully, especially with advances being made in the science of human immune response systems.

In 1971 Callender received a special postdoctoral fellowship at the National Institutes of Health, the U.S. government agency that serves as a research hub for ground breaking medical technology. He spent much of his two years at various medical centers that were making great

strides in organ transplant medicine, including the University of Minnesota, where Callender studied under Dr. John Najaraian; he was also able to work with Dr. Samuel Kountz, the first African-American doctor to specialize in the field. Callender went on to the University of Pittsburgh, where he trained with Dr. Thomas Starz, a liver transplant specialist. Returning to the Washington, D.C. area in 1973, he was awarded an assistant professorship at Howard University Hospital's medical school and founded the Howard University Hospital Transplant Center. It was the first such minority-operated center in the United States. He also founded a transplant center in the Virgin Island city of St. Thomas, which bears his name.

Over the next decade, Callender strove to make his Howard University Hospital Kidney and Liver Transplant Center one of the leading sites for minority transplant medicine. Part of his work has involved research into antigens, which are carried by the donor organ into the recipient's blood system and then stimulate an immune response in the recipient; this natural way that the body rejects a foreign presence is one of the major obstacles to successful organ transplants. Callender's Transplant Center has conducted important research into antigen-matching and immunogenetics to help correct this problem. In 1983 he testified about organ donor programs and the minority community in Senate hearings on the matter.

Cultural Taboos

Still, Callender realized that perhaps the greatest obstacle in the organ-transplant field was the scarcity of donor organs, and he became increasingly aware that African Americans registered as organ donors at a far lower rate than white Americans. There were several reasons for this discrepancy, which Callender learned by conducting extensive research into the matter among the African American populace: some held fears that blacks who needed organs would be neglected in favor of white patients; there were also conflicts about organ donations because of deep-seated religious beliefs—the idea that it is disrespectful to enter or otherwise disturb a body after death; and finally, there was a concern that a white physician might be too quick to declare an African American legally dead in order to make his or her organs available for transplant. "When I first got started in this, I didn't realize what an emotional issue it was for blacks," Callender told Paul Delaney in the *New York Times* in 1991. "We're dealing with myths, but to the people who believe them, the myths are real."

Callender set out to solve this problem and increase minority awareness and support of organ donor programs. African Americans suffer from higher rates of kidney failure and hypertension, while in many cases a donor organ from their own ethnic group yields the best match for a minority patient. In order to take his ideas to the general public, Callender courted funding from the Dow Chemical Company for his "Take Initiative" program. For this awareness campaign, Callender led seminars in which he, a transplant recipient, a donor or member of the donor's family, and someone on a waiting list for an organ share their views with African-American audiences. Callender then passed out organ donor cards, which many enthusiastically signed. As reported in *Contemporary Black Biography,* he told *Jet* magazine, "If you take the problem to the Black community and give them an opportunity to become sensitive and give them the knowledge to open the door . . . they will rally behind the issue."

A Marked Gain in Donors

By 1990 Callender's efforts had yielded impressive results: there was an increase of nearly threefold in the registered number of African-American organ and tissue donors in just five years. As the leading medical professional on minority organ-transplant medicine, Callender has also been an active player in a $6 million program launched by National Institutes of Health in 1991 to found the Minority Organ Tissue Transplant Education Program (MOTTEP), a program that aims to increase the number of donors among all minority groups in the United States. He has also campaigned for an increase in federal funding for community education programs for organ donor awareness programs. From 1990 to 1991, the Bush Administration increased spending for such programs threefold, to $1.5 million, but Callender told the *New York Times* that more was needed. "This country spent billions of dollars to fight a war in the Persian Gulf and surely it can spare a few million for such an important task," Callender told Delaney.

In 1994, Callender spoke at the United Network for Organ Sharing symposium about the number of African Americans on waiting lists for donor kidneys, a number higher than that of other ethnic groups in the United States. Callender has argued that the antigen-matching guidelines then in place discriminated against African-Americans, forcing members of this minority group on the list for kidney transplants to wait almost twice as long as whites. Since then, the parameters for antigen-matching have been revised, and Callender has since used his prominent position to speak out for reforming the way in which available organs are allocated at the national and local levels.

Controversy in D.C.

In the spring of 1996 Callender's MOTTEP teamed with the American Medical Association and two other professional organizations to launch a campaign to increase registered organ donors in the United States; basketball star Michael Jordan served as the focal point of an advertising campaign for this. Callender has also defended the practice of using organ-preserving drugs on near-death patients, which in some cases accelerates the process of dying. In 1997 this procedure was legal in Washington, D.C., where Callender's transplant center at Howard University Hospital is located. "We're giving families the option to say 'yes' or 'no,'" Callender told *Washington Post* reporter Rick Weiss. "If you don't preserve, you have taken away that option." Furthermore, Callender noted that the District of Columbia city council had not passed the law in 1996 without first gleaning the opinion of local citizens through an outreach and education program.

In 1996 Callender became the Lasalle D. Leffall Professor at Howard University, named after the first African-

American president of the American College of Surgeons. that same year, Callender also succeeded the actual Dr. Leffall as chair of surgery for Howard University's Medical School. He has been inducted into the Hunter College Alumni Hall of Fame, and is the author of over 70 scientific papers. He married Fern Marshall in 1968, with whom he is parent to three children: Joseph, Ealena, and Arianne.

Further Reading

Contemporary Black Biography, volume 3, Gale, 1993.
Hawkins, Walter L. *African American Biographies 2: Profiles of 332 Current Men and Women,* McFarland & Co., 1994.
Notable Twentieth-Century Scientists, Gale, 1995.
New York Times, November 6, 1991.
Washington Post, December 19, 1997.

Roberto de Oliveira Campos

Brazilian economist and diplomat Roberto de Oliveira Campos (born 1917) struggled for most of the latter half of the twentieth century to promote what he called pragmatic, democratic nationalism in his socialist homeland that, during the early 1960s, had been flirting with Communism.

C ampos was born in Cuiabá, in the rural state of Mato Grosso, Brazil, on April 17, 1917. In reference to his humble background, Campos often referred to himself as "a Brazilian hillbilly." He initially planned to enter the priesthood, and received degrees in Philosophy and Theology from the Catholic Seminary of Guaxup. For his graduate work, however, he turned to economics, and studied at George Washington University, Columbia University, and New York University, all in the United States. In 1939, at the age of 22, Campos entered the Brazilian foreign service.

Frustrations with Foreign Service

From the foreign service, Campos moved to a number of important national and international posts, serving on the Brazil-U.S. Economic Development Committee and the National Development Council, and acting as a delegate to General Agreement on Trade and Tariffs (GATT) and other international conferences during the 1950s. Campos was often openly critical of the United States' treatment of Latin American countries. In 1958, the *New York Times* reported that Campos, speaking as president of Brazil's National Bank for Economic Development, accused the United States of treating Latin America as "less important than Europe for public investment," adding that the U.S. had "lost much goodwill as the result of its former opposition to the creation of an inter-American [including both North and South America] financial agency," an idea Campos supported.

Despite his criticism of U.S. policy, the Brazilian press considered him too pro-American. After a conflict with

Brazilian president Juscelino Kubitschek over the president's plan to print new money to finance government programs, he set up a management consultant firm with former Finance Minster Lucas Lopes. The firm encouraged and advised foreign clients on establishing industry in Brazil—a position that earned Campos the nickname "Bob Fields," an English translation of Roberto Campos.

In 1961 a new president, Joao Goulart, called Campos back to the government to serve as ambassador to the United States, hoping to gain U.S. favor and aid. Goulart's regime failed to fulfill many of its promises, however, and became increasingly corrupt; although Goulart had promised agrarian reform he amassed more and more private land, becoming, by far, the country's greatest landholder. Brazil's high rate of economic growth gave way to stagnation and decline. As Goulart repeatedly sacrificed national economic security to political pressures, the U.S. grew frustrated and cut off aid to Brazil.

After Goulart disavowed Campos' agreements with foreign investors and fired his fourth finance minister in less than three years, Campos resigned the ambassadorial post as a form of protest in 1964. *Newsweek* reported that Campos had "grown weary of serving as an apologist for a nation characterized by 'financial irresponsibility and disregard for social equity.'" He criticized Goulart for his "purely demagogic and utopian tendencies," adding that Brazilians tended to blame their troubles on foreign exploitation, "as if there were no lack of discipline or waste in government spending and no tax evasion or intemperance in private finance." Campos returned to Brazil hoping to run for congress, in order to facilitate change. "I was so tired of trying to interpret policy," he told *Business Week,* "so I decided I wanted to help make it."

Revolution Led to Opportunity

Change came more quickly than he had expected. As Goulart lost one after another source of domestic support, Brazilians began to fear he would resort to a coup d'tat to solidify his power. As election time drew near and serious challengers to Goulart's increasingly authoritarian presidency began to fade, tensions ran high. In April 1964, three months after Campos' resignation, a revolution took place, and the Goulart government collapsed without a fight. Army Marshal Castelo Branco reluctantly accepted the post of interim president, and Campos was appointed minister of planning, the top policymaking post in Brazil.

The problems Campos faced were staggering. Inflation was going up at the rate of 114 percent a year; in the first four months of 1964, the rate was 120 percent. The gross national product could not even keep up with the rate of population growth. Adding to his difficulty was President Branco's tendency to cave into pressure from right-wing extremists, driving the administration toward an increasingly reactionary policy and making significant changes hard to implement.

Campos' own style also undermined his efforts. As he later admitted, he struggled with translating economic ideas into terms ordinary people could understand. "One of my main problems," he said in *Newsweek,* "has been my ex-

cessive rationalism, my horror of instincts. It has reduced my ability to communicate with the people." He also demanded stringent austerity from a government and people accustomed to the spendthrift regimes of the past. When he got rid of federal subsidies for wheat and gasoline, bread prices and bus fares soared. Campos' bold Action Plan, driven by what he called his "congenital recklessness," was supported by President Branco and the U.S. government, but was tremendously unpopular among the Brazilian people.

He was not without successes, however. In the first hundred days of the Action Plan, the congress passed two tax-reform bills, a banking-reform bill, housing legislation, and a sweeping agrarian-reform bill designed to support family-size farms. By the end of 1965, the inflation rate had been cut by more than half, down to 42 percent. Noted for his shrewd bargaining skills, he persuaded a reluctant World Bank to grant Brazil a loan, and he continued to push U.S. manufacturers to invest in their Brazilian subsidiaries, resulting in hundreds of millions of new dollars for expansion or initiation of Brazilian industry.

Left Office still Unpopular

Nevertheless, when Campos retired from the position in 1967, along with President Branco, he was still without the respect of many of his countryman. "Most Brazilians consider him an aloof, insensitive man who has shown himself to be more interested in techniques than in people," *Newsweek* reported. When he made his final report to the Brazilian Congress, one congressman told him, "We consider your presence here today meaningless.

Despite this treatment, he continued to be drawn to national service. In *Reflections on Latin American Development,* Campos corrected critics who accused him of a lack of national interest: "I shall continue considering myself a pragmatic nationalist. I renounce the temptation of mobilizing resentment in order to gain the authority to plan development. I would rather strengthen the national entrepreneur than merely antagonize the foreigner. I would want the State not to do what it cannot do, in order to do what it should do. I prefer to love my own country rather than to hate the others."

Campos continued through the rest of the 1960s and 1970s to serve on such committees as the Inter-American Committee for the Alliance for Progress and the Inter-American Council of Commerce and Production, still committed to helping South American countries learn and benefit from North American prosperity. During this period, he also turned more of his attention to publishing his ideas in such books as *A tenica e o riso* (Technique and Laughter), *A nova economia brasileira* (A New Brazilian Economy), and *Funcao de empresa privada* (The Function of Private Enterprise). Whether addressing economic theory or Brazilian nationalism, Campos maintained his position that the future of Brazil's economy would depend on a reduction in government spending, the substitution of private businesses for government services, and the encouragement of foreign investors.

Returned to Congress as Senator

In 1975 Campos returned to an official government post to serve as the Brazilian Ambassador to the United Kingdom. Among his successes in this term as ambassador was a multimillion dollar loan for equipment to modernize and electrify Brazilian railroads. When he left his diplomatic position and returned to Brazil in 1982, he had become popular enough to win a seat in the Brazilian Congress. A 1996 poll included Campos as one of Brazil's top 10 most influential congressmen.

Despite his influence, he continued to struggle to win acceptance for his ideas. In 1995, *The Economist Survey* quoted Campos repeating his mantra to a still-uncertain audience: "Privatize, privatize, privatize." In 1997, Campos was still in congress pushing his country to open its doors to foreign business. When U.S. President Bill Clinton visited Brazil, Campos took the opportunity to promote Brazil's participation in a global economy. In a speech so vehement that it brought opponents to tears, he declared that "Brazil should exchange the clichs of nationalistic discourse—based on reactions (such as those of the politicians) that are mere posturing, and not supported by reality—for a coherent and sustainable attitude towards the opening up of its economy, with the objective of becoming fully integrated into the new world order." Many Brazilians, and much of the influential Brazilian press, still objected to his position.

Nevertheless, Campos is likely to be remembered in Brazil with admiration. As one of his critics told *Newsweek* in 1967, "Campos was like a Napoleon. Some people will remember his victories and some his defeats, but no one will forget he existed."

Further Reading

Campos, Roberto de Oliveira, *A nova economia brasiliera*, Crown Editores Internacionais, 1974.
Campos, Roberto de Oliveira, *Reflections on Latin American Development,* Institute of Latin American Studies, 1967.
Business Week, June 13, 1964.
Newsweek, February 24, 1964; March 20, 1967.
New York Times, December 3, 1958.
Times (London), December 15, 1976.
Washington Post, March 14, 1995.
"The Power in Brazilia," http://www.brazzil.com (March 15, 1998).
"Slimming the State: The Many Virtues of Privitization," *The Economist Survey,* http://www.demon.co.uk (March 15, 1998).
"Brazil, USA and the New Order," *Banco Icatu S.A.,* http://www.icatu.com.br (March 15, 1998). □

Pierre Cardin

Pierre Cardin (born 1922) came from obscurity but very quickly became one of the top fashion designers in the world and was the trailblazer for the soft and floppy fashion look of the 1950s and 1960s. He developed the first line of clothes for men by a courtier and continually changed and expanded the world of fashion with his creations over the years. He is considered a living legend in the fashion industry.

ierre Cardin was born at his parents vacation home at San Andrea da Barbara near Venice, Italy on July 7, (some sources say July 2) 1922. In 1926, his parents moved back to their native France where Cardin grew up in the industrial town of St. Etienne in the Department of Loire in southeast France. His parents were wealthy wine merchants who had always hoped their son would become an architect, but by the age of eight Cardin was showing an ability and aptitude for fashion design by designing dresses for the dolls of his neighbor's child. In 1936, Cardin began apprenticing in Vichy, France for a tailor named Manby and would stay on until almost the end of World War II. At Manby's, Cardin learned the art of tailoring suits that would show in the rest his work.

Designs In Paris

Cardin quit Manby's with the war almost over and got a job with the French Red Cross. This job brought him to Paris in late 1944. The 17-year-old Cardin stayed in Paris, the fashion capital of the world, and began working for French fashion designer Paquin. While working for Paquin, Cardin met many French intellectuals and heads of society. Using these connections, Cardin began designing and making the elaborate costumes for theatrical presentations and motion pictures.

In 1946, Cardin's work could be seen in French film director Jean Cocteau's *Beauty and the Beast.* Cocteau was very impressed with the young Cardin and introduced him to designer Christian Dior. Dior was an internationally recognized fashion designer preparing to release his latest *House of Dior* collection. Cardin was soon working for the Dior house and became one of the "team of thirteen" that would design so much of Dior's line over the next years and become associated with fashions post-war "New Look." While at Dior's, Cardin designed his famous and much publicized "Bar" line that featured tight jackets and long black skirts. He soon came to the notice of fashion observers and buyers as the natural successor to Dior.

House of Cardin

In 1949, Cardin left the *House of Dior* and in 1950, with the help of Marcel Escoffier, struck out on his own and became a costume designer in an attic shop where he would design many costumes for the French capital city's numerous balls and create his own line of suits for a clientele that would continue to expand. His work was widely seen and loved and he designed costumes for many other French designers, including Dior. He was widely believed to be the best suit designer in Paris and by 1953, Cardin had purchased the entire building on Rue Riche Panse where he had started barely three years earlier.

In 1953, he moved his operations into a six-story eighteenth-century mansion on the very fashionable Faubourg Saint-Honore and established the *House of Cardin.* As part of the purchase agreement, Cardin was obliged to continue a conservative men's shop that had occupied the building's ground floor. Unwilling to associate with traditional men's shirts and ties, Cardin divided his elegant house into two separate boutiques in 1954: one was called "Adam" and the other "Eve." He then set about designing avant-garde ties, sweaters and suit jackets that became enormously popular in Europe.

In 1957, Cardin was still regarded as a suit designer and costume maker. He wanted to break out of this mold into the world of total fashion design. To do this, Cardin presented his first full fashion collection of over 120 styles in the summer of 1957 in Paris. The show was an immediate success and Cardin soon became a member of the Chambre Syndicale de la Couture (Couture Employers' Federation) as one of the best designers in France. His show in 1958 proved that he was not a one-hit wonder and he solidified his reputation in the fashion world.

Shows America His Designs

Throughout the 1960s Cardin continues to design clothes for both men and women that became increasingly fanciful and replete with bright colors. But, knowing that some of his customers would not wear many of the avant-garde creations that he was producing, he soon began designing a separate and more traditional lines for a department store in Paris. In 1961, he was allowed to distribute these lines himself outside of Paris. His designs of ready-to-wear fashions that were semi-fitted became increasingly

popular throughout Europe and he decided to travel to the United States to show his fashions.

In 1966, Cardin traveled to New York City to show his women's fashions to American customers and designers and upon arriving at the airport in New York, he saw the bright colors of the automobiles in the parking lot. He later remarked to an interviewer that: "It confirms my instinct that color—lots of it—is the most essential thing in today's world." His designs for women were and immediate success and would lead him to open a store dedicated to these fashions in the city. He also launched a line of children's clothes which became almost as popular as his designs for adults. For these and other designs, he was awarded the Golden Spinning Wheel Award by the town of Krefeld, Germany in 1966.

Following his successes in America, Cardin traveled to Japan with the same success. His fashions were highly popular and their easy fit and bright colors became popular with Japanese women. Cardin liked the more traditional lines of Japanese clothing and their influence would continue to make an impression on him throughout the years. Their influence would be seen in many of his later creations as models often wear Japanese hairpieces. He has returned to Japan several times, once at the invitation of the Japanese government.

Highly Decorated Designer

By the 1970s, Cardin was regarded among one of the top fashion designers in the world and was awarded many times for his designs. In 1973, Cardin received the Basilica Palladiana Award for the most successful Venetian that year. In 1974, Cardin was awarded the EUR Award, which is the equivalent of an Italian Academy Award, for his varied and successful enterprises in the world of entertainment. In 1977, Cardin received the Golden Thimble of French Haute-Couture Award, made by Cartier, as designing the most creative collection of the season. He would go on to win this award two more times, once in 1979 and again in 1982. It was also in 1977 that he purchased the Maxim's chain of stores and turned them into a unique line of boutiques to sell his designs.

In 1980, Cardin celebrated 30 years in the industry at the Metropolitan Museum of Art in New York City and opened a new office building in New York City to handle his growing American enterprises. In 1985, Cardin was awarded the Fashion Oscar at the Paris Opera and later, was named as a Commander of the Order of Merit by the President of France. In 1988 he was awarded the Grand Order of Merit by the Italian Republic and, in 1991, was promoted to Officer of the Legion of Honor in France. It was also in 1991 that he was promoted to an officer in the Legion of Honor in France and received the Gold and Silver Star of the Japanese Sacred Treasure, that nations highest honor. In 1992, Cardin accepted a seat in the French Academy of Fine Arts as the nations highest-ranking fashion designer.

Sportif

To commemorate the XXVI Olympic Games being held in Atlanta, Georgia, Cardin presented a fashion show starring his new *Sportif* designs. The *Sportif* line of clothes for men and women was a tremendous success and spawned a line of *Sportif* fragrance for men. later that year, Cardin put on an exhibition by painter Daniel You called *Les Dieux de Olympe.*

In 1996, Cardin was awarded the France-Italie Prize by the Italian chamber of commerce in France. Cardin was also asked by the Chinese government to design uniforms for it's public servants in 1996. Soon the People's Liberation Army as well as railway, airline and post office workers were sporting Cardin designs at their job. In January of 1997, Cardin was decorated as a Commander of the Legion of Honor in France, that nations highest honor.

Cardin lives and works in Paris, constantly designing and innovating his many lines of clothing, footwear, perfume and hats. His designs and his commercial success have made him one of the living legends among French fashion designers.

Further Reading

Contemporary Designers, St. James Press, 1997.
Contemporary Fashion, St. James Press, 1995.
Chicago Tribune, March 19, 1996.
Daily News Record, June 5, 1996.
Women's Wear Daily, January 7, 1994; February 24, 1995; October 27, 1997.
"Cardin, Pierre," *A & E Biography Website,* http://www.biography.com (March 18, 1998).

Fernando Henrique Cardoso

Brazil inaugurated Fernando Henrique Cardoso (born 1931), a world-renowned sociologist, president in 1995. Cardoso's success in that office prompted a constitutional amendment to allow him to run for a second term in 1998.

Fernando Henrique Cardoso's political career lurched to an inauspicious start in 1978. Though no stranger to political thought as an academic, Cardoso, by his own admission, ran "an amateur campaign" his first time before the electorate. However, it was remarkable that he was able to run at all.

As a young intellectual with leftist leanings, Cardoso ran afoul of the government in 1964. In March of that year, President Joao Goulart was forced from power by a military coup as corruption and mismanagement threatened Brazil with chaos. Though Cardoso's father and grandfather both had been respected generals, the young sociologist irritated the new regime. Faced with certain imprisonment, Cardoso chose exile, first to Chile and then to France. After a short return to the University of Sao Paulo in 1968 and 1969, Cardoso packed his bags again for a shuttle career between the United States, Britain, and France.

By 1978, Brazil's ruling generals had relaxed after years of record growth and relative tranquillity. Citizens and for-

eign diplomats alike clamored for a return to civilian rule, and the military permitted congressional elections. As more of a protest than a serious bid, Cardoso ran for a Senate seat under the banner of the Brazilian Democratic Movement, an opposition party created during military rule to create the illusion of a two-party system. Though he attracted 1.5 million votes, Cardoso lost the election to Franco Montoro and returned to his academic career.

By a quirk of fate and Brazilian electoral law, Cardoso inherited the Senate seat in 1983 after Montoro moved on to become the Governor of Sao Paulo. The consummate academic became a rookie Senator, and at first embodied the clash between two polar-opposite cultures. Accustomed to worshiping ideas, Cardoso quickly learned to bow to a different god.

"As a politician, your responsibility is to change reality and not just to defend principles," said Cardoso, as reported by Alan Riding in the *New York Times.* "If you're committed to change, you cannot turn an ethical position into an obstacle for action. The problem is that, as an academic, you're trained to tell the truth, but a politician is taught to lie, or at least to omit. As a politician, if you say everything you want, you never get everything you want."

Academic Origins

Cardoso, born June 18, 1931 in Rio de Janeiro, earned his doctorate from the University of Sao Paulo in 1961. After a post-graduate course in sociology at the University of Paris, he returned home and raised enough of a political

rumpus to attract the disfavor of the generals newly in charge of Brazil's government. While his friends suffered torture and imprisonment at home, Cardoso served as Professor of Developmental Sociology at the Latin American Institute for Economic and Social Planning in Santiago, Chile.

During this period, he collaborated with Enzo Faletto to write what would become his best known work, *Dependencia y desarrollo en Amrica Latina, (Dependency and Development in Latin America)*. In this work, Cardoso and Faletto examined the tendency of developing post-war Latin American countries to throw off political and economic dependency on foreign powers only to reestablish a new economic dependency on international capitalists and multinational corporations. This academic analysis proved a valuable backdrop for Cardoso's eventual political career, which grew from an intimate understanding of the vagaries of international business and their effects on Brazil's domestic economy.

In 1967 Cardoso accepted a position as Professor of Sociological Theory at the University of Paris-Nanterre for one year, and thence moved home again for a year as Professor of Political Science at the University of Sao Paulo. Finding his career there was still hobbled by political disfavor in his homeland, Cardoso went into self-imposed exile again, first to Stanford University, then to Cambridge University, and finally back to Paris in 1977. Back in Brazil in 1978, Cardoso was the natural choice of the Brazilian Democratic Movement for his ill-fated run for Senate, since he had served both at home and abroad as an advocate for democracy and an advisor to the Brazilian political opposition.

Failing in his first bid for the Senate, Cardoso swung through the international academic world once more, this time as Associate Director of Studies at the Institute for Higher Studies in Social Sciences in Paris and at the University of California.

An Academic Turned Politician

Though chastened by his first foray into the Senate in 1983 and forced to adapt his speech and thinking quickly to survive, Cardoso was drawn to his new role. In 1985 Cardoso thrust himself before voters again, running this time as a social democrat for Mayor of Sao Paulo against Brazil's former President, Jnio Quadros. He ran another inept campaign and lost, too often answering questions as a professor rather than as a politician. Observers noticed he approached meetings with masses of poor, dispossessed voters with barely disguised distaste, unable to reconcile his leftist social consciousness with his sheltered social prejudices.

Though defeated for mayor, Cardoso remained in the Senate and won reelection in 1986. In 1988 he helped found the Brazilian Social Democratic Party (PSDB). In 1993, when President Fernando Collor de Mello was ousted for corruption, his Vice President, Itamar Franco, took over. Franco appointed Cardoso foreign minister, in a move to enlist the support of the new PSDB. Within months, after impressing Franco during cabinet meetings, Cardoso was shifted to the more prestigious job of finance minister. By

the next general election, Cardoso had gained recognition for his program to reign in hyperinflation, then running at 50 percent per month, and the neophyte politician was a natural choice to become a candidate for president.

Brazilians were naturally weary of inflation, having watched prices increase 22 billion fold in 34 years. Economic plans and currencies had come and gone—five currencies in the eight years preceding the 1994 elections—so voters were both cynical and hopeful when Finance Minister Cardoso announced his "Real Plan." Business leaders felt a strong incentive to make this plan work, since only a strong Cardoso could defeat his popular left-wing opponent, Luis Incio Lula da Silva.

Introduction of the Real Plan was intended to give it enough time to work but not enough to fail before the election. Before its introduction, da Silva held a sizable lead. By October 3, however, with inflation reduced to between 2 and 3 percent per month, the tables turned, and Cardoso won by a 2-to-1 margin. Opponents warned that inflation would soar again just after the election, but their predictions proved false. While 64 percent of registered voters rejected Cardoso by casting their lot with his competitors or filing blank or otherwise invalid ballots, 53 percent of the valid votes swept him into office with what appeared an impressive mandate. In an interview with James F. Hoge, Jr., editor of *Foreign Affairs* magazine, President Cardoso stated that "Leftist politicians were virtually excluded from the political life of Latin America under authoritarian rule . . . This situation has changed. . . . If the goal of a socialist regime is forgotten, the notion of a strong state as the main instrument of development is still alive. Perhaps this is what explains why the left is now a major force among public civil servants and has developed corporate interests in several areas of the state." The alliance which endorsed Cardoso also sent a majority to Congress, though that fact would prove only a mixed blessing later.

The First Term

Cardoso took office on January 1, 1995, and seemed to meet the prayers of the broadest of constituencies. Business leaders, the oligarchy, and foreign powers counted on the new leader to put Brazil's economic house in order, while the economically disenfranchised trusted that the once leftist social scientist would correct the country's social ills. Social inequities in Brazil were staggering, with the richest 20 percent of the population earning 26 times that of the poorest 20 percent. In addition, Brazil suffered high infant mortality, short life expectancy, low literacy rates, poor educational opportunity, high incidence of serious disease, and a nearly non-existent infrastructure.

Foreign investors, upon whom Brazil depended for its growth, demanded domestic economic austerity which would make social programs impossible. Much to the pleasure of the business community and the dismay of his traditional allies on the left, Cardoso proposed to privatize previously nationalized industries, opening vast opportunity for entrepreneurs in communications, mining, energy, and heavy industry. In a risky move, Cardoso used the revenues from privatization to fund social projects beyond the reach of the government's meager resources.

Beyond this strategy, the president worked to tighten the collection of taxes, which posed an unfair advantage for the wealthy. Cardoso vowed to change that. He also tried to retain a greater proportion of the revenues collected for the use of the central government, instead of distributing 65 percent of it to the states as in the past. Since the states had few spending responsibilities, much of that revenue had been frittered away in corruption.

Despite a crisis in Latin America caused by economic disasters in Mexico, Brazil's economy grew healthier, with inflation in check and a gross domestic product increasing at five percent. While the business community complained of bank failures, increasing costs due to rising wages, and a swelling budget deficit, others faulted Cardoso for not moving fast enough toward social reform. Cardoso's popularity grew elsewhere, though, as unemployment dropped and the government initiated education reforms and rural projects which would benefit some of Brazil's poorest citizens. Writing for *Current History,* Carlos Eduardo Lins da Silva commented that the "new Brazilian president is a professional intellectual in the contemporary meaning of the word; not the 'humanist' of the sixteenth century or the 'philosopher' of the eighteenth and nineteenth, but someone who contributes to the production, confirmation, and dissemination of values, or what might be called 'world visions,' in his or her society."

Cardoso remained responsive to the business community, but leftist critics took comfort that the person with easiest access to his ear was unlikely to forsake social reform. That advisor was anthropologist Ruth Corra Leite Cardoso, Brazil's first lady. Some have likened her to Eleanor Roosevelt of the United States. Many of those least patient with the pace of change under Cardoso remained assured that his wife would not let him forget the ideals of their youth.

A Second Term?

Such was the confidence Cardoso inspired—many claimed he was that country's last hope to head off a return to authoritarianism—that a constitutional amendment was introduced and passed to allow presidents a second term in office. Though Cardoso had been elected to serve only until the end of 1998, he instantly became the leading contender for the term running through 2002. Unfortunately, the El Nino phenomenon brought a drought to northeast Brazil in 1998, and Cardoso was blamed for not taking enough action. Commenting on the president's status in May of that year, Cable News Network (CNN) online stated: "[the] front-runner to win the October elections, has seen his star dim in recent weeks as unrest mounts over millions starving in a severe drought while cost-cutting reforms languish in Congress." Yet, it appeared that the unlikely, awkward politician would still become Brazil's most successful president of his generation.

Further Reading

Business Week, October 10, 1997; June 30, 1997; February 17, 1997; June 10, 1996; October 10, 1995; October 3, 1994.
Current History, February, 1995.
Forbes, June 17, 1996.
Foreign Affairs, July/August, 1995.
Macleans, October 3, 1994.
New York Times, March 14, 1988.
US News and World Report, April 24, 1995.
CNN interactive, http://cnn.com/WORLD/americas (May 19, 1998).□

Ben Carson

American doctor Ben Carson (born 1951) overcame poverty, racism, and a violent temper to become a world-renowned neurosurgeon.

In 1987, neurosurgeon Ben Carson successfully performed an operation to separate Siamese twins who were born joined at the head. It was a milestone in neurosurgery, but was far from the only noteworthy achievement of Carson's career. He also performed groundbreaking surgery on a twin suffering from an abnormal expansion of the head. Carson was able to relieve the swelling and remove the surplus fluid—all while the unborn twin remained in its mother's uterus. This too was a first, and in other instances Carson has performed operations which have greatly expanded scientific knowledge of the brain and its functions. His "can-do" spirit, combined with his medical expertise, has made him the surgeon of choice for parents with children suffering rare neurological conditions.

If Carson seemed destined for any position when he was a child growing up on the streets of Detroit, he appeared most qualified for the role of putting someone else in the hospital—or even the morgue. In his profile on the American Academy of Achievement website, it was noted that Carson "had a temper so violent that he would attack other children, even his mother, at the slightest provocation." No doubt some of his anger stemmed from the conditions of his childhood. Carson's father left his mother, Sonya, when he was only eight; his mother, who had only a third-grade education, was faced with the daunting task of raising her sons Ben and Curtis by herself. She worked as a maid, sometimes holding two or even three jobs to support her family. The family was poor, and Carson often endured the cruel taunts of his classmates.

A further source of frustration in Carson's life was his poor performance as a student. During a two-year period when his family lived in Boston, he fell behind in his studies. By the time he returned to elementary school in Detroit, he was, according to his profile on the American Academy of Achievement website, "considered the 'dummy' of the class." It was a position for which he "had no competition," he related in his book *Gifted Hands.*

After Carson brought home a report card of failing grades, his mother quickly limited her sons' television view-

ing and required them to read two books a week. The boys then had to give written reports to their mother on what they read. While other children were outside playing, Sonya Carson forced her boys to stay inside and read, an act for which her friends criticized her, saying that her sons would grow up to hate her. Carson later realized that because of her own limited education, his mother often could not read her sons' reports, and was moved by her efforts to motivate them to a better life.

Before long, Carson moved from the bottom of the class to the top. However, there was resentment from his classmates at the predominantly white school. After awarding Carson a certificate of achievement at the end of his freshman year, a teacher berated his white classmates for letting an African-American student outshine them academically. In his high school years and later, Carson faced racism in a number of situations, but as he said in his 1996 interview with the American Academy of Achievement, "It's something that I haven't invested a great deal of energy in. My mother used to say, 'If you walk into an auditorium full of racist, bigoted people . . . you don't have a problem, they have a problem.'"

Despite his academic improvement, Carson still had a violent temper. In his interview with the American Academy of Achievement, he recalled trying to hit his mother over the head with a hammer because of a disagreement over what clothes he should wear. In a dispute with a classmate over a locker, he cut a three-inch gash in the other boy's head. However, at the age of 14, Carson reached a turning point

after he nearly stabbed a friend to death because the boy had changed the radio station.

Terrified by his own capacity for violence, he ran home and locked himself in the bathroom with the Bible. "I started praying," he said in his American Academy of Achievement interview, "and asking God to help me find a way to deal with this temper." Reading from the Book of Proverbs, he found numerous verses about anger, but the one that stood out to him was "Better a patient man than a warrior, a man who controls his temper than one who takes a city." After that, he realized he could control his anger, rather than it controlling him.

With his outstanding academic record, Carson was in demand among the nation's highest-ranking colleges and universities. He graduated at the top of his high school class and enrolled at Yale University. He had long been interested in psychology and, as he related in *Gifted Hands,* decided to become a doctor when he was eight-years-old and heard his pastor talk about the activities of medical missionaries. College would prove difficult, not just academically but financially, and in his book Carson credits God and a number of supportive people for helping him graduate successfully with his B.A. in 1973. He then enrolled in the School of Medicine at the University of Michigan.

Carson decided to become a neurosurgeon rather than a psychologist, and this would not be the only important decision at this juncture of his life. In 1975 he married Lacena Rustin whom he had met at Yale, and they eventually had three children. Carson earned his medical degree in 1977, and the young couple moved to Maryland, where he became a resident at Johns Hopkins University. By 1982 he was the chief resident in neurosurgery in Johns Hopkins. In his 1996 interview on the American Academy of Achievement website, Carson noted that being a young, African American made things different in the work setting. He recalled that in his early days as a surgeon, nurses would often mistake him for a hospital orderly, and speak to him as such. "I wouldn't get angry," he remembered. "I would simply say, 'Well, that's nice, but I'm Dr. Carson.'" He continued, "I recognize[d] that the reason they said that was not necessarily because they were racist, but because from their perspective . . . the only black man they had ever seen on that ward with scrubs on was an orderly, so why should they think anything different?"

In 1983, Carson received an important invitation. Sir Charles Gairdner Hospital in Perth, Australia, needed a neurosurgeon, and they invited Carson to take the position. Initially resistant to the idea, as he related in *Gifted Hands,* the choice to go to Australia became one of the most significant of his career. The Carsons were deeply engaged in their life in Australia, and Lacena Carson, a classically-trained musician, was the first violinist in the Nedlands Symphony. For Ben Carson, his experience in Australia was invaluable, because it was a country without enough doctors with his training. He gained several years' worth of experience in a short time. "After several months," he wrote in *Gifted Hands,* "I realized that I had a special reason to thank God for leading us to Australia. In my one year there I got so much surgical experience that my skills were honed tremendously, and I felt remarkably capable and comfortable working on the brain.''

Carson drew upon his previous experiences after he returned to Johns Hopkins in 1984. Shortly thereafter in 1985, and only in his early 30s, Carson became director of pediatric neurosurgery at Johns Hopkins Hospital. He faced several challenging cases, the first being four-year-old Maranda Francisco. Since the age of 18 months, the little girl had been having seizures, and by the time her parents brought her to Johns Hopkins, she was having more than 100 of them a day. In consultation with another doctor, Carson decided to take a radical step: a hemispherectomy, the removal of half the patient's brain. It was a risky procedure, as he told the girl's parents, but if they did nothing, Maranda would probably die. In *Gifted Hands* he described the painstaking surgery, which took more than eight hours and at the end of which the tearful Franciscos learned that their daughter would recover. Carson went on to perform numerous successful hemispherectomies, and only lost one patient; but that loss, of an 11-month-old, was devastating.

Carson described numerous other important operations in his book, *Gifted Hands,* but one which attracted international attention was the case of the Binder Siamese twins, Patrick and Benjamin. The Binders were born to German parents on February 2, 1987, and they were not merely twins: they were joined at the head. Ultimately the parents contacted Carson, who performed the 22-hour surgery on September 5 with a team of some 70 people. Although the twins would turn out to have some brain damage, both would survive the separation, making Carson's the first successful such operation. Part of its success owed to Carson's application of a technique he had seen used in cardiac surgery: by drastically cooling down the patients' bodies, he was able to stop the flow of blood. This ensured the patients' survival during the delicate period when he and the other surgeons were separating their blood vessels.

This type of surgery was in its developmental stages in the 1980s and early 1990s. When Carson and a surgical team of more than two dozen doctors performed a similar operation on the Makwaeba twins in South Africa in 1994, they were unsuccessful, and the twins died. Perhaps more representative of Carson's cases is the one chronicled in the July 1995 issue of *US News and World Report,* entitled "Matthew's Miracle." Matthew Anderson was five-years-old when his parents learned that their son had a brain tumor. According to the article, right before the little boy was to begin radiation treatments, a friend recommended the autobiography of a brain surgeon "who thrived on cases that other doctors deemed hopeless." After the Andersons read *Gifted Hands,* they decided that they wanted Carson to operate on their son. Carson performed two surgeries, one in 1993, and one in 1995. Ultimately, Matthew Anderson recovered.

According to the *US News and World Report* article, Carson performs 500 operations a year, three times as many as most neurosurgeons, a fact for which he credits his "very, very efficient staff." He works with the music of Bach, Schubert, and other composers playing, "to keep me calm," he told the magazine. In 1994, *US News and World Report*

rated Johns Hopkins Hospital the finest specialty institution in the country, ranking it above such highly respected hospitals as Mayo Clinic and Massachusetts General.

Because Carson's career has represented a triumph over circumstances, he has become a well-known inspirational writer and speaker. He is not short on advice for young people. In his 1996 American Academy of Achievement interview, he commented, "We don't need to be talking about Madonna, and Michael Jordan, and Michael Jackson. I don't have anything against these people, I really don't. But the fact of the matter is, that's not uplifting anybody. That's not creating the kind of society we want to create.'' He has noted that the most important thing is to bring value to the world through improving the lives of one's fellow human beings. Carson has done this through perseverance and example.

Further Reading

Carson, Ben, with Cecil Murphey, *Gifted Hands,* Zondervan, 1990.
Black Enterprise, October 1993, p. 147.
Christianity Today, May 27, 1991, pp. 24-26.
People, fall 1991 (special issue), pp. 96-99.
Readers Digest, April 1990, pp. 71-75.
US News and World Report, July 24, 1995, pp. 46-49.
"Dr. Benjamin S. Carson," *American Academy of Achievement,* http://www.achievement.org (February 27, 1998).
"Skull Basher to Brain Healer," *Connection Magazine,* http://www.connectionmagazine.org (February 27, 1998).

Catherine of Aragon

Catherine of Aragon (1485-1536) was to represent a political union between a strong and powerful Spain and the up-and-coming England; instead, she became a paragon of virtue. She was the first wife of King Henry VIII who never gave up the crown even after her husband had forsaken her in his quest for a male heir.

Catherine of Aragon was the last child born to the two reigning monarchs of Spain, King Ferdinand of Aragon and Queen Isabella of Castile. She was born in the Castle of the Archbishop of Toledo where her mother took refuge after engaging in combat with the Moors. Catherine's childhood was filled with battles and celebrations as her parents worked to expand the realm of their influence.

Catherine's mother ascended the throne unexpectedly without the benefit of a formal education; she therefore brought scholars into Spain in an effort to give her daughters a broad knowledge of the world. Catherine was an attentive student who was capable of speaking Latin, French, Spanish, and later English. As a balance the girls were also trained in law, genealogy and domestic life, including embroidery, household management, dance, and music. The belief that a pious Christian life could be led within the world of the monarchy was passed to Catherine by her devoutly Catholic mother.

Knowing that the union of their daughters to other powerful nations could strengthen their foothold in Europe the King and Queen chose these alliances carefully. The Treaty of Medina del Campo in 1489 contained the promise of a bride for Prince Arthur of England, son of Henry VII. The daughter chosen was Catherine, but the actual treaties of marriage did not occur until August 1497 at Woodstock, England. In May 1499 the first of the wedding ceremonies occurred in Worcestershire after a Papal dispensation allowed Arthur, who was below the age of consent, to make his vows.

Life as Princess of Wales

A second proxy marriage occurred in 1500 in Ludlow, but it was not until the summer of 1501 that Catherine finally arrived in England as the Princess of Wales. The trip was physically difficult for her, but she was welcomed in England with great fanfare. Her final marriage vows were said in November 1501 in St. Peter's Cathedral, and a mere five months later, the Prince of Wales died. Until her death Catherine insisted that this marriage to Arthur was never consummated, a fact that her second husband was never able to publically deny.

The comforts that Catherine had enjoyed as a new bride were soon stripped as King Henry VII refused to support her household because her complete dowry had never been paid. In humiliation she was forced to live

meagerly at court. She worried about her women in waiting who had accompanied her from Spain and for her own future as well. For seven years she continued in a state of limbo as the Princess Dowager (widow) of Wales, no longer under the care of her father and refused care by her father-in-law.

Life as Henry VIII's Queen

The death of Henry VII and the ascension of Henry VIII brought Catherine new hope of a marriage and the chance to take her rightful place as Queen of England. The king's council preferred a Hapsburg or a French marriage, as was the wish of Henry VII when he betrothed his son to the child Eleanor of Austria. Catherine insisted to those in her household that her marriage to Henry would occur although privately worried about her fate. Those fears were put to rest when Henry VIII went against council and took Catherine as his bride, a mere six weeks after ascending the throne. They were married in a church outside Greenwich Palace on June 11, 1509. The King was 18 years old and Catherine was five years his senior.

Speculation exists about why he chose her when he could have made a marriage with a number of women. According to *The Lives of the Kings & Queens of England*, edited by Antonia Fraser, as he was dying, Henry VII advised his son to marry Catherine "to preserve the Spanish alliance." Other historians dispute this deathbed promise as unfounded, particularly given the poor treatment Catherine suffered at the hands of Henry VII. Another theory is that the new king wanted to quickly secure a successor. All indications suggest however, that Henry chose Catherine for the sake of romance. He could easily have been smitten with her as she was one of the few women that he had been able to speak with during his adolescence. Catherine was "dainty and graceful, with fine eyes." In regards to the young king, Fraser added that Henry "was young enough to be in love with love" and "became captivated by the Princess it was his duty to wed."

Further proof that he loved Catherine is exhibited by the fact that they shared a coronation day, which was highly unusual at the time. Normally a queen consort was coronated only after she bore an heir as had happened with the king's own mother. Instead Henry broke with tradition and Catherine rode with him through the city of London in lavish carriages and clothing as part of a joyous celebration. Catherine was well received by the English subjects as their Queen.

Catherine loved her young, athletic, charming husband. She wanted to please him and as a devoted wife, was determined to give Henry an heir. Their first child was a stillborn daughter in 1510. A son, Henry was born in January 1511 but sadly only lived 52 days. Catherine miscarried in October 1513 and in February 1515, had a stillborn son. In February 1516, there was happiness as Princess Mary was born. There was joy in the sign that Catherine could bear a vital child which kept alive the hope of a son. Sadness accompanied the birth as the Queen was finally informed of her father's death two weeks prior. In 1518 Catherine had another stillborn daughter and there would be no more children.

Catherine was comforted by Henry at each loss. In the beginning of their marriage Henry was not the heartless man that he is portrayed as later in his life. He showed open affection for Catherine as he jousted in her colors as Sir Loyal Heart. A love knot with their intertwined initials was emblazoned on his armor. Goblets were made with this same emblem of unity. Catherine also had her own personifying fertility and her own Spanish upbringing. Although Catherine adapted well to her role as English Queen, she still was bound to her land of origin.

While Henry was at war he named Catherine as the Queen Regent of the Kingdom which showed the great faith that he had in her. Given her upbringing amidst war she was well equipped to serve in the regent capacity. Reminiscent of her mother she addressed the English army as they prepared for an invasion by the Scots. Catherine sent Henry the bloodied coat of the Scot King who was killed in the battle as proof of her devotion and service to him.

As was customary of the time, Henry and Catherine maintained two separate households with large suites near one another. With over 140 persons attending her Catherine still insisted on embroidering the king's shirts herself. Catherine was also devoutly religious and defended the Catholic faith as evidenced by her title *Fidei Defensor*. Her piety increased with her age as did her interest in scholars for the continued improvement of herself and for the training of her daughter. Learning among women became fashionable much from the influence of Catherine. She was a benefactor of St. John's College in Cambridge, Queens College, Cardinal College in Oxford, and Corpus Christi.

Rejected by Henry

As time passed, it became more clear that two groups were present in the English court, those who were French-minded in their speaking, socializing, and dress, and those who were scholars and theologians. The King associated with both groups but Catherine isolated herself with the scholars. She presided in state functions but declined to participate in the dancing and antics of the court.

In June 1519, Henry's mistress, Bessie Blount, a maid in the court, gave birth to a son. This event did not bother Catherine until 1524 when the illegitimate child was given the title Duke of Richmond by Henry along with rights for ascension to the throne behind Princess Mary. Henry loved his daughter Mary and his later poor treatment of her was viewed as only a punishment to Catherine. In 1518, at the age of two, Mary was betrothed to the Dauphin of France which did not please her mother. Catherine campaigned for an alliance with her nephew Holy Roman Emperor Charles V (was also King Charles I of Spain) instead and began the instruction of Mary as Queen of Spain. Henry counted on this alliance for political gain and was furious when Charles married another.

A king with no male heir feared for the succession of his throne. It was around this time that Anne Boleyn, a lady in waiting to Catherine, caught Henry's eye. Anne refused to be anything less than queen, so Henry needed a way out of his marriage. In 1527, Henry used a passage of Leviticus from the bible as proof that his marriage to his brother's wife was not viewed favorably by God and therefore was cursed with no sons. He claimed his conscience could not allow him to continue in the marriage and requested what in modern terms would be an annulment. Cardinal Wolsey set-up an official court to investigate the validity of the marriage. The Pope refused to allow the English court to try the case since a papal dispensation had been issued in 1509 at the time of the marriage, but delayed in making a decision for many years. Wolsey tried to get all the English bishops to agree that the marriage was invalid to force the hand of the Vatican but John Fisher, Bishop of Rochester (who was later executed by Henry VIII) refused.

End of her Life

Catherine refused to withdraw from public life and retire to a nunnery. She firmly believed that her marriage to Henry was divinely ordained and to interfere with this would jeopardize her soul. Another concern to Catherine was the legitimacy and safety of her daughter. She was encouraged by some to invoke the aid of her nephew, Charles V, as many believed he controlled the pope. Others hoped he wouldn't stand for his aunt being cast aside and would return her to her rightful position, but Catherine refused. It is questionable whether he would have obliged and Catherine believed that a war would harm the citizens of England. The Catholic Church also attempted to pressure Charles V into re-instituting Catherine's claim as Queen, but that may have had more to do with keeping power in England rather than concern for a queen.

In 1531, Princess Mary and her household were removed to Ludlow by the King which greatly saddened Catherine. She was told that she could travel to be with Mary only when she accepted that her marriage to Henry was not valid. Catherine refused to deny her marriage and continued to view herself as Queen of England. Since Catherine refused to leave her husband he moved the entire court without her and secretly married Anne Boleyn. Before the birth of his first child by Anne, Catherine was moved to Bickden Palace in Huntingdonshire. In 1533 her marriage was declared invalid by the Archbishop of Canterbury and by order of the King she was to return to her title of Princess Dowager of Wales (meaning she was the widow of Prince Arthur).

In 1534 the Pope found for Catherine and validated her marriage but this made little difference as the King was preparing for the birth of his second child by Anne Boleyn. Henry officially broke away from the Roman Catholic Church and the Archbishop Lee of York and Bishop Tunstall of Durham brought the Oath of Succession for Catherine to swear to, which named Henry as head of the Church of England, her as Dowager to Prince Arthur, and Henry's children by Anne as his rightful heirs. Catherine refused. Parliament soon passed the Act of Supremacy, which made Henry head of the Church of England.

In the end, Henry was cruel to Catherine, forcing her to live in seclusion and refusing to allow her to see their daughter. She died at Kimbolton Castle near Huntington in 1536. In the end she was maintained less in the style of royalty and more like a nun. She had been stripped of her jewels by order of the King years earlier. Catherine was buried in Peterborough Cathedral under the emblem of Wales and Spain, not of England. Henry continued to seek an heir and in his rush to marry his third wife, his marriage to Catherine was eventually re-affirmed and his second marriage was deemed invalid.

Further Reading

Fraser, Antonia, *The Wives of Henry VIII,* Knopf, 1993.
Fraser, Antonia, ed. *The Lives of the Kings & Queens of England,* University of California Press, 1995.
Luke, Mary M.,*Catherine, the Queen,* Coward-McCann, Inc., 1967.
Mattingly, Garrett, *Catherine of Aragon,* Little, Brown and Company, 1941.
Catherine of Aragon—The Six Wives of Henry VIII (videocassette series), BBC TV, New York: Time-Life Media, 1976.

Lynn Russell Chadwick

One of the leading sculptors in Britain after World War II, Lynn Chadwick (born 1914) is well known for both abstract and figurative works that embodied the tensions of the post-war era. His precariously balanced, spiky, insect-like figures and more monumental geometric works have brought him international renown as a successor to Henry Moore and Barbara Hepworth.

Like many of his contemporaries, Chadwick followed a relatively indirect path to sculpture. He was born in London in 1914, the son of Verner Russell Chadwick, an engineer, and the former Marjorie Brown Lynn. He attended the Merchant Taylor's School in London, where his mentor K. P. F. Brown taught him oil and watercolor painting. Though his family appreciated the arts and had artist friends, they dissuaded Chadwick from pursuing formal training in sculpting, pointing out the difficulty of making a living through the arts in Depression-era England. In 1933 Chadwick began training as a draftsman and joined the firm of Rodney Thomas in 1937.

During World War II, Chadwick volunteered in the Fleet Air Arm of the Royal Navy and was sent to the United States and Toronto for training. In Canada, he met his first wife, Ann Secord, whom he married in 1942. Chadwick was commissioned as a pilot and flew missions over the North Atlantic protecting convoys from submarine attacks. Some critics have speculated that Chadwick's wartime flying experience fueled his interest in the movement of forms in space—which would become a repeated theme in his work—and imbued his early sculptures with their characteristic anxiety.

Back in London after the war, Chadwick began to design textiles, furniture, and exhibition stands in addition to his drafting work. In March, 1946 he won a textile design prize sponsored by Zika and Lida Ascher, which brought him enough small commissions for him to quit his architectural job and work independently. He moved his family from London to Fisher's College, near Edge, Stroud, and a year later moved to Pinswell, near Cheltenham.

Began with Mobiles

Chadwick's first sculptures were mobile constructions of balsa and aluminum wire, designed primarily for exhibition stands. They incorporated elongated fish-like or wing-like shapes, which led many critics to conclude that Chadwick was influenced by the mobiles of American sculptor Alexander Calder (1898-1976). Chadwick, however, insists he had not yet seen Calder's work when he began constructing his own mobiles, but was intrigued by his colleague Rodney Thomas's constructions of thin balanced shapes.

Interest in Chadwick's work grew, and in June, 1950, Gimpel Fils in London gave him his first one-man show. The British Council liked the exhibition so much that they commissioned three mobiles for the 1951 Festival of Britain, and Chadwick received other large commissions as well. In order to create larger sculptures, though, Chadwick had to learn new techniques. He studied welding at the British Oxygen Company's Welding School in Cricklewood during the summer of 1950, and then began executing large pieces such as his iron and copper mobile *Fisheater* (1951) and the iron mobile *Dragonfly* (1951). With these works, Chadwick began to explore more overtly animalistic subjects, which he developed over the next several years in solid sculptures suggesting weird birds, insects, or beasts.

"The Geometry of Fear"

Chadwick entered the international limelight when the British Council invited him to contribute four pieces to the Venice *Biennale* in 1952. Critics were tremendously impressed with the show, which showcased the vitality of British sculpture and also included Armitage, Butler, Paolozzi, and Turnbull. Art critic Herbert Read, in his *Exhibition of Works,* pointing out that these artists had moved away from the classical serenity of earlier times, commented that "These new images belong to the iconography of despair, or of defiance" and created a "geometry of fear." But Read also acknowledged a playful element in Chadwick's work that coexisted with its more disturbing subconscious allusions. In the welded iron *Barley Fork* (1952), for example, the spiky tines of the fork grip two smaller, sharp pieces reminiscent of an animal trap—an image both menacing and witty. Chadwick is always concerned with geometry and tension in a work and he strives to invest his pieces with a vital quality.

In 1953, Chadwick entered the International Sculpture Competition on the theme of "The Unknown Political Prisoner" organized by the Institute for Contemporary Arts in London. His entry, a welded iron maquette (a small model from which a sculpture is elaborated) suggested a harsh, geometric enclosure of attached triangular shapes. The work received an honorable mention, which prompted Chadwick to concentrate more seriously on solid sculpture.

Always interested in technical innovations, Chadwick began experimenting with a new casting technique in 1953. He constructed elaborate armatures, or frames, of multiple welded iron rods over which he applied an artificial stone compound of gypsum and iron powder called "Stolit." When this dried, it could be worked or left to weather. One of the first pieces made with this process was *Ideomorphic Beast* (1953), an angular, bat-like figure which displays a peculiarly fossilized quality in the rough surface that fills in the complex frame. Though this new process was time consuming and made it impossible to make multiple copies of a piece, Chadwick enjoyed the fresh possibilities that the approach offered. Fascinated by pure abstract shapes, he found that his new casting method enabled him to start with such forms and then add on the quirkier elements—legs, beaks, wings—that so interested him.

Beats Giacometti

By the mid-1950s, Chadwick's reputation was at its peak. His work was being bought by private collectors and by leading museums throughout the world. In 1955 his work was included in the Museum of Modern Art's "The New Decade" show, and the next year he was given his own exhibition room at the Venice *Biennale.* He showed 19 pieces completed between 1951 and 1956, including *The Inner Eye* (1952), an iron and glass sculpture in which clawlike spikes grip a chunk of crystal within an iron rib-cage, *Ideomorphic Beast,* and the iron and Stolit *The Seasons* (1955), a piece that symbolizes the conflict between new birth and decay by the juxtaposition of a gnarled bare tree form with a bold triangular shape. At Venice, Chadwick was awarded the International Prize for Sculpture, becoming, at age 41, the youngest major prize recipient since World War II. Many in the art world were shocked at Chadwick's selection, having assumed that Swiss sculptor Alberto Giacometti (1901-1966) would win. Though Chadwick felt his prize did not affect his relations with fellow sculptors, it may have alienated critics who had favored Giacometti, especially among the British art establishment.

By this time, distinct aspects of Chadwick's work were evident. In addition to more abstract, allusive pieces like *The Inner Eye,* he was developing his interest in paired structures through the exploration of dancing figures and coupled forms. *Teddy Boy and Girl* (1955), a bronze, contains both abstract and naturalistic elements. The piece achieves a formal tension by the juxtaposition of two strongly contrasting shapes, one male and one female. Although the geometric shapes are abstracted, the sculpture also suggests the curvature and volume of human bodies. *Winged Figures* (1955), a bronze comprising two standing forms, continues Chadwick's move toward less aggressive imagery and his interest in the relationship between multiple figures in space.

In 1957 Chadwick was invited to create a memorial to commemorate the successful double crossing of the Atlantic in 1919 by the airship R34, to be placed at London's Heathrow Airport. Chadwick again used the theme of the double, creating a two-headed winged figure, with one face looking in each direction. Later, he modified the wings into a more truncated, blockish shape which implies both movement and solidity. Though the memorial committee approved the design, it was strongly opposed by the Guild of Air Pilots and was ultimately rejected. Chadwick later cast the bronze figure *Stranger III* (1959) in an edition of four.

After *Stranger III,* Chadwick began to explore the spatial possibilities of three-part groups in works like *The Watchers* (1960), a bronze group of three upright figures with geometric bodies perched on spindly legs. By the early 1970s he sometimes experimented with groups of four, five, or six male and female figures. He also moved away from the rougher surfaces of his early work, experimenting with highly polished surfaces in pieces such as his *Elektras,* a series of bronze female figures in which sections of torsos or heads are polished to a mirror smoothness.

Eclipsed by New Generation

In 1964, Chadwick was made a Companion of the British Empire, but his career had already begun to wane. New movements such as pop art, minimalism, and conceptual and performance art attracted attention while Chadwick's work was neglected. Though he continued to exhibit widely in Europe, he rarely showed new work in Britain until 1974, when Marlborough Fine Arts gallery held the first London exhibition of Chadwick's work in eight years. Critics were disappointed, judging that Chadwick's work had lost its impetus. One observed that the anxiety and tension found in Chadwick's early skeletal pieces had been weakened in the use of smoother surfaces and less aggressive imagery. Another found Chadwick's use of pyramid shapes to be stale, merely stylized rather than dynamic. Four years later, the Marlborough mounted another Chadwick show at which critical response was similar. Though some pieces—notably the three bronze works *Three Sitting Watchers* (1975), *Pair of Walking Figures—Jubilee* (1977), and *Cloaked Figure IX* (1978)—were praised as forceful, mythic images, others were faulted for using abstraction as a decorative rather than integral element. Charles Spencer, writing for *Contemporary Artists,* asserted that even into the 1990s, Chadwick's work "has shown little development . . . formulas of pyramid shapes or wingspans have now been reduced to anecdotal, almost sentimental symbols; seated couples, walking figures, or standing forms, reminiscent of the gentler imagery of his contemporary, Kenneth Armitage."

Through the 1970s, Chadwick continued his exploration of paired groups, working with the theme of the cloaked couple or single figure. This image allowed Chadwick to suggest the movement of wind through hair or drapery—possibilities that continued to interest him for the next decade. Earlier pieces dealing with this theme emphasize semi-abstracted fan or wing-like shapes swirling out behind angular figures, while the bronze *High Wind* (1984) demonstrates in the subtle modeling of the female figure a more naturalistic approach.

Much of Chadwick's work is in the collections of major museums throughout the world, including the Tate Gallery, London; National Museum of Wales; Scottish National Gallery of Modern Art; Musee Nationale d'Art Moderne, Paris; Peggy Guggenheim Collection (The Solomon R. Guggenheim Foundation), Venice; Galleria Nazionale d-Arte Moderna e Contemporanea, Rome; Museum of Modern Art, New York; and the Smithsonian Institute, Washington, DC. Several of Chadwick's pieces are also owned by private collectors.

Chadwick's first marriage, which produced one son, ended in divorce. In 1959, he married Frances Mary Jamieson, with whom he had two daughters before her death in 1964. The following year he married photograher Eva Reiner; they have one son. Since 1958, Chadwick has lived at Lypiatt Park, an old estate in Gloucestershire, which the artist has restored over the years.

Further Reading

Arnason. H. H. *History of Modern Art: Painting, Sculpture, Architecture, Photography,* third edition, Prentice-Hall, 1986.

Bowness, Alan, *Lynn Chadwick, Art in Progress,* Methuen, London, 1962.

Contemporary Artists, Fourth edition, St. James Press, 1996.

Farr, Dennis and Chadwick, Eva, *Lynn Chadwick, Sculptor,* Oxford University Press, 1990.

Read, Herbert, "New Aspects of British Sculpture," *Exhibition of Works by Sutherland, Wadsworth; Adams, Armitage, Butler, Chadwick, Clarke _ Turnbull,* XXXVI Biennale, Venice, 1952.

Seuphor, Michel, *The Sculpture of This Century,* George Braziller, Inc, 1960.

Tamplin, Ronald, editor, *The Arts: A History of Expression in the 20th Century,* Oxford University Press, 1991.

Chadwick, Lynn, "A Sculptor and His Public," *The Listener,* October 20, 1954, p. 671.

British Contemporary Sculpture/Lynn Chadwick, http://www.sculpture.org.uk/biography/chadwick.html

Eric Patrick Clapton

In the 1960s graffiti appeared on London and New York City streets proclaiming "Clapton is God." For the next 30 years, Eric Clapton (born 1945) forged out a career as an extraordinary guitar player, singer, and songwriter, becoming a musician of legendary proportion.

Eric Clapton's musical roots were formed by American blues artists such as Muddy Waters, Robert Johnson, and Sonny Boy Williamson. During his career, he experimented with many musical forms, including rock, pop, reggae, and even techno-jazz. However, he always seemed to find his way back to his beloved blues where his music is fueled by a life filled with personal struggles and tragedies.

The First Guitar

Clapton was born on March 30, 1945, in Surrey, England. He was the illegitimate son of Patricia Molly Clapton and a Canadian soldier stationed in England named Edward Fryer. When Fryer returned to his wife in Canada, Clapton's mother left him to be raised by his grandparents, Jack and Rose Clapp. (He received his surname from his mother's first husband, Reginald Clapton.) Clapton was told his grandparents were his parents and his mother was his sister. He did not find out the truth until he was nine years old.

Clapton was an above-average student who excelled in art, but played the guitar more often than he studied. He received his first guitar as a present from his grandmother on his thirteenth birthday. As Clapton moved through adolescence, his love for the guitar and American blues music grew. Influenced and inspired by many of the great American blues artists, Clapton began playing almost full time. In the process, at age 17, he failed out of Kingston College of Art, where he was studying stained glass design. He moved to London, took a manual labor job, convinced his grandparents to buy him an electric guitar, and began playing in clubs and pubs.

Early Bands: Roosters, The Yardbirds, and Bluesbreakers

Soon Clapton joined his first band, the Roosters, which quickly disbanded. He played with several other British blues bands until 1963 when he joined The Yardbirds, with whom he would achieve international fame. Clapton came into the band on the recommendation of lead vocal for the band, Keith Relf, Clapton's former classmate from art college. Clapton recorded two albums with The Yardbirds, *Five Live Yardbirds,* a live album released in 1964, and *For Your*

Love, the title track reaching number two in England in 1965. During his stint with the band, Clapton came to be known by his nickname "Slowhand" for his string-bending blues riffs. *For Your Love* found eager audiences in both England and the United States, and it marked The Yardbirds intentional move away from the blues in an attempt to break into the pop charts. Clapton, who wanted to remain a blues artist, barely played on the album, and in 1965 quit the band.

Almost immediately, Clapton joined John Mayall's Bluesbreakers. Mayall gave Clapton the freedom to explore his blues style, and soon Clapton's searing blues guitar was the driving force behind the band's popularity. In 1966 the band released *Bluesbreakers: John Mayall with Eric Clapton.* This album, which reached number six on the British pop charts, propelled Clapton into the spotlight and, at the age of 21, marked him as a guitar virtuoso. It was during his stint with the Bluesbreakers that fanatical fans started the chant "Clapton is God."

Supergroups: Cream and Blind Faith

Clapton left the Bluesbreakers in July 1966, to form Cream with bass player Jack Bruce and drummer Ginger Baker. Clapton desired to break out of the standard forms of rock and blues to create a new sound that allowed more experimentation and improvisation. He wanted to start a revolution in music, and the super trio of Cream did just that. After three albums (*Fresh Cream, Disraeli Gears,* and *Wheels of Fire,*) and an extensive tour of the United States, the members of Cream became superstars in the order of the Beatles and the Rolling Stones. From these albums came legendary rock hits such as "White Room," "Sunshine of Your Love," and "Crossroads."

Much to the dismay of their fans, the members of Cream announced in 1968 that they would part ways. Tension and strife created by three strong, creative personalities, intensified by the drug use of all three, proved to be too much for Cream. Before disbanding, Cream went on a farewell tour and, in 1969, released one last album, *Goodbye,* which went to number two on the charts in the United States.

Clapton's next band, Blind Faith, became yet one more short-lived supergroup. Made up of Clapton, ex-Cream member Ginger Baker, ex-Traffic member Steve Winwood, and bassist Rick Grech, Blind Faith released just one self-titled album in July 1969. They quickly made their presence known in the music world by staging a free concert for 100,000 people in London's Hyde Park. But, after a six-week tour in the United States, the band called it quits. Clapton's most lasting work with Blind Faith is the song "Presence of the Lord." After the demise of Blind Faith, he briefly played with John Lennon and Yoko Ono's Plastic Ono Band, and then he moved on to record his first solo album, self-titled *Eric Clapton.* Although generally disappointing as a debut solo album, Clapton did find an audience for the song "After Midnight," which made it into the Top 40.

Derek and the Dominos

In the spring of 1970, Clapton brought together a new band, Derek and the Dominos. They toured throughout England during the summer of 1970. By fall, they had released a double album, *Layla and Other Assorted Love Songs.* Much of the album was inspired by Clapton's love for Patti Harrison, the wife of his good friend, ex-Beatle George Harrison. For example, the song "Have You Ever Loved a Woman" contains the lyrics: "Have you ever loved a woman / And you know you can't leave her alone? / Something deep inside you / Won't let you wreck your best friend's home." Clapton also sings about his love for Patti in the title track, "Layla," a song that became a Clapton classic.

By the early 1970s, Clapton's heroin addiction was becoming unmanageable. His drug use was fueled by the trauma of losing two of his closest friends. Slide guitar player, Duane Allman, who collaborated with Derek and the Dominos, was killed in a motorcycle accident, and Jimi Hendrix died of a drug overdose. Finally, after hitting the depths of his addiction, Clapton kicked his heroin habit using a controversial electro-acupuncture treatment.

With drugs behind him, Clapton staged a comeback concert in London in January 1973. In 1974 he released his second solo album, *461 Ocean Boulevard.* The album went to number one on the charts as did his remake of the Bob Marley song "I Shot the Sheriff." Through the rest of the 1970s, Clapton released a succession of albums. The most successful of these projects was *Slowhand* (1977), which included hits "Cocaine," "Lay Down Sally," and "Wonderful Tonight."

In 1979 Clapton married Patti Harrison (who in 1974 had divorced George Harrison and moved in with Clapton). Unfortunately, Clapton had traded one addiction for another, and this period marked his fall into a serious drinking problem. During the first half of the 1980s Clapton managed to release five solo albums, *Just One Night* (1980), *Another Ticket* (1981), *Money and Cigarettes* (1983), *Behind the Sun,* (1985), and *August* (1986). Each album was only marginally successful.

Clapton's life changed forever in 1986 when Italian actress Lori Del Santo gave birth to Clapton's son, Conor. Although this event brought great happiness to Clapton, it also marked the end of his marriage to Patti who moved out and subsequently filed for divorce. Clapton renewed his effort to give up alcohol, entered a rehab center, and became a member of Alcoholics Anonymous. At the same time, his popularity rose again dramatically after the release of the box set *Crossroads* (1988) and a new album *Journeyman* (1989).

Tragedy and "Tears in Heaven"

Although 1990 brought Clapton his first Grammy Award for "Bad Love" off the *Journeyman* album, 1990 and 1991 were marred by tragedy for Clapton. First, in 1990, Clapton once again lost close friends when guitar virtuoso Stevie Ray Vaughan and two members of Clapton's road crew died in a helicopter crash. Then, in 1991, Clapton was getting ready to pick up his then four-year-old son Conor for lunch when he received the news that the boy was dead after falling from a fifty-third-story window of a Manhattan high-rise apartment.

Clapton responded to this tragedy by writing the super hit, "Tears in Heaven," as a tribute to his son. The song was featured in the sound track of the movie *Rush.* It also appeared on the acoustical album *Unplugged* (1992), which turned out to be Clapton's biggest selling album and swept the 1993 Grammy Awards. With the success of *Unplugged,* Clapton found the courage to return to his beloved blues, and in 1994, released the blues album *From the Cradle.* The album was both commercially successful and critically acclaimed.

After releasing a four-CD box set, *Crossroads 2: Live in the '70s,* in 1996, Clapton became involved in a new age, techno-jazz duo with Simon Climie called T.D.F. Clapton, who used only the pseudonym "x-sample," and Climie released *Retail Therapy* in 1997. Although this experimental recording received mixed reviews, Clapton was still doing well on the pop charts. He claimed two Grammy Awards in 1997 (record of the year and best male pop vocal performance) for his collaboration with Babyface on "Change the World," which appeared on the soundtrack for the movie *Phenomenon.*

In March 1998, Clapton released his latest project to date, *Pilgrim.* The album is filled with almost all original Clapton songs; most noticeable are two songs that pay tribute to Clapton's son Conor, "Circus" and "My Father's Eyes," both written in 1992. Although those looking for the Clapton of Cream found the introspective, sometimes melancholy tone of *Pilgrim* disappointing, others have embraced Clapton's ever-changing style of mixing blues, rock, and his own painful soul into the songs that have aged as gracefully as the singer.

Further Reading

Rees, Dafydd, and Luke Crampton, *The Encyclopedia of Rock Stars,* DK Publishing, 1996.
Schumacher, Michael, *Crossroads: The Life and Music of Eric Clapton,* Hyperion, 1995.
Guitar Player, November, 1994.
People, March 1, 1993.
"Bluesman Eric Clapton Mixes Styles on Upcoming LP," *Addicted To Noise,* the on-line rock & roll magazine, http://www.addict.com (March 10, 1998).
"Eric Clapton," *All-Music Guide,* http://www.allmusic.com (March 10, 1998).
"Eric Clapton," *Celebsite,* http://www.celebsite.com (March 10, 1998).
Hoffman, Evan, "Eric Patrick Clapton," *Geocities,* http://www.geocities.com (March 10, 1998).
Wild, David, "Eric Clapton," *Rolling Stone Network,* http://www.rollingstone.com (March 10, 1998). □

Arthur C. Clarke

Known as one of the modern masters of science fiction, English novelist Arthur C. Clarke (born 1917)

created the immensely popular *2001* series, which became the basis for a classic film in 1968.

Arthur C. Clarke is the architect of some of the 20th Century's most enduring mythology. A futurist and science fiction writer, Clarke has penned over 600 articles and short stories, as well as dozens of novels and collections. His work has been translated into over 30 languages and adapted on television and in Hollywood movies, most notably in the classic 1968 film *2001: A Space Odyssey.* That Stanley Kubrick movie helped make Arthur C. Clarke an international celebrity. It won a whole new audience for his visionary tales about the possibilities of science and the wonders of space exploration, and solidified his reputation as one of the modern masters of science fiction.

Discovers Science Fiction Early

Arthur Charles Clarke was born on December 16, 1917 in the seaside town of Minehead, Somerset, England. His parents, Charles Wright and Nora (Willis) Clarke, were farmers. Clarke was educated at Huish's Grammar School in Taunton, Somerset. He first began reading science fiction at the age of 12, when he first discovered the pulp magazine *Amazing Stories.* It soon became his principal passion. "During my lunch hour away from school I used to haunt the local Woolworth's in search of my fix," he told *The New York Times Book Review,* "which cost threepence a shot, roughly a quarter today."

As a teenager, Clarke began writing his own stories for a school magazine. When poverty forced him to drop out of school in 1936, he moved to London to work as a civil servant auditor for the British government. He kept up his interest in outer space by joining the British Interplanetary Society, an association of sci-fi hobbyists. He wrote articles on space exploration for the Society journal and got to know other science fiction writers and editors. He would later use these contacts to secure the publication of his first stories.

When World War II broke out, Clarke joined the Royal Air Force (RAF), where he worked as a radar instructor and earned the rank of flight-lieutenant. During this time, Clarke served as a technical officer on the first Ground Control Approach radar. In 1945, he wrote an article, "Extraterrestrial Relays," which proposed using satellites for communications, something which would become quite common in later years. After the war ended he returned to London and enrolled at King's College. He graduated in 1948 with a bachelor of science degree. His honor subjects were mathematics and physics.

Becomes Prominent Futurist

In 1946, Clarke became the chairman of the British Interplanetary Society. That spring saw the publication of his first two science fiction stories, "Loophole" and "Rescue Party" (both published in *Amazing Science Fiction* magazine). During this period, he often wrote under pen names, which included Charles Willis and E.G. O'Brien. His early stories were known for their tidy construction and sound scientific basis.

In 1949, Clarke returned to hard science, joining the staff of *Physics Abstracts* as its assistant editor. But he continued writing about outer space as well. His first novel, *Prelude to Space* was published in 1951. Another book, *The Sands of Mars* followed later that year. While many reviewers found the prose in these novels a bit stiff, they did offer an optimistic view of the potentials of science in the space age. *Islands in the Sky* (1952), about a boy in an orbiting space station, was another representative early book.

Sentinel of Things To Come

In 1952, Clarke received the International Fantasy Award for his early work. The next year, he published *Expedition to Earth,* a collection of short stories which included "The Sentinel." This tale, which involves the discovery by humans of a mysterious alien monolith, was to form the basis of the 1968 film and novelization *2001: A Space Odyssey.* It also marked the introduction of metaphysical and religious themes into Clarke's work. Many readers saw "The Sentinel" as an allegory about man's search for God. Certainly it expressed Clarke's belief in the power of science in helping mankind understand the universe.

Clarke continued to explore these themes in his next two books. *Against the Fall of Night* (1953) follows a young protagonist in his attempts to escape from the controlled environment of a utopian city of the future. *Childhood's End* involves an attempt by aliens to tutor mankind in the ways of cosmic transcendence. Both stories so gripped Clarke's imagination that he spent many years revising and rewriting

them under various titles. Both novels are highly conceptual and contain many mystical, visionary passages. They are considered two of his finest achievements and helped break new ground in the science fiction genre.

Man of Many Interests

Clarke maintained other interests during this fertile period as well. On June 15, 1953, he married Marilyn Mayfield. In 1954, he took the first the first step in what would become a lifelong effort to explore and photograph the Great Barrier Reef of Australia and the coast of Sri Lanka. He took up residence in Sri Lanka (known at the time as Ceylon) in 1956. An avid skin diver, Clarke wrote many non-fiction books and articles about his experiences.

Clarke continued to write prolifically throughout the 1950s. His work came to embrace many topics that went beyond the conventions of genre science fiction. *The Deep Range* (1954) concerned the possibility of farming under the sea in the future, managing to combine Clarke's interests in science and underwater exploration. *The Star* (1955) was another powerful allegorical story about a star put in the sky by God to herald the birth of Jesus. It won a Hugo award, the science fiction community's highest honor.

In the 1960s, Clarke began to concentrate on non-fiction. His writings on the nature of science won him the UNESCO Kalinga Prize in 1962. In 1963, he published his first non-science fiction novel, *Glide Path,* about the origins of radar. As space travel became more reality than fiction, Clarke began to write and speak extensively on the subject. He became well-known around the world as a television commentator for CBS covering the Apollo 11, 12, and 15 missions.

Becomes an International Figure

Clarke's fame took a quantum leap with the release of Stanley Kubrick's film *2001: A Space Odyssey* (1968). This adaptation of Clarke's short story "The Sentinel" redefined science fiction filmmaking. It eschewed the cowboy conventions of earlier, Western-influenced movies about space exploration. Instead, *2001* followed Clarke's lead in using science fiction as a bridge to the consideration of mystical and religious themes. The limits of technology were also explored, in a scene where a space station's super computer, known as HAL 9000, goes berserk and attempts to kill its human users. The picture was a hit with moviegoers and made Clarke the most recognizable science fiction writer on the planet. He penned a novelization of the film which expanded upon the characters and themes contained in "The Sentinel."

Clarke used his newfound international celebrity to secure a lucrative new book contract. A collection of his non-fiction science writing, *The Exploration of Space* received the International Fantasy Award in 1972, A new novel, *Rendezvous with Rama* appeared in 1973. It explored many of the same themes as *2001* and was awarded all the major science fiction prizes. *Imperial Earth: A Fantasy of Love and Discord* (1975) got a decidedly mixed reception from critics. But Clarke bounced back with *Fountains of Paradise* (1979), which won the Hugo Award for Best Novel. Clarke disappointed many of his fans, however, when he announced it would be his last book of fiction.

Reneges on Promise

By 1982, despite his previous statements, Clarke was ready to write another novel. He produced a sequel, *2010: Odyssey Two,* which was made into a popular film two years later. It was followed in 1986 by *2061: Odyssey Three,* solidifying the ''Sentinel'' mythos into a full-blown series. Also in 1986, Clarke was the recipient of a Nebula Grand Master Award for his contributions to science fiction.

Now in his seventies and a certified living legend, Clarke showed no signs of slowing down. With help from co-author Gentry Lee, he produced sequels to *Rendezvous with Rama* in 1989, 1991, and 1994. In 1989, his memoir, *Astounding Days: A Science Fictional Autobiography* appeared. The entertaining account of his life contains many fascinating anecdotes about other writers Clarke had known. The solo novel *The Ghost from the Grand Banks* (1990), about attempts to raise the Titanic in the near future, was dismissed by reviewers as too spare. But *3001: The Final Odyssey* (1997) returned Clarke to familiar and beloved territory. The sprawling conclusion to the saga begun in ''The Sentinel'' some 45 years earlier read like a summation of the visionary writer's life and philosophy.

Clarke's critics have said his work lacks warmth, that he concentrated on science to the detriment of the ''human element'' that is so necessary to good fiction. But critics sympathetic to Clarke's viewpoint see in his work a vision that transcends the limitations of ''nuts and bolts'' sci-fi. That vision, wrote Eric S. Rabkin in his study *Arthur C. Clarke,* is ''a humane and open and fundamentally optimistic view of humankind and its potential in a universe which dwarfs us in physical size but which we may hope some day to match in spirit.''

Further Reading

Contemporary Authors, New Revisions, Volume 55, Gale, 1997.
The Encyclopedia of Science Fiction, edited by John Clute and Peter Nichols, St. Martin's Press, 1993.
Hollow, John, *Against the Night, The Stars: The Science Fiction of Arthur C. Clarke,* Harcourt Brace, 1983.
Rabkin, Eric S., *Arthur C. Clarke,* Starmont House, 1979.

Jacqueline Cochran

Jacqueline Cochran (1910-1980) rose from childhood poverty to become an aviation pioneer. She was the first woman to fly in the Bendix Trophy Transcontinental Race in 1935, winning it in 1938, and was the first woman to ferry a bomber across the Atlantic Ocean in support of the war effort in 1941. By 1961, she had become the first woman to break the sound barrier and held more speed records than any other pilot in the world.

The achievements of Jacqueline Cochran would be remarkable for anyone but are even more spectacular considering her humble beginnings and the fact she chose to compete in an arena not readily open to women of her time. An orphan, Cochran's exact birth date is uncertain. While she was raised with the name of her foster family, Cochran later picked from a phone book the name she would make famous. Early years offered little comfort. Cochran recounted in her autobiography *Jackie Cochran: An Autobiography* how she didn't have shoes until buying her own when she was eight. ''Food at best consisted of the barest essentials—sometimes nothing except what I foraged for myself in the woods of the Northern Florida sawmill towns my foster family called home. . . . I've often heard that if you want someone to really enjoy the pleasures of heaven, then just pitch her into hell for a spell. Perhaps that's why I enjoyed my life to the brimful.''

Childhood in Poverty

Cochran attempted to leave the squalor of her childhood by running away with the circus. The circus left without her, but it wasn't long before she found another way out. In her early teens she moved in with a Jewish family that owned hair salons. Underage, Cochran worked mixing dyes when she secured a promotion by threatening her employer with disclosure to child labor authorities. A year later, Cochran moved to Montgomery, Alabama, to work in another salon. There, a prominent client secured her admission to nursing school. She recalled that ''the formal academic requirements for entry had been waived for me, as prom-

ised," Cochran wrote in her autobiography. "I'm certain that hospital had never admitted a second-grade dropout to the program before." Following training, Cochran abandoned hope of passing the state board exam. "My handwriting alone, not to mention my rudimentary arithmetic, would never have allowed me to pass." She went to work for a Florida country doctor where a license wasn't a necessity. Fearful the quality of treatment she and the doctor were providing was worse than none at all, Cochran left medicine and moved to Pensacola, Florida, where she became part owner of a beauty shop. There she picked "Cochran" out of the phone book.

In 1929 she moved to New York City and blustered Charles of the Ritz into offering her a salon job she ended up turning down. "I was so stubborn." Cochran went to work in a Saks Fifth Avenue salon. In 1932 on a trip to Miami, she met Floyd Odlum, the successful businessman whom she would marry in 1936. "Every orphan dreams of marrying a millionaire, but I had no idea at first that Floyd Odlum was worth so much money." Cochran confided her idea of becoming a traveling cosmetics saleswoman. His mind on the Depression, Odlum said success could only come from covering a large territory. "Get your pilot's license," he told her. In the year they met, the two made a wager: if Cochran could get her license in three weeks, Odlum would pay the $495 course fee. Cochran won the bet.

Took to the Skies Immediately

Emboldened by her success, Cochran set out on a solo flight to Canada, learning compass navigation from a helpful fellow aviator along the way. A commercial pilot's license followed, as did Cochran's entry in her first race in 1934, the MacRobertson London-to-Australia race. With a great deal of effort by Cochran and others working on her behalf, she secured a plane with which to enter the race, one manufactured by the Granville Brothers called a Gee Bee. "There were few pilots who flew Gee Bees and then lived to talk about it. Jimmy Doolittle was one. I was another." Cochran flew the race with copilot Wesley Smith. Malfunctioning flaps put the pair down in Bucharest, Rumania, and out of the race.

One year later, in 1935, Cochran entered her first Bendix Trophy Cross-Country Air Race, a race that is "to aviators what the Kentucky Derby still is to horse breeders," Cochran wrote. The year before she had managed to get the race open to women but didn't make it to the starting line herself. Cochran finished third in the 1937 Bendix and won the famous race in 1938; the same year First Lady Eleanor Roosevelt awarded her the first of 15 Harmon Trophies she would win. That first trophy was her recognition for setting three speed records. After winning the 1938 Bendix race from Burbank, California, to Cleveland, Ohio in 8 hours, 10 minutes and 31 seconds in a Seversky Pursuit, Cochran set a new women's west-to-east transcontinental record of 10 hours, 7 minutes, 10 seconds.

Always A Lady

Women could compete with and often surpass men, but being ladylike also was a Cochran priority. Before stepping from the cockpit, she usually paused to apply lipstick. No longer a teen-ager mixing hair dye in someone else's beauty parlor, Cochran set about building her own cosmetics empire. "I told Floyd that I wanted my own beauty business so I could end up at the top. I had started at the bottom and supervising shampoos and permanents was not for me anymore." In 1935, the same year she entered her first Bendix race, Jacqueline Cochran Cosmetics began manufacturing operations. A popular product was Cochran's "Perk-Up" cylinder, a container holding enough makeup for any woman traveling light. "I would take one on all my trips, all my races."

There were many more races, victories and records. In 1939, Cochran established a women's national altitude record and broke the international open-class speed record for men and women. The following year she broke the 2,000 km international speed record and the 100 km national record. During this time one of Cochran's dearest friends was fellow aviator Amelia Earhart, who Cochran met in 1935.

Lost Famous Friend to Skies

Cochran assured readers of her autobiography she and Earhart were not competitors. Earhart flew for distance; Cochran was after speed, but she later did pursue distance and altitude. Earhart shared in Cochran's interest in parapsychology, first sparked by Odlum. Cochran and Earhart used what they considered extra-sensory powers to locate the crash sites of downed aircraft. Earhart's husband, George Putnam, was skeptical and someone Cochran considered less than a friend. "I didn't like that man at all." But Putnam called on Cochran for help when Earhart failed to arrive at a planned stop on her 1937 quest to encircle the globe. Cochran wrote she "saw" Earhart after her plane went down over the South Pacific. "'Circling—cannot see island—gas running low' were the last words anyone heard from Amelia, including me. That still hurts," Cochran wrote.

In spite of the achievements of Cochran and others, women aviators had to fight for the right to serve their country during World War II. Cochran was in the forefront of the battle. In June 1941, Cochran became the first woman to pilot a bomber across the Atlantic Ocean. However, because she had some difficulty operating the plane's hand brake during practice flights, she was forced to turn the controls over to a male pilot on take-off and landing. The flight was a milestone male pilots fought all the way. Cochran was accused of wanting to make the flight for publicity reasons. Male pilots also charged that allowing women to fly bombers would take work away from themselves. Someone tried to prevent Cochran's flight by holding up a required visa. "In a contest of power and friends, I knew I could win, so I contacted the American consul in Montreal, who called the Passport Department in D.C. and, *voilà* the visa arrived sooner than someone else ever predicted."

Organized Women for War

Seeing British women ferrying planes for their country's war effort gave Cochran the idea to start a similar program in the United States. She told President Franklin D. Roosevelt her plan over lunch. Cochran was against integrating women aviators into the U.S. war effort on a piecemeal basis. "I felt that a few good women pilots amidst all the men would simply go down as a flash in the historical pan. I wanted to make a point with my planned program." Perhaps she did have extra-sensory powers; it would be many years after the war before women aviators would receive recognition for their contributions.

In preparation for a larger effort in the United States, Cochran organized a group of 25 female American aviators to ferry planes for Great Britain's Air Transport Auxiliary. "More than a month before Pearl Harbor brought World War II to America, I was off on my own wartime project—a project that would take me away from Floyd and home for nearly three years." The British program was a success, and the United States decided a similar program also would work. In 1942, Cochran was assigned the task of training 500 women pilots. The number would eventually grow to more than 1,000. A bill had been introduced in Congress to militarize Cochran's pilots and incorporate them into the Army Air Corps, giving them military benefits. This is what Cochran wanted as she saw plans for a separate Air Force. She fought attempts to make her pilots part of the Women's Army Corps. In 1943, the Women's Airforce Service Pilots (WASPs) was formed, and Cochran was named director of women pilots.

"The Women's Airforce Service Pilots program really proved something," WASP member Margaret Boylan is quoted saying in Cochran's autobiography. "It was a marvelous period of history, made possible by Jackie Cochran. When you consider how competitive this woman was with other women equal to her, it's amazing that she worked so hard for our benefit." Among the obstacles the women pilots and Cochran overcame was the belief women's flying ability was affected by their menstrual cycles. More than 25,000 women applied for WASP training; 1,800 were accepted and 1,074 graduated. The women aviators flew about 60 million miles for the Army Air Forces with only 38 fatalities, about one to every 16,000 hours of flying.

Cochran lost the battle to have the WASPs militarized in 1944, denying the women pilots military benefits including the GI bill. The WASP program was deactivated at the end of 1944. In 1977, Congress passed a bill giving the WASPs honorable discharges and declaring them veterans. It took two more years to make it official.

Broke Her Own Records

Cochran's aviation career continued well after the war, as did other activities. She was the first woman to enter Japan after the World War II, and she traveled to the Far East as a correspondent for *Liberty* magazine. In 1956 she ran, unsuccessfully, for a California congressional seat, campaigning by flying her plane around her own district.

In 1953, Cochran was the first woman to break the sound barrier and received a Gold Medal from the Fèdèration Aèronautique Internationale. She was president of the organization, holding two terms, from 1958 to 1961. In 1962 she established 69 inter-city and straight-line distance records for aircraft manufacturer Lockheed and was

the first woman to fly a jet across the Atlantic. The same year Cochran set nine international speed, distance and altitude records in a Northrop T-38 military jet. In 1963, Cochran set the 15-25 km course record in a Lockheed F-104 Starfighter, going 1,273.109 mph, and broke the 100 km course record with a speed of 1,203.686 mph. The following year she began resetting her own records in the Lockheed F-104G Starfighter. In the 15-25 km course she set a record of 1,429.297 mph; for the 100 km course her record was 1,302 mph; and for the 500 km course she set a record of 1,135 mph.

Not only was Cochran competitive with herself; she was competitive with others. When she was a child, Cochran was forced to give a cherished doll, her only doll, to a younger sister in her foster family. When they were adults, the younger sister sought Cochran's aid in New York City. Cochran gave it but demanded her childhood doll as payment. At Cochran's insistence, she was buried with that doll following her death in 1980 at her Indio, California home.

Further Reading

Cochran, Jacqueline, *The Stars at Noon,* Ayer, 1979.
Cochran, Jacqueline, and Maryann Bucknum Brinley, *Jackie Cochran: An Autobiography,* Bantam Books, 1987.
Fisher, Marquita O., *Jacqueline Cochran: First Lady of Flight,* Garrard, 1973.
McGuire, Nina, Sammons, Sandra Wallus and Sandra Sammons, *Jacqueline Cochran: America's Fearless Aviator,* Tailored Tours, 1997.
Smith, Elizabeth Simpson, *Coming Out Right: The Story of Jacqueline Cochran, the First Woman Aviator to Break the Sound Barrier,* Walker & Co., 1991.
Wayne, Bennett, *Four Women of Courage,* Garrard, 1975.
Los Angeles Times (Orange County Edition) October 2, 1996.
Stamps, February 24, 1996; March 30, 1996.
USA Today, October 14, 1994.
U.S. News & World Report, November 17, 1997.
"Jacqueline Cochran," *Allstar Network,* http://www.allstar.fiu.edu/aero/cochran1.htm (March 6, 1998).
"Jacqueline Cochran," *First Flight,* http://www.firstlflight.org/shrine/jacqueline_cochran.html (March 6, 1998).
"Jacqueline Cochran," *Motor Sports Hall of Fame,* http://www.mshf.com/hof/cochran.htm (March 6, 1998). □

William S. Cohen

William S. Cohen (born 1940) has been active in United States government since the mid-1970s, serving in both houses of Congress in subsequent terms. He was named Secretary of Defense in 1997.

Former Senator William S. Cohen of Maine, nominated for the position of 20th Secretary of Defense in January of 1997, has after 24 years in national governmental service a reputation as a "maverick," a person who places ideals and morality above party loyalties. "Cohen won the label in 1974, when, as a 33-year-old freshman Congressman, he was the first Republican on the House Judiciary Committee to oppose Richard Nixon on the question of providing 'edited' transcripts of Oval Office plotting in the Watergate cover-up," explained *Nation* contributor Doug Ireland, "and was one of seven Republicans who voted for Nixon's impeachment." President Clinton nominated Cohen for the position because of his reputation as a moderate-to-liberal Republican and because of his extensive record of service on the Senate Armed Services Committee.

Cohen was born in Bangor, Maine, to an ethnically and religiously mixed set of parents. His father was a Russian-Jewish immigrant, while his mother was of Irish Protestant extraction. At his father's wish he was raised Jewish, attending Hebrew school and preparing for the Bar Mitzvah examination. When he was told that he would have to undergo a conversion ceremony, however, he decided not to follow through with the Bar Mitzvah. Instead, he followed his mother's example in refusing to convert to Judaism and became a Christian.

By the time Cohen entered Bowdoin College in 1958 he had developed a reputation as an athlete, excelling in basketball. He had been co-captain of Bangor High School's basketball team and had earned Maine All State honors during his senior year. He originally majored in Latin, with the idea of becoming a teacher following graduation. After receiving his bachelor's degree, however, Cohen entered Boston University's Law School in 1962 to study for his law degree. He passed the Maine state bar exams in 1965 and the same year entered the Bangor law firm of Paine, Cohen, Lynch, Weatherbee, & Kobritz, Inc., eventually becoming a partner. In 1972 he took advantage

of Maine's Representative William Dodd Hathaway's decision to run for a Senate seat to launch his own campaign for national office. He was elected by the Second Congressional District to the House of Representatives that year.

Elected to House of Representatives

As a freshman representative, Cohen was assigned to a position on the House Judiciary Committee a position regarded by many of his colleagues as a political dead-end, because he could not use it to benefit his constituents directly. However, "Fate played its ultimate trick on me," Cohen related in his memoir *Roll Call: One Year in the United States Senate,* "and turned my assignment to the Judiciary Committee into a rendezvous with history." Only a few months later, Congress instructed the Judiciary Committee to investigate whether or not there were grounds to impeach President Richard M. Nixon. When a vote to inform the president that he had failed to answer the committee's subpoena for tapes and documents came before the committee in May of 1974, Cohen sided with the Democrats in favor of the motion instead of with his fellow Republicans. He later sided with the Democrats again to vote in favor of impeachment.

Sought Higher Office

Although Cohen's cross-party voting record on these important issues angered some of the Republican constituents who had elected him, the Representative was able to use his new reputation to seek higher office. "In 1978," Ireland reported, "he won the first of three Senate terms by knocking off moderate Democratic incumbent William Hathaway with a demogogically nationalist campaign in which Cohen 'mov[ed] briskly to his right,' as the Associated Press noted that year, attacking Hathaway and the Carter Administration on the Panama Canal treaties, strategic arms negotiations with the Soviet Union and neutron weapons." During his succeeding terms Cohen cemented his reputation as a conservative on defense issues, helping to create and sponsor the G.I. Bill of 1984 and the Goldwater-Nichols Defense Reorganization Act of 1986. He also worked for the Council on Foreign Relations, including a stint as the chair of the Middle East Study Group in 1996. Cohen became a published author during his terms as Senator, completing a volume of memoirs, several collections of poetry, some nonfiction works, and a couple of novels, including one *The Double Man* co-written with then-fellow Senator Gary Hart.

In 1996 Cohen announced his retirement from the U.S. Senate. In part, Ireland suggested, this was because of "his recent marriage to longtime girlfriend Janet Langhart, a former Marshall Field runway model and TV weather announcer who went on to a lucrative career as a talk-show host and now works for Black Entertainment Television." On December 5, 1996, however, President Clinton announced Cohen's nomination as Secretary of Defense. On January 22, 1997, Cohen was confirmed by the Senate, and he was sworn into office on January 24th.

Assumed Post of Secretary of Defense

As Secretary of Defense, Cohen has faced many problems concerning the nature of military life and making military training fair for both male and female recruits. During his first year in office, he had to confront the issue of sexual harassment in the military. Following the conviction of an Army drill sergeant of using his position of authority to demand sexual favors from female recruits, Cohen appointed a panel to investigate the military's policy of mingling male and female recruits during training. In December of 1997, the panel recommended segregating the genders for at least the first twelve weeks of training. Cohen also faced criticism for his support of General Joseph Ralston as successor to Joint Chiefs of Staff chair John Shalikashvilli. Ralston confessed to having an adulterous affair with a civilian woman while he was separated from his wife.

At the same time, Cohen has led the military toward more aggressive prosecution of sex offenders in the armed services. "Three Army sergeants were given prison terms for raping female recruits," wrote Johnathan S. Landay in the *Christian Science Monitor,* "and their commander, Major General John Longhouser, resigned . . . after admitting to having an adulterous affair years ago." Landay added that both an Army general and a Navy admiral "were stripped of their commands during investigations for alleged adultery and sexual harassment respectively." At the same time, the Army's chief noncommissioned officer and the Air Force's first female B-52 pilot both left the armed services to avoid prosecution for sex-related offenses.

As Secretary of Defense, Cohen faces the challenge of preparing the United States' armed services for work in "a world where the only constant is change," noted Linda D. Kozaryn quoting Cohen in a report for the *American Forces Press Service,* "where threats to American interests can erupt anywhere at any time . . . where rogue states and freelance terrorists can spread fear and death with a truck full of fertilizer, a vial of volatile liquid or a homemade nuclear device. It is a world that demands American leadership and a strong, capable and ready American military force." Future plans, Kozaryn reported, "include continuing to reduce Russia's remaining 20,000 nuclear weapons, continuing the Partnership for Peace program, enlarging [the North Atlantic Treaty Organization (NATO)] and stabilizing Bosnia."

Further Reading

Cohen, William S., *Roll Call: One Year in the United States Senate,* Simon & Schuster, 1981.
Cohen, William S., and Gary Hart, *The Double Man,* Morrow, 1985.
Cohen, William S., *One-Eyed Kings: A Novel,* Nan A. Talese/Doubleday, 1991.
Cohen, William S., *Easy Prey: The Fleecing of America's Senior Citizens And How to Stop It,* Boomer Books/Marlowe, 1997.
Christian Science Monitor, June 6, 1997, p. 3.
Nation, January 6, 1997, pp. 17-20.
New York Times, April 12, 1978.
New York Times Book Review, March 1, 1981; May 5, 1985.
Time, November 20, 1978; May 6, 1985.
Washington Post, December 22, 1987.
"Biography of William S. Cohen," http://www.defenselink.mil/bios/secdef_bio.html (December 16, 1997).
"Biography: William S. Cohen," *American Forces Press Service,* http://www.dtic.dla.mil/afps/news/9701238.html (November, 1997).
"Senator William S. Cohen (R-Me)," http://www.bates.edu/~jwallace/reps/billcohen.html (November, 1997).

Nadia Comaneci

Nadia Comaneci (born 1961) is one of the most-celebrated gymnasts in the history of the sport. At the 1976 Olympic Games in Montreal, Quebec, Canada, she was the first person in Olympic history to score a perfect 10 in gymnastics. In all, she earned seven perfect scores at the 1976 games.

The future Olympic star was born on November 12, 1961, in Onesti, Romania, to Gheorghe, an auto mechanic, and Stephania Comaneci. By the age of six, she was already hooked on gymnastics. Then she was discovered by famed Romanian gymnastics coach, Bela Karolyi. He and his wife were looking for youngsters for the National Junior Team and he decided she had potential. She began to train two to three hours a day with Karolyi and he was impressed with her work ethnic.

Even great talent and a strong work ethnic did not guarantee results. Comaneci remembered that in early gymnastic competitions, she fell a lot, and that motivated her to keep practicing. In 1969, at the age of seven, she entered her first official competition, the Romanian National Junior Championship. She finished in thirteenth place. The following year, she won the competition. When she turned 12, she went to live and train at a state-run gymnastics training school. She trained with Karolyi eight hours a day, six days a week.

Comaneci continued to get better and she started to win her competitions regularly. At the time, her role model was the dominant woman in gymnastics, Soviet star Olga Korbut. She continued to win competitions and in January of 1975, became eligible for senior level international competitions. She entered the European championships in May of that year and won four gold medals and one silver medal.

The summer Olympic games were approaching, and Comaneci wanted to be ready. As a warm-up, she competed in the American Cup competition in New York City in March of 1976. In the competition, one male and one female gymnast represent each country in the meet. She won the competition. Standing next to her on the winners' stand after they both won silver cups was an 18-year-old American, Bart Conner, who was also heading for the Olympics. A photographer, thinking the blond, handsome American and the tiny dark-haired wisp of a girl would make a nice picture, asked Conner to kiss her. He obliged with a peck on the cheek. Although Conner, now her husband, says he remembers the moment, Comaneci says never thought much about it.

Comaneci arrived at the 1976 Olympic Games, in Montreal, with her reputation firmly established. On the first night of the competition, July 18, she became the first person in Olympic history to earn a perfect score (a 10.00 on the uneven bars) in gymnastics. The following night she continued her streak, earning perfect scores for her performances on the uneven bars and balance beam. A few nights later, she again received perfect scores for her balance beam and uneven bar performances. In all, Comaneci earned seven perfect scores and won gold medals for the all-around competition, the balance beam, and the uneven bars. The Romanians also won the silver medal in the team competition. Comaneci became the darling of the gymnastics world and was on the cover of several magazines. After the Olympic competition, the Comaneci family got a one month vacation and a new car from the Romanian government.

The times after the 1976 Olympic Games were tough for Comaneci. Her parents divorced and Romanian sports officials separated her from Karolyi and made her train with another coach. Upset by the turn of events, Comaneci swallowed bleach to get attention. The government then allowed her to train with Karolyi once again. In 1979, Comaneci allegedly became involved in with the son of Romanian dictator Nicolae Ceausescu. Reflecting the turmoil in Comaneci's personal life, her performance at the 1980 Olympics in Moscow, Russia, didn't measure up to her personal standards. Although she did win two gold medals and one silver medal, she fell off the uneven bars, considered her best event.

Back home in Romania, life was becoming difficult for Comaneci. First, her beloved coach, Karolyi, defected to the United States in 1981. His revolt was a protest against the oppressive government of Ceausescu. Comaneci was the first to discover his absence, and although she thought about following him, she felt that she could not leave her family. At the age of 19, she participated in her last major competition. Shortly before attending the 1984 Olympic Games (as an honored guest who traveled with the Romanian delegation) that were held in Los Angeles, California, she officially retired from gymnastics.

Because Romania's government regarded her as a valuable Communist model of domination in sports and because it feared that she might defect to the United States, they no longer allowed her to travel to Western countries. For the next several years, she was literally out of sight to the Western press. In the meantime, officials kept a watchful eye on her whereabouts, read her mail, and even tapped the phone in the eight-room house that had been provided for her and her family. Although her fame gave her an easier life than most of her countrymen, Comaneci more and more thought about defecting.

Finally, in late 1989, the 27-year-old found a way. She met Romanian-born Constantin Panait, a roofer who lived in Florida, and learned that he helped people escape to America. Her mind made up, she told only her brother of her plans. She later said she was afraid her parents would

have a heart attack if she told them. With five other Romanians, she made a dangerous six-hour walk through the cold of winter to the Hungarian border, where they were stopped by Hungarian police who immediately recognized Comaneci. At first they asked her to stay in their country, but they did let her go on. The group headed for the Austrian border and the American Embassy. Soon they were on a plane to New York City.

The former Olympic star arrived in the United States overweight and heavily made up. Americans were shocked at her appearance and rumors started to hit the press. They charged that Panait, who was now posing as her manager, was a married man with children and that Comaneci was having an affair with him. She denied any such relationship and claimed that Panait was in fact controlling her life and her money and she felt helpless to escape from this new kind of bondage.

Lucky for Comaneci, the world of gymnastic competitors is a tight community. Some of her old friends, including Conner and former Romanian rugby coach Alexandru Stefu, living in Montreal, began to think that she was in trouble. Stefu lured the elusive Panait, along with Comaneci, to a meeting, where she admitted that he was mistreating her. The next day, Panait disappeared with her money. It was a hard lesson, but she was free at last.

Comaneci went to Montreal to live with Stefu and his family. There she returned to gymnastic form and kept up her budding friendship with Conner, who was living in Norman, Oklahoma. When Stefu died in a snorkeling accident, Comaneci moved to Norman. She lived with Paul Ziert, Conner's coach and a friend of her former coach, Bela Karolyi, and his family. Comaneci and Conner began dating, and together they performed in a number of gymnastic competitions. They also worked at the Bart Conner Gymnastics Academy opened by Conner and Ziert. The academy had 37 coaches and 1,000 students.

Besides teaching and performing, Comaneci signed several product endorsement contracts. In 1994, Conner proposed to her while the couple was in Amsterdam. In April of 1996, they were married in an elaborate wedding in Bucharest, Romania, which *Sports Illustrated* described as "the gymnastics world's version of a royal wedding." She had introduced him to her family in Romania the year before, the first time she had seen her father in five years. (Her mother had previously visited her in the United States.) The government treated them like royalty (Ceausescu had been killed in an overthrow of the Communist government shortly after Comaneci defected), and they were given the use of the Parliament House for the reception.

Comaneci has made a new life for herself in the United States. She and her husband travel extensively throughout the country for exhibitions and commercial appearances, besides their work at the academy in Norman. She hasn't forgotten the dark times, but she doesn't like to talk about them. She is pleased, however, when people stop and talk about her Olympic performances. People still remember how Comaneci captivated fans, judges, and viewers at the 1976 Olympics, and how she changed the world of gymnastics forever.

Further Reading

International Gymnast, February 1991; February 1995; June/July 1996.
Life, March 1990.
New York Times, April 5, 1996.
Oklahoma Family, January 1998.
People, December 18, 1989; November 26, 1990; March 27, 1995; July 15, 1996.
Sports Illustrated, December 11, 1989; May 6, 1996.
Texas Chronicle, August 5, 1987.
USA Today, October 18, 1994.
"Nadia Comaneci," http://www.nadiacomaneci.com (May 15, 1998).

Sean Connery

From humble beginnings as a school dropout, Sean Connery (born 1930) became a major movie star at the age of 32 when he was cast as the sophisticated secret agent James Bond. Connery went on to distinguish himself in a number of major motion pictures, including his Oscar-winning performance in *The Untouchables.*

An unlikely candidate to play Ian Fleming's snobbish 007, Connery became so well known as this character that he nearly didn't break out of the mold. Despite his many years of work on the stage and screen, Connery was still being thought of as "the guy who played James Bond" into the early 1980s. But throughout his career, the stubborn Scot has taken on movie roles that interested him, regardless of how they fit his image. As a result of this shrewd thinking, he now has quite an impressive list of roles in his repertoire and critics talk more about his exceptional acting ability than his inability to break out of a role. With more than 60 movies to his credit, Connery has become one of the world's most prominent movie stars.

A Depression-Era Childhood

Thomas Sean Connery began his life in the humblest of surroundings. He was the eldest of two sons, born in an Edinburgh, Scotland, tenement to Joseph and Euphamia Connery. During World War II, when he was 13, he dropped out of school to help support his family. "The war was on, so my whole education was a wipeout," Connery reminisced in *Rolling Stone.* "I had no qualifications at all for a job, and unemployment has always been very high in Scotland, anyway, so you take what you get. I was a milkman, laborer, steel bender, cement mixer—virtually anything." After several years of this, Connery decided to better his lot, and he joined the British Royal Navy. He received a medical discharge three years later, when he came down with a case of stomach ulcers.

Returning to Edinburgh, Connery began to lift weights and develop his physique. He became a lifeguard and even modeled for an art college. Then in 1953, the toned Connery traveled to London to compete in the Mr. Universe competition. This trip was to mean more to him than the third place prize he won. While he was there, he heard about auditions for the musical *South Pacific.* He decided he wanted to try out, took a crash course in dancing and singing, and was cast for a role in the chorus.

Chose Acting over Soccer

This small part became a crucial turning point for Connery. At the time, he was teetering between wanting to be an actor and a professional soccer player. But actor Robert Henderson, who was also in *South Pacific,* encouraged him to consider a career in acting. Connery took Henderson's advice: as a soccer player, one is limited by age; a good actor could play challenging roles forever.

The unschooled Connery looked up to Henderson as a mentor. He commented in *Premiere* that "[Henderson] gave me a list of all these books I should read. I spent a year in every library in Britain and Ireland, Scotland and Wales. . . . I spent my days at the library and the evenings at the theater." He also went to matinees and talked to a lot of other actors, people he met over the year-long touring run of *South Pacific.* "That's what opened me to a whole different look at things," said Connery. "It didn't give me any more intellectual qualifications, but it gave me a terrific sense of the importance of a lot of things I certainly would never have gotten in touch with." It is also where he picked up his stage name, Sean Connery. When asked how he wanted to be billed for the musical, he gave his full name, Thomas Sean Connery. After being told that was too long, he opted for Sean Connery, not knowing how long he was going to be an actor. The name stuck.

After *South Pacific,* Connery began broadening his horizons by working on the stage. He was also notable in his first television role, a British production of Rod Serling's *Requiem for a Heavyweight.* After garnering critical acclaim for this role, he received several film offers. In the years from 1955 to 1962, he made a string of B movies, including *Action of the Tiger* (1957).

It was there he met Terence Young, who was to be the director of the Bond films. Young recalls in *Rolling Stone* that *Action of the Tiger* ''was not a good picture. But Sean was impressive in it, and when it was all over, he came to me and said, in a very strong Scottish accent, 'Sir, am I going to be a success?' I said, 'Not after this picture, you're not. But,' I asked him, 'Can you swim?' He looked rather blank and said, yes, he could swim—what's that got to do with it? I said, 'Well, you'd better keep swimming until I can get you a proper job, and I'll make up for what I did this time.' And four years later, we came up with *Dr. No.*''

Bond, James Bond

Connery was still doing B movies when he was called in to interview for *Dr. No,* the first James Bond film. But he had matured quite a bit as an actor and exuded a kind of crude animal force, which Young compared to a young Kirk Douglas or Burt Lancaster. Producer Harry Saltzman felt that he had the masculinity the part required. In the course of a conversation he punctuate his words with physical movement. Everyone there agreed he was perfect for the role. Connery was signed without a screen test.

Dr. No was an instant success, propelling the little-known Connery into fame and sex-symbol status virtually overnight, a situation that the serious-minded and very private Connery did not like. Equally distressing to him was the way the media handled his transition into the role. He commented in *Rolling Stone:* ''I'd been an actor since I was twenty-five but the image the press put out was that I just fell into this tuxedo and started mixing vodka martinis. And, of course, it was nothin' like that at all. I'd done television, theater, a whole slew of things. But it was more dramatic to present me as someone who had just stepped in off the street.''

Connery also performed many of his own stunts in *Dr. No.* He has continued this practice in many of his movies because it often speeds up the production. One of the stunts in *Dr. No* almost killed him. They had rehearsed a scene where he drives his convertible under a crane. At a slow speed, his head cleared by a few inches. When they actually shot the scene, the car was going 50 m.p.h., bouncing up and down. Luckily for Connery, the car hit the last bounce before he went under the crane and he emerged unhurt.

In 1962 Connery married his first wife, Diane Cilento. She was also an actress, having played the part of Molly in *Tom Jones.* Apparently their relationship was loving, yet tempestuous. Connery's friend Michael Caine reported in *Rolling Stone:* ''I remember once I was with them in Nassau. Diane was cooking lunch, and Sean and I went out. Of course, we got out and one thing led to another, you know,

and we got back for lunch two hours later. Well, we opened the door and Sean said, 'Darling, we're home'—and all the food she'd cooked came flying through the air at us. I remember the two of us standin' there, covered in gravy and green beans.'' The couple divorced in 1974 and their only son, Jason, is now a movie actor.

Between 1962 and 1967, Connery made five James Bond movies—*Dr. No, From Russia with Love, Goldfinger* (which was, at that time, the fastest money-maker in movie history, netting more than $10 million in its first few months), *Thunderball,* and *You Only Live Twice.* He was tiring of the grueling pace of producing a new feature every year, and of the constant publicity and invasion of privacy. During the filming of *Thunderball* Connery was working long days and doing press interviews at night.

He was also arguing with the Bond movies' producer, Albert (Cubby) Broccoli, because he wanted to slow the pace of the series—completing a feature every 18 months instead of each year. He threatened to cut out of the contract after completing *You Only Live Twice,* and agreed to accept a salary that was lower than normal.

But the nation was Bond-crazy and the films were a gold mine. Connery agreed to star in *Diamonds Are Forever* in 1971, demanding a salary of $1.25 million, plus a percentage. At that time, it was an unprecedented sum of money for such a role. After completing the film, Connery said ''never again'' to Bond roles and donated all of his salary to the Scottish International Education Trust, an organization he'd founded to assist young Scots in obtaining an education. (This is not the only example of Connery's generosity to charities. In 1987, he donated 50,000 British pounds to the National Youth Theatre in England after reading an article on the failing institution.)

Life After Bond

After his split with Broccoli, he continued to pursue a variety of movie roles with his main concern being that he find them interesting. He would also do films if he felt his help was needed. He reportedly offered to be in *Time Bandits* for a very modest salary because he heard the producer was running into financial difficulties. With a few exceptions, however, most of the films Connery did in the decade following *Diamonds Are Forever* were not noteworthy.

Then, in the early 1980s, a strange thing happened. At the age of fifty-three, Connery was asked to reprise the role he had made famous, in *Never Say Never Again.* The movie rights to this film had been won in a long court battle by Kevin McClory, an enterprising Irishman whom Connery admired a great deal for being able to beat the system. The movie was also scheduled to go head-to-head with *Octopussy,* a Broccoli Bond epic featuring the new 007, Roger Moore. It seems that twist was too much to resist, and Connery signed up. Another possibility is that Connery's second wife, Micheline Roquebrune, whom he had met on the golf course in Morocco in 1970 and married in 1975, convinced him to give the role another try.

Connery drew rave reviews as an aging Bond trying to get back in shape for a daring mission. ''At fifty-three, he may just be reaching the peak of his career,'' reported Kurt

Loder in *Rolling Stone.* "Connery reminds you anew what star quality is all about. A good deal of that quality is on display in *Never Say Never Again,* a carefully crafted and quite lively addition to the lately listless Bond series." Instead of furthering any Bond typecasting by doing this film, Connery seemed to squash it.

Roles Increased with Age

In the years since, his performances seem to be getting better and better. In *The Untouchables,* Connery took the supporting role of Malone, a world-weary, but savvy, street cop. "It's a part that gives him ample opportunity to demonstrate his paradoxical acting abilities," wrote Benedict Nightingale in the *New York Times,* "his knack for being simultaneously rugged and gentle, cynical and innocent, hard and soft, tough and almost tender." For his portrayal of Malone, Connery won an Academy Award.

Connery was also very strong in *Indiana Jones and the Last Crusade,* where he played the scholarly father of the ever-adventurous Jones, entangling himself in a lot of adventure and intrigue. Peter Travers commented in *Rolling Stone* that "Connery, now fifty-eight, has been movie-star virility incarnate. Here in his scholar's tweeds, with an undisguised horror of creepy-crawly things . . . and armed only with an umbrella and a fountain pen, Connery plays gloriously against type."

Similarly, in his other recent roles—a monk in *The Name of the Rose* (1986), a deranged Russian submarine commander in *The Hunt for Red October* (1990), the knowledgeable police detective in *Rising Sun* (1993), an aging attorney in *Just Cause* (1995), King Arthur in *First Knight* (1995)—Connery continues to prove his versatility and maturity as an actor. Even as he passed age 65, Connery showed he can hold his own against Hollywood's hottest upstarts with his role as the ex-con who had once escaped from Alcatraz in the 1996 action thriller *The Rock,* costarring Nicolas Cage and Ed Harris.

Connery has worked hard throughout his career and taken professional risks with his roles. For these efforts, he has become a greatly respected actor, almost a legend in the screen world. Patrick commented that "You suddenly realize [Connery is] the closest thing we now have to Clark Gable, an old-time movie star. Everyone knows him and likes him. It's shocking—every age group, men and women. There's something very likable about him on screen." In 1998 Connery received the Fellowship Award, the British Academy of Film and Television Arts highest honor. Yet, in spite of this, he remains a very conscientious worker, always trying to improve the movie he's in rather than sabotage others' performances to make himself look better. When asked whether he can now write his own ticket when he decides to star in a movie, he replied in "*Premiere*": "I have enough power in terms of casting approval and director approval. But I don't think it's something someone can brandish like a sword. I sense myself as much more a responsible filmmaker in terms of what's good for the overall picture, and for the actors as well, because I have had all this experience, and I've seen a lot of waste."

Further Reading

The Film Encyclopedia, Harper, 1990.
American Film, May 1989.
Entertainment Weekly, February 17, 1995.
Interview, July 1989.
Newsweek, June 8, 1987; May 29, 1989.
New York Times, November 12, 1965; June 7, 1987.
Parade, May 20, 1992.
People, October 17, 1983.
Premiere, April, 1990; February 1992; August 1993.
Rolling Stone, October 27, 1983; June 15, 1989.
Time, November 1, 1982; August 2, 1993.
Vanity Fair, June 1993.

Francis Ford Coppola

Schooled in low-budget filmmaking, Francis Ford Coppola (born 1939) has gone on to direct some of the most financially successful and critically acclaimed movies in U.S. cinematic history.

Francis Ford Coppola, director of *The Godfather* and its two sequels, would be considered one of the masters of modern cinema based on those credits alone. But the writer/director/producer has been behind the scenes on numerous commercial and critical successes outside the gangster genre. Coppola's uncommon craftsmanship has enabled him to make a dizzying variety of films, from low-budget labors of love to mainstream Hollywood crowd-pleasers. All his projects have the earmarks of a Coppola production: a respect for storytelling and a passionate commitment to the filmmaker's art. It was these qualities that led David Thomson, in his *Biographical Dictionary of Film,* to say of Coppola: "No one retains so many jubilant traits of the kid moviemaker."

Raised in Show-Business Family

Coppola was born in Detroit, Michigan on April 7, 1939. His father, Carmine, was a concert flautist who played with Arturo Toscanini's NBC Symphony Orchestra. His mother, Italia, was an actress who at one time had appeared in films. Coppola's younger sister Talia would later follow in her mother's footsteps into the world of film acting, changing her name to Talia Shire and starring in the film *Rocky* alongside Silvester Stallone. A few years after his birth, Coppola and his family moved to the suburbs around New York City, where he would spend most of his childhood.

All the Coppola children were driven to succeed in show business and the arts. Leading by example was Coppola's father, who had achieved success as a musician for hire but longed to compose scores of his own. Francis seemed the least likely to redeem his father's promise, however. He was an awkward, myopic child who did poorly at school. At age nine, he was stricken with polio. The illness forced him into bed for a year, a period during which he played with puppets, watched television, and became lost

Establishes His Reputation

Coppola submitted his next film, *You're a Big Boy Now* (1966), as his master's thesis at UCLA. The sweet coming-of-age drama anticipated the style and themes of *The Graduate* and received many positive reviews. Warner Brothers selected the promising young filmmaker to direct their big-budget musical *Finian's Rainbow*. But the subject matter took Coppola away from his strengths and the film was savaged by critics. *The Rain People* (1969) represented Coppola's attempt to return to "personal" (not to mention low-budget) moviemaking. A somber travelogue about a housewife on the run, the movie was made up as the crew went along, evidence of Coppola's flair for the experimental.

Coppola might have remained in an avant-garde rut were it not for his next project. As co-writer of the mega-hit biopic *Patton,* Coppola earned an Academy Award and added considerable luster to a tarnished reputation. Paramount Pictures next asked him to take the reins on its screen adaptation of Mario Puzo's bestselling novel *The Godfather.* It would prove to be Coppola's greatest triumph.

Glory Gained from *Godfather*

Filming *The Godfather* posed many challenges. Coppola fought hard to retain control of casting decisions. He also resisted studio attempts to cut his budget and make the setting more contemporary. Italian-American groups protested the depiction of organized crime in the original screenplay. Even Coppola's own crew at times lost faith in his ability to control the mammoth project. Nevertheless, he steered the movie to completion.

The Godfather tells the sweeping story of the Corleone crime family, focusing on the ascension of young Michael Corleone to control of the family's empire. It is a violent epic on the scale of classic American films like *Gone with the Wind*. Propelling the drama forward are powerful performances by Marlon Brando and newcomer Al Pacino. At its release in 1972, critics were floored by the film's depiction of America's criminal underworld. The film became a sensational hit with moviegoers as well, and the *The Godfather* swept the Academy Awards that year. Coppola was a winner in the Best Director and Best Screenplay categories; suddenly he was the toast of Hollywood.

Now a wealthy man thanks to the success of *The Godfather,* Coppola could at last pick and choose his own projects. In 1974 he made *The Conversation,* an edgy drama about secret surveillance. He returned to the world of organized crime with 1974's *The Godfather Part II,* which continued the Corleone family saga through the 1950s and, via flashback, to the early 1900s. The intricate storyline resonated once again with critics and moviegoers alike. Coppola accepted a second Academy Award statuette as Best Director of 1974. The haunting score, by Nino Rota and family patriarch Carmine Coppola, also took home an "Oscar."

in an inner fantasy world. After his recovery, he began to make movies with an eight millimeter camera and a tape recorder.

Interest in Film Sparked in High School and College

While a student at Great Neck High School on Long Island, Coppola began to study filmmaking more formally. He soon became enamored with the work of Soviet director Sergei Eisenstein. Coppola also trained in music and theater to round out his education. In 1956 he enrolled at Hofstra College in Hempstead, New York on a drama scholarship. Here he acted in and directed student productions, and founded his own cinema workshop. So determined was Coppola to direct his own pictures that he once sold his car to pay for a 16-millimeter camera.

After graduating from Hofstra, Coppola moved to the West Coast to attend film school at the University of California—Los Angeles (UCLA). But he was impatient to escape the classroom and start making his own films. He signed on to direct an adult movie, which caught the attention of low-budget impresario Roger Corman. Corman hired Coppola to work on his movies as a jack-of-all-trades. Coppola's strong work ethic prompted Corman to allow him to direct his own picture. The result was *Dementia 13* (1963), a gory horror movie Coppola had written in three days and shot for $40,000. That year, Coppola married Eleanor Neil, his set decorator on the picture.

Apocalypse and Aftermath

Coppola's next project was *Apocalypse Now,* an ambitious film about the Vietnam War. But the expensive production was bedeviled by bad weather, budget overruns, and the bizarre behavior of its star, Marlon Brando. The release date was pushed back repeatedly as Coppola struggled to come up with an ending for the film. When it finally reached the screen in 1979, the film was hailed by many critics as a visionary masterpiece. It was nominated for several Academy Awards and did well at the box office. But many in Hollywood never forgave Coppola for letting the project get so out of control. For many years, Coppola could not get funding from a major studio to make his movies.

Unable to make mainstream movies, Coppola instead crafted independent films which he released through his own Zoetrope Studio. These pictures, including *Rumble Fish* (1983) and *The Cotton Club* (1984), received mixed reviews and had many wondering if Coppola was a spent force in the industry. He did manage to create a hit with the offbeat *Peggy Sue Got Married* (1985), about a woman who travels back in time to her own high school days, but the project seemed like a work-for hire. Closer to Coppola's heart was *Tucker: The Man and His Dream,* a 1988 biopic about a maverick automaker who could have been a stand-in for the director himself.

Return to Prominence via *Godfather III*

In 1990 Coppola completed *The Godfather Part III.* While not as lavishly praised as the previous two installments, it nevertheless was a box office success and won back the confidence of the major studios. While receiving mixed critical response, his *Bram Stoker's Dracula* (1992) helped solidify Coppola's comeback. This lush, gory version of the horror classic was undermined by some poor performances but widely praised for its visual style. Audiences flocked to see stars Winona Ryder and Keanu Reeves, made the film a major hit, and returned Coppola to the ranks of "bankable" directors.

As the 1990s rolled on, Coppola continued to turn out Hollywood productions. The comedy *Jack* (1994) utilized the talents of Robin Williams, while *The Rainmaker* (1996) adapted the work of best-selling novelist John Grisham. Finally out of debt and at ease working for the major studios, Coppola in his late 50s seemed content with his cinematic legacy. He expanded his interests into publishing in 1997 with *Zoetrope Short Stories,* a magazine dedicated to literary, not Hollywood, material. "Coppola is hoping to revive the literary tradition of Ernest Hemingway, F. Scott Fitzgerald, . . . and maybe make a good movie in the process," noted Leslie Alan Horvitz in *Insight on the News.* In 1998 Coppola helped launch the first Classically Independent Film Festival in San Francisco, California; films shown included *One Flew Over the Cuckoo's Nest* and *Diner.* Outside the film industry, Coppola is the owner of a California winery that produces wine under the Niebaum-Coppola label.

Further Reading

Contemporary Literary Criticism, Volume 16, Gale, 1981.
Contemporary Theatre, Film, and Television, Volume 13, Gale, 1995.
Cowie, Peter, *Coppola: A Biography,* Scribner, 1990.
Dictionary of Literary Biography, Volume 44: *American Screenwriters, Second Series,* Gale, 1986.
Lewis, Jon, *Whom God Wishes to Destroy: Francis Coppola and the New Hollywood,* Duke University Press, 1995.
Thomson, David, *The Biographical Dictionary of Film,* Knopf, 1994.
American Film, April 1983.
Chicago Tribune, January 18, 1982; February 11, 1982; October 5, 1986; March 3, 1989; December 15, 1990.
Entertainment Weekly, February 7, 1997.
Film Quarterly, spring 1986.
Insight on the News, May 12, 1997.
Los Angeles Times, December 19, 1988; January 26, 1990; December 30, 1990.
New York Times, August 12, 1979; August 15, 1979; March 18, 1980; March 21, 1980; November 23, 1980; February 11, 1982; April 16, 1982; May 3, 1987; March 1, 1989; March 12, 1989; December 23, 1990; December 25, 1990.
Premiere, September 1996.
Time, April 17, 1995.
Times (London), January 21, 1988; November 14, 1988; February 11, 1989.
Vanity Fair, June 1990; December 1995; July 1996; April 1998.
Variety, November 17, 1997; January 26, 1998. □

Artur da Costa e Silva

Artur da Costa e Silva (1902-1969) played a prominent role in the Brazilian military, affording him considerable political influence. He subsequently served as Brazil's 22nd president from March 1967 until a stroke ended his career two years later.

Artur da Costa e Silva spoke few lines on the Brazilian political stage, but his influence on the course of history in the second half of the twentieth century casts him among the major players. He was no stranger to political intrigue at any time during his military career. As a young lieutenant in 1922, he was imprisoned for his part in a failed revolt. Forty-two years later, when the leftist civilian government of João Goulart fell to a military coup, Costa e Silva emerged as the most prominent leader of the new regime. Though disdaining the office of president in 1964, Costa e Silva played an important role behind the scenes and was only too happy to assume a leading role in 1967.

As the regime's second president, Costa e Silva attempted to win over Brazil's middle class by casting the outgoing president, Humberto Castelo Branco, as responsible for the country's economic problems. Costa e Silva initially proposed rolling back the most odious of the regime's economic policies. However, his actions failed to match his rhetoric. Costa e Silva was able to calm the fears of the populace while continuing the policies of his predecessor—policies which he had been instrumental in planning behind the scenes.

A genial man, Costa e Silva laughed along with the swarm of jokes which gave his early months as president a human touch, but he laughed only as long as it suited his purposes. As pressures mounted on his presidency and the military officers in his power base grew restive, Costa e Silva gradually lost his cultivated sense of humor. Journalists and political critics, who had previously enjoyed considerable freedom, found themselves under attack with a zeal unknown in the previous three decades of Brazilian politics.

Though the president attempted to maintain the appearance of civilian rule, the fate of the government after his debilitating stroke in August 1969, left no doubt that the military remained in charge. A trio of generals ran the country for two months until a suitable successor could be installed, despite constitutional provisions that the vice president would assume control in the event that the president became disabled.

Middle Class Origins

Artur da Costa e Silva was born in Tarquarí in the state of Rio Grande do Sul on October 3, 1902, to Aleìxo Rocha da Silva and Almerinda da Costa. Following common practice in Brazil, his parents blended their two names to form a new surname for their nine children. Costa e Silva's parents were descended from Portuguese colonists who had settled in Brazil's southern farmlands. His father ran a general store owned by his wife's father. Second of the children, Costa e Silva's first teacher was his older sister.

By the age of ten, Costa e Silva's military career passed from child's games to reality at the Military School of Porto Alegre. He quickly rose to the top of his class and was graduated in 1917 as commander of the student body. His sub-commander, by an ironic twist of fate that would persist throughout their lives, was the awkward young Humberto Castelo Branco—later destined to become the 21st president of Brazil.

Costa e Silva ended his late teens at the Brazilian Military Academy at Realengo, graduating third in his class at the country's premier military school. At that time he noticed the ten-year-old daughter of one of his teachers and decided she would be his future wife. "She'll grow up," he explained to a friend.

A Military Career

In 1922, Costa e Silva joined a cadre of junior officers opposed to the controlling influence of wealthy landowners in the national government. A rebellion he helped to initiate was quashed immediately, and Costa e Silva found himself imprisoned on a freighter anchored in Guanabara Bay. With time on his hands to pine, he arranged to have a note smuggled to his former teacher, General Severo Barbosa, asking permission to marry his daughter. The suitor was disappointed with the General's reply—"You have some nerve!" His future father-in-law eventually relented and Costa e Silva was permitted to marry Iolanda Barbosa in 1925. Six months after the failed rebellion, Costa e Silva won his freedom. He served as an instructor in military schools during the rest of the decade.

In 1930, Getúlio Vargas launched a successful coup and created what was described as a mild, semi-Fascist dictatorship in which the influence of landowners was greatly reduced. Costa e Silva rose through the ranks rapidly—first as an aide to a Vargas cabinet minister and later as one of a group of pro-democratic officers who succeeded in removing Vargas from power in 1945. Vargas would be reelected in 1950, only to be confronted four years later by another group of officers who were discontent with his corrupt and dictatorial government. This time Vargas shot himself rather than step down, and his party returned to leadership under Juscelino Kubitschek.

Kubitschek oversaw years of growth and prosperity, culminating in uncontrolled inflation and corruption. When his successor, Jânio Quadros, attempted to control spending, the state militia in Sao Paulo rebelled in protest over a pay freeze. Costa e Silva enhanced his prestige when he defied the rebels and halted their action. Quadros moved increasingly toward the political left, however, to the dismay of Brazil's military. He was eventually forced to flee the country under threat of another coup. Quadros's vice president, Joâo Goulart, took control of the country but failed to halt the slide into economic chaos. By 1963, corruption was rampant, the annual increase in the cost of living had risen to 81 percent, foreign investment had dropped in response to government nationalization of industries, and Brazilians took to the streets in huge protest marches.

Path to the Presidency

This was too much for the army to bear. Generals deposed Goulart in 1964, to the delight of investors in the United States, and handed control of the military to Costa e Silva. Brazil's state governors asked him to assume the Presidency, but Costa e Silva deferred to Castelo Branco—preferring to let his protégé take the blame for imposing necessary austerity measures such as cutting government spending, increasing income taxes, and placing a cap on wages. As a result of these actions money again poured into the country, the gross national product soared, and inflation dropped to 41 percent.

Meanwhile, Costa e Silva established himself as a buffer between constitutionalists and right-wing, hard line revolutionaries in the military while positioning himself in the public consciousness as the humanist answer to the hardships of Castelo Branco's economic austerity program. He was elected to succeed Castelo Branco by Congress rather than by a popular vote, much to his predecessor's dismay. Castelo Branco and his cabinet, who had lobbied the military for a civilian successor, feared that Costa e Silva would undo much of what they had labored to accomplish. However, their fears proved groundless.

Spouting "social humanism," Costa e Silva was elected president on his 64th birthday, and quickly amused his followers by publicizing his love of bad television, card games, small bets on horses, flirting at dinner parties, short work days, and long naps. The dark glasses he wore to avoid eye irritation were a boon to political cartoonists, who portrayed him as a bumbling simpleton. He chuckled along with his detractors when they suggested a terrorist might destroy his government by hurling an alarm clock into his bedroom.

Laugh he might, for he had manipulated the military into loyal support with pay raises and hardware during his tenure as Castelo Branco's war minister, bought the loyalty of the masses with promises of social and economic relief, and ensured foreign support by pledging his allegiance to the United States business community.

Political Support Wanes

The laughter grew thin by the end of 1967 and stopped in 1968, as Costa e Silva's populist, bumbling image crumbled and he metamorphosed into one of the most repressive dictators in Brazil's recent political memory.

Brazil's great natural and human resources give it great potential, but its social problems challenge even the most adept politician. As the fifth largest nation with the eighth largest population in 1967, more arable land than in all of Europe, and immense reserves of minerals and timber, economic prosperity seemed inevitable. But Costa e Silva inherited a country with the highest child mortality rate, the third highest illiteracy rate, and the third lowest per capita income in South America. Add that to low life expectancy, rampant disease, hyper-inflation, and growing income inequities, and Costa e Silva found himself at the helm of a country impatient for change.

Though much of the impetus needed for social change resided in the military, sectors of that institution also vigor-ously defended the accumulation of wealth by the upper classes and the well-being of the business community. Costa e Silva had come to the presidency promising to satisfy all sectors of Brazilian society and ended up satisfying none. By late 1968, those who had looked to the new president for salvation had become deeply disillusioned. Students, mollified by some of the president's pro-university decrees, mounted protests. United States diplomats signalled their shift from enthusiasm to displeasure. Brazil's moderate middle class began to clamor for a return to civilian rule.

Slide into Repression

Discontent reached a head in September 1968, when Márcio Moreira Alves, an opposition politician, attacked Costa e Silva's government from the floor of the Chamber of Deputies. The military demanded that Moreira Alves face charges for insulting its institution. Though the Congress served at the pleasure of the military, the lawmakers refused to lift their colleague's immunity from prosecution. Faced with rumors that he would be removed from power by the military if he did not take a firm stand, Costa e Silva dissolved Congress on December 14, suspended the constitution, and assumed dictatorial powers. Many of his outspoken opponents were imprisoned.

Thus began a downward spiral into severe repression. Brazil's newspapers, which had enjoyed relative freedom early in Costa e Silva's government, were now censored. The president assumed the right to intervene in any state or municipality, to withdraw the political rights of any citizen, to suspend habeas corpus for political offenses, and to expel students for anti-government protests. Political murder became a feature of life.

Though United States diplomats voiced their displeasure, foreign businessmen were perversely pleased by developments. Inflation dropped below 20 percent, the gross national product jumped, as did industrial growth, and the balance of payments improved. Though economic aid had been suspended in protest against the crackdown, restrictions were quietly lifted under pressure from the U.S. business community.

Career Ends Abruptly

In late August 1969, the Costa e Silva suffered a debilitating stroke. Witnesses reported that he took up a pen when he found he could not speak, and then hurled the pen across the room in tears when he found he also could no longer write. As he lay in his bedroom in the presidential mansion, three generals who had taken over his government issued decrees from a room directly below. Costa e Silva's vice president, who had the constitutional right to assume the presidency, disappeared from public view and was placed under virtual house arrest.

Costa e Silva died on December 17, 1969. Few mourned his passing. Under temporary leadership, Brazil's government veered to the right and its 23rd president, Emílio Garrastazu Médici was quickly installed as his successor. The economy grew at an unprecedented rate during the following five years, and by the end of the 1970's steps were initiated to restore civilian democracy and lift political repression.

Further Reading

Atlantic Monthly, April, 1969.
Commonweal January 10, 1969.
New Republic, August 2, 1969; September 10, 1966.
Newsweek, September 15, 1969; December 23, 1968; May 8, 1967; January 31, 1966; August 8, 1966; October 10, 1966.
New York Times, December 18, 1969.
Time, December 27, 1968; March 24, 1967; April 21, 1967; April 29, 1966; January 13, 1967; November 12, 1965.
U.S. News and World Report, October 17, 1966.

Aleister Crowley

Misunderstood and even feared during his lifetime, Aleister Crowley (1875-1947) channelled his brilliance into the black arts, believing that he was the greatest of the world's magicians, brought back to life.

Aleister Crowley (the surname rhymes with "slowly") was an iconoclast among iconoclasts. In an era noted for decadence and rife with religious experimentation and deviation from the rigid Christian strictures suffocating Victorian society, he diverged from even the more bizarre religious factions through his insatiable lust for sensation. Beginning what would become a lifelong study of the occult while still a child, Crowley's thirst for knowledge would cause him to travel the world, studying the Eastern mystics as well as the pagan religions of the ancients. Finally believing that he had achieved a kind of spiritual nirvana, he wrote his *The Book of the Law,* which has been studied as a primer by students of the occult since its publication in the early 1900s. Crowley's excesses extended to drug use; his health gradually declined after he reached the age of fifty and he spent his final years in relative obscurity, reviled for his outrageous activities and impoverished by the financial extravagances of his youth. His bizarre reputation has earned him a posthumous following: rock and roll performers Ozzie Osborne and Jimmy Page are long-term fans of Crowley's Satanic leanings.

Father's Zeal Proves Early Influence

Crowley was born in Warwickshire, England, in October of 1875. He was the son of a brewer and part-time preacher in the church of the Plymouth Brethren whose zeal for his religion as the only true form of Christianity prompted him to train young Aleister to preach alongside him from an early age. When the boy rebelled, his mother reacted by dubbing him "the beast," implying that her son's rejection of their faith was somehow motivated by the devil. It was an implication that Aleister took to heart; a fascination with non-Christian religions and the black arts would consume much of his adult life.

As a young man, Crowley attended Trinity College, Cambridge, where he wrote poetry, publishing his first book, *Aceldama, a Place to Bury Strangers In. A Philosophical Poem. By a Gentleman of the University of Cambridge.* His academic pursuits, however, did not fully interest him. He left before receiving his degree, opting instead to devote himself to mastery of the occult. He joined the Hermetic Order of the Golden Dawn, the first order, or lowest tier, of the secret Great White Brotherhood of Rosicrucians. The Order, led by Samuel Liddel MacGregor Mathers, included elements of astrology, the tarot, alchemy, and magick in its rites; other members of this group included the British poet William B. Yeats. After joining the London chapter of the Golden Dawn on November 18, 1898, Crowley dubbed himself Count Vladimir and began moving up through each successive level of ability. He eventually graduated from the first order and sought entry into the second, the Order of the Red Rose. Crowley ran afoul of certain leaders of the Golden Dawn, however, who prevented his advancement because of jealousy. After being attacked by several henchmen, Crowley decided to leave England for a period, to travel and study independently.

Continues Move up Religious Ranks

In addition to being intelligent and fascinated by his new course of study, Crowley was also very ambitious, with a desire to be in a highly visible role. After traveling from England to Asia in 1900, where he disciplined his approach to mysticism through studying the physical and mental aspects of Tantric yoga and gained an appreciation for other religions of the Far East, he returned to London, determined to expand the vision of the Order of the Great White Brotherhood. However, not surprisingly, there was resistance on the part of the existing leadership, and Crowley still found his efforts to move up the ranks thwarted. At one point, it is reported that he attempted to stage a coup, appearing at a meeting of the Second Order wearing a black mask and carrying a dagger. His growing dissatisfaction was fueled by his wife, Rose Kelly, whom Crowley had married in 1903. While she originally had no interest in the occult, she began falling into trance-like states shortly after her honeymoon trip to Egypt; she convinced Aleister that Horus, the Egyptian god of light, was trying to communicate with him. Crowley saw no reason to be skeptical of his wife's assertions and, in April of 1904, went into retreat for three days. When he emerged, he had with him *The Book of the Law,* which he maintained that his guardian spirit, the devil-god Aiwaz, an agent of Horus, had narrated to him.

The Book of the Law, a three-part long poem, would prove extremely influential among fellow occultists. It maintained that the age of Horus was upon mankind, ushering in the age of "Thelema," a Greek word meaning "will." Crowley, as the receiver of the word of Horus, must, then, be the prophet for this new age, as well as the interpreter of its laws. The central tenet of *The Book of the Law* is "Do what thou wilt shall be the whole of the law." While some have interpreted this to justify a life of self-indulgence, Crowley placed a different interpretation on the words, seeing in the term "will" the ability to control the actions of others or create a change in one's surroundings through one's psychic powers. Breaking with the teachings of the Golden Dawn, he determined to dedicate the remainder of his life to developing his Thelemic philosophy, including this development of will, which he referred to as "magick." The number 666 gained in significance in his teachings, and he began to call himself "The Great Beast." The reputation for wickedness that this name provoked from most people only added to his growing sense of self-esteem and empowerment.

Joins Ordo Templi Orientis

In 1906 Crowley founded his own chapter of the third order of the Great White Brotherhood, known as the Astron Argon or Silver Star. Four years later, he was contacted by Theodore Reuss, leader of a German cult of Freemasons called the Ordo Templi Orientis (OTO). They too were deeply involved in magick, and Crowley joined, eventually becoming the head of the Order. He restructured the OTO to conform to his Thelemic principles, and broke with the Freemasons, thereafter allowing men and women to join. From 1909 to 1913 he also published *The Equinox,* a newspaper that exposed the secret rituals used by the rival Golden Dawn as well as Crowley's verse.

As Crowley gained in power in the OTO, he also gained in notoriety. In 1923, he was exiled from Cefalu, Sicily, where he had formed a branch temple, after a scandal involving several prostitutes broke out. But he took the event in stride, bragging thereafter that he had been "expelled from Italy." Rumors grew about his leadership of

rituals involving animal sacrifice, celebration of the Black Mass, hallucinogenic drugs, and outlandish sexual conduct, but Crowley continued his Order unabated. During the 1920s he published several books, including *Clouds without Water, Confessions, The Herb Dangerous,* and *The Winged Beetle,* although their circulation remained clandestine due to their subject matter. Continuing to add fuel to his reputation as a Satanist, he blithely remarked in one essay that "for nearly all purposes, human sacrifice is best." Such comments, when made public, did little to endear him to most English people, although he continued to draw to him a small but loyal band of converts.

Reduced to Obscurity in Later Years

In 1929 Crowley married his second wife, Maria Ferrari de Miramar, and published *Moonchild,* a novel that depicts the efforts of rival magicians to create the miracle child predicted to be the future leader of their craft. While critical of its plot, *Survey of Modern Fantasy Literature* contributor Brian Stableford called *Moonchild* valuable "as part of a psychological case study. What value it has rests in whatever insight it provides into the character of [its author], an actor for whom the stage of life itself was too confined." By the mid-1930s, reality caught up with the author of this fantasy fiction. His lavish lifestyle had extended far beyond his thirty thousand pound inheritance, and a heavy drug addiction did little to stabilize a failing financial picture. By 1939 Crowley's creditors were forced to take a small percentage of the money owed following bankruptcy proceedings. The following decade would prove to be a black one for Crowley, who supported himself through royalties off such published books as *Diary of a Drug Fiend, The Book of Thoth,* and *Magick in Theory and Practice,* and whose home had been reduced to a room in a boardinghouse. His popularity in the United States had been slight on the heels of the pro-German propaganda he released there during World War I; in World War II he shocked and alienated even more people by commenting that "Before Hitler was, I am." The atrocities of the Nazi government diminished Crowley's past activities by comparison, and such a comment reduced him to a pathetic, jealous, disturbed man. He died in Hastings, England, on December 1, 1947, shortly after his physician had refused to supply the morphine on which Crowley had become dependent. He was seventy-two.

After his death, two schools of thought rose up about Crowley. In some appraisals, he has been considered perhaps the greatest magician of the twentieth century. Others, however, have portrayed him as a hedonistic egomaniac, bent on acquiring power over others and addicted to sex and a multitude of mind-altering drugs. His greatest influence has been felt in the arts, particularly in the rock music of Ozzie Osborne and Led Zeppelin, as well as in the art of Austin Osman Spare and filmmaker Kenneth Anger. Crowley also served as the basis for the character of Oliver Haddo in William Somerset Maugham's 1908 novel, *The Magician.* A recording of Crowley's teachings titled *The Beast Speaks* was release on compact disk in 1993 and sold upward of eight thousand copies. And the OTO, while splitting into rival factions following Crowley's death, would enjoy a revival of sorts, particularly in England, during the later part of the twentieth century.

Further Reading

The Beast Speaks (recording), Virgin Records, 1993.
Cammell, Charles Richard, *Aleister Crowley: The Man, the Mage, the Poet,* New York University Press, 1962.
DuQueste, Lon Milo, *The Magick of Thelema: A Handbook of Rituals by Aleister Crowley,* S. Weiser, 1993.
Guiley, Rosemary Ellen, *Encyclopedia of Witches and Witchcraft,* Facts on File, 1989, pp. 75-77, 157-59.
Magill, Frank N., editor, *Survey of Modern Fantasy Literature,* Volume 3, Salem Press, 1983.
Suster, Gerald, *Legacy of the Beast,* W. H. Allen, 1988.
Symonds, John, *The Great Beast: The Life and Magic of Aleister Crowley,* Roy, 1952, revised as *King of the Shadow Realm,* Duckworth, 1989.
Aleister Crowley Homepage, http:/www.crl.com/ thelema/ crowley.html (March 15, 1998). □

Eve Curie

The daughter of Nobel award-winning scientist Madame Curie, Eve Curie (born 1904) would gain fame on her own terms: as a concert pianist and journalist during World War II.

The youngest child born to Pierre and Marie (Sklodowska) Curie, discoverers of radium and Nobel Prize recipients, Eve Curie's interests and talents were more musical, literary, and political than scientific. Encouraged by her mother, Curie developed her early skill in music, and her first career was as a concert pianist. Later she would turn her talents to writing, lecturing, and international advocacy on behalf of Free France during World War II. During the 1950s and 1960s, Curie worked for the North Atlantic Treaty Organization (NATO), and for the United Nations' Childrens' Fund in Greece.

Raised Alone by Marie Curie

Curie was born in Paris, France on December 6, 1904. She had one older sister, Irène, who shared her parents' scientific bent. The younger Curie barely knew her father; she was less than two years old when he was tragically killed. Pierre Curie died instantly in an accident on April 6, 1906 when he was pulled under the wheels of a carriage while attempting to cross a Paris street; his cranium was crushed by the force. Eve's mother lost her partner in marriage as well as science, and could never bear to talk of Pierre to her daughters after his death. Marie Curie's father-in-law, Dr. Eugène Curie provided support to her and her young daughters until his death in 1910.

Forced to raise her children alone, and determined to continue the work she had begun with husband, Pierre, Marie Curie also wished to spare her children some of the difficulties and fears she had been subject to as a child growing up in Poland. With the aid of governesses, she created lessons encouraged to stimulate both of her daugh-

ters' minds and bodies. She watched with great interest as each of the girls developed interests and skills in diverse areas. Music became the subject in which young Eve first excelled from a young age.

Physically, the girls were also encouraged in many areas. Despite all types of weather, they would take long walks. Marie Curie had gymnastic equipment installed in their garden at Sceaux and both girls earned first prizes from a local gymnasium for their skills. They learned cooking, gardening, and sewing. Along with their mother, they went on outings on bicycle, and during the summers, Marie Curie taught them how to swim. The one area in which their mother did not specifically attempt to give them direction, was in spiritual matters. She was unwilling to impose dogmas upon her daughters that she no longer believed.

During 1911, when Eve was less than seven years old, she and older sister, Irène both accompanied their mother to Poland, to visit Marie Curie's sister, Bronya, at the sanatorium. In Poland the sisters learned to ride horses and trekked into the mountains for several days, staying at mountaineering cabins during the nights.

Accompanies Mother to United States

In the spring of 1921 Eve, then 16 years old, and Irène travelled to New York with their mother on the ship, the Olympic, for Eve's first trip to the United States. Marie Curie was received with much fanfare by the people of the United States, and the two young women acted as bodyguards and also filled in for their famous mother at various social engagements for which she was highly in demand. In addition to meeting President Warren G. Harding while in Washington, D.C., the Curies also visited Niagara Falls, and took the Sante Fe line through Texas to enjoy the vistas of the Grand Canyon. The younger Curies couldn't resist the call of the Colorado River, and trekked into the canyon on mules. They returned to Paris on June 28, 1921.

Eve graduated with honors with two degrees from the Sévigné College: bachelor degrees in both science and philosophy. She also studied piano for many years, and in 1925 performed her first concert in Paris. In addition to giving many concerts in Paris, she also performed in Belgium and in the provinces of France.

Older sister Irène married Frédéric Joliot in 1926. Curie continued sharing the large, rather cold, and unadorned apartment with her mother in Paris after her older sister's marriage. Now adults, both daughters remained devoted to their mother: Irène and husband Joliot shared Marie Curie's scientific world, while Eve was a support to her mother at home, sharing evening meals and talking of the world. Curie sometimes accompanied her mother on Marie Curie's many trips to Italy, Belgium, Switzerland, and throughout France. Mother and daughter also travelled across Spain with then-President Masaryk in 1932.

Eve was quite different from her famous mother in many ways, and Marie Curie gave up trying to impose her ways upon her daughter, especially in matters of fashion. The younger Curie, attractive, elegant, and dark haired, was interested in matters that baffled her mother. Marie Curie always seemed amazed and curious about daughter Eve's dressing up, wearing high heels and makeup, which held no interest for the elder Curie, who dressed simply in her signature black dresses. Both Curies shared a love of literature, and although here also their tastes diverged, they shared a love of Kipling and Colette. Curie attended her mother during her many bouts of ill health, and was at her mother's bedside on July 4, 1934 when Marie Curie died.

Writes Biography of Marie Curie

Following her mother's death, Curie turned her talents to writing, and decided to write a biography about her famous mother. To this end, she lived in a small apartment in Auteuil, collecting and sorting various documents and letters left by Marie Curie. Eve Curie also journeyed to Poland during the fall of 1935, where some family remained, searching for additional information about her mother's youth. The information, letters, and photographs she obtained were used in the writing of Marie Curie's biography, *Madame Curie*, published simultaneously around the world in 1937 in France, England, Italy, Spain, the United States, and in other European countries.

Curie received much acclaim and high praise for the personal and definitive account of Marie Curie's life and work. Translated into English by Vincent Sheean, it became a best seller in the United States. The *New Yorker* called the biography a rare book, "which reconciles us to belonging to the human race." Mrs. Franklin D. Roosevelt said, "I have read it with great thrill. The simplicity and beauty of the style and the understanding and love for her mother are in them-

selves wonderful." The *Philadelphia Record* agreed, calling it "One of the outstanding publications of the season." Curie also won the National Book Award for non-fiction in 1937 for *Madame Curie.* In 1943 the biography was adapted by M.G.M., and released as a film.

In addition to writing her mother's life story, Curie also wrote as a music critic under a pseudonym for several years for the weekly *Candide,* and authored articles for other Parisian publications on theatre, music, and movies. She translated and adapted the American play, *Spread Eagle,* written by George S. Brooks and Walter B. Lister, for stage production in France in 1932. The play enjoyed a long run under the name, *145 Wall Street.* In 1940, after the fall of France, she travelled to England working for the cause of Free France. She would later become an officer of the women's division of the army and serve in Europe with the Fighting French.

Appointed to Diplomatic Position

Following the outbreak of World War II, Curie was appointed by former novelist and playwright Jean Giraudoux, who had become the French Information Minister, to the position as head of the feminine division of the Commissariat of Information. Between 1939 and 1949 Curie lectured across the United States on seven separate tours. During 1940 then-First Lady of the United States Eleanor Roosevelt hosted Curie at the White House in Washington, D.C. Following this visit, Curie would launch one of her tours across the United States, on the topic of *French Women and the War,* beginning in Kalamazoo, Michigan, stopping in many places across the country. She was articulate and elegant, and as official spokesperson for the women of France during World War II told White House correspondents during her visit that, "Peace will not come soon, and it will not come at all while the Hitler regime remains in Germany because the French are determined that when this war ends there will be no more fighting in Europe for a long time." Also in May 1940, her essay on *French Women and the War,* was published in *Atlantic Monthly.*

In 1943 the personal account of Curie's travels to the fronts during World War II, *Journey among Warriors,* was published by Doubleday. Sponsored by Allied Newspapers, Ltd. and the Herald Tribune Syndicate, and beginning in November 1941, Curie had toured Africa, the Near East, Russia, India, China, and Iran covering the major battlefields of the war. *Journey among Warriors* was generally positively received, with the primary negative comment being about excess length. Clifton Fadiman of the *New Yorker* called it "One of the best jobs of world reporting evoked by the current conflict."

Curie was also the co-publisher of the daily newspaper, *Paris-Press,* in Paris, France from 1945-49. In 1952 she was appointed as the Special Advisor to the Secretary General of NATO; she held this position on its international staff until 1954. On November 19, 1954 Curie married Henry Richardson Labouisse who was the U.S. ambassador to Greece. Curie served as the executive director of the United Nations' Childrens' Fund, Greece from 1962-65. She and Labouisse travelled extensively to more than 100 of the developing nations who were beneficiaries of UNICEF relief.

Among Curie's other interests during her long and varied life have been skiing, skating, and swimming. She speaks Polish, as well as some Greek and Spanish. Both of her books have been translated into various languages. Curie makes her home in New York City.

Further Reading

Curie, Eve, *Madame Curie,* Doubleday, 1937.
New Yorker, May 8, 1943.
Time, February 12, 1940, p. 25.

D

Dorothy Dandridge

Dorothy Dandridge (1922-1965) was the first African American woman to receive an Academy Award nomination for best actress for her performance in the 1954 film *Carmen Jones*. Her glamorous image and turbulent life have inspired many to compare her to another equally tragic Hollywood figure, Marilyn Monroe.

One of the most strikingly beautiful and charismatic stars ever to grace Hollywood, Dorothy Dandridge blazed a number of significant trails during her short but noteworthy career as the first African American actress to achieve leading-role status. Yet hers was also a deeply troubled life, marked by the scars of a miserable childhood, a string of failed personal relationships, numerous career setbacks, and ongoing struggles with drug and alcohol abuse. Racism was also one of the demons with which she had to contend, for Dandridge came of age in an era when the entertainment world was rife with demeaning racial stereotypes.

A native of Cleveland, Ohio, Dorothy Jean Dandridge was born in 1922 to Ruby Dandridge and her estranged husband, Cyril. As children, Dorothy and her older sister, Vivian, traveled to schools and churches around the country performing in song-and-dance skits scripted by their mother, who longed for a career in show business. By 1930, Ruby Dandridge had left Cleveland with her daughters to seek her fortune in Hollywood. There the family survived on what Ruby could earn playing bit parts in the movies or on radio, usually as a domestic servant—the kind of character role typically offered to black actors and actresses at that time. Meanwhile, Dorothy was subjected to years of physical, sexual, and emotional abuse at the hands of her mother's female lover.

Achieved Early Fame in Nightclubs

Around 1934, Dorothy and Vivian teamed up with another singer named Etta Jones and, billed as the Dandridge Sisters, began touring with a popular band. Their talents eventually landed them a regular spot at the famous Cotton Club in Harlem, New York where white audiences flocked to see a wide variety of black performers. Dorothy went on to make her Hollywood debut in 1937 with a bit part in the classic Marx Brothers film *A Day at the Races,* followed a couple of years later by an appearance of the Dandridge Sisters with jazz trumpeter Louis Armstrong in *Going Places.* By 1940, however, the trio had disbanded, and Dorothy set out on her own.

In 1941 and 1942, Dandridge worked in several musical film shorts and Hollywood features before marrying Harold Nicholas of the celebrated Nicholas Brothers dance duo. While he pursued a film career, she temporarily set aside her ambitions to await the arrival of their first child in 1943. However the marriage was an unhappy one almost from the start, due to Nicholas's philandering. The couple's difficulties were compounded when their daughter, Harolyn (known as Lynn), was diagnosed as being severely mentally retarded due to brain damage suffered at birth. She was eventually institutionalized. For the rest of her life, Dandridge blamed herself for Lynn's condition.

Dandridge and her husband finally divorced in 1949. Deeply depressed over what she perceived as her failure as a wife and as a mother, she decided that the best way to cope with her sad situation was to keep busy. She took

singing, acting, and dance lessons to regain her confidence and soon hit the road with a nightclub act that eventually took her all over the world. In 1951, she became the first African American to perform in the Empire Room of the Waldorf-Astoria Hotel in New York City. That same year, she also broke attendance records at the Mocambo in Hollywood. Despite her success, Dandridge constantly battled insecurities about her looks and her talent and such anxiety often left her feeling physically ill before, during, or after a performance. Additionaly, she absolutely detested the cigarette smoke, the drinking, and the often obnoxious male patrons she had to endure on the nightclub circuit.

Launched Film Career

Before long, however, Dandridge's film career began to blossom. In addition to some bit parts, she played an African princess in the 1951 movie *Tarzan's Peril* and a teacher in 1953's *Bright Road*. In 1954, she won the lead role in the movie that would make her a star—*Carmen Jones,* a lavish musical based on the nineteenth-century French opera *Carmen* by Georges Bizet that tells the story of a beautiful but fickle gypsy girl whose seductive ways lead to tragedy. In director Otto Preminger's updated version, set in Florida during World War II, Bizet's gypsy girl is transformed into a sultry black factory worker who corrupts a young black soldier, betrays him, and then pays the ultimate price for her actions. Featuring an all-black cast that, in addition to Dandridge, included Harry Belafonte, Pearl Bailey, and Diahann Carroll, *Carmen Jones* proved to be a critical and commercial success. It not only established

Dandridge as a bona fide sex symbol, it also earned her the honor of being the first African American to receive a best actor or actress Academy Award nomination.

Dandridge almost did not get to play Carmen Jones. When she first auditioned for Preminger, she struck him as being far too elegant and ladylike for the part. She, however, was determined to become a movie star, so she acquired an authentic-sounding southern accent, put on a tight skirt and low-cut blouse, applied heavy eye makeup and tousled her hair, and headed off for a second audition. This time, Dandridge electrified Preminger with her grasp of the character and won the part on the spot. She also captivated the director personally, but their liaison was an unfortunate one that caused Dandridge a great deal of sorrow.

Although Dandridge did not win the Oscar for *Carmen Jones,* which went to Grace Kelly for her role in *The Country Girl,* she still became the toast of Hollywood. Reporters and photographers trailed in her wake. Articles about her appeared in black as well as white publications, including a cover story in *Life* magazine that described her as one of the most beautiful women in America. Even the foreign press lavished her with attention. For a while, it looked as if Dandridge would be the one to force the movie industry to acknowledge the reality of racial integration.

Challenged Racial Stereotypes

Despite receiving such acclaim, Dandridge waited in vain for more demanding film roles to come her way. Instead, she was usually offered parts that were little more than variations on the Carmen Jones character—that is, lusty young women of dubious morality who meet with tragic ends. It was a frustrating turn of events for Dandridge, who took pride in working hard at her craft only to see herself locked into a racial stereotype. Sadly, studio bosses believed that white moviegoers would not accept African American actresses in roles other than that of the domestic servant or the trampy seductress.

As a result, three years passed before Dandridge starred in another film. This one, too, generated headlines, but not just for her performance. *Island in the Sun* (1957) was a daring foray into interracial romance that paired Dandridge with a white leading man. It was the first time a major American film had depicted such a relationship, and some audiences reacted with shock despite its extremely cautious approach to the subject matter. In the wake of the controversy, a number of theaters (mostly in the South) refused to show *Island in the Sun.* Nevertheless, it was a hit at the box office, and Dandridge went on to make several other movies dealing with the same theme, including *The Decks Ran Red* in 1958, *Tamango* in 1960 (a French production that could not obtain distribution in the United States), and *Malaga* in 1961.

Dandridge's final film triumph came in 1959 in the all-black musical *Porgy and Bess,* which many consider her finest performance. For her skillful portrayal of Bess (opposite Sidney Poitier as Porgy), Dandridge received a Golden Globe Award nomination for best actress in a musical.

Struggled against Depression

With the dramatic roles she wanted to play in short supply, Dandridge resumed her singing career after *Porgy and Bess* was released. It was while she was on tour in Las Vegas that she met white restaurateur Jack Denison, who, in 1959 became her second husband. Much like her first marriage, this one was a failure almost from the very beginning. Always fearful of poverty, Dandridge had saved much of the money she had earned as an actress, but soon lost everything after making a series of bad investments in her husband's business. Denison then took off, leaving her alone, broke, and depressed; she divorced him in 1962 and was forced to declare bankruptcy the following year. An attempt to revive her acting career went nowhere, and before long Dandridge had turned to pills and alcohol to ease her despair, which took a heavy toll on both her mental and physical well-being.

For a brief period in early 1965, it seemed that Dandridge might succeed in getting her life back in order. She left Hollywood for Mexico, where she checked into a health spa and worked at getting in shape. Several deals were in the works, including starring roles in a couple of new movies. However, on September 8, 1965, just a few days after returning to Hollywood, the forty-two-year-old Dandridge was found dead in her apartment of an overdose of antidepressant medication. Authorities could not determine whether it was an accident or suicide.

In January 1984, Dandridge finally received the recognition she had long deserved when her gold star was unveiled on Hollywood Boulevard's Walk of Fame. A crowd of fans of all ages attended the ceremony, joined by a number of prominent black actors and actresses, including her former co-stars Belafonte and Poitier. As her biographer, Donald Bogle, noted in *Essence,* they had gathered there to honor "a pioneer" who "cleared a path for so many to follow" with her determination to make something more of herself than society was ready to accept. "After all these years," concludes Bogle, "there still has never been another woman in American motion pictures quite like Dorothy Dandridge."

Further Reading

Bogle, Donald, *Dorothy Dandridge: A Biography,* Amistad Press, 1997.

Mills, Earl, *Dorothy Dandridge: A Portrait in Black,* Holloway House, 1970.

Notable Black American Women, Gale, 1992.

Ebony, September 1986, pp. 136-146; August 1997.

Essence, October 1984; May 1997, p. 114.

Jet, February 6, 1984, p. 55.

New Yorker, August 18, 1997, pp. 68-72.

People, July 28, 1997.

Premiere (special issue on women in Hollywood), winter 1993, pp. 85-89.

Time, September 1, 1997, p. 73.

John-Hall, Annette, "Brief Flame," *Philadelphia Online,* http://www3.phillynews.com/packages/history/notable/dot26.asp (April 1, 1998).

Wayne, Renee Lucas, "Rediscovering the Black Bombshell: Maybe Dorothy Dandridge Will Finally Get Her Due," *Phila-delphia Online,* http://www.phillynews.com/daily_news/97/Sep/18/features/DAND18.htm (April 1, 1998).

Erasmus Darwin

The grandfather of evolutionist Charles Darwin, Erasmus Darwin (1731-1802) was a prominent English physician and poet whose interests included biology, botany, and technology.

Darwin was born December 12, 1731, at Elston Hall, near Newark, in the county of Nottingham. The son of Robert, a retired lawyer, and Elizabeth Hill Darwin, he was educated at Chesterfield School from 1741 to 1750 and studied at Cambridge University from 1750 to 1754. Darwin attended medical school at Edinburgh University from 1750 to 1756 and afterward opened a medical practice in Lichfield, near Birmingham. His medical skills quickly earned him a wide reputation that extended even to London, where King George III is reported to have sought his services as a personal physician. Throughout his career Darwin maintained a thriving medical practice and treated impoverished patients at no charge.

Darwin married Mary Howard in December of 1757. Together they had five children, three of whom survived into adulthood. Their third son, Robert, became the father of the naturalist Charles Darwin. Erasmus Darwin's wife died in 1770, and he continued to live in Lichfield, where he fathered two illegitimate children by a woman named Mary Parker. The two daughters were raised in Darwin's household, and he later helped them establish a school for girls in Ashbourne. In the late 1770s Darwin began cultivating a botanical garden in Lichfield and formed a local botanical society to pursue his interests in that discipline. He moved from Lichfield to Derby following his marriage to a young military widow, Elizabeth Pole, in 1781.

An avid inventor, Darwin often pursued proof of current scientific theories and as a result of his efforts made notable contributions to such areas of study as physics, meteorology, and geology. According to his biographer Desmond King-Hele, Darwin's achievements as a mechanical inventor included a "speaking machine that astonished everyone . . . [and] a superb copying machine." In addition, his sketches reveal unrealized designs for such advancements as "canal lifts, an 'artificial bird,' and multimirror telescopes." On the strength of his research into the physical properties of gases and steam, Darwin was elected a fellow of the Royal Society in 1761.

By the mid-1760s Darwin was at the center of a circle of eminent philosophers and inventors that formed in Birmingham. Among the members of the coterie were the inventor James Watt, the manufacturer Matthew Boulton, and the potter Josiah Wedgwood. One of the original members of the society, William Small, whom Darwin had met through his acquaintance with Benjamin Franklin, had formerly been a teacher to Thomas Jefferson. The group for-

gained approval among leading English intellectuals. Published in two parts as *The Loves of the Plants* in 1789 and *The Economy of Vegetation* in 1792, the poem is also notable for introducing such terms as "oxygen," "hydrogen," "convoluted," "iridescent," and "frenzied" into the English language. While King-Hele himself has described Darwin's verse as "smooth and skillful," in the *Dictionary of Literary Biography* he quoted the contemporary opinions of such notable commentators as William Cowper and Horace Walpole. Cowper, in the *Analytical Review* of May 1789, assessed Darwin's couplets as having "a boldness of projection . . . unattainable by any hand but that of a master," while Walpole, in private correspondence dated April 1789, hailed Darwin's work as "the most delicious poem upon earth."

In a similar fashion, Darwin's *The Temple of Nature* traces the development of life and offers his views on evolutionary theory. Posthumously published in 1803, the work had originally been called *The Origin of Society,* a title the publisher considered too inflammatory as it could be construed as antireligious. In the work Darwin held that all life originated in the sea and can be traced back to a single common ancestor. He also outlined how species diversified in response to environmental factors. *The Temple of Nature* reads, in part, "Organic life beneath the shoreless waves/ Was born and nurs'd in ocean's pearly caves;/ First forms minute, unseen by spheric glass,/ Move on the mud, or pierce the watery mass;/ These, as successive generations bloom,/ New powers acquire and larger limbs assume;/ Whence countless groups of vegetation spring,/ And breathing realms of fin and feet and wing."

Many of Darwin's ideas on evolutionary theory were earlier discussed in the treatise *Zoomania, or, the Laws of Organic Life,* published in two volumes in 1794 and 1796. Containing an outline of Darwin's extensive medical knowledge, the first volume considers a number of biological and medical subjects, including sleep and instinct, and offers a discussion of evolutionary principles. Darwin investigated such aspects of the problem as how organisms pass through transitional stages, how sexual competition impacts the development of species, and how one species can give rise to another. In the second volume of *Zoomania* Darwin classified diseases and recommended methods of treatment for each.

malized their meetings under the title the "Lunar Society," a name derived from their habit of meeting on the evening of a full moon so as to be assured of light for the way home. The "Lunaticks," as they became known, were credited with initiating or advancing many technological developments of the Industrial Revolution. Members of the society discussed scientific and technological issues, inventions, and theories. Chemist Joseph Priestly joined the group in 1780, and his experiments, according to King-Hele, "gave the meetings a chemical focus." In the *Dictionary of Literary Biography* King-Hele asserted, "The Lunar group was perhaps the strongest intellectual driving force of the Industrial Revolution in Britain, and Darwin did much to keep up their enthusiasm for improving technology."

Combines Science and Poetry

Active in the Cathedral Close literary circle in Lichfield, Darwin later gained considerable literary fame as a poet during the early 1790s. At the height of his fame he was ranked with such significant literary figures as poet John Milton, and in 1797 Samuel Taylor Coleridge called Darwin "the first literary character in Europe, and the most original-minded Man." Darwin's best-known works treat scientific subjects within the formal conventions of verse. Among his most recognizable works is *The Botanic Garden,* which was inspired by his translations of the botanical writings of Swedish botanist Linnaeus into English. The work, which began as a rendering of Linnaeus's botanical catalog in rhyming couplets, reveals Darwin's early acceptance of Continental developments in chemistry that had not yet

Reputation and Legacy

Darwin's chief contributions to the development of life science are perhaps found in his relationship to the advancement of evolutionary theory, in particular to that of his grandson Charles Darwin, and in his participation in the Lunar Society, a group which fostered many of the leading scientific minds of the era. According to King-Hele, "Darwin celebrated the idea of progress via the march of science and technology. He was the laureate of the Industrial Revolution, glorifying the entrepreneurs and engineers . . . [a]nd ignoring the grief and grime of the factories." In addition, in *From Soul to Mind: The Emergence of Psychology from Erasmus Darwin to William James,* Edward S. Read has credited Darwin with repositioning psychology in the sciences, driven in part by his view that all mental states derive from the motion of particles in the brain.

As a poet, too, Darwin's influence was significant. His presentation of a humanity integrated with nature influenced the Romantic poets William Blake, William Wordsworth, and Samuel Taylor Coleridge, among others. Darwin was also the author of the social reform treatise *A Plan for the Conduct of Female Education in Boarding Schools*, 1797, and *Phytologia, or the Philosophy of Agriculture and Gardening*, 1800. He died following a heart attack in Derby on April 17, 1802.

Further Reading

Dictionary of Literary Biography, Volume 93: *British Romantic Poets, 1789-1832,* Gale, 1990.
Dictionary of National Biography, Volume V, Oxford University Press, pp. 534-36.
Hassler, Donald M., *Erasmus Darwin,* Twayne Publishers, 1973.
Read, Edward S., *From Soul to Mind: The Emergence of Psychology, from Erasmus Darwin to William James,* Yale University Press, 1997.
Los Angeles Times, July 14, 1997.
New Republic, June 12, 1995, p. 42.
"Erasmus Darwin—Champion of Oxygen," http://ci.mond.org/9522/952215.html (March 24, 1998).
"Prairie Pen: Reflections in Natural History," http://www.prairienet.org/gpf/gould.html (March 29, 1998).
"Wilkins Lecture—Erasmus Darwin, the Lunaticks and Evolution," The Royal Society Online, http://www.royalsoc.uk/st_lect5.htm (March 29, 1998).

Rupert Davies

British character actor Rupert Davies (1916-1976) often played amiable, reassuring authority figures, none more famous than his signature role, Inspector Jules Maigret.

A bluff, burly man with an unruly mop of crinkly brown hair, Rupert Davies was an instantly recognizable character player in movies of the 1950s and 1960s. Gentle in demeanor, he often played priests, detectives, and other authority figures. But he is best known to audiences in his native Great Britain for his portrayal of Inspector Jules Maigret, a pipe-puffing Parisian sleuth, on a television series in the early 1960s. Later in his career he became a valuable supporting actor in low-budget horror movies, often starring Vincent Price or Christopher Lee.

Rupert Davies was born in Liverpool, England in 1916. He did not take up acting until he was an adult. When World War II broke out, Davies joined the British naval air force. After his airplane went down off the coast of Holland during the early days of the conflict, Davies was captured by the Germans. He was placed in a prisoner of war camp, where he spent the next five years of his life. To keep up morale and entertain his fellow inmates, Davies performed in camp shows. After the war, Davies continued acting in provincial repertory companies. He made his film debut in

1949 in *Private Angelo*. Three years later, Davies played Page, a resident of Windsor whose wife helps to trick Sir John Falstaff, in a television production of Shakespeare's *The Merry Wives of Windsor*.

In the 1950s, Davies' movie career began to take off. He had a small role in *The Dark Avenger* (1955), a swashbuckling adventure starring screen legend Errol Flynn and British actor Christopher Lee, with whom Davies would work on many subsequent pictures. After a brief stint on the British Broadcasting Company (BBC) television series *Quatermass II*, about an intrepid scientist who routinely saves the world from alien threats, he worked alongside Lee again in the 1957 spy drama *The Traitor*. Davies' other supporting roles in this period came in *Danger Tomorrow* and *The Criminal*, both in 1960.

Wins Signature Role

In 1960, the BBC signed Davies to a two-year contract to play Inspector Jules Maigret, a pipe-smoking French detective, in a television drama series. Maigret, a fictional Parisian detective, was the creation of Belgian-born novelist Georges Simenon. Maigret's adventures have been translated into English and scores of other languages almost since they first started to appear in 1931. There are 75 Maigret novels and 25 short stories.

The colorful part was perfectly suited to Davies' affable screen demeanor. Maigret was to become the actor's signature role. The show was a huge hit with viewers in Britain, and Davies' unforgettable portrayal earned him British Actor of the Year honors in 1961. With only a limited number of Maigret novels to work from, the series eventually ground to a halt.

Returns to Big Screen

After *Maigret's* cancellation, Davies found it hard to land other parts in television. For years his most memorable work in that medium came as a commercial pitchman for Flora margarine. In need of steady work, Davies returned to making movies. Now in his late 40s, Davies settled for supporting roles, invariably playing a comforting authority figure. The most popular of these releases was the 1965 film *The Spy Who Came in from the Cold,* an adaptation of John Le Carre's best seller about a disenchanted undercover agent. Davies played George Smiley, the career spy later essayed by Sir Alec Guinness in the TV production of Le Carre's *Tinker, Tailor, Soldier, Spy.* Davies' other mainstream features during this period were *The Uncle* (1966) and the West German production *Das Geheimnis der gelben Mnche,* also in 1966.

Horror Movie Fixture

In the late 1960s, Davies found a niche in the horror and fantasy genre. He appeared in a succession of low-budget films in the United States and Great Britain. *The Brides of Fu Manchu* (1966) cast him opposite horror icon Christopher Lee in an adaptation of Sax Rohmer's classic book series. Lee and Davies were reunited in *Five Golden Dragons* (1968), a fantastic crime adventure set in Hong Kong. George Raft, Robert Cummings, and Klaus Kinski rounded out the international cast. Davies took a break from the fantasy genre for his next film, *Submarine X-1* (1968). The World War II adventure, about a Royal Navy officer who takes on the German battle fleet with midget submarines, also starred James Caan and William Dysart.

Davies returned to horror movies with his next project, *Witchfinder General* (1968), a creepy witchhunting tale featuring another of the genre's stalwart stars, Vincent Price. He paired again with Christopher Lee for the 1968 film *Dracula Has Risen from the Grave,* the fourth installment in Hammer Films' gory vampire cycle. Davies plays Monsignor Ernst Muller, a virtuous cleric who sacrifices himself to destroy Lee's pasty prince of darkness. Davies again played a vicar, again opposite Lee, in the 1968 film *The Crimson Cult,* an adaptation of the H.P. Lovecraft story "The Dreams in the Witch House." The low-budget production features one of the final performances by 81-year-old horror legend Boris Karloff. Davies' next film, *The Oblong Box* (1969) was loosely based on the work of Edgar Allen Poe. It starred Vincent price as a depraved aristocrat who keeps his disfigured brother locked in a tower in his house. Complications ensue when the deranged man escapes and begins murdering villagers.

Last Years

By the end of the 1960s, the market for low-budget horror movies had largely dried up. Davies found it difficult to make the transition back to mainstream drama. He had a small role as Lord Gordon in *Waterloo* (1970), an epic about Napoleon's disastrous final campaign that starred Rod Steiger as the French general. And he supported Max Von Sydow in the 1970 film *The Night Visitor* about an ingenious murderer who keeps escaping from his asylum cell. Davies' other films of this period are *The Firechasers,* a crime drama about an arsonist, and *Zeppelin* (1971), about espionage on board a balloon over pre-World War I Europe.

Davies' fortunes took a turn in 1972, when the BBC cast him in the role of Count Rostov in its 20-part serialization of Leo Tolstoy's classic novel *War and Peace.* The programs were handsomely produced and well-received by the public. They helped remind viewers what an engaging presence Davies could project on the small screen. That same year, Davies played Cerdig, Chief of the Saxons, on the BBC series *Arthur of the Britons.* The historical drama, starring Oliver Tobias in the title role, depicted Arthur not as a grand king but as the chief of a small Celtic tribe in Dark Ages Britain.

Davies last screen appearance came in *Frightmare,* a 1974 British horror feature. The gory film cast Davies against type as one half of a cannibal farm couple. It was released on video under the title *Frightmare 2.* Rupert Davies died of cancer in London, England on November 22, 1976. He was 59 years old.

Further Reading

Quinlan, David, *Quinlan's Illustrated Directory of Film Character Actors,* Bath Press, 1995.
New York Times, November 23, 1976.
Time, December 6, 1976.

William Robertson Davies

Robertson Davies (1913-1995) enjoyed a distinguished career as a journalist, playwright, and novelist, helping to enhance the literary standing of his native Canada.

Robertson Davies was a writer of grand ideas and fertile imagination who excelled in a variety of literary disciplines. As a journalist, his humorous observations about life amused newspaper readers over two decades. His comic plays addressed the plight of the Canadian artist to great effect. His sprawling, intellectually rich novels, including the acclaimed Deptford and Cornish trilogies, set a high standard for all Canadian authors who wish to follow him. With his bushy white beard and flowing mane of hair, Davies looked the part of a grizzled, ancient storyteller—which to his millions of devoted readers is exactly what he was.

Privileged Upbringing

William Robertson Davies was born on August 28, 1913 in the village of Thamesville, Ontario, Canada. He came from a very old and prominent family. The family of his mother, Florence Sheppard McKay Davies, had moved to Canada from England in 1785. His father, William Rupert Davies, hailed originally from Wales, but made his name as a Canadian publisher and politician. Davies also had two older brothers.

Davies developed an interest in drama early in life. At the age of three, he made his stage debut in the opera *Queen Esther.* He maintained a diary throughout his school years in which he wrote out his reactions to the stage performances he saw.

When Davies was five years old, his family moved to Renfrew, Ontario, a rural village in the Ottawa Valley. He spent his childhood years attending country schools and living the life of a typical country boy. When Davies was 12, his family uprooted again, this time moving to the city of Kingston. In this way, Davies gained his intimate knowledge of urban and rural life in Canada. From 1928 to 1932 he attended Upper Canada College in Toronto. His favorite activities during this period included music, theater, and editing the school newspaper.

Works at Old Vic

Davies next moved on to Queen's University in Kingston. He spent three years there, marked by his participation in the Drama Guild. He completed his higher education in 1938 at Balliol College, Oxford, where he earned a literature degree. His thesis, entitled *Shakespeare's Boy Actors,* attracted the attention of Sir Tyrone Guthrie, a legendary drama teacher. Guthrie hired Davies to work him at London's famous Old Vic theater.

Davies spent a year there working at a variety of jobs, from bit player to stage manager. He gained valuable stage experience on productions of Shakespeare, working along-

side world-renowned actors including Ralph Richardson and Vivien Leigh. He also fell in love with the Old Vic's stage manager, Australian-born Brenda Mathews, whom he married on February 2, 1940. The couple honeymooned in Wales, then returned to Canada, where Davies took a job as literary editor of the Toronto magazine *Saturday Night*. The couple had their first child in December of 1940.

Begins Writing Professionally

After two years with *Saturday Night,* Davies took a position with the Peterborough *Examiner.* He would remain with that paper for the next 20 years. In the early days there he wrote a whimsical column under the guise of "Samuel Marchbanks." These witty observations were later collected into the books *The Diary of Samuel Marchbanks* (1947), *The Table Talk of Samuel Marchbanks* (1949), and *Marchbanks' Almanack* (1967). Another of his regular columns, "A Writer's Diary," consisting of observations on the literary scene, helped establish Davies as a major new voice in criticism.

The 1940s were a fertile period for Davies. Besides his weekly columns, he was also writing and directing plays at the Peterborough Little Theatre. In 1946 his one-act comedy *Overlaid* was awarded a prize by the Ottawa Drama League. The fantasy *Eros at Breakfast* (1948) won the Gratien Gelinas Prize for best Canadian play at the Dominion Drama Festival. Other one-acts Davies crafted during this time were *The Voice of the People* (1948), *At the Gates of the Righteous* (1948), and *Hope Deferred* (1948).

The year 1948 saw the production of Davies' first full-length play. *Fortune, My Foe* deals with the plight of the Canadian artist and was awarded the Gratien Gelinas Prize at the 1949 Dominion Drama Festival. Another three-act, *At My Heart's Core,* dealt with similar themes. It was set in provincial Canada in 1837 and shows Davies' growing mastery of historical material.

From Dramatist to Novelist

Frustrated by his inability to get his plays produced outside of Canada, Davies turned to novel writing in the 1950s. His first novel, *Tempest-Tost,* was published in 1951. Set in the small Canadian town of Salterton, the book details the reactions of townsfolk to a troupe of Shakespearean actors in their midst. *Leaven of Malice* (1954) is set in the same locale, and revolves around the confusion that ensues when an erroneous engagement announcement is printed in a local newspaper. The final book in the Salterton trilogy, *A Mixture of Frailties* (1958) concerns a young girl who returns to the town after a sojourn studying music in Europe. The books received many positive critical notices and established Davies' reputation as a novelist.

Even as he switched media, Davies never lost his love for the stage. He helped found the Stratford Shakespeare Festival, served on its Board of Directors, and hired Tyrone Guthrie as creative director. In 1960, Davies adapted his novel *Leaven of Malice* for the New York stage. Directed by Guthrie using experimental techniques, the play failed with critics and folded after six performance. Disappointment over this experience all but drove Davies away from theater, though he did continue to write and lecture on the subject.

As his creative reputation grew, Davies found himself in demand for academic appointments. He served as a visiting professor at Trinity College from 1961 to 1962 and was named to the Master's Lodge at Massey College, a graduate wing of the University of Toronto, in 1963. He quit his newspaper post at the *Examiner* in 1962 to concentrate on these teaching endeavors.

Writes Deptford Trilogy

In 1970, Davies published a new novel, *Fifth Business,* the first installment of his "Deptford Trilogy." The book chronicles 60 years in the life of Dunstan Ramsey, an assistant headmaster at a Canadian prep school. Davies weaves into the story many religious and psychological themes, prompting L.J. Davis of *Book World* to brand the novel "a work of theological fiction that approaches Graham Greene at the top of his form." Its rich plot helped make it a bestseller in America, cementing Davies stature as an international author of the first rank.

Davies followed *Fifth Business* with another Deptford novel, *The Manticore* (1972). Again set amongst the Canadian upper classes, the book follows David Staunton, an alcoholic attorney, on a spiritual odyssey of self-discovery. Davies' dry, analytic style put off some readers, while others found his command of symbols and allusions masterful. Another highbrow hit with readers, *The Manticore* received the Canadian Governor General's Award for excellence.

Rounding out the Deptford trilogy was *World of Wonder* (1975). Comprising the story of Paul Dempster, a character who had appeared in the previous two novels, the book was judged "a novel of stunning verbal energy and intelligence" by Michael Mewshaw of the *New York Times Book Review*. Readers and reviewers generally found it a satisfying conclusion to the trilogy.

1980s and Beyond

In the 1980s, Davies completed another trilogy of novels, revolving around the biography of Francis Cornish. The so-called "Cornish Trilogy" was another dense, erudite chronicle of upper class Canadian life. The second installment, *What's Bred in the Bone* (1985) earned Davies the 1986 Canadian Author's Association Literary Award for best fiction, as well as the New York National Arts Club's Medal of Honor for Literature. The other books in this series are *The Rebel Angels* (1982) and *The Lyre of Orpheus* (1988).

Davies also wrote novels outside the trilogy format. These included *High Spirits* (1983) and *Murther & Walking Spirits* (1991). *The Cunning Man* (1994), a novel in the form of a memoir by an aging physician, was called "as substantial and entertaining as any he has written" by Isabel Colegate in the *New York Times Book Review*.

Davies retired from teaching in 1981, but maintained his membership in various literary and academic societies as he worked on his various novels. He died of a stroke on December 2, 1995. His last book, a collection of non-fiction essays entitled *The Merry Heart: Reflections on Reading, Writing, and the World of Books,* was published posthumously in 1997.

Further Reading

Anthony, Geraldine, *Stage Voices: 12 Canadian Playwrights Talk about Their Lives and Work,* Doubleday, 1978.
Contemporary Novelists, 5th edition, St. James, 1991.
Dictionary of Literary Biography, Volume 68, edited by W.H. New, Gale Research, 1988.
Grant, Judith Skelton, *Robertson Davies,* McClelland & Stewart, 1978.
Grant, *Robertson Davies: Man of Myth,* Penguin, 1994.
Peterman, Michael, *Robertson Davies,* Twayne, 1986.
Interview, March 1989.
New York Times, December 4, 1995.
New York Times Book Review, December 20, 1970; November 19, 1972; April 25, 1976; February 14, 1982; December 15, 1985; October 30, 1988; January 8, 1989; November 17, 1991; December 1, 1991; February 5, 1995.
Maclean's, December 18, 1995.
Time, December 18, 1995.

Bette Davis

Considered by some to be unappealing in her first screen tests, Bette Davis (1908-1989) went on to become one of Hollywood's greatest actresses. She won two Best Actress Academy Awards and was nominated eight other times.

Bette Davis's career, which spanned some 60 years, included 86 films and 15 television movies. In addition to the countless honors and awards, she earned the respect and admiration of audiences and colleagues alike. She was best known for playing strong and often scheming characters. Her large, expressive eyes, exaggerated mannerisms, distinctive voice and diction, and ubiquitous cigarettes became her trademarks. She is often credited with broadening the range of roles available to actresses as well. Her fans can still recite her most memorable lines, such as when Davis, portraying an aging stage legend in *All About Eve,* (1950) tells her guests to "fasten your seatbelts, it's going to be a bumpy night!"

The elder daughter of Harlow Morrell, a lawyer, and Ruth (Favor) Davis, she was christened Ruth Elizabeth, but was called Bette as a child and kept the name throughout her career. Davis was born in Lowell, Massachusetts, on April 5, 1908. After her parents divorced in 1916, she and her sister Barbara moved frequently throughout New England while their mother pursued a photography career.

Both girls attended boarding school in the Berkshires and high school in Newton, Massachusetts. Davis graduated from a finishing school, Cushing Academy, in Ashburnham, Massachusetts, with an idea that she might try acting. Not the so-called conventional beauty of the day, she received little encouragement, but in what would become typical Davis style, she made up her own mind and headed for New York City.

Her experience in New York City was not encouraging either. In fact, Davis was rejected when she tried to enroll in the famed acting school of Eva Le Gallienne, noted actress, director, and producer. Le Gallienne told her to study some other field. Undaunted, Davis was admitted to the John Murray Anderson's drama school instead. She got a role with George Cukor's stock company in Rochester, New York.

For the next four years, she hung around New York City and the Cape Playhouse in Dennis, Massachusetts, where she worked as an usherette in between playing bit parts. Her first major role was in an off-Broadway production of *The Earth Between* (1928). After a brief tour in *The Wild Duck*, Davis reached Broadway. The comedy *Broken Dishes* opened in November of 1929 and ran for six months. That led to a 1930 production of *Solid South,* which led to a screen test in Hollywood. She failed the screen test.

Critics who viewed Davis's 1930 screen test at Goldwyn studios said she had no audience appeal. So, she tested at Universal and was hired, even though it was said that studio boss Carl Laemmle also didn't think she had appeal. However, she was cast in two films in 1931, *Bad Sister* and *Seed.* The critics ignored her in both.

With her strong resolve about to cave in and force her to leave Hollywood, Davis got a break when George Arliss offered her the part opposite him in *The Man Who Played God* from Warner Brothers. She won good reviews and a long-term contract. Thus began a succession of films with Warner, most mediocre and unmemorable. But poor as the films were, the talent and unique quality of Davis began to emerge so that critics started to praise her while panning her movies.

Fighting the studio for better roles became a way of life for Davis as she clawed her way to the top of the film world. She fought for and won the right to be loaned out to RKO in 1934 to play Mildred, the selfish waitress who manipulates an infatuated medical student, in John Cromwell's *Of Human Bondage.* Suddenly, the world was introduced to a brilliant new actress.

One might have thought that Davis's career was on the upswing, but Warner continued to cast her in poor quality films. There were two exceptions. In *Dangerous,* Davis played a failed actress who tries to murder her husband. For this role, she won her first Best Actress Academy Award in 1935. She also appeared with Humphrey Bogart and Leslie Howard (her co-star in *Of Human Bondage*) in *The Petrified Forest* in 1936. Growing disgusted with the studio's offerings, Davis refused any more roles and was suspended without pay. She sued. Warner Brothers and the movie world were astounded; this was not expected behavior of the time. Although Davis lost her battle in court, Warner Brothers apparently got the message for they paid her legal fees and began offering her more suitable roles.

The stature of Davis, the actress, continued to grow. Ty Burr of *Entertainment Weekly* noted that "Davis was a top box office draw throughout the '30s and '40s, and in 1948 she was the highest paid star in Hollywood." Among her memorable roles in the 1930s and 1940s were: *Jezebel,* 1938, for which she won her second Academy Award for her portrayal of "a witchy Southern belle" according to Burr; *Dark Victory,* 1939, which she once told Harry Bowman of the *Dallas News* was her favorite film; *The Private Lives of Elizabeth and Essex* and *Juarez,* also 1939; *All This and Heaven Too* and *The Letter,* both 1940; *The Little Foxes,* 1941; *Now Voyager,* 1942; *Watch on the Rhine,* 1943; *The Corn Is Green,* 1945; *Deception* and *A Stolen Life,* both 1946; and the delightful *June Bride,* (1948) which showed her comic touch.

Despite the praise and awards, by the end of the 1940s, Davis's career seemed to be slowing down, mainly for lack of good material. But in true Davis style, she came through with perhaps the greatest performance of her career as the troubled, aging star, Margo Channing, whose life and career are being taken over by a cunning newcomer, Eve, played by Anne Baxter in *All About Eve* (1950). It was a biting satire on the world of the theater. Davis won the New York Film Critics best actress of the year award.

After a number of films in the 1950s, Davis's career seemed to slow down again. But she was back on top in the early 1960s, with two shockers. In 1962, Davis appeared in the smash *Whatever Happened to Baby Jane?,* playing opposite Joan Crawford. Crawford played the physically handicapped sister at the mercy of her demented sister, Baby Jane Hudson (Davis), a former child star. It was ghoulish and audiences loved it. This was followed by *Hush, Hush, Sweet Charlotte,* (1965) with Davis (co-starring Olivia de Havilland and Joseph Cotton) playing a recluse who is haunted by the unsolved murder of her lover many years earlier.

During the 1970s and 1980s, Davis continued to appear in films, mainly on television. As she marched cantankerously into old age, she appeared on many talk shows, delighting her audiences with her feisty, undaunted in the face-of-aging spirit. She was the fifth recipient of the American Film Institute's Life Achievement Award in 1977, the first woman to be so honored. In 1979, she won an Emmy Award for *Strangers: The Story of a Mother and Daughter.* One her best features became the inspiration for a number one pop song, "Bette Davis Eyes," in 1982.

Davis wrote two autobiographies, *The Lonely Life* (1962) and *This 'N That* (1987), the latter to refute her daughter's (Barbara Davis [B.D.] Hyman) 1985 tell-all book *My Mother's Keeper,* which portrayed Davis as an abusive alcoholic. She was also married four times. In 1932, she married Harmon Oscar Nelson, Jr.; they divorced in 1938. Her second marriage was to Arthur Farnsworth, a businessman from Boston who died in 1943. She married and divorced artist William Grant Sherry in 1945; they had a daughter named Barbara. In 1950, she married actor Gary Merrill, whom she met while making *All About Eve.* They adopted two children, Michael and Margot, and were divorced in 1960.

In the last five years of her life, Davis had a mastectomy, suffered with cancer and had several strokes. She probably was not kidding when she, according to an on-line biography commented, "Old age is not for sissies." Davis died on October 6, 1989, in Neuilly-sur-Seine, France, outside of Paris. She had just attended the San Sebastian Film

Festival in Spain where she had been honored for a lifetime of film achievement. In the late 1990s, her son Michael created the Bette Davis Foundation and awarded American actress Meryl Streep the first ever Bette Davis Lifetime Achievement Award.

Further Reading

Davis, Bette, and Michael Herskowitz, *This 'N That,* Putnam, 1987.
Hadleigh, Boze,*Bette Davis Speaks,* Barricade Books, 1996.
Chicago Tribune, October 9, 1989.
Dallas News, March 20, 1974.
Entertainment Weekly, August 13, 1993; Fall 1996.
Los Angeles Times, October 7, 1989.
Modern Maturity, July/August 1994.
New York Times, October 8, 1989.
''Bette Davis,''*All-Movie Guide,* http://205.186.189.2/cgi-win/AVG.exe?sql = 2P_IDP 17295 (May 14, 1998).
''Bette Davis,'' *Database—Katz Biography,* http://www.tvgen.com/movies/katz/1789.sml (May 14, 1998).
''Bette Davis,'' *Internet Movie Database,* http://us.imdb.com (May 14, 1998).
''Bette Davis,''*Welcome to the Golden Years—the Superstars,* http://www.geocities.com/Hollywood/9766/davis.html (May 14, 1998).
''Connery, Streep, Davis Honored,'' (April 17, 1998), http://www.mrshowbiz.com/ (May 14, 1998).

John Dodge

Dodge Brothers

The Dodge brothers, John Francis (1864-1920) and Horace Elgin (1868-1920), were among the earliest and most successful automotive pioneers of the twentieth century.

John Francis Dodge and Horace Elgin Dodge worked together around the turn of the twentieth century in the field of transportation—specifically in the newly formed auto industry. Originally working from a small machine shop in Detroit, Michigan, the pair contributed to the success of several famous automakers, including Ransom Olds and Henry Ford, before designing and beginning to manufacture their own Dodge Brothers automobile. They were also famous for the fortunes they built from their automotive empire, which they used to make Detroit into a world-renowned center of art, music, and architecture.

John and Horace Dodge were both born and grew up in the western Michigan town of Niles in the years following the Civil War. John was born October 25, 1864, and Horace was born May 17, 1868. Their father, Daniel Rugg Dodge, ran a foundry and machine shop, where he built and maintained engines for the river boat traffic. ''The boys spent much of their free time puttering around their father's foundry, learning the skills of the forge and machine shops,'' explain Jean Maddern Pitrone and Joan Potter Elwart in *The Dodges: The Auto Family Fortune and Misfortune.* ''Since the boats that navigated the St. Joseph River provided the Dodge shop with most of its business, the boys soon became familiar with the intricacies of the marine engines their father and uncles repaired.'' The family business provided a living but very few conveniences for the family. The boys and their older sister Della ''had no shoes even in early winter when Maria [their mother] sent them to the brick schoolhouse down the road from their home,'' explain Pitrone and Elwart. Despite these handicaps, both Della and John graduated from high school in Niles, while Horace completed his education in his father's shop.

Ironically the transportation revolution that swept the United States during the nineteenth century—and which culminated in the development of the automobile—contributed to the Dodge family's poverty. By 1882, when John graduated from high school, ''the railroad had developed into a booming new transportation medium in the past few years, and as Niles was emerging as a railroad link of its new industry between Chicago and Detroit,'' explain Pitrone and Elwart, ''the Dodge business, dependent in great part on the obsolescent river traffic, continually worsened.'' Soon after John's graduation the family moved to Port Huron in search of better opportunities. Within four years, however, they had moved again. ''In 1886 when the Dodge family moved to Detroit,'' say Pitrone and Elwart, ''the Detroit River was rivaling the Suez Canal in the amount of tonnage passing through its channels.'' The brothers went to work at first in marine engineer Tom Murphy's Boiler Shop, then in 1892 moved to the Dominion Typography

Company across the river in Windsor, Canada, where they not only produced machines that nearly perfectly cut type for printing, but also contributed to the company's Maple Leaf bicycle, which was successful largely because of Horace's patented ball-bearing device. They also married—John in September 1892 to Ivy Hawkins, Horace in 1896 to Christina Anna Thomson.

Failures and Successes

The Dominion Typography Company was not suited to the manufacture of bicycles and soon collapsed. The Dodges saw the failure of their employer as a chance for them to go into business for themselves. "In 1896, when the failing Canadian typography company was listed for sale," writes Pitrone in *Tangled Web: Legacy of Auto Pioneer John F. Dodge,* "the Dodges took every dollar they could drain from their family budgets to lease the company's building and fixtures." "Obtaining the lease, the brothers started operating their own business, but it survived only a short time," the critic continues. Instead of trying to maintain the company through a failure, John and Horace sold the business to another Canadian firm, which manufactured bicycles using the Dodge patent. "The brothers," say Pitrone and Elwart, ". . . had expected to receive substantial royalty payments from the buyer for their ball-bearing bicycle invention. But the company, beginning to fail, had reneged on royalty payments. As soon as the Canadian company made plans to dispose of its assets, the Dodge brothers canceled

Horace Dodge

their claims against the firm in exchange for their pick of the machinery in the Windsor plant."

This second-hand Canadian machinery formed the nucleus of the Dodge Brothers Machine Shop which John and Horace founded in the Boydell Building in Detroit in 1902. Their earliest contracts came from stove manufacturers, but soon they contracted with Ransom Olds, producer of the single-cylinder Oldsmobile, to build transmissions. The Dodges' success in creating high-quality parts that Olds used to assemble his cars brought the brothers both profits—which they invested in their business—and fame. Soon they were approached by budding auto designer Henry Ford. "Near the end of 1902," write Pitrone and Elwart, "the Dodge brothers produced in their machine shop the automobile that was to be the basis for Ford's successful business." Early in 1903, John and Horace abandoned their contract with Olds in favor of investing in the Ford prototype Model A automobile, a car that was produced almost entirely in their own shop.

Although the Dodges delivered the nearly completed cars they had contracted for on schedule, Ford and his two partners, the coal dealers Alexander Malcomson and James Couzens, found themselves unable to pay. Instead, the partners offered the brothers fifty shares of stock in the newly formed Ford Motor Company apiece. "By October of that first year," state Pitrone and Elwart, "Ford expanded the assembly plant, and the Dodges, who contracted to deliver 755 more chassis in the first five months of 1904, made a personal profit of more than $75,000." "By June 1904, less than one year from the date the company had begun selling its first cars," the writers explain, "dividends of 98 percent were paid to its stockholders. The Dodges received $9,800 in dividends on their original $10,000 investment in stock." "In June 1905, the Dodges received another $10,000 in dividends, plus an additional $10,000 the following month—dividends which were only a faint indication of the millions of dollars they would receive within the next several years," they conclude.

The Dodge Reputation

John and Horace quickly began investing their new wealth in their business and in their families. They expanded their shop in order to keep pace with the demands of the Ford contract—in 1910, they moved to a new and larger facility in the enclave of Hamtramck—and they started construction on palatial estates: John on Boston Boulevard in Detroit, Horace in Grosse Pointe. John, whose wife Ivy had died in 1901 from tuberculosis, also remarried, choosing as his next wife his former secretary Matilda Rausch. The two brothers also indulged themselves in trying to recapture some of their earliest interests. John bought the first of the farms that eventually made up the Meadow Brook estate near Rochester, Michigan, while Horace began construction of the first of what would become a fleet of yachts on Lake St. Clair and the Detroit River. Horace also became the primary sponsor of the new Detroit Symphony Orchestra, contributing heavily to the construction of its permanent home at Orchestra Hall.

John attracted less favorable attention in 1911, when newspaper headlines announced that he and his friend Robert Oakman had insulted and beaten handicapped attorney Thomas J. Mahon in a brawl at Schneider's Bar in Detroit. Both brothers were heavy drinkers, prone to belligerence when under the influence of alcohol, and they had a reputation in the city saloons for aggressive behavior. After the Mahon incident, however, "the escapades of the Dodges, which had been looked on by some with an admiring tolerance," state Pitrone and Elwart, "were suddenly viewed differently." The suit Mahon filed against Dodge and Oakman was eventually dropped, but the damage to John's reputation could not be undone.

The Dodges may have sought consolation in alcohol in part because of their frustration over their relationship with Ford and his associates. Although profits from the association were tremendous, the brothers disapproved of the way Ford treated his partners and his employees. In 1906, Ford squeezed his former partner Malcomson out of the Ford Motor Company. He also tried to reduce the payment of dividends to stockholders. "The squeeze play that had forced Malcomson—along with some other minor original stockholders—out of the company had demonstrated to the Dodges that Ford had no loyalty to those whose time and labor had brought him success," explain Pitrone and Elwart. The brothers' own sense of loyalty to their employees and friends was legendary. In addition, they had begun to make plans to build and manufacture their own car, realizing that to rely on Ford as their sole major source of income would prove to be a serious mistake. "In August of 1913," says Pitrone, "John Dodge resigned from the vice-presidency of the Ford Motor Company to avoid a conflict of interests as he and Horace began enlarging their Hamtramck factory for the production of their own car. . . . Newspapers across the country carried the announcement of John Dodge's resignation from Ford Motor Company's board of directors, and of the brothers' intention to manufacture a Dodge car in 1914. Since the automobile world recognized the Dodges' contributions to the success of Ford automobiles, the brothers' revelation that they would build a moderately priced, four-cylinder Dodge car received respectful attention in the nation's journals."

The car that emerged from the Hamtramck plant on November 10, 1914, represented a significant improvement on the Ford cars for which the brothers had been making parts only the previous year. The Dodge Brothers auto had a self-starter that only rarely relied on cranking, making it easier for women to drive. It also had a hand-controlled fuel pump that "made it possible for the Dodge car to climb a steep hill without forcing the driver to put his car into reverse gear and to ascend the hill backwards, as drivers of some Model T Fords had to do," says Pitrone. "By the end of 1914, John and Horace were planning for major production of Dodge cars in 1915, introducing a two-passenger roadster with rear luggage compartment, and a first closed car—a center-door sedan." The solid, dependable Dodge autos won recognition from General John J. Pershing in his mechanized-cavalry campaign in Mexico in 1916. "The Dodge cars swayed and lurched along in low gear," declare Pitrone and Elwart, "belching steam and grinding their way

through the sand so successfully that, less than three months later, Pershing requested another 250 Dodges from the War Department, putting out an order that only Dodges would be used by his staff in Mexico's rugged territory." Dodge cars and trucks were also used extensively by the American forces during World War I.

By the war's end, the Dodge Brothers plant ranked fourth in production among American car producers. When Horace and John left Detroit for the 1920 National Automobile Show, their prospects were bright. "In the summer of 1919," say Pitrone and Elwart, "their factory had produced 500 cars each day and still ran behind the volume of orders received from dealers." However, within the week, Horace Dodge fell very ill. Rumors circulated that he had fallen victim to a bad batch of illegal liquor, but the doctor's diagnosis was "grippe"—the influenza that in 1918-19 had killed more than 500,000 Americans. John Dodge, who camped outside his brother's sickroom door, soon was taken sick as well. John had suffered from tuberculosis more than twenty years previously, and it had damaged his lungs. He died on January 14, 1920. Although Horace recovered from the flu, he was a broken man without his older brother and partner. He died of cirrhosis of the liver on December 10, 1920. The Dodge brothers left behind them two tremendous fortunes that caused much family squabbling, a legacy of contributions to the city of Detroit, and a reputation for making solid, dependable cars and trucks that survives to this day.

Further Reading

Pitrone, Jean Maddern, and Joan Potter Elwart, *The Dodges: The Auto Family Fortune and Misfortune,* Icarus Press (South Bend, IN), 1981.

Pitrone, Jean Maddern, *The John Dodge Story,* Meadow Brook Hall Publications, Oakland University (Rochester, MI), n.d.

Pitrone, Jean Maddern, *Tangled Web: Legacy of Auto Pioneer John F. Dodge,* Avenue Publishing (Hamtramck, MI), 1989.

Andrea Doria

In the Mediterranean world of the late Middle Ages, Andrea Doria (1466-1560) was both famous as an adventurer and feared as a ruler. His seafaring skills made him one of the principal maritime commanders of his day, and his alliances with popes and a succession of kings helped make him rich.

"Doria's accomplishments illustrate some of the main themes of Genoese history," noted Steven A. Epstein in *Genoa and the Genoese, 958-1528*. History has not always treated Doria kindly, however, and a reputation as somewhat of a despot remains as a result of his firm control over the city of Genoa during the later years of his career. Yet Genoa was a warring, fractious city-state where democratic ideals often yielded chaos. A member of one of the city of Genoa's oldest aristocratic families, Doria was born in 1466 in Oneglia, in the Duchy of Milan (now Italy). The Dorias were a prominent and powerful force in the Republic of Genoa, in what is present-day Liguria and stretching several hundred miles along the Mediterranean coast from Monaco to the Italian city of Lerici. Its strategic importance on the Mediterranean coast, wedged between territories held by the rival powers of France and Spain, made it a much-coveted ally.

Mediterranean Power

The seaport city of Genoa itself had been a free commune since the tenth century, and during the intervening centuries had become one of Europe's major urban hubs. It was an important trade center, and rivaled Venice as a maritime power on the seas. The Genoa of Doria's day was a winding, medieval city organized by neighborhoods and ruled by a strong internal political culture. It was a city with an extremely stratified social structure, including a large class of laborers and artisans, and at times its various quarters had even battled one another for political power.

The Genoese themselves, however, were anything but insular: their dialect contained elements of the Portuguese language, and a colony on the Black Sea had been established and at times governed by members of the Doria family. Several famous explorers, including Christopher Columbus, were Genoese by birth; the Vivaldis navigated the West African coast and still others ventured out into the Atlantic to discover the Azores and Canary islands. But the Genoese also enjoyed a reputation as tyrants as well: their ships brought back Muslims from the eastern edge of the Mediterranean, who were then purchased by Genoa's

noble families as slaves, and there was a law stipulating that Jewish people could remain no more than three days in the city. They also held the island of Corsica for over 500 years.

The Dorias

Andrea Doria's ancestors had been political leaders in Genoa as far back as 1134. In 1270, Oberto Doria had established a two-family system of government for Genoa with a member of another influential family, the Spinolas. Other Doria forebears were celebrated sailors or statesmen; the cartographer Domenico Doria served as the Mongols' ambassador to Europe in the late thirteenth century. There were also some Dorias who achieved fame through less than admirable methods: one ancestor, Branca Doria, had allegedly murdered his father-in-law, which earned him mention as a resident of hell in Dante's *Inferno*. The political power of the Dorias lessened for a time after a series of late fourteenth-century popular revolts which effectively ended the dominance of the noble families. A political system with an elected magistrate known as a doge, as in Venice, replaced it from 1384 to 1515. The Dorias, however, continued to achieve renown in sea battles against rival Venice.

Andrea Doria was orphaned as a child, and journeyed to Rome as a teenager to serve in the papal army of Pope Innocent VIII, a fellow Genoese, who battled the Turks until his death in 1492. Doria made a pilgrimage to the holy city of Jerusalem in 1495, which was a somewhat rare feat at the time, for it involved an arduous and even perilous trek. As he entered adulthood, he became a mercenary, or soldier-for-hire. He fought for King Ferdinand I, ruler of the Holy Roman Empire, as well as for Genoa's powerful Casa San Georgia, a private financial collective that held great power. He also assisted Domenico Doria, his uncle, in subduing an anti-Italian revolt on the island of Corsica in 1506.

Condottiere

Through his thirties and forties, Doria accumulated much of his wealth by battling corsairs, or pirate ships, along the coast of North Africa, and fighting Turks; both were standard ways by which Genoese nobles earned distinction. These men were known as *condottieres,* or commanders-for-hire, and sailed the Mediterranean in manned galleys. In 1519 Doria won a decisive victory over a Turkish force at Pianosa, which further enhanced his reputation. Back home, however, trouble brewed, and the Holy Roman Emperor Charles V seized Genoa in 1522. The city was mercilessly sacked, and its pro-French rulers were ousted. In response, Doria entered the service of French regent Francis I, Charles V's foe. Francis I gave Doria command of the French fleet on the Mediterranean, and with it Doria scored a decisive victory at Marseilles in 1524. The following year, however, the French were vanquished, and Francis I was seized and put in prison.

Doria then went into the service of Francis I's ally, the Medici Pope Clement VII, who was taken prisoner himself in 1527, the same year Francis was freed. Doria again led a French incursion, and helped retake Genoa from the Holy Roman Empire. Because of France's new policies governing Genoa, Doria became discontented with Francis I, and switched allegiances. In the service of Charles V, he recaptured Genoa for the Empire in September of 1528, and reentered the city greeted by cheering masses of his fellow Genoese. Historians note that Doria's decision to side with the Empire was a savvy one, since in the end it allowed Genoa to maintain some sovereignty instead of being subsumed by France; it also gained the Republic the protection of powerful Spanish kings.

Led Genoa for Three Decades

Doria was now the de facto ruler of the Republic of Genoa, and held the tittle of Grand Admiral of the fleet of the Holy Roman Empire, which Charles V bestowed upon him because of his services to the Empire. He was also granted the princedom of Melfi. His position allowed him the exclusive rights to supply both Charles V and Spain's Philip II with ships, which tied Doria to sailing fortunes then being made across the Atlantic Ocean. Genoa's new ruler was known as a shrewd businessman—preferring, for example, to hire slaves as oarers on his ships: one free oarer cost 13 scudi annually, but a slave could be purchased for 40 scudi and worked for a decade.

As the leader of the city of Genoa, Doria displayed a comparable astuteness. First, he imposed laws that rid the city of its fractious political rivalries, and instituted an oligarchic form of government that returned political power to the aristocrats. Under the terms of a constitution that went into effect under Doria (and lasted until 1797), Genoa was ruled by its four main families, granted a certain number of commoners noble status every year, and was headed by a doge with little actual power. Genoa's political decisions were instead made in two council chambers, the Maggiore Consiglio and the Minore Consiglio. The latter elected the city officials, the doge, and appointed its financial and legal ministers. Supervising this structure were five syndics, of whom Doria was "perpetual prior." His rule, which began in 1528 and endured over thirty years, has been considered a virtual dictatorship; hints of political opposition were sometimes ruthlessly extinguished.

Doria, now a wealthy, powerful, but older man, built a Palazzo del Principe for himself at Fassolo, situated just west of the city walls. He shared it with his wife, the Princess Peretta Uso di Mare. The structure was designed so that he could see every ship entering and departing Genoa's port. Inside, the lavish paintings and frescoes depicted him as a heroic figure from classical mythology, and celebrated him as the one who brought peace. Indeed, Doria did not rest on his laurels in his palace: he still led several naval battles against the Turks well into his sixtieth decade, including a victorious one at Tunis in 1535. Yet his power in Genoa had also earned him enemies, and pro-French families tried to undermine his rule by carrying out a plot that resulted in the murder of his nephew Giannettino Doria in 1547. An investigation uncovered the culprit, and Doria extracted harsh retribution.

At the age of 84 Doria was still sailing in anti-pirate expeditions on the Mediterranean. When war broke out between France and Spain, Doria allied with the Spaniards and captured Corsica from the French. He retired in 1555 from his admiral duties, passing on his post to another grandnephew, Giovanni Andrea Doria. He died on November 25, 1560, just a few days before his 94th birthday; he outlived many of the great names of his era. Perhaps because of the looting of the city by Holy Roman Empire armies in 1522, the portrait of Doria that hangs in one of the city's museums, attributed to Jan Massys, is the first depiction of any of Genoa's rulers. In the twentieth century, a luxury liner was named after him. Unfortunately, the ship bearing his name collided with another ship off the coast of Massachusetts in 1956, resulting in the loss of 44 lives.

Further Reading

Epstein, Steven A. *Genoa and the Genoese, 958-1528,* University of North Carolina Press, 1996.

Daphne du Maurier

In a writing career that spanned over four decades and brought her international renown, Daphne du Maurier (1907-1989) published in a number of different genres. Among her most popular works were those that spun tales of mystery, suspense, and drama, including the classic Gothic novel *Rebecca*.

Daphne du Maurier was born in London, England, in 1907. The du Mauriers were a privileged and prosperous family. Her father, Gerald, was a well-known actor and theater manager whose own father, George, had been an artist and a writer. Her mother, Muriel Beaumont, was an actress until the birth of her third child in 1911. Du Maurier had both an older sister, Angela, and a younger sister, Jeanne.

Gerald du Maurier was a devoted and affectionate father, especially to Daphne. His longing for a son prompted her to dress like a boy, cut her hair short, and adopt an alter ego she named "Eric Avon." As a member of a theatrical family, she found that such imaginative flights of fancy met with encouragement rather than resistance. Upon reaching puberty, however, du Maurier put "Eric" aside. She later referred to this repressed side of herself as "the boy-in-the-box."

Du Maurier was privately educated at home by governesses. Maud Waddell, nicknamed "Tod," was her favorite. She was one of several older women who served as role models for the young girl and tried to make up for her rather cool and distant biological mother. An avid reader from early childhood, du Maurier was especially fond of the works of Walter Scott, W.M. Thackeray, the Brontë sisters, and Oscar Wilde. Other authors who strongly influenced her include R.L. Stevenson, Katherine Mansfield, Guy de Maupassant, and Somerset Maugham. Du Maurier herself began writing during her adolescence as a way to escape reality and in the process discovered more about herself and what she wanted in life. At the age of 18, she completed her

first work, a collection of 15 short stories entitled *The Seekers.*

Attended Finishing School in France

In early 1925, just before her eighteenth birthday, du Maurier left England to attend finishing school at Camposena, a village near Meudon, outside of Paris, France. Life at Camposena was spartan—there was no heat in the rooms and no hot water. But these inconveniences were bearable given the school's close proximity to Paris, which allowed du Maurier to make frequent trips into the city to visit the Louvre, the Opera, and other points of interest.

In 1926, the du Mauriers purchased a vacation home called Ferryside in the town of Fowey, a harbor town on the rocky southwestern coast of Cornwall, England. Daphne had enjoyed previous family holidays to Cornwall during her childhood, and there she cultivated many interests that became lifelong passions. In Fowey she took long walks with her dog, learned to sail, enjoyed swimming, and went dancing. She also found the quiet seaside environment perfect for writing.

Yearned for Independence

After leaving school in France, du Maurier struggled to find her place in the world. Her father's doting attention had turned oppressive; he was suspicious of any young man in whom she expressed an interest. Furthermore, she found the constant entertaining in the family home in London ex-

tremely distracting as she tried to establish her writing career. She longed for financial independence. In the autobiographical work *Daphne du Maurier: Myself When Young,* she recalled the thoughts that went through her mind as she reflected on her plight: "It's no use. I must make money and be independent, but how can I ever make enough? Even if my stories are published they can only bring in a very little. . . . I won't go on the films, that would merely be slaving to no purpose, for I should never have time for anything else."

Eventually du Maurier convinced her family to allow her to live at Ferryside, where she could work undisturbed. She was 22 when she published her first short story, "And Now to God the Father," in the *Bystander.* Her mother's brother, Willie Beaumont, had helped her make the necessary contacts, and she was well aware that her family name was something of an advantage, too. Although the payment she received was modest, it encouraged her to continue writing.

Discovered Inspiration in Rundown Mansion

It was around that same time that she first came across the abandoned estate of Menabilly, near Fowey, which would play such a prominent role in both her personal and professional life. As she later wrote in *Daphne du Maurier: Myself When Young,* "the place called to me." Hidden from view and overgrown with ivy, Menabilly had been empty for many years and was full of dust and mold. But du Maurier was intrigued by the atmosphere of secrecy and decay that enveloped the house and grounds. Visiting the estate stimulated her vivid imagination and left her wondering about those who had lived and died there. Menabilly eventually served as the model for a number of her fictional locales, most notably Manderley in *Rebecca.*

During her early twenties, du Maurier was bursting with ideas for stories. Many of these came to her while on holiday. (She traveled extensively.) Commenting in her diary early in her career on the method of construction she often used in her stories, she noted "how often I seem to build a story around one sentence, nearly always the last one, too." She greatly admired Katherine Mansfield, who may have been her greatest literary influence.

In 1931 du Maurier published her first novel, *The Loving Spirit.* (The title was inspired by lines from an Emily Brontë poem.) The book's success finally made it possible for her to gain financial independence from her family.

First Novel Led to Romance

Among the many fans of *The Loving Spirit* was Major (later Lieutenant-General) Frederick Arthur Montague Browning, a member of the Grenadier Guards. Determined to meet the novel's author, he sailed his boat, the *Ygdrasil* (meaning "Tree of Fate"), into Fowey harbor several times before he could arrange for a neighbor to deliver a note to du Maurier asking if she would like to go out for a sail. The couple first met on April 8, 1932, and were immediately attracted to one another. They were engaged by June, and on July 19, 1932, they married in the Lanteglos Church near

Fowey. In true romantic fashion, the new Mr. and Mrs. Browning then set off in the *Ygdrasil* to begin their life together.

Also in 1932, du Maurier published her second novel, *I'll Never Be Young Again.* It was very different from her first book in that it dealt with sexual issues, which was considered very racy for that time. Another novel, *The Progress of Julius,* followed in 1933. Although neither were as popular as *The Loving Spirit,* they made it clear that du Maurier would not be easily pigeonholed into one genre.

A little over a year after her marriage, du Maurier gave birth to her first child, a daughter named Tessa. (Du Maurier had hoped for a boy, so the arrival of a girl was a source of considerable disappointment.) After Gerald du Maurier's death from colon cancer in 1934, his daughter wrote his biography, which proved to be very successful upon its publication later that same year. This was followed by another novel, *Jamaica Inn,* a suspenseful, melodramatic adventure story set in Cornwall complete with smugglers and villains in a style similar to R.L. Stevenson's *Treasure Island.*

In March 1936 du Maurier sailed to Alexandria, Egypt, to join her husband at his new post, but she hated it and ended up returning to England in January 1937. There she gave birth to her second daughter, Flavia, in April of 1937. That same year, du Maurier published a biographical work on her famous family entitled simply *The Du Mauriers.*

Rebecca Earned Many Accolades

The year 1938 marked the publication of du Maurier's most acclaimed novel, *Rebecca.* Considered a classic work of Gothic fiction, it is a suspenseful psychological mystery that takes place on a ''secretive and silent'' estate known as Manderley. The novel's opening line—''Last night I dreamt I went to Manderley again. . . .''—ranks among the most memorable in modern literature and is typical of du Maurier in that she begins her story with the ending. *Rebecca* was a huge success; compared by some critics to Charlotte Brontë's *Jane Eyre,* it sold over a million copies and was made into a movie directed by Alfred Hitchcock and starring Laurence Olivier and Joan Fontaine. (It went on to win the 1940 Academy Award for best picture.) But du Maurier herself never quite understood its popularity.

On November 3, 1940, du Maurier gave birth to a son, Christian. Another one of her fondest wishes came true in 1943 when she finally signed a lease on her beloved Menabilly. She then proceeded to spend a great deal of money restoring the property, an expense many considered foolish given the wartime shortage of manpower and materials as well as the fact that she did not actually own the house. Du Maurier ignored such comments and went ahead with her plans. She remained at Menabilly for more than 25 years until she was forced to vacate the estate in 1969 when her landlord decided he wanted to live there instead. Du Maurier then settled nearby at Kilmarth, a seaside home in the village of Par.

Throughout her life, writing served as a form of therapy for du Maurier; her days were structured around her various routines, which she found were as important to her creative process as inspiration. From the 1940s through the 1970s, she published many more novels, novellas, biographies, autobiographies, and short-story collections. Du Maurier's growing interest in the supernatural was reflected in some of her later work in particular, which blended her usual suspense with a touch of the macabre. The combination translated well to the screen; in addition to *Rebecca,* seven of her novels and one short story, ''The Birds,'' were made into movies.

In 1967, du Maurier branched out into yet another genre when she and her son collaborated on a travel book about the Cornish countryside entitled *Vanishing Cornwall.* It featured du Maurier's text accompanied by Christian Browning's photographs. In 1971 Browning made a film of their joint effort that also proved to be a great success.

Du Maurier spent her later years walking, traveling, and writing. She eventually lost her appetite for life after her creativity and imagination began to fail her. By the late 1980s her health had declined to the point that she required nursing care, and on April 20, 1989, she died in her sleep at the age of 81 at her home in Par.

Further Reading

Contemporary Authors, Volumes 5-8, First Revision, Gale, 1969.
Contemporary Literary Criticism, Volume 6, Gale, 1976.
du Maurier, Daphne, *Myself When Young: The Shaping of a Writer,* Doubleday, 1977.
Forster, Margaret, *Daphne du Maurier: The Secret Life of the Renowned Storyteller,* Doubleday, 1993.
New York Times, April 20, 1989, sec. 2, p. 13.

E

Umberto Eco

Umberto Eco (born 1932) is a best-selling author of mystery novels that reflect his many intellectual interests and wide-ranging knowledge of philosophy, literature, medieval history, religion, and politics. His academic work in semiotics, the science of signs by which individuals and cultures communicate, has made important contributions to studies of popular culture as well as to communication science and information theory.

Umberto Eco was born in a small town in northwest Italy, the only son of an accountant. When World War II broke out, his family fled to the country to escape the bombing. There he observed conflicts between the Fascists and the partisans and experienced wartime deprivations that would later become a part of his second novel, *Foucault's Pendulum.* After the war, he entered the University of Turin to study law, but soon switched to medieval philosophy and literature. Partly as a result of his involvement with Italy's national organization for Catholic youth, he wrote a dissertation on St. Thomas Aquinas and in 1954 was awarded a doctorate of philosophy.

After graduation, Eco worked for Italian state television as "Editor for Cultural Programs," which gave him an opportunity to observe modern culture as a journalist. He published his first book, *The Aesthetics of Thomas Aquinas,* in 1956 and began lecturing at the University of Turin. Following a brief period of military service, when he pursued further studies in medieval philosophy and aesthetics, he published a second book, *Art and Beauty in the Middle Ages,* which established him as a leading medieval scholar. After losing his job, Eco became an editor for Casa Editrice Bompiani, a prominent publisher in Milan, and began writing a monthly column of parodies for an avant-garde magazine. In 1962 he published *The Open Work,* which outlined his developing view that because modern art is ambiguous and open to many interpretations, the reader's responses and interpretations are an essential part of any text.

Throughout the 1960s, Eco's academic work began to focus on semiotics, a discipline which holds that all intellectual and cultural activity can be interpreted as systems of signs. He also continued to write for a wide variety of scholarly and popular publications and taught at universities in Florence and Milan while broadening his interests to include the semiotic analysis of non-literary forms such as architecture, movies, and comic books. In 1971 he became the first professor of semiotics at Europe's oldest university, the University of Bologna, and in 1974 he organized the first congress of the International Association for Semiotic Studies. At this meeting he summarized his view that semiotics was a "scientific attitude" that he had begun to use in examining subjects as diverse as James Bond, the literature of James Joyce, and revolutionary comic books from China. In 1976 he published a systematic examination of his views in *A Theory of Semiotics.*

In 1978, however, Eco's career took a dramatic new turn. At a friend's invitation, he decided to write a detective story. He also decided to make it a demonstration of his own literary theories of an "open text" that would provide the reader with almost infinite possibilities for interpretation in the signs and clues the protagonist must decode in order to solve a mystery. Set in a fourteenth-century monastery, *The Name of the Rose* is the story of a monk who tries to solve

several murders while struggling to defend his quest for the truth against church officials. A main theme of the novel is Eco's own love of books, and the solution to the murders ultimately lies in coded manuscripts and secret clues in the abbey's library. Dense with learned references and untranslated Latin, it is both an exhaustively detailed murder mystery and Eco's semiotic metaphor for the reader's own quest to derive meaning on many levels from the signs in a work of art. Its publishers expected to sell no more than 30,000 copies, but the novel became an international bestseller. In 1986 it was made into a film starring Sean Connery and Christian Slater.

Eco's second novel, *Foucault's Pendulum*, is an even more ambitious attempt to incorporate Eco's ideas of the limits of interpretation into a mystery story. Three editors who work for a seedy publisher in contemporary Milan concoct a fake conspiracy theory that the medieval Knights Templar had devised a plan for harnessing all the energy in the universe. With the aid of a computer, they invent an elaborate web of links between the Templars and numerous other figures and events, gradually reinterpreting all of history. Eventually, the editors begin to believe their own fabrications, in the end becoming the victims of their own imagined conspiracy. Published in 1988, this book also became a bestseller, although critical reception was mixed. Clyde Haberman, writing in the *New York Times,* called it "a kitchen sink of scholarship," while Salmon Rushdie in *The Observer* called it "mind-numbingly full of gobbledygook of all sorts." The Vatican's official newspaper denounced it for its "vulgarities," and the Pope condemned Eco as "the mystifier deluxe."

In 1994 Eco published *The Island of the Day Before,* which pays homage to Robinson Crusoe. It is the story of a seventeenth-century Italian castaway, marooned on a ship in the South Pacific, who recalls fragments of his past as he explores the deserted vessel. That same year he also published *The Search for the Perfect Language,* an account of historical attempts to reconstruct a primal language, and *Role of the Reader: Explorations in the Semiotics of Texts,* in which he describes the "model reader" as "one who plays your game" and accepts the challenge of interpreting complex ideas. In an interview with the *Washington Post,* Eco declared that he considered it a compliment for his work to be described as difficult: "Only publishers and television people believe that people crave easy experiences."

In recent years Eco has become increasingly involved in debates of how electronic media and computer technologies will affect culture and society. At the International Center for Semiotic and Cognitive Science in San Marino in 1994, he organized a seminar on the future of the book that attracted hypermedia experts from around the world. His own observations on the Internet, virtual reality, and hypertext have appeared in *Encyclomedia,* a CD-ROM history of philosophy that he helped to develop. Recently he has become involved with the Multimedia Arcade, a complex in Bologna offering Internet access, a computer training center, and a public multimedia library.

Eco believes that although the Internet and CD-ROMs will change the way we read and write, the fundamental problem posed by the new media is the sheer volume of unfiltered information. Broadcasting live over the Internet at Columbia University in 1996, he outlined a hope that computer technology will make possible hypertexts which are unlimited and infinite. "We are marching toward a more liberated society in which free creativity will co-exist with textual interpretation," he said, but we will need a "new form of critical competence . . . "a new kind of educational training, a new wisdom" to cope with the sheer quantity of information.

In spite of advances in hypertext and other means of recombining information electronically, he is optimistic that books as we know them will remain the fundamental currency of language. Writing in *The Nation,* he asserted that "books still represent the most economical, flexible, wash-and-wear way to transport information at very low cost." Books will remain essential not only for literature but for "any circumstance in which one needs to read carefully, not only to receive information but also to speculate and reflect about it." In his opinion, a device which allows us to invent new texts has nothing to do with our ability to interpret pre-existing texts.

Eco is an avid book collector who has apartments in Milan, Bologna, and Paris, as well as a summer home near Rimini. In addition to running the Program for Communication Sciences at the University of Bologna, he travels frequently to speak and teach. He continues to publish scholarly treatises, which number almost two dozen, and to contribute to several foreign and Italian newspapers. He also edits a weekly column for the magazine *L'Espresso.*

Further Reading

Bondanella, Peter, ed.,*Dictionary of Italian Literature,* Greenwood, 1996.
Bondanella, Peter, *Umberto Eco and the Open Text: Semiotics, Fiction, Popular Culture,* Cambridge University, 1997.
Capozzi, Rocco, ed., *Reading Eco: An Anthology,* Indiana University, 1997.
Civilization, June 1997.
Harper's, January 1995; October 1996.
The Nation, January 6, 1997.
Newsweek, September 29, 1986.
New York Review of Books, February 2, 1995.
New York Times, December 13, 1988; October 11, 1989; December 10, 1989; October 22, 1995; Novemer 28, 1995.
New Yorker, May 24, 1993.
Le Nouvel Observateur, October 17, 1991.
Observer, October 15, 1989.
Time, March 6, 1989.
US News and World Report, November 20, 1989.
Washington Post, December 19, 1993.
Wired, March 1997.
"Biblio Feature," *Biblio,* http://www. bibliomag.com (April 8, 1998).
"Eco: Internet Will Not Replace Books," *Columbia University Record,* http:// www.columbia.edu/cu/record (April 9, 1998).
"A Conversation on Information," *Multimedia World* interview, http://www.cudenver.edu (April 9, 1998).
"Umberto Eco," *Porta Ludovica,* http://www.rpg.net/quail/libyrinth/eco (March 24, 1998).
"Umberto Eco," http://www4.ncsu.edu/eos (April 4, 1998). □

Nora Ephron

The daughter of successful Hollywood screenwriters, Nora Ephron (born 1941) herself won acclaim during the 1980s for such screenplays as the Academy Award-nominated *Silkwood* and the highly successful comedy *When Harry Met Sally.* In the 1990s Ephron turned to film directing with such works as *This Is My Life* and the romantic comedy *Sleepless in Seattle.*

Success has marked every phase of Nora Ephron's career as a journalist, novelist, screenwriter, and movie director. Viewing her life and the lives of others, particularly intimates, as material for her works, she is famous for her observations of other people's lives, as well as for her own personal revelations. Ephron was a pioneer of "new journalism" in the 1970s, writing bold essays about social issues of the day, as well as other writers' views. The novel and movie *Heartburn* turned the very public breakup of her second marriage into a best-seller. Such screenplays as *Silkwood* and *When Harry Met Sally* followed and became box office hits. Destined to be in the director's chair, she directed *Sleepless in Seattle,* the 1994 romantic comedy blockbuster.

The daughter of screenwriters Henry and Phoebe Ephron, Ephron and her three sisters grew up in Beverly Hills, amid its glamorous people and surroundings. Her parents had started their careers in New York collaborating on plays, but when Ephron was three, they decided to try parlaying their successes on stage to the screen and moved West. They were among the top screenwriters of the day, and such actors as James Cagney, Marilyn Monroe, Katharine Hepburn, and Spencer Tracy starred in movies they wrote. With such hits as *Carousel, There's No Business Like Show Business,* and *What Price Glory,* the Ephrons set high standards for excellence for their four daughters. Phoebe Ephron, especially, had high expectations and a determined, no-nonsense approach to life—yet, she added to that an infectious sense of humor. In an interview with *Vanity Fair,* Nora Ephron reminisced about her childhood, remembering singing rounds at the dinner table and playing charades afterward. "There was always a great deal of laughter," she said. The atmosphere was electric with creativity and famous people, as well as the daily traumas of raising a family of four.

A Mind of Her Own

As writers, the Ephrons thoroughly processed the rich material of everyday life and drew upon their experiences, as well as their children's—especially Nora's—for inspiration. Talking, often telling stories around the dinner table became a family ritual. More than her sisters, Ephron enjoyed and thrived in the nightly competitions to tell the best story. That environment helped her polish a budding hu-

mor, which in turn helped her compensate for being a skinny, dark-haired flatchested teen in Beverly Hills High School—a place where appearance was of utmost importance. A classmate recalled in *Vanity Fair,* "Her wit made up for not having the beauty; it was 'Don't mess with me.'" Later, Ephron's letters home from college became the basis for *Take Her, She's Mine.* Family lore has it that Ephron was named for Henrik Ibsen's feminist protagonist in *A Doll's House,* her parents perhaps foreseeing their first born's gift as an outspoken, independent thinker.

Ephron learned how to make the best of what life offered. According to Leslie Bennetts in *Vanity Fair,*" 'No matter what happens,' her mother was fond of saying, 'It's all copy.'" Years later Ephron told a reporter for *New Statesman & Society,* "I think what I learned from my mother was a basic lesson of humor, which is, if you slip on a banana peel, people will laugh at you; but if you tell people you slipped, it's your story—you are in fact the heroine of slipping on the banana peel."

Comedy or Tragedy

From beneath the laughter, a dark side began to emerge. As Bennetts commented in *Vanity Fair,* it took the girls years to realize that their mother drank too much. Life became increasingly chaotic with their father suffering from manic-depression, and their mother suffering from alcoholism and cirrhosis of the liver, which took her life at 57. The youngest daughter, Amy, added, "Mommy was this sort of closet alcoholic, where her best friends didn't know she drank . . . father was drinking, and it was horrible; my parents used to scream all night. I remember Nora coming home from college one year and she suddenly realized what was going on. We got different parents; she got the upswing, and I got the downswing." Ephron recalled visiting her mother in the hospital near the end and hearing her say, "Take notes, Nora, take notes."

Ephron was determined to leave the West Coast and assert her independence. "I grew up in L.A. knowing that if I didn't get out of there I would die," she later recalled. From Wellesley she headed straight to New York, where she started honing her craft as a reporter at the *New York Post.* Soon she was making the rounds to magazines and getting assignments from *Esquire* and *New York.* On the surface, it appears that she intended to follow the career path of her parents, but the opposite is true. Going into journalism as far away as she could from Hollywood, movies, and screenwriting was her form of rebellion. She became one of the wittiest essayists of the 1970s, challenging the wisdom of luminaries of the day, including Betty Friedan and Brendan Bill. No subject—or person—was off limits; she described male oppression in an article on women in magazine publishing, and took public the stories of famous women betrayed by their husband's infidelity. She gained stature as a respected writer, and notoriety for her no-holds-barred approach. One of her greatest pleasures was criticizing celebrity journalists. During this time her marriage to humorist Dan Greenburg ended acrimoniously after she learned he was having an affair with her best friend.

Then, in an ironic twist of fate, Ephron married the epitome of celebrity journalists, Carl Bernstein, who, along with Bob Woodward, wrote the famous Watergate expose of then President Richard Nixon. The popular "perfect couple" made headlines. It appeared as if they had it all—until the day Ephron learned, after everyone else, that her husband was having an affair with the wife of the British ambassador. To make matters worse, Ephron was pregnant with their second child. In addition to feeling angry, hurt, and humiliated, she felt—and was made to look—stupid. She told *Vanity Fair'* s Bennetts, "I think probably the feeling I like least in the whole world is feeling dumb. I think it was foolish and pathetic of me to have thought it could have worked." The lessons of her youth paid off; she had learned how to take whatever cards life dealt and turn them into a winning hand. She vowed to regain control of her life and not to be a victim.

A Return to Independence

In the wake of her failed second marriage, Ephron returned to home base, which she considered to be New York, re-established herself, and settled in to exorcise this episode from her life by writing the novel *Heartburn.* An article in *Time* summarized: "The humiliation described in the novel is that she, the witty observer of other people's lives, was unaware of what was going on in her own. The book was her way of ending up knowing more than anyone else. . . ." She evidently hit a nerve because her (by then) ex-husband Bernstein spent years in court trying to prevent her from making the book into a movie. Eventually a watered-down version was made into a film that had mediocre box office results. In the end, Ephron succeeded—she got the satisfaction of revenge and made money on the book and movie.

As a single mother, financial security became a primary concern, and Ephron turned to screenwriting hoping it would prove to be as lucrative for her as it had been for her parents. She began collaborating with Alice Arlen, with whom she wrote *Silkwood* and *Cookie,* among others, but saved the screenplay of *Heartburn* as a solo venture. *When Harry Met Sally,* another independent project, was a huge success. Vindicated personally and professionally, she decided to risk marriage a third time. In 1981, Ephron married author and screenwriter Nicholas Pileggi.

The more time Ephron spent shepherding her work from paper to film, the more she yearned for full control. She set her sights on directing, and in 1992 broke through Hollywood's gender barrier to direct her first movie, *This Is My Life,* co-written with her sister Delia. Somewhat surprisingly for a woman with two bitter divorces under her belt, the film that solidified her reputation as a director was the 1994 romantic comedy *Sleepless in Seattle.* When asked by a reporter from *Rolling Stone* how she managed to remain a believer in romance, she replied, "If I weren't a romantic, why would I keep doing it? There's no one who's more romantic than a cynic."

It's All Copy

Directing provides Ephron with long-sought professional fulfillment. She admitted in *Rolling Stone* that some friends even say her sharp tongue is mellowing and attribute the change in disposition to Pileggi. Others partially agree, but add, "She's a very hungry woman. . . . hungry for all the things her parents had—ability, power, the right friends." However, as a commentator in *Time* noted, if Ephron listens to herself, she'll remember that one of the themes in *Heartburn* "is that no one can have it all, that life unravels faster that you can weave it back together." So, make the most of today.

Further Reading

New Statesman and Society, June 30, 1995, p. 32.
New York, April 11, 1994, p. 7.
Rolling Stone, July 8, 1993, pp. 73-75.
Time, January 27, 1992, pp. 62-63.
Vanity Fair, February, 1992, pp. 76-90.

M. C. Escher

M.C. Escher (1898-1972) produced work that remains among the most widely reproduced and popular graphic art of the twentieth century. His brain-teasing prints use interlocking shapes, transforming creatures, and impossible architectures to challenge the viewer's perceptions of reality. Expressing what he called a "keen interest in the geometric laws contained by nature around us," his finely crafted compositions combine precise realism with fantastic explorations of pattern, perspective, and space.

Maurits Cornelis Escher (who called himself M.C.) was the youngest son of a hydraulic engineer but showed no early aptitude for mathematical concepts. He was such a poor student, in fact, that he twice had to repeat a grade. He did show some artistic talent and so was encouraged by an art teacher to pursue his interests in woodcuts and drawing. His father then sent him to the School for Architectural and Decorative Arts in Haarlem to study architecture. Within a few days of his arrival, a graphics instructor named Samuel Jesserun de Mesquita recognized that his talent lay not in architecture but in the decorative arts. Escher soon transferred to a graphic arts curriculum and within two years had become such an accomplished printmaker that de Mesquita encouraged him to leave academia in favor of professional work. Escher considered his teacher such an important influence that he kept a photograph of him on his cupboard for the rest of his life.

Early Works Inspired by Italian Landscape

In 1921 Escher first visited Italy with his parents and discovered the Italian landscapes and architecture that he would depict in his prints for the next fifteen years. The steep slopes and clustered dwellings of the Amalfi coast and the stark Abruzzi mountains provided his first inspirations for exploring the illusions of perspective and spatial structure. On a trip to Spain the following year he visited the Alhambra Palace for the first time. Its complex Moorish ornaments and highly abstract designs had a profound effect on his later work. On his next trip to Italy in 1923, he met the woman who would become his wife, Jetta, and moved with her to Rome. For the next few years he regularly traveled to rugged areas of Italy, Corsica, and Sicily, often in the company of other artists, to sketch and record his impressions. During this time he began to show his prints and develop a reputation as a graphic artist, but he was principally supported by his family. One of his first prints to draw critical attention was *Castrovalva,* a lithograph of a small town in the Abruzzi region.

By the early 1930s, the rise of fascism was beginning to make life in Italy uncomfortable for the Eschers, who now had two young sons. In July of 1935, they moved to Chateau d'Oex in Switzerland. From May to June in 1936, Escher and Jetta made their last study trip by freighter along the coast of Spain. Escher received free passage in exchange for prints of the sketches he would make along the route. On this trip he made detailed sketches of the Alhambra and of the mosque La Mezquita in Cordoba. This exposure to the repeating motifs and complex abstract patterns of Islamic design, which contains no recognizable human or animal forms and is created from a center outward, inspired the pursuit which occupied the rest of his creative life—the regular division of a plane. From this point on, his work turned dramatically from landscapes to invented images and the mathematical principles which underlie nature. After 1936 he used natural elements only in the service of more abstract explorations and subjects.

As war threatened Europe, Escher decided to move closer to his homeland, so in 1937 the Eschers moved to Belgium. By this time Escher had begun a systematic study of periodic surface division and tessellation, the creation of a pattern of shapes that continuously covers a surface. He also discovered a mathematical paper on plane symmetry groups and began to incorporate its principles into his work, even though he did not fully understand many of the abstract concepts it described. One of his most famous prints, *Day and Night,* was produced during this same period and illustrates his interest in dualities and transformations. In it, a flat surface of farmland gradually is transformed into mirror images of two flocks of black and white geese who migrate east and west simultaneously, confusing the viewer with a two-dimensional image which appears to be three-dimensional.

In 1941 Escher moved to Baarn, Holland, where he remained for the rest of his life. During the war, he visited the deserted house of his teacher de Mesquita and salvaged the prints that had been scattered there when German troops took the family away to a concentration camp, where they died. From this time on he lived quietly and continued to explore such concepts as capturing infinity within a single plane, self-similarity, and the relativity of perspective, as in *High and Low,* which depicts the same scene from above and below. He also developed an interest in purely geometric figures and crystals. In the mid-1950s he began producing so-called impossible figures, visual riddles which follow the logic of pictorial representation yet could not possibly exist in reality.

International Recognition in the 1950s

By the early 1950s Escher's work had begun to draw the attention of scientists and the public, although he was largely ignored by art critics. He exchanged ideas with mathematicians, although he claimed to be "absolutely innocent of training or knowledge in the exact sciences," and in turn influenced them. Articles on his work were published in *Time* and *Life,* and his work began to be displayed in galleries. Recognition from the art world finally arrived in a 1951 article in *The Studio,* which referred to Escher as "a remarkable and original artist who was able to depict the poetry of the mathematical side of things in a most striking way." In 1954, his work was exhibited in a large show as part of an international mathematics conference in Amsterdam. During this time he continued exploring approaches to infinity and in 1956 produced *Print Gallery,* which he considered the pinnacle of his expression as an artist and thinker.

In the 1960s, Escher's visual illusions and paradoxes found a new audience among academics who were questioning conventional views of human perception and exploring alternative views of nature. Escher's work was seen as relevant to new views of geology, chemistry, and psychology as well as to more inclusive views of the physical relationships of time and space. His work was even more popular among college students and in the counterculture, which was questioning accepted views of normal experience and testing the limits of perception with hallucinogenic drugs. He became a cult figure whose images were reproduced on so many different ordinary objects and became so much a part of popular culture that the Escher Foundation, formed late in his life, spent much time and effort trying to control the unauthorized use of his work.

Although he was flattered by his following among young people, he did not encourage their mystical interpretations of his images, saying, "I have had a fine old time expressing concepts in visual terms, with no other aim than to find out ways of putting them on paper. All I am doing in my prints is to offer a report of my discoveries." To a woman who claimed to find illustrations of reincarnation in *Reptiles,* he replied, "Madam, if that's the way you see it, so be it." Far from symbolic, his work is the "pictorial representation of intellectual understanding," according to Bruno Ernst in The Magic Mirror of M.C. Escher, and is "strictly rational; every illusion . . . is the result of a totally reasoned construction" and the endpoint of a quest to discover new insights into how space can be depicted on a flat surface. Although his imagery became part of a cultural trend toward transcending the limits of rationality, Escher's goal was to "testify that we live in a beautiful and orderly world, not in a chaos without norms." Far from challenging sanity itself, he

wanted merely to demonstrate "the nonsensicalness of some of what we take to be irrefutable certainties."

In the 1960s critics began to place Escher among the great thinkers of art for whom the act of seeing and reproducing visual images required careful examination of the fundamentals of perception. In *Jardin des Arts,* Albert Flocon wrote in 1965 that his work "teaches us that the most perfect surrealism is latent in reality, if only one will take the trouble to get at the underlying principles of it." A retrospective of Escher's work was held in the Hague in 1968, and the government of the Netherlands commissioned a film about him in 1970. Even though his work had begun to sell well, he continued to live frugally late in life and gave away much of his income. In 1969 he created his last great print, *Snakes,* and was forced by declining health in 1970 to move to a nursing home for artists in Laren, Holland. He died on March 27, 1972.

In the 1980s, Escher's work reached another audience with the publication of a Pulitzer Prize-winning book by Douglas Hofstadter that used many features of his work as examples of "Strange Loops," intricate structures and forms that paradoxically represent an endless process in a finite way. As in some musical compositions or computer programs, the Strange Loops of Escher's images draw the viewer into a system with many coexisting levels of structure which may be part of an infinite cycle that only leads back to the starting point. Escher's work also began to be used in the classroom for hands-on demonstration of geometric and mathematical principles. In 1995 the National Gallery of Canada held an exhibition of his work that was accompanied by a forum to investigate how Escher's work could be used to integrate teaching of the visual arts, mathematics, and music.

Centenary Celebrations

To celebrate the centennial of Escher's birth, the National Gallery of Art held a retrospective exhibition in 1997-98 which included many rare early works as well as his most famous images. The *New York Times* critic wrote of it that "the viewer is presented with little more than a reasonable facsimile of the art experience, one that is challenging without being demanding, magical without being genuinely mysterious, that tickles the mind without genuinely stirring the emotions." Other critics, however, agreed with the public that Escher's well-crafted images "tease the mind in a way that's comfortable and inviting." In the *Washington Post,* Henry Allen observed: "Escher is for people who savor the infinities implied by master craftsmanship and enjoy spending an hour or so in the pristine gloaming and mathematical mortalities and mischief of Planet Thought."

An international congress of scholars in Italy celebrated Escher's multifaceted contributions in 1998 with noted speakers from mathematics, science, art, education, psychology, and other disciplines. Commemorative exhibitions were also held in Greece, Great Britain, the United States, and elsewhere. Escher's prints have become prized by collectors, and many books, articles, and CD-ROMs exploring his legacy have been produced since his death. New generations of enthusiasts continue to respond to his playful, imaginative manipulations of reality whose aim, he wrote, was above all to "awaken wonder in the minds of my viewers."

Further Reading

Coxeter, H.S.M., ed., *M.C. Escher, Art and Science: Proceedings of the International Congress on M.C. Escher, Rome, Italy, 26-28 March 1985,* Elsevier, 1986.

Ernst, Bruno, *The Magic Mirror of M.C. Escher,* Random House, 1976.

Hofstadter, Douglas R., *Gödel, Escher, Bach: An Eternal Golden Braid,* Vintage, 1979.

Locher, J.L., ed., *Escher: The Complete Graphic Work,* Thames and Hudson, 1992.

Locher, J.L., ed., *M.C. Escher: His Life and Complete Graphic Work,* Abrams, 1982.

Schattschneider, Doris, *Visions of Symmetry: Notebooks, Periodic Drawings, and Related Work of M.C. Escher,* W.H. Freeman, 1990.

Chronicle of Higher Education, December 19, 1997.

Insight on the News, March 23, 1998.

New York Times, January 15, 1989; September 15, 1996; January 21, 1998.

School Arts, October, 1995.

Scientific American, February, 1993; November 1994.

Washington Post, October 26, 1997.

"Escher98: The Centennial Congress," *Centennial Congress on M.C. Escher,* http://www.mat.uniroma1.it (April 4, 1998).

"M.C. Escher: A Centennial Tribute," *National Gallery of Art Escher Exhibit,* http://www.nga.gov (March 26, 1998).

"Biography of M.C. Escher," *Thames and Hudson's Escher Interactive,* http://www.thameshudson.co.uk (April 4, 1998).

"An Invitation from the National Gallery of Canada," http://www.umanitoba.ca/cm (April 4,1998).

F

Herbert Feigl

Austrian-born American philosopher of science Herbert Feigl (born 1902) is a major influence in the field of modern philosophy.

Herbert Feigl has achieved renown in the realm of modern twentieth-century philosophical currents, initially as a member of one well-regarded movement centered in Vienna in the 1920s; he would later be credited for transporting much of its ideology and spirit to American shores when he immigrated from Austria as a young academic at that decade's close. Feigl, whose main interests lie in the philosophy of science and epistemology—the branch of philosophy concerned with the origin and nature of knowledge—founded the Minnesota Center for Philosophy of Science in 1953. Since then the Center has become a distinguished nucleus for the discussion and development of new threads in the field of modern philosophy.

Feigl was born in Reichenberg, Austria, in December of 1902; though it would later become the Czech Republic, Reichenberg was situated in what was then the Austro-Hungarian Empire. After the end of the first World War, this area became a part of Czechoslovakia known as the Sudetenland. Feigl's father, Otto, was an industrialist, and as a youth Feigl proved himself especially gifted in academics and planned to become a chemist. When he was 16, however, he discovered a treatise on Albert Einstein's theory of relativity, and, intrigued, set out to disprove it. Published in 1905, Einstein's famous theory posited a new view of space and time: the physicist argued that absolute motion did not exist, instead only relative motion between two systems or

frames of reference was crucial. Space and time were seen as interconnected and making up a four-dimensional continuum Einstein named "Space-Time."

The University of Vienna

Inspired by such new ideas, Feigl took up the study math and physics with a vigor. He chose the renowned University of Munich for further study, and headed there in 1921 to spend a year as a student of professors who were either already well-established and influential in their fields, or would later gain such distinction. After reading a work by Edgar Zilsel, Feigl decided to pursue a degree in philosophy. One of his mentors during this first year was Moritz Schlick, and when Schlick took a teaching post at the University of Vienna, Feigl followed him there. He spent a good part of the 1920s at the Austrian university, where he studied math, psychology, and theoretical physics. He also penned his first significant paper while still a student: "The Philosophical Significance of Einstein's Theory of Relativity," which won a 1922 prize.

In 1924 Feigl joined a weekly discussion group with Schlick and others that became known as the "Vienna Circle." He would remain an integral member of the group until his immigration to the United States in 1930, and played a not unimportant role in the formulation of its ideology. Rudolf Carnap and the mathematician Kurt Goedel were, along with Schlick, the leading names of the Vienna Circle and the school of philosophy to which it would become closely linked, logical positivism. Another term for this concept is "scientific empiricism," and it arose out of the modern, early twentieth-century writings of philosophers Bertrand Russell, Ludwig Wittgenstein, and G.E. Moore.

135

Logical Positivism

At their weekly gatherings, Feigl and other members of the Vienna Circle gave form to logical positivism as a school of philosophy. It was an attempt to bring the methodology and precision of the mathematical sciences to the study of philosophy, much as the recently developed movement in philosophy known as "symbolic logic" had replaced ordinary language with mathematical terms. Logical positivism offered the idea that metaphysical speculation (in other words, the "unknowable," or to a religious believer, the "divine") was invalid and absurd as a philosophical concept. The group also argued that logical and mathematical propositions were tautological, or easily clarified in the most simplistic terms ("Either the sun will shine today, or it will not shine") and that any statements regarding morals or values were merely a reflection of human emotion. Finally, the Vienna Circle held that the function of philosophy was to interpret ideas and theories in both everyday and scientific language.

Feigl and the Vienna Circle were greatly influenced by the aforementioned Wittgenstein and his *Tractatus Logico-philosophicus* of 1921. This work argued that an intertwined relationship existed between language, thought, and the world. Wittgenstein wrote that in order to "understand" a sentence, the listener must first discern the reference of its various parts, both to one another and to what is real. The philosopher also posited that language could indeed testify to an area beyond itself, that it could express things that were not tangible or demonstrable, and furthermore, maintained that nonsensical statements could yield philosophical insight. These latter ideas allowed for the possibility of the metaphysical, and it was at this point that Wittgenstein and the logical positivists diverged.

Feigl, still a University of Vienna student, and the already established Wittgenstein were known to enter into spirited debates at Schlick's home during Vienna Circle meetings. In 1927, Feigl earned his Ph.D. with the dissertation "Chance and Law: An Epistemological Investigation of Induction and Probability in the Natural Sciences." His first teaching job was at Vienna's Volkshochschule ("People's Institute"), a select continuing education curriculum for adults, where his first class in 1927 was on the fundamentals of astronomy. Eventually he became an instructor in philosophy and his classes grew quite popular. The post allowed him to pursue the further development of his own ideas, and in 1929 his first book was published, *Theorie und Erfahrung in der Physik* ("Theory and Experience in Physics"). The work received a favorable mention from Einstein.

Feigl and Bauhaus

During the late 1920s Feigl became acquainted with the Bauhaus school of art and architecture in Germany, a controversial movement that was sometimes vilified in its day but later respected as an integral force in twentieth-century design. In classes at the Bauhaus, instructors such as Laszlo Moholy-Nagy and Marcel Breuer taught students how to apply the machine-age concepts of the industrial revolution to craftsmanship. It was a spirit and way of thinking which fit naturally into the Vienna Circle's ethos, and

Feigl cultivated particular ties with the painters Paul Klee and Wassily Kandinsky.

Feigl arrived in the United States at the behest of the Rockefeller Foundation, which had made him a fellow for the academic year 1930-1931. He spent part of it at Harvard University, and the following year wed psychologist Maria Kasper. The couple would have one child, Eric Otto. Feigl was then hired by the University of Iowa, where he began as a lecturer in 1931, and was promoted to assistant professor the next year. He was made associate professor of philosophy in 1938, and spent the next two years in this capacity. He had already become a naturalized U.S. citizen in 1937. Another Rockefeller Foundation fellowship in 1940 enabled him to work at Columbia and Harvard universities as part of his investigations into the methodology of scientific explanation. To accomplish this he held discussions with many great minds in philosophy at Harvard at the time, including Bertrand Russell. His growing reputation attracted the attention of the philosophy faculty at the University of Minnesota at Minneapolis, and he was hired as a professor of philosophy in 1940. He would spend the rest of his academic career there, and his and other well-known names in the field became virtually synonymous with the university's philosophy department and its outstanding reputation.

Founded Center

Part of that standing was the result of Feigl's founding of the Minnesota Center for Philosophy of Science in 1953. This institute, for which he served as director for decades, invited distinguished international names in philosophy for seminars and discussions, and soon gained a reputation as an important nucleus in the study of philosophy. Moreover, the Center was known for its cordial ambiance, despite the serious and dissenting opinions argued there. Feigl's Center, it was noted, seemed to carry on the spirit of the Vienna Circle, which disintegrated with the rising threat of Nazism in Austria, Germany, and the rest of Europe. "The atmosphere at the Center," wrote Paul K. Feyerabend in the introduction to *Mind, Matter, and Method: Essays in Philosophy and Science in Honor of Herbert Feigl,* "and especially Feigl's own attitude, his humor, his eagerness to advance philosophy and to get at least a glimpse at the truth, and his quite incredible modesty, made impossible from the very beginning that subjective tension that occasionally accompanies debate and that is liable to turn individual contributions into proclamations of faith rather than into answers to the questions chosen."

Feyerabend also offered laudatory words about Feigl's oratorical talent: "His wit and his ability to put complex problems in simple language have convinced many doubters among scientists (who are often likely to frown upon what they think is useless mental gymnastics) and among laymen that philosophy cannot be such a monster after all, and he has also done a great deal to ally the fairly prevalent impression that an empiricist is bound to be a dry and unimaginative bore."

The University of Minnesota named Feigl a Regents Professor in 1967, and bestowed upon him the honor of professor emeritus in 1971. The numerous books published under his name include *Readings in Philosophical Analysis,* a 1949 tome written with Wilfrid Sellars; a treatise co-authored with Grover Maxwell in 1962, *Scientific Explanation, Space, and Time; The "Mental" and the "Physical,"* published in 1967; and *Inquiries and Provocations: Selected Writings, 1929-1974,* published in 1981. During his long career Feigl has served as vice president of the American Association for the Advancement of Science, and president of the American Philosophical Association.

Further Reading

Contemporary Authors, Permanent Series, Volume 1, Gale, 1975.
Mind, Matter, and Method: Essays in Philosophy and Science in Honor of Herbert Feigl, edited by Paul K. Feyerabend and Grover Maxwell, University of Minnesota Press, 1966.
Thinkers of the Twentieth Century, second edition, edited by Roland Turner, St. James Press, 1987.

Howard Ferguson

A composer, musician and musicologist, Howard Ferguson (born 1908) is perhaps best known for his compositions which are characterized by lyricism and integrity of structure; as well as his editing of early keyboard music.

Howard Ferguson's musical career is notable in that he made significant contributions in several areas of music. He was a performer, a composer, and an editor of music. His music has ranged from orchestral works to pieces for choir; yet all of his work was characterized by lyricism, good use of structure and harmony, and an adherence to the classical model of music.

Ferguson, through his editing, resurrected early keyboard works which had laid dormant for years. He also had the wherewithal to know when he was done with composition; he stopped composing midway through his career claiming that he'd said all he wished to say.

Education and Musical Premier

Ferguson was born in Belfast, North Ireland in 1908 to Stanley (a banker) and and Frances (Carr) Ferguson. When Ferguson was 13, his piano playing was noticed by the musician Harold Samuel, who offered to direct Ferguson's music education. With the consent of his parents, he relocated to London to receive a general education at Westminster School between 1922-1924. From 1924-1928 Ferguson continued his musical education at the British Royal Conservatory of Music, where he studied conducting (under Sir Malcolm Sargent), composition (with O.R. Morris) and piano (with Samuel).

In the musical world, Ferguson was first noticed and taken seriously in 1932, when his *Violin Sonata No. 1* was performed by Menges and Samuel. Ferguson continued to receive recognition when his *Octet* was first performed in

November 1993, and when his *Two Ballads for Baritone and Orchestra* were performed at the Three Choirs Festival in Gloucester in 1935.

Ferguson continued to compose in a steady fashion until 1959, when he decided that he'd reached a point where he'd "said everything he needed to say." His last two compositions were also written for the Gloucester Three Choirs Festival; including *Amore langueo* (composed in 1956) and *The Dream of the Road* (1959).

Ferguson's musical career was partly devoted to instruction. Between 1948-1963 he taught composition at the Royal Academy of Music; many of his students ended up becoming accomplished composers in their own right.

After Composing Came Editing

With the cessation of composing, Ferguson began to concentrate on editing early keyboard music. His love of musical craftsmanship and his experience as a performing pianist prepared him well for this transition. He compiled anthologies of early keyboard music that appealed to accomplished musicians and amateurs alike. In 1975 he authored and published the book *Keyboard Interpretation.*

Ferguson continued to perform recitals during and after his composing career. He collaborated and performed with the pianist Denis Matthews and the Violinist Yfrah Neaman and performed worldwide. He was also instrumental in organizing daily wartime concerts at London's National Gallery between 1939-1946.

Lyric Music with Craftsmanship

Ferguson's works continued to be re-recorded and released. In an *American Record Guide,* review of some Ferguson compositions, the reviewer noted that Ferguson composed with "style and warmth" and was at least as good a song writer as Finzi or Samuel Barber. In another *American Record Guide* review of an Ferguson Octet, the reviewer referred to the music as a "cow-pat" style of British music; music that evoked pastoral images rather than being difficult to listen to.

Another reviewer from *American Record Guide* referred to Ferguson's *Four Short Pieces* as having melodic expression and rhythmic vitality. His work has also been characterized as having clarity and economy of expression. This style was developed in his early composing career and he used it over and over, with originality and success. Ferguson composed a total of 24 works, including four symphonies or orchestral works, 13 works for chamber orchestras, six choral or vocal works, and one piece for ballet. In his later years, Ferguson has made his home in Cambridge, England.

Further Reading

Arnold, Denis, editor, *New Oxford Companion to Music,* Oxford University Press, 1983.
Contemporary Authors, Permanent Series, Gale Research, 1975.
Contemporary Composers, St. James Press, 1992.
American Record Guide, July-August 1995; November-December 1995; September-October 1996.
American Record Review, January-February 1993.

"Howard Ferguson," *Guild Music Home Page,* http://www.guildmusic.com/composer/fergusoh.htm (May 7, 1998).

Carlos Roberto Flores Facussé

It was his "New Agenda" platform that helped to sweep Carlos Roberto Flores Facussé (born 1950) into the presidency of Honduras in December of 1997.

Oscar A. Flores and his wife Margarita Facussé de Flores became parents for the first time on March 1, 1950. They named their son Carlos Roberto Flores Facussé. As was the custom in Honduras, he would have both his father's surname, Flores, and his mother's, Facussé. The future political leader of Honduras was born in the capital city of Tegucigalpa. Almost a half a century later, thousands would cheer for him in the same city as he took the presidential oath of office.

Like most of his nation, Flores was born into a Catholic family. He was not born into the same poverty, however, that had much of Honduras in its grip. Even by the 1990s, the average annual income for Hondurans was estimated at $650 in U.S. currency—one of the lowest in the western hemisphere. An estimated 80 percent of the population was reported to be in poverty in the 1990s.

The poor economic conditions of Honduras spawned a history of political unrest. Flores' father, Oscar, was part of that turmoil. Ruling in the 1950s was Julio Lozano Diaz. In 1956, despite a democratic process, Diaz did not want to turn control of the government over to new president Ramon Villeda Morales. The newspapers, including *El Pueblo* of which Oscar Flores was editor, recognized Villeda as the rightful president. Flores, Villeda, and another Liberal Party official were rounded up the next day without warning and exiled to Costa Rica. Later in the year, Diaz was himself deposed by the military, and Villeda was made president in 1958.

The incident left its mark on both Oscar Flores and young Carlos Flores. As Carlos Flores remarked in *World Profile, the Making of a President,* an alumni report for Louisiana State University, "Because of the hardship that [my father] had been through in leaving us when we were little—these were difficult times for us—he got the sense afterwards that politics wasn't worth it." Oscar Flores eventually abandoned the political arena and co-founded what became the popular Honduran newspaper, *La Tribuna.*

A Tiger in College

Carlos Flores was educated in the American school system in Honduras. The combined influence of the American schools and his mother had Flores speaking English from an early age. When it came time for college, Oscar

Flores encouraged his son to go to school in the United States. Carlos Flores selected Louisiana State University (LSU) in Baton Rouge, Louisiana. The school had drawn Central American students for decades, partly because of its agriculture department. Flores chose to study industrial engineering.

Flores' leadership abilities started to emerge when he began his studies at LSU in the late 1960s. The school, nicknamed the Tigers, heard a roar from Flores as he chartered the school's first and only fraternity for Hispanic students, Phi Iota Alpha. He was also an active president of the Honduran Student Association.

In 1970, while still an undergraduate, Flores met fellow student Mary Carol Flakes. Also a senior at LSU, she had a roommate who had visited Honduras over the summer and had met Flores. When school resumed in the fall, Flores went to see the roommate in the dormitory. He instead made the acquaintance of Flakes. They began dating and were married in 1974. The couple eventually had two children, Mary Elizabeth and Carlos David.

Before Flores married Flakes, however, he completed his education. After earning his bachelor of science degree in industrial engineering, Flores entered graduate school at LSU. In 1973, he earned a masters degree in international trade and finance. During this time, Flakes had also earned a bachelor's degree, although her field was textiles and marketing.

Business and Political Leader Emerges

Flores and his wife returned to Honduras after their marriage in 1974. At that time, Flores became involved in the private sector by serving on various boards of directors, including the Central Bank of Honduras. He also taught part-time at the National University. In 1979, Flores joined with his father in founding the newspaper, *La Tribuna*. Flores took over as president and chief executive officer of the newspaper after his father's death. The publication was sympathetic to the Liberal Party of Honduras. Unlike many Central American countries, the Liberal Party, along with its main rival, the National Party, had survived since early in the century.

Although the parties had endured, there had been military regimes until 1982 when a new constitution was drafted. Flores was instrumental in the writing of the document, beginning in 1980. In the years following, he was elected to the national congress as a Liberal Party candidate for three terms. Flores became a prominent figure in political circles, serving in the ministry of president Roberto Suazo Córdoba from 1982 to 1984.

Road to the Presidency

With the backing of one of the country's largest newspapers—*La Tribuna*—Flores was ready for the next step. He campaigned for the presidency in 1988. Flores won the primary, but it came at a cost. He had 35.5 percent of the total vote from a bruising primary election.

As the Liberal Party's presidential candidate, Flores faced some personal scandal. He was trying to distance himself from an earlier episode, which involved the National Corporation of Industrial Development, or CONADI. The program, designed to help launch private businesses, was funded with American aid. A number of projects were never completed, and rumors of corruption followed those who participated in the CONADI program. In the book *The United States, Honduras, and the Crisis in Central America,* Donald E. Schulz and Deborah Sundloff Schulz noted that the Facussé family, including Flores' uncle Miguel Facussé, had been involved with CONADI.

Still, Flores waged an active battle for the presidency. The National Party candidate, Rafael Leonardo Callejas, won with 50.9 percent of the vote, while Flores drew 43.1 percent. The Nationalists also won control of the Congress. Flores reflected on the loss almost a decade later in the *World Profile, the Making of a President:* "We [the Liberal Party] had been in office for three consecutive terms. The people wanted to alternate power and give the other party the opportunity to govern."

The tables were turned four years later when the Liberal Party and its new president, Roberto Reina, were back in power. Following the national presidential campaign, Flores had been reelected to congress in 1993. A popular politician, he became the president of the National Congress of Honduras, the second most powerful position in the Honduran government. From 1993 to 1997, the Honduran Congress, under Flores' leadership, ratified a number of reforms to the civil service, judiciary, and military sectors.

One of the more far-reaching changes was to the military, which became a force based on voluntary service. Going into the 1997 elections, Flores was perhaps most proud of the fact that the 1982 constitution was still intact and gaining more acceptance with the public.

Flores was again named as the Liberal Party's candidate in the elections of 1997, less than a decade after his first run. He campaigned on a "New Agenda" platform, vowing to move Honduras past its image of being primarily a banana and coffee exporter. Under the "New Agenda," Flores promised to promote education for low-income families by creating scholarships and developing partnerships with the private sector, to adjust salaries in order to keep pace with inflation, and to fight domestic violence and set up nurseries for working mothers. He committed to the development of a mixed private and public pension system. Foreign investment would be encouraged through the privatization of some state enterprises and by providing access to the country's natural resources. Flores also pledged to promote sustainable development while protecting the country's rich ecological diversity. Throughout the campaign, Flores made a plea for unity toward the future and the new millennium to achieve success for an "independent and dignified nation."

Critics were less impressed with Flores plans than the general public. They noted that Flores' message was short on details. Many suggested that it would be unlikely he would achieve much of what he had promised. Critics noted, for instance, that the state of the Honduran tax system needed to be revamped. Flores might be unwilling or unable, however, to carry out tax reform. Without an effective tax system, resources to promote education, health, and pension reform would be wanting. Wage increases would need to be accompanied by increases in productivity in order to prevent inflation. Without investing in education, health, and infrastructure, it would be unlikely that productivity would increase. In addition, foreign debt renegotiation, subsidies and low interest loans from industrialized countries, an increase in the tax base, and foreign investments would be needed in order to generate the revenues required to develop a pension system and provide greater opportunities for women who wanted to enter the work force.

Despite the criticism, Flores' message sounded with the electorate. With the political support of former president Suazo, Flores vied for his party's nomination. He distanced himself from the Reina administration, and successfully portrayed himself as an opposition candidate from the same party as the incumbent president. Flores was able to capitalize on his record as president of Congress and on the poor economic performance of the Reina administration. He won the Liberal Party's nomination, and on November 30, 1997, he won the national election. He polled 53 percent of the vote in the election, thus defeating his opponent, National Party candidate Nora Gunera de Melgar, the first woman to be nominated to the Honduran presidency.

On January 27, 1998, Flores was installed as president while 30,000 supporters cheered for him at a stadium. "Honduras is a country that does not tolerate the misery of underdevelopment," Flores declared, as quoted in the Associated Press. "With the help of God and the people, today we undertake a new agenda for Honduras." In addition, the new leader vowed to fight rising crime and government corruption as well as improve wages and stimulate investment in his nation.

Flores' "New Agenda" served as the centerpiece of his administration. The plan called on Hondurans to recover the faith and initiate a search for a more prosperous future. It also proposed ten central themes for the first four years of his administration to increase growth, reduce unemployment, and stabilize the economy. Flores' plan was faced with challenges as early as the spring of 1998. In April of that year, the United States, under the administration of President Bill Clinton, leveled a $5 million trade sanction against Honduras as a result of the Central American nation's failure to protect copyright properties, including American television shows. In a United Press International report, Flores called the decision "unfair and unfortunate." Also in April, one of Flores' cabinet ministers escaped being shot while traveling in a rural northern part of the nation.

The early incidents served to remind both Flores and Hondurans that challenges, some severe, would probably follow the nation through Flores' administration and beyond into the twenty-first century. But Flores maintained that a stable government could accomplish much. As he noted in *World Profile, the Making of a President,* "We have had four consecutive constitutional presidents. That is very positive. . . . People have learned to respect the constitution as a permanent guarantee of principles. They have the conviction that the system works, that government will respond to their expectations."

Further Reading

Honduras, A Country Study, Federal Research Division, Library of Congress, 1994.

Martz, John D., *Central America, the Crisis and the Challenge,* University of North Carolina Press, 1959.

Schulz, Donald E., and Deborah Sundloff Schulz, *The United States, Honduras, and the Crisis in Central America,* Westview Press, 1994.

World Profile, the Making of a President (alumni report), Louisiana State University, 1995.

Associated Press, December 1, 1997; January 27, 1998.

United Press International, April 2, 1998.

"Biography and New Agenda," www.partido-liberal.hn (March 30, 1998).

"Hondurans Vote In Lackluster Presidential Poll," November 30, 1997 (March 30, 1998); "Gunmen Attack Honduran Minister, One Wounded," April 4, 1998 (April 4, 1998). *CNN Interactive,* http://cnn.com,

Honduras This Week, www.marrder.com, November 30, 1996 (March 30, 1998). □

Dario Fo

Italian playwright Dario Fo (born 1926) is known for his satirical and often controversial works. He was awarded the 1997 Nobel Prize in Literature.

Although he has been hailed by critics worldwide for his acting abilities and especially for his artful, satirical works that convey his leftist ideology, Italian playwright Dario Fo was an unexpected winner of the 1997 Nobel Prize in Literature. Fo, who according to the press release from the Swedish Academy, "emulates the jesters of the Middle Ages in scourging authority and upholding the dignity of the downtrodden," was by his own admission "amazed" to learn that he had won the prestigious award, according to an article by *Chicago Tribune* contributor Tom Hundley. The Nobel committee's choice was indeed unpopular among many segments of the world population, especially with the Italian government and with the Roman Catholic Church, which have both been favorite targets of Fo's in such works as *A Madhouse for the Sane* and *Mistero buffo.* According to an article by the *New York Times'* s Celestine Bohlen, "the Vatican newspaper *L'Osservatore Romano* said it was flabbergasted by [Fo's] selection. 'Giving the prize to someone who is also the author of questionable works is beyond all imagination,' the paper said."

Fo was born on March 24, 1926, in San Giano, a small fishing village in northern Italy where his father, Felice, was a railroad stationmaster and part-time actor. His father and the local storytellers provided the young Fo with his first lessons in the art of dramatic presentation, and he emulated their animated gestures and vocalizations in his own acting performances. He attended the Academia di Belle Arti (Academy of Fine Arts) in Milan, but left without earning a degree, instead opting to write plays and perform with sev-

eral improvisational theatre groups. Fo's first success as a playwright came with his 1953 work, *Il dito nell'occhio* (*A Finger in the Eye*), which was a social satire that presented Marxist concepts with a circus-like backdrop.

Early Works Prove Controversial

Fo became an outspoken opponent of the Italian government with his 1954 play, *I sani de legare* (*A Madhouse for the Sane*), which charged several government officials with being fascist sympathizers; the government ordered Fo to cut some of the original material from his script and mandated the presence of state inspectors at each performance of the play to ensure that Italian libel laws were not being broken. Between 1956 and 1958 Fo worked as a screenwriter in Rome, but he returned to the stage and began to produce, along with his wife, actress and playwright Franca Rame, a less conspicuously political variety of satirical plays. Of the works produced during this period of his career, Fo's best is considered by many to be 1959's *Gli arcangeli non giocano a flipper* (*Archangels Don't Play Pinball*), which was the first of his plays to be staged outside of Italy.

In 1968 Fo and Rame, with the support of the Italian communist party, formed Nuova Scena, a nonprofit theatre organization whose works were aimed at the working class audience; the couple's decision to form the group was prompted by their rejection of the theatrical establishment. Nuova Scena productions were marked by an intensely radical tone and dealt with political issues of the time. In one such work, 1968's *Grande pantomima con bandiere e pupazzi piccoli e medi* (*Grand Pantomime with Flags and Small and Medium-Sized Puppets*), Fo took a satirical look at Italy's political history following World War II, depicting the way in which he believed the communist party had given in to the temptation of capitalism; the Italian communist party withdrew its support of Nuova Scena following the production of *Grand Pantomime*, and Fo and Rame formed Il Colletive Teatrale La Comune, known as La Comune, in 1970.

Mistero buffo Produced

Fo was highly popular during the 1960s, perhaps due to the prevailing feelings of social and political upheaval that marked that decade and provided him with exposure to a much broader audience than any with which he had previously been acquainted. *Mistero buffo* (*The Comic Mystery*), considered by many to be Fo's foremost work for the stage as well as his most controversial, was first produced in 1969. Although the actual script is improvised and thus changes with each performance, the narrative always involves a depiction of events based upon the gospels of the Bible's New Testament presented in a disparaging manner that accuses the Catholic church, landowners, and the government of persecuting the masses. Fo took the idea for this play from the Middle Ages, when traveling performers known as *giullari* would enact medieval mystery plays in the streets; in Fo's production, a single actor Fo himself performs the series of sketches on an empty stage, introducing each segment with a short prologue and linking them

together, portraying as many as a dozen characters at one time. The parables from the gospels portrayed in *Mistero buffo* include the resurrection of Lazarus, with pickpockets who steal from those who witness the miracle, the story of a crippled man who avoids Jesus' healing power because he makes a good living as a beggar, and a scornful depiction of the corrupt activities of Pope Boniface VIII.

Mistero buffo was broadcast on television in 1977, and, according to an *Atlantic Monthly* article by Charles C. Mann, the Vatican proclaimed the work to be "the most blasphemous" program ever televised; Fo was, as Mann reported, delighted with the church officials' response. Despite the church's disapproval, or perhaps because of it, *Mistero buffo* was a popular success throughout Europe; when it was performed in London in 1983, the revenue brought in by the play was enough to save the theatre in which it was produced from financial ruin. Fo and Rame were eventually given permission to enter the United States in 1986, after having been denied visas in both 1980 and 1984 because of reports that they had helped to raise funds to support an Italian terrorist organization; the couple denied taking part in any such activities. *Mistero buffo* opened in New York City in the spring of 1986, and was hailed by the *New York Times'* s Ron Jenkins as "a brilliant one-man version of biblical legends and church history" whose humor "echo[es] the rhythms of revolt."

In response to the premature death of anarchist railway worker Giuseppi Pinelli in 1969, Fo composed the absurdist play *Morte accidentale di un anarchico* (*Accidental Death of an Anarchist*), which was the only one of his plays produced during his La Comune period to become an enduring favorite and a popular success. Pinelli's death was, Fo believed, the result of a plot by right-wing extremist members of the Italian military and secret service to undermine the credibility of the Italian Communist party by executing a string of bombings and making it appear that they were the work of leftist terrorists. Pinelli was charged with the 1969 bombing of the Agricultural Bank of Milan, one of the most devastating of the bombings that killed numerous innocent bystanders. At some point during the time in which the railway worker was held for interrogation by police in Milan, he fell later it was argued that he was pushed from a window on the fourth floor of police headquarters.

In *Accidental Death of an Anarchist,* Fo's play based on the events surrounding Pinelli's death, Fo uses a character known as the maniac to reveal the attempts by the police to cover up the truth. In an article in *American Theatre,* Fo observed: "When I injected absurdity into the situation, the lies became apparent. The maniac plays the role of the judge, taking the logic of the authorities to their absurd extremes." In this way, Fo was able to demonstrate that Pinelli was murdered, and could not have died accidentally as the police maintained. *Los Angeles Times* contributor John Lahr reported that around the time *Accidental Death of an Anarchist* was first staged Fo was assaulted and imprisoned and Rame was kidnapped and brutalized as punishment for their part in exposing the police cover-up.

Fo Popular in Europe

Accidental Death of an Anarchist was enormously popular in Italy, and attracted large audiences during the four years following its first production. In a review of the play in *New Society,* John Lahr proclaimed it "loud, vulgar, kinetic, scurrilous, smart, [and] sensational. . . . Everything theatre should be." Although the play was also popular in London, where it ran successfully for two and a half years, it failed to win over audiences in the United States in 1984, when it opened and closed within a matter of months.

Most commentators assert that Fo's plays are not as popular with American audiences as they are with European audiences because they are loosely translated into English or performed in Italian, and because they are based upon historical, political, and social events that even if they are known to Americans are not as significant to them as they are to Europeans. *New York Times* contributor Mel Gussow contended that "dealing with topical Italian materials in colloquial Italian language . . . presents problems for adapters and directors." Specifically, critics faulted as distracting the use of an onstage translator during an American performance of *Mistero buffo,* and characterized a production based upon the English translation of *Accidental Death of an Anarchist* as considerably less effective than the original Italian production. The *New York Times'* s Frank Rich declared that the insertion of puns based on contemporary American occurrences into the script of *Accidental Death* by adapter Richard Nelson served to "wreck the play's farcical structure and jolt both audience and cast out of its intended grip."

During the 1980s Fo collaborated extensively with Rame, and the couple produced several plays with distinctly feminist themes. Their most successful of these plays was *Tutta casa, letto e chiesa,* which is comprised of eight monologues that focus on women's position in a male-dominated society. The work, which includes a varying number and combination of the eight monologues in each production, was performed in England and the United States under several different titles, including *Woman Plays, Female Parts,* and *Orgasmo Adulto Escapes from the Zoo.* According to the *Washington Post'* s David Richards, who reviewed an American production of the play, although the play is admirably candid, because it depicts a brand of sexism practiced more commonly in Italy, the play "may have lost some of its punch crossing the Atlantic," noting that to American audiences "the women in *Orgasmo* seem to be fighting battles that have long been conceded on these shores." Another of Fo and Rame's woman-centered plays, 1974's *No se paga! No se paga!* (*We Won't Pay! We Won't Pay!*), concerns a group of homemakers who organize a boycott of their local supermarket to protest its outrageous prices; this play was a moderate success in the United States when it was produced Off-Broadway in 1980 and enjoyed a fairly lengthy run.

Fo has continued to produce works that provoke anger and controversy. His 1992 play, *The Pope and the Witch,* which has as its subject a news conference during which the Pope, as described by *New York Times* contributor Celestine Bohlen, "confuses a children's gathering in St. Peter's Square with an abortion rights rally," incited fury among Catholics worldwide. His 1997 play, *Devil with Boobs,* is, according to Bohlen, "a comedy set in the Renaissance featuring a zealous judge and a woman possessed by the devil." Fo has also continued to appear in productions of his works, and his acting style has been compared to that of the members of the comedy troupe Monty Python, but most often Fo as an actor is "compared to the comedian Lenny Bruce for his activism, scatological humor, sarcasm and barely submerged bitterness," as *New York Times* contributor Rick Lyman related. Nevertheless, Lyman continued, a comparison between Bruce and Fo "ignores a chameleonlike aspect to [Fo's] performances that recalls [comedian] Sid Caesar. In a style reminiscent of Mr. Caesar's double-talk routines, Mr. Fo uses a gibberish called 'grammelot,' often accompanied by a 'translator.' The language is a jumble of syllables that evokes, without actually simulating, Italian, French and American technological jargon."

Fo Awarded Nobel Prize

Because his works have invited such tremendous controversy throughout the world, and because although some of his plays have been successful outside of Italy he is by far more popular and well-known to Italians than to the rest of the world, it was a shock to many when it was announced that Fo would receive the 1997 Nobel Prize for Literature. The announcement, according to the *New York Times'* s Bohlen, was greeted with "the guarded amazement of Italy's literary establishment and the outright dismay of the Vatican." In its press release, published on the Nobel Prize Internet Archive, the Swedish Academy declared that Fo's plays "simultaneously amuse, engage and provide perspectives. . . . His is an oeuvre of impressive artistic vitality and range." Despite the furor surrounding his selection as a Nobel laureate, Fo has maintained his characteristic irreverence; as related in an unsigned article in the *Chicago Tribune* covering his news conference to discuss his prize, Fo remarked on the controversy surrounding his selection: "God is a jester because he bitterly disappointed a lot of people, including the Vatican newspaper. I feel almost guilty, but it was a great joke on them." Fo's plans as a Nobel laureate have included using his status to promote the fight for civil rights in such countries as China, Algeria, Turkey, and Argentina, and donating portions of his $1 million prize to the movement to ban the use of land mines and to aid the legal defense of three men Fo has steadfastly proclaimed their innocence prosecuted for the 1971 murder of the police officer who was in charge of interrogating Giuseppe Pinelli, the railway worker whose death was the inspiration for Fo's *Accidental Death of an Anarchist.* At the time he announced his intentions for his prize money, Fo had already outlined a sequel to *Accidental Death* based upon one of the accused men's struggle to prove his innocence.

Further Reading

American Theatre, June 1986.
Atlantic Monthly, September 1985.

Chicago Tribune, October 9, 1997; October 10, 1997; October 11, 1997; November 6, 1997.

Los Angeles Times, January 16, 1983; January 21, 1983.

New Society, March 13, 1980, pp. 559-60.

New York Times, December 18, 1980; April 17, 1983; August 5, 1983; August 14, 1983; August 27, 1983; February 15, 1984; October 31, 1984; November 16, 1984; May 29, 1986; May 30, 1986; May 9, 1987; November 27, 1987; October 10, 1997.

Washington Post, August 27, 1983; November 17, 1984; January 17, 1985; June 12, 1986.

Nobel Prize Internet Archive, http://www.almaz.com (October 9, 1997).

Swedish Academy Press Release, The Permanent Secretary, Nobel Prize Internet Archive, http://www.almaz.com (October 9, 1997). □

Hiram Leong Fong

The son of immigrant plantation laborers, Hiram L. Fong (born 1907) became a self-made millionaire and the first person of Chinese descent to serve in the United States Congress.

Hiram L. Fong capped a life spent blazing trails when he was sworn in as Hawaii's first United States Senator on August 24, 1959. Fong earned the designation "senior Senator" through sheer luck—he won a coin flip with Senator Oren Long—but the moderate Republican achieved almost everything else in life through hard work and political tenacity. The son of plantation workers worked his way through Harvard Law School and founded Honolulu's first multiracial law firm before embarking on a successful career in politics. He served with distinction in the U.S. Senate until his retirement in 1977.

Worked His Way Up

Hiram Leong Fong was born in Honolulu, Hawaii on October 1, 1907. He was originally given the name Yau, but as a young man he changed his name to Hiram out of regard for the Hawaiian missionary Hiram Bingham. Fong was the seventh of 11 children born to Lum Fong and Lum Fong Shee, both immigrants from China's Kwantung Province. Both of Fong's parents worked as indentured laborers on a sugar plantation, earning $12 a month between them. To help support his large family, Hiram worked as a shoe shine boy, newspaper seller, and golf caddy. He attended Kalihi Waena Grammar School and, later, McKinley High School, a large public school in Honolulu.

As a young adult, Fong lacked the money to attend college. He worked for three years as a clerk in the Pearl Harbor Naval Shipyard to save enough money for tuition. He entered the University of Hawaii and graduated with honors in just three years, working all the while at various odd jobs to keep up with expenses. While at the university he also edited the school newspaper, played volleyball, and joined the debating team. After graduation, Fong wished to attend law school, but again found his dreams deferred because of lack of funds. He worked full-time for another two years—this time with the Suburban Water System—and saved up enough to enter Harvard Law School in 1932. He graduated, in 1935, broke but thoroughly educated. He returned to Honolulu and found work as a city clerk and then as deputy city attorney.

Early Career

In 1935, Fong founded Fong, Miho, Choy, and Robinson, a law firm consisting of Chinese, Japanese, Korean, and Caucasian partners. The multiracial venture was the first of its kind in Honolulu and proved wildly successful. Fong used his portion of the profits to invest in a variety of business interests that eventually made him a millionaire. In 1938, the progressive Republican was elected to Hawaii's territorial House of Representatives, where he would serve for 14 of the next 16 years. On June 25, 1938, he married Ellyn Lo, a fellow Chinese-American, in Honolulu.

Fong's victory was a major step for Chinese-Americans, helping to break the stranglehold on Hawaiian politics held by the so-called "plantation elites." But Fong's own political ascent was briefly interrupted by World War II. He served in the Army Air Corps as a judge advocate—known in military parlance as a "JAG"—for the 7th Fighter Command, earning the rank of major. Returning to Honolulu after the war, he resumed his position in the territorial legislature. In an unusual move for a Republican at that time, Fong forged an alliance with a major labor union, the International Longshoreman's and Warehouseman's Union (ILWU). The group's clout helped Fong win election as

Speaker of the Hawaiian territorial legislature, in 1948. He served three terms in that position before being ousted, in a close election, in 1954. Fong fell only 31 votes shy of re-election in that contest.

The Senate and Statehood

Though out of office, Fong remained involved in politics. He served as a delegated to the Republican National Conventions in 1952 and 1956. He also continued to diversify his business interests, founding Finance Factors Limited in 1952. He managed his personal assets until they totaled several million dollars by 1960. But his principal cause during these years was statehood for Hawaii, which was finally achieved, in 1959. That June, Fong was selected by Republican voters as their candidate for one of Hawaii's two United States Senate seats. He ran against Democrat Frank F. Fasi and relied on his labor connections and personal success story for support. On July 28, 1959, Hawaii's voters elected Fong by just over 9000 votes.

When Hawaii was formally admitted as America's 50th state on August 21, Fong and his Democratic colleagues, Oren E. Long and Daniel K. Inouye, stood in line to be sworn in as the island's first congressional delegation. Fong won a coin flip with Long to be granted the designation "senior senator," thereby achieving a lifelong dream for himself and his state.

Moderate Voice in Senate

During his first term in the Senate, Fong served on the Interior and Insular Affairs Committee and the Public Works Committee. In October of 1959, to improve relations with Asia, he embarked on a 45-day tour of that continent. He received a warm welcome from the Chinese communities in the various countries he visited.

Fong soon began became a leading voice in the moderate faction of the Republican Party. During the administration of John F. Kennedy, he often sided with the Democratic president on issues of civil rights, aide to education, and civil service reform. In March of 1963 Fong was one of seven Republicans to introduce a package of civil rights legislation in the Senate. On foreign policy issues, however, Fong sided more consistently with the conservative majority in his party,

After winning reelection in 1964, Fong continued on the same track in his second term—moderate on domestic issues, "hawkish" on foreign affairs. He supported President Lyndon Johnson's Voting Rights Act, in 1965, and worked to eliminate immigration restrictions against Asians. He spoke out in favor of control and applauded Johnson's proposal to set up a special Administration on Aging. But Fong defied the president, in opposing his nominee for Chief Justice of the Supreme Court, Abe Fortas, in 1968. On the war in Vietnam, Fong was an early and enthusiastic supporter—a position which often put him in hot water with his Asian-American constituents.

Rightward Turn

In 1968, Fong endorsed former Vice President Richard M. Nixon in his race for president. His support signaled a pronounced conservative tilt and more partisan stance from Hawaii Republican. Following Nixon's election, Fong became one of his most ardent backers, in the Senate. He consistently voted the for president's large defense budgets and spoke out loudly in defense of Nixon's Vietnam policy. Other programs Fong supported during this period included the Anti-Ballistic Missile System (ABM) and supersonic transport (SST).

Fong's rightward turn may have strengthened his position within the Republican Party, but it cost him support from the voters of Hawaii. In 1970, he won election to a third term by a narrow margin. When he returned to the Senate for the 92nd Congress, in January 1971, he moderated his positions somewhat. Key positions of Fong's third term were his support of the Equal Rights Amendment (ERA) and his opposition to forced busing to achieve school integration. Most damaging to Fong was a bribery scandal involving one of his long-time aides. While no blame was ever assigned to Fong, he nevertheless declined to seek a fourth term, in 1976. Spark M. Matsunaga, a former Democratic representative, succeeded Fong in the U.S. Senate.

Retirement and Riches

In 1977, Fong retired to a 725-acre botanical garden on the Hawaiian island of Oahu. Here he farmed his land and oversaw his various business interests. By 1993, Finance Factors Ltd. which he had founded in 1952, saw its sales grow to $44.5 million. Fong used part of his fortune to found three charitable organizations. He donated $100,000 annually to mostly local causes. In 1995, Fong was inducted into the Hawaii Business Hall of Fame. Speaking to the magazine *Hawaii Business* soon after his induction, he gave the following advice to aspiring entrepreneurs, "No. 1, get as much education as you can. No. 2, find someone established that you can apprentice yourself to."

Further Reading

Biographical Directory of the American Congress 1774-1996 CQ Staff Directories, Inc., 1996.
Political Profiles: The Johnson Years edited by Nelson Lichtenstein, Facts on File, 1976.
Political Profiles: The Kennedy Years edited by Nelson Lichtenstein, Facts on File, 1976.
Political Profiles: The Nixon/Ford Years edited by Eleanora W. Schoenebaum, Facts on File, 1979.
Hawaii Business, January 1995.

Henry Stuart Foote

Henry Stuart Foote (1804-1880) bucked the tide of public opinion as an opponent of secession and the expansion of slavery in Civil War-era Mississippi.

The career of Henry Stuart Foote is a profile in political courage—or at the very least, political stubbornness. For Foote swam against the tide of public opinion and defied the wishes of the political establishment in opposing southern secession and the expansion of slavery in the years before the outbreak of the Civil War. Serving Mississippi as its senator, governor, and even, paradoxically, as a representative of the Confederate Congress, Foote argued consistently for peace and against the inevitability of war between the states. His stubbornness in political convictions was an outgrowth of his personal character, which was marked by a propensity to engage in feuds and duels with his rivals.

Henry Stuart Foote was born in Fauquier County, Virginia, on February 28, 1804. His parents, Richard Helm Foote and Jane Stuart, were cousins of English and Scottish descent. Henry undertook a course in classical studies at Washington College (today Washington and Lee University) in Lexington, Virginia and graduated in 1819 at the age of 15. He then began the study of law and was admitted to the Virginia bar at the state capital of Richmond in 1823.

After passing the bar, Foote moved to Tuscumbia, Alabama, where, in 1825 he began plying the legal trade. The following year he moved on to Jackson, Mississippi, which would be his home base for the next 28 years. Foote practiced law in the cities of Natchez, Vicksburg, and Raymond, specializing in criminal cases. According to many historians, Foote had no equal in Mississippi when it came to trying criminal cases. Foote also edited newspapers during this period.

Foote began his political career in 1832, by campaigning for a spot in the Mississippi constitutional convention. While that effort was unsuccessful, it enhanced his state-

wide reputation. Turning to national politics in 1835, Foote, then a Democrat, took to the stump to defend the policies of President Andrew Jackson. As a reward, he was named to the office of United States surveyor-general south of Tennessee, but resigned that post in 1839 to run for—and win—a seat in the Mississippi state legislature. Representing Hinds County, Foote showed an interest in regional issues as well. He visited Texas in 1839 and took up the cause of independence for that state. The result was his book, *Texas and the Texans*, published in 1841.

In 1847, Foote was elected to the United States Senate as a Democrat, and served with distinction as chairman of the Committee on Foreign Relations in the 31st and 32nd Congresses. Foote became well-known for his skill as a public speaker and for his engaging conversation, but he could just as easily rub people the wrong way and got into a number of celebrated feuds. Foote is said to have engaged in four formal duels, twice facing off against Representative Sergeant S. Prentiss of Mississippi. He was wounded three times in these encounters. Often it was political arguments that prompted the physical confrontations. Foote once tussled in the aisles of the Senate with one of his opponents, Senator Simon Cameron of Pennsylvania. Another time, he threatened to hang New Hampshire Senator John P. Hale if he ever set foot in Mississippi.

However, it was Foote's position on slavery that proved most controversial. He earned the everlasting ire of his Mississippi brethren by supporting the Compromise of 1850, a measure which severely restricted the slave trade. When Senator Thomas Hart Benton obstinately refused to back the legislation, Foote castigated him on the floor for weeks. Finally, Benton had had enough. He confronted Foote in a rage, prompting Foote to draw a pistol from his pocket. "Let the assassin fire!" Benton is said to have bellowed, tearing open his vest. Foote later claimed that he drew his weapon only because he suspected that Benton was armed as well.

Foote's defense of his maverick views extended even to his own Mississippi colleagues, including the state's senior senator, Jefferson Davis. The two men clashed for years over the right of the south to secede from the union. The conflict eventually came to blows, with Foote and Davis at one point exchanging punches at the boarding house they shared. Before long, Foote was a pariah among his fellow legislators and the Mississippi legislature passed a resolution censuring him for his views on slavery. Four years into his six-year term in the senate, Foote seemed destined for the political graveyard.

In 1852, Foote ran for governor, this time on the Unionist ticket, against Jefferson Davis. The popular tide seemed to be against him, but his ability as a public speaker helped him carry the race in a shocking upset. It was the last time a pro-Union Whig would win a political contest in pre-Civil War Mississippi. However, the old conflicts over slavery and secession continued to bedevil Foote, and his administration split into factions. Frustrated, Foote left office in 1854, five days before his term expired. He moved to California, where he hoped to continue his political career in a state more receptive to his anti-secession views.

Foote had difficulty establishing a foothold outside of Mississippi. He ran for the United States Senate from California in 1856, but lost in a tight race. He briefly returned to his home state, settling in Vicksburg, but still found his views out of step with the political establishment. In 1859, he moved to Tennessee, serving as a delegate to the Southern convention held in Knoxville in that year. He later settled near Nashville.

With America on the brink of civil war in 1861, Foote found himself in the unlikely position of secessionist legislator. He was elected to terms in the lower house of the First and Second Confederate Congress, but he refused to moderate his views on disunion. He repeatedly criticized the war policies of the Confederate president, his old enemy Jefferson Davis, and lobbied for a peaceful settlement, but when President Abraham Lincoln's peace overtures were rejected by the Confederate Congress, Foote resigned in disgust. He was detained briefly by Confederate authorities, but eventually made his way onto Northern soil.

Foote hoped to find a receptive audience to his peace overtures in the Lincoln administration, but when the president and his secretary of state, William Seward, responded coolly to his plans for a settlement, Foote left his native land for Europe. Here he worked on his memoir of the war years, *The War of the Rebellion* (1866), which stated his case that conflict between north and south was not inevitable and could have been avoided. Other books by Foote appeared in the post-war period, including *Casket of Reminiscences* (1874), a commentary on his times and contemporaries, and the legal tome *The Bench and Bar of the South and Southwest* (1876).

After the war, Foote returned to Washington and resumed the practice of law. He became an ardent Republican, supporting the administrations of Presidents Ulysses S. Grant and Rutherford B. Hayes. In 1878, Hayes appointed him superintendent of the United States mint at New Orleans, Louisiana. He served almost two years in that post and died in Nashville, Tennessee, on May 20, 1880. He is buried in Mount Olivet Cemetery.

Further Reading

Biographical Annals of the Civil Government of the Unted States, James Anglim, 1876, reprint, Gale 1976.
Biographical Dictionary of Southern Authors, Martin & Hoyt Co., 1929, reprint, Gale, 1978.
Biographical Dictionary and Synopsis of Books Ancient and Modern, Werner Co., 1902, reprint, Gale, 1965.
A Dictionary of American Authors, Houghton Mifflin Co., 1904, Gale, 1969.

Shelby Foote

American novelist and historian Shelby Foote (born 1916) is best known for his three-volume history of the Civil War. Envisioned as a one-volume work, Foote's effort grew into a monumental project that took two decades to complete.

Shelby Foote was born November 17, 1916, in Greenville, Mississippi, to Shelby Dade Foote, a business executive, and Lillian (Rosenstock) Foote. His father came from a long line of illustrious Mississippians. One of his ancestors, Isaac Shelby, was a frontier leader during the American Revolution and the first governor of Kentucky. His great-grandfather, Captain Hezekiah William Foote, fought for the Confederacy at Shiloh and went on to become a judge. His grandfather, Huger Lee Foote, was a Washington County planter who gambled away what would have been a substantial inheritance. His son, Shelby's father, was employed as an executive with Armour and Company. He died in 1922, when his son was almost six years old. There were no other children. His mother never remarried.

Restless Youth

In a September 11, 1994, *Booknotes* television interview with C-SPAN's Brian Lamb, Foote claimed that he was frequently in trouble during his childhood. As editor of his high school paper, for example, he dedicated himself to "giving the principal a hard time." According to Foote, the principal retaliated by urging the University of North Carolina to reject his application. This was in 1935—when there were few students—and the university relented. Although he enjoyed studying English and history and writing short stories and poetry for the campus literary magazine, he ignored mathematics and other courses that bored him. Foote left college in 1937 without earning a degree. Between 1935 and 1939, he worked on an intermittent basis for Hodding Carter's *Delta Star,* which became the *Delta*

Democrat-Times. Carter often chided Foote for writing fiction instead of tending to his newspaper responsibilities.

In October 1939, Foote joined the Mississippi National Guard and, with the mobilization of his unit the following year, became a sergeant in the regular United States Army. After the United States entered World War II, he was sent to Europe, where he served as a battery commander of field artillery, rising to the rank of captain. His army career ended abruptly, however, when he was dismissed by court-martial in Ireland after traveling two miles beyond the official limit to see his girlfriend. In 1944 he married his Irish girlfriend, Tess Lavery. He returned to the United States and worked on a local desk of the Associated Press for about six months before joining the Marine Corps. He was in the Corps for a year as an enlisted man assigned to combat intelligence, but the war ended before he was shipped overseas.

Kindred Souls

Foote did not begin writing about the Civil War until 1954, when he was about 37 years old. His fascination with the subject began when he was growing up in Greenville, Mississippi. One of his best friends was Walker Percy, who became a novelist and essayist. Walker's uncle and guardian, William Alexander Percy, had a profound influence on the boys. "He was the greatest teacher I have ever known, because he thought about books and talked about them in a way that made you want to read them," Foote said in a July 6, 1982 interview in the Jackson, Mississippi, *Clarion Ledger.* In 1931, Percy began his writing career as gossip columnist for the Greenville (Mississippi) High School *Pica.* His first item was about the "desperate affair" of his best friend, "G.H.S.'s own playboy, Shelby Foote." The friendship survived Percy's adolescent wisecracks and Foote's later criticism of Percy for his religiosity. It survived, in fact, for six decades. Their correspondence is contained in *The Correspondence of Shelby Foote and Walker Percy.*

Following his discharge from the Marine Corps in November of 1945, Foote worked as a construction worker, as a copywriter for a radio station in Memphis, Tennessee, and as a reporter for the *Delta-Times Democrat.* In 1946, Foote sold his first short story to the *Saturday Evening Post,* and he returned with renewed vigor to the novel he had begun while still in the army. One publisher after another rejected it. After being rewritten, he eventually sold it to Dial Press. Published as *Tournament* in 1949, the novel is a character study of a Delta planter who gambles away the family fortune (much as his own grandfather had done). It was greeted by critics as a promising first novel.

In his second novel, *Follow Me Down* (1950), Foote used multiple points of view to unfold the story of a fanatically religious Mississippi farmer who murders a teenage girl for whom he has abandoned his wife and family. Critics acknowledged Foote's talents but criticized the repetition of events as seen through the eyes of eight characters.

Civil War Studies

In *Shiloh* (1952), his first historical novel, Foote described the chaos of this 1862 Civil War battle through the eyes of several soldiers from both the Union and the Con-

federacy. Foote's *Jordan County* was published in 1954. It consists of seven stories taking place in reverse chronological order from 1950 to 1797.

In December 1953, Foote left Greenville to settle in Memphis, Tennessee. There he began researching and writing a history of the Civil War. The project began with an invitation from Bennett Cerf of Random House to prepare a brief history of the Civil War. "I didn't think a summary would hold my interest, but I told Mr. Cerf I was willing to go whole hog and do a three-part thing on it," he said in a 1990 interview with *People* magazine. "There was silence for about a week, and then he wrote back and said to go ahead. I thought it would take me about three years, but it took me 20." He spent a decade on the 1,100-page third volume alone.

The trilogy was widely praised for enticing the reader into the sectional conflict with its vivid imagery and strong characterization. Some academics, however, deprecate *The Civil War* as the work of a college dropout. They found its absence of footnotes appalling and pointed out that Foote had ignored the causes of the war and had provided only a sketchy political, diplomatic, or economic background. He was also criticized for relying too heavily on secondary sources. He does, however, claim to have based his research on no fewer than 350 books on the Civil War, all of which are in his personal library. He claims to have read each and every one. The first volume, *The Civil War: A Narrative: Fort Sumter to Perryville,* was published by Random House in 1958. Other volumes in the trilogy include *Fredericksburg to Meridian,* published in 1963, and *Red River to Appomattox,* published in 1974.

Return to Fiction

After devoting 20 years of his life to the four-year Civil War, Foote returned to fiction with *September, September* (1978), in which a group of whites plot to kidnap a black child for ransom. The drama takes place in a 30-day period in 1957 and is played against the background of white resistance to racial integration in Little Rock, Arkansas. Adapted for television, *September, September* was retitled *Memphis.*

Civil War Documentary

In 1985, Foote received a call from Ken Burns, a documentary-film maker whom he admired for his treatment of the life of the former governor of Louisiana and senator Huey Long. Burns invited Foote to be part of the Civil War documentary he was preparing for the Public Broadcasting Service. Upon meeting Foote, Burns was soon moved to make him "the presiding spirit" of the documentary. "He provides the painful recollection of the South's loss without any of the old animosity and the old excuses," Burns said in an October 15, 1990, *People* magazine interview. Fourteen million Americans discovered Shelby Foote in the fall of 1990, when he appeared as the principal guide through the hugely successful 11-hour PBS Civil War series. The appearance turned him into a video folk hero, and he has been in much demand for public appearances ever since. For a man who had always jealously guarded his privacy, the sudden attention was disruptive. Foote told *People* magazine: "I'm looking forward to when my fifteen minutes of Andy Warhol fame are over. What I do requires steady work and isolation from all this hoorah." Foote told Margaret Carlin of the Scripts-Howard News Service: "I've got to have quiet time, because I'm slow. . . . I compose with a dip pen—the kind that used to be in the post office. I studied German, so I write in that kind of Gothic script. Using that kind of pen slows me down so I can get my thoughts right. Then I type the manuscript on big 10-by-14-inch yellow sheets, making changes as I go."

A Sin As Great As Slavery

Foote believes that the conflict that ended in 1865 still has a bearing on our lives. "It was the last great romantic war and the first horrendous modern war," he told *People* magazine. "It fascinates us because it is still the central event of our history. So many of the questions that still plague us, particularly concerning race relations and the power of central government, can be better understood if we see how they arose and how we attempted to solve them." In the August 1996 issue of *Smithsonian Magazine* Foote is quoted as saying: "Right now I'm thinking a good deal about emancipation. One of our sins was slavery. Another was emancipation. It's a paradox. In theory, emancipation was one of the glories of our democracy—and it was. But the way it was done led to tragedy. Turning four million people loose with no jobs or trades or learning. And then, in 1877, for a few electoral votes, just abandoning them entirely. A huge amount of pain and trouble resulted. Everybody in America is still paying for it."

Foote told the Lexington *Herald-Leader* in a 1997 interview: "I learned to love my country, in two ways. I began to learn the geography of the South—the mountains, the rivers, the valleys. The other thing was the incredible heroism on both sides. It's hard to believe men were as brave as those men were. Somehow sense of honor was stronger than fear. God knows, they felt fear. I would really like it to be stressed that my work helped me to love my country. I hope my work does that for other people, learning both our virtues and our vices."

Further Reading

Contemporary Authors, New Revision Series, Volume 45, Gale, 1991.
Dictionary of Literary Biography, Gale, Volume 2: *American Novelists since World War II, First Series,* 1978, Volume 17: *Twentieth-Century American Historians,* 1983.
Phillips, Robert L., *Shelby Foote: Novelist and Historian,* University Press of Mississippi, 1992.
Tolson, Jay, editor, *The Correspondence of Shelby Foote and Walker Percy,* Center for Documentary Studies, 1997.
Chicago Tribune, November 18, 1990; May 12, 1994.
Clarion Ledger (Jackson, MS), July 6, 1982.
Commonweal, January 9, 1959.
People, October 15, 1990, p. 60.
Smithsonian Magazine, August, 1996.
Virginia Quarterly Review, winter 1998.
C-SPAN *Booknotes* transcript, http://www.booknotes.org (March 15, 1998).
"Historian loves his nation, and his nation loves him," *Herald-Leader,* http://www.kentuckyconnect.com (March 24, 1998).
"Meet The Modern Library Board/Shelby Foote," http://www.randomhouse.com/modernlibrary/authors/foote.html (March 24, 1998).

Edsel Bryant Ford

Edsel Bryant Ford (1893-1943), the only child of Ford Motor Co. founder Henry Ford, grew up with America's nascent auto industry and, for a time until his death at 49, ran the car company. His most notable contributions were to automobile styling. With his father, Ford established the philanthropic Ford Foundation.

During his youth, Edsel B. Ford enjoyed a close relationship with his father that became strained in his adulthood. While the senior Ford generally supported his son and spoke highly of his abilities, Ford's stewardship of Ford Motor was tightly contained by the will of his father.

According to a Ford Motor biography, Ford was six weeks old when his father tested the first Ford engine in the family's kitchen. When he was three years old, his father took him for a ride in his first successful car on June 4, 1896.

Ford Motor was founded in 1903, the same year Ford was making his first car sketches. Later as a student at Detroit's University School, young Ford wrote essays on automobiles and manufacturing them. After school he visited the Ford factory and helped out in the office, licking stamps, carrying mail, and learning how cars were made. When he was 12, Ford had his own Model N Runabout, and his interest in car design drove him to formulate a number of car designs, including the Model T Torpedo Runabout. Ford introduced his father to his University School manual arts teacher, Clarence W. Avery. Avery soon signed on with Ford and is generally given the main credit for developing the moving assembly line.

Entered Company Early

The Ford Motor Company's biography differs from other accounts on why young Ford did not attend college after completing Detroit University School in 1912 but instead went to work for his father. The company suggests the decision was Edsel Ford's own and stemmed from his wish to be different. However, Eastern Michigan University's George S. May, writing on Ford in *The Encyclopedia of American Business History and Biography* offered another explanation: "Henry Ford, whose formal education had been confined to a one-room country school, was convinced his son would learn all he needed by working for the Ford company. This was perhaps the first major instance in which Ford interposed his authority to prevent his son from doing what he wanted to do." May does note, though, Ford may have bypassed college of his own free will. He had

certainly showed great enthusiasm for the company, and there was never a doubt he would work at Ford eventually.

At the company, Ford demonstrated management ability and an understanding of all aspects of the business. While his rise to power within the company was clearly driven by his father, Ford's pleasant personality won him much respect and affection from Ford employees.

On November 1, 1916, Ford married Eleanor Lowthian Clay, niece of Joseph L. Hudson, who owned Detroit's largest department store and was a leader of the Hudson Motor Car Co. Ford's parents approved of the union, but as Ford's wife came from older money, she was able to introduce her husband to Detroit society, a fact that would later come between Ford and his father. While Ford's parents hoped the couple would be neighbors to the Ford family Fair Lane estate, Ford and his wife chose to live in Detroit's fashionable Indian Village section. The couple's first son, Henry Ford II, was born in 1917, followed by Benson in 1919, Josephine in 1923, and William Clay in 1925. In the late 1920s, the family moved to the elite Detroit suburb of Grosse Pointe Shores and lived in a home more elaborate than Fair Lane, further straining father-son ties.

Rose in Ranks Quickly

When the post of company secretary opened up following the 1915 resignation of James Couzens, Ford was appointed at the age of 21. He also was named to the company's board of directors. Couzens had quit in objection to the senior Ford's antiwar pronouncements following

the war's outbreak in Europe the preceding year. Young Ford would never stand up to his father like that. Although Ford had said after the United States entered the war in 1917 he was willing to be drafted; his father insisted on an exemption, which Ford sought and received. His work was said to be essential to the war effort, and he was married with a dependent child. Nonetheless, some thought Ford a draft dodger, the result of his complying with his father's wishes.

In January 1917, Ford became vice president of the company. "From the beginning he assumed responsibility for the business side of the company, sales, purchasing, advertising and the numerous details of the daily routine," the Ford Motor biography said. "His father was free to concentrate on engineering and manufacture." Ford saw a good deal of success during his early years at the company. He helped bring the Fordson tractor to market, supervised automobile sales and foreign operations and assisted in managing the company's wartime production.

Henry Ford suddenly resigned the presidency of Ford in December 1918, and Edsel Ford was elected to succeed him. The senior Ford had been angered by minority stockholders, particularly the Dodge brothers, who had sued for increased dividends. Early the next year, Henry Ford said he would form a new company and produce a car to rival the famous Model T. Made skittish by the threat to the value of their Ford shares a Model T competitor would pose, minority shareholders sold their shares to agents secretly working for the Fords. Edsel Ford is said to have been instrumental in this ruse of his father's, which brought complete ownership of Ford Motor back to the Ford family. The charade led to Edsel Ford's ownership of 41 percent of the company's stock that had been in non-Ford hands. Henry Ford remained the majority stockholder—seemingly forgetting his plan for a Model T rival—while his son remained Ford president.

"The commercial side of the company was Edsel's domain," the Ford Motor biography said. "The overseas operations were of special interest to him and he worked to expand Ford facilities in foreign places. He encouraged and supervised Ford participation in public events such as the World Fairs of the 1930s. He constantly emphasized quality and service as the prime factors in Ford sales. In business and administration it was Edsel behind the scenes who held the company together."

Presidency Brought Pressures

But as a number of executives left Ford, those who remained tended to be loyal to Henry Ford. Edsel Ford sought, and for a time found, an ally in his brother-in-law, Ernest Kanzler, an attorney who had been hired to manage the Ford tractor business. Kanzler had ascended to a vice presidency when Henry Ford determined Kanzler was trying to drive a wedge between him and his son. Kanzler and Edsel Ford agreed Ford was in need of management policy changes. Kanzler's downfall came after he petitioned Henry Ford to discontinue the Model T and replace it with a more modern car. When Edsel Ford returned from a European trip, Kanzler was gone; he'd either been fired or resigned. According to May's biography of Edsel Ford, the son never attempted to challenge his father over Kanzler's departure although he himself had been arguing for a Model T replacement. During his tenure at the top of the company, Ford had a number of his decisions reversed by his father, reversals he is said to have accepted quietly and without complaint.

One area where Edsel Ford's talents were allowed to soar unfettered was automobile design. While the younger Ford enjoyed modest success in persuading his father to revamp the venerable Model T with smoother lines and choice of colors, he wielded considerable influence over the Lincoln cars. When Henry Ford agreed to buy the failing Lincoln Motor Co. in 1922, he saw himself acquiring a canvas for his son's design artistry. Edsel Ford transformed Lincoln into a leading luxury car in a market well populated with fancy models. When the time finally came to replace the Model T, the Model A, introduced in 1927, had an elegant look, thanks to Edsel Ford. The Lincoln Zephyr followed in late 1935 and was regarded as the first successful streamlined car. The Lincoln Continental came in 1939 and was architect Frank Lloyd Wright's choice for most beautiful car of all time. Other designers managed development of the Zephyr and Continental, but Edsel Ford was a supervisor and close collaborator.

Tastes Differed from Father's

Ford's artistic interests revealed themselves again in tastes more sophisticated than his father's. He supported painter Charles Sheeler's studies of the Ford Rouge plant and in the early 1930s financed Diego Rivera's Detroit Institute of Art murals, also centered on the Ford Rouge operations. Ford became an avid art collector and principal benefactor of the Detroit Institute of Arts. His father's collections of Americana spawned Henry Ford Museum and Greenfield Village.

Aviation also caught the fancy of Edsel Ford. He bought the Stout Metal Aircraft Co. to produce the famous Ford trimotor plane. Ford's aircraft division pioneered the establishment of airlines and flew U.S. mail. Ford also mobilized engineers and technicians to develop a conveyor system for mass production of World War II bombers with interchangeable parts.

During the 1930s, Henry Ford ignored the advice of his son and enlisted the aid of Harry Bennett and his strong-arm tactics to thwart attempts to unionize Ford plants. Edsel Ford argued in 1937 the company would eventually be forced to recognize a union, and that finally happened in 1941.

The war effort and its pressures are said to have contributed to Ford's early demise at 49. Others hold the main detriment to his health was the stress of running the company and pressure from his father. When Ford had surgery for a stomach ulcer in 1942, doctors discovered rapidly spreading cancer, news they kept from their patient. Later that year, Ford contracted undulant fever from drinking unpasteurized milk from the Ford farms. Despite this widely publicized illness, May asserts in his biography it must have been the cancer that killed Ford in the spring of 1943.

Edsel Ford lent his name, posthumously, to Ford Motor's infamous Edsel models of the late 1950s. Year-long efforts to name the new car line had included polls, contests and suggestions from a poet such as Mongoose Civique, Pastelogram, and Resilient Bullet. Finally, Ford Chairman Ernest Breech suggested "Edsel." Edsel Ford's three sons balked, but the name stuck. Out of touch with the times, the Edsel was a huge failure, mechanically and aesthetically. Naming such a car after a Detroit "car man" known for his design sense and modern thinking was indeed a dubious tribute.

Further Reading

Johnson, Thomas H., editor, *The Oxford Companion to American History,* Oxford, 1966.

May, George S., *Encyclopedia of American Business History and Biography, the Automobile Industry, 1920-1980,* Facts on File, 1989.

"News Release: Edsel Ford," Ford Motor Company, 1998.

"Chronology of Henry Ford's Life," *Henry Ford Museum & Greenfield Village,* http://www.hfmgv.org/histories/hf/chrono.html (March 6, 1998).

"Ford's Big Mistake—The Edsel," *Your Mining Co. Guide to Vintage Cars,* (June 13, 1997) http://vintagecars.tqn.com/library/weekly/aa061397.htm (March 6, 1998). □

Anna Freud

Anna Freud's (1895-1982) pioneering efforts in establishing the theory and method of child psychoanalysis expanded the legacy of her father, Sigmund Freud, while it applied psychoanalytic discoveries to practical problems of child care and development in her innovative child care and study centers. As an investigator, speaker, teacher, and writer, she established a training method and body of scientific work that greatly influenced the study of children in the late twentieth century.

Anna Freud, the youngest of Sigmund Freud's six children and the only one who became a psychoanalyst, was born in Vienna in 1895. In the same year, Sigmund Freud published *Studies on Hysteria,* regarded as the first work of what would come to be known as psychoanalysis. From her earliest years, she identified closely with her father. Freud's mother was more attached to the other children, however, and the youngest daughter seems to have envied her beautiful older sister Sophie. Throughout her life, Freud had a difficult and distant relationship with her mother, who was famously skeptical of psychoanalysis. The elder Freud later praised her intellectual interests, but he did not send her to schools that could prepare her for university. Instead she was sent to the Cottage Lyceum, a school for teachers.

In 1914, Freud was visiting England when World War I broke out. Helped by friends in the diplomatic community, she returned to Austria where, stimulated by the ideas of Maria Montessori, she began her career as an elementary

school teacher. She taught in her old school during the war, but abandoned teaching soon afterwards to begin working more closely with her father. She briefly considered becoming a doctor but was dissuaded by him.

Freud increasingly assumed a role as her father's assistant, secretary, and proponent. In 1918, she entered analysis with the elder Freud. That same year she attended her first meeting of the Vienna Psychoanalytic Society. She became immersed in the development of psychoanalysis and began attending psychoanalytic meetings, translating papers, and analyzing patients. In 1922, she delivered her first paper to the Vienna Psychoanalytic Society and soon afterwards was accepted as a member.

The period from the mid-1920s to 1938, when the Freuds were forced by the Nazi occupation of Austria to leave Vienna, was a period of rich intellectual activity and rapid development in psychoanalytic thought. Freud's first patients were adults, but she soon began treating children. Her work as a teacher served as a bridge to what was emerging as her life's work—the psychoanalytic study of the child. Her interest in working with the Berlin Clinic promised to grant her a degree of independence from her father, but she decided to remain in Vienna after her father narrowly escaped bleeding to death after outpatient surgery. In 1923, he was diagnosed with cancer and from then on Freud became his primary caretaker, secretary, and intellectual companion. In that year she also established her own private practice. During this time she also assumed increasingly responsible positions in the leadership of the Vienna

Psychoanalytic Society and the International Psychoanalytic Association.

In 1925, she met Dorothy Burlingham, who had brought her children to Vienna for analytic treatment. Their friendship eventually deepened into a lifelong bond. During this time she also began a private analytically-oriented nursery school together with several other analysts, and also set up what is now regarded as the first modern day care center for underprivileged infants. The city of Vienna asked her in 1926 to train nursery workers and elementary teachers in applying the new analytic knowledge to education theory. That year she delivered four lectures, published as *An Introduction to the Technique of Child Analysis,* which marked the recognition of child analysis as a legitimate sub-specialty. In 1929, she first warned childcare professionals against mistaking professional child care for mothering. Throughout her career, Freud continued to stress that child care and analysis itself cannot substitute for the early parental attachments which shape personality development.

The elder Freud defended his daughter against the differing views of Melanie Klein and others and came to admire her intellectual independence. In 1931, she became editor of the *Journal of Psychoanalytical Education,* a forerunner of *The Psychoanalytic Study of the Child.* By the early 1930s, however, opposition to Freud's ideas was growing among extremists in the Nazi Party in Germany, and in 1933 his books were burned in Berlin.

Her efforts at this time to define normal child development led her to expand on her father's ego theory in her influential work *The Ego and the Mechanisms of Defense,* published in 1936. The principal defense mechanism, she claimed, is repression, which develops as children learn that some impulses are harmful and cannot be acted upon. Child analysis was the best means, she believed, for examining the functions of the ego and the instinctual drives, since children respond to their own internal pressures and the demands of the external world with a wider and more creative range of defenses than do adults. Considered a classic, this work contained one of the first comprehensive examinations of the conflicts of adolescence and outlined her views of the structure and unity of the human personality.

In 1938, after Freud was interrogated by the Nazi Gestapo in Vienna, the family emigrated to England. In England, Freud went back to seeing patients and founded a nursery at her family's house for children who had been separated from their parents by the war. The Hampstead Wartime Nursery for Homeless Children provided a natural laboratory for Freud's views on the influence of parental separation on childhood development. In two books and a series of reports collected as *Infants Without Families,* Freud and Burlingham, who also had become an analyst, outlined a program of service and research to prevent further harm to the children, conduct research on the fundamental needs of children, and develop an ideal nursery environment that could provide a model for peacetime education. A fundamental conclusion from these works was that separation from family could have a more detrimental effect than the war itself.

Freud consistently sought to apply the theories of psychoanalysis to the practical problems of children. The children of the war nurseries included the blind, handicapped, and deprived as well as those troubled by minor problems. Her observations convinced her of the importance of the parental bond to both normal and abnormal childhood development. The immediate effect of the nurseries was to shift childcare policy in favor of supporting children in their families rather than sending them away to institutions. She also initiated a form of core training for the war nurseries staff.

Others were also applying psychoanalysis to the treatment of children at this time, but a number of major differences soon emerged after Freud's arrival in England. A lifelong rift developed in the British Psychanalytic Society between Freud and Melanie Klein, who believed that techniques could be equally applied to children and adults. Freud held, however, that analysis of children must make allowances for children's unique developmental stages and fluid individuality. She believed in a reality-based and practical application of educational devices for both parents and children. She also disagreed that child analysis was beneficial to all children, and she objected to over-interpretation of children's movement and expression in play as signs of underlying conflict. Freud argued instead that a wide range of behavior could be considered ''normal'' and relied, more heavily than her counterparts, on direct observation and on the clues provided by children's drawings, play, and daydreams.

Like her father, Freud believed that analysis was essentially a talking cure, and children could not therefore be analyzed until they could talk. Children cannot be trusted to control the impulses set free by analysis, she argued; they must be controlled by the parents or by the analyst acting as ''auxiliary ego.'' Child analysis, Freud concluded, aims to strike a balance between freeing and restricting the child's impulses in the process of educating them. And no therapy of children can succeed without parental support. With her practical focus and humanistic outlook, Freud played a major part in maintaining unity among British psychoanalysts who often held widely differing points of view.

The nurseries were succeeded in 1947 by the Hampstead Child Therapy Course and Clinic, which she founded with a number of other prominent analysts. It would become the world's largest and most comprehensive child analytic training and treatment center. It provided analytic therapy, counseling, and a renowned training course for many American child psychologists and other practitioners and served as a model for similar centers throughout the world. For the next 40 years, Freud served as a training analyst, supervisor, and consultant to the clinic while speaking internationally and publishing on a wide variety of subjects. Freud continued her collaborations with pediatricians, social workers, and teachers, combining models of service to children with rigorous scientific investigation.

In the early 1960s, Freud began a collaboration with the Yale Child Study Center, contributing to seminars on family law and child placement conflicts. In the resulting books, Freud argued that the child's perspective must be paramount in determining child care decisions and that the ''least detrimental alternative'' should be pursued that will allow the child to maintain a stable parental relationship. She also argued for minimizing the state's intrusion into family life. In her final years, she extended this work to examining the uses and misuses of experts in resolving custody and placement conflicts.

In her final years, Freud believed the future of psychoanalysis lay in examining each developmental path that led to adulthood. Instead of seeking the origin of disturbances in earliest life, she proposed a number of ''developmental lines'' of normal development in which disturbance could occur. Psychic disturbance, she believed, may have many origins and take forms in childhood and adulthood which are not necessarily causally related or even similar. A later major work, *Normality and Pathology in Childhood*, focused on assessing childhood developmental stages and establishing norms for childhood development.

Freud came to believe that modern analysis had wrongly shifted attention from unearthing repressed past childhood experiences to dealing solely with the patient's present relations with the therapist. She also disagreed with the modern shift from a father-centered to mother-centered approach. When asked about her views on the subject of mothering, Freud replied that she had never written of mother-daughter relations because she knew nothing about them. A striking irony of her life was that she never married or had children of her own; and in spite of her lifelong dedication to the care of children, she refused to be identified as a universal mother figure.

Although Freud never acquired advanced academic degrees, her accomplishments were widely recognized in the many honorary degrees awarded her in England, Europe, and the United States. As the last link to the origins of psychoanalysis, she embraced her father's ideas while forging her own theories of normal and abnormal child development and psychology and creating a coherent therapeutic technique. Freud suffered a stroke in 1982 and died later that year. Clifford Yorke, a fellow psychoanalyst, wrote that her death ''brought to a close the distinguished career of one of the great scientific leaders of our time, and one whose impact and influence will continue to be felt as long as a science of the mind survives.''

Further Reading

Coles, Robert, *Anna Freud: The Dream of Psychoanalysis,* Addison-Wesley, 1991.

Freud, Anna, *Writings of Anna Freud [8 volumes],* International Universities Press, 1964-1980

Peters, Uwe H., *Anna Freud: A Life Dedicated to Children,* Schocken Books, 1985.

Sayer, Janet, *Mothers of Psychoanalysis: Helene Deutch, Karen Horney, Anna Freud, and Melanie Klein,* Norton, 1991.

Young-Bruehl, Elizabeth, *Anna Freud: A Biography,* Norton, 1994.

Women in Psychology: A Bio-Bibliographical Source Book, edited by Agnes N. O'Connell and Nancy F. Russo, Greenwood, 1990.

American Journal of Psychiatry, December 1983, p. 1632; May 1995, p. 784.

American Psychologist, February 1985, p. 230.
Journal of the American Academy of Child Psychiatrists, 1984, p.233
London Times, October 11, 1982, p. 12.
Psychoanalytic Study of the Child, 1984, p. 31.

Millard Fuller

Millard Fuller (born 1935) is the founder of Habitat for Humanity International, an organization staffed by volunteers that was created to help those in need purchase a home of their own.

Millard Fuller was a millionaire by the age of 29, and has experienced the "American Dream." But more importantly, he has made it his life's work to pass that dream on, especially through his work with Habitat for Humanity International. This need to serve came upon him when he almost lost his family and his health to the rigors and pressures of the business world. Although the *Atlanta Constitution* once identified Fuller as the lowest paid among the top executives of the country's one hundred largest charities, it does not seem to bother him in the least.

Fuller, who holds a B.S. in economics and a law degree, had a strong entrepreneurial streak in him from the beginning. As a child in Lanett, Alabama, he fattened and sold a pig, and then used the profits to buy and sell more small livestock. Certain experiences in his childhood also seemed to foreshadow his future. His mother, Estin Cook Fuller, died when he was three years old. His father, Render Alexander Fuller, later married Eunice Stephens. His father and stepmother had two sons and owned a grocery store. When Millard was about ten, his father bought 400 acres of farmland. An elderly couple lived in a small, rickety building on the land. One of the first things that Fuller's father did was to purchase materials and help the couple rebuild their home. In a way, this was Millard Fuller's first brush with destiny.

Fuller continued his entrepreneurial ways in high school, raising beef cattle and earning enough to pay for his college expenses. He graduated from Auburn University in Auburn, Alabama, in 1957. He then went to law school at the University of Alabama. There, he was joined in his entrepreneurial ventures by friend and a fellow law student, Morris S. Dees, Jr. They ran a direct mail fund raising operation that sold items to schools and nonprofit organizations that they could in turn sell for more money to earn a profit. They also invested in real estate near the school, buying, repairing and then renting out a number of buildings. The two were earning up to $50,000 a year between them before they even finished law school. During this time, in 1959, Fuller also married his college sweetheart, Linda Caldwell. They eventually had four children: Christopher, Kimberly, Faith, and Georgia.

Fuller served a brief stint in the United States Army in 1960, the same year he received his LL.B. and passed the Alabama bar exam. Shortly thereafter, Fuller and Dees started their own law office in Montgomery, Alabama. Still, they put more energy into their entrepreneurial projects than their legal ones. They began publishing cookbooks, starting with *Favorite Recipes of Home Economics Teachers* (1963), and eventually started their own imprint, The Favorite Recipes Press. After two years, they folded their legal practice and were the largest publisher of cookbooks in the United States.

Things were not idyllic in the Fuller household, however. Fuller had a severe breathing disorder, among other health problems, which his doctors believed were stress-related. By November of 1964, he realized his symptoms had spread into his relationship with his family as well. His wife abruptly left for New York City to seek the counsel of a pastor and examine her commitment to her marriage. That event was Fuller's wake-up call. He followed his wife to New York and they had many soul-searching conversations.

The couple finally decided they would sell almost everything they owned. According to the Shirley Barnes of the *Chicago Tribune*, they returned home to Montgomery to "sell their home and give away their possessions, donating the proceeds to mission projects worldwide and church-related organizations." Fuller also sold out his share of the business to his partner, and donated the proceeds of that sale to humanitarian causes. Dees eventually followed Fuller's lead; he sold the business and cofounded the Southern Poverty Law Center in 1971.

The Fuller family moved to Koinonia Farm, "Koinonia" taken from the Greek word for "fellowship." The farm was founded in 1942 to be a space for racial equality and the common sharing of material goods. Residents had only enough possessions to support a meager lifestyle. Fuller met Clarence Jordan, a Bible scholar and author of "The Cotton Patch Gospel," at the farm. Jordan was soon to wield great influence on Fuller's life.

Beginning in 1966, Fuller was a fund-raiser for Tougaloo College, a small, church-funded, and predominantly African-American school in Tougaloo, Mississippi. Though based in New York, Fuller traveled frequently for the school. He also took a two-month leave of absence to visit Africa with a group from the Church of Christ. The burgeoning city of Mbandaka, Zaire, made an impression on him at this time.

In 1968, the Fuller family returned to Koinonia Farm to find it much-changed due to the harassment of neighbors. Only six inhabitants remained. Yet, the Fullers and Jordan resolved to rebuild the community somehow. They decided to start a housing partnership plan which would build small houses on plots of one half-acre each. The homes were to be built on a corner of the 1100 Koinonia parcel, and were to be sold to poor, rural families.

Additionally, their faith dictated they follow the biblical edict in Exodus 22:25: "If you lend money to any of My people who are poor among you, you shall not be like a moneylender to him; you shall not charge him interest." The money would come from Linda Fuller's business, as well as charitable donations, interest-free loans from donors, and later, small mortgage payments from the homeowners themselves.

Fuller and Jordan began building in 1969, but unfortunately, Jordan was unable to see the project through. He passed away that same year. The Fullers and the other residents of Koinonia kept the dream alive, erecting 27 houses by mid-1972. Thirty-two homes were scheduled to be built on another site as well.

With the great success of the Koinonia community, the Fullers remembered the citizens of Mbandaka, Zaire, and decided to turn their attention in that direction. They spent six months preparing for their stay in Zaire, including three months in Paris to brush up on their French, which was the official language in Zaire. Fuller became the Church of Christ's Director of Development for the entire equatorial region of Zaire. First, his team constructed several small cement-block homes. While not luxurious by any means, they were far superior to the crumbling huts the natives had previously inhabited. The Fullers and their church group also raised money for prosthetic limbs and eyeglasses for the people of Mbandaka who desperately needed them.

In 1976, Fuller and his family returned to Koinonia Farm, determined to use their experience for even bigger and better purposes. As Fuller later commented to Barnes of the *Chicago Tribune,* "We want to make shelter a matter of conscience. We want to make it socially, politically, morally, and religiously unacceptable to have substandard housing and homelessness." They founded Habitat for Humanity International, an organization which was to raise money and recruit volunteers to build homes for those in need. Government help would be enlisted for land acquisition and utilities, but the houses themselves were to be built from the donations of individuals.

Habitat homes are sold to families or individuals living in substandard housing who do not earn enough to buy a home through conventional channels. Some people mistakenly believe that Habitat gives people free homes, but as a Habitat volunteer commented to *Christian Science Monitor,* "We give away nothing but a great opportunity." A small down-payment is required, as is a low monthly mortgage. The mortgage payments go into a fund that perpetuates the program. Additionally, all buyers invest a set number of labor hours in their own home. Fuller calls this "sweat equity" and points out that it builds a sense of pride and ownership in the individuals.

The organization has grown each year: in 1980, the organization had eleven U.S. affiliate groups and five projects running overseas. Fourteen years later, they boasted 1,108 affiliate groups in the United States, plus 331 college chapters in North America, and over 160 affiliate groups in Hungary, Poland, Central and South America, the Caribbean, Africa, Asia and the Pacific region. In their first 15 years of operation, Habitat for Humanity built 10,000 homes. They built their next 10,000 homes in just two years' time, and a subsequent 10,000 homes in the next year and a half. The organization ranked seventeenth in the home construction business in 1995.

The Fullers and Habitat have also generated support from people of all walks of life and every side of the political fence: former President Jimmy Carter and Rosalyn Carter, President Bill Clinton, leading Republican Newt Gingrich, actor Paul Newman, entertainer Bob Hope, and singer Amy Grant. The Fullers were joined by the Carters for a rebuilding effort of 20 homes in parts of riot-torn Los Angeles in 1995.

Fuller has written a number of books which both set forth his philosophies and detail the histories of his various contributions. *Bokotola* (1977) was inspired by the Fullers' time in Zaire; *The Theology of the Hammer* (1994), and *A Simple, Decent Place to Live: The Building Realization of Habitat for Humanity* (1995) in which he discusses Habitat for Humanity and the theology the inspired and continues to inspire it. In *The Theology of the Hammer,* Fuller explained, "The idea or concept of the theology of the hammer is that our Christian faith (indeed, our entire Judeo-Christian tradition) mandates that we do more than just talk about faith and sing about love. We must put faith and love into action to make them real, to make them come alive for people. . . . True faith must be acted out."

Fuller continues to refuse large yearly salaries, yet, his rewards are great. He has received 15 honorary doctorates, the Council of State Housing Agencies Outstanding Achievement Award (1986), the Common Cause Public Service Achievement Award (1989), and the Martin Luther King Jr. Humanitarian Award, from both the King Center (1987) and the Georgia State Holiday Commission (1992). In late 1996, President Clinton awarded him a Medal of Freedom. Millard and Linda Fuller have jointly won a few awards as well, including the 1994 Harry S. Truman Public Service Award.

In a May 1995 interview with Barnes of the *Chicago Tribune,* Fuller remarked, "You are looking at a very happy man. Very busy, but Linda and I work together now and I derive much more joy making money for other people than I ever did from making it for myself."

Further Reading

Fuller, Millard, *The Theology of the Hammer,* Myth and Helwys, 1994.

Atlanta Journal, "Habitat Leader Tries to Set an Example in Refusing Large Salary," April 28, 1992, p. A4.

Atlanta Journal/Constitution, "A Firm Foundation," July 28, 1996, section M, p. 1.

Chicago Tribune, "Building New Hope: Couple Find Each Other by Trading Their Millions for Hammer and Nails," May 14, 1995, section 6, p. 3.

Christian Science Monitor, August 7, 1987, p. 21.

Ebony, November 1996, p. 28.

Time, "A Bootstrap Approach to Low-Cost Housing," January 16, 1989, pp. 12-13.

Habitat for Humanity, http://www.habitat.org (December 29, 1997).

G

John Galt

Scottish author John Galt (1779-1839) wrote extensively during the early 1800s, producing novels as well as works of drama, poetry, art criticism, and biography. He also worked as a lobbyist and founded settlements in Canada. Galt's style of novel writing contributed to the development of the realistic Scottish novel in which characters were depicted in their day-to-day lives in the Scottish countryside, speaking in colorful local idioms.

John Galt was born on May 2, 1779, in the Scottish seaport town of Irvine, in the county of Ayrshire. Born to John Galt, captain of a merchant ship, and Jean Tilloch Galt, he was the oldest of four children. His health was fragile as a child, and he spent much of his time reading and helping his mother garden. Galt's mother was a major influence on him, and her use of metaphorical language and mastery of Scottish dialect would later be reflected in his novels. His family moved to another seaport town, Greenock, a little farther north in western Scotland when he was ten years old. From this port his father expanded his mercantile business, which included trading with Jamaica. Although bookish, and displaying ability in writing couplets from age six, Galt was taught subjects considered useful in business, including math, astronomy, penmanship, English, and French.

At a young age he was apprenticed in business. He worked as a clerk in Greenock between 1795 and 1804, first at the customshouse and later in another commercial enterprise. At age 25, in 1804, Galt moved to London to enter the business world. His first partnership with another young man failed after he discovered his partner was bankrupt. His next business venture with his brother, Tom, lasted a short time before his brother left for Honduras. Although several of his business ventures during his first five years in London were unsuccessful, it was at this time Galt began his writing career. In 1804 he published *The Battle of Largs: A Gothic Epic, with Several Miscellaneous Pieces* and wrote numerous articles on a range of subjects for the *Greenock Advertiser* and the *Scots Magazine*. Other early works included publications in the newspaper the *Star,* and an article entitled, "Statistical Account of Upper Canada," published in October of 1807 in *Philosophical Magazine.*

In 1809, at about 30 years old, Galt planned to reside in Lincoln's Inn and study for a career in law. After spending the next two years travelling, however, Galt abandoned his plans to become a lawyer. During his time abroad in the Mediterranean and Near East, he met English author George Gordon, Lord Byron, with whom he travelled from Gibraltar to Malta in 1809. Soon Galt became involved in yet another unsuccessful business venture. This plan was designed to thwart Napoleon's decrees blocking British ships from trading with Europe. Galt's scheme had been to move merchandise into Europe via Turkey, after the goods had been stored secretly on a Greek island. Although a business failure, the correspondence he had with a friend, James Park, became the cornerstone for Galt's first book. *Voyages and Travels in the years 1809, 1810, and 1811* was published in January of 1812. He also served as editor for *Political Review* later that same year.

Held Variety Of Business Positions

Galt married Elizabeth Tilloch, daughter of Dr. Alexander Tilloch who owned the *Philosophical Magazine,* on

During the years 1820 to 1825, Galt wrote ten novels about life in West Scotland. He chronicled daily existence during the period of social and economic change brought on by the Industrial Revolution in the late eighteenth and early nineteenth centuries. Some scholars considered four of his novels, *Annals of the Parish* (1821), *The Ayrshire Legatees* (1821), *The Provost* (1822), and *The Entail* (1822), his best works detailing English and Scottish society during this period. Galt used realistic depictions, including local vernacular, in his novels, and those unfamiliar with the dialect might find a glossary of Scottish idioms and terms useful.

Founded Settlements In Canada

After four years as agent for the United Empire Loyalists, a large group of settlers in Upper Canada (now Ontario) for whom he had lobbied Britain's Colonial Office, he failed to recover their losses from the British government. Instead of giving up, he sought another means of gaining financial remuneration for his clients. Through a complex turn of events, the Canada Company was formed in 1825 with Galt as one of its commissioners. The company planned to develop a million acres of government-owned woodlands located between Lake Huron and Lake Ontario for settlement and then resell at a profit. That same year, Galt made his first voyage to North America. During this trip, he organized the takeover of extensive acreage which would later be sold to settlers. He also visited New York State in the United States to study methods of settling land and plan for new towns, before returning to London in June 1825.

Galt made a second trip to Canada in 1826. His *Autobiography* (1833) chronicles his travels with William "Tiger" Dunlop throughout Canada, and is considered an excellent resource about the usual weather patterns, system of roads, methods of shipping, and social life of the day. And although Galt stopped writing novels during his time in Canada, in 1826 *The Last of the Lairds* was published in London while he was in North America.

Initially this venture to develop settlements in Canada looked promising. On Galt's return visit in 1826, he was made superintendent. He was instrumental in founding the towns of Guelph and Goderich in today's Ontario, Canada. He had plans for other colonies, too. Galt even brought his wife and three sons to Canada in 1828, intending to settle there permanently. But by April 1829, he lost his profitable position due to what the company called "mismanagement." Forced to return to England, he landed in Liverpool in May of 1829. Unfortunately he had not left trouble behind in Canada. Galt had left considerable debt behind in England, and upon his return, his creditors sought payment. Unfortunately, Galt had used the money to educate his sons, and he could not repay the amount owed. Because of non-payment of his debts, he was arrested on July 15, 1829, and served in the King's Bench debtors' prison until November 10, 1829. While in prison, his health began to fail.

April 20, 1813. By then, Galt had also published a biography about Thomas Cardinal Wolsey (1812) which he had researched at Jesus College, Oxford. Additional books about his travels included an autobiography, and *Letters from the Levant,* which was published in 1813. From 1814 to 1815 he was editor for *New British Theatre* (a monthly periodical), as well as the author of several published plays. He was also a frequent contributor to the *Monthly Magazine* during the years 1817-1823.

By 1818 Galt had moved to Glasgow, Scotland. He was well-connected politically, and used his influence as a lobbyist for several causes. Beginning in 1819 he worked for a year for the Edinburgh and Glasgow Union Canal Company, promoting the Glasgow-Edinburgh canal. Later clients he lobbied for included the United Empire Loyalists, a group of Canadian settlers who sought money from the British government for their losses incurred when American soldiers had crossed into Canada during the War of 1812.

Although Galt continued his lobbying activity, beginning in 1820 he started gaining recognition as a novelist. At that time, his association with William Blackwood, the publisher of *Blackwood's Magazine* benefitted both men. Blackwood found the novelist he had sought for his publication, and Galt found a outlet for his early novels. From mid-1820 to the end of 1822, *Blackwood's Magazine* published a great deal of Galt's writing, including book reviews and other articles as well as installments of *The Ayrshire Legatees* and *Annals of the Parish,* both of which were later released as complete novels.

Wrote Extensively from Debtor's Prison

Although Galt had written little in Canada, during his four months in prison he produced many commercial articles for magazines as well as several books. He wrote the novel, *Lawrie Todd; or, The Settlers in the Wood,* which was published in 1830, and depicted life in a settlement in the United States. Also published in 1830 was a biography about Lord Byron, and a romantic novel, *Southennan,* set in the sixteenth century during reign of Mary Queen of Scots. Numerous articles appeared in *Fraser's Magazine,* including "The Hurons, a Canadian Tale," "Canadian Sketches," "American Traditions," and "Guelph in Upper Canada."

The success of *Lawrie Todd* eased his financial difficulties. Additionally, after the increase of the Canada Company's stock value, Galt's management skills were looked upon favorably again, and he was hired by the British-American Land Company in 1831 as its secretary. He continued writing about his experiences in Canada, and 1831 the novel, *Bogle Corbet; or, The Emigrants,* was published. He wrote articles about the country for several publications, including *Fraser's, Tait's,* and *Blackwood's.*

In 1832 Galt suffered the first in a series of three strokes. The second occurred in 1834, and last in 1836. By then he had returned to his native Scotland and, due to his extensive efforts at writing, was debt free. In spite of Galt's abrupt departure from Canada, the family remained respectable there, and his son, Thomas, became a judge in the country, while another would become Sir Alexander Tilloch Galt, the nation's prime minister. Although Galt wrote with great difficulty during his last years, he continued publishing articles and books, many concerned with the topic of Canada. Some of his last works were dictated to his son, and although considered by many critics to be inconsistent and verbose, they were are also recognized as informative to students of early life in Canada. Among these were *The Demon of Destiny; and Other Poems* (1839) and *The Literary Life and Miscellanies of John Galt* (1834). Galt died on April 11, 1839, in Greenock, Scotland.

Contributed Realism In Scottish Novels

During his lifetime, Galt produced over 40 volumes of material. He wrote novels, biography, travel, poetry, and art criticism. Ian A. Gordon noted in *Novelists and Prose Writers,* that a distinction should be made between works written under financial pressure and others. Gordon commented, "Galt's major contribution to the novel was his sensitive and yet ironic portrayal of the rural Scotland of the late eighteenth century, a period when agricultural society was giving way to the new industrial growth." Galt considered *The Provost* his best effort. The story of a man's personal advancement in a Scottish town, the work had also been praised by his contemporary, Samuel Taylor Coleridge. In his biography, *John Galt: The Life of a Writer,* Gordon declared Galt "a novelist of considerable power, with an assured niche in literary history."

Further Reading

Daiches, David, *A Critical History of English Literature, Volume II,* second edition, Ronald Press, 1970.
Gordon, Ian A., *John Galt: The Life of a Writer,* University of Toronto Press, 1972.
Dictionary of Literary Biography, Gale, Volume 99: *Canadian Writers before 1890,* 1990; Volume 116: *British Romantic Novelists, 1789-1832,* 1992; Volume 159: *British Short-Fiction Writers, 1800-1880,* 1996;
Vinson, James, editor, *Novelists and Prose Writers,* St. Martin's Press, 1979. □

James Galway

A master flutist whose playing style has become the measure by which others are judged, James Galway (born 1939) is credited with elevating the status, stature, and performance standards of his chosen instrument.

James Galway's illustrious musical career boasts a number of critical as well as popular successes. Even before he reached his teens, for instance, he had been named a champion flute player in Ireland. Later, after studying with flute masters in Paris and London, he performed with the London Symphony Orchestra and served for years as the principal flutist with both the Royal Philharmonic Orchestra and the Berlin Philharmonic Orchestra. Galway then sought to increase public awareness and appreciation of the flute through various international tours and television programs. He has also reached out to a new generation by teaching master classes. As Galway declared in a 1994 interview with Philip Kennicott available online at www. futurenet.com, "I've set the standard. . . . I think I've inspired a lot of kids to really try to do something better with the flute."

Galway was born on December 8, 1939, in a working-class neighborhood of Belfast, Northern Ireland. He developed his interest in all things musical at a very early age. His father, a shipyard riveter who was also named James, was a flutist and accordion player in a local band, while his mother, Ethel, a textile mill worker, was a self-taught piano player. When he was a just a young child, Galway began to try out a variety of instruments, picking up the harmonica, violin, and penny whistle before settling on the flute, which he quickly decided was his favorite.

At about the age of nine, Galway began taking informal flute lessons from both his father and grandfather. He also learned how to read music from the leader of the local flute band. When he was ten, he entered an Irish Flute Championship contest and won the three solo contests he entered. By the time he turned 12, he knew he wanted his career to be in music.

Awarded Prestigious Scholarship

While attending Mountcollyer Secondary Modern School, Galway met Muriel and Douglas Dawn, both of whom made sure the promising youngster had every opportunity to realize his goals. Muriel Dawn, a flutist with the British Broadcasting Corporation's (BBC) Northern Ireland Symphony Orchestra, taught him the basic skills involved in playing the flute. Douglas Dawn found him a job as a piano tuner's apprentice, sought out opportunities for him to per-

form with Belfast-area orchestras, and helped persuade the Belfast Education Committee to award Galway a scholarship to study at the Royal Academy of Music in London.

Galway studied for three years at the Royal Academy of Music under the tutelage of John Francis before he moved on to the Guildhall School for Music. There he was instructed by Geoffrey Gilbert, whom he credits with being one of the major technical influences in his career. The early 1960s saw Galway move to Paris and study under Gaston Crunelle at the Conservatoire National Superieur de Musique.

In between his studies and his appointments to various international orchestras, Galway married his first wife, Claire. They had one son. Galway married his second wife, Anna Renggli, in 1972. The couple had twin daughters.

Despite the fact that he never graduated from any of the musical academies he attended, Galway managed to impress a number of London-based conductors and easily found work in their orchestras and ensembles when he returned to the United Kingdom from Paris. His first job was with the Wind Band of the Royal Shakespeare Theatre at Stratford-upon-Avon. He then moved on to the Sadler's Wells Opera Orchestra, where he played both the flute and piccolo. His next job was with the Royal Opera House Orchestra, once again as a flutist and piccolo player. Galway then joined the London Symphony Orchestra, serving as the principal flutist for the 1966-67 season before accepting the same position with the Royal Philharmonic Orchestra, also in London. He remained with the Royal

Philharmonic for two seasons, resigning in 1969 to become the principal solo flutist for the Berlin Philharmonic Orchestra.

Galway's tenure with the Berlin Philharmonic was not an especially happy one. Feeling unfulfilled and underutilized, he began accepting engagements that allowed him to perform apart from the orchestra. During the summer of 1975, with the encouragement of Michael Emmerson, a former talent scout who offered to become his manager, Galway resigned from the Berlin Philharmonic to seek his fortune as a full-time solo instrumentalist.

Gained International Prominence

The gamble paid off handsomely. Galway appeared in more than 120 concerts over the next year at venues throughout the world, including stints with all four of the major orchestras in England. He also recorded his first four albums and even found time to teach a semester course in advanced flute studies at the Eastman School of Music in Rochester, New York.

In his solo work, Galway has always sought to broaden the traditionally limited classical repertoire of flute music by transcribing whatever captures his fancy. His new arrangements for the flute range from classical pieces originally written for other instruments (such as *The Four Seasons* by Vivaldi and Khachaturian's concerto for violin) to popular tunes of the day done in classic Galway style. Nothing is beyond his scope—jazz, country, show tunes, and the folk music of both Ireland and Japan all figure prominently in his repertoire. In addition, Galway often commissions new flute pieces from contemporary composers such as Lorin Maazel, Joaquin Rodrigo, and Thea Musgrave.

One of Galway's most famous arrangements is his cover of folksinger John Denver's "Annie's Song." Released in 1978, this highly acclaimed and wildly successful instrumental piece not only won him legions of new fans but also encouraged him to collaborate with other popular performers of the day, including singer Cleo Laine and composer Henry Mancini.

Yet as Kennicott notes, "Galway's high profile as a crossover artist, popular entertainer, and restless raider of popular classics not written for the flute, naturally alienates the purists. With dozens and dozens of recordings of Vivaldi's 'Four Seasons,' why would anyone want to hear it transcribed for flute? Galway argues that musical practice of the time included a great deal of shifting about among instruments, and that composers such as Bach regularly reworked material for different instruments. He's right of course, but the popularity of his crossover and transcription discs doesn't rest on any such historical premise. They're popular because Galway is performing them, and flute lovers are grateful for almost anything he performs."

Galway has further cemented his widespread appeal by making frequent television appearances. Besides his own specials, he has been featured on the critically acclaimed children's program *Sesame Street* and other American public television shows as well as a wide variety of regular network shows. And in 1989, Galway decided to resume teaching master classes in the flute. He works with students at his home in Switzerland and in many of the cities he visits while on tour.

Recordings Brought Acclaim

Ever the consummate perfectionist, Galway has typically refused to release any recording with his name on it until he was completely satisfied with the results. This fastidious attention to detail is in no small way responsible for the many honors he has garnered throughout his career. He was awarded the Grand Prix du Disque for his recordings of Mozart's concertos and also received kudos for his recordings of Vivaldi. His album sales have netted him several gold and platinum records. He has received record of the year awards from both *Billboard* and *Cashbox* magazines. In 1977, he was named a member of the Order of the British Empire (OBE), a commendation by Queen Elizabeth II that recognized Galway's musical contributions to society. And in 1997, *Musical America* named him musician of the year.

Given his tireless quest for innovation, his flair for improvisation, and his ability to secure critical acclaim as well as commercial success, Galway has unquestionably earned the distinction of being the premiere flutist of his generation. The charismatic performer is well aware of his appeal and makes good use of his abilities as a showman to broaden the audience for flute music. As he told Kennicott, "I know who's got the best chops—me."

Further Reading

Contemporary Musicians, Volume 3, Gale, 1990, pp. 87-89.
Galway, James, *Autobiography,* enlarged edition, Chivers, 1980.
"James Galway," http://www.cameratapacifica.org/galway.html (March 3, 1998).
"The James Galway Flute Page," http://www.classicalmus.com/bmgclassics/galway/bio.html (March 3, 1998).
"James Galway," http://www.futurenet.com/classicalnet/artists/galway/interview.html (March 3, 1998).

Roberto Crispulo Goizueta

Since taking over as CEO (chief executive officer) of the Coca-Cola Company in 1981, Roberto Goizueta (1931-1997) brought market value of his company's stock from $4 billion to over $150 billion. During his tenure, Coca-Cola became the world's biggest trademark, dominating the international soft drink market.

A patrician-looking but gentle-ruling capitalist, Roberto Goizueta was admired by both business competitors and his own company's shareholders (whom he referred to as "shareowners.") He made it his only priority to pull the Coca-Cola ("Coke") Company out of its 20-year decline and into global stardom. His success was tracked around the world. Diversifying internal investments while pushing for overseas expansion, Goizueta and his hand-picked management team quickly gained domin-

ance for Coke in the world market, and enhanced the company's share value by more than $148 billion. In 1996 alone, shareholders realized a remarkable 43 percent return on their investments. Goizueta's own personal wealth, starting with 100 shares of company stock, multiplied by the millions. However, he believed that big business had a responsibility to the community in which it thrived (whether local or global), and he donated most of his personal wealth to major charities.

An Unlikely Candidate

Born in Havana, Cuba, Goizueta was the son of Crispulo and Aida Goizueta. His mother was an heiress to a sugar fortune and his father was an architect who had attended the University of Pennsylvania. As a teenager, he was sent to New England to attend school. A shy intellectual educated at Yale University in chemical engineering, Goizueta made a pivotal decision in 1954 to join Coke's technical subsidiary in Havana, Cuba, rather than return to his family's sugar plantations. The job offer followed Goizueta's response to Coke's newspaper advertisement for employment opportunities. After joining the company as a technician, he borrowed money from his father to purchase 100 shares of company stock.

Fleeing Fidel Castro's revolution, Goizueta brought his family to the United States in 1961 with $40 in his pocket and the 100 shares of Coke stock. He continued with Coca-Cola, first in Miami, Florida, then at corporate headquarters in Atlanta, Georgia. After several career promotions, he

entered executive management in 1974 as senior vice-president of Coke's technical division.

Goizueta did not fit the historical profile of corporate executive ranks. The Coca-Cola Company was founded and headquartered in the southern United States, and its management was top-heavy with Southern gentry. Conversely, the cigar/cigarette-smoking Goizueta spoke English as a second language, though he became an United States citizen in 1969. Nonetheless, he was well-bred, well-educated, and well-thought-of. Most of all, he had drive and integrity, and his style caught the attention of Robert Woodruff, then-head of the Coca-Cola Company. He offered Goizueta the CEO position in 1981, an offer which was modestly but enthusiastically accepted. Although Goizueta had virtually no experience in marketing, a necessary skill to lead a major company, he did hold one advantage over other vice presidents who were considered. From his years in the technical division, Goizueta had "the knowledge." He was reportedly only one of two people in the company who knew Coke's secret formula.

Formula For Success

Even before Goizueta was offered the CEO job, he had outlined his perception of its duties in a two-page paper, along with another outlining his vision for the company's future and his objectives for making such vision a reality. He kept that mission statement in his top desk drawer for his entire tenure as CEO, periodically updating it as needed. Goizueta also knew that his greatest strength was that of a think-tank, therefore, he would need a strong team to put his ideas into action. His only request upon being offered the CEO job was that he could choose his team. Given full reign to do so, he then named his colleague, Don Keough, as president and chief operating officer (COO), giving him comprehensive authority across the organizational structure. Keough, an extroverted, strong-willed, charismatic leader, was the perfect compliment to Goizueta's quiet management style. Together, they forged ahead to turn around the company's fate: Goizueta up in his Atlanta office, brainstorming new markets, products and strategies—and Keough out in the field, making it all happen.

At the time Goizueta took over Coke in 1981, the company had been declining in growth and profit, and was fighting to keep its market share away from the new cola on the block, "Pepsi Cola." Coke's holdings at that time also included many businesses which had strayed outside the parameters of the soft drink market, including a shrimp farming business. The company was considered conservative in its spending, forecasting, and growth potential.

Goizueta made it known immediately that he intended to change all that. He had a singular objective: to increase investor wealth/earnings. And his plan for achieving his objective was equally focused. As he told *Fortune* interviewers, "You borrow money at a certain rate and invest it at a higher rate and pocket the difference. It's simple."

And that's exactly what Goizueta did. First, he analyzed the existing corporate holdings and got out of the shrimp business, putting the money back into what the company knew best: soft drinks. Within the first twelve

months in office, he had put his new product, Diet Coke, on the market, and money into his investors' hands. Next came an updated version of the old Coca-Cola formula, which was marketed as "New Coke." Although technically a failed product, New Coke only made things better for the staged marketing return of the "Coke Classic," using the original 100-year old fountain-drink recipe concocted by an Atlanta, Georgia, pharmacist. As of 1997, Coke Classic remained the company's biggest seller. Then came "Cherry Coke," another nostalgic money-maker. Eventually, Goizueta brought the bottling companies in-house. He was putting money into his investors' hands, year after year. Coke gained an unequivocal market advantage over Pepsi.

Next, Goizueta and Keough planned their global expansion. Goizueta viewed the United States market as representing about five percent of the potential world market. The world's taste for Coke actually began during World War II when, during Woodruff's reign, Coke was provided to American G.I.s overseas. Early on, Goizueta realized the strength of Coke's trademark in foreign markets. Coke's team forged into Europe, Australia and Japan. After Russia came China and India. According to *Fortune,* as of 1997, clearly 80 percent of Coke's profits came from overseas markets.

Only once did Goizueta stray outside the soft drink market entirely. In 1982, he purchased Columbia Pictures. Unfortunately, shortly after the purchase, Columbia released *Ishtar,* a movie hardly even remembered by persons outside the film industry. However, during Coke's ownership of Columbia Pictures, the movie, *Ghostbusters* was also released, and when Goizueta sold Columbia to Sony in 1989, he had pocketed over $800 million in profits for his "shareowners."

Husband, Father and Dog-Lover

Goizueta married Olga Casteleiro in 1953, with whom he had three children, Roberto, Olga, and Javier. He lived in Atlanta, Georgia, close to company headquarters. Very fond of his prize Welsh Corgi, "Just Enuff of the Real Thing," Goizueta's idea of a nice afternoon was to attend a dog show with his wife. He vacationed at the same rental place on Sea Island for 20 years. Although a heavy cigarette-smoker, Goizueta was otherwise formal and conservative in his manner and appearance, seldom, if ever, seen in public in casual attire. He often engaged in public speaking at colleges and universities, where he proudly shared his formula for success.

Having been greatly influenced by the thinking of his maternal grandfather, Marcelo Cantera, a self-made businessman, Goizueta would often inject into his speeches little Spanish proverbs used by his grandfather. He believed that big business was responsible for creating a "civil society," and he encouraged his audiences, as well as fellow CEOs around the world to be active in charities and non-profit organizations which addressed social problems. An article in *Newsweek* noted that in 1997, Goizueta donated $38 million of Coca-Cola stock to an anonymous Atlanta, Georgia foundation.

Preparing For the Future

To Goizueta, there was no end in sight on the horizon of new markets. The quintessential planner and strategist, he constantly reviewed demographic and geographic market research data to streamline his products or direct their entry into the most promising areas. His advertising campaigns often focused upon a youthful market, targeting countries with huge younger populations, such as China. He also considered warm climates like that in the Pacific as potentially better markets, although in the mid-1990s, Iceland remained one of Coke's highest consumption countries. Additionally, Goizueta often referred to the untapped market within the human body itself, remarking that Coke consumption was a mere fraction of the total fluid intake per person per day, leaving plenty of room for increase. He constantly tested the price of his products in the marketplace, preferring lower prices with high volume business over more exclusive or higher-priced products.

Goizueta believed in rich rewards for company performers. He had little turnover in his hand-picked top management, and he made them millionaires. He also traded his company's Triple-A debt rating for more market adventure and risk, borrowing more money than any other CEO, but likewise, making more profit than any other. He never lost focus of his objectives to bring his shareowners great returns on their investments, and he was described as "monomaniacal" in that regard. Importantly, he also made sure that at least three or four others were trained and capable to take over his job at any time. Thus, he had secured perpetuity in the character and personality of his company, although, in actuality, he remained as CEO until his sudden death from lung cancer on October 28, 1997, at the age of 65.

Further Reading

Economist, October 25, 1997, p. 97.
Financial World, April 5, 1988, p. 89; April 4, 1989, p. 74.
Forbes, January 11, 1988, p. 86.
Fortune, May 31, 1993, p. 44; May 30, 1994, p. 123; December 11, 1995, p. 80 and p. 96; October 13, 1997, p. 88.
Newsweek, September 29, 1997, p. 31.
New York Times, September 9, 1997; October 19, 1997.
U.S. News & World Report, June 9, 1997, p. 50.

Thomas Gold

Throughout his career as an astronomer, Thomas Gold (born 1920) has been no stranger to controversy. He has argued for a "steady-state" theory of the origin of the universe rather than the more popular big bang theory. He has also postulated a geological origin of petroleum rather than the traditional biological one. Though he has been overruled by the majority of the scientific community on both counts, he continues to stand by his theories.

A Childhood In Vienna

Gold was born on May 22, 1920, in Vienna, Austria. His father, Max Gold, was the director of Austria's largest mining and smelting company, and his mother, Josefine, was a former child actress. Gold recalled having a very comfortable childhood and noted that his parents were active in their children's lives. All that ended when Europe entered a depression. Sensing that the company he ran would suffer in the economic downturn, the elder Gold accepted a senior partnership in a metals trading firm in Berlin, Germany. However, they left Berlin in 1933 as Adolf Hitler (Gold's father was Jewish) gained more power.

For the next four years, Gold's parents traveled throughout Europe. After spending much time in Italy, they finally settled north of London in 1937. For many years later, Gold reminisced, the family carried with it acquired table silver and original renaissance art from Italy and Spain as a hedge against losing all their wealth in the turmoil surrounding World War II.

School Days

Gold attended boarding school in Switzerland, from the age of 13 until he joined his family in England at age 17. He then enrolled in Trinity College of Cambridge University, where he earned his bachelors degree in mechanical sciences in 1942 and his masters degree in 1946. It was there at the close of his student career, though he'd studied

physics and astronomy, that he proposed and won a fellow-ship to study the detection of sounds by the inner ear.

Because of the war, Gold's years at Cambridge were somewhat chaotic. At the beginning of World War II, he was interned for nine months because of his nationality and sent to a camp in Canada. When he was released, he rejoined his degree program, and graduated after attending only two of the normal three years. While still in school, he joined friends working for the British Admiralty Signals Establishment developing radar. Though he had trouble at first getting clearance for the top-secret work, he eventually became chief of a laboratory developing anti-jamming devices and Doppler radar which would display only moving targets.

During his tenure at the radar lab, Gold noticed that devices developed for creating images of ships and airplanes could be adapted to reveal the inner structure of his hand. He applied for a grant to refine the first sonography, but was turned down since, the laboratory claimed, it had no room for additional research. The same idea was pursued by others a decade later.

Following completion of his masters degree, Gold worked another year at the Cavendish Laboratory. The associations he formed during an unexciting magnetron assignment helped Gold between 1947 and 1949 as he studied the mammalian ear, completing work on his Trinity College prize fellowship by 1951. Also during this period, Gold developed the steady-state theory of the expanding universe with Hermann Bondi and Fred Hoyle. Though that theory fell out of favor with the increased acceptance of the "big bang" theory, its influence is still felt since it raised basic questions and stimulated essential research in cosmology.

Astronomy

After a stint as university demonstrator in physics at the Cavendish Laboratory from 1949 to 1952, Gold took a position as senior principal scientific officer with the Royal Greenwich Observatory. As chief assistant to the Astronomer Royal, Gold oversaw the varied research departments of the observatory. He became most involved with research on the sun and magnetic fields, and later coined the term 'magnetosphere' to describe the field associated with a star or planet. Gold's work with positional astronomers led to his important contribution to *Nature* in 1955, entitled "Instability of the Earth's Axis of Rotation." In that article, Gold noted that the position of the rotational pole on the earth's surface can change without affecting the direction of the axis in space, thus causing an apparent change of latitude of points on the earth's surface. He speculated that such changes could result from a redistribution of matter or angular momentum in the rotating earth. The theory was confirmed four decades later.

When the mantle of Astronomer Royal passed to a new man Gold decided to leave. He first accepted a professorship at Harvard University in 1957, and then deciding he preferred country living, moved to Cornell University. He was chair of the astronomy department until 1968, director of the Center for Radiophysics and Space Research from 1959 to 1981, and Assistant Vice President for Research

from 1969 to 1971. Gold retired in 1986, and then became arguably even more active as professor emeritus at Cornell. Also in 1986, he was named an honorary Fellow of Trinity College. Other honors bestowed on Gold included the John F. Lewis Prize of the American Philosophical Society in 1972, the Alexander von Humboldt Prize in 1980, and the Royal Astronomical Society's Gold Medal in 1985.

Beyond Astronomy

By the time Gold retired, he was widely recognized for his habit of questioning the most basic assumptions underlying scientific dogma in any field. Gold once insisted, "It wasn't that I was particularly contrary. I look at what is known about a case and what is the best explanation for it. I refuse to take anybody's word for it." His willingness to question, he said, grew out of his wide-ranging interests and his penchant for finding errors in textbooks he read as background for further study. In explaining his credo, Gold quoted Hungarian physicist Albert Szent-Gyrgyi: "Discovery consists of seeing what everyone has seen and thinking what nobody has thought."

Simon A. Cole, in an analysis of Gold's brand of science published in *Social Studies of Science,* wrote, "Gold endorses a broad, interdisciplinary model of science, which integrates evidence from disparate disciplines . . . Gold's model of science resembles Thomas Kuhn's: specialists are best qualified to carry out 'normal science,' but it takes an outsider to challenge the very foundations of a field, to effect a scientific revolution."

Nowhere was this propensity more evident than in Gold's challenge to the entire petroleum industry. He insisted that the geological dogma which states that natural gas, oil, and coal are all derived from fossilized organic matter is simply wrong. Instead, Gold postulated a cosmic origin for hydrocarbons, dating to the very formation of the earth.

To prove his point, the cosmologist-turned-geochemist inspired the drilling of an oil well 6.6 km deep where a petroleum geologist might least expect to strike oil, into the granite of Sweden over the traces of an ancient meteorite impact. To Gold, the results were conclusive, proving his hypothesis beyond a doubt. To others, oil and microbes found in the well looked more like contamination than proof.

Tempers flared and charges flew. Some claimed that Gold was simply a charlatan and that he profited from the drilling in Sweden at the expense of investors. When a book published by the United States Geological Survey containing an article by Gold was published, 34 prominent geologists signed a letter demanding it be withdrawn, charging Gold's work was unscientific. Gold countered by suing the author of the letter for libel. He later dropped the suit after receiving a formal apology.

If anything, the dispute made Gold even more determined to make his point. After his initial theory on the origins of hydrocarbons, he plunged into speculation on the concentration of minerals by the movements of hydrocarbons through the earth's mantle and crust, the prediction of earthquakes, and the origins of life.

Several years into his retirement, Gold showed no sign of reducing his scientific output. With over 280 publications under his name, Gold challenged his detractors in an *Omni* article by Anthony Liversidge. Quoting Tolstoy, Gold commented, "Most men . . . can seldom accept even the simplest and most obvious truth if it obliges them to admit the falsity of conclusions which they have delighted in explaining to colleagues, which they have proudly taught to others, and which they have woven thread by thread into the fabric of their lives."

Further Reading

Wilson, J.P., and D.T. Kemp, *Cochlear Mechanisms,* Plenum Publishing Corporation, 1989.
American Scientist, July/August 1984; September/October 1997.
Lingua Franca, December/January 1998.
Nature, March 26, 1955; January 4, 1969; December 23/30, 1993; January 5, 1995.
Omni, June 1993.
Proceedings of the National Academy of Sciences, July 1992.
Scientific American, November 1987.
Social Studies of Science, 1966, p. 733-766.
Thomas Gold, interviews by Alan Morse, March 26, 1998; March 30, 1998.

Ekaterina Gordeeva

From triumph to tragedy and back, Ekaterina Gordeeva (born 1971) is not only a champion ice skater, but also a symbol of grace, strength, and courage.

At age 11, Ekaterina Gordeeva (called Katia by her friends) became one of a pair—a pair of "G's"—Gordeeva and Grinkov. In their 13 years of skating together, Gordeeva and Sergei Grinkov were first co-workers, became friends, then fell in love, married, became parents, and won four World championships and two Olympic gold medals. However, in 1995, the magic tragically ended when Grinkov died of a heart attack. At only 24, Gordeeva became a widow, a single mother, and solo skater. As she told *Time* writer Steve Wulf, "Skating was the only thing that could bring back my confidence because it's the only thing I can do. I'm so happy to have a place to express my feelings." Fans worldwide, including former Olympic champion and commentator Dick Button were also happy again. Button, in *Time,* described Gordeeva as "a very elegant snowflake, but one that is made of steel."

Gordeeva was born in Moscow, Russia, in 1971. Her father, Alexander Alexeyevich Gordeev, a folk dancer for the Moiseev Dance Company, wanted Gordeeva to become a ballet dancer. Her mother, Elena Levovna, was a teletype operator for the Soviet news agent Tass. Gordeeva's parents both worked hard and traveled so much that Gordeeva and her sister, Maria, often stayed with their grandparents. Gordeeva's grandmother read Grimm's fairytales to Gordeeva, not knowing that's how Gordeeva would later describe her life—like a fairytale. Gordeeva, in *My Sergei,*

also commented that "I was the luckiest girl on earth, wanting for nothing." At four, too young to try out for ballet as her father had wanted, Gordeeva was invited by a trainer at the Central Red Army Skating Club in Moscow for a skating tryout. By the time she turned five years old, Gordeeva was practicing four times a week. In *My Sergei,* Gordeeva remembered, "I can't miss it. It's my job." However, pushed by her father, Gordeeva did try out for ballet school at age ten, but failed. She continued skating and one year later was paired with Grinkov.

Gordeeva and Grinkov—"G & G:" The Fairytale Begins

In December 1983, after a coaching change and just one year of training, Gordeeva & Grinkov finished sixth in the Junior World Championships. The next year, they won. Gordeeva was 13 and began to see Grinkov as more than just her skating partner. In *My Sergei,* Gordeeva recalled, "I remember becoming aware that I found him attractive, and that it was nice to be with him." However, they never spent much off-ice time together. In 1985, Gordeeva & Grinkov had to endure another coaching change. However, this new coach was a tyrant. Stanislav Zhuk, head coach at the Central Red Army Skating Club, pushed Gordeeva & Grinkov too hard, overtraining them while he drank every day. In spite of this, in their first senior level skating competition, Gordeeva & Grinkov finished second. A few months later, at the European Championships, they won. They then also won the World Championships. Yet, Gordeeva was not happy. In *My Sergei* she reviewed their performance, "we just proceeded from element to element without feeling, intent only on not making mistakes." In 1986, after petitioning the Central Red Army Skating Club to remove Zhuk as their coach, Gordeeva & Grinkov found joy once again in their skating with their new coach, Stanislav Leonovich.

In 1987, Gordeeva & Grinkov continued their winning streak by placing first at the Russian Nationals. However, they were disqualified at the European Championships because they refused to reskate their long program after a problem with their music. They quickly rebounded however, successfully defended their world title and then began their first American tour with skating promoter Tom Collins. Finally, much to the happiness of Gordeeva, Gordeeva & Grinkov spent off-ice time together. In *My Sergei* Gordeeva remembered a trip to Disneyland, "Sergei bought me some ice cream. A couple of times he he hugged me after a ride, or put his arm around me when we were standing in line. He had never done this before, and it made me excited. This was a wonderful day for me."

Gordeeva & Grinkov's first Olympics in 1988 was filled with nerves, homesickness, and sickness—Sergei had the flu. However, the nerves did wear off, Grinkov recovered, and they skated both their short and long programs successfully and won the gold medal. However, Gordeeva being just 16, was left behind when Grinkov, 21, celebrated with his older friends. In *My Sergei*, Gordeeva stated, "I don't remember Sergei . . . probably because I was so wrapped up in the competition."

In the fall of 1988, Gordeeva was diagnosed as having a stress fracture in her right foot. Gordeeva was sad that she could not skate. Yet Grinkov came up with an idea. As Gordeeva remembered in *My Sergei*, "Sergei asked, "So you like to skate? Come on. I'll give you a little ride." Grinkov picked up Gordeeva and carried her in his arms as he skated their program. By now they were both falling in love and on New Year's Eve, they finally kissed. Because of Gordeeva's stress fracture, they did not skate in the European Championships that year. However, they did skate at the World Championships in Paris—they won and everyone, friends, fans, and judges alike, saw how much they were in love.

Husband and Wife

In 1990, Gordeeva turned 18 and while she had to adjust to a new grown-up body, Grinkov had to live with pain in his shoulder. At the European Championships, skating to "Romeo and Juliet," Gordeeva & Grinkov won another title. They next won the World Championships, but skated weakly, feeling burnt out. Hoping for more off-ice time together, they rejoined the Tom Collins skating tour. However, tragedy struck—Grinkov's father died of a heart attack. A few months later, Grinkov suggested to Gordeeva that they turn professional. They did and by 1991 they had won their first of three World Professional Championships. However, winning skating competitions was not the only joy in their lives. The couple married on April 28, 1991.

After Grinkov's shoulder surgery, they returned to the skating tour and began their new life together on the road. However, that life was about to change. In January of 1992,

Gordeeva discovered she was pregnant. The couple continued to skate for four months, then awaited the birth of their daughter. Five months later, on September 11, 1992, Daria was born. In *My Sergei*, Gordeeva recollected, "Daria weighed five pounds, four ounces, and was in perfect health. The fact that she had no hair drove me crazy. I was such a sad, funny little mom."

Just 19 days after Daria's birth, Gordeeva was back on the ice. By October, after deciding to leave their daughter with Gordeeva's mother in Moscow, Gordeeva & Grinkov began rehearsals for the Stars on Ice skating tour in Lake Placid, New York. Two months later, Gordeeva & Grinkov successfully defended their World Professional Championship title, but they missed Daria's first Christmas.

Gordeeva & Grinkov returned home to Moscow in May 1993. After petitioning the International Skating Union to reinstate their amateur status, they began training for their second Olympics. With their new long program, Beethoven's *Moonlight Sonata,* they won the Russian Nationals and the European championships. Gordeeva & Grinkov were ready for the 1994 Olympics. However, at the Olympics, they did not skate perfectly—Grinkov had done a single instead of a double jump—still they won their second gold medal. Yet even with their performance not being perfect, Gordeeva stated in *My Sergei* that she was happy because, "the first gold medal we had won for the Soviet Union. This one we won for each other."

Life After The Olympics

After the Olympics, Gordeeva & Grinkov returned to the professional ice skating world and toured in the United States. However, this tour was different because they had finally found a home in Simsbury, Connecticut. In December of 1994, Gordeeva & Grinkov won their third and last World Professional Championship. The couple took the spring off when Grinkov hurt his back. As they trained later that summer, Grinkov's back continued to hurt, yet Gordeeva & Grinkov completed a tour with Stars on Ice. They then returned to Lake Placid, New York, to practice a new program—a program Gordeeva would never skate with Grinkov.

On November 20, 1995, Gordeeva & Grinkov began a run-through of their new program, but Grinkov had not put his arms around Gordeeva for their lift. In *My Sergei*, Gordeeva said she thought it was his back again, but Grinkov shook his head then "bent his knees and lay down on the ice very carefully." At 28, Grinkov died of a heart attack. In *My Sergei*, a few days later at Grinkov's wake, Gordeeva remembered telling 1984 Olympic gold medalist Scott Hamilton, "It was too perfect, maybe. It's only fairytales that have happy endings. Everything was too good with me and Sergei for it to end happily."

A New Life: Skating Solo

On February 27, 1996, Gordeeva began her new life as a solo skater in a televised tribute to Grinkov, *A Celebration of a Life.* Author E.M. Swift in *Sports Illustrated* described her performance: "Gordeeva exposed her soul with such gentleness and pathos and strength that no one watching could remain unmoved. This was a rarity: sport, art, and tragedy fused into one." In *My Sergei,* after her performance, Gordeeva remembered speaking to the audience: "I'm so happy I was able to show you my skating. But I also want you to know that I skated today not alone. I skated with Sergei. It's why I was so good. It wasn't me."

The Gordeeva & Grinkov fairytale has ended. However, Gordeeva continued to not only skate in professional competitions and TV specials like *Beauty and the Beast* and *Snowden on Ice,* as well as in the Stars on Ice tour, but she also wrote *My Sergei,* a memoir of her and Grinkov's life together. In February of 1998, CBS televised an adaptation of this memoir with Gordeeva as narrator. This TV movie showed both the on- and off-ice magic of "G & G" and offered one last look at their fairytale. In May, her second book, *A Letter for Daria,* was published and the Target department store launched its "Katia" fragrance line.

Gordeeva has become a symbol of grace, strength, and courage not only for ice skating fans, but also for her daughter, Daria. In *My Sergei,* Gordeeva promised Grinkov, "I will always take good care of her. She'll be the happiest girl ever." Gordeeva also believes, as she told Joanna Powell in *Good Housekeeping,* that Daria "is a gift from God. When Sergei died she was such a help because she needed attention and I had to take care of her. I think she drove me back to a normal life." As Gordeeva continues to live this normal life, she offered this advice in *My Sergei* to everyone, "Try to find happiness in everyday. At least once, smile to each other everyday. And say just one extra time that you love the person who lives with you. Just say, 'I love you.'"

Further Reading

Gordeeva, Ekaterina, with E.M. Swift. *My Sergei: A Love Story,* Warner Books, Inc., 1996.
Good Housekeeping, November 1997, pp. 104-107.
Newsweek, December 23, 1996, pp. 56-59.
Sports Illustrated, February 28, 1994, p. 48-49; Dec. 30, 1996-Jan. 6, 1997, p. 74.
Time, December 4, 1995, p. 89.

Pamela Gordon

The daughter of a prominent legislator, Pamela Gordon (born 1955) used her family name and her own political skills to become Bermuda's first woman premier in 1997.

W hen Pamela Gordon was sworn in as the premier (prime minister) of Bermuda on March 27, 1997, she became the first woman and the youngest person ever to hold that post. At the age of 41, she had already lived an eventful life—giving birth to a child at the age of 16 and overcoming the economic obstacles posed by early motherhood by working in a variety of jobs. However, Gordon had two things going for her: she was the daughter of one of the founding fathers of Bermuda politics, and she had considerable political skills of her own. She

used these resources in steering the United Bermuda Party to victory.

An Unconventional Family

Pamela Gordon was born on September 2, 1955 in Hamilton, Bermuda. She was the youngest of five children born to Mildred Layne Bean and Dr. E.F. Gordon, a prominent labor leader and member of Bermuda's parliament in the late 1940s and early 1950s. E.F. Gordon was known as a champion of unheralded causes. Born in Trinidad, he became a physician, moved to Bermuda, and spent his time campaigning against segregation and improving conditions for the working class. He urged black participation in the colony's government and challenged the white power structure to cede some of its authority. Dr. Gordon and Mildred Layne Bean never married, as Gordon was a Roman Catholic and, according to a strict interpretation of church laws, forbidden to divorce his first wife, Clara. They did live together during his last years, however, and she was pregnant with Pamela when he died on April 21, 1955.

Gordon was herself baptized as a Catholic. She grew up at "Beulah," the Gordon family estate, where her father used to hold meetings with his political supporters. Without him around to pay the bills though, life was a struggle for Gordon and her sisters Olympia and Patricia and brothers Keith and Edgar. Her mother worked as a switchboard operator to support the family.

While Gordon never knew her father, she is said to have inherited some of his headstrong temperament. "She

was always sweet and demure," commented her sister Patricia to the *Bermuda Sun*, "But she always spoke her mind." Her father's legacy to her included a passionate commitment to her own views no matter what other people might think. "Dr. Gordon was strong willed," Mildred Layne Bean remarked to the *Bermuda Sun*. "My daughter isn't much different."

Teen Mother

Growing up, Gordon attended Central School and Berkeley Institute. However, she had to leave school at the age of 16, when she became pregnant by Ronald Furbert. She gave birth to a daughter, Veronica, and resumed her studies at another institution. It could have been a major setback to Gordon's career aspirations, but she had the support of her family to fall back on. "She had a teenage pregnancy," Gordon's mother told *The Bermuda Sun*. "Everybody wanted to put her down. Yes, she made a youthful mistake." Instead of shunning her, however, Gordon's mother helped take care of the baby while she attended college in Ontario, Canada. When she returned to Bermuda, she married Ronald Furbert. The couple subsequently had a son, Ronald, and later divorced.

With a family of her own to support, Gordon began working at odd jobs while she continued to attend college classes. For a time, she owned and managed a restaurant, The Moonglow, in St. George's, where her mother also worked. In 1983, she took a job as a sales accountant at St. George's Club, a hotel. Despite not having accounting accreditation, she worked her way up to the post of controller. She finally earned her college degree in commerce from Queen's University and began studying for a master's degree.

Remarkable Political Ascent

Always one to speak her mind, Gordon found herself complaining more and more about public policy in Bermuda. That bluntness about the issues impressed Sir John Swan, Bermuda's premier, whom Gordon met through her sister Patricia. Swan convinced Gordon that the best way to work for change was by joining the United Bermuda Party (UBP). It was the first step in Gordon's political career.

In 1990, Gordon won a seat in the Bermuda Senate. In March of 1992, Premier Swan appointed her to his cabinet as Minister of Youth Development. She later served as Minister of the Environment, Planning, and Recreation in the cabinet of Premier David J. Saul. In October of 1993, Gordon was elected to Bermuda's House of Assembly as the representative for Southampton West.

In March of 1997, Premier David J. Saul shocked the colony—and the ruling UBP—by announcing his resignation. Saul may have been swayed by polls that showed him losing the next election to the candidate for the Progressive Labor Party (PLP). A contest for the leadership of the UBP now ensued. The stakes were high because, in a parliamentary system, the winner of the party vote would also assume the post of premier. Undeterred by the odds against her candidacy, Gordon immediately threw her hat into the ring.

The contest was hard-fought. Twenty-one UDP parliament members were eligible to vie for the $89,000-a-year post, but many senior members shied away, afraid that Bermuda's voters were looking for "new blood." Gordon and Irving Pearman quickly emerged as the front runners. At first, Pearman appeared to have the votes to win. Gordon even announced that she would pull out of the race if that were true in order to preserve party unity, but by March 24, 1997, the tide had turned. She was the unanimous choice for party leader. "Pam seems to be the one," a senior UBP cabinet member told Reuters. "She's the only real choice."

First Woman Premier

Now the head of Bermuda's ruling party, Gordon was duly sworn in as premier by Governor Lord Waddington on March 27, 1997. The orderly transition of power pleased Bermuda's business community. "International business is moving our economy and we look forward to working with Premier Gordon to promote Bermuda and its attractive business environment," announced Arthur B. Sculley, Chairman of the Bermuda Stock Exchange, in a press release issued by the Bermuda International Business Association (BIBA). For her part, Gordon promised economic and political stability in the run-up to general elections to be held some time within the next 18 months.

In the tradition of her father, Pamela Gordon did not waste any time in challenging the powers that be—including the British government, the colonial masters of Bermuda. In January of 1998, she accused Great Britain of violating international agreements by denying Bermudans the right to live in Britain. Other colonial powers, such as the United States and the Netherlands, give citizenship rights to their Caribbean dependencies. Gordon also butted heads with the government in London over the issue of capital punishment, which Britain put pressure on Bermuda to abolish in 1998. "The only way they can force us to do anything is by them going through their own parliament," Gordon told Reuters in February of 1998. Capital punishment remains on the books in Bermuda, and is popular with voters, though it has not been invoked since the late 1970s.

By the spring of 1998, Gordon was shoring up her political support, especially among blacks and labor unions, for what was expected to be a hotly contested election campaign. Now a member of the African Methodist Episcopalian Church, she remained single following her divorce and maintained a close relationship with her daughter Victoria and son Ronald. She lived with her mother in the family home at Beulah until her election to the premiership. Her mother remains convinced that Gordon's father would approve of her taking over the "family business." "He would have been absolutely delighted," Mildred Bean told the *Bermuda Sun*. "He would have said: 'Although you [the establishment] didn't want me, now my daughter is in charge.'"

Further Reading

The Bermuda Sun, March 21, 1997; March 27, 1997.
The Daily Telegraph, January 27, 1998.
Reuters, March 24, 1997; March 25, 1997; February 13, 1998.

Kate Greenaway

The English illustrator Kate Greenaway (1846-1901) dramatically changed the art of the picture book. For many modern critics, her work represents the essence of a Victorian childhood.

For over a hundred years, Kate Greenaway's works have been honored as representing the essence of illustrations for children. Her relatively simple line drawings and colored pictures of young boys and girls at play influenced generations of writers and illustrators for children. Her seminal role in creating the form of the modern child's picture book was recognized in 1955, when the Library Association of Great Britain established the Kate Greenaway Medal. The award is given annually to the British artist who has produced the most distinguished illustrations in works of literature for children.

Kate Greenaway's romantic conception of childhood was based in part on her own experiences. She was born on March 17, 1846, in Hoxton, a community in what is now Greater London, England. "She was the second daughter of John Greenaway, a draughtsman and engraver," writes Bryan Holme in *The Kate Greenaway Book,* "and of Elizabeth Greenaway, a Miss Jones before the marriage." "I had such a very happy time when I was a child," Greenaway is reported as saying in M. H. Spielmann and G. S. Lanyard's 1905 biography *Kate Greenaway,* "and, curiously, was so very much happier then than my brother and sister, with exactly the same surroundings. I suppose my imaginary life made me one long continuous joy—filled everything with a strange wonder and beauty. Living in that childish wonder is a most beautiful feeling—I can so well remember it. There was always something more—behind and beyond everything—to me. The golden spectacles were very very big."

Her earliest artistic desires found their expression in drawing and in dressing up her dolls. "A strong bond existed between father and daughter," Holme reports. "He had nicknamed her 'Knocker' because when she cried her face used to look like one—or so he had teasingly told her. As soon as Kate's fingers had strength enough to hold pencil, John Greenaway had encouraged her to draw—and this he continued to do up to and through her student years." Some of these pictures were of contemporary events, including the Great Indian War in 1857, in which many English women and children were killed. "At the time of the Indian Mutiny I was always drawing people escaping," Greenaway revealed in *Kate Greenaway.* "I could sit and think of the sepoys till I could be wild with terror, and I used sometimes to dream of them. But I was always drawing the ladies, nurses, and children escaping. Mine always escaped and were never taken." Other inspirations for her art work were the family vacations taken in rural Rolleston, Nottinghamshire. "Here Greenaway was touched by the commonplace sights of old-fashioned England," states Lundin: "villagers in their antiquated eighteenth-century dress; men working in the fields in embroidered smocks dyed blue; women wearing their Sunday best of frilly lace and large poke bonnets; and roads edged with primroses or fields filled with poppies."

A Career as an Illustrator and Designer

Greenaway's doll-dressing talents may have had their origins in Elizabeth Greenaway's occupation. "Her mother was a seamstress and milliner, who opened a shop in Islington when her husband's business waned," explains Anne H. Lundin in the *Dictionary of Literary Biography.* "Certainly Kate Greenaway's taste for 'dressing up' found its major expression at the drawing, [but] . . . in her childhood it had through her love of dolls," states Holme. Even after she had been sent to school at what would become the Royal Academy of Art in 1858, and after she had won local and national awards for her work in 1861 and 1864, she continued to work with dolls and fabric. In 1868, at the age of 22, she had an exhibition of her watercolors at the Dudley Gallery in Piccadilly. She created these pictures by first making the clothing, then dressing model in the clothes. The significance of the pictures in terms of her career, however, was that they "caught the eye of an editor and led to a commission for illustrations for *People's* magazine and later for Christmas cards and valentines for Marcus Ward," declares Lundin. "In 1870 she received a commission to illustrate an edition of *Madame D'Aulney's Fairy Tales.* She also began contributing to *Little Folks,* the *Illustrated London News,* and *Cassell's* magazine, and she exhibited for the first time at the Royal Academy in 1877."

Greenaway's largest influence on her art work at this time came from the artists of the Pre-Raphaelite Brotherhood, which was formed in 1848 by William Holman Hunt, John Everett Millais, and Dante Gabriel Rossetti. "This trio of artists," writes Holme, "protested the ravages of modern industry, but their plea for a return to simplicity, sincerity, and respect for nature had no bearing beyond the immediate world of British art. Yet in that world, within a decade, they became gods." Many of her early cards and valentines, such as those that appeared in *The Quiver of Love: A Collection of Valentines* (1876) show the Pre-Raphaelite influence on her work. John Ruskin, the first British art critic to recognize the contributions of the Pre-Raphaelites, later became a close friend of Greenaway. Their correspondence continued until the critic's death in 1900.

Much of Greenaway's earliest work appeared in the publications of Marcus Ward & Company, which published her art work on their cards, calendars, and books. "Over the years," writes Holme, "hitherto unknown books containing one or more Greenaway illustrations have turned up in the rare-book market." Her "earliest free-lance work also included odd jobs for Messrs. Kronheim and Company, the giant color printers of Shoe Lane," the critic continues. The Kronheim connection led to the publication of her first illustrated book: *Diamonds and Toads* (1871). "This slim paper-bound volume, a popular little tale pointing to the moral that 'cross words are as bad dropped from the mouth as toads and vipers, while gentle words are better than roses and diamonds' was printed by Kronheim," Holme concludes, "and destined to number in Aunt Louisa's London Toy Book Series under the imprint of Frederick Warne and

Company." Other books featuring Greenaway illustrations published in the early 1870s included *The Children of the Parsonage, Fairy Gifts; or, A Wallet of Wonders,* and *Topo.*

Under the Window **and Other Works**

The artist's aspirations, however, went beyond simply illustrating books written by other people. "Greenaway's ambition was to publish a book of her own verses and drawings based on her memories of Rolleston, street rhymes, and favorite childhood stories," explains Lundin. "She dressed her characters in the old-fashioned clothing so common in Rolleston: high-waisted gowns, smocks, and mobcaps. She accompanied these drawings with her own verse, based on nursery-rhyme morals and make-believe." Her father, John Greenaway, shared the unfinished manuscript with a colleague named Edmund Evans. Evans was "a pioneer color printer who had already created successful productions of Walter Crane's toy books and had recently engaged Randolph Caldecott for a similar series," states Lundin. The volume that Evans published became the first and most popular of Greenaway's books, *Under the Window: Pictures and Rhymes for Children.* Evans's original printing of 20,000 copies quickly sold out and Evans had to print another 50,000 to satisfy the demand for the book. One-third of the profits went to Greenaway. The sales made her comfortably well-off, if not wealthy, and her name became familiar in households throughout the British Empire and the United States. "Throughout the 1890s *Under the Window* was listed as a perennial seller," says Lundin, "along with Greenaway's three other most popular works: *Kate Greenaway's Birthday Book for Children* (1880), *Mother Goose; or, The Old Nursery Rhymes* (1881), and *A Painting Book* (1884)."

These four books marked the pinnacle of Greenaway's critical and commercial success. However, her reputation was further spread by a series of yearly almanacs, published first by Routledge and later by Dent. "The almanacs were booklets with variant bindings that contained monthly calendars and in which the surprise from year to year was in Greenaway's choice of decorations for the seasons," writes Lundin. Their sales were more erratic than those of Greenaway's major books—except in the United States, Lundin says, where "the almanacs had a greater following . . . with sales often twice that of the British market." The *Almanack for 1883,* the best-selling of her collection, sold 90,000 copies throughout Great Britain, the United States, France, and Germany. The almanacs appeared yearly from 1882 to 1895; the publisher skipped 1896, and the last of Greenaway's almanacs was published in 1897.

Commercial Success

These almanacs and Greenaway's other publications brought out a "Greenaway Vogue" that began shortly after the publication of *Under the Window* and continued for some time. "Numerous imitations, piracies, and spinoffs were produced without her permission, an onslaught that popularized her name by adversely affected her livelihood and stature," says Lundin. Even clothing styled after the patterns she had developed in her illustrations was created.

At one point Greenaway was approached by a shoe manufacturer who wanted to market a "Kate Greenaway shoe." Greenaway herself told another anecdote about an acquaintance who had been exposed to the vogue: "The lady who has just left me, has been staying in the country and has been to see her cousins. I asked if they were growing up as pretty as they promised. 'Yes,' she replied, 'but they spoil their good looks, you know, by dressing in that absurd Kate Greenaway style'—quite forgetting that she was talking to me!"

Although Greenaway maintained her reputation throughout the late nineteenth century, by the dawn of the twentieth century her popularity began to wane. Despite the loss of her parents and her friend John Ruskin, she never lost the dedication that characterized her earliest work. However, by early 1901 Greenaway was complaining of chronic pain, which was diagnosed as "acute muscular rheumatism," but which modern critics believe was actually breast cancer. She died on November 6, 1901, and was buried in her family's plot at Hampstead cemetery. "Her work," concludes Lundin, "remains a part of folk culture as well as a landmark in the history of children's bookmaking."

Further Reading

Arbuthnot, May Hill, and Zena Sutherland, *Children and Books,* 4th edition, Scott, Foresman, 1972.

Dictionary of Literary Biography, Volume 141: *British Children's Writers, 1880-1914,* Gale Research, 1994.

Ernest, Edward, and Patricia Tracy Lowe, editors, *The Kate Greenaway Treasury: An Anthology of the Illustrations and Writings of Kate Greenaway,* World Publishing, 1967.

Holme, Bryan, *The Kate Greenaway Book,* Viking Press, 1976.

Meigs, Cornelia Lynde, et. al., editors, *A Critical History of Children's Literature,* Macmillan, 1953.

Moore, Anne Carroll, *A Century of Kate Greenaway,* Warne, 1946.

Spielmann, Marion Harry, and George Somes Layard, *Kate Greenaway,* A. & C. Black, 1905.

Yesterday's Authors of Books for Children, Gale Research, 1976.

□

Pope Gregory XII

In 1406 an aged Italian cardinal named Angelo Correr (c. 1327-1417) was elected pope; calling himself Gregory XII, he had a bedeviled nine-year tenure as head of the Roman Catholic Church. His ascension to the Holy See came during a tumultuous crisis in Christian Europe usually referred to as the Great Schism, a conflict that divided clerics, royals, and the faithful for several decades. At one period of Gregory XII's rule, there were two other popes elsewhere vying for authority, but his own eventual assent to a compromise helped end the Schism.

Very little is known about the life of Angelo Correr, the man who would later take the name Gregory XII. Sources place his date of birth around 1327, and it is known that his family was among Venice's wealthy and influential clans. At the time, the lagoon city on the Adriatic Sea was a powerful sovereignty that controlled and profited from the busy shipping trade of the Mediterranean. Correr, however, opted for the priesthood, and in 1380—by then in his early sixties—he was made bishop of Castello, a city near Perugia. Ten years later, he was elevated to the title of Latin Patriarch of Constantinople, the Roman Catholic Church's representative in what is now Istanbul. Since 1054 the Eastern Orthodox Church, allied with the Byzantine Empire, had been separated from the Roman Catholic Church. The pope in Rome was known as the Patriarch of the West. In 1404 that pontiff was Innocent VII, a Neapolitan named Cosimo dei Migliorati.

A Church Divided

Innocent VII made Correr an apostolic secretary, and then legate, or papal emissary, of Ancona, another Italian port on the Adriatic. In 1405 Correr became a cardinal, the highest position a priest could achieve in the Church before the papacy itself—indeed, popes were elected by the college of cardinals from amongst themselves. Yet over the last century both the Church and the papacy had experienced inner discord. This began in 1309 when a French pope, Clement V, relocated the Holy See to Avignon, France. In 1378 it was returned to Rome by another Gregory, Gregory XI, ending what became known as the Babylonian Cap-

tivity. Upon this pope's death, the cardinals chose Urban VII, who berated them for the luxury in which many of them lived. At the time, the Church was a corrupt institution, more often than not in the service of Europe's kings, and profited handsomely from selling all kinds of spiritual services to illiterate believers.

Urban VII was thought to be insane, and his violent rages were well-documented. Historians believe he may have murdered several cardinals after some of them convened elsewhere, declared him an antichrist, and elected a Swiss, Robert of Geneva, as Pope Clement VII. This occurred just four months into Urban VII's rule, and set in motion the Great Schism. Urban VII remained in Rome, was succeeded in 1389 by Boniface IX, whose successor upon death was Innocent VII, the pope who would become Gregory XII's mentor. Innocent reigned from 1404 to 1406, and like his predecessors, had little luck in resolving the papal crisis. Meanwhile, a series of popes remained firmly entrenched back in Avignon; the intervention of kings, future saints, and philosophers had little effect upon the situation.

"Anathema to the Schismatics!"

At next papal election in Rome in 1406, convened upon the death of Innocent VII, every cardinal made a solemn promise that if he were to be elected, he would abdicate, provided that the Avignon pope also resigned, which would allow the two separate colleges of cardinals to reconvene and elect a pope of a united Western church. Correr was elected partly because of his character: he was elderly, and rather severe and pious in demeanor. His fellow cardinals thought him a good candidate for keeping his word. He was elected on November 30, 1406, and took the name Gregory XII. "Anathema to the Schismatics!" he proclaimed to the cardinals, according to Marzieh Gail's *The Three Popes,* " . . . Anathema upon me also if I do not use all my efforts to end the deplorable division which harms and dishonors Christianity."

Thirteen days after his election, Gregory XII formally notified the Avignon pope, Benedict XIII, of his own intention to resign. The two decided to arrange to meet, the first step in the process, so that they could negotiate the dual resignation—yet could not agree upon a place. Gregory XII made a younger relative one of his envoys for this task, "an unfortunate choice as the nephew had every reason for prolonging his uncle's pontificate," wrote L. Elliott Binns in *The History of the Decline and Fall of the Medieval Papacy.*

Gregory XII and Benedict XIII discussed and rejected a number of cities between Rome and Avignon, including Siena, Lucca, Nice, and Genoa. They finally agreed upon Savona, and complex negotiations ensued to set terms: each wanted bring along as much military force as possible, but were limited to eight galleys and a hundred crossbowmen. Their number of servants would also be equal, and each was to have free reign over half of Savona and half of its harbor. Benedict XIII arrived in Savona at the end of September 1407. Gregory XII journeyed to Lucca, a city not far from Pisa, and sent word suggesting they change the venue to Pisa. It never happened.

Unwilling to Abdicate

It is thought that the aging Gregory XII came under undue influence from his family, who wished to see their kin in the prestigious office. A powerful Italian leader, King Ladislaus of Naples, was also interested in seeing Gregory XII remain on the papal throne. In May of 1408 Gregory XII named four new cardinals—all of them his nephews. He was in Lucca at the time, and the incident marked a turning point in opinion against him. Notices began appearing in the city, according to *The Three Popes*. "They summoned the Pope to appear on a certain day to be degraded," wrote Gail. "They accused him of being a shedder of blood, a drunkard, a man of dishonor, a slave to carnal appetites, a hypocrite, madman, heretic, even one who sought to overthrow the Church."

The cardinals who had elected Gregory XII in good faith were now angry. Nine of them left and traveled to Pisa for what became known as the Council of Pisa. Several cardinals dissatisfied with Benedict XIII's rule also participated. The Council was convened, though not quite legally according to church law, in June of 1409. The cardinals ordered both Gregory XII and Benedict XIII to stand before them, but neither appeared. They then declared both popes invalid and elected a third, Peter of Candia, who took the name Alexander V. Thus began the era of the three popes—one in Rome, another in Avignon, and a third seated in Pisa. In response, Gregory XII created more cardinals to replace those who had convened the Council of Pisa, and summoned them to his own Council at Cividale. There they declared both Benedict XIII and Alexander V wrongful popes.

A popular saying arose among European Christians—"one Pope is too much for the Catholic world, no Pope would be even better," according to Gail in *The Three Popes*. The historian also wrote that public opinion had very nearly turned against the Church itself as a result of the three decades of discord and its inability to resolve the Schism from within. As the division spiraled out of control, its ramifications were felt in other parts of Europe. In Prague, for instance, the rector of its university, Jan Hus, supported Alexander V, while his archbishop was loyal to Gregory XII. For this—as well as Hus's criticisms of the abuses of the clergy—Hus was excommunicated. Later, he was invited to the Council of Constance (1414-18, the massive, pan-European meeting that eventually ended the Schism) to defend his views, but there he was burned as a heretic.

Malatesta and Sigisimund

Alexander V died in 1410—thought to have been poisoned—and then a corrupt cardinal named Baldassare Cossa was chosen as his successor to the Pisa papacy. Cossa, who came from a pirate family, was Bologna's notorious tyrant ruler. His "election" as pope occurred when he told the cardinals to bring him the stole of Peter and that he would put it upon the man most deserving—and then put it on himself. Cossa took the name Pope John XXIII. Meanwhile Gregory XII, now well into his eighties, had grown weary of the Schism and its unending intrigues. His friend and protector, Charles Malatesta, helped sway his mind by

appealing to Gregory's religious convictions, reminding him that he had once sworn to do his part to end the Schism.

The Holy Roman Emperor and King of Hungary, Emperor Sigisimund, was the authority who finally compelled all sides to come to the table. Sigisimund forced John XXIII to summon the Council of Constance in December of 1413. It met for the first time in the lakeside German city on November 5, 1414. An ecumenical council of massive proportions, its numbers probably included, according to *The Three Popes*, 2,300 princes, knights, and deputies, 18,000 clergy, 242 bankers, 83 tavernkeepers who brought Italian wines along, and 700 prostitutes.

Delicate Bargaining

The Council's first order of business was to unseat the Pisan pope, John XXIII, which it did on May 29, 1415. It then named Gregory XII the rightful heir to the Holy See. In return Gregory XII sent a letter to Council of Constance that reconvoked it officially. Yet he refused to travel to Constance in person, fearing imprisonment or even death. During this time, he prayed with a relic dear to him, a tooth that was allegedly the late Catherine of Siena's. Forty years before, Catherine had persuaded the other Gregory, Gregory XI, to return the papacy from Avignon to Rome.

When the Council of Constance accepted Gregory XII's official convocation, it was also tacit recognition of his legitimacy among the three popes. In return for the favor, he abdicated on July 4, 1415. Benedict XIII still remained pope in Avignon, but the Council of Constance eventually declared him guilty of heresy in July of 1417. The Constance cardinals then elected Martin V, and since then the papacy has remained in relatively stable condition, with the exception of one other antipope's claim in 1439 that came about as the result of Jan Hus's martyrdom in Constance. In gratitude, Gregory XII was made bishop of Porto and legate of the March of Ancona, both for life. He died in Recanati, Italy, on October 18, 1417. According to *The Three Popes*, his last words were: "I have not understood the world, and the world has not understood me."

Further Reading

Binns, L. Elliott, *The History of the Decline and Fall of the Medieval Papacy*, Archon Books, 1967.
Brusher, Joseph, *Popes Through the Ages*, Van Nostrand, 1959.
Gail, Marzieh, *The Three Popes*, Simon & Schuster, 1969.
New Catholic Encyclopedia, Volume VI, McGraw-Hill, 1967.

Andrew S. Grove

For 30 years, American businessman Andrew S. Grove (born 1936) has served in a variety of high-level posts at Intel Corp., considered one of the most powerful microprocessor manufacturers in the world.

From humble beginnings in Hungary, Grove went on to become chief executive officer (CEO) and chairperson of one the most powerful microprocessor manufacturing companies in the world, Intel Corp. He is highly regarded both as a physicist in the field of semiconductors as well as an expert in management. With Intel, he has helped to usher in an information revolution unmatched by anything since the invention of the printing press. As noted by Walter Isaacson in *Time*: "*Time* chooses as its 1997 Man of the Year Andrew Steven Grove, chairman and CEO of Intel, the person most responsible for the amazing growth in the power and innovative potential of microchips."

Early Life

Andrew Steven Grove was born András Gróf in Budapest, Hungary, on September 2, 1936. His father, George, was a dairyman, and his mother, Maria, worked as a bookkeeping clerk. The family was of Jewish descent and World War II proved to be a difficult time; Grove would see nothing but trouble until he departed from Europe. At the age of four, a wave of scarlet fever swept through Hungary. Grove was not spared, and over the course of the illness, his hearing was seriously damaged. The following year, his father was removed to a Nazi work camp. Grove and his mother changed their names and moved in with Christian acquaintances, who hid them during the Nazi pogroms of 1944. After the war, his father miraculously reappeared, though weakened by typhus and pneumonia. Grove, hoping to attend college in a few years, dabbled in journalism

and took voice lessons, dreaming of perhaps becoming an opera singer. Political circumstances again intervened, however, in 1956, when Soviet tanks arrived in Budapest to put down the Hungarian Revolution. His father's occupation, as a private business owner, made Grove a potential dissident in the eyes of the communists. So, rather than face the possibility of prison, Grove and a friend fled to Austria.

From there, Grove made his way to the United States, where he moved in with an uncle who had immigrated to New York in the early 1930s. He enrolled in the City College of New York (CCNY), studying chemical engineering and waiting tables to pay his tuition. In the summer of 1957, he met a woman named Eva, who became his wife the following year. Grove graduated from CCNY in 1960, after which he and Eva relocated to California, where he entered the Ph.D. program at the University of California, Berkeley. There, as at CCNY, he performed spectacularly. Upon his graduation in 1963, he went to work for Fairchild Semiconductor, a small company which had recently been created by a few of the more forward-thinking engineers on the West Coast. He also began teaching at Berkeley, a side career he has continued to the present day.

At Fairchild, along with the head of the research department, Gordon Moore, and two other colleagues, Bruce Deal and Edward Snow, Grove helped create the first marketable silicon-based integrated circuit. This was a major step for the computer industry, which, until then, used transistors as switching elements in their products. To be sure, transistors were far better than their predecessors, vacuum tubes. Vacuum tubes were bulky, and they generated a tremendous amount of heat and consumed an equally large amount of electricity. The transistor was considerably smaller, and required no heating element. The drawback was that they had to be used individually. In order to move forward, the industry required that more than one transistor occupy a single unit. The solution to this dilemma came as early as 1959, but it would take several years, and the particular combination of talents that existed at Fairchild, under the leadership of general manager Bob Noyce, to create a reliable, mass-produced integrated circuit. That accomplishment stood poised to revolutionize the industry, and thereafter, the world.

Grove Moves to Intel

None of this made much of an impact on the top executives of Fairchild—they displayed the same lack of vision that kills so many high-technology companies even today. So, in 1968, frustrated with the state of affairs, Noyce secured the support of Arthur Rock, a prominent high-tech investor, and with Gordon Moore's help, started a company called Intel (short for Integrated Electronics). With these three men, the company looked unsinkable. Their decision to employ Grove as director of operations was, however, in the words of Tim Jackson's history of Intel, "so bizarre that it mystified most of the people who were watching the new business take shape." Up to that point, Grove had virtually no manufacturing experience at all, plus he was decidedly unusual. Jackson continued, "Grove spoke English with an accent that was almost incomprehensible. Over his head, he wore an awkward hearing-aid device that looked like a product of Eastern European engineering." Furthermore, he had a severe temper, and an equally severe manner of maintaining discipline and control. None-the-less, Noyce and Moore admired his intelligence and drive, and they believed he was the right man. Grove tacitly agreed, leaving Fairchild almost immediately.

The doubts held by onlookers concerning his abilities were quickly put to rest. Grove guided the development of manufacturing processes first for the company's computer memory products, then for its first general-purpose microprocessor (the component that serves as the "brain" of modern desktop computers), outstripping all competitors and even the company which had licensed their technology to provide the "second-source" so important to computer companies at that time. The early years of the company were particularly hectic, as the demands of the high-tech sector tended to change dramatically and unpredictably. Thus, despite the concentrated talent at their disposal, Intel found itself constantly changing gears, and struggling to keep up with the latest developments. Grove's force of will aided the company greatly during this period, but an insight of Moore's was necessary for long-term stability. Moore's Law, as the insight came to be known, was that chip power would continue to double roughly every 18 months for the foreseeable future. Thus, Intel was able to chart its course ahead of the fact rather than leaping after changes in demand.

Moore's Law did not, however, eliminate all difficulties. The first major crisis began in the mid-1970s, when Japanese companies, who could manufacture memory chips at much lower costs, began dumping large quantities of cut-rate chips on American markets, seriously reducing demand for Intel's products. This was a major blow for the company, whose business relied at that time primarily on the sale of memory. They responded by shifting their emphasis to microprocessors, but many rival American companies collapsed under the pressure. In 1981, the chip market took another nosedive, and once again, many companies were caught unprepared. Grove, rather than laying off employees, ordered them to work 25 percent overtime for free. The strategy succeeded, and Intel survived.

Grove's hard work and demanding management style, while criticized by many, brought ever-increasing profits for Intel, and in 1979, he was made president of the company. Four years later, he published his second book, *High Output Management,* which was subsequently translated into 11 languages (his first volume, *Physics and Technology of Semiconductor Devices,* was published in 1967 during his tenure at Fairchild). His third book, *One-on-One with Andy Grove,* was published in 1987. He also wrote a regular management column which appeared in several newspapers, as well as occasional pieces for the *Wall Street Journal, Fortune,* and the *New York Times.* He became the CEO of Intel in 1987. The decade of the 1980s brought him recognition outside of the company as well. He received honorary doctorates from the City College of New York and from Worcester Polytechnic Institute in 1985 and 1989, respec-

tively. Furthermore, he was honored in 1987 with the Engineering Leadership Recognition Award.

The Half-Billion Dollar Mistake

Intel's biggest stumbling block came abruptly in 1994, with the release of the company's Pentium processor. The chip was flawed slightly, performing math calculations incorrectly. The error was small, and would not have affected the vast majority of users—only people running math-intensive programs like those required for nuclear research or astrophysics. Grove decided that there would therefore be no reason to order a recall. Those who called in to ask about the problem were simply told not to worry. Intel's customers didn't see the matter the same way, and in short order, the flaw was suddenly the topic of technology columns in newspapers around the world. After much deliberation, Grove backed off his position, and Intel began replacing the faulty chips. The crisis cost the company half a billion dollars, but in the end the decision to switch courses wound up bolstering their image. Intel was stronger than ever.

As noted by Isaacson in *Time,* Intel controls 90% of the microprocessor market. They also face little in the way of competition, although the combined efforts of IBM, Apple, and Motorola are beginning to have some effect. Grove, certainly not one to rest on his laurels, has made the 1990s a productive decade for himself as well. His fourth book, *Only the Paranoid Survive: How to Exploit the Crisis Points that Challenge Every Company and Career,* was published in 1996, and several more awards have been forthcoming as well. In 1993, he received a Medal of Achievement from the American Engineering Association, and, in March of 1994 he was elected a Fellow of the Academy of Arts and Sciences. The following year, he was awarded the Heinz Family Foundation Award for Technology and the Economy. Finally, *Time* magazine named him their Man of the Year in 1997.

The challenges in Intel's future are many. The increasing popularity of sub-$1000 computers could prove damaging to the company's flagship product, the high-end Pentium II. Also, Intel has had to cope with increasing scrutiny from the U.S. Federal government, which has grown uneasy with the monopolistic characteristics of Intel and its chief ally, Microsoft. Grove's level of participation in these issues is definitely declining, however. In 1996, he was diagnosed with prostate cancer, and although treatment was successful he began actively grooming a successor, Craig Barrett. In March of 1998, Grove stepped down as CEO, though he remains chairperson. Outside the corporate world, he teaches a class in the business school at Stanford University. A modest man, Grove commented in the *Wall Street Journal,* "One position says you ought to put some effort into making sure that people know what you do. The opposite is, look, you'll never get 100 percent credit, so just do your stuff. Advertising your achievements will probably make you look like a jerk anyway. I lean toward the second view."

Further Reading

Grove, Andrew S., *High Output Management,* Vintage, 1995.

Grove, Andrew S., *One-On-One With Andy Grove: How to Manage Your Boss, Yourself, and Your Co-Workers,* Penguin, 1989.

Grove, Andrew S., *Only the Paranoid Survive: How to Exploit the Crisis Points That Challenge Every Company and Career,* Currency Doubleday, 1996.

Grove, Andrew S., *Physics and Technology of Semiconductor Devices,* Wiley, 1967.

Jackson, Tim, *Inside Intel,* Dutton, 1997.

Business Week, April 13, 1998.

Fortune, April 27, 1998; May 11, 1998.

Time, December, 1997, p. 46

U.S. News and World Report, April 6, 1998.

Intel Corp., ''Executive Bio—Andrew S. Grove,'' http://www.intel.com/pressroom/kits/bios/grove.htm (March 31, 1998).

Veronica Guerin

Irish investigative reporter Veronica Guerin (1959-1996) believed in revealing the truth about drugs and crime in Ireland, continuing to write her revealing articles even in the face of numerous threats. She was assassinated while sitting in her car on a Dublin street in 1996.

On June 26, 1996, a tough investigative reporter named Veronica Guerin became the twenty-fourth journalist that year to die in the line of duty, according to figures compiled by the Committee to Protect Journalists. She was a relative newcomer to the field, having only practiced her craft for some six years. Yet she was already one of its brightest stars, celebrated worldwide for her willingness to track down and publish the kind of information that certain people preferred to keep quiet. And when she died at the hands of a professional killer, presumably to ensure her silence, Guerin was elevated to the status of a national heroine.

Guerin, who acquired the nickname ''Ronnie'' during her childhood, was one of five children born to a Dublin-based accountant and his wife. She received her education in the Catholic schools of Dublin's north side, where she became an accomplished athlete in camogie (a game similar to lacrosse), soccer, and basketball. Soccer, in fact, remained a lifelong passion of Guerin's; she was a fanatic supporter of England's Manchester United professional soccer team.

Switched Careers from Accounting to Journalism

After studying accounting at Trinity College, Guerin joined her father's firm but left upon his death in 1983 to form her own public-relations company. Seven years later, she took up journalism, first as a business writer for Dublin's *Sunday Business Post* and then as a news reporter for the city's *Sunday Tribune.* In 1994, Guerin became an investigative reporter for the *Sunday Independent,* the largest-circulation weekend newspaper in Ireland.

As a member of the *Sunday Independent* staff, Guerin specialized in crime stories. She soon made a name for herself in international journalism circles for hard-hitting pieces that sought to expose the truth about Dublin's burgeoning drug trade and the part that increasingly violent and ruthless organized gangs played in it. Guerin was outraged by the mob activity she documented and frustrated by the inability of the police to bring the crime bosses to justice, so she launched a virtual one-woman crusade to bring down the gangs. ''She had no basic training [as a reporter],'' an editor at the *Sunday Business Post* later recalled. ''She just had a very simple philosophy that she wanted to get the truth.''

Guerin's investigative style was a combination of tenacity and boldness. She typically worked out of her car rather than an office, staying on a story for weeks and weeks—long after many other reporters would have given up. Sometimes she even camped out on a person's doorstep for days until he would agree to talk to her. And she didn't rely strictly on police sources for her information. Instead, she went directly to the criminals themselves, persuading many of them to talk to her and detail their activities. Mindful of strict Irish libel laws that make it illegal for reporters to identify suspected wrongdoers by name, she was careful to identify the subjects of her articles only by their street names or by colorful pseudonyms such as ''The Monk,'' ''The Coach,'' and ''The Penguin.''

Investigative Reporting Proved Dangerous

In October 1994, Guerin experienced the first serious repercussions from one of her stories when two bullets were fired through the window of her home as she played with her young son. The incident occurred only a month after she had written an article on the life of a high-living Dublin drug kingpin known as "The General" who had been found shot to death in his car.

Just a couple of months later, in January 1995, Guerin opened the door to her home and came face-to-face with a man who pointed a handgun at her head, then lowered it and shot her in the thigh instead. The man fled and was never identified. She later speculated that the shooting was in retaliation for an article she had written about the theft of $4.4 million from a supposedly secure depot near the Dublin airport—the largest cash robbery in Irish history. Guerin interviewed a known con man who was reportedly the chief suspect in the heist and described him as the local head of a crime syndicate.

After leaving the hospital, Guerin still on crutches had her husband, Graham Turley, take her to see every crime boss she knew "just to let them know I wasn't intimidated," she later revealed in an interview. Her employer had a security system installed in her house and arranged for her to have a round-the-clock police escort once she returned to work, but she canceled it after only a few days because she felt it hindered her efforts to gather information for her articles.

In September 1995, Guerin paid a visit to a horse farm owned by a prominent ex-convict named John Gilligan, a known leader in the Dublin underworld. She questioned him about how he was able to afford such a luxurious lifestyle with no apparent income. He responded by ripping open her shirt to look for hidden microphones and then beating her. During a subsequent telephone conversation, he threatened to rape her son and kill her if she published anything about him in the newspaper.

Guerin's friends later recalled that although she had always been fearless in her dealings with organized crime figures, she was especially frightened by Gilligan's outburst because he had mentioned the possibility of harming her son. Nevertheless, she pressed on with her work, confident that her familiarity with the mobsters she covered lent her an air of invulnerability; after all, she surmised, they would probably find it very difficult to kill someone they knew. In December 1995, Guerin's bravery and persistence in the face of such attempts to intimidate her into remaining silent earned her the prestigious International Press Freedom Award from the Committee to Protect Journalists.

Guerin's Death Affects Nation

On the afternoon of June 26, 1996, Guerin was alone in her car when she stopped at a traffic light in suburban Dublin and made a quick call to a friend on her cellular phone. Two men on a motorcycle pulled up alongside her car. One of them opened fire, shooting Guerin five times in the neck and chest, killing her almost instantly. The men

then sped off into traffic and escaped before anyone nearby had even had a chance to react.

The Irish responded to Guerin's assassination with shock, sorrow, and outrage. On the day of her funeral, the small chapel near the Dublin airport where she and her family regularly worshipped was packed with mourners, including Ireland's president, prime minister, and head of the armed forces; others watched the service on television. On July 4, the day labor unions across Ireland had called for a moment of silence in her memory, people on trains and buses, in stores and on the street, sat or stood quietly and bowed their heads in tribute. Admirers lined up in front of the offices of the *Sunday Independent* to leave flowers and sign a condolence book.

From the very beginning, there was little doubt that Guerin had been the victim of a professional hit, most likely ordered by one of the criminals she had already written about or planned to write about. Police immediately launched a full-scale investigation of the crime but admitted that they expected it would be quite some time before anyone was apprehended if ever. In October 1996, however, Irish police charged a man named Paul Ward with conspiracy to murder in the death of Veronica Guerin. His was the first in what law enforcement officials hoped would be a series of arrests in the case.

Most of the suspicions have centered around Gilligan, who left Ireland for Amsterdam the day before the murder. Several months later, in September 1996, he was scheduled to board another flight from London to Amsterdam when a search of his luggage turned up $500,000 in cash. He claimed he had won the money gambling, but authorities didn't buy his explanation. He was arrested on charges of trying to launder profits from selling illegal drugs.

Since Guerin's assassination, a number of events have suggested that she did not die in vain. First of all, amid criticism that they did not do enough to protect her, officials of the *Sunday Independent* announced that they were considering offering journalists working on dangerous stories more and better protection. Secondly, the Irish Parliament convened a special session to discuss anti-crime legislation aimed at cracking down on organized crime and making it easier for police to pursue cases against mob bosses. The tough new measures caused some members of Dublin's underworld to flee the country to avoid arrest.

Perhaps most important of all, Guerin's death prompted a period of soul-searching in Ireland, the likes of which had not been seen for quite some time. Citizen groups sprang up in some of Dublin's poorest neighborhoods, where the drug trade thrived, and people demanded change.

On May 2, 1997, at a ceremony in Arlington, Virginia, the name of Veronica Guerin and those of 38 other international journalists who died in the line of duty in 1996 were added to the Freedom Forum Journalists Memorial. (Ironically enough, Guerin had been scheduled to speak at a Freedom Forum conference on the subject of journalists in peril just two days after she was killed.) Her husband addressed the audience, noting the pride both he and his son felt at seeing Guerin honored in such a way. "Veronica stood for freedom to write," Turley observed. "She stood as light, and wrote of life in Ireland today, and told the truth. Veronica was not a judge, nor was she a juror, but she paid the ultimate price with the sacrifice of her life."

Further Reading

Chicago Tribune, January 19, 1997.
GQ (Gentlemen's Quarterly), March 1997.
Irish Times (online edition), October 19, 1996; June 21, 1997.
Knight-Ridder/Tribune News Service, July 11, 1996.
Nation, June 30, 1997.
New York Times, June 27, 1996, p. A4; July 8, 1996, p. D8; October 19, 1996; November 23, 1996; February 5, 1997.
People, July 22, 1996, pp. 40-43; February 24, 1997, p. 90.
Washington Post, July 9, 1996.
World Press Review, December 1996; December 1996, p. 22.
Committee to Protect Journalists, http://www.cpj.org (January 19, 1998).
Freedom Forum and the Newseum, http://www.newseum.org (January 19, 1998).
Guardian newspaper (online edition), June 27, 1996; June 28, 1996; available at http://www.guardian.co.uk (January 20, 1998).

Cathy Lee Guisewite

Creator of the syndicated cartoon, *Cathy,* which humorously chronicles the ups and downs of a single woman's life, Cathy Guisewite (born 1950) has created an endearing character whose thoughts, words and actions are humorously paralleled in the lives of millions of people (mostly women) who appreciatively follow her cartoons in over 1600 different newspapers around the world.

Cathy Guisewite's immense and sustained success is partly due to the fact that she fashions her comic-strip character's adventures after her own life's experiences, which, in turn, reflect those of the population at large. Thus, *Cathy* readers can readily relate to "bad hair days," Saturday nights without a date, or maybe a credit-card shopping spree. When another cartoon character asks "Cathy" what she is doing for lunch, she responds, "Writing a presentation, paying my bills, having a root canal, going to the bank and picking up my cleaning!!"

The Brainchild of an Achiever

Guisewite, an Ohio native, originally started a career in advertising after her graduation in 1972 from the University of Michigan, with a degree in English. She became a writer for the Campbell-Ewald agency in suburban Detroit, Michigan, then joined Norman Prady, Ltd. in 1973. Shortly thereafter, she moved to the advertising firm of W. B. Doner & Company in Southfield, Michigan, where she advanced from a group supervisor's position into the executive ranks in 1976. That same year, Guisewite negotiated a long-term

contract for her newly-created *Cathy* with Universal Press Syndicate in Mission, Kansas (later in Kansas City, Missouri).

Guisewite's first cartoon book, *The Cathy Chronicles,* (1978) was an instant success. The timely appeal of her cartoons' subject-matter is apparent in the titles of her equally successful subsequent books, including *What Do You Mean, I Still Don't Have Equal Rights??!!,* (1980); *What's a Nice Single Girl Doing with a Double Bed??!,* (1981); *It Must Be Love, My Face Is Breaking Out,* (1982); *Cathy's Valentine's Day Survival Book, How to Live through Another February 14,* (1982); *How to Get Rich, Fall in Love, Lose Weight, and Solve all Your Problems by Saying "NO",* 1983; *Eat Your Way to a Better Relationship,* 1983; *Climb Every Mountain, Bounce Every Check,* 1983; *Thin Thighs in Thirty Years,* 1986; *Why Do the Right Words Always Come Out of the Wrong Mouth?,* 1988; *$14 in the Bank and a $200 Face in My Purse,* 1990; and *Revelations from a 45-Pound Purse,* 1993.

Guisewite also created three Emmy award-winning *Cathy* television specials. *Cathy* has also appeared on calendars, coffee mugs, sweatshirts, mouse pads, and pajamas around the world. The staying power of *Cathy* owes as much to the familiarity of her face and image across the media as it does to the constant resourcefulness of Guisewite's humor and insight.

During Guisewite's 1993 acceptance speech for the prestigious National Cartoonist Society's Reuben Award, *Editor & Publisher* reported that she told the audience, "A lot of my material comes from my mother, and a lot of my sense of humor about my mother comes from my father!'' She also admits to bouncing material off her sister, Mickey Guisewite, a talented writer and advertising executive. Guisewite illustrated her sister's book, *Dancing Through Life in a Pair of Broken Heels.* Guisewite also credits Charles Schulz, the artist of *Peanuts* fame, and Mort Walker, the creator of *Beetle Bailey* and *Hi & Lois,''* for "paving the way" for her and other cartoonists into syndication. Although Guisewite was a finalist for the Reuben award in the three previous years, she shared the honor of being only the second female to actually receive the award since its inception in 1946. (Lynn Johnson, creator of *For Better or For Worse,* was a prior recipient of the award.)

According to writer Tony Case of *Editor & Publisher,* Guisewite told attendees at a 1995 American Society of Newspaper Editors (ASNE) convention that when she first created *Cathy,* young females dreamed of becoming "housewives." However, Guisewite added, the average woman today wants to be "a dynamic businessperson, financial wizard, nurturing homemaker, enlightened and involved parent, environmental activist, physical fitness expert, low-fat chef, champion of human rights, alluring and responsible partner, community activist and a size five, all at once."

Cathy vs. Cathy

Guisewite reportedly told the same audience that if she had to do one thing over, she would not have given her comic-strip character the same name as her own. Guisewite stated that she found it humiliating that readers might assume they were reading about the "less-than-perfect" moments in her own personal life. "Of course," she advised the audience, "it's even more humiliating when they *are* reading about the less-than-perfect moments in my own life."

The *real* Cathy moved to California in 1980 and has her own studio set up in her Los Angeles ranch house. She starts her day early, with her dog, Trolley, underneath her drawing desk, and a jar of M&M candies at her side. Drawing from her own family experiences, Guisewite works with India ink on a layout pad stretched across her wooden desk, creating workplace scenarios, kitchen disasters, or mother-daughter exchanges between cartoon-Cathy and her cartoon-mom. "I think the truest thing in the comic strip is Cathy's relationship with her mom," Guisewite told *Redbook'* s Carole Saline. "It's a rich tangle of devotion, anxiety, friendship, love, a need for dependence, and a need for independence. . . . Around [my] Mom, I still behave like a six-year-old."

In real life, Guisewite's mother began collecting wedding silver for her daughter when Guisewite was still a baby. When Guisewite remained single at the age of 35 years old, her mother gave up all hope and handed the collected pieces to her, assuming she would continue being a single career woman just as in *Cathy.* Her mother didn't have to wait much longer. In 1992, Guisewite adopted a daughter named Ivy, and in 1997, she married screenwriter Chris Wilkinson in a private Los Angeles, California, ceremony. However, she intends to keep her creation "Cathy" single, advising *Good Housekeeping's* Charlotte Latvala, "I was

single a long time, so I don't have to be single to write about it."

Further Reading

Guisewite, Mickey (illustrations and introduction by Cathy Guisewite). *Dancing Through Life in a Pair of Broken Heels,* Bantam Books, 1993.
Biography, April 1998, pp. 48-52.
Editor & Publisher, October 20, 1990, p. 42; May 15, 1993, p. 43; January 28, 1995, p. 36; April 29, 1995, p. 50.
Good Housekeeping, November 1997, p. 27.
New Woman, March 1990, p. 90.
Publishers Weekly, April 19, 1993, p. 43.
Redbook, April 1997, p. 104.
Savvy Woman, January 1988, p. 50.

Thom Gunn

For more than 40 years, award-winning poet Thom Gunn (born 1929) has concentrated on traditional form and, in contrast, on modern themes like LSD, panhandlers, and homosexuality. Born in England, he has spent most of his life in America, writing in traditional verse about American issues and subjects.

Thom Gunn was born Thomas William Gunn in Gravesend, England. His father, Herbert Smith, and his mother, Ann Charlotte Thompson Gunn, were both journalists; they divorced when Gunn was nine. Gunn traveled with his father, moving from town to town, and served in the British Army for two years, from 1948 to 1950. After serving in the army, Gunn lived in Paris for a year, beginning to write there, then moved to Trinity College at Cambridge, where he focused seriously on writing poetry.

California Liberated Style

Gunn published his first collection of poems, *Fighting Terms,* in 1954, the same year he began graduate study at Stanford University with poet Yvor Winters, who was known as a stern poetic rationalist. Gunn decided to settle in San Francisco, and became a resident of California in 1954. Gunn studied at Stanford from 1954 to 1955 and again from 1956 to 1958, publishing his second collection, *The Sense of Movement,* in 1957.

His new home became an essential part of his work; the discipline and structure that characterized his early work began to combine with "Californian 'with it' subject matter," according to *New York Review of Books* critic Stephen Bender. In a *San Francisco Chronicle* interview, Gunn said coming to America "changed everything for me." He began reading free verse—Wallace Stevens and William Carlos Williams—and embraced American culture. "I saw there were other things you could do. I started out with heroic stuff; full of Shakespearean-like heroes. Gradually, by the time I was living in San Francisco, I could write a poem called 'Taylor Street' about an old man sitting in a doorway." But Gunn's focus on form remained: "Whether describing the countryside of his native England or an acid trip in his adopted California, Gunn's poems have a singular purity of measure and tone," reported *Publishers Weekly*.

The Movement

My Sad Captains, published in 1961, marked a turning point in Gunn's work from metrical to more lyrical language, and a turn towards the subject of nature. *My Sad Captains* is frequently regarded as his best-known early collection. Originally, Gunn was associated with Philip Larkin and other poets of the Movement, who began to publish during the fifties and who rejected the Romantic excesses as well as the modernist revolution led by Ezra Pound and T.S. Eliot. The Movement, according to the *Norton Anthology of Modern Poetry,* "sought greater concreteness and a less high-flown diction for poetry."

The link between Gunn and the Movement, however, Gunn himself referred to as "categorizing foolishness." In an interview with *Contemporary Authors,* Gunn proclaimed that he was "not a member of the Movement, and I don't think the Movement was a movement; I think it was simply a period style that extended way beyond the people who were supposed to be involved with it." Throughout his career, Gunn has clearly defied any kind of easy categorization.

Counter Culture Influenced Poetry

Settled in San Francisco, Gunn continued to write, and began teaching at the University of California, Berkeley in 1958 after graduate studies at Stanford. Aside from occasional trips to England and a year teaching in San Antonio, Texas, Gunn has taught at Berkeley and lived in San Francisco ever since.

"In the 1960s and '70s, Gunn was part of the pleasure-seeking culture of the hippies and gay liberation," wrote *San Francisco Chronicle* reporter Jesse Hamlin. This culture included experimentation with LSD, which Gunn believes "increased the subject matter" of his poetry, giving him "more of an accepting attitude towards the world."

Writing About AIDS

When AIDS struck San Francisco, Gunn lost many friends to the disease. He voiced his opinion and vision of the epidemic in the clear and unsentimental manner characteristic of his work, particularly in poems like "The Man With Night Sweats" and "In Time of Plague." *Poetry*'s David Spurr wrote that Gunn "follows erotic impulse as well as disease—the pleasures and pains of the body—as a kind of corporeal index to the news of life and death." But the poet did not actually plan to write "The Man With Night Sweats." As he confessed to Hamlin, "I was writing about friends as they were dying, but I didn't realize the poems would have the impact they all did coming together. I was so impressed by the way people face death. So few people

feel sorry for themselves, or whimper. I hope I can have such bravery, whatever kind of death I eventually have."

But Gunn resists being identified with any particular group. According to William Logan of the *New York Times Book Review,* Gunn writes "of America without being of America." Gunn said, "Being English is very important to me since I spent my first twenty-five years in England. On the other hand . . . living in America is very important to me too, since I have spent more than half my life in this country." Interestingly, after more than 40 years of living in America, Gunn has chosen to remain a resident alien, perhaps attesting to his firm desire to remain an outsider. However, he does show preference for the writing of his adopted home: "I find most English poetry terribly timid," he told *Contemporary Authors.* "American poetry is much more interesting."

Collected Poems is Acclaimed

With the release of 1994's *Collected Poems,* Gunn seems to have "made a peace with art, its beauty and inherent artifice," according to *Publishers Weekly.* The collection reads as a personal retrospective of San Francisco. Especially at the beginning of the collection, Gunn "brings to demotic experience his finely-honed meter and incisive rhymes," wrote Tillinghast. "The balanced caesuras, the Augustan assurance of verse, are worthy of Alexander Pope, the subject matter is Big Brother and the Holding Company territory." Halfway through the book, though, Gunn began experimentation with free verse that was indicative of the chaotic, wild atmosphere of San Francisco in the 1970s.

When Gunn began to write about AIDS in the 1980s, his work became more compassionate, yet still unsentimental, and clear-headed. Tillinghast observed that "the poet is human enough to feel consoled, while at the same time having enough wry self-knowledge to undercut that consolation." And *Publishers Weekly* opined that Gunn "avoids both naive realism and modernist self-referentiality." Most remarkable about this collection of poetry is the "care, both in the making of the poem and in the concern for people." He addresses both the city of San Francisco and its citizens with "an intelligence and a warmth superior to those of virtually any other gay poet," observed *Booklist.* The people who inhabit Gunn's poems, however, are a part of the world he seeks to subvert. In the *Los Angeles Times Book Review,* poet Donald Hall wrote that he did "not find [Gunn] pledging allegiance to anything except his own alert, unforgiving, skeptical independence."

Further Reading

Contemporary Authors, New Revisions, Volume 33, Gale 1991.
Booklist, April 15, 1994, p. 1503.
New York Times Book Review, November 15, 1992; May 29, 1994.
Poetry, February 1995, p. 289.
Publishers Weekly, February 28, 1994, p. 77.
San Francisco Chronicle, April 8, 1996, p.D1.

H

Uta Thyra Hagen

From *The Sea Gull,* her 1938 Broadway debut, to the 1995 off-Broadway hit *Mrs. Klein,* Uta Hagen (born 1919) keeps bringing down the house. Many critics consider her the first lady of theater.

Uta Hagen was born to Oskar Frank Leonard and Thyra A. (Leisner) Hagen in Gottingen, Germany, on June 12, 1919. Her brother, Holger Hagen, later became an actor in Germany. Hagen's father taught art history at the local university and also directed the Gottingen Handel festivals after World War I.

In 1924, as a Carl Schurz Foundation Professor, Hagen's father traveled to Wisconsin in the United States. He founded the art history department at the University of Wisconsin in Madison. Offered the position as head of the department, he accepted and moved his family to the United States.

For many years during her childhood, Hagen had accompanied her parents to the theater both in the United States and abroad since the family made numerous trips back to Germany. It appeared that acting was already in her blood. In 1936, she graduated from the University of Wisconsin High School and entered the university itself, but she left after just one term. A semester of study at the Royal Academy of Dramatic Art in London convinced Hagen that acting was the right career choice and caused her to leave the University of Wisconsin for the uncertainties of the theater.

In 1937 she was on stage as Ophelia in a production in Dennis, Massachusetts. The title role of Hamlet was played by Eva Le Gallienne, one of Broadway's leading actresses. Le Gallienne, born in London in 1899, had founded the famed Civic Repertory Theatre in New York in 1926, becoming director and producer as well. With Le Gallienne's nurturing, Hagen skipped the usual route of small parts and made her stage debut on March 28, 1928. She was 19 when she made her debut as Nina in *The Sea Gull* at the Shubert Theatre.

In 1938, Hagen met the actor who would become her husband. They became acquainted in a rather unusual way. During a summer stock production of *The Latitude of Love,* in Ridgefield, Connecticut, Hagen was required to knock the leading man unconscious every night. However, José Ferrer survived, and they married on December 8, 1938. During their ten years of marriage, Hagen and Ferrer performed in many productions together, as well as separately. They became one of the very few teams of co-starring spouses to achieve stardom together. They had one daughter, Leticia.

Hagen kept busy over the next few years. She returned to Broadway in 1939, playing Edith in *The Happiest Days* and then appearing in *Key Largo,* the powerful Maxwell Anderson drama at the Ethel Barrymore Theatre. Audiences applauded her Desdemona in *Othello* in 1942. The cast featured Paul Robeson in the title role and Ferrer as Iago. Later that year, she and Ferrer played in *Vickie,* a comedy at the Plymouth Theatre. Perhaps the key performance of Hagen's career occurred in 1943, again as Desdemona in the Theatre Guild's production of *Othello,* and once again with Robeson and Ferrer. The show ran for 295 performances.

After World War II and fears of the Soviet Union and communism were running high. Because Hagen and Ferrer were so closely associated with Robeson, an African-Ameri-

179

can actor well-known for his leftist views, they were eventually called to Washington, D.C., to be questioned about their own beliefs. Ferrer denied any connection to leftist views, and Hagen was never asked to give her views at all. Despite that, Hagen ended up being blacklisted from television and Hollywood movie roles.

In 1947, Hagen co-founded an acting school with actor/director Herbert Berghof and began teaching acting classes. Early in 1948, Hagen starred with Ferrer again in a production of *Angel Street,* and that June, they divorced. She married Berghof in 1951.

In the late 1940s and early 1950s, Hagen truly came into her own as one of Broadway's most respected and admired stars. She replaced Jessica Tandy on Broadway as Blanche DuBois in Tennessee Williams's *A Streetcar Named Desire.* She received enthusiastic reviews from critics. She next portrayed Georgie, the dowdy wife in the Clifford Odets' play, *The Country Girl.* Hagen won her first Antoinette Perry Award (Tony Award) for best dramatic actress for this role.

Hagen kept busy in summer stock in 1954, touring in *The Lady's Not for Burning* and *The Deep Blue Sea.* After her appearance in *Island of Goats* at the Fulton Theatre in 1955, Hagen left Broadway for a period of seven years. She had decided to wait for the perfect part.

Hagen returned to Broadway on October 13, 1962. Playing the ruthless Martha, a college professor's wife, in Edward Albee's searing drama, *Who's Afraid of Virginia Woolf?,* Hagen earned her second Tony Award as well as

the critics award for best dramatic actress of the year. Her co-star, Arthur Hill, portraying the husband who cannot live up to his wife's expectations, also won a Tony Award and the critics award. The play, as well as the film (with Richard Burton and Elizabeth Taylor in the lead roles) was a bit of a shock to audiences in the 1960s, not only for the way it laid open the ugly realities of a failed marriage, but also for its liberal use of obscenities.

Hagen has written two books, *Respect for Acting* in 1973 and *A Challenge for the Actor* in 1991. According to her biography on the *Women's International Center* website, the books "grew out of decades of collaboration and exploration of the actor's craft." She also continued to teach at the Herbert Bergof Studio, although her husband, the school's namesake, died in 1990. According to Marjorie Rosen of *People,* her students, who have included Academy Award winners Whoopi Goldberg, Jack Lemmon, and Geraldine Page, as well as Golden Globe winner Christine Lahti, "regard Hagen as the quintessential drama teacher." Lemmon commented that "Hagen taught him the 'truth about character behavior.'" Hagen responded to Rosen, "I try to teach actors to bring a human being onstage, not an actor."

From the 1960s through the early 1990s, Hagen made television and film appearances, most notably *The Boys from Brazil* in 1978, an episode of *The Twilight Zone* television show in 1985, and *Reversal of Fortune* in 1990. She was also inducted into the Theatre Hall of Fame in 1981. In 1995 at the age of 76, Hagen again received critical acclaim for her portrayal of psychoanalyst Melanie Klein in the off-Broadway production *Mrs. Klein.* Lloyd Rose of the *Washington Post* commented, "A legend is playing a legend when Uta Hagen appears in the title role of 'Mrs. Klein.'"

Further Reading

Hagen, Uta, *A Challenge for the Actor,* Scribner, 1991.
Hagen, Uta, *Respect for Acting,* revised edition, Macmillan General, 1979.
Back Stage West, July 10, 1997.
People, February 5, 1996.
Time, November 20, 1995.
Washington Post, September 20, 1996.
"Uta Hagen," *Internet Movie Databank,* http://us.imdb.com (May 18, 1998).
"WIC Biography - Uta Hagen," *Women's International Center,* http://www.wic.org/bio/hagen.htm (May 18, 1998).

David Halberstam

American journalist and author David Halberstam (born 1934) was awarded the Pulitzer Prize in 1964 for his international reporting of the Vietnam War.

D avid Halberstam is a versatile author who has published more than 16 books on diverse subjects such as civil rights, the world economy, the auto industry, and the war in Vietnam. He also writes about sports topics, such as basketball, baseball, and amateur rowing. Halberstam's best-selling books are characterized by voluminous research and an anecdotal, novelistic narrative style. His work has been reproduced for television and has been used as reference material and as text in the classroom.

David Halberstam was born April 10, 1934, to Charles A. and Blanche (Levy) Halberstam. His father was a surgeon and his mother worked as a teacher. The family moved around frequently when Halberstam was a child, following Charles Halberstam's military career. David Halberstam spent his youth in such cities as El Paso, Texas, Rochester, Minnesota, and Winsted, Connecticut. After his father's return from service in Europe during World War II, the family again relocated, this time to Westchester County in New York. Halberstam attended Roosevelt High School in Yonkers, New York, participating in track and writing for the school newspaper. He graduated in 1951 and was accepted at Harvard University as an undergraduate.

Halberstam did not have the best grades as a student at Harvard, but he did achieve the prestigious assignment of managing editor of the *Harvard Crimson,* the school's daily newspaper. The paper was published on a demanding deadline six days a week for an intellectual readership; it was a good beginning for the student journalist. When he graduated from college in 1955, Halberstam admitted he wanted to improve his interviewing skills. He told Brian Lamb, the host of C-Span's *Booknotes,* "I had to learn how to go out and interview ordinary people." He did that working at the West Point, Mississippi, *Daily Times Leader.*

His modest beginning at the smallest daily in Mississippi taught Halberstam how to "deal with ordinary people, to listen to them, to see the value in people who didn't agree with the same things I agreed and how they worked, what their lives were," he recounted to Lamb.

Within a year Halberstam moved to the *Nashville Tennessean* where he continued to hone his skills by modeling himself upon the best reporters. He covered civil rights issues and was enthralled by a sense of violence. Halberstam told *People Weekly* writer Christopher P. Andersen, "Trucks would try and run us off the road, we'd be threatened with guns." In general he felt his experience in Tennessee was worth it "because it validated all the reasons anybody becomes a reporter in the first place."

Halberstam left the *Nashville Tennessean* in 1960 as a confident reporter. He accepted a position with the *New York Times.* In his first months with the well-known paper he covered Washington and within his first year there he was transferred to cover the war in the Congo. By 1962, Halberstam was in Vietnam.

Foreign Correspondent

Initially, Halberstam supported the United States' involvement in Vietnam. As told to *People Weekly* writer Andersen, "We were there to help another country against encroachment from within, and I did not dissent. I believed in the cause that was at stake and in the men who were fighting it." But when the Vietnam policy became more controversial, when Washington ignored assessments reported by their advisers, Halberstam started to question and criticize. Journalist William Prochnau covered the Vietnam War for *The Seattle Times.* He met Halberstam in Vietnam and described him to Lamb of *Booknotes* as "a brilliant brat" who was working for "the dominant and most prestigious newspaper in the world." Prochnau further explained to Lamb, "He was twenty-eight years old. He was a man of great passions, great angers. He felt the government was deluding itself as much as deluding the American people. It drove him to fits." Halberstam's courage enabled him to report both sides of the Vietnam experience. He was awarded the Pulitzer Prize for international reporting in 1964.

Author

About this time Halberstam began his career as a nonfiction author. He published *The Making of a Quagmire: America and Vietnam During the Kennedy Era* in 1965. This is his first nonfiction attempt to analyze American involvement in Vietnam. In 1967, Halberstam left the *New York Times.* He pursued a position as contributing editor of *Harper's* magazine. Then he published *The Unfinished Odyssey of Robert Kennedy* in 1969. By the time he published *Ho* in 1971, Halberstam knew the Vietnam war was lost. He returned to the subject that was an essential part of his life for several years and published *The Best and the Brightest* in 1972. Halberstam asked how the gifted leaders assembled by the Kennedy and Johnson administrations could have allowed such a tragic involvement in Vietnam. The book is his first best-seller.

The Powers That Be

In 1974, Halberstam had been a journalist for 20 years. The Watergate scandal was widely reported and Halberstam perceived, "that in both Vietnam and Watergate the principal antagonists were not the president and the Congress, or the president and the opposition party but the president and the media." Sharing his opinion with *BOMC Today* he added, "How that had happened seemed to me a rich question in its possibilities." Halberstam's speculation grew into another best seller, *The Powers That Be*, published in 1979. The book concentrates on four news reporting giants: CBS, *Time*, the *Washington Post*, and the *Los Angeles Times*. Halberstam contends that the media helped shape opinion and recent politics. He pointed out to *People Weekly* writer Andersen, why he chose those four reporting companies. "CBS was, and probably still is, the best network. *Time* is the most important opinion-shaping magazine. The *Washington Post* uncovered Watergate. And the *Los Angeles Times* invented Richard Nixon."

The Amateurs

Halberstam is a talented writer who can work on more than one project at a time. While conducting research for a major work in progress he will take a break and direct his strong investigative reporting skills to another passion: sports. Halberstam has been described as the ultimate fan. In 1981 he published *The Breaks of the Game*, a book about professional basketball and followed that in 1985 with a book about non-professional rowing called *The Amateurs*. Halberstam got his inspiration for the book while watching a pre-Olympic event on television. Amazed by the hype surrounding the athletes, Halberstam wondered if amateur athletics meant only money, endorsements, or fame. He set out to find athletes that were involved in sports for the love of the sport and not on a quest for fame or fortune. He found what he wanted in a group of amateur rowers. Sculling is an obscure sport and the success of the book surprised and pleased Halberstam who confided to Lamb on *Booknotes*, "I have a small book that I did about four young men rowing for an Olympic medal that I really love." He said *The Amateurs* "is my inner, secret favorite."

The Reckoning

While delivering *The Breaks of the Game* and *The Amateurs*, Halberstam researched and wrote *The Reckoning*. Published in 1986, *The Reckoning* was "by far the hardest book I have ever done," Halberstam told *BOMC Today*. "I wanted to do a comparative study of an American and a Japanese auto company." The book also includes the economic and cultural differences between the two countries. True to his style, Halberstam interviewed everyone in the auto industry. "I came to like the auto men of Detroit. I found these men interesting, reflective and generous with their time." He spent eight months in Tokyo, a country that, in his opinion, is receptive to receiving information but is reluctant to disclose it. "The burden was not one of language but of culture. At first I found the Nissan officials unreceptive and only superficially cooperative to what I was doing."

The Summer of '49

In 1989 Halberstam took a look at the last radio era in baseball and published *The Summer of '49*. The book chronicles the 1949 pennant race between the Boston Red Sox and the New York Yankees in a time before television and before the superstar contracts. "When you hear a game on the radio and you form a mythic vision of a DiMaggio or a Williams," Halberstam recalled to Lamb on *Booknotes*, "They live larger because you create the myth for them in the fantasy of your mind."

The Next Century

Working with material he researched for *The Reckoning* Halberstam delivered an essay in 1991 called *The Next Century*. This essay is about Americans' complacent attitude toward declining education and economic productivity. Critics consider the title a misnomer because, the essay concentrates on America since Vietnam and makes no predictions for the coming century.

Social Historian: *The Fifties*

Having told the story of America under pressure, Halberstam moved to a time when America was rich and everything seemed to work. *The Fifties*, published in 1993 includes sections on politics, civil rights, and the McCarthy period. Also covered is the impact television made on society. "There was an innocence about television," Halberstam explained to Lamb on *Booknotes*. "It really changed everything." As television developed, the pace of life suddenly sped up. There were commercials and politicians and the ideals of someone's vision of the American family coming into peoples homes. Of the time frame, *Wall Street Journal* writer Dorothy Rabinowitz recalls, "We are speaking here of a decade whose creative ferment, and level of art and culture, has never since been equaled."

Halberstam discussed with Lamb on *Booknotes* the phenomenon that "When people talk about America in the '50s . . . they talk about it as an innocent time. . . . Yet the '50s were not that innocent." The *Wall Street Journal* writer Rabinowitz contends, "This is the era now routinely described as the age of conformity, the time of hula hoops and tail fins, and sterile obedience."

October 1964: Baseball History

Moving ahead to the 1960s Halberstam returned to baseball in *October 1964*, published in 1994. Here he covers the World Series competition between the St. Louis Cardinals and the New York Yankees. The story relates the rise of the St. Louis team and the decline of the Yankee dynasty. Some historians concur that the history of baseball offers insight into labor law, race relations, urban history, and the development of a leisure industry. *October 1964*, among other books, is required reading for a history class at the University of South Florida.

The Children

While the 1960s was a decade of rich sports anecdotes it is also the decade of real social revolutions. His book titled *The Children,* published in 1998, chronicles the lives of some of the kids who challenged social order. Halberstam was a witness to the first sit-in in his early years as journalist for the *Nashville Tennessean* and regularly covered the civil rights movement for the paper. Speaking to Lamb on *Booknotes,* Halberstam said, ''The first sit-ins started there, and it was a very interesting group of young black kids.'' Halberstam was close to the kids in age and earned their trust. He tracked their lives and tells of their experiences then and now. In a *Booklist* review, Mary Carroll noted, ''*The Children* is both a survey of five central years of the civil rights movement (1960-65) and a sterling example of the genre with which Halberstam is most closely identified: collective biography.''

Halberstam's typically long books are always well-researched and maintain a narrative flair that holds a reader's interest. His book topics develop from within himself. Halberstam said to *BOMC Today*, ''My books have always been the result of my own curiosity: the questions I answer for other people are the questions I seek to answer for myself.''

Further Reading

Contemporary Authors, New Revision Series, Volume 45, Gale, 1995.
Lamb, Brian, *Booknotes,* Times Books, 1997.
Booklist, January 1, 1998.
People Weekly, November 4, 1985.
Wall Street Journal, November 24, 1997.
''Booknotes Transcript,'' *C-Span,* July 11, 1993, http://www.booknotes.org/transcripts/10198.htm (April 1998).
Halberstam, David, ''David Halberstam Talks about *The Reckoning*,'' *BOMC Today,* 1987, http://www.bomc.com/ows-bin/owa/rr_authorsintheirownwords_sub?intid=12&uid= (April 1998).

Suzan Shown Harjo

Suzan Shown Harjo (born 1945) is one of the leading Native American activists in the United States. She has raised public awareness about issues of concern to Native Americans by working on legislation to protect their rights, preserve their languages and traditions, reduce their high levels of poverty, alcoholism and unemployment, and safeguard their sacred lands.

Through a multitude of activities—lobbying legislators, speaking to the media, and writing numerous articles for general circulation and Native American publications—Suzan Shown Harjo has been able to exert her influence and raise the consciousness of a not-always-receptive public. Her most important activity, however, is serving as president and director of the Morning Star Institute in Washington, D.C., the oldest and largest Native American advocacy group in the country. That organization, which Harjo founded in 1984 in memory of her late husband, Frank Harjo, reminds the federal government of the treaty rights promised in return for land cessions. It also tries, in the face of constant budget cuts to get the government to honor the education, housing, and health benefits promised to Native Americans.

In addition, Harjo is a founding trustee of the National Museum of the American Indian, which opened its first facility in New York City in 1994. The main museum will be built in Washington, D.C. on the Capitol Mall sometime after the year 2000. To educate young Americans about Native American concerns, she helped develop ''Red Thunder,'' a Native American rock band, and Indian rock music videos, including ''Makoce Wakan: Sacred Earth,'' a special that runs often on VH-1, a music video cable station. Harjo has appeared on the *Oprah Winfrey Show, Larry King Live,* CNN's *Talkback Live,* C-SPAN's *Washington Journal,* and many others.

The Early Years

For the first 11 years of her life, Harjo grew up on a farm in an Oklahoma reservation, much aware of her Native American heritage and the obstacles faced by her people. Like so many others on the reservation, the Harjo family was poor; their modest home was without indoor plumbing and electricity. At that time, young Suzan's idea of wealth was to be able to put ice cubes in her drinks, the way they did at the drugstore in town.

A citizen of the Cheyenne and Arapaho tribes, she was born with the spirit of a fighter, which her difficult early circumstances could not destroy. As a girl, she was deter-

mined to carry on the legacy of her great-grandfather, Chief Bull Bear, who was a leader in the Cheyenne resistance against government oppression during the latter half of the 1800s. Harjo also showed early literary promise, writing poetry from the time she was a young girl.

Between the ages of 12 and 16, Harjo lived with her family in Naples, Italy, where her father was stationed in the U.S. Army. Later, she told reporters that she found a familiar tribal feeling in the Italian neighborhoods where people had known each other for generations, as they had on her Oklahoma reservation.

Moving Toward Her Mission

After her return to the U.S., Harjo worked in radio and theater production in New York, where she met her husband-to-be and the father of her two children, Frank Ray Harjo. The roots of her activism date back to struggles of the mid-1960s for religious freedom and civil rights. She and her husband co-produced "Seeing Red," a bi-weekly radio program on WBAI-FM in New York City, the first regularly-scheduled Indian news and analysis show in the United States.

In addition to her duties as a journalist, she served as the station's director of drama and literature and produced hundreds of plays and other programs for broadcast. Also while in New York, Harjo helped to found the Spiderwoman Theater Company, an improvisational group. She played various roles in repertory company productions and sang in Gilbert and Sullivan performances. But, as the years, passed, she felt a growing obligation to help Native Americans.

In 1974, Harjo moved to Washington, D.C., where she served as a legislative liaison for two law firms which were involved with Native American rights. Then, in 1978, President Jimmy Carter appointed her a congressional liaison for Indian Affairs, a job in which she helped plan and draft legislation, including laws that would protect Indian lands and tribal governmental tax status. She also worked for the National Congress of American Indians (NCAI), an organization devoted to safeguarding the rights of Native Americans.

When the 1980s ushered in a new president whose Republican agenda was far different than that of his predecessor, Harjo's activities shifted to battling proposed budget cuts in Indian programs and attempts to turn over control of tribal and federal schools to the states. She also continued to champion legal cases involving treaty rights, individual civil liberties, land claims, environmental protection, and restoring federal recognition to tribes that lost their official status as Indians as a result of the government's termination policies of the 1950s.

In 1984, Harjo returned to the NCAI, this time as the organization's executive director. Over the next six years, she provided the leadership for the NCAI's national policy activities, focusing in particular on legislative and litigation efforts and cultural concerns. She lobbied on behalf of the nation's nearly two million Indians who faced massive cuts in their federal funds during the Reagan administration. One of Harjo's biggest concerns was the decline in health clinics on reservations; poor health care led to a higher mortality rate among Native Americans, who already suffer high incidences of cancer, diabetes, suicide and alcoholism.

Morning Star

The year 1984 also marked the beginning of her role as founder and president of The Morning Star Institute. The organization focuses on protecting sacred lands and developing cultural rights policies to protect tribal names, symbols, history and music. In addition, the organization conducts programs and sponsors events in the areas of Native arts, cultural and traditional rights, youth, the environment, and leadership training. In addition, Harjo is the co-founder and vice president of Native Children's Survival, dedicated to "the healing of Mother Earth and her children."

Since the 1970s, Harjo has proven to be not only a high-profile spokesperson for Native Americans, but she also is a savvy lobbyist who has been able to deliver the goods. She has been instrumental in securing the return of one million acres, including holy lands, to the Cheyenne, Arapaho, Lakota, Zuni, Taos, Mashantucket, and other Indian nations. She also has conducted more than 450 successful legislative efforts, including extending the amount of time a Native American can sue for damages against third parties, creating protections for Native American children, and instituting protective measures for Indian lands and tribal governmental tax status.

Battles Fought

Among the general public, Harjo may best be known for filing a lawsuit with the U.S. Patent and Trademark Office to stop the Washington Redskins from using that name and logo, which Harjo and six other prominent Native Americans claim is demeaning to their culture. The football franchise declared a First Amendment "free speech" defense against the lawsuit, but the trademark board agreed with Harjo that the case merited further study.

Harjo and other Native Americans were successful in stopping the University of Oklahoma from using the "Little Red" mascot and name; the Dartmouth University Indians also changed their name as a result of pressure from the group. Several colleges and high schools around the country have stopped using names and mascots that refer to American Indians. "I am really heartened [by the name changes]," Harjo told the *Los Angeles Times* during a 1994 interview. "That is a really good sign of America growing up and shining a light on racism."

Another area of concern for Harjo is television and movies. She has spoken out against the portrayals of Native Americans in films such as *Dances With Wolves, Last of the Mohicans,* and *Cheyenne Autumn.* She did, however, praise the characterizations of Native peoples in the television series, *Northern Exposure.*

"The problem with most movies is that they are still about the good-hearted, good-looking white guy," Harjo told the *Los Angeles Times.* "The stories are secondarily about Indians. And they use a whole different language to refer to us." She continued, "We don't eat corn—we eat maize. We don't walk, skip, or jump—we roam. We don't have music or songs—we have chants. We don't have church services—we have rites. All that suggests we are either not here or we are so different that we don't fit in any place."

Harjo also has stood up against the federal government in a fight to allow Indians to acquire eagle feathers and body parts for use in religious ceremonies. While federal laws make it illegal to kill bald eagles because the bird is a threatened species, the laws do allow exceptions for Indians to use feathers and body parts, which they obtain from a federal repository set up to take in carcasses from eagles electrocuted by power lines, hit by automobiles or killed illegally. Under special circumstances, Indians can get permits to kill eagles. In 1997, however, an Indian man in New Mexico was prosecuted for shooting a bald eagle for a religious ceremony. Harjo spoke out, telling the government, "Stop prying. You don't need to delve into the details of this particular man's religion."

Harjo, the mother of an adult son and a daughter, has explained that her efforts are fueled by one thing: protecting the cultural heritage of her children and grandchildren. "What I do is for them," she said. "My parents did stuff for me. We're always doing things several generations out to protect the rights of our people, through our families. That's really how I define myself. I'm a mother."

Further Reading

Malinowski, Sharon, *Notable Native Americans,* Gale, 1995.
North American Indian Landmarks: A Traveler's Guide, (forward by Suzan Shown Harjo) Gale, 1994.
Dallas Morning News, October 11, 1992.
Indian Country Today, September 8, 1994.
Lear's, July/August 1989.
Los Angeles Times, November 27, 1994.
Morning Star Institute, fact sheets and press releases. April 3, 1998.
Native Peoples, winter 1994.
Newsweek, Fall/Winter 1991.
New York Times, April 2, 1986.
Washington Post, November 6, 1994.
"The National Museum of the American Indian—A Promise America is Keeping—Story by Suzan Shown Harjo," *Native Peoples Magazine,* (Fall 1996) http://www.nativepeoples.com/np_features/np_articles/1996_fall_article/nmai_article.html (May 21, 1998).

Frances Ellen Watkins Harper

African American writer, lecturer, abolitionist, and women's rights activist Frances Ellen Watkins Harper (1825-1911) was a notable voice in social reform in the nineteenth century. She captivated black and white audiences alike with dramatic recitations of her antislavery and social reform verse.

Dubbed the "Bronze Muse" in honor of her skills as both a writer and lecturer, Frances Ellen Watkins Harper is regarded as one of the most extraordinarily accomplished African American women of the nineteenth century. She was, for example, a respected poet whose ten volumes of verse sold well enough to provide her with a modest income. In 1859, she became the first black woman to publish a short story. And her only novel, *Iola Leroy; or Shadows Uplifted* (1892), was the first book by a black writer to depict the life of African Americans in the Reconstruction-era South. (Many colleges and universities across the United States still feature it as part of their women's studies and black literature courses.) But it was as a lecturer that Harper had her greatest impact, beginning in the antebellum period as an antislavery activist and ending up as a crusader for women's rights and moral reform.

Harper was born of free parents in September of 1825, in Baltimore, Maryland. She was raised there by an aunt and uncle after being orphaned at an early age. She attended a private school run by her uncle until she was 13, when she went to work as a housekeeper for a family that owned a bookstore. Harper's employer encouraged her to spend her free time reading and writing, and before long the young woman was composing her first poems and essays. Her first book, *Forest Leaves* (also known as *Autumn Leaves*), a compilation of poetry and prose, was published about 1845.

After leaving Maryland in 1850, Harper taught school for a while in Ohio and Pennsylvania. It was in Pennsylvania that she became active in the Underground Railroad.

She also launched her career as an antislavery lecturer during this period, traveling extensively throughout New England, New York, Ohio, and eastern Canada to speak as often as three or four times a day. On May 13, 1857, for example, she addressed the New York Antislavery Society. In an excerpt of what is believed to be the only surviving example of one of Harper's antislavery lectures, as quoted from *Outspoken Women: Speeches by American Women Reformers, 1635-1935,* Harper called for an end to slavery: "A hundred thousand newborn babes are annually added to the victims of slavery; twenty thousand lives are annually sacrificed on the plantations of the South. Such a sight should send a thrill of horror through the nerves of civilization and impel the heart of humanity to lofty deeds. So it might, if men had not found out a fearful alchemy by which this blood can be transformed into gold. Instead of listening to the cry of agony, they listen to the ring of dollars and stoop down to pick up the coin."

The 1850s proved to be a productive time for Harper, and in addition to her public speaking engagements, she also published several volumes of poetry. In much of her writing, Harper argued for social change and in support of her beliefs. One of her most critically acclaimed works, the abolitionist poem "Bury Me in a Free Land," was published in 1854 in her popular book *Poems on Miscellaneous Subjects.* This collection saw print in over 20 editions. "Mrs. Harper's verse is frankly propagandist, a metrical extension of her life dedicated to the welfare of others," commented Joan R. Sherman in *Invisible Poets: Afro-Americans of the Nineteenth Century.* "She believed in art for humanity's sake."

In 1860, Harper married Fenton Harper, a farmer, and briefly retired from public speaking. The couple had one daughter, Mary. After her husband's death in 1864, Harper returned to the lecture circuit. She also published what many critics believed to be her best work, *Moses: A Story of the Nile,* a collection of poems and an essay, under the name Mrs. F.E.W. Harper around this time. An extended biblical allegory written in blank verse and lacking overt racial references, *Moses* tells the story of the Hebrew patriarch by focusing on his self-sacrifice and leadership skills. "The poem's elevated diction, concrete imagery, and formal meter harmoniously blend to magnify the noble adventure of Moses' life and the mysterious grandeur of his death," judged Sherman in *Invisible Poets.* "Mrs. Harper maintains the pace of her long narrative and its tone of reverent admiration with scarcely a pause for moralizing. *Moses* is Mrs. Harper's most original poem and one of considerable power."

After the American Civil War, Harper continued to lecture on behalf of the women's movement and the Women's Christian Temperance Union. Her top priority, however, was the race issue; while on a lengthy tour across the South during the late 1860s and early 1870s, she saw firsthand that former slaves endured conditions nearly as intolerable as those that had existed before the war. (And as lynchings and other forms of racial intimidation became more commonplace, the lives of Southern blacks took on an increased sense of desperation.) Consequently, like many of her fellow black activists, she felt that securing rights for women could wait until African Americans were guaranteed certain basic freedoms. Harper addressed this very topic on February 23, 1891, at a meeting of the National Council of Women. Her remarks were originally published in 1891 in *Transactions* and later reprinted in *Black Women in Nineteenth-Century American Life: Their Words, Their Thoughts, Their Feelings.* In her introduction, Harper declared: "I deem it a privilege to present the negro, not as a mere dependent asking for northern sympathy or southern compassion, but as a member of the body politic who has a claim upon the nation for justice, simple justice, which is the right of every race, upon the government for protection, which is the rightful claim of every citizen, and upon our common Christianity for the best influences which can be exerted for peace on earth and goodwill to man."

In the same speech, Harper appealed to women of all colors to work towards social equality: "[T]here are some rights more precious than the rights of property or the claims of superior intelligence: they are the rights of life and liberty, and to these the poorest and humblest man has just as much right as the richest and most influential man in the country. Ignorance and poverty are conditions which men outgrow. Since the sealed volume was opened by the crimson hand of war, in spite of entailed ignorance, poverty, opposition, and a heritage of scorn, schools have sprung like wells in the desert dust. It has been estimated that about two millions have learned to read. . . . Millions of dollars have flowed into the pockets of the race, and freed people have not only been able to provide for themselves, but reach out their hands to impoverished owners."

At the Columbian Exposition in Chicago in 1893, Harper delivered a speech entitled "Women's Political Future." In this presentation, she reiterated her belief in the ability of women to exert a strong moral force for social change. Her address was published in May Wright Sewall's 1894 book entitled *The World's Congress of Representative Women.* "The tendency of the present age, with its restlessness, religious upheavals, failures, blunders, and crimes, is toward broader freedom, an increase of knowledge, the emancipation of thought, and a recognition of the brotherhood of man; in this movement woman, as the companion of man, must be a sharer," declared Harper. "So close is the bond between man and woman that you can not raise one without lifting the other. The world can not move without woman's sharing in the movement, and to help give a right impetus to that movement is woman's highest privilege."

Harper also presented her ideas on suffrage in this speech, favoring an educated voter of either sex over the then-current system of only men being allowed to vote in the United States: "I do not believe in unrestricted and universal suffrage for either men or women. I believe in moral and educational tests. I do not believe that the most ignorant and brutal man is better prepared to add value to the strength and durability of the government than the most cultured, upright, and intelligent woman. I do not think that willful ignorance should swamp earnest intelligence at the ballot box, nor that educated wickedness, violence, and fraud should cancel the votes of honest men. The unsteady hands of a drunkard can not cast the ballot of a freeman. The hands of lynchers are too red with blood to determine the political character of the government for even four short years. The ballot in the hands of woman means power added to influence. How well she will use that power I can not foretell. Great evils stare us in the face that need to be throttled by the combined power of an upright manhood and an enlightened womanhood; and I know that no nation can gain its full measure of enlightenment and happiness if one-half of it is free and the other half is fettered. China compressed the feet of her women and thereby retarded the steps of her men. The elements of a nation's weakness must ever be found at the hearthstone."

Harper continued to write and lecture for social reform until her death on February 22, 1911, in Philadelphia, Pennsylvania. Among the notable posts she held during her life included director of the American Association of Education of Colored Youth, executive member of the National Women's Christian Temperance Union, and founding member and vice-president of the National Association of Colored Women. Eugene B. Redmond, discussing Harper's writing in *Drumvoices: The Mission of Afro-American Poetry, A Critical History,* noted: "Up until the Civil War, Mrs. Harper's favorite themes were slavery, its harshness, and the hypocrisies of America. She is careful to place graphic details where they will get the greatest result, especially when the poems are read aloud." He continued: "Critics generally agree that Mrs. Harper's poetry is not original or brilliant. But she is exciting and comes through with powerful flashes of imagery and statement." W.E.B. DuBois, writing an editorial for *Crisis* after Harper's death, opined: "It is, however, for her attempts to forward literature among colored people, that Frances Harper deserves to be remembered. She was not a great singer, but she had some sense of song; she was not a great writer, but [what] she wrote [was] worth reading. She was, above all, sincere. She took her writing soberly and earnestly; she gave her life to it."

Further Reading

Anderson, Judith, *Outspoken Women: Speeches by American Women Reformers, 1635-1935,* Kendall/Hunt, 1984.
Foner, Philip S., editor, *The Voice of Black America: Major Speeches by Negroes in the United States, 1797-1971,* Simon & Schuster, 1972.
Lerner, Gerda, editor, *Black Women in White America: A Documentary History,* Pantheon Books, 1972.
Loewenberg, Bert James, and Ruth Bogin, editors, *Black Women in Nineteenth-Century American Life: Their Words, Their Thoughts, Their Feelings,* Pennsylvania State University Press, 1976.
Redmond, Eugene B., *Drumvoices: The Mission of Afro-American Poetry, A Critical History,* Anchor/Doubleday, 1976.
Sewall, May Wright, editor, *The World's Congress of Representative Women,* Rand, McNally, 1894.
Sherman, Joan R., *Invisible Poets: Afro-Americans of the Nineteenth Century,* University of Illinois Press, 1974.
Crisis, April 1911.

Pamela Harriman

Pamela Harriman (1920-1997) enjoyed the acquaintance of a number of world leaders and international men of wealth and influence. At various times married to the son of Winston Churchill, to a Hollywood and Broadway producer, and to a former governor of New York, Harriman was at first noted for her personal charm and ability to attract powerful men. However, in the final decade of her life she made significant contributions to the Democratic Party and served as the U.S. ambassador to France.

Pamela Digby Churchill Hayward Harriman led an extraordinary life among the world's rich and powerful. She parlayed an aristocratic British lineage into social position, political prominence, and tremendous wealth. Initially fueled by youthful determination to escape country life in Dorset, the rebellious, high-spirited girl settled in London after coming out before King George VI and then spending the requisite year "finishing" on the Continent. Shortly after arriving, a series of events and opportunities presented themselves that, once taken, shaped the course her life would take: she took a job as a translator in the Foreign Office; Great Britain declared war on Germany; and she met and married Randolph Churchill, son of Prime Minister Winston Churchill. Although the marriage soon failed, the prime minister, who genuinely liked her, recognized her charm and ability to gain the attention of influential men. Under his tutelage she learned politics, while hosting the "Churchill Club" to help the prime minister foster Anglo-American relations.

An Independent Woman

After the war, Harriman used the Churchill name as an entree to the socially elite first in France and Italy, and later in the United States. Men were reportedly mesmerized by her. During what has been called the "courtesan" years, her name was linked romantically with millionaire diplomat Averell Harriman, playboy Jock Whitney, Prince Aly Khan, Fiat heir Gianni Agnelli, Baron Elie de Rothschild, and Greek shipping magnate Stavros Niarchos, among others. She was known for attaching herself to smart, wealthy men, and devoting her time and energy to supporting their interests. In 1960, she met and married Hollywood producer Leland Hayward; and after his death 11 years later, married one of her first loves, Averell Harriman. In an odd twist of fate, by marrying Harriman, her focus returned to politics—this time in the United States. Her new husband was a diplomat, one of the country's preeminent statesmen, a former governor of New York, and a scion of the Democratic Party. She dedicated herself to advancing her husband's interests and by so doing became a unifying force in the Democratic Party.

In the 1980s, Harriman organized a political action committee to revitalize the party after it suffered humiliating losses to the Republicans led by Ronald Reagan. Her efforts were credited with much of the turnaround that led to Bill Clinton's election as president in 1992. In return, Clinton appointed her ambassador to France. She gained the grudging respect of her detractors as a skilled diplomat and mediator, and was finally known for her own ability rather than that of her man. At her death in 1997, President Clinton remembered Harriman, saying, "She was one of the most unusual and gifted people I ever met. . . . She was a source of judgment and inspiration to me, a source of constant good humor and charm and real friendship. I am here in no small measure because she was there."

From Country Charm to City Sophisticate

Born Pamela Digby in Farnborough, England, Harriman was the oldest daughter of the eleventh Baron Digby who served in the House of Lords and as the governor of Dorset. She enjoyed growing up at Minterne, the family's 1,500-acre estate, she but as an adolescent became impatient with country life. Like so many of the upper classes, the Digbys were land rich but cash poor. Once her "finishing" was complete, she realized she would have to work if she wanted to live in London. Through family connections (nine members of the family were serving in parliament) she easily got a job at the Foreign Office. She was ambitious, but also plump and a bit self-conscious—not yet the beauty she was to become—when she accepted a blind date with Randolph Churchill. He was 26, a strong-willed journalist and lieutenant, also known to be unreliable, a drinker, and a gambler. In the wartime fervor, he was determined to get married before leaving London again. Caught up in the moment, Digby said yes when he proposed two weeks later.

By the age of 20, she was pregnant, and her husband had been called into service. The elder Churchills insisted she move into 10 Downing Street, thus placing her at the center of power and politics. *Time* reported that the prime minister doted on her, played bezique with her, kept her up all night listening to him brood over the delayed invasion of Sicily, and introduced her to anyone he received. "The experience colored my whole life," she said. "It seemed natural for me to be entertaining General Marshall or General Eisenhower."

Meanwhile, her husband began sending his gambling debts to her with the expectation that she pay them without telling his father. She went to Max Aitken, Lord Beaverbrook—a newspaper publisher and member of Churchill's War Cabinet. According to an article in *New York* by Michael Gross, Beaverbrook bailed her out—paid the debt, let her put her child at his country home, found her a job, and a place to stay in the Dorchester Hotel. The Churchills' marriage was over, though they did not divorce until 1947.

Tex McCrary, an American journalist in London during the war, told Gross in *New York* how Beaverbrook taught her to be a catalyst. He said, "It was part of Pamela's job to know Americans. . . . Beaverbrook's intelligence system was unparalleled." She met Averell Harriman, President Roosevelt's special liaison to Britain, within a week of his arrival. According to *People,* both were smitten, and an affair began that lasted until Harriman left London. The young Mrs. Churchill, as she was then known, blossomed during those years, both as a vivacious beauty and as an intelligent hostess. She co-created the Churchill Club, humorously dubbed "Eisenhowerplatz," a place where top officials could meet informally. Rudy Abramson, Averell Harriman's biographer, added, "the hostess was always the main attraction." After Harriman left, she had relationships with other powerful men, including radio broadcaster Edward R. Murrow.

Nonconformist Abroad

After the war, Harriman wrote articles for Beaverbrook's *Evening Standard* from all over the world. She settled in Paris, her son in a Swiss school; and, as Gross said in the *New York* story, "She moved in many worlds." Jet-setter John Galliher added, "When she came to Paris, she was a star." To the political elite, she added the international social set, and the worlds of art, fashion, and theater. She was subsequently supported by wealthy men, including Gianni Agnelli, heir to the Fiat fortune; Elie de Rothschild, head of Chateau Lafite vineyard; and Stavros Niarchos, Greek shipping magnate. Sally Bedell Smith, author of *Reflected Glory: The Life of Pamela Churchill Harriman,* has asserted, "for nearly 20 years she lived as a courtesan in the precise, centuries old definition of the word."

Harriman began spending more time in the United States, and in 1960 met mega-agent and producer Leland Hayward, whose film credits included *South Pacific* and *Gypsy,* and who represented Fred Astaire, Clark Gable, and Judy Garland. Hayward's marriage was already troubled; he proceeded to get a quick divorce, and they were married a year later. According to *Time,* they were social stars of the mid-sixties. Again, she adapted her world to his and turned their home into a place where producers, publishers, and other opinion makers met. By all accounts, the Haywards had a happy marriage. In 1971 Leland Hayward died after a series of strokes. Hayward's son, Bill, later commented, "Pamela was very fearful and, I'm sure, resentful about having to fend for herself." While she was not broke, she had to pay another husband's debts, and she and his children ended up fighting over a small estate.

Harriman said of that time, "It was like starting all over again." Ironically, Averell Harriman's wife of 40 years died about the same time. Shortly thereafter, they were invited to the same dinner party, and within six months were married. He was 79; she was 51. Kitty Hart, a friend of both said, "The marriage brought her all she cared about: love, lovely things, and the political arena." For his wedding gift, she presented her U.S. citizenship papers to him. As reported in *New York,* even her many detractors eventually had to admit that she added years to Harriman's life by keeping him active and involved.

On Her Own

It was a Republican era in Washington, D.C., and the Harrimans took the lead pulling Democrats together. "No one else was left with that eminence, authority, historical reach, social class, and policy credentials," said Tony Podesta, a lobbyist. In 1980, she was named Democratic Woman of the Year. It was also a year in which Democrats lost badly, and she decided to start a political-action committee, Democrats for the '80s, which at first was derisively dismissed as "PamPac." As the organization evolved, it was patterned after the Churchill Club. She began hosting successful "issue dinners" to bring the old guard together with newcomers and to raise money. She and the organization soon gained respect, and when Averell Harriman died in 1986, she became the doyenne of the Democratic Party, working tirelessly to raise Democrats' spirits as well as fill their coffers.

When Bill Clinton won the presidency in 1992, Speaker of the House Tom Foley said, "No one in this country can take greater credit for winning the White House than Pamela." As recognition and reward, Clinton appointed her ambassador to France. The French were extremely pleased, and she proved herself a hard-working and effective diplomat. Historian Michael Beschloss commented, "She understands domestic policy better than any ambassador to France since Sargent Shriver under Johnson." After a life of living for and through men, she finally came into her own.

As in life, Pamela Digby Churchill Hayward Harriman's death was uncommon. She suffered a stroke while swimming in the pool of the Ritz hotel and died two days later. The French expressed their admiration by making her a Commander of the Order of Arts & Letters, the first time an active foreign diplomat was honored in such a way.

Further Reading

Ogden, Christopher, *Life of the Party.*
Smith, Sally Bedell, *Reflected Glory: The Life of Pamela Churchill Harriman,* Simon & Schuster, 1996.
Detroit News, February 5, 1997.
Economist, January 4, 1997, p. 82.
New York, January 18, 1993, pp. 25-34; May 19, 1997, pp. 20-21.
People, April 26, 1993, pp. 39-41; December 2, 1996, pp. 29-30.
Time, July 5, 1993, pp. 52-54; January 22, 1996, p. 32; November 11, 1996 pp. 95-98.

LaDonna Harris

Since the 1960s, activist LaDonna Harris (born 1931) had been an outspoken advocate on issues of concern to Native Americans, women, children, and the mentally ill. In 1970 she founded Americans for Indian Opportunity (AIO), and continued to lead that organization nearly two decades later.

As a member of the Comanche tribe whose father and husband of many years were non-Native Americans, LaDonna Harris has the benefit of experience in several different cultures. During the 1960s and 1970s, her work as an activist took her around the world, and she gained an even wider perspective. Her chief interest, however, has remained with her own people—not just the Comanche tribe, but all native peoples of the Americas.

"Indian 101"

In a 1997 profile of Harris, *New Mexico Business Journal* quoted her sardonic reference to the difficulties she repeatedly encountered in explaining the painful situation of Native Americans to white politicians in Washington. The article mentioned the "endless explanations of Indian history" which she has been required to give, explanations which Harris refers to as "Indian 101." Her own early experience was certainly an education, made doubly so by the fact that her father was a white Irish-American, and her mother a Comanche. Not long after Harris's birth in Temple, Oklahoma, on February 15, 1931, her father left her mother, in part because of the constant hostility they faced as a racially mixed couple.

Harris's grandparents raised her, and through their influence she grew up educated in both white and Indian culture. Her grandmother was a Christian, whereas her grandfather—a former Indian scout at Fort Sill, Oklahoma—was a tribal medicine man. But the two showed by their example of mutual respect for each other's beliefs that two cultures could exist side by side in harmony.

Harris's education, both in the larger American culture and in her own Native American one, continued when she entered elementary school. Until the age of six she spoke only the Comanche language, but when she entered public

school she had to learn English. Meanwhile, in her home the primary influence remained the Comanche tradition.

Years later, in high school, she met the young man who would become her husband. Fred Harris was not a Native American, but like her, he had experienced poverty and hardship as the son of a sharecropper. He wanted to go to law school and run for public office, and after they were married, she helped put him through college and law school. The Harrises had three children: Kathryn, Byron, and Laura. Fred was elected first to the Oklahoma state senate, then to the U.S. Senate.

To Washington and Beyond

With Fred's election in 1965, the Harrises began to divide their time between Washington, D.C., and their home in Oklahoma. Perhaps this experience helped to expand Harris's vision to encompass national issues, because in 1965, she began an effort that mirrored the civil rights movement then making great strides on behalf of African Americans in the Southeast. But she was working in the Southwest, and she undertook her activities on behalf of Native Americans.

Operating from a base in the Oklahoma town of Lawton, Harris sought to bring together the state's tribes to combat segregation. This period saw the birth of an organization called Oklahomans for Indian Opportunity, which had members from 60 tribes. The group defined a set of goals which equated economic priorities with political ones, placing an emphasis on improvement of economic

conditions for Native Americans while remaining committed to securing civil rights for them. Harris's work on this organization's behalf helped earn her recognition as "Outstanding Indian of the Year" for 1965.

Meanwhile, back in Washington, D.C., Harris's activities expanded. She became a nationally recognized advocate on behalf of Native Americans, and numerous groups sought her involvement in projects designed to assist the Indian population in achieving greater civil rights. Harris became involved with the National Rural Housing Conference, the National Association of Mental Health, the National Committee against Discrimination in Housing, and the National Steering Committee of the Urban Coalition, which she chaired.

In 1967 President Lyndon B. Johnson appointed Harris to lead the National Women's Advisory Council of the War on Poverty, an organization charged with assisting all Americans in enjoying the benefits of civil rights and economic prosperity. Johnson's administration created the National Council on Indian Opportunity, and in 1968 the president appointed Harris to a position with the new commission. Clearly Harris had come a long way from her humble beginnings in Oklahoma, and the coming years would see the expansion of her vision from a national to a global one.

A Global Vision

Harris's appointment to the National Council for Indian Opportunity coincided with the end of Johnson's administration and the beginning that of President Richard Nixon. In fact, the council did not actually meet for the first time until a year into Nixon's presidency—in January of 1970. Harris began to believe that Vice President Spiro Agnew, whose responsibility the council was, did not feel any great sense of urgency with regard to the issues it was intended to address. Finally she decided to leave the council.

During the early 1970s Harris became heavily involved in work both at home and abroad. A founding member of the National Women's Political Caucus, in 1970 she also founded Americans for Indian Opportunity (AIO), and assisted women's and Native American grassroots organizations in their efforts on behalf of their constituency groups. Another cause of interest to her was that of the mentally ill. Harris also became interested in the needs of native or indigenous peoples around the world, and travelled to Latin America, Africa, and the former Soviet Union as a representative of the Inter-American Indigenous Institute. In this capacity, she participated in a number of conferences on world peace.

In 1975 President Gerald R. Ford named Harris to the U.S. Commission on the Observance of National Women's Year. But Harris's husband was retiring from the Senate, and the family decided that it was time to leave Washington, D.C. Instead of returning to Oklahoma, however, the Harrises moved to New Mexico, and the AIO relocated its offices with them. While concentrating her efforts more fully on the AIO, Harris also maintained her global vision. Thus when Cyrus Vance, secretary of state under President Jimmy Carter, offered her an appointment to the United Nations Education, Scientific, and Cultural Organization (UNESCO), she accepted.

In line with her interest in the cause of native peoples as a global and not merely national phenomenon, Harris had become interested in the U.S. Peace Corps as an effective instrument to assist in local development for indigenous peoples around the world. When President Carter appointed her to serve as special advisor to Sargent Shriver, who directed the Office of Economic Opportunity, she was able to realize this vision. The "Peace Pipe Project" trained Native Americans in skills necessary to assist in development of communities, then sent them to work in indigenous communities throughout the Western Hemisphere. The value of the Peace Pipe Project, which remained a limited effort, was that native peoples in other countries were more likely to trust the advice of another indigenous person than they were a white official.

Continued Commitment

While working with the Office of Economic Opportunity, Harris also introduced another initiative of interest specifically to Native Americans in the United States. Called the Council for Energy Resources Tribes, the program assisted tribes in acquiring the best possible monetary returns for the natural resources located on tribal lands. The council, which was not without its critics, also helped tribes protect those resources if the tribe chose not to exploit them.

In the 1980s and 1990s, Harris remained active with the AIO. She founded the National Indian Housing Council and the National Indian Business Association, but continued with the AIO as director, although daughter Laura Harris Goodhope also assisted with those responsibilities. According to a profile in the *New Mexico Business Journal*, Harris lived on the Santa Ana reservation near Bernalillo, outside of Albuquerque, New Mexico. Her home, owned by the reservation, also doubled as the main office of AIO. Divorced from her politician husband, Harris devoted most of her time to the organization.

Among the AIO's achievements in the 1990s was its work to strengthen tribal organizations for groups located as far apart as Alabama, Wisconsin, and Nebraska. Concern for the environment continued, and the AIO hosted regional meetings on that subject. With the greatly increased traffic on the "information superhighway" in the early 1990s, the AIO was quick to establish a significant Internet presence on behalf of Native Americans. It founded INDIANnet, which helps tribes and other groups set up Web pages and make the best possible use of the Internet's resources. The AIO, according to its own INDIANnet Web site, facilitated Harris's participation in the United States Advisory Council on the National Information Infrastructure, a group headed by Vice President Al Gore.

According to the *New Mexico Business Journal,* among the projects most important to Harris was the American Indian Ambassadors Program, funded by Kellogg's, the cereal manufacturer. Each year, advisors to the program choose some 30 young professional men and women from tribes throughout the United States. Each of the selectees serves as "ambassador" for a year, during which time he or she goes to Washington, D.C., and learns about the political process. The selectees also tour reservations around the country, and visit a selected tribal group in Central or South America.

Commenting on gaming, the federal policy that allows Indian reservations to operate casinos as a means of economic development, Harris has remained cautious. "I hate to see gaming of any kind used to support regular government," she told an interviewer for *New Mexico Business Journal.* "But the tribes have no other method that commands this degree of success." After 30 years as an activist, Harris remains positive about the future of Native Americans: "Exasperated—yes. Tired—maybe. But not angry," concluded the interviewer. "Despite years of dealing with Washington bureaucracy, despite funding cuts, run-arounds and red tape, Harris remains soft-spoken, optimistic, and certain that change for her people can occur."

Further Reading

Harris, LaDonna, Margaret A. Fiore, and Jackie Wasilewski, editors, *Overcoming the Barriers to the Effective Participation of Tribal Governments in the Federal System,* American Institute for Interactive Management, 1989.
Notable Native Americans, Gale, 1995.
Schwartz, Michael, *LaDonna Harris,* Raintree Steck-Vaughn, 1997.
New Mexico Business Journal, January 1997, p. 78.
Americans for Indian Opportunity, Inc., http://indiannet.indian.com (April 3, 1998).

Edith Head

Edith Head (c. 1898-1981) is widely viewed as Hollywood's most successful costume designer, as well as one of its most colorful personalities. Head was nominated for 35 Academy Awards, won eight, and designed the costumes for several hundred films.

E dith Head's birthdate was probably October 28, 1898. All records of that time period were destroyed in a courthouse fire, and Head publicly claimed to have been born in 1907 or 1908. However, since she definitely had graduated from college, married, divorced, and worked as a teacher for several years by 1923, the later birthdates are not possible. Even her family name is uncertain; Head was the name of her first husband. One biographer, Paddy Calistro, determined that her parents were probably of Jewish heritage, which Head never acknowledged. Similar uncertainty about the details of many events continued throughout Head's long life. In a *Vanity Fair* feature story, Amy Fine Collins reported that the designer "obstinately refused to talk about her background except in the vaguest of terms. Edith admitted, 'I have in my mind a special room with iron doors. The things I don't like I throw in there and slam the door.'"

What does seem factual about Head's childhood is that she was born in California, and then lived with her mother and stepfather in an isolated area of Nevada until she was about 12, when the family moved to Los Angeles. In her autobiography, *The Dress Doctor,* Head describes how her best friends were animals—dogs, cats, and donkeys—which she dressed in scraps of material. She also was interested in gymnastics, a sport for which her small frame (five-feet-one-inch at adulthood) was well suited.

Won First Studio Job by Deception

Head graduated from the University of California at Berkeley with a major in French, before going on to receive her master's from Stanford. Then she became a teacher, first at an exclusive finishing school and then at the Hollywood School for Girls, where she taught the children of many famous film personalities. When she was asked by her school to teach an additional course in art, she enrolled in night classes, where she met the sister of the man who would become her first husband, Charles Head. "After 15 years of marriage," reported Collins, "Edith sued Charles for divorce in 1938, complaining that her husband 'indulged in the use of intoxicating drinks,'" causing her "'great mental anguish.'" Although Head made only a passing reference to this husband in her autobiography, she used his name professionally for her entire life.

In 1923, desperately in need of a higher-paying job after her divorce, Head answered an advertisement for a costume design artist at Paramount Studios. The chief designer, Howard Greer, was greatly impressed by the variety of work in Head's portfolio—everything from fashion designs to interior decoration plans. It was only after she had taken the job, which paid $50 per week (double her teacher's salary), that Head confessed she had "borrowed"

this work from other art school students. By then, however, Greer had decided that Head's own work was good enough for her to stay on at Paramount—where she remained until 1967 following sale of the studio, moving for her final career years to Universal Studios.

Became First Woman Design Head at Major Studio

The year after Head joined Paramount, Travis Banton was added to the design staff. He and Greer became notorious for their wild lifestyles, and in 1927 Greer left Paramount to open an exclusive shop on what is now Rodeo Drive. Banton became Head's mentor, and he began to give her the sole responsibility for designing costumes when he was too busy to do the work himself, or when he did not particularly like the actress.

Head was assigned the designs for Lupe Velez in *Wolf Song* (1929), but her first major project was to create gowns for Mae West in *She Done Him Wrong* (1933), while Banton was busy with a Paris buying spree. The tight-fitting outfits designed by Head probably contributed to the film's huge success. Afterward, West frequently requested that Head design her costumes, noting that she loved the "insinuendo" in them. When West made her film comeback in *Myra Breckinridge* (1970), she insisted that her contract specify Head as her designer. Another notable Head design of the 1930s was a clinging sarong made for Dorothy Lamour in *The Jungle Princess* (1936). This creation became an instant fashion hit among women of all shapes and sizes.

By the late 1930s Head's popularity was increasing, and her success was almost guaranteed when she began to outfit Barbara Stanwyck (a reportedly difficult-to-fit actress handed down to Head by Benton). Head became Stanwyck's confidante (a role she replayed with many other actresses over the years), and Stanwyck insisted that Head be written into all of her contracts, even outside of Paramount. Head's mentor Benton decided to leave Paramount for Universal Studios in 1938, and Head was selected as his successor to run the design department—a first for a woman at a major film studio. As a reward, Paramount sent Head on a trip to Europe (her first, despite her French language background and 15 years at the studio). By that time she was designing costumes for as many as 50 films per year, and routinely worked 16-hour days. As reported in *The Annual Obituary,* Head said she was "a combination of psychiatrist, artist, fashion designer, dressmaker, pincushion, historian, nursemaid, and purchasing agent."

Second Husband Became Lifelong Companion

In the early 1930s Head met the Paramount art director Wiard (Bill) Ihnen, himself the winner of two Academy Awards. In 1940, apparently on a whim, Head (42) and Ihnen (52) chartered a small plane, flew to Las Vegas, and were married, much to the surprise of all who knew them. Ihnen had never married and was known as a "confirmed bachelor" (a code often used at the time to refer to a gay man). In turn, by then Head had adopted her unusual trademark appearance: large-framed dark glasses, inconspicuous tailored suits, and long bangs on her forehead. However, according to her entry in *The Annual Obituary*, Head admitted that at night she wore "wild colors and evening pants, anything I want, but when I'm at the studio, I'm always little Edith in the dark glasses and the beige suit. That's how I survived." Ihnen and Head shared the remainder of their lives together, most of it living at a Los Angeles hacienda named Casa Ladera, which Ihnen decorated in bright Mexican style. Head had a separate bedroom, furnished in the French Provincial style that she had used in her previous home. She and Ihnen maintained a companionable relationship until he died in 1979, at the age of 91.

Won Eight Academy Awards

The Academy of Motion Picture Arts and Sciences decided to institute a "best costume" Oscar for films released in 1948. Head arrived at the award ceremonies, assuming that she would receive the award for the elegant costumes she had created for *The Emperor Waltz*. She was stunned when the award went instead to the designers for *Joan of Arc*. However, Head made up for this defeat, winning four Oscars in the following three years.

Head won the 1949 Oscar for Olivia De Haviland's mid-19th century costumes in the black-and-white film *The Heiress*. In 1950 Head won two Oscars: one for Cecil B. DeMille's color biblical spectacle, *Samson and Delilah* (a project she had thoroughly detested because DeMille insisted that costumes be approved by a group of designers); and the other for the black-and-white film *All About Eve*, for which she had designed Bette Davis's costumes. The 1951 Oscar for best black-and-white costume design went to Head for outfitting Elizabeth Taylor in *A Place in the Sun.* A strapless bouffant dress worn by Taylor in the film became an immensely popular outfit when it was sold to the public under the Edith Head label. (This film also marked the beginning of a long friendship between Head and Taylor, who reportedly lived with Head and Ihnen when her marriage to Richard Burton was in trouble).

In 1953 Head won another Oscar for the film *Roman Holiday*, in which Head worked with the rising star Audrey Hepburn. The following year Head won another Oscar for a Hepburn film, *Sabrina*. This award led to controversy over who actually designed some of the costumes. Hepburn had chosen to wear several costumes created by the young Paris designer, Hubert de Givenchy, rather than let Head design everything. Givenchy was shocked to see that he received no credit in the final film; and, when Head received her award for the film, she did not mention him. In fact, she repeatedly claimed that she had designed dresses actually made by Givenchy.

After *Sabrina*, Head did not receive another Oscar until 1960, for *The Facts of Life*. Her eighth and final Oscar came after she had switched to Universal Studios, for *The Sting* (1973), the first film for which she received an award for outfitting male stars, Paul Newman and Robert Redford. Head has won more Academy Awards than any other woman. Actress Arlene Dahl stated in *Vanity Fair* that Head "referred to her Oscars as 'my children.'"

In addition to these award-winning films, Head worked on hundreds of other films, earning a total of 35 Academy Award nominations. One of her most notable partnerships was with Alfred Hitchcock, with whom she worked on 11 films. These included designs for Grace Kelly's costumes in *Rear Window* and *To Catch a Thief,* and for Kim Novak's in *Vertigo*. Head considered Kelly and *To Catch a Thief* her favorite star and film.

Remained Active While Elderly

During the 1950s Head became a fashion commentator on the Art Linkletter television show, *House Party*. "She was my dress doctor," recalled Linkletter in the *Vanity Fair* piece. "The first time Edith was on she was so introverted. . . . Then I coached her until she felt comfortable . . . It was remarkable to see this shy, retiring designer suddenly become a national personality!" By the late 1950s, Hollywood had moved away from elaborate costume dramas, and Head was working on only a few films per year. She used some of her time to move into new areas. In 1959, she wrote *The Dress Doctor,* a retelling of her career that became an instant best-seller. However, some details of the book remain questionable. According to *Vanity Fair*, it is even acknowledged now that the sketches in the book, attributed to Head, were drawn by her assistant, Grace Sprague.

After she moved to Universal Studios in the late 1960s, Head's film work was further reduced. She began new work, such as writing a syndicated fashion column and serving as president of the Costume Designers Guild for three years (1966-1969). With her friend June Van Dyke, Head began to hold costume fashion shows, supposedly with original costumes from films. However, numerous sources insisted that many of these costumes were reproductions, and that some were not even Head's designs.

In 1970 Head was diagnosed with a rare bone marrow disease and her husband also was in poor health. However, Head continued to work through the following decade. Her final film work was for *Dead Men Don't Wear Plaid*, which was released in 1982 after her death. Head's husband died in 1979, and Head herself finally succumbed to her illness on October 24, 1981. Her funeral was attended by crowds of Hollywood stars, as well as costume fitters and studio guards. Bette Davis (who kept a Head gown from *All About Eve* on permanent display in her home) gave the eulogy, calling Head "the queen of her profession."

Further Reading

Epstein, Beryl Williams, *Fashion Is Our Business,* J.B. Lippincott, 1945.

Head, Edith, and Jane Kesner Ardmore, *The Dress Doctor,* Little, Brown and Company, 1959.

Head, Edith, and Paddy Calistro, *Edith Head's Hollywood,* Dutton, 1983.

LaVine, W. Robert, *In a Glamorous Fashion,* Charles Scribner's Sons, 1980.

Podell, Janet, editor, *The Annual Obituary 1981,* St. Martin's Press, 1982.

Vanity Fair, March 1998.

Internet Movie Database, http://us.imdb.com (March 4, 1998).

Thor Heyerdahl

Through his oceanic expeditions on primitive rafts and boats, documented in books, films, and television programs, Norwegian anthropologist Thor Heyerdahl (born 1914) has popularized ideas about common links among ancient cultures worldwide.

Since his voyage across the Pacific on the *Kon-Tiki* in 1947, Thor Heyerdahl has been the modern world's most renowned explorer-adventurer. He has made four oceanic trips in primitive vessels to demonstrate his theories that ancient civilizations may have spread from a common source through sea voyages. His expeditions to sites of ancient stone statues in the Pacific Ocean and pyramids in Peru have also attracted great interest. More than a dozen books about his adventures have sold tens of millions of copies worldwide. Heyerdahl's work has included several documentary films and hundreds of articles for journals and magazines. But while he has gained more popular attention than any contemporary anthropologist, the scientific community largely has rejected his controversial theories.

Early Love of Nature

Heyerdahl was born into an upper-class family in the coastal village of Larvik, Norway, in 1914. His father, Thor, was president of a brewery and a mineral water plant, and his mother, Alison Lyng Heyerdahl, was chairman of the Larvik Museum. His mother, an ardent atheist, studied zoology, folk art, and primitive cultures, and influenced her son greatly. His father was an avid outdoorsman. By age seven, young Thor had started his own zoological museum, filled with specimens of sea shells, butterflies, bats, lemmings, and hedgehogs. It was housed in an old outhouse at his father's brewery.

Heyerdahl and his parents spent summer holidays at a log cabin in the wilderness, where Thor made friends with a hermit and learned much about nature. He also made many winter camping trips by sled and ski to remote locations with his schoolmates. According to his school friend Arnold Jacoby, in his book *Senor Kon-Tiki,* "Thor was convinced that modern man had . . . an over-loaded brain and reduced powers of observation. Primitive man, on the other hand, was an extrovert and alert, with keen instincts and all his senses alive. . . . Civilization might be compared with a house full of people who had never been outside the building." Throughout his early life, Heyerdahl was determined to go "outside the building" and live in a more primitive setting.

In 1933, Heyerdahl entered the University of Oslo and specialized in zoology and geography. In Oslo, he spent a lot of time in the home of a wealthy wine merchant and family friend who had a huge library of Polynesian artifacts. With his girlfriend Liv Torp, Heyerdahl decided to quit college and make an expedition to the South Seas. His father agreed to finance the trip. Heyerdahl and Torp were married

on Christmas Eve in 1936, and the next day they set out for Fatu Hiva in the Marquesas Islands, their hand-picked Garden of Eden. On the island Heyerdahl discovered evidence that Peruvian aboriginal voyagers had visited the islands. The inhabitants told him stories of Kon-tiki, a bearded, white sun king who arrived over the sea. Heyerdahl's stay on Fatu Hiva is recounted in his 1996 book, *Green Was the Earth on the Seventh Day.*

Daring Raft Voyage

In 1938, the Heyerdahls returned to Norway and settled in a log cabin in a mountain wilderness near Lillehammer. He wrote a book in Norwegian about their expedition to Fatu Hiva, *Pa Jakt efter Paradiset (On the Hunt for Paradise).* The couple had two sons, Thor and Bjorn. Heyerdahl did field research among American Indian tribes in British Columbia in 1939 and 1940, trying to support his theory that two waves of migration from the Americas had settled Polynesia, one from the northern hemisphere and one from the south. During World War II, Heyerdahl trained as a wireless radio operator in Canada and was active for a few months in the Norwegian resistance behind German lines.

After the war, Heyerdahl found little acceptance of his ideas in academic circles. He planned a dramatic experiment to convince his critics that a voyage by ancient peoples from Peru to Polynesia was possible. In 1947, he and a crew traveled to Peru and built a raft made of nine balsa logs, which they named the *Kon-Tiki.* Following the Humboldt Current, the voyagers covered 4,300 miles of ocean in 101 days. Heyerdahl detailed the extraordinary journey in his book, *The Kon-Tiki Expedition.* The book was "the first great post-war adventure story to catch the imagination of the world," according to biographer Christopher Ralling. It was translated into dozens of languages and sold more than 20 million copies. Heyerdahl's documentary movie of the voyage won him an Academy Award in 1951. "That film won the Oscar because it was so badly shot they knew it couldn't have been faked," Heyerdahl told Pope Brock of *People.* "It was done after 20 minutes instruction from a Bell & Howell dealer, and I filmed at the wrong speed."

Brock noted that the book and film created a global audience for Heyerdahl's adventures: "They saw a Ulysses, the last of the bold and bearded seafarers. Ever since then, Heyerdahl has shown that same genius for attracting followers and funding; he has transformed a crabbed and insular science into world theater." But while the *Kon-Tiki* voyage captured public attention, it was met with scientific disdain. To advance his theories further, Heyerdahl wrote an 800-page scholarly work, *American Indians in the Pacific: The Theory behind the Kon-Tiki Expedition,* published in 1952.

While Heyerdahl was achieving fame, his constant travels had weakened his marriage. The couple divorced, and he married Yvonne Dedekam-Simonsen in 1949. They had three daughters, Anette, Marian, and Elisabeth, and in 1958 settled in a remote Italian Alpine village. They divorced in 1969.

Explorations Worldwide

In 1953, Heyerdahl went to the Galapagos Islands, off the South American coast. There, he and his companions found evidence that indigenous people of South America had visited the islands long before the Incan Empire. In 1955, Heyerdahl led an expedition to Easter Island, the remote Polynesian island where enormous stone statues of unknown origin had been discovered in 1722. His team found a carving of a reed ship at the base of one of the statues and much other evidence that the island had been populated by at least three migrations from South America, the earliest in the fourth century. He wrote about this expedition in two books, *Aku-Aku: The Secret of Easter Island* and *The Archaeology of Easter Island.*

Heyerdahl was among a group of scientists called "diffusionists," who believed that ancient cultures had come from a common source through land and sea migrations. The opposing camp, called "isolationists," thought that civilizations had cropped up around the world independently of one another. The isolationist theory has remained the dominant one, and Heyerdahl's work did not disprove it. Still, as writer Thomas Morrow noted in *U.S. News & World Report,* Heyerdahl "has turned up a surprising amount of convincing evidence suggesting sea contacts among remote ancient cultures, for which he gets little credit."

As a proponent of a single global prehistorical culture, Heyerdahl also became, through his work and notoriety around the globe, a symbol of multiculturalism. He learned to speak fluent Spanish, English, French, German, and Italian as well as his native Norwegian.

In 1969, Heyerdahl organized a new expedition. In Egypt, he and a multinational six-man crew built a papyrus reed boat which they named *Ra,* after the Egyptian sun god. Under the flag of the United Nations, they sailed across the Atlantic, a voyage of 2,700 miles, but the boat broke apart 600 miles short of Barbados. The next year, Heyerdahl tried again, sailing the *Ra II* all the way from Morocco to Barbados in 57 days. His account of these expeditions is found in his 1970 book *The Ra Expeditions.* It is also documented in a 1971 Swedish Broadcasting Corporation film. To Heyerdahl, the voyages were evidence that Egyptians or other sailors could have crossed to the Americas several thousand years before Columbus.

His voyages led Heyerdahl to become active internationally in fighting pollution of the oceans. In *Green was the Earth on the Seventh Day,* Heyerdahl wrote about how his voyage on the *Kon-Tiki* had increased his awareness of threats to the environment: "My childhood fear of the ocean had left me on the balsa raft. My fear was now instead that man should destroy the ocean. A dead ocean meant a dead planet." He wrote eloquently about the poisoning of ocean plankton and its effects on the food chain: "What the farmers and the housewives spray out of plastic bottles, the fishermen and the middlemen serve us on our own plates."

New Challenges

In 1977, at the age of 62, Heyerdahl took up another challenge. He went to Iraq and with a crew of 11 men and built a reed ship, the *Tigris.* They sailed it down the Tigris River, through the Persian Gulf and across the Indian Ocean to the mouth of the Indus River in Pakistan, then westward to Djibouti at the mouth of the Red Sea on the eastern African coast. This 4,200-mile, five-month-long voyage was an attempt to show that the ancient civilizations of Egypt, the Indus Valley, and Mesopotamia could have sprung from a single source. Ironically, Heyerdahl's *Tigris* trip ended in political turmoil in the Gulf of Aden region, and Heyerdahl burned the ship in protest. In a message to the United Nations Secretary General, Heyerdahl wrote: "There is a desperate need for intelligent co-operation if we are to save ourselves and our common civilization from what we are turning into a sinking ship." The Tigris expedition became a BBC documentary film in 1979.

In 1982, Heyerdahl and several archaeologists undertook an expedition to the remote Maldive islands off the coast of India. There, Heyerdahl was fascinated by stone statues which bore a striking resemblance to the monoliths of Easter Island. His discoveries led him to conclude that the Maldives also had been involved in prehistoric ocean trading and migration. Heyerdahl's 1986 book, *The Maldive Mystery,* was hailed by some as a great detective story. It, too, was made into a film, as had been his expeditions to the Galapagos and Easter Island.

In 1988, Heyerdahl returned to Peru to explore 26 pre-Incan pyramids at ruins named Tucume. In 1990, Ralling wrote a biography, *Kon-Tiki Man,* which quotes extensively from Heyerdahl's previous accounts of his travels. A reviewer in *Publishers Weekly* called the book "a stimulating chronicle of curiosity and wanderlust." A television series was made to accompany the book.

In *Green Was the Earth on the Seventh Day,* Heyerdahl wrote movingly of the mysteries which fascinated him all his life. "Sailing on a raft in a black night through an explosion of blinking stars and plankton, our horizons widen," he wrote, referring to the *Kon-Tiki* voyage. "We live in a fairy tale world and carry heaven and hell within us." Writing about his opposition to nuclear arms and advanced technology, Heyerdahl noted: "At a time when we plunge into the technological era with fairy-tale visions of a manmade environment, science itself begins to see that nature is totally superior to man in its incredible composition of the world's ecosystem. Destroy it, and no brain and no money in the world can put it together again."

In the same book, Heyerdahl composed an eloquent testament for his children and their generation: "You are now to take over this planet; take good care of it. We did not, when we borrowed it before you. . . . Forgive us for the forests we have depleted. For the waters we have polluted. For the horrible arms we have in store. . . . Forgive us for the holes we have torn in the ozone layer. . . . We have narrowed our horizons by hiding ourselves behind walls and blinded the heavenly bodies with neon lights. We have worshiped dead things. . . . Help to heal the system we have wounded. . . . All that walk and crawl and swim and fly are members of our extended family."

In one interview, Heyerdahl told Brock of *People:* "We have the egoistic idea that we in the 20th century are the civilized ones. That people living 1,000 years ago, not to mention 5,000 years ago, were greatly inferior to us. I am opposed to that. The people back then were physically and mentally our equal—if not in many ways better. . . . We couldn't survive using our brains, as ancient people did. But they would certainly have been capable of watching a television."

Further Reading

Contemporary Authors, New Revision Series, Volume 22, Gale, 1988.
Heyerdahl, Thor, *Green Was the Earth on the Seventh Day,* Random House, 1996.
Heyerdahl, Thor, with Christopher Ralling, *Kon-Tiki Man,* Chronicle Books, 1990.
Atlantic, December 1989.
Booklist, March 1, 1996.
Modern Maturity, February-March 1992.
People, December 11, 1989.
Publishers Weekly, September 6, 1991.
U.S. News & World Report, April 2, 1990.

Sir Anthony Hopkins

Sir Anthony Hopkins (born 1937) acted on stage and in film for over 30 years before receiving his first Academy Award, which he won for his portrayal of Dr. Hannibal Lecter in the 1991 film *Silence of the Lambs.* Since that time, Hopkins has become a true Hollywood superstar.

Over the course of his acting career, Hopkins has added extensive acting credits to his name. From his early career in the British theatre to his long list of movie parts, Hopkins has had his share of critical and box office failures and successes.

Humble Beginnings

Anthony Hopkins was born in the small working-class town of Port Talbot, Wales, on December 31, 1937, the only child of Richard Hopkins, a baker, and his wife Muriel. Hopkins had an emotionally tumultuous childhood during which time he often felt isolated and lonely. He admitted to *People,* that he was "hopeless, pathetic, an idiot. I thought I was nuts. I felt so weird." Although he studied piano and could draw well, Hopkins did not excel in the classroom at Cowbridge Grammar School.

An early turning point in Hopkins' life came when he met the famous actor Richard Burton, also a Port Talbot native. Hopkins, then 15, went to Burton's home to get his autograph. As he recalled, in an interview with *US* magazine, he thought, "I've got to get out of this place. I've got to become what he is. And I think something deep in my subconscious mind, or whatever it was, set the target. I thought, I'm going to be famous."

Despite his newfound commitment to making his way out of Port Talbot, Hopkins continued to struggle socially and academically. At age 17 he dropped out of school, and, at the urging of his father, he enrolled in a drama class held at a local YMCA. Well skilled at the piano, Hopkins then earned a scholarship to the nearby Cardiff College of Music and Drama, where he studied for two years. After two years of military service, Hopkins worked in the Manchester Library Theatre and the Nottingham Repertory Company. In 1961, he decided to pursue formal training as an actor. He received a scholarship to the Royal Academy of Dramatic Art, in London. He graduated in 1963.

Over the span of the next two years, he worked with the Phoenix Theatre in Leicester, the Liverpool Playhouse, and the Hornchurch Repertory Company. In 1965, he applied for membership in the National Theatre under the direction of Laurence Olivier. Hopkins was invited to join the company where he remained a member for seven years, until 1973. He began with understudy work and supporting roles, but soon moved into the role of leading man. Hopkins's stage work earned him critical acclaim, and he was compared to both Burton and Olivier.

Personal Troubles

In 1968, Hopkins began his film career, playing Richard in the movie *The Lion in Winter.* Over the next 30 years, Hopkins would make at least one movie almost every year, and some years as many as six. As his stage and film career began to evolve in the 1960s, Hopkins's personal life was falling more and more into turmoil. He quickly earned a reputation for his temper and his excessive drinking. He gained notoriety for walking out in the middle of a performance of *Macbeth* while he was a member of the National Theatre.

Hopkins married actress Petronella Barker, in 1967, but the marriage was brief. By the time Hopkins's only child, a daughter named Abigail, was 18 months old, the couple had split. Hopkins married again, in 1973, this time to Jennifer Lynton, a film production assistant.

In 1974, Hopkins and his wife moved to New York City where Hopkins earned critical acclaim for his portrayal of the psychiatrist in the Broadway production of *Equus*. He quickly gained fame for his temper in the United States, when he stopped a performance to berate latecomers. After *Equus*, Hopkins moved to Hollywood, hoping to find the fulfillment to his childhood dream of becoming truly famous. However, at this time, Hopkins was drinking heavily, even suffering blackouts. "I went around for years thinking I was some kind of fiery, Celtic soul," Hopkins told MSNBC's Joe Leydon. "But I wasn't—I was just drinking too much." After waking up in a Phoenix hotel room with no recollection of how he got there, Hopkins realized that his destructive lifestyle would eventually cost him his career and his wife. In 1975, Hopkins quit drinking.

Ten Years in Hollywood

At the same time, Hopkins was accepting acting jobs with little regard to the quality of the script. Hopkins admitted to *People* that he made little attempt to save his career, and in fact accepted less desirable roles in an attempt to reject his formal Shakespearean upbringing in the British theatre. He acted, he says, "out of perverseness and sheer rebellion toward the English Establishment. I was saying, 'That's all crap over there.' That was my cynical way of protesting too much." For ten years, from 1975 to 1985, Hopkins undertook over 25 movies made for either television or theatrical release. During this time, he earned an Emmy Award for his portrayal of Bruno Hauptmann, in the 1976 television movie *The Lindbergh Kidnapping Case* and for his portrayal of Hitler in the 1981 television movie *The Bunker*. While he received recognition for these two projects, the majority of the movies Hopkins made during this time period were less than memorable. These movies included *The Girl from Petrovka,* (1974), *Audrey Rose,* (1977), *International Velvet,* (1978), and *A Change of Seasons,* (1980). In 1985 Hopkins played Neil Gray in the much criticized television miniseries *Hollywood Wives.*

In 1985, at the urging of his wife, Hopkins reluctantly moved back to London, and he returned to the stage. A self-proclaimed workaholic, Hopkins attacked the British theatre, playing Shakespeare's Lear and Anthony on two different stages for a total of 200 performances over a 17-month period. In 1987, Hopkins became a Commander of the British Empire (CBE). In 1988, he received an honorary degree of Doctor of Letters, from the University of Wales. In 1993, he was knighted.

Silence of the Lambs

His desire for international critical acclaim and recognition came in 1991, when he earned an Academy Award for best actor in the box office hit *Silence of the Lambs.* Hopkins played Dr. Hannibal "The Cannibal" Lecter, a demonic, but brilliant serial killer known for eating his victims. Jodie Foster played a Federal Bureau of Investigations agent looking to Lecter for clues to catch another serial killer still at large. Hopkins's portrayal of Lecter was decidedly dark, menacing, and evil. Although Hopkins only appeared in 27 minutes of the movie, this role finally made him an actor of Hollywood superstar status.

After *Silence of the Lambs,* Hopkins did not slow his movie-making pace, acting in four films released in 1992, and five in 1993, plus a television movie in both 1992 and 1993. His body of work during these two years included *Bram Stoker's Dracula* (1992), *Freejack* (1992), *Howards End* (1992), *Shadowlands* (1993), and *The Trial,* (1993). His most noticed film was *The Remains of the Day,* (1993) for which he received an Academy Award nomination and a Golden Globe nomination for his portrayal of the reserved butler, Stevens. In 1994, Hopkins appeared in *Legends of the Fall* and *The Road to Wellville.*

In 1995, Hopkins played the part of United States president Richard M. Nixon in controversial director Oliver Stone's movie *Nixon.* The casting of Hopkins, a British actor, as Nixon was questioned by much of the entertainment media. In fact, Hopkins himself was skeptical. However, he took the part and, for his performance, earned both an Academy Award nomination and a Golden Globe nomination.

Fame and Fortune

Although not all Hopkins's movies, in the first half of the 1990s, were box office hits, Hopkins found himself working with high profile actors, such as Brad Pitt, Debra Winger, Emma Thompson, and Foster. The roles had become more challenging, and Hopkins earned respect in the acting community for his ability to play any part, from Hannibal the Cannibal to Richard Nixon. Hopkins also played the title role in *Surviving Picasso,* which was released in 1996.

After starring in *The Edge,* which was released in 1997 and co-starred Alec Baldwin, Hopkins found his next major role. He was cast as another United States president, John Quincy Adams, in director Steven Spielberg's historical drama *Amistad.* In the movie, former president Adams defended a group of Africans charged with murdering the crew of a slave ship. For his performance, Hopkins received an Academy Award nomination for best actor.

Hopkins turned 60 in 1997 and commanded over five million dollars per movie and he has not slowed his pace. He has two movies opening in 1998 with yet another in production. In 1998, Hopkins appeared in the remake of the classic *The Mask of Zorro,* co-starring Spanish actor Antonio Banderas. He also starred in 1998's *Meet Joe Black.* In *Instinct* (formerly called *Ishmael*), he played an anthropologist working in Africa who was convicted of murdering a group of white men who had killed a family of gorillas.

In some ways Hopkins has changed little since his time in Port Talbot. He was still a loner, choosing to take long road trips in his car, by himself, to relax. He has maintained his intense, driven personality that pushes him to continue to take on movie projects at an exceptional pace. However, he has also learned to not push too hard. Finally, after more than 30 years, he found what he knew he wanted at age 15: fame and fortune. He told *Vanity Fair,* "It can't get better than this. Years ago I wanted to be rich and famous, and it all happened to me. . . . They pay me a lot of money, more money than I ever dreamed of. It just cannot get better than this."

Further Reading

Callan, Michael Feeney, *Anthony Hopkins: The Unauthorized Biography,* Charles Scribner's Sons, 1994.

Falk, Quentin, *Anthony Hopkins, The Authorized Biography,* Interlink Books, 1993.

Moser, James D., editor, *International Motion Picture Almanac,* 68th edition, Quigley, 1997.

Vincendeau, Ginette, editor, *Encyclopedia of European Cinema,* Facts on File, 1995.

Hola!, December 1997.

US, February 1998.

Vanity Fair, October 1996.

Jerome, Jim, "Anthony Hopkins is the Scariest Film Killer Since Bruce, the Jaws Shark," *People Online,* http://www.people.com (March 4, 1998).

Leydon, Joe, "Anthony Hopkins' Supreme Confidence," *MSNBC Living,* http://www.msnbc.com (March 4, 1998).

"Nominated for Best Actor," *People Online,* http://www.people.com (March 4, 1998).

John Winston Howard

John Winston Howard (born 1939), the prime minister of Australia, has established himself as a pro-business labor reformer and has voiced support for strengthened ties with Europe and America while integrating his nation's economy with neighboring Asian nations.

When John Winston Howard became prime minister, he brought with him extensive experience in government, leading the opposition against the political party in power. In Australia, as in many nations with a parliamentary form of government, the party with the majority in parliament runs the country. As leader of the minority Liberal Party, Howard was often the voice for the out-of-power factions and a critic of the majority Labor Party. In the March 1996 national elections, Howard's Liberal Party, in a coalition with another minority faction, the National Party, succeeded in removing the Labor Party from power. Subsequently, Howard became the political leader of the nation and has characterized himself as being in touch with the average Australian. Yet the pro-business measures he has taken as prime minister have led some to question his awareness of the problems of Australia's blue-collar workers.

Lifelong Ambition

John Winston Howard was born in the summer of 1939, the youngest of four boys, in a working-class neighborhood of Sydney called Earlwood. His father was an automobile mechanic who ran his own small shop. The younger Howard attended the Earlwood Primary School and Canterbury Boys' High School. Classmates later recalled that, even as a young boy, he talked about being a politician. Once he bet a friend that he would be prime minister. After graduating from high school, he attended the University of Sydney. His instructors remembered him as a serious student. He was also an active member of the conservative, yet confusingly named, Liberal Party and participated in student politics at the university. Howard graduated with a Bachelor of Laws degree in 1961. He was then admitted as a solicitor of the supreme court in the Australian state of New South Wales in July 1962 and worked for a private law firm.

Howard's political career did not begin until 1974 when he won a seat in parliament representing the northwestern Sydney district of Bennelong. He has been returned to parliament in every election since then. At age 36, he became known nationwide when he was appointed the minister for business and consumer affairs during the administration of Liberal Australian Prime Minister Malcolm Fraser. In this position, Howard rewrote the Australian

Trade Practices Act, which prohibited boycotts on businesses and trade unions. He also served as minister for special trade negotiations and treasurer of the commonwealth for five years. From 1977 to 1983, when the opposition Labor Party was in power, he served as finance minister. In 1982, he was elected deputy leader of the Liberal Party and, three years later, became leader of the Liberal Party. By 1987, he led his party in national elections and was, for the first time, in a position to become the next prime minister of Australia. The influential *Sydney Morning Herald*, however, warned that "a Howard government would be a leap in the dark" and came out in support of Howard's opponent, Robert Hawke. During the election campaign, critics of Howard questioned how he would pay for the income tax cuts he had proposed. Not surprisingly, Howard lost the election. Two years after that, he lost his position as party leader, but he remained a coalition spokesman. On January 30, 1995, however, he was returned as leader of the opposition by a unanimous vote of his colleagues.

Ousting the Established Leaders

Upon his reelection as party leader, he worked vigorously to unseat the ruling Labor Party, which had been in power since 1983. Howard gave the impression that the Labor Party and its leader, Prime Minister Paul Keating, were out of touch with the Australian people. He often pointed out Australia's economic condition. At the time, the country had amassed a record foreign debt of $180 billion and was experiencing high unemployment. He appealed to blue-collar workers who had grown disenchanted by the Labor Party. He made campaign promises that would cost six billion dollars and told voters he would ignore trying to balance the Australian budget if it meant breaking his promises. Although he talked about the issues and refrained from personal criticisms of Keating, the campaign became notable for the viciousness of the attack ads on Australian television by both sides. Nevertheless, most Australians agreed that a change needed to be made to their government. Howard's victory in the 1996 national election was the biggest for the Liberal Party since it had formed in 1944. Also, the Liberal National coalition won the biggest majority of any party in 21 years.

Howard claimed the landslide was an mandate to change 15 years of Labor Party rule. He then set about reforming labor laws that weakened labor unions and increased the power, flexibility, and efficiency of businesses. Compulsory union membership was outlawed, unfair dismissal laws were abolished, and union-negotiated pay awards were replaced with contracts negotiated at individual workplaces. The monopoly of the Maritime Union on shipping was ended. Tougher requirements were developed for those people collecting unemployment pay. Many political observers believed Howard's solutions to Australia's economic problems were rooted in his experiences as the son of a small-business owner. When accused of declaring war on organized labor, Howard responded that he had no intention of destroying trade unions but was determined to give the highest priority to policies supported by his Liberal Party.

Economic Reformer and Staunch Monarchist

Howard also said the Labor Party had left the country's finances in tatters and announced a series of economic measures. He promised to increase job opportunities and reduce the unemployment rate, which hovered above eight percent; the youth unemployment rate was 28%. Then he proposed spending cuts of eight billion dollars, the sale of the government's 50.4% stake in the Commonwealth Bank of Australia, and the sale of Telstra, a publicly-owned communications company. In addition, he promised a tax rebate for people who used private health insurance, rather than a government health plan, and proposed a new one billion dollar fund to deal with environmental problems. Yet he also angered environmentalists when he lifted the ban on the exporting of Australia's uranium reserves and attempted to raise revenue by selling uranium to Indonesia, Korea, and Japan for nonmilitary purposes.

The election of Howard also slowed Australia's growing republican movement, which supported a change in the nation's constitution that would sever Australia's links to the British monarchy. An Australian-elected head of state would replace the British monarch, the figurative head of Australia. Howard, however, is a monarchist. He believes the current relationship with the United Kingdom works well and sees no reason for change. This is in spite of opinion polls that show most Australians are against retaining the monarch as head of state.

Howard has pledged to strengthen ties with Europe and the United States but has also reassured Australians that he does not intend to reverse foreign policy. During his successful election campaign, he accused Prime Minister Keating of ignoring Europe and North America. He claimed Keating had shifted Australia's foreign policy, which had been centered around relations with the United Kingdom, Western Europe, and the United States, to one that centered on the Asian-Pacific region. He has recently made it clear, however, that he is not anti-Asian. He has stated that closer relations with Europe and the United States do not exclude the integration of Australia with Asia, pointing out that two-thirds of Australia's foreign trade is with Asia and that relationship is important. Nevertheless, he has mentioned human rights abuses in Asia, such as the existence of sweatshops where children are overworked under hazardous conditions, and has stated that Australia would not sacrifice its values and principles simply for better trade relations. He has scheduled summit meetings with Asian leaders in an attempt to open lines of communication and has had cordial relations with Malaysian Prime Minister Mahathir Mohamed, who had been a vocal critic of Australian policies when Keating was in power.

Outside politics, Howard is an enthusiastic sports fan. He takes in an occasional cricket or rugby match and enjoys playing golf and tennis. He married his wife, Janette, a teacher, in April 1971. They have three children Melanie, Tim, and Richard.

Further Reading

Bernell, David, "John Howard," *Current Leaders of Nations,* Gale Research, 1996.
McLean's, March 4, 1996.
New York Times, July 10, 1987.
Wall Street Journal, September 16, 1985; October 5, 1988.
"Honorable John Howard," *PM's Homepage,* http://www.pm.gov.au/athome/pmbio.htm (March 13, 1998).
"John Howard Story," *News Scripts,* http://www.abc.net.au (March 13, 1998).
Stephens, Tony, "Howard the man who wins the last battle," *Sydney Morning Herald,* http://www.smh.com.au (March 20, 1998).

Fred Hoyle

British astronomer and cosmologist Sir Fred Hoyle (born 1915) is best known as the champion of the steady-state theory of the nature of the universe. He also has made significant contributions to the study of stellar evolution and has published more than 40 books, including science fiction.

Fred Hoyle was born in Bingley, Yorkshire, England, on June 24, 1915. His fascination with mathematics and astronomy was evident at an early age. He taught himself the multiplication tables before he was six and would often stay up all night looking through a telescope he received as a gift.

Hoyle was educated at Emmanuel College and St. John's College, Cambridge. He spent six years during World War II with the British Admiralty working on radar development. In 1945, he returned to Cambridge as a lecturer in mathematics. Three years later, in collaboration with the astronomer Thomas Gold and the mathematician Hermann Bondi, he announced refinements to the steady-state theory first put forward by Sir James Jeans in about 1920. Within the framework of Albert Einstein's theory of relativity, Hoyle formulated a mathematical basis for the steady state theory, making the expansion of the universe and the creation of matter interdependent.

Bondi, Gold, and Hoyle found the idea of a sudden beginning to the universe—the so-called big bang theory—philosophically unsatisfactory. They devised a model derived from an extension of the "cosmological principle" that had been used for previous theories. It stated that the universe appeared the same from any location, but not necessarily for all times. They proposed that the decrease in the density of the universe caused by its expansion is exactly balanced by the continuous creation of matter condensing into galaxies that take the place of the galaxies that have receded from the Milky Way, thereby maintaining forever the present appearance of the universe.

Controversy Over Steady-State Theory

In the late 1950s and early 1960s, controversy over the steady state theory grew. New observations of distant galaxies and other phenomena, supporting the big bang theory, weakened the steady state theory, and it has since fallen out of favor with most cosmologists. Although Hoyle was forced to alter some of his conclusions, he attempted to make his theory consistent with new evidence.

Hoyle was elected to the Royal Society in 1957, a year after joining the staff of the Hale Observatories (now the Mount Wilson and Palomar observatories). In collaboration with William Fowler and others in the United States, he formulated theories about the origins of stars as well as about the origins of elements within stars. He directed the Institute of Theoretical Astronomy at Cambridge (1967-73), an institution he was instrumental in founding. Hoyle received a knighthood in 1972.

In 1976, Hoyle and Chandra Wickramasinghe, a fellow professor at the University of Cardiff with whom Hoyle often collaborated, speculated that microorganisms or biochemical compounds from outer space are responsible for originating life on Earth and possibly other parts of the universe.

In 1981, the two coauthored *Diseases from Space* in which they hypothesized that viruses and bacteria fall into the atmosphere after being incubated in the interiors of comet heads, and that people become ill by breathing this infected air. They supported their theory by stating that the spread of disease is frequently far too rapid to be attributable solely to person-to-person contact. Their theory, known as panspermia, was widely derided.

AIDS From Outer Space?

In December 1988, Hoyle wrote to the *Daily Telegraph* of London explaining his theory that AIDS originated in outer space. It was immediately dismissed by most British AIDS experts. Many viewed the theory as proof that Hoyle had overstepped the limits of acceptable scientific eccentricity. His letter claimed that viruses from outer space are also responsible for many other epidemics in Britain, including Legionnaires' disease and meningitis. "A small comet disintegrating low in the atmosphere could lead to pathogens being brought down in rainstorms that are geographically localized," Hoyle claimed. "The comets responsible for new diseases such as AIDS are admittedly rare objects, but the sudden injection into the human population of at least three disjoint viruses point decisively to an input that is external to the Earth," Hoyle wrote. "We think it most likely in each instance primary entry was secured through infected rainwater entering lesions in feet in the mainly barefoot populations of the Third World with subsequent transmissions proceeding through human contact. Hoyle urged that a major international effort was needed to carry out "a rigorous and continuous microbiological surveillance of rainwater and of groundwater on a worldwide scale. The survival of our species may well be contingent upon this." His ideas were largely viewed as fantasy by other scientists.

In 1996, however, the National Aeronautics and Space Administration (NASA) announced that a small asteroid it had been studying possibly contained fossil remains of primitive life. This finding rekindled speculation about the extraterrestrial "seeding" of life on Earth. Other recent discoveries in astronomy, biology, and chemistry have tended to support the idea first proposed by Hoyle and Wickramasinghe some 20 years earlier. Other scientists, however, remain skeptical. Under closer scrutiny, the evidence turned out to be ragweed pollen and furnace ash. If NASA's microfossils really are the remnants of past life on Mars, then the implications for life and how it got started are profound. The first thing that would have to be explained is why ancient microorganisms on Earth and on Mars are apparently so similar. Some scientists, such as Ian Crawford of University College London, believe that the resemblance may be only superficial.

An Iconoclast

Hoyle has published numerous books challenging many of the basic tenets of modern cosmology. In his 1951 book, *The Nature of the Universe,* Hoyle rejects the long-standing big bang theory of the origin of the universe in favor of the steady state theory. He expounds further upon the steady state and other theories in *The Intelligent Universe: A New View of Creation and Evolution,* published in 1977. In it, he dismisses one piece of orthodox science after another, replacing each with ingenious alternatives. He also presents an argument against Darwin's theory of evolution, claiming that "living organisms are too complex to have been produced by chance." Hoyle suggests, instead, that "we owe our existence to another intelligence which created a structure for life as part of a deliberate plan." In describing the attributes of an intelligence superior to ourselves, Hoyle admits that we may have to use the word forbidden in science, "God." He said he found his atheism greatly shaken after calculating the chance that carbon, "uniquely designed to make life possible," would have precisely the required resonance to permit it to form in sufficient abundance in the universe. "A common sense interpretation of the facts suggests that a super intellect has monkeyed with physics, as well as with chemistry and biology, and that there are no blind forces worth speaking about in nature. The numbers one calculates from the facts seem to me so overwhelming as to put this conclusion almost beyond question." His scientific works for a lay audience include *Highlights in Astronomy* (1975). He has also written science-fiction, including *The Black Cloud* (1957), and an autobiography, *The Small World of Fred Hoyle* (1986).

Hoyle and Wickramasinghe were among the first to argue against the theory that life on Earth originated in a so-called "prebiotic soup." The theory is based on a famous experiment by Stanley Miller in 1953. Deciding to test an earlier hypothesis by Alexander Oparin and John Haldane, Miller started with a sealed mixture of gases thought to be constituents of the primitive Earth's atmosphere. The gases—water vapor, hydrogen, ammonia, and methane—were subjected to an electric discharge, simulating lightning, and the products were found to contain certain amino acids that are building blocks of proteins. This experiment led to the theory that living organisms originated from a prebiotic soup formed in the above manner. This theory soon became the textbook model to describe the origins of life. Hoyle and Wickramasinghe pointed out that the primitive Earth could not have had the hydrogen-rich atmosphere postulated for a prebiotic soup.

Science Fiction

Hoyle has remained controversial. In 1981, he and others made the erroneous claim that a famous Archaeopteryx fossil in the British Museum was a fake. In 1990, he coauthored a theory linking influenza pandemics and sunspot outbreaks. While noting that Hoyle's theses are sometimes far-fetched, reviewers often express their admiration for the author's writing style, statistical data, and its richness in classical quotations. Hoyle has also authored over a dozen science fiction novels, more than half of which have been co-written with his son, Geoffrey Hoyle. Several critics suggest that Hoyle's highly technical and scientific background enhances the credibility and appeal of his novels.

Among the numerous awards and distinctions bestowed on him are the UN Kalinga Prize, the Royal Medal of the Royal Society, and the Gold Medal of the Royal Astronomical Society. In 1997, he was awarded the highly prestigious Crafoord Prize by the Swedish Academy in recognition of outstanding basic research in fields not covered by the Nobel Prize. Hoyle is a Fellow of the Royal

Society and a Foreign Associate of the US National Academy of Sciences. He has published over 40 books, including technical science, popular science, and science fiction. Hoyle is an Honorary Fellow of both Emmanuel College and St. John's College Cambridge and an Honorary Professor of Cardiff University in Wales.

Further Reading

Contemporary Authors, Volume 55, Gale, 1991, p. 234-237.
Alberta Report, September 23, 1977, p. 35.
Chicago Tribune, September 4, 1985; December 18, 1986.
Independant, September 18, 1997, p. 3.
Reuters, August 7, 1996.
Scientific American, August, 1996.
The World and I, September 1, 1997, p. 218.
"Sir Fred Hoyle Homepage," Cardiff University, http://www.cf.ac.uk/uwcc/maths/wickramasinghe/hoyle.html (April 1998).

L. Ron Hubbard

The story of L. Ron Hubbard (1911-1986) is also the story of a movement—the Church of Scientology. Founded by L. Ron Hubbard, Scientology claims millions of devoted members worldwide and, beyond all controversy, it cannot be denied that the movement retains its influence around the world even after Hubbard's death.

Lafayette Ronald Hubbard was born on March 13, 1911, in Tilden, Nebraska. He was the son of Harry Ross, a naval officer, and Dora May (Waterbury de Wolf) Hubbard. He attended George Washington University in the early 1930s and studied at Princeton University in 1945. The years in between undergraduate studies were spent as a free-lance writer. During World War II, he served in the U.S. Navy as a lieutenant though he was not "extensively decorated" as church brochures would later claim. After two unsuccessful marriages, Hubbard married Mary Sue Whipp on October 30, 1952. The couple had four children: Diana Meredith de Wolfe, Mary Suzette Rochelle, L. Ron Hubbard, Jr. (changed name to Ronald DeWolf), and Arthur Ronald Conway.

Pulp Fiction

Hubbard first came to public attention as a writer for the pulp magazines of the 1930s. During the next two decades he turned out a host of westerns, mysteries, sea adventures, and science fiction stories under his own name and several pseudonyms. *Xignals* reported that at his peak he wrote "over 100,000 words a month." Hubbard's writing, Martin Gardner explained in his *In the Name of Science,* "is done at lightning speed. (For a while, he used a special electric IBM typewriter with extra keys for common words like 'and,' 'the,' and 'but.' The paper was on a roll to avoid the interruption of changing sheets.)" Hubbard published nearly 600 books, stories, and articles during his lifetime.

His fiction volumes sold over 23 million copies, while his nonfiction books sold over 27 million copies.

Birth of a Movement

During the late 1940s, Hubbard began to synthesize concepts from Eastern religions and modern psychology into a new system for mental health. Called Dianetics, after the Greek word for thought, this system promised to cure all mental disorders and psycho-somatic physical ailments. "The hidden source of all psycho-somatic ills and human aberration has been discovered," Hubbard explained in his manuscript *Dianetics: The Modern Science of Mental Health,* "and skills have been developed for their invariable cure." Dianetics sees the human mind as "blocked" by traumatic emotional memories called engrams. By talking over these emotional memories in a process similar to conventional psychoanalysis, a patient can remove the engrams and "clear" his mind. Hubbard believed that a treated patient—called a "clear"—was "to a current normal individual as the current normal is to the severely insane," and claimed that those treated by Dianetics had higher IQs, healed faster, had better eyesight, and never got colds. "The clear is, literally, a superman—an evolutionary step toward a new species," Gardner summarized. A writer for *Fantasy Review* saw a parallel between Dianetics and Hubbard's outer space adventures, claiming that "like the quasi-superman heroes of most of Hubbard's fiction, initiates were encouraged to believe their mental powers were unlimited."

Bought at first by Hubbard's science fiction fans, the manuscript soon became a national best-seller when it was published by Hermitage House in 1950. Groups were formed to learn and practice Dianetics, especially on college campuses and among the Hollywood set. In 1947, Hubbard actually opened an office in Los Angeles to "[test] the application of Dianetics" among the Hollywood elite. Hubbard left freelance writing in 1950 to promote Dianetics, writing a score of books on the subject in the following decade, delivering some 4,000 lectures, and founding a string of research organizations to spread the word. The Church of Scientology, founded by Hubbard in 1954, became the largest and best-known of these groups.

Essentially the bible of Scientology, *Dianetics* describes a program of self-improvement and spiritual awakening. As a journalist in *People* described it, "basically it is the use of a crude lie-detector-type device called an 'E-meter' to diagnose an individual's emotional state, followed by lengthy and expensive Dianetics counseling sessions to deal with the 'problems' the meter detects—and it is the basis of the church's wealth."

Hubbard's ideas continued to be popular throughout the 1960s and 1970s. The church has over 700 established churches, missions, and groups around the world and membership reached its peak at around six million. *Dianetics* has sold over eight million copies and still sells nearly 400,000 copies a year. A 1991 *Time* cover story characterized the movement as at best a money-making scam and at worst a terrorist organization. As Cult Awareness Network director Cynthia Kisser has stated, "Scientology is quite likely the most ruthless, the most classically terroristic, the most litigious and the most lucrative cult the country has ever seen."

Bringing New Members to the Fold

To a church that runs on that kind of money, the need for ongoing new members is crucial. *Time* has listed various ways in which Scientologists would recruit. In many cases, targeted individuals were often led to believe that they were enrolling in a self-help or professional organization, with church affiliations never mentioned initially. There was, for instance, the HealthMed chain of clinics, which *Time*'s Richard Behar said promoted "a grueling and excessive system of saunas, exercise and vitamins designed by Hubbard to purify the body. Experts denounce the regime as quackery and potentially harmful, yet HealthMed solicits unions and public agencies for contracts." Then there was a drug-treatment program, Narconon, "a classic vehicle for drawing addicts into the cult." There was also The Concerned Businessmen's Association of America, another Scientology-linked group that, according to Behar, held "antidrug contests and [awarded] $5,000 grants to schools as a way to recruit students and curry favor with education officials."

Indeed, members of Scientology are reportedly subjected to mental and even physical abuse while paying exorbitant prices for an unending series of texts and programs. The recollections of Edward Lottick attest to the pull and power of Scientology. Seeking spiritual guidance, Lottick's 24-year-old son, Noah, had joined the movement in

1990. Just months later, drained of his money and intimidated to the breaking point, Noah leapt to his death from a 10th-floor window. "The Lotticks [wanted] to sue the church for contributing to their son's death, but the prospect [had] them frightened," commented Behar. "For nearly 40 years, the big business of Scientology has shielded itself exquisitely behind the First Amendment as well as a battery of high-priced criminal lawyers and shady private detectives."

Because of Scientology's legal problems, Hubbard went into seclusion in the early 1980s, reportedly living on his yacht in international waters, in one of his homes in England, and on a ranch in rural California. But Hubbard seemed unable to avoid the legal battles of the time. In 1982, Hubbard's son Ronald DeWolf tried to have his father declared legally dead or incompetent. He further charged that Scientology officials had stolen millions of dollars from his father's estate and described his father as "one of the biggest con men of the century." At the same time, Hubbard's wife, Mary Sue Whipp Hubbard, was sentenced to prison for her part in covering up Scientology break-ins at Federal offices.

"2000 hours, the 24th of January, AD36"

Hubbard's death from a stroke on January 24, 1986, was officially announced by church officials several days later, after Hubbard's body had been cremated and his ashes scattered in the Pacific Ocean. In accordance with Hubbard's will, "no autopsy was performed," according to the *Chicago Tribune,* and the bulk of his estate—"estimated at tens of millions of dollars," according to Mark Brown of the *County Telegram-Tribune* —was given to the Church of Scientology.

Hubbard's death was a Scientology event described by the authors of *L. Ron Hubbard: Messiah or Madman?* As they reported, a missive dated January 27, 1986, ordered all Scientology churches and missions worldwide to close their doors for the day. In the Los Angeles area, Commander David Miscavage addressed a packed audience at the Hollywood Palladium. As he told the mourning group, as quoted in *L. Ron Hubbard: Messiah or Madman?:* "For many years Ron had said that if given the time, . . . he would be able to concentrate on and complete all of his researches into the upper OT level [for Operating Thetan, a Scientology spiritual state]. . . . Approximately two weeks ago, he completed all of his researches he set out to do." The book noted an audience reaction of approval. Then Miscavage continued: "He has now moved on to the next level of OT research. It's a level beyond anything any of us ever imagined." According to Miscavage, Hubbard had achieved a state so pure, the body was no longer needed: "Thus at 2000 hours, the 24th of January, AD36 [signifying the 36th year after the publication of *Dianetics*], L. Ron Hubbard discarded the body he had used in this lifetime for 74 years, 10 months and 11 days."

Further Reading

Corydon, Bent, and L. Ron Hubbard, Jr., *L. Ron Hubbard: Messiah or Madman?*, L. Stuart, 1987.
Gardner, Martin, *In the Name of Science,* Putnam, 1952, published as *Fads and Fallacies in the name of Science,* Dover, 1957.
Hubbard, L. Ron, *Dianetics: The Modern Science of Mental Health,* Hermitage House, 1950, reprinted, Bridge Publications, 1984.
Miller, Russell, *Bare-faced Messiah: The True Story of L. Ron Hubbard,* Holt, 1988.
Chicago Tribune, January 30, 1986.
County Telegram-Tribune, January 30, 1986.
Fantasy Review, February 1986.
Maclean's, November 17, 1997.
People, January 24, 1983.
Reason, April 1996.
Time, May 6, 1991; February 10, 1997.
Xignals, April/May 1986.

Dolores Huerta

Dolores Huerta (born 1930) is a labor activist who worked with the late Cesar Chavez to organize and run the United Farm Workers.

Cofounder and first vice president of the United Farm Workers, Dolores Huerta (sometimes referred to as Dolores "Huelga," Spanish for "strike") is the most prominent Chicana labor leader in the United States. For more than 30 years she has dedicated her life to the struggle for justice, dignity, and a decent standard of living for one of the United States' most exploited groups—the men, women, and children who toil in the fields and orchards picking the vegetables and fruits that stock grocery stores. The recipient of countless awards from community service, labor, Hispanic, and women's organizations as well as the subject of *corridos* (ballads) and murals, the vibrant and charismatic Huerta is a much-admired role model for Mexican American women.

Born April 10, 1930, in the small mining town of Dawson in northern New Mexico, Dolores Fernandez Huerta was the second child and only daughter of Juan and Alicia (Chavez) Fernandez. On her mother's side of the family, Huerta is a third-generation New Mexican. Huerta's father was also born in Dawson but to a Mexican immigrant family. The young couple's marriage was a troubled one, and when Huerta was a toddler, her parents divorced. Her mother moved her three children first to Las Vegas, New Mexico, and then to Stockton, California, where Huerta spent the remainder of her childhood.

As a single parent during the Depression, Alicia Chavez Fernandez had a difficult time supporting her young family. To make ends meet, she worked as a waitress during the day and in a cannery at night, relying on her widowed father, Herculano Chavez, to watch her children. Despite the hardships, it was a loving and happy household. The gregarious Huerta was very close to her grandfather, who called her

"seven tongues" because she talked so much. (Such verbal skills would serve her well later in life.) As she once recalled in an interview, "My grandfather kind of raised us. . . . He was really our father. . . . [His] influence was really the male influence in my family." But Huerta also maintained sporadic contact with her father, a miner and migrant worker whose own political and labor activism later proved inspirational to his daughter.

The family's economic fortunes took a turn for the better during World War II. Alicia Fernandez ran a restaurant and then purchased a hotel in Stockton with her second husband, James Richards, with whom she had another daughter. During summers in particular, Huerta and her brothers helped manage these establishments, which were located on the fringes of skid row and catered to a working-class and farm-worker clientele. She relished the experience and believed it taught her to appreciate all different types of people. "The ethnic community where we lived was all mixed," she explained. "It was Japanese, Chinese. The only Jewish families that lived in Stockton were there in our neighborhood. . . . There was the Filipino pool hall . . . , the Mexican drug stores, the Mexican bakeries were there."

In the early 1950s, Alicia Fernandez Richards divorced her husband, whose strained relationship with Huerta had been a source of tension, and married again, this time to a man named Juan Silva. Their union was a happy one that produced another daughter and endured until Alicia's death. Huerta speaks admiringly of her mother's entrepreneurial and personal spirit and her expectations for her children. "My mother was always pushing me to get involved in all these youth activities. . . . We took violin lessons. I took piano lessons. I took dancing lessons. I belonged to the church choir. . . . I belonged to the church youth organization. And I was a very active Girl Scout from the time I was eight to the time I was eighteen." Mother and daughter enjoyed a caring relationship that extended into Huerta's adult years.

Although Huerta counted her mother and grandfather as the primary influences in her life, she also credits her father with inspiring her to be an activist. Like most people in Dawson, Juan Fernandez worked in the coal mines. To supplement his wages, he joined the migrant labor force, traveling to Colorado, Nebraska, and Wyoming for the beet harvests. The inferior working conditions, frequent accidents, and low wages he encountered as a farm worker sparked his interest in labor issues. Leaving Dawson after his divorce from Huerta's mother, Fernandez continued his activism, becoming secretary-treasurer of the Congress of Industrial Organizations (CIO) local at the Terrero Camp of the American Metals Company in Las Vegas, New Mexico. In 1938, using his predominately Hispanic local union as a base, he won election to the New Mexico state legislature. There he worked with other sympathetic members to promote a labor program, including a piece of legislation known as the "Little Wagner Act" and a wages-and-hours bill. Due to his outspoken independence on many issues, Fernandez lasted only one term in the state house.

After her parents' divorce, Huerta saw her father only occasionally. Once she reached adulthood, however, she met up with him more frequently, especially after he settled in Stockton. There he lived in a labor camp for a while, worked in the asparagus fields, held other odd jobs, and returned to school for a college degree. Huerta remained proud of her father's union activism, political achievements, and educational accomplishments, and he in turn supported her labor organizing. But their relationship remained aloof and distant, partly because he disapproved of her personal lifestyle.

After graduating from Stockton High School, Huerta—unlike most Hispanic women of her generation—continued her education at Stockton College. A brief and unsuccessful marriage that produced two daughters prompted her to abandon her studies for a while, but after divorcing her husband, she returned to college and earned her associate's degree with financial and emotional support from her mother.

Huerta held a variety of jobs in Stockton before, during, and after her marriage. Before her marriage, for example, she managed a small neighborhood grocery store that her mother had purchased. (It eventually went bankrupt.) Then she obtained a job at the Naval Supply Base as the secretary to the commander in charge of public works. During and after her divorce, she worked in the sheriff's office in records and identifications. Dissatisfied with these kinds of jobs, Huerta resumed her education and earned a provisional teaching certificate. Once in the classroom, however, she quickly grew frustrated by how little she could really do for those students who didn't have proper clothing or enough to eat.

Huerta's frustration eventually found an outlet in the Community Service Organization (CSO), a Mexican American self-help group that first took shape in Los Angeles in the years after World War II and then spread across California and the Southwest. She joined up during the mid-1950s and became very active in the CSO's many civic and educational programs, including registering voters, setting up citizenship classes, and lobbying local government officials for neighborhood improvements. Huerta showed particular talent for the latter, so much so that the CSO soon hired her to handle similar duties for the group at the state level in Sacramento.

During the course of these activities, Huerta met and married her second husband, Ventura Huerta, who was also involved in community affairs. Their relationship produced five children but gradually deteriorated because of incompatible temperaments and disagreements over Dolores Huerta's juggling of domestic matters, child care, and civic activism. "I knew I wasn't comfortable in a wife's role, but I wasn't clearly facing the issue," she later remarked in the *Progressive.* "I hedged, I made excuses, I didn't come out and tell my husband that I cared more about helping other people than cleaning our house and doing my hair." A series of trial separations eventually led to a bitter divorce, and once again, Huerta turned to her mother for financial and emotional support so that she could continue her work for the CSO.

During the late 1950s, as Huerta was struggling to balance a failing marriage, her family, and a job with her commitment to social activism, she found herself drawn to the plight of Mexican American farm workers. She soon joined a northern California community interest group, the Agricultural Workers Association (AWA), which had been founded by a local priest and his parishioners. It later merged with the American Federation of Labor-Congress of Industrial Organizations (AFL-CIO)-sponsored Agricultural Workers Organizing Committee (AWOC), for which Huerta worked as secretary-treasurer.

It was around this same time that Huerta first met Cesar Chavez, another CSO official who shared her concern for migrant workers. The two worked together to bring rural labor issues to the attention of the more urban-oriented CSO. When they could not interest the CSO in expanding its focus, both Chavez and Huerta left the group to devote their time to organizing this overlooked segment of American society. In 1962, from their base in the town of Delano, they changed the course of agricultural and labor history in California when they founded the National Farm Workers Association (NFWA), the precursor to the United Farm Workers (UFW).

The full extent of the Chavez-Huerta collaboration has only recently been documented as correspondence between the two and others becomes available. For instance, in a 1962 letter to activist Fred Ross, his CSO mentor, Chavez remarked, "Dolores was here [in Delano] for one and a half days. I filled her in on all the plans and asked her to join the parade. . . . While here we did some work on the list of towns to work in throughout the valley. . . . Also she,

Helen [Chavez's wife], and I decide [sic] on the name of the group. 'Farm Workers Assn.'"

Ever since the founding of the union, Huerta has held decision-making posts and maintained a high public profile. As second in command to Chavez until his death in 1993, she exerted a direct influence on shaping and guiding the fortunes of the UFW. In the famous 1965 Delano strike (the one that first attracted national attention to the union and launched the table grape boycott), she devised strategy and led workers on picket lines. She was also responsible for setting up the UFW's contract negotiation department and served as its director in the early years.

In these and other positions in the union, Huerta had to battle both gender and ethnic stereotypes. Commenting on her uncompromising and forceful personality, for example, one grower declared, "Dolores Huerta is crazy. She is a violent woman, where women, especially Mexican women, are usually peaceful and calm." But she was able to hold her own against hostile Anglo growers who resented the fact that any Mexican American—and a woman, no less— would dare challenge the status quo.

Another major undertaking for Huerta involved running the table grape boycott in New York City in the late 1960s, an effort that eventually expanded to include the entire east coast, the primary distribution point for grapes. The leadership she provided in 1968 and 1969 as the east coast boycott coordinator greatly contributed to the success of the national boycott. Huerta mobilized other unions, political activists, Hispanic associations, community organizations, religious supporters, peace groups, student protestors, and concerned consumers across racial, ethnic, and class lines in a drive to show support for farm workers and keep media attention focused on their cause. Their efforts finally paid off in 1970 when the Delano growers agreed to contracts that ended the five-year-old strike.

It was also while she was living and working in New York that Huerta met feminist Gloria Steinem, who made her aware of the emerging women's movement. Huerta then began to incorporate a feminist critique into her human rights philosophy.

During the early 1970s, Huerta once again found her expertise in demand in New York, where she directed not only the continuing grape boycott but also boycotts against lettuce and Gallo brand wine. As before, the strategy was to maintain nationwide pressure to force changes in California. Victory came in 1975 when the California state legislature passed the Agricultural Labor Relations Act (ALRA), the first law to recognize the collective bargaining rights of farm workers in California.

In the midst of her busy schedule, Huerta began a third relationship, this time with Richard Chavez, Cesar's brother. Their liaison produced four children. Reflecting on the sacrifices all 11 of her children have had to make given her frequent absences from home, Huerta admitted, "I don't feel proud of the suffering that my kids went through. I feel very bad and guilty about it, but by the same token I know that they learned a lot in the process."

During the late 1970s, Huerta assumed the directorship of the UFW's Citizenship Participation Day Department (CPD), the political arm of the union. In this role, she lobbied the California state legislature to protect the new farm labor law. During the 1980s she became involved in another ambitious UFW project, the founding of KUFW-Radio Campesina, the union's radio station. Meanwhile, Huerta also continued to devote a great deal of her time to various other UFW activities, including speaking engagements, fund raising, publicizing the renewed grape boycott, and testifying before state and congressional committees on a wide range of issues, including pesticides, health problems of field workers, Hispanic political issues, and immigration policy.

Huerta's activism has come at great personal cost to her and to her family. Besides the extensive travel that keeps her away from home most of the time, she has been arrested on more than 20 occasions. In 1988, she suffered a life-threatening injury at a peaceful demonstration against the policies of George Bush, who had made a stop in San Francisco during his campaign for the presidency. Rushed to the hospital after a clubbing by baton-swinging police officers, Huerta underwent emergency surgery for removal of her spleen. (She also suffered six broken ribs in the incident.) She later sued the city and settled out of court, receiving a record financial settlement. In addition, as a direct result of the assault on Huerta, the San Francisco police department was forced to change its rules regarding crowd control and police discipline.

After recovering from her injuries, Huerta gradually resumed her work for the farm workers in the 1990s. It was an especially difficult time for the UFW; the political climate had shifted more toward the conservative point of view, the farm workers' cause no longer seemed as pressing, and the union itself was in turmoil as it went through a process of internal reassessment and restructuring. The sudden death of Cesar Chavez in 1993 was also a severe blow, one that some people thought might signal the end of the UFW as well.

Huerta insists, however, that the UFW legacy remains strong in the Hispanic community and beyond. She herself continues to commit her energies to the union as an outspoken leader, executive board member, administrator, lobbyist, contract negotiator, picket captain, and lecturer. And she is very proud of what has been accomplished so far and is still hopeful for the future. "I think we brought to the world, the United States anyway, the whole idea of boycotting as a nonviolent tactic," Huerta once told an interviewer. "I think we showed the world that nonviolence can work to make social change. . . . I think we have laid a pattern of how farm workers are eventually going to get out of their bondage. It may not happen right now in our foreseeable future, but the pattern is there and farm workers are going to make it."

The current president of the United Farm Workers, Arturo Rodriguez—who happens to be married to Cesar Chavez's daughter—agrees that the road ahead is challenging. The union has had a tough time holding on to contracts in the grape vineyards and citrus orchards, but it is fighting to reorganize there while also reaching out to new groups such as the rose and mushroom workers. Like his father-in-law before him, Rodriguez depends on Huerta's tireless enthusiasm to help boost membership and hammer away at the growers on issues such as pesticide use. "Early in 1970, Cesar Chavez said [Huerta] is totally fearless, both physically and mentally," Rodriguez recalled in a chat with a reporter for *Hispanic* magazine. "A quarter of a century later she shows no sign of slowing down. [Huerta] is an enduring symbol of the farm worker movement."

Further Reading

Day, Mark, *Forty Acres: Cesar Chavez and the Farm Workers,* Praeger, 1971.

De Ruiz, Dana Catharine, *La Causa: The Migrant Farmworkers' Story,* Raintree Steck-Vaughn, 1993.

Dunne, John Gregory, *Delano: The Story of the California Grape Strike,* Farrar, 1976.

Levy, Jacques, *Cesar Chavez: Autobiography of La Causa,* Norton, 1975.

Matthiessen, Peter, *Sal Si Puedes: Cesar Chavez and the New American Revolution,* Random House, 1969.

Perez, Frank, *Dolores Huerta,* Raintree Steck-Vaughn, 1996.

Telgen, Diane, and Jim Kamp, editors, *Notable Hispanic American Women,* Gale Research, 1993.

Delano Record, April 28, 1966, p. 1.

Hispanic, August, 1996.

Ms., November, 1976, pp. 11-16.

Nation, February 23, 1974, pp. 232-238.

Progressive, September, 1975, pp. 38-40.

J

Ruth Prawer Jhabvala

Whether producing her award-winning novels or working as the screenwriting member of Merchant-Ivory, the film industry's longest-lasting creative team, Ruth Prawer Jhabvala (born 1927) contributes a respected voice to modern literature.

Ruth Prawer Jhabvala's perspective as a creative writer is one born of the conflict between East and West, a conflict that mirrors her life as a citizen of both worlds. Born in Germany to Polish parents, Jhabvala, the daughter of a lawyer, began writing stories at age six. In the prewar days, she and her brother attended segregated Jewish schools, which "wasn't pleasant," as Jhabvala told *People* reporter Harriet Shapiro. "Other children would scream after us and throw stones."

Jhabvala and her family left Germany for England in 1939, where they survived the London Blitz—the constant *blitzkreig* bombing of the city by German war planes. But tragedy was to follow: as Shapiro noted, Jhabvala's father, depressed by the loss of many of his relatives to the concentration camps, committed suicide in 1948.

A new life in India

At the time of her father's death, Jhabvala was a student of Queen Mary College. That same year, she attended a get-together in London, where an attentive young Indian man "stayed by my side for the entire party," as the author recalled to Shapiro. While she admitted that his accent made conversation a challenge, Ruth Prawer and architect Cyrus Jhabvala completed a long-distance courtship and were married in 1951, after Ruth had completed her master's degree in English literature.

The new bride relocated to New Delhi with her husband; she later described her first impression of India as "the most wonderful place I had ever been in my life. India was a sensation. It was remarkable to see all those parrots flying about, the brilliant foliage and the brilliant sky." Indeed, Jhabvala had seen the India of travelogue—"I never noticed the poverty," she added in the *People* interview.

The circumstance under which Jhabvala arrived in India—her marriage—is not usually the kind that propels other westerners to the Asian continent. In short, as *Time* writer Paul Gray remarked, the young woman was not "a do-gooder, a foreign-service careerist or a spiritual pilgrim. But her European background and natural desire to sympathize with her adopted land made her an acute observer."

Writing from "the Inside"

Her adopted country provided Jhabvala with the impetus to begin her literary career. "I was 24," she told David Streitfeld in a *Washington Post Book World* interview, "and just at the age when one really starts to write seriously. There was so much subject matter for me. I hardly finished a book before I started a new one. I was so full of energy, I immediately wrote as if I were an Indian, from inside." But even that kind of enthusiasm couldn't mask an underlying conflict: "I wasn't even really anything when I was in India, because I was a foreigner there. People are always asking where my roots are, and I say I don't have any."

Jhabvala's first novel, *To Whom She Will* (published in the United States as *Amrita*) was released in 1955. In a *New York Herald Tribune Book World* review, Nancy Wilson Ross welcomed the publication as "a fresh and witty novel about modern India." Jhabvala's Jane Austen-like take on

As Jhabvala explained in *People,* "India became more and more an alien place. It is not a place that you can be indifferent to. It absorbs you against your will. You can't live there and eat and be comfortable when you see how others have to live." And so in 1975 the author moved to a New York City apartment. Her husband, who remained in India, is a frequent visitor to New York, while the couple's three grown children live in India, England, and California.

Now in the United States, Jhabvala was not lacking in challenging work opportunities. As a longtime collaborator with the filmmaking team of producer Ismail Merchant and director James Ivory—indeed, the two were even neighbors, living in the apartment below Jhabvala, as Shapiro's article reported—she produced scripts on an average of almost one per year through the 1980s and 1990s. Merchant-Ivory Productions gained fame as a leading proponent of period dramas, many of them bearing the stamp of India as provided by Jhabvala.

A Thriving Film Career

Beginning with *Shakespeare Wallah* and *Bombay Talkie,* and continuing through *Autobiography of a Princess, Heat and Dust,* and *A Passage to India* from the E.M. Forster novel, Merchant-Ivory pictures brought to the world Jhabvala's visions of the East. But as successful as those films were, the moviemaking trio would gain their largest audiences with more "mainstream," Western-themed productions, including the smash hit *A Room with a View.* This tale of a naive-but-pragmatic young Englishwoman torn between her hot-blooded true love and her dull, sensible fiancee struck a chord with audiences and critics, whose acclaim helped propel the independent film to three Academy Awards, including one for Jhabvala in adapting another Forester book to the screen.

A Room with a View ushered in an era of Merchant-Ivory-Jhabvala films that caught popular attention. The release of *Howards End* (1992) prompted *Time* columnist Richard Corliss to dub the three artists "a nuclear family, a multinational corporation and a tight little island of quality cinema." Corliss also noted that Merchant-Ivory films "have often been admired, and reviled, for their dogged gentility, the Masterpiece Theatricality of their style. Even the soggy films proceed at a confidently leisurely pace." But with Jhabvala's tight script for *Howards End,* he added, "you get the sense of an entire novel, its characters and character, unfolding in 140 minutes."

Kazou Ishiguro's 1988 novel, *Remains of the Day,* was the basis of another well-received Merchant-Ivory film. In adapting the story of a butler whose lifetime of selfless dedication to the denizens of Darlington Hall is tested when Lord Darlington becomes allied with the Nazi Party during World War II, the filmmakers also faced industry gossip. "As is widely known, a screenplay by Harold Pinter was discarded in favor of one by Ruth Prawer Jhabvala," as Stanley Kauffmann reported in a *New Republic* review. "Jhabvala is certainly no crude hack, but she has underscored some matters and has altered the tone of the original." That sits fine with Corliss, who wrote in his *Time* review that with this film the creative team has "gone their source one better, or

the mores of middle-class Indians found favor with many critics and readers, and *Amrita* paved the way for a collection of insightful novels and short stories with an Indian theme.

One of the best-known Jhabvala novels is the 1975 work *Heat and Dust,* which the author also adapted for film. This story of a young British woman recreating the India journey of her grandfather's wife contains "social comedy . . . as funny and as sympathetic as it is in Jhabvala's earlier novels, even though she has departed from her more usual theme of middle-class Indian life," according to *Times Literary Supplement* critic Brigid Allen. A critical and popular success on both sides of the Atlantic, *Heat and Dust* won Britain's prestigious Booker Prize for fiction.

"More and More an Alien Place"

After two decades in India, Jhabvala faced a growing problem: she was finding it increasingly difficult to write about a country that she was living in. Reviewers began commenting on an ambivalence toward India in her work that was particularly apparent in her short story collection *Out of India.* One reviewer of this 1986 work, Michiko Kakutani of the *New York Times,* wrote that "bit by bit, the stories in *Out of India* darken, grow denser and more ambiguous." In this way, Kakutani concludes, Jhabvala "gradually moves beyond the tidy formulations of the comedy of manners, and a strain of melancholy also begins to creep into her writing."

one quieter: the film is more discreet . . . than the book." Also in agreement is *National Review* writer John Simon: "It is to Jhabvala's credit that she has managed to objectify and animate what in the novel is mostly internalized, point-of-view reflection."

Less successful for Merchant-Ivory Productions was the team's 1995 film, *Jefferson in Paris.* Simon, in another *National Review* article, singled out Jhabvala as "culpable" for what he termed a lifeless study of Thomas Jefferson's years as an ambassador.

In the view of Owen Gleiberman of *Entertainment Weekly,* Merchant-Ivory-Jhabvala "have turned civility into a kind of middlebrow fetish. Their films have come most alive when the characters are most repressed." With another adaptation, *Surviving Picasso* (1996), the filmmakers "have now achieved a certain slickness and fluency, but without the spark of inspiration that makes the whole world kin," in the words of John Simon. This film dramatizes the affair between the aging Pablo Picasso and his young protégé, Francoise Gilot. "Never less than watchable," said Gleiberman, the production "is also a cinematic paradox, a movie that works to capture Picasso from every angle yet somehow misses the fire in his belly."

However the critics may react to their films, there is no denying the success of the Merchant-Ivory-Jhabvala partnership—in fact, the three were cited in one reference source as the longest-lasting filmmaking team ever. Discussing their formula for success with *People*'s Harriet Shapiro, Ivory singles out Jhabvala's contributions. "Most screenwriters are not fueled by any real creative gifts as writers. They are not proper storytellers. Unlike so many people who adapt classic novels, Ruth is not down on her knees before them, not daring to change anything."

Further Reading

Contemporary Literary Criticism, Gale, Volume 4, 1975, Volume 8, 1978, Volume 29, 1984.
Entertainment Weekly, September 27, 1996.
National Review, December 13, 1993; May 1, 1995; November 11, 1996.
New Republic, December 6, 1993; April 24, 1995.
New Statesman & Society, April 9, 1993.
New York Herald Tribune Book Review, January 15, 1956.
New York Times, August 30, 1973; July 19, 1983; September 15, 1993; August 2, 1984; August 5, 1984; March 7, 1986; May 17, 1986; July 5, 1986; August 6, 1987.
People, September 28, 1987.
Publishers Weekly, July 17, 1995.
Time, May 12 1986; March 16, 1992; November 8, 1993.
Times Literary Supplement, May 20, 1965; November 7, 1975; April 15, 1983; April 24, 1987; November 13, 1987; April 16, 1993.
Washington Post Book World, September 12, 1976; September 18, 1983; May 25, 1986; February 21, 1993; March 28, 1993.

Alfred Jodl

Alfred Jodl (c. 1892-1946) was a top German military officer during World War II and part of the leadership cadre around Nazi leader Adolf Hitler. **For his military strategies and orders that led to deaths of enemy troops and civilians throughout Europe, Jodl was arrested in 1945 and hanged a year later with several other top Nazis as a war criminal.**

S ources place Alfred Jodl's date of birth around 1892, and there is little information about his life prior to his military career. Jodl's official public record began with his service during World War I in the Bavarian Army, where he was an artillery expert. At the war's end, imperial Germany was soundly defeated, and the Treaty of Versailles dictated that its armed forces would be limited to 100,000 men; the treaty also curtailed Germany's use of heavy artillery, tanks, submarines, and the famed Luftwaffe (air force). Jodl remained in the service of the military, though a leadership vacuum and a near-revolution had made mutinies quite common among the demoralized armed forces in the final months of the war.

Advanced Through Ranks

During the 1920s Jodl served the newly-created Weimar Republic in Germany's Ministry of War and in the intelligence service. He was perhaps fortunate to have a steady post, for the country's economy was in ruins and the unemployment rate was dangerously high. Such conditions gave rise to a political movement called National Socialism, a right-wing fascist movement led by another World War I

veteran, Adolf Hitler. By 1932 Jodl had returned to service in the Army itself and was head of its Operations Department. Hitler became German Chancellor early the next year.

Jodl served as head of Army operations until 1935. During this period Hitler was consolidating power and winning support for an economic course that brought some measure of stability and prosperity. Yet the Nazi political platform blamed its Jewish citizens for many of Germany's economic woes, and imposed an increasingly drastic series of laws that restricted the civil rights of German Jews. Hitler also began violating the terms of the Versailles treaty by rearming. By 1936 Jodl had advanced to the rank of colonel and to the post of head of the National Defense Section in the High Command of the Armed Forces.

Outbreak of War

In 1938 the German border to be defended widened considerably when Austria was annexed and became part of the country—an act that took place with almost no resistance. From 1938 to August of 1939 Jodl served as Artillery Commander of the 44th Division, and was posted in both Vienna, the Austrian capital, and Brno, a city in the former Czechoslovakia. In the late summer of 1938 German troops were massing on Germany's border with Czechoslovakia. Jodl had planned the specifics of the invasion, but alarmed European leaders signed a peace agreement with Germany a few weeks later that allowed Hitler to simply annex part of Czechoslovakia. A year later, an increasingly bellicose Germany invaded Poland, an act that launched World War II. Hitler had signed a non-aggression pact with the Soviet Union, and with his eastern flank protected—as well as a standing alliance with a fascist dictatorship in Italy—Germany launched air attacks on Britain. German troops successfully invaded France, Norway—which Jodl himself strategized—Denmark, Holland, Belgium, Yugoslavia, and Greece.

At this point Jodl began to take on an even more decisive role in Germany military matters. In August of 1939, now a general major, he became Chief of Operation Staff of the High Command of the Armed Forces, essentially Hitler's liaison between the Wehrmacht, or armed forces, and the puppet Nazi Cabinet. One of the youngest among Hitler's inner circle, Jodl was the German officer in charge of negotiations at Salonika regarding Greece's capitulation to Nazi forces in the spring of 1941. Later that spring, Germany invaded the Soviet Union. Troops marched though Poland, where many of the concentration camps constructed to annihilate European Jewry were located; meanwhile, the outside world had little idea of the extermination policies that had been signed into action by Hitler and Jodl's colleagues at the top levels.

Germany's invasion of Russia proved its fatal error, however. Wehrmacht troops made it as far as Moscow and Leningrad by the end of 1941, but the Soviet army proved a tough foe. On an order dated October 7, 1941, Jodl's signature appears under the directive that Hitler would reject Russia's possible surrender of Moscow and Leningrad in the event of a negotiation; it declared that the cities should be leveled. Furthermore, problems among his top aides and advisors plagued Hitler during the war years. This dissension led to an assassination attempt on his life in July of 1944, and Jodl was wounded by the bomb. A secret landing of American troops in France and successful routing of the Germans spelled the end of the war. In April of 1945 Russian and American troops took Berlin (the German capital), and Hitler committed suicide. He passed on his command to Karl Doenitz, the admiral of the German Navy.

Signed Surrender

The Wehrmacht's official surrender came in the northeast French city of Reims. Jodl was sent on Doenitz's behalf, and over two days in early May of 1945, Jodl stalled with Allied negotiators from the staff of American General Dwight D. Eisenhower, commander of the Allied forces in Europe. Eisenhower himself refused to negotiate with Jodl personally. Doenitz had given orders to delay the signing as long as possible to enable German soldiers in the east of Europe to turn back and surrender to Allied forces instead of Russians, who were inflicting dire retribution upon their vanquished. Eventually Eisenhower became incensed at Jodl's tactics, and threatened to close the front in the West, which would leave the retreating German troops stranded in the east. Jodl signed the surrender at 2:38 a.m. on May 7, 1945. It was estimated that because of the delay almost a million Germans were able to evade the Russians.

Jodl then went to the north German city of Flensburg, where Doenitz was. Jodl was arrested there with his superior on May 23. In October of 1945, an International Military Tribunal (IMT) in Nuremberg issued an indictment against Jodl and several other top Nazi leaders, including Doenitz; Minister of Armaments and War Production Albert Speer; Luftwaffe chief Hermann Goering; Fritz Sauckel, head of the Nazis' forced labor operations; and foreign minister Joachim von Ribbentrop. The Russians had demanded that Jodl's name be included on the War Criminals list in part for his stalling at Reims and for once issuing an order of Hitler's that German units in Russia could act with heedless brutality.

Tried at Nuremberg

Other evidence that survived the end of World War II linked Jodl to serious transgressions, including a plan of action regarding the destruction of the United States and Britain. Jodl also had made a speech on November 7, 1943, about slave labor—for which the genocidal camps, such as Auschwitz and Treblinka, were ostensibly designed—asserting that ''remorseless vigor and resolution'' was critical regarding German actions in Denmark, France, and Belgium, according to Alfred D. Low's *The Men Around Hitler: The Nazi Elite and Its Collaborators*. That same year Jodl gave orders that citizens should be evacuated in the north of Norway and their homes burned so that they could not provide assistance to an imminent Russian invasion. Other documents show that Jodl knew that thousands of civilians had been forcibly deported from France to work in German munitions factories.

The trial for Jodl and the nineteen other defendants began in November of 1945. In contrast to some of the other defendants, such as the visibly unstable Sauckel and the eloquent, repentant Speer, Jodl was known for his stoic demeanor on the stand. His wife left flowers for him on the witness box at the start of his testimony on June 3, 1946. Luise Jodl, once a secretary at the offices of the German High Command, had married Jodl after the death of his first wife, Anneliese, in 1944. She walked to Nuremberg from Berchtesgaden, and her interventions helped Jodl obtain the services of a well-known attorney, Franz Exner from the University of Munich.

Among the many incidents about which Jodl was questioned were his orders to bomb the Dutch city of Rotterdam. In his defense, Jodl asserted that this and other actions that he ordered were not "criminal" in the sense that they violated international standards of military conduct during warfare. On the stand, he also hinted that much of the blame for the war lay in the maneuvers of German politicians, not the actions of loyal officers. He claimed to have known nothing of the death camps at which nearly six million European Jews met their death. In his cell, he spoke with Gustave Gilbert, the prison psychiatrist at Nuremberg who later wrote a book on his experiences. Jodl told Gilbert that he had sometimes hated Hitler, because of "his contempt for the middle class, with which I identified myself, his suspicion and contempt for the nobility, to which I was married, and his hatred of the General Staff, of which I was a member," Gilbert reported in *Nuremberg Diary*.

Last-Minute Appeal

During this time, Luise Jodl sent telegrams to England's wartime Prime Minister Winston Churchill, attempting to appeal to his own sense of military duty and the officers' code of conduct to carry out orders, that he might intervene on her husband's behalf. She asked that Churchill "give your voice of support to my husband, Colonel General Jodl, who, like yourself, did nothing but fight for his country to the last," according to Joseph Persico's *Nuremberg: Infamy on Trial*. She also sent similarly worded missives to English Field Marshal Bernard Montgomery and General Eisenhower. None stepped in, however, and unlike a few of the other defendants, the IMT did not find any "mitigating factors" regarding Jodl's actions during the war, and sentenced him to death.

Jodl was hanged in a gymnasium at the Nuremberg prison on October 16, 1946. He was cremated, and his ashes later taken to the Munich suburb of Solln, and then scattered into a tributary of the Isar, which in turn carried them to the Danube and then out to sea. According to Persico's *Nuremberg: Infamy on Trial,* in his cell at Nuremberg Jodl kept a timeworn picture of a woman holding an infant. When a prisoner of war came in to give him a shave and inquired as to who the two were, Jodl said that it was his mother and himself as a baby, and then reflected, "it's too bad I didn't die then. Look how much grief I would have been spared. Frankly I don't know why I lived anyway."

Further Reading

Fest, Joachim C. *The Face of the Third Reich: Portraits of the Nazi Leadership,* translated from the German by Michael Bullock, Pantheon, 1970.

Gilbert, G. M., *Nuremberg Diary,* Farrar, Straus, 1947.

Low, Alfred D., *The Men Around Hitler: The Nazi Elite and Its Collaborators,* East European Monographs, 1996.

Persico, Joseph, *Nuremberg: Infamy on Trial,* Viking, 1994.

Shirer, William L. *The Rise and Fall of the Third Reich: A History of Nazi Germany,* Simon & Schuster, 1960.

Speer, Albert, *Inside the Third Reich: Memoirs,* translated from the German by Richard and Clara Winston, Macmillan, 1970.

New York Times, October 16, 1946, p. 21.

Elton John

Once famed for his campy outrageousness and string of successful pop songs, English musician Elton John (born 1947) has more recently made a name for himself as a humanitarian with a particular interest in supporting AIDS research.

Ever since he first burst on the music scene in the early 1970s, Elton John has been alternately adored, abhorred, commended, and criticized. At one time, his image was that of a flamboyantly over-the-top "glam rocker" with an undeniable gift for crafting memorable pop tunes. His spectacular theatrics may have earned him legions of fans and a generous income, but they also thrust him into the media spotlight on numerous occasions as reporters scrutinized his sexual orientation, his lavish lifestyle, his addictions to drugs and alcohol, and his bulimia.

As he approached middle age, however, John began to take stock of his life and career. He toned down the glitz and glitter both on stage and off, overcame his dependencies and eating disorder, and turned his attention to concerns other than himself. Since the early 1990s, he has donated all of the royalties from the sales of his singles to charity (most notably AIDS research) in both the United Kingdom and the United States. (His poignant tribute to his friend Diana, Princess of Wales, who died in a car crash during the summer of 1997, became the number-one selling single of all time, with proceeds earmarked for the charitable trust established in Diana's name.) As a result, John has finally been able to lay to rest much of the controversy and negative press that dogged him earlier in his career.

John was born Reginald Kenneth Dwight on March 25, 1947, in the town of Pinner in the Middlesex region of England. An only child who was somewhat overweight and wore glasses, he was acutely sensitive to his appearance and how others perceived him. "Image" thus became an obsession of John's at a young age and remained an issue well into his adulthood.

Decided on a Career in Music

John embarked on a musical career in the early 1960s. He was just two weeks away from taking his final exams and

Logged His First Big Hit

The advent of the 1970s saw John's fortunes improve dramatically. His self-titled second album spawned his first hit single, "Your Song," which climbed into the top ten in both America and the United Kingdom. But the watershed year for John was 1972. "Rocket Man" was his first number-one single in America. (It topped out at number two in England.) Other smash singles soon followed, including "Daniel" and "Crocodile Rock," both of which appeared on the album *Don't Shoot Me, I'm Only the Piano Player*—John's first number-one album in both the United States and the United Kingdom. The seminal double album *Goodbye Yellow Brick Road* was released in 1973. Besides the classic title track, it contained "Candle in the Wind," a winsome ode to Marilyn Monroe. That same year, John launched his own record label, Rocket Records.

As his sales soared, John cultivated a colorfully outrageous and campy stage persona that drove audiences wild and provided plenty of fodder for the tabloids. Outlandish glasses (the more bizarre the better) and elaborate costumes featuring rhinestones and feather boas soon came to define him as a performer, and he was dubbed the "Queen Mum of Pop." He also lived a private life of luxury and excess that included a fleet of pricey cars, expensive shopping sprees, several lavish homes, and relationships with both men and women, all of which was recounted in detail by the media.

By the mid-1970s, however, John's popularity had begun to decline a bit after he released a series of less-than-stellar albums. In 1975, he starred as the Pinball Wizard in the film adaptation of the Who's rock opera, *Tommy*. The following year, he charted his first British number-one single, "Don't Go Breaking My Heart," a duet with Kiki Dee.

Turned His Back on the Music Business

In 1976, John decided to retire from the music business and focus his energies on running a soccer team he had purchased, the Watford Football Club. Around this same time, he publicly admitted his bisexuality. The ensuing controversy took its toll on John personally and professionally. As he remarked to *People* magazine reporters Fred A. Bernstein and Laura Sanderson Healy, "the gay business really hurt me. A lot of radio stations stopped playing my records." And when he attended Watford's soccer matches, he told Bernstein and Healy, "twenty thousand people would sing, 'Elton John's a homosexual, tra-la-la.'" To help him deal with the pressures of fame and the pain of depression, he turned to alcohol and cocaine, which he continued to abuse throughout the rest of the 1970s and 1980s.

In 1978, having grown bored and restless with his new lifestyle, John sought to return to the pop arena. But finding the right collaborator proved to be a struggle until he once again hooked up with Taupin in 1983. It was during the studio sessions for an album he made that year, *Too Low for Zero*, that John met Renate Blauel, a German-born recording technician. John courted her while working on his album and, after a five-day engagement, married her in Australia on Valentine's Day in 1984.

graduating from the London Academy of Music when he quit school to pursue his dream. He first went to work for a music publishing house, where he served as a messenger and tea server. To supplement his income, John also played the piano in bars and clubs and eventually joined forces with a band called Bluesology.

Bluesology had some success backing up soul artists such as Doris Troy and Patti LaBelle until around the mid-1960s. It was during this same period that John picked up his stage name, which was a combination of the middle name of Bluesology's singer, Long John Baldry, and the first name of the saxophone player, Elton Dean. Much later in his life, John added the middle name Hercules.

In 1968, an advertisement in the British music magazine *NME* seeking writers and performers brought John together with Bernie Taupin, the man who would become his on-again, off-again songwriting collaborator. One of their earliest pieces managed to land on the short list for the British entry to the 1969 Eurovision contest. Even though they lost out when it was not chosen to be performed, they continued to write and record new material, including the early singles "Skyline Pigeon" and "Lady Samantha," which sold moderately well. In 1969, John released his debut album, *Empty Sky*, which was a commercial flop. That same year, he played piano on the classic Hollies single, "He Ain't Heavy, He's My Brother."

The union was doomed from the start. The British press viciously attacked both the marriage and John, dwelling primarily on his checkered sexual history. After less than five years, the estranged couple amicably divorced. In a 1992 *Los Angeles Times* interview quoted by Caren Weiner of *Entertainment Weekly,* John explained that he had married Blauel while in a drug-induced stupor. "Even though I knew I was gay," he explained, "I thought this woman was attractive and that being married would cure me of everything wrong in my life. . . . When you take that amount [of drugs and alcohol] you can't have any relationship."

Set New Priorities

The early 1990s saw John undergo treatment for alcoholism, drug abuse, and bulimia. Once he was clean and sober, he publicly acknowledged his homosexuality and refocused his energies and talents toward helping others. Starting in 1990, he donated all of his royalties from the sales of his English singles to charity, mostly those involved in AIDS research or in offering assistance to people with AIDS. Two years later, he did the same for the royalties from his single sales in America. "It's about time I got off my backside . . . ," John told Melinda Newman of *Billboard.* "We have a long way to go." In 1992, he established the Elton John AIDS Foundation to further his philanthropy.

As the 1990s progressed, John garnered increasing respect as both an artist and a humanitarian. He began accumulating numerous awards, including ASCAP honors as songwriter of the year (with his longtime collaborator Taupin) in 1994, induction into the Rock & Roll Hall of Fame in 1994, a lifetime achievement citation at the Brit Awards in 1995, the Royal Swedish Academy of Music's Polar Prize in 1995, Grammy Awards in 1995 and again in 1998, and an Academy Award in 1995, among others. In 1996, John was named Commander of the Order of the British Empire (CBE) by Queen Elizabeth II.

Tragedy followed in 1997, however, when he lost two good friends in quick succession—fashion designer Gianni Versace, who was murdered in mid-July, and Diana, Princess of Wales, who died in a car accident in late August. John performed a reworked version of "Candle in the Wind" at her September funeral (which he vowed never to sing in public again), then released it as a single. Within just a short time it became the top-selling single of all time, with more than 30 million copies sold in 1997 alone. John donated all of the proceeds from the recording (which amounted to more than $47 million by the end of 1997) to the charitable trust established in Diana's name.

The phenomenal success of "Candle in the Wind 1997" earned John even more accolades, including Billboard awards for single of the year, singles artist of the year, and singles sales artist of the year. In early 1998, he was named favorite male adult contemporary artist at the American Music Awards, and at the 1998 Grammy Award ceremonies, he took home the trophy for best male pop vocal for "Candle in the Wind 1997." And to top it all off, he was knighted by Queen Elizabeth II in 1998 for his achievements in music and contributions to charity. John reflected on this honor in an Associated Press report published in the *Toledo Blade,* remarking that "I've had a long career and worked hard. But I think the turning point came in 1990, when I got sober and started to do some charity work, particularly for the AIDS problem. A knighthood is the icing on the cake."

Further Reading

Newsmakers, 1995 Cumulation, Gale, 1995.
Billboard, October 17, 1992; May 21, 1994; May 20, 1995.
Entertainment Weekly, February 14, 1997, p. 76; December 26, 1997.
Maclean's, March 13, 1995, p. 62; December 22, 1997, p. 11; January 12, 1998, p. 9.
People, February 27, 1984, p. 79; November 12, 1984; September 8, 1986; December 5, 1988, p. 85.
Time, March 13, 1995.
Toledo Blade (Toledo, Ohio), February 25, 1998, p. 15.
"Elton John," http://grove.ufl.edu/devseeff/bigpicture.html (March 3, 1998).
"Elton Hercules John," http://www.public.usit.net/artboy/ejfan.html (March 3, 1998).
"Elton John," http://www.roughguides.com/rock/entries/ELTON_JOHN.html (March 3, 1998). □

Lynn Beverley Johnston

Award-winning cartoonist Lynn Johnston (born 1947) took over where *Family Circus* and *Blondie* left off with her comic strip, *For Better or for Worse,* which presents a modern-day view of family life. The strip has apparently struck a chord, as it appears in 87 of the 100 largest papers in the United States and is consistently voted one of the top five comics by readers.

Lynn Beverley Johnston was born May 28, 1947, in Collingwood, Ontario, Canada, to Mervyn and Ursula Ridgway. Her father was a jeweler and watchmaker who loved comics and cartoons and instilled in his daughter an enthusiasm for those same things. He also taught her to analyze the value of timing and setting in comedy and cartoons. Johnston's mother was an illustrator and calligrapher whose talents inspired the young Lynn. Johnston's love of drawing and cartooning was a natural outgrowth of her parents' influence, and she developed her skills as a child, using art as an outlet for her emotions.

As a young adult, Johnston enrolled in the Vancouver School of Art. She left before earning a degree, having taken jobs as an animator and illustrator. She moved to Ontario after marrying her first husband, Doug, at the age of 20. In 1968, she found a job at McMaster University in Hamilton, Ontario, as a medical illustrator. The University trained her, and she went through the first year of medical school, taking anatomy courses and dissecting alongside the medical students. She very much enjoyed her job, but her happiness was yet to be complete.

First Child, First Cartoons

In 1972, Johnston's son Aaron was born, but the joyous event was overshadowed by her crumbling marriage. Her husband divorced her and moved back to Vancouver six months after Aaron's birth. Johnston, who had quit her job at McMaster during her pregnancy, began working as a freelancer. Johnston told Rob Colapinto in *Chatelaine*, "My life was in the toilet. It was up and down, dating these duds, having this kid who was a spinning top, and no money."

Somehow, Johnston managed to make enough to pay the mortgage. Her first work was for her obstetrician, who asked her for some cartoons to post on the ceiling above his examining tables. Eventually, she'd drawn enough cartoons for a book. That first book, featuring the 80 cartoons she'd drawn for her obstetrician, *David! We're Pregnant!* was very successful, eventually selling 300,000 copies. She wrote two more books after that, as well: *Hi Mom! Hi Dad!* and *Do They Ever Grow Up?*

See You in the Funny Pages

More success was soon to follow. In 1978, the submissions editors at Universal Press Syndicate had seen her books and contacted her, proposing Johnston produce a four-frame comic. They accepted her initial submissions and gave her a syndicated strip that would appear daily. With their one-year development contract, she was able to create a year's worth of comic strips to be published the following year. At the end of that first year, she was given a 20-year contract.

Just before this career-energizing year with Universal Press Syndicate, Johnston met the man who was to become an important part of her life, and by extension, her comic strip. She had taken young Aaron to look at the planes at a nearby airport, and ran into John Roderick ("Rod") Johnston, a dental school student and amateur pilot. The two married in 1977, and Rod adopted Aaron. Two years later, their daughter Kate was born. About the time Lynn Johnston sent her first proposal to Universal Press Syndicate, Rod Johnston graduated from dental school and the new family moved north to Manitoba.

The Johnstons now live in a two-story log house in Corbeil, Ontario. In her spare time, Lynn Johnston enjoys travel, doll collecting, and playing the accordion, as well as co-piloting and navigating aircraft. Her husband, in addition to his love of being a pilot, is a train enthusiast and has a small model train that runs by Johnston's studio window where she works almost daily to produce *For Better or for Worse*. Their hobbies enrich not only their lives, but Johnston's imagination, and therefore, the comic strip.

Johnston plans her strip week by week by developing a script and story line before she begins drawing. The story line has continued to grow and blossom since its inception. Originally, the characters were based on her own family, with bits and pieces of extended family and friends thrown in.

The Pattersons, the family in *For Better or for Worse,* are Canadian. Elly Patterson, the mother in the comic strip, was initially based on a childhood friend who passed away. Some of Johnston's own traits, including a propensity for trying to "fix" people and situations, crept in as well. John Patterson, the father, is loosely based on Rod Johnston in that both are dentists and pilots. The Patterson's first two children, Michael and Elizabeth, are three years younger than the Johnston children. And, the Johnstons once owned an English Sheepdog named Farley. The characters have all taken on a life of their own, however, and that separate life is very real to their creator.

In *Authors and Artists for Young Adults* Rod Johnston is quoted on the blurring of reality his wife often experiences with her characters. "You can ask her what Elly's wearing today, and she'll tell you. If you ask about their house, she'll describe the sun room at the back and the driveway and all the junk in the garage."

In the fall of 1996, Johnston was diagnosed with torsion dystonia, a neurological disorder, the symptoms of which include involuntary muscular spasms. Johnston told Colapinto that her illness was hereditary and isn't likely to get worse. "Luckily," she said, "my rendition of *The Exorcist*'s demon child mainly happens when I'm lying down." While her illness has not found it's way into the comic strip, many other events and concerns in her life have.

"I use my life and surroundings as a source of inspiration, that's all," she told Colapinto. "[At the same time it is] a fiction where I can undo wrongs that have been inflicted on me or others."

Controversies in the Comic Strip

In 1991, when Johnston wanted another child, but realized that at the age of 45 it wasn't a high probability, she instead created a new baby April in *For Better or For Worse*. She also dealt with the death of the Pattersons' family dog, Farley, much to the chagrin of fans. The strip was true-to-life as ever, though. Farley was old, growing deaf, and slowing down. In the spring of 1995, she had the beloved comic strip pet die of a heart attack after rescuing little April from a river.

Perhaps her most controversial story line in the strip occurred in 1993, when she addressed the subject of homosexuality through the strip's character Michael, the high-school age son, and his best friend, Lawrence Poirier. In the series, Lawrence tells his family that he is gay. His parents don't accept the news and eventually kick him out. The story is based partly on Johnston's brother-in-law, Ralph, who is gay, and partially on a homosexual friend of Johnston's who was murdered. The reports of the murder, Colapinto pointed out, emphasized her friend's homosexuality as if that was all there was to tell about his life and that bothered Johnston immensely. "There were so many other ways to describe him," Johnston commented.

The story line ran from March 26 to April 24, 1993, and stirred up a great deal of controversy among both readers and newspaper editors. While the strip was canceled permanently or temporarily at several newspapers, over 50 more picked up the comic strip as a result of the publicity.

"Peanuts" cartoonist Charles M. Schulz defended his friend's controversial series in *Editor & Publisher:* "I thought it was quite mild and handled with great taste. We should all have the flexibility to experiment once in a while. I'm glad that she tried it."

Johnston told David Astor in *Editor & Publisher,* "People should be judged by how kind and honest and trustworthy they are, not by their sexual orientation." The series itself had more supporters than detractors, however, and in the end it earned Johnston a 1994 Pulitzer Prize nomination.

On September 29, 1997, Johnston left Universal Press Syndicate and began work for United Feature Syndicate Inc., who offered her a seven year contract with a three year option. Johnston's Universal contract would have expired in March 1998. Johnston told *Editor & Publisher,* "More than anything, United's enthusiasm for my work rekindled my enthusiasm for my work. I needed a change. I wanted to be new again."

Sid Goldberg, president of United Media, the conglomerate to which United Feature Syndicate, belongs, shared Johnston's enthusiasm. He told *Editor & Publisher,* "We're absolutely delighted. 'For Better or For Worse' is one of the greatest comics of all time."

In 1986, Johnston became the first woman to win the Reuben Award presented by the National Cartoonists Society for "Outstanding Cartoonist of the Year." In 1992, she was appointed to the Order of Canada. Five years later, she became one of a few living comic creators to be inducted into the International Museum of Cartoon Art's Hall of Fame in Boca Raton, Florida.

Further Reading

Authors & Artists for Young Adults, Volume 12, Gale, 1994.
Contemporary Authors, Volume 110, Gale, 1984.
Chatelaine, March 1997, p. 41.
Editor & Publisher, April 3, 1993, p. 32; April 10, 1993, p. 34; March 11, 1995, p. 40; June 17, 1995, p. 34; September 30, 1995, p. 30; September 13, 1997, p. 36.

Erica Mann Jong

Since publishing her grounding-breaking first novel, *Fear of Flying* in 1973, best-selling American feminist writer Erica Jong (born 1942) has published fiction, collections of poetry, and countless articles about the lives of women, focusing on stories of sex, love, possibilities, and adventure.

Erica Jong grew up on Manhattan's Upper West Side, in a house of artists. Jong's mother was a portrait painter whose parents had immigrated from Odessa in Russia in the early twentieth century. Her father was a songwriter who became a businessman so he could support the family. "We had all the problems of a New York Jewish intellectual family," Jong commented in a *Washington Post* interview in 1997. "It was hard to get a word in at the dinner table. When I first saw Woody Allen's *Hannah and Her Sisters,* I thought he was writing about me."

Always Circling Back to Writing

Jong attended New York's public High School of Music and Art in the 1950s, concentrating on art and writing. She read voraciously, especially Russian novels, and wrote poems, reading them aloud to whomever would listen. As an undergraduate at Barnard College, Jong intended to become a doctor, "to support herself while she wrote on the side, 'like William Carlos Williams'" she noted in a 1997 *New York Times Book Review* article. Instead, she eventually majored in writing and literature, studying with biographer James Clifford and poet Robert Pack, both of whom helped her to think of herself as a writer. "Don't worry, Erica," Jong remembered Pack saying after she expressed worry about her zoology classes, "you're a poet." Exhibiting her typical, lifelong energy for the arts, Jong also edited the Barnard literary magazine and produced poetry programs for the Columbia University campus radio station. In 1963, she graduated from Barnard, Phi Beta Kappa and magna cum laude. She was also briefly married to her first husband, Michael Werthman, around this time.

Jong studied eighteenth-century English literature at Columbia, and received her M.A. in 1965. She married Allan Jong, a child psychiatrist, the following year. Continuing her education as a post-graduate, Jong studied poetry at Columbia's School of the Arts with Stanley Kunitz and Mark

Strand. About this time, she published two books of poetry, *Fruits and Vegetables* and *Half-Lives*. "Welcome Erica Jong," declared James Whitehead in his *Saturday Review* critique of *Fruits and Vegetables,* "and welcome the sensuality she has so carefully worked over in this wonderful book. . . . Clearly she has worked hard to gain this splendid and various and serious comic vision." Immersed in the world of academia, however, Jong continued her studies in the doctoral program at Columbia, intending to become a professor. "I was such an academic," she commented in the *New York Times Book Review.* "I don't recognize myself when I look back. I knew exactly how to write tedious, footnoted tomes, and never suspected I would do anything else."

The *Fear of Flying* Phenomenon

But Jong was always drawn back to creative writing. Half way through the doctoral program, she left to try her hand at writing a novel about a woman's sexual experience. Jong once explained: "Males were writing about the bedroom. Why not women? Why not me? But we were still undiscovered country. No one had written about what goes on in a woman's head with any nakedness." *Fear of Flying* was published in 1973 in hardback to critical acclaim, including praise from such writers as John Updike and Henry Miller, who called it "a female *Tropic of Cancer*." Explicit in its descriptions of sex from a woman's point of view, it tells the story of Isadora Wing, a woman who seeks sexual and emotional fulfillment. "Isadora Wing was a creature of sexual delight, huge appetite, and no guilt whatsoever about

infidelity and promiscuity," declared a reviewer in the *New York Times Book Review.* Erica Jong "was the first woman to write in such a daring and humorous way about sex," Karen Fitzgerald noted in *Ms.* "She popularized the idea of a woman's ultimate sexual fantasy . . . sex for the sake of sex."

Buoyed by initial praise, the book was received as a literary feat. "*Fear of Flying* is essentially a literary novel, a Bildungsroman with strong parallels to the *Odyssey,* Dante's *Inferno,* and the myths of Daedalus and Icarus," judged Emily Toth in the *Dictionary of Literary Biography.* But when the novel came out in paperback and was available to a more general audience, the reception changed to one of scandal. Jong once noted, "There was a media frenzy. . . . Here was this young woman coming out of nowhere to talk about sex . . . the book became (popular) for extraliterary reasons." In the America in the 1970s, *Fear of Flying* gave voice to many readers' experiences and emotions in a way no book had before, and despite the scandal surrounding its publication, *Fear of Flying* became the first of Jong's best-sellers, and perhaps the book for which she is the most well-known. The volume remains a perennial favorite, and has been translated into many languages.

After her initial success as a novelist, Jong returned to her original genre, poetry, and published her third poetry collection, *Loveroot,* in 1975. Two years later, as a sequel to *Fear of Flying,* Jong released *How to Save Your Own Life.* Continuing the story of Isadora Wing and her adventures, the second book did not reach the same acclaim as the first. John Leonard, writing in the *New York Times Book Review,* noted that *How to Save Your Own Life* lacks the "energy and irreverence of *Fear of Flying.* . . . Whereas the author of *Fear of Flying* was looking inside her own head, shuffling her fantasies, and with a manic gusto playing out her hand, the author of *How to Save Your Own Life* is looking over her shoulder, afraid that the critics might be gaining on her." Switching back to poetry, Jong then published two more books of verse, *At the Edge of the Body* (1979), a collection of metaphysical poems, and *Ordinary Miracles* (1983), a book about childbirth based on her own experience with the birth of her daughter Molly in 1979. Jong had divorced Allan Jong by that time, and married Jonathan Fast, a writer, in 1977.

Experimenting with Forms of Writing

Jong never forgot her love of eighteenth-century English literature from her doctoral-candidate days and used her knowledge of the times in her third novel, *Fanny, Being the True History of the Adventures of Fanny Hackabout-Jones* (1980). The volume, according to Jong, was a response to the hypothetical question "What if Tom Jones was a woman?" *Fanny* is "a picaresque of intelligence, buoyant invention and wonderful Rabelaisian energy," opined Michael Malone in the *New York Times Book Review.* The book gained Jong attention as a satirist. According to Toth, "Jong uses the eighteenth-century novel form to satirize both Fanny's century and her own." "At heart," noted *Chicago Tribune* contributor James Goldman, "this novel is a vehicle for Jong's ideas about Woman and Womanhood." Ever prolific and experimental with creative forms, Jong later adapted the novel into a musical produced by the Manhattan Theater Club in New York. *Fanny* was followed by Jong's fourth poetry collection, *Witches*, published in 1981. Paintings by Joseph A. Smith illustrated this book, which was a study of the figure of the witch as a historical reality and archetype.

Soon after her divorce from her third husband, Jonathan Fast, Jong published *Megan's Book of Divorce* (1984), illustrated by Freya Tanz. The book originally had the title *Molly's Book of Divorce*, but Fast threatened court action over the title, stating that it violated a divorce decree stipulating that Jong refrain from using the name of their then-five-year-old daughter, Molly, in her works. The book was published later than expected that year, under a changed title; it was intended both for children and adults. Written from the viewpoint of a child, the volume is about what it is like to be four years old and live through parents' divorce. According to the *New York Times Book Review*, *Megan's Book of Divorce* "smoothly glosses over the considerable pain and trauma small children suffer" in divorce. The book was reissued in 1996, and Molly Jong-Fast later recorded the Audiobook version.

Isadora Wing Lives On

Later in 1984, Jong's fourth novel, *Parachutes and Kisses*, emerged as the third book in the Isadora Wing trilogy. In this volume, Isadora Wing is 39 and has been through three divorces. But in the typical Isadora fashion audiences had come to know and appreciate, she still has a strong appetite for sex and adventure. According to the *New York Times Book Review*, Isadora Wing "discovered men in their mid-20's with energy levels to match or, with luck, to surpass her own. She especially falls for men who have read her books. . . . Miss Wing is one long advertisement for herself." The title of the book, *Parachutes and Kisses*, is taken from a poem by Pablo Neruda, a poet Jong admired and of whom she sometimes wrote. *Parachutes and Kisses* met with some critical success, but, like *How to Save Your Own Life*, it was not met with nearly the same overwhelming success as *Fear of Flying*.

Jong's fifth novel, *Serenissima: A Novel of Venice*, was released in 1987, and, like her earlier novels, quickly became a best-seller. In this volume, beautiful, 40-something movie star Jessica Pruitt travels to Venice to make a movie of Shakespeare's *Merchant of Venice*. She becomes ill and somehow travels back in time to the sixteenth century. Among other adventures, Jessica meets and falls in love with a young William Shakespeare, the English author of the *Merchant of Venice*. In the *New York Times Book Review*, reviewer Michael Malone stated: "As she proved in *Fanny*, . . . Erica Jong can write a historical novel that both honors its tradition with affectionate parody and creates its own full fictional reality."

The novel *Any Woman's Blues* was published three years later and one year after her marriage to attorney Kenneth David Burrows. *Any Woman's Blues* tells the story of Leila Sand, a mother and artist, who succeeds in ending an addictive relationship with a younger man to achieve peace and self-knowledge. The preface of the book reveals that the volume is actually the work of Isadora Wing, the character who had originally captured the imaginations of millions of readers. And "with this news comes lessons," noted Benjamin Demott, reviewer from the jury of the 1989 National Book Awards. "If Leila (of *Any Woman's Blues*) is Isadora 17 years later, it follows (for moralists) that sin and abomination don't pay."

Reflecting on a Life of Writing, and Looking Forward

Two memoirs followed *Any Woman's Blues: The Devil at Large: Erica Jong on Henry Miller* in 1993 and *Fear of Fifty* in 1994. *The Devil at Large* chronicled Jong's long-standing friendship with author Henry Miller which began when Miller sent Jong a letter of praise for *Fear of Flying*. Miller's letter also included discussions about literary censorship and sexual politics. *Fear of Fifty* was lauded as a "funny, blistering mid-life memoir that assesses how far women have—or have not—traveled since the explosion of feminism in the late sixties and early seventies," as noted on the *Erica Jong Web Page*. Lynn Freed, writing in the *Washington Post Book World*, called *Fear of Fifty* "a funny, pungent, and highly entertaining memoir of [Jong's] growing up, her men, her marriages, her motherhood, her writing, her successes and her failures on all fronts. And she has done so . . . with all her customary candor." The novel was a world-wide best-seller.

Jong published her seventh novel, *Inventing Memory: A Novel of Mothers and Daughters,* in 1997. This volume is a four-generational story about a Jewish family in America, and as with many of her other novels, quickly became a best-seller. The novel was met with critical acclaim, especially in terms of the focus on Jewish identity. Many reviewers also praised Jong's heroines as examples of the changing role of women. For Jong, the writing of her books, such as *Inventing Memory*, has been a very personal experience. "It's a very profound self-analysis. It's like meditation," Jong commented to Dana Micucci of the *Chicago Tribune*. "I try to tell a certain truth about the interior of my life and other women's lives. If you're writing the kinds of books I write, you come out a changed person."

Erica Jong has long been known as an energetic supporter of other writers, including her daughter Molly Jong-Fast. An advocate of artists' and authors' rights, she served as President of the Authors' Guild from 1991 until 1993, and she continues to serve on the advisory board as well as the advisory board of the National Writers Union. In 1996, Jong and her fourth husband, Kenneth David Burrows, helped to endow Barnard College's writing program. Jong also maintains a homepage on the World Wide Web that includes Erica Jong's Writers' Forum, a place for anyone to submit writings, on which fellow writers comment. Jong herself is a frequent participant in the discussions about fledgling writers' work.

Further Reading

Contemporary Literary Criticism, Gale, Volume 4, 1975, Volume 6, 1976, Volume 8, 1978, Volume 18, 1981, Volume 85, 1994.

Dictionary of Literary Biography, Gale, Volume 2: *American Novelists since World War II,* 1978, Volume 5: *American Poets since World War II,* 1980, Volume 28: *Twentieth-Century Jewish-American Fiction Writers,* 1984.

Jong, Erica, *Witches,* illustrated by Joseph A. Smith, Abrams, 1981.

Templin, Charlotte, *Feminism and the Politics of Literary Reputation: The Example of Erica Jong,* University of Kansas Press, 1995.

Chicago Tribune, April 25, 1990, sec. 7, pp. 11-13; April 25, 1993, sec. 6, p. 3; July 31, 1994, sec. 14, p. 3; August 18, 1994, sec. 5, pp. 1-2.

Interview, July 1987.

Ms., November 1980; July 1981; July 1986; June 1987.

New York Post, August 7, 1997.

New York Times Book Review, March 20, 1977; August 12, 1973; November 11, 1973; March 5, 1978; August 17, 1980; December 27, 1981; March 8, 1984; July 1, 1984; August 5, 1984; October 10, 1984; March 3, 1985; April 19, 1987; January 28, 1990; June 10, 1992; June 21, 1992; February 14, 1993; July 24, 1994; September 20, 1996; July 20, 1997.

Saturday Review, December 18, 1971; April 30, 1977; August 1980; November 1981; December 1981.

Washington Post Book World, July 31, 1994, p. 5; February 9, 1997.

"About Erica Jong," *Erica Jong Web Page,* http://www.ericajong.com (March 19, 1998).

Percy Lavon Julian

As the inventor of synthetic cortisone, fire-extinguishing Aero-Foam, and drugs to treat glaucoma, Percy Lavon Julian (1899-1975) made life-enhancing and life-saving products more affordable. Despite facing racial prejudice and segregation at nearly every step of his career, Julian became the first African American to be named director of research at a white-owned firm, and he eventually founded his own Julian Laboratories and Julian Research Institute, where he continued as director until his death.

Percy Lavon Julian was born in Montgomery, Alabama, on April 11, 1899; his father was a railway mail clerk, and his grandfather had been a slave. He credited his strict father with providing the discipline and high standards necessary to his success. *Reader's Digest* reported that when as a young boy Julian proudly brought home a math test with a grade of 80, his father responded, "A son of mine must not be satisfied with mediocrity. After this make it 100!"

As a teenager, Julian moved with his family to Greencastle, Indiana, home of DePauw University. All six of the Julian children, including Percy, studied there. Although he was required to enter the university as a "sub-freshman," in 1920 he graduated Phi Beta Kappa, as class valedictorian. He hoped to continue his education and become a research scientist in the field of organic chemistry, but his mentors dissuaded him. Although one of his chemistry professors

made inquiries to graduate schools on Julian's behalf, they all replied negatively. "Discourage your bright young colored lad," one school advised. "We couldn't get him a job when he was done, and it'll only mean frustration. Why don't you find him a teaching job in a Negro college in the South? He doesn't need a Ph.D. for that."

Despite his father's suggestion that he go into medicine, where he could be more independent, Julian persisted in chemistry. He went to Fisk University in Nashville, a school for African Americans, where he taught until 1923. The talent of his students encouraged him to pursue his own dream, and he applied for a research fellowship at Harvard. He earned his Master's degree in a year, finishing in the top group of his class. Had he been white, Harvard would have rewarded him with a post as a teaching assistant, but, as they explained to Julian, they feared that white students from the South would not accept him as a teacher. He stayed at Harvard on minor research fellowships, then returned to the South to teach at all-black schools West Virginia State College and Howard University, where after one year he was appointed head of the chemistry department.

Invented Drug for Glaucoma

Julian's research at Harvard served him well later. He had begun to repeat the experiments of the Austrian chemist Ernst Spth, who had learned to synthesize chemicals such as nicotine and ephedrine—rather than studying these compounds as they appeared in nature, Julian experimented on making these chemicals himself. With the financial backing of a wealthy Harvard classmate, he went to Vienna to study with Spth. Spth welcomed Julian into his household, initiating a father-son relationship and working closely together on synthesizing a variety of naturally occurring chemicals. Through his work with Spth, Julian received his Ph.D. at the University of Vienna in 1931. With his Ph.D., he returned to Howard, and then went again to DePauw, where he both taught and researched, but was denied the title of professor because of his race.

Although he would make one of his most important discoveries at this time, Julian's students remembered him as a committed teacher. Chemist J. Wayne Cole recalled in *Ebony* magazine, "He was obviously involved in his laboratory work but was essentially an instructor—first and foremost. It was the shaping of the student that appealed to him the most. And believe me, he never tolerated laziness or disinterestedness."

While carrying his teaching load, Julian pursued the problem of synthesizing physostigmine, a chemical known to help in the treatment of glaucoma. Despite years of effort, chemists had not been able to make the chemical in the laboratory. With fundraising help from his former professor Dean William Blanchard, Julian's research progressed rapidly and attracted international attention as he reported his findings in the *Journal of the American Chemical Society.* When he finally succeeded, he was universally acknowledged as leader in the field of chemistry. Dean Blanchard moved to appoint Julian as the head of DePauw's chemistry department, to make Julian the first professor of chemistry at any traditionally white university in America, and to make DePauw, as *Reader's Digest* reported, "a chemical Mecca." Blanchard's colleagues refused, calling the appointment "inadvisable."

Soybean Research Enabled More Innovations

With his academic career apparently at a dead-end, Julian received a timely invitation from Chicago's Glidden Company to direct soybean research. While there, he developed a process for isolating and preparing soya protein, which led to a number of important inventions. Among the most highly praised was his "bean soup," commercially known as Aero-Foam, which the Navy used during wartime to put out fires; he also developed a soy protein for coating paper at a fraction of the cost of the previously used milk casein.

Even more important was his discovery of a technique by which he could mass-produce the hormones testosterone and progesterone. Testosterone was then touted as an anti-aging drug for men, while progesterone helped prevent spontaneous abortion in pregnant mothers. While these hormones were available in nature, they were difficult to get, with the supply limited to the brains and spines of cattle that had been slaughtered. Although German chemists had extracted hormones from soybean oil, the technique they used was expensive and could not provide them in commercial quantities. Julian discovered away to make the oil porous, enabling chemists to create mass quantities of the hormones.

The invention of Compound S, however, is considered Julian's biggest scientific achievement. Natural cortisone was a recognized treatment for rheumatoid arthritis and other illnesses causing muscle pain; to get it, however, the bile from nearly 15,000 oxen would be required to treat a single patient for a year. The limited supply of cortisone made it impractical as a treatment option. Again using soybean oils, Julian created a drug—Compound S—that could mimic the effects of natural cortisone in the body. His synthesized cortisone resembled natural cortisone in every way, except that it lacked an oxygen atom in a crucial position. Because the body itself could replace that atom when the drug was used, the therapeutic result was the same. Julian's discovery made the benefits of cortisone economically feasible for all patients.

Racial Discrimination Did Not Deter Him

Julian patented these and nearly 130 other chemical innovations, enabling him to earn make a living much larger than that available to most blacks. In 1950, shortly after he had been named "Chicagoan of the Year" in a *Chicago Sun-Times* poll, Julian moved into the white, middle-class suburb of Oak Park, Illinois. He purchased an ornate, 15-room house and planned extensive landscaping and improvements, but even before he and his family moved in, they received threats and were the victims of an attempted arson. The water commissioner refused to turn on their water, until the family threatened to go to court. Julian was compelled to hire a private guard to patrol the property 24 hours a day. He told *Time,* "We've lived through these things all our lives. As far as the hurt to the spirit goes, we've become accustomed to that."

Julian continued to confront racism in his professional life as well. In 1951, when the Research Corporation of New York City invited Julian, along with 34 other scientists, to hear a talk at the Union League Club of Chicago, the club's manager contacted the organization and informed them that Julian would not be permitted to enter the building. The *New York Times* reported that the club's directors had issued "explicit instructions" forbidding Julian's attendance. By 1956, he had become more actively involved in opposing racial injustice. He became the first black man to chair the General Council of Congregational Christian Churches' Council for Social Action. The council voted to raise litigation funds for a delegate who had been refused admission to an American Legion Post, and, according to the *New York Times,* called on members to "support nonsegregated practices in selling, buying, and leasing property."

In 1967, Julian and North Carolina Mutual Life Insurance Company president Asa Spaulding organized a group of 47 wealthy business persons and professionals to raise money for the NAACP Legal Defense and Educational Fund. The group, calling itself the National Negro Business and Professional Committee for the Legal Defense Fund, announced in the *New York Times,* "This means the Negro millionaire is coming of age and taking a responsible place in the community." The committee planned to raise $1 million a year for cases involving voting rights, school desegregation, and job discrimination. Julian had been connected with the NAACP since 1947, when he won their Spingarn Medal Award.

Founded His Own Laboratories

Julian's financial success also enabled him to leave Glidden in 1953 and found Julian Laboratories. In addition to his suburban Chicago laboratory, he established subsidiaries in Mexico and Guatemala, which studied the possible medical benefits of the Mexican yam. These pharmaceutical businesses were so successful that eventually Julian, approaching his mid-60s, found the pressure to be too much, and in 1961 he sold them for nearly $2.4 million. In 1964, he retired as president from Julian Laboratories, then became director of Julian Research Institute and president of Julian Associates.

In 1974, Julian became increasingly ill, and was diagnosed with cancer of the liver. Despite a lack of energy and a difficult schedule of treatment, Julian continued to work and give speeches. In November of that year, he was honored by Sigma Xi, a society of research scientists, with the Procter Prize for extraordinary service to science and humanity. As *Ebony* reported, in his acceptance speech he discussed the benefits and drawbacks of scientific advancements: "Many of these successes have been abused, he acknowledged, while others have been the subjects of material applications having little implication for the enrichment of the spirit; man has treasured them as weapons or employed them as gadgets." Despite this, he said, he "shares the humanistic faith in an ordered, purposeful and meaningful reality."

Shortly before his death, Julian announced that he was satisfied with his life's work. "I have had one goal in my life," he said, "that of playing some role in making life a little easier for the persons who come after me." He died in April of 1975. In addition to many academic honors and citations he received during his lifetime, he was honored in 1993 by the U.S. Postal Service with a postage stamp in the Black Heritage Series. He was also honored by the city of Oak Park, Illinois, which named a middle school after one of its first residents.

Further Reading

Contemporary Black Biography, vol. 6, Gale, 1994.
Ebony, March 1975.
Jet, June 3, 1985; January 29, 1990.
New York Times, January 18, 1950; July 19, 1951; June 28, 1956; March 20, 1967; April 21, 1975.
Reader's Digest, August, 1946.
Stamps, February 13, 1993.
Time, December 4, 1950.
"Percy Julian School," http://kato.TheRamp.net/julian/bio.html (March 20, 1998).

K

Laurent Kabila

Laurent Kabila (born 1939) is the president of the central African nation called Democratic Republic of Congo (formerly Zaire).

Few figures emerge on the world stage as suddenly as Laurent Kabila did in the last months of 1996. It is a measure of the speed with which he made his appearance that there were literally hundreds of magazine and newspaper articles about him in the United States and Britain during the first half of 1997—but almost no pieces whatever for the five years preceding that time. In October of 1996, he entered the limelight as the leader of Zairian forces rising up against the corrupted regime of dictator Mobutu Sese Seko. Less than six months later, troops under his command took control of the capital, Kinshasa, and Kabila became the leader of the country, now renamed Democratic Republic of Congo. With its location at the center of Africa, its physical size (as large as Western Europe), and its troubled past, Congo occupies a strategic position in Africa, and suddenly leaders all over the world were asking "Who is Laurent Kabila?" The answer to that question lies beneath layers of mystery, and indeed analysts are far from agreement as to who he is or what he intends for his country's future.

Kabila was born in 1939, in Shaba Province, part of the region then called Belgian Congo. This was the same land described memorably by Joseph Conrad in his novel *Heart of Darkness* (1902), a vast stretch of jungles, rivers, and mountains nearly one million square miles in area. Belgian rule in the Congo became legendary for its cruelty, but by the time Kabila reached maturity, there were few colonial empires left in Africa. One legacy of the Belgians was the French language; therefore when it came time for Kabila to receive a university education, he went to France and studied political philosophy.

Kabila Entered Politics

By the time Kabila returned home, the Congo was in a state of turmoil. It had gained its independence from Belgium in 1960, but that was far from the end of the new nation's troubles; in fact, those had only really begun. By now the old struggle of the European colonial empires was an artifact of history, and the new battle over Africa was the Cold War conflict between the Soviet Union and the United States. The Soviets supported Marxist Prime Minister Patrice Lumumba, and so did Kabila, who became a pro-Lumumba member of the North Katanga Assembly, a provincial legislature. The United States, on the other hand, supported Lumumba's chief opposition, an army officer named Joseph Dsir Mobutu.

A bloody civil war ensued, and in 1961, Mobutu allegedly had Lumumba killed. Kabila fled to the Ruzizi lowlands, and tried to wage war against the government from there, but was defeated. In 1963, he formed the People's Revolutionary Party, and set up operations on Lake Tanganyika, at the country's eastern edge. Two years later, he was joined by one of the twentieth century's most prominent revolutionary leaders, a man who in 1959 had helped Fidel Castro take power in Cuba, Ernesto "Che" Guevara. Guevara kept a diary during the six months of 1965 that he spent in Africa, released in English as *Bolivian Diary [of] Ernesto "Che" Guevara* (1968). In the volume, he complained bitterly about Kabila's lack of commitment, and his penchant for spending time away from the front, "in the best hotels, issuing communiques and drinking Scotch in the

222

cally, and did mining. Then they smuggled the ivory and diamonds and gold through Burundi."

Kabila Redefines Position as Revolutionary Leader

Burundi was one of three small countries on Zaire's eastern border, and events in the other two nations—Uganda and Rwanda—led to a dramatic change in fortunes for Kabila, who all but disappeared from view by 1988. Tensions began to mount between Rwanda's two main ethnic groups, the Hutus and the Tutsis, in the late 1980s and early 1990s, and because the Hutus were in power, Tutsi refugees were spread throughout Uganda and Zaire. Kabila moved to Uganda in the early 1990s, and became associated with a group of Tutsis who helped a rebel leader named Yoweri Museveni take power in that country. When civil war broke out in Rwanda in 1994 following massacres of Tutsis by Hutus, two things happened: Museveni's Tutsi associate Paul Kagame became the vice president and de facto leader of Rwanda, while fleeing Hutus flooded Zaire.

As the Rwandan civil war spread over into Zaire, Mobutu attempted to conduct a campaign of ethnic cleansing against his country's Tutsi minority. The latter, supported by Kagame in their homeland, began an uprising, and as they took town after town, they were joined by Zairians eager to throw off Mobutu's rule. By October of 1996, Kabila emerged as the leader of the group, which he called the "Alliance of Democratic Forces for the Liberation of Congo-Zaire."

Journalists described Kabila, a large man with a bald head, as jovial in manner, though this was certainly no cause for relief, since Uganda's notorious Idi Amin had been described the same way 25 years before. And it did not help that he refused to speak much about his past: "When he is asked about himself or his family," the *New York Times* reported on April 1, 1997, "Mr. Kabila—a stout man with an easy laugh—invariably changes the subject with a deep chuckle and a wave of the hand." Other journalists, most notably Philip Gourevich of the *New Yorker,* were apt to give Kabila the benefit of a doubt and so too were representatives of the United Nations, the United States, and the continent's most noted political leader, Nelson Mandela of South Africa.

Mobutu was out of power by May of 1997—he died in September of that year, ironically in the same week as Princess Diana and Mother Teresa—and Kabila was the new president. Kabila assumed leadership of the country, which he renamed the Democratic Republic of Congo, on May 29, 1997, and the months that followed did not appear to confirm the high hopes many had expressed for the nation's future. Kabila's troops engaged alternately in lawless robbery, or in strict enforcement of repressive social codes, such as a ban on miniskirts. His foreign minister justified clampdowns on demonstrations, claiming they were unnecessary. Kabila stalled United Nations teams attempting to investigate allegations regarding massacres of Hutus, and he had the chief opposition leader, Etienne Tshisekedi, jailed briefly.

company of beautiful women." Though admitting that Kabila was young (26 years old) and therefore capable of change, Guevara wrote, "for now, I am willing to express serious doubts, which will only be published many years hence, that he will be able to overcome his defects."

By the end of 1965, it became clear that Mobutu was about to win the war, so Guevara left in disgust. In 1966, Mobutu took power and declared himself head of the nation, which he renamed Zaire in 1971. He also gave himself a new name, the abbreviated form of which was Mobutu Sese Seko, which in full meant something like "the rooster who leaves no hens alone." Zaire came under Mobutu's domination, and he made himself one of the world's richest men while keeping his people in extreme poverty.

Kabila Lived in Exile

Kabila's life during the three decades between the mid-1960s and the mid-1990s are somewhat of a mystery. In the early 1970s, his People's Revolutionary Party established a "liberated zone" in Kivu Province, and spent the next 20 years in periodic fighting with the government. Kabila himself went into exile in neighboring Tanzania in 1977, and from there he continued to lead guerrilla attacks against the increasingly repressive and corrupt Mobutu regime. While Mobutu stole both from his people and the Western nations who gave him financial aid, Kabila engaged in some questionable dealings himself, not the least of which was the kidnapping of hostages—including some Americans. In addition, Congo expert Gerard Prunier told *ABC News,* "[Kabila] and his supporters killed elephants, quite ecologi-

The people of Congo had pinned their hopes on Kabila, who used the same middle name as Mobutu once had: Dsir, which means "the one hoped for" in French. But by September 18, 1997, the *Christian Science Monitor* was reporting that hopes for genuine change were ebbing. People even claimed nostalgia for the Mobutu era, since as one Zairian said, the soldiers under Mobutu could be counted on to spare people who bribed them—unlike the loose cannons of the Kabila regime.

Yet there was still hope to be found in the person of Kabila's backer and mentor, Museveni. The latter has enacted democratic and pro-market reforms in Uganda, exerts enormous sway throughout Africa, and has urged a pro-Western stance on the part of his allies. This may be a pragmatic response to a situation in which there is little choice, as the *New Republic* observed in a June 16, 1997, assessment of the new Kabila regime entitled "The End and the Beginning": with the Cold War over, Africa is no longer a staging ground for superpower conflict, and African leaders cannot count on Western dollars to prop up their regimes. Observers who wish for genuine positive change in the country formerly known as Zaire, a place rich in natural resources and poor in its history of freedom, can only hope that the West will maintain a policy of constructive engagement with Kabila and the other leaders of the Democratic Republic of Congo.

Further Reading

Hansen, Carlos P. and Andrew Sinclair, translators, *Bolivian Diary [of] Ernesto "Che" Guevara,* introduced by Fidel Castro, J. Cape (London), 1968.

Waters, Mary-Alice, translator, *The Bolivian Diary of Ernesto Che Guevara,* Pathfinder (New York), 1994.

Christian Science Monitor, November 25, 1996, p. 7; March 31, 1997, p. 6; May 30, 1997, p. 6; September 18, 1997, p. 8.

National Review, June 16, 1997, p. 16.

New Republic, June 16, 1997, pp. 7, 15-18.

Newsweek, December 15, 1997, p. 37-39.

New Yorker, May 19, 1997, pp. 7-8; June 2, 1997, pp. 50-53.

New York Times, April 1, 1997, p. A1; June 28, 1997, p. A3; July 8, 1997, p. A3; July 13, 1997, section 1, p. 9.

Time, May 12, 1997, pp. 52-55.

World Press Review, June 1997, p. 15.

"Kabila Was Addicted to Women and Drink," *Sunday Times on the Web,* http://lacnet.org/suntimes (November 26, 1997).

"Laurent Kabila, President of the Democratic Republic of Congo," *ABC News,* http://www.abcnews.com (November 26, 1997).

"President Laurent Kabila of the Democratic Republic of Congo," *MBendi: Information for Africa,* http://mbendi.co.za (November 24, 1997). □

Wilhelm Keitel

German Field Marshal General Wilhelm Keitel (1882-1946), Adolf Hitler's senior military advisor during World War II, was the individual who personally conducted the armistice agreement with the French. He was eventually convicted for crimes against humanity at the Nuremberg Trials and subsequently hung as a war criminal in late 1946.

Wilhelm Bodewin Johann Gustave Keitel was born on September 22, 1882 in the village of Helmschrode, which was located in Harz Mountains portion of the Braunschweig province of Germany. He was born into a family with a long and rich military history. In his early years, Keitel wasn't much of a student, but he did enjoy hunting and farming. He joined the German army in 1901 as a member of the artillery corps. Gradually, he rose through the ranks of the officers, and was generally considered to be a good soldier. A year after he joined the army, he was made a second lieutenant. It would be another eight years before he received a promotion to the rank of first lieutenant. Keitel married Lisa Fontaine, the daughter of a well-to-do brewer on April 18, 1909. In *Memoirs of Field-Marshal Keitel,* Walter Gorlitz, editor, noted that "she [Keitel's wife] was probably the stronger and certainly the more ambitious partner of the marriage." Gorlitz added that Keitel "was just an average officer, whose only secret ambition was to be a farmer." The Keitels had three sons and two daughters.

During World War I, Keitel served as an artillery and General Staff Officer in the Ministry of War. By this time, he had been promoted to a captain. He was severely wounded during the war, but managed to successfully recover from his injuries. Family papers shed light on Keitel's views regarding the first world war. According to Gorlitz, "he was

duty-bound to hope piously for a German victory, but at the same time deep down there was a dejected conviction that, in fact, all they could do now was grimly hold on." Gorlitz elaborated further and commented "How similar was his attitude to the Second World War!" Eventually, Keitel was well and able enough to join the Freikorps in 1919 after the war had ended and Germany was defeated.

Rising Through the Ranks

In 1920, Keitel was named as the instructor of the Reichswehr Cavalry School. He held this post for the next two years. A promotion to the rank of major, in 1923, led to his tenure at the Reichswehr Ministry. Keitel was a member of the Reichswehr Ministry from 1925 to 1927. Two years later, he was made a lieutenant colonel. Also in 1929, Keitel was named as head of the Army Organization Department. He held this post for the next five years.

The year 1931 saw Keitel promoted again. This time, he had achieved the rank of colonel. It was around this time that Keitel first met Adolf Hitler, although he later claimed they didn't meet until 1938. As noted by Gorlitz, in a family letter dated July 1933, Keitel's wife shared her husband's impressions of Hitler. She wrote, "He has spoken at length with Hitler, he has been up to his cottage, and is full of enthusiasm about him. His eyes were fabulous, and how the man could speak!"

Keitel's next promotion was to the rank of major general. This promotion occurred in 1934. Also around this time, Keitel was made responsible for commanding the 4th Infantry Division, which had its headquarters in Bremen.

Hitler's Chief of Staff

Keitel was named Chief of the Wehrmacht Armed Forces Office of the Ministry of War in late 1935. This department, which Keitel was in charge of for the next three years, served to form the basis for the creation of the Wehrmacht High Command. As a result of this, Keitel gained access to Hitler as a member of Hitler's inner circle. During his tenure as the head of the Wehrmacht Armed Forces Office of the Ministry of War, Keitel was promoted to the rank of artillery general.

On February 4, 1938, Keitel was named as the Chief of Staff of the Supreme Command of the Armed Forces. He succeeded General Werner von Blomberg, although Keitel's new position, unlike the position held by von Blomberg, was mostly administrative and lacked genuine authority. In this role as the German government's most senior ranking military official, Keitel gained increased access to Hitler as a member of the Cabinet for Defense of the Reich. Keitel then became Hitler's militaristic chief of staff. Keitel's unwavering loyalty to the Reich was rewarded with a promotion to the rank of colonel general on November 10, 1938.

"Lakaitel"

As Hitler's favorite general, Keitel not only earned the trust and respect of the Führer [Hitler], but he also earned the intense distrust and abhorrence of the rest of the General Staff who derided and dismissed Keitel as a "lakaitel,"

which was an army term for lackey. It was Keitel who had coined the phrase the "greatest military commander-in-chief of all time" in regards to Hitler and his so-called military genius.

While Keitel had a hand in all of the strategic military plans and policies in Germany's Third Reich, he was limited in his authority to influence them because he lacked the authority to command. Thus, his post was mostly of a ministerial function, although he was able to implement the decrees by virtue of his position in the government and by the necessity of having his signature on the commands issued by the National Socialist (Nazi) government in Germany.

Keitel was responsible for not only signing and authorizing various Nazi edicts, but he was also in charge of implementing them as well. He was responsible for enforcing Hitler's order to execute large numbers of the Polish population, and he was also responsible for rationalizing the work of the Einstazgruppen Special Action SS Groups, who systematically mass executed the Russian civilian population. Keitel also implemented the "terror fliers policy" which authorized shooting down American and English fighter planes and executing the crews. He was also responsible for enforcing the "Nacht und Nebel" (Night and Fog) decrees which permitted the covert arrest of any person who was thought of as posing a threat to the national security of Germany, including military POWs, who were executed without a trial or court martial. (These "Night and Fog" decrees had a major negative impact on his defense during the Nuremberg Trials.)

His favored status in Hitler's cabinet was evidenced by the fact that Keitel joined the Führer on a number of Hitler's most important missions in 1938, including a trip to Rome, the Munich Conference, and a meeting with the English Prime Minister Neville Chamberlain. As a result, historians have noted that Keitel became a rather mindless and obedient servant of the Führer. Keitel also sought to suppress others who dissented and objected to Hitler's policies and practices in the General Staff. This led not only to a severe breakdown in the communication between the members of the General Staff, but also a disintegration of the decision-making process.

Keitel was partly responsible for the German army smashing through the Maginot Line, because he had helped to persuade Hitler to concentrate the efforts of the army on the Western Front. He also tried, unsuccessfully, to persuade Hitler not to launch an aerial assault on Britain during the summer of 1940.

The crowning glory of Keitel's military career occurred in June, 1940 when France was defeated by the Germans. A tremendous indication of his closeness to the Führer was evidenced in the fact that Keitel was the individual who was allowed to read the armistice agreement which highlighted the capitulation of the nation of France to the Germans and detailed the terms for peace. This historic moment took place in a railway car on the edge of the Compiegne Forest and served as a rather potent indicator of the highly venerated status of Keitel as not only the spokesperson on all militaristic matters, but as a trusted and honored advisor of Hitler.

As a result of the capitulation of France, Keitel was promoted to the rank of Field Marshal in July, 1940. In October of that same year, Keitel assumed the control of the Axis-African command. The following year saw him take command of the Russian Front as well.

His role as the Chief of Staff of the Supreme Command of the Armed Forces and as an intermediary between the Wehrmacht and the German government, gave Keitel the authority to be the person who signed the unconditional surrender of Germany on May 8, 1945. This was also furthered by the fact that Hitler had committed suicide not long before the capitulation of Germany at the hands of the Allied powers.

Keitel was arrested five days after he signed the unconditional surrender of Germany. In his memoirs, he described himself in a preliminary interrogation in August 1945: "At the bottom of my heart I was a loyal shield-bearer for Adolf Hitler." Gorlitz added, "For Keitel, Hitler—both the man and the Führer—was always an enigma."

Keitel was imprisoned before being brought before the International Military Tribunal at Nuremberg in 1946. He was found guilty of crimes against humanity and was charged with being directly responsible for the planning of war at the highest levels. Keitel maintained that he was only following orders and requested to be shot as a soldier. His request was denied and he was hung at Nuremberg Prison on October 16, 1946.

Further Reading

Encyclopedia of the Third Reich, Macmillan, 1991, p. 493.
Harper Encyclopedia of Military Biographies, Harper Collins, 1992, p. 397.
Keitel, Wilhelm, *Memoirs of Field Marshal Keitel,* edited by Walter Gorlitz and translated from German by David Irving, William Kimber and Company, Limited, 1966.
"Nuremberg Trials," http://www.mtsu.edu/baustin/trials3.html (March 23, 1998).

Thomas Keneally

Thomas Keneally (born 1935) is an Australian novelist and nonfiction writer who gained worldwide attention when his best-known work, the Holocaust novel *Schindler's List,* was adapted into an Academy Award-winning motion picture in 1993.

Keneally was born in Sydney, Australia, in 1935. The son of Roman Catholic parents of Irish descent, he was educated at St. Patrick's College in Strathfield, New South Wales, and later studied for the priesthood from 1953 to 1960. While Keneally left the seminary before being ordained, he later drew on his experiences as a seminarian in his early novels *The Place at Whitton* (1964) and *Three Cheers for the Paraclete* (1968). He taught high school in Sydney during the early 1960s, and from 1968 to 1970 served as a lecturer in drama at the University of New

England in New South Wales. During this time Keneally gained recognition as a historical novelist with the publication of *Bring Larks and Heroes* (1967), a consideration of Australia's early history as an English penal colony.

Early Novels

Keneally's early works tend to reflect his interests in spiritual matters and contemporary social issues. In the allegorical novel *A Dutiful Daughter* (1971), which Garry Wills of the *New York Times Book Review* called "an extraordinary book in every way," Keneally drew a nightmarish portrait of a close-knit family coping with the sudden and incomprehensible transformation of the parents into creatures half-cow and half-human. While the college-age son begins to turn away from his extraordinary family situation, his sister becomes increasingly defined by it. Angela Carter, in the *New York Times Book Review,* described the novel as a "spirited expressionist performance" that displayed "a diabolical ingenuity." Muriel Haynes, in the *Saturday Review* found the work "modeled loosely on the Christian legend of redemption" and judged it "the boldest expression yet of [Keneally's] war against moribund doctrine and its crippling of living religious faith."

Racism and violence, two social issues that figure prominently in many of Keneally's works, are closely examined in his acclaimed early work *The Chant of Jimmie Blacksmith* (1972). In the novel Keneally depicted an incident that occurred in New South Wales in 1900 in which a mixed-race aborigine exploded into a murderous rage following persistent racist treatment by white settlers. Re-

viewer Anthony Thwaite wrote in the *New York Times Book Review* that the novel blends "history, psychological insight and an epic adventure with great skill. *The Chant of Jimmie Blacksmith* echoes in the head long after it has been put down." The novel, which is based on contemporary newspaper accounts of the tragedy, is also considered an early expression of Keneally's antiassimilationist views of race relations. It won the Heinemann Award of the Royal Society of Literature in 1973.

With Keneally's next work, *Blood Red, Sister Rose: A Novel of the Maid of Orleans* (1974), he turned from writing local history to world history and introduced a recurring interest in warfare into his oeuvre. Keneally's portrait of Joan of Arc in *Blood Red, Sister Rose* is considered objective and human, emphasizing her everyday qualities within the uncommon context of fifteenth-century warfare. A. G. Mojtabai, in the *New York Times Book Review,* commented on Keneally's unusual choice in retelling such a well-known story. According to Mojtabai, "We all know the story, the big scenes: the Voices, the Dauphin's court, Orleans, Rheims, Rouen, the pyre.... It would seem foolhardy to attempt to revive these worn tales again. Yet Australian novelist Thomas Keneally has done it and carried it off with aplomb. St. Joan lives again, robustly, in a way we have not known her before." Comparing Keneally's portrait of Joan with the religious presentation of her as saintly and with Bernard Shaw's humanizing dramatic rendering as earthy and pragmatic, Melvin Maddocks noted in *Time* that Keneally "thoughtfully reconstructs a whole Joan, less spectacular than the first two but decidedly more convincing and perhaps, at last, more moving."

Novels of the Late 1970s

A Victim of the Aurora (1977) combines the adventure of Antarctic exploration with the intrigue of a classic murder mystery. In a favorable review of the novel in the *Spectator,* Peter Ackroyd noted that Keneally "astutely aligns the imaginative content of historical fiction with the pert structure of the detective thriller, and by conflating them creates a new thing." Praising *A Victim of the Aurora* in the *Listener* Neil Hepburn located the importance of the novel in "Keneally's clear-sighted view of how vulnerable conventional men are to the poisoned authority of great leaders, and of how calmly the best of us can be led to sanction abominations in the name of the common good."

The setting of *Passenger,* another of Keneally's novels of the late 1970s, is perhaps "the most exotic," according to Blake Morrison in the *New Statesman.* The narrator of the novel is the unborn child of a historical novelist who is researching an eighteenth-century convict ancestor who was transported to Australia from Ireland. Morrison characterized the device as "the Romantic idea of insightful childhood pushed one step further—the wise womb," and Hermione Lee, writing in the *Observer,* called the novel "a witty variant on the picaresque tradition."

Historical War Novels

In addition to the balanced portrait of Joan of Arc, *Blood Red, Sister Rose* drew critical praise for its realistic depiction of the brutality of medieval warfare. In a number of subsequent works Keneally approached the subject of war from varying perspectives, including the thoughts of a World War I peace negotiator in *Gossip from the Forest* (1975), the activities of a doctor involved with partisans during World War II in *Season in Purgatory* (1977), and the preparations of American Civil War soldiers for battle in *Confederates* (1979). *The Cut-Rate Kingdom* (1980), set in Canberra in 1942, considers the moral character of military and political leaders in wartime Australia.

In *Gossip from the Forest,* Keneally offered a concentrated fictional presentation of the peace talks that took place in the forest of Compiegne in November 1918, focusing on the highest-ranking German negotiator, Mattias Erzberger, a liberal pacifist. According to the *New York Times Book Review'* s Paul Fussell, *Gossip from the Forest* "is a study of the profoundly civilian and pacific sensibility beleaguered by crude power.... it is absorbing, and as history it achieves the kind of significance earned only by sympathy acting on deep knowledge." Robert E. McDowell in *World Literature Today* concluded that "with *Gossip from the Forest* Keneally has succeeded better than in any of his previous books in lighting the lives of historical figures and in convincing us that people are really the events of history."

Confederates is counted among Keneally's most ambitious historical undertakings in its faithful representation of the military life of a band of southern soldiers preparing for the Second Battle of Antietam in the summer of 1862. Covering a range of characters, including slaves, farmers, and aristocrats, the novel, in the opinion of Jeffrey Burke of the *New York Times Book Review,* "reaffirms Mr. Keneally's mastery of narrative voice."

Schindler's List

While the film version of *Schindler's List,* brought world fame to Keneally, the work had already brought literary fame—as well as controversy—when it won the Booker McConnell fiction prize in 1982. Like many of Keneally's works, the novel is based on historical events during wartime, and in the case of *Schindler's List,* reflects the testimony of surviving participants who were interviewed by Keneally for the book; some critics argued that for that reason it should be excluded from the fiction category. Published in England as *Schindler's Ark,* the work resulted from Keneally's chance encounter with Leopold Pfefferberg, one of the 1,300 Jewish factory workers saved by Schindler. Keneally was shopping for a new briefcase when he entered a Los Angeles store owned by Pfefferberg, who related the Schindler story to Keneally and subsequently assisted him in interviewing dozens of other survivors of the group now known as *Schindlerjuden.* Like Keneally's earlier portraits of historical individuals, the depiction of Oskar Schindler is considered complex and human. An opportunistic businessman who prospered during the war, Schindler owned an armaments factory that supplied war materials to the German army and drew laborers from nearby concentration camps. By convincing Nazi authorities—through "[b]ribes and bluff, cognac and con-man effrontery," according to Peter Kemp in the *Listener*—to allow him to establish his own labor camp he saved the lives of his workers. According to A. N. Wilson in *Encounter*, Schindler "was a swindler, a drunkard, and a womaniser. And yet, had he not been these things, he would not have been able to rescue hundreds of Jews from the concentration camps." Similarly, Lorna Sage noted in the *Observer* that as "Keneally presents him in the novel Schindler becomes, by almost imperceptible stages, a three-dimensional 'good' man, at once alive and in love with life, without ever seeming 'fated' or heroic or unnatural." In a 1995 interview with Sybil Steinberg of *Publishers Weekly*, Keneally himself commented: "I was convinced of the moral force of the story. . . . Stories of fallen people who stand out against the conditions that their betters succumb to are always fascinating. It was one of those times in history when saints are no good to you and only scoundrels who are pragmatic can save souls."

After the success of *Schindler's List* Keneally focused on another aspect of Holocaust subject matter in his 1985 novel *A Family Madness*. Based on the mass suicide of a family of five in suburban Sydney in July 1984, the novel traces the legacy of guilt that impairs the lives of Nazi collaborators and their children. John Sutherland, comparing the novel to *Schindler's List* in the *London Review of Books*, proclaimed *A Family Madness* "better than its applauded predecessor." Discussing *A Family Madness* in *Contemporary Novelists*, Keneally commented that the novel's contemporary setting is "significant. . . . I believe the historic phase is nearly over for me and was merely a preparation for the understanding of the present."

Later Works

Keneally turned to contemporary warfare with his 1989 novel *To Asmara: A Novel of Africa*, a fictional consideration of civil strife in Ethiopia during the 1980s. The novel depicts the struggle of the Eritrean Peoples Liberation Front to overcome Ethiopian domination as witnessed by the narrator, an Australian journalist. In a favorable assessment in the *New York Times Book Review*, Robert Stone asserted that "Not since *For Whom the Bell Tolls* has a book of such sophistication, the work of a major international novelist, spoken out so unambiguously on behalf of an armed struggle."

In a departure from works based in fact and drawing broad portraits of war and its impact on individual lives, Keneally's 1991 novel *Flying Hero Class* confines its scope to events taking place on an airplane hijacked en route from Frankfurt to New York. *Woman of the Inner Sea* (1992) returns to fact-based fiction with its portrayal of a woman who seeks to redefine herself in the Australian outback after losing her husband to another woman and her children in a fire. The 1995 novel *A River Town* draws on the experiences of Keneally's Irish ancestors in portraying the difficulties encountered by turn-of-the-century Irish immigrants to Australia. The novel's protagonist, the grocer Tim Shea, who extends generous credit to his neighbors and ends up bankrupt, is based on Keneally's grandfather, Tim Keneally, who settled in Kempsey, New South Wales. Writer Brian

Bethune in *Maclean's* noted that "Shea's self-destructive nobility is at times maddening, yet Keneally's nuanced portrayal ultimately renders the character endearing." According to David Willis McCullough in the *New York Times Book Review*, *River Town* is a "finely told novel. . . . fired with the passion and hidden poetry that only a sure and experienced novelist can bring to fiction."

Career in the 1990s

Keneally's reputation rests primarily on his prolific fiction output, yet he has also written a number of nonfiction works on Australia as well as the travel books *Now and in Time to Be: Ireland and the Irish* (1992) and *The Place Where Souls Are Born: A Journey into the Southwest* (1992).

Keneally lived in the United States and taught at the University of California at Irvine during the early 1990s. An advocate of Australian separation from the British Commonwealth, he founded and chaired the Australian Republic Movement, a political group devoted to that end. During the mid-1990s he was researching the lives of escaped Australian transportees who fled to the United States and established new lives. He was also planning a sequel to *A River Town* and hoped eventually to trace the Shea family through the World War I era. Assessing Keneally's strengths in *Publisher's Weekly*, Steinberg wrote: "In ancient times, Tom Keneally would have been a Celtic bard, such is his gift for wielding narrative and anecdote, witty quip and resonant observation. While his books never scant on storytelling brio, however, his work also reflects a concern for life's ambiguous challenges, glancing ironies and opportunities for moral behavior."

Further Reading

Brown, Susan Windisch, ed.,*Contemporary Novelists,* 6th ed., St. James Press, 1997.
Contemporary Authors, New Revision Series, Volume 50, Gale Research, 1996.
Encounter, February, 1983, pp. 65-71.
Listener, September 22, 1977, pp. 382-83; October 14, 1982, p. 31.
London Review of Books, November 7, 1985, pp. 24-6.
Maclean's, August 28, 1995, p. 50.
New Statesman, January 19, 1979, p. 88.
New York Times Book Review, September 12, 1971, p. 53; January 16, 1972, p. 20; August 27, 1972, pp. 3, 24; February 9, 1975, p. 7; April 11, 1976, p. 8; October 5, 1980, pp. 3, 28; October 1, 1989, pp. 1, 42; May 14, 1995, p. 12.
Observer, January 21, 1979, p. 35; October 17, 1982, p. 33.
Publishers Weekly, April 3, 1995, p. 40.
Saturday Review, July 24, 1971, p. 52.
Spectator, September 3, 1977, pp. 19-20.
Time, February 10, 1975, p. 76.
World Literature Today, winter, 1977, pp. 157-58.

Nannerl Overholser Keohane

Nannerl Overholser Keohane (born 1940), a professor of political science, is the first woman to become the president of both a U.S. women's college, Wellesley, and a major research university, Duke.

Dr. Nannerl Overholser Keohane has broken the glass ceiling in the academic world by becoming the first contemporary woman to become the president of both a women's college, Wellesley, and a major research university, Duke. In 1992, when she was named Duke's eighth president, she became the second woman ever in the United States, after Hannah Gray of the University of Chicago, to take the helm of a prominent research university. She has not, however, rested on her laurels, as she continues to work to improve educational opportunities not only for the students at Duke, but also for women and minorities throughout the country.

Early Influences

Keohane was born in Blytheville, Arkansas, the daughter of James Olverholser, a Presbyterian minister, and Grace Olverholser White, a high school and college English teacher. The family later moved to Texas and then to South Carolina. She graduated Phi Beta Kappa with honors in political science from Wellesley College in 1961, where she had been a Durant Scholar. During the two years following her graduation, Keohane was awarded a Marshall scholarship to travel to England and attend St. Anne's College at Oxford University. There she earned a B.A.-M.A. degree with first class honors in philosophy, politics, and economics. Returning to the United States, she completed her Ph.D. at Yale University on a Sterling fellowship in 1967, earning her doctorate in political science.

After completing her education, Keohane was appointed a lecturer and assistant professor at Swarthmore College in Pennsylvania from 1967-73. Between 1970 and 1972 she was also a visiting lecturer at the University of Pennsylvania. She left Swarthmore in 1973 to become a professor at Stanford University. During her tenure there, she was chair of the faculty senate and won the Gores Award for Excellence in Teaching. While at Stanford, Keohane served as associate editor of *Signs: Journal of Women in Culture and Society*, an interdisciplinary journal that publishes articles about feminism and women's studies. In 1970, while at Swarthmore, Keohane married a fellow political science professor, Robert Owen Keohane. The marriage was her second, and the couple went on to have four children. Robert Keohane would eventually become the James B. Duke Professor of political science and professor in the Nicholas School of Environment at Duke University.

Keohane left Stanford University in 1981 to serve both as president of Wellesley College and as a professor of political science, positions she held until 1993 when she assumed her responsibilities as the president of Duke University. In her inaugural address after taking the helm at Duke, Keohane spoke optimistically of the responsibilities of a research university. "It is surely not beyond our powers," she said "to rebuild an intellectual community where scholars of all ages share in the partnership of learning, and feel a responsibility to one another in doing so."

Accolades along the Way

Keohane has been recognized for her numerous contribution to the educational sphere over her three decades of service. She has received honorary degrees from over ten schools, including Harvard University, Dartmouth College, and Smith College. She has been a fellow for the Center for Advanced Study in the Behavioral Sciences and for the American Academy of Arts and Sciences, and won Yale University's Wilbur Cross Medal. In 1995 she was inducted into the National Women's Hall of Fame, a national membership organization founded in 1969 that honors and celebrates the achievement of American women. The organization cited Keohane's distinction of being the first contemporary woman as president of Wellesley College and Duke University, as well as her contributions to increasing minority student enrollment and improving faculty diversity at Duke as their reasons for honoring her.

Publications

Keohane is the author *Philosophy and the State in France: The Renaissance to the Enlightenment* (Princeton University Press, 1980) and the co-author of *Feminist Theory: A Critique of Ideology* (University of Chicago Press, 1982). Her articles have appeared in a wide variety of publications, including *Political Theory, Journal of Politics,* and *College Board Review,* as well as in several other books. Several of her speeches were compiled and published in book form as *A Community Worthy of the Name* (1995).

Promoting Educational Equity

In an article that Keohane wrote for Duke University's Community Service Center Newsletter, she stated that "beyond self-interest, we have the obligation to contribute to the larger community in which we reside." As an educator, she has lived by those words, consistently striving to make the United States a more equitable place for all of its citizens, especially when it comes to educational opportunities. Likewise, as president of Duke University, Keohane has taken a strong stance on improving race relations on the campus. In the spring of 1997, Duke found itself embroiled in racial controversy. First there had been two student publications which had published stories that many people considered racist. And not long after that, Duke police arrested a male African American student who was mistakenly identified as a burglar. In August of 1997, after surveying 56,000 students, the *Princeton Review* ranked Duke ninth worst among universities in interaction between students of diverse backgrounds. Keohane immediately sought a remedy to the problem, and in fact, personally apologized to the young man who had been unjustly arrested.

As she addressed the incoming freshmen that fall, Keohane challenged the new students to consider race on a day-to-day basis. "you have chosen a university in the American South, with a legacy of slavery followed by decades of rigid segregation. . . . So race is relevant here in ways that it may not have seemed relevant in the societies from which some of you have come. . . . And one of the ways it is relevant is in daily interactions and experiences in the lives of every one of you." She went on to tell her audience that this was good news, "because race is so clearly a powerful factor in this historically Southern region, it is harder to ignore it than it is in some other places. This makes it, paradoxically, perhaps easier to do something significant about making connections among people of different races and ethnic backgrounds."

Columnist William Raspberry applauded Keohane's efforts to address racial issues, but, writing in the *Philadelphia Inquirer,* concluded that "it will take a good deal more than freshmen being nice to each other, even trying hard to make friends across racial lines. I think it will take a critical mass of students *and* faculty who believe inclusive community is worth the effort it takes to create—and who will get busy creating it."

In November 1997, Keohane was one of seven educators to address the seven-member Commission on Race appointed by President Clinton to advise him about racial and ethnic issues. The group of educators, led by Keohane, took exception with the current trends to cut back affirmative action programs. While opposing quotas or set-asides, the group, instead, stressed the need for college admission policies to take ethnicity, race, and gender into account. Said Keohane, "As an educator, I assert unequivocally that diversity is a powerful force for education. We, as educators, are best qualified to select those students—from among many qualified applicants—who will best enable our institutions to fulfill their broad educational purposes."

Keohane has not limited the issue of educational equity to just women and minorities. She also believes that income should not be a hinderance for those students who are ready to apply themselves. "The principle of accessibility to a Duke education is both a moral and prudential commitment," she told the Faculty Forum at Duke in January of 1997. "If we believe that the best education is one that includes diverse companions to open the mind and enrich the spirit of all students, it is important that we not people Duke University only with the children of the well to do.

Keohane has also been concerned that waning government support for higher education would be harmful to our country. She was quoted in the *Wall Street Journal* saying that, "Scaling back our nation's investment in science and research runs counter to our very purpose of balancing the budget: strengthening the economy and ensuring a prosperous future for our country." Yet, she has remained optimistic about higher education's ability to help all students. Writer Robert Cole, in *George* magazine, listed her as one of the "20 most fascinating women in politics." He wrote that "With universities now subject to brutal government budget cuts, many believe the American academy's golden era is

over. Keohane is one of the few college presidents who refuses to bow to such pessimism."

Service to the Community

Besides working tirelessly for equity in education, Keohane has also served on the board of directors of IBM Corporation and on the boards of trustees of the Colonial Williamsburg Foundation, the Center for the Advanced Study of the Behavioral Sciences, the National Humanities Center, and the Doris Duke Charitable Foundation. She has served on the editorial boards of both *Ethics* and *American Political Science Review,* and was a member of the executive editorial committee for *Political Theory.* A member of the Rockefeller Commission on the Humanities and the American Political Science Association, Keohane also served as vice president of the latter association.

More recently, she has served on the boards of the North Carolina Progress Board and the Research Triangle Foundation of North Carolina. In November 1997, she was named "City of Medicine Ambassador" by Durham Mayor Sylvia Kerckhoff. The honor is given to distinguished citizens who have made significant contributions in their professional and community endeavors.

Creating diversity among the students and faculty at Duke will continue to be an important endeavor for Keohane, as will her commitment to opening the doors to educational opportunities for all citizens of the United States. Certainly, her role at Duke as well as her longstanding support and work with other organizations will allow her numerous opportunities to continue her mission.

Further Reading

George, September 1996.

Duke University Chronicle, August 30, 1996.

Duke University Community Service Center Newsletter, fall, 1996.

Philadelphia Inquirer, September 12, 1997.

Wall Street Journal, January 20, 1997.

"A Brief Biography of Nannerl Overholser Keohane," Duke President's Home Page, http://www.oit.duke.edu/president/president.html (July 9, 1997).

Convocation Speech to Incoming Freshmen, August 28, 1997, http:www.inform.und.edu/EdRes/Topics/Diversity/response/web/newsroom/newsletter/duke.html (March, 1998).

Nando Times Delegation Notes, http://wedge.nando.net.nt/Elex96/insider/notes8.html (March, 1998).

"Nannerl O. Keohane," National Women's Hall of Fame. http://www.sbaonline.sba.gov/womeninbusiness/fame.html (March, 1998).

"Teaching in the Research University," Duke University Inaugural Address, http://www.aas.duke.edu/teach/pos/teachinru.shtml (October 23, 1993).

"University Research in the News," Tulane University Research, http://www.Tulane.edu/~aau/ures1.18-24.97.html (January 18-24, 1997).

Maxine Hong Kingston

Maxine Hong Kingston (born 1940) is one of the first Asian American writers in the United States to achieve great acclaim for both her nonfiction and fiction. With her vivid portrayals of the magic of her Chinese ancestry and the struggle of Chinese immigrants to the United States, she makes the Asian American experience come alive for her readers.

On September 29, 1997, President Bill Clinton awarded Maxine Hong Kingston a National Humanities Medal for her work as a writer and a supporter of both the California and Hawaii Councils for the Humanities. In his remarks that day, Clinton praised Kingston's talent for revealing "a world we've never seen but instantly recognize as authentic." Through her work, he said, she had "brought the Asian-American experience to life for millions of readers and inspired a new generation of writers to make their own unique voices and experiences heard."

Both of Kingston's parents, Tom and Ying Lan (Chew) Hong, immigrated to the United States from China, but not together. Tom Hong, a scholar and a poet, arrived in 1924 and went to New York City, while Ying Lan Hong, who received training during his absence as a doctor and midwife, joined him there about 15 years later. (Two children

they had had before he left died before Tom Hong could arrange for his family's passage to America.) The couple eventually settled in California, where Tom Hong worked in a laundry and managed a gambling house. Like her husband, Ying Lan worked in a laundry; she also toiled as a field hand. Kingston was the oldest of their six American-born children.

Fascinated by Mother's Stories of China

As a youngster, Kingston was profoundly influenced by her parents' struggle to deal with the difficulties of assimilation and their need to remind their children and themselves of their rich cultural heritage. She recalls listening intently to her mother's "talk-stories" about her ancestors and also delighted in hearing her recount mystical Chinese folk tales. In particular, Kingston was drawn to the narratives about women who had been considered especially privileged or damned. These women haunted her as she later sought to give voice not only to their experiences but also her own.

Kingston has said that she thinks she was a storyteller from the moment she was born because she very much wanted to write down everything her mother told her. While she was intrigued by the myth and magic of China, she was deeply disturbed by the family secrets revealed in her mother's stories. Learning about the adversity that so many of her relatives had known in their lives also troubled her. Writing thus became her way of understanding their pain and working toward some sort of resolution.

Kingston attended the University of California at Berkeley on a scholarship and served as the night editor for the *Daily Californian.* She graduated in 1962, the same year she married her husband, Earll Kingston, an actor. After the birth of their son, Joseph, in 1964, the couple taught at Sunset High School in Hayward, California, during the 1966-67 school year. In 1967, they moved to Hawaii. There Maxine Hong Kingston taught at a private school, Mid-Pacific Institute, and later at the University of Hawaii.

Bridged the Gap Between Two Worlds

Growing up as she did feeling the pull of two very different cultures, Kingston has sought a reconciliation of sorts through her writing. Her goal has always been to incorporate the mystery of China in her work without fostering the stereotypical exotic image that appeals to so many white Americans. She believes that such an image "cheapens real mystery," as she remarked to journalist Bill Moyers in an interview published in *Bill Moyers: A World of Ideas II.*

Her first book, a combination novel and memoir entitled *The Woman Warrior: Memoirs of a Girlhood Among Ghosts* (1976), explores the lives of women who have had the strongest impact on Kingston throughout her life—women whose voices have never been heard. One of the most poignant stories deals with her aunt, who gave birth to an illegitimate child. Because having a child outside of wedlock was absolutely taboo and thus a threat to the community's stability, her whole village rose up against her, forcing her to kill not only herself but also her child. From then on, even mentioning her name was forbidden; for all intents and purposes, it was if she had never existed. By writing about her aunt, however, Kingston felt that she was able to rescue the unfortunate woman from oblivion and give her back her life. *Time* magazine named *The Woman Warrior* one of the top ten nonfiction works of literature of the 1970s.

Kingston was also interested in giving voice to the male side of her family. In 1980, she published *China Men,* another blend of fact and fantasy that won the 1981 American Book Award for nonfiction and was runner-up for the Pulitzer Prize. Based on the experiences of her father and several generations of other male relatives, the book explores the lives of Chinese men who left their homeland to settle in the United States. It contains stories of loneliness and discrimination as well as determination and strength, enhanced and embellished by Kingston's own formidable imagination. The project also inspired a unique dialogue between father and daughter. In the Chinese translation of the book, Kingston invited her father to note his own comments in the margins of each page, a tradition in ancient Chinese literature. She is especially proud of this edition, because it allowed her father to be recognized and honored once again for his writing.

Kingston's third book, *Tripmaster Monkey: His Fake Book,* earned the 1989 PEN West Award in fiction. In this book, Kingston examines the life of a young, fifth-generation Chinese American named Wittman Ah Sing (a tribute to poet Walt Whitman). Somewhat of a hippie who believes in doing what you please no matter what the consequences, Wittman majors in English in college during the 1960s and then sets out to find his place in the world. He ends up in Berkeley, California, where he struggles to make a go of it as a playwright.

Many readers and critics have found Wittman to be an especially annoying character. While Kingston admits that Wittman means to be offensive at times, she has been dismayed by the negative reaction to him. As she told Moyers, "What's sad is that when many people tell me that they don't like Wittman and his personality, what they're also telling me is that they don't like the personalities of a lot of actual Asian American men out there." Kingston *wants* Wittman to offend people; she believes that it is his way of making himself his own man. "He does know how to be charming," she explained to Moyers. "Minority people in America all know how to be charming, because there are very charming stereotypes out there."

Kingston has also published numerous poems, short stories, and articles in her career. *Hawaii One Summer,* a book of 12 prose essays, was published in a limited edition in 1987. In 1991, she co-authored *Learning True Love: How I Learned and Practiced Social Change in Vietnam,* essentially a compilation of talks given by a Vietnamese Buddhist nun who has spent her life in service to the poor of her country. That same year, fire raged through Kingston's home in Oakland, California, and destroyed the manuscript of *The Fourth Book of Peace,* a project she had been working on that was inspired by the Chinese legend of the three lost books of peace. She has since completed *The Fifth Book of Peace,* which attempts to imagine in realistic rather than utopian terms what a world of peace might be like.

Classroom Techniques Combined East and West

After teaching at the University of Hawaii and Eastern Michigan University, Kingston joined the faculty of the University of California at Berkeley in 1990. Many of the same qualities of Eastern and Western culture and folklore that appear in her writing also surface in her classroom. For example, while discussing traditional Western literature, Kingston has been known to introduce concepts of Zen meditation.

Kingston is hopeful that the day will soon come when she is no longer considered "exotic." She would like to be viewed as someone who writes and teaches about Americans and what it means to be human. As she told Moyers, "I think I teach people how to find meaning." She encourages her readers as well as her students not to hesitate to reexamine the past and find new meaning in events that took place long ago.

For Kingston herself, meaning changes as she grows older. Looking back over her earlier works, she realizes there are additional details that she wishes she had incorporated into her stories. In the case of *The Woman Warrior,* for instance, she pointed out to Moyers that "the earlier meaning was we feminists have masculine powers, too. We can go into battle and lead armies." But the passing years have altered her perspective a bit. "This new meaning I'm finding from that myth is that war does not have to brutalize us," she said. "In that sense I want to rewrite it, to bring in these new meanings that I've discovered in my life."

Further Reading

Contemporary Authors, New Revisions, Volume 13, Gale, 1984.

Moyers, Bill, *Bill Moyers: A World of Ideas II—Public Opinions from Private Citizens,* edited by Andie Tucher, Doubleday, 1990.

Clipper, Marguerite, "UC Berkeley's Woman Warrior," *Daily Californian,* http://www.dailycal.org/archive (October 30, 1997).

Scalise, Kathleen, "President Clinton pays tribute to UC Berkeley's Maxine Hong Kingston, author of 'Woman Warrior,'" University of California News Release, http://www.urel.berkeley.edu (September 29, 1997).

Soderstrom, Christina K., "Voices from the Gaps: Maxine Hong Kingston," University of Minnesota, Department of English and Program in American Studies, http://english.cla.umn.edu (February 19, 1998).

White House, Office of the Press Secretary, "Remarks by the President at Arts and Humanities Ceremony," http://ofcn.org/cyber.serv/teledem/pb/1997/Sep/pr19970929f (September 29, 1997).

Viktor Klima

Viktor Klima (born 1947) who became Chancellor of Austria in 1997, promised to streamline his govern-

ment and lead his nation in cooperation with a united Europe.

Viktor Klima came to head the executive branch of the Austrian government after a long period of apprenticeship in the business world and in several government ministries. He succeeded his mentor, Franz Vranitzky, who resigned after bitter wrangling in the Austrian parliament over privatization of government industries and banking. With the threatened demise of Vranitzsky's coalition government, Klima stepped in with promises to streamline government and heal the wounds of the past.

Klima faces many challenges in Austria, known since the end of World War II for its strict neutralist policies. With pressures from both the European Union (EU) and the North Atlantic Treaty Organization (NATO), as well as domestic social and political problems, Klima treads carefully in order to protect his country's interests and his party's needs in a changing European scene.

Personal History

Born in 1947 in Vienna, Klima studied economics and business information at the Vienna Technical University and the University of Vienna. For more than twenty years, he worked for Osterreichische Mineralol-Verwaltungs AG (OMV), a huge oil and gas consortium, as a manager and business analyst. At OMV, Klima was known as a capable

manager who streamlined the organization and worked to make the company more effective in international markets.

Klima was not directly involved in politics during this time although he did join the Social Democratic Party (SPO), the rough equivalent of the Labor Party in Great Britain. SPO leadership soon began think of tapping Klima for a government ministry position.

As Chancellor, Klima is a hard-working politician, and according to a *Nando.net* article, has been called "charming," "smart," and "tough" by political commentators. The *Financial Times* has compared him to British Prime Minister Tony Blair because of his practical approach to government, his attractive appearance, and his ease with the media. Klima is married, with two children from a previous marriage. He and his wife Sonja enjoy jungle safaris in their leisure time.

Rising Through the Ranks

Klima was first appointed to a government position in April 1992. As Minister of Transport and State Industry, he applied his business expertise to the gradual privatization of many state-run companies. He oversaw this important change from state control to private ownership, convincing many skeptical industrialists of the virtues of private enterprise. In 1996, Chancellor Vranitzky appointed Klima to the position of Finance Minister. Klima's main focus in this ministry was to bring Austria's monetary system into compliance with the European Monetary Union.

Unlike his predecessor, he was able to negotiate a state budget with the People's Party (OVP), also called the Christian Democrats, the conservative junior partner in the coalition government. Klima also undertook to cut government expenses, especially for social services. In general, he was seen as a leader with excellent political skills and a practical sense of what could and could not be accomplished.

Particularly hard to accomplish was a reform of the banking industry. Much controversy surrounded the proposed government sale of its shares in Austria's second-largest bank. OVP members refused to agree to the SPO plan to merge the country's two largest banks, and the resulting political stalemate threatened the health of the Austrian economy. In January 1997, Vranitzky gave up his efforts at compromise and resigned as chancellor, asking Klima to succeed him.

A Popular New Leader

Klima's first task as chancellor was to negotiate with the OVP to stave off a power grab by the far-right Freedom Party (FPO). He was able to put together a new SPO-OVP coalition government, with the support of OVP leader Wolfgang Schussel, and was inaugurated chancellor on January 28, 1997. According to a political commentator in the *Economist,* Klima "promises to be tougher, more energetic and more decisive" than Vranitsky, as well as "more charming and more clever" and "better versed in economics" at a time when Austria is preoccupied with getting into the European Monetary Union.

He may need all of his political and personal skills to counter a growing rightist (some say neo-fascist) movement in the country, led by the colorful Jorg Haider of the Freedom Party. In the 1996 European parliament elections, the Freedom Movement took an unprecedented 28 percent of the votes. Haider is a charismatic politician who has capitalized on the economic uncertainty brought about by the growing power of the EU and fears of increased immigration. According to an on-line article from the *Socialdemocratic News from Austria,* Klima considers Haider's ideal for Austria "isolated, barricaded, stuffy and nationalistic," in contrast to the SPO's model of "an economically competitive, peaceful, just and humane state within a unified Europe."

In addition to his plans for Austria to take a fuller role in European affairs, Klima unveiled the rest of his program at a federal congress of the Social Democrats, held in of April 1997. In a speech on the "Next Millennium," (on-line article from the *Socialdemocratic News from Austria,*) he praised the SPO's "courage, energy, and . . . vision of a better Austria." Klima addressed his hopes of creating full employment by a productive melding of government and private efforts, proposed a reform of the social system to help those in poverty, advocated more cooperation among generations and sexes, and explored ways in which government could be more responsive on the local level.

Klima also spoke about improvements in education, environmental issues, the dissemination of more cultural projects to the public, the necessity of cooperation in government, and the need for openness and tolerance. His own tolerance did not extend to the Freedom Party, however, which (from the *Socialdemocratic News from Austria,*) he called "[a] party which is always against something but never actually for anything, which plays on fears, seeks out scapegoats, and has a sloppy relationship to the issue of national socialism [Nazism]."

Challenges of the Future

Klima faces the paradox of a traditionally neutralist Austria which also wishes to integrate more fully with the EU. Following the Allied occupation of Austria after World War II, Austria agreed to join neither the North Atlantic Treaty Organization (NATO) or the Warsaw Pact, making it a neutral bridge between Cold War enemies. The OVP has been urging Austria to join NATO, as have several of the western allies.

To many observers, Austria was a perfect candidate for NATO; it had, after all, been a part of the EU since 1995, and in February of 1998 it became one of eleven European nations to agree to a single currency by January 1, 1999. Klima at first vacillated on the NATO issue but in the end reverted to a neutralist stance, asserting to the *Washington Post* that "Austria will not become a member of any military bloc." Klima's political sense is good, despite the puzzlement of many in the West: a clear majority in his country opposes joining NATO, partly because of Austria's current lean defense budget. In March of 1998, Klima denied that staying outside NATO would adversely affect Austria's abil-

ity to cooperate in security responsibilities, including peacekeeping efforts in Bosnia.

Klima faces many more challenges in the near future. Although the inflation and unemployment rates are low in Austria, the country continues to have problems related to deregulation of industries, which Claus Raidl, an Austrian industrialist said was similar to a "change from a communist economy to a market economy on a small scale." With government interference in business still fairly high in Austria, according to British commentator William Hall in the *Financial Times,* "the traditional cosy political relationships which used to characterise corporate Austria do not score high marks with international investors."

Austria will also be tested as it takes over the presidency of the EU in the second half of 1998. As Klima leads the country more and more into international trade, Austria will be pressured to open its political system as well as its markets. Moreover, in the EU, Austria will have to help nations sort out the imminent question of the single currency. Several of smaller countries of central Europe would also like to be considered for EU membership; if they are admitted, many see economic difficulties, including pressure to admit many more immigrants, on the borders of Austria. Austria as temporary leader of the EU will have to mediate between those who favor and those who fear EU expansion.

Klima seems to have the right combination of political skills and personal traits for effective leadership in post-Cold War Europe. He has reorganized government, pacified disputing parties, kept his country economically sound, and, most important, encouraged Austria's participation in European affairs. As Klima commented to *ArabicNews.com,* "Austria really believes that a state of peace in Europe will only be possible by [a] process of European unification."

Further Reading

Chicago Sun-Times, February 28, 1998, p. 28.
Daily Telegraph, October 18, 1997, p. 12.
Economist, January 25, 1997, p. 47.
Financial Times, January 20, 1997, p. 2; December 1, 1997, pp. 1-2; March 16, 1998, p. 3.
Los Angeles Times, December 11, 1997, p. A1.
New York Times, October 14, 1996, p. A9.
Washington Post, March 15, 1998, p. A28.
"Austrian Information," http://www.austria.org/feb97/klima.html (March 22, 1998).
"Austria's New Finance Minister Has Political Savvy," *Nando.net,* http://nando.net/newsroom/ntn/world/010396/world6_.html (March 22, 1998).
"Federal Chancellor Viktor Klima Elected Chairman of the SPO," Current Affairs—Federal Press Service, Vienna, 1997-98, http://www.austria.gv.at/e/aktuell/berichte/spvorsitz.htm (March 22, 1998).
"Klima: Talks Constructive, Israeli Pullout from Golan Imperative," *ArabicNews.com,* http://arabic news.com (March 22, 1998).
"News from Austria," http://www.austria.gv.at/e/aktuell/info14/03-98.htm (March 22, 1998).
"Preparing for the Next Millennium: the SPO's 35th Federal Party Congress," *Socialdemocratic News from Austria,* http://iis.spoe.or.at/is/02_97/art01.htm (March 22, 1998).

C. Everett Koop

C. Everett Koop (born 1916), one of America's most outspoken surgeons general, served two terms in the 1980s. Koop's appointment angered liberals. However, the conservative Christian doctor later alienated social conservatives by refusing to compromise his common-sense approach to health issues for the sake of politics.

Brooklyn, NY-born Koop graduated from Dartmouth College in 1937 and earned his M.D. degree from Cornell Medical College in 1941. Following an internship, he pursued postgraduate training at the University of Pennsylvania School of Medicine, Boston Children's Hospital, and the Graduate School of Medicine at the University of Pennsylvania, from which he earned a doctor of science degree in medicine in 1947.

Koop became a professor of pediatric surgery at the University of Pennsylvania's School of Medicine in 1959 and professor of pediatrics in 1971. Koop also was surgeon-in-chief of Children's Hospital of Philadelphia from 1948 until he left academia in 1981. At the hospital, Koop gained renown for success in repairing birth defects, including the separation of conjoined twins. He also was editor-in-chief of the *Journal of Pediatric Surgery* from 1964 to 1976.

Koop was appointed Deputy Assistant Secretary for Health of the U.S. Public Health Service under the Reagan administration in March 1981 and was sworn in as surgeon general November 17, 1981. He held the post for two terms, serving under presidents Ronald Reagan and George Bush, until resigning October 1, 1989. In that time, Koop's willingness to speak out—and speak out boldly—on public health issues earned him much media attention and the enmity of a number of former allies.

Refused to Compromise on Health Matters

Koop saw fit to wear the traditional braided uniform of the surgeon general, a decision some derided, calling him an admiral without any ships. While traveling, the uniform once caused him to be mistaken for an airline crew member. A more significant departure from the style of previous surgeons general was Koop's decision to ignore advice he had been given upon arriving in Washington. That advice was, "Keep your head down and your mouth shut," he wrote in *Koop: The Memoirs of America's Family Doctor.* While the uniform confused some, the man wearing it left no doubt where he stood on numerous public health issues.

Koop took on the American tobacco industry, a bountiful source of campaign contributions for a number of congressional Republicans, when he called for a smoke-free society by 2000. Koop also pushed then-president Ronald Reagan to publicly address the AIDS crisis. In addition he weathered a storm of criticism over positions on abortion and contraception many conservatives said were in conflict with Koop's own beliefs. During the course of his tenure he

was shunned by conservative former associates and embraced by liberal former detractors.

Koop became a Reagan nominee largely based on his anti-abortion activism. The devout evangelical Koop had delivered his pro-life message through a number of books, films and lectures nationwide. One film shows Koop surveying a sea of naked dolls, intended to symbolize aborted fetuses, and saying, "I am standing on the site of Sodom, the place of evil and death." Liberals challenged Koop's appointment, delaying Congressional confirmation for eight months. Once Koop took office, though, liberals and conservatives each would do a turnabout.

Shortly after becoming the nation's top doctor, Koop began speaking out against tobacco and pressed for legislation to strengthen warning labels on cigarette packs. He later called for smoke-free work environments. As a result, the ten-year period encompassing Koop's tenure is said to have seen the greatest decline in smoking by Americans ever.

Safe Sex Proponent

In an October 1986 report to the president, Koop argued sex education and condoms were the most effective way to combat the AIDS epidemic. In 1987, Koop was the lone administration dissenter from a plan calling for widespread AIDS testing. His rationale was that the prevailing stigma against people with AIDS made mandatory testing unfair and impractical. He argued that compulsory testing would force those potentially infected with AIDS or HIV, the virus that causes AIDS, further away from medical treatment and education that could prevent spread of the disease.

Conservatives found Koop's views on AIDS so unpalatable they attempted to sabotage a Washington testimonial dinner held in his honor in May 1987. Of the dinner's original sponsors, 11 boycotted the event, including then Republican presidential hopefuls Senator Robert Dole and Congressman Jack Kemp. As pickets demanding his ouster marched outside, Koop thanked those in attendance. "There has never been a time in my life when I wanted or appreciated such a show of friendship." According to a 1987 *Time* magazine report, Koop was discouraged by the loss of conservative supporters. "They don't listen to what I've said, but they criticize me about what somebody told them they think I've said."

One weapon in Koop's anti-AIDS arsenal was information. The surgeon general was responsible for developing an eight-page booklet on the disease and its communicability at a cost of $17 million. *Understanding AIDS* was mailed to 107 million households in 1988 following a year and a half of debate over what the pamphlet would and would not say. Social conservatives were angered by the pamphlet's content as it included information on condom use. The AIDS prevention effort had two sides: Prevent the spread of the disease, of course, but also prevent the spread of panic over the disease. "Trying to estimate your chances of catching the virus based on the latest magazine article or newspaper story is like playing Russian roulette," Koop said at the time of the pamphlet's release.

Unexpected Abortion Report

Koop was routinely caught in the crossfire when medicine and politics clashed, as when President Reagan called upon the surgeon general to report on the psychological effects of abortions on women who have them. One might have guessed the outcome of a conservative president asking a conservative, staunchly anti-abortion doctor for such a document. All bets were off, however, when in early 1989 Koop wrote to the president saying data he had gathered were inconclusive; he could not determine whether women who had abortions suffered psychologically. Koop's response to President Reagan did not go unnoticed by either side of the abortion debate.

Writing in the liberal journal *New Republic*, John B. Judis commented at the time, "The antagonism generated by the report will only reinforce the reversal over the past eight years in Koop's constellation of friends and enemies. The New Right, which once championed him as a bearded Ahab who would slay the white whale of liberalism (and which helped him get his job), now denounces him as an instrument of immorality. Meanwhile, the liberals, feminists, and public health lobbyists who once called him 'Dr. Kook' sing his praises."

A commentator in the conservative *National Review* suggested that the thinking behind Koop's abortion letter was in conflict with principles underlying his stance on other public health issues. "Koop's tentative tone on [abortion] contrasts sharply with his own strong statements of yore that abortion does harm women," according to a

1989 article in the magazine. "Nor is he averse to making stern moral, as opposed to merely medical, statements against smoking. On abortion, as on AIDS, he has learned to assume properly enlightened attitudes."

In an interview following delivery of his letter to President Reagan, Koop articulated his frustration with social conservatives and reiterated his philosophy on health policy. "What has given me so much trouble in this job from the right is that I separate ideology, religion and other things from my sworn duty as a health officer in this country."

When Koop resigned as surgeon general, he did not put the abortion debate behind him. Instead, as he did in a 1991 *Good Housekeeping* magazine article, he lamented the politicization of an issue that came to life as concern for the unborn and the health of women. "I wonder if they have forgotten what originally prompted the debate: the innocent unborn child, the agonized pregnant woman. Many opposed to abortion have been notoriously unhelpful to unwed pregnant women; they must be more forthcoming with their time and money to help pregnant women in hardship. And those who call themselves 'pro-choice' ought to make more of adoption as a clear choice."

Remained in Debate

Although no longer surgeon general, Koop retained a voice in the debate of public health issues during the administration of Democrat Bill Clinton. He did not keep quiet during the Clinton administration's aborted attempt to reform the health care and health insurance industries and lent his support to some Clinton initiatives.

Koop was not immune to controversy even during his early eighties. When President Clinton granted Koop a waiver in 1994 for burial at Arlington National Cemetery, congressional Republicans thought they smelled a conspiracy and suggested Koop was granted the waiver in exchange for his support of health care reform. Precedent did exist for granting a waiver to a surgeon general who had not served in the armed forces. President Reagan had approved an Arlington burial for Dr. Luther Terry, the surgeon general who first publicized the link between smoking and cancer. Koop later declined the waiver. "I do this without rancor and with an understanding of and respect for the special place that burial at Arlington has in the hearts of the American people," a Koop statement at the time said.

In 1997, Koop co-chaired a task force on tobacco that recommended a hefty increase in the tax on cigarettes to discourage teenagers from smoking. Koop also was an opponent to granting tobacco companies immunity from further liability in conjunction with a government settlement with the industry over the cost of smoking-related illnesses. The prospect of revenue from a tobacco settlement being used to fight cancer and improve public health must have been gratifying to Koop. Indeed, a Koop remark reported by Reuters in 1998 suggested that the former surgeon general saw similarities between tobacco's reversal of fortune and his own during the 1980s. "The public is now fully aware that the tobacco industry has lied to them. This has enraged a number of Americans and has disgusted a number of people in Congress who were for years the best friends of tobacco.''

Koop has written more than 200 articles and books on medicine and surgery, biomedical ethics and health policy. He is married to the former Elizabeth Flanagan and has three living children and seven grandchildren.

Further Reading

Bianchi, Anne, *C. Everett Koop: The Health of the Nation,* Millbrook Press, 1992.

Easterbrook, Greg, *Surgeon Koop,* W.W. Norton & Company, 1991.

Koop, C. Everett, M.D., *Koop: The Memoirs of America's Family Doctor,* Random House, 1991.

Koop, C. Everett, *The Right to Live: The Right to Die,* Life Cycle Books, 1981.

Koop, C. Everett, *Whatever Happened to the Human Race,* Crossway Books, 1983.

Koop, C. Everett, and Johnson, Timothy, *Let's Talk: An Honest Conversation on Critical Issues: Abortion, AIDS, Euthanasia, Health Care,* Zondervan, 1992.

Koop, C. Everett; Virgo, John M., editor, *Exploring New Vistas in Health Care,* International Health Economics, 1985.

Koop, Everett C.; Elizabeth Koop; and Koop, C. Everett, *Sometimes Mountains Move,* Zondervan, 1995.

Christian Century, January 26, 1994.

Good Housekeeping, September, 1991.

JAMA: The Journal of the American Medical Association, November 24, 1989.

Los Angeles Times, December 23, 1997.

National Review, February 10, 1989.

New Republic, February 1, 1988; January 23, 1989; October 23, 1989.

Playboy, May, 1989.

Time, June 8, 1987.

U.S. News & World Report, May 16, 1988; May 30, 1988.

Heinz Awards, 1995 Recipients, http://www.awards.heinz.org/koop.html (March 6, 1998).

Stanley Kubrick

Although he first won acclaim for films he made during the 1950s such as *Spartacus* and *Lolita*, director Stanley Kubrick (born 1928) is best known for his later work, including *Dr. Strangelove, 2001: A Space Odyssey, A Clockwork Orange, Barry Lyndon, The Shining,* and *Full Metal Jacket.*

D uring his long and distinguished career as a filmmaker, Stanley Kubrick has earned a reputation as a control-obsessed perfectionist who often reshoots scenes hundreds of times, driving actors and actresses to distraction. Yet a number of his films are considered classics of postwar American cinema, including the one critics most often point to as his masterpiece, the black comedy *Dr. Strangelove, Or: How I Learned to Stop Worrying and Love the Bomb*. Kubrick himself for the most part ignores what people have to say about both him and his movies, believing that his work speaks for itself.

Born in New York City in 1928, Stanley Kubrick grew up in one of the more prosperous families of his Bronx neighborhood. Yet his childhood was rather bleak and unhappy. His father, a doctor, tried his best to stimulate his son's interest in learning. He made books from his library readily available, for example, and also taught the boy to play chess. But Kubrick was a poor student throughout his school years; nothing his teachers presented in class seemed to be able to hold his attention. ''I never learned anything at all in school and didn't read a book for pleasure until I was 19 years old,'' he is quoted as saying in *The Making of Kubrick's 2001*. When he turned 13, however, his father bought him a still camera as a birthday present. As time would tell, it was probably the most significant gift he ever received.

Although young Kubrick took a dim view of school, he was an avid moviegoer with a keen sense of what worked and what didn't. ''One of the important things about seeing run-of-the-mill Hollywood films eight times a week was that many of them were so bad,'' biographer Vincent LoBrutto reports Kubrick told a writer for the *New York Times*. ''Without even beginning to understand what the problems of making films were, I was taken with the impression that I could not do a film any worse than the ones I was seeing. I also felt I could, in fact, do them a lot better.''

Experimented with Still Photography

But it was still photography, not film, that brought Kubrick his first commercial success. Rarely without his camera, he made a hobby of taking pictures to document

the events unfolding around him. One such occasion presented itself following the death of Franklin Delano Roosevelt in 1945. Kubrick, who was then only 17, came upon a newspaper dealer at his stand surrounded by headlines trumpeting news of the president's death. His subject's dejected posture and mournful facial expression captured the eye of the young photographer, who snapped his picture. But as LoBrutto observed, "Stanley didn't just take the man's picture, he made the situation into a piece of photojournalism." Editors at *Look* magazine recognized the nascent artistry in his work and bought the photograph for publication. It was the first picture Kubrick had ever sold.

Not long after that, Kubrick landed a job as a staff photographer for *Look.* He remained in the job for several years and traveled all over the United States. Many of his assignments were simply routine, but some allowed him more freedom to exercise his creativity.

Kubrick's travels eventually inspired him to enroll at Columbia University as a non-matriculating student. In his spare time, he often attended films shown at the New York Museum of Modern Art. And those childhood chess matches with his father finally paid off when he began playing the game for money from time to time in several New York City venues.

Tried His Hand at Filmmaking

In 1951, at the age of 23, Kubrick financed his first film with his own savings. His 16-minute documentary, entitled *Day of the Fight,* was about boxer Walter Cartier, the subject of one of his *Look* magazine photo assignments. Kubrick served as director, cinematographer, editor, and sound technician for the film, which RKO bought for its *This Is America* series. It played at the Paramount Theatre in New York.

Kubrick soon quit his job at *Look* to pursue filmmaking on a full-time basis. With an advance from RKO, Kubrick made a short documentary, *The Flying Padre* (1951), about a priest named Father Fred Stadtmueller who traveled around his New Mexico parish in an airplane. Two years later, Kubrick made his first color film, a 30-minute industrial documentary entitled *The Seafarers.*

Kubrick raised $13,000 from relatives to help finance his first feature-length film, *Fear and Desire* (1953). The plot centers around four soldiers trapped behind enemy lines who kill four of their adversaries while trying to escape only to discover they've killed their own doubles. (Kubrick's first wife, Toba Metz, whom he married when he was 18, was one of the crew members on the project.) In later years, Kubrick disowned the film, calling it amateurish. On more than one occasion, he has even prevented it from being shown in public.

Kubrick's next film was *Killer's Kiss* (1955), financed with $40,000 raised from friends and relatives. It tells the story of an aging boxer who becomes involved with a gangster's girlfriend. He followed this with *The Killing* (1956), which focuses on a gang of small-time hoods and their elaborate plan to rob a racetrack. Widely regarded as an above-average crime thriller, it is the film Kubrick himself

reportedly considers the true beginning of his filmmaking career.

Scored First Cinematic Triumph

In 1957, Kubrick directed *Paths of Glory* (1957), an adaptation that he, Calder Willingham, and Jim Thompson wrote of the best-selling Humphrey Cobb novel of the same name. No studio had been willing to take on this particular project until Kirk Douglas agreed to star. Filmed in Germany, *Paths of Glory* is about three soldiers tried for cowardice; it is regarded as one of the best films ever made about the insanity of war.

Despite the kudos he received for *Paths of Glory,* Kubrick ran into some difficulties with his next few projects, which never even reached the production stage. His fortunes took a turn for the better, however, when the original director of *Spartacus,* Anthony Mann, was fired and producer Kirk Douglas offered Kubrick the job, making the 32-year-old filmmaker the youngest person ever to direct a Hollywood epic. It took 167 days to shoot, employed some 10,000 people, and cost more than $12 million, an astronomical sum in those days. Although *Spartacus* was a hit upon its release in 1960 and attracted some Academy Award attention, it left Kubrick feeling as if he had had too little creative control. As a result, he later sought to disassociate himself from the film.

Having acquired the rights to Vladimir Nabokov's controversial novel *Lolita* with its themes of sexual obsession and pedophilia, director Kubrick and producer James B. Harris headed to England to do the film. The two men ended up rewriting Nabokov's script, leaving only about 20 percent of the original (by Nabokov's own estimate). The novel's subject matter was handled very subtly in the film, primarily through looks and double-entendres. But this toned-down version left many moviegoers and critics disappointed because they felt it was not true to the frank eroticism of the original story.

Ever since making *Lolita,* the thrice-married Kubrick has called England home; he even refuses to leave the country to work elsewhere. Notoriously reclusive, he lives in a semi-rural manor house in Childwickbury, near St. Albans. He rarely grants interviews, but when he does, he demands total control over the circumstances and the result. "He doesn't like people much; they interest him mainly when they do unspeakably hideous things or when their idiocy is so malignant as to be horrifyingly amusing," Kubrick biographer John Baxter quoted Kubrick's onetime collaborator Calder Willingham as saying. That assessment would seem to be supported by Kubrick's next film, *Dr. Strangelove, Or: How I Learned to Stop Worrying and Love the Bomb.*

Tackled Diverse Themes

Dr. Strangelove was released in 1964, two years after the Cuban missile crisis led the United States and the Soviet Union to the brink of nuclear war. Based on Peter George's novel *Red Alert,* it is what some consider the blackest comedy in movie history. The film is both a suspenseful Cold War thriller and a wicked farce that lampoons both the military and political establishments. It was a resounding hit, with Kubrick receiving Academy Award nominations as co-author, director, and producer.

Kubrick next hired science fiction writer Arthur C. Clarke to develop a story about man's encounter with extra-terrestrial intelligence. The result was the landmark *2001: A Space Odyssey* (1968). It netted Kubrick more Academy Award nominations for writing and directing and his only Academy Award for designing and directing the movie's complicated special effects. Critics generally panned *2001,* but audiences loved it. Regarded as a technological triumph of filmmaking, it is also noteworthy for the fact that it contains fewer words than any other commercial sound film of its length in history (about 40 minutes' worth over the course of nearly 3 hours). "The feel of the experience is the important thing, not the ability to verbalize it," Kubrick once explained, as reported online at *Criterion's The Films of Stanley Kubrick.* "I tried to create a visual experience."

In 1971, Kubrick adapted Anthony Burgess' novel *A Clockwork Orange* for the screen and also filled his custom-ary roles of producer and director. Controversial because of its violent scenes, the film initially garnered an "X" rating in the United States. Kubrick nevertheless wound up with three Academy Award nominations (for writer, producer, and director) as well as the New York Film Critics' Best Picture and Best Director honors. It played in England for nearly a year to sellout crowds before Kubrick and Warner Brothers removed it from theaters in the wake of several crimes that appeared to be modeled on acts of violence depicted in the film.

Kubrick's next film, *Barry Lyndon* (1975), represented quite a departure from his previous works. Based on the eighteenth-century novel by William Makepeace Thackeray, it was an expensive, meticulously detailed cos-tume drama that did not do well at the box office. But it was a hit with critics and with Kubrick's fellow filmmakers, who nominated it for seven Academy Awards. Three of those were for Kubrick himself as the movie's writer, director, and producer.

Five years later, Kubrick adapted Stephen King's novel *The Shining* for the screen. Although it was a financially successful film, it left critics unmoved and angered King, who deeply resented the changes Kubrick had made to his original story. King eventually bought back the rights to *The Shining* and approved a 1997 television remake that he felt was more in line with how he himself envisioned the char-acters and themes.

In 1987, Kubrick released *Full Metal Jacket,* based on Gustav Hasford's novel *The Short-Timers.* A brutal look at Marine basic training and the subsequent combat experi-ences of a group of recruits sent to Vietnam, the film tackled one of Kubrick's favorite themes—dehumanization, partic-ularly amid war and violence. But some moviegoers and critics took issue with the fact that he insisted on shooting the movie in London rather than in a more appropriate locale. To make his sets look as authentic as possible, Kubrick demolished a number of 1930s-era buildings to create his own rubble, brought in palm trees from Spain,

and imported over 100,000 plastic tropical plants from Hong Kong.

Scheduled for release in late 1998, *Eyes Wide Shut* took nearly two years for Kubrick to complete. Based on a novel by Frederic Raphael, it is a tale of jealousy and sexual obsession involving a married couple who are both psychia-trists. Problems plagued the project almost from the begin-ning. Star Tom Cruise reportedly balked at having to reshoot so many of his scenes and was furious that the delays finally forced one of his co-stars, Harvey Keitel, to quit due to a scheduling conflict. His departure meant that six months' worth of work had to be scrapped.

Despite his eccentricities, Kubrick is an acknowledged master of the modern cinema. His thought-provoking, care-fully crafted films address timeless themes such as the absurdity of war, the nature of crime and punishment, ob-sessive love, madness, and even the enigma of humankind's evolution. The fact that he has not yet had a blockbuster success during his career is of no concern to him; he aims to please himself above all, which is perhaps the source of his perfectionism. As Kubrick remarked in a 1997 speech upon accepting the D.W. Griffith Award from the Director's Guild of America, a transcript of which is available online at http:// pages.prodigy.com, "although [directing a film] can be like trying to write *War and Peace* in a bumper car in an amusement park, when you finally get it right, there are not many joys in life that can equal the feeling."

Further Reading

Agel, Jerome, editor, *The Making of Kubrick's 2001,* New Ameri-can Library, 1970.

Baxter, John, *Stanley Kubrick: A Biography,* Carroll & Graf, 1997.

Ciment, Michael, *Kubrick,* Holt, 1984.

Falsetto, Mario, editor, *Perspectives on Stanley Kubrick,* G.K. Hall & Co., 1996.

Kagan, Norman, *The Cinema of Stanley Kubrick,* Continuum, 1993.

LoBrutto, Vincent, *Stanley Kubrick: A Biography,* Donald I. Fine Books, 1997.

Nelson, Thomas, *Kubrick: Inside a Film Artist's Maze,* Indiana University Press, 1982.

Entertainment Weekly, December 15, 1995; April 11, 1997.

Film Comment, September-October 1996.

New Statesman, October 3, 1997.

Omni, May 1993.

People Weekly, January 27, 1997; June 9, 1997.

"Criterion's The Films of Stanley Kubrick," http:// www.voyagerco.com/criterion/indepth.cgi? (March 4, 1998).

"Stanley Kubrick's Videotaped DGA Acceptance Speech," http:/ /pages.prodigy.com/kubrick/dgaspe.htm (May 19, 1998).

"Stanley Kubrick: The Master Filmmaker," http:// pages.prodigy.com/kubrick (May 19, 1998).

Milan Kucan

Milan Kucan (born 1941), first president of the inde-pendent Republic of Slovenia, has set the tone for democratic reform in the former Yugoslavian states.

The first president of an independent Slovenia, the northernmost former Yugoslavian state, Milan Kucan has led his new nation in economic and political progress unrivalled in eastern and central Europe in the period following the breakup of the Soviet Union. He is a popular politician who, according to the "Central Europe Online" website, believes in "supraparty politics" and encourages the participation of all the citizens of Slovenia. The first former Yugoslav state to enter negotiations for admittance to the European Union (EU) and one of the first considered for possible future admittance to the North Atlantic Treaty Organization (NATO), Slovenia is western-oriented and free from the strong ethnic divisions of neighbors like Bosnia and Serbia. Kucan's leadership has helped to keep his country moving toward full participation in the new Europe.

Personal Life

Kucan was born January 14, 1941, in a Prekmurje village, the son of a teacher. He was raised a Protestant. During World War II, when Kucan was very young, his father was killed by the Nazis. After the war, Kucan attended grammar school in the town of Murska Sobota. Later he went to law school in Ljubljana, graduating in 1963. He married and had two children. His daughter Ana has a master's degree from Harvard University, while his other daughter Spela is studying ethnology and Spanish.

Early Political Career

Kucan's first political experience was in youth organizations in the old Communist-dominated Yugoslavia. He later held positions in other political organizations and in 1971 helped to prepare the Yugoslav constitutional amendments which brought about decentralization in the former Yugoslav federation. He became president of the Slovene Assembly in 1978 and held several more government positions following Marshall Josip Tito's death in 1980.

Kucan's experiences in government convinced him that the diverse ethnic groups in Yugoslavia needed better relations and that political power should be spread to more citizens. In 1986, after becoming president of the League of Communists of Slovenia (ZKS), he worked to make the organization more reformist. The ZKS soon initiated the multi-party system which brought more democracy to Slovenia. In several important speeches, Kucan spoke eloquently about individual freedom and democracy. He saw that the old system was doomed if people were not granted a political voice. "The freedoms of an individual are limited solely by the boundaries of equal rights and the freedoms of others," he stated in a July 1986 political speech.

Kucan and the New Slovenia

By 1988, Slovenia was gaining a reputation as a forward-looking state with more political freedoms and more industrial base than most of its Slavic neighbors. The first multi-party elections were held in 1990, when Kucan became president of the Republic of Slovenia. In 1991, as the old Soviet Union was breaking up, Slovenia declared itself independent of Yugoslavia after a ten-day "war," perpetrated mostly by Serbians who wished to dominate the region. Border posts were seized and some bombing raids were initiated, but relatively few people were killed or injured before a cease-fire was initiated. Slovenia soon became a new nation independent of Yugoslavia, with Kucan as its new president.

As Kucan commented to *World Statesman,* "Slovenia avoided . . . bloodshed . . . because, of all the former Yugoslav republics, it is the most ethnically homogeneous." He also cited the "special character" of his country, which he said had never really been a Balkan state like Bosnia or Croatia. Slovenia's border with Italy and Austria has always been one of the most open in Europe. Slovenia's interest in the European Union and its cooperation with western interests mark it as a central, not an eastern, European country, according to its president. No longer a Communist, Kucan was re-elected in 1997.

Independence for Slovenia did not come without frustration noted an article in the *Toronto Globe and Mail.* The United States and several other major western European states were slow to recognize Slovenia, fearing the instability brought about by the breakup of Yugoslavia. Widespread unrest in the other former Yugoslav states in fact brought over 100,000 refugees to Slovenia; economic conditions deteriorated since more than 30 percent of Slovenia's industrial output had formerly gone to the Yugoslav federation; inflation soared; Slovenian assets in other former Yugoslav states were confiscated; and foreign investment and tourism slowed. With Kucan's leadership, however, inflation has been brought to a reasonable level, and economic growth has resumed through trade with the EU and other western countries.

Looking Toward the Future

Kucan continues to speak strongly for increased ties with the EU and with the United States and also favors cooperation with other central European states such as the Czech Republic, Poland, Slovakia, and Hungary. In 1997, in a speech at the International Economic Conference on the 50th anniversary of the postwar Marshall Plan for European recovery, he warned against antidemocratic movements such as the one which has caused all the bloodshed in Bosnia-Herzegovina and said that leaders of the new Europe need to "realise the free community of European countries, which will be founded on social stability, competitive cooperation in the common economic area, the rule of human rights and other values of the Euro-American democratic tradition."

Seeking to allay fears in the West about increased trade with less prosperous eastern neighbors, Kucan became one of the most outspoken central European leaders, favoring opening western Europe more and more to central and eastern states. At the opening session of the World Economic Forum in 1996, Kucan asserted, "Cooperation has now become realistic because the countries of Europe are no longer committed to ideologies."

Several obstacles remain to be overcome, however. Kucan has spoken out strongly against the policy of neutrality maintained by many countries in the West regarding the "ethnic cleansing" by Serbian forces in Bosnia and other Balkan states over the last several years. "[This situation]," he commented to World Statesman in 1996, "began and unfolded as neither a civil nor as a religious conflict: it was an offensive war with a known aggressor, and a known victim. . . . If the Europeanisation of these states has not succeeded . . . by the end of the millennium, Europe will enter the next century with smouldering battlefields."

Another disappointment for Slovenia came in October 1997, when three other central European nations (Hungary, Poland, and the Czech Republic) were approved as prospective members of NATO, while Slovenia and Romania were rejected. Although the latter two countries were praised for their steps toward democracy, many NATO leaders, including U.S. President Bill Clinton, felt that Slovenian and Romanian political systems were too new and untested. However in his 1997 speech at the International Economic Conference Kucan stated, "To leave anyone from Central Europe standing outside the gates to the EU and NATO means to maintain or renew the European divisions." By March of 1998, President Clinton in fact had begun to urge the U.S. Congress to look favorably on increased NATO expansion.

Slovenia has had better luck seeking involvement in the EU. Kucan argued that the European Union is no longer simply an economic community, but one which "represents the institutional framework" for the return of nations which had been isolated by the Iron Curtain following World War

II. In June of 1996, Slovenia became an associate member of the EU. In December of 1997, at a summit of European leaders in Luxembourg, Slovenia and four other former communist countries—Poland, the Czech Republic, Hungary, and Estonia, along with the divided island of Cyprus—were invited to start entry negotiations toward full membership.

Although the EU is preoccupied with the question of a common currency rather than with admission of new members, the nations under consideration expect to be admitted within the next four to six years. Slovenia is first in line among the nations slated for admission. As Kucan commented to World Statesman in 1996, "Slovenian membership [in] the EU is not only in the interests of our economic, security, defence, cultural and other ties, but also in Europe's interests." Kucan has stressed the unifying and stabilizing result of including the new European states in an overall economic and political plan for European development.

More Work to Be Done

Despite Slovenia's forward strides on the world scene in its brief life as a nation, Kucan has many more goals to accomplish. According to the Toronto Globe and Mail, he wants to continue to strengthen Slovenia's economy, increase tourism, and lead his country to more participation in European and world affairs. In the brief span of Slovenian democracy, the country has increased representative government dramatically, expanded human rights, and privatized more than ninety percent of its former socialist economy.

Kucan continues to be very popular among his constituents and also with western leaders. In his 1997 speech at the International Economic Conference, he maintained the hope that "Europe is destined to cooperation and not to division." If his brand of leadership, combining old-world realism with contemporary progressivism, prevails, the new nations of central and eastern Europe can hope to play important parts in what former U.S. President George Bush called the "new world order" which has followed the fall of communism.

Further Reading

A Matter of Fact, Vol. 17, Pierian Press, July-December 1992, pp. 349-50; July-December 1996, p. 515.

Baltimore Sun, October 24, 1997, p. 2A.

Christian Science Monitor, December 15, 1997, p. 7.

Economist, January 18, 1992, pp. 48-49.

National Review, July 29, 1991, pp. 18-19.

New York Times, November 12, 1996, p. A9.

Newsday, March 21, 1998, p. AO4.

Newsweek, July 8, 1991, pp. 32-34.

"NATO Invites Three ex-Communist Countries to Join," Knight-Ridder/Tribune News Service (Washington Bureau), July 8, 1997.

Toronto Globe and Mail (Scripps Howard News Service), November 21, 1997.

Washington Times, August 24, 1997, p. A6.

"Daily News Home Page," Central Europe Online, http://www.centraleurope.com (March 15, 1998).

''Discussion by the President of the Republic of Slovenia, Milan Kucan, at the Opening Session of the World Economic Forum,'' (November 11, 1997) *Republic of Slovenia—Government Centre for Informatics,* http://www.sigov.si/http://www.sigov.si:90/upr/ang/salz-an.htm (March 15, 1998).

''Expectations of a Growing Together in Europe,'' (November 12, 1997) *Republic of Slovenia—Government Centre for In-*formatics, http://www.sigov.si/http://www.sigov.si:90/upr/ang/mplan-a.htm (March 15, 1998).

''SloWWWenia,'' *Slovenia—A Guide to Virtual Slovenia,* http://www.ijs.si/slo (March 15, 1998).

''The Rising Star: Slovenian President Milan Kucan,'' (Fourth Quarter 1996) *World Statesman,* http://www.kenpubs.co.uk/worldstatesman/Archive/Kucan.html (March 15, 1998).

L

Jonathan Larson

In February of 1996, the musical _Rent,_ created by Jonathan Larson (1961-1996) and billed as "The Rock Opera of the Nineties," opened in New York City. The show moved to Broadway on April 29, and later that year it would win the Pulitzer Prize for Drama, as well as two Antoinette Perry ("Tony") Awards. But Larson would not be there to accept his awards: on January 25, 1996, the young playwright and composer died of an aortic aneurysm.

Evelyn McDonnell and Katherine Silberger, authors of the text that accompanied the libretto of _Rent_ in a 1997 book published by Morrow, summed up this ironic alignment of events by noting that "it's hard not to think of this story, ultimately, as a tragedy." Yet Larson, who had supported himself as a waiter for the ten years prior to _Rent'_ s first production, left an enormous legacy. John Lahr in the _New Yorker,_ while noting that Larson was far from the first composer to attempt the marriage of rock and the Broadway musical, noted that he may have been the first to succeed. Larson's "gift for direct, compelling, colloquial lyrical statement," Lahr wrote, "seems to prove that the show tune can once again become pertinent and popular."

Singing in His Diapers

Larson was raised in White Plains, New York, and enjoyed what _Entertainment Weekly_ called an "idyllic Jewish middle-class childhood." Music was important to him from the beginning, according to his father. The latter told McDonnell and Silberger: "I was changing his diaper, so he had to be pretty young, and he started singing 'Yellow Bird.' In tune."

In an interview with John Istel for _American Theatre_ shortly before his death, Larson named several musical figures who had been important influences on him. Later in life, he had come to appreciate Kurt Cobain of Nirvana, he said, along with fellow "alternative" musician Liz Phair. As a teen, his influences had included the Police and the artist who at that time went by the name of Prince. Still earlier, he had enjoyed the Beatles and the Who's Pete Townsend, the latter known for his rock opera _Tommy_ that would have an impact on Larson's later work.

But Larson also appreciated composers Leonard Bernstein and Stephen Sondheim, whose work would not normally be found among the typical American teenager's favorites. Sondheim, who wrote the lyrics for Bernstein's _West Side Story_ (1957) and composed the musicals including _A Little Night Music_ (1973) and the Pulitzer Prize-winning _Sunday in the Park with George_ (1984), would eventually become Larson's mentor. Still another influence lay even further in the musical past. When Larson was a child, he was taken to see a children's version of _La Boheme,_ Giacomo Puccini's opera about a group of struggling young artists, or "Bohemians." From that seed, the idea that would become _Rent_ slowly germinated over the next two decades.

Acting Student Turned Composer

After high school, Larson attended Adelphi University in Garden City, New York on an acting scholarship. Recalling his college experience in his _American Theatre_ interview, Larson said, "Adelphi was a lousy place to go to school in the sense that it's in suburbia and that's where I grew up." But, he went on to say, he was fortunate to study

under Jacques Burdick, who had been strongly influenced by theatre critic Robert Brustein. Burdick had established what Larson described as an undergraduate version of the prestigious drama school program at Yale University.

Under Burdick's direction, Larson studied works by a wide range of playwrights. Even more important, he had his first opportunity to write plays. Four times a year, the university theatre program put on "cabarets," and they were always in need of writers. Thus, Larson said, by the time he finished school he had written "eight or ten" shows.

Following graduation in 1982, Larson moved to New York City. Because he had performed in summer stock productions, he was able to obtain his Actor's Equity card, and started going to auditions. He also had an opportunity to meet his hero, Stephen Sondheim, and this coincided with a change in his career plans. Larson's father Al later explained to *People* magazine: "Sondheim told him there were a lot more starving actors out there than starving composers."

The Struggling Artist

Larson already had some experience writing musicals. Late in his time at Adelphi, he had written a show based on George Orwell's novel about a nightmare police state of the future, *1984*. The musical attracted attention, he told Istel, primarily because it was 1982, and the year 1984 was fast approaching. It was almost produced, but in the end nothing happened with the musical, which Larson said "was a

good thing . . . because it was not a very good show. But it was my first attempt to write a big show."

Sondheim encouraged him to become involved with the American Society of Composers, Authors, and Publishers (ASCAP). Larson described ASCAP as "a sort of 12-step meeting for people who write musicals" but, he told *American Theatre*, his experience with other composers he met through the organization gave him greater confidence in his work. By the time he had written some 100 songs, he said, he knew when to accept and when to reject the comments of a would-be critic—even Sondheim.

During the 1980s and early 1990s, Larson stayed very busy. In 1985 or 1986, he began working as a waiter in a restaurant called Moondance, located in New York City's fashionable SoHo district. The job gave him a reliable income, and he would support himself this way for the next decade, up until the eve of *Rent's* first stage production. He also earned money through freelance work, composing songs for the children's show *Sesame Street*. Larson created a thirty-minute children's video called *Away We Go*, produced with the financial backing of a restaurant patron who had learned of his composing talents from an article in *New York* magazine.

Larson continued to work on other projects, which satisfied his creative urge even if they did not "pay the rent." Among these were the musicals *J. P. Morgan Saves the Nation* and *Superbia*, as well as a rock monologue called *Tick, Tick . . . Boom!*, which Larson performed himself. He obtained a number of grants for his productions, including a Richard Rodgers Development Grant and a Stephen Sondheim Award, both for *Superbia*. He also became involved with the New York Theatre Workshop, the company that would eventually produce *Rent*.

The Road to *Rent*

Through a mutual friend in the theatre, Larson met writer Billy Aronson, who he described in his *American Theatre* interview as "a sort of Woody Allen type." Aronson had an idea for an updated version of *La Boheme* as a comedy set on New York's Upper West Side with yuppie characters, and he wanted Larson to write the music. Larson, in turn, said he liked the basic concept, having been influenced by Puccini's opera as well; however, he envisioned the musical as a serious one. On Aronson's urging, Larson wrote three songs for the proposed musical: "Santa Fe," "I Should Tell You," and what would become the title composition, "Rent."

The two men made a demo tape and shared it with people they knew. The music received a positive response, but the libretto did not. Therefore, Larson said, "we just put it on hold. I loved the concept, but I didn't have a burning reason to go back to it. And then I did."

In the early 1990s, several of Larson's friends discovered they had the Human Immunodeficiency Virus (HIV) linked with AIDS. Devastated, he began to re-conceive the *La Boheme* story as one involving characters with AIDS. He went to Aronson and asked the latter to let him proceed with resurrecting the defunct musical on his own. Aronson agreed. In 1992 Larson and James Nicola of the New York

Theatre Workshop began working together on the production, and two years later, they obtained a $50,000 Richard Rodgers award. By early 1996 *Rent* and its author were on the verge of success.

Triumph and Tragedy

The plot of *Rent* is, by many accounts, a complex one, a set of eight stories revolving around a rent strike in a New York apartment building. Among the characters are Roger, a punk rocker and former heroin addict whose former lover committed suicide when she discovered she had AIDS; his roommate Mark, a filmmaker; Maureen, a performance artist and Mark's girlfriend—until she leaves him for a lesbian affair with Joanne, described in *Maclean's* as "a lawyer slumming as a stage manager in the Village." Tom Collins is a gay African American assaulted on the street and helped by a transvestite named Angel. Both are HIV-positive, and they fall in love. Roger, too, falls in love, with a character named Mimi (one of the central characters of the original *La Boheme* also had this name), who is dying of AIDS.

John Bemrose of *Maclean's* described *Rent's* plot as "a hodgepodge of lover's quarrels, with the unusual twist (at least for a mainstream musical) that several of the lovers are of the same sex." The stage design, too, was unusual: as the show begins, "the uncurtained stage gives the impression that the show is far from ready. . . . there is no scenery in sight: a catwalk crosses in front of a brick wall, while a few red folding chairs are scattered around a long metal table. Nearby looms an enormous abstract sculpture containing, among other things, pieces of a shopping cart and several bicycles. It looks like a windmill rearranged by a hurricane."

What made *Rent* a success, according to Bemrose and other critics, were songs such as "Without You," a ballad; and "Out Tonight," which Bemrose described as a "raunchy" number. Lahr wrote that three songs from the show were "as passionate, unpretentious, and powerful as anything I've heard in the musical theatre for more than a decade." Jack Kroll of *Newsweek* praised *Rent* as a "rousing, moving, scathingly funny show" which "has brought a shocking jolt of creative juice to Broadway."

Larson would never read these accolades. Late in 1995, he left his job to work full-time on *Rent;* but in January of 1996, three weeks before *Rent* opened at New York's Nederlander Theatre, he began experiencing chest pains. He went to the emergency room of one hospital, where he was treated for food poisoning. When this did not help, he went to another emergency room, and there was diagnosed with a viral infection. On January 25, the day of the last dress rehearsal, Larson died from a foot-long tear in his aorta. New York State would ultimately fine both hospitals for their negligence, and according to *Time* magazine, Larson's family planned to sue the institutions for $250 million.

Though nothing would bring Larson back to life, death could not silence the effect of his work. Later in 1996, his sister accepted the Pulitzer Prize on his behalf. *Rent* became a Broadway sensation, and attracted fans around the United States and the world. As for Larson's ultimate musical legacy, it seems clear that he made great strides toward his goal

of redefining the American musical, but fans can only wonder what he might have done if he had lived longer. Sondheim told *Entertainment Weekly* that when he last spoke with Larson about a month before his death, "He was learning to swallow his pride. . . . He felt pleased with himself for growing up."

Further Reading

Contemporary Authors, Volume 156, Gale, 1997.
Contemporary Literary Criticism, Volume 99, Gale, 1998.
Larson, Jonathan, *Rent,* with interviews and text by Evelyn McDonnell with Kathy Silberger, Morrow, 1997.
American Theatre, July/August 1996, pp. 13-16.
Entertainment Weekly, May 30, 1997, pp. 64-65.
Maclean's, December 15, 1997, p. 60.
Newsweek, May 13, 1996, pp. 54-59.
New Yorker, February 19, 1996, pp. 94-96.
People, April 22, 1996, p. 59.
Time, December 23, 1996, p. 20.
Village Voice, December 3, 1996, p. 48.

Alexander Ivanovich Lebed

A former paratrooper in the Russian Army, General Alexander Lebed (born 1950) served briefly as Russia's national security chief under president Boris Yeltsin before moving on to become one of Yeltsin's most probable successors. He is regarded as a fierce nationalist and an outspoken critic of corruption in Russian business and government.

With a strong showing in the 1996 Russian presidential elections, Alexander Lebed has shown himself to be one of the nation's most popular politicians. Building on an admirable 25-year military career, he has captured the interest of a population weary of corruption and political strife, promising renewed strength, unity, and prosperity for Russia. He is a harsh critic of Russian business and government leaders, a nationalist hero who brought an end to a costly civil war in Chechnya, and a brusque, dry-witted politician with powerful populist appeal.

Early Life and Military Career

In his autobiography, *My Life and My Country,* Lebed claims that he knew from a very early age that he wished to serve as a pilot in the Russian air force. As his book makes clear with its many accounts of brawls and resulting injuries, he was a competitive and aggressive youth, well-suited to his military ambitions. When he was old enough, he applied to aviation school and was rejected, ironically, due to the many operations he had undergone as direct results of his combative nature. Lebed recovered from this setback quickly, applying shortly thereafter to the Komsomol Ryazan Higher Airborne Command School—a school for paratroopers. "Although I wouldn't be in the pilot's seat," he said, "I'd still be in the sky."

As a cadet at the Komsomol School, Lebed developed interests in chess and boxing. He excelled in the latter, advancing to the heavyweight semifinals of the school's boxing championship in his second year. Upon graduating, he remained at the school, first as a training platoon commander, then as a company commander, until 1981.

Itching for a change of pace, the civil war in Afghanistan gave Lebed his first real opportunity. He was placed in command of the 1st Battalion of the 345th Detached Airborne Regiment. He spent a year there, building combat experience, after which, he entered the M.V. Frunze Military Academy in Narofominsk, Russia. He graduated with honors in 1985, and, with the newly acquired rank of major, was placed in command of the 331st Airborne regiment, stationed in the city of Kostroma.

From there, Lebed rose quickly. In 1986 he was promoted to lieutenant colonel and was assigned the post of executive officer of the 76th Airborne Division in Pskov. Two years later he was given the rank of full colonel and placed in command of the Tula Airborne Division. These promotions took place during a time when the entire Russian military was undergoing great change, as a consequence of the political upheaval—the dissolution of the Soviet Union and the collapse of its Communist leadership—which was also taking place at that time. His years in the Tula assignment would prove, due in part to this political unrest, to be among the most decisive of his career.

Most of the incidents in which Lebed was involved over the years 1988 to 1995 involved ethnic clashes in the former Soviet republics. Lacking the strong guiding hand of the Soviet government, many of these states were disintegrating as long-suppressed conflicts rose to the surface. Thus, very shortly after his promotion to colonel, Lebed found himself attempting to intervene in hostilities between Azerbaijanis and Armenians in the region of Baku, in southern Russia. The experience may have helped bolster his already strong nationalist streak. He remarked, "There, for the first time since Afghanistan, I saw burned-out trucks and buses, charred houses, and people's hair, naturally black, turned white from the horrors they had seen . . . all this, in my country—as it was at the time."

There was to be much more of this. The year 1989 brought him and his division to Tblisi, Georgia—also in southern Russia. This was followed shortly by renewed unrest in Baku. At the conclusion of this last event, he was promoted to major general, and soon after, he was appointed deputy commander of Airborne troops for combat training and military schools. As his star continued to rise, however, the political situation in Russia seemed only to worsen, culminating on August 1991 in an attempted coup by hardline communist elements within the government. Lebed was called upon to organize a defense of the Supreme Soviet building in Moscow, and the coup failed in a matter of days.

Lebed's military career took one more turn, in the summer of 1992, when he was called in to quell an ethnic conflict in the Dniester Moldovan Republic. Although his sympathies in this episode lay with Dniester's Russian population, he performed his duties with detached coolness, and the episode was widely recognized as his greatest achievement as a military commander. Shortly thereafter, he was given his last appointment—commander of the 14th Guardian Army in Dniester. In June 1995, at the age of 45, he retired from service in the Russian Army.

Political Life

Lebed's involvement in politics began quite some time before his military career ended. In 1990, he was elected by the 51st Tula Airborne Regiment to serve as their delegate to the 28th Congress of the Communist Party of the Soviet Union, which turned out, due to the sweeping political changes of that time, to be the founding congress of the Communist Party of Russia—the Soviet Union by that time had ceased to exist. He rose quickly to prominence, and his performance there resulted in his being elected to the Central Committee of the Communist Party. The chaotic and self-defeating nature of both these assemblies instilled in him a great distrust for the Russian political system. "I listened to the screaming and the useless fights," he says of the plenary meetings he attended, "I observed the open, no-holds-barred struggle of various factions to get their people in the party hierarchy. . . . I was an eyewitness to the double, or even triple, standards of morality that were endemic to the Party." This rude awakening was, by his own admission, a turning point in his life, "My faith in authority came tumbling down. I became convinced that all men are opportunists and fallible."

Regardless of these opinions, he was not dissuaded from pursuing a second career in politics. In 1993, he won a seat in the Supreme Soviet of the separatist Dniester Moldovan Republic, capturing 88 percent of the vote. This post was short-lived. In October of 1993, following a violent confrontation between Russian President Boris Yeltsin and the Russian Supreme Soviet, he resigned to protest Dniester's decision to send soldiers to oppose Yeltsin (Lebed preferred neutrality in this matter).

After this experience, Lebed departed the political scene until his retirement from the army. In 1995, he was elected in Tula as a deputy of the State Duma. The following year, he was nominated as a Presidential candidate. In June, running in third place, he withdrew from the race, backing Boris Yeltsin, who was subsequently elected. Yeltsin, in turn, appointed him Secretary of the Russian Federation Security Council. In this role, he brought about an end to the lengthy and bloody war in Chechnya. This may well have been the most decisive accomplishment in Lebed's life thus far. Discarding the standing government policy—violent repression of separatist elements in Chechnya—he brokered a peace which postpones a final decision on the Chechan independence question until 2001.

However much this bold move may have impressed watchers at home and abroad, his term in Yeltsin's cabinet was short-lived, ending with his expulsion in October 1996. Since that time, he has strived to cultivate a political following in Russia, forming his own political party, Honor and Motherland, to further that end. In February of 1998, he made a bid for the governorship of the region of Krasnoyarsk. He won this election in May of that year, and all indications are that he will run for president again in 2000.

Lebed has long been an outspoken critic of the "crony capitalism" (the selling of former state industries to political insiders at cut rates) which he claims is "bleeding the country." According to a website biography, he also has harsh words for his government's tax policy, which he says "is making everyone, every single entrepreneur, every single businessman, a criminal." He frequently refers to Russia's leadership as criminal, and in a turn of phrase so particularly characteristic of his style, he calls for the Old Guard to step aside, "Let them keep their orders, their medals, their diplomas, and let them fish and let them grow strawberries."

He is no less turbulent on the military front. Despite the keen fear and hatred of NATO held by so many of his countrymen, Lebed advises acceptance of the organization in a spirit of post-Cold War cooperation with the West. He seems compelled in this regard by a danger about which many Russian politicians refuse to speak—the fate of the U.S.S.R.'s nuclear arsenal. Lebed angered the Yeltsin government in 1997 by claiming, on U.S. television, that 84 tactical nuclear warheads had gone missing from the Russian stockpile.

To be sure, Lebed is not without his critics, both outside and within Russia. According to a website biography, the Russian press has referred to him as a "cheap populist," while those in the West have emphasized his blustering nationalism and communist sympathies. He was noted early in his political career for his approval of former Chilean dictator General Augusto Pinochet, which support he abruptly shifted to General Charles de Gaulle of France, after observing the effect of his remarks in democratic nations.

Either way, no-nonsense reformer or aspiring demagogue, there can be no doubt that Lebed is a force to be reckoned with in Russia. Whether he will continue to influence events past the presidential elections of 2000 remains to be seen.

Further Reading

Lambeth, Benjamin, *The Warrior Who Would Rule Russia*, Brassey's, 1997.

Lebed, Alexander, *My Life and My Country*, Regnery Publishing, Inc., 1997.

Polushin, Vladimir, *General Lebed: zagadka Rossii*, Vneshtorgizdat, 1996.

Christian Science Monitor, February 24, 1997.

East European Markets, February 14, 1997.

Forbes, January 12, 1998, p. 56.

New Perspectives Quarterly, Spring 1997, p. 30.

New Times, June 1996, p. 13.

Newsweek, July 1, 1996; October 28, 1996.

Time, February 27, 1995; July 1, 1996.

U.S. News & World Report, October 9, 1995.

Wall Street Journal, November 20, 1996, p. A22.

Washington Post, October 9, 1996, p. A19.

"Alexander Lebed," http://www.cs.indiana.edu/hyplan/dmiguse/Russian/albio.html (March 24, 1998). □

Bruce Lee

At the time of his sudden and mysterious death in 1973, actor and martial arts expert Bruce Lee (1940-1973) was on the verge of international superstardom. Rooted strongly in both Oriental and Western cultures, Lee brought to the ancient Chinese fighting art of kung fu the grace of a ballet dancer. He was an actor as well, and infused his performances with humor and a dramatic sensibility that assured a place for king fu films as a new form of cinematic art.

R aised in San Francisco, California, Hong Kong, and Seattle, Washington, Lee had gained his first American audience with a groundbreaking role on the 1966-67 television series *The Green Hornet*. Eager to challenge Hollywood's stereotypical images of Asian Americans, he returned to Hong Kong and ultimately developed his own style of kung fu. On the strength of his film, *Enter the Dragon* (1973), Lee returned to the attention of American audiences and posthumously ushered in a new era of cinematic art. Stars such as David Carradine, Chuck Norris, Jean-Claude Van Damme, Steven Seagal, and fellow Hong Kong martial artist Jackie Chan would follow his example, making Lee the father of an enduring style of action hero.

The "Strong One"

In 1939 Lee's father, a popular Chinese opera star, brought his wife and three children with him from Hong Kong to San Francisco while he toured the United States as a performer. At the end of the following year, on November 27, 1940, another son was born to the Lees. In accordance with Chinese tradition, they had not named him, as his father was away in New York; therefore the mother took the advice of her physician and called the boy Bruce because it meant "strong one" in Gaelic. Lee reportedly had a number of Chinese names, but it would be by the name of Bruce that he would become famous.

Stardom began early, with his first film appearance at age three months in a movie called *Golden Gate Girl.* By then it was 1941, and though their native Hong Kong was occupied by Japanese troops, the Lees decided to return home. According to Chinese superstition, demons sometimes try to steal male children. Out of fear for the young boy's safety, they dressed him as a girl, and even made him attend a girl's school for a while. Meanwhile Lee grew up around the cinema, and appeared in a Hong Kong movie when he was four. Two years later, a director recognized his star quality and put him in another film. By the time he graduated from high school, Lee had appeared in some twenty films.

As a teenager, he became involved in two seemingly contradictory activities: gang warfare and dance. As a dancer he won a cha-cha championship, and as a gang member he risked death on the streets of Hong Kong. Out of

fear that he might be caught at some point without his gang, helpless before a group of rivals, Lee began to study the Chinese martial arts of kung fu. The style that attracted his attention was called wing chun, which according to legend was developed by a woman named Yim Wing Chun, who improved on the techniques of a Shaolin Buddhist nun. Lee absorbed the style, and began adding his own improvements. This proved too much for the wing chun masters, who excommunicated him from the school.

Lee's film career continued, and he was becoming a popular actor in the Hong Kong film scene. Producer Run Run Shaw offered the high schooler a lucrative contract, and Lee wanted to take it. But when he got into trouble with the police for fighting, his mother sent him to the United States to live with friends of the family.

Teacher and Actor

Lee finished high school in Edison, Washington, near Seattle. He then enrolled as a philosophy major at the University of Washington, where he supported himself by giving dance lessons and waiting tables at a Chinese restaurant. As a kung fu teacher instructing fellow university students, he met Linda Emery, whom he married in 1964.

The newlyweds moved to California, and Lee—who had begun developing a new fighting style called jeet kune do—ultimately opened three schools in Los Angeles, Oakland, California, and Seattle. He also began to pursue his acting more seriously, and landed a part in the TV series *The Green Hornet.* The show was based on a 1930s radio program, and Lee played the role of the Hornet's Asian assistant, Kato. He virtually created the role, imbuing Kato with a theatrical fighting style quite unlike that which Lee taught in his schools. The show would be cancelled after one season, but fans would long remember Lee's role.

After the end of *The Green Hornet,* Lee made guest appearances on TV shows such as *Longstreet* and *Ironside.* His most notable role during this time was in the film *Marlowe* (1969) with James Garner, when he played a memorable part as a high-kicking villain. Clearly Lee had the qualities of a star; but it was just as clear that an Asian American faced limitations within the Hollywood system, which tended to cast Oriental actors in stereotypical roles. Therefore in 1971, the Lees, including son Brandon (born 1965), and daughter Shannon (born 1967) moved to Hong Kong.

Dramatic Rise, Tragic End

Back in Hong Kong, Lee soon signed a two-film contract, and released the movie known to U.S. audiences as *Fists of Fury* late in 1971. The story, which featured Lee as a fighter seeking revenge on those who had killed his kung fu master, was not original in itself; but the presentation of it was, and the crucial element was Lee. He combined the smooth, flowing style of jeet kune do that he taught in his schools with the loud, aggressive, and highly theatrical methods he had employed as Kato. With the graceful, choreographic qualities of his movements; his good looks and charm; his sense of humor and his acting ability, Lee was one of a kind—a star in the making.

Fists of Fury set box-office records in Hong Kong which were broken only by his next picture, *The Chinese Connection,* in 1972. Lee established his own film company, Concord Pictures, and began directing movies. The first of these would appear in the U.S. as *Way of the Dragon.* Lee was enthusiastic about his future, not merely as a performer, but as an artist: "With any luck," he told a journalist shortly before his death, "I hope to make . . . the kind of movie where you can just watch the surface story, if you like, or can look deeper into it." Unfortunately, Lee would not live to explore his full potential as a filmmaker: on July 20, 1973, three weeks before his fourth film, *Enter the Dragon,* was released in the United States, he died suddenly.

Lee's death became a source of controversy. Officially the cause of death was brain swelling as a reaction to aspirin he had taken for a back injury. But the suddenness of his passing, combined with his youth, his good health, and the bizarre timing on the verge of his explosion as an international superstar, spawned rumors that he had been killed by hit men. Some speculated he had run afoul of the Chinese mafia and other powerful interests in the Hong Kong film industry, and had been poisoned. Throughout his life, Lee had been obsessed by fears of his early death, and some believed that the brilliant young star had some sort of bizarre "curse" on him.

According to legend and rumor, when Lee bought a house in Hong Kong shortly before his death, he incurred the wrath of the neighborhood's resident demons. The curse is said to last for three generation. Tragically, the notion of a curse gained eerie credence on June 18, 1993—a month and two days before the 20th anniversary of Lee's death—when Brandon Lee died under equally strange circumstances. While filming a scene for the movie *The Crow,* he was shot by a gun that supposedly contained blanks but in fact had a live round lodged in its chamber. Like his father, Brandon Lee was on the verge of stardom.

Lee gave the world an enormous artistic legacy, in the process virtually creating a new cinematic art form. By the 1990s, *Enter the Dragon* alone had grossed more than $100 million, and Lee's influence could be found in the work of numerous Hollywood action heroes. In 1993, Jason Scott Lee (no relation) appeared in *Dragon: The Bruce Lee Story,* directed by Rob Cohen. Actress Lauren Holly played Lee's wife Linda, and Holly became friends with Lee's daughter Shannon.

Shannon Lee once told *People* that she had not inherited any of her father's or brother's fighting abilities. Although she became host of a TV show featuring martial arts competitions, she has said in most respects she was quite unlike her father.

Further Reading

Contemporary Theatre, Film, and Television, Volume 15, Gale, 1996.
Hoffman, Charles, *Bruce Lee, Brandon Lee, and the Dragon's Curse,* Random House, 1995.
International Dictionary of Films and Filmmakers, Volume 3: Actors and Actresses, St. James Press, 1992.
Jahn, Michael, *Dragon: The Bruce Lee Story,* Jove Books, 1993.
Lee, Linda, *The Life and Tragic Death of Bruce Lee,* Star Books, 1975.
Notable Asian Americans, Gale, 1995.
Uyehara, M., *Bruce Lee: The Incomparable Fighter,* Ohara Publications, 1988.
Maclean's, May 10, 1993.
People, October 23, 1995.
Time, May 17, 1993.

Ursula K. Le Guin

Science-fiction writer Ursula K. Le Guin (born 1929) created fantastic worlds in which the author's strong-willed, feminist protagonists have increasingly taken center stage.

An understanding of both anthropology and varied cultures informed the highly acclaimed science fiction writing of Ursula K. Le Guin. In such books as the *Earthsea Trilogy, The Lathe of Heaven,* and *The Left Hand of Darkness,* she created what Nancy Jesser in *Feminist Writers* called "an anthropology of the future, imagining whole cultural systems and conflicts." Eschewing the "pulp" aspects of most science-fiction—brawny male heroes, compliant women, and over-the-top technology as both cause and solution to the world's problems—Le Guin was known for skillfully telling a story containing many layers of meaning beneath its calm exterior. Her *Earthsea* novels have been cited by several reviewers as characteristic of her work; an essayist in *Science Fiction Writers* commented that, as it was "constrained neither by realistic events nor by scientific speculation, but only by the author's moral imagination," the Earthsea books showed such characteristic themes from "questing and patterning motifs to [her] overall emphasis on 'wholeness and balance.'" Echoes of Taoism, Jungian psychology, ecological concerns, and mythos resonate throughout her written works.

Inspired by Parents' Example

Le Guin was born in Berkeley, California, on October 21, 1929. Her father, anthropologist Alfred L. Kroeber, was noted for his studies of the Native American cultures of California. Her mother, Theodora Kroeber Quinn, was a psychologist and, in her later years, a writer; she would be a particularly strong influence on her daughter, both as a writer and as a feminist.

Raised in an intellectually stimulating environment, Le Guin excelled at academics. After graduating from high school, she enrolled at Harvard University's Radcliffe College, where she received her bachelor's degree, in 1951, and was a member of Phi Beta Kappa national honorary. Course work in New York City, at Columbia University, followed. Le Guin was named a faculty fellow, in 1952, and received a Fulbright fellowship to study in Paris, in 1953, having earned her master's degree in romance literature of the Middle Ages and Renaissance from Columbia, the previous year.

The year after she earned her master's degree at Columbia, Le Guin married the historian Charles A. Le Guin. The couple made their home in Portland, Oregon. They had two daughters and one son. Prior to raising her family, she got a job as a French instructor at Mercer University, in Macon, Georgia, before moving on to the University of Idaho for a brief period, in 1956.

Short Fiction Set Stage for Novels

Le Guin's first written efforts consisted of poetry and short fiction. Her first published work was the story "April in Paris," which appeared in *Fantastic* magazine, in 1962, when she was 33 years old. Le Guin's first novel, *Rocannon's World,* would be published by Ace Books, in 1966. It was the first of many science-fiction works she would write in the following decades, and the first of her five-volume "Hainish" series of novels. In the Hainish novels—*Rocannon's World, Planet of Exile, City of Illusions, The Left Hand of Darkness,* and *The Word for World Is Forest*—the author allowed readers to follow the physical and emotional journeys taken by her protagonists as they were confronted with cultures that had rules and systems radically different from their own. The Hainish were a race of beings from the planet Hain who have colonized all planets of the Universe that will sustain them. As each colony adapted to its new, unique environment, it developed differently, evolving distinctive physical and cultural traits in relation to other Hain colonies. Le Guin's protagonists must become, in a sense, amateur anthropologists in their attempts to understand and exist within new worlds as

they journey between colonies, re-evaluating their own cultural assumptions in the process.

Novels Explored Universal Themes

While most science fiction has traditionally been dismissed by critics, as well as serious students of literature, Le Guin's sophisticated, well-studied, yet immensely readable novels have been able to break the barrier and gain a mainstream audience and mainstream attention, perhaps because of her ability to weave fantasy elements into her gentle, often dispassionate prose. After the publication of the highly acclaimed *The Left Hand of Darkness* in 1969, 1971's *The Lathe of Heaven,* and 1974's *The Dispossessed: An Ambiguous Utopia,* Le Guin's work began to be taken seriously, even within academic circles.

With these novels, the author seriously explored the influence of gender roles and race on cultural attitudes, and focused on such backlashes as sexism and oppression in all of their forms. The juxtaposition of contrasting societies was a familiar motif: one society off balance, characterized by violence, injustice, and inequality; the other stable, just, and peaceful. This duality related to the universal duality reflected in such sources as the Christian belief in heaven and hell, or the Taoist philosophy of balanced opposites, the yin and yang. Le Guin's focus on this universal duality has allowed her fiction to speak to mainstream readers, particularly those not inducted into the heavy-duty technological concerns addressed in so-called "hard science fiction."

In her works after the Hainish novels, Le Guin began to broaden her talents, writing poetry, the short play *No Use to Talk to Me,* two volumes of literary criticism, and several children's books. In her imaginative *Catwings* and *Catwings Return,* she entertained younger readers with imaginary worlds containing flying cats and kittens. In Le Guin's adult novels written after the mid-1970s, she also began to stretch the boundaries of her so-called science fiction, creating the quasi-history of an anonymous nineteenth-century country in 1979's, *Malafrena,* and again in the short stories collected in *Orsinian Tales,* and combining music (via an accompanying cassette), verse, anthropologist's notations, and stories in 1985's, *Always Coming Home,* a book about the Kesh, future inhabitants of California who establish a new society after ecological Armageddon.

Fantasy Fiction as Effective Allegory

Whether set in the past or future, each of Le Guin's novels actually addressed the present. Imbedded within the plot of her 1972 novel *The Word for World Is Forest,* thoughtful readers could easily discover solemn parallels to the Vietnam War era, as well as telling commentary about the destruction of the world's rain forests. The novel told of the reaction of the colonizing culture—the Terrans—to the peaceful, forest-dwelling tribes—the Athsheans (read "indigenous tribes of South America and Indonesia") that they encountered in their new home. Because they fear the ways of the Athsheans, the Terrans react violently, destroying the homes of the forest dwellers in an effort to exterminate them and reap financial rewards.

Award-winning Quartet

Spanning Le Guin's career as a writer were her four award-winning *Earthsea* novels, which have been praised by critics as some of her most enjoyable works. Beginning with 1968's *A Wizard of Earthsea*, readers met the goat herder Ged, who lives on one of a kingdom of islands known as Earthsea, as he trains to become a practitioner of magic. In later novels in the series—*The Tombs of Atuan* (1970) and *The Farthest Shore* (1972)—Ged matured as both a man and a wizard, grappling with hubris, then flattery, before sacrificing his own powers to save his world. In 1990s, *Tehanu: The Last Book of Earthsea*, which concluded the series and which Le Guin wrote as a response to criticism by feminists that her male protagonists were all powerful, and female characters merely helpers, an elderly woman and a young girl were featured. According to Charlotte Spivack in her appraisal, *Ursula Le Guin*, "Earthsea is a convincingly authenticated world, drawn with a sure hand for fine detail. [It is a] mature narrative of growing up, a moral tale without a moral, a realistic depiction of a fantasy world."

In addition to her prolific career as an author, Le Guin has taught writing workshops at numerous colleges around the United States, as well as in Australia and Great Britain. She has also revised several of her early works, updating them in response to her growing feminist leanings. She has also been involved in the adaptation of several of her novels into motion pictures. The Public Television production of *The Lathe of Heaven*, in 1980, benefited from her adaptation of her own novel—the story about a man whose dreams alter reality—as well as her on-the-set production assistance. Le Guin's positive appraisal of the resulting film was a marked contrast to most authors' feelings about their work after a film crew gets through with it. The recipient of numerous awards, she continued to make her home in Oregon.

Further Reading

Bittner, James, *Approaches to the Fiction of Ursula K. Le Guin*, UMI Research Press, 1984.
Bleiler, E.F., editor, *Science Fiction Writers*, Scribner's , 1982.
Cogell, Elizabeth Cummings, *Understanding Ursula K. Le Guin*, University of South Carolina Press, 1990.
Feminist Writers, St. James Press, 1997.
Greenburg, Martin H., and Joseph D. Olander, *Ursula Le Guin*, Taplinger, 1979.
Slusser, George Edgar, *The Farthest Shores of Ursula K. Le Guin*, Borgo Press, 1976.
Spivack, Charlotte, *Ursula Le Guin*, Twayne, 1984.
Science-Fiction Studies, March 1976.

Vivien Leigh

To legions of movie fans, Vivien Leigh (1913-1967) will best be remembered as the defiant and beautiful Scarlett O'Hara, heroine of the 1939 movie classic *Gone With the Wind*.

Vivien Leigh had only a brief career on the British stage and screen when she was plucked out of relative obscurity for the female lead in what would become one of the greatest movies ever made. Playing opposite the charismatic Clark Gable, Leigh became an instant celebrity after her role as Scarlett O'Hara, and remained so for the rest of her relatively short, yet sometimes turbulent life.

An International Upbringing

Leigh was born Vivian Mary Hartley in India, in the cool mountain region of Darjeeling in 1913. Her stockbroker father, Ernest Richard, and her mother, Gertrude, spent half the year in England and half in India, which was then under British control. Enrolled in a convent boarding school outside of London at the age of five, Leigh first appeared on stage three years later in *A Midsummer's Night's Dream*. She recalled after that experience that she couldn't remember when she didn't want to be an actress. The stage would have to wait, however, as she finished her education. She attended a finishing school in Paris, studied languages in Italy, and attended a girls' seminary in Bavaria. When she was 18, her parents sent her to the Royal Academy of Dramatic Arts.

The Early Career

In 1932, Leigh decided to get serious about her stage career. Married that year to a London barrister, Herbert Leigh Holman, she took his middle name, slightly changed the spelling of her first name. She gave birth to a daughter,

Suzanne, in 1933, and got a part in a British film called *Things Are Looking Up* in 1934. For Leigh, they were looking up. She landed small parts in several movies and then won her first stage role in 1935 for a production of *The Green Sash*. Although the play never got to London's famed theater district, her performance caught the attention of Sydney Carroll, a West End producer. She opened later that year in his *The Mask of Virtue*. The critics were smitten; some said as much by her astounding beauty as her acting ability. However, this role led to her "big break" and she was signed to a five-year film contract.

Although she worked steadily over the next several years, Leigh's career never brought her top status. From 1936 to 1939, Leigh appeared in a number of British stage and screen productions. She was the Queen in *Richard II*, an Oxford University student drama production directed by John Gielgud, who would become one of England's greatest stage performers. She played Anne Boleyn in *Henry VIII* and Jessica Morton in *Bats in the Belfry*. In 1937, she was invited by the Danish government to play Ophelia to Laurence Olivier's Hamlet. She also appeared on the London stage in the title role of *Serena Blandish*.

Leigh was busy on the British silver screen as well. Cast again with Laurence Olivier, she played a lady in waiting to Queen Elizabeth in *Fire Over England,* in 1937, followed by *Dark Journey* and *Storm in a Teacup*. In 1938, she played opposite American screen idol Robert Taylor in *A Yank at Oxford*, a film that really only boosted Taylor's career. She also appeared with Charles Laughton that year in *St. Martin's Lane*, which was released in the United States in 1940 as *The Sidewalks of London*. This role was a bit of a change for Leigh, as she was cast to play a mean and unscrupulous heroine.

The Scarlett Legend Begins

Leigh came to the United States in 1938, where she visited Olivier on the set of *Wuthering Heights*. Sir Laurence Olivier (who was knighted in 1947) was regarded as one of England's greatest stage actors, noted especially for his Shakespearean roles. Leigh and Olivier had become attracted to each other during the filming of *Fire Over England,* and their well-publicized romance became a main topic of gossip, especially since they were both already married.

While Leigh and Olivier were spending time together, waiting for their divorces so they could marry, David O. Selznick was looking for a star. It was January 1939, and he was still without an actress to play the most publicized, sought-after role in movie history—Scarlett O'Hara, the extraordinary southern belle who is the main character in *Gone With The Wind.*

Even without Scarlett, the movie was already in production. Selznick had cast the other important roles: Clark Gable as Rhett Butler, who proves to be more than a match for Scarlett; Leslie Howard as the quiet, gentlemanly Ashley Wilkes, whom Scarlett believes she loves; Olivia de Havilland as the gentle Melanie Hamilton, whom Wilkes marries; and Hattie McDaniel as the black servant who runs Tara with a blustery but devoted sense of duty. Even though

many actresses, including Joan Crawford and Lucille Ball, tested for the part, Selznick still had not found the right person.

As noted in the "Pre-Production" section of the *Gone With the Wind Homepage,* Selznick's brother Myron, a talent agent, showed up on the set as they were filming the scene of the burning of Atlanta. He told his brother, "I want you to meet Scarlett O'Hara." According to the website, "The shadowy figure stepped forward, green eyes glinting in the half-light. Selznick always maintained that from the moment he first saw Vivien Leigh, the flames of Atlanta playing across her face, he had known she was Scarlett. She was later given a screen test, but it was only a formality. The part was hers—a storybook ending to a legendary search." As noted in the website, Leigh later commented, "There were dozens of girls testing and I did not seriously consider that I might actually play the part."

The filming of *Gone With the Wind* was officially completed about five months later. According to the "Post-Production" section of the *Gone With the Wind Homepage,* Leigh had worked almost non-stop for five months and was totally exhausted. However, she would soon reap the benefits of her dedication to the project.

Critics called Leigh's performance flawless and brilliant, and she went on to win the Academy Award for Best Actress. The film won several other Academy Awards, including Best Picture, and over the years its fame has hardly diminished. From relative obscurity, the name of Vivien Leigh became known worldwide.

Life After Scarlett

In 1940, Leigh and Olivier starred in *Romeo and Juliet* in New York, but they did not get good reviews. The disappointment was forgotten a few months later when the couple finally wed in August. That December they sailed for wartorn England where Olivier served in the Royal Navy and Leigh worked for the equivalent of the American USO. The couple made the film *That Hamilton Woman* in 1941. According to the *Times,* Leigh had "hoped to join the Old Vic Company (a highly respected repertory company) on her return to England. . . . the director was of the opinion that her new celebrity would make it impossible for her to fit in."

Leigh continued to bask in the adoration of her fans for her memorable portrayal of Scarlett O'Hara, but she received praise for other work as well. In 1945, she played a 16-year-old Cleopatra in *Caesar and Cleopatra* and then appeared in the London production of *The Skin of Our Teeth,* directed by her husband.

Soon after the play opened, Leigh's illness forced its closing for a time while she recuperated. According to her biography on a *Gone With the Wind* website, "Always frail, Leigh saved her limited stamina for her frequent stage appearances. Bouts of physical illness and mental breakdowns also cast a tragic shadow over the brightness of her many achievements.

Leigh once again found success when she portrayed Blanche Du Bois, the female lead in Pulitzer Prize winning play by Tennessee Williams, *A Streetcar Named Desire.* In the London stage production, she was directed by Olivier. In the film version, she was directed by Elia Kazan, and in 1951, Leigh won her second Academy Award for the role. Also in 1951, Leigh and Olivier appeared at the St. James in London, during the Festival of Britain. According to the *Times,* "when this theatre was about to be demolished six years later, she led a vigorous if unsuccessful movement to save it, interrupting a debate in the House of Lords in order to protest."

Leigh and Olivier divorced in 1960, but she continued to work in the theatre. In 1963, she made her Broadway musical debut in *Tovarich.* She made her last film, *Ship of Fools,* in 1965, and died on July 8, 1967, in London. According to the *Times,* "on the night of her death all theaters in the West End extinguished their exterior lights for an hour as a sign of mourning."

As noted by her biography on a *Gone With the Wind* website, Leigh will be best remembered for her portrayals of Scarlett O'Hara and Blanche Du Bois. Her biography states, "Although she was British, she played the part of the Southern belle to perfection. . . . Those two sterling performances alone would qualify her for immortality, and she won Academy Awards for Best Actress in both of them."

Further Reading

Bridges, Herb, *'Frankly, My Dear . . . ': Gone With the Wind Memorabilia (Motion Pictures),* Mercer University Press, 1995.

Bridges, Herb, and Terryl C. Boodman, *Gone With the Wind: The Definitive Illustrated History of the Book, the Movie and the Legend,* Fireside, 1989.

Katz, Ephraim, *The Film Encyclopedia,* Harper, 1990.

Walker, Alexander, *Vivien: The Life of Vivien Leigh,* Grove Press, 1989.

Times (London), July 10, 1967.

Gone With the Wind Homepage, http://www.geocities.com/Hollywood/Set/3070 (April 23, 1998).

"Vivien Leigh," *Sherrie's Gone With the Wind Page,* http://www.ladyrulz.tierranet.com/gwtw/vivien.html (April 23, 1998).

Vivien Leigh, (VHS tape) Americans Talk Issues, 1992.

Vivien Leigh: Scarlett and Beyond, (VHS tape) Theatre Communications Group, 1991.

Madeleine L'Engle

American fiction writer Madeleine L'Engle (born 1918) is the accomplished author of numerous plays, poems, novels, and autobiographies for children and adults. She is perhaps best known for her children's book, *A Wrinkle in Time,* written in 1962 and winner of the 1963 Newbery Medal for Children's Literature. Two later works, *A Wind in the Door* and *A Swiftly Tilting Planet,* continue the theme and form a trilogy about time.

onald R. Hettinga, in *Presenting Madeleine L'Engle,* wrote of the author: "Her vocation is that of storyteller and story itself is part of her story." As a young girl, L'Engle used writing to make sense of things. "Her fiction, while not rigidly autobiographical as, for example, Ernest Hemingway's," Hettinga continued, "is yet informed and sometimes shaped by the experiences of her life."

Influenced by Artistic Parents

Madeleine L'Engle Camp was born November 29, 1918, in New York, New York, the only child of artistic parents who fed her imagination and encouraged her creativity. She was named for her great grandmother, who was also named Madeleine L'Engle but went by the nickname Mado. L'Engle's father, Charles Wadsworth Camp, arrived home from World War I when Madeleine was less than a year old. He had been a newspaper reporter—a drama and music critic for the *Herald-Evening Sun*—but his lungs were so damaged by mustard gas that he quit his job after the war. He then focused his energies on writing short stories, movies, and plays in his small office in New York's Flatiron building.

L'Engle's mother was a pianist. Madeleine Hall Barnett Camp was almost 40 years old when she gave birth to Madeleine. She and her husband had wanted a child for a long time, but when Madeleine finally arrived, they disagreed on how to raise her. In the end, it was a strict upbringing, replete with governesses and boarding schools.

Nannies and Boarding Schools

L'Engle spent her first years with her parents and her English nanny, Mrs. O'Connell, in a two bedroom apartment on 82nd Street in New York. The city provided many opportunities for her to experience the arts, and her parents often entertained musicians, artists and writers in the evenings. This atmosphere fostered her creativity and imagination, inspiring her to write her first story at the tender age of five. She continued her interest in writing throughout her school years, and used her hobby to combat the loneliness she often felt. "It never occurred to me that [writing] was something you were supposed to worry about," L'Engle told Claire Whitcomb in *Victoria*. "You learn by doing it."

In fifth grade, L'Engle won her first poetry contest. The teacher accused her of plagiarizing the poem, though, stating flatly that L'Engle wasn't bright enough to have written it. Her mother intervened, bringing the teacher a stack of L'Engle's poems and stories from home. The following year, her parents sent her to a new school, Todhunter, where her teacher, Margaret Clapp, encouraged her love of reading and writing. Years later, Clapp became the first woman president of Wellesley College.

During the winter of 1930 to 1931, Charles Camp developed pneumonia and his doctors encouraged him to leave New York as soon as he recovered. The family moved to Switzerland, and L'Engle was sent to Chatelard, a girls' boarding school in Montreaux, Switzerland. At Chatelard, she and a friend experimented with dream states as inspiration for writing. The two girls had read about poppies and opium in books and learned that the flower would enhance their dreams. So, they planted poppies, ate them in sandwiches, and kept their dream journals at their bedsides. "While L'Engle soon determined that she did not need to eat poppies to dream," Hettinga explained, "she does credit this experience with awakening a sensitivity to the world of the subconscious, a sensitivity that is crucial to her as a writer."

When L'Engle was 14, her grandmother, Dearma, became seriously ill and the Camps moved to Florida to be with her. That fall, L'Engle was sent to Ashley Hall Boarding School in Charleston, South Carolina. She was an active student, participating in plays and serving on the student council. From 1936 to 1937, she served as student council president. Earlier in 1936, her father died. L'Engle graduated from Ashley Hall the following June. In the fall, she attended Smith College, majoring in English.

Writer Takes Up Acting

Following her graduation with honors from Smith in June of 1941, L'Engle returned to New York City and worked as an actress. As the author herself noted in the *About the Author* website, "I took an apartment in Greenwich Village with three other girls, two of whom were aspiring actresses. Because I wanted to be a writer, I was the lucky one to get jobs in the theater (I thought it was an excellent school for writers and it is)." L'Engle enjoyed New York. While there, she acted on Broadway and wrote her first novel, *The Small Rain* (1945). She also met a man who would have a great impact on her life while acting in Russian playwright Anton Chekhov's *The Cherry Orchard*. He was actor Hugh Franklin. Around this time, L'Engle had several of her plays produced, including *18 Washington Square, South: A Comedy in One Act* (1940) and *How Now Brown Cow* (1949).

Marriage, Children, and Crosswicks

On January 26, 1946, during Franklin's tour with *The Joyous Season*, the two were married in Chicago, Illinois, in a spur-of-the-moment ceremony with just two friends present as witnesses. The following spring, they purchased a 200-year-old farmhouse near Goshen, Connecticut. As they were renovating the house, they talked about starting a family. In June of 1947, L'Engle gave birth to a daughter, Josephine. For several years after, they spent their summers at the Connecticut home they called Crosswicks, and their winters in New York.

Franklin had continued to tour with acting companies, often being away most of the year. When L'Engle became pregnant again in 1951, however, Franklin decided to get a job near Crosswicks and the family moved there permanently. On March 24, 1952, their son, Bion, was born. Franklin still hadn't found a job, but the General Store in Goshen was up for sale. The young family bought it, and began handling both mail and groceries for the small town.

In 1956, L'Engle and Franklin adopted a friend's seven-year old daughter, Maria. The friend had passed away that November, one year after her husband's death. The Franklin family was thus completed. When all the children were off at school, L'Engle began to write *Meet the Austins,* a book inspired by her own family. The work was to be one of the first of a successful series for L'Engle. *Meet the Austins* even earned its place on the list of the American Library Association's Notable Children's books of 1960. Additional titles in the series included *The Moon by Night* (1963), *The Twenty-Four Days before Christmas: An Austin Family Story* (1964), *The Young Unicorns* (1968), and *A Ring of Endless Light* (1980).

A New Wrinkle, A New Direction

By 1959, the family was ready for a change. They sold the General Store and opted to again use Crosswicks as a summer home and return to New York for the winter months. First off, though, they took a ten-week camping trip. During this vacation, L'Engle got some ideas for a new book. She jotted them down, and as soon as she got back to Crosswicks, she began writing. The result was her classic novel for young adults, *A Wrinkle in Time*. The fantasy world of the book included time travel and a heroine with extrasensory perception (ESP).

L'Engle was discouraged when the book was rejected by 26 publishers, but she kept sending out her manuscript. Finally, the work was purchased by Farrar, Straus, and Giroux and published in 1962. The book was a great success, winning several honors, including the Newbery Medal, the American Library Association's Notable Book Award, the Lewis Carroll Shelf Award, and the Hans Christian Andersen Runner-up Award. Writing in *A Critical History of Children's Literature*, Ruth Hill Viguers called *A*

Wrinkle in Time a " book that combines devices of fairy tales, overtones of fantasy, the philosophy of great lives, the visions of science, and the warmth of a good family story. . . . It is an exuberant book, original, vital, exciting. Funny ideas, fearful images, amazing characters, and beautiful concepts sweep through it. And it is full of truth." Three sequels, *A Wind in the Door* (1973), *A Swiftly Tilting Planet* (1978), and *Many Waters* (1986) formed what is popularly known as the Time Fantasy Trilogy.

Hugh Franklin began acting again soon after the sale of the store, eventually settling into the role of Dr. Charles Tyler on the television program *All My Children.* L'Engle continued to write, more prolific than ever, and broadened her scope to non-fiction and religion. Franklin's death in 1986 inspired a book about her life with him, *Two Part Invention: The Story of a Marriage,* published in 1988. Other works from around this period included *Dragons in the Waters* (1976) and *A House like a Lotus* (1984), both sequels to L'Engle's 1965 volume *The Aim of the Star Fish.* L'Engle also wrote several collections of poetry, such as *The Weather of the Heart* (1978) and *Cry like a Bell* (1978). In 1982, she published a sequel to *The Small Rain,* called *A Severed Wasp.*

L'Engle served as writer in residence at *Victoria* magazine in 1995. At the beginning of her residence there, Whitcomb interviewed her at Crosswicks, reporting that L'Engle was the "centerpiece of a very extended family." In addition to her three children and five grandchildren, L'Engle has 19 godchildren with whom she keeps in close contact. She also served as writer-in-residence at the Cathedral of St. John the Divine in New York, where she had also been a librarian for over 30 years.

In 1998, L'Engle received the Margaret A. Edwards Award, sponsored by the *School Library Journal,* in honor of her lifetime contribution to adolescent literature. On the "Tesseract" website, Jeri Baker, chair of the Edwards Award Committee noted, "L'Engle tells stories that uniquely blend scientific principles and the quest for higher meaning. Basic to her philosophy of writing is the belief that 'story' helps individuals live courageously and creatively."

L'Engle continues to write and to lecture, teaching writing workshops at universities and churches. Her works in the 1990s include *The Glorious Impossible* (1990), *Certain Women* (1992), *Troubling a Star* (1994), *A Live Coal in the Sea* (1996), and *Penguins and Golden Calves: Icons and Idols* (1996). L'Engle also writes on religious topics, publishing such works as *Sold into Egypt: Joseph's Journey into Human Being* (1989), *Anytime Prayers* (1994), *Glimpses of Grace: Daily Thoughts and Reflections* (1996), and *Bright Evening Star: Mystery of the Incarnation* (1997). In 1997, L'Engle released *Friends for the Journey: Two Extraordinary Women Celebrate Friendship* and *Mothers and Daughters.*

"It's a full life she draws on—ranging from her days as a young actress to those as a Connecticut mother with a houseful of young children," commented Catherine Calvert in *Victoria.* "[Hers is] a life informed by unabashed optimism and faith in humankind and steadied by a strong religious sense." Her continued popularity as an author is evidence of her ability to entertain both young readers and adults. "L'Engle's writing could well be called timeless rather than timely," noted Marygail G. Parker in the *Dictionary of Literary Biography.* "Her warm portraits of caring families, her fervent belief in the dignity and creativity of each individual, and her sense of the universal importance of particular acts give her work a peculiar splendor."

Further Reading

Chase, Carole F., *Madeleine L'Engle, Suncatcher: Spiritual Vision of a Storyteller,* LuraMedia (San Diego, CA), 1995.

Dictionary of Literary Biography, Volume 52: *American Writers for Children since 1960: Fiction,* Gale, 1986.

Gonzales, Doreen, *Madeleine L'Engle,* Dillon Press,1991.

Hettinga, Donald R., *Presenting Madeleine L'Engle,* Twayne, 1993.

Meigs, Cornelia, editor, *A Critical History of Children's Literature,* Macmillan, revised edition, 1969, p. 481.

Booklist, September 1, 1992; April 15, 1994; August 1994; May 1, 1996; May 15, 1996.

Children's Literature in Education, winter 1975; summer 1976; winter 1983; spring 1987.

Horn Book, August 1963; December 1983.

Library Journal, May 1, 1996.

People, December 7, 1992; November 28, 1994.

Victoria, January 1995, pp. 26-29.

"Madeleine L'Engle," *About the Author,* http://www.wheaton.edu/learnres/arcsc/collects/sc03/bio.htm (March 17, 1998).

Blocher, Karen Funk, "The Tesseract: A Madeleine L'Engle Bibliography in 5 dimensions," http://members.aol.com/kfbofpq1/LEngl.html#bio (March 15, 1998).

Greene, Dave, "The Artist," *The Christian: A Portrait of Madeleine L'Engle,* http:www.windwords.org/virtual/books/lengle.html (March 17, 1998).

Little Wolf

Famed Cheyenne chief and leader of the Bowstring Warriors, Little Wolf (c. 1818-1904) defied the U.S. government and led 300 Cheyenne from an Indian reservation in Oklahoma back to their homeland in southeastern Montana. In the course of this journey, the group eluded some 13,000 U.S. troops for more than half a year before finally surrendering.

In the late 1870s, Little Wolf, along with Dull Knife, led 300 Native Americans from the Cheyenne Indian Reservation near Fort Reno, Oklahoma, resulting in a lengthy chase by the U.S. Cavalry through Kansas, Nebraska, South Dakota, and into Montana. The leadership Little Wolf demonstrated during this incident, as well as his courage and skill in battles covering a period of over 45 years prior, contributed to his reputation as a great Cheyenne warrior. Although this reputation was diminished among his people in his later years due to his murder of a fellow tribesman, many of the white soldiers who fought and chased him over the high plains remembered him with admiration long after his death.

Early Life

Very little is known of the early life of Little Wolf. He was born some time between 1818 and 1820, probably closer to the latter year, in southeastern Montana, the home of his tribe, the Northern Cheyenne. He is mentioned as a good warrior as early as 1837, during which time the Cheyenne were involved frequently in inter-tribal warfare. By 1838, he was the chief of the Bowstring Warriors, one of the six military societies—including the Fox Soldiers, the Blue Soldiers, the Dog Men, the Red Shields, and the Crazy Dogs—which comprised the fighting segment of the Northern Cheyenne people.

By 1851, treaties with the United States government had brought an end to the conflicts between the tribes, for the most part. Little Wolf effectively disappeared from the historical record for a lengthy period. He always preferred peace, so until 1865, there was little reason to take notice of him. In that year, he led an assault on U.S. troops to avenge the massacre of 150 Cheyenne at Sand Creek, Colorado, the year before. Three years later, he and his warriors drove troops out of Ft. Kearny, Nebraska, burning it to the ground after it was abandoned.

These were, however, isolated incidents. Later in 1868, Little Wolf and 13 other Northern Cheyenne and Northern Arapaho chiefs signed a treaty with the U.S. government granting them the option of settling with the Southern Cheyenne south of the Arkansas River, or with the Sioux on the Great Sioux Reservation. It is perhaps an indicator of Little Wolf's great desire to make peace with the U.S. government

that he was willing to tarnish his own reputation among his people by agreeing to this treaty. When he returned to his tribe, he was greeted with anger for signing it without consulting the other tribal leaders first. While he could perhaps be faulted for this, his status among whites as a peacemaker grew. Some time after the treaty signing, he traveled to Washington, D.C., to receive a peace medal from United States President Ulysses S. Grant.

The Darlington Reservation

In 1877, relations between the U.S. government and the Northern Cheyenne changed. Lieutenant H. W. Lawton of the U.S. Fourth Cavalry arrived in Red Cloud, Montana, with orders to escort the Northern Cheyenne to Darlington, Oklahoma, where they would join their southern brethren on a reservation there, near Fort Reno. Peaceful as always, the Cheyennes in Red Cloud agreed to the move, and they began to arrive at their new home in August of that year, continuing throughout the fall.

The conditions in Darlington, unfortunately, were not what they had been promised. Indian agent John D. Miles was charged with caring for all of the Cheyenne and Arapaho people on the reservation, but in this role he was either woefully inadequate or entirely corrupt, as many believed. Before long, several chiefs were complaining to Lieutenant Lawton that they were being given starvation rations. The buffalo herds in the region had been systematically decimated by careless hunters, so the Native Americans on the reservation depended on their caretakers for the bare necessities for survival. Lawton and a trader named Philip McCusker alleged that Miles was charging the Northern Cheyennes up to 300 percent of the normal prices for goods, and that he played favorites among the traders in the area.

None of this much pleased the Northern Cheyennes, who began squabbling over minor issues with the southerners already on the reservation, as well as with Miles. Cheyenne chiefs Dull Knife and Wild Hog refused to send their children to the Native American school Miles had set up, and in the spring, they refused to plant crops and settle down. The winter was extremely hard on the nearly 1,000 Northern Cheyennes who had relocated to the camp. Being used to the dry climate of the high plains of Montana, they were defenseless against disease in the more humid southern region. Forty-seven Cheyennes died that first winter in Oklahoma.

The Dull Knife Outbreak

By September of the following year, the crisis was coming to a head. Small numbers of Cheyenne males began to leave the group, heading back north to their home in Montana. When Miles confronted Little Wolf and demanded aid in recovering these fugitives, Little Wolf refused. Shortly after, on September 10th, approximately 350 Northern Cheyennes left Darlington and headed north. They were led by Dull Knife, Wild Hog, Crow Indian, Chewing Gum, Old Bear, Squaw, Black Horse, Day, Red Blanket, and Little Wolf.

The group had not traveled far, perhaps just under a hundred miles, when they were overtaken at the Little Medicine Lodge River by troops from Fort Reno with Arapaho scouts. A brief fight ensued, in which three soldiers and one Arapaho were killed. The Cheyennes barely paused, driving north with great intensity. Though the band was comprised mainly of women, children, and elderly men, with only about 60 warriors in the whole group, General P. H. Sheridan of the U.S Indian Bureau apparently considered them a significant threat. He immediately ordered his subordinate, General Crook, to capture or kill the renegades. Fearing perhaps that the Cheyenne's success might spur other tribes to desert the reservations, Crook mobilized over 13,000 troops to apprehend Little Wolf, Dull Knife, and the others.

Still the determined group pushed onward. A series of battles were fought through the fall, at the Cimarron River, south of the Arkansas River, then again north of the Arkansas. Despite being outnumbered and forced to move relentlessly over open country where there were no opportunities to hide and rest, the Cheyennes fared well under Little Wolf's great tactical skill. In all of the battles fought during that period, they lost only half a dozen men, with another half dozen wounded. Furthermore, they made tremendous progress, fighting their battles as quickly as possible and then moving on, or even fighting while on the march. In this way, they were able to cover over 700 miles before winter.

Before reaching their winter destination, however, Dull Knife's group split off from that of Little Wolf, somewhere near the Platte River. Dull Knife headed west, toward Fort Robinson, Nebraska. He and his band were soon captured without a fight. Little Wolf, with about 114 remaining Cheyennes pressed on until he reached the Sand Hills. Here, game was plentiful, and there were plenty of places to hide from pursuers. He and his followers entered winter quarters and effectively disappeared.

In the spring they continued on to the Powder River. Here they were met by Lieutenant W. P. Clark, known to the Cheyenne as White Hat, a friend to Little Wolf. When Clark found Little Wolf, he shook his hand and assured him that the group would not be harmed. Wishing only peace for his people, Little Wolf surrendered. He followed Clark to Fort Keogh, where Little Wolf and many of his followers signed on to help U.S. troops fight the Sioux. Although Little Wolf's band had far outlasted Dull Knife's, the chase from Darlington to Red Cloud is now known as the Dull Knife Outbreak.

Late Life

Some time after these events—probably in the 1880s, Little Wolf murdered a fellow Cheyenne, Starving Elk, who had been paying too much attention to his daughter. Murder within the tribe was extremely rare, though not unprecedented, and was considered to be an unforgivable crime. Little Wolf's reaction was to give up all his property, including his horses, and commit himself to exile. He was no longer a chief, and he went with his family to the Tongue River Indian Reservation in the southeast corner of Montana, near his original home. There he lived out his years. Although he had long been expected to die in battle, he instead grew old, eventually going blind. He died in 1904.

It is arguable whether Little Wolf ever achieved his dream: "a springtime when the Cheyenne were once more warm, a well fed, a straightstanding people." Considering the tremendous forces in play at that time, he probably never could have succeeded unequivocally. He brought his people home, but on terms dictated by the U.S. government. Furthermore, he permanently disgraced his own name within his tribe. It is therefore a testament to the overwhelming power of his memory, the sheer force of his personality, that George Bird Grinnell, a one-time U.S. cavalryman who wrote a two-volume history of the Cheyenne tribe in 1923, said of Little Wolf that he was "the greatest of modern Cheyennes."

Further Reading

Berthrong, Donald J., *The Cheyenne and Arapaho Ordeal: Reservation and Agency Life in the Indian Territory, 1875-1907*, University of Oklahoma Press, 1976.

Grinnell, George Bird, *The Cheyenne Indians: Their History and Ways of Life*, Yale University Press, 1924.

Grinnell, George Bird, *Fighting Cheyennes*, University of Oklahoma Press, 1915.

Sandoz, Mari, *Cheyenne Autumn*, McGraw-Hill, 1953.

Stands in Timber, John, and Margot Liberty, *Cheyenne Memories*, Yale University Press, 1967.

Svingen, Orlan J., *The Northern Cheyenne Indian Reservation, 1877-1900*, University Press of Colorado, 1993.

Frank Loesser

Frank Loesser (1910-1969) is one on America's major lyricists, having written the lyrics to hundreds of songs for films and army shows. He is most famous for writing the musical comedy scores for *Where's Charley?*, *Guys and Dolls*, *The Most Happy Fella*, and *How to Succeed in Business Without Really Trying*.

Precocious From the Start

Francis Henry Loesser was born on June 29, 1910 in New York, New York. His father Henry was a Prussian piano virtuoso, and his mother Julia was Bohemian. His half-brother Arthur was in his teens by the time Loesser and his sister Grace were born. Arthur was a gifted pianist and was often away on concert tours. *Time* writer Richard Corliss intimated, "Friends of the family were surprised that Frank, not Arthur, achieved top musical renown; they affectionately called him the 'evil of the two Loessers.'"

Loesser was a rebel from an early age, refusing to speak German, the family's language of choice, and he took great pleasure from playing practical jokes. Although raised in a genteel home filled with serious music, he never studied under his parents. He was a natural musician but to restless to settle down for lessons. By age four, he could play any tune he heard and was able to spend a great amount of time at the piano.

A bright student, Loesser was accepted at Townsend Harris, a three-year high school for gifted children. He was expelled, however, because of his practical jokes and he did not graduate. Loesser was 15 when he was accepted at City College of New York, but because he failed every subject except English and gym, Loesser dropped out.

When his father died in 1926, his mother made a living lecturing on contemporary literature and his brother quit touring and accepted a position as the head of the piano department of the Cleveland Institute of Music. Loesser took a series of odd jobs and in this way contributed to the family income. To soothe his creative spirit, he began writing silly couplets. Encouraged by friends, he began writing song lyrics and occasionally, selling a song.

Resolved to Succeed

Loesser was determined to succeed as a lyricist. Often though, he was compelled to accept other employment to supplement his income. He sold classified ads for the *Herald Tribune,* was the knit-goods editor for *Women's Wear,* and was editor of the *New Rochelle News,* a trade publication. As related by his daughter Susan in the biography *A Most Remarkable Fella,* Loesser was not satisfied at any of those jobs. He confided to his brother in a letter, "And so I have gone back to the song business. Although I have been writing them five years or more, I have never stuck to the trade for more than a year at a time. Not because I got tired of it, but because every once in a while some "money-making" idea comes up which takes me off the track, in the hope that I can make a better living in it than with music."

In the early 1930s, Loesser wrote lyrics for the Leo Feist Music Publishing company. He was under contract for a year at $100 a week for all the songs he could write. He collaborated with composer Joe Brandfon and then with his friend William Schuman. They established an unusual writing pattern that enabled them to work on two songs at the same time. Together they would outline the two songs, then Schuman worked out the tune on one song while Loesser worked on the lyrics for the second. When they were ready to switch, Schuman would take the lyrics Loesser had worked out and put them to music and Loesser drafted lyrics to the tune Schuman composed. Remembering Loesser, Schuman recalled to Corliss for *Time* that, "He was an intellectual who'd go to the ends of the earth to hide that from anybody." Schuman went on to become a distinguished classical composer and president of the Lincoln Center.

Always pushing to sell his lyrics, Loesser transformed himself to blend with the group in control of Tin Pan Alley. He developed his pendant for local dialect preferring the accent and slang of the street. His daughter recalled, "Early on he cultivated a brassy, New York, blue-collar accent, sprinkled with a little Yiddish for ethnic flavor."

Hollywood

By 1935, Loesser and Irving Actman were collaborating on music and performing their songs nightly in a small New York club. The team was discovered by a movie studio scout and in 1936, Loesser and Actman signed a six-month contract with Universal Studios and moved to Hollywood, California. Loesser was picked up by Paramount when the Universal contract ran out. In 1937 he began writing lyrics with Manning Sherwin. He had done well enough as a lyricist that he signed an individual contract with the studio. As his music became more popular his income grew and Loesser was on his way.

Between 1936 and 1942, the American Society of Composers, Authors and Publishers (ASCAP) catalog listed over a hundred songs with lyrics by Loesser. These songs were composed for the movies in collaboration with various music writers and included: *Small Fry, Heart and Soul, Jingle, Jangle, Jingle,* and *Two Sleepy People.* Part of the charm of Loesser lyrics was the phrasing. They were written the way people talked. Loesser picked up phrases from all over and incorporated them in songs. His music can be used as a reference to dialect. Wilfrid Sheed pointed out for *GQ,* "'Murder He Says' (music by McHugh) remains the best guide we have to the slang the kids were using during World War II. And then there's 'I get the neck of the chicken/ I get the rumble-seat ride' (McHugh again), which conveys not only the sound of middle-American life but the whole texture of it."

One inspiring phrase came from an army chaplain who had said, "Praise the Lord and Pass the Ammunition." Loesser knew the phrase was jaunty but not irreverent. As related by Sheed for *GQ,* the phrase seemed to say, "We're a God-fearing nation, but we're not pantywaists, by golly." Meeting the challenge of 1941 for a patriotic song, Loesser used that phrase and created a tune to help establish the rhythm of the verses as he wrote them. The song was part hymn and part animated folk and it was a success. It gave Loesser another artistic vein to tap and that is all he needed to compose his own music. World War II gave him the inspiration for the verses.

War Years

In 1942 Loesser enlisted in the army. Initially he was stationed at a base in Santa Ana, California. He, along with other military people, produced many songs for the Army. He was transferred to the Army's Special Services Unit in New York in 1943. There he wrote scripts and music for the *Blueprint Specials.* In addition to producing material for the war effort, Loesser was involved in several motion pictures for Hollywood until his discharge from the army in 1945.

Loesser returned to California after his army discharge eager to try new material. In 1948, he agreed to write the score for *Where's Charley?* the George Abbott adaptation of the Victorian farce *Charley's Aunt.* The musical was a surprise smash hit. Loesser's daughter recalled, "It ran for two years on Broadway, went on the road with the original cast, was made into a movie by Warner Brothers, and is still performed regularly in stock and amateur productions and revivals all over the world."

Guys and Dolls

Guys and Dolls is a musical masterpiece based on *The Idyll of Miss Sarah Brown,* a story by Damon Runyon. It is full of comedy, romance, gangster dialogue and music.

Loesser teamed with Abe Burrows and together they crafted the show. Sheed remarked for *GQ* about the production, "It is one of the minute number of musicals without a single weak tune. It is also a superb piece of theatrical construction, with a great opening and a dandy close and maybe the best first act curtain in musical history."

Francis Davis writing for the *Atlantic* commented on Loesser's talent, "Musical comedy is a stylized art form that reached its peak in Frank Loesser's 'Guys and Dolls.'" The original show opened in 1950, and ran for 1,200 performances on Broadway. Loesser won a New York Drama Critics Award and an Antoinette Perry Award (Tony Award) for the score. *Guys and Dolls* was made into a movie in 1955, produced by Samuel Goldwyn and starring Frank Sinatra and Marlon Brando. The musical celebrated a Broadway revival in 1992 and ran for 1,143 performances. The 1992 performance was awarded four Antoinette Perry Awards, including Best Revival, and won a Grammy Award for the cast recording (revival cast).

The Most Happy Fella

In 1951 while working on music for Goldwyn's *Hans Christian Andersen,* Loesser began looking for his next challenge. He found it in *The Most Happy Fella.* The new musical was based on Sidney Howard's play *They Knew What They Wanted.* Loesser actually adapted the play, writing the script, the music and the lyrics. According to *Time* writer Corliss, *The Most Happy Fella* turned out to be, "A rich and deeply felt pastiche of popular and operatic vocabularies. The show has an emotive force rare on Broadway; the feeling is big enough to fill an opera stage." Loesser was awarded the New York Drama Critics Award for the musical score in 1957.

Greenwillow

Loesser's next project was *Greenwillow,* a musical adaptation of the B.J. Chute novel. For Loesser, this undertaking included writing the show, the music and lyrics, as well as, managing all aspects of the production. In 1960, the production opened in Philadelphia, but received poor reviews. Loesser, despite reservations, took the show to New York where it ran for only 95 performances.

Greenwillow has been rewritten and produced by writers Walter Willison and Douglas Holmes. The revised musical opened in 1997. Jay Handelman reviewer for *Variety* suggested that, "Fans of the original cast album and of musical theater in general may well rejoice over the job that Douglas Holmes and Walter Willison have done in taking Loesser's beautifully varied score and fitting it into a magical story that is both touching and funny."

How to Succeed in Business Without Really Trying

In 1961, Loesser was approached by old friends Abe Burrows, Cy Feuer and Ernest Martin to write the score for *How to Succeed in Business Without Really Trying.* Based on the book by the same name, *How to Succeed in Business Without Really Trying* was a satire about rising to the corporate top. The original production was the longest running of

Loesser's musicals. It earned Loesser and Burrows a Pulitzer Prize in 1962. After 1,417 performances the show closed in 1965.

A revival production opened the same year. Writing for *The New Yorker,* John Lahr commented, "The success of 'How to Succeed' comes primarily from the pit, thanks to Loesser's music and lyrics which shrewdly send up the rituals and cliches of office life circa 1961."

Loesser was a chronic overachiever who experienced success in everything he put his mind to. Collaborator Hoagy Carmichael found Loesser to be, "so packed with ideas, he was overloaded." However, Loesser's last years were frustrating. His health was failing and his musical plots would not connect. *GQ* writer Sheed summarized "*How To Succeed in Business Without Really Trying* now figured as the last of the great post-World War II musicals born of depression, war and jazz, and everything since simply has to be called something else." Loesser died of lung cancer in 1969 in New York at the age of 59. His music and lyrics will long survive him.

Further Reading

Contemporary Authors, Volume 112, Gale, 1985.
Loesser, Susan,*A Most Remarkable Fella*, Donald I. Fine, Inc., 1993.
The Atlantic, March 1993.
GQ-Gentlemen's Quarterly, September 1997.
The New Yorker, April 24, 1995.
Time, September 16, 1991.
Variety, July 21-27, 1997.

Sophia Loren

The acting career of Sophia Loren (born 1934) has covered over 50 years and more than 100 films. Her work has earned virtually every major acting award the international film community has to offer.

Growing up

Born as Sofia Scicolone on September 20, 1934 in Rome, Italy, she was the illegitimate child of Romilda Villani and Riccardo Scicolone. Sofia grew up in Pozzuoli, near Naples, Italy. Her mother, Sofia, and eventually her sister Maria, lived with her maternal grandparents, aunts and uncles in a two room apartment.

Sofia said "the two big advantages I had at birth were to have been born wise and to have been born in poverty." Her mother's unmarried status lead to a life of poverty. Sofia was so undernourished as a child she was called Sofia Stuzzicadente or "Sofia the toothpick." By all accounts she was a thin, shy, fearful and unattractive girl.

World War II

Sofia recalls the war as a time of cold, starvation and sickness. Her grandfather and uncles worked in a munitions factory which supported the family briefly. The plant, however, was a frequent target of bombings. During bombing raids Sofia remembers hiding in train tunnels but leaving them before the morning trains started.

Italy was devastated following the end of the war. Food, jobs and money were scarce, particularly for unmarried mothers. One way women could make money was by participating in beauty pageants. Sofia, who had blossomed from 'the toothpick' into a lovely teenager entered such a pageant as a teenager and was a finalist. After this contest, Sofia's mother learned extras were needed for the film *Quo Vadis*. Hoping for employment, her mother packed their belongings and headed for Rome.

The Movies—Bit Parts

Sofia and her mother were hired as extras for *Quo Vadis*. When the film was over they were unemployed. Her mother headed back home but Sofia remained in Rome. During the early 1950s she secured work modelling for fumetti magazines. Comic-like, these magazines used actual photographs. The dialogue bubbles were called fumetti—hence the popular name.

Fumettis were quite popular throughout Italy and Sofia was in demand. She used this recognition to get bit parts in movies. Under her real name she made eight films. One director suggested she change her name to Sofia Lazzaro, which she did for three films.

Carlo Ponti and His Influence

Sofia's luck changed due to an encounter at a night club holding a Miss Rome contest. A stranger asked her to enter the contest but she refused. The stranger returned a second time and told Sofia one of the judges, Carlo Ponti, suggested she enter. She entered the contest and won second prize. More important she also won a screen test with Ponti, one of Italy's leading film directors.

Ponti gave her bit parts in films, believing there was something worthwhile there. Borrowing Marta Toren's last name, she changed the spelling of her first and her last name to Sophia Loren. She quickly made several films while taking drama lessons.

The Big Break

In 1953, producers were filming *Aida* with Gina Lollobrigida. The concept was to have a beautiful actress lip-synch the opera's arias which would be performed by one of Italy most famous opera singers, Renata Tebaldi. Lollobrigida backed out when she learned about the lip synching. Ponti suggested Loren as a replacement. Appearing completely painted black, Loren made the film.

Her success in *Aida* lead Loren to parts in nine films that year. One was *Anatomy of Love* which co-starred Marcello Mastroianni and Vittorio De Sica, two men she would successfully continue to work with over time. By the mid-1950s Loren had established herself as an Italian sex symbol. Loren once commented, "Sex-appeal is 50 per cent what you've got and 50 per cent what people think you've got."

Sex Symbol to Serious Actress

In 1954 Loren again teamed up with De Sica for *The Gold of Naples*. This time de Sica was directing the film. Sam Shaw, in *Sophia Loren: In the Camera Eye*, noted "De Sica taught her [Loren] the craft of acting. Secrets of interpretation, restraint. It took a director like him to get the talent out of her." Loren agreed, claiming "the second man of my life is Vittorio De Sica."

De Sica once stated to an interviewer, "She was created differently, behaved differently, affected me differently from any woman I have known. I looked at that face, those unbelievable eyes, and I saw it all as a miracle." He considered her "the essential Italian woman." Loren had a box-office success when she teamed up with Mastroianni, in *Too Bad She's Bad*, with De Sica directing. In *The Films of Sophia Loren*, Tom Crawley noted *Too Bad She's Bad* was the "genesis of the most successful partnership in Italian movies." Loren explained this success, "The three of us were united in a kind of complicity that the Neapolitans always have among themselves. The same sense of humor, the same rhythms, the same philosophies of life, the same natural cynicism. All three of us did our roles instinctively."

The Marriage Scandal

In 1957 Loren appeared in her first English-speaking film, *The Pride and the Passion*, with Cary Grant. Despite the fact that Grant was married, romance was rumored between the stars. This concerned Ponti, who was Loren's agent and manager. Ponti, despite a wife and two children, was also in love with Loren. From all accounts it seemed Loren was also in love with Ponti. "What nobody could understand then and still can't is the extraordinary power of the man," Loren once claimed in an interview.

This relationship was troublesome in Italy which did not recognize divorce. Loren found herself embroiled in a scandal, when Ponti obtained a Mexican divorce from his wife. Loren and Ponti were married by proxy in Mexico on September 17, 1957. The Vatican refused to recognize the divorce and subsequent marriage and labeled the couple public sinners. After a hearing, warrants were issued for Carlo (as a bigamist) and Loren (as a concubine).

Hollywood at Last

Loren's first Hollywood film was the 1958 *Desire Under the Elms.* During this year she worked with Peter Sellers in another film from which they recorded an album. One single from the album "Goodness Gracious Me" topped the charts in England.

Over the next years Loren worked on ten films. Two of the most important were *El Cid* and *Two Women. El Cid* with Charlton Heston is probably the largest grossing film of Loren's career. *Two Women* achieved greater importance in Loren's life. Loren received numerous Best Actress awards, including an Academy Award for her depiction of a mother struggling during war. This was the first Academy Award ever given to a foreign actress in a foreign language film.

Personal Life

In 1963 the Pontis were charged with public bigamy and their marriage was annulled. Hoping to resolve this problem, the Pontis moved to France where they became citizens. In 1965 the French court granted a divorce to Giuliana, Ponti's wife. On April 9, 1967 Loren remarried Ponti in a small French civil wedding.

While Loren enjoyed a successful career, she also attempted to become pregnant. She suffered two miscarriages after which she underwent a series of tests. When Loren again became pregnant her doctor ordered complete bed rest. On December 28, 1968, Hubert Leoni Carlo Ponti, Jr. (known as Cipi), was born. Loren had spent almost the entire pregnancy in bed.

Five years later on January 1, 1973, Eduardo Ponti arrived. Again several months of bed rest were ordered by her physician. Despite the lengthy confinements, Loren was overjoyed. In a *Good Housekeeping* interview with Heather Kirby, Loren claimed childbirth "is something women are born for, the continuation of life." During this period an Italian appellate court also dismissed all bigamy charges against Ponti.

The early to mid-1970s proved to be a very productive time for Loren. She made ten films and wrote a cookbook, *In the Kitchen with Love,* published in 1972. Unfortunately these good times were not destined to last.

Financial Problems

On February 8, 1977, Italian police searched the Pontis' private home and business offices. The government believed Ponti was guilty of income tax evasion, the misuse of government subsidies, and the illegal export of Italian funds. A warrant was issued for Ponti's arrest. Loren was charged as an accomplice.

In 1979 the government tried the couple, in absentia. Ponti was found guilty and sentenced to four years in prison, and fined 22 billion lire (about 24 million dollars). Loren was acquitted. Ponti was eventually cleared of all charges in 1987.

Other Endeavors

Loren continued making films, but she also began other endeavors. She published *Sophia: Living and Loving, her own story,* written with A.E. Hotchner. She also moved into marketing when she became the first female celebrity with her own perfume. "Sophia" a combination of jasmine and roses was manufactured by Coty. In 1981 she partnered with Zyloware to market the Sophia Loren Eyewear collection.

Loren was asked to be the first female grand marshall of the annual Columbus Day Parade in New York City, a parade celebrating Italian-Americans, which she did in 1984. She also published her second book, *Sophia Loren on Women and Beauty.*

All these activities were interrupted by legal problems. A tax court sentenced Loren to a 30 days jail term for income tax evasion on a 1966 filing. Loren promised to return once work obligations were completed. She began the sentence May 19, 1982. She served 17 days at a women's prison and was paroled early.

Later Work

Since the mid-1980s Loren has continued making films, shifting towards television movies. She used her celebrity status on behalf of charity projects such as the Statue of Liberty, protecting Greco-Roman ruins and drought-relief work for Somalian refugees.

In 1991, she received a Special Academy Award, for as the Academy noted, being "one of the genuine treasures of world cinema who, in a career rich with memorable performances, has added permanent luster to our art form." Sadly though, Loren also experienced a great loss with the death of her mother that year. In an interview, Loren said "I think when a mother dies the whole world collapses because she's the anchor that you don't have anymore."

Sixty-Plus

After turning 60 in 1994, Loren received a Hollywood Walk of Fame star and numerous lifetime achievement awards. *Entertainment Weekly* selected her as one of The 100 Greatest Movie Stars of All Time in 1996. She appeared in *Pret-a-Porter* (Ready to Wear), which marked her fifteenth and final pairing with Mastroianni, who died shortly after.

Fans seemed to agree with Sam Shaw when he stated, "Whatever she does on screen is right. She can do ordinary pictures; and still she remains an international superstar, still she grows as a human being." With accolades like this Sophia Loren will be a presence for sometime to come.

Further Reading

Crawley, Tony, *The Films of Sophia Loren,* Citadel Press, 1976.
Harris, Warren G. *Sophia Loren,* Simon & Schuster, 1998.
Shaw, Sam, *Sophia Loren: In the Camera Eye,* Exeter Books, 1979.
ArtNews, March 23, 1998.
Chicago Tribune, October 7, 1990.
Esquire, August 1994.
Good Housekeeping, August 1994.
Houston Chronicle, February 2, 1994.
New York Times, August 18, 1983; August 25, 1984.
Orange County Register, February 19, 1994.
People, March 11, 1988.
San Diego Union-Tribune, July 8, 1988.
Washington Post, May 20, 1982.
"Sophia Loren," *CelebSite,* http://www.celebsite.com (March 25, 1998).
"Contemporary Authors-Sophia Loren," http://galenet.gale.com (March 24, 1998).
"The Epitome of Woman ... Sophia Loren," http://www.spyderempire.com/sophia (March 25, 1998).

Trent Lott

Trent Lott (born 1941) has served in the United States government for over three decades. He was elected to both houses of the United States congress and served subsequent terms as a member from the state of Mississippi.

A U.S. Senator from Mississippi, Trent Lott is a major political figure in the nation's capitol. He first came to Washington as a Democratic congressional aide in the early 1960s. Known for his conservative views, however, Lott served as a Republican in both the House of Representatives and the U.S. Senate. Lott was recognized for his leadership skills in Congress and was able to organize support for important issues among both Republicans and Democrats. Paul Weyrich, a radio news commentator, once described Lott "as a wily Southerner. He likes to make deals, but sometimes, when he feels a great principle is at stake, he can be tough as nails." A skillful politician, the U.S. Senator from Mississippi was elected by fellow senators as Senate Majority Leader on December 3, 1996.

Born on October 9, 1941, in Grenada County, Mississippi, Chester Trent Lott, moved with his family to the costal town of Pascagoula. As an only child, Trent received the full attention and love of his parents. His father, Chester, worked as a shipyard worker who later tried his hand in the furniture business. In a *U.S. News & World Report* interview with Gloria Borger, Lott described his father as "handsome and outgoing, and I always thought he might actually run for office someday."

Lott's mother, Iona, was a schoolteacher and bookkeeper. Iona Lott recalled to *Time* contributor Dan Goodgame, "People used to say an only child would be spoiled and selfish. And I was determined he wouldn't be that way." She insisted that he share everything, even the pony she and Lott's father gave him before he was ten. Lott was exposed to politics at any early age, as one grandfather was a justice of the peace, and the other grandfather a county supervisor. Lott also had an uncle who was a tax assessor and a state senator.

The family moved to Pascagoula when Lott was in the seventh grade. He adapted to the new location quickly and wasn't afraid to participate in a wide range of activities. During his school years, he played tuba in the band and was a member of the drama club. He also worked part-time at a local rootbeer stand. Among his classmates, Lott was popular and well-respected. In high school, he was elected president of the drama club, president of the student body, homecoming king, most popular, most likely to succeed, and most polite. Goodgame quoted a high school friend who recalled that Lott found time for everyone "from shy girls to the guys we would describe these days as gang members."

With money earned from summer jobs and support from his parents, Lott entered the University of Mississippi (Ole Miss) in the fall of 1959. While at Ole Miss, Lott had his first real experience at politics. His freshman year, he pledged the Sigma Nu social fraternity. While he participated in Sigma Nu activities, Lott also made many friends among members of other fraternities and independent student groups. Eventually, he was elected as president of both Sigma Nu and the university's interfraternity council. Cheerleaders at Ole Miss were also elected positions, and running for cheerleader provided Lott another opportunity to gain political skills in forming political blocks, cutting deals and doing door-to-door precinct work.

No African American students attended the University of Mississippi when Lott first entered the school. During Lott's senior year, on September 30, 1962, Air Force veteran James Meredith, protected by armed U.S. marshals, enrolled at Ole Miss. The small group was confronted by rock-throwing students and non-student protestors in violent demonstrations. By the time the violence ended, two people had been killed and many others injured and arrested. Lott worked to keep Sigma Nu fraternity members from taking part. At the same time, he used his campus influence to call for peaceful campus integration. In *National Review*, Rich Lowry quoted Lott as saying, "Yes, you could say that I favored segregation then. The main thing was, I felt the Federal Government had no business sending in troops to tell the state what to do."

Graduating with a bachelor's degree in Public Administration in the spring of 1963, Lott enrolled in the Ole Miss law school. He subsidized his graduate education with a federal student loan and also obtained a job with the university's recruitment office. Later, he was able to work for the alumni association as a fund raiser, a position that enabled him to make valuable political connections throughout his native state.

While Lott attended law school, the Vietnam War was expanding in scope and troop commitments. Like other college students Lott received a student deferment from the draft. By the time he graduated from law school in 1967 Lott had married Patricia (Tricia) Thompson of Pascagoula and, under Selective Service rules, obtained a hardship exemption due to the birth of their first child, also named Chester.

After graduating from the Ole Miss law school, Lott and his family returned to Pascagoula. For a brief period Lott worked in a private law firm, leaving after less than a year when he was offered a top staff job by Congressman William M. Colmer, a Mississippi Democrat. The Lott family moved to Washington, D.C., in 1968. Tricia Lott explained to Lowry that the family went to Washington "to stay a couple of years and see if we liked it." Political skills learned at Ole Miss in organizing and influencing people earned Lott a reputation as an effective and able congressional aide.

Elected to House of Representatives

When Congressman Colmer announced his retirement from the House of Representatives in 1972, Lott announced his candidacy as a Republican to seek the vacant office. Lott was able to win Colmer's endorsement and support. According to Lowry, Lott explained his party switch by vowing to "fight against the ever increasing efforts of the so-called liberals to concentrate more power in the government in Washington." Lott had a well-organized and tireless campaign. With the aid of the landslide re-election of President Richard Nixon he was able to win the House seat with a vote margin of 55 percent.

Arriving in Washington as a freshman Representative, Lott was appointed to membership on the House Judiciary Committee. As the youngest member of this committee Lott became involved in the 1974 hearings to impeach President Nixon. The president had been implicated in the break-in of the Democratic National Committee headquarters at an office complex called Watergate. After the President released tape recordings and transcripts indicating his involvement and a cover-up of the crime, Lott reversed his position as a staunch supporter and joined others in the call for the President's resignation, which occurred less than a week later.

Although Lott had vowed to fight against increased government controls from his seat in the House, he actually supported more federal spending for entitlement programs, farm subsidies, public works projects, and the military. During his 16-year tenure in the U.S. House of Representatives, Lott was never credited with authoring any major legislation. However, he won praise for his work on tax and budget reform. He was an active member of the House, and served on the powerful House Rules Committee from 1975 to 1989. With the support of his fellow Representatives, Lott was elected and served as Minority Whip from 1981-89. As Minority Whip, he was the second ranking Republican in the House of Representatives. He was also named chair of the Republican National Convention's platform committees in 1980 and 1989. Lott, however, did not always support the legislative agenda of his political party. When President Reagan proposed a tax reform bill in 1985, Lott used his political power as Minority Whip to oppose the measure. Two years later, Lott joined with Democrats to override a presidential veto of a highway spending bill which included several highway projects in his home district.

Joined United States Senate

When the Mississippi Democratic Senator, John Stennis, retired in 1988, Lott announced that he would seek the vacant Senate seat. He won the Senate position with a 54 percent majority. As a Senator, Lott continued to focus his political talents on building coalitions and was appointed as a member of the Ethics Committee. He was later appointed as a member of the powerful Senate Budget Committee. Continuing his climb through the ranks of the Senate, Lott was elected as the secretary of the Senate Republican Conference in 1992. In 1994 he won the election for Senate Majority Whip by a one vote margin, making him the first person to be elected Whip in both houses of Congress.

Lott's experiences as House Minority Whip helped him to establish a highly-organized whip system in the Senate. Individual members of Congress were drafted to organize and track colleagues on a regional basis. These regional whips provided daily briefing to Lott on crucial votes. One of the regional whips was also tasked to be on the Senate floor at all times. Lott's ability to work with both parties helped to end what was described in the popular press as budget gridlock. During 1997 budget negotiations, Richard Stevenson, writing in the *New York Times*, described him as

"Trent Lott the bad cop" and as "Trent Lott the good cop." Stevenson reported that Lott's message to both parties was, "I'm going to urge that we not waste time talking about what we disagree on. Let's see where we can find some commonality, where we can begin to come up with agreements that will help the quality of life for all Americans." When the Senate Majority Leader, Bob Dole, announced his plans to retire from the Senate in order to run for President, Lott used his well-controlled whip organization to campaign for the vacant Majority Leader position. His organizational and political skills were rewarded, and he was elected Senate Majority Leader on June 13, 1996.

Campaign financing became the focus of national attention after the re-election of President Clinton in 1996. With reports of improper fund-raising activities by the Democrats, many Republicans called for in-depth investigations of campaign practices. While some called for major campaign reforms, Lott had other views. In an interview with *New York Times* contributor Katharine Seelye, Lott described his position on this issue, commenting that "I support people being involved in the political process. . . . I think for them to have the opportunity to do that is the American way."

The Senator's stance on other major issues facing the nation were widely known. He articulated his views on numerous radio and television interview shows. He also took advantage of the electronic media and maintained an internet home page stating his position on key political and national issues. In regards to a balanced national budget, Lott declared, "I understand the concerns regarding the Balanced Budget Amendment and want to assure you that I do not take amending our Constitution lightly. However, having watched many futile attempts to reduce the deficit through legislation, I am convinced that an amendment to our Constitution is necessary." Lott also described his position concerning prayer in public schools on this site: "I have consistently advocated strong legislative action in support of the rights of students who wish to participate in voluntary prayer in their schools."

Lott's personal beliefs reflect those of his constituency, and his election to both houses of Congress show his successful representation of the people in his home district and home state. In Congress, his ability to mobilize his fellow Representatives and Senators in support of key legislation was recognized with prominent positions in both houses— as Minority Whip in the House of Representatives, and in the Senate as Majority Whip and later Senate Majority Leader. Lott has the distinction of being the first Southerner to be House Minority Whip and the first person to be elected Whip in both houses of Congress.

Further Reading

National Review, June 30, 1997, pp. 20-23.
New York Times, February 8, 1997; February 21, 1997.
Time, March 10, 1997, pp. 38-39.
U.S. News & World Report, February 24, 1997, pp. 22-24.
Direct Line with Paul Weyrich (live broadcast on radio station KIUSA), December 3, 1996.
Issue Positions, http://www.senate.gov (November 10, 1997). □

Ada Byron Lovelace, Countess of Lovelace

In her 1843 translation of an article on Charles Babbage's Analytical Engine, Ada Byron Lovelace (1815-1852) added notations three times the length of the original text. The "Notes" earned her a place in computer history when they were later recognized as the first detailed description of a computer, including what is now considered a software program. In recognition of her enlightened ideas that were over 100 years before their time, the United States Department of Defense named its Ada programming language after her in 1980.

Though she was born the daughter of the notorious English Romantic poet, Lord Byron, Ada Byron Lovelace chose to pursue the more objective field of mathematics. She proved to be her father's daughter, though, for her sense of passion was arguably as strong as her father's, despite her mother's attempts to suppress any "Byronic" tendencies in her. She went against traditional Victorian society by studying mathematics which was a discipline few women attempted. The height of her passion for mathematics can be seen in her "Notes" on Charles Babbage's Analytical Engine, a calculating device that was never actually built. She wrote with tremendous insight and her ideas about the capabilities of an analytical engine became reality in 20th century computers which earned her a place in the history of mathematics and computer science.

Lord Byron's Legitimate Daughter

Augusta Ada Byron was born on December 10, 1815 in London, England, and was Byron's only legitimate child. Five weeks after her birth, her mother, Lady Byron, left her abusive husband. On April 24, 1816 a deed of separation was signed and Lord Byron left England for good. Ada never saw her father again for he died eight years later in Greece. However, he did correspond with Lady Byron regarding her well-being and her studies. He also wrote of her in his poetry. The line, "ADA! sole daughter of my house and heart," can be found in *Childe Harold's Pilgrimage*, Canto III.

After Lord Byron's departure, Lady Byron took control of her daughter's upbringing. This control included the suppression of any undesirable traits that may have inherited from her father. In her book, *The Calculating Passion of Ada Byron*, Joan Baum notes, "Lady Byron had insisted on the cultivation of mathematics primarily because its discipline represented for her the direct opposite of everything associated with her depraved husband: dangerous fancy, melancholy moods, evil, even insanity." Baum also stated that "Mathematics was first for Lady Byron a mode of moral discipline. Accordingly, she arranged a full study schedule for her child, emphasizing music and arithmetic—music to

be put to purposes of social service, arithmetic to train the mind."

A Passion for Numbers

By her early teenage years, Ada realized she had a true passion for numbers not unlike that of her father's passion for poetry. Lady Byron provided tutors of high distinction for her such as William Frend, a Cambridge mathematician, who instructed Ada in the areas of astronomy, algebra and geometry. Another tutor, Augustus De Morgan, was the first Professor of Mathematics at the newly founded University of London. He described Ada as "an original mathematical investigator, perhaps of first-rate eminence" according to Dorothy Stein in her book, *Ada: A Life and a Legacy.* "Indeed, it was a desire for mathematical glory, rather than a particular kind of mathematics, that compelled Ada," concluded Baum.

This passion continued throughout the rest of her life as Stein demonstrates in a quote from an 1843 letter Lovelace wrote to Babbage, "I hope another year will make me really something of an Analyst. The more I study, the more irresistible do I feel my genius for it to be. I do not believe that my father was (or ever could have been) such a Poet as I shall be an Analyst, (& Metaphysician)."

The Countess of Lovelace

On July 8, 1835, Ada Byron married William King who was then the eighth Baron King. In 1838, he became the 1st Earl of Lovelace and she became the Countess of Lovelace.

The following year, Lord Lovelace also became lord lieutenant of Surrey. Her husband was 11 years older than she and considered to be somewhat reserved. He did, however, take pride in his wife's mathematical talents and supported her endeavors. His approval was quite fortunate for Ada Byron Lovelace as few women of her station in Victorian England were encouraged to pursue academic interests of any kind. In fact, those of the aristocracy considered it to be beneath them to practice a profession. For that reason, Lovelace only signed the initials, "A.A.L." to her "Notes." Consequently, she was limited by her class status as much as by her gender with regard to her passion for mathematics.

Charles Babbage and the "Notes"

Lovelace first met Babbage when she was 18 at a dinner party hosted by Mary Fairfax Somerville, the 19th century's most prominent woman scientist. Despite the fact that he was 23 years her senior, Babbage became her good friend and intellectual mentor. She was immediately intrigued when she first saw Babbage's Difference Engine and plans for the Analytical Engine in 1834. The perfect opportunity for Lovelace to study the Analytical Engine came after Babbage's 1840 lecture in Turin, Italy. An Italian military engineer by the name of Luigi Federico Menabrea wrote an article on the lecture that was printed in a French publication in 1842. Lovelace's translation of Menabrea's article from French to English and her accompanying notations were published in the prestigious *Taylor's Scientific Memoirs* the following year.

Lovelace labeled her seven "Notes" with the letters A through G. The word "computer" did not mean in the 19th century what it came to mean in the 20th century. Rather, it referred to a device that only did arithmetic or a person whose job was to add up numbers. Therefore, Lovelace never used the word in her "Notes."

"Note A" distinguished between Babbage's Difference Engine and his Analytical Engine. This note was significant in that it described a general purpose computer that would not be invented for more than 100 years. In "Note B," Lovelace looked at the concept of computer memory and the ability to insert statements to indicate what is happening to the person looking at the program. This idea is similar to the current practice of using REM or non-executable remark statements in a program.

Lovelace expanded on a method called "backing" in "Note C." This allowed for the operation cards to be put back in the correct order so that they could be used again and again like a loop or subroutine. "Note D" was a very complex explanation of how to write a set of instructions or a program to accomplish a set of operations. "Note E," aptly stated by Baum, clearly "emphasize[d] the versatility of the Analytical Engine and suggests, in its brief description of operation cards which designate cycles, modern-day function keys."

"Note F" explained how the Analytical Engine could solve difficult problems and eliminate error. This would allow for the solving of problems that were prohibitive due to the constraints of time, labor and funds. Baum also noted that Lovelace wondered "if the engine might not be set to investigate formulas of no apparent practical interest . . . as computers are used today, to find problems rather than to solve them."

The last and probably the most mathematically complex and most quoted of Lovelace's notations was "Note G." In this note, she stated what some have referred to as "Lady Lovelace's Objection" or, in the more modern phrasing, "garbage in, garbage out." Basically, she was saying that the computer's output is only as good as the information it is given. "Note G" also included an actual illustration of how the engine could produce a table of Bernoulli numbers.

Personal Difficulties

Lovelace faced numerous illnesses throughout her life. As a child, she had bouts with both measles and scarlet fever. Byron received a report on Lovelace's health stating that she "had symptoms of fullness of the vessels of the head . . . varying in degree during different parts of the day, never very severe but never or scarcely ever totally absent" according to Doris Langley Moore in her book, *Ada, Countess of Lovelace: Byron's Legitimate Daughter.* Byron had had the same affliction, possibly migraine headaches which can be hereditary, until he was 14.

In 1829, Lovelace suffered an unidentified ailment that left her unable to walk for many months. She was also subject to convulsive fits and there was speculation that they may have been due to a mental rather than a physical condition. None of these conditions, though, caused any permanent disabilities. In fact, Lovelace was an accomplished dancer, horseback rider and gymnast. Only uterine cancer would prove to be insurmountable for her.

Lovelace's life was also fraught with difficulties of her own making. She not only had a passion for mathematics, she had a passion for men of mathematics. She was known to have had affairs with several men whose attention she initially sought on an intellectual level. Her affair with John Crosse proved to be the most devastating. She pawned the Lovelace diamonds to pay his gambling debts, and it is possible that he was blackmailing her as well. Lovelace, too, fell victim to the vice of gambling and enlisted the help of some of her male friends to place bets for her.

A Place in History

Lovelace's passions far exceeded her body's limits. She died on the evening of November 27, 1852 of uterine cancer at the age of 36, the same age at which her father had died. At her request, she was buried beside her father in the Byron vault at Hucknall Torkard, near Newstead Abbey, the ancestral home of the Byrons in Nottinghamshire. This last request was prompted by a visit in 1850 to Newstead Abbey where Lovelace finally made peace with her father's memory.

Though Lovelace's "Notes" were well received by those who knew her, there is no indication of how they were taken by the general public. In fact, she did not obtain widespread recognition until the historian, Lord B.V. Bowden, rediscovered her "Notes" in 1952 and had them reprinted the following year, 110 years after their original publication.

Posthumous mathematical glory was probably not what Lovelace had in mind when she was alive. However, she would have undoubtedly been pleased with a fourth-generation programming language being named after her. In the words of Baum, Lovelace "was the world's first extensive expositor of a computing machine. She was also a fascinating woman, interesting as much for her motives as for her work, illustrating as she does the theme of creative energy in collision with suppressed desire."

Further Reading

Baum, Joan, *The Calculating Passion of Ada Byron,* Archon Books, 1986.
Moore, Doris Langley, *Ada, Countess of Lovelace: Byron's Legitimate Daughter,* Harper & Row, 1977.
Stein, Dorothy, *Ada: A Life and a Legacy,* The MIT Press, 1985.
"Ada Byron Lovelace: The First Computer Programmer," *AIMS Education Foundation,* http://www.aimsedu.org (March 15, 1998).
"Augusta Ada Byron, Countess of Lovelace," *Sonoma State University,* http://www.sonoma.edu/Math/faculty/Falbo/adabyron.html (March 15, 1998).

Yuri Luzhkov

Russian politician Yuri Luzhkov (born 1936) has proven to be a popular mayor of Moscow. He has ushered in reforms to the economy and infrastructure that have increased the prosperity of the nation's capital.

Yuri Luzhkov, mayor of Moscow since his appointment by Boris Yeltsin in 1992, is a reformer who directly involves city government with the interests of private economic enterprises. Perhaps more important, he seems to have an intuitive sense of knowing what issues to champion, which people to support, and when to be in the public eye. He has made it clear to his subordinates and to Muscovites alike that he is the man in charge of the city. At times, he appears to be the ruler of a near-independent city-state. He has used his position to refuse the federal government's plan to privatize state assets in his city; as a result, Moscow now controls all federal property within its boundaries. He has also made efforts to develop the infrastructure of the city. A popular official, Luzhkov received approximately 90 percent of the vote in the 1996 mayoral election.

Son of a Carpenter

Yuri Mikhailovich Luzhkov was born in Moscow on September 21, 1936. His father was a carpenter, but Luzhkov preferred mechanical engineering and studied at the Gubkin Institute of Oil, Gas, and Chemical Industries. Soon, however, he became more interested in government. By combining his education with his interests, he landed a job in the Ministry of the Chemical Industry in 1964. For the next 13 years, he occupied a series of managerial positions

told *U.S. News & World Report* writer Christian Caryl. "Luzhkov said, . . . 'I'm just a builder.'"

City residents admire many of Luzhkov's more conspicuous efforts. "He is known to Muscovites simply as 'The Boss,'" noted Charles Piggott and Askold Krushelnycky in the *European.* Under Luzhkov's direction new subway stations have opened, rutted roads have been paved, and Moscow is now surrounded by a ten-lane superhighway. He has also had an estimated 32 million square feet of new apartment space built each year. His pet projects include the construction of a World War II memorial; the development of Luzhniki Stadium, which will be Europe's largest roofed stadium; and the reconstruction of the nineteenth century Cathedral of Christ the Savior that dictator Joseph Stalin tore down in 1931. Government officials claim that Luzhkov gets the money for such expensive, and some say extravagant, projects through privatization. In 1994, Yeltsin gave Luzhkov control over Moscow's inventory of state property. In 1997, Moscow took in $1 billion in privatization revenues. In addition, as noted in the *Economist,* Moscow receives "[t]wo-thirds of foreign investment into Russia, and four-fifths of all Russian capital."

Luzhkov has become such a powerful Russian leader that he has even gotten involved in affairs outside Moscow. In early January of 1997, for example, he traveled to Sevastopol, the Crimean port in the Ukraine, where he promised to have housing built for the sailors of the Russian Black Sea fleet. The housing was to be funded by the Moscow city government. He also announced that the port should be returned to Russia, infuriating Ukrainian government officials and embarrassing Yeltsin. In addition, Luzhkov has come out in support of union with Belarus, the small former Soviet republic in east central Europe. At the end of 1997, he criticized the United States and the International Monetary Fund (IMF) for trying to negatively influence Russian economic development.

Successful and Supportive Governing Style

Luzhkov runs Moscow by defining clear duties among his team, and he prohibits city officials from encroaching on each other's area of responsibility. Consequently, factions have not developed that can potentially disrupt the operation of city government. Although Luzhkov has issued public reprimands to his team leaders, he will support them during times of controversy. He is not only a technically good city manager, owing, in part, to his background in engineering, but he is considered a good manager of people. Among his advisors is Vladimir Yevtushenkov the head of a joint-stock company called the Moscow City Committee for Science and Technology. In addition, Yevtushenkov is an old friend of Luzhkov's wife, Yelena Baturina, who is also an adviser on many issues and a successful businesswoman in her own right.

Alleged Ties to Crime

Although credited with much of the reform occurring in Moscow, Luzhkov is also being blamed for the increasing crime in the city. Luzhkov has responded to this criticism by

in the ministry. In 1987, he became first deputy chairman of the Moscow Executive Committee and head of the Moscow Agro-Industrial Committee during which he ran the city's food distribution system. Yet his desire to advance to increasingly more responsible job levels was being thwarted in the Communist system of Soviet Russia. Leadership positions usually went to party officials, and Luzhkov had no strong connections to the party. During the last days of Communism in Russia, however, he worked for Boris Yeltsin, who was a Moscow party boss.

Luzhkov's opportunities to advance were improved after the fall of the Soviet Union when he was appointed deputy to Gavril Popov, the first mayor of Moscow in post-Communist Russia. After a year, it was apparent that Popov was more interested in politics than the management of Moscow. By default, Luzhkov handled the day-to-day operations of the city. Once his old boss, Yeltsin, became president of Russia, Luzhkov was made mayor by decree when Popov resigned in 1992.

Staying Power

Currently, Luzhkov is a major political leader in Russia. He has thrived in an environment in which many other politicians have risen and quickly faded. Luzhkov is also extremely popular with the ten million residents of Moscow. Muscovites admire him because he is seen as a leader who can accomplish his goals. He won re-election in June of 1996 with nearly 90 percent of the vote. "His popularity began when people began to get tired of politics," Andrei Klochkov, an analyst at the Russian Socio-Political Center putting approximately 5,000 law-enforcement volunteers on the streets of the city. Still, many critics note that law enforcement is weak, and police allegedly take bribes. The presence of organized crime has resulted in more frequent reports of kickbacks, car bombs, and contract murders. In 1996, an American businessman, entangled in a legal dispute with a city agency over hotel property, was killed on the street.

Luzhkov's image is threatened further by his friendship with people such as Iosif Kobzon, a businessman and singer who, according to foreign law-enforcement agencies, is closely tied to organized crime in Russia. Yet such allegations have not discouraged Luzhkov's supporters. "Perhaps Luzhkov is on the take," a Russian anti-corruption politician told *Time* contributor Paul Quinn-Judge. "But he is getting this place into shape. So why should I waste my time on him? Others do nothing but steal."

Another blemish on Luzhkov's mayoral record is Moscow's growing homeless population, officially numbering approximately 100,000 in 1997 but probably much higher. Luzhkov has overseen mass expulsions of the homeless from the city and the alleged "roughing-up" of the darker-skinned minorities. This has resulted in criticism from international human-rights groups. Yet Moscow has become a busy city with well-stocked grocery stores; consequently, many residents believe crime and homelessness are a part of progress. "For all its crime and corruption and bureaucracy, Moscow has by far the best-developed infrastructure in Russia, and a government that understands roughly how laws and markets work," noted the *Economist*.

Politician's Dance

With such power and popularity among Muscovites, Luzhkov appears to be a logical choice for prime minister or president of Russia in the twenty-first century. Yet his rise to the country's top spots is not guaranteed. He cannot afford to antagonize incumbent leaders, yet he must distance himself from them and many of their policies. In the early 1990s, Luzhkov was a staunch supporter of President Yeltsin. He allied himself with other reform leaders in August 1991 when he joined them in the Russian White House in anticipation of an attack by coup leaders. More than anything else, this earned him Yeltsin's gratitude.

Luzhkov has continued to profess admiration for Yeltsin and supported him against unpopular voices within the remains of the Communist party. Yet, at times, he distances himself from the president. In 1997, for example, the weekly Moscow newspaper, *Obshchaya Gazeta*, reported that Luzhkov had said that Yeltsin was not fully in control of the country. Luzhkov has also distanced himself from many unpopular reforms supported by Yeltsin, has criticized ministers and their mistakes, and has publicly disclosed corrupt practices. Still, he maintains access to all Russian leaders.

Luzhkov continues to expand his public image into the international arena. A new Moscow television and radio station recently went on the air with substantial funding from the city. In order to broaden his appeal to those outside Moscow, Luzhkov is trying to make the television station national. In September of 1994, he signed an agreement with 20 heads of Russian regions that established direct economic and cultural links between Moscow and the provinces. Leaders in the Russian hinterland have been suspicious of Luzhkov and jealous of Moscow's new prosperity. Yet, Pavel Bunich, a Luzhkov adviser and member of parliament, told David Hoffman of the *Washington Post* that envy would recede "once people see there are no potholes on the roads."

Luzhkov is becoming more aware that his age might be a political liability. By 2000, he will be 64 years old, the same age of Yeltsin in 1996 when Russia's government was at a standstill as it waited out the president's fight with poor health. Moscow observers speculate that Luzhkov's rival for the presidency may be his deputy, Boris Nikolsky, who is more than two decades younger than Luzhkov. Thus, the mayor frequently shows off his athleticism and good health by playing soccer and fishing. Every winter, he breaks the ice in the Moscow River and plunges in for a supposedly healthy swim. The media even reported on his appearance at a local circus where he was practicing on the trapeze until he fell and injured his leg.

During the 850th anniversary celebration of Moscow in 1997, Yeltsin publicly commented on Luzhkov's energy and accomplishments. On December 14, 1997, elections for the 35-seat City Duma, Moscow's representative body, resulted in the most votes for candidates who supported Luzhkov. The Duma had been perceived as a governing body unwilling to challenge Luzhkov, resulting in Luzhkov's ability to run the city unhindered. The December elections were seen as an informal referendum on Luzhkov's potential as a presidential candidate. As noted by Caryl, "The mayor is the only Russian politician whose popularity has steadily risen in recent years and continues to do so."

Further Reading

Economist, April 20, 1996; February 8, 1997; August 9, 1997; April 11, 1998.
European, February 2, 1998.
McLean's, July 15, 1996, p. 35.
New Statesman, September 12, 1997.
Sydney Morning Herald, September 13, 1997.
Time (Australia), October 6, 1997, p. 53.
Times (London), May 31, 1995.
U.S. News & World Report, May 19, 1997, p. 19.
Washington Post, February 24, 1997, p. A1.
"Yuri Mikhaylovich Luzhkov," Centre for Russian Studies Database, http://www.nupi.no/cgi-win/Russland/personer.exe/513 (March 18, 1998).
"Russia: Future of Democracy," Close Up Foundation, http://www.closeup.org (March 20, 1998).
"Boris Yeltsin fires premier, majority of Russian cabinet," CNN Interactive, http://www.cnn.com (March 23, 1998).

M

Wangari Muta Maathai

A visionary environmentalist, Wangari Maathai (born 1940) created a successful reforestation program that began in Kenya and was adopted in other African nations and the United States. Maathai was recognized world-wide for her achievements, although she was denounced as a traitor and a rebel in her home country.

Wangari Maathai is perhaps best known for creating the Green Belt Movement of Kenya, a program recognized all over the world for combining community development and reforestation to combat environmental and poverty issues. Maathai excelled at mobilizing people for a very simple goal—reforestation—which also impacted poverty and community development in Kenya. Maathai believed that people needed to help with environmental issues and should not rely upon the government. Maathai clashed with the Kenyan government, often at risk to her own life, when she opposed destructive governmental initiatives and when she forayed into politics personally.

Turmoil Early On

Maathai was born in Kenya in 1940. Attending college in the United States, she went on to earn a B.S. from Mount St. Scholastica University, in Kansas and a M.S. from University of Pittsburgh, in Pennsylvania. She then earned a Ph.D. from the University of Nairobi. She was the first woman in Kenya to earn a Ph.D. and at age 38, she held the first female professorship (in Animal Science) at the Univer-

sity of Nairobi. She credited her education with giving her the ability to see the difference between right and wrong, and with giving her the impetus to be strong.

Maathai's life was not without turmoil and hurdles, which she described as God-given. She married a politician who unknowingly provided the basis for her future environmental activities when he ran for office in 1974 and promised to plant trees in a poor area of the district he represented. Maathai's husband abandoned her and their three children later, filing and receiving a divorce on the grounds that she was "too educated, too strong, too successful, too stubborn and too hard to control." Maathai maintained that it was particularly important for African women to know that they could be strong, and to liberate themselves from fear and silence.

Visionary Reforestation Program

In 1977 Maathai left her professor position at the University of Nairobi and founded the Green Belt Movement on World Environment Day by planting 9 trees in her backyard. The Movement grew into a program run by women with the goal of reforesting Africa and preventing the poverty that deforestation caused. Deforestation was a significant environmental issue in Africa and was resulting in the encroachment of desert where forests had stood. According to the United Nations in 1989, only 9 trees were replanted in Africa for every 100 trees that were cut down. Not only did deforestation cause environmental problems such as soil runoff and subsequent water pollution, but lack of trees near villages meant that villagers had to walk great distances for firewood. Village livestock also suffered from not having vegetation to graze on.

Women in the Kenyan villages were the people who first implemented Maathai's Green Belt Movement.

269

"Women," Maathai explained, "are responsible for their children, they cannot sit back, waste time and see them starve." The program was carried out with the women establishing nurseries in their villages, and persuading farmers to plant the seedlings. The movement paid the women for each tree planted that lived past three months. Under Maathai's direction in its first 15 years, the program employed more than 50,000 women and planted more than 10 million trees. Other African nations adopted similar programs based on the Green Belt Movement model. Additionally, the government stepped up its tree planting efforts by twenty times.

More Than Planting Trees

The Greenbelt Movement that Maathai conceived was not limited solely to tree planting. The program worked in concert with the National Council of Women of Kenya to provide such services to Kenyan women and villages including: family planning, nutrition using traditional foods, and leadership skills to improve the status of the women. By 1997 the Movement had resulted in the planting of 15 million trees, had spread to 30 African countries as well as the United States, and had provided income for 80,000 people.

Maathai had strong beliefs about how she carried out environmental activism. She warned that educated women should avoid becoming an elite, and instead, should do work for the planet. Nobody could afford to divorce themselves from the earth, she believed, because all human had to eat and depend on the soil. Activism, she felt, was most effective when done in groups rather than alone. She

credited her success with the Green Belt Movement to keeping the goal simple. The program provided a ready answer for those who asked, "What can I do?" Planting trees, in this case, was the simple solution.

Clashes with Government

Maathai continued to oppose modernization that collided with her environmental beliefs; this often put her at odds with government. She admitted that "You cannot fight for the environment without eventually getting into conflict with politicians." As an example, she was thrown out of her state office in 1989 when she opposed the construction of a 62 story skyscraper in Uhuru Park in Nairobi. Maathai claimed that the building, which was to house government offices and a 24 hour TV station, would cost 200 million dollars. The money, she claimed, could be better spent addressing serious poverty, hunger and education needs in the country. Her opposition succeeded in frightening off foreign investors and they withdrew their support; the skyscraper was never built. In Nairobi, Maathai also opposed the deforestation of 50 acres of land outside the city limits to be used for growing roses for export.

Politics and environmental activism continued to interweave in Maathai's life even before she attempted to run for office. She helped found the Forum for the Restoration of Democracy, a group that was opposed to the leadership of then-president Daniel arap Moi. She advocated for the release of political prisoners and led a hunger strike on 1992 with the mothers of these prisoners. During one of these protests, she was beaten by police until unconscious.

In January 1992 she was arrested for her political protest activities when more than 100 police raided her Nairobi residence. Later in 1992, she was charged with spreading rumors that then-president Moi planned to turn government power over to the military in order to prevent multi-party elections. While Maathai awaited trial for the latter charge, she was refused medical treatment in jail; even though she was experiencing difficulties due to a history of heart problems and arthritis.

Political Campaigns

In 1992 Maathai was approached to run for the Presidency by a cross section of the Kenyan population. She declined, preferring to try and unite the fractured opposition parties against President Moi. Her efforts failed and Moi was again elected.

In 1997 Maathai responded to pressure from supporters and friends and announced that she was running not only for a Parliament seat, but for the Presidency under the Liberal Party of Kenya (LPK) in an attempt to defeat President Moi. She got a late start in the process and did not announce her intentions until a month before the election. Maathai explained that she was "finding it increasingly difficult to turn away those who approach me stating that the time has come for me to practice what I preach in the Green Belt Movement . . . honesty, vision, courage, commitment and genuine concern for all people." She denounced the current corruption in the government, and urged that the time had come to restore Kenyan people's dignity, self respect, and human rights. The government that she proposed was a people centered operation, or an "enabling political environment to facilitate development." Central to her vision was a Kenyan society where people acknowledged their cultural and spiritual background as they participated in government.

However, Maathai released no party manifesto prior to the election, claiming that the Green Belt Movement would provide the direction for her platform. At least one political analyst of the *Africa News Service,* saw this as troubling, claiming that Maathai might focus only on environmental issues and that the LPK already had a manifesto. Maathai countered such fears by claiming that her leadership would focus not only on the environment (which was, in her mind, tied to other issues like hunger), but on infrastructure issues, poverty, disease, and the empowerment of the oppressed.

Maathai found fault with the current political system which required candidates to acquire extremely large amounts of money in order to carry out campaigns. This situation, she claimed, made it difficult for many visionary hopefuls like herself to even have a chance at making a difference in Kenya. A few days prior to the December 1997 election, the LPK leaders withdrew Maathai's candidacy without notifying her. Her bid for a Parliament seat was also defeated in the election; she came in third. Moi again emerged as the presidential victor. She continued to be admired world-wide, however, for her visionary work in the environmental arena.

Further Reading

Africa News Service, October 27, 1997; January 5, 1998.
E Magazine, January 11, 1997.
Inter Press Service English News Wire, December 10, 1997.
Time, April 23, 1990; April 29, 1991; April 27, 1992.
Women in Action, January 1, 1992.
"Africa Prize Laureates, Professor Wangari Muta Maathai," *The Hunger Project,* www.thp.org/thp/prize/maathai/maathai.htm. (April 13, 1998).
"Awareness Raising; Wangari Maathai Comes From Kenya," *BBC World Service,* www2.bbc.co.uk./worldservice/BBC_English/women/prog14.htm. (April 13, 1998).
"Wangari Maathai Biography," sosig.esrc.bris.ac.uk/schumacher/maatbiog.html. April 13, 1998).
"Women's One World, Women Who Dare: Celebrating Women's Her-story," *World Citizen News,* (February/March 1997) www.worldcitizen.org/issues/febmar97/womens.html. (April 13, 1998).

Hazrat Mahal

Hazrat Mahal (c. 1820-1879) was one of the primary Indian leaders in the struggle known variously as the Great Mutiny or the Indian War (1857-58).

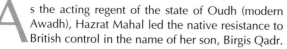

As the acting regent of the state of Oudh (modern Awadh), Hazrat Mahal led the native resistance to British control in the name of her son, Birgis Qadr.

The Indian War was one of the most significant colonial wars of the nineteenth century because it brought India, which had been ruled by agents of the British East India Company, directly under the control of the British Crown. It also united Hindus and Muslims in ways that would never happen again. This led directly to the Indian independence movement and the creation of the modern nations of India and Pakistan. Hazrat Mahal was the only major leader never to surrender to the British, and she maintained her opposition through twenty years of exile in Nepal until her death in 1879.

Hazrat Mahal's origins are unclear. Apparently she was born into a poor family in the city of Faizabad, located in the state of Oudh. Her parents were obscure; most sources written in English only know her family name, which they say was Iftikarun-nisa. The name may indicate that she was of Iranian descent; the state of Oudh, writes Rudrangshu Mukherjee in *Awadh in Revolt 1857-58: A Study of Popular Resistance,* had been established in 1722 by a Persian adventurer. Local traditions maintain that she was educated as a dancing-girl and attracted the attention of the king of Oudh, Wajid Ali Shah. He called her to his court in his capital city of Lucknow, received her into his harem, and, according to P. J. O. Taylor in *A Companion to the 'Indian Mutiny' of 1857,* "when she gave birth to a son, raised her to the rank of one of his wives, under the title Hazrat Mahal."

Background of the Indian War

The conflict that led to Hazrat Mahal's resistance was one of a series of similar conflicts happening across India between the Indian states on the one hand and the British East India Company on the other. By the time Hazrat Mahal's son was born, around 1845, the state of Oudh had been virtually independent from the Moghul Emperor in Delhi for nearly a hundred years. By the 1850s, most of the states that made up the former empire paid only lip service to Bahadur Shah Zafar, the titular Moghul Emperor. The East India Company encouraged these states in their quest for independence in the name of profit. The Company, by offering individual rulers arms and the use of its own independent army, won trading concessions from the local rulers. It also encouraged them to go into debt and, when the rulers proved unable to pay, forced new concessions from them or even confiscated their lands.

Wajid Ali Shah, Hazrat Mahal's husband, faced a similar situation in 1856. He had gotten into debt to the East India Company, and his administration was proving too corrupt to manage his debts. Traditionally, the right to collect taxes in Oudh was sold to the highest bidder, usually one of a small number of important men. This tax collector then squeezed the most money possible from the taxpayers in order to turn a profit on his investment. In many cases, the tax collector also kept part of the money that was due to the government and slipped bribes to government officials to cover their tracks. Whether or not this widespread corruption included Wajid Ali Shah himself is not known.

Foreclosure on a Country

Late in 1855 the Court of Directors, the governing body of the East India Company, came to the conclusion that Wajid Ali Shah was either unwilling or unable to repay his debts. They instructed their representative in Lucknow, Lieutenant General Sir James Outram, to begin the process of annexation. Begum Hazrat Mahal (Begum being a title of respect bestowed upon Muslim women of high rank), as well as the king's brother, were both opposed to annexation. On February 7, 1856, the British took control of the kingdom of Oudh. Five weeks later, on March 13, the king himself left Lucknow for exile in Calcutta. He left his eleven-year-old heir Birgis Qadr and Hazrat Mahal, acting as regent for her son, in charge.

Outram had some sympathy for the position of the former king's family, but his successor had very little. The British placed a new representative, C. Coverley Jackson, in Lucknow to protect their interests and to supervise the transfer of power from the former royal family to the East India Company. Jackson was only stationed in Lucknow for a year, from March 1856 to March 1857, but in that period he managed to alienate the Begum, her son, and many of the major political figures of Oudh. The man that replaced him, Sir Henry Lawrence, was a much better politician, but he proved unable to repair the damage done by Jackson before the Great Mutiny broke out in Delhi on May 11, 1857.

Background of the Great Mutiny

The Indian War had its roots in the resentment that Indians, both Muslims and Hindus, had toward the East India Company and its growing power in the subcontinent. Both groups felt that the British were intolerant of their faiths and customs, and wanted only to convert them forcibly to Christianity. Early in 1857, rumors began spreading among the various native troops making up the bulk of the Company's army in India that the new cartridges issued for use in army guns had been greased with pork and beef fat. Since the cartridges were designed so that the soldiers had to tear them open with their teeth, this meant that the native troops would be forced to eat some of the grease. Pork was a forbidden meat to Muslims, while the cow was sacred to Hindus. Native troops believed, whether rightly or wrongly, that the grease on their cartridges was a calculated insult by the British meant to humiliate them.

In the period immediately preceding the Mutiny, Hazrat Mahal was busily at work consolidating her son's position as his father's rightful heir. She convinced the emperor Bahadur to name Birgis Qadr regent for Oudh, confiscated the property of corrupt officials and used it to pay her own troops, and recruited respected Hindus to join her largely Muslim administration. Rajah Jai Lal Singh, who became her primary military commander, brought with him most of the local Hindu soldiers and threw their support behind the Begum and her son. "The boy was only twelve years old: it was assumed, though not explicitly, that Hazrat Mahal should rule in his name," explained Taylor. "She did, and from that moment she had great power."

From late June through the middle of September, the Begum exercised her power against the British in Lucknow.

Most of the 600 Europeans still living in the city found shelter from Indian guns in the 37-acre compound called the Residency. Hazrat Mahal and her generals placed the Residency under siege, bombarding the building and placing snipers to pick off unwary residents. Sir Henry Lawrence himself was one of the first casualties, hit by a fragment from an artillery shell on July 2. The siege of the Residency made great headlines in the contemporary British press and attracted world attention to Lucknow and the state of Oudh.

"It was not until September 23, after 90 days of siege," writes James Morris in *Heaven's Command: An Imperial Progress,* "that the defenders heard gunfire on the other side of the city, and two days later there burst into the compound a column of Highlanders." Their generals were Henry Havelock and James Outram. Although the British force was too weak to evacuate the compound, it did provide some protection for the civilians trapped there until General Colin Campbell forced his way into the city in November. Campbell relieved the siege of the Residency and left a sizeable force under Outram's command at the Alambagh just outside the city.

Hazrat Mahal's Resistance

Hazrat Mahal was very unhappy with her commanders' performance. Part of the reason that the Indian troops were unable to capture the Residency during the siege was because of arguments between her generals. In addition, the British were offering pardons and favorable terms for Indians who could prove they were not responsible for the deaths of British citizens. Many *talukdars,* the important landowners of Oudh, were beginning to take advantage of the British terms. When Campbell finally relieved the siege in November, her patience snapped. She summoned a *durbar,* or high council, and addressed her army in terms of reproach. "The whole army is in Lucknow, but it is without courage," Taylor quotes her as saying. "Why does it not attack the Alambagh? Is it waiting for the English to be reinforced and Lucknow to be surrounded? How much longer am I to pay the sepoys for doing nothing? Answer now, and if fight you won't, I shall negotiate with the English to spare my life."

Although Hazrat Mahal's commanders made six separate assaults on Outram's forces between Christmas day, 1857, and late February, 1858, they failed to move the British. On March 16, 1858, the British recaptured Lucknow and forced the Begum and her army out of the city. She kept an army in the field throughout the year, but she was never able to reestablish herself and her son in Lucknow. Despite her desperate condition, she remained defiant of the British. When Queen Victoria issued a proclamation taking the British East India Company's possessions in India under Crown control on November 1, 1858, the Begum responded with an announcement of her own. She criticized the British offers as misleading, lacking in substance, and as breaking treaties and promises. She further accused the British of using discontent among the native people as a pretense for taking over the country, and demanded the restoration of her family as rightful rulers.

Despite her defiance, by the end of 1859 Hazrat Mahal had lost most of her adherents and was forced to seek shelter with the Maharajah of Nepal, Jung Bahadur. She remained in Nepal, refusing all offers of terms from the British government, until her death in 1879. She was the last free leader of the Mutiny.

Further Reading

Bhatnagar, G. D., *The Annexation of Oudh,* Volume 3: *Uttaara Bharati,* [n.p.], 1956.

Bhatnagar, G. D., *Awadh Under Wajid Ali Shah,* Bharatiya Vidya Prakashan, 1968.

Morris, James, *Heaven's Command: An Imperial Progress,* Harcourt Brace Jovanovich, 1973.

Mukherjee, Rudrangshu, *Awadh in Revolt 1857-58: A Study of Popular Resistance,* Oxford University Press, 1984.

Pemble, John, *The Raj, the Indian Mutiny, and the Kingdom of Oudh,* Fairleigh Dickinson University Press, 1976.

Stokes, Eric, *The Peasant Armed: The Indian Revolt of 1857,* edited by C. A. Bayly, Clarendon Press, 1986.

Taylor, P. J. O., *A Feeling of Quiet Power: The Siege of Lucknow 1857,* HarperCollins, 1994.

Taylor, P. J. O., general editor. *A Companion to the 'Indian Mutiny' of 1857,* Oxford University Press, 1996.

Louis Malle

French director Louis Malle (1932-1995) was both a part of and separate from French cinema's new wave. By showing audiences the humanity beneath his characters' moral failings, Malle became one of the most celebrated directors of postwar cinema. His films, in French and English, won acclaim and sparked controversy in his native France and America.

Malle was one of eight children born to a wealthy family in northern France. His mother's family owned a giant sugar concern, and his farther, a former naval officer, ran the family's sugar factory. Wealth provided Malle with private tutors at the family's chateau in Thumeries, France. He spent his summers in Ireland and became fluent in English. Malle was eight when World War II broke out and his family went to Paris. Rebelling against his religious education and bourgeois upbringing, Malle sought refuge in the cinema.

Career Began Undersea

At the end of World War II, Malle studied political science; however, against the wishes of his family, he soon switched to the Institut des Hautes Etudes Cinematographiques. Malle's 40-year career began with his direction of the 1956 undersea documentary *Le Monde du silence,* or *The Silent World.* He had left school to assist undersea explorer Jacques-Yves Cousteau aboard his boat, the Calypso. Malle shot footage in 1954 and 1956 to create *Silent World.* The film captured the Palme d'Or at the 1956

Cannes Film Festival and won an Academy Award for best documentary in 1957. "When I started out, it infuriated me that people seemed to think I could never be anything but a dilettante - that I was riding on my family's money. It was not true," Malle told a writer for French newspaper *Le Monde.* Having something to prove perhaps inspired Malle to work all the harder.

Sexual Themes Caused Controversy

Malle became famous with his film *Les Amants,* (also known as *The Lovers;* 1958) about the sexual awakening of a middle-class woman. With *Lovers,* Malle broke taboos about on-screen eroticism. An Ohio theater was convicted of obscenity charges for showing the film. The success was followed by *Zazie dans le metro* (also known as *Zazie in the Underground;* 1960), a comedy about an eleven year old girl's visit to Paris with her uncle. Other films in French followed, including the documentary *Calcutta L'Inde Fantome* (also known as *Phantom India;* 1969), a seven-part television series made from film shot during Malle's six-month sojourn in India.

Lacombe, Lucien (1974) sparked the career of at least one filmmaker: Jodie Foster. "As a young moviegoer and aspiring filmmaker, I left my first Louis Malle film that day and said, 'That's it. That's what I want to do,'" Foster wrote in a tribute to Malle in *Premier* magazine following his death. Foster's directorial debut, *Little Man Tate,* was inspired by Malle's *Murmur of the Heart* (1971). She continued, "I loved the awkwardness, complexity, and pain of the adolescent boy in the film. He wasn't just a cute little prop filled with ironic witticisms. He was suffering and became impossible because he couldn't name his fears."

Murmur of the Heart (also known as *Le Souffle Au Coeur;* 1971) is the story of an incestuous encounter between a mother and her son while the two are away at a spa for treatment of his heart murmur. Malle countered conventional ideas of morality and incest by having the boy walk away from the tryst emotionally unscathed. "I'm always interested in an aspect of the truth which goes against preconceived ideas, including mine. So I end up working on material that often has something controversial about it," Malle once said.

Childhood Shaped Work

Many of Malle's films tell their stories through the eyes of children whose perspective is shared by the audience. Malle had three of his own. Malle's first marriage to Anne-Marie Deschodt ended in divorce. It wasn't until Malle was in his mid-40s that he married American actress Candice Bergen in 1980. The couple's daughter, Chloé, was born in 1985 in New York. Malle also fathered two children during the 1970s by actresses Gila von Weitershausen and Alexandra Stewart.

Malle wrote, produced and directed *Lacombe, Lucien* (1974) nearly 30 years after World War II, and it was inspired, in part, by a pivotal childhood event he would later document in another film set during World War II, *Au revoir les enfants*. The part of Lucien is played by Pierre Blaise, a woodsman who had never acted before. As is evidenced by casting in *Au revoir* and *Murmur*, Malle preferred using child and young actors with little or no experience. "With very few exceptions, professional child actors are so gimmicky, they're like little monkeys, they scare me," he commented in *Horizon* magazine.

Pretty Baby (1978), Malle's first American film, is another initiation story with controversial sexual content. American actress Brook Shields, in her first important film role, portrays Violet, a young girl reared in a brothel in the New Orleans' Storyville section. The story was inspired by a 1970 New York Museum of Modern Art exhibition of photographs of prostitutes taken by Ernest James Bellocq around 1912 around New Orleans' infamous red light district. Violet's eyes are also those of the audience to whom the world of her prostitute mother is revealed as Violet moves through the brothel and the streets of Storyville. *Pretty Baby* was criticized for having no moral point of view, an assessment Malle disagreed with in a 1990 *Newsday* interview. "This was a true story that fascinated me. There was nothing graphic about the movie."

Atlantic City (1980) garnered Malle an Academy Award nomination for best director in 1982. The film was nominated for best picture and it is another Malle film in which the transformation of characters happens against the backdrop of their changing environment. *My Dinner with Andre* (1981) was the filmed conversation over dinner between two actors who wrote and improvised their dialogue. Despite its static setting, the film won Malle much acclaim in America. Less successful were subsequent efforts *Crackers* (1983) and *Alamo Bay* (1985).

Goodbye Children

Perhaps Malle's most noteworthy film and certainly his most personal is *Au revoir les enfants* (also known as *Goodbye, Children*), released in 1987. This film marked Malle's return to French filmmaking after years in America. Written and directed by Malle, the film is based on a childhood event that haunted the artist all his life, one which took years to commit to film.

Malle was eleven when his Jesuit boarding school sheltered three Jewish boys from the Nazis. Set in the German-occupied France of 1944, the film tells the story of friendship between one of the boys, Jean Bonnet, and Julien Quentin, a wealthy young Catholic boy and the character representing Malle as a child. In the film and in reality, the boys and the school's priest-director were betrayed to the Nazis and arrested by the Gestapo. As the Germans took the four away to be executed in the Nazi death camps, the school director turned to Malle and the other remaining students and said, *"Au revoir, les enfants . . . á bientôt"* (meaning "Goodbye, children . . . see you soon").

Malle revealed in an interview for *Le Monde,* that his friendship with the real Bonnet never existed. "I was the good student, the star pupil. He was bigger, stronger, better than me. I hated him. We did not know that our days together were numbered. Afterward, I could never get rid of the idea that all of us, I and the others, were a little guilty of his death—maybe just because we belonged to the human race. More than 40 years later, I finally wanted to tell Bonnet that I liked him." *Au revoir* gave Malle's career a boost in the United States where it won larger audiences than those typically attending art house films. The film won the Golden Lion at the Venice Film Festival, the Prix Louis-Dellec in 1987, and the Felix Award from the European Film Awards in 1988; *Au revoir* was also nominated for an Academy Award for best original screenplay and for a British Academy of Film and Television Arts Award for best director.

Among Malle's last work is the production *Vanya on 42nd Street* (1994), a filming of a rehearsal performance of David Mamet's reworking of Anton Chekhov's *Uncle Vanya*. Stage actors recreate the play in their street clothes, and the film's dialogue is interwoven with that of the play. Malle's other films include *Ascenseur Pour L'Echafaud* (*Frantic*), 1957; *Vie Privee* (*A Very Private Affair*), 1961; *Le Feu Follet* (*The Fire Within*), 1963; *Viva Maria*, 1965; *Le Voleur* (*The Thief of Paris*), 1966; *Histoires Extraodinaires* (*Spirits of the Dead*), 1967; *Humain, Trop Humain*, 1973, a documentary; *Black Moon*, 1975; *And the Pursuit of Happiness*, 1986, a documentary; *Milou en mai* (*May Fools*), 1990; and *Damage*, 1992.

Malle died November 23, 1995, at 63 of complications from lymphoma; he was buried in France. "For me, his work opened up a glimpse into humanity that I had never seen before, an eye toward forgiveness that no other person, place, or thing had ever presented to me," actress Jodie Foster wrote in her tribute to Malle.

Further Reading

Malle, Louis, *Malle on Malle,* Faber & Faber, 1992.

American Film, July 1990.
Detroit News, November 25, 1995.
Entertainment Weekly, December 8, 1995.
Horizon, January-February, 1988.
Newsday, November 25, 1995.
New York Times, November 25, 1995; December 3, 1995;
    March 1, 1996.
Premiere, February 1996.
San Francisco Chronicle, November 25, 1995.
Time, January 4, 1993.
Time International, March 22, 1993.
U.S. News & World Report, February 15, 1988.
Variety, November 27, 1995.
Vogue, June 1990.
World Press Review, January 1988.

Henry Mancini

The composer, pianist, and theme song scorer Henry Mancini (1924-1994) was a major figure in American music from 1954 until his death. He spearheaded a change in film scoring, replacing the use of symphonic arrangements with elements of jazz, tin pan alley, and popular music.

Henry Mancini composed a legacy of famous and enjoyable film music which moved beyond film's former use of symphonic scores and incorporated elements of jazz and popular music. Mancini won many awards for his music, including four Oscars, 20 Grammys, and two Emmys. Much of his music became even more well known as film soundtracks; he produced over 50 albums and published over 500 of his compositions. His music was characterized by clean melody lines, usually on piano, with a background of French horns and strings. His theme songs for film, including *Moon River* and *The Pink Panther* are some of his most well known accomplishments.

Working Class Musical Roots

Mancini was born on April 16, 1924 in Cleveland, Ohio. His family later relocated to Aliquippa, Pennsylvania, a factory town. His father, a steelworker, was a musician who played flute in the Sons of Italy Band. He encouraged young Mancini to take up music as a way to rise above the options of working for a factory. As a child, Mancini was exposed to such composers as Puccini and Rossini; he played and took lessons in flute and piano. He also studied with a theater conductor and began arranging music in his teen years. Mancini discovered early on that he had a knack for arranging music. He took a job arranging for Benny Goodman, but later remarked that "it didn't take long for both Benny and me to find out I wasn't ready for such an ambitious assignment."

Mancini attended college and studied composition and theory at Julliard, but dropped out to serve in the military during World War II. After the war, he moved into the musical arena again, working as a pianist and arranger for the Glenn Miller-Tex Beneke orchestra. He married Ginny

O'Connnor, the vocalist for the Mel-Tones band, in 1947. They had three children together.

Hollywood Start

Mancini broke into Hollywood in 1952 when he was given a small two week job at Universal Studios to arrange the music for the Abbott and Costello comedy *Lost in Alaska.* He continued to work at Universal for the next six years where he arranged or part-scored music for over 100 films. Notable during this period was the popular score that he created to *The Glenn Miller Story* (1954), which incorporated his background in jazz. One of his first outstanding scores was for the Orson Welles film *Touch of Evil* (1958). *Touch of Evil* was unique in that it was one of the first films to use source music, or music that didn't just play in the background but actually came from a visible source in the film story, such as a radio or a nightclub. In the film Mancini used jazz, Latin, and rock tunes. *The Glass Menagerie* (1987) was another example of a Mancini scored film that uses both source and regular music.

At this point in Mancini's career, he caught the attention of movie producer Blake Edwards, who asked Mancini to score the music for the television series *Peter Gunn* (1958). The Edwards/Mancini collaboration was to extend into a partnership that spanned the rest of Mancini's life and included 28 films. Some of their work together included: *The Great Race, The Days of Wine and Roses, 10, S.O.B,* and several of the *Pink Panther* comedies.

Music Made a Difference

Th e popular music for *Peter Gunn* was another breakthrough that served to get Mancini more widely recognized and stood apart as an example of a television show where the music really had an impact. The music was notable in its jazzy sparseness, a style that record companies had caught onto but was in its infancy in movie studios. Mancini remarked that "It was the score I wrote for the Peter Gunn TV series that was the big break for me. That use of the jazz idiom, applied dramatically to the story, put music on everybody's mind as far as TV is concerned." Mancini's work for *Peter Gunn* won him a number of awards, including two Grammys and Best Jazz Record of the Year (in a *Down Beat* poll).

Mancini continued to produced creative and award winning film music. The score and a theme song (*Moon River*) to the Edwards film *Breakfast at Tiffany's* (1961) earned Oscars for Mancini, even though *Moon River* was almost cut out of the film during production.

Contributed to Musical Trends

Mancini's contribution to film music occurred during a time when changes were shaping the film industry and American culture. In the early 1950s and 1960s, in part due to Mancini's influence, studios began to move away from the traditional symphonic sounds that had served as the backdrop for films. Mancini contributed to this trend by offering jazzy and popular alternatives that were more sparsely scored instrumentally. By the early 1960s, studios were facing increased competition from television and the musical scene in America was hugely impacted by the evolution of rock and roll. Mancini responded well to the changes and took advantages of opportunities to compose for new media, as in his work for television series such as *Peter Gunn* and *Mr. Lucky.*

In his studio work, Mancini made an effort to break down pre-existing barriers and to introduce and jazz and contemporary influences to film music that had in the past been predominantly influenced and served by classical musicians. Mancini made a point to bring young musicians of varying backgrounds and interests to film scoring sessions. Mancini was able to see the bigger picture in film production, caring not only about the music but about the quality of the rest of the film making process. Due to his foresight and efforts, his music worked not only for films, but as soundtracks that were sold separately and successfully. He recorded music for the soundtrack so that for listeners, the music stood by itself even without the film. Mancini had the foresight to collaborate with talented lyricists such as Johnny Mercer, which added to the popularity of music such as *Moon River.*

During his time at Universal, Mancini had opportunities to compose music for a diversity of films. Some of these included: *Man Afraid* (1957), *Summer Love* (1958), *Creature from the Black Lagoon* (1954), and *It Came from Outer Space* (1953). In 1961 he scored the film *Breakfast at Tiffany's,* another musical breakthrough in his career which resulted in an Academy Award for the song *Moon River* from the film. The song used folk influences and was easy to sing. Mancini continued to receive recognition and fame for his film theme songs such as music from the film *Days of Wine and Roses* (1962) and the well known *Pink Panther* theme song. No other film composer received as much recognition for theme song composition until *Star Wars* was released in the 1970s.

Mancini had an appreciation of the art of scoring music to films. A reviewer from the *Journal of Popular Film and Television* claimed that Mancini's music for the films *Touch of Evil* (1958) and *White Dawn* (1974) showed a side of Mancini that many had not seen; the music, in this reviewer's opinion was well composed even though it hadn't been a hit commercially. In later life, Mancini remained busy with the scoring for *Victor/Victoria* (1982), as well as scores for television shows such as *The Thorn Birds* (1983), *Hotel, Newhart,* and *Remington Steele.*

Personal Traits

As a professional musician, Mancini was known to be modest and unpretentious. He made no time for musical elitism, claiming that he had written *Moon River* in a half hour and that his Italian background helped him musically. Mancini had strong feelings about the role of music in film; he saw the film score as something which facilitated the film rather than standing on its own. Less was more, in his opinion. He hoped that he could "paint pictures with his music." Mancini also felt that his success with such popular compositions as *The Pink Panther* theme song overshadowed some of his better work; which included the score for *Experiment in Terror* (1962), *Wait Until Dark* (1967), and *White Dawn* (1974).

In his last interview, Mancini claimed that music writing was his therapy, because when he wrote, he thought of nothing else. He continued conducting an average of 30 pops concerts a year and producing albums even after being diagnosed with cancer. He also continued work on the score for an upcoming stage version of *Victor/Victoria.* Mancini died in 1994 at the age of seventy, from complications of liver and pancreatic cancer. When he died, he left behind a legacy of popular and artistic film music.

Further Reading

Gannett News Service, June 14, 1994.
Independent, June 16, 1994; June 27, 1994.
Journal of Popular Film and Television, March 1, 1996.
Knight-Ridder/Tribune News Service, March 3, 1994.
USA Today, June 15, 1994. □

Vilma Socorro Martinez

Since the early 1970s, Mexican American attorney and activist Vilma Martinez (born 1943) has been a leading advocate for the civil rights of Hispanic Americans, especially at the ballot box.

Growing up as a Mexican American in Texas during the 1940s and 1950s, Vilma Martinez experienced the effects of racial prejudice firsthand. Later, also because of her ethnicity, she was discouraged from trying to obtain a college education, but she ultimately graduated from a distinguished law school. While still in her twenties, she participated in an important civil rights case that came before the U.S. Supreme Court. Martinez subsequently served for nearly a decade as head of one of the most prominent advocacy organizations in the country. More recently, her work as a lawyer in private practice has focused on resolving labor disputes.

Vilma Martinez was born in San Antonio, Texas, in 1943. As a Mexican American, she was often treated like a second-class citizen. Even though she was an honor student in high school, for example, she found herself steered away from academics by a counselor who tried to convince her that someone of her background would be better off attending a trade school than a major university. Martinez ignored that advice and instead enrolled in the University of Texas at Austin.

While working her way through college in the biochemistry lab, Martinez met a professor who recognized her potential. In marked contrast to her high-school counselor, the professor insisted that Martinez not only belonged in the world of higher education, but that she should go on to obtain a graduate degree—preferably out east, far from the state of Texas and its history of prejudice against Mexican Americans. Thus, after receiving her bachelor's degree,

Martinez went on to Columbia University in New York City, where she studied law.

Joined NAACP Staff

By 1967, Martinez had earned her law degree from Columbia. She soon went to work for the Legal Defense and Educational Fund of the National Association for the Advancement of Colored People (NAACP). In her job, she defended a number of poor and minority clients. She also served as the attorney for the petitioner in the case of *Griggs v. Duke Power Company,* a landmark action that ultimately went before the U.S. Supreme Court and helped establish the doctrine of affirmative action.

The Griggs case tested the limits of Title VII of the Civil Rights Act of 1964, which had prohibited employers from using race, sex, religion, ethnicity, or national origin as a factor for consideration in hiring. In issuing its decision, the Supreme Court found that a company's practice could be discriminatory even if it did not intend to perpetuate racial imbalance by that policy. Thus, if a company hired candidates solely or chiefly on the basis of their training and it could be proven that minorities had in the past been prevented from receiving such training, then the training requirements for the job were discriminatory. In 1972, partly in response to the Griggs decision, the federal government under President Richard Nixon enacted Executive Order 11246, which mandated a nationwide policy of affirmative action.

After spending several years with the NAACP, Martinez left in 1970 to serve as an equal opportunity counselor for the New York State Division of Human Rights. In this role, she created new rules and procedures governing the rights of employees. In 1971 she joined the firm of Cahill, Gordon & Reindel in New York City, where she worked as a labor lawyer.

Assumed Presidency of MALDEF

It was during her stint at the law firm that Martinez and one of her colleagues, Grace Olivarez, became the first women to join the board of the Mexican American Legal Defense and Educational Fund, or MALDEF, which was patterned after its counterpart at the NAACP. Soon afterward, in 1973, Martinez was hired as the advocacy organization's general counsel and president. Thus began a new era in both her life and in the history of MALDEF.

MALDEF had been founded in San Antonio in 1968 in response to years of discrimination and civil-rights violations against Mexican Americans. When Martinez came aboard, the fledgling group's mission was fairly clear but its financial stability was in doubt. In fact, she and other MALDEF staff members wondered if it could stay solvent from month to month since there was no regular source of funding. Thus, one of Martinez's most significant accomplishments as head of MALDEF was developing an operating framework that enabled it to grow and support a broader array of activities.

By the time she left in 1982, MALDEF had an annual budget of nearly $5 million, thanks to an increase in the number of corporate sponsors and foundation grants. As of

1998, MALDEF had become a large national nonprofit organization with 75 employees, including 22 attorneys. Its headquarters had moved from San Antonio to Los Angeles, and it boasted regional offices in San Francisco, Chicago, and Washington, D.C., as well as satellite and program offices in Detroit, El Paso, Sacramento, Fresno, and Santa Ana. Hence MALDEF could truly claim—as its site on the World Wide Web declared—to "protect and promote the civil rights of over 26 million Latinos living in the United States."

Spearheaded Historic Legal Challenges

On the legal front, MALDEF made U.S. civil rights history during Martinez's tenure as general counsel and president when she directed a program that helped secure an extension of the Voting Rights Act to include Mexican Americans among the groups it protected. When first passed by Congress in 1965, the Voting Rights Act had been aimed primarily at protecting black voters in the South, who were often harassed, intimidated, or forced to pass unconstitutional voting tests to keep them away from the ballot box. The only other group specifically protected by the act were Puerto Ricans, but Martinez and others were aware of voting-rights abuses involving Mexican Americans as well. Many of these were similar to the threats and tricks used on blacks and played on the additional factor of the language barrier. Therefore MALDEF began urging Congress to extend the purview of the Voting Rights Act to include Mexican Americans.

In pursuing this aim, Martinez and her colleagues faced opposition from various white and conservative groups as well as from an unexpected foe—the NAACP. Its director, Clarence Mitchell, maintained that expanding the Voting Rights Act to include other groups would weaken its protection of blacks, and therefore he opposed MALDEF's efforts. But other African American groups, most notably the Congressional Black Caucus, threw their support behind the idea. In 1975, the movement met with success when Congress finally agreed to extend the existing provisions of the Voting Rights Act and expand it to include Mexican Americans.

Another important legal victory that occurred during Martinez's decade at MALDEF was the 1974 ruling guaranteeing that non-English-speaking children in public schools could obtain bilingual education. And near the end of her tenure, she became involved in the landmark case of *Plyler v. Doe*. At issue was a Texas law that denied free public education to children of illegal aliens. Under the law, the parents of those children had to pay $1,000 tuition per year. Not only was it unlikely that anyone would come forward and identify himself or herself as an illegal alien, but few undocumented immigrants—most of whom survived on menial labor jobs—had the money to pay such an amount. Martinez argued that the children of illegal immigrants were in essence Americans by virtue of the fact that they had lived in the country for years, even if they were not citizens in the legal sense. In 1982, the courts finally agreed, and the tuition payment requirement was lifted.

Broadened Her Scope

While she was working with MALDEF, Martinez participated in a number of other activities on behalf of Mexican Americans. From 1975 to 1981, for example, she served as a volunteer consultant to the U.S. Census Bureau. Among the achievements of the panel that she chaired was the addition of a question to the census form asking if the respondent was Hispanic. This change had far-reaching effects, including the redrawing of some electoral districts.

In 1976, Martinez accepted an invitation from California Governor Jerry Brown to join that state's Board of Regents. She remained with the board until 1990, at one point serving a two-year term as chairman. From 1977 until 1981, during the presidency of Jimmy Carter, Martinez also was a member of an advisory board that reviewed appointments to ambassadorial positions around the world.

Martinez's personal life was equally busy during the 1970s. Early in the decade, she married a fellow attorney named Stuart Singer. They eventually had two sons, Carlos and Ricardo.

Entered Private Law Practice

In 1982, after spending nearly a decade at the helm of MALDEF, Martinez was ready to make a change. She stepped down from her position as president and considered a variety of options that included running for elected office or teaching law. She ultimately settled on a position with a prestigious Los Angeles law firm, Munger, Tolles & Olson. In her new role, Martinez specialized in resolving labor disputes.

In addition to her work as an attorney, Martinez has been a popular speaker at educational institutions around the United States, including Harvard Law School, Yale University, the University of Notre Dame, and her alma mater, the University of Texas, which honored her with its distinguished alumnus award in 1988. Martinez has received a number of other awards and has been invited to sit on numerous civic and corporate boards, among them Shell Oil Company. She has also played an important role with the federal government as a consultant to the U.S. Commission on Civil Rights and as a lawyer delegate to the Ninth Circuit Judicial Conference.

Throughout her career, Martinez has been cited as proof that a person from humble beginnings can become a success. Even children have looked to her for inspiration as they deal with the many challenges of living in a diverse culture. For instance, in a 1997 essay contest sponsored by Project Wisdom, a nationwide program to encourage excellence in students (described online at www.projectwisdom.com), a seventh-grader named Shara of Bondy Intermediate School in Pasadena, Texas, tied for first place with her reflections on Martinez's approach to life. ". . .If more people had the same attitude as Vilma Martinez," wrote Shara, "our country wouldn't have as many homeless, unemployed, or people financially aided by the government."

Further Reading

Coduye, Corinn, *Vilma Martinez*, Raintree/Steck Vaughan, 1989.

Dictionary of Hispanic Biography, Gale, 1996, pp. 528-30.

Notable Hispanic American Women, Gale, 1993, pp. 261-263.

The Hispanic-American Almanac, Gale, 1993, p. 243.

"MALDEF: Background/Mission Statement," http://www.maldef.org/mission (April 3, 1998).

"Presidential Records, 1973-1982," *Research Guide to the Records of the Mexican/American Legal Defense Fund*, http://www-sul.stanford.edu/depts/spc/guides/m673 (April 3, 1998).

"Project Wisdom—Winning Essays," *Project Wisdom*, http://www.projectwisdom.com (April 3, 1998).

"Vilma Martinez Elected to Shell Oil Company Board of Directors," *Shell Oil Company*, http://ms.shellus.com/news/press120996 (April 3, 1998).

Spark M. Matsunaga

Born in Kukuiula, Hawaii, Spark M. Matsunaga (1916-1990) served as a member of the U.S. House of Representatives and then the U.S. Senate, where he devoted himself to the cause of peace and the task of seeking redress for Japanese Americans interned during World War II. He died in Toronto, Ontario, Canada.

As one who was well acquainted with the devastating effects of war, Spark M. Matsunaga made peace the focus of his career in the United States Congress. For nearly two decades, he lobbied his colleagues to establish a National Academy of Peace and Conflict Resolution, which he envisioned as a place young Americans could go to learn how to resolve domestic and international disputes without resorting to violence. He also championed the creation of a cabinet-level Department of Peace. In addition, Matsunaga was committed to seeking redress for a special group of war victims the tens of thousands of people of Japanese descent who were unjustly held in U.S. prison camps during World War II. On this front, too, he battled long and hard, joining with a number of his colleagues to achieve the justice that had been denied to him and many others on account of their race."

Spark Masayuki Matsunaga was born in Hawaii to Kingoro and Chiyoro Fukushima Matsunaga, both of whom had emigrated from Japan. He and his five siblings grew up amid extreme poverty, yet their parents instilled in them the belief that hard work would bring them success. In fact, Matsunaga held a variety of jobs while still in high school and also worked his way through the University of Hawaii, graduating with honors in 1941. Postponing his plans to go on to law school, he joined the U.S. Army and was commissioned a second lieutenant. But fate soon intervened; on December 7 of that year, the Japanese bombed Pearl Harbor and brought the United States into World War II.

In the weeks and months following the attack, Japanese Americans even those who were U.S. citizens became targets of prejudice, fear, and hatred by those who questioned their loyalty to America. On February 19, 1942, President Franklin D. Roosevelt issued Executive Order 9066, which called for the evacuation of some 120,000 Japanese Americans (about two-thirds of whom were U.S. citizens) from the West Coast to large "relocation centers" in isolated areas of Arizona, Arkansas, inland California, Colorado, Idaho, Utah, and Wyoming. (A number of smaller camps were also set up in about fourteen other states.) By and large, Japanese Americans living elsewhere in the United States and in Hawaii were not affected by the order. As a member of the military, however, Matsunaga was considered suspect, even though he had given no cause for anyone to doubt his allegiance. So he, too, was shipped off to an internment camp in Wisconsin.

But Matsunaga and many other young Japanese American men desperately wanted the chance to fight for their country and prove their loyalty. Before long, they began petitioning the U.S. government to allow them to serve in the armed forces. Finally, in January of 1943, the War Department announced that it would accept fifteen hundred Japanese American volunteers for a new unit, the 442nd Regimental Combat Team. Matsunaga joined up and fought for the 100th Infantry Battalion in Italy, where he was wounded twice. The now-legendary 442nd went on to become the most decorated unit in U.S. military history; Matsunaga himself returned home as a captain with many medals and commendations.

After the war, Matsunaga enrolled in Harvard University and earned his law degree in 1951. He then headed back to Hawaii, where he worked as a prosecutor in Honolulu until 1954 and then entered politics as a member and later majority leader in the Territorial House of Representatives. He was also active in the administrative ranks of the Democratic party, serving as an executive board member of the state organization and a delegate to county and state conventions. When Hawaii became a state in 1959, the immensely popular and personable Matsunaga known as "Sparky" to his friends in recognition of his lively, sunny disposition was elected to its new senate.

In 1962, Matsunaga made the leap to national office when he was elected to the U.S. House of Representatives. He went on to serve seven consecutive terms in that body before being elected to the U.S. Senate in 1976. While his impact on legislation was not as great as that of his fellow Democratic senator from Hawaii, Daniel K. Inouye, Matsunaga's devotion to his causes peace, nuclear arms control, safeguarding the environment, securing redress for Japanese Americans interned during World War II was never in doubt. Beginning almost from the moment he first arrived in Washington in 1963, for example, Matsunaga lobbied for the creation of a cabinet-level Department of Peace, which he felt would institutionalize at the federal level "our nation's commitment to the goal of global peace." While he was not the first to propose such an idea, he was certainly one of its most ardent supporters.

As outlined by Matsunaga, one of the major responsibilities of the Department of Peace would be to establish and maintain another cherished dream of his, the National Academy of Peace and Conflict Resolution. It was envisioned as a place where young Americans could go to master "the art of peace." Explained Matsunaga: "The United States wields all economic, social, cultural, and political power over the world that is unequaled in history. I believe that [the Academy of Peace and Conflict Resolution] will enable our nation to bring this power to bear directly on the problems of war and on those related problems that plague the lesser developed countries. . . . I submit that peace, like war, is an art which must be studied and learned before it can be waged well. . . ."

It was not until 1984, however, that Matsunaga's idea finally met with a measure of success. While he was unable to persuade his colleagues to establish a Department of Peace within the cabinet, he did manage to secure approval for the creation of the U.S. Peace Institute. It awards graduate degrees to those who help resolve disputes in the national and international arena.

Another significant and highly personal achievement of Matsunaga's legislative career involved obtaining redress for those Japanese Americans who were victims of injustice during World War II as a result of the infamous Executive Order 9066. Ostensibly imprisoned for their own "protection," these men, women, and children of all ages and backgrounds had not been accused of any crime, yet they spent as long as three years imprisoned in tar-paper shacks behind barbed wire and guarded by armed military police. Many had been forced to give up everything they owned. But the greatest blow was to their dignity and sense of security; they could not comprehend why their loyalty

was being questioned and why the government they respected and admired was so willing to cast aside their constitutional rights.

On August 2, 1979, Matsunaga co-sponsored a bill known as S. 1647 that proposed creating a commission to investigate the wartime relocation of Japanese Americans and determine what, if any, compensation was owed to them for the losses they had suffered both emotionally and economically. "Many unanswered questions remain about the detention of Japanese Americans during World War II . . . ," noted Matsunaga during Senate hearings on the bill held in early 1980. "Passage of S. 1647 will be just one more piece of evidence ours is a nation great enough to recognize and rectify its mistakes."

S. 1647 sailed through the Senate on May 22, 1980, and, after the House and Senate reached agreement on a final version, it was signed into law by President Jimmy Carter on July 31. On July 14, 1981, the Commission on Wartime Relocation and Internment of Civilians (CWRIC) began gathering testimony from others with something to say about this dark episode in American history. In all, more than seven hundred people appeared before the CWRIC, which in 1983 published a report of its findings entitled *Personal Justice Denied.*

In this document, members of the commission condemned the relocation of Japanese Americans, insisting it was done not out of military necessity but as a result of "race prejudice, war hysteria and a failure of political leadership." The CWRIC later issued several recommendations for redress, including an apology from Congress and the president acknowledging the injustice done to Japanese Americans and a payment of $20,000 to each of the estimated sixty thousand survivors of the camps.

On April 19, 1988, a bill known as S. 1009 proposing that the CWRIC's recommendations be adopted finally made it to the floor. Matsunaga, who had shepherded the measure through the Senate with a number of impassioned speeches urging its approval, faced his colleagues yet again, this time to head off attempts by opponents to eliminate cash compensation to former internees. While few legislators had a problem with the idea of apologizing to Japanese Americans, some questioned the fairness of holding present-day taxpayers responsible for wrongs committed decades earlier and raised the prospect that approving such payments would open the door to similar claims from African Americans and other groups.

Addressing his fellow senators, Matsunaga noted that "in the life of every individual, and every nation, there are certain events which have a lasting, lifelong impact and which change the shape of their future. . . . For Americans of Japanese ancestry who are over the age of forty-five years, the single, most traumatic event, the one which shaped the rest of their lives, is the wholesale relocation and incarceration in American-style concentration camps of some 120,000 Americans of Japanese ancestry and their parents and grandparents. . . ."

The debate over S. 1009 continued the next day, April 20. Matsunaga again rose to speak in support of the bill and against any attempts to remove provisions that awarded monetary damages to former internees. Shortly before a vote was taken, Matsunaga addressed his colleagues one last time. Newspaper accounts noted that he wept and momentarily faltered as he recalled the suffering of some prisoners, especially an elderly man whose innocent game of catch with his grandson ended in tragedy when their ball landed too close to the camp's fence and a guard shot and killed the man as he went to retrieve it.

"The stigma of disloyalty has haunted Japanese Americans for the past forty-five years," declared Matsunaga, "and it is one of the principal reasons that they are seeking congressional action to remove that cloud over their heads.... The sponsors of the bill do not pretend that history can be erased, but the measure would provide for the first time an official acknowledgement of the grave injustice which was done, and it would provide token monetary compensation to those who suffered irreparable losses.... Its passage ... will prove that our beloved country is great enough to acknowledge and correct its past mistakes."

Later that same day April 20, 1988 the Senate voted 69 to 27 in favor of S. 1009, including the provision awarding a $20,000 payment to former internees. After President Ronald Reagan signed it into law in August, Matsunaga was hailed for almost single-handedly bringing about its passage.

In addition to his interest in conflict resolution and securing redress for Japanese Americans, Matsunaga supported legislation aimed at safeguarding the environment. He backed efforts to investigate alternative sources of energy, including planes fueled by hydrogen instead of petroleum-based products and commercial ships powered by the wind. His last official act as a U.S. senator was to cast a vote in favor of extending the Clean Air Act.

Matsunaga also harbored a love of space exploration and envisioned a day when international cooperation would lead to a manned flight to the planet Mars. And his interest in poetry (he himself wrote haiku) led him to push for the naming of a national poet laureate, a proposal that gained legislative approval in 1985.

In January of 1990, Matsunaga announced that he was suffering from prostate cancer that had spread to his bones. He began treatments immediately but died three months later while hospitalized in Toronto, Canada. "He will be remembered most for his vision of peace and his faith in the human heart," noted Hawaii Governor John D. Waihee in a statement issued after news of the popular senator's death was made public. "Sparky warmed our state and country with his humanitarianism."

Further Reading

Commission on Wartime Relocation and Internment of Civilians Act: Hearing Before the Committee on Governmental Affairs, United States Senate, 96th Congress, Second Session, U.S. Government Printing Office, 1980.

Congressional Record, 100th Congress, 1st Session [and] 2nd Session, U.S. Government Printing Office, 1988.

Daniels, Roger, *Concentration Camps USA: Japanese Americans and World War II,* Holt, 1972.

Hosokawa, Bill, *JACL: In Quest of Justice,* Morrow, 1982.

Matsunaga, Spark M., *To Establish the United States Academy of Peace,* U.S. Government Printing Office, 1981.

Matsunaga, Spark M., *The Mars Project: Journeys Beyond the Cold War,* Hill & Wang, 1986.

National Academy of Peace and Conflict Resolution: Hearings Before the Subcommittee on International Operations of the Committee on International Relations, House of Representatives, 95th Congress, 2nd Session, U.S. Government Printing Office, 1978.

Personal Justice Denied: Report of the Commission on Wartime Relocation and Internment of Civilians, U.S. Government Printing Office, 1983.

Christian Science Monitor, September 16, 1987.

Los Angeles Times, April 16, 1990, p. A24.

New York Times, April 21, 1988; April 16, 1990, p. D10.

Washington Post, April 16, 1990, p. D6.

Carson McCullers

One of America's most unique writers, Carson McCullers (1917-1967) wrote about isolation, loneliness and failures in human communication in popular novels and plays set in the Southern United States, mostly in the 1940s.

Carson McCullers is considered to be a member of the "Southern gothic" tradition in American literature, and is often compared to writers like Eudora Welty and Flannery O'Connor. Her characters include tortured adolescents, homosexuals, and outcasts from conventional society. Several of her novels were popular, but critics have disagreed about her achievements. Because of her fluid, nuanced prose, she is most appreciated by other writers. Gore Vidal said her "genius for prose remains one of the few satisfying achievements of our second-rate culture." Playwright Tennessee Williams spoke of the "intensity and nobility of spirit" in her writing.

Lonely Heart

Lula Carson Smith was born in 1917 in Columbus, Georgia. She was a precocious child encouraged by an indulgent mother to pursue her talents. She began piano lessons at age five and became an awkward and isolated prodigy. During her school days she was often harassed by children who called her a freak.

At 17, she entered the prestigious Julliard School of Music in New York City, but poor health prevented her from going to classes. Instead, she took a series of odd jobs by day and studied writing at Columbia University at night. She was a failure at earning a living by any means other than writing. "I was always fired," she once told an interviewer. "My record is perfect on that. I never quit a job in my life."

Her first published story was a thinly disguised autobiographical piece called *Wunderkind.* It tells the story of a girl who realizes at age 15 that she is not the musical prodigy her parents told her she was. She quits music and loses her friends and her parents' affection. In New York in 1937, she married Reeves McCullers. But neither was suited to heterosexual monogamy, and theirs was a difficult union. They divorced in 1940 but remarried in 1945.

Critic Robert F. Kiernan once noted that McCullers was "an eccentric, self-centered woman, preoccupied with money, with literary success, and with the satisfaction of her own emotional needs. . . . But the failings of M.'s life were the material of her art, and all of her characters share her egocentricity and suffer the pangs of its attendant loneliness."

The "air of stark, existential angst" which Kiernan noted in her work was present from the very start. In her first novel, *The Heart Is a Lonely Hunter,* published in 1940, when she was only 23, McCullers told a desperately sad story about a deaf-mute, John Singer, who cares for a mentally impaired deaf-mute, Spiros Antonatoulos. Four townspeople adopt Singer as their confidante. They believe Singer is sympathetic, but in fact he listens merely to be polite and does not understand them. Antonatoulos is sent to an insane asylum, and Singer commits suicide.

The novel explores the inability of human beings to soothe others' loneliness. None of the characters are capable of giving the love and understanding the others need. One of the characters is a black doctor who is frustrated at his inability to make progress in race relations in the Southern town. Another is an adolescent girl who dreams of becoming an orchestra conductor but is doomed by her family's poverty to a lifetime of working in a dime store; the character is modeled after McCullers.

Critics loved the way McCullers recreated the closed-in atmosphere of a Southern small town. They also admired how sympathetically the characters were portrayed despite their obvious failings. In her later work of collected essays and stories, *The Mortgaged Heart,* McCullers explained her themes: "Love, and especially love of a person who is incapable of returning or receiving it, is at the heart of my selection of grotesque figures to write about—people whose physical incapacity is a symbol of their spiritual isolation."

Defying Convention

The Heart Is a Lonely Hunter was a best-seller and instantly established McCullers on the American literary scene. Critics hailed her as a major emerging talent. Her second novel, *Reflections in a Golden Eye,* shattered expectations, mostly because of its unconventional subject matter. The homosexual nature of the relationship between the two deaf-mutes in her first novel was only implied. In *Golden Eye* the characters' non-standard sexual behavior was obvious. Set on an army base in the South in the 1930s, the novel is about the relationships among Captain Penderton, a bisexual, sadomasochistic, impotent man; Major Langdon, who is having an affair with Penderton's wife; the two wives; a homosexual houseboy, Anacleto; and Private Williams, who has relations with a horse. The novel is full of perverse scenes and ends with a murder. Most critics found the characters grotesque and unsympathetic.

McCullers's second novel was written as her marriage fell apart. She had taken a female lover, and her husband

had taken a male lover. After finishing the book, McCullers moved to New York to live with book editor George Davis. In 1942, McCullers was awarded a Guggenheim fellowship. She was awarded another in 1946. She also got a National Institute of Arts and Letters grant in 1943.

That same year, she completed her long novella, *The Ballad of the Sad Cafe.* Cast in terms of a folk tale with a nameless narrator, it is the story of a female giant, Amelia Evans, who is in love with Lymon, a hunchback. Evans runs a cafe in a small Southern town. Her husband, Marvin Macy, returns from prison and starts a relationship with Lymon. The story ends in a brawl between the married couple and the destruction of the cafe. Many critics considered the story McCullers's finest work, approaching the level of myth. Tennessee Williams said it was "among the masterpieces of the language."

In 1946, the novel *The Member of the Wedding* was published. McCullers had been working on the story off and on since 1940. Again set in a small Southern town, it concerns an awkward, lonely adolescent girl, Frankie Adams. She tries to become a member of her brother's wedding party to overcome her isolation, but her father prevents her from riding in the newlyweds' car. More realistic than her previous two works, *The Member of the Wedding* is a sympathetic portrayal of adolescent misery. It won a great reception from critics and the public. McCullers adapted it for the stage, and it had a successful run of 501 performances in New York in 1950, winning several important awards. In 1952, it was made into a film of the same name, starring Julie Harris.

Challenges and Decline

McCullers's health was never good, but by the time she was 30 it began to seriously hamper her career. In 1947, she suffered a series of strokes which left her blinded in the right eye and partially paralyzed. She could type with only one hand, and produced only a page a day. In 1948, in despair over her physical condition, McCullers attempted suicide but failed; she never tried again. But her husband was also suicidal because of his lack of success in a career and their unstable marriage. In 1953 he suggested a double suicide while they were living in Europe. She fled to the United States, and a few weeks later he killed himself in a hotel in Paris. McCullers returned to live with her mother, who died in 1955.

Her personal difficulties greatly diminished her literary output. In 1953 she wrote a television play, *The Invisible Wall,* for CBS. Her second and last stage play, *The Square Root of Wonderful,* was a failure in 1958. Her final novel was published in 1961. Titled *Clock without Hands,* it returns to the themes of homosexuality and racial bigotry McCullers first raised in *The Heart Is a Lonely Hunter.* A critical and commercial failure, *Clock without Hands* is the story of the bigoted Southern patriarch Judge Clane, who is raising his orphaned grandson Jester. The judge, who still believes in the principles of the old Confederacy, wants to send Jester to a military school, but Jester is more interested in music and flying and in his grandfather's mixed-race male secretary, Sherman Pew.

The same year *Clock without Hands* was published, McCullers had breast cancer surgery. In 1964, her second and last television screenplay, *The Sojourner,* aired on NBC. That year, her book of poems for children, *Sweet as a Pickle and Clean as a Pig,* was published. Another children's book, *Sucker,* was published posthumously in 1986.

In 1967, McCullers suffered another stroke and soon died at the age of 50. That same year, *Reflections in a Golden Eye* was released as a Hollywood feature film. Directed by John Huston and starring Marlon Brando and Elizabeth Taylor, the movie was a flop despite its big names. The following year, a film version of *The Heart Is a Lonely Hunter,* starring Alan Arkin, won a little more attention.

The Mortgaged Heart: The Previously Uncollected Writings of Carson McCullers, came out in 1971. Another volume of short stories, *Collected Stories,* was published in 1987. In 1989, *The Member of the Wedding* enjoyed a revival at the Roundabout Theater in New York. McCullers's tale of suburban alcoholism in the 1950s, *A Domestic Dilemma,* became part of a 1991 HBO television anthology, *Women and Men 2,* starring Andie McDowell and Ray Liotta. That same year, *Ballad of the Sad Cafe* was made into a film, with Vanessa Redgrave as the giant woman and Keith Carradine as her husband. The film was a failure.

A Mixed Legacy

Critics disagree strongly on McCullers's standing in American literature. Stanley Kauffmann, reviewing the film version of *Ballad of the Sad Cafe* in the *New Republic,* blasted the story as a "fashion whose vogue is well over." Kauffmann said McCullers was overrated: "Nowadays it's hard to believe that some of the writers of the so-called Southern Gothic school. . . . were taken so seriously." Except for O'Connor and Welty, Kauffmann said, McCullers and the others were merely "Spanish moss hanging on the tree of American literature—once perhaps atmospheric but gone gray and dry." Kauffmann blasted *Sad Cafe* as "almost an epitome of in-grown artiness that depends for its reception on, in a way, browbeating readers: humbling them into acceptance of all this rampant sensibility at the risk of being thought philistine otherwise. Couch that sensibility in grotesquery, as is done here, add a dollop of Loneliness and the Need for Love, and you're home free."

But others have hailed McCullers as one of the giants of American literature. In 1994, playwright David Willinger adapted *The Heart Is a Lonely Hunter* for the stage in a play he also directed at the Theater for the New City in New York. With little dialogue to work with, Willinger constructed a kind of extended physical style for his actors, rejecting the idea of using pantomime or dance to convey script points. A deaf actor, Bruce Hilbok, played John Singer. A non-deaf actor, Ralph Navarro, played Spiros Antonatoulos. "I don't know if McCullers is underrated, but I think of her as on a par with Hemingway," said Willinger.

McCullers's career was short, but it was filled with daring and unusual work. Critics may disagree on her place in American literature, but clearly her writings were unique in their treatment of isolation, loneliness and people who were outcasts from conventional society. "No one has writ-

ten more feelingly than her about the plight of the eccentric," Kiernan contended, "and no one has written more understandingly than she about adolescent loneliness and desperation."

Further Reading

Carr, Virginia Spencer, *The Lonely Hunter: A Biography of Carson McCullers,* Doubleday, 1975.
Contemporary Authors, New Revision Series, Volume 18, Gale, 1986.
James, Judith Giblin, *Wunderkind: The Reputation of Carson McCullers, 1940-1990,* Camden House, 1995.
Malinowski, Sharon, editor, *Gay and Lesbian Literature,* St. James Press, 1994.
Back Stage, May 20, 1994.
Los Angeles Times, August 21, 1987.
New Republic, May 20, 1991.
New York Times, July 14, 1987.
People, August 19, 1991.

Vladimir Meciar

As one of the most prominent of politicians in a newly de-Communized Eastern Europe, Slovak leader Vladimir Meciar (born 1942) has been called the "architect of his country's independence," but has also faced criticism for his role in the breakup of the former Czechoslovakia.

Vladimir Meciar, a lawyer and onetime Communist, rose to political power after the "Velvet Revolution" of 1989 that ousted decades of socialist, pro-Soviet leadership in Czechoslovakia. Held as a heroic figure among some segments of the Slovak electorate, Meciar has held the prime minister position for the majority of the years since its split into the independent nation of Slovakia.

Meciar was born in 1942 in Zvolen, Czechoslovakia—in the Slovak region of the country—into a proletariat family where his mother, even after the rise to prominence of her son, worked as a janitor in a factory. He attended Comenius University in Bratislava, the Slovak capital, and first became involved in politics in 1959 when he was appointed to a clerk's position at the District National Committee for the community of Ziar nad Hronom.

From 1962 to 1968, he rose through Communist Party ranks in a number of bureaucratic jobs with the Slovakia Union of Youth. During this era, Meciar, like many young Czecholovaks, became a staunch supporter of the democratic reforms of Alexander Dubcek, the Communist Party's extremely popular reformist leader. That spirit of change was crushed when Russian tanks rolled across Czechoslovakia's borders in 1968 and Dubcek was ousted.

Death of Communism

Meciar, too, was ousted from the Communist Party after a purge in 1968 that targeted liberal-leaning communists. At this point, he began studying law, and worked at an industrial job, as many similarly-fired bureaucrats were forced to do during the 1970s. After 1973 he was employed as a clerk, then a lawyer, for a firm called Skloobal, located in Nemsova. It was a post he held until his re-entry into politics in 1989.

Czechoslovakia's Velvet Revolution occurred not long after the fall of the Berlin Wall and the ousting of Communist leadership in East Germany. During the tumultuous weeks that followed, Meciar became active in a Slovak group called Public Against Violence, one of the two main organized forces behind a peaceful change in government for Czechoslovakia. The once-jailed playwright Vaclav Havel, along with other prominent artists and writers who were members of the other main opposition group, the Civic Forum, stepped in to fill the leadership vacuum left by the ouster of the Communists.

In 1990, Meciar became a deputy in House of Nations for the new-era Czechoslovak Federal Assembly, and was also appointed Minister of Interior and Environment for Slovakia, which at this point was still one-half of the nation now known as the Czechoslovak Federation. When the first free elections were held in June of 1990, Meciar campaigned for and won the post of Slovakia's prime minister.

A Nation Divided

As its top statesperson, Meciar soon became the point-person for the Slovak state's long-simmering problems with the neighboring Czech republic. The two Slavic ethnic groups were closely related by language, but divided culturally, and Czechoslovakia itself had only been in existence as a nation since the end of World War I. For centuries the Czechs had often tied their fortunes to the rest of Western Europe, especially to Germany, their next-door neighbor. Its capital, Prague, was a Baroque treasure and center for the country's spirited intellectual and artistic movements.

Slovakia and its people, on the other hand, were more closely allied with the rest of the true Eastern Europe. It possessed rich agricultural lands, and during the years of Communist rule was sometimes treated shabbily by the leadership in Prague. The landscape of Slovakia was heavily industrialized during this era, but still retained its "peasant" character. Indeed, Slovaks were often the butt of Czech jokes, while the Czechs were viewed by Slovaks as arrogant and untrustworthy.

These long-simmering tensions came to a crisis point in the early 1990s, when Meciar and other politicians from each side tried to chart a course for their new nation. The Czechs wished for faster de-communization and heartily welcomed Western-style free-market capitalism. They were also eager to lure lucrative foreign investment, which some patriotic Slovaks were loathe to see in their part of the country.

By this point Meciar had began to earn criticism for his sometimes heavy-handed political style that mimicked the excesses of authoritarian Communist rule. It was alleged he had ties to right-wing movements, and had been able to have his internal-security police files destroyed during his stint as interior minister. Later, when the man who suc-

ceeded him in the post moved to eradicate the secret police—counterparts to the Soviet KGB—Meciar told him to resign, and when he refused, Meciar sharply curtailed the minister's authority. He also threatened to step away from his prime minister's post, but received an outpouring of public support.

Still, Meciar's opponents voted him out of power in April of 1991, but he won a resounding share of votes in the 1992 elections as leader of a new political party, Movement for a Democratic Slovakia (Hnutie za Demokraticke Slovensko, known as HzDS). This party campaigned for independence from Czechoslovak Federation, and found fault with the new Prague-based Czech leadership—an administration viewed with suspicion by less-politically aware Slovaks. With their arms factories closing and many out of work for the first time in their lives, the Slovaks faced economic hardships as a result of the fall of Communism and the Soviet Union. This was highly in contrast to the heady new Prague, where Western advertising agencies were opening offices and sports bars catered to a large American expatriate community. The idea of self-determination, for an independent Slovakia, grew in power over the next year. The Czechoslovak Federation came to an end officially on January 1, 1993, when the Slovak Republic came into being.

Meciar and the Hungarians

Another important zone of Slovak politics that has served Meciar's political career well is the country's border with Hungary, which is home to most of the ten percent of ethnic Hungarians in Slovakia. "In Slovak politics, nationalist prejudices and ethnic tensions are never far below the surface," wrote Bruce Wallace in *Maclean's*. "Meciar knows exactly how to fuel those emotions."

Tensions between the two lands had existed for a thousand years, with the Hungarians usually prevailing, but during Meciar's era Slovakia seemed to be collecting a past-due debt. The Hungarian populace in Slovakia was a legacy from the days of the Austro-Hungarian Empire. Prior to the empire's fall in 1918, neither Slovakia nor Czechoslovakia existed as independent nations, but were simply subjects of the Empire; the Hapsburg leaders in Vienna had instituted a "Magyarization" plan in the decades prior to that as its authority slid into decline. Under this homogenization program, the Slovak language was forbidden.

A peaceful co-existence and tolerance was apparent in the actual Slovak towns and villages that were heavily Hungarian, but Meciar's agitating of dormant ethnic rivalries ended that era. During Meciar's 1992-94 term, he forbade the use of the Hungarian language on any official documents, and even ordered that Hungarian road signs be removed. Furthermore, the region's desire for less inference in local affairs from Bratislava—the government seat of Slovakia—was sometimes seen as a push for increased autonomy there.

"An Excellent, Evil, Political Mind"

Meciar has also slandered the Gypsies, a common target of ethnic prejudice in Eastern Europe. These and other actions caused him, once again, to be ousted from his prime minister position in March of 1994 by a coalition of his political foes. The anti-Meciar block then fell apart, leaving a leadership vacuum by which Meciar again profited. In October of that year, he and the HzDS received a majority of the vote in the general elections. He campaigned under the slogan, "Slovakia—Go for It," and the party made a music video that featured he and other HzDS candidates singing in a type of "We Are the World" anthem called "Vivat Slovakia." Despite the MTV-style television ads, Meciar's biggest support base lies with Slovakia's older generation; political analysts have even dubbed his most ardent fans the "Democratic Grandmothers"—babushka-clad women who turn out in full force at his public appearances. Once, a few of them even attempted to thrash some liberal journalists who had written unfavorably about Meciar.

A member of the renowned human-rights group Charter 77 told Maclean's journalist Wallace, that Meciar "has an excellent, evil, political mind." In 1996, the son of his political foe, Slovak president Michal Kovac, was kidnapped, and it was suspected that the Slovak Intelligence Service was involved, which one of Meciar's top aides is also the head of. Yet Meciar's HzDS party retains firm control of Slovakia's state-run television network, and its news reports aired allegations that the whole abduction was a publicity stunt by the Kovac family when it was verified that the kidnapped had landed in legal trouble and was the target of a fraud investigation in Germany.

Meciar's authority has also extended into attempts to censor media outlets that have criticized him and the HzDS. In 1997 he tried to increase the value-added tax on magazines and newspapers—except for those that carry less than ten percent advertising in its page content, such as his party's organ, Slovenska Republika. That same year, the independent station Radio Twist went off the air for a day after its transmission was halted by the state-controlled telecommunications agency. The agency asserted that Radio Twist was behind in its transmission fees—but the state-run television station was in far greater arrears.

That same year, Meciar proposed to his Hungarian counterpart that minorities be exchanged, a move that was roundly criticized by the international community. Because of these engineered tensions, Slovakia was not asked to join the North American Treaty Organization (NATO). Still, such actions do not appear to diminish Meciar's popularity at home. He has won more general elections than any other new-era leader in post-communist Europe, a remarkable accomplishment in a part of the world where newly-democratic citizens are still testing out their political clout at the ballot box.

Meciar's autocratic style has seemed to be an increasing thorn in Slovak politics, however, and his popularity may be on the wane. He attempted to consolidate his power by taking over the presidential post in March of 1998 after Kovac resigned. The Slovak Parliament voted for a number of candidates to succeed Kovac, but none received a majority. In the intervening weeks Meciar held presidential power himself, and fired most of the staff of the executive office. Another of his presidential decrees granted amnesty to the suspects jailed for the kidnapping of Michael Kovac Jr.; this

and other acts were protested in peaceful street demonstrations.

Further Reading

Detroit Free Press, January 15, 1997.
Economist, November 15, 1997, p. 54; February 7, 1998, p. 55.
Interpress Service, May 21, 1996.
Maclean's, October 10, 1994, p. 28.
New York Times, October 12, 1997.
Prague Post, April 8, 1998.
Sydney Morning Herald, March 7, 1998.

Duong Van Minh

General Duong Van Minh (born 1916) was the first and last of a string of leaders who governed South Vietnam in the dozen years between the overthrow of President Diem and the fall of Saigon.

In 1963, Duong Van Minh represented pro-American, anti-communist values. By 1975 he remained the only figure of stature who could negotiate with North Vietnamese forces and avert a bloody end to the Vietnam War. Duong Van Minh's military career spanned decades of conflict. He gained an early reputation for bravery, honesty, and leadership in the field and quickly rose to national prominence. In his later career, however, power remained just beyond his reach and he was eventually forced into exile.

French Colonial Era

Minh was born into a wealthy Vietnamese family on February 19, 1916, in the Mekong River delta village of My Tho in Long An Province, just 35 miles southwest of Saigon. After graduating from a high school run by the French, Minh enlisted in the colonial army in 1940 and was commissioned a second lieutenant. He continued to serve under the French during World War II until Vietnam surrendered to Japan. At that point he joined a resistance group which was soon quashed. The young officer was taken prisoner for two months and tortured, having half of his teeth knocked out. For the rest of his life, his gold tooth-lined grin would be his trademark. Standing 5 foot 10 inches tall and athletic, he developed a pronounced stoop, supposedly from constantly leaning over to talk to his shorter companions. Minh was known fondly as "Beo" (fat boy) to his fellow soldiers. Americans later dubbed him "Big Minh" to distinguish him from another South Vietnamese official by the same name.

After his release by the Japanese, Minh returned immediately to the French, but was imprisoned for joining the resistance. He was jailed for an additional three months, this time in a crowded dark cell with no toilet. Driven nearly to insanity by the subhuman prison conditions, Minh won his freedom with the help of another prisoner, Nguyen Ngoc Tho, who would later become the premier of his country.

Minh's nationalist spirit grew during his incarceration, but he agreed upon release to serve the French for another

four years under the puppet government of Emperor Bao Dai. When a Vietnamese army was created in 1952, two years before independence, Minh jumped at the chance to join. Soon he was on his way to the École Militaire in Paris for further training, the first Vietnamese officer to be so honored. By the end of the French war against the Vietnamese nationalists, Minh was commander of the Saigon-Cholon garrison.

South Vietnam Army

After the French withdrew from Vietnam, Ngo Dinh Diem became president of the Republic of Vietnam. Minh went to work for Diem's new regime, first earning the gratitude of his people in 1955 by vanquishing a gangster syndicate and later pacifying two religious cults. Minh distinguished himself by his respect for these sects' temples, even while giving no quarter to their fighters. His actions would put him in sharp contrast years later Diem, who showed no such regard when attacking Buddhist dissidents.

After his success in these campaigns, Minh was sent for yet more training at the U.S. Army Command and General Staff College at Fort Leavenworth, Kansas. Upon his return, Diem chose Minh in 1958 to become the first commander of field operations in the developing war against Viet Cong guerrillas. Minh's success and popularity with his troops would later prove his downfall in Diem's eyes, however. As dissatisfaction among Vietnam's generals mounted, the president grew suspicious of Minh's loyalty. Though not openly critical of Diem, Minh privately questioned the wisdom of fighting a war against the communists without

greater popular support in South Vietnam. Finally, Diem removed Minh's command and named him military advisor to the president. This effectively removed Minh from any direct power in the army and gave Diem a fleeting sense of security.

Diem became more erratic, tyrannical, and dangerously detached from his people in the early 1960s. Rumors circulated that he was secretly negotiating with Ho Chi Minh's North Vietnam to unify the country and declare neutrality. United States support, critical to Diem's survival, grew thin. There were whispers of a coup, and Minh seemed a logical choice to lead it, but the general insisted he had no stomach for politics but was content to play tennis, read French and American magazines, and tend to his orchid garden. He stated his commitment to preserving civil instead of military control in South Vietnam's government. Minh's dedication had impressed American advisors years earlier, however, when he had reportedly mortgaged his home and sold his car and furniture to finance under-funded army intelligence operations. It was clear the Americans were not content to let Minh continue raising orchids.

In November 1963, Minh led a military coup that toppled the Diem government, with the tacit approval of the United States. Minh offered him safe conduct if he surrendered within five minutes, but Diem reportedly hung up and attempted to flee dressed in the robes of a Catholic priest. Diem and his brother Ngo Dinh Nhu were later captured and killed, on orders from Minh, according to some accounts. Friends of Minh said he had acted out of patriotism and outrage at Diem's attacks on Buddhist temples, not personal ambition. The Kennedy administration showed little surprise or regret, but simply remarked that it would have preferred to have the brothers survive in exile.

The Junta

The same qualities which endeared Minh to his people—his slow, diffident approach; his bashful, gawky demeanor; his honesty and integrity—quickly led Americans behind the scenes in Saigon and Washington to grow impatient. Under Minh, South Vietnam drifted into a serene normalcy, but this did not satisfy Americans who had hoped the pro-U.S. general would launch a tough offensive against communist insurgents. When Minh demonstrated reluctance to play the role which American advisors deemed essential to secure the South Vietnamese countryside, kingmakers grew impatient.

President Lyndon Johnson sent Minh a pointed New Year's greeting, both pledging support and warning the general not to become soft on communism: "The United States will continue to furnish you and your people with the fullest measure of support in this bitter fight. We shall maintain in Vietnam American personnel and material as needed to assist you in achieving victory . . . The U.S. government shares the view of your government that 'neutralization' of South Vietnam is unacceptable." Neutralization, or a compromise settlement with the communists, was precisely what Minh favored. On January 30, 1964, Minh was toppled in a bloodless coup by General Nguyen Khanh, who soon received another message from Johnson: "I am glad to know that we see eye to eye on the necessity of stepping up the pace of military operations against the Viet Cong."

Exile

Bitter at the sudden withdrawal of American backing, Minh refused to cooperate for several days and was detained in his home. Students demonstrated in the streets demanding his return to power. Eventually he agreed to join Khanh's government as a figurehead. Before long, he was sent on a goodwill tour to Thailand and then refused reentry into Vietnam, effectively exiling him from his homeland. By the end of 1964, he had been forcibly retired from the military.

Though Minh received a pension which allowed him to live well with his wife in Bangkok—raising orchids, writing memoirs, playing tennis, and receiving visiting dissidents from Vietnam—he was far from content. In May 1965, he attempted to fly back to Vietnam but was humiliated when the Saigon airport refused him permission to land. In 1967, Minh tried another tack. He filed papers at the embassy in Bangkok to run for president of Vietnam from exile. Though this ploy was unsuccessful, he was allowed to return in 1968, as a gesture of goodwill. Though Minh kept a low profile, he continued to talk with dissidents and quietly proposed a "people's congress" to find a way out of the war and back to a government which reaffirmed the democratic ideals that prompted his coup against Diem. Minh came to symbolize hopes for a negotiated compromise with the North Vietnamese.

A Brief Run for President

In 1971, Americans pressured both Minh and Vice President Nguyen Cao Ky to run against Nguyen Van Thieu in presidential elections. The U.S. government seemed more concerned with appearances than with promoting real democracy, and desperately sought to sign up and retain both men as candidates. Both went through the motions, but the campaign soon turned into a circus. Ky maintained that Thieu had "an excessive attachment to power," and both candidates complained that the contest was patently rigged. The campaign gave Minh some opportunity to put forth his views on democratic reform and possible means to end the war, but the retired four-star general openly expressed fears that he could be sent back into exile if he advocated a coalition government with Ho Chi Minh.

Both opposition candidates eventually withdrew. In doing so, Minh said, "I cannot put up with a disgusting farce that strips away all the people's hope of a democratic regime and bars reconciliation of the Vietnamese people." Ky said he simply didn't want to be a clown.

Robert Shaplen, in the *New Yorker,* analyzed the debacle later: "The consensus is that by his antic and frantic efforts to guarantee his reelection, President Thieu has, for once, outsmarted himself. One way or another, his days are numbered."

Minh gradually increased his criticism of Thieu. In 1973, he openly deplored the government's repressive tactics. In 1974, he called Thieu's government "violence-

thirsty," and in 1975 he said, "The Government is now nothing but a tyranny." Minh demonstrated how he had earned his reputation for patience. As one friend said, "To grow one orchid takes four years. You cannot grow orchids in haste."

Saigon Fell

By April 1975, it was clear that South Vietnam would fall. Americans had lost their taste for pursuing the endless war and North Vietnamese troops stood poised just miles outside the capital. Thieu resigned on April 21, and was replaced by Vice President Tran Van Huong, Minh's old teacher and mentor. The concern in South Vietnam was no longer with winning the war, but simply with losing it as gracefully and safely as possible. In a last attempt to place a man in power who could negotiate with the communists, the National Assembly turned to Minh.

Minh took over on April 28. In his inaugural address he said, "The coming days will be very difficult. I cannot promise you much." Minh was on the radio reassuring his people two hours after the last American helicopter took off from the roof of the U.S. embassy, but the war was over. On April 30, he ordered his troops to lay down their arms. Minh was placed in detention by the victorious North Vietnamese. In 1983, he was allowed to emigrate to France.

Further Reading

Business Week, November 9, 1963.
Newsweek, November 11, 1963; November 17, 1969; August 2, 1971.
New Yorker, September 11, 1971.
New York Times, November 2, 1963; November 3, 1963; November 15, 1963; December 28, 1963; February 8, 1964; August 17, 1964; August 28, 1964; September 4, 1964; October 27, 1964; December 23, 1964; June 28, 1964; April 28, 1975; April 29, 1975; May 4, 1975.
Time, November 8, 1963; September 27, 1968; August 2, 1971; July 26, 1971; November 21, 1969; May 5, 1975.
U.S. News and World Report, November 18, 1963.

Patsy Takemoto Mink

While representing Hawaii for nearly 20 years in Congress, Representative Patsy Takemoto Mink (born 1927) has made great strides toward peace, women's rights, civil rights, equality and justice.

On January 3, 1965, Patsy Takemoto Mink was the first Japanese American woman and the first woman of color to be elected to the United States Congress. Breaking new ground for women and ethnic groups, though, was nothing new for her. The road to Congress was paved with many firsts such as being elected the first female class president in her high school and being the first Japanese American woman to practice law in Hawaii. Mink's dedication to helping others has resulted in legislative reforms in health care, education, women's rights, civil rights, conservation, employment and environmental affairs.

Trouble in Paradise

Patsy Takemoto Mink was born on the Hawaiian island of Maui on December 6, 1927. She grew up in the small town of Hamakuapoko where she lived with her parents and brother. Early on, she noticed the inequality between the *haole* or white people who owned the island's plantations and the plantation workers who were mostly Japanese or Filipino. After the bombing of Pearl Harbor on December 7, 1941, she experienced even more inequality and injustice when her father was taken for questioning because of his Japanese heritage even though he had been born in Hawaii. Fortunately, he was released but many others were not. This event left a lasting impression on Mink. In Sue Davidson's book, *A Heart in Politics,* she recalled that the "experience was an important part of my development. It made me realize that one could not take citizenship and the promise of the U.S. Constitution for granted."

A Change in Plans

Mink was an excellent student and became the first female class president. She graduated from Maui High School at 16 and was valedictorian of the class of 1944. She then went on to the University of Hawaii where she wanted to study medicine. With the end of World War II, she was able to travel to the U.S. mainland and decided to transfer to Wilson College in Pennsylvania. Unfortunately, Wilson did not offer the classes she needed to prepare for medical school so she transferred to the University of Nebraska in Lincoln. Illness, though, took her back to Hawaii where she graduated with a degree in zoology and chemistry from the University of Hawaii.

Her dream of going into medicine was not to be realized. She was turned down by all of the medical schools to which she applied. At the time, she thought the problem was with her grades or that she was a Japanese American. Later, she realized it was her gender that excluded her. With no other options, Mink had to choose a different career. According to Davidson, Mink believed "the highest achievement is to find a place in life that permits one to be of service to people." With that in mind, she decided to become a lawyer and was admitted to the University of Chicago in 1948.

The Road to Washington

While attending the University of Chicago, she met John Mink who was studying geology. They were married on January 27, 1951 in the campus chapel. On March 6, 1952, their daughter, Gwendolyn Rachel Matsu Mink, was born. When their baby was six months old, the family moved to Honolulu where Mink became the first female Japanese American woman to pass the Hawaii bar exam. Yet again, she ran into sexism and was forced to open her own practice when no law firm would hire her. She also started teaching business law at the University of Hawaii. She was in her tiny law office when a friend called and invited her to a meeting about reforming Hawaii's lagging

Democratic Party. The meeting ended up being the beginning of an entirely new career for Patsy Takemoto Mink.

Mink was convinced that the only hope for revitalizing the Democratic Party was the involvement of young people. She organized the Young Democrats throughout Hawaii and became the national vice-president for the organization. Her first big success was on November 7, 1956 when she was elected to the House of Representatives for the Territory of Hawaii. Then in 1959, she was elected to the territorial Senate. In March of the same year, Hawaii became the 50th state and she was out of a job. She decided to run for Congress but was defeated by the war hero, Daniel Inouye.

Mink did not run for office again until 1962 when she ran for a seat in the Hawaii Senate and won by a great margin. In 1964, she ran for Congress again and this time she won a seat in the House of Representatives which she retained for six terms until 1977. On the eve of her first term, Davidson reported that Mink told *Life,* "What I bring to Congress is a Hawaiian background of tolerance and equality that can contribute a great deal to better understanding between races."

Congresswoman Mink

From her first day in Congress, Mink was not afraid to take a stand. She and a few others protested the seating of the representatives from Mississippi to demonstrate their opposition to voting practices in that state that excluded African Americans. Mink also took a stand against the Vietnam War. When asked later if she considered that her views against the war might have hurt her career, Davidson noted her response was, "It was a case of my living up to my own views and conscience. If I was defeated for it, that's the way it had to be. There was no way in which I could compromise."

One thing Mink did agree on was President Johnson's war on poverty. She took an interest in more than sixty programs that were developed between 1965 and 1967. Some of her greatest efforts were in the area of education which fulfilled a campaign promise. She wrote bills for the benefit of needy children from pre-school through college and succeeded in getting many of them passed.

Mink also focused on women's rights. She felt that she not only represented her district; she represented all of the women in America since there were so few women in politics to voice women's issues. In 1970, Mink's objection to G. Harrold Carswell's nomination to the U.S. Supreme Court based on his sexist beliefs resulted in the Senate turning him down. Mink also chose to push the idea of women in politics. In 1971-72, she ran for president in order to make Americans consider the possibility of a woman president.

In the fall of 1973, Mink took a position that she knew would be very unpopular with a great number of people. She asked Congress to begin the impeachment process of President Nixon so that the American public would finally know the truth about his actions. Four months later, the House brought impeachment charges against Nixon who resigned instead of facing the proceedings. President Ford's subsequent pardon of Nixon angered Mink greatly because she saw it as an injustice to Americans and she spoke out strongly against it.

In 1976, Mink decided to run for the U.S. Senate. She was defeated by another war hero, Masayuki "Spark" Matsunaga, who could be counted on to stick to the popular party opinions. In January of 1977, after 12 continuous years in Congress, Patsy packed up her Washington, D.C. office which had seen much activity. Davidson cited "halting nuclear weapons testing, ending the Vietnam War, amnesty for evaders of military draft; support of civil rights and liberties . . . family assistance programs, federal funding of daycare centers, federal aid for abortions, conservation, [and] environmental protection" as some of the issues she had tackled. Mink did have a new job, though. The newly-elected President Carter had asked her to be the Assistant Secretary for Oceans and Environmental Affairs. The high position was thought to be a breakthrough for the women's movement. Unfortunately, the job offered very little decision-making power and Mink resigned after less than a year.

Upon her return to Hawaii, Mink resumed her law practice and teaching at the University of Hawaii. However, it wasn't long before she got back into politics. In 1983, she won a seat on the Honolulu City Council and was re-elected for a second term. She also ran for Governor of Hawaii in 1986 and Mayor of Honolulu in 1988 but was defeated both times. In 1990 the tide turned, as Matsunaga died in office and Representative Akaka was appointed to Matsunaga's seat in the Senate. A special election was then held to fill Akaka's seat in the House. Mink won the seat and found herself back in Congress in 1991.

Back to Washington

Mink's return to Congress found her picking up many of the issues she had dealt with before. Once again, she confronted the military. This time, she opposed a planned military base on the island of Kauai in her district. She also found herself, along with the other women of the House, demanding an investigation of Supreme Court nominee, Clarence Thomas, who was accused of sexual harassment. Unlike Carswell, the Senate approved the appointment of Thomas. In 1994, Mink sponsored more than one of the healthcare proposals being considered by Congress. When asked by *Time* why she was doing so, she replied, "I want to make sure that we have a bill."

Mink has also continued her earlier work for the rights of Native Hawaiians and others of Asian descent. In February of 1997, she introduced a bill that would speed up the naturalization process by eliminating literacy and civics tests for certain categories of legal immigrants. The *Northwest Asian Weekly* quoted Mink as saying that "their patriotism and loyalty to the U.S. should be rewarded rather than hindered by delays in the naturalization process." Mink was also one of the founding members of the Congressional Asian Pacific Caucus which she has chaired since 1995. As chairperson, she has placed health, immigration, affirmative action, and "English-only" legislation among the agenda items of the caucus.

No matter what position Patsy Takemoto Mink holds, her constituents can count on her to fight for their best interests. Alethea Yip in *Asian Week* quoted former Representative Norman Mineta as saying, "Her principle, her courage, and her committed leadership will serve the Asian Pacific American community well." Mink's strong and outspoken leadership has taken her far in politics and there seems to be no stopping her. In his book of poetry, *Believers in America*, Steven Izuki said it best, "Criticism never stops Patsy Mink / From doing what she thinks is right. / She forges ahead against all the odds, / Refusing to give up the fight!"

Further Reading

Davidson, Sue, *A Heart in Politics: Jeannette Rankin and Patsy T. Mink,* Seal Press,1994.
Hoobler, Dorothy and Thomas Hoobler, *The Japanese American Family Album,* Oxford University Press, 1996.
Izuki, Steven, *Believers in America: Poems about Americans of Asian and Pacific Islander Descent,* Childrens Press, 1994.
Asian Week, October 6, 1995.
Northwest Asian Weekly, February 21, 1997.
Rocky Mountain News (Denver, Colorado), May 12, 1997.
Time, February 21, 1994.
"U.S. Congresswoman Patsy T. Mink Biographical Data," personal documentation from Patsy Mink, 1998.

Susan Molinari

Former U.S. Congresswoman Susan Molinari (born 1958), the highest ranking woman elected to a position of leadership in the House of Representatives (as vice chair of the Republican Conference, 1996), left politics in 1997 for a career in television broadcasting.

Susan Molinari seemed destined for politics. Her grandfather, S. Robert Molinari, was a member of the New York State Assembly and her father, Guy V. Molinari, was a member of Congress and Staten Island Borough President. In 1996, shortly before Molinari quit, she had reached a high point in her political career as the keynote speaker at the Republican National Convention. She was hailed as one of the bright new stars on the Republican political scene by many, including such periodicals as *Time*.

Growing Up Political

Susan Molinari was born in Staten Island, New York, on March 27, 1958, to Guy V. and Marguerite (Wing) Molinari. As a child, she attended political rallies with her father. Raised in the state of New York, Molinari later attended the State University of New York in Albany. In 1981, having graduated cum laude in communications, with a master's in political communications, she decided to move to Washington, D.C., to pursue a career. Molinari was very familiar with politics, and broadened her knowledge while an undergraduate by serving as an intern for State Senator Christopher Mega.

After arriving in Washington, D.C., following her graduate studies, Molinari worked for the Republican Governors' Association as a financial assistant. Beginning in 1983, she served a year as the ethnic-community liaison with the Republican National Committee. She moved back to New York to campaign for public office in the mid-1980s. Her efforts were successful and, at the age of 28, Molinari was elected to the New York City Council. She earned two distinctions with that election: recognition as the youngest-ever council member and the title of council minority leader. A leader of one, it would turn out, as Molinari was the sole Republican to sit on the council. With this position also came a $20,000 tax-payer-financed stipend and a chauffeur-driven car. It was a promising start for a woman not yet 30.

In 1990, Molinari was elected to the U.S. House of Representatives from the 14th New York District, which consisted of Staten Island and parts of Brooklyn. The area was reconfigured into the 13th Congressional District by the time she ran for and won reelection in 1992. During these years in political office, she saw her first marriage to John Lucchesi, a Staten Island limousine company owner, come to an end. Married in 1988, by 1992 the couple had separated and divorced. In 1994, Molinari married fellow politician William Paxon, a congressman from Buffalo, New York. He had proposed the previous year while kneeling on the floor of the U.S. House of Representatives. According to Craig Bromberg of *People,* Molinari's response to the proposal was, "You're not doing this *here?*" When it became clear that Paxon was indeed proposing then and there, Molinari hastily agreed: "Yes, but *get up!*" The couple would have one daughter, Susan Ruby.

Molinari, a moderate Republican, was known for her stance on women's rights. In the *New Yorker,* Judith Shulevitz, a policy analyst at the NOW Legal Defense and Education Fund, asserted that Molinari's "reputation as an urban moderate rests largely on a commitment to abortion rights." In December of 1994, Rich Lowry's profile of Molinari appeared in the *National Review.* He reported that Molinari "was one of four Republicans . . . to join 68 Democrats this June in signing a letter to House Speaker Tom Foley warning that a 'health care reform that does not include coverage of abortion treats women as second class citizens.'" Meryl Gordon later quoted Molinari in a *Harper's Bazaar* interview: "I have friends who had abortions and in some cases it probably saved their lives in terms of mental stability."

In 1995, Molinari was considered the highest-ranking woman in the House. By the age of 32, she had won the vice-chairmanship of the House Republican Conference, and was then described by Shulevitz as "No. 5 in [House Speaker] Newt Gingrich's inner circle." On the surface, this powerful woman worked hard for women's rights. She continually pushed for stronger domestic-violence laws and the Gender Equity Act, which included, among other things, an emphasis on promoting gender equity in college sports. She was proud of what Lowry would call a "signature contribu-

tion to the Violence Against Women Act, a provision making it easier for judges to admit into evidence previous *unproved* allegations against defendants in sex-crime cases." All of these policies would make Molinari a Republican that women could empathize with and support. In an article which appeared in *Newsday,* Mary Voboril quoted Frank Luntz, a Washington Republican communications consultant: "She appeals particularly well to working women, and she's got a bubbly sense of enthusiasm that Republicans so often lack. They often seem so dour and depressing."

In 1996, Molinari was chosen to deliver the keynote address at the Republican National Convention. The keynote speaker at a political convention presents the issues relevant to the assembly, and also sets the convention tone, inspiring unity and enthusiasm. Molinari did just that. She did cause controversy, however, when she refused to mention abortion in her speech. She defended her choice by commenting to Voboril in the *Newsday* article that the purpose of the convention was to unify and that abortion "is an issue that divides Republicans, divides Democrats and, frankly, divides probably every family in America." As noted in *Commonweal,* Molinari was the ideal choice as a keynote speaker for the Republicans: "Molinari is a Catholic ethnic of the baby-boomer generation who is a) pro-choice, b) divorced, and c) a mother with a professional career. . . . [B]oth parties are trying to appeal to voters with similar profiles."

Is There Life After Politics?

Molinari startled a good many people when she announced her retirement from politics in 1997, leaving Congress before her term of office had ended. Although many speculated that her decision was family related, Molinari claimed to be pursuing a life-long desire to be in front of the television camera. As *Newsweek* contributor Jonathan Alter declared: "What's so striking about her decision is that instead of explaining it as a way to spend more time with her 1-year-old daughter, . . . she says the move is the fulfillment of a personal dream." In an article for *Family Circle* Molinari noted, "Having majored in communications, I'd always dreamed of a position in broadcast news, but never thought it a possibility. Suddenly, the opportunity to join CBS presented the best of all worlds. In a different context, I could remain involved in national affairs and pursue a lifelong passion. Although my new job will be challenging, I expect to have somewhat more predictable hours, allowing me more time with my daughter."

Molinari was named news co-anchor on the program *CBS News Saturday Morning* in May of 1997. The broadcast premiered in September of that year, and was met with positive reviews. Molinari has commented that her congressional background gives her an advantage as a television news reporter, and her skills in evading questions as a political figure will help her recognize the tactic in guests, making her a sharp interviewer. With co-anchor Russ Mitchell, Molinari provides viewers of *CBS News Saturday Morning* an intelligent alternative to cartoons.

Maintaining a busy schedule even though no longer in Congress, Molinari commutes to Manhattan every week from the Washington, D.C., area. In 1998, she published her memoirs, *Representative Mom: Balancing Budget, Bill, and Baby in the U.S. Congress*. Written with Elinor Burkett, the volume presents Molinari's years in the political arena. A reviewer in *Booklist* noted, "Perhaps more interesting, though, than Molinari's personal story is the insider's look she provides at the U.S. Congress." When asked about her decision to leave the House of Representatives, Molinari was quoted in the *National Review* as saying: "As an American I am sorry. As a wife and mother I couldn't be happier."

Further Reading

Booklist, March 15, 1998.
Commonweal, September 27, 1996.
Harper's Bazaar, May 1995, pp. 73-74; November 1997, pp. 52-53.
Family Circle, November 18, 1997, p. 152.
National Review, May 1995; April 6, 1998.
Newsday, July 17, 1996, p. A6; August 1, 1996, p. A22; August 10, 1996, p. A6; August 12, 1996, p. B4; August 16, 1996, p. A4.
Newsweek, June 9, 1997.
New Yorker, February 26, 1996.
Parade, October 5, 1997, pp. 5-6.
People, October 25, 1993.
Time, August 19, 1996; June 9, 1997; April 27, 1998.
CBS News, http://199.173.162.17/news/saturdaymorning/bios/smolinari.shtml (May 14, 1998).

Lady Mary Wortley Montagu

Well known throughout polite society for her wit and verse, English world traveller Lady Mary Wortley Montagu (1689-1762) also worked to introduce the practice of inoculation against smallpox to the medical establishment of eighteenth-century Britain, despite their resistance to taking advice from a woman.

In an age noted for its wit, Lady Mary Wortley Montagu outshone many of her contemporaries. While education was not considered mandatory for young women, Montagu channelled her enthusiasm, curiosity, and intellect into numerous areas, including the arts, language, history, and even science, sharing her insights and humor with others through social interactions, published writings, and letters to family and friends.

Born the Honorable Mary Pierrepont on May 26, 1689, Montagu was the daughter of Evelyn Pierrepont, the Duke of Kingston. As a young girl she would miss the companionship of her mother, Mary Fielding, who died in 1694 when Mary was five, and the lack of supervision that resulted from her mother's absence created a streak of eccentricity that lasted into Montagu's adult life. The loss of a supervisory

parent would be replaced by the company of books, as Montagu's father confined her to the house, which included a large library. Academically inclined, Montagu devoured the many volumes of classics and contemporary literature available to her as the daughter of a member of the landed gentry, and also taught herself several languages, including Latin, with the encouragement of an uncle and Bishop Burnet, a family friend. Among her close childhood friends was Mary Astell, who, sharing Montagu's independent spirit and intelligence, would grow up to become one of England's first feminists.

Socializes with Reigning British Intellectuals

In addition to her exposure to many of the intellectual lines of inquiry of her time, Mary's good looks, intelligence, and pleasant personality encouraged Montagu's father to expose his daughter to an active social life from an early age. Her social circles included some of the most noted thinkers and writers of the day, including novelist Henry Fielding (a nephew of her late mother) and poet Alexander Pope (author of "The Rape of the Lock"). Pope became one of her closest friends until that relationship was derailed years later by a series of quarrels, the root of which can only be speculated but likely stemmed from his unrequited declaration of love in 1722. Later in her life, Pope would prove to be one of her strongest critics, defaming her character as "dirty, avaricious, heartless, and eccentric to the point of insanity," according to *British Authors before 1800*.

Accompanies Husband on Dangerous Trip to Turkey

Throughout her teenage years, Mary exchanged numerous letters with friend Anne Montagu, a correspondence that would be taken up by Anne's brother, Edward, after Anne's death in 1709. Edward Wortley Montagu, a Cambridge graduate who had been called to the bar in 1699, was at first impressed by Mary's ability to quote Roman poet Horace; as the couple's letter-writing continued, that respect ripened into love. Upon reaching the age of marriageability, however, Mary's hand was promised by her father to a rich lord; as she was on her way to the home of her intended husband, Mary and Edward eloped. The year was 1712, Mary was twenty-three, and the young couple lived together in relative poverty for the next four years while Edward's political fortunes floundered during Tory rule. Fortunately, with the death of Queen Anne in 1714, his Whig party once again came into prominence. Edward was elected to Parliament and, in the winter of 1716, with his young wife only recently recovered from a case of smallpox that had left her beautiful face permanently scarred, he was assigned to the task of ending hostilities between Turkey and Austria. As his wife, Mary willingly accompanied her husband on the long journey to his post at Constantinople (since renamed Istanbul), the seat of the Ottoman Turks.

A busy port, the city of Constantinople was the center of the ancient kingdom of Byzantium and the former home of Emperor Constantine the Great. Amid the ruins of this ancient culture, Mary Wortley Montagu soaked up the history, culture, and language around her, and busied herself with travel, study, and writing. Her activities were supported by her husband, who was a strong believer in the then-radical concept of an educated woman. It would be during her stay in Constantinople that Montagu would write her *Turkish Embassy Letters,* a collection of witty correspondence that, when published after her death, would become her major contribution to English literature. The Montagus remained in Turkey until 1718. Upon her return to England in the fall of that year, Montagu worked to popularize a method of inoculation (rather than vaccination) against smallpox that she had discovered while abroad, hoping to save others from the illness she had battled three years earlier.

Return to England Brings Rise, Then Fall in Fortunes

Home once more in England, the Montagus made a new home at Twickenham, near London and in the vicinity of Pope's home. The increased sophistication gained through her travels made Montagu now shine even more brightly in court. She was actively sought as a guest at numerous social functions, both with friends and through her husband's administrative capacity. Her vivaciousness and popularity made her even more attractive to Pope, who had a portrait of her painted and hung in a prominent place in his home. Pope, along with Horace Walpole, another leading literary figure of the day, was struck increasingly by her charms but spurned into anger after a declaration of his love for her resulted in rejection. The attractions of other

men were of little interest to Montagu, who at this point devoted her time to her writing, to her friends, and to her growing family. A son, Edward Wortley Montagu Jr., had been born in 1713, and a daughter, also named Mary, had been born to the couple while stationed in Turkey. As a child, young Edward proved to be troublesome, and his parents were forced to send him to a tutor on the Continent, although his continued attempts to run away proved costly. As an adult, he would become notorious for marrying a succession of women, with nary a divorce between each marriage.

Between 1730 and 1750 several volumes of Montagu's poems were published, including *Town Eclogues,* which had been circulated without her permission in 1716 as *Court Poems by a Lady of Quality* and reprinted in its authorized edition in 1747 with additional verses. After 1727 her battle with Pope intensified, fueled by her participation in fellow poet Lord Hervey's *Verses Addressed to the Imitator of Horace,* a 1733 volume that directly attacked Pope. Pope responded by attacking Hervey as a homosexual and by publishing such poems as "Epistle to Dr. Arbuthnot" and "The Dunciad," which served to ostracize Montagu socially and affect her husband's political career by implying that he was a dullard, a miser, and that his wife was repeatedly unfaithful to him. Between 1737 and 1738 she published, anonymously, a newspaper titled *The Nonsense of Common-Sense.* Running for approximately nine issues, its contents satirized the Tory-sponsored *Common-Sense* and helped to support her husband's Whig party. While Montagu continued to write, it was unfashionable for a woman of society to lower herself by publishing her works, so much of her writing remained privately held by friends.

Lives Abroad Independently

In 1739, shortly after organizing her daughter's wedding to the Earl of Bute, Montagu left her husband and her home in England and moved abroad. Some have surmised that her self-exile was a way of distancing herself from the negative public sentiment generated by Pope and Walpole and thus freeing her husband from its shadow, while others maintained that it was an effort to join the Italian author Francesco Algarotti, who was rumored to be her lover. While she would never see Edward Wortley Montagu again, the correspondence between Montagu and her husband showed that the couple remained full of affection for one another; indeed, without his wife's presence, Edward Wortley Montagu withdrew from friends and family and became miserly in his old age (by the time of his death, he had amassed almost a million and a half pounds, a considerable fortune for the period). Fifty years of age when she left England, Montagu did not join Algarotti, but lived alone, spending her middle years travelling in France and Italy and engaging in a voluminous correspondence with several people, most particularly her husband and her daughter, Lady Bute. Much of her time on the continent was spent in Brescia, a walled commune located at the foot of the Italian Alps, home to the Palazzo della Loggia and many Roman remains. Montagu remained away from England for twenty-three years, returning after her husband's death to spend her remaining time with her children. Unfortunately, her own death was imminent; she died of cancer, August 21, 1762, in London, at the age of seventy-three.

Turkish Letters Result in Lasting Fame

Despite the criticism heaped upon her by Pope and Walpole during her lifetime, Montagu was remembered for both her quick wit and her letters; even such a harsh critic as French writer Voltaire found her correspondence delightful. Dr. Samuel Johnson also enjoyed her prose, while historian Edward Gibbon would write, "What fire, what ease, what knowledge of Europe and Asia" upon reading her letters from Turkey. Her poetry, written in imitation of the style popularized by Pope, was collected in 1768 as *Poetical Works;* her *Embassy Letters,* written while she was in Turkey, escaped efforts by her family to acquire and destroy them and were released to great acclaim; a complete collection of her written works, containing both poetry and letters, was published in 1837; and a biography and an edited collection of Montagu's collected correspondence were published during the mid-twentieth century. Unfortunately, Montagu's personal diary was burned by her daughter in 1794 due to concerns that its nature would reflect poorly on the daughter's own social standing in the court of George III.

Further Reading

Dictionary of Literary Biography, Gale, Volume 95: *Eighteenth-Century British Poets, First Series,* 1990, Volume 101: *British Prose Writers, 1660-1800, First Series,* 1991.

Drabble, Margaret, editor, *Oxford Companion to English Literature,* fifth edition, Oxford University Press, 1985.

Halsband, Robert, *Life of Mary Wortley Montagu,* Oxford University Press, 1960.

Kunitz, Stanley, and Howard Haycroft, editors, *British Authors before 1800,* H.W. Wilson, 1952.

Bear, Richard, transcriber and annotator, *Selected Prose and Poetry of Lady Wortley Montagu,* http://www.darkwing.uoregon.edu (March 15, 1998).

Jim Morrison

Lead singer for the rock group the Doors, Jim Morrison (1943-1971), personified the mind-bending, uninhibited lifestyle of the 1960s, in his brief but brilliant career.

Like few bands other than the Beatles, the influence of the Doors has eclipsed the generation that first carried it to fame. Like the band, its leader, poet and visionary, Jim Morrison, continued to inspire fascination. Morrison has become a legendary figure, both in rock music and in popular culture, fueled to prominence by a score of books and articles, as well as by a major motion picture, *The Doors,* that recounted the musician's brief but tumultuous life.

First Creative Outlet in Film

Morrison was born in Melbourne, Florida, on December 8, 1943. His father, a career Navy officer, was transferred from base to base during his son's childhood, but, by his son's early teens, the family had settled in Alexandria, Virginia. After finishing high school in Alexandria, Morrison took several classes at St. Petersburg Junior College and Florida State University before pulling up roots in 1964, and heading for the West Coast. By 1966, the 22-year-old Morrison was enrolled in film classes at the Universtiy of California at Los Angeles (UCLA) but a friendship with fellow student Ray Manzarek would sideline any plans he had of becoming a film maker.

While the two young men had known each other only casually as fellow students, they ran into each other one day by accident, on a Venice beach. As Manzarek later recalled in an interview for a television show transcribed on the *American Legends* web site, Morrison "knew I was a musician. I knew he was a poet.... So he sat down on the beach, and he dug his hands into the sand.... And he began to sing ... in this really haunting kind of voice. It was soft—a soft but powerful voice.... I thought—Wow. Those are great lyrics. And he continued the song, and I thought this is one of the best Rock & Roll songs I've ever heard.... As Morrison was singing, I could hear the things that I could play behind it."

The Doors

Manzarek, an organist, along with Morrison, guitarist Robbie Krieger, and drummer John Densmore decided to form their own rock band to put those songs to music. The young men decided to call their group the Doors, a name inspired by a quote from nineteenth-century English poet William Blake: "If the doors of perception were cleansed every thing would appear as it is, infinite." As Morrison was fond of saying, "there are things known and things unknown and in between are the Doors."

Although his new lifestyle as a rock musician was a radical break from growing up in the uneventful fifties or life as a college student, images of his past, particularly his childhood, haunted many of Morrison's works, including his poetry and song lyrics. In *Peace Frog,* recorded on the album *Morrison Hotel,* he recalls an event from childhood, singing of "Indians scattered on dawn's highway bleeding/ Ghosts crowd the young child's fragile eggshell mind." Imagery involving Native Americans would surround Morrison even in adulthood; in fact he was nicknamed "the electric shaman" by fans hypnotized by Morrison's on-stage energy and powerful charisma. His growing relationship with girlfriend Pamela Courson would also inspire song lyrics; the couple lived together in a somewhat loose relationship, from 1966 on, although they never married.

Meanwhile, a long-term gig at the Whiskey-a-Go-Go on Hollywood's Sunset Strip allowed the Doors to develop their stage presence, and it eventually drew the attention of talent scouts searching for new recording acts. Not the least of the group's attractions was Morrison, who sang in a husky baritone, wore skin-tight pants, and went even further than Elvis Presley had in incorporating sexually suggestive movements into his on-stage performances. With lyrics like "Come on baby, light my fire," Morrison held young women enthralled.

Band Signed with Elektra

Although they had signed a record contract with Columbia, the label showed little interest in the new band. In 1966, their luck changed when the Doors were offered a recording contract with Elektra Records. They accepted, and, under the management of Bill Siddons, released their self-titled debut the following year. In Morrison's Elektra biography, released in conjunction with the group's debut album, he stated, "I like ideas about the breaking away or overthrowing of established order. . . . It seems to me to be the road toward freedom—external revolt is a way to bring about internal freedom. Rather than starting inside, I start outside—reach the mental through the physical." Such ideas reflected the attitude of a generation raised under the repressive conventions of the 1950s and rebelling against what they viewed as unwarranted hostilities of an older generation in Vietnam. Morrison and his message tapped a very large nerve.

The Rise of the Lizard King

After the release of *The Doors,* the group went back into the studio and cut *Strange Days,* which also came out in 1967. Other albums would include *Waiting for the Sun*

(1968), *The Soft Parade* (1969), *Morrison Hotel* (1970), *Absolutely Live* (1970), and *L.A. Woman* (1971). Morrison, caught up in Native American lore and the images of the American deserts, dubbed himself the "Lizard King" and wrote several songs, including "Celebration of the Lizard," in reference to his reptilian alter ego.

Caught up in a wave of popularity, the young band found itself carried into a new world, where drugs, alcohol, and sex played a major role. Morrison, whose status as a celebrity had begun almost overnight, found it difficult to handle the change: his growing dependence on alcohol would dim his talent in the years that followed, and the superstar status made him believe he was immune from normal authority. In one instance, an altercation with a police officer who accidentally attempted to arrest the star for loitering backstage during a concert in New Haven, Connecticut, resulted in Morrison's arrest while on stage after the rock singer began antagonizing the police posted in the concert arena.

Concert in Miami Sparked Controversy

On March 1, 1969, Morrison and the Doors were booked for a concert at Dinner Key Auditorium, in Coconut Grove, in Morrison's home state of Florida. Late for his scheduled flight to Miami, Morrison waited in the airport lounge, drinking heavily, until the next flight was called. When he missed the stop over flight in New Orleans, he again spent the time in the airport bar. By the time Morrison arrived in Miami, he was barely able to stand. During his performance before thirteen thousand screaming fans, Morrison, totally inebriated, exposed himself briefly, to the audience. Nothing was done until pressure from disgusted Miami-area residents forced local police to issue a warrant for Morrison's arrest. The singer, who had been vacationing out of the country, turned himself in to the Federal Bureau of Investigation (FBI) and returned to Miami, where he went on trial on August 12, 1970. Found guilty of a misdemeanor for profanity and drunkenness, he was sentenced to six months hard labor, although the sentence was stayed, while his attorney appealed the conviction. Morrison would not live to see the outcome of that appeal.

Trial Served as Coda to Life

After the trial in Miami, Morrison's life grew more chaotic, his relationships with band members more strained. His fifth-a-day drinking habit continued unabated, and he began to consider leaving the group to return to film studies. Searching to recover a sense of himself, he went back to the poetry that he had loved while a college student. In 1970, he published his first book of verse, *The Lords* [and] *The New Creatures,* which had been privately printed the year before. During an interview with Tony Thomas of the Canadian Broadcast Company (CBC), despite the toll drugs and alcohol had taken on him, Morrison presented himself as an insightful student of life, philosophy, and modern culture: "When I was in high school and college," he noted, "the kind of protest that's going on now was totally unheard of. At that time, to be a teenager, to be young, was really nothing, it was kind of a limbo state, and I think it's amazing, just in the last five years. What's happened is young people have become increasingly aware of the power and the influence that they have as a group. It's really amazing."

On July 3, 1971, Morrison was found dead in his bath tub, by his girlfriend. The cause of death was determined to be a heart attack, although an autopsy was never performed. He was buried at the Pere-Lachaisse Cemetery, in Paris. His death was kept secret until after the funeral, to eliminate the crowds of saddened fans that would likely have attended.

Further Reading

Hopkins, Jerry, *The Lizard King: The Essential Jim Morrison,* Collier, 1993.

Kennealy, Patricia, *Strange Dreams: My Life with and without Jim Morrison,* Dutton, 1992.

Riordan, James, and Jerry Prochickey, *Break on Through: The Life and Death of Jim Morrison* Quill, 1991.

Rocco, John, editor, *The Doors Companion: Four Decades of Commentary,* Schirmer, 1997.

Crawdaddy, January 1968; April 1969.

Down Beat, May 28, 1970.

Rock, September 27, 1970.

Rolling Stone, October 2, 1969.

American Legends Home Page, http://www.americanlegends.com/morrison (March 15, 1998).

The Doors' Home Page, http://www.the_doors.com (March 15, 1998).

"Morrison, Jim, interview with Tony Thomas, May 27, 1970," http://gyoza.com/frank/html/05/Morrisonspeak/html (March 15, 1998).

Constance Baker Motley

The first African American woman appointed to a federal judgeship in the United States, Constance Baker Motley (born 1921) has repeatedly blazed new trails for women in the judiciary, as well as in politics.

Constance Baker Motley led a distinguished career as both a civil rights attorney and a jurist on the federal bench. Representing the voice of both minorities and women during her decades as a practicing attorney, she had also addressed the rights of these same groups from her position on the U.S. District Court of New York State. An energetic, dedicated woman who had devoted her life to the practice of law, she had transcended many stereotypes levelled against members of her sex, earning a reputation as a somewhat uncompromising jurist with little patience for lawyers who overstep their bounds. Upon receiving the Distinguished Alumna Award from Columbia Law School's Women's Association, Motley was cited as "a symbol of success . . . at a time when there was enormous discrimination against woman, and even more against black women."

Early Involvement in Community Yields Benefits

Motley was born in New Haven, Connecticut, on September 14, 1921, the daughter of emigrants from the West Indies. Motley's father worked as a chef on the campus of Yale University, thus ensuring that his daughter would be exposed to an academic environment. As a child, Motley learned about the history of African Americans through her local Sunday School class, in which teachers sought to address the large number of African-Americans in the community.

During her high school years she exhibited both initiative and strong leadership skills, serving as president of the city's Youth Council and as secretary for New Haven's Adult Community Center. These early experiences would serve Motley well after high school graduation; although the financial demands of tuition put college out of reach, she was still able to obtain a good job with the National Youth Administration (NYA) due to her strong clerical and administrative skills and her public service background. Among Motley's tasks at the NYA was addressing topics of interest at the city's public forums. At one such forum, a talk she presented so impressed local businessman Clarence Blakeslee that he offered to put Motley through college.

Motley took Blakeslee up on his offer and enrolled at Fisk University, transferring to New York University after a few semesters and graduating with a degree in economics in 1943. Columbia Law School would be next; Motley received her LL.B. from that institution in 1946. That same

year, on August 18, she would marry a local insurance broker named Joel W. Motley, with whom she would eventually have a son.

Devotes Early Career to Quest for Civil Rights

In 1945, even before completing her law degree at Columbia, Motley began the search for a position as a clerk in a local law firm, the typical first step in the career path of freshly minted young lawyers. However, after a few interviews in which she barely got past the outer office, the young black woman realized that, because of her gender and her race, it would be next to impossible for her to be given a job in a private law firm. She decided, instead, to apply for a position as law clerk at the Legal Defense and Education Fund of the National Association for the Advancement of Colored Persons (NAACP), a legal aid society overseen by attorney Thurgood Marshall during the years prior to his 1967 appointment to the U.S. Supreme Court.

Marshall would become a mentor to the young law student, and Motley would remain at the Fund for the next twenty years, becoming assistant counsel in 1950, and the organization's principal trial lawyer in the decade that followed. She was called to the bar of the State of New York in 1948.

As principal legal counsel for the NAACP's Legal Defense and Education Fund, Motley was almost exclusively involved in the litigation of civil rights cases, working to end discrimination against African Americans in areas of education, housing, employment, transportation, and public accommodations. In 1954 she wrote the briefs presented to the U.S. Supreme Court arguing the plaintiff's side in *Brown v. Board of Education,* a landmark civil rights case that resulted in the elimination of the "separate but equal" clause that had allowed the continued segregation of many of the nation's public schools.

In the years that followed, Motley would be asked to argue many cases involving the issues raised in *Brown,* appearing in state and federal courts around the country. Ten of her cases would be argued before the U.S. Supreme Court; of those, she won nine. During her travels, she gained experience working with many judges, one of the most notable of whom was Ohio justice Florence E. Allen, the first woman to sit on the bench of either a state supreme court or a U.S. Court of Appeals. In 1995 Motley would be the recipient of the New York Women's Bar Association's Florence E. Allen award. The award held a special meaning for Motley; as she told the *Columbia University Record,* "My role model as a female judge was Florence Allen."

In tandem with her work for the NAACP, Motley began a part-time career in government as a member of the New York State Advisory Council on Employment and Unemployment Insurance, a position she held from 1958 to 1965. Her government job became full-time in 1963 when she served out the unexpired term of New York State Senator James Watson. The following year she was elected to the state senate in her own right, and introduced and supported legislation to establish much-needed low- and middle-income housing in New York's urban areas before resigning the following year to pursue another opportunity in politics. In February of 1965, Motley was elected by the New York City Council to fill a one-year vacancy as president of the Manhattan borough, and she still holds the record as the only woman to yet occupy that position. Her success in that capacity earned her a full four-year term in office, during which time Motley developed a program for the revitalization of Harlem and East Harlem, winning the city $700,000 in funds to plan much- needed improvements for impoverished areas of New York City.

Gains Historic Judgeship

In 1965, on the advice of Supreme Court Justice Ramsey Clark, who had been impressed by Motley's arguments before his court, President Lyndon B. Johnson nominated Motley for a seat on the U.S. Court of Appeals for the Second Circuit, the bench that hears all cases arising out of the federal trial courts in Connecticut, New York, and Vermont. However, opposition to this nomination was so vocal that Johnson withdrew Motley's name and appointed her, instead, as one of twenty-eight U.S. District judges for the Southern District of New York. This post, which was confirmed by the Senate in 1966, made her the first African American woman to serve as a federal judge. While Motley had to work twice as hard as her white male colleagues to earn the respect of attorneys and her fellow justices, she eventually gained a reputation as a respected and fair-minded jurist.

After serving the court as district judge for over a decade and a half, in 1982 Motley advanced to the position of Chief Justice, holding this post until 1986 with her appointment as Senior Justice. As a justice on the federal judicial circuit, Motley has been privileged to hear cases involving diverse, often sophisticated points of law dealing with issues regarding the U.S. Constitution, federal statutes, and disagreements between residents of different states, many of them large corporations.

In 1982 she sentenced six Croatian nationalists to prison terms of over twenty years for murder, arson, and extortion; in 1991, in *Basic Books v. Kinko's Graphics Corp.,* the issue of copyright infringement prompted a ruling by Motley that stores that photocopy and sell excerpts of textbooks for inclusion in course packets were required to pay royalties to publishers, despite the fact that such photocopies were for educational purposes; and in 1994, in a case involving Vassar College, Motley ruled that the denial of tenure to a former biology professor was because she was married—and thus discriminatory—rather than because of poor evaluations. In her lengthy written opinion, Motley noted that the evidence presented at trial showed a pattern of denying tenure to all women educators in the area of the sciences that extended back over three decades, and that marriage was looked upon by the college as synonymous with needing time off to raise children.

In a 1987 decision, Motley addressed the issue of probable cause in detaining individuals suspected of violating the law, ruling that, without exceptional circumstances, suspects cannot be detained by police for more than twenty-four hours without a court ruling that sufficient evidence exists to justify the arrest. New York Legal Aid Society attorney Caesar Cirigiano, who had filed the suit on behalf of the plaintiff, was quoted in the *New York Times* as calling Motley's ruling "the most important decision in the area of defendants' rights in the last ten years."

Long Career Brings Deserved Recognition

In appreciation for her long career in the law, Motley has received many honors and accolades. She was the recipient of the 1984 Candace Award from the National Coalition of One Hundred Black Women, and, in 1988, was asked to address an audience at the University of California at Los Angeles as part of the Thurgood Marshall Lecture series. Her topic, "Thurgood Marshall: The Early Years," recalled the period she worked alongside the esteemed jurist at the NAACP Legal Defense Fund. In the fall of 1997 she served as jurist-in-residence at the Indiana University School of Law.

Further Reading

Hine, Darlene Clark, *Black Women in America,* Carlson, 1993.
Almanac of the Federal Judicial, Volume 1, 1998, pp. 66- 68.
American Lawyer, June 1991.
Columbia University Record, June 9, 1995.
New York Times, July 7, 1987, p. 12.
Wall Street Journal, May 17, 1994.
Yale Law Journal, November 1991.

Louis Francis Albert Victor Nicholas Mountbatten

Louis Mountbatten (1900-1979) was one of the last of Britain's great war heroes. After his assassination by the IRA in 1979, the world joined Britain and India in mourning the loss of one of the most celebrated military men of the twentieth century.

A great-grandson of Queen Victoria was born June 25, 1900, on the grounds at Windsor Castle, and one month later was christened Louis Francis Albert Victor Nicholas. He was Prince Louis of Battenberg, born to Prince Louis and Princess Victoria (granddaughter of Queen Victoria), and his family had a rich and proud history of military service. Louis of Battenberg not only lived up to his family expectations, he surpassed them.

Two popular anecdotes from his early years followed Battenberg the rest of his life. The first was how as an infant he knocked the spectacles off his great-grandmother, Queen Victoria just moments before his christening. The second was how he received his nickname, "Dickie." From early on his family referred to him as "Nicky," but a visit from Czar Nicholas of Russia prompted a change to Dickie, and the name stayed with him for life.

Early in His Career

Prince Louis of Battenberg was mostly home-schooled during the early years and attended Lockers Park preparatory boarding school before entering Osborne Naval Training College (the Royal Navy) at age 13; he entered Dartmouth Naval College a year later. In 1916 he served in Admiral Sir David Beatty's flagship H.M.S. *Lion* as a Midshipman.

At this time, Battenberg was making friends with Winston Churchill, his cousin "David," (the future King Edward VIII) and most of the women he met. Soon he had the reputation of a playboy. Early on, it wasn't evident that Battenberg would be a success. His academic performance was only marginal, and he hadn't made a name for himself anywhere else. A shake-up in his family in regards to their heritage (and name) sobered his outlook.

During World War I, everything German and German-related was vilified in England. King George V, the grandson of the half-German Queen Victoria and the German Prince Albert, feared the wave of anti-German hysteria could reach the British Royal Family. Because of his German lineage, the senior Prince Louis of Battenberg was stripped of his title and position in the navy, and as a result, the title of "prince" was lost for the younger Louis as well. His father became the first Marquess of Milford Haven, and the family anglicized their name to Mountbatten. With newfound determination, Mountbatten gradually climbed the ranks through the navy.

In the summer of 1922 Mountbatten married Edwina Cynthia Annette Ashley. She was the heir to a sizable for-

tune, providing the couple with a comfortable lifestyle for the rest of their lives. Two years later, they had a daughter, Patricia. Another daughter, Pamela, was born seven years later. Anne Edwards, a biographer of Queen Elizabeth II, noted in her book *The Royal Sisters* that Mountbatten was "fond of children . . . a devoted father . . . and a concerned uncle to his sister's . . . son, Philip." (Philip, who later married the future Queen Elizabeth II, and his family were members of the exiled royal family of Greece.)

His Contributions to the Royal Navy

Mountbatten was successful in his professional life as well as his personal life. He created a device that bore his name and became standard equipment for all ships in the Royal Navy. The device enabled ships to keep an assured, clear distance from one another while steaming in line. He also pushed for arming British ships with machine guns. These guns provided excellent defense aerial attacks during World War II.

In 1939 he was promoted to Captain. Two years later Prime Minister Winston Churchill appointed Mountbatten Chief of Combined Operations with rank of Acting Vice-Admiral. He was in charge of planning the European Invasion. He also directed the invasion of Madagascar and commando raids on Norway and France. These raids became known as "butcher and bolt" raids and often left more casualties than success.

In 1943 Churchill and Roosevelt named Mountbatten the Supreme Allied Commander for Southeast Asia. He served in that capacity until 1946 and was responsible for the recapture of Burma from Japan. In 1945 he accepted the Japanese surrender at Singapore.

Throughout the war Mountbatten's wife worked near her husband, working for the welfare of the wounded, and after the war, she aided many prisoners of war. Together the press referred to Mountbatten and his wife as "The Fabulous Mountbattens," and their popularity with servicemen and crew.

After the war, Mountbatten served as the last viceroy (governor of a country who rules as the representative of his king) of India from March through August of 1947. He oversaw the creation of India and Pakistan through negotiations with the Hindus and the Moslems. Although Britain was weakened from the war and could no longer hold onto India, many of the upperclass in England viewed Mountbatten as a traitor to his class and country for being instrumental in the dissolution of the British Empire.

During this time the title Lord Mountbatten of Burma was created; he also served as Governor-General of India for a year, from 1947-1948. He also, according to Edwards, attended "the wedding that had been his lifelong dream— his nephew Philip [married] the future Queen of England" in November, 1947. Edwards noted that it really wasn't a secret that "from early in his youth, Philip had been a pawn in his uncle's ambitions . . . and was being groomed for the future role of Prince Consort."

The next year Mountbatten was promoted to Vice-Admiral. The rank of Fourth Sea Lord followed in 1950. He

also served as Chief of the North Atlantic Treaty Organization (NATO) forces in the Mediterranean. Promotions continued—to Admiral the following year—and he attained the height of his professional career on April 18, 1955, when he was named First Sea Lord. This was the exact title stripped from his father all those years ago. The following year he was promoted Admiral of the Fleet. In these capacities Mountbatten oversaw numerous changes in Britain's defense system, such as guided missile ships and nuclear submarines.

It was also around this time that he became the confidant of his great-nephew, Prince Charles, the future king of England. According to the A & E Biography profile *Prince Charles: Born to be King,* Charles turned to Mountbatten for "support and guidance," and viewed him as a "honorary grandfather."

Throughout his career, Mountbatten was known to be ruthless. He used his status to get his way, and often publically and privately criticized his peers. He also enjoyed both recognition for his successes and ceremonies where he could dress in his military uniform, adorned in medals and honors. In his obituary, *The New York Times* attributed the following quote to Mountbatten, "I am the most conceited man I have ever known." This attitude often alienated Mountbatten from his peers and simultaneously made him popular with commoners.

The End of His Life

His wife died in 1960, and Mountbatten retired five years later, though he remained a confidant to Queen Elizabeth II and his nephew, Prince Philip. He also continued to advise Prince Charles, according to the A & E profile, encouraging Charles to join the Royal Navy and "to play the field and have lots of affairs before he settled down." Although he was often considered irritating and annoying, Mountbatten was respected by both royalty and ordinary people, and was almost universally loved.

In 1979, a bomb demolished his fishing boat in waters off the northwest coast of Ireland near his family summer home, on August 27. Mountbatten, his 14-year-old grandson, and a friend of his grandson were all killed instantly. He became the IRA's most famous victim. A member of the Provisional wing of the Irish Republican Army (IRA) was later convicted of his murder.

Mountbatten's funeral at Westminster Abbey was considered the most-outstanding tribute to any military personnel since the Duke of Wellington was buried in 1852. His great-nephew, Prince Charles, was one of many who paid tribute to him at the funeral. He was buried in an abbey at Romsey near his Hampshire home. After 50 years of service to the Royal Navy, he was buried facing the sea.

Further Reading

Butler, David, *Lord Mountbatten: The Last Viceroy,* Methuen, 1985.
Edwards, Anne, *The Royal Sisters,* Jove Books, 1991.
Hough, Richard, *Mountbatten,* Random House, 1981.
New York Times Biographical Service, August 1979, p. 1099.

Prince Charles: Born to be King, Arts & Entertainment (A & E) Television Network (April 13, 1998).

Audie Murphy

Born near Kingston, Texas, Audie Murphy (1924-1971) won fame as the most decorated soldier in U.S. military history.

During World War II and for many years afterward, Audie Murphy personified heroism on the battlefield. His death-defying exploits were the stuff of legend, but to many Americans Murphy is a virtual unknown. As Don Graham observed in his biography of Murphy, "we prefer video fantasy—*Rambo*—a kind of MTV celebration of American machismo. . . . [But] Audie Murphy was the real thing. . . . And the real thing is always more interesting."

Audie Leon Murphy, the seventh of twelve children of Emmett "Pat," a sharecropper, and Josie Murphy, was born June 20, 1924, in a Texas cotton field. Leon, as Audie was known until he went into the army, had chores to do at an early age, and when he was five years old, he was hoeing and picking cotton alongside his parents and siblings. There was no time for play and not much time for school, either. Murphy recalled years later, "It was a full-time job just existing."

Yet nearly everyone who knew Murphy during his childhood noted his intelligence and his determination to "be somebody." He loved to read and enjoyed listening to his uncles recount their experiences in World War I. To Murphy, it all seemed very glamorous and exciting.

In 1939, at the age of fifteen, Murphy dropped out of school for good and left home to seek work that would help the family. He held a series of low-paying odd jobs. Then, in 1940, his father walked out on the family, leaving them in dire straits. This turn of events took a heavy toll on Murphy's mother, and in May 1941, she died.

Murphy was devastated by his mother's death and bitterly resented his father. As he looked at his own life, however, he realized that he was headed down a similar path. His lack of education and opportunity meant that he would probably never be able to escape the poverty that had entrapped his family.

A war got Murphy out of Texas. Less than seven months after his mother died, the United States entered World War II following the bombing of Pearl Harbor on December 7, 1941. Like so many other eager young men, seventeen year old Murphy tried to enlist in the military. But at only 5'5" tall and 112 pounds, the baby-faced teenager (who looked even younger) was rejected by both the marines and the army because of his age. He tried again after he turned eighteen. The marines still weren't interested, but on June 30, 1942, he was officially inducted into the army and immediately sent to boot camp for combat infantry training.

There he excelled at marksmanship and quickly developed into a well-disciplined soldier.

In late January 1943, Murphy shipped out to North Africa. Assigned to Company B, 1st Battalion, 15th Infantry Regiment, 3rd Division, he was sent to the island of Sicily on July 10. It was there that he began to compile his remarkable service record. Aggressive and audacious, yet levelheaded, Murphy proved to be the ideal soldier.

Murphy quickly discovered that war was not quite what he had expected it to be. "Ten seconds after the first shot was fired at me by an enemy soldier, combat was no longer glamorous," he later observed. "But it was important, because all of a sudden I wanted very much to stay alive." Fear was always beside him, and he could sometimes feel his insides twist into knots. But as Murphy noted after the war, "Sometimes it takes more courage to get up and run than to stay. You either just do it or you don't. I got so scared the first day in combat I just decided to go along with it."

Murphy and his battalion headed north through Sicily. Their first enemy encounters were with Italian troops who proved to be easy to subdue. Then they came face-to-face with tougher and well-trained German soldiers. From his experiences in Sicily he gained what he termed "a healthy respect" for his German counterparts. By mid-August of 1943, however, Sicily was in Allied hands.

After a brief rest period near Naples in late November and early December of 1943, the 3rd Division received its next orders, an amphibious landing at Anzio, to be followed by a quick thrust north to Rome. Murphy missed the actual landing but he rejoined his division as they waited on the beachhead for reinforcements. The delay proved costly, however; within days, the Germans had moved some 125,000 troops into position.

The Germans showered Allied ground troops with artillery fire, but nineteen year old Murphy distinguished himself when he stepped up to lead his men after his company commander was wounded. However, the Allies were no match for the Germans, and they were finally forced to retreat. They took refuge in cold, muddy foxholes and trenches for some five months while under constant fire. Meanwhile, Murphy was promoted to platoon leader.

Murphy earned his first medal, the Bronze Star, in March of 1944 for singlehandedly knocking out a German tank. He received two more awards in May, the Combat Infantryman Badge, which set him apart from soldiers who had not been under fire, and the 1st Oak Leaf Cluster to the Bronze Star Medal, which recognized his "exemplary conduct in ground combat against an armed enemy."

The 3rd Division's next assignment was to land on the coast of southern France to start driving north along the country's eastern border. Beginning August 15, 1944, the story of Murphy's exploits becomes "simply incredible," to quote his biographer.

Murphy encountered a hill dotted with German machine-gun nests that were protecting a big gun aimed at the coast. He headed up the hill alone, methodically destroying several of the machine-gun nests along the way. Suddenly, his best friend in the unit appeared at his side and insisted on staying with him. Then, as Murphy and his buddy engaged enemy troops in a gun battle, the Germans indicated they were ready to surrender. Murphy was suspicious, but his friend stood up to acknowledge the gesture and was immediately gunned down. In a burst of fury, Murphy killed the Germans who had shot his friend and continued on his rampage up the hill, taking out another machine-gun nest and eventually securing the area for the Allies. For his actions, he won the Distinguished Service Cross, the second-highest U.S. Army medal for valor.

From then on, Murphy absolutely craved action and sought it out whenever and wherever possible. He astounded his fellow soldiers by volunteering for one dangerous assignment after another; he was especially adept at stalking and killing snipers. On September 15, 1944, he was wounded for the first time, but after just a few days in the hospital for treatment, he was back on the front lines. Offered a promotion to second lieutenant in the wake of his heroics, Murphy turned it down, expressing embarrassment about his lack of formal education and indicating his desire to remain with the men he had fought with for so long.

In eastern France during the fall of 1944, Murphy earned two Silver Stars. The first was for saving his commanding officer. His second was awarded for actions he took to destroy a well-camouflaged machine-gun and sniper outpost. In the end, Murphy received a promotion to second lieutenant, which he accepted on the condition that he could remain with his company.

Murphy was wounded for a second time on October 26, 1944, when a shot from a sniper glanced off a tree and struck him. Three days passed before he could be evacuated, and by the time he made it to the hospital, the wound had become gangrenous. He spent the next two months out of action, but was back on the front lines by mid-January of 1945, during the coldest and snowiest winter Europe had seen in twenty-five years.

When Murphy rejoined his regiment, it was preparing to clear the Germans out of a much-disputed territory on the border of Germany and France. The task proved to be an arduous one; American ground troops were ill-equipped to endure the harsh weather. Meanwhile, Murphy sustained his third war wound. The injury did not require medical attention, so he kept fighting. He was placed in command of Company B after its first lieutenant was badly wounded. With that, Murphy became the sole officer in a company that had once numbered over 200 men but was now down to only 18.

On January 26, 1945, Murphy's courage under fire earned him the nation's highest honor for personal bravery and self-sacrifice in combat, the Congressional Medal of Honor. Murphy and his men were ordered to take up a position and hold it. Less than two dozen Americans protected by two tank destroyers then squared off against some 200 enemy soldiers backed up by six tanks. In the opening minutes of the battle, Company B's machine-gun squad was wiped out, one of its tank destroyers slid into a ditch and had to be abandoned, and the other tank destroyer was hit by artillery fire. Murphy figured the end was near as he realized how outnumbered he and his men were.

Ordering his men to retreat, Murphy stayed and directed artillery fire into the area while emptying his gun at the advancing Germans. He then spotted the burning tank destroyer about ten yards away and noticed that its machine gun appeared to be undamaged. He ran over, jumped on the tank destroyer's turret, and started firing the machine gun as he continued to direct the ongoing artillery barrage. He kept up this attack on his own for at least thirty minutes and perhaps as long as an hour, killing or wounding some fifty enemy soldiers. Finally, the Germans were forced to withdraw. After being knocked unconscious momentarily, Murphy came to and started walking, weak, exhausted, and in a bit of a daze, but miraculously unscathed except for a slight reinjury to his legs. From a distance, he heard the tank destroyer explode.

Murphy then threw himself back into battle, hammering at the Germans as they retreated east toward the Rhine River. By February, most of the enemy forces that were still west of the Rhine had surrendered. This gave the 3rd Division some time to relax a bit, followed by another couple of weeks of rest well behind the lines. During this period, Murphy was promoted to first lieutenant. At the end of the month, training began for an invasion of Germany.

Murphy did not join his men on the front lines this time. To keep him out of combat, his superiors had assigned him to serve as a liaison officer with the 15th Infantry. (The Army did not want to see one of its Congressional Medal of Honor winners die in battle.) Murphy nevertheless managed to involve himself in some dangerous situations from time to time, including one instance in which he raced to the front lines to lead his beloved Company B out of danger.

Murphy spent the remaining weeks of the war engaging in similar operations that suited his taste for action and thrills. The end of the conflict found him on a train to the French Riviera, where he had hoped to enjoy a little rest and relaxation before resuming command of Company B at its headquarters just outside Salzburg, Austria. It was there that Murphy officially received his Congressional Medal of Honor on June 2, 1945, a few weeks shy of his twenty-first birthday. The ceremony capped a truly remarkable two years that saw him become the most decorated soldier in U.S. history. Murphy was ultimately awarded a total of thirty-seven medals, eleven of which were for valor.

Murphy returned to the United States a larger-than-life hero, a shy Texan whose smiling face adorned the covers of news magazines. He marched in victory parades and made personal appearances before cheering crowds. Yet Murphy's postwar life was notable for its modest successes and major troubles. Restless, he couldn't seem to find his niche and took little pleasure in an ordinary existence. In late 1945, he headed to Hollywood to pursue a film career. Although he appeared in a string of low-budget westerns and war movies over a twenty-year period, he turned in only a couple of truly noteworthy performances. In 1951, he played a young Civil War soldier in *The Red Badge of Courage* that garnered him his best reviews. Four years later, in 1955, he played himself in the movie version of his autobiography, *To Hell and Back,* which proved to be a hit with critics and at the box office. In the early 1960s, he dabbled in songwriting and produced a number of country-western tunes.

Murphy's personal life was also unsettled. Plagued by recurring nightmares, he slept with a loaded gun under his pillow for many years. He suffered tremendous guilt about the war and agonized over friends who never made it back. He became hooked on prescription drugs. Gambling, womanizing, and involvement in various business schemes caused him to lose most of his money. By the late 1960s, Murphy's many setbacks had left him bankrupt. One of the lowest points in his life came in 1970 when he was charged with assault after he beat up a man and fired a shot at him during an argument. He was eventually acquitted, but the negative publicity generated by the case proved tough to live down.

On May 28, 1971, Murphy died along with five others in a plane crash while on a business trip. In a ceremony befitting the hero that he had once been, he was buried at Arlington National Cemetery with full military honors. Yet his passing went almost unnoticed by the media. To a nation that was torn by the Vietnam War, there was little respect for the kind of traditional military valor that a soldier like Murphy represented.

Further Reading

Graham, Don, *No Name on the Bullet: A Biography of Audie Murphy,* Viking, 1989.
Murphy, Audie, *To Hell and Back,* Henry Holt, 1949.
Whiting, Charles, *Hero: The Life and Death of Audie Murphy,* Stein & Day, 1990.
Chicago Tribune, October 8, 1996.
New York Times, June 1, 1971.
Texas Monthly, June 1989.

Joseph Murray

Born in Milford, Massachusetts, Joseph Murray (born 1919) was a pioneer in the field of organ transplantation and, in 1954, was the first to successfully transplant a human kidney. For his efforts he was awarded the 1990 Nobel Prize in Physiology or Medicine.

On December 23, 1954, Richard Herrick became the first human to receive a successful organ transplant when he was given a kidney from his identical twin brother, Ronald, at Boston's Brigham and Women's Hospital. Joseph Murray was the thirty-five-year-old surgeon who presided over the five and one-half hour operation and took this momentous step in medical science. Today, over 50,000 organ transplants are done yearly in the United States, with seventy-five percent of them involving kidneys, according to the *Detroit Free Press.* These remarkable procedures developed by Murray and the lives that they save would never have been possible without Murray's groundbreaking efforts. In acknowledgement of this contribution to humankind, Murray was honored with the Nobel Prize (shared with E. Donnall Thomas, a pioneer in bone marrow transplants).

Joseph Edward Murray was born April 1, 1919, in Milford, Massachusetts, to William Andrew and Mary (DePasquale) Murray. His father served as a district court judge and his mother was a teacher. Both parents instilled in Murray the values of a good education and service to others. With this in mind, Murray always knew that he wanted to be a doctor. In 1936, after graduating from high school, where he had been a baseball star, a good swimmer, tennis player, and an exceedingly good science student, he set out for the College of the Holy Cross in Worcester, Massachusetts. He received his B.A. in humanities in 1940 and went on to attend Harvard University Medical School, graduating in 1943.

After receiving his medical degree, Murray took a surgical internship at a Harvard-affiliated hospital, Peter Bent Brigham Hospital (now Brigham and Women's Hospital) in Boston. In 1944, he was given a commission in the U.S. Army Medical Corps and served at Valley Forge General Hospital in Pennsylvania as a plastic surgeon under James Barrett Brown and Bradford Cannon. In this post, he worked on soldiers coming back from the battlefields of World War II, including a childhood friend from his own hometown whose face had been damaged by a defective shell. He performed over 1,800 surgeries during this period, specializing in the reconstruction of hands and eyes of burn victims. "We took care of thousands of casualties, many with

severe burns," he told Michael D. Lemonick of *Time.* "I was performing skin grafts and became interested in why skin wouldn't graft permanently."

At this time, the typical procedure for treating burned skin involved grafting—or transplanting—unburned skin from other parts of a patient's body to the burned areas. But often, the patient was so severely burned that there was not enough skin to be grafted. In these cases the doctors would practice allografting, in which they used the skin of another person to cover the burned areas. In the 1940s, allografting was not a permanent solution because the patient's body would soon reject the foreign skin and it would fall off. Murray's mentor, Brown, had studied this problem in the 1930s and discovered that the only allografts that were successful were those between identical twins. At that time, the common theory of organ rejection, proposed by French surgeon Alexis Carrel, suggested that the body attacked foreign tissue or skin as if it were fighting off, or resisting, a disease.

As Murray was becoming more deeply involved in issues of organ transplantation, he was also starting his own family. In 1945 Murray married singer and pianist Virginia Link. They would eventually have six children. Two years after his marriage, Murray left military life and returned to Boston's Brigham and Women's Hospital. He became a member of the hospital's team of doctors studying end-stage renal (kidney) disease. One of the processes this team was studying was the practice of kidney transplantation. Murray had originally hoped to specialize in plastic surgery, but this was a very young discipline in the late 1940s, and he was

encouraged by others to go into general surgery while keeping plastic surgery as a sideline specialty. He soon won a reputation among his colleagues for his neck and head surgical reconstructions on cancer patients as well as gaining recognition for the field of plastic surgery. His assignment within the Brigham group, however, was to find a competent surgical procedure for kidney transplants. After working on dogs for many years, he gradually developed a technique that is still used today of placing the transplanted organ in the lower abdomen. Before then, no one knew how long a kidney would be able to survive outside the body or the complicated surgical techniques of attaching a donated kidney to the recipient's blood vessels and extremely precise urinary system.

Murray and the Brigham team had their first chance at a successful kidney transplant in 1954. A patient who was suffering with kidney failure had an identical twin brother who was willing to donate one of his kidneys. Even after fifteen previous failures in which the transplanted organ was rejected within hours or days, Murray felt that the transplant was the only way to save the man's life. With this in mind, Murray told the *Los Angeles Times,* "we were struck with the moral problem of removing a healthy organ from a healthy person." The doctors in the team consulted the clergy and were even granted a special decree from the Massachusetts Supreme Court that allowed the operation to proceed. The operation was a success and the patient lived eight additional years before dying from congestive heart failure brought on by the same kidney disease that had necessitated the transplant. "Kidney transplants seem so routine now," Murray told Gina Kolata in the *New York Times.* "But the first one was like Lindbergh's flight across the ocean."

In the late 1950s, Murray and his team continued to perform transplants, but at a slow rate. Between 1954 and the early 1960s only a dozen transplants were performed. Murray shifted the focus of his research to study the body's immune system, which would attack a foreign transplanted organ as an invader. He eventually developed drugs and techniques to reduce the body's own fight against transplanted organs and thus curb the rejection of those organs. He began studying transplants in fraternal twins, often using low doses of X-rays to help suppress the patient's immune system. It was also during this period that Murray had one of his greatest successes in transplantation with the longest-living kidney transplant recipient, Edith Helm. Helm received a kidney from her sister in May of 1956 and continued to correspond with Murray into the 1990s.

During the 1950s, significant advances were being made in pharmaceutical research, especially in the area of manipulating the immune system. In 1951 two scientists out of the Burroughs Wellcome Research Laboratories developed a drug called 6-MP (6-mercaptopurine). Initially used to treat leukemia, a form of cancer, 6-MP was found to inhibit the immune system from reacting to a foreign substance in the body. Later tests by British researcher Roy Calne and Boston hematologists Robert Schwartz and William Dameshek of kidney transplants in dogs using 6-MP found that the drug reduces the body's rejection of transplanted organs. The two scientists from Burroughs, Gertrude B. Elion and George H. Hitchings Jr., were awarded the Nobel Prize in 1988 for their work.

In 1961, Murray and other researchers at Brigham (including Elion, Hitchings and Calne, who had moved to Boston to collaborate with Murray) developed Imuran (azathioprine), an immunosuppressive drug still in use today. The next year, they used the drug successfully for the first time in a kidney transplant from an unrelated donor. This was the first time an operation of this type had worked. By 1965, the survival rates after receiving a kidney transplant from an unrelated donor were exceeding sixty-five percent. Later drugs, including cyclosporine and FK-506, pushed the survival rate even farther using the basic principles developed by Murray and his team at Brigham. As Murray's successes rapidly became known worldwide, other physicians began experimenting with organ transplantation.

Beginning with his days working on burned soldiers at Valley Forge General Hospital, Murray continued to develop his interest and skills in plastic surgery. After working primarily in the field of organ transplantation for years, he switched back to plastic surgery. One of his most notable efforts in this field involved children, specifically devising new ways to correct inborn facial defects. From 1951 to 1986 he worked in the plastic surgery division of Brigham and Women's Hospital, retiring as chief of plastic surgery.

During that same period, from 1972 to 1985, he also served as a plastic surgeon at Children's Hospital Medical Center in Boston. Murray retired from active surgery at Brigham in 1986 but remained on staff as chief emeritus of plastic surgery at Brigham. He has also been on the staff at Harvard University since 1970 as a professor of surgery.

In 1990, Murray shared the Nobel Prize for Physiology or Medicine with bone marrow transplant pioneer and friend E. Donnall Thomas. They were credited with making discoveries "crucial for those tens of thousands of severely ill patients who either can be cured or given a decent life when other treatment methods are without success," the Nobel committee's citation read, as quoted in *Time*. Murray donated his half of the award, approximately $700,000, to Harvard University Medical School.

Further Reading

Detroit Free Press, October 9, 1990, p. A3; October 16, 1990, p. C3.

Los Angeles Times, October 9, 1990, p. A23.

New York Times, October 9, 1990, p. C3; December 19, 1993, pp. WC8-9.

Science, October 19, 1990, p. 378.

Time, October 22, 1990, p. 62.

"Joseph E(dward) Murray," *A&E Network Biography*, http://www.biography.com (December 11, 1997).

N

Ogden Nash

Ogden Nash (1902-1971) was arguably one of the most commercially successful English-language poets of the twentieth century.

Nash's verse skewered the pretensions of the modern middle class existence and gave voice to the inner seethings of the average, besieged-by-life individual—and he did it with a cunning, swift humor. Though sometimes the object of criticism from literary purists, Nash's talent for composing verse using the common American vernacular earned him great success over a four-decade period.

Nash was born Frediric Ogden Nash in Rye, New York, to Edmund Strudwick and Mattie (Chenault) Nash in 1902. His father was in the import-export business, but the Nash family's ancestry was a distinguished American blueblood one. Their roots in North Carolina stretched back to the American Revolutionary era, and the city of Nashville, Tennessee, was named in honor of another forbearer. Nash himself grew up in various East Coast communities, and also lived in Savannah, Georgia, during his youth. He was accepted to Harvard College, but dropped out after a year in 1921.

Found Success in Advertising

From there Nash held a variety of jobs, none for very long. He worked on Wall Street as a bond salesperson, but admittedly sold only one bond, to his godmother, and instead spent his afternoons in movie theaters. He was a schoolteacher for a year in Rhode Island at his alma mater, St. George's School, and from there was hired as an advertising copywriter for streetcar placards, a job in which he finally discovered his calling. In 1925 he was hired at the publishing house of Doubleday in their marketing department, and did well enough that he eventually moved on to its editorial department as a manuscript reader.

Nash has said that it was the abysmal quality of the manuscripts he read that compelled him to take up the pen himself as a writer. He tried his hand at serious verse in the style of the eighteenth-century Romantic poets, but soon came to realize his own limitations. There were, however, some creative efforts that he was not hesitant to share with others—his scribbled comic verse that he frequently crumpled and lobbed across the office to the desks of colleagues. This led to a collaborative effort with friend Joseph Alger to produce a 1925 children's book, *The Cricket of Carador*. A few years later, he teamed with two Doubleday colleagues to produce *Born in a Beer Garden; or, She Troupes to Conquer*, which lampooned the canon of classic literature.

An Overnight Success

In 1930, Nash's career as a published poet began in earnest when he wrote a poem called *Spring Comes to Murray Hill* and submitted it to the *New Yorker*, considered one of the most respected, well-read periodicals of the day. Nash had been gazing out his office window and contemplating his own particular spiritual burden:

"I sit in an office at 244 Madison Avenue And say to myself you have a responsible job, havenue? Why then do you fritter away your time on this doggerel? If you have a sore throat you can cure it by using a good goggerel If you have a sore foot you can get it fixed by a chiropodist And you can get your original sin removed by St. John the Bopodist."

The *New Yorker* published *Spring Comes to Murray Hill,* and invited Nash to continue to submit; his regular appearances, in turn, led to a contract for his first work, *Hard Lines,* published by Simon & Schuster in 1931. It was a tremendous success, and catapulted Nash into a certain, albeit unique, place in American letters. "In comparing Ogden Nash to [seventeenth-century English poet John] Milton we should have to go over to the Public Library and do a good deal of reading, so we won't compare him to Milton. The great thing about him is that he doesn't really compare with anyone," opined William Rose Benét in the *Saturday Review of Literature* in 1931. Another critic, Lisle Bell of *New York Herald Tribune Books,* also bestowed plaudits: "Any one who is under the impression that the English language is not sufficiently flexible should study 'Hard Lines,'" Bell asserted. "It demonstrates that our mother tongue can be made to behave in a manner hardly becoming a mother, but irreproachably amusing." Bell concluded by granting that while Nash's work appears at first reading rather superficial in subject matter, some examples hint of Nash's more contemplative side as an artist: "A very definite attitude toward life underlies the most skittish of verses," Bell noted. "They have a flavor apart from their pattern and from their infectious novelty."

Hard Lines went into seven printings its first year alone—at the height of the financial hardships of the Great Depression—and Nash soon quit his Doubleday job. Over the next few years, he contributed to the *New Yorker* and a number of other periodicals, and penned a prolific amount of verse for additional books. For a brief period in 1932 he was on the staff of the *New Yorker,* but never again held a day job after that. As a writer of comic verse, Nash found great success with his own unique brand of anti-establishment humor; his ability to express incredulity and dismay at the foibles of modern American life fit in perfectly with the mood of many Americans, who saw their financial catastrophes as perhaps the product of unknown forces within banking and financial sectors of the economy. Elsewhere in his poetry Nash offered trenchant observations on American social mores, or lambasted religious moralizing and pompous conservative senators. He was also skilled at presenting the common citizen amusingly beleaguered by the intricacies of the English language. He once observed, in non-verse form, that barbed sentiments could be better, less maliciously expressed in rhyme.

Nash and the *New Yorker*

Another example of Nash's talents came with the publication of *The Primrose Path* in 1935. Critiquing it for the *New York Times Book Review,* C. G. Poore called Nash "still fundamentally and magnificently unsound." A 1938 work, *I'm a Stranger Here Myself,* featured the comic travails of the much-harried Ballantine, an attorney. During this era, Nash was a regular contributor to *Life, Saturday Evening Post, Harper's, Vogue,* the *New Republic,* and *McCall's,* among others. Yet it was his decades-long association with the venerable *New Yorker* that essayist Reed Whittemore cited as his greatest impact on American letters: in contrast to the serious, classical-form poetry written by the magazine's roster of earnest bards, "Nash was the one who practically singlehandedly kept the verse department of the magazine in the business that the rest of the magazine was in, of commenting with intelligence, wit and asperity upon the contemporary American scene—its fads and fashions, its promotional and rhetorical excesses, its varied social and cultural crises," Whittemore declared in the *New Republic.*

During the 1930s and 1940s, Nash was praised as the heir of the revered American humorist Will Rogers, and he was also fixed among the pantheon of cutting American satirists such as Ring Lardner, Dorothy Parker, Robert Benchley, and H. L. Mencken. Still, Nash referred to himself simply as a "worsifier," in comparison to a "versifier." British reviews of his work were sometimes scathing in their assessments, for he was known to take great liberties with spelling and rhyme. One of his more famous examples is the line: "If called by a panther/Don't anther." In another poem, he offered his own assessment of "serious" works of prose: "One thing that literature would be greatly the better for/would be a more restricted use of simile and metaphor," he quipped.

Mined the Minds of Children

Nash had married Frances Rider Leonard in 1931, with whom he had two daughters. His experiences with fatherhood provided more comic fodder for his verse, evident in the 1936 collection *The Bad Parents' Garden of Verse.* He offered this observation as a result of a party, comparing his children and their companions to tribal warriors: "Of similarity there's lots/Twixt tiny tots and Hottentots." Nash also satirized the country-club set to which he belonged, and like other acclaimed writers of his generation, spent some time in Hollywood as a screenwriter. His efforts there included screenplays for three Metro-Goldwyn-Mayer films— *The Firefly* (1937), *The Shining Hair* (1938), and *The Feminine Touch* (1941). In California he met another well-known scribe, S. J. Perelman, who had written for the Marx Brothers films. They collaborated on a musical, recruiting the German-born composer of satirical operas, Kurt Weil, to write the score. The result, *One Touch of Venus,* was a huge success on Broadway during the 1943 season.

Nash was a celebrity during his day, appearing on radio and later television programs as a panelist. He was inducted into both the American Academy of Arts and Sciences and National Institute of Arts and Letters. During the 1950s, he wrote more frequently for the children's market, finding success with such titles as *The Boy Who Laughed at Santa Claus* (1957), *Custard the Dragon* (1959), and *Girls are Silly* (1962). He also wrote lyrics for television programs, such as adaptations of *Peter and the Wolf* and *The Sorcerer's Apprentice.* Though his children were grown, he maintained contact with the juvenile state of mind through his grandchildren, and often wrote humorously about his experiences babysitting them. He was also prone to illness, and recounted his experiences with the medical establishment in a number of poems that were later published in an entire volume, 1970's *Bed Riddance: A Posy for the Indisposed.*

Nash died a year later on May 19, 1971. Several collections of his work were published posthumously, including *I Wouldn't Have Missed It* (1975) and *A Penny Saved Is Impossible* (1981). Fellow poet Morris Bishop eulogized Nash in *Time* magazine with these lines: "Free from flashiness, free from trashiness/Is the essence of ogdenashiness./Rich, original, rash and rational/Stands the monument ogdenational."

Further Reading

Contemporary Authors, New Revision Series, Volume 34, Gale, 1991.
Contemporary Literary Criticism, Volume 23, Gale, 1983.
Dictionary of Literary Biography, Volume 11: *American Humorists, 1800-1950,* Gale, 1982.
Nash, Ogden, *The Bad Parents' Garden of Verse,* Simon & Schuster, 1936.
Reference Guide to American Literature, second edition, St. James Press, 1987.
New Republic, October 21, 1972, pp. 31-34.
New Yorker, 1930.
New York Herald Tribune Books, January 18, 1931, p. 7.
New York Times Book Review, February 17, 1935, p. 4.
Saturday Review of Literature, January 17, 1931, p. 530.
Time, May, 1971. □

Paul Newman

Born in Cleveland, Ohio, Paul Newman (born 1925) is one of the most distinguished twentieth-century American actors. Drama, however, is not Newman's sole passion; he is a professional race car driver, owns a food business that donates all proceeds to charity, and is an outspoken proponent of various liberal causes.

Paul Newman has been described as the quintessential American on-screen male. His sometimes gruff, sometimes duplicitous, nearly always captivating characterizations have earned him a place in the pantheon of celebrated and beloved American film stars. In a 1994 assessment of Newman's career, *Newsweek* writer David Ansen mused that "the great mystery of his stardom is how he has managed to play so many heels—driven, ambitious, solipsistic men—that the audience falls in love with."

Paul Leonard Newman was born to Arthur and Theresa Newman in Cleveland, Ohio, on January 26, 1925. He was raised in Shaker Heights, a well-to-do suburb, where the family enjoyed a comfortable middle-class lifestyle. His father was a partner in a sporting goods store which Newman was expected to eventually take over. As a child, however, Newman was far more interested in extracurricular activities than in achieving good grades and acquiring a head for business. He loved sports and dreamed of becoming a professional athlete. Around this time, he began acting. At the age of ten, he won the lead role in a production of *St. George and the Dragon* at the Cleveland Playhouse. Still, to Newman his flaws were numerous: "When I was a kid, I

was not a good scholar, and I really wanted to be one," Newman once said to *Esquire*. "I was not a good athlete, and I really wanted to be one; I was not a good conversationalist, and to this day I have difficulty talking."

An injury ended Newman's dream of a sports career. When he graduated from high school in 1943, in the midst of World War II, he enlisted in the U.S. Naval Reserve. Newman had hoped for the heroic role of a fighter pilot, but this dream also disappeared when it was determined that he was slightly colorblind. Newman instead served as a radioman in the South Pacific for three years. After his discharge, he returned to Ohio and enrolled at Kenyon College on the G.I. Bill, which provided tuition assistance to returning veterans. Once more, Newman displayed a proclivity for everything but academics, running a lucrative beer and laundry business that was a hit with Kenyon students. He also began to contemplate a career on the stage at this point and devoted much of his energy to roles in Kenyon's drama department productions.

Newman graduated in 1949 and joined a summer stock company in Wisconsin, then an Illinois repertory theater. He also married fellow actress, Jacqueline Witte, that same year; the couple would have three children. When Newman's father passed away, he returned to the Cleveland area to take over the sporting goods store. It was a life and career path to which he was deeply averse. Fortunately for him, the store was sold and he took his wife and growing family to New Haven, Connecticut, where he was accepted at the prestigious Yale School of Drama.

At Yale, Newman honed his stage skills and sold encyclopedias on the side for cash. His talents landed him a place with the acclaimed New York drama workshop, the Actors Studio, where he studied with such luminaries of the craft as Lee Strasberg and Elia Kazan in the early 1950s. Soon Newman found work in television plays, then a fresh and innovative union of the two arts that was attracting stellar writers, directors, and performers. His success in this medium led to Broadway work, and, in 1953, he was cast as the understudy for the lead in the play *Picnic*. Hungry for a chance to prove himself, Newman asked the director if he could play the part on the road, to which the director, Joshua Logan, refused. Newman, Logan said, did not possess the sexual charisma required for the character.

Crushed, Newman adopted a new attitude. He began working out, but more importantly, he began observing others and their behavior. It was also around this time that he met actress Joanne Woodward, and the chemistry between the two dissolved Newman's first marriage. Film seemed the next logical career move, but he was wary. He finally accepted the lead in the 1955 biblical drama *The Silver Chalice*. It was a disastrous move and almost ended his acting career in one fell swoop. Newman played a Greek slave who hammered the cup from which Jesus and the apostles allegedly drank at the Last Supper. "That I survived that picture is a testament to something," Newman declared in an interview with *New York* writer Lynn Hirschberg. He wore a short toga through most of it. When a network bought *The Silver Chalice* and planned to broadcast it,

Newman bought newspaper advertisements urging people not to watch.

Newman returned to New York and devoted his energies to more gratifying stage work. He was next cast alongside James Dean in a teleplay, but when Dean died in a car crash in September of 1955, Newman was asked to take the lead. He hesitated, but his role in the adaptation of a story by Ernest Hemingway revived his reputation and his faith in his abilities. Hollywood beckoned again, but this time with an offer to play the boxer Rocky Graziano in *Somebody Up There Likes Me*. The 1957 hit made the actor into an overnight sensation, and Warner Brothers signed Newman to seven-year contract.

Newman's next film, *The Long Hot Summer*, also starred his new wife, Woodward, in the tale of small town Southern politics and a malevolent drifter. The role would come to typify the characterization in which the tougher, now battle-scarred actor would excel and build his career upon. Other films included *Cat on a Hot Tin Roof*, which was also released in 1958 and earned him his first Academy Award (Oscar) nomination, and another biblical drama, *Exodus*. Still, Newman was unhappy with the Hollywood system and managed to be released from his contract through the help of his savvy agent. Now an independent actor not influenced by studio whims, he was able to take a role that offered a well-written dramatic challenge: the smooth talking pool shark Fast Eddie Felson in *The Hustler*. The 1961 role brought Newman his second Academy Award nomination.

Similar roles followed, with similar results. For the 1963 drama *Hud* and the mournful prison picture *Cool Hand Luke*, one of 1967's biggest box-office successes, Newman again won nominations, but did not win the Oscar in either instance. Subsequent roles in period pieces, such as 1969's *Butch Cassidy and the Sundance Kid* and 1973's *The Sting*, again teamed him with Robert Redford and did phenomenally well. Later in the decade, Newman's career took a slight downturn. His only admirable portrayal came as a vicious minor league hockey coach in the 1977 cult classic *Slap Shot*.

Personal tragedy also visited Newman. In 1978, his son from his first marriage, Scott, died of a drug and alcohol overdose. Newman would later fund a drug rehabilitation facility in Los Angeles in honor of his son. The veteran actor also began to take an active role in other issues of personal significance to him, most notably liberal politics. Though he had always been politically active, by marching in civil rights protests and publicly supporting Democratic presidential campaigns, Newman grew more outspoken. President Jimmy Carter appointed him as his delegate to nuclear disarmament talks at the United Nations, and Newman once took on fellow actor and noted Republican Charlton Heston in a television debate.

In 1995, Newman bought a controlling interest in *The Nation*, a liberal political journal, and even began writing for it occasionally. One essay spoke out against a prominent United States senator who had supported dictatorial regimes in Latin America, for example. Newman is also on the board of Cease Fire, a gun control group funded by prominent celebrities. He also sponsors an annual free speech award by the writers' organization PEN. "Your sense of yourself comes from what you're doing today, not what you did yesterday," Newman told Hirschberg in the *New York* interview.

Newman continued to command respect with his film roles as well, especially with the 1981 drama *Absence of Malice,* for which he earned his fifth Oscar nomination. The role of a wretched alcoholic lawyer in 1982's *The Verdict* landed him his sixth. His Oscar losing streak became a joke among Newman and his circle of family and friends. "I had this wonderful scenario worked out in my head that somehow I would never win," Newman confessed to Hirschberg, "and then, finally, in a terrible state of physical disrepair, I'd be nominated and I'd win and I'd be carried up by two paramedics on a stretcher. . . ." When he was nominated for reprising his "Fast Eddie" role in the sequel to *The Hustler,* the 1986 Tom Cruise movie *The Color of Money,* he didn't even travel to Los Angeles for the ceremony. This time, he won.

Newman remains grounded on the East Coast, far away from the celebrity glamour of Hollywood. "Hollywood breeds insecurity," Newman told *New York'* s Hirschberg. "When I was a young actor, I delighted in the dailies," referring to the unedited footage from the a movie shoot. "I used to bathe in the idea of watching that image on the screen. I'm uneasy about it now. I'm afraid I will be so critical that I will be immobilized for the next day's shooting." He and Woodward, with whom he has three daughters, live in a 200-year-old farmhouse in Connecticut and also keep a home on New York's Upper East Side. The actor is well-known personality on the automobile racing circuit, and owns an Indy car competitor with a partner. He is also a famed prankster feared by his film set colleagues. He once had a Porsche demolished, wrapped, and sneaked into Robert Redford's house. Film director Robert Altman was paid back for exploding nine feet of popcorn in Newman's dressing room on a film set with a series of attacks that included 200 live chickens installed in Altman's personal trailer.

Perhaps Newman's proudest achievement, however, is the food company he launched in the 1980s with his friend A. E. Hotchner, a writer. "Newman's Own" began with their bottling of a vinaigrette they concocted that had been a hit with friends. "Giving the profits away was a philosophy that evolved with the company," Newman told Pam Janis for *USA Weekend,* noting that he was strongly urged by all involved to lend his name and visage to the label. "With that, it would be tacky *not* to give the money away." Over the next decade, Newman's Own expanded to over 40 different products, including salsa, lemonade, and the prank inducing popcorn. His daughter, Nell, and her devotion to organic foods helped launch a second line. All proceeds are donated to charitable organizations. By 1997 Newman's Own had given more than $80 million away to projects chosen by the actor and his wife, such as a school for children of migrant laborers and AIDS research.

Newman continues to choose outstanding film roles when he does enter into the Hollywood sphere. One such effort was the critically acclaimed 1994 drama *Nobody's Fool.* His character, wrote Ansen in *Newsweek,* "is a classic Newman type, the older relative of all the intransigent outsiders he played in the '50s and '60s." Ansen likened Newman's tragicomic Sully to the "rebellious rakes who cut themselves off from women, from family, from community to pursue their private dreams and demons. . . . Sully's selfish, self-involved and a loser. He's also, like all Newman antiheroes, enormously likeable." Newman admitted that *Nobody's Fool* and his role as Sully, who learns to connect when he establishes a shaky relationship with his grandson, tapped into some emotional defenses that were not altogether unfamiliar to him. "An actor who's successful develops a certain shield to protect that part of his life which isn't up for public examination," he told Bonnie Churchill in the *Christian Science Monitor.* "It bleeds over into your private life."

Further Reading

Contemporary Theatre, Film, and Television, Volume 14, Gale, 1996.
Newsmakers, 1995 Cumulation, Gale, 1995.
Christian Science Monitor, December 27, 1994, p. 14; March 5, 1996, p. 8.
Good Housekeeping, May 1995, p. 147.
Newsweek, December 19, 1994, pp. 56-62.
New York, December 12, 1994, pp. 36-45.
Sunday Times (London), June 22, 1997.
USA Weekend, October 17-19, 1997.
Wall Street Journal, November 20, 1997, p. B1. □

Antonia Novello

In 1990 Antonia Novello (born 1944) became the first female United States Surgeon General; she was also the first Hispanic in history to win the appointment to this nationally prominent government office. During her three-year term, Novello won praise for her campaigns targeting America's youth, especially her crusade against underage tobacco use. The former pediatrician used her post to voice criticism of tobacco companies and their marketing strategies; a few years after Novello's tenure, strict legislation was enacted to drastically curb teenagers' access to cigarettes.

N ovello's own youth was marked by hardship and medical trauma. She was born Antonia Coello in Fajardo, Puerto Rico, the first of Antonio and Ana Delia Coello's three children. Shortly after the birth of their daughter in 1944, the Coellos were informed that Antonia suffered from congenital megacolon, an abnormality of the large intestine. This required periodic visits to the hospital for treatment, because of her body's inability to rid itself of waste; one side effect was a periodically swollen abdomen.

Compounding Novello's burden was the death of her father when she was eight. Her mother—a teacher who later became a high school principal—was told that her daughter could have an operation to correct the procedure. Yet it never happened. "The university hospital was in the north, I was 32 miles away, my mother could only take me on Saturday, so the surgery was never done," Novello explained in an interview with *Saturday Evening Post* writer Carol Krucoff. "I do believe some people fall through the cracks," Novello continued. "I was one of those. I thought, when I grow up, no other person is going to wait 18 years for surgery."

A Standout Student

Still, Novello is grateful to her mother for not allowing her to feel sorry for herself because of her condition. Instead of pampering her, Ana Flores—who had remarried—pushed her child to succeed academically, and Novello graduated from high school at the age of 15. She then enrolled at the University of Puerto Rico at Rio Pedras, and it was there that she finally grew weary of her long-term condition. The hospital treatments remedied her occasionally distended stomach—but as she explained to the *Saturday Evening Post,* "By the time I was 18, it was not good to have those big bellies one month that are, in the next month, flat."

Novello's first surgery, however, was not a complete success, and she suffered from complications for another two years. Finally, at the age of 20 she traveled to the renowned Mayo Clinic for a final operation, which was

successful. By this time Novello's exposure to the medical establishment had strengthened her own ambitions—she had dreamed of becoming a pediatrician since her childhood, and her academic achievements brought the realization that such a goal was indeed possible. After earning her undergraduate degree from the University of Puerto Rico in 1965, she applied to its school of medicine—but was afraid to tell her mother, since female doctors were still such a rarity. Once informed, however, her mother vowed to provide the financial support toward her daughter's aspiration, and Novello received her medical degree in 1970. That same year she wed Joseph R. Novello, a Navy flight surgeon who later became a psychiatrist.

Too Compassionate

Soon after their marriage, the newlyweds won residencies at the University of Michigan Medical Center in Ann Arbor, Michigan. Novello's was in pediatrics, and she completed further training in her specialty, pediatric nephrology, at Georgetown University Hospital in 1975. Her childhood illness had made her an unusually compassionate physician, but would also be her undoing. For a time in the mid-1970s, she had a pediatric practice specializing in kidney health, but took her job to heart. "When the pediatrician cries as much as the parents do, then you know it's time to get out," Novello recalled in an interview with *People* in 1990.

In 1978, Novello considered joining the U.S. Navy, but was discouraged by a male recruiter. Instead she signed on with the U.S. Public Health Service in 1979. The PHS is a quasi-military corps of doctors, nurses, and other medical personnel who conduct research, serve in areas where there are shortages of doctors (such as on Native American reservations), and assist in national disaster relief. Novello joined the PHS's National Institutes of Health, and began as project officer in the Institute for Arthritis, Metabolism, and Digestive Disease. By the early 1980s, she was a serving as a Congressional fellow, lending her expertise to the staff of Capitol Hill legislators drafting health-related legislation.

Nominated as Surgeon General

In 1982, Novello earned a degree in public health from Johns Hopkins University in Baltimore. Four years later she was promoted to deputy director of the National Institute of Child Health and Human Development in 1986, which effectively combined her pediatrics training with a desire to assist and act for those who could not. In her new job, she became a prominent activist for pediatric AIDS research, and executed her duties with zeal and zest for the job, certain that her post was the apex of her ambitions. Yet when Novello's name was mentioned to fill the vacant Surgeon General slot during the presidency of George Bush, she realized she could do even more.

Traditionally, the sitting U.S. president nominates the Surgeon General from among a list of accomplished physicians to serve as director of the U. S. Public Health Service. That honoree is also charged with raising public awareness on health issues and serving as the administration's spokesperson for such matters. On March 9, 1990, Novello was sworn in as U. S. Surgeon General, after a Senate confirmation hearing that was markedly dissimilar to that of her controversial predecessor, Dr. C. Everett Koop. She was the fourteenth physician to hold the job, but its first female and its first minority. "Today West Side Story comes to the West Wing," Novello joked in her swearing-in speech at the White House, referring to the Broadway musical about Puerto Rican immigrants and the section of the American president's mansion used for public ceremonies.

Not surprisingly, in her new role Novello initiated campaigns designed to raise awareness for America's children and their health-care needs. She was an advocate of the necessity for preschool immunization programs to reduce infant mortality rates, and espoused increased research and funding into providing better health care services for America's minorities, women, and children—all traditionally underserved by a medical establishment skewed to provide the best care only to fully employed Americans with job-provided health insurance. Novello and her Surgeon General's office also launched a "Spring Break '91" campaign that targeted the rising number of binge drinkers among American college students; she undertook a speaking tour of college campuses herself to make her point. Her office also implemented AIDS awareness programs.

Novello and Joe Camel

But perhaps Novello's greatest impact during her three-year tenure as Surgeon General came as a result of her vehement opposition to teen smoking. She was the most prominent government official to target the "Joe Camel" advertising campaign by tobacco giant R.J. Reynolds, whose cartoon "spokescamel," Novello bluntly declared in 1992, was a clear ploy aimed at luring new underage smokers. Backing her up were statistics showing that though the number of adult smokers had declined, three thousand teens were picking up the habit on a daily basis.

By 1998 such imagery was prohibited by federal law, vending machines were banned, and stores that sold tobacco products were responsible for checking the identification of any potential purchasee who appeared to be less than 28 years old. The rising rates of lung disease among American women—attributable to a much higher rate of smokers over the last two decades—focused Novello's attention on the tobacco companies and their marketing strategies as well; in the "women's lib" era, cigarette smoking was positioned as a "liberated" act, since it had been looked upon with such censure for so many decades. "Call it a case of the Virginia Slims woman catching up with the Marlboro Man," *People* reported her as saying.

Novello's stint as Surgeon General also found fault with alcohol advertising aimed at teenagers. One particular target of her wrath was a high-alcohol sweet wine called Cisco; Novello spoke publicly against it and its maker, alleging it was aimed at teenagers since it resembled Kool-Aid. She excoriated other beverage companies and their advertising agencies that tied in their product with sports in the context of their marketing campaigns, which she asserted gave teens a confusing message that alcohol use was somehow both adventureous and healthy.

Such deeds helped make Novello one of the most popular Surgeon Generals in history. She was also far less controversial than her successor, Dr. Jocelyn Elders, who was forced to step down during the Clinton Administration for her frank pronouncements. She continues to play an active role in public-health issues, especially pediatric-related topics, and works for UNICEF (United Nations International Children's Emergency Fund) as a special representative for health and nutrition. A professor of medicine at Georgetown University since 1986, Novello resides in the Washington area still with her husband, a prominent psychiatrist whose brother is comedian Don Novello, most famous for his occasional appearances on the long-running NBC program *Saturday Night Live* as Father Guido Sarducci. The sense of humor, presumably, is a shared one: "I survived many times in my life by learning to laugh at myself," Novello told the *Saturday Evening Post*'s Krucoff. "That's the best medicine. But I also became very self-assured and capable of saying that if I could do that, I can do anything."

Further Reading

Detroit Free Press, October 30, 1990.

Newsweek, October 30, 1990.

People, December 17, 1990.

Saturday Evening Post, May/June 1991.

USA Today, April 30, 1991.

Washington Post, October 18, 1989; October 24, 1989; May 8, 1990.

"Dr. Antonia Novello - The Hall of Public Service," *Academy of Achievement,* http://www.achievement.org/autodoc/halls/ser (May 4, 1998). ☐

O

Chukwuemeka Odumegwu Ojukwu

Nigerian-born military leader Chukwuemeka Odumegwu Ojukwu (born 1933) headed the unsuccessful move by Biafra to secede from Nigeria.

Oxford-educated Chukwuemeka Odumegwu Ojukwu joined the Nigerian army, against his wealthy father's wishes, hoping to play an integral role in the nation's affairs once Nigeria had gained independence from Britain. Instead, due to his ethnic loyalties and to political events, he became the leader of the Biafrans during a bloody civil war in Nigeria. Although claiming some early victories, his forces were fighting against troops backed by Britain, Russia, and most of Europe. For three years, Odumegwu Ojukwu fought to keep Biafra from being annihilated. With supply lines cut, an estimated eight million Biafrans slowly starved to death. After the civil war ended in 1970, Odumegwu Ojukwu lived in voluntary exile. He was invited back to Nigeria in 1982, and Nigerian leaders have sought his counsel as the African nation charts its future.

Privileged Child

Chukwuemeka Odumegwu Ojukwu was born in 1933 in Zungeru, a community in the northern part of Nigeria, which was then a colony of Britain. He was the son of Sir Louis Philippe Odumegwu Ojukwu, one of the most successful businessmen among the Ibos, the largest ethnic group in Nigeria. Consequently, the younger Odumegwu Ojukwu received the best education money could buy. His primary education was at a private Catholic school in the Nigerian city of Lagos. Before he was ten years old, he was enrolled at nearby King's College as the youngest pupil in the institution's history. Two years later, Odumegwu Ojukwu's father transferred him to a school in Surrey, England, called Epson College, to finish secondary studies. Odumegwu Ojukwu had a natural athletic ability and, during his years in England, he honed his skills on the playing field when not attending classes. In school-sponsored sports he served as captain of the rugby and soccer teams. He also set the All England Junior record in the discus throw.

In 1952, Odumegwu Ojukwu was admitted to Oxford University. He majored in history, graduating in 1955 with honors. As an undergraduate, Odumegwu Ojukwu continued to pursue his love of athletics while developing outside interests in drama and journalism. He served as a leader in the Oxford branch of the West African Students Union during this time. In addition, he was known for his flashy sports cars, which he frequently drove at high speeds between Oxford and London. It was at Oxford that he met a female law student named Njideka; she eventually became his wife.

Away from the Sheltered Life

With a degree from Oxford University and a wealthy father, Odumegwu Ojukwu was guaranteed access to the highest levels of British colonial Nigeria. Rather than relying on his father, however, he chose to enter the workforce. Odumegwu Ojukwu was hired by the Nigerian civil service and became the assistant district officer in the town of Udi, overseeing community development in rural areas. He later served in the same position in the towns of Aba and Umuahia. As a community development leader, he gained a

311

reputation for his quick understanding of complex issues and was respected for his fair recommendations.

In 1957, again in an attempt to distance himself from his privileged upbringing, he joined the army. His father was so against this decision that he did not speak to his son for the next two and a half years. Meanwhile, the younger Odumegwu Ojukwu completed officer training in England at the Officer Cadet School at Eaton Hall and was commissioned a second lieutenant. After attending the Infantry School in Warminister, England, the Small Arms School in Hythe, England, and the Royal West African Frontier Force Training School in Teshie, Ghana, he returned to Nigeria in 1958 and was assigned to the Fifth Battalion in Kaduna.

Once Nigeria had gained independence from Britain in 1960, Odumegwu Ojukwu was quickly promoted; he held the rank of major by 1961. As one of his assignments, he served with the Nigerian First Brigade in the Congo as part of a United Nations peace-keeping program. Later, he attended the Joint Services Staff College in the United Kingdom as the first Nigerian officer ever to do so. In 1963, Odumegwu Ojukwu, as a lieutenant colonel, became the first Nigerian quartermaster-general in the Nigerian Army. His first independent command came in 1965; he was assigned as commanding officer to the Fifth Battalion of the Nigerian Army in Kano.

Fragile Independence

The early years of Nigerian independence were difficult for the country. Political turmoil, riots, and ethnic ri-

valries resulted in a civil war in the latter half of the 1960s. Members of the largest ethnic group, the Ibos, were murdered in great numbers during the chaos, and more than a million (some sources say over four million) survivors fled back to their homeland in eastern Nigeria. Odumegwu Ojukwu, the military governor of the region, assumed control in the mid-1960s in an attempt to strengthen the bargaining power of the Ibos. He first argued against secession from Nigeria by the Ibos and, instead, urged easterners to accept a loosening of ties with the rest of Nigeria. A 1968 article in *Time* magazine stated, "[Odumegwu Ojukwu] was a calm and reasoned voice pleading for a united Nigeria long after other powerful Ibos had angrily given up hope of preserving the union." Critics felt that because most of Odumegwu Ojukwu's inheritance from his father was in Lagos, he had a personal stake in keeping Nigeria together.

Odumegwu Ojukwu changed his stance, however, and sided with the separatists on the issue of safety for the Ibos. At one point, he and Nigerian army chief of staff Yakubu Gowon, also in control of the central Nigerian government, appeared to be nearing a compromise that would have allowed the Ibos a measure of autonomy while staying within the Nigerian federation. But Gowon was unwilling to let the eastern region maintain a separate army, and Odumegwu Ojukwu was unsure of the ability of the Nigerian central government to protect the Ibos. Odumegwu Ojukwu reluctantly demanded independence for the easterners. He formally proclaimed the independent Republic of Biafra on May 30, 1967, during a reception in the regional capital of Enugu. At the time, he also hinted that the Nigerian central government had played a role in the genocide of the Ibo people. He then built up his army and expelled northerners from Biafra, telling them that, because of the flood of Ibo refugees, non-easterners should leave for their own safety.

Civil War

At the onset of conflict in 1967, Odumegwu Ojukwu received little sympathy or support from the international community. Nigeria, however, was backed by Britain, the Soviet Union, and most of Western Europe. The Nigerian central government first established a naval blockade along the Biafran coast then sent troops, composed mostly of Muslims from the northern part of the country, to the east where they were met by Odumegwu Ojukwu's rebel forces. Initially, the Biafrans took control of strategic points in the midwestern region of Nigeria and the oil-rich Niger River delta. The central government retaliated by sending in more armed forces, which escalated the conflict into a full-blown civil war. Odumegwu Ojukwu directed the overall strategy for Biafra in the war, but he left most of the tactical decisions to his brigade commanders and often sought advice from Ibo elders. He downplayed his role in the civil war, although the Nigerians frequently called the conflict "Ojukwu's war" and depicted the military leader as a power-mad Hitler who was shattering the unity of the new Nigeria. Odumegwu Ojukwu told *New York Times Magazine* reporter Lloyd Garrison, "Independence is not one man getting up and declaring it. Freedom without substance is meaningless."

By the end of 1967, Nigerian forces had regained control of the midwest and had cut off Biafran access to the sea. Although they had encircled the Biafrans, they were unable to penetrate the Ibo heartland. The Biafrans, however, were crowded into mangrove swamps and hardwood forests, unable to provide themselves with the materials of daily existence. Meanwhile, Soviet-built warplanes, many flown by hired Egyptians and British pilots, cut supply lines and inflicted heavy casualties during raids on Biafran urban centers.

Consequently, Biafrans were starving to death at a rate conservatively estimated to be approximately 1,000 people a day, according to *Time.* Other sources estimate that as many as 8,000 people a day died of starvation in the region during this time. Despite the hardship, the Ibo people continued to support the war effort. Odumegwu Ojukwu thus began waging a public-relations campaign to receive badly needed supplies from the rest of the world. He sent out press releases and photos showing starving Biafrans. He persuaded several countries, including Czechoslovakia, The Netherlands, and Belgium, to cut off weapons supplies to Nigeria. Odumegwu Ojukwu hoped for airlifts, which he considered a symbol of the world helping a besieged people. But by October of 1969, realizing that he would receive little foreign support, he appealed for United Nations mediation to obtain terms for a cease fire and to begin peace negotiations. The Nigerian central government, however, was not inclined to accept anything less than surrender and seemed to consider starvation a weapon of war that would preclude its having to send soldiers into battle. At about this time, Odumegwu Ojukwu told *Time* correspondent James Wilde, "What you are seeing now is the end of a long, long journey. It began in the far north of Nigeria and moved steadily southward as we were driven out of place after place. Now this path has become the road to the slaughterhouse here in the Ibo heartland." By the end of the year, 120,000 Nigerian troops had divided Biafra in half. The rebel nation collapsed in January of 1970.

After the civil war, under Gowon's supervision, the Nigerian central government took steps to ensure that the Ibos would be treated as fellow citizens rather than defeated enemies. Programs were developed to reintegrate the Ibos into a united Nigeria. Many Biafran military officers rejoined the central government as part of a general amnesty. Odumegwu Ojukwu, however, opted for voluntary exile and went to the Ivory Coast on the invitation of that nearby African nation's president. He justified his actions at the time by declaring, as quoted in *Newsweek,* "[W]hilst I live, Biafra lives." Odumegwu Ojukwu was invited back to Nigeria by Shehu Shagari of the Nigerian government in 1982. Since then, the former Biafran leader has become active in the National Party of Nigeria. Although he was unsuccessful in a bid to be elected to the national senate, his advice is often sought by factions of the Nigerian and greater African community. He has encouraged the military to support Nigeria's slow transition toward democracy. In 1993, he publicly supported Nigeria's Republican Party because he thought it would be the best guarantor of eastern interests in national politics.

Further Reading

Dostert, Pierre Etienne, *Africa,* Stryker-Post Publications, 1990.

Hatch, John, *Nigeria: Seeds of Disaster,* Henry Regnery Company, 1970.

Schultz, John, *Nigeria . . . in Pictures,* Lerner Publications, 1988.

America, February 8, 1969, p. 162.

Newsweek, March 24, 1969, p. 55; January 26, 1970, p. B49.

New York Times Magazine, June 22, 1969, p. 7.

Time, August 23, 1968, p. 20.

"Biafra versus the Federal Military Government of Nigeria: Oil and War," *ICE Case Studies,* http://gurukul.ucc.american.edu/TED/ICE/BIAFRA.HTM (March 13, 1998).

"Lt. Col. C. O. Ojukwu," *NewJan Communications,* http://www.nigeriangalleria.com/portrait/bios/ojukwu.htm (March 13, 1998).

"Chief Chukwuemeka Odumegwu-Ojukwu," http://freeweb.pdq.net/qualitech/ (March 9, 1998).

Ransom E. Olds

Ransom E. Olds (1864-1950) was an automotive industry pioneer whose company developed, manufactured, and sold one of the first affordable cars in mass production in the United States. His $650 "runabout," popular in the early 1900s, came about partly as a result of his experiments with perfecting a gasoline-burning engine at his family's machine shop. Though Olds was only active during the automobile industry's formative years, the influence he exerted on others—both colleagues and competitors—as well as the numerous patents granted to this gifted inventor marked him as one of the field's most important founders.

Ransom Eli Olds, whose ancestry stretched back to Puritan-era New England, was born in Geneva, Ohio, on June 3, 1864. His father, Pliny Fisk Olds, was at various times a blacksmith, manager of an ironworks facility, farmer, and pattern maker before moving to Lansing, Michigan, and opening a machine shop when "Ranny," the fourth of his sons, was in his teens. Two older Olds brothers were many years Ranny's senior, and had by then struck out on their own, but the third son, Wallace, joined his father in the family business, P. F. Olds and Son; while still in school Ransom Olds also began working at the shop, which both manufactured and repaired steam engines.

Clever Machinist

Olds had learned a great deal from observing the ups and downs of his father's business ventures, and soon proved to be an adept third manager from the launch of P. F. Olds and Son in 1880. He also demonstrated a talent for machining, pattern making, and general mechanical tinkering, the first two learned directly from his father; he later credited Pliny Olds with providing him the most valuable

training of his career. Olds did not finish high school, but did take courses at Lansing Business College around 1882. Three years later, his father made him a partner in the shop, and the business soon became a great deal more successful with the fruits of Ransom Olds's experiments: he developed a steam engine with a gas burner, which worked far more efficiently than others that burned coal or wood. Within five years, their company had sold 2,000 of the engines and was turning a healthy profit.

Olds was an avid boater, and began experimenting with other uses for his gas-burning engine. He tried one out in a boat, but also installed one on a carriage—in a horse's stead—perhaps as early as 1887. The taciturn Pliny Olds, according to George S. May's *R. E. Olds: Auto Industry Pioneer,* reportedly told someone, "Ranse thinks he can put an engine in a buggy and make the contraption carry him over the roads. If he doesn't get killed at his fool undertaking, I will be satisfied." Olds soon found that by installing a pair of engines on a carriage, he could get the vehicle up to 15 miles per hour. An 1892 article in *Scientific American* aroused the interest of a British patent-medicine firm who bought Olds's experimental vehicle and transported it to India—making this perhaps the first sale of a self-propelled vehicle in the United States, and certainly the first exported for foreign sale. Automotive historians have tried with little success to determine the fate of that motorized carriage, but surmise that it did not even reach Bombay at all and went down at sea.

Granted Historic Patent

Olds attended the Chicago World's Fair in 1893, where the gasoline engines displayed by a Grand Rapids firm likely spurred him to switch his company's focus away from the steam-gasoline engine and to instead perfect a fully gas-powered device. By June of 1896 the Olds firm had an internal-combustion engine in production, a patent application pending, and Olds returned to his horseless carriage experiments. He managed to reach a top speed of 25 miles per hour in his prototype vehicle, and later that year applied for the first patent granted in the United States for an "automobile carriage." Olds's company teamed with a carriage-maker to build their product, about which there appeared to be great consumer excitement.

To expand his facilities in order to meet this demand, Olds sought investors and found one in a Lansing real-estate mogul named Edward W. Sparrow. With Sparrow's capital the Olds Motor Vehicle Company was launched, of which Sparrow held the presidency, but there were problems from the start in 1897. By the following year the company had yet to make more than a handful of vehicles, and there were continual problems between the money-minded investors and the less pragmatic Olds. It nearly went under several times, but then in 1899 Pliny Olds's original, still-profitable engine-manufacturing firm was merged into a new venture called the Olds Motor Works. It was backed by a friend of Sparrow's, a retired Michigan copper-mine mogul, Samuel L. Smith.

Smith, a Detroiter, and other local stockholders insisted that the Olds Motor Works locate in Detroit, which was already a thriving manufacturing center for carriages, stoves, and other products. At this point, another Detroiter, Henry Ford, was still attempting to launch his own motor-vehicle manufacturing operation; he had incorporated one in 1899, but it failed a year later. The newly-built Olds Motor Works plant and offices on the Detroit River were the city's first permanent auto manufacturing enterprise. Olds and the board of directors finally agreed to concentrate first-year production on the "runabout," an open-air vehicle with a lightweight carriage. Olds himself was responsible for the car's unique "curved dash," which kept passengers warm, but more importantly, gave it a distinct profile that set it apart from competitors. The company advertised the car nationally—and were the first to market the product as a convenience to women and doctors—and had orders for 300 of them at $650 a piece when production began in 1901.

Factory Fire

Production ceased, however, in March of 1901 when Olds and his family—he had married Metta Ursula Woodward in 1889, with whom he had two daughters—were returning from a California visit to the now-retired Pliny Olds and his wife Sarah. Olds was on a streetcar back to his home on Detroit's Edmund Place, and spotted a newspaper headline announcing his factory had been destroyed by fire that day. Fortunately the conflagration occurred on a Saturday afternoon, and no one was killed. The plant, however, was ruined, and the fire would enter the annals of American automotive history as an apocryphal, though not altogether true, tale. Olds would later say that all the plans and patterns had been destroyed in the fire (which was not true), and that only one model had been saved by a brave worker—his curved-dash runabout (actually, this and several other prototypes emerged safely from a fireproof vault). The company recovered quickly from the setback, farming out light assembly work to supplier facilities while insurance money financed the reconstruction of the plant.

Over four hundred runabouts were produced in 1901, a healthy comeback for the Olds company, but its founder suffered health problems as a result of the stress and was hospitalized that spring. The company would eventually relocate some of its production back to Lansing—with Olds moving back to manage its plant there—and by 1905 the Olds Motor Works was producing 5,000 cars a year. Olds worked tirelessly to promote the car himself, and was a well-known American business celebrity in his day. He raced the car at a track at Daytona Beach, Florida, in 1902 (where he had real estate investments), and his name and visage often appeared in national advertisements.

A New Start

In time, the Olds company was troubled by Olds's conflict with Frederic Smith, son of Samuel L. Smith. The younger Smith, who usually held the title of company president, handled sales and began questioning production techniques when runabout buyers complained of problems; he claimed that Olds was uninterested in improving the car or certifying that it was free from mechanical defects when it left the plant. The split between the two came when Smith set up an experimental engineering shop without Olds's knowledge, and by 1904 Olds had sold nearly all of his stock and exited the company for good. He was just forty years old, however, and far from eager to retire. Instead he founded the R. E. Olds Company in Lansing in August of 1904; the Detroit Olds Motor Works threatened to sue for use of the name, and so Olds changed it to one with his initials, the Reo Motor Car Company.

Olds's new venture produced the Reo, which was introduced in 1905, and its plant would turn out a record number of cars between 1905 and 1909. They also sold a runabout for around $650, and a more powerful touring car for almost twice that amount. Yet once again, Olds came into conflict with his investors, and once he had proven to his detractors that he could indeed launch and make profitable his own automobile manufacturing operation, he seemed to lose interest. His second company had eclipsed that of the Smith's Olds Motor Works, which was taken over in 1908 by a newly-created General Motors Corporation. Over the next two decades, Olds devoted more of his energy to his real estate and banking holdings, and also enjoyed yachting in both Florida and on the Great Lakes.

Olds only became actively involved again in his company briefly in 1934 during the midst of the Great Depression, but by 1936 he had formally retired and the Reo Company had halted its car manufacturing operations. It concentrated instead on truck production, but faced receivership, sit-down strikes during the labor-union era of the late 1930s, and continual problems with New York stockholders. For a time, the company survived from truck contracts from the U.S. military during World War II, but in the postwar era concentrated on lawn-mower and marine engines. It was sold twice in the 1950s, switched its focus to nuclear-device testing, and existed in the late 1990s as the Nucor Corporation of Charlotte, North Carolina.

Ransom E. Olds died at his Lansing home in August of 1950; his wife fell at his funeral and died a few weeks later. He had been a well-known figure in Lansing's social and business community, and for years the city officially feted him on his birthday. George S. May, writing in the *Encyclopedia of American Business History and Biography: The Automobile Industry, 1896-1920*, praised Olds for his impact on the automobile industry as a catalyst, for "the role he had played in stimulating and encouraging others to enter the field." Several who had worked for Olds went on to found their own car or supplier firms (Roy Chapin and the Hudson Motor Company was one), two others who made sheet metal for him founded a company that was eventually subsumed into Chrysler, and his engine-maker, Henry Leland, would go on to co-found the Cadillac nameplate; Olds also worked with the Dodge Brothers in Detroit and, according to May, proved to Henry Ford "that there was money to be made in producing a low-priced car."

Further Reading

Encyclopedia of American Business History and Biography: The Automobile Industry, 1896-1920, edited by George S. May, Bruccoli Clark Layman/Facts on File, 1990.

Fucini, Joseph J., and Suzy Fucini, *Entrepreneurs: The Men and Women behind Famous Brand Names and How They Made It,* G. K. Hall, 1985.

May, George S., *R. E. Olds: Auto Industry Pioneer,* William B. Eerdmans Publishing Company, 1977.

Niemeyer, Glenn A., *The Automotive Career of Ransom E. Olds,* MSU Business Studies, 1963.

Raleigh News & Observer, September 21, 1997.

Michael Ondaatje

Once a highly regarded denizen of a burgeoning Canadian literary scene in the early 1970s, Michael Ondaatje (born 1943) has since gone on to achieve international renown for his poetry and fiction. His 1992 novel, *The English Patient,* was made into a motion picture four years later that won an array of industry awards.

Philip Michael Ondaatje was born in 1943 in Ceylon (now Sri Lanka), a large island located off the southern tip of India. He later wrote of his unusual childhood in *Running in the Family,* a 1982 memoir. In it, Ondaatje explains that his family were British colonists who possessed a large tea plantation—as well as a spirit of adventure that this large extended family and their lavish colonial life passed on to him. The work won critical acclaim for the beautiful imagery which Ondaatje, by then an established poet, used to tell his predecessors' tales—such as the story of his grandmother attending a formal dance with fireflies sewn into her gown. "The book was praised by critics as much for its re-creation of a particular society," wrote Ann Mandel in the *Dictionary of Literary Biography*, "as for its stylistic exploration of the relationship between history and the poetic imagination."

Yet Ondaatje's childhood, as some of *Running in the Family* recollects, was less than idyllic; his father drank to excess, and so before he was ten his parents' marriage had ended. As a result, Ondaatje went to London, England, with his mother in the early 1950s, and eventually studied at Dulwich College. Ondaatje, however, found the English educational system constricting. He subsequently left to join his brother, already living in Quebec, and enrolled in Bishop's University in the early 1960s. He completed his undergraduate work at the University of Toronto, receiving a B.A. in 1965. Graduate work was undertaken at Queen's University in Kingston, Ontario, from which Ondaatje earned a master's degree in 1967.

Ondaatje entered academia, becoming an instructor in English at the University of Western Ontario until 1971; when his superiors pressured him to earn a Ph.D., Ondaatje left and took a post in the English department at York University's Glendon College in Toronto. There was little reason for him to add a title to his name, since by then he was already an established poet: *The Dainty Monsters*, its title borrowed from a poem by Charles Baudelaire, was his

first published volume. Its first half poeticized some fantastical beasts and otherworldly animals, such as the mythological beast known as a manticore (human head, lion's body, dragon's tail) that populated Toronto's sewer system in one poem. Its second half, "Troy Town," featured interrelated poems based on tales from classical literature. *The Dainty Monsters* was extremely well-received for a small edition by an unknown poet, and made Ondaatje an important figure in Canada's acclaimed new generation of young writers; the work has never gone out of print.

Ondaatje's next few works were also published by his first press, Toronto's acclaimed Coach House, and he has worked for them as an editor as well over the years. These early titles offered more examples of his poetry and included 1969's *The Man with Seven Toes*, and his nonfiction look at Canadian singer/songwriter *Leonard Cohen*, published in 1970. What has been termed Ondaatje's best-known volume of poetry, *The Collected Works of Billy the Kidd: Left-Handed Poems*, appeared in 1970. In it, Ondaatje placed himself in both the third-person and the first with the inner monologues of the outlaw Kidd himself to re-create his unusual life story and to speculate on the motivations behind this icon of the American Wild West.

"The book continues thematically his exploration of the ambiguous and often paradoxical area between biology and mechanization, movement and stasis, chaotic life and the framed artistic moment," wrote Mandel in the *Dictionary of Literary Biography*. When *Billy the Kidd* received one of Canada's top literary prizes in the poetry category in 1971, there was some grumbling from the Canadian political establishment that the Governor-General's award had been given to a work that reflected some very American subject matter. Ondaatje's verse was adapted into a script and staged at the legendary Stratford Festival Theatre in 1973.

Matured, Ventured into Other Forms

Ondaatje had married and begun a family in the mid-1960s, and the poems and often whimsical imagery contained in 1973's *Rat Jelly* reflect the blended family he and artist Kim Jones created. The writer also ventured into film-making, such as a 1972 short work that chronicled the tale of the abduction of Wallace, the family's basset hound. His first foray into fiction came with the 1976 title *Coming through Slaughter*, classified as "a biographical novel." In London years before, Ondaatje was intrigued by a newspaper article about a New Orleans musician early in the twentieth century who had what apparently was a breakdown while playing in a parade. He began to research the life of cornetist Buddy Bolden, an actual figure who spent the last twenty-plus years of his life in a mental ward. Bolden is credited with pioneering a playing style that gave birth to what is now known as Dixieland jazz. No recordings were ever made of him, and little is actually known about the man or his tragic life. Ondaatje traveled to New Orleans in 1973 to work on the book, which takes a non-chronological form as part narrative, part interior monologue. "Ondaatje succeeds in giving us a sense of how Bolden actually played," wrote *Canadian Literature*'s Roy MacSkimming.

"The texture of the book itself has that fertile, driving, improvisational quality, rich with its own pleasure in language and human complexity."

During the 1970s, Ondaatje continued to write poetry, edit the works of others for Coach House, and experiment with blending fact, fiction, and verse. Volumes which further enhanced his reputation include: *There's a Trick with a Knife I'm Learning to Do: Poems, 1963-1978,* published in 1979, *Claude Glass,* another volume of poetry published that same year, and the aforementioned memoir published in 1982, *Running in the Family.* In order to write the last work, Ondaatje journeyed to Sri Lanka and spent time with his relatives there. His own family in Canada underwent transformation during the early part of the next decade, when Ondaatje's relationship with Jones ended. The poems in *Secular Love,* published in 1984, reflect this change in his life, chronicling the difficulty of coming to terms with the end of a long-term coupling, as well as the joys of beginning a new one. Its title comes from the following poem: "Seeing you/I want no other life/and turn around/to the sky/and everywhere below/jungle, waves of heat/secular love." Again, Ondaatje won kudos for his work among the members of the literary establishment. The critic Liz Rosenberg, writing for the *New York Times Book Review* called Ondaatje "an oddity—a passionate intellect—and his book is alternatingly exasperating and beautiful."

Now in his forties and still teaching at Glendon College, Ondaatje returned to the quasi-novel format with the 1987 work *In the Skin of a Lion.* To construct a plot about the life of a young man coming of age in Toronto during the 1920s and 1930s, the author built upon the facts of a real-life incident from that time—the mysterious disappearance of a well-known millionaire. The novel is as much about the search for the missing tycoon, the hero's involvement in the potentially lucrative quest, and his ensuing mix-up in radical politics of the era, as it is about Toronto's immigrant communities and their role in building the city. Its focal point is an actual viaduct at Bloor Street that was indeed constructed by laborers who spoke a polyglot of languages. *In the Skin of a Lion* was adapted into a play staged that same year. A *Times Literary Supplement* reviewer, Michael Hulse, compared Ondaatje's achievement in painting a portrait of a growing city to that of James Joyce's *Dubliners* or Alfred Doeblin's *Berlin Alexanderplatz.* Hulse commended the way by which Ondaatje mixed "psychological sensitivity and physical sensuality with a meticulous fidelity to factual detail," and termed it "his most ambitious work to date."

The English Patient

Ondaatje became a household name, however, with the 1996 film adaptation of his 1992 novel *The English Patient.* Set in a Tuscan villa at the end of World War II, the story took Ondaatje eight years to write. It begins with a Canadian nurse, Hana—in time, the reader learns she is the daughter of the protagonist of *In the Skin of the Lion* —who is left almost alone in a bombed-out former convent. She has stayed behind at the former military hospital with a badly burned patient who has been brought there to pass his remaining days. Nameless, he was rescued from an air crash in the North African desert, and appears to be English. Hana reads to him, gives him morphine, and ministers to his charred skin. "Hipbones of Christ, she thinks. He is her despairing saint," Ondaatje writes of Hana, who is washing the body. "He lies flat on his back, no pillow, looking up at the foliage painted onto the ceiling, its canopy of branches, and above that, blue sky."

Ondaatje introduces two other characters into the novel—one, a Canadian who has spied for the Allies and lost his thumbs for it, and a Sikh Indian who is a "sapper," or bomb disposal expert. The Canadian ascertains that the "English patient" is actually a Hungarian noble and one-time Nazi spy. Through the course of the novel, the quartet of characters recount their pasts, all of which are emotionally wrenching. "Isolated together, they invent for a brief while an improbable and delightful and fearful civilization of their own, a zone of fragile intimacy and understanding that can't—of course—survive," wrote Lorna Sage in a *Times Literary Supplement* review. The novel concludes as the characters learn that an atomic bomb has been dropped on Japan, a betrayal that Kip, the Indian bomb-defuser, feels more keenly than the others: he spent years working in the rubble of London and the minefields of Tuscany in the service of the West, who in turn use their technological "superiority" to annihilate an Asian nation.

The screen version of *The English Patient* was adapted from the novel by director Anthony Minghella and won the Academy Award for Best Picture of 1996. Ondaatje's novel version was awarded Britain's top literary honor, the Booker Prize, in 1992.

Further Reading

Contemporary Literary Criticism, Gale, Volume 14, 1980, Volume 29, 1984, Volume 51, 1989, Volume 76, 1993.
Contemporary Poets, Gale, 1985.
Dictionary of Literary Biography, Volume 60: *Canadian Writers since 1960,* Gale, 1987.
Canadian Literature, summer, 1977.
New York Times Book Review, December 22, 1985.
Times Literary Supplement, September 4, 1987; September 11, 1992.

P

Itzhak Perlman

Itzhak Perlman (born 1945) is accepted and celebrated by many as one of the greatest classical violinists of the twentieth century. Overcoming polio and its crippling effects, Perlman was a distinguished musician in his native Israel prior to entering his teens. He travels around the world performing and teaming with other great musicians and he has brought a new style, individuality and technical ability to classical music and the violin.

Itzhak Perlman was born on August 31, 1945 in Tel Aviv, then the largest city in Palestine (a few years later it became the nation of Israel) to Chaim and Shoshana Perlman. His parents, both natives of Poland, had immigrated to Palestine in the mid-1930s before meeting and marrying. Perlman had wanted to be a violinist after hearing a concert performed on the radio when he was a mere three-years-old. His father worked as a barber and bought his young son his first violin from a second-hand shop shortly thereafter for approximately six dollars. Perlman practiced intensely every day before facing one of is toughest challenges.

When Perlman was four-years-old, he was stricken with polio, which would forever leave him disabled. He continued to practice for the full year it took for him to recover and was soon able to walk using the aid of leg braces and crutches. Upon being released from the hospital, Perlman enrolled at the Tel Aviv Academy of Music where he studied under the famed Madame Rivka Goldart on a scholarship from the American-Israeli Cultural Foundation.

By the time he was seven-years-old, he was making regular appearances with the Ramat-Gan Orchestra in Tel Aviv and the Broadcasting Orchestra in Jerusalem, Israel. In 1955, at the age of ten, he gave his first solo recital and was widely considered a music prodigy in Israel.

Moves To America

In 1958, at the age of 13, Perlman was brought to New York City, by the Columbia Broadcasting Corporation's (CBS) *Ed Sullivan Show* for two performances during the show's "Cavalcade of Stars." His rendition of Rimsky-Korsakov's *Flight of the Bumblebee* and Wieniawski's *Polonaise Brillante* made Perlman a star in America and he soon decided to stay for good. After being joined by his parents, Perlman toured American and Canadian cities performing under the sponsorship of the Zionist Organization of America which soon aided Perlman in gaining admission into the famed Juilliard School of Music in New York City. Perlman, under a special arrangement with the New York City board of education, finished his secondary education during his five years in Juilliard's preparatory division. He then enrolled in their regular division studying under Ivan Galamian and Dorothy Delay and would eventually earn a diploma.

On March 5, 1963, Perlman made his Carnegie Hall debut in New York City with Wieniawski's *Violin Concerto No. 1 in F Sharp Minor.* New York City was in the midst of a newspaper strike and the concert received no coverage, but Perlman came to the attention of famed violinists Zino Francescatti, Isaac Stern and Yehudi Menuhin. Stern introduced Perlman to impresario Sol Hurok, who would manage his career.

On April 21, 1964, Perlman won the 23rd-annual Edgar M. Leventritt Foundation competition at Carnegie

318

In 1965 and 1966, Perlman performed in 30 cities during his first major concert tour of America. In Chicago, his performance was so compelling that the *Chicago Daily News* stated "It was possible to imagine that Itzhak Perlman was born with a violin protruding from his left clavicle and never had to learn to play it, and more than he had to learn to breathe." In February of 1966, he played again with the National Symphony Orchestra. His performance of Karl Goldmark's *Violin Concerto in A Minor* at the Philharmonic Hall left the crowd breathless both there and at Toronto's Massey Hall, where he played Paganini and Prokofiev a few days later with the Toronto Symphony under Seiji Ozawa.

Marathon Touring

In 1967 and 1968, Perlman went even further with performances in 50 American cities and trips abroad. The highlight of the 1967 tour was his Honolulu, Hawaii, performance of Stravinsky's rare *Violin Concerto* with the composer himself conducting. Perlman would go on to rack up performances in Philadelphia and Pittsburgh, Pennsylvania; Los Angeles, California; Portland, Oregon; Denver, Colorado; Dallas, Texas and Kalamazoo, Michigan in 1967 before moving on to hugely-attended shows at the Berkshire Music Festival in Tanglewood, Massachusetts, the Hollywood Bowl in Hollywood, California, the Merriweather Post Pavilion in Washington, D.C. and the Ravina Festival in Chicago, Illinois.

Earlier that year, on January 5, 1967, Perlman married Toby Lynn Friedlander, a native New Yorker and fellow Juilliard violinist he met in 1964 while performing at a summer camp concert. In 1968, Perlman performed in Portugal, Italy, Scotland, England, France, Sweden, The Netherlands, Switzerland and Israel. The constant touring and his exceptional performances quickly made Perlman one of the most-recognized classical musicians in the world.

Individualized Music

Hoping to individualize his performances and make them more challenging to perform, in April of 1969, Perlman gave a special interpretative performance of Paganini's *Violin Concerto No. 1 in D* in New York City. This performance, as well as other such performances, set Perlman apart from other musicians of renown as one that not only could play technically well, but could also change arrangements to make them fit the performer instead of the other way around.

His 1970 performances included stops in Toronto and Stratford, Ontario and a special performance in Washington, D.C. alongside conductor George Szell. His constant search for new or rare works to perform led him to a 1971 performance of Dvorak's *Violin Concerto* in Washington, D.C. and New York City. A performance of Alban Berg's *Violin Concerto* in New York City over the summer of that year garnered him even more renown as an individually-minded classical musician.

In 1972, Perlman performed in England and Israel along with performances in New York City and at the Kennedy Center Concert Hall in Washington, D.C. In 1973,

Hall in New York City. He was the youngest of the 19 contestants and performed Bach, Mozart, Tchaikovsky and Wieniawski compositions before an all-star panel of judges. This is the same music competition that helped launch the careers of popular classical musicians such as Van Cliburn and Pinchas Zukerman, and Perlman would be the next name on that list of great musicians.

Performs Around the World

The Edgar M. Leventritt Foundation competition is one of the most prestigious and demanding international musical competitions and Perlman's winning of its Memorial Award, and the $1,000 that went along with it, guaranteed him solo appearances all over the nation. In 1964 and 1965, he traveled to Cleveland, Ohio; Detroit, Michigan; Pittsburgh, Pennsylvania; Denver, Colorado; Buffalo, New York and New Haven, Connecticut performing for sold-out crowds.

In 1964, Perlman performed twice again for CBS's *Ed Sullivan Show* before traveling to Washington, DC to perform Tchaikovsky's *Violin Concerto* alongside the National Symphony Orchestra. In October of that year he repeated this performance alongside the Israel National Youth Symphony before traveling back to his birthplace in January of 1965 for the first time since 1958. Perlman performed eight concerts throughout Israel and culminated with a performance of Tchaikovsky pieces at the Mann Auditorium in Tel Aviv for which he received a 15-minute ovation.

despite a telephone death threat called in to him at the theater, Perlman performed flawlessly at New York's Museum of Modern Art. In 1974, Perlman performed in New York City with the Baltimore, Maryland and Philadelphia, Pennsylvania orchestras and gave two Carnegie Hall chamber music concerts with Isaac Stern. He also continued his large-scale touring with extensive performance dates in both Canada and the United States.

On January 30, 1975, Perlman gave a performance of *Chiaroscuro,* a piece that had been specially composed for him by Robert Mann, at Carnegie Hall in New York City. His performance was widely hailed and the *New York Times* wrote that Perlman "now has taken the quantum leap into a tiny group of artists—the names of Rubinstein and Segovia come most quickly to mind—who make audiences fall deeply in love with them."

After 1975, Perlman would perform all of his 100-plus annual concerts with a $60,000 Stradivarius violin he discovered after a comprehensive search. A fan of other genres of music, in 1975 Perlman and Andre Previn released an album of Scot Joplin ragtime compositions on Angel Records. This was not Perlman's first album, he had been recording standard classical arrangements for the RCA Victor and London Records labels since his earliest days following his win at the Edgar M. Leventritt Foundation competition.

In 1986, Perlman was awarded the Medal of Liberty for his efforts in promoting classical music across international boundaries. As a result of this touring, Perlman has played with almost every symphony orchestra in the world. He has also been awarded honorary degrees from Yale, Harvard and Brandeis Universities as well as one from Hebrew University in Jerusalem, Israel.

Perlman lives in New York City with his wife and their five children. He continues to tour extensively and, in 1998, toured in the United States and Japan as well as performing for Public Broadcasting System (PBS) classical music television specials. In 1975, he started teaching private students and also participates in the Aspen Music Festival in Colorado. He continues to amaze audiences and other artists alike continually improving his technical ability and changing his style to best fit his individuality to remain the "fiddler's fiddler."

Further Reading

Schwarz, Boris, *Great Masters of the Violin,* Simon and Schuster, 1987.
Billboard, September 28, 1996.
Chicago Daily News, November 29, 1965.
Esquire, June, 1968.
Glamour, March 1987.
Houston Post, January 9, 1989.
New York Times, March 8, 1970; February 1, 1975.
Newsweek, April 14, 1980.
People, May 26, 1980; June 8, 1981; August 11, 1997.
Seattle Times, October 21, 1988.
Time, January 15, 1965.
"Classics World Biography - Itzhak Perlman," *BMG Classics,* http://classicalmus.com/composers/perlman.html (May 7, 1998).

Jacques Piccard

One of a remarkable family of record-setting explorer/scientists, Jacques Piccard (born 1922) is one of the fathers of marine exploration and a pioneer of ocean engineering.

E xplorer Jacques Piccard comes from a family known for their daring achievements and has added to the family name through his own record-setting feats. In 1960, Piccard and a co-pilot took a vessel developed by Piccard's father to the deepest spot on earth, the Marianas Trench in the western Pacific, in a record seven-mile descent that has never been duplicated. He then went on to develop other submarines for research, salvage, and recreation. The Piccard family has the unique distinction of having made both the highest flight and the deepest dive of all time.

Jacques Ernest Jean Piccard was born July 28, 1922, in Brussels, Belgium. His career as an ocean engineer and explorer began with the aeronautical exploits of his father, Auguste, a physicist who became interested in balloons as a way of studying cosmic rays in the upper atmosphere. In 1931, Auguste reached a record altitude of 50,000 feet in a balloon equipped with the first pressurized cabin, becoming the first person to reach the stratosphere and return safely. Having developed a method for surviving the low pressures of the upper atmosphere, Auguste Piccard then turned to inventing a submersible device for withstanding the immense pressures of the deep ocean. The result was a bathyscaphe, a balloon-like vessel which used the same principles of buoyancy that governed balloon flight. On descent, lighter-than-water gasoline from an external flotation tank was released and replaced with seawater, which provided enough negative buoyancy to sink the vessel. To ascend, heavy ballast was released from the ballast tanks. The bathyscaphe was in effect a pressurized diving bell which was towed to its destination and then dropped.

Jacques Piccard began studying economics at the University of Geneva in 1943 but interrupted his studies to serve in the French First Army during World War II. He then taught at the University of Geneva while continuing to help his father improve the bathyscaphe and demonstrate its potential for operating in deep waters. The first working model was built with money from a Belgian scientific foundation in 1948. After a successful unmanned trial descent to 4,600 feet, it was damaged in heavy seas and had to be redesigned. Another was built in 1953 and purchased by the French Navy. At the request of the city of Trieste, Italy, a third vessel was built in 1954 and taken by the Piccards to a record depth of 10, 355 feet in the Mediterranean off the island of Ponza, Italy. With this success, the younger Piccard abandoned economics to collaborate with his father on further improving the bathyscaphe and demonstrating its practicality for exploration and research.

In 1956, Piccard sought outside financial support from the U.S. Navy, which was exploring the potential uses of submersibles like the bathyscaphe in underwater research.

Jacques Piccard (right)

He was invited to bring the vessel, now named *Trieste,* to San Diego to work with scientists there on the biological and acoustical properties of deep scattering layers, areas of sound reflection that seemed to vary at different depths and in different lighting conditions. Two years later, the Navy bought the vessel and hired Piccard as a consultant. Recognizing the strategic value of a workable submersible for submarine salvage and rescue, the Navy began testing *Trieste* at greater and greater depths. In her first 17 months as a naval vessel, the *Trieste* made 22 descents and broke three depth records.

Following a successful descent to 24,000 feet, Piccard and his colleagues planned an even greater challenge—a voyage to the bottom of the sea. Early on January 23, 1960, Piccard and Lt. Don Walsh, a submarine officer, boarded the vessel in rough seas near Guam and began a descent to 36,000 feet in a chasm of the Marianas Trench known as Challenger Deep. The bathyscaphe carried no equipment and planned no experiments; the mission's purpose was merely to prove that the depth could be reached. The descent progressed without incident until 30,000 feet, when the crew heard a loud crack. They continued the dive, however, finally touching down in "snuff-colored ooze" at 35,800 feet. To Walsh, the experience was like "being in a big bowl of milk."

When they finally settled on the featureless seabed, they saw a flat fish as well as a new type of shrimp. Marine biologists later disputed their observations, claiming that no fish could survive the 17,000 psi pressure at such depths. After discovering cracks in the viewing windows, Piccard cut the voyage short. After a 20-minute stay on the bottom, they began dumping ballast for their return to the surface, and the damaged vessel returned to its escort ships without incident.

The historic dive received worldwide attention, and Piccard wrote an account of it, *Seven Miles Down,* with Robert Deitz, a renowned geologist who had help plan the mission. A planned return expedition, however, never occurred. The *Trieste* was expensive to maintain and operate. It was incapable of collecting samples and could not take photographs and so had little scientific data to show for its voyages. The original vessel was retired in 1961, although a rebuilt version later located the lost remains of two lost nuclear submarines, *Thresher* and *Scorpion.*

Following the success of the bathyscaphe, Auguste and Jacques then began developing a "mesoscaphe"—a ship that could operate at depths of up to 2,000 feet. Piccard envisioned it as a tourist submarine, and the first mesoscaphe, *Auguste Piccard,* carried more than 30,000 passengers into Lake Geneva at the Swiss National Exhibition in 1964-65. Working with the Woods Hole Oceanographic Institution, Piccard then developed a second vessel, the *Ben Franklin,* for the Gulf Stream Mission, which studied the physical and biological features of the Gulf Stream on its month-long voyage from Florida to Nova Scotia in 1969. His account of that voyage was published in *The Sun Beneath the Sea.*

During the 1970's, Piccard formed the Foundation for the Study and Preservation of Seas and Lakes and began warning about the dangers of pollution and overfishing. His new submersibles included *Forel,* launched in 1979, which made more than 700 dives in European lakes for scientific, industrial, and recovery missions. Although he continued his research for governments, universities, and the police, his efforts in later years included developing passenger vessels. He developed more than 40 innovative designs for commercial sightseeing submersibles, of which half a dozen were built. Piccard also became a founder of the Exploration Society of America, an international travel group.

Piccard wrote in 1961: "That man is headed for ultimate adventure at the basement of earth, there is no doubt at all." Today he acknowledges that he expected too much in the 1960's. Political attention and funding were soon diverted from ocean exploration to the space race, and the benefits of deep-sea expeditions were not believed to offset their enormous costs. He remains optimistic, however, that a new generation of deep-sea exploration technology may enable humans to return to the Challenger Deep: "We opened the door, and now we must go and see what's behind the door." The Japanese unmanned submersible Kaiko approached Piccard's depth record in another part of the Marianas Trench in 1995, and several international efforts are in progress to take innovative new manned craft to the Challenger Deep before the end of the century.

Piccard continues to develop and build submersibles, partly as a way of increasing awareness of environmental threats to the world's seas. "For me," he says, " the more people discover the sea, the greater the chance of bringing marine issues into public view and the better off we will all be." In 1996, he expressed a concern that the sea is now severely endangered and can only be saved by widescale changes in attitudes toward overfishing and pollution. Meanwhile, the Piccard family legacy of adventure and exploration is being continued by his son Bertrand, who received international attention in 1997-98 for his participation in several team attempts to circle the globe by balloon. The family was also featured in a 1997 public television series, "The Adventurers." Piccard lives in Cully, Switzerland.

Further Reading

Baker, Daniel B., editor, *Explorers and Discovers of the World,* Gale, 1993.

Piccard, Jacques, and Robert Dietz, *Seven Miles Down: The Story of the Bathyscaphe Trieste,* Putnam, 1961.

Piccard, Jacques, *The Sun Beneath the Sea,* Scribner, 1971.

Japan 21st, October 1996.

Los Angeles Times, October 22, 1989.

National Geographic, July 1960.

New York Times, August 20, 1969; June 17, 1971; June 23, 1991.

Newsweek, July 5, 1993.

Oceanus, winter 1988-89.

San Diego Tribune, May 19, 1984.

San Francisco Chronicle, November 12, 1995.

Time, August 14, 1995.

Times Newspapers, June 14, 1990.

"The Piccards: To the Ends of the Earth," *The Adventurers,* http://www.pbsonline.org (March 24, 1998).

"The Abyss," *Dateline,* NBC News Transcripts, September 12, 1997.

"Deep Flight: What Is It?," http://www.deepflight.com (March 23, 1998).

"RV Trieste," *Historic Naval Ships Visitors Guide,* http://www.maritime.org (March 27, 1998). □

Arthur Wing Pinero

Though English writer Arthur Wing Pinero (1855-1934) was an extremely successful playwright of his era, a century later his body of work was known almost only in the literary histories of his craft. Pinero first rose to prominence in the 1880s with the comedies, farces, and, later, serious dramas he wrote for the London stage, many of which exposed contemporary social ills and attracted not a small degree of scandal as a result.

Arthur Wing Pinero was born into a fairly well-to-do family of Portuguese heritage in London in 1855. Both his grandfather and father were solicitors, or lawyers, and it was expected that he, too, would enter the

firm as a young man. As preparation, he began working there when he was just ten. It was a job the young Pinero grew to dislike, and it strengthened his desire to avoid its more permanent chains. An avid theatergoer as a teen, Pinero dreamed instead of a career on the stage. At the age of 15, he enrolled in London's Birkbeck Literary and Scientific Institution to study elocution. For four years from 1870 to 1874, he trained in stagecraft there; the classes staged their own plays as part of the curriculum, and even made tours of several English cities.

Rejected an Assured Future

In 1874, the 19-year-old Pinero joined the Theatre Royal Company in Edinburgh, Scotland. He was a minor player, appearing in its repertoire of classic and contemporary plays that ranged from Shakespeare to Edward Bulwer Lytton. After a fire gutted the venue, he obtained a similar post, called a "utility actor," in the Royal Alexandra Theatre in Liverpool, and through his work there came to the attention of an influential name in London theatrical circles, the actor and agent Henry Irving. By this time Pinero had forever quit the law, and with Irving's good word won a role in a London production, which led to a place with the Lyceum Theatre in 1876.

Perhaps realizing his limitations as an actor and foreseeing a more rewarding career on the other side of the curtain, Pinero had begun to write short plays for the stage. These were one-acts, called "curtain-raisers," and his production, *Two Hundred a Year,* premiered at London's Globe Theatre on October 6, 1877. Its plot and setting

would characterize much of Pinero's later body of work: romantic relationships among well-to-do middle- to upper-class scions of Victorian England. In *Two Hundred a Year,* the male protagonist needs to find a well-heeled wife to support him; the woman who chooses him, on the other hand, does so because she wishes to have a man at her mercy.

Skewered Hypocrisy of Victorian Era

Over the next few years, until he quit the stage permanently in 1885, Pinero belonged to the ranks of respected London actors—he had departed the Lyceum in 1881 to join the Haymarket Theatre—and devoted much of his spare energy into writing the curtain-raisers and seeing them into production. He often acted in them as well. The staging of one of these early works, *Daisy's Escape* in September of 1879, was responsible for introducing Pinero to his future wife, Myra Moore, whom he married in 1883. As a playwright, Pinero expressed some decidedly progressive attitudes about women and the difficult burdens that society, religion, and economics placed upon them. His male leads were often overshadowed by intelligent, witty women, and his plot structures usually revolved around a woman who was constrained by the strict morals of the Victorian era and the all-important need to maintain her "respectability." Pinero was also fond of turning the traditional symbols of "decency," such as the exalted war hero, into comic figures.

Pinero's first full-length comedy, *The Squire,* was produced at St. James's Theatre in 1881. The male lead, Thorndyke, is a rake who desires to find a woman who will support him; Kate Verity is a liberated character who runs her own farm—a radical means of self-sufficiency for a woman. Their eventual marriage remains a secret to the world. When Kate becomes pregnant, however, a woman claiming to be Thorndyke's wife appears; in the end, the bigamy is but a misunderstanding, and he retains a degree of dignity when it comes to accepting his wife's largesse. The work was the controversy of the London season, however, for Pinero was accused of pilfering its plot from Thomas Hardy's *Far from the Madding Crowd* of the previous decade. The scandal worked to *The Squire*'s advantage, though, and the play enjoyed a successful run.

Pinero was soon a popular and critically-acclaimed dramaturge. He often directed many of his own plays, and was known for exhibiting lawyer's attention to detail. A number of his works—*The Magistrate* (1885), *The Schoolmistress* (1886), and *Dandy Dick* (1887) in particular—enjoyed long and successful runs. Like many of his plays during this era, they mirrored a popular form of stagewriting known as the *piece bien faite,* French for "well-made play." These were usually spirited comedies that relied on a tangled, though decisively resolved, plot structure. *The Schoolmistress* features a heroine who leads a double life as a proper Victorian woman by day as director of a girls' finishing school, but supports her wastrel husband by working as an actress in the evening. *Dandy Dick* concerns a man of the cloth who becomes addicted to racetrack gambling. Martin Banham, writing in the *International Dic-*

tionary of Theatre, singled these plays out as "brilliant examples of their craft . . . all powered by plots of splendid English dottiness, which gives them a style and eccentric verve that distinguishes them" from their French counterparts.

Pinero credited another English dramatist whose career preceded his own, Tom Robertson, as a much greater influence on his writing than the French comedies. Robertson had introduced more realistic sets and abandoned conventional dramatic devices, such as the soliloquy and the aside, in his successful works, and Pinero carried on these innovations in his own work. He paid homage to Robertson in the 1898 work *Trelawny of the "Wells."* This and other works featured trademarks of Pinero's style, with their colloquial dialogue and reliance on the talents of a well-rehearsed ensemble, rather than the imposing presence of a well-known star.

The Second Mrs. Tanqueray

Pinero began to move away from the light fare of the *piece bien faite* around 1889, and evidence of his more serious approach came with the *The Profligate,* which debuted at London's Garrick Theatre in April of that year. The play featured a corrupt protagonist and charted his sad decline, and though the production ran for a 129 performances it was not considered a success. He enjoyed better luck with *The Second Mrs. Tanqueray,* which debuted at London's St. James's Theatre in May of 1893. The production ran for 225 performances, and critics started to hail Pinero the best English playwright in two hundred years; the play also made a star of its lead actress, Mrs. Patrick Campbell.

The plot of the *The Second Mrs. Tanqueray* was considered somewhat risqué in its day—Paula Tanqueray's less-than-virtuous past comes to light when her new stepdaughter becomes engaged to one of her former beaus. The revelation shakes her marriage to the well-to-do, respectable George Tanqueray. She faces public disgrace and, in the end, commits suicide; meanwhile, Pinero's male characters face no such censure or scorn as a result of their affairs. Because of the finale, later critics would condemn Pinero—they pointed out that Paula Tanqueray and other heroines always seemed to suffer in the end, accepting punishment for their ways. Other reviewers contended this was the playwright's way of first shocking, then playing into the moral attitudes of the era. Yet in the *Dictionary of Literary Biography,* the critic J. P. Wearing wrote of *The Second Mrs. Tanqueray* and its relevance: "If the play seems tame to modern viewers, it should be remembered that Pinero managed to induce society audiences to watch a play which condemned the hypocrisy of which they were culpable."

Changing Times

These and other mid-career works put Pinero in line with other contemporary dramatists writing for the European stage, such as Henrik Ibsen, Gerhart Hauptmann, and Maurice Maeterlinck. Many of Pinero's works seemed especially comparable to Ibsen, for they dramatized contemporary social ills within their plots. Victorian society's double standard was incriminated by Pinero's pen in other works, including *The Notorious Mrs. Ebbsmith* (1895), *Iris* (1901), *Letty* (1903), and *His House in Order* (1906). This latter work is a *Rebecca*-like tale about a new wife haunted by the reputation of her predecessor, a supposedly good-hearted, virtuous woman; then it is discovered that the first wife had carried on an affair under her husband's nose for years.

Pinero was knighted in 1909—only a few years after his fiftieth birthday—and was an important figure in the London theater world. He served as secretary and provident of the Benevolent Fund for Actors, chaired the Royal General Theatrical Fund, acted as an examiner at his alma mater, which became Birkbeck College and part of the University of London, and sat on the Council of the Royal Academy of Dramatic Arts for 20 years. During World War I he chaired the First Battalion of the United Arts Rifles of the volunteer Central London Regiment. He found less success with his later plays, however: after the war, popular tastes ran to the vulgar, and his works were suddenly out of step. Pinero died on November 23, 1934, after emergency surgery. His manuscripts and letters are housed in the British Library, the University of Texas at Austin, and several other British and North American repositories.

Further Reading

Contemporary Authors, Volume 153, Gale, 1997.
Dawick, John, *Pinero: A Theatrical Life,* University Press of Colorado, 1993.
Dictionary of Literary Biography, Volume 10: *Modern British Dramatists, 1900-1945,* Gale, 1982.
Dunkel, Wilbur Dwight, *Sir Arthur Pinero; A Critical Biography with Letters,* Kennikat Press, 1967.
International Dictionary of Theatre, Volume 2: *Playwrights,* St. James Press, 1994.
Lazenby, Walter, *Arthur Wing Pinero,* Twayne, 1972.

Christian de Portzamparc

In 1994, Christian de Portzamparc (born 1944) became the first French architect to receive the prestigious Pritzker Prize, architecture's equivalent to the Nobel Prize. This honor placed Portzamparc's name among the ranks of some of the world's most renowned practitioners in his field.

Though he belongs to a younger, postwar generation of design philosophers, he has won acclaim for a style that melds centuries-old classical forms, modernist radicalism, and postmodern quirkiness. "My point of view can be summed up by Lao-Tzu," Portzamparc explained to *Artforum'* s Lauren Sedofsky. "My house is not the wall, or the floor, or the roof, but the emptiness between."

Christian de Portzamparc was born in Casablanca, Morocco in 1944, into a family of French Breton heritage. He attended the Ecole Nationale Superieure des Beaux-Arts in Paris from 1962 to 1969, a traditionalist school where he studied architecture, and spent a year at Columbia University in 1966. He opened his architectural firm in Paris in 1970. Over the next few years, France and French culture underwent major social upheavals, much of which either had given cause to or was the result of the student riots and national strikes in 1968.

Trod New Ground

As a result, most architects of Portzamparc's generation veered to a more radical, leftist philosophy, and among them some had even began to believe that architecture could not be an mechanism for social revolution at all, that it was an inherently bourgeois art. Portzamparc's philosophy is a realistic merging of pragmatism and politics. "Architects participate in the positive construction of the world," Portzamparc told *Artforum'* s Sedofsky. "Once you have a program to realize, you participate in a society that implicitly recognizes the power that organizes it, the power that governs it. You have to take responsibility for this 'constructive' aspect, to dirty your hands in making the world and impacting on the quantity of order or disorder."

Grounded by just such ideas, within a short span of years Portzamparc was winning acclaim for his designs. In 1975 he was commissioned by the French New Architectural Program, and received accolades for his ballet school in Nanterre, France, which opened in 1987. It featured rehearsal studios, a performance hall, video library, dance club, and residence hall for students. He also designed the Cafe Beaubourg, opposite the famed Centre National d'Art et de Culture Georges-Pompidou, which houses the country's stellar collection of modern art and also goes by the name the Palais Beaubourg. His patron for the project was Gilbert Costes, who was embroiled in a rivalry with his brother. The sibling had hired another famed French architect, Philippe Starck, to design to Cafe Costes not far away from the Beaubourg, and both became 1980s-era hangouts for an arty, intellectual crowd. In the end, however, Cafe Beaubourg's design—in part done with Portzamparc's wife, Elizabeth Jardim Neves—emerged the victor when Cafe Costes became a clothing boutique.

Acclaimed Public Housing

Another work that vaulted Portzamparc to the attention of the international design community was his 1979 Rue des Hautes-Formes housing project, near the Rue Nationale in the southeast section of Paris. Its phases included a redesign for what had been typical block-style government-subsidized housing, a depressing, fortress-like space. One of the changes Portzamparc made was to add balconies and awnings to each apartment. "I shall never forget the happy faces of the first people to move into the rue des Hautes-Formes," Portzamparc told Marie Christine Loriers in the Dutch architectural magazine *Archis.*

Later Portzamparc won a commission to add to the complex, and constructed new low-rise residences on the Rue Nationale, adjacent to a new school and community center which he also designed. He united the space with an arch for its entrance-way, and revamped the roofs that oversee the central courtyard to redirect sunlight on the space onto which the apartments overlook. All of the new elements, wrote Herbert Muschamp in the *New York Times,* "give the place the serenity of an enclave without disconnecting it from the city outside."

Cite de la Musique

In 1983 Portzamparc took first prize in the French government's "Grand Projets" competition for a cultural complex to be located in northeast Paris. The Grand Projets, or Grand Travaux, were a planned series of massive architectural public works, similar to imperial building projects in past centuries. The concept became the cultural beacon of the Socialist presidency of Francois Mitterand, elected in 1981, who with state funding launched and shepherded them to creation before leaving office in 1995. Among the other Grand Travaux were a new opera house at the Bastille and a controversial national library. Portzamparc's design was chosen for the Cite de la Musique, a complex situated in Paris's Parc de la Villette in what was once a meatpacking district. For this, Portzamparc designed two concert halls, administrative offices, a museum for France's collection of 4000-plus instruments, and dormitories for students at the National Conservatory of Music and Dance.

The $120 million Cite project was started in 1984 and opened in successive phases though 1995, and unlike some of the Grand Travaux, was hailed as a success. Portzamparc's National Conservatory, for instance, featured an elliptical concert hall, spiral lobby, and other unusual design elements that reflect the architect's fascination with blending historical and futurist forms. Elsewhere, a smaller organ recital "hall's design fuses intimacy with grandeur," wrote Muschamp of the *New York Times.* "The ceiling, a soaring yellow cone paneled with wooden acoustical baffles, holds players and listeners within one radiant embrace, conferring a sense of ritual at once familiar and urbane." Muschamp was in the hall during an informal rehearsal that day, and wrote it was not just the string quartet's arrangement he sensed—"it was the sound of a city that has sheltered civilization for centuries, rehearsing to pass it on."

In Tune With Asian Aesthetics

Portzamparc's particular reliance on space and light as integral design elements has won him prized commissions in Asia. These have included the National Museum of Korea in Seoul, and a 1991 apartment complex in Fukuoka, Japan. This latter project is remarkable for the way in which Portzamparc linked the buildings together with bridges and canals. He has also designed the bank offices of Credit Lyonnais in Lille, France—a skyscraper built above a railroad station—and was the architect of New York City's LVMH Tower. For this skyscraper—which serves as offices for the luxury-goods cartel Louis Vuitton-Moet Chandon-Hennessy—Portzamparc explained to Sedofsky in *Artforum* that "what was requested was a building that differed as much as possible from the Chanel building next door."

For such works Portzamparc has won several honors in his field, including being made a Commandeur de L'Ordre des Arts et des Lettres in 1989. In 1990 he and two other prominent French architects, Philippe Stack and Jean

Nouvel, were selected for the French pavilion at the Venice Biennale, a space customarily given to esteemed visual artists who work within more accessible mediums of paint or clay. That same year he also won the Grand Prix d'Architecture de la Ville de Paris, and in 1993 he was honored with a medal from the French Academy of Architecture.

The Pritzker

Such awards and prestigious commissions are dwarfed, however, by Portzamparc's achievement in being selected as the Pritzker Laureate for 1994. The esteemed Pritzker Prize for Architecture, with its $100,000 purse, is bestowed by the foundation started by Chicago's Pritzker family of the Hyatt Hotels chain. It was created in part because of the absence of architecture as a "field of endeavor" category in the Nobel Prizes. Past Pritzker recipients include Phillip Johnson, I. M. Pei, Frank Gehry, Aldo Rossi, and Robert Venturi. Portzamparc won out over an entry list of 500 similarly acclaimed nominees to become the first architect of the postwar generation to win the honor. He learned the news on his fiftieth birthday, for which his wife had planned a surprise party at the Cafe Beaubourg. Instead of an intimate gathering of friends and family, France's Minister of Culture showed up and the attendees sang "the first French Pritzker" to the tune of "Happy Birthday."

The Pritzker jury called him "a powerful poet of forms ... who is aware of the past, but true to himself and his time," according to *Architecture.* Another design magazine, *Graphis,* quoted Pritzker panelist Ada Louise Huxtable's assessment—she termed Portzamparc's style "a joyful architecture which leaves the rigidity of modernism and the cartoonish decoration of post-modernism far behind." Portzamparc has also won the Equerre d'Argent award twice, and in 1996 France's Centre Pompidou hosted a retrospective of Portzamparc's work.

Reality to Form, Forethought to Future

Portzamparc continued to win prestigious, historically significant commissions. One of these was a new French Embassy to Germany, constructed in the newly reunited country's redesignated capital of Berlin. Situated at the formerly unremarkable Pariser Platz, Portzamparc's diplomatic headquarters stands opposite both the American and British embassies, a symbolic nod to the post-World War II nations who occupied a divided West Germany and three-quarters of a divided Berlin before the fall of the Berlin Wall in 1989. The Embassy, also near the celebrated Hotel Adlon, is slated to open in 2000 along with several other noteworthy structures in the revitalized city.

Portzamparc is the author of two books, 1983's *La Spatialite n'est plus interdite* ("Spatiality Is No Longer Prohibited") and *Genealogies des Formes/Genealogy of Forms,* a bilingual work published in 1997. He lives in Paris with his wife and two sons, keeps his office in the Montparnasse neighborhood, and continues to use his own unique language of forms to conceptualize his designs. "I'm moving toward the moment when we'll be able to quit Cartesian coordinates," Portzamparc told *Artforum*'s Sedofsky, referring to the centuries-old mathematical system of using *x* and *y* axes to represent spatial relationships. ''The ellipse is an extremely subtle form, with two axes, the perception of which changes your position. We haven't lived much in ellipses.''

Further Reading

Amsoneit, Wolfgang, *Contemporary European Architects,* Benedikt Taschen, 1991.
Archis, May 1996.
Architectural Record, March 1995, p. 13.
Architecture, June 1994, p. 23.
Art International, summer 1990, p. 87.
Artforum, May 1996.
Graphis, November/December 1994.
Japan Architect, autumn 1991.
New York Review of Books, April 6, 1995, pp. 18-21.
New York Times, June 16, 1994, p. C1.
Opera News, May 1996, p. 23.
Progressive Architecture, July 1987, p. 88.

Beatrix Potter

Beatrix Potter (1866-1943) wrote and illustrated some two dozen children's books that are now considered classics, including *The Tale of Peter Rabbit.*

Although Beatrix Potter's name may not be a household word, that of her first artistic creation, Peter Rabbit, certainly is. An entire industry has sprung up around this beloved character; one can find his image on everything from tea towels to toys. In 1993, when *The Tale of Peter Rabbit* marked the one-hundredth anniversary of its official publication, people around the world commemorated the event with parties and other celebrations. Given their enduring appeal, he and Potter's other memorable animal characters will likely live on for many generations to come.

Helen Beatrix Potter was born on July 28, 1866, in Bolton Gardens, Kensington, England. Her father, Rupert, was a wealthy barrister who derived his most of his fortune (as did his wife's family) from the Lancashire cotton industry. Even though Potter's parents left her mostly in the care of governesses and servants, they nevertheless exerted tight control over her life. She was educated at home and had virtually no contact with other children until her brother, Bertram, was born when she about five. But even he was soon sent to boarding school, which meant that their time together was limited mostly to the summer holidays, which the family typically spent in Scotland or the English Lake District.

Other than her brother, Potter's only friends were her animals. She had a deep interest in and love for all creatures and kept several as pets, including mice, frogs, bats, rabbits, and even a hedgehog. Her strong affinity for animals was not merely sentimental, however; she was a naturalist at heart, with a sharp eye for scientific detail. She enjoyed exploring the outdoors, especially during the summer when she and Bertram had the rare opportunity to roam around in relative freedom.

Artistic Bent Revealed in Childhood

Potter also displayed an early talent for drawing. Her own pets as well as the animals she discovered while on vacation were often the subjects of her illustrations. Her governesses encouraged her to practice her drawing, as did her parents, who harbored an interest in art and sometimes allowed their daughter to accompany them to exhibitions.

Another interest of Potter's was science, especially mycology, the study of fungi. The British Museum of Natural History was near Potter's house in London, and she spent many hours there learning about various fungi and sketching them. (Fungus-hunting was also one of her favorite summertime activities.) When she was in her late twenties, Potter decided to illustrate a book on fungi and made hundreds of precise drawings based on her observations. Her uncle presented them to the director of the Royal Botanical Gardens on her behalf, but no one took them seriously.

Potter even made an actual scientific discovery and wrote a paper about it entitled ''The Germination of the Spores of Agaricineae'' for the Linnaean Society of London. Since women were not allowed to attend the society's meetings, her uncle appeared before the members and read her paper. The fact that she was a woman and a novice in the field put her at a distinct disadvantage, however, and eventually she gave up any serious attempts to draw or write about fungi.

From the time she was 14 until she was 31, Potter kept a journal that she wrote in secret code. (It was finally decoded by Leslie Linder and published for the first time in 1966 and again in 1989.) The entries show her reluctant acceptance of her parents' dominance over her life during her teens and a gradual build-up of resentment as she moved through her twenties. Bouts of depression and occasionally poor physical health plagued her as well. Despite these obstacles, she was determined to make something of her life, noting in her journal, "I *must* draw, however poor the result. . . . I *will* do something sooner or later."

The year 1890 marked Potter's debut as a published illustrator. Her animal drawings accompanied verses written by Frederic Weatherley in a book entitled *A Happy Pair*. Potter remained virtually anonymous, however, by virtue of the fact that she signed her name simply as "H.B.P."

Peter Rabbit Launched Writing Career

Three years later Potter wrote a letter to five-year-old Noël Moore, the seriously ill son of one of her former governesses. To help cheer him up, Potter included in her letter the story of Peter Rabbit in words and pictures. Friends who saw what she had done encouraged her to turn her ideas into a book.

Unable to find a publisher who would accept her work, Potter had the first version of *The Tale of Peter Rabbit* privately printed in 1900. She had it reprinted in 1902, the same year she arranged for the first private printing of her second book, *The Tailor of Gloucester*.

By this time, Potter had begun to attract some attention in publishing circles. Frederick Warne & Co. offered to publish *The Tale of Peter Rabbit* on the condition that she supply color illustrations. Potter complied, and the book proved to be very successful. As she produced additional titles, her popularity as a children's author grew. Potter maintained her relationship with Frederick Warne & Co. for many years, turning out around two dozen books in all.

Potter's association with Frederick Warne & Co. became personal as well as professional when she became romantically involved with Norman Warne, whose father operated the firm. Much to the chagrin of her domineering parents, she accepted Warne's proposal of marriage in 1905. Sadly, her fiance died of leukemia only a month or so after they announced their wedding plans.

Found Happiness at Hill Top Farm

That same year, Potter bought a farm near the village of Sawrey in the English Lake District, home to some of her fondest childhood memories. She visited the property, which she named "Hill Top," as often as she could given the fact that she still lived with her parents and was subject to their control. Gradually, she was able to spend more and more time there. As a result, the years from 1906 until 1913 marked an especially productive phase of Potter's career.

Among the many classic works she wrote during this period are *The Tale of Jemima Puddle-Duck, The Story of Miss Moppet, The Tale of Mr. Jeremy Fisher, The Tale of Tom Kitten,* and *The Tale of the Flopsy Bunnies.* These charming animal stories were typically written in an unpretentious and often witty style. Sometimes they would take the reader to the edge of something a bit scary or dark, but Potter would always retreat to safety and a happy ending.

In addition to writing and illustrating her books, Potter directed their production and design. She insisted that they be kept small to fit comfortably into a child's hands and that only a few words appear on each page. She also liked to challenge her readers now and then with a surprisingly sophisticated vocabulary in the belief that children delighted in learning new words. Potter took an active interest in the merchandising possibilities of her books as well, pointing out to her publisher the need to copyright her characters and suggesting games and other items that could be based on them.

Gave Up Writing for Farming

During the course of business transactions related to her farm, Potter met a lawyer named William Heelis, whom she married in 1913. Able at last to leave her parents' house, she moved with her new husband to Hill Top, where they lived for several years before buying a large sheep farm in 1923.

Potter's writing career basically ended when she married Heelis and began devoting her time to being a wife and a farmer. As she had noted years before in her journal entry for June 12, 1894, "I hold an old-fashioned notion that a happy marriage is the crown of a woman's life." Although she published a few more books, including *Johnny Town-Mouse,* for which she created new illustrations, her output slowed considerably, especially after she started losing her eyesight in 1918.

By 1930 Potter had given up writing entirely. She was not interested in fame and regarded people who praised her work with suspicion. According to Brian Alderson in his *Times Educational Supplement* review of the book *Beatrix Potter's Letters,* she told journalist John Stone in 1939, "I hate publicity, and I have contrived to survive to be an old woman without it, except in the homey atmosphere of Agricultural Shows."

Indeed, farming took second place only to her marriage once Potter reached her fifties. By the time she was in her sixties, she had become an accomplished sheep breeder, held in high enough esteem by her peers that she was elected president of the Herdwick Sheep-Breeders' Association shortly before her death. Potter was also active with the National Trust and worked to preserve open land for future generations.

Potter died of complications from uterine cancer on December 22, 1943, in Sawrey, England. She bequeathed several thousand acres of land, including Hill Top farm, to the National Trust; her previous Lake District home became a museum. But her true legacy consists of the wonderful stories and illustrations that live on in innumerable ways. In 1988, for example, the Pierpont Morgan Library held an exhibition entitled "Beatrix Potter: Artist and Storyteller." Two years later, she was the subject of the British Broadcasting Company television show "Beatrix." And in 1994, the

Royal Ballet performed "The Tales of Beatrix Potter." Her stature and influence in the world of children's literature thus remains considerable.

It is her books, of course, that continue to captivate children around the world. Writing in the *American Journal of Psychiatry,* Sophia Vinogradov reflected on what she and undoubtedly many others remember about favorite characters such as Peter Rabbit, Jemima Puddle-Duck, and Squirrel Nutkin. "Even now those names evoke for me the set of tiny hardback books from my childhood," she wrote. "I can still recall the smell and feel of the smooth papierglace pages, with their delicate, exquisite drawings: rabbits, frogs, mice, cats, ducks—all fully developed personages, with serious, thoughtful faces, old-fashioned waistcoats, bonnets, shoes with buckles." In short, declared Vinogradov, "Beatrix Potter was a remarkable woman who triumphed over life's adversities. . . . [She] transformed her struggles into stories that have fascinated readers of many different cultures for the entire twentieth century."

Further Reading

Grinstein, Alexander, *The Remarkable Beatrix Potter,* International Universities Press, 1995.
Lane, Margaret, *The Magic Years of Beatrix Potter,* Frederick Warne, 1978.
MacDonald, Ruth K., *Beatrix Potter,* Twayne, 1986.
Potter, Beatrix, *Beatrix Potter's Letters,* selected and introduced by Judy Taylor, Frederick Warne, 1989.
Potter, Beatrix, *The Journal of Beatrix Potter, 1881-1897,* transcribed from her coded writings by Leslie Linder, Frederick Warne, 1989.
Wilson, Katharina M., Paul Schlueter, and June Schlueter, editors, *Women Writers of Great Britain and Europe: An Encyclopedia,* Garland, 1997.
American Journal of Psychiatry, December 1996.
Times Educational Supplement, November 17, 1989.
Washington Post, October 5, 1997. □

Dith Pran

Dith Pran (born 1942) became known to moviegoers in the West as his story was portrayed in *The Killing Fields* (1984). When the Communist forces of the Khmer Rouge took control of his homeland in 1975, Pran and his compatriots experienced almost unimaginable suffering. Four years later he was able to escape and ultimately become a crusader for justice in Cambodia.

As a guide and interpreter working with members of the United States media in his country during the early 1970s, Pran got to know *New York Times* journalist Sydney Schanberg. The two worked together, became close friends, and witnessed firsthand the horrors of the Cambodian government's war with the Khmer Rouge. Yet those horrors would be overshadowed by much greater ones that ensued when the Khmer Rouge took power in

April of 1975. Schanberg would return to the U.S., where he earned a Pulitzer Prize for his work on Cambodia, but Pran would be forced to stay behind, victim of the madness that swept his country for four years. The story of his later escape, and the reuniting of the two friends, would prove an inspiring one; yet before it could be written, Dith Pran would have to endure a great deal.

The War Next Door

Dith Pran was born on September 27, 1942, in the town of Siem Reap. At that time, the Japanese army occupied Cambodia, which belonged to French Indochina, but Pran's home was far from the center of the occupying force's power. He grew up near the ruins of the vast complex of temples called Angkor Wat, built centuries before in northwestern Cambodia. His father was a senior public-works official, and Pran attended local schools, where he learned French. He learned English on his own, and after finishing high school in 1960, went to work as an interpreter for the U.S. Military Assistance Command.

From the end of World War II, neighboring Vietnam—formerly a part of French Indochina as well—had been involved in a civil war. A coalition of nationalists and Communist insurgents, led by Ho Chi Minh, had fought the French colonizers. In 1954 they were able to drive French forces out of Vietnam. The Communists suppressed all other factions to gain control over the north, and with the support of the Soviet Union and China, began waging war with anti-Communist forces in the south, which were supported by the U.S. Cambodia, meanwhile, remained in a state of rela-

tive peace. But as American bombing raids increased, North Vietnamese troops—along with South Vietnamese Communists, called Viet Cong—began using the neighboring country as a place of refuge. In 1965, Cambodia's government severed its relations with the U.S. amid charges that American troops had entered the country's borders to pursue their Communist enemies.

For Pran, the withdrawal of the Americans meant the end of a job he had held for five years. He went to work as an interpreter for a British film crew, then moved to a position as a receptionist at a hotel near Angkor Wat. In 1970, a U.S.-backed dictator, Lon Nol, seized power in the Cambodian capital of Phnom Penh. War broke out between Lon Nol's forces and those of a frightening new enemy: the Khmer Rouge.

Darkness Descends on Cambodia

The name "Khmer Rouge" means simply "Red Cambodian," signifying the group's Communist and nationalist roots. Their leadership was a clique of some 20 intellectuals, called *Angka Loeu,* or "The Higher Organization." Educated in France during the 1950s, the *Angka* had absorbed an amalgam of doctrines from philosophers such as Jean Jacques Rousseau, who maintained that science and technology had corrupted mankind's natural goodness, and melded these theories with the Communist ideologies of Marx, Lenin, Stalin, and Chairman Mao of China. But the rank-and-file of the Khmer Rouge, led in the field by the infamous Pol Pot, knew little of these theories. Mostly illiterate peasants and young people, they had little experience with the sophisticated city life of Phnom Penh, let alone Paris. The *Angka Loeu* leadership had determined that the answer to Cambodia's problems was a return to subsistence farming and destruction of anything that hinted of the West or the twentieth century. This message had particular appeal to the rank-and-file soldiers of the Khmer Rouge.

Because the civil war had virtually destroyed the tourist trade, and in part because of his desire to tell the world about the war sweeping his country, Pran moved his family to Phnom Penh to work as a journalist. There he met Craig Whitney, Saigon bureau chief for the *New York Times,* and he worked with a number of journalists as guide and interpreter. In 1972, Pran made one of the most important friendships of his life. *New York Times* writer Sydney Schanberg had been operating in Singapore, but he became fascinated by the war in Cambodia, and arranged for a transfer to Phnom Penh. He had contacted Pran, who met him at the airport with a list of contacts and ideas for stories. From that day, the two were close friends and, by 1973, Pran worked exclusively with Schanberg.

Both men were dogged in their pursuit of their work, a fact which had as much to do with their circumstances as their personalities. As the war with Lon Nol's forces continued, the Khmer Rouge, operating from strongholds in the hinterlands, became an ever more hardened and fanatical fighting force. Meanwhile the U.S. had pulled its troops out of Vietnam, which was subsequently overrun by Communist forces. On April 12, 1975, American personnel evacuated Phnom Penh as well. With Khmer Rouge victory

imminent, thousands of Cambodians scrambled for any possible means of escape.

Pran put his wife, Ser Moeum, and their four children on a truck operated by the U.S. military, but he chose to stay and help Schanberg report the story of the Khmer Rouge takeover. Both men assumed that once the Khmer Rouge had achieved victory, they would behave responsibly. As the first troops began to enter the city between April 12 and April 17, it indeed seemed possible that peace had come. But the Khmer Rouge soon began to display their true intentions.

Year Zero Begins

Historian Paul Johnson, in his *Modern Times,* offers a chilling account of what followed: "On 17 April over 3 million people were living in Phnom Penh. They were literally pushed into the surrounding countryside. The violence started at 7 a.m. with attacks on Chinese shops; then general looting. The first killings came at 8:45 p.m. Fifteen minutes later troops began to clear the Military Hospital—driving doctors, nurses, sick, and dying into the streets. An hour later they opened fire on anyone seen in the streets, to start a panic out of the city." Many were slaughtered in these first attacks, and many more killed in the forced exodus from the city, which involved some 60 percent of Cambodia's entire population of 5 million.

Pran, Schanberg, and two other journalists went to a hospital to investigate the casualties. As they were leaving, they were accosted by a group of armed Khmer Rouge. Suddenly Pran sprang into action, beseeching the soldiers on his friends' behalf. The troops ordered them to get into an armored vehicle, and the Westerners complied, but Pran stayed behind, still speaking to the soldiers. In his 1985 book *The Death and Life of Dith Pran,* Schanberg recalled that he thought "For God's sake, Pran, get inside. . . . if you go on arguing, they'll shoot you down in the street." Finally Pran got in, and they were released several hours later. Schanberg learned that Pran had not been hesitant to get in the armored vehicle—on the contrary, the Khmer Rouge were trying to keep him away, because they intended to kill the foreigners.

Pran had saved Schanberg's life. Now Schanberg, along with the other Western journalists who had remained behind in the city, tried to save Pran's. With their close Cambodian associates, the Westerners had taken refuge in the French embassy. Under an ordinary government, no matter how repressive, the Cambodian nationals would have been safe inside the foreign embassy; but the Khmer Rouge "government" was not an ordinary one. The soldiers ordered Pran and all Cambodians to leave the embassy. Schanberg and other journalists tried to create a fake passport for him. It did not work, and Pran was forced to leave the embassy.

Schanberg soon returned to the United States, where he looked after Pran's wife and children in New York City. (The *New York Times,* in fact, helped to support the family financially.) Through intermediaries at border camps in Thailand, Schanberg circulated photographs of his lost friend. Pran, meanwhile, was absorbed in the new Cambodia, or "Kampuchea" as the Khmer Rouge had renamed it.

Sizing up the situation, he quickly realized that anything which hinted of the West or of wealth was a liability, not an asset. Therefore he discarded the items with which he had intended to bribe the Khmer Rouge, dressed himself like a peasant, adopted a limited vocabulary, and pretended to be a simple villager. It was a wise decision. The Khmer Rouge had orders to execute as "intellectuals" and "foreigners" anyone who wore eyeglasses, perfume, makeup, watches, or other evidence of non-traditional influences. Everything that was not agrarian and Cambodian would be eradicated, and the Khmer Rouge were determined to remake their country from scratch. As a symbol of the fact that Cambodia was starting over, they designated 1975 as "Year Zero."

The Killing Fields

In accordance with his strict Buddhist faith and its belief that a name is sacred, Pran kept his. But under the persona of his peasant alter-ego, a taxi driver, he made his way to a village 20 miles from Siem Riep. He and the other villagers, many of them evacuees from Phnom Penh, were put to work in the rice paddies. Their days consisted of back-breaking labor, while their nights were filled with political indoctrination.

Though they were growing food, literally at gunpoint, the ration of rice was reduced to just one spoonful per day. Starving, Pran and other villagers ate anything they could find: bark, snakes, snails, rats, and other vermin. Some even dug up dead bodies—one of the few products in abundant supply under the new regime—and gnawed human flesh. Pran was so weak he could barely walk, and his face was becoming swollen from malnutrition while he began to lose his teeth. One night he dared to sneak out to a rice paddy and try to eat some raw rice. For this he was beaten, under guards' orders, by a dozen of his fellow villagers wielding bamboo-cutting blades. He was left outside in a rain storm, and there he prayed to Buddha for survival.

Ultimately the Khmer Rouge would be responsible for the slaughter of between 1.5 and 2 million of their compatriots, an act of genocide which—given the fact that Cambodia only had 5 million people to begin with—was proportionately greater than the atrocities committed by Hitler, Stalin, or Mao. But while this holocaust continued, the rest of the world remained largely silent. Having withdrawn completely from Southeast Asia, America had turned its attention to other concerns, and there were few protests of Khmer Rouge atrocities on U.S. college campuses. But Sydney Schanberg did not forget. Receiving a Pulitzer Prize in 1976 for his Cambodia reporting, he accepted it on behalf of Pran as well, and continued to search for his friend.

In the fall of 1977, Pran was granted permission to relocate—a rare privilege in Kampuchea. He became a house servant for a commune chief in the village of Bat Dangkor. The chief, a disillusioned Khmer Rouge officer, allowed Pran far greater freedom than he had experienced at the slave-labor camp. In January of 1979, the Vietnamese invaded Cambodia and overthrew the Khmer Rouge. Pran made his way to Siem Riep, and there he found that some 50 members of his family had been killed. The village wells were filled with skulls and bones, and the land was covered with graves. Nicknamed "killing fields," these were easily distinguished from the nearby ground by the fact that the grass was greenest over them.

Death and Life

Pran was given a position as village administrative chief by the Vietnamese, who had no idea that he had been a journalist. When a group of reporters from Eastern Europe came to visit, he managed to get a message to Schanberg through a member of the East German media. But the Vietnamese learned that Pran had been involved with the press himself, and he decided to escape before they began to question him more closely about his past.

On July 29, 1979, Pran set out with several other men on a 60-mile journey past land mines, traps, and the forces of the Vietnamese and Khmer Rouge. He arrived at the Thai border after almost two months, and entered a refugee camp there on October 3. He asked an American relief officer to contact Schanberg, who met him on October 9.

Their emotional reunion and the saga that had led them there would be depicted by Haing S. Ngor and Sam Waterston in Roland Joffe's 1984 film *The Killing Fields*. By that time, Schanberg had assisted Pran in relocating to the United States, where he was reunited with his family. The *New York Times* gave him a job as a reporter, and Pran became a U.S. citizen in 1986.

Pran began to devote all of his spare time to activities on behalf of his fellow Cambodians who had suffered under the Khmer Rouge. He would ultimately take several trips back to his homeland, and would attempt to bring the Khmer Rouge to justice before the World Court. His example is Elie Wiesel—who helped keep alive the memories of the Nazi genocide. Remarried, Pran and wife Kim DePaul operate the Dith Pran Holocaust Awareness Project, Inc. Among the other projects in which his group assists is a photographic archive on the Internet to assist Cambodians looking for missing family members. In the early 1990s, he interviewed 29 people who had suffered in the Khmer Rouge camps, and published the results in 1997 as *Children of Cambodia's Killing Fields: Memoirs by Survivors*.

For Pran, the ghosts of Cambodia remain, and the memories are "Still alive to me day and night," he said in an online interview at "The Site. "When I'm too busy, I can try to forget a little bit, but if I have nothing to do, it bothers me so much because my mind goes back and forth. . . . It's unbelievable what [the Khmer Rouge] did to the Cambodian people."

Further Reading

Johnson, Paul, *Modern Times: The World from the Twenties to the Eighties,* Harper & Row, 1983, pp. 654-657.
Notable Asian Americans, Gale, 1995, pp. 318-321.
Pran, Dith, compiler, *Children of Cambodia's Killing Fields: Memoirs by Survivors,* edited by Kim DePaul, Yale University Press, 1997. □

Schanberg, Sydney H., *The Death and Life of Dith Pran,* Viking, 1985.

New York Times, September 24, 1989, section 6, p.125.

New York Times Book Review, May 25, 1997, p. 21.

Reader's Digest, May 1997, p. 60.

"Dith Pran," *The Site,* http://www.zdnet.com/zdtv/thesite (March 26, 1998).

"MSNBC TV: Dith Pran with Brian Williams," *The Dith Pran Holocaust Awareness Project, Inc.,* http://www.dithpran.org (March 26, 1998).

Otto Preminger

The bombastic Austrian-born film director and producer Otto Preminger (1906-1986) had a long Hollywood career making movies that defied conventions of the time.

Nicknamed "Otto the Terrible" for his legendary tantrums on Hollywood sets, Otto Preminger cajoled countless stars in dozens of films from the 1930s through the 1970s. His movies ranged from the delicately crafted suspense classic *Laura,* to the colossal epic *Exodus,* and included many commercial and critical successes as well as failures. Preminger had no single specialty, but his films ranged over a wide variety of styles and subject matters. His trademarks were his staunch independence and fierce control over all aspects of his films.

Early Years

Preminger's father, Marc, was a lawyer and onetime attorney general of the Austro-Hungarian Empire. Otto and his brother Ingo both earned law degrees in Vienna, the latter of whom ended up as a Hollywood agent. Otto was a teenager when he first started acting in plays in Vienna. At 17, he starred as Lysander in a production of *A Midsummer Night's Dream,* and at 19, he was already managing a Vienna theater. By 20, he was mostly bald and had earned his law degree. He spent his twenties becoming one of Europe's most successful theatrical producer-directors and at 26, he directed his first film, *Die Grosse Liebe.*

Preminger was Jewish, and in 1935, he thought it wise to leave Austria to escape the Nazi threat and take up an invitation to direct Broadway plays in the United States. In New York, he directed *Libel,* a minor success and the next year went to Hollywood to make the films *Under Your Spell* and *Danger, Love at Work* for Daryl F. Zanuck's 20th-Century Fox.

After clashes with Zanuck, Preminger returned to New York and directed the plays *Outward Bound,* which had a 19-month Broadway run, and *Margin for Error,* in which Preminger also acted—playing a Nazi official. By 1941, Zanuck was in the Army and Preminger was invited back to Hollywood and remained under contract with Fox as a director, producer and actor until 1952. In 1942, Preminger played Nazi heavies in *The Pied Piper* and *They Got Me Covered,* and the next year, he directed and acted in a film version of *Margin for Error.* In 1944, he directed the comedy *In the Meantime, Darling.*

Hollywood Studio Days

Relations between Zanuck and Preminger remained cool until 1944, when Preminger persuaded the studio head to let him produce and direct the suspense story *Laura.* Starring Clifton Webb, Dana Andrews, and Gene Tierney, *Laura* was a critical and commercial success. Many considered it Preminger's finest film. *Halliwell's Film Guide* calls *Laura* "a quiet, streamlined little murder mystery that brought a new adult approach to the genre and heralded the mature *film noir* of the later forties." Preminger received an Academy Award nomination for *Laura.*

During the rest of his tenure with Fox, Preminger churned out a number of films, few of them notable. Tallulah Bankhead starred in his 1945 costume drama *A Royal Scandal.* It was followed by *Where Do We Get from Here* in 1945, *Centennial Summer,* and *Fallen Angel* in 1946, *Forever Amber* and *Daisy Kenyon* in 1947, *That Lady in Ermine* in 1948, *The Fan* in 1949, *Whirlpool* and *Where the Sidewalk Ends* in 1950, *The Thirteenth Letter* in 1951, and *Angel Face* in 1952.

Taking on the Censors

In 1953 Preminger, who had grown to resent Hollywood, quit 20th Century Fox and formed his own company, Carlyle Productions. For the rest of the decade Preminger produced and directed several taboo-breaking films.

Preminger had directed a highly successful stage production of Hugh Herbert's light sex comedy *The Moon Is Blue,* and he made it into his first independent movie in 1953. Starring William Holden and David Niven, the film was notable only for defying the strict Hollywood production code. Preminger insisted on the play's original dialogue being used in the film, including words like "virgin," "pregnant," and "seduce," terms that were taboo in films of that era. *The Moon Is Blue* was the first commercial feature to be released without a seal of approval from the Motion Pictures Association of America, and it earned a "condemned" rating from the powerful Roman Catholic Legion of Decency. It also was banned by local censorship boards until Preminger won a U.S. Supreme Court case ordering the film to be shown.

In 1954, Preminger directed two movies: *River of No Return,* a successful Western with Marilyn Monroe and Robert Mitchum, that was one of the first features shot in wide-screen Cinemascope, and *Carmen Jones,* a musical adaptation of Bizet's opera *Carmen,* with an all-black cast, including Dorothy Dandridge, Harry Belafonte, and Pearl Bailey. In 1955, he brought to the screen *The Court Martial of Billy Mitchell,* a military justice drama with an all-star cast including Gary Cooper, Rod Steiger, and Ralph Bellamy.

In 1956, Preminger directed Frank Sinatra as a junkie in *The Man With the Golden Arm.* It was Hollywood's first serious look at drug addiction and included sensational scenes of Sinatra's character going "cold turkey" to kick his habit. The film was banned in Boston among other cities, but again Preminger went to the courts and beat the censors. Though it caused a sensation, critics didn't think much of the way Preminger had lightened up his subject and tacked on a happy ending. Diana Willing in *Films in Review* called it "a very inferior film. . . . The script is inexcusably clumsy, the sets are unbelievable, and the casting is ridiculous." Nonetheless, Preminger's challenge to the studios' rating system proved a success. In the late 1950s the code was liberalized, and Preminger's films paved the way for directors to tackle formerly taboo subjects frankly and openly.

He followed *The Man With the Golden Arm* in 1957 with *Bonjour Tristesse,* based on a novel by Francoise Sagan, was about a teenage girl who becomes enmeshed in his father's womanizing and ends up causing a death. David Niven, Deborah Kerr and Jean Seberg starred in the film. Seberg also appeared that same year in Preminger's film of George Bernard Shaw's play about Joan of Arc, *Saint Joan.* Shot in Great Britain and adapted for the screen by Graham Greene, the film was a flop, and Seberg's performance was universally panned.

Master of the Set

By the late 1950s, Preminger had developed a reputation as a tyrant. He kept firm control over all aspects of his film company, including scripts, casting, advertising, and even camera equipment. In 1959, Preminger brought another all-black musical, *Porgy and Bess,* to the screen, starring Sidney Poitier, Sammy Davis Jr., and Diahann Carroll. Samuel Goldwyn's Columbia Pictures produced the film. On the set, Preminger and Goldwyn argued about every detail.

Also in 1959, he produced and directed the box-office smash *Anatomy of a Murder,* a riveting courtroom drama starring James Stewart. Preminger got the film publicity during its filming by firing its star, Lana Turner, and replacing her with Lee Remick; by casting in the role of the judge a non-actor, Joseph N. Welch, who was famous as the Army's chief counsel during the televised anti-communism hearings of Senator Joseph McCarthy; and by bringing jazz great Duke Ellington onto the set to liven up the score. Donald Chase noted in *Film Comment* that *Anatomy of a Murder* had "a buzzing low-key energy that never falters over 2 hours and 40 minutes." The film also provoked controversy for its realistic rape scene, and was nominated for an Academy Award for Best Picture of 1959.

In 1960, Preminger unleashed his epic *Exodus,* based on Leon Uris's best-selling novel about the founding of the state of Israel. Preminger again displayed his knack for publicity. To cast a mob scene, he sold lottery tickets to 30,000 people and delayed the prize drawing until morning, to keep the extras around all night. The prizes turned out to be tickets to the opening of *Exodus.* He also made headlines by using as his screenwriter Dalton Trumbo, who had been blacklisted by Hollywood since the McCarthy hearings. With a cast of thousands, including Paul Newman, *Exodus* was a big-budget, 220-minute extravaganza which failed to impress audiences or critics.

In 1961 Preminger directed the successful *Advise and Consent,* a political thriller adapted from a best-seller by

Allen Drury. *Entertainment Weekly* critic Tim Purtell termed it "a hornet's nest of a drama about United States senators squabbling over a controversial cabinet nominee. . . . one of the savviest of all films about politics."

Hits and Misses

Preminger's pace had begun to slow. In 1963, he brought out *The Cardinal,* a long-winded but visually arresting film about a young priest's rise to power in the Catholic Church. Andrew Sarris, author of *Confessions of a Cultist,* noted that "Preminger is much better with image than with actors." Two years later, Preminger directed *In Harm's Way.* In *A World on Film,* critic Stanley Kauffmann called it "one more guts-and-glory naval saga complete with John Wayne as a crusty commander and an ensign son who finally does him proud." Kauffmann added that Preminger "has a reputation—deserved—for intelligence and cultivation, and another reputation—equally deserved —for shrewd exploitation of mass tastes."

Preminger clearly was fading in the late 1960s. In 1967, he directed *Hurry Sundown,* a melodramatic story about race relations with Jane Fonda and Michael Caine. In 1968, he made *Skidoo,* considered a feeble attempt to appeal to the counter-culture of the era. In 1970, Preminger followed with what was regarded as another flop, *Tell Me That You Love Me, Julie Moon.* Starring Liza Minnelli, it was the story of a disfigured girl, a gay paraplegic and an introverted epileptic who live together. Writer Elaine May penned *Such Good Friends,* which Preminger released in 1972, a "satiric parable which alternates between sex comedy and medical expose," according to *Halliwell's.* Preminger's next film, the 1975 release *Rosebud,* about Middle Eastern terrorists, was ignored by the public, as was his final film, *The Human Factor,* released in 1979.

In his personal life, in 1971 after the death of stripper Gypsy Rose Lee, Preminger revealed he was the father of her son, Erik Kirkland, who became his chief assistant. In 1986 at the age of 80, Preminger died of cancer at his home in Manhattan. Critics sharply disagree on his legacy. Sarris noted: "His enemies have never forgiven him for being a director with the personality of a producer." And Purtell contended: "Of all big-name Hollywood directors, possibly none has had as bad a rep as Otto Preminger. Admired in the '50s by French critics and new-wave filmmakers, he was largely dismissed in this country for what were perceived to be superficial, self-important films. . . . He deserves better. . . . Preminger made intelligent, literate entertainments that were models of screen clarity."

Further Reading

Halliwell's Film Guide, Eighth Edition, Harper Collins, 1991.
Kauffmann, Stanley, *A World on Film,* Harper, 1966.
Sarris, Andrew, *Confessions of a Cultist,* Simon & Schuster, 1970.
Entertainment Weekly, July 29, 1994; February 14, 1997.
Film Comment, September/October 1994.
Films in Review, January 1956.
New York Times, April 28, 1986.
Time, May 5, 1986.

Andre Previn

German-born American composer Andre Previn (born 1929) has received acclaim in every musical venue explored during his exceptional career, and has refused to be typecast along the way.

When Andre Previn began his professional musical career, few could have imagined, much less predicted, the circuitous route and dimension his journey would take. Just when one path seemed certain, when he received acclaim in one discipline and success was assured, the determined artist changed course. Endowed with a magnitude of talents, Andre Previn is a richly decorated and world-renowned musician: a highly sought conductor of the world's most prestigious orchestras, an award-winning composer for all media—orchestra, chamber ensemble, stage, and film productions; classical and jazz pianist; recording artist; as well as author and educator.

The Gift

Born Andreas Ludwig Priwin in Berlin, Germany, on April 6, 1929, Previn was the youngest child of a prosperous Jewish family. His father, Jacob, was a respected attorney, as well as an accomplished amateur pianist. Music was an important part of family life, and young Andre, wanting to participate, asked for lessons. After testing revealed that he had perfect pitch, he was enrolled in the Berlin Conservatory of Music at the age of six. As the threat of World War II loomed, life under Nazi rule became increasingly difficult, and in 1938 the family fled to Paris. He studied at the Paris Conservatory of Music until they immigrated to the United States.

Life in Los Angeles, California, was different from life in Berlin and Paris in almost every way possible—from the climate and architecture to the language spoken and career opportunities available. Upon arrival to the U.S., none of the family spoke English, including Previn's father, which made practicing law impossible. To make ends meet, he gave music lessons at home—yet nothing stood in the way of young Previn's musical education. He studied piano, theory, and composition from the best instructors available, Joseph Achron and Mario Castelnuovo-Tedesco.

Versatile Talent

Previn became an American citizen at the age of 14, about the same time he became captivated by the most American of all musical formats—jazz. The great African-American jazz pianist, Art Tatum, was his inspiration. Previn began splitting time between his classical studies and jazz, and word of his talent spread. Eager to supplement the family's income, Previn quickly followed up when he heard that MGM needed someone to do a jazz arrangement. That led to writing more arrangements, at first sporadically and then more regularly, several times a week after school. Throughout high school, he managed to make time to continue his serious musical studies, while exploring and developing as a jazz pianist, and working part-time. Seduced by Hollywood's glamour, he signed a contract with MGM when he turned 18. He also made his first recording on the Sunset label while still in his teens.

Previn worked his way up Hollywood's music world, gradually moving from playing rehearsals and writing arrangements to composing original movie scores—all while making a name for himself as a jazz pianist. By 1950, his recordings on the RCA label were hits. Even though writers and musicians were at the bottom of the studio hierarchy, being under contract to the world's biggest studio had its perks and he loved being part of it.

Virtuoso

During this time, the Korean War was creating uncertainty for men his age, so Previn joined the national guard as a self-protective measure. After basic training, he was assigned to the Sixth Army Band unit in San Francisco where he was able to study conducting with Pierre Monteux, as well as pursue his passion for jazz with a new friend, drummer Shelly Manne. After the service, he returned to Los Angeles and continued an exhaustive exploration of music, including film composing, arranging, and conducting at MGM, as well as chamber music and jazz. During this time, he married and divorced his first wife, and in 1959, married his second wife, Dory Langdon, a lyricist with whom he collaborated on numerous projects.

Previn's career flourished in the late 1950s and early 1960s with musical hits that he adapted from the theatrical stage for films, and original scores he composed and conducted for other musicals and dramas. He became musical director at MGM, was nominated for 16 Academy Awards, and won four. There were performances with his own jazz combo and the Jazz at the Philharmonic All-Stars. He collaborated with top jazz musicians, such as Benny Goodman, Herb Ellis, Ella Fitzgerald, and Shelly Manne with whom he recorded a jazz version of *My Fair Lady*. In addition to becoming a best seller, the album triggered the popularity of jazz based on Broadway musicals.

Another part of his musicality was calling, however. According to his own account in *No Minor Chords, My Days in Hollywood,* he longed to be part of the inner circle of what he regarded as the legitimate world of classical music. Hollywood was not the place to write and perform serious music. He wrote in his autobiography, "The truth is I was, in the sixties, somewhat of a misfit in Hollywood, or at least that's how I increasingly came to view myself." He had gotten a valuable practical education, but now he wanted more. Although he performed as a concert pianist, composed chamber music, and began devoting more time to conducting, his focus was divided. In 1965, he began recording with the London Symphony Orchestra, and from 1967 to 1970, he was conductor-in-chief of the Houston Symphony Orchestra.

In 1969, while still married to Langdon, Previn began to be seen with actress Mia Farrow, ex-wife of popular crooner Frank Sinatra. She gave birth to their twin sons, Matthew and Sascha in early 1970. The ensuing scandal resulted in Previn leaving the Houston Symphony Orchestra. Langdon and Previn divorced and he married Farrow shortly thereafter. They had another child, Fletcher, and adopted three other children, Daisy, Lark Song and Soon Yi. Due to career conflicts, they divorced in the late 1970s.

Accession to Maestro

Life changed gradually until he accepted the appointment of principal conductor with the London Symphony Orchestra in 1969. In London he became a popular personality, appearing frequently on television to talk about music. He also toured throughout Europe and the United States with the London Symphony, and became especially well-known for his interpretations of British and Russian symphonic repertoire.

Throughout his active conducting career—with the Pittsburgh Symphony Orchestra (1976-1984), the Los Angeles Philharmonic (1985-1989), and the Royal Philharmonic (Music Director: 1985-1988; Principal Conductor: 1988-1991), and Conductor Laureate of the London Symphony (since 1993)—he has continued to compose. Compositions included: a Symphony for Strings; "Four Outings," for brass quintet; a piano concerto, commissioned by Vladimir Ashkenzy; a cello sonata, written for Yo-Yo Ma; a song cycle, written for Dame Janet Baker; a music drama, *Every Good Boy Deserves Favour*, written in collaboration with playwright Tom Stoppard; a set of orchestral song settings, "Honey and Rue," for Kathleen Battle, commissioned by Carnegie Hall as part of its centennial celebration in 1992; and an opera based on Tennessee William's *A Streetcar*

Named Desire, commission by the San Francisco Opera in 1998.

His many other pursuits include regular piano performances; playing and recording chamber music, especially at festivals such as Caramoor (New York), the South Bank Festival (London), and the La Jolla (California) Chamber Music Festival; and writing and teaching. In addition to many jazz and chamber music recordings, he has recorded complete cycles of Vaughan-Williams, Elgar, Rachmaninoff, Shostakovich, and Prokofiev, and is known for late Romantic and early twentieth century music. Not ashamed of his past in popular music, he also composed scores for the musicals *Coco* and *The Good Companions*.

In 1982, he married Heather Hales and they have one child. In the early 1990s, Previn returned to one of his first loves—jazz. He resumed recording, and formed the Andre Previn Jazz Trio, which toured Japan, North America, and Europe in 1992 and 1993.

Further Reading

Previn, Andre, with Antony Hopkins, *Music Face to Face,* Hamilton, 1971.
Previn, *No Minor Chords, My Days in Hollywood,* Doubleday, 1991.
The New Grove Dictionary of Jazz, Grove, 1994.
The New Grove Dictionary of Music, Grove, 1992.
Boston Globe, February 14, 1997; July 28, 1997.
G. Schirmer Publicity Releases, March 1998.
New York, June 10, 1996.

R

Prince Rainier III of Monaco

Scion of one of Europe's oldest extant monarchies, Prince Rainier III (born 1923) became the thirty-first ruler of Monaco in 1949. In the years since he has maintained the tiny Mediterranean principality as a prosperous slice of a bygone era, attractive to the rich and idle for its sunshine, lavish casino, and absence of income tax.

Rainier Louis Henri Maxence Bertrand de Grimaldi was born May 31, 1923 to Princess Charlotte, daughter of Monaco's reigning prince, Louis II. Rainier's father, Comte Pierre de Polignac, hailed from a venerable line of French aristocrats, but incited little but rancor in Louis II, a stern, military-loving monarch. Such intrafamilial conflicts were nothing new to the Grimaldi line, who possessed a long history of internal tumult. De Polignac and Charlotte's first child, Princess Antoinette, would one day conduct her own underhanded machinations in an attempt to seize power.

Treacherous Roots

At the time of Rainier's birth Monaco enjoyed a reputation as an opulent, though somewhat amoral, playground on the Riviera. Just eight square miles of rocky land wedged between France and Italy on the Mediterranean Sea, Monaco's main attraction was the Monte Carlo Casino, where many a new or old fortune had been squandered since its opening in 1865. The ornate building was the showpiece of the resort and had given it international notoriety, though Monaco itself dated back to ancient times as a port. It had been in possession of Grimaldis since 1297, when Francois Grimaldi seized control of it from the Genoese. This Grimaldi forebear was of a successful sea-trading family in Genoa, a clan sometimes referred to in less euphemistic terms as "pirates." By the late nineteenth century, with the popularity of the casino among Europe's elite, Monaco was known as a hideout for jewel thieves and the more debauched members of European society.

Rainier grew up in the Palace de Princier primarily under the care of his English nanny. Tensions within the family were exacerbated by his parents' divorce in 1929. De Polignac was then banned from Monaco for life by Louis II, while Princess Charlotte grew increasingly eccentric over the years. In time, she would be constantly surrounded by a brigade of seven small terriers who bit the heels of anyone who tried to approach. Later, one of France's most notorious jewel thieves would be paroled by authorities into her custody; he was her chauffeur, bodyguard, and paramour.

"Fat Little Monaco"

Beginning in 1934, Rainier was sent abroad for his secondary education. That year he arrived at Summer Fields in Oxford, England. This was a misnomer for a boarding school of the roughest, most gothic order. The Riviera-bred Rainier found himself in an elite but frigid, damp setting where privacy was nonexistent, the toilet was outside, and students were regularly caned. He was called "Fat Little Monaco" by the other students. Nobody in his family visited him there, and after his 1935 term came to an end, he announced his refusal to go back. He then ran away from another school, and the disappearance made headlines—it

335

Rainier's future became increasingly unavoidable in the spring of 1949 when Charlotte officially renounced her rights to the throne as Louis II's health worsened. His austere grandfather died in May of that year, and after the stipulated period of mourning Rainier was formally installed as Prince of Monaco in a lavish public ceremony in April of 1950. Over the next few years, he became known as avid sportsman who loved car racing, deep-sea diving, and skiing. His romance with Gisele Pascal ended after she resumed her acting career in 1953 after a three-year hiatus.

Meanwhile, a financial crisis involving the embezzlement of casino funds nearly left Rainier tainted by scandal, while his sister Antoinette schemed to depose him through it. She was having an affair with a member of Monaco's National Council, and the pair hoped to place Antoinette's young son on the throne by giving Rainier unsound advice. In the end, Rainier used his own money to replenish the national assets and restore confidence in his rule. When he discovered the plot, he might have had Antoinette arrested or even banned from Monaco for life.

Instead Rainier took advice from Greek shipping tycoon Aristotle Onassis, who was part-owner of the casino. Onassis pointed out that a united family gave the whiff of stability to lure investors and companies, which would benefit Monaco's economic livelihood in the end. The powerful shipping magnate, whose permanent home, the yacht *Christina,* was anchored in Monte Carlo's harbor for years, also advised Rainier to find a wife. Thus not long after the casino crisis Rainier was introduced to American film star Grace Kelly, who was in nearby Cannes for its film festival in May of 1955. A photo opportunity was arranged for the actress through a Paris magazine, and after a meeting for which Rainier appeared almost an hour late, the pair began corresponding secretly.

Fairy-Tale Wedding Makes Headlines

Kelly had just won an Academy Award for her lead in *The Country Girl,* and despite her acting career otherwise fit the shoes of a possible Princess of Monaco: she was a Roman Catholic, unmarried, and hailed from a well-to-do Philadelphia family. By October of 1955, Rainier had decided he wanted to marry her, and traveled to America for the first time in his life that December to meet the Kellys. Rainier gave Grace a twelve-carat diamond engagement ring, and obtained a pledge from her that she would give up her film career permanently. Kelly was also faced with a Monaco law that stipulated should the marriage come to an end, the Prince would receive custody of any children. Though they appeared very much in love, such legal arrangements and the media-circus atmosphere made for a shaky wedding day in April of 1956.

Leader, Dealmaker, Father

Rainier and the new Princess Grace produced an heir to the throne with the birth of Caroline Louise Marguerite Grimaldi in January of 1957. Fourteen months later, those rights were ceded to the first male when her brother, Albert Alexander Louis Pierre, entered the world. Grimaldi family

was thought he might have been kidnapped—but he was easily spotted by authorities at the local train station.

The posh Le Rosey School in Switzerland was Rainier's next stop, and there he fared much better. Often referred to as "the school of kings" because of the panoply of international royalty among its alumni, Le Rosey was entirely relocated to the ski resort of Gstaad each winter for the benefit of its students. After graduation, Rainier enrolled at France's University of Montpelier. Shortly after his arrival there in August of 1939, war broke out in Europe and he did not return to Monaco until Easter of 1942. On that visit, he attended a theater performance by actress Gisele Pascal; he and the French divorcee, who was a few years his senior, began corresponding. After he received his degree from Montpelier in June of 1943, he enrolled in Paris's Ecole Libre des Sciences Politiques in order to carry on the romance with her.

Rainier enlisted in the Free French Army after his twenty-first birthday. With France now liberated from the Germans and battling them along the shared border, Rainier saw combat as a lieutenant and received the Croix de Guerre for bravery. He remained in uniform until early 1947, and then resumed life in Monaco in his own villa, as well as his affair with Gisele Pascal. The actress, of humble birth, was despised by the women in his family, and his sister Antoinette circulated gossip that Pascal was unable to bear children, which would have made it impossible for her to wed Rainier.

life was best described as idyllic. A third child, Stephanie Marie Elisabeth, was born in 1965, and the family divided their time between the Palace de Princier and a beloved farmhouse, just over the border with France, that they came to call Roc Agel. Unlike his own parents, Rainier took an active role in his children's lives from the start, and photographs from the era depict a regal, yet doting couple and their attractive, spirited offspring.

Rainier remained intensely involved in affairs of state, however, and over the next few years, Monaco would be rocked by minor political and economic cataclysms that required a decisive hand. In 1959 he learned that his sister's lover was still working behind the scenes against him, trying to sway others to campaign for a constitutional monarchy that would give the Grimaldi line far less power. In response, the Prince declared virtual martial law in January of 1959 by issuing several firm edicts that banned demonstrations, suspended the constitution, and dissolved National Council upon which his nemesis sat. After restoring stability, he then managed to oust Onassis, whose control over the casino and Monaco's finances he had grown to resent.

Monaco Flourishes

Rainier's ejection of Onassis launched a new and even more prosperous era for Monaco, and the Prince grew to be a savvy manager of Monaco's assets and development. It remained a luxury tourist draw, but he also lured major companies to headquarter there because of its absence of taxes. There was no unemployment, but Monaco did grow crowded as a result of the boom. Rainier launched a project to reclaim land from the ocean, and sometimes faced criticism for allowing so many high-rise hotel and condominium developments along the shore. Unlike his European counterparts, however, Rainier enjoyed absolute power—a holdover from the medieval era and perhaps one more symbol of Monaco's seemingly perpetual good fortune.

That lucky streak began to unravel as the royal offspring grew into teenagers. Caroline proved headstrong and was plagued by paparazzi as a young adult living in Paris in the 1970s, who trailed behind her incessantly as she went club hopping. At one point, Rainier even threatened the tabloid papers with lawsuits, saying that the constant hounding was putting undue pressure on his eldest. In 1977, Caroline announced that she wanted to marry a raconteur/investment banker nearly twenty years her senior. Her parents reluctantly acquiesced—fearing she might elope anyway—and the marriage to Philippe Junot ended just eighteen months later.

A Lonely Twilight

Two years later, with equally headstrong daughter Stephanie alongside, Princess Grace was driving her Land Rover from Roc Agel into Monaco and suffered what may have been a stroke. The car careened down a steep embankment, Stephanie emerged from the wreck hysterical and pleading with stunned onlookers for help, and Grace died the next evening—September 14, 1982—at the second-rate Princess Grace Hospital after being removed from life sup-

port. The funeral was an extremely difficult experience for the Prince, who sat shaken between Caroline and Albert.

Yet over the next few years, the aging Prince came to rely heavily on a newly-mature Caroline, who, it is said, has stepped in to fill her universally revered mother's shoes quite admirably. In 1983, Caroline married Italian industrialist Stefano Casiraghi; the couple had three children before he was killed in a speedboat accident off Monaco's coast in 1990. The heir apparent, Albert, has yet to find a suitable bride and produce an heir, which would allow Rainier to abdicate. Meanwhile, the youngest of Rainier's children has been in the public eye far more than her father may have wished. Stephanie had two children out of wedlock with one of her bodyguards and finally married him with her father's approval in 1995. She filed for divorce just over a year later.

Like his son Albert, Rainier is often linked with some of the most beautiful and accomplished European women of his generation. Yet it is unlikely that the Prince, who was 73 when Monaco celebrated the 700th anniversary of Grimaldi rule in 1997, would remarry. He remains an active monarch and still enjoys sailing and hunting, though he underwent heart-bypass surgery in 1994. Press photographs clearly show a doting, much-loved grandfather with his five grandchildren. "I would like to be remembered as the person who got rid of the bad image and bad legend of Monaco," Rainier once said, according to a 1988 *People* magazine article.

Further Reading

De Massy, Baron Christian and Charles Higham, *Palace: My Life in the Royal Family of Monaco,* Atheneum, 1986.

Edwards, Anne, *The Grimaldis of Monaco,* William Morrow, 1992.

Lacey, Robert, *Grace,* G.P. Putnam's Sons, 1994.

Robinson, Jeffrey, *Rainier and Grace: An Intimate Portrait,* Atlantic Monthly Press, 1989.

Cosmopolitan, August, 1993, pp. 192-195, 252.

People, June 13, 1988, pp. 46-47; February 12, 1996, pp. 144-147; September 30, 1996, pp. 70-76.

Peyton Randolph

American patriot Peyton Randolph (1721-1775), president of the first Continental Congress, was instrumental in securing independence for the United States of America.

At the time of Peyton Randolph's birth, the future United States of America was an assortment of 13 separate colonies ruled from far away England. But, by the time of his election as president of the first Continental Congress in 1774, these colonies had begun to see themselves as one united nation that could rule itself independently. Randolph was an early patriot who pushed for independence and his contributions to the movement for American independence and democracy were significant and long-lasting.

Peyton Randolph was born in the Tazewell Hall section of Williamsburg, Virginia, sometime during September of 1721 to Sir John and Susanna (Beverly) Randolph. Randolph's father was very prominent in Virginia politics as the King's attorney for the colony of Virginia. His father was also a diplomat and speaker of the Virginia House of Burgesses located in Williamsburg. His grandfather, Colonel William Randolph came to Virginia from England in 1674 and was also a prominent figure in the colony's early social and political life.

Colonial Education

With his father's prominent position, young Randolph could be educated at home by private tutors hired by his father. This practice was especially common among the upper classes of southern colonials and was the only way to secure a quality education for their children in the days before publicly funded schools became available or popular. George Washington and Thomas Jefferson were other early colonial leaders that benefited from this type of private education.

In 1739, Randolph began studying at the College of William and Mary in Williamsburg and, later that year, traveled to London to study law at the Inner Temple (also called Middle Temple). He graduated from the College of William and Mary in 1742 and, following in his father's

footsteps, was admitted to the Virginia bar on February 10, 1745, becoming a practicing attorney. He married Elizabeth Harrison in Williamsburg on March 8, 1745; they had no children.

Early Political Career

In 1748, Randolph was appointed as the King's attorney for the colony of Virginia, taking over his father's former position. He would stay on as the King's attorney for the colony of Virginia until 1766, when his political beliefs made it impossible for him to continue on at the post. He was also elected to represent Williamsburg in the Virginia House of Burgesses in 1748, but served only one year before returning in 1752 to represent the College of William and Mary until 1758. In his first visit to the House of Burgesses, Randolph had came to prominence while objecting to taxes scheduled to be attached to deeds on new land purchases.

In 1754, Randolph traveled to London to plead his case and was partially successful in getting some of the taxes revoked. His campaign against these taxes had brought him into conflict with Virginia's governor, Robert Dinwiddle, and, even though he was seen by his compatriots as having somewhat moderate political opinions, his reputation as being pro-colonial was made. In 1758, Randolph was back at his seat in the House of Burgesses representing Williamsburg and continued to serve there until his death. Randolph also became a visiting professor of law at the College of William and Mary that year and helped revise early Virginia laws to better correspond to the times.

During the French and Indian War (1754-1763), many inhabitants of the British colonies in North America felt threatened by the large numbers of hostile French and Native Americans spread out along their western frontier. Following the 1754 defeat of British General Edward Braddock's 1,900-strong force on the way to Fort Duquesne (Pittsburgh, Pennsylvania) in the western Virginia wilderness, Randolph led a small company of Virginia volunteers against a Native American force that had allied itself with the French. This only strengthened his reputation among Virginians as a man of value and worth.

Valuable Colonial Leader

In 1765, the British Parliament passed the Stamp Act to help pay some of the expenses incurred fighting the French in North America and throughout the world. The act required colonists to pay a tax in the form of a stamp that would be placed on all official documents such as wills, deeds and marriage certificates as well as on things like playing cards and newspapers. Randolph had already taken a side on the proposed act a year earlier when he helped draft a remonstrance in the Virginia House of Burgesses against the proposed act.

With the Stamp Act's passage in 1766, Randolph saw that he was in fundamental disagreement with Parliament and resigned from his very lucrative post as the attorney for King George III in Virginia. In November of 1766, Randolph was elected as speaker for the Virginia House of Burgesses due to his popularity and his belief that the Stamp Act must be opposed. He held this post almost uninterrupted until his death in 1775.

The Stamp Act was repealed late in 1766 but was almost immediately replaced with the Townshend Act of 1767 which sought to tax everyday commodities used in the colonist's homes. In 1773, Randolph was chosen as the chairman for the committee of correspondence which sought to find some remedy to the problems between the colonies and Great Britain so that conflict could be averted.

The passage of the Townshend Act helped lead to the 1773 opposition by citizens of Boston in the *Boston Tea Party.* The British government reacted by passing the Coercive Acts in early 1774. These acts closed the port of Boston and put British regulars in the homes of many Bostonians. In response, the Virginia House of Burgesses called for a day of fasting and prayer in support of Boston and was promptly dissolved by Virginia's new governor, Lord Dunmore. Randolph and many others were alarmed by this and called for a convention of former Virginia delegates to meet in Williamsburg on August 1, 1774 to propose a course of action for, as a broadside of the day stated, the "Preservation of the Common Rights and Liberty of British America." More than 100 delegates attended the first convention and this initial meeting would be the first of five such meetings that would determine Virginia's stance toward Great Britain.

Randolph's staunch opposition to the Coercive Acts put him soundly in the patriot camp and he was respected and sought for council on many occasions by other leaders such as George Washington and Patrick Henry. Randolph is considered such an important figure in colonial politics, that it has been said that a young Thomas Jefferson patterned himself after him. His calm judgment and abundant legal knowledge made him well-known and respected among rebel leaders throughout the continent.

President of the Continental Congress

In early August of 1774, Randolph was elected as the chairman of the Virginia delegation to the first Continental Congress. On August 10, 1774 he called a meeting of citizens of Williamsburg to call for their support for the resolutions recently passed by the Virginia delegation that called for them to resist economically the efforts of Great Britain to pass taxes on Virginians without their approval. For this the government of Great Britain put a mark against his name.

On September 5, 1774, upon his arrival at Carpenter's Hall in Philadelphia to attend the first meetings of the Continental Congress, he was elected its first president. He presided over the Continental Congress and heard debate from all sides on the troubles with Great Britain. There were some delegates that felt open war and a declaration for independence were warranted, while others felt reconciliation and a return to the pre-Stamp Act era were best.

Throughout the six days that the convention met, Randolph kept the body calm and did not malign any opinions, however unpopular with the rest of the assembled representatives. The end result was a series of resolutions in which the colonies pledged to support Boston and the colony of Massachusetts. They also pledged not to import any British manufactured goods after November 1, 1774. If this alone did not have the desired effect of lifting the Coercive Acts, the delegation pledged to go a step farther and refuse to export American goods to Great Britain as of August of 1775.

At the conclusion of the first Continental Congress, Randolph returned to his native Virginia to gauge the mood of its citizens. On March 21, 1775 he called a meeting of citizens in Richmond, Virginia to debate the recent efforts of the Continental Congress and hear discussions on their effectiveness. On April 20, 1775, Lord Dunmore, had the gunpowder removed from the armory in Williamsburg and placed on board an English vessel sailing off the coast without paying the colony for it. This action infuriated many Virginians and a mob in Williamsburg set upon the antagonists to demand payment. Randolph calmed the mob and eventually exacted payment for the gunpowder from Lord Dunmore.

During the summer of 1775, Randolph was again in the Virginia House of Burgesses serving as its speaker and calling for resistance to British tyranny. But, as the summer turned to autumn, Randolph traveled again to Philadelphia to attend the second Continental Congress and was again chosen as its president. It was here that he died on October 22, 1775 from apoplexy at the age of 54. In respect for all that he had done for Virginia, his body was transported to Virginia and buried beneath the chapel at the College of William and Mary.

Further Reading

Johnson, Rossiter, *The Twentieth Century Biographical Dictionary of Notable Americans,* Gale, 1968.

Knight, Lucian Lamar, *Biographical Dictionary of Southern Authors,* Gale Research Company, 1978.

Reardon, John J., *Peyton Randolph, 1721-1775: One Who Presided,* Carolina Academic Press, 1982.

Treese, Joel D., *Biographical Directory of the American Congress, 1774-1996,* Congressional Quarterly Staff Directories, Inc., 1997.

"The First Virginia Convention," *Let America Speak—Our Voice as Our Vote,* http://www.history.org/other/teaching/voteasvoice/convention.html, (March 17, 1998).

Robert Redford

When Robert Redford (born 1937) appeared in the 1969 hit motion picture *Butch Cassidy and the Sundance Kid,* he was already well on his way to becoming an American motion picture icon. Known for his good looks, intelligence and commercial success, Redford's successes in writing, directing and producing motion pictures, as well as his establishment of the Sundance Institute, has made him a household name throughout the world.

Charles Robert Redford, Jr. was born on August 18, 1937 in Santa Monica, California to Charles, Sr. and Martha (Hart) Redford. His father was a milkman who worked long hours in Redford's early years. After World War II, Redford's father got a job at the Standard Oil Company as an accountant and the family moved to nearby Van Nuys, California where Redford attended high school along with his brother, William. Redford was not happy in Van Nuys, which he called "a cultural mud sea," and was soon engaging in activities designed to break the unending boredom and conformist attitudes he felt closing in around him. He climbed high buildings in the Hollywood area and stole hub caps off of automobiles.

Fortunately for Redford, he also excelled in athletics, and upon his graduation in the spring of 1955, he accepted a baseball scholarship from the University of Colorado in Boulder, Colorado. Although Redford seemed to have the world by the tail and a bright future, 1955 was also the year that his mother died suddenly. This shocked and stunned Redford deeply and it would take him years to come to terms with her death.

Early Academic Failure

Redford commenced his studies at the University of Colorado in late 1955, but he soon became disillusioned with college life. Although Redford joined a fraternity and tried to become interested in college curriculum he was uninterested by most of his courses with the exception of some art classes. He started skipping classes and practices and took up drinking as way to ease his unhappiness. It was

for his drinking that he was kicked off of the team, losing his scholarship.

While Redford was at the University of Colorado, a friend suggested that he should travel to Europe. He moved to Los Angeles, California and began working in the nearby oil fields to pay his bills and save enough money to travel to France so that he could study painting. Once there, he hitchhiked from country to country and stayed in youth hostels. Redford eventually found a sympathetic teacher in Florence, Italy, but later when that teacher criticized him for his slow progress, he decided to return home.

Redford hitchhiked from the east coast of the United States back to Los Angeles where he became increasingly discouraged and began drinking heavily again. In 1958, Redford met Lola Jean Van Wagenen who was living in the same apartment building where he rented. A Mormon from Utah, Van Wagenen encouraged Redford to resume his study of the arts. Van Wagenen's effect on Redford was so profound that they were married on September 12, 1958 and she left college to travel with him to New York.

With a new outlook and encouragement from his wife, Redford moved to Brooklyn, New York to study painting at the Prat Institute late in 1958. Redford was aware that he might need a sideline career to fall back on in case painting did not pay the bills. He decided to study theatrical set design at the American Academy of Dramatic Arts in New York as a sideline.

Starts Acting

Redford received complimentary reports on his designs and came to the attention of Mike Thoma, the stage manager for the Broadway comedy *Tall Story* which had opened on January 2, 1959. Thoma was responsible for recruiting replacements when actors left the cast. Thoma invited Redford to audition for a small part in the production. Redford auditioned and was hired on the spot. When *Tall Story* ended its run on May 2, 1959, the agent who had signed Redford recommended him for a role in *The Highest Tree.* The production opened on November 4, 1959 at the Longacre Theatre in New York City but ran only a few weeks. The experience was not a total loss for Redford, as he had found an occupation in which he was capable and enjoyed.

With the prospect of not being able to find another acting job until the next season opened in early 1960, Redford returned to Los Angeles to try his hand at television. Los Angeles was overflowing with acting jobs and Redford played half a dozen roles within six months. The most notable of these parts was as a Nazi lieutenant in *In the Presence of Mine Enemies* in 1960. In the autumn of 1960, Redford returned to New York to take part in a production of *The Iceman Cometh.* His first child, Shauna, was born shortly thereafter. Redford was then cast in a production of *Little Moon of Alban* which opened on December 1, 1960 but had only twenty performances.

Redford had his first leading role in a production of *Sunday in New York* on Broadway. It ran until May of 1962, but during breaks in the production Redford would appear with small parts on such television shows as *Route 66, The*

Twilight Zone, Alfred Hitchcock Presents and *Naked City.* He also made his motion picture debut in the 1962 film *War Hunt,* which was hailed by critics despite its low budget. Redford also became a father for the second time when his son, David James, was born.

Redford returned to California following the close of *Sunday in New York* to work in television. He was noticed by actor and comedian Mike Nichols who was to direct a production of Neil Simon's *Barefoot in the Park.* Nichols demanded that Redford be cast in the production and when it opened in New York on October 23, 1963, it was an overnight success. The tediousness of doing the same performance eight times a week soon bored Redford and he withdrew from the cast on September 5, 1964, never returning to the stage.

Early Movies

Instead of stage, Redford concentrated on motion pictures. His first four motion pictures were not very successful and a less determined actor might have given up. Redford stuck it out through 1965 with *Situation Hopeless - But Not Serious,* and *Inside Daisy Clover,* opposite Natalie Wood. *Inside Daisy Clover* earned him a Golden Globe award for the most promising male newcomer. The 1966 films *The Chase* and *This Property Is Condemned* were not received much better by critics or the public, so Redford decided to vacation with his family in Spain and Crete until the right role came along.

Redford returned to Hollywood to do a film version of *Barefoot in the Park.* His performance was widely hailed and earned him a spot in what was to become one of his greatest successes, *Butch Cassidy and the Sundance Kid.*

Mainstream Success

After negotiations with three other well-known actors failed, Redford was offered the part of the Sundance Kid opposite Paul Newman in 1969. Initially rejected by the head of Twentieth Century-Fox for the role, Redford worked and made it his own. *Butch Cassidy and the Sundance Kid* became one of the most successful westerns of all time and made Redford a household name. The movie is widely regarded as one of the pinnacle motion pictures about the American west and the men who lived in and through it. It won four Academy Awards and made Redford a bankable movie star.

Hoping to cash in on Redford's success in *Butch Cassidy and the Sundance Kid,* Paramount hurried *Downhill Racer* into theaters in November 1969. Redford starred in and co-produced the motion picture and, although it was hailed by critics, the public did not react as strongly as the had to *Butch Cassidy and the Sundance Kid.* The same fate awaited *Tell Them Willie Boy Is Here,* which had been rushed into theaters in December 1969. Redford's role as a good samaritan cowboy earned him the British Film Academy's 1970 award for best actor and in May of that year his daughter, Amy Hart, was born.

Redford made *The Hot Rock* and *The Candidate* in 1972, but it was the last of the films he made that year, *Jeremiah Johnson,* that remains his favorite of his own films.

The film, the story of a trapper trying to survive in the Utah wilderness of the nineteenth century, was initiated by Redford in his search for good roles. *The Way We Were,* a story concerning the Hollywood witch-hunts of the 1950s, followed in 1973. That year also saw his reunion with Newman in *The Sting.* The story of two gangsters out for revenge in the 1930s in Chicago earned the motion picture seven Academy Award nominations and Redford his first nomination for best actor.

Redford followed up with *The Great Gatsby,* the motion picture adaptation of the F. Scott Fitzgerald novel, in 1974. He acted in *The Great Waldo Pepper* and *Three Days of the Condor* in 1975 before making one of his most acclaimed motion pictures, *All the President's Men,* in 1976. Redford took an active part in the movie by convincing Watergate reporters Carl Bernstein and Bob Woodward to write a motion picture script relating their experiences during the last days of Richard Nixon's presidency instead of a book. *All the President's Men* was awarded four Academy Awards and was second on the list of top ten money-makers for that year.

Redford had only a small role in the 1977 film *A Bridge Too Far,* opting to spend more time with his family. It was not until *The Electric Horseman* (1979) that he returned to play a leading role in a motion picture. His ever-growing social conscience was evident in *Brubaker* (1980). This motion picture was seen by many critics as more of a lecture on social politics than as entertainment, but Redford rebounded with one of his greatest accomplishments on film, *Ordinary People.*

Released in 1980, *Ordinary People,* was the story of a suburban family whose life unravels following the death of a child. Redford had made the transition from actor to director, and would be rewarded highly for his efforts. He received the Director's Guild of America Award for the outstanding motion picture director of 1980, an Academy Award for the best director of 1980, the National Board of Review Award for best director of 1981 and a Golden Globe Award for the best director of 1981 for his direction in *Ordinary People.*

Founded Sundance Institute

In 1981, Redford founded the Sundance Institute near his summer home in Utah to help promote the art of motion picture making and to provide financial funding for artists developing unique visions of their own. The Institute, named after the role that made Redford famous, has since expanded to incorporate a yearly film festival and a theater company that produces original works.

Redford returned to motion pictures in 1984 with his role as an aging baseball player in *The Natural.* He acted in the 1985 Academy Award winner for best picture, *Out of Africa,* but told *New York* that this experience ranked among the least satisfying of his career. After that, with a divorce from his wife later that year, his movie roles became less frequent. He appeared in only six motion pictures, *Legal Eagles* (1986), *Havana* (1991), *Sneakers* (1992), *Indecent Proposal* (1993), *Up Close And Personal* (1996), and *The Horse Whisperer* (1998), over the next twelve years.

Instead, he concentrated his efforts more on creating and directing quality motion pictures for other actors. He directed *The Milagro Beanfield War* in 1988, *A River Runs Through It,* in 1992, and *Quiz Show,* (1994), which won him the Cecil B. DeMille Award for best picture and established the Sundance Institute as a creative force in the motion picture industry. For all of his efforts in promoting the art of movie making and for his achievements in film, he was awarded the 1995 Screen Actors Guild Lifetime Achievement Award.

Further Reading

Authors & Artists for Young Adults, volume 15, Gale Research, 1995.
Contemporary Authors, volume 107, Gale Research, 1983.
Entertainment Weekly, Fall 1996; September 5, 1997.
Interview, September 1994; January 1997.
McCall's, April 1996.
New York, December 10, 1990.
Premiere, February 1998.
Rolling Stone, October 6, 1994.
''Celebsite: Robert Redford,'' *CelebSite,* http://www.celebsite.com (March 18, 1998).
''E! Online - Fact Sheet - Robert Redford,'' *E! Online,* http://eonline.com (March 18, 1998).
''Robert Redford,'' *The Network for Entertainment Fans—fansites.com—Index,* http://www.fansites.com (March 18, 1998).
Sundance Institute, http://www.sundance.net/institute/ (March 18, 1998).

Christopher Reeve

Christopher Reeve (born 1952) is an actor who has worked on behalf of those with disabilities ever since he suffered an injury that left him a quadriplegic.

Inspirational, brave, determined this is how actor and activist Christopher Reeve has been described ever since a devastating accident in 1995 left him paralyzed from the neck down. Best known for his starring role in four *Superman* movies, Reeve saw his life change forever in a mere moment. His tireless efforts to secure funding for spinal cord research may one day lead to a cure for paralysis. ''I think God sent Chris to be the man to do this because of his heart and courage and awareness and fight,'' declared his longtime friend and fellow actor Mandy Patinkin in *People* magazine. ''The ironies are unbelievable. He's more than Superman.''

A native of Manhattan, Reeve was the oldest of two sons born to Franklin D. Reeve, a novelist, translator, and university professor, and Barbara Pitney Lamb Johnson, a journalist. Reeve's parents were divorced when he was about four years old and he moved with his mother and brother to Princeton, New Jersey. Although he grew up there amid affluence, following his mother's remarriage to a

stockbroker, he nevertheless had to cope with the lingering anger and tension that characterized his parents' relationship.

Reeve would often pass the time away during his youth playing the piano, swimming, sailing, or engaging in some other solitary activity. And while he was still just a child around ten or so the stage began call. His very first role was in a Princeton theater company's production of Gilbert and Sullivan's *The Yeoman of the Guard,* and after that experience, Reeve was hooked. Later, as a gawky teenager lacking in self-confidence, he found that acting helped him overcome his feelings of clumsiness and inadequacy. ''[My life] was all just bits and pieces,'' Reeve explained to *Time* magazine reporter Roger Rosenblatt. ''You don't want to risk getting involved with people for fear that things are going to fall apart. That's why I found relief in playing characters. You knew where you were in fiction. You knew where you stood.''

Reeve starred in virtually every stage production at his exclusive private high school and also spent the summer months immersed in the theater, either as a student or an actor. By the time he was sixteen, he was a bona fide professional with an Actors' Equity Association membership card and an agent.

After graduating from high school in 1970, Reeve attended Cornell University, where he earned a bachelor's degree in English and music theory in 1974. Meanwhile, he continued his drama education, serving as a backstage observer at both the Old Vic in London and the Comedie-

Francaise in Paris before enrolling in the Juilliard School for Drama in New York City to pursue graduate studies.

Reeve's first major acting assignment came shortly after his graduation from Cornell when he joined the cast of the television soap opera "Love of Life." He remained with the program for two years, during which time he also performed on stage in the evenings with various New York City theater companies, including the Manhattan Theater Club and the Circle Repertory Company. Reeve made his Broadway debut in 1975 in the play *A Matter of Gravity,* an offbeat comedy starring Katharine Hepburn. Even though it received lackluster reviews and closed after only a few weeks, it provided Reeve with the opportunity to learn valuable lessons about his craft from one of the greatest actresses of the century.

Later that same year, Reeve headed to California and won his first movie role, a bit part in a 1978 nuclear submarine disaster movie titled *Gray Lady Down.* But when no other work was forthcoming, he returned to New York City and appeared in an off-Broadway play that opened in January 1977.

Then, to Reeve's surprise, Hollywood came calling with an offer to try out for the role of Superman in an upcoming film of the same title. (After approaching several big-name actors who turned them down or who just didn't suit the part, the project's producers and director had decided to go after an unknown.) At first, Reeve thought the idea was downright silly and very un-theatrical, but then he read the script and loved it. So when he was invited back for a screen test, he was determined to beat out the other hopefuls for the part. Reeve prepared for two solid weeks, experimenting with complete makeup and costume changes for both Superman and Clark Kent. He aced the screen test and the part was his.

Filming on *Superman* began in the spring of 1977 and took about eighteen months to complete, partly because of its technical complexity and certain logistical problems. When it premiered in December 1978, it met with almost universal critical acclaim and astounding box-office success. Suddenly, Reeve was a megastar with all of the baggage that entailed, including countless demands on his time, a total loss of privacy, and the danger of being typecast forever as the hunky "Man of Steel."

Deluged with offers, Reeve accepted a part in a low-budget romantic drama as his next project. *Somewhere in Time,* which also starred Jane Seymour and Christopher Plummer, was released in 1980 to less-than-enthusiastic reviews and a lukewarm reception at the box office. Since then, however, it has developed a cult-like following among those who find its dreamy quality and pretty scenery irresistible.

Reeve's next project was *Superman II,* which he had agreed to do when he signed on for the first film. It, too, was spectacularly successful upon its debut in mid-1981, setting what was then a record by taking in five million dollars on a single day. The critics also liked it, with some even saying that it was better than the first movie.

Throughout the 1980s and early 1990s, Reeve enjoyed an increasingly busy film career. Besides reprising his most famous role in *Superman III* (1983) and *Superman IV: The Quest for Peace* (1987), which he also helped write, Reeve appeared in about a dozen other pictures, including *Deathtrap* (1982), *Noises Off* (1992), *The Remains of the Day* (1993), *Speechless* (1994), and *Village of the Damned* (1995). Reeve was also involved in a number of television productions during this same period, among them the movies *Anna Karenina* (1985), *The Rose and the Jackal* (1990), *Death Dreams* (1991), *The Sea Wolf* (1993), and *Above Suspicion* (1994). In addition, he appeared in several documentaries for which he served as host and narrator. He also appeared on *Faerie Tale Theatre* in a production of "Sleeping Beauty" and in an episode of *Tales from the Crypt.*

In between working in film and television, Reeve often returned to the stage, both on and off-Broadway and in regional venues such as the Williamstown (Massachusetts) Theatre. During the summer of 1980, for example, he appeared in Williamstown in *The Cherry Orchard, The Front Page,* and *The Heiress.* Later that same year, he opened on Broadway in the hit drama *Fifth of July* and remained with the cast for five months. He then returned to Williamstown in the summer of 1981 to perform in *The Greeks.* Reeve's subsequent stage appearances included *The Aspern Papers* in London in 1984 and New York productions of *The Marriage of Figaro* (1985) and *Love Letters.* In Williamstown, he performed in *Holiday, John Brown's Body* (1989) and *The Guardsman* (1992).

On May 27, 1995, Reeve's world was shattered in a matter of seconds when he was thrown from his horse head first during an equestrian competition in Virginia. The impact smashed the two upper vertebrae in his spine, leaving him completely paralyzed from the neck down and able to breathe only with assistance from a ventilator. Reeve remained in intensive care for five weeks as he fought off pneumonia, underwent surgery to fuse the broken vertebrae in his neck, and weathered several other life-threatening complications of his injury. Doctors initially gave him no more than a fifty percent chance of surviving. Once he was stabilized, he was then transferred from the hospital to a rehabilitation facility for six months of therapy and learning how to adjust to his paralysis.

With his characteristic grit and determination, Reeve set about the task of putting his life in order. He mastered the art of talking between breaths of his ventilator. He learned how to use his specialized wheelchair, which he commands by blowing puffs of air into a straw-like control device. Always hungry for the smallest sign of progress, he did countless exercises, competing against himself to improve and grow stronger. All the while, he later recalled, "You're sitting here fighting depression. You're in shock. You look out the window, and you can't believe where you are. And the thought that keeps going through your mind is, This can't be my life. There's been a mistake.'"

Reeve astounded his friends and admirers by making his first public appearance on October 16, 1995, less than six months after his accident. The occasion was an awards dinner held by the Creative Coalition, an actors' advocacy organization he had helped establish. Reeve joked with the audience about what had happened to him and immediately put everyone at ease, then introduced his old friend Robin Williams, who was being honored for the work he had done on behalf of the group.

The awards dinner was just the beginning for Reeve, who has since channeled his considerable energies into a wide variety of endeavors. In March 1996, he appeared before a worldwide television audience at the Academy Awards to introduce a special segment on movies that display a social conscience. In August of that same year, Reeve was in Atlanta to serve as master of ceremonies at the Paralympic Games and then went on to Chicago, where he delivered an emotional opening-night speech to the Democratic National Convention. Reeve has also kept busy with countless speaking engagements, delivering motivational talks to eager audiences all over the country.

During the spring of 1996, Reeve took on his first acting job since his accident when he agreed to do the voice of King Arthur in an animated feature entitled *The Quest for Camelot.* Later that year, in the fall, he made a cameo appearance in the television movie *A Step Toward Tomorrow* playing a disabled patient who offers psychological support to a young man injured in a diving mishap. And in April 1997, Reeve demonstrated his talents behind the camera when he made his debut as a director of the Home Box Office (HBO) movie *In the Gloaming* about a family struggling to cope with the impending loss of a son to AIDS. Before his accident, Reeve was an activist on behalf of children's issues, human rights, the environment, and the National Endowment for the Arts. He has since assumed the role of national spokesman for the disabled especially those people who, like him, have suffered spinal-cord injuries. As a famous actor and one of the most visible disabled people in the United States, Reeve is using his celebrity status not only to secure financial support for research but also to lobby for insurance reforms that would increase the lifetime benefits cap for catastrophic illnesses or injuries in employer-sponsored health plans from the industry average of $1 million to at least $10 million. He is also the founder of the Christopher Reeve Foundation, which raises funds for biomedical research and acts as an advocate for the disabled, and serves as chairman of the American Paralysis Association.

Meanwhile, Reeve continues to cope with the daily trials and occasional triumphs related to his quadriplegia. "You don't want the condition to define you," he once commented, "and yet it occupies your every thought." While he may never be completely free of his respirator, he does manage to go without it for several hours at a time. He can move his head and shrug his shoulders, and he reports some sensation in one of his legs and one of his forearms. He exercises regularly to keep his body flexible and to prevent his muscles from atrophying, noting that "the more I do, the more I can do." Yet Reeve must also deal with unpredictable spasms that send his body into embarrassing and potentially dangerous contortions, and in 1997 he was hospitalized twice for blood clots.

Reeve is determined to walk again; one of his fondest dreams, has him standing up on his fiftieth birthday in the year 2002 and offering a toast to all of the people who helped him get to that point. "When John Kennedy promised that by the end of the 1960s we would put a man on the moon," Reeve told Rosenblatt of *Time,* "everybody, including the scientists, shook their heads in dismay. But we did it. We can cure spinal-cord injuries too, if there's the will. What was possible in outer space is possible in inner space."

Further Reading

Reeve, Christopher, *Still Me,* Random House, 1998.
Chicago Tribune, April 13, 1993; June 3, 1996.
Entertainment Weekly, November 15, 1996.
Good Housekeeping, August 1997.
Ladies' Home Journal, April 1996.
McCall's, September 1987; January 1991.
Newsweek, June 12, 1995, p. 43; July 1, 1996, p. 56.
New York Times, June 1, 1995; June 2, 1995; June 6, 1995; October 17, 1995; June 2, 1996; October 31, 1996.
People, June 12, 1995; June 26, 1995, pp. 55-56; December 25, 1995-January 1, 1996, pp. 52-53; April 15, 1996; December 30, 1996, p. 71; January 27, 1997, pp. 82-86.
Time, August 26, 1996, pp. 40-52. □

Frederic Remington

The works of 19th-century American sculptor and illustrator Frederic Remington (1861-1909) recall the rough-hewn frontier life of the American West.

F rederic Remington is the artist most closely identified with subjects of the American West during the closing decades of the 19th century. His drawings, paintings, sculptures, and writings present realistic and highly detailed depictions of many aspects of frontier life, including cowboys taming broncos, cavalry soldiers engaged in battle, and Native American warriors and scouts. According to Harold McCracken in his *Frederic Remington's Own West,* "The name of Frederic Remington has become synonymous with the realistic portrayal of our Old West. His impressive paintings, drawings and works of sculpture of the early day frontiersmen, cowboys and Indians are today well established as pictorial documentations of the most colorful and virile, as well as the most popular chapter in American history."

Born in Canton, New York, in 1861, Remington was the only child of Clara B. Sackrider and Seth Pierre Remington, a journalist who served as a Union cavalry officer during the American Civil War. In 1873 the family moved to nearby Ogdensburg, a port city on the St. Lawrence River, where Seth Remington became a customs official. Young Remington was educated at Vermont Episcopal Institute in Burlington and later attended the Highland Military Academy in Worcester, Massachusetts. Although he had expressed some interest in pursuing a journalistic career, Remington entered Yale University as a student in the

School of Fine Arts in 1878. While he was determined to pursue a career as an illustrator, he chafed under the constraints of formal art training and particularly resisted the academic practice of drawing from plaster casts rather than from nature. At Yale, in addition to his studies, Remington participated in boxing and football as a member of the 1879 team, then captained by Walter Camp, later known as the "father of football."

First Experiences in the West

Remington left Yale in 1880 when his father died. Acting on a long-held fascination with the frontier, he made his first extended trip into the West—specifically to the Montana Territory—in 1881 and on his return East sold his first sketches to *Harper's Weekly*. In a 1905 article in *Collier's* he later recalled his early inspiration for depicting Western subjects, stating: "I knew the wild riders and the vacant land were about to vanish forever. . . . And the more I considered the subject, the bigger the forever loomed. Without knowing exactly how to do it, I began to try to record some facts around me, and the more I looked the more the panorama unfolded . . . I saw the living, breathing end of three American centuries of smoke and dust and sweat."

With a $9,000 inheritance from his father, the 21-year-old Remington travelled West again, determined to seek his fortune. He bought a sheep farm in Kansas in 1883, but this venture proved a failure, and Remington sold it the spring of 1884. He next embarked on a sketching trip to the Southwest, returning to Kansas City to invest in a saloon. He married his Ogdensburg neighbor Eva Adele Caten, whose

father had earlier refused a proposal by the unemployed artist, and with her settled in Kansas City. However, Remington's investment in the saloon proved an unfortunate one, and within months Eva Remington had returned to her parents' home. Remington set out on another tour of the Southwest, sketching subjects in Arizona and in the Indian Territory.

Career as a Magazine Illustrator

In late 1885 Remington sold two sketches to *Harper's Weekly* owner Henry Harper, and he settled in New York City to pursue a career as a magazine illustrator. He reunited with his wife and enrolled in the Art Students League in 1886 to refine his technical skills. The following summer Remington returned to the West, but on this occasion his trip was financed by *Harper's,* which commissioned a series of illustrations covering the Indian Wars. These works, depicting clashes between U.S. troops commanded by General Nelson Miles and their Native American opponents, were published weekly in the magazine and proved highly popular with readers. As a magazine illustrator, Remington's reputation grew quickly. Among his chief subjects were cowboys, cavalry soldiers, Native Americans, and settlers, whom he depicted in realistic war scenes as well as engaged in the ordinary activities of camp life.

In 1888 *Century* magazine commissioned a series of sketches and articles focusing on the adjustment of Native Americans to reservation life. Beginning with these reports, Remington became a regular and well-recognized writer on Western subjects both in journalism and in fiction. He subsequently served as a journal correspondent during the Indian Wars of 1890-91, in Russia and Algiers in 1892 and 1893, and in Cuba during the Spanish-American War. His principal writings include *Pony Tracks* (1892), the short-story collections *Crooked Trails* (1898), *Sundown Leflare* (1899), and *Men with the Bark On* (1900), and the novels *John Ermine of the Yellowstone* (1902) and *The Way of an Indian* (1906). In 1897 Theodore Roosevelt, who had admired Remington's illustrations since they accompanied Roosevelt's own documentary series "Ranch Life and the Hunting Trail" in *Century,* praised Remington's literary skill in a letter quoted by McCracken in *Frederic Remington's Own West,* a collection of Remington's stories and journalism. Roosevelt told Remington: "You come closer to the real thing with the pen than any other man in the western business. . . . Somehow you get close not only to the plainsman and soldier, but to the half-breed and Indian. . . . Literally innumerable short stories and sketches of cowboys, Indians, and soldiers have been, or will be written. Even if very good they will die like mushrooms, unless they are the very best, but the very vest will live and will make the cantos in the last epic of the Western Wilderness. . . . Now, I think you are writing this 'very best' . . . . You have struck a note of grim power."

A Shift to Painting

Also in the mid-1880s Remington moved from illustration to water-color and oil painting. The transformation from magazine illustrator to fine artist required Remington to apply himself to learning the intricacies of color, a task he found daunting. He remained devoted to Western subjects, using photography and studies produced on numerous excursions into the frontier as guides for more permanent works, which he completed in his studio in New Rochelle, New York. His oil *A Dash for the Timber* (1889), which depicts cowboys fleeing on horseback from Native warriors, is seen to demonstrate many of the notable qualities of Remington's art of this period, including strong narrative content, masculine energy, and realistic detail. After 1900 he experimented with a subtler and more limited palette in such nocturnal scenes as *The Old Stagecoach of the Plains.* In 1903 he was awarded an exclusive contract with *Collier's* to provide a painting for each monthly issue of the magazine, and this agreement provided Remington with a secure income. Commenting on his paintings in 1903, Remington told Edwin Wildman in *Outing:* "Big art is a process of elimination. . . . Cut down and out—do your hardest work outside the picture, and let your audience take away something to think about—to imagine. . . . What you want to do is just create the thought—materialize the spirit of a thing." The final years of Remington's life saw the production of a number of impressionistic works, but he never fully adopted the techniques of Impressionism or eliminated the narrative element from his works.

Begins Work in Bronze

In 1895 Remington began sculpting in bronze, a medium that he believed would prove more lasting than illustration or painting. He wrote to his friend the novelist Owen Wister at the time, "My oils will all get old mastery—that is, they will look like *pale molasses* [sic] in time—my watercolors will fade—but I am to endure in bronze—even rust does not touch.—I am modeling—I find I do well—I am doing a cowboy on a bucking bronco and I am going to rattle down through all the ages." The work he described, *The Bronco Buster* (1895), won immediate praise from contemporary art reviewers, and Remington produced another 24 sculptures in the remaining years of his career. Among the most recognized of these is the 1902 multifigured work *Coming through the Rye,* which was based on Remington's earlier drawing *Cowboys Coming to Town for Christmas.* Depicting four exuberant horsemen riding close together in obvious revelry, the work has, in the words of Michael Edward Shapiro in his *Frederic Remington: The Masterworks,* "become an icon, and its emblematic role transcends its flaws. Etched into popular consciousness in a way that is rare in the annals of American sculpture, it has been widely accepted as an image of the untrammeled life of the West."

Legacy and Contribution

In addition to numerous trips into the American West, Remington also visited Canada and Mexico in pursuit of the subjects of his art. He produced nearly 3,000 drawings and paintings, 25 sculptures, and eight volumes of writings throughout his career. He died December 26, 1909 following an emergency appendectomy that was performed at his home in Ridgefield, Connecticut.

Remington's works are housed in the Remington Art Memorial, in Ogdensburg, New York, as well as in such institutions as the Art Institute of Chicago, the Metropolitan Museum of Art, the Amon Carter Museum of Western Art, and the Whitney Gallery of Western Art, among others. According to Peter Hassrick in *The Way West: Art of Frontier America,* "The scope of Remington's art was truly remarkable," and he noted that "In his career after 1900, Remington served also as a bridge between the tradition of narrative Western art and a new sensitivity toward the quiet passing of the frontier." McCracken, recognizing Remington's continuing appeal to Western enthusiasts and art collectors in the later 20th century, concluded, "In his pictures and his writings, Remington left for the benefit of the generations that follow him, what is beyond doubt one of the most comprehensive documentary records of our Old West and its transition into the limbo of history—and for this alone he deserves our everlasting gratitude."

Further Reading

Baigell, Matthew, *Dictionary of American Art,* Harper, 1979.
Contemporary Authors, Volume 108, Gale, 1983.
Dawdy, Doris Ostrander, *Artists of the American West: A Biographical Dictionary,* Sage Books, 1974.
Hassrick, Peter, *The Way West: Art of Frontier America,* Abrams, 1977.
Hodge, Jessica, *Frederic Remington,* Barnes & Noble, 1997.
Remington, Frederic, *Frederic Remington's Own West,* edited by Harold McCracken, Promontory Press, 1960.
Shapiro, Michael Edward, and Peter H. Hassrick, editors, *Frederic Remington: The Masterworks,* Abrams/St. Louis Art Museum, 1988.

Cal Ripken Jr.

Cal Ripken, Jr. (born 1960) holds many records in professional baseball, but it is his breaking of Lou Gehrig's record of 2,131 consecutive games played that especially endears him to his admirers, who call him the "Iron Man" of baseball. The perseverance, endurance and everyday work ethic that Ripken has exhibited throughout his 17 seasons with the Baltimore Orioles has made him one of the most popular professional athletes in all of sports.

Calvin Edwin Ripken, Jr. was born on August 24, 1960 in the small Maryland town of Havre de Grace to Calvin, Sr. and Viola Ripkin. His father had been with the Baltimore Orioles as a minor-league catcher since 1957, and after a shoulder injury dashed his hopes of a major-league career, the elder Ripken stayed on with the club as a coach and manager at both the minor and major-league level. While the family made their home in Aberdeen, Maryland, Ripken's father traveled around from Wisconsin to South Dakota before finally managing the Orioles minor-league team in North Carolina.

His father would also work extra jobs in the summer to help the family keep their heads above water. During the summers, the family would leave Aberdeen, about 30 miles north of Baltimore, and travel with their father during the baseball season. Even with all of the traveling alongside his father, Ripken never saw much of him because of the long hours he put in at the ball park. He soon came to the conclusion that the only way he would be able to see his father was if he played baseball.

Interest in Baseball Grows

Sitting in the stands watching his father coach, the young Ripken learned the finer points of the game that would one day be his life. After the games, he would spend what little time he had with his father discussing the games. At the age when most young children dream of becoming a fireman or an astronaut, Ripken had already decided what his future career would be. "I've always been serious about baseball," Ripken told the *Washington Post.* "From eight or nine on, I knew sports were my life. The teachers would say, 'Write down what you want to be,' and by eleven or twelve, I had narrowed it to baseball." By the time Ripken was 12-years-old, he was taking batting and in-field practice with his father's team and idolizing his favorite minor-league player, Doug DeCinces, who he would one day replace in the Orioles line-up.

In 1976, Ripken's father was promoted to a coaching position with the Orioles in Baltimore and Ripken was a constant presence pitching and hitting during batting practices, retrieving balls, getting advice from major-league stars

like Brooks Robinson and dreaming of becoming a Baltimore Oriole. After games, Ripken would quiz his father further about the day's game, picking up more knowledge about the intricacies of the game. A two time letter-winner in soccer, it was baseball that was Ripken's first love during high school and he made the varsity team as a freshman. Ripken played in the Mickey Mantle World Series in Texas in 1977, and won the Harford County batting title with an amazing .492 batting average his senior year. Behind his play, his high school team was crowned state Class A champions in 1978 and, soon after, Ripken was selected by the Orioles in the second round of the annual baseball draft. His dream was complete, as he was now a member of the Baltimore Orioles baseball team.

Begins Play for the Orioles

Ripken was employed by the Orioles amateur-league team in Bluefield, West Virginia, where he decided to play shortstop instead of pitcher. He reasoned that if he failed as a shortstop, he could instead try out as a pitcher. His first season with the Orioles organization was not an amazing success, he had a mediocre .264 batting average and led the league in errors with 33. Soon after, he was moved to the Oriole's Florida Instructional League team in Miami and improved to a .303 batting average.

At the end of the 1979 season, he was promoted to a spot on the Oriole's AA team in Charlotte, North Carolina and had a .180 batting average after only 61 at-bats. In 1980, he had a .276 batting average and hit 25 home runs after hitting only eight in his previous two seasons. Behind this performance, he was named the Southern League's all-star and was soon moved up the ladder again, this time to the Oriole's AAA team in Rochester, New York in 1981. He continued to develop in Rochester, with a batting average of .288 and 23 home runs, before being called up to the Orioles in August of 1981.

Learns to be Himself

Ripken had a batting average of only .128 in 39 at-bats during his first season with the Orioles, but his second season would prove to be a watershed. The Orioles had traded former third baseman Doug DeCinces, who had been with the club since 1977, to the California Angels believing that third base would be Ripken's ultimate spot on the team. Although he had started out switching back and forth between third base and shortstop, Oriole manager Earl Weaver placed Ripken at third base to start his second season. After hitting a home run during his first at-bat his second season, Ripken's performance declined to a mere .117 batting average.

After consulting his father and future baseball hall of fame star Reggie Jackson, Ripken's performance improved to a .264 batting average with 28 home runs and he was selected as the American League's Rookie of the Year. "[Reggie Jackson] told me to just be myself and everything would fall into place. . . . After that, everything seemed to click," Ripken told the *Sporting News.* With the club struggling during the playoff race at the end of the 1982 season, Ripken was moved to shortstop, a position many thought him too young and too tall, at six-feet-four-inches, to play effectively. The Orioles eventually lost the eastern division championship to the Milwaukee Brewers, but Ripken had played well and Jackson's advice had worked. Ripken would continue to play shortstop until 1996 before moving back to third base.

Success and Defeat

In 1983, with Ripken firmly in place and comfortable, he helped the Orioles win the World Series against the Philadelphia Phillies. For his efforts he was voted the American League's most valuable player for the series and the *Sporting News* player of the year. Earlier that year, he also helped captain the American League all-star team to its first victory since 1971 over the National League.

In 1984, Ripken signed a new four-year contract, but even with going on to set record after record, his team finished only in fifth place. In 1985, the Orioles finished in fourth place, but Ripken had a respectable .282 batting average. In 1986, the Orioles finished last in their division, the first time this had happened in team history. In response the team fired their manager and hired Ripken, Sr.

At the beginning of the 1987 season, there were three Ripkens in the Orioles training camp, Cal, Sr. and Jr. and Billy, Cal, Jr.'s younger brother, who would play second base. Ripken had only a .252 batting average that year but led American League short stops in assists and later that year signed a new one-year contract worth $1.75 million. At the end of the 1987 season, Ripken married his longtime girlfriend, Kelly Greer. During the 1988 season, Ripken's father was fired as the Orioles had the worst record in baseball history. However, Ripken was seen by fans and management as a player the team could not afford to be without, and he soon signed a new four year contract worth $8.4 million.

Record Breaker

During the 1989 season, Ripken was slowly taking over as the team's leader, as Eddie Murray, who had been traded to the Los Angeles Dodgers, was no longer there. Despite losing the divisional title to the Toronto Blue Jays, Ripken committed only eight errors and hit 21 home runs. This made him the first shortstop to have eight 20-homer seasons. On June 12, 1990, Ripken moved into second place for the record of most consecutive games played as he appeared in his 1,308th consecutive game, surpassing Everett Scott's mark. Ripken also broke Scott's record for the most games played in one position. "It wasn't a goal coming to the big leagues that I wouldn't miss a game," Ripken told the *New York Times*. "You just try to prepare yourself each and every day and go there. Eight years later, it had evolved into this."

Unfortunately, Ripken's batting average had declined every year since 1983 and many wondered if his insistence to play every game was wearing him down. But, his defensive play was improving and in the 1990 season, he made only three errors. He also set a record for shortstops by playing 95 games without committing an error. In 1990, the Orioles finished only in fifth place, but Ripken continued to hit over 20 home runs and was runner-up for the Gold Glove award. In 1991, Ripken won the American League's most valuable player award for the second time and was voted the major-league player of the year by the *Sporting News* and the Associated Press. That year he would win the Gold Glove award for the best defensive player and was named the most valuable player for the all-star game.

The opening of the 1992 season saw Ripken bogged down in contract talks with Orioles management. Although he continued to play, his batting average dropped dramatically from the previous year. The fans showed their support and empathy by making him the leading vote-getter in the all-star balloting. On his thirty-second birthday, the talks with management were resolved and Ripken signed the richest deal in baseball history with a five-year contract worth $30.5 million. The deal improved his playing, as he had a batting average of .300 for the 1993 season and in 1994 surpassed Brooks Robinson as the all-time Orioles run-scorer.

Iron Man

On September 6, 1995, Ripken became baseball's "Iron Man" as he surpassed Lou Gehrig's all-time consecutive games played record of 2,130. He had not missed a game since May 30, 1982 and when the game became official in the fifth inning, the capacity crowd at Baltimore's Camden Yards roared its approval. During a speech after the milestone game, Ripken underplayed his achievement and showed the humility that had become his trademark. "Tonight I stand here, overwhelmed, as my name is linked with the great and courageous Lou Gehrig. I'm truly humbled to have our names spoken in the same breath."

On May 29, 1996, Ripken hit his 334th home run for first-place on the Orioles all-time list. On June 14, 1996, he played in his 2,216th consecutive game. This mark surpassed the record of Sachio Kinugasa of the Hiroshima Carp of Japan's Central League and gave Ripken the world record. After moving to third base, he helped lead the Orioles into the playoffs for the 1997 season.

Ripken is signed to a contract extension to play for the Orioles through the 1999 season and lives with his wife and two children, Rachel and Ryan in Reistertown, Maryland. In the spring of 1996, Ripken helped open the Ripken Museum in the town hall at Aberdeen, Maryland and he is extensively involved in various charity organizations throughout Baltimore and Maryland.

Further Reading

Rosenfeld, Harvey, *Iron Man: The Cal Ripken, Jr. Story,* St. Martins Mass Market Paperback, 1996.
Inside Sports, April 1984.
New York Times, June 11, 1990.
Sport, June 1997.
Sporting News, November 29, 1982; March 9, 1998.
Sports Illustrated, March 22, 1984; April 2, 1984; June 18, 1990; July 29, 1991; June 28, 1993; August 7, 1995.
Washington Post, March 22, 1992.
Cal Ripken, Jr.—Homepage—CBS Sportsline USA, http://www.2131.com (April 28, 1998).

"Orioles Online," *Orioles Online Home Page,* http://the-orioles.com (April 28, 1998).

Alice M. Rivlin

Founding director of the Congressional Budget Office, economist Alice M. Rivlin (born 1931) has leveraged her financial savvy into a key post with the Democratic administration of President Bill Clinton.

Considered to be one of the foremost analysts of the U.S. economy, Alice M. Rivlin has never been known to look at the country's financial forecast wearing rose-colored glasses. Independent-minded, Harvard-educated, and with years of experience in both the public and private sector, Rivlin has been credited with molding the fledgling Congressional Budget Office (CBO) into a respectable government agency responsible for long-term analysis and planning of the nation's government spending. Attempting to balance the usual optimism surrounding economic forecasts by the executive branch of government, Rivlin has been careful to act as a counterbalance, employing a conservative, even pessimistic, outlook in the economic projections she generates upon congressional request. Appointed the founding director of the CBO in 1975, Rivlin has worked in the administrations of presidents Lyndon Johnson, Jimmy Carter, Gerald Ford, Bill Clinton, and Ronald Reagan, moving from the CBO to the second most powerful government position associated with the nation's economy: that of assistant chairman of the Federal Reserve Board.

Rivlin was born March 4, 1931, in Philadelphia, Pennsylvania. The daughter of Allan and Georgianna Mitchell, she and her family soon moved to Bloomington, Indiana, where her father held a professorship in nuclear physics at the University of Indiana. Returning to Pennsylvania after high school, she was accepted by Bryn Mawr College and graduated in 1952, magna cum laude. Rivlin went on to obtain an M.A. in 1955 and a Ph.D. in economics from Harvard University's Radcliffe College in 1958. In 1955 she married attorney Lewis A. Rivlin, and relocated to Washington, D.C. The Rivlins would have three children: Catherine Amy, Allan Mitchell, and Douglas Gray, before divorcing in 1977. She was married for a second time, to Sidney G. Winter, in 1989, and still makes her home outside the nation's capitol.

In 1955, while still studying for her doctorate at Radcliffe, Rivlin joined the staff of the Economic Studies Division of the Brookings Institution, a prestigious, liberal "think tank" located in Washington, D.C., as a research fellow. After graduating from Radcliffe, she served that organization until 1993, moving up to senior staff economist in 1963, and senior fellow from 1969 to 1975. Embarking on a full-time career in government in the mid-1960s when she was thirty-five, Rivlin took absences from the Brookings Institution from 1966 to 1969 to work as deputy program coordinator, then assistant secretary for planning and evalu-

ation, for the newly created U.S. Department of Health, Education, and Welfare (H.E.W.), a part of President Johnson's visionary Great Society program, and from 1975 to 1983 to serve as founding director of the Congressional Budget Office established by the Congressional Budget and Impoundment Control Act of 1974 as a reaction to the domination of congressional spending by the executive branch during the presidency of Richard M. Nixon. The CBO allows Congress to have independent forecasts that can enable them to view economic predictions issuing from the White House with greater scrutiny.

While some policymakers feared that Rivlin would use her new position in the CBO as a launching ground for her own pet social and economic policy programs—Maine senator Edmund Muskie reportedly called Rivlin on several occasions, criticizing even informational bulletins issuing from her office that were not specifically authorized by the congressional act—it was soon made clear that she would run the CBO as a neutral office responding to the directives of both House and Senate—functioning as what she has termed the "official purveyor of bad news to the Congress." Her service to other organizations has included acting as consultant to the House committee on education and labor in 1961, as chairman of the National Academy of Sciences/National Research Council's committee on federal agency evaluation research, as trustee for numerous public service organizations, and as a member of the board of directors of such corporations as Union Carbide and Unysis.

Publishes in Many Aspects of Economics

In addition to her work for both the Brookings Institution and the federal government, Rivlin also wrote several books during the 1960s and 1970s. An outgrowth of her job with the H.E.W., a discussion of federal subsidies of undergraduate and graduate education titled *The Role of the Federal Government in Financing Higher Education* was published in 1961, along with several other relatively technical books on budget, tax, and other public policy issues. Other books have included *Microanalysis of Socioeconomic Systems* (1961), a lecture series made at the University of California, Berkeley, and published as *Systematic Thinking for Social Action* (1971), and *Economic Choices,* a book coauthored with others and published in 1982. In 1971 she wrote a regular column published in the *Washington Post* and contributed her insights into economic and public policy topics in articles for a variety of magazines and newspapers.

Weathers Reaganomics in the 1980s

In 1982, after Rivlin ran afoul of newly elected President Ronald Reagan by doubting the accuracy of his projected budget deficit, several congressmen attempted to remove her from the position at the CBO; while such efforts were unsuccessful, she decided to voluntarily step down in 1983. During the remainder of the 1980s, while the presidency was held by Republicans Reagan and George Bush, Rivlin returned to the Brookings Institution, where she served as director for economic studies between 1983 and 1987. She was awarded a MacArthur Foundation Prize fellowship in 1983 and was elected national president of the American Economic Association in 1986. She also wrote and published the 1988 work *Caring for the Disabled Elderly: Who Will Pay?,* and *Reviving the American Dream,* a proposal regarding altering the way in which the federal government relates to the U.S. economy that she released in 1992.

In *Reviving the American Dream,* which Rivlin wrote from the point of view of a "fanatical, card-carrying middle-of-the-roader," she cited the budget deficit as "the biggest single impediment to reviving the American economy" and addressed the drop in real income of U.S. families despite rising income levels. To bolster the U.S. economic future, she outlined a plan that would allow the states to assume a greater portion of the responsibility for economic policy-making. *New York Review of Books* contributor Robert M. Solow commented at length upon Rivlin's proposals, and while commending her approach, detected some weaknesses. Her plan, he noted, makes two questionable assumptions: the first, that state governments have evolved to the point where they can "take on and carry out additional responsibilities without the parochialism, racism,and corruption that justified the growth of federal power in the first place"; second, that U.S. voters will support taxes only when they can clearly see the results of their votes and their tax dollars. "History does not justify much confidence," noted Solow, adding that while Americans demand a balanced budget, they are less sure about which taxes they would be willing to accept to see their demands fulfilled.

Gains Appointment by Clinton

Rivlin served as First Professor of Public Policy at George Washington University during the 1992-93 academic year. When Bill Clinton won election to the presidency in 1992, Rivlin was ready to step back into politics. In January of 1993 she was appointed by President Clinton to a post as deputy director of the Office of Management and Budget, under the directorship of California Congressman Leon Panetta.

After confirmation by the Senate, Rivlin remained OMB's deputy director for a year before being promoted to director in response to Panetta's move to the position of White House Chief of Staff; her appointment was confirmed by the U.S. Senate in October of 1994. Contrasting the then 63-year-old Rivlin with her predecessor, the *Congressional Quarterly* quoted observers as noting that, unlike the gregarious Panetta, "Rivlin . . . is comparatively shy and reserved . . . She's not a politician, she's an analyst."

Despite Rivlin's criticism of several of his policies, including his plan for a deficit reduction trust fund, which she dubbed a "display device," President Clinton continued to express confidence in her abilities and insight. On April 12, 1996, she was nominated for the position of vice-chairman of the Federal Reserve System, the central bank of the United States. This new position would place her immediately under that of Federal Reserve director Alan Greenspan, a man whom many have called the most powerful man in the world due to his control of the U.S. economic system via interest rates and the money supply.

While Rivlin continued to draw confidence from liberal Democrats, partisanship dictates that Republicans would take her economic policies to task. Criticism of her policies has ranged from her continued advocacy of large central governments (either state or federal) as controlling policymakers in lieu of private industry, and her lack of support for tax cuts that would boost investment spending. "For all her distinguished public service . . . and as OMB director . . . Mrs. Rivlin refuses to peer into the twenty-first century," maintained *New Republic* commentator Lawrence Kudlow. "She does not yet grasp that the public believes the Federal Government is too big, costly, and wasteful, controlling too much of daily life." Despite such criticisms, which were reflected in the limited support given her by Republican senators during her FRB confirmation, Rivlin's nomination passed by a vote of 57-41, placing her in line to assume the position of director of the Federal Reserve when Greenspan's term expires in the year 2000.

Further Reading

Schick, Allen, *Congress and Money,* Urban Institute, 1980.
Congressional Quarterly Weekly Report, July 2, 1994, p. 1770; October 1, 1994, p. 2769; June 22, 1996, p. 1746.
Forbes, November 21, 1994, p. 26.
Fortune, June 29, 1992, pp. 25-26.
National Review, November 21, 1994, p. 30.
New York Review of Books, March 25, 1993, pp. 12-18.
Washingtonian, October, 1992, pp. 33-41.

Eddie Gay Robinson

Eddie Robinson (born 1919) brought Louisiana's Grambling State University eight black college football championships during his 56 seasons of coaching. At the time of his retirement, the legendary Robinson had won 408 games, more than any other football coach in history, college or professional.

The son of sharecroppers, Eddie Robinson was born in Jackson, LA, but grew up in Baton Rouge. Across the street lived the Williams family, whose son John, 15 years younger than Robinson, would later become the mayor of Grambling. Young Eddie organized sandlot games and was fascinated from an early age with coaching. His heroes were legendary college coaches Bear Bryant and Amos Alonzo Stagg. "Being coach, it's all I ever wanted to be," Robinson later said.

Putting Grambling on the Map

Robinson completed his bachelor's degree from now-defunct Leland College in 1940. He got a job at a feed mill for 25 cents an hour. Later he would complete a master's degree in science from the University of Iowa. In 1941, Robinson married his college sweetheart Doris and landed the job of his dreams. That year, he coached his first football game at the Louisiana Negro Normal and Industrial Institute in the little northern Louisiana town of Grambling. The school's name was later changed to Grambling State.

In those days black players weren't allowed on most white college teams, especially in the segregated South. The school's president, Ralph Jones, wanted the tiny, underfunded college to gain a national reputation through its football program. That way it would be able to recruit nationwide and survive. Jones and Robinson worked together at this goal for decades.

Robinson became vice-president of athletics and built a strong athletic program from scratch. At first, Robinson coached football, basketball and baseball, for a monthly salary of $63.75. He led the drill team at halftime of football games, put the chalk lines on fields himself, and even wrote game stories for the local paper.

In Robinson's second season, his football team went undefeated and held its opponents scoreless in all nine games. Jones soon succeeded Robinson as baseball coach and created a school band. Robinson was left to concentrate on football, but it wasn't always easy fielding a team. Once, two brothers who were his star players had to leave the team to help their family pick cotton. Robinson and the rest of his players pitched in to help them.

From the start, Robinson stressed a well-rounded education. "The first thing he'd do, he'd assemble the players, tell them they had to get their education, had to get more out of this than football," recalled Fred Hobdy, who played for Robinson in the 1940s and was his athletic director from 1989 to 1996. Robinson inaugurated an Everyday Living course at the college to teach the unsophisticated students the manners of social life.

With the help of school sports information director Collie Nicholson, Grambling soon became a byword in the national black media. Grambling played games all over the country and as far away as Tokyo. In 1968 in Yankee Stadium in New York, the team drew a crowd of 60,000 people. "The Grambling mystique developed until we really did have a national black following," Nicholson said. "President Jones was a genius at opening doors. Of course, the doors wouldn't have stayed open for anybody if Eddie hadn't won."

Hands-On Coaching

Throughout his long career, Robinson remained eager to learn. He attended one to five coaches' clinic each season for 57 years. He borrowed plays liberally from others and drilled his team endlessly to perfect them. Robinson did more than win games. He helped put Grambling on the map and helped put scores of black football players in the professional ranks. And he educated countless youngsters to become constructive citizens. He claimed an 85 percent graduation rate among his players, and coached an estimated 4,500 students.

Robinson groomed more than 200 Grambling players who went on to professional careers in the National Football League, including four Hall of Famers: Buck Buchanan, Charlie Joiner, Willie Brown, and Willie Davis. Seven of his players were first-round draft picks by NFL teams.

Robinson's coaching style was full of emotion. "Robinson was always a master motivator, theatrical and preachy," wrote Richard Hoffer of *Sports Illustrated*. Doug Williams, a Grambling star who became an NFL quarterback and later coach at Morehouse College, recalled: "He'd cry before a big game. He'd cry so hard that you'd be crying. Oh, would he cry." Williams was the first black quarterback to be named Most Valuable Player in a Super Bowl. Robinson had also coached James Harris, the first black man to be a quarterback on any NFL team.

Robinson believed in practice rather than theory, and he always interacted closely with his players. "He's as hands-on as you can get," noted Hoffer. "He takes a player aside to teach him the proper footwork. He makes the offense run Merry-Go-Round, a carnival play that involves three reverses and a pass, over and over." His teams were always squeaky clean. Robinson forbade profanity and made players run sprints if they used any words he considered inappropriate.

During his career, Robinson's Tigers won or shared 17 Southwestern Athletic Conference championships. Among black colleges, Robinson's football teams were dominant for decades. Grambling's growing national reputation attracted star athletes, but Robinson himself was the key. As a recruiter, he was a superb salesman for his college's program.

The small town of Grambling was a family place, and despite his growing national reputation, Robinson never had any desire to go anywhere else. He and his wife Doris had two children: Lillian Rose and Eddie Jr. His son eventually joined him as an offensive and backfield coach, serving as his assistant for 15 years.

"Grambling," wrote Bill Minutaglio of the *Sporting News,* "has always been defined by Eddie Robinson. . . . Every year—with one raw young man after another nervously stepping off the bus from . . . all the rural outposts buried in every corner of Louisiana. For decades they have come to the hidden town of 4,000 because of Eddie Robinson. In the segregated South, Robinson had a sanctuary. And, because the pro scouts also knew their way, Robinson had the promise of a way out."

Difficult Exit

Robinson never wanted to do anything other than coach football at Grambling, and in his advancing years he refused to even consider stepping down. The result was a controversial final few seasons. Because he had opened so many doors for black athletes, Grambling was no longer the only opportunity for talented high school players. The program began to lose some of its luster. The 1994 season ended with a loss to South Carolina State in the Heritage Bowl, a post-season event Grambling always had dominated. The next year, his players threatened to walk out because they hadn't received their Heritage Bowl rings.

In 1996, some Grambling alumni, including some of his former players, launched a movement to get rid of Robinson, whom they felt had lost his grip at age 77. Many observers agreed that Robinson stubbornly had stayed on too long. For the first time in his tenure, Robinson's team had suffered two losing seasons in a row. Five Grambling players pleaded guilty to lesser charges after being accused in the rape of a teenage girl after a game. Grambling was under investigation for the fixing of football players' grades. The program was put on probation for two years for minor infractions, including violations by Eddie Robinson Jr.

Robinson asked for one more season to clean things up and end his career on a better note, and university president Raymond Hicks obliged. "I want to prove I can still win at this age," Robinson told Tim Layden of *Sports Illustrated.* "I ain't ready to sit in a rocking chair and wait for death to come calling on me."

Frank Lewis, a Robinson player who went on to the Pittsburgh Steelers, told Minutaglio: "I don't think he ever had, in his dreams, the thought of retiring. He was going to coach until he passed away." Lewis said Robinson did more for black athletes than anyone would ever know. "With all the good and wonderful things this man has done, he should have been able to set his own date for leaving."

Asked if he was bitter at being turned out of his longtime job, Robinson told Minutaglio: "I have been here all my life. I have had one job, one wife. I had a chance to coach some of the finest players who ever played the game. I've been working at Grambling for 56 years and my paycheck has never been late. Do I need to say anything else?"

Robinson's last game was a 30-7 loss to Southern University in the Bayou Classic on November 29, 1997. He finished with a record of 408 wins, 165 losses and 15 ties. "These 56 years, I've been about the happiest man in the world for coaching the best athletes in the world," Robinson said at a press conference after his final game. In 1997, the Football Writers Association of America renamed its college coach of the year honor the Eddie Robinson/FWAA Coach's Award. Robinson will be remembered among the greatest football coaches in history.

Further Reading

Hawkins, Walter L., ed., *African American Biographies,* McFarland & Co., 1994.

Porter, David L., ed., *African-American Sports Greats,* Greenwood Press, 1989.

Jet, October 20, 1997; December 15, 1997.

Sporting News, October 2, 1995; August 25, 1997.

Sports Illustrated, December 23, 1996; December 1, 1997. ☐

Fred McFeely Rogers

American minister Fred Rogers (born 1928) is the host and creator of the popular and critically acclaimed *Mister Rogers' Neighborhood.* The program is the longest running children's television program on the Public Broadcasting Service (PBS).

For more than forty-five years, Fred Rogers has been entertaining, enlightening, and informing preschool children with his warm and sincere messages of love and acceptance, which serve to validate and reinforce feelings of self-worth among children of all ages. He accomplishes this through his masterful use of television, books, records, and videotapes. Generations of young people have come of age knowing that they are special and loved by the soft-spoken, kindly man who wears sneakers and a cardigan sweater. His Public Broadcasting Service (PBS) program is viewed by more than eight million people in the United States alone. Rogers's endearing appeal is due to the fact that he never talks down to or belittles his audience, rather he relates to them and their lives on their level. This realistic and honest approach has won him legions of fans and numerous awards, including Peabodys, Emmys, and honorary doctorates.

Fred McFeely Rogers was born March 20, 1928, in the western Pennsylvania industrial town of Latrobe, which is about one hour away from Pittsburgh. The city's claim to fame was that it was the home of the Rolling Rock Beer Company. His parents, James and Nancy McFeely Rogers, named him after his maternal grandfather, Fred McFeely. Rogers's father was the president of the McFeely Brick Company, one of Latrobe's largest companies. He was an only child until the age of eleven, when his parents adopted a baby girl.

A lonely, sickly, and shy child, Rogers contented himself by playing the piano and with his puppets. He looked forward to spending quality time with his grandfather McFeely, who encouraged Rogers to be all that he could be and

loved him unequivocally. This deep love was evidenced one day as their visit was drawing to a close, and Rogers's grandfather told him something that would profoundly change his life. Rogers related to *Life* magazine that his grandfather had said, "You know, you made this day a really special day. Just by being yourself. There's only one person in the world like you. And I happen to like you just the way you are." This reaffirming message became the guiding principle in all of Rogers's work.

After graduating from high school in 1946, Rogers attended Dartmouth College to study music. He left after one year and enrolled in Rollins College in Winter Park, Florida. Rogers graduated magna cum laude from Rollins with a bachelor's degree in music composition in 1951. He married fellow Rollins classmate, Sara Joanne Byrd, on July 9, 1952. The couple had two sons.

When he was home on spring break from Rollins in 1951, Rogers was watching television and saw a slapstick, pie-in-the-face comedy routine. This program compelled him to go into television, because Rogers thought that the new mass communication medium of television was not living up to its full potential. Shortly after he graduated from Rollins, he obtained a job at the National Broadcasting Company (NBC) in New York City where he worked as an assistant producer and floor director for such programs as the *Your Lucky Strike Hit Parade,* the *Kate Smith Hour,* the *Voice of Firestone,* and the *NBC Opera Theatre.*

In 1953, Rogers gave up a promising career as a network television producer at NBC and moved back to Penn-

sylvania, where he helped to establish the nascent Pittsburgh public television station WQED. Of the rather abrupt career shift, Rogers told *Broadcasting and Cable,* "[it] seemed to be the way to go for me." Initially Rogers was reluctant to get involved with children's programming, but he picked it up when no one else at the station was willing to do it. With children's programming he found a ready-made outlet for his puppetry when he, along with Josie Carey, produced the hour-long show the *Children's Corner* for National Educational Television (NET) in 1954. This show gave birth to a number of Rogers's beloved puppet friends, including Daniel Striped Tiger and King Friday XIII. During his seven-year stint as the behind-the-scenes puppeteer, writer, and co-producer of the show, Rogers started to work part-time on his master of divinity degree at the Pittsburgh Theological Seminary. He eventually earned his degree in 1962 and was subsequently ordained as a Presbyterian minister by the Pittsburgh Presbytery.

It was also during this time that Rogers started to forge a lifelong association and friendship with his mentor, Dr. Margaret McFarland. McFarland had helped Dr. Benjamin Spock establish the child care development program at the University of Pittsburgh in 1952. It was through her work guiding and shaping the department's program that Rogers had met McFarland. She had served as a mentor to him when he was enrolled in graduate work in the child care development program. After his studies they had stayed in close contact, and McFarland became an informal consultant to Rogers and subsequently his show until she died in 1988. Rogers informed the *Los Angeles Times* that McFarland had told him once to "'offer the kids who you really are because they'll know what's really important to you.' She was always encouraging me to go to the piano on the program [*Mister Rogers' Neighborhood*]. She said, 'they'll find their own way, but show them that there's a way that really means something to you.'"

In 1962, Rogers was offered the opportunity to create a fifteen-minute children's program for the Canadian Broadcasting Corporation (CBC) in Toronto, Ontario. The show was named *Misterogers* by the head of the CBC's children's programming department. This program, which he not only developed but produced as well, marked the first appearance of Rogers in front of the camera. The fifteen-minute segments were hosted by Rogers and incorporated many of the elements that later would be found in *Mister Rogers' Neighborhood.* Two years later he left the CBC and moved back to Pittsburgh and to WQED.

Rogers had obtained the broadcast rights to the *Misterogers* episodes from the CBC and began to combine them into half hour segments called *Mister Rogers' Neighborhood.* The new show was broadcast on WQED and distributed through the Eastern Educational Network from 1965 to 1967. In 1967, the Sears-Roebuck Foundation agreed to fund *Mister Rogers' Neighborhood,* thus making it available to all the public television stations throughout the United States. *Mister Rogers' Neighborhood* was first broadcast across the country in early 1968. Rogers has served as host and executive producer of the show since its inception. In the early 1970s, he established Family Communications,

Inc., a nonprofit organization which was committed to producing family-oriented materials for mass distribution.

Mister Rogers' Neighborhood has differed from many other children's television programs because Rogers has actively sought to converse with his preschool audience, not to talk at them. He also speaks to them on their level and holds a genuine interest and concern in their lives and problems. The focus and emphasis of each show is on children and their individual needs and feelings. Just as his grandfather McFeely had done for him, Rogers has sought to validate the preschoolers' existence and lives. He has endeavored to do this by constantly reinforcing their positive images of self-worth and reminding them that they are special individuals who are well loved.

The pace of *Mister Rogers' Neighborhood* is leisurely, and things happen in real time as opposed to the hyperkinetic jump-starts and flashy cuts and edits of most other programs aimed at young people. There is an established, comfortingly simple routine which starts off each episode of *Mister Rogers' Neighborhood*. Rogers enters the set and begins to sing the show's theme song, a folksy, whimsical tune that urges everyone to join in and become a neighbor. The theme song of *Mister Rogers' Neighborhood* is one of his most famous self-penned songs. As he sings, Rogers changes from his business attire of dress shoes and a sport coat into the more comfortable sneakers and cardigan sweater which has become one of his most identifiable and endearing trademarks. His look has become such a part of American popular culture that one of the cardigans that his mother knitted for him hangs in one of the permanent collections of the Smithsonian Museum in Washington, D.C.

The show's guests and neighbors drop by *Mister Rogers' Neighborhood* and help to deal with the issues of the program. This shows the children in the audience that their feelings and concerns are shared by many others who have also been scared, frightened, apprehensive, alone, happy, and sad, to name but a few emotions. Also part of the show is the daily journey by trolley to the "Neighborhood of Make-Believe" where puppets like Daniel Striped Tiger, King Friday XIII, Queen Sara, and Lady Elaine help to deal with the day's issue in a fantasy-like setting. In this portion of the program, Rogers is content to let the puppets do the explaining and remains offscreen.

During the 1960s and early 1970s, Rogers branched out and released six children's music albums. He also has written several books for and about his preschool-aged audience. The books deal with such diverse, real-life events and episodes as going to the doctor, going to school, going to day care, step families, cancer, and death. These issues and the assorted feelings and emotions which arise in response to them have formed the basis of many of the more than 700 episodes of *Mister Rogers' Neighborhood*. Many of the shows have been rebroadcast over the years (especially the first day of school series), although Rogers has tried to create about fifteen or so new episodes annually to make sure that the show remains relevant and in touch with the youth of today. He has also produced the PBS programs

Old Friends . . . New Friends which aired from 1978 to 1981 and *Fred Rogers' Heroes* which aired in 1994.

Rogers told the *Boston Globe* that the essence of *Mister Rogers' Neighborhood* is "talking about how important the inside [of a person] is in comparison to the outside. Whether the children can use that message right then, at least they can hear it and in some way be comforted by it." Rogers believes that the real test of the show's merit and worth comes when the television is turned off and the show's message is put into practice in the preschooler's day-to-day interactions in the real world.

The strength of *Mister Rogers' Neighborhood* is its constant focus on building and nurturing the self-esteem of young children. According to the official Mister Rogers PBS website, Rogers achieves this by "repeatedly stressing the unique value of each human being—the traits that make us who we are and no one else."

In recognition of his many years of tireless effort to improve the quality of children's broadcasting, Rogers has been honored with numerous awards, including two Peabody Awards, three Emmy Awards, the Ralph Lowell Award from the Corporation for Public Broadcasting in 1975, and a special Christopher Award in 1984. In addition, he has received thirty honorary doctorates from universities and colleges throughout the United States. Child study experts have praised him for his natural ability to effectively relate to preschoolers. He was also honored with a star on the Hollywood Walk of Fame in 1998. In the *Tribune-Review* website, Rogers mentioned the epitaph he would like to be remembered by: "somebody who cared for his neighbor and his neighbor's children."

Further Reading

Boston Globe Sunday Magazine, August 25, 1996, p. 14.
Broadcasting & Cable, July 26, 1993, p. 115.
Christian Century, April 13, 1994, pp. 382-84.
Life, November 1992, pp. 72-82.
Los Angeles Times, January 17, 1993, p. 5.
"Fred Rogers Speaks Out On," *Tribune-Review,* http://www.tribune-review.com/features/cities/mrogers2.html (January 9, 1998).
"Mister Rogers: About Fred Rogers," http://www.pbs.org/rogers/about.html (January 14, 1998).
"Mister Rogers: Welcome to the Series," http://www.pbs.org/rogers/series.html (January 9, 1998).
Williams, Candy C., "Our Favorite Neighbor," *Tribune-Review,* http://www.tribune-review.com/features/cities/mrogers.html (January 9, 1998). □

Anastasia Nicholaievna Romanov

Anastasia Romanov (1901-1918) has become one of the most romanticized figures in history, due to her noble birth, playful personality, and the tragic, mysterious circumstances of her death.

To understand Anastasia Romanov, one must understand the world "Her Imperial Highness the Grand Duchess (equivalent to a princess) Anastasia Nicholaievna Romanov" entered at birth. She was the youngest daughter of Czar (equivalent to an emperor or king) Nicholas II, who, as progenitor of the Romanov dynasty (autocratic rulers of Russia for almost three hundred years), believed he inherited the God-given right to rule. The Romanovs embodied Russia and maintained inseparable ties to the Orthodox church. Many of their subjects, especially peasants, looked to them as demigods.

When Anastasia was born in 1901, Russia was the largest, richest country in Europe. Great wealth was concentrated among the aristocracy and a small upper class, while eighty percent of the population lived in poverty. The opulence and grandeur of imperial Russia outshone the remaining royal courts of Europe, most of which had lost absolute power by 1900, and had accepted redistribution of land as a new reality. *Anastasia: The Lost Princess,* describes the gulf between Russian rulers and their subjects, which began with small revolutionary reform groups during the mid-nineteenth century. Even though reformers within the nobility attempted to make changes, the imperial rulers' attitudes and traditions remained largely unchanged. Conflict was inevitable.

Early Life

Despite her privilege and status, Anastasia grew up to be a remarkably warm, down-to-earth young woman with a spirited personality. She was the darling of the family, popular with the Russian people, and world press. When imperial rule ended with the family's brutal execution, loyalists to the crown—and others around the world—grasped at the possibility of her survival. A woman named Anna Anderson, claiming to be Anastasia, kept the fantasy of her escape and survival alive until 1994 when it was definitively disproved.

The first years of Nicholas II's reign were peaceful. By all accounts, the czar and czarina's primary interest was their family. They spent a great deal of time with the children, and kept them as far away from the social whirl of the court as possible. For Anastasia and her older sisters—Olga, Tatiana, and Marie—and later her brother, Alexei, home within the Winter Palace's 1,000 rooms was the family's private apartment. Less opulent and imposing, the chambers reflected Alexandra's English upbringing with her grandmother, England's Queen Victoria. An observer noted, "English was the language which she always spoke and wrote to the Emperor. . . . the Empress always thought of herself an English woman."

Russia Under The Czars describes Nicholas "as handsome, charming, gentle to the point of weakness, and religious to the point of mysticism." When he met the beautiful, and equally religious and mystical, Princess Alix of Hess-Darmstadt (Germany), they were immediately drawn to one another. The match was as unpopular as it was strong. Russia was on unfriendly terms with Germany, and the czar's family disliked Alexandra's English upbringing. As time went on, and she had not produced the requisite male heir, she retreated from public life.

Both parents agreed that discipline was important; hence, the children slept on hard camp cots with no pillows, made their own beds, and took a cold bath every morning just as their father had done as a boy. Their studies included four languages, in addition to music, drawing, and needlework. Nobility had its rewards, as well; the family traveled aboard a blue imperial train or royal yacht when they went to Tsarskoe Selo, the "tsar's village." The imperial couple preferred the seclusion of Alexander and Catherine Palaces; and the children loved the relative freedom they had to roam around the palatial grounds, which included a small lake with an island where they had a playhouse.

An Evil Spirit Arrives

The joy over the birth of Alexei in 1904 faded when it was learned that he had inherited hemophilia, an incurable disease that prevents blood from clotting. Specialists were consulted, and the czar and czarina prayed for a miracle. A year later they were introduced to Rasputin, a religious pilgrim of immense physical size. With his hypotonic eyes and inexplicable powers to stop Alexei's bleeding, Rasputin gradually gained a dangerous control over Alexandra and her fears. In time, he also dominated Nicholas and exerted his influence on matters of state as well as Alexei's health.

Other than close family friends, the children grew up playing among themselves without much interaction with the outside world. In addition to the czar and czarina's distaste for court life, keeping Alexei's illness secret was crucial to maintaining strong Romanov rule. The nursery years were spent playing with many dolls and toys, each under the supervision of a personal nurse. Even at the age of three, Anastasia knew that Alexei's illness was a secret.

As Anastasia grew older, she and her sisters followed a prescribed routine of visiting their mother in the morning, attending classes, playing, and then joining both parents for afternoon tea. Anastasia, with her golden hair, sparkling blue eyes, and impish playfulness, exerted her head-strong personality and great energy. Nicknamed shvibzik, meaning "imp," Anastasia was mischievous, and loved making others laugh. She delighted in mimicking pompous guests, as well as instigating pranks on nurses and tutors. In his memoirs, her French tutor, Pierre Guillard, wrote, "She was the imp of the whole house and the glummest faces would always brighten in her presence, for it was impossible to resist her jokes and nonsense."

Anastasia did not enjoy most of her schoolwork. According to Hugh Brewster, author of *Anastasia's Album,* her English teacher remembered her trying to bribe him with flowers so he would raise her poor marks. When he refused, she gave them to her Russian teacher. She adored creative subjects, however, and wrote, "I excelled at composition. I must say that all my poems were satires, lampoons, from which no one was safe." Her drawings, paintings, and photographs are well documented in family albums. She often spent hours illustrating letters with drawings, and hand-coloring photographs to highlight a special aspect.

Anastasia was easily bored, and always ready for breaks in the routine. Every March the family boarded the imperial train to go to their retreat on the Black Sea. Photographs portray a simple, informal life filled with swimming and long walks. The family's happiest times were when they were away from duty and the public eye. Journal entries and photographs during summer cruises, vacations at their beachfront dacha (summer villa), and private island show a relaxed family enjoying hikes, picnics, games, and sports. In a letter to her Russian teacher when she was about ten years old, she reported, "We take long walks with Papa. One day we walked around the whole island—twelve miles. . . . Marie and I recited our French dialogues, everybody liked it very much. Today I went swimming after tennis. . . . We had cinematograph twice. We are so comfortable here on the yacht."

The War Years

Elsewhere revolutionary forces were beginning to rumble again. In 1904, Russia became involved with a disastrous and unpopular war with Japan. A year later an Orthodox priest organized workers to present work grievances to Nicholas. As they approached the Winter Palace, government troops opened fire. Thousands were killed on "Bloody Sunday," a general strike ensued, and discord raged for months. Finally Nicholas was convinced to support the establishment of an elected legislature, and in 1906 the Duma was founded in Russia's first national election. Although Russia was behind the rest of Europe, the country began to prosper and was moving into modernity when World War I exploded in 1914. By that time, Rasputin's word ruled, and for a time he ran the government when Nicholas was at the front.

In the hope of saving Russia, a group of concerned Romanov supporters killed the despised cleric in December 1916. But it was too late. Millions of Russian soldiers were dying; unrest was growing against the war and the czar. The Duma formed a separate government that was joined by many of the czars soldiers, and in an effort to quell rioting, asked Nicholas to give up the throne. On his way back from military headquarters, he abdicated. From March 1917 until July 1918, the Romanovs were prisoners in their own country.

Anastasia was thirteen when the war began. While her mother and two older sisters trained as nurses and worked in military hospitals, Anastasia and Marie visited soldiers at a small hospital near Alexander Palace. She wrote often to her father who was away at military headquarters, "I sat today with one of our soldiers and helped him to learn to read. Two more soldiers died yesterday. We were still with them."

While the children realized conditions were worsening, they were astounded by their arrest. At first little changed; the close knit family banded together, and hoped they would be allowed to live at on one of their small estates. As time passed, however, less friendly forces seized power and sent the Romanovs to Siberia, where they lived from August 1917 until May 1918. Shortly after Vladimir Lenin came to power, the family was separated—Nicholas, Alexandra, and Marie were taken to Ekaterinburg in the Ural region, and Anastasia, Olga, Tatiana, and Alexei were left in Tobolsk, Siberia. Two months before their execution, the family was reunited. Anastasia turned seventeen that June.

The Secret Execution

Historians can only surmise exactly what happened during the early morning hours of July 16, 1918. The family was ordered to go to the basement of the house, called the "House of Special Purpose." Most experts agree that Nicholas was shot first, then the rest—Alexandra, the children, the family's doctor, and three servants—in the mayhem that followed. The White Army (loyalists to the Czar) concluded Bolsheviks had killed the family, burned, and buried the bodies in a mass grave. Years passed before their remains were found in a forest nearby. Russians leaders were afraid, if found, the Romanov's bones might be considered religious relics by loyalists to the throne, and no further investigation was conducted.

A Mystery Emerges

A year later a woman who could not be identified was found trying to jump off a bridge in Berlin. She was hospitalized, and rarely spoke during her long recovery. Many people tried to identify the mystery woman, but failed. To everyone's surprise, when she was released from the hospital, she announced that she was Anastasia. In the years that followed, she told stories about imperial family secrets in amazing detail. Speculation about Anastasia's survival exploded. Even after Romanov relatives visited and declared her not to be Anastasia, speculation continued and various benefactors came to her rescue.

Eventually the woman assumed the name Anna Anderson, and became increasingly eccentric and reclusive. Legal battles were waged between her and the Romanov family, but neither side could prove or disprove her identity conclusively. She died in 1984 still claiming to be Anastasia.

Hollywood did its part to keep the romantic story of Anastasia alive. In 1956, Ingrid Bergman played the title role in *Anastasia* and won an Oscar for her performance. In 1986, Amy Irving starred in the television movie *Anastasia: The Mystery of Anna*. In 1997, Disney brought the story to life with the animated feature *Anastasia*. These movies loosely supported the claims that Anastasia survived the massacre of her family.

When Russia opened up politically in the 1980s, the government excavated what was believed to be the burial site. Scientists confirmed the remains were those of the Romanovs, but of the eleven people known to have been executed, only nine bodies were found. The two smallest bodies, thought to be Alexei and Anastasia, were missing.

The question of Anna Anderson's identity remained unanswered. In 1993, *People,* reported that DNA tests comparing a sample of Anderson's body tissue, which had been saved after an operation, with a blood sample from England's Prince Philip, a distant cousin of Anastasia, proved that they were not related. Anna Anderson could not have been Anastasia. One mystery was solved, but the question of Anastasia's and Alexei's whereabouts lingered until scientists matched old photos with skulls exhumed from the grave. Russia's chief forensic expert told *U.S. News and*

World Report in 1994 that computer modeling matched five skulls precisely with photos of Nicholas, Alexandra, and their daughters Olga, Tatiana, and Anastasia. The myth of Anastasia's survival ended, but the whereabouts of Alexei and Marie remain unknown.

Further Reading

Brewster, Hugh, *Anastasia's Album,* Hyperion Madison Press, 1996

Kurth, Peter, *Anastasia: The Riddle of Anna Anderson,* Little Brown & Co., 1985.

Lovell, James Blair, *Anastasia The Lost Princess,* Regnery Gateway, 1991.

Moscow, Henry, *Russia Under The Czars,* American Heritage Publishing, 1962.

Electronic World Communication, 1994.

People, July 26, 1993.

Publishers Weekly, October 7, 1996.

Reader's Digest (Canadian), April 1996.

Sunday Times, June 26, 1994; October 9, 1994.

U.S. News & World Report, September 19, 1994.

S

Susan Sarandon

Susan Sarandon (born 1946) is an American actress who has appeared in almost 50 films. Ben Yagoda, in *American Film,* suggests "Sarandon *is* a character actor, in the best sense of the word, with attributes that don't necessarily translate into the traditional notion of stardom." As an actress and a political activist, Sarandon presents an important side of American cinema.

Born to Phillip, an advertising executive, and Lenora Marie Crisicione Tomalin, Sarandon was the eldest of the couple's nine children. Growing up in a Welsh/Italian household she was raised Catholic. As a teenager in the 1960s Sarandon was active in the civil rights and anti-war movements and was arrested in high school for participating in protests.

After graduating from high school, she attended Catholic University in Washington D.C. She graduated from college with a degree in Drama in 1969. While in college she met Chris Sarandon who shared her love of acting. They were married on September 16, 1967. Following graduation, Chris Sarandon went to a casting call and asked Susan along to read scenes with him. Both Sarandons ended up with parts in *Joe.* With this debut, Susan Sarandon began a long career in film.

The Film World

Chris Baker, on his webpage, suggests Sarandon "is an intelligent and versatile actress having built a reputation for portraying strong, independent women on the screen." Yet many critics define her early films as her 'ingenue' period. Following her debut in *Joe,* Sarandon appeared in a number of soap operas, some television episodes, movies and miniseries. From 1970 through 1978, many of Sarandon's roles were minor parts. In 1975 she starred as Janet in the great classic cult film *The Rocky Horror Picture Show,* which is quite possibly her most watched film.

Following her divorce from Chris Sarandon in 1979, Susan Sarandon went on to work with director Louis Malle in *Pretty Baby* and *Atlantic City.* She received critical acclaim for both films and was nominated for an Oscar for *Atlantic City.* In an interview with Eleanor Blau, for the *New York Times,* Sarandon said "I try for parts that frighten me or seem impossible. So to survive, I will have to learn something and overcome it." She is well known for taking acting risks as illustrated by these two films. In *Pretty Baby* Sarandon plays a prostitute whose child (played by Brooke Shields) also grows up to be a prostitute. She took another risk in one of the opening scenes of *Atlantic City* by bathing her bare breasts with lemons in front of an open window. In *The Hunger,* 1993, Sarandon has a same-sex love scene with Catherine Deneuve.

A Theatrical Detour

Another risk Sarandon took in the early eighties was to work in theater. She formed an improvisational company with friends. In 1981 she appeared off-Broadway in *A Coupla White Chicks Sitting Around Talking,* with Eileen Brennan and received favorable reviews. She followed this with a well-received performance in *Extremities.* The play deals with an attempted rape and what occurs when in a surprising twist the intended victim captures her would-be rapist. As Sarandon explained to Blau, "*Extremities* is a metaphor about the animal in you. And it's about power. Not

sex—that's not what rape is about; it's the rage a rapist feels and the power he is exercising. She's learning from him about power. The play is about the contagion of violence."

In an interview with Christian Williams, for the *Washington Post,* she compared theater to film. "Movies don't provide any instant gratification at all. Making them is very slow, and there's a lot of waiting around. But on a stage it's overwhelming. You and the audience become completely involved, laughing and crying together and if when it's over they applaud, there's no way to avoid believing that you contributed to it."

During this time Sarandon gave birth to her daughter Eva Maria Livia Amurri. Eva's father is writer-director Franco Amurri, Sarandon's partner at the time, but the relationship did not last.

Political Activist

Gloria Jacobs in *Ms.* magazine claims that for Sarandon "political activism is not a pastime but an inherent part of her life—part of her soul." As she told Clarke Taylor, in the *Chicago Tribune,* "It's a matter of extending one's sense of responsibility to others, and to the rest of the world. It's not altruism, it's understanding that we really are all connected. We're not isolated. We are the world. And understanding this is the basis of hope for the world."

As Baker noted, "she remains one of Hollywood's most visible activists, lending her name, time and presence to many political, cultural and health organizations." She was an early supporter of AIDS activism, particularly working

with ACT UP. In 1984 she went to Nicaragua on behalf of MADRE, an organization which provides aid to war victims there and in El Salvador. She has been a longtime supporter of women's reproductive rights and the Equal Rights Amendment, as evidenced by her participation at numerous marches, rallies, and a stint as a guest columnist for *USA Today* on April 10, 1989. She has worked on issues facing the homeless and mentally ill. She also works closely with the Center for Constitutional Rights.

Throughout the years she has continued to oppose violence, supporting efforts towards nuclear disarmament. She was publicly opposed to the Persian Gulf war, which many others viewed as a risky professional stance. Her anti-violence work stems from her desire to teach her children that violence is an inappropriate way to accomplish goals. When Claudia Dreifus asked Sarandon about the impact on her career, in *The Progressive,* Sarandon replied "whenever anybody asks me that, I always say 'It's a little like worrying whether your slip is showing while you flee a burning building.' I don't know. I can't dwell on it. Maybe it has. Maybe being outspoken can cost you work. It's a very subjective business."

Where possible Sarandon has incorporated the issues into her work. In 1984 she narrated *Talking Nicaragua,* a documentary discussing U.S. involvement with Nicaragua. She has produced Public Service Announcements on the First Amendment. In 1995 she participated in the film, *The Celluloid Closet,* which discussed Hollywood's treatment of gays and lesbians in the movies. In 1995 she narrated two documentaries, *Tell the Truth and Run: George Seldes and the American Press* and *School of Assassins* a one hour documentary on the School of the Americas.

Since 1988 she has participated in many of these activities with her partner, actor/writer/director Tim Robbins. She and Robbins became involved following their work together in *Bull Durham.* Later, the pair had two children, Jack Henry and Miles. Both share a commitment to activism, perhaps best illustrated in their 1996 film *Dead Man Walking.* Sarandon persuaded Robbins to write and direct the film, based on the true story of Sister Helen Prejean. The film is a commentary on the use of capital punishment. Sarandon won an Academy Award for Best Actress for this role, and continues to work on this issue with the National Coalition to Abolish the Death Penalty.

Sarandon once told Nancy Mills in an interview for the *Los Angeles Times,* "I may not have control over whether my films are good or bad, but I certainly can turn down those with excessive violence, those that link sex and violence or those that propagate certain cliches about women. I think you can make a difference if you bring your own values to your work."

Feminism, Sarandon and Film

In an interview with Claudia Dreifus, for *New Woman* Sarandon noted, "People just don't know how to write stories about women. If you're an actress who cares about playing characters with some dimension, finding scripts is a problem." As Sarandon has moved into more starring roles she has had the opportunity to select roles which reflect the diversity of women's experiences. In addition to the parts noted above, she has played a journalist, *Compromising Positions* and *Bob Roberts;* prisoner of war, *Women of Valor;* medical researcher, *The Hunger;* fortuneteller, *King of the Gypsies;* music teacher, *The Witches of Eastwick;* college professor, *Bull Durham;* waitress, *White Palace* and *Thelma & Louise;* attorney, *The Client;* linguist, *Lorenzo's Oil;* mother, *Little Women* and *Safe Passage;* and a wife, *Sweet Hearts Dance.*

Vincent Canby, in a *New York Times* piece suggested Sarandon was an example of the new breed of "women's" movies. "These women are active forces in the environments that contain them. They aren't passive little creatures who accept their fates without question. They play roles more often associated by movies with men. They do things." This seemed evident in *Thelma & Louise.* At the time of its release the movie sparked a national debate over violence, women, and feminism. Some saw the film as a feminist manifesto, others claimed the film gloried male-bashing, and still others saw the film somewhere between these extremes. Sarandon noted in an on-line interview she "was surprised that the film struck such a primal nerve. I knew when we were filming that it would be different, unusual and hopefully entertaining. But shocking? I guess giving women the option of violence was hard for a lot of people to accept."

Sarandon clearly connects with the roles she has chosen. As she told Nina Darnton, of the *New York Times,* "There are really two kinds of actresses. Either you play essentially the same part over and over, playing whatever it is that endears you to the public as an actress, or you lose yourself in the character and let the character dictate the part. It's easier to be a star the first way. But it's also easier to become a caricature of yourself. To me, the whole point of acting is to experiment and learn—it's like living hundreds of lives in one lifetime."

Further Reading

American Film, May, 1991.
Chicago Tribune, June 14, 1987.
Editor & Publisher, November 12, 1994.
Los Angeles Times, June 21, 1988.
Mother Jones, February, 1989.
Ms., January/February, 1996.
National Catholic Reporter, May 3, 1996.
New York Times, January 14, 1983; September 1, 1985; November 10, 1985.
New Woman, September, 1988.
Progressive, October, 1989.
Washington Post, April 20, 1981.
"Chris Baker's Susan Sarandon Site," http://www.geocities.com/ Hollywood/Hills (March 30, 1998).
Gerosa, Melina, "A Woman of Substance," *Ladies Home Journal,* http://lhj.com (March 30, 1998).
Glickman, Simon, "Susan Sarandon," *Contemporary Newsmakers,* http://galenet.gale.com (March 24, 1998).
Internet Movie Database, "Biographical Information for Susan Sarandon," http://us.imdb.com (March 30, 1998).
"Susan Sarandon Fact Sheet," *E! Online,* http://e1.eonline.com (March 30, 1998). □

Betty Bone Schiess

Betty Bone Schiess (born 1923) helped spark a national controversy when she emerged as one of the "Philadelphia Eleven," a group of Episcopalian women who were ordained as priests in a Philadelphia church ceremony. It was an act of defiance since the church hierarchy was still debating whether or not to allow women to enter the priesthood.

Schiess was born in Cincinnati, Ohio in 1923, the daughter of Evan and Leah Bone. In 1945 she received her undergraduate degree from the University of Cincinnati, and then journeyed to New York's Syracuse University for a master's degree, which she earned in 1947. That same year she married William Schiess, and like most American women of her generation, settled down to a role as homemaker and, in time, mother to their two children. Yet during the 1960s, Schiess—like other educated, primarily middle-class women of her day—found a new direction with the burgeoning feminist movement. Launched in part by their participation in the civil-rights struggle, the publication of a myth-shattering book (Betty Friedan's *The Feminine Mystique*), and the formation of the National Organization for Women (NOW), thousands of women like Schiess began rejecting the limitations placed upon them by institutions, the workplace, and social customs. They began agitating for the repeal of discriminatory laws, or called for legislation that would placed them on equal ground with American men.

The Episcopal Church in America

Schiess became head of the Syracuse chapter of the National Organization for Women by the late 1960s. She also became an important force in a movement within the Episcopal Church of America to eradicate discriminatory practices. With over three million members at the time, American Episcopalians were certainly not the largest sect of the Protestant faith, but perhaps the most influential. The creed represented the American version of England's Anglican Church, and its origins as a separate entity from the Church of England dated back to 1784. It was also the religion of the East Coast elite—America's venerable, old-money families were usually Episcopalian; so were a disproportionate number of American presidents.

The Episcopalian Church was organized into geographic dioceses, who in turn sent representatives to a General Convention every three years. Lay people served in the House of Deputies, lesser in status to the House of Bishops. The issue of allowing women to become Episcopal priests had first been raised in the 1940s, when dioceses began sending women representatives to General Conventions as deputies. Though the first of these was allowed to take her seat on the convention floor, subsequent women deputies at later conventions were not. Nearly 20 years later, the Convention finally resolved the controversy and voted to allow

women into the House of Deputies in 1967. By then, devout Episcopalian women had pushed for and been granted admission to Episcopalian seminaries. Other changes had occurred as well: in 1965, the General Convention abolished the celibacy rule for deaconesses. These were Episcopalian women who trained at special church schools, then undertook charity, social, or educational work under the auspices of the Church; over time, they were allowed to read in church and assist in ceremonies. The 1965 General Convention bestowed on them a more equal status to men and abolished the rule of celibacy. Five years later, they were allowed as full members of the diaconate with an investiture ceremony that recognized their clerical status.

At that same General Convention of 1970, a vote was held for the first time about ordaining women into the priesthood, and did not pass. It did serve to launch an organized movement within the Episcopal Church, however: the Episcopal Women's Caucus was formed in late 1971 as a feminist-action group. Many of its members were women who had earned degrees from Episcopal divinity schools. Schiess had earned a master's in divinity in 1972 from the Rochester Center for Theological Studies. They were buoyed by the fact that many other Protestant faiths— Methodist, Lutheran, and Presbyterian, among others—had allowed women to become priests.

The Philadelphia Eleven

On July 29, 1974, Schiess and ten other women became the first to be ordained in a formal ceremony at an inner-city Episcopal church in Philadelphia. It was a rene-

gade act, however. They had been ordained by three retired bishops, who possessed the ecclesiastical authority to ordain priests, but had not followed Church procedure and allowed the names of the potential candidates for priesthood to be approved by a diocese committee.

The other women ordained with Schiess were similarly accomplished women in their respective congregations and dioceses. They were Merrill Bittner, Alla Bozarth-Campbell, Allison Cheek, Emily Hewitt, Carter Heyward, Suzanne Hiatt, Marie Moorefield, Jeanette Piccard, Katrina Swanson, and Nancy Wittig. Swanson's father was one of the ordaining bishops, the Right Reverend Edward R. Wells. The other two sympathetic elders were the Right Reverend Daniel Corrigan and the Right Reverend Robert DeWitt. As retired bishops, they faced less censure from Church authorities for the act.

According to David E. Sumner in *The Episcopal Church's History: 1945-1985,* Schiess and her ten colleagues issued a statement of their aims, and expressed gratitude toward the bishops who conducted the ceremony: "We rejoice in their courage and feel privileged to join them in this action of Christian obedience. We are certain God needs women in the priesthood to be true to the Gospel understanding of human unity in Christ. Our primary motivation is to begin to free priesthood from the bondage it suffers as long as it is characterized by the categorical exclusion of persons on the basis of sex."

A House Divided

The next day, on July 30, Schiess and Bittner were suspended by respective dioceses. Schiess's bishop, the Right Reverend Ned Cole, sent a letter to the clergy of the diocese of central New York that declared the ordination had been "a mutinous use of episcopal power," according to the *New York Times,* and that Schiess's involvement in the renegade act "shall always hamper the ministry which would be hers." In response, Schiess refused to put her signature to a statement accepting the suspension, asserting she would wait for the judgment of an ecclesiastical trial.

The controversy divided the church and achieved national attention. Those opposed to the ordination of women as priests pointed out that the Philadelphia ordination had not taken place via the proper avenues, with the women first being approved by a diocese committee. A few weeks later, a special meeting of the House of Bishops condemned the ordination by a vote of 128 to 9 for the same reasons. Conversely, other Episcopalians asserted that those same bishops may not have even possessed the authority to declare the ordination of Schiess and the others invalid.

Another supporter of Schiess's cause was Dr. Charles Willie, a prominent African-American academic and vice president of the House of Deputies. He had delivered the sermon at the Philadelphia ordination and, after the August vote by the House of Bishops, resigned his post in protest. At a sermon in Schiess's hometown of Syracuse at Grace Episcopal Church, Willie found fault with his colleagues for toeing the line too narrowly on the issue. "In the Christian religion, concern for personhood always takes precedence over concern for procedures," Willie explained. "A state of social pathology exists whenever individuals are sacrificed by others for the benefit of an institution."

Filed Discrimination Charges

In January of 1975, that same congregation asked Schiess to become its associate priest. At the time, she was the director of a senior citizens' center. Her superior, the Right Reverend Cole, refused to grant her an officiating license. He was of the opinion that the matter should be decided at the next General Convention. In response, Schiess filed suits with both the federal Equal Employment Opportunity Commission (EEOC) and the New York State Division of Human Rights charging employment discrimination on the basis of gender, a violation of Title VII of the federal Civil Rights Act of 1964. This was a somewhat radical move, since tenets and laws of religious creeds enjoyed fairly sacrosanct protection under the First Amendment.

Time in a story headlined "Sue Thy Bishop," expressed the opinion that "Schiess's decision to accuse her bishop of sex discrimination through secular channels is likely to do the women's cause little good within the church, and it could well create a backlash. The article even cited a New Testament passage that condemned any Christian who brought suit against his "brother." In her complaint, Schiess pointed out that the Episcopal Church had ordained women as priests in Hong Kong, and that no specific law in the Church prohibited women from becoming priests. Furthermore, her complaint cited one particular prior court case as providing a legal basis for her charge of discrimination, in effect giving the government jurisdiction over the matter: a court had ruled that if a church body holds a vote on the matter, it is technically not part of its religious belief and thus cannot be protected by the First Amendment.

Stalemate Resolved

On September 16, 1976, the General Convention voted to allow women to join the priesthood, and it became Section 1 of Title III, Canon 9. This decision came about, in part, because the Episcopal Church was so bitterly divided over the issue. Some bishops and deputies felt that to deny the women once more would bring about a permanent rift. In early 1977, after the withdrawal of her EEOC complaint, Schiess was ordained by Cole according to Episcopal guidelines. She went on to an accomplished career within the church, serving as chaplain of Syracuse University from 1976 to 1978, and holding the same post at Cornell University from 1978 to 1979. For five years she served as rector of Grace Episcopal Church in Mexico, New York, and was also a member of the New York Task Force on Life and Law from 1985 onward.

Schiess's story is told in the 1996 work *A Still Small Voice: Women, Ordination, and the Church.* She is the author of *Take Back the Church, Indeed the Witness,* (1982), *Creativity and Procreativity: Some Thoughts on Eve and the Opposition and How Episcopalians Make Ethical Decisions* (1988). Schiess belongs to the Religious Coalition for Abortion Rights, the Council on Adolescent Pregnancy, and is a trustee of the Elizabeth Cady Stanton Foundation.

She has received a Governor's Award as Women of Merit in Religion, served as president of the International Association of Women Ministers from 1984 to 1987, and was inducted into the National Women's Hall of Fame in 1994.

Further Reading

Sumner, David E. *The Episcopal Church's History: 1945-1985,* Morehouse-Barlow, 1987.
New York Times, July 31, 1974; August 19, 1974; March 8, 1976, p. 28; November 14, 1976, p. 51.
Time, August 16, 1975, p. 36.

Oskar Schindler

German businessman Oskar Schindler (1908-1974) saved Jews in Poland and Czechoslovakia from death at the hands of the Nazis during World War II by employing them in his factory.

Oskar Schindler was the unlikeliest of heroes—indifferent to religion and politics, partial to gambling and drinking, and not averse to skirting the law in his many business ventures. Yet to the eleven hundred Jews whose lives he saved during World War II, he was nothing less than a saint. Until the 1980s, his name was barely known outside the world of Holocaust survivors. Thanks to a book and then a movie about his exploits, however, he has taken his place among those the Israelis call "Righteous Gentiles"—non-Jews who took great risks to ensure the safety of Jews doomed by the Nazis' "Final Solution."

Schindler was born in 1908 in the industrial city of Zwittau, Moravia, then a German province of the Austro-Hungarian Empire and now part of the Czech Republic. Also known as the Sudetenland, the region was home to several million ethnic Germans, including the Schindler family. It was there that Oskar grew up (his father owned a farm-machinery factory) and attended a German-language school. Among his childhood playmates were the two sons of a local rabbi.

During the 1920s, Schindler worked in sales for his father. In 1928, however, the young man's marriage to a woman named Emilie caused a rift in the relationship between the two men. Schindler subsequently left his father's employ and became a sales manager for a Moravian electric company. His new job often took him to Poland on business, and over time he developed a strong affinity for the city of Krakow, the ancient seat of Polish kings.

Meanwhile, the political landscape in Europe was undergoing major changes, especially in Germany, where Adolf Hitler assumed the post of chancellor in 1933. Hitler's vision of a new German empire included the Sudetenland, which had been annexed by the fledgling Republic of Czechoslovakia at the end of World War I in 1918 following the destruction of the Austro-Hungarian Empire and the German Empire. Hitler began stirring up ethnic passions

among the Sudeten Germans, pointing out that their "rightful" ties were with Germany, not Czechoslovakia.

By 1935, Sudeten Germans who wanted to avoid being labeled as Communists or Social Democrats joined the pro-Nazi Sudeten German Party. One of those who jumped on the bandwagon was Schindler—not out of any love for the Nazis, but because it made business sense to go along with the prevailing wind. In 1938, Hitler forced an international crisis over the fate of the Sudetenland when he threatened war if the region was not turned over to Germany. The leaders of Great Britain and France acquiesced, and Hitler annexed the Sudetenland without a struggle.

Within weeks of the annexation, officials of the *Abwehr,* or German military intelligence, approached Schindler about gathering information on Polish military activity during his frequent visits to Krakow. A gregarious, attractive, and charming person who always found it easy to get people to talk to him, he agreed to pass along whatever he could to the *Abwehr.* In exchange for his help, he was exempted from military service.

On September 1, 1939, Hitler invaded Poland, prompting Great Britain and France to declare war on Germany. Within a week, Schindler arrived in Krakow, eager to find a way to profit from the conflict in one way or another. Fortuitously, in mid-October, the city became the new seat of government for all of Nazi-occupied Poland. Schindler quickly cultivated friendships with key officers in both the *Wehrmacht* (the German army) and the SS (the elite armed

Nazi unit), plying them with black-market goods such as cognac and cigars.

It was around this same time that he also made the acquaintance of Itzhak Stern, a Jewish accountant who served as his liaison with the local Jewish business community. With capital he borrowed from some of the men he met through Stern, Schindler purchased a bankrupt enamel kitchenware factory, renamed it Deutsche Emailwaren Fabrik, and opened it in January 1940. Stern hired on as the bookkeeper and soon established a bond with his employer that proved to be tremendously influential in the difficult years ahead.

Relying on his legendary panache as well as his willingness to bribe the right people, Schindler secured numerous German army contracts for his pots and pans. To staff his factory, he turned to Krakow's Jewish community, which, Stern told him, was a good source of cheap, reliable labor. At the time, some 56,000 Jews lived in the city, most in the ghetto (a neighborhood that was traditionally reserved for Jews). By the spring of 1940, however, the Nazi crackdown against Jews had begun. Schindler was ordered to pay his Jewish employees' wages directly to the SS rather than to the workers themselves. In August, Nazi authorities issued a new regulation ordering all but "work-essential" Jews to leave the city. This touched off a panic that sent Jews scrambling for work deemed "essential." (At Stern's urging, Schindler hired about 150 of them to work in his factory.) And by the end of the year, all of Krakow's Jews were ordered to wear a four-inch wide white armband emblazoned with the Star of David.

Near the end of 1941, Schindler was arrested by the SS for dealing in black market goods. With the help of his high-ranking Nazi friends (not to mention a few well-placed bribes), he was quickly released to return to work. On April 29, 1942, however, he was arrested again and jailed, this time for violating the Nazis' "Race and Resettlement Act." The charge stemmed from a kiss he had given a young Jewish girl at the factory during his birthday party the day before. Once again, Schindler secured his release within a short time thanks to his connections in the SS and the *Abwehr.*

In June of 1942, the Nazis began deporting Krakow's Jews to labor camps. Some of Schindler's workers, including his office manager, were among the first group of people ordered to report to the train station. Furious at what he regarded as unwelcome SS interference in his business affairs, Schindler raced to the station and argued with an SS officer about how essential his workers were to the war effort. (It became his standard argument when dealing with similar situations over the next few years.) By dropping the names of some of his Nazi friends and making a couple of threats, he was finally able to rescue the workers and escort them safely back to his factory. But Schindler could only do so much; by the end of 1942, deportations had reduced the ghetto's population of around 17,000 to about 4,000 or so. And the warnings he personally delivered that fall to leaders of the Jewish community in Budapest, Hungary, about what was going on in Poland fell on deaf ears—they could not believe that the Germans were capable of such actions.

In early 1943, the Nazis ordered the final "liquidation" of the Krakow ghetto. The man put in charge of the operation was a young SS officer named Amon Goeth, the commandant of the Plaszow forced labor camp just outside the city. Those Jews who were healthy and could work went to Plaszow; the rest were sent off to death camps or executed on the spot. Goeth then met with Schindler and other industrialists in the area to convince them to relocate their factories inside the camp. But Schindler had a somewhat different idea. He proposed establishing a labor subcamp within his factory that would continue to employ his own workers. He would run it, and the Plaszow guards would not be allowed on the premises without his permission. Schindler secured Goeth's support for this unusual plan after making it clear that cooperation would be generously compensated.

Schindler's Emalia Camp, as it was known, thus served as a haven for Krakow's Jews, at least for a few months. There they knew they would not be beaten or executed. Despite widespread food shortages, they could also count on eating much better than those imprisoned in the main camp at Plaszow because their boss regularly purchased his supplies on the black market at exorbitant rates. Nor did they have to endure the degrading living conditions in the main camp, because they were housed right in the factory. To make sure his camp stayed open, Schindler regularly handed out bribes to selected SS officers.

In early 1944, however, Plaszow's designation was changed from that of a labor camp to a concentration camp. This meant that its prisoners were suddenly earmarked for transport to death camps such as Auschwitz. Then came word in the summer that the main camp was to be closed and Schindler's factory dismantled. In anticipation of these changes, his workers were moved from the subcamp into the main camp. Once again, however, the canny businessman offered a counterproposal. He approached Goeth about moving his factory and his workers to Czechoslovakia so that they might continue to supply the Third Reich with vital munitions. After some money exchanged hands, the SS officer agreed to throw his support behind the plan and told Schindler to draw up a list of those people he wanted to take with him.

It is impossible to pinpoint the exact moment when Schindler ceased to be merely an exploiter of cheap labor to become a rescuer of those condemned to certain death. There probably was no single incident that brought about his transformation; more than likely, it was the cumulative effect of many different events that ultimately led him to take bold action. From the earliest days of the war, he had displayed a sense of humanity and concern for his workers (whom he referred to as his "children") that set him apart from most of the other Germans the Jews of Krakow encountered. But now, faced with the task of actually having to name those he wanted to save, Schindler realized that his choices were quite literally a matter of life and death for people he had come to know and respect. No longer could he act solely out of self-interest as a war profiteer. So he came up with a list containing some eleven hundred names, including all the employees of Emalia Camp and a number of others as well.

During the fall of 1944, Schindler made the necessary arrangements (and paid the necessary bribes) to begin the process of moving his factory to the town of Brunnlitz, Czechoslovakia, not far from his hometown of Zwittau. The liquidation of the Plaszow camp began that October. Shortly after around eight hundred men were shipped out in boxcars bound for Brunnlitz, three hundred women and children who were supposed to join them there were mistakenly routed to Auschwitz instead.

Meanwhile, Schindler had been arrested in Czechoslovakia and questioned about his relationship with Goeth, who had been jailed for various black market activities. The ever-wily businessman managed to convince the authorities (with some help from his friends in high places) that he was innocent of any wrongdoing. Once released, Schindler immediately set about retrieving those on his list who had been sent to Auschwitz. Armed with diamonds as bribes, he told the SS that the women and children they were holding were essential to the war effort because their smaller fingers allowed them to polish the insides of anti-tank shells. The SS believed his story, and the women and children were sent on to Brunnlitz.

Over the next seven months, Schindler's factory never produced a single useful shell. He attributed it to "start-up difficulties"; in reality, he had deliberately undermined the manufacturing process to make sure that the shells failed quality-control tests.

Finally, on May 8, 1945, the war came to an end after Germany surrendered to the Allies. Schindler gathered all of his workers together on the factory floor to pass along the good news. He then asked them not to seek revenge for what had been done to them and called for a moment of silence in memory of those who had perished. He also thanked the members of the SS who were present and encouraged them to go home peacefully and without further bloodshed.

As Schindler prepared to leave, his workers (who referred to themselves with pride as *Schindlerjuden*, or "Schindler Jews") gave him a letter they had written attesting to his good deeds in case he was captured and needed it to defend himself. In addition, they presented him with a special gift—a gold ring (made from the bridgework of one of the prisoners) inscribed in Hebrew with a verse from the Talmud, "He who saves one life, it is as if he saved the entire world." Along with his wife, Schindler then fled west to avoid Russian troops advancing from the east. (He preferred to take his chances with the approaching American forces instead.) A couple of days later, the twelve hundred or so *Schindlerjuden* were liberated by a lone Russian officer who rode up to the factory on horseback.

Much like his life before the war, Schindler's postwar life was marked by a string of failed business ventures, profligate spending, and plenty of drinking and womanizing. In 1949, after receiving a substantial sum from the Jewish Distribution Committee in appreciation for his wartime efforts as well as a large settlement from the West German government to compensate him for the loss of his

Czechoslovakian property to the communists, he moved to Argentina and purchased a farm. By 1957, however, Schindler had gone bankrupt and was relying on the charity of the Jewish organization B'nai B'rith to survive.

In 1958, Schindler abandoned his wife and returned to West Germany to live. Once again, the Jewish Distribution Committee and several grateful individuals came through for him with money he used to start a cement business in Frankfurt. It failed in 1961, and from then on, he lived mostly off funds provided by the *Schindlerjuden* as well as a small pension the West German government granted him in 1968.

The same year he lost his cement business, Schindler was invited to visit Israel for the first time. He was delighted with the cordial reception he received, which contrasted sharply with how he was usually treated at home. (Many of his countrymen despised him for saving Jews and testifying in court against Nazi war criminals.) Every spring for the rest of his life, he returned to Israel for several weeks to bask in the admiration of the *Schindlerjuden* and their offspring, whom he regarded with great affection as his own family.

Shortly after his fifty-fourth birthday in 1962, Schindler was officially declared a "Righteous Gentile" and invited to plant a tree on the Avenue of the Righteous leading up to Jerusalem's Yad Vashem Museum, a memorial to the Holocaust. Upon his death from heart and liver problems in 1974, he was granted his request to be buried in Israel. About five hundred *Schindlerjuden* attended his funeral and watched as his body was laid to rest in the Catholic cemetery on Mount Zion in Jerusalem. Thanks to Oskar Schindler, more than six thousand Holocaust survivors and their descendants were alive in the 1990s to tell the remarkable story of "Schindler's List" and of the equally amazing man who compiled it.

Further Reading

Brecher, Elinor J., *True Stories of the List Survivors,* Dutton, 1994.
Keneally, Thomas, *Schindler's List* (historical novel), Simon & Schuster, 1982.
American Health, June, 1994.
Christian Century, February 16, 1994.
Entertainment Weekly, December 17, 1993.
Knight-Ridder/Tribune News Service, December 28, 1993.
Maclean's, January 17, 1994.
People, March 21, 1994, pp. 40-44.
Saturday Night, April, 1994.
Time, December 13, 1993, pp. 75-77.
Schindler's List (motion picture), Amblin Entertainment, 1993.

Selena

Selena (1971-1995), often called the "The Mexican Madonna," was from very humble beginnings but used her raw talent and sultry voice to become one of popular music's fastest rising stars. Although cut down very early in her career as she was preparing to make the transition from Spanish-language to En- glish-language chart success, her legacy has been one of ever broader exposure for Tejano music and the artists that create it.

Selena Quintanilla-Perez was born on April 16, 1971 to Abraham, Jr. and Marcella Quintanilla in Lake Jackson, Texas, where her father worked as a shipping clerk for Dow Chemical Company. Her father had led a band in the 1950s and 1960s called Los Dinos (Spanish for "the boys") that played early rock 'n' roll favorites mixed with traditional Mexican music. This music would later be called Tex-Mex or Tejano music and, with its three-part vocal harmonies and accordion and horn sections, would became very popular throughout the southwest United States and Mexico. Abraham eventually gave up his music career to settle down and start a family.

Selena, the youngest of the three Quintanilla children, attended O.M. Roberts Elementary School in Lake Jackson, a small town approximately 55 miles south of Houston, Texas, and soon showed a flair for entertaining. When she was six years-old, her father noticed her talent while teaching her older brother, Abraham III, to play a few chords on a guitar and Selena broke out into song. Her father soon converted the family garage into a music studio where her brother played bass guitar and her sister, Suzette, played drums while Selena sang.

The family band practiced almost every day after school and in 1980, her father left his job at Dow Chemical

Company and opened a restaurant, Papagayo's, in Lake Jackson. The restaurant had a small stage and dance floor where the band would play on weekends. The band, now called "Selena y Los Dinos," or "Selena and The Boys," eventually added two guitarists and a keyboard player and garnered a local following of fans.

Initially concentrating on English pop songs and old Spanish favorites, her father soon began to write original Spanish-language songs for the band to perform. Selena's first language was English, and she had to learn the words to the Spanish-language songs phonetically. In only a few years though, the Texas oil industry dried up and so did the family restaurant's business. Her father moved the family to his hometown of Corpus Christi, Texas and began taking them on long road trips criss-crossing the state to perform their music. Selena often missed classes at West Oso Junior High School in Corpus Christi due to her touring with the band. Her father pulled her from classes permanently when she was in the eighth grade so that she could concentrate music. She took correspondence courses through the American School in Chicago, the same school that educated the Osmond family, and earned her General Education Diploma (GED) in 1989.

The constant touring paid off with an opening slot for the Tejano band, Mazz, at the Angleton, Texas fairgrounds in 1983. Mazz was one of the most popular Tejano acts of the time and Selena, only eleven-years-old, took the stage by storm, putting on a show impressed the assembled crowd.

Early Recordings

Taking time out from touring and opening up for other more established Tejano bands, Selena recorded *Mis Primeras Grabaciones* in 1984 for Corpus Christi's Freddie label. Freddie was one of the oldest and most established Spanish-language record companies in Texas, but the album and its only single, *Ya Se Va,* did not sell well. Within a year the band had moved to the Cara label and then to the Manny label. Selena's albums for Manny did not sell much better than before and the band continued to tour, living in a van while they traveled around the southwest United States opening for larger Tejano acts and playing shows at small clubs and fairgrounds.

Due to the diverse crowds that the band played to, they learned to perform many different styles of music, rhythm and blues-based music for audiences in the larger cities, like Houston, and more traditional accordion-style Tejano music for fans in the small western Texas crowds they performed for. In 1988, Selena was popular enough among Tejano fans that she was voted the female artist of the year at the Tejano Music Awards in San Antonio, Texas. She would go on to win this award consecutively for the next seven years as her popularity increased every year.

Chart Success

In 1989, Selena was signed to EMI Records and suddenly she had the weight and distribution system behind her to make her a giant star. She was spotted by the head of the label's new Latin music division, Jose Behar, as she performed at the Tejano Music Awards. Upon first spotting Selena, Behar knew that she could be a great cross-over artist, appealing not only to traditional fans of Tejano music, but also to the larger pop music market in the rest of the United States. Selena would be the first artist signed by Behar and in 1991, her duet with Alvaro Torres, *Buenos Amigos,* became her breakthrough hit. The song went to number one on Billboard's Latin chart and introduced her to audiences throughout the United States. Her next hit song, *Donde Quiero Que Estes,* would also be a duet, this time with the Latin group the Barrio Boyzz.

Donde Quiero Que Estes was more tropical-influenced than most traditional Tejano music, and this song exposed Selena to an even wider market. On April 2, 1992, Selena married 22-year-old Christopher Perez, the lead guitarist for her band and they soon moved into a house in the La Molina neighborhood of Corpus Christi between her parents and her brother's family.

In the early 1990s, Selena's biggest following had begun to be in Mexico. This was due to the more international sound of the songs that her father was now writing for her to perform. The songs had an Afro-Caribbean sound that more-traditional Tejano artists shied away from, but which Selena accepted with open arms. These new songs were not only popular in Mexico, but also began to be heard throughout the United States in Miami, New York, Los Angeles and even outside its borders in South and Central America. This wider audience soon came to be reflected in the size of the crowds that she attracted to her shows.

In February of 1993, Selena performed for a record crowd of 57,894 at the Houston Astrodome. One year later, on February 1994, she would break her own record, as 60,948 came to the Astrodome to see her perform during the Houston Livestock Show and Rodeo. In August of 1993, a crowd of over 20,000 watched her perform in Pasadena, California, an area that she had previously been almost unknown in. In March of 1994, her album *Selena Live* won a Grammy award for the best Mexican-American album.

In July of 1994, Selena released *Amor Prohibido. Amor Prohibido* would give Selena four number one singles and replaced Gloria Estefan's *Mi Tierra* as the top Latin selling album of that year. The album would go on to sell over a million copies worldwide and led to Selena being listed as one of the most successful Latin entertainers in the world by *Hispanic Business Magazine* and winning the Tejano Music Award's album of the year.

Posthumous English-Language Success

In December of 1993 Selena was moved to EMI's SBK label. SBK was primarily an English-language label, and Selena was eager to make an album in her first language. Often compared to other English-language artists such as Madonna, Janet Jackson and Mariah Carey, Selena was enthusiastic about having the same kinds of success that these artists had. She began recording English-language songs for her new album and continued touring throughout 1994 and 1995. On February 26, 1995, Selena would set the third straight record for attendance at the Houston Astrodome when an audience of 61,041 saw her perform on-stage alongside Emilio Navaira, the Tejano Music Awards male vocalist for that year.

On March 31, 1995, Selena was shot and killed by the president of her fan club, Yolanda Saldívar, in a hotel room in Corpus Christi, shortly after a confrontation about missing business funds. (Saldívar was later convicted of murder but has since proclaimed her innocence). *Dreaming of You,* the album released posthumously in 1996, contained five tracks sung in English as well as remixes by her father of *Bidi Bidi Bom Bom, Como la Flor, Techno Cumbia* and *Amor Prohibido.* The album also featured two tracks with Selena singing traditional Tejano songs alongside a Mexican mariachi band and *God's Child,* a song she recorded in 1994 alongside musician David Byrne for the motion picture *Don Juan DeMarco,* in which she had a small role. The album went straight to the number one spot on the Billboard chart and sold over a million copies. The crossover success that Selena had always hoped for had finally come and the album's success brought Tejano music to millions of fans who previously knew nothing about this genre of music.

Further Reading

Houston Chronicle, April 1, 1995.
New York Times, July 27, 1995; July 30, 1995.
People, April 17, 1995.
Washington Post, April 1, 1995; April 2, 1995.
"Selena," *Selena - the Movie,* http://www.selena - the movie.com/main.html (April 28, 1998).
"Selena's Page," *The Unofficial Selena's Web Site,* http://www.ondanet.com:1995/tejano/selena.html (April 28, 1998).
The Selena Foundation, http://www.neosoft.com/selena/ (April 28, 1998).

Jane Seymour

Jane Seymour (1509-1537) was the third wife of King Henry VIII of England. She is remembered as being a good, quiet and conservative wife. More importantly to Henry, she gave birth to his first male heir, the future King Edward VI.

Jane Seymour, the daughter of Sir John Seymour and Margery Wentworth, was twenty-five in 1535 when Henry VIII began to show an interest in her. He was visiting her family's home, Wolf Hall, in Wiltshire. Hers was a country family of the higher classes, descended from Edward III. She was intelligent, but quiet and the very example of purity. She was known equally for her porcelain skin—despite her love of gardening and the outdoors—and her kind heart.

Jane served as a lady-in-waiting to both of her predecessors, Catherine of Aragon, beginning in 1529, and then Anne Boleyn. As Francis Hackett wrote in *Henry the VIII: The Personal History of a Dynast and His Wives,* "Jane was the very reverse of her former mistress: where Anne was sparkling, she was still; where Anne was challenging, she was meek. She was maidenly, sentimental, and fortunately inarticulate."

It was not just Jane's beauty and innocence that attracted Henry, however. She also came with a handsome dowry: 104 manors in 19 counties, five castles and several chases and forests. The Seymour family stood to gain as well. Her brother Edward had served as a page in the household of Mary Tudor, and soon after Henry noticed Jane, Edward was named Gentleman of the Privy Chamber (a member of the King's advisory council). Both Edward, and the youngest of the Seymour brothers, Thomas, stood to gain great standing with the court as a result of the King's affection for their sister. At one brief and awkward point, there were three women in Henry's life, but it soon became clear, that Jane Seymour would soon be the one true queen.

Catherine of Aragon, Henry's first wife, died at the age of 50 on January 7, 1536 of what one report called "cardiac dropsy." The only abnormality found by the embalmer was that her heart had turned completely black and had a round black growth protruding from it. Some suggested she may have been poisoned. One author, modern day biographer of the Royals of Britain, Antonia Fraser, suggested in *The Wives of Henry VIII* it might have been "a broken heart." Henry was unrepentant for any wrong he may have done Catherine to contribute to her demise. He is said to have dressed entirely in yellow, with a huge white plume in his hat, the day after her passing. Anne Boleyn dressed likewise.

The fall of Anne Boleyn came soon after Catherine's death. In late January, upon hearing that Henry was knocked unconscious after falling off his horse, Anne gave birth to a stillborn boy. Henry and Anne already had a daughter, Elizabeth, born in 1533. She would later serve as Queen Elizabeth I. The unfortunate death of their son was the end for Anne.

The first divorce had been damaging to the public view of the throne, so a second divorce was not to be risked. Henry had broken away from the Catholic Church and created the Church of England to be with Anne, and these changes had led to turbulence throughout England. These changes colored private as well as public affairs for the royal family. For instance, a coronation was postponed for Jane, on the one hand, because of the plague in London and, equally, on the other, because of public outrage at Henry VIII's quick succession of wives.

On May 19, 1536, Anne was beheaded after a farce of a trial in which the verdict had been decided from the outset. She was accused of many crimes that were false, including adultery, incest, witchcraft, and attempting to poison Henry. Thomas Cromwell, the Henry's chief minister, is thought to have engineered the plan to get rid of Anne.

Henry and Jane were betrothed at Hampton Court in a secret ceremony on May 20. They wed less than two weeks after Anne's execution—May 30, 1536. The wedding took place in "the Queen's Closet" at York Place—the same place Henry had married Anne Boleyn only a few years prior, in January 1533.

Jane's portrait was painted by Hans Holbein a few months later. (It now hangs in the Belvedere Gallery in

Vienna.) The King showed off his new bride at the Whitsun festivities that June, as well. Henry and Jane followed a procession of barges, his lords sailing ahead, and it is reported that shots were fired in honor and celebration as they passed. That summer, "the Queen's badge" that was hung in several windows of the royal suite were changed from those of Anne Boleyn to those of Jane Seymour. Jane's badge featured a panther, conveniently placed over Anne's leopard, along with a phoenix rising from a castle. This latter symbol indeed foreshadowed Henry's return to favor with his public.

Catherine's motto had been "humble and loyal," and Anne's had been "the most happ[y]," both of them true enough, and at the same time bitterly ironic in the end. Jane's motto, however, had a little more gravity and far less irony about it: "bound to obey and serve."

Jane's brothers greatly benefited from their sister's marriage to Henry. Edward was given the title Viscount Beauchamp, put on the Privy Council the following year, and the next year was named the Earl of Hertford. Edward was thus in position to serve as a leader if something should happen to the King. Thomas succeeded to the Privy Chamber after Edward. Following the announcement that his sister was with child, he was given the stewardship of Chirk Castle and other border castles on Wales. The following year, he was given the manor of Holt in Cheshire. (Thomas's connections to royalty continued over the years in other ways as well. In May 1547, he secretly wed Henry's widow, Catherine Parr.)

One gift Henry gave Jane was a gold cup, weighing 65.5 ounces, twice engraved with her motto, designed by Holbein. Henry also gave her several medallions, with her own arms and the "crown imperial." Another gift from Henry designed for her by Holbein was an emerald and pearl pendant.

Jane was very traditional and she used this trait to her advantage. For example, Fraser noted that she asked her ladies to wear "suitable gowns of black satin and velvet," with high necklines. Some have surmised that this dress code had been designed to keep Henry's eyes on her. On another level, the things she did dare to challenge Henry about were matters of tradition. First, she wanted to make sure that Catherine's daughter Mary was reinstated in the court. Second, she asked the King to return England's monasteries. She was successful on the first account, but not the latter.

Mary was convinced to write a letter to the King that June, denouncing her mother as well as her right to the throne. This, she had been told, was the only was to win the King's favor, and avoid possible execution if his wrath were incited. Jane and Henry visited Mary shortly thereafter. Jane presented Mary with a diamond ring and the Henry gave her a 1,000 crowns. Jane and Mary continued to exchange gifts and became close confidantes. On the subject of the monasteries however, Jane was warned to keep her opinions to herself. Henry issued a threatening reminder to her to be mindful of the fate of her predecessor.

Happier occasions were to come, however. In January 1937, it was announced that Jane was pregnant. The cele-bration of the "quickening" of the unborn child was held on May 27th—"Trinity Sunday."

Most important to Henry, and perhaps to the kingdom as well, Jane gave birth to a son, the long-awaited male heir. Jane went into labor on October 9, and Prince Edward was born on the twelfth of October 1537. The baby was named Edward both to honor his great-grandfather, Edward III, and because he entered the world on the eve of the Feast of St. Edward. Three days later, the tiny prince was christened, with Mary serving as Edward's godmother.

Two thousand guns were shot from the Tower in celebration, and the whole day long bells sounded from all the churches. The happiness of the kingdom was short-lived, however, as the beloved Jane died shortly thereafter, on the 24th of October, from complications. She was only 28 years old, and had served as Henry's queen for less than eighteen months. She was buried in St. George's Chapel, Windsor.

"Everything points to the fact that Henry VIII mourned Jane Seymour with a genuine sense of loss," wrote Fraser, "the 'entirely beloved' wife who has presented him with his heart's desire at the cost of her own life." And some historians believe Henry VIII paid Jane Seymour the highest honor upon his own death. As Fraser noted in *The Lives of the Kings & Queens of England,* "When ten years later he was called to his Maker he [Henry VIII] ordered that his coffin should be laid beside hers, for Jane had given him, after twenty-eight years of ruling, the Prince he had wanted, Edward, Prince of Wales."

Further Reading

Fraser, Antonia, *The Wives of Henry VIII,* Alfred A. Knopf, 1993.
Fraser, Antonia, ed. *The Lives of the Kings & Queens of England,* University of California Press, 1995.
Hackett, Francis, *Henry the VIII: The Personal History of A Dynast and His Wives,* Liveright Publishing Corporation, 1945.
Starkey, David, ed. *The Lives and Letters of the Great Tudor Dynasties: Rivals in Power,* Toucan Books Ltd., 1990.
Jane Seymour—The Six Wives of Henry VIII, (videocassette series) BBC TV, New York: Time-Life Media, 1976.

Muriel Siebert

Known as the First Lady of Wall Street, stockbroker Muriel Siebert (born 1932) made history in 1967 when she became the first woman to own a seat on the New York Stock Exchange. She also owns and operates the only female-owned brokerage firm on the exchange.

Outspoken, smart, and determined, Muriel Siebert has made a career out of taking risks. The founder and president of the national discount brokerage firm that bears her name, Siebert became the first woman member of the New York Stock Exchange (NYSE) in 1967. With offices in California and Florida, Muriel Siebert & Co.

remains the only female-owned brokerage firm on the exchange. In all of her business dealings, Siebert continues to view risk as opportunity and chides her colleagues for not being more daring. "The men of the top of the industry and government should be more willing to risk sharing leadership with women and minority members who are not merely clones of their white male buddies," she was quoted as saying in a press release available online at www.msiebert.com. "In these fast-changing times we need the different viewpoints and experiences, we need the enlarged talent bank. The real risk lies in continuing to do things the way they've always been done."

Siebert, the youngest daughter of dentist Irwin J. Siebert and his wife, Margaret, was born and raised in Cleveland, Ohio, where she was known to her friends as "Mickie." (She still prefers her childhood nickname to her given name of Muriel.) She enrolled at Western Reserve University (now Case Western Reserve University) in 1949 with the intention of obtaining a degree in accounting. Unfortunately, her father was diagnosed with cancer during her junior year, and the family's finances would not allow her to complete her education as planned.

Headed to New York City

Rather than follow other women of her generation down the traditional path—marriage to a man who could support her while she raised a family—Siebert opted for a different course. In 1954, at the age of 22, she drove a used Studebaker 700 miles from Cleveland to Manhattan and began knocking on doors. With only $500 in savings, she

knew that she had to find a job quickly or face having to return home.

After Merrill Lynch rejected her because she lacked a college degree, Siebert decided to stretch the truth a bit. During her interview at the brokerage firm of Bache & Co. for an entry-level research analyst position, she answered "yes" when asked if she had a degree, figuring that she could eventually make up whatever credits she lacked. Siebert got the job at Bache and proceeded to learn the brokerage business from the ground up. (She never did find the time to complete her degree.) Given accounts that none of the more experienced analysts wanted, she used her knack for interpreting financial reports—quarterly and year-end earnings statements, annual reports, and balance sheets—to predict where certain industries were headed financially. Her analyses proved to be accurate, and Siebert began to rise through the ranks.

Compared to the men around her, however, Siebert felt she was on a slow track despite her undeniably savvy business sense. So she left Bache in 1957 and spent the next decade working for a variety of Wall Street firms. But it was a world where all of the other women she met were secretaries, not brokers. Banned from investment clubs because of her gender, she could not gain access to the places where the best deals were made. But Siebert was smart and ambitious. She discovered that using the initial "M" in place of "Muriel" on her resume got her in the door at many firms; her experience, intelligence, and can-do attitude then convinced prospective employers to give her a try. She worked briefly at Shields & Co. and Stearns & Co. before joining Fickle & Co. as a partner from 1962 to 1963 and Brimberg & Co. from 1965 to 1967.

Obtained Coveted Seat on the Exchange

Although she had risen to the level of partner, Siebert didn't like having to deal with a lot of red tape before she could make a financial decision. Independent by nature, she was determined to go off on her own. But such a move would involve finding a member of the New York Stock Exchange to sponsor her and persuading a bank to lend her 70 percent of the $445,000 she needed to purchase her own seat—things that no woman had ever tried to do in the history of Wall Street.

Siebert's search for a sponsor was met with suspicion and, on one occasion, ridicule. She was rejected nine times before she found a willing backer. Obtaining financing proved to be just as difficult, but ultimately she was victorious when Chase Manhattan Bank agreed to support her. On December 29, 1967, at the age of 35, Siebert was finally elected to a seat on the New York Stock Exchange, shattering a longstanding gender barrier. A decade would pass, however, before she was joined by any other women.

Two years after gaining her seat on the exchange, Siebert founded the brokerage firm that bears her name. While this step represented another important first for a woman, it once again required her to battle sexism in the financial world. Clients used her services but were notoriously hesitant to publicize what she had been able to do for them. Still, she persevered.

As a result of her determination to succeed, Siebert was in a good position to restructure her company as a discount brokerage after the U.S. Congress granted brokers the right to charge flexible rather than fixed commissions for financial transactions and other services. The day after the federal regulations were lifted—May 1, 1975—she ran a full-page newspaper ad that showed her cutting a $100 bill in half with a pair of scissors. While the ad got the attention of potential customers, it also raised the ire of her clearinghouse, which gave her 60 days to take her business elsewhere. This she managed to do, though not without some difficulty.

Entered Public Service

In 1977, Hugh Carey, the Democratic governor of New York, offered Siebert, a staunch Republican, a government position as superintendent of banking. Welcoming the challenge and appreciative of Carey's recognition of her accomplishments, Siebert took a five-year leave of absence from her firm to put the banks of the state of New York on solid financial footing during an era of double-digit inflation, double-digit interest rates, and an alarming number of bank failures.

By demolishing the inefficient bureaucratic obstacles blocking her path and relying on then-radical techniques such as salary cuts, mandatory reorganizations, and inter-bank mergers, Siebert made sure that not a single bank in the state failed. This success prompted her to compete for the Republican nomination for the U.S. Senate from the State of New York in 1982. She lost in the primary, however, coming in second among the three candidates.

Returning to the private sector, Siebert spent the rest of the decade getting her brokerage firm back on track. As the tumultuous 1980s gave way to the bullish 1990s, she looked for new directions in which to grow her company. In 1996 she merged with Brooklyn-based furniture retailer J. Michaels, creating a holding company, Siebert Financial Corporation, to facilitate the transaction. Later that same year she acquired several key partners of Grigsby Brandford Co., a California firm specializing in municipal bonds. The acquisition of individuals with expertise in the sale of municipal bonds broadened the scope of business Siebert was able to draw via Muriel Siebert & Co.

Made Giving Back to the Community a Priority

In recognition of the battles yet to be waged by other fledgling organizations—especially those owned by women—Siebert has devoted a significant portion of her financial resources in recent years to various nonprofit, civic, and women's organizations. In 1990 she established the Siebert Entrepreneurial/Philanthropic Plan (SEPP), a program that donates to charity 50 percent of the net commission revenues Muriel Siebert & Co. earns on sales of new-issue equity, municipal, and government bonds. (As of 1997, total contributions from the SEPP topped five million dollars.) And when many small shopkeepers lost their businesses during the 1992 Los Angeles riots, Siebert gave money to women entrepreneurs to help them get back on their feet.

In addition to funneling money to the causes she supports, Siebert has been generous with both her time and her expertise. She was, for instance, the first female director of the Manhattan Savings Bank and the first woman to chair the annual fund drive for the local chapter of the Boy Scouts of America. She serves on the boards of the Metropolitan Museum of Art business committee, the Guild Hall Museum, New York's State Business Council, and the Boy Scouts of Metro New York. She is also active in such women-centered organizations as the National Women's Business Council, New York's Minority and Women-Owned Business Enterprise Advisory Board, the United Way of New York City, the International Women's Forum, and Deloitte & Touche's Council for the Advancement of Women. Additionally, Siebert is the founder and former president of the Women's Forum and founder of the WISH List, an organization supporting the political candidacy of pro-choice Republican women. As time permits, she continues to honor requests to serve as a director or board member for other organizations.

Many observers might be inclined to wonder how she has managed to accomplish so much in her life, particularly when she encountered such fierce resistance at nearly every turn. But as Siebert herself suggested to interviewer Ed Leefeldt in *Bloomberg Personal Magazine,* it's a matter of exploiting your natural talents. "Don't ask me to paint. Don't ask me to sing," she declared. "But I know a balance sheet. I can understand cash flow and depreciation. . . . I'll stay until it's not fun."

Further Reading

Herera, Sue, *Women of the Street: Making It on Wall Street—The World's Toughest Business,* Wiley, 1997.
Bloomberg Personal Magazine, October 1994.
Fortune, October 28, 1996, p. 170.
New York Times, December 22, 1991, p. 10; February 11, 1996, p. 1.
Wall Street Journal, May 27, 1997, p. B13.
Working Woman, April 1986, p. 4; December 1992, p. 20.
Muriel Siebert & Co., Inc. Website, http://www.msiebert.com.

Hernán Siles Zuazo

Hernán Siles Zuazo (1914-1996) served as president of Bolivia for four years in the 1950s and was returned to his nation's highest office for an additional three years in the 1980s. As one of the leaders of the 1952 revolution and through his continuing political activities, Siles Zuazo played a major role in 20th century Bolivian history.

Hernán Siles Zuazo was born into a prominent Bolivian family in the capital city of La Paz in 1914. He attended school at the Methodist Church's American Institute in La Paz, although he was a Roman Catholic. His father, Hernando Siles Reyes, had served as president of Bolivia from 1926 until 1930. Despite this promising background, his early years were not easy. As Edward Schumacher wrote in the *New York Times*, Siles Zuazo "began life with the odds against him," because the former president never married Siles Zuazo's mother. Although in later life father and son remained on friendly terms, they were never very close.

The entire Siles Zuazo family demonstrated forthrightness and great political skill. His mother was a strong-minded woman. When Siles Zuazo became president she would occasionally scold her son if she believed he had failed to keep promises. A half-brother, Luis Adolfo Siles Salinas, was to serve as Bolivia's president for five months in 1969.

War Against Paraguay

In 1932, Bolivia battled neighboring Paraguay in a territorial dispute known as the Chaco War. Although the Bolivian army was better trained and equipped, it was badly defeated; land was lost and national pride was shattered. Siles Zuazo fought as a volunteer. Serving as a sergeant, his left arm was badly injured, leaving some of his fingers immobile for the rest of his life. As a result, Siles Zuazo was awarded several medals for bravery.

After the war, Siles Zuazo earned a law degree from San Andres University in La Paz. He later set up a private law office in that city. In 1938, he married Maria Teresa Onmecha. They had three daughters, Marcela, Ana María, and Isabel.

The Chaco War defeat turned the Bolivian people against their leaders. Many in the nation also blamed international oil companies, as well as wealthy mine owners and land-holders. Bolivians felt that the interests of all citizens, including the very poor and the Indians, were not being equally represented. In the wake of the Chaco War, a large number of political parties were established to challenge the existing structure. Siles Zuazo was an important part of that challenge.

New Political Party

In 1941, the Nationalist Revolutionary Movement (MNR) was founded by Siles Zuazo and Victor Paz Estenssoro. Their party, like many others, became caught up in the revolutionary fervor which swept Bolivia during World War II. The seeds of the MNR's eventual division were sown by its ill-defined mixture of European Marxism and fascism—an ideology that suppressed opposition and encouraged nationalism and racism.

That oppressive strain was evident in 1943, when an army major was installed as president by a military movement aided by the MNR. That administration proved to be repressive and was overthrown by a popular uprising in 1946. The major was lynched in front of the presidential palace. Consequences for supporters, such as Siles Zuazo, were not as severe—he fled to exile in Argentina and Chile.

The uprising served as an alarm to party members, including Siles Zuazo. They rebuilt their party and introduced a reform agenda. From exile, Paz Estenssoro ran for president and Siles Zuazo for vice president. They won a plurality of the vote in the 1951 election, but the military prevented Congress from installing them in office. The tin miners protested, beginning a national revolution in 1952. Siles Zuazo returned to Bolivia and was soon able to take office as vice president.

Strains in Party Coalition

The factions that made up the MNR were diverse, creating an "uneasy alliance," according to historian Eric Selbin. Working class members, who had been oppressed for years, demanded strong reform. Upper class members tended to be more moderate in their views and were often reluctant to embrace change.

In the years following the 1952 revolution, reforms were passed. The major tin mines, owned by foreign companies, were nationalized. Voting reform was instituted, creating universal suffrage. Perhaps the greatest reform was the abolition of a feudal landholding system, which had been in place for hundreds of years. This agricultural reform, however, was begun by rural workers and peasants seizing land. As with many other reforms, the MNR followed the peasantry. When it was clear that such reform was becoming a reality, the new ruling party was forced to accept it and try to take credit for it.

Although the reforms were striking, increased inflation was driving many Bolivians further into poverty. When Siles Zuazo was elected president in 1956, he sought to improve the economic health of the country by acquiring loans from the International Monetary Fund and requesting aid from the United States. These measures came with a large cost, however. IMF loans required the adoption of an austerity plan that placed the severest burdens on the working and poor classes. Siles Zuazo froze wages, reduced social services, and invited American oil companies to return to Bolivia. These were all policies harshly criticized by leftist citizens.

The president also was forced to confront labor unrest among the very workers who had helped install him in office. In response to strikes, Silas Zuazo countered with his own personal hunger strikes. In later years, he would employ the same method with varying effectiveness. One incident highlights the bravery of the man and the dilemma into which he had been placed. When Siles Zuazo met with a group of striking miners, he was handed a lighted stick of dynamite. Siles Zuazo simply took it, but refused to extinguish the fuse. A panicked miner grabbed the dynamite from his hand and threw it away moments before it exploded.

The courage of Siles Zuazo, however, was not enough to alter the divisions within his party. Years after 1952 the rebellion had taken firm hold on Bolivian soil, but had not sprouted and flowered. As historians J. Domínguez and C. Mitchell have written in *Comparative Politics*, the establishment of the revolution "proved to be a hollow accomplishment."

Moved Leftward in Exile

After completing his four-year term as president, Siles Zuazo served as ambassador to Paraguay and Spain in the government of Paz Estenssoro. But a 1964 coup forced him to leave Bolivia once again.

During his years exile, Siles Zuazo moved further to the left. In 1971, he established the Leftist Nationalist Revolutionary Movement (MNRI), a group that enjoyed broad support from the Bolivian peasantry.

In 1979, Siles Zuazo won another presidential election and returned from exile in triumph. However, a violent military uprising forced him into exile once again. Many leftist leaders were tortured and killed. The escape by Siles Zuazo was accomplished by disguising himself as a peasant and crossing Lake Titicaca by boat to Peru.

During the period of military rule that followed, the economy grew worse. Bolivia defaulted on its foreign debts. In 1982, the military handed the government back to Siles Zuazo. He was inaugurated on October 10, 1982.

New Challenges

"We are going to construct a democracy with absolute liberty," Siles Zuazo said in his inaugural address. "Those who do not believe in democracy and have interrupted it many times, depriving people of their liberties, should reflect and understand that their time has come to end."

The problems facing the Siles Zuazo government proved to be overwhelming. Prices rose by more than 24,000 percent during his tenure, due to a miscalculation in an austerity program. In addition, the worldwide price for tin plunged in 1985, crippling the nation that had once been the most important tin producer in the world.

Political divisions worsened the situation. As the austerity program increasingly hurt the very poor, leftist leaders and workers demanded that foreign debt payments end, that refinancing be handled on more favorable terms, and that negotiations with the IMF cease.

Kidnapped Amid Economic Crisis

In May 1984, Siles Zuazo suspended payments of foreign debt until refinancing arrangements could be made. This action infuriated rightists, who demanded the president's resignation. An attempted coup led to the abduction of Siles Zuazo. Surprisingly, even the military spoke out against this action. As a reporter for *Time* magazine wrote, "The show of loyalty to democracy was impressive." In less than 10 hours, he was released unharmed.

The administration of Siles Zuazo was crippled by clashes of the left and right and by his inability to reconcile them. As the historians James Malloy and Eduardo Gamarra have noted in *Revolution and Reaction: Bolivia, 1964-1985*, "Siles was to begin and end his presidency essentially the political prisoner of both [left and right]. . . . On numerous occasions the central government for all practical pur-

poses came to a standstill as Siles exhausted himself juggling personalities and factions."

The president took decisive action, however, in combating terrorism. Immediately after assuming office in 1982, his police arrested one of Italy's most wanted right-wing terrorists. In addition, his administration was instrumental in the capture of Klaus Barbie, the former Nazi who was returned to Israel to stand trial.

Drug Trafficking Scandal Weakens Government

Upon assuming the presidency, Siles Zuazo "wasted no time in taking the broom to the country's corrupt, cocaine-fueled politics," wrote Barry Came in *Newsweek* magazine. Siles Zuazo tried to cooperate with the United States in controlling drug traffic, but resistance was strong in his impoverished nation. At that time, the cocaine industry was earning approximately $2 million per year.

In 1984, a scandal hastened the end for Siles Zuazo. It was alleged that he had authorized a meeting between the head of his antidrug agency and the prime exporter of cocaine in Bolivia, Robert Suárez Gomez. At that meeting the drug dealer supposedly offered to pay off some or all of the nation's debts. When the Congress learned of this, it reprimanded the president.

In 1985, amid worsening conditions, a general strike was ignited by a walkout of tin miners. For the first time in his administration, Siles Zuazo deployed riot police and army troops against crowds of strikers. Although a bloody clash was avoided, "the looming confrontation was sad testimony to the deterioration of the political system in Bolivia," wrote Malloy and Gamarra.

By that summer, Siles Zuazo had decided to step down, one year before the end of his term. The Congress named Paz Estenssoro to succeed him.

Exactly 11 years after he stepped down as president, Siles Zuazo died on Bolivia's independence day. After a long illness, he died from a lung embolism in Montevideo, Uruguay.

Further Reading

Alexander, Robert J., *Bolivia: Past, Present, and Future of Its Politics*, Praeger, 1982.

Barton, Robert, *A Short History of the Republic of Bolivia*, Werner Guttentag, 1968.

Klein, Herbert S., *Bolivia: The Evolution of a Multi-Ethnic Society*, Oxford University Press, 1992.

Morales, Waltraud Queiser, *Bolivia: Land of Struggle*, Westview Press, 1992.

Malloy, James M. & Eduardo Gamarra. *Revolution and Reaction: Bolivia, 1964-1985*, Transaction Books, 1988.

Selbin, Eric, *Modern Latin American Revolutions*, Westview Press, 1993.

Comparative Politics, Volume 9, number, 2, 1990.

Newsweek, October 25, 1982, p. 87.

New York Times, October 19, 1982; August 8, 1996.

Time, July 9, 1984, p. 58.

"Bolivia: A Proud History," http://jaguar.pg.cc.md.us/historia.html (April 1998).

"Destination: Bolivia," www.lonelyplanet.com/dest/sam/boliv-ia.htm (April 1998).

"History of Bolivia," http://www.latinsynergy.org/boliv-iainfo.htm (April 1998).

"Latin American History, Modern Andean History," http://www.emayzine.com/lectures/Modern~1.htm (April 1998).

"The Lure of Easy Money," http://www.fieldingtravel.com/dp/dangerousplaces/bolivia/main.html (April 1998).

McFarren, Peter, "Hernan Siles Zuazo, Former Bolivian President and Revolutionary, Dies," http://www.sddt.com (April 1998).

Morris, Harvey, "Death of a President," http://ourworld.compuserve.com/homepages/Harvey_Morris/bo-livia.htm (April 1998).

U.S. Department of State, Bureau of Inter-American Affairs, "Background Notes: Bolivia," http://www.state.gov (April 1998).

Neil Simon

Pulitzer Prize-winning playwright Neil Simon (born 1927) has become America's most prolific and popular dramatist. His tragicomic plays expose human frailties and make people laugh at themselves.

One of America's favorite playwrights, Neil Simon has been relieving audiences of their anxieties, fears, and worries by making them laugh at their own foibles for almost forty years. His portrayals of individual angst and dysfunctional family relationships, while exaggerated, manage to hit a nerve every time. Simon takes the audience through laughter to tears and back, as he explores life's emotional truths. A prolific writer, he has written and had produced more Broadway hits than any other American playwright, making him the wealthiest dramatist in history. Numerous Antoinette Perry (Tony) Awards and nominations, and special achievement awards have followed. His contribution to the arts and to popular culture in the twentieth century was recognized in 1995 when he received Kennedy Center Honors from President Bill Clinton. As part of his tribute to Simon the President said, "He has written a string of magnificent hit plays unprecedented in the history of the American theater. Audiences found them so funny that, at first, few people noticed the gentle, deep, and sometimes sharp truths behind the comedy. . . . We saw the flaws and foibles and faults, but always, through them all, the indomitability of the human spirit."

Marvin Neil Simon was born in the Bronx, in New York, on the Fourth of July in 1927. The Great Depression brought difficult times for the family. His father, a garment salesman, periodically disappeared, leaving his wife to support their two sons by working at Gimbel's department store and relying on family and friends. After they divorced, Simon lived with relatives in Forest Hills, in the Queens borough of New York City. Simon and his older brother developed a very close relationship, and during their teens wrote and sold material to standup comics and radio shows. It was his brother who encouraged him to pursue writing while in the United States Army Air Force Reserve program

He attended college also at this time. His childhood fixation with comedy stuck, and he learned to write comedy by studying the work of his favorite comics—Robert Benchley and Ring Lardner.

After being discharged from the army, Simon got a job in the mailroom of Warner Brothers thanks to his brother who worked in the publicity department. They began collaborating again, and from 1947 to 1956 worked as a team writing comedy for television hits such as the Jackie Gleason and Phil Silvers Shows. Simon continued writing comedy for four years after his brother quit to become a television director. Some of television's top shows were showcases for his work, including the Sid Caesar and Garry Moore Shows. The pleasure was fading, however, and he turned his energies to playwriting in 1960.

Simon's first play, *Come Blow Your Horn,* was a modest hit; but it was followed shortly thereafter with *Barefoot in the Park,* a runaway hit that ran on Broadway for four years. His third play, *The Odd Couple,* introduced two characters that have become American icons—Felix and Oscar, two men estranged from their wives who move in together to save money, and find that they have the same problems living with each other as they did with their wives. The story lines usually presented conflicts between two people, and were filled with funny one-liners that brought the house down. While not entirely autobiographical, Simon makes no secret about using personal experiences or those of his friends for material. *Come Blow Your Horn* was about two brothers who moved away home and shared a bachelor apartment (just as Simon and his brother did); *Barefoot in the Park* was the story of newlyweds adjusting to married life (reminiscent of his own marriage); and, of *The Odd Couple* Simon once commented, "[the story] happened to two guys I know—I couldn't write a play about Welsh miners." *The Odd Couple* had a two-year run on Broadway, won Simon his first Tony Award, and has been adapted to television and film several times.

Critics often belittled Simon's work on the basis that he sacrificed character and plot development for laughs, to the extent that some plays were hardly more that a series of one-liners. In the 1970s, he made a conscious effort to add depth to his work by treating serious issues within a comic framework. He presented tragicomedies such as *The Last of the Red Hot Lovers*, the story of a man in a mid-life crisis who seeks solace in extramarital affairs; and *The Gingerbread Lady*, in which a one-time singer, who is now an alcoholic, struggles to make a comeback; and *The Prisoner of Second Avenue*, which witnesses the nervous breakdown of a recently fired executive. Some applauded his new "real life honesty," while others still criticized his characterizations as being superficial.

Simon continued to depict characters grappling to handle their feelings in difficult situations, and releasing tension with humor. He began to share more of himself and his life, including boyhood fantasies of escape from the emotional turmoil of his family, and the frustration and despair of coping with his wife's terminal illness. In a 1996 interview with Randy Gener for *American Theatre*, Simon commented, "I was writing plays that made people laugh. I wanted a response from the audience that would make up for whatever it was that was missing from those formative years of mine." For him, laughter provided a sense of comfort, fulfillment, and approval to replace insecurity, fear of abandonment, and later the futility of loss. During this period he wrote *The Sunshine Boys, The Good Doctor, California Suite,* and *Chapter Two,* whose leading character, a widower, feels guilty and miserable over falling in love and remarrying much as Simon had.

The 1980s took the intermingling of honesty and humor to new levels of intimacy. With the advent of *Brighton Beach Memoirs,* the first in a trilogy of semi-autobiographical plays, Simon develops the stories and conflicts among several characters, rather than presenting a one-on-one confrontation. The series begins telling the story of an adolescent middle-class Jewish American boy growing up amid a dysfunctional family and yearning to escape. *Biloxi Blues,* chronicled the boy's coming of age and the stunning reality of facing anti-Semitism while in the army —again mirroring some of Simon's personal experiences. The third, *Broadway Bound,* took audiences into the boy's young adulthood as he struggled to establish his career, and saw with new clarity the problems in his parents' relationship—Simon claimed writing the play was instrumental in resolving the relationship with his mother.

Simon uses writing as a coping mechanism for life's ups and downs, and explores a variety of mediums. When his third marriage broke up, he wrote *Rumors,* a farce, and *Jake's Women,* in which he introduces "ghosts"—good and bad experiences of two marriages and their impact on the

third. Meanwhile, he has found time to write original screenplays, as well as many adaptations of his plays for the screen. His screenplays include: *The Heartbreak Kid; The Goodbye Girl,* which won an Academy Award nomination in 1977 and a Golden Globe Award for best screenplay the following year; *Seems Like Old Times; The Lonely Guy;* and *The Slugger's Wife.*

The playwright keeps pealing away layers of psychological insight. He began the 1990s with *Lost in Yonkers,* a painfully funny story of the long lasting impact an abusive mother has on her grown children. William Henry III, writing in *Time,* noted: "At the heart is . . . a mother who was physically and psychologically abusive and four middle-aged children who still suffer the weaknesses she inflicted in teaching them to be strong." In many plays the hardened protagonist has a soft heart underneath; not the mother in *Lost in Yonkers.* She never responds to the pleas of her retarded child for affection; she turns her back and walks out the door without a word—a poignant and sad ending for a playwright known for "schtik" comedy. The play was a success, and in 1991 earned both the Antoinette Perry Award for best play and the prestigious Pulitzer Prize in drama.

His next works turned back in time to reflect and reminisce about the days of writing comedy for legends such as Mel Brooks, Carl Reiner, and Sid Caesar. *Laughter on the 23rd Floor* is a far cry from the dramatic characterizations in *Lost in Yonkers* and *Jake's Women.* The play is a behind-the-scenes look at writing comedy by committee, as a group of men shout fast one-liners, each trying to top the other. While funny, critics had a field day talking about the lack of plot and depth of these characters.

In a similar, though much less superficial vein, Simon wrote a book entitled *Rewrites* in 1996. The book is a memoir of his early career during which time he wrote hits such as *Barefoot in the Park,* and enjoyed an extremely happy marriage that ended too early when his wife lost her battle with cancer. The book received mixed reviews; *People Weekly* commented that it "doesn't live up to the creativity it documents." As Simon has often found, his own work is a hard act to follow.

Simon continues to explore new terrain in his writing. In 1997, he further developed the ghost devise first used in *Jake's Women,* and introduced his first major Black character in *Proposals.* In an interview with David Stearns for *USA Today* he said, "It is one of the most loving plays I've ever written. There's also a lot of anger. Because love is the main theme in the play, I was trying to cover all the aspects of it—those who get it and those who don't." As President Clinton remarked when presenting the Kennedy Center Honors to Simon, "he challenges us and himself never to take ourselves too seriously. Thank you for the wit and the wisdom."

Further Reading

American Theatre, October 1996.
Newsweek, March 4, 1991.
People Weekly, December 16, 1996.
Time, March 4, 1991; December 6, 1993.
USA Today, October 2, 1997.

Alvaro Siza

Alvaro Siza (born 1933) is considered Portugal's greatest living architect and possibly the best that country has ever produced. His works are internationally renowned for their coherence, clarity, and what Siza calls simplism—a quality that recognizes the complexity and contradictions of a project without trying to impose artificial control over them.

Siza was born in the town of Matosinhos, near Oporto, Portugal, in 1933. He studied architecture at the Escola de Belas Artes in Oporto from 1949 to 1955, and his first design was built in 1954. From 1955 to 1958, he worked with architect Fernando Tavora. Through the 1950s, Siza developed several projects in Matosinhos, including private houses, a Parochial Center, a Tourist Office, and a low-cost housing project as well as the acclaimed Boa Nova restaurant (1958-63; renovated 1992) and a public swimming pool in Leca da Palmeira (1958-65). These early projects indicated Siza's characteristic ability to integrate his designs with the distinct qualities of their environments.

"Embracing the Rhythm of the Air"

Siza's work, though linked to Minimalism, is considered rooted in Expressionism. These roots can be seen in the formal structures of his designs, which, according to Oriol Bohigas, are "always based on unity of space and volume" and possess "an absolute coherence of function and form." These qualities are already apparent in the Boa Nova project, chosen in a competition sponsored by the Matosinhos City Council in 1958. The building's dramatic site on a rocky coastline is integral to Siza's spectacular design. The completed work, which was restored in 1992, inspired the poem "Alvaro Siza's Restaurant in Boa Nova" by Eugenio de Andrade: "The musical order of the space,/ the manifest truth of stone,/ the concrete beauty/ of the ground ascends the last few steps,/ the contained/ and continuous and serene line/ embracing the rhythm of the air,/ the white architecture/ stripped/ bare to its bones/ where the sea came in."

In 1966, Siza joined the faculty at the School of Architecture in Oporto (ESBAP), and in 1976 he was appointed Assistant Professor of Construction. Through the 1960s and early 1970s, he continued to design private houses as well as commercial buildings near Oporto. His second swimming pool for Leca da Palmeira displays his brilliant use of space. The design uses a natural rock formation to complement the man-made sides of a large pool placed as if carved out of the sand and rock of the coastline. A smaller children's pool, changing building, and cafe are also included, and the building is set below the level of the access road to provide an uninterrupted view of the ocean. José Paulo dos Santos has noted in his *Alvaro Siza: Works & Projects 1954-1992* that the design contains formal references to Finnish architect Alvar Aalto and to neoplasticist architecture.

Public Housing and Urban Design

Since the mid-1970s, Siza has been involved in numerous designs for public housing. At that time, overcrowding and lack of sanitary facilities plagued many old sections of Oporto, and after Portugal's revolution against dictator Salazar in 1974, the political group SAAL (servicio de apoio ambulatorio local) responded to urban problems by planning designs to remedy slum conditions. In 1974, Siza worked on renovations for the Bouca quarter that would both resolve the problems that had been characteristic of the antiquated buildings and also fit within the historical context of the site. He used a vertebral wall to screen the project from adjacent railroad tracks. Perpendicular to this wall were four linear terraces of double maisonettes, forming long courtyards reminiscent of the type of neighborhood the new project replaced.

Siza worked with SAAL again in a design for the rehabilitation of the Sao Victor district of Oporto, then embarked on the enormous subsidized housing project in Quinta de Malagueira, Evora, in 1977. This design included 1,200 housing units as well as institutional and commercial facilities, with a raised service duct, similar to the Renaissance aqueduct that had fed the old city, supplying utilities. "Without grand polemic," wrote dos Santos, "the scheme touches on the attitudes and formal achievements of European Modernist settlements but rejects their isolation from their contexts. The absorption of the cultural aspirations of different social classes, the pressures placed on the public space by the car, and the ambivalent requirements for communal identity are convincingly resolved in this scheme."

Forming a Whole with Ruins

Siza's interest in urban design soon brought him to projects outside of Portugal. In the late 1970s he worked on an urban renewal design in the Kreuzberg district of Berlin, and in 1984 he won first prize in the International Building Exhibition (IBA) for the rehabilitation of an entire block in the same district. The project (Schlesisches Tor) was to have maintained the block's mix of residential and commercial space, but, because of financial considerations, the developer made several changes in the design. The finished project, though, does retain the curved, wave-like facade of the corner building. Doug Clelland commented in *Architectural Review* that the scheme knits together the existing fabric of the site well, but "lacks the presence and assurance of the decayed nineteenth century block across the street." Indeed, Siza himself has remarked that "The problem is to form a whole with ruins." This attention to the past, according to Kenneth Frampton in *Design Quarterly*, is a quality that distinguishes Siza's approach from that of many contemporaries. He emphasized that in all of Siza's collective housing projects there is the "potential for establishing a critical interaction between the new and the ruined."

Among several other public housing projects are Siza's design for the Guidecca district of Venice, which was first in the 1985 international competition for controlled-cost subsidized housing in the Campo di Marte, and his design for 106 low-cost units in The Hague. The Netherlands project, noted dos Santos, refers to the brick tradition of such architects as Michel de Klerk and J. J. P. Oud, but also shows the influence of Mendelsohn.

During the 1980s, Siza expanded his international repertoire when he was invited to enter several international competitions, including the Expo 92 in Seville in 1986; Un Progretto per Siena, Italy, in 1988; Bibliotheque de France, Paris, 1989-90; and the Helsinki Museum, 1993. He obtained first place in the Schlesisches Tor, Kreuzberg, Berlin in 1980; restoration of Campo di Marte, Venice, in 1985; redevelopment of the Casino and Cafe Winkler, Salzburg, 1986, and La Defensa Cultural Centre, Madrid, 1988-89. During this period, he also worked on several institutional and commercial projects. His Banco Borges & Irmao in Vila do Conde, Portugal, is notable for its vertical identity and its dramatic rotational character, with all the interior floors visually related as in Le Corbusier's Carthage villa. "João de Deus" kindergarten in Penafiel, Portugal, is built on a plinth to respond to challenges of site and to integrate the structure's various uses.

Wide Range of Concerns

Siza's range of architectural interests remains especially broad, from residences to churches, schools, shopping centers, libraries, museums, and even, most recently, furniture. His design for the Oporto Faculty of Architecture, a monumental project, is nearing completion. This comprises several buildings placed along the banks of the River Douro in an arrangement that, according to one critic, suggests an allusion to the Acropolis. Another has noted the influence of Austrian and German architecture in this design, pointing out that Siza's precision of scale is complemented by the architect's "subtle understanding of the surroundings." In fact, Siza vigorously opposed a plan to construct a major automobile throughway along the riverbank, arguing that unobstructed river frontage is integral to the Faculty of Architecture's overall design.

Among Siza's other unusual projects are a water tower for the University of Aveiro (1988-89), designed as a reinforced concrete slab and parallel cylinder which rise out of a reflecting sheet of water, and the cylindrical meteorological center for the Barcelona Olympic Village (1989-92), built on the beach of the city's Olympic Port. Critics admired the way in which the design for the meteorological center "has both presence and autonomy with respect to the grand dimensions of the neighbouring volumes and the scale of the Port's quays and harbor wall."

Other projects of the late 1980s and early 1990s include La Defensa Cultural Centre, Madrid (1988); the Museum of Contemporary Art, Santiago de Compostela, Spain (1988-93); the Rector's Office and Law Library for the University of Valencia (1990); the Vitra office furniture factory, Weil-am-Rhein, Germany (1991); and the Contemporary Art Museum, Casa de Serralves, Oporto (1991).

One of Siza's most important ongoing projects is the reconstruction of Lisbon's historic Chiado district. This area, the principal civic and commercial space for the neighborhood, was heavily damaged by fire in 1988. Seventeen buildings had to be redesigned based on historic plans. The project was complicated by damage from tunnel excavation under the site, which badly weakened the foundations of several buildings, especially the ancient ruins of the Carmo Convent. Siza has been active in seeking solutions for this damage.

International Renown

In addition to his major design projects, Siza remains deeply committed to teaching. He has participated in numerous conferences and seminars throughout Europe, North and South America, and Japan. He has been a visiting professor at the Ecole Polytechnique of Lausanne, the University of Pennsylvania, the Los Andes School, the University of Bogota, and Harvard University's Graduate School of Design as Kenzo Tange Visiting Professor. He continues to teach at the Oporto School of Architecture.

Siza's distinguished work has been widely recognized. In 1982, he was awarded the Prize of Architecture from the Portuguese Department of the International Association of Art Critics, and in 1987 he received an award from the Portuguese Architects Association. In 1988, Siza received the Gold Medal for Architecture from the Colegio de Architectos, Madrid, the Gold Medal from the Alvar Aalto Foundation, the Prince of Wales Prize in Urban Design from Harvard University, and the European Architectural Award from the EEC/Mies van der Rohe Foundation, Barcelona. In 1992, he was awarded the prestigious Pritzker Prize from the Hyatt Foundation of Chicago, for lifetime achievement. That same year, Siza was also named Doctor Honoris Causa at the University of Valencia. In 1993, he won the National Prize of Architecture from the Portuguese Architects Association and was named Doctor Honoris Causa at the Ecole Polytechnique Federal de Lausanne. In 1996, he received the honorary title of Fellow, American Institute of Architects.

In May 1996, a major retrospective of Siza's work opened in his home town of Matosinhos. "Alvara Siza— Buildings and Projects" included models of many of the architect's projects since 1980, as well as pieces of his furniture, drawings, sketches, and photographs. Portuguese President Jorge Sampaio attended the exhibit's opening ceremonies. The show, which was scheduled to travel to Tenerife, Sardinia, Brussels, Brazil, and the United States, was expected to draw more than 150,000 people.

Further Reading

Contemporary Architects, third edition, St. James Press, 1994.
Testa, Peter, *Alvaro Siza,* Birkhauser, 1996.
Doug Clelland, ed., "West Berlin 1984: The Milestone and the Millstone," *Architectural Review,* September, 1984, pp. 40/9-41/9.
Dos Santos, José Paulo, ed., *Alvaro Siza: Works and Projects 1954-1992,* third edition, Editorial Gustavo Gili, S.A., Barcelona, 1993.
Frampton, Kenneth, *Design Quarterly,* summer, 1992, pp. 2-5.
"Alvaro Siza," SALA Gallery, http://www.clr.toronto.edu:1080/~nives/intro.html.
Editorial Blau, http://www.cidadevirtual.pt/blau/siza.html.

William Joseph Slim

English General William Joseph Slim (1891-1970) was involved in some lesser-known but still critical battles of World War II. He later served as head of the Imperial General Staff, Britain's top military post, and governor-general of Australia.

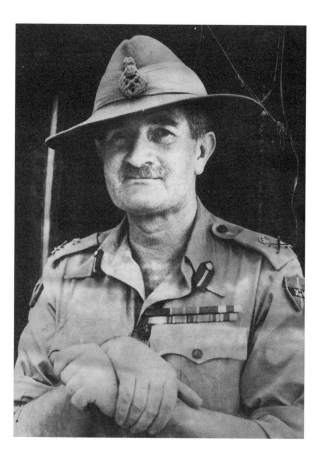

As a boy, William Joseph Slim had always wanted to be a military officer. During World War II, he took command of allied forces defeated and demoralized by advancing Japanese troops that had overrun Burma and were threatening to invade India. Slim made it his priority to improve the morale of his men, rebuild their confidence, and teach them to adapt to the jungles of southeast Asia. Consequently, he regained the offensive and reconquered Burma.

Boyhood Dream

William Joseph Slim had always dreamed of becoming a soldier. He was born October 6, 1891, in Bristol, England. The son of John Slim, an iron merchant in Bristol, he moved with his family to Birmingham at the turn of the century. There, he attended St. Philip's Catholic School and then King Edward's School, where his favorite subject was literature. At the time, he was a member of the Officers Training Corps, and he often told people that his great ambition was to be an army officer. But in early 20th century England, the army did not financially support those in officers training, and Slim's parents could not pay for their son to pursue his ambition. Consequently, after leaving school, Slim worked as a clerk and a teacher. Also, he was a foreman at an engineering firm. When World War I began, his military dream was abruptly realized. England was desperate for soldiers to fight against the Germans. Slim was commissioned in the Royal Warwickshire Regiment, a territorial troop similar to the National Guard in the United States. He joined the regiment as a private, but when his troop was made part of the regular British army, he was promoted to lance-corporal. He was later demoted to private for drinking from a jug of beer while marching with his men as they marched through Yorkshire on maneuvers. It was the only demotion Slim ever received.

He first saw action when his regiment was sent to Mesopotamia (modern-day Iraq), followed by an engagement in the Battle of Gallipoli in Turkey, where he was so seriously wounded that it seemed unlikely that he would ever return to active service. However, through a series of subterfuges that Slim never entirely revealed, he was able to rejoin the army and fought in France and Belgium before rejoining his old troops in Mesopotamia. He was wounded again in the battle to capture Baghdad and was evacuated to India.

When World War I ended, he joined the Sixth Ghurka Rifles of the Indian Army and learned to speak their language. From 1917 to 1920 and again from 1929 to 1933 he was part of the General Staff of the Indian Army. During this period he graduated from the Indian Army Staff College in Cambalay and later was an instructor at the college. He returned to England briefly to attend the Imperial Defence School. During the 1930s his effectiveness as a teacher was recognized by British and Indian military leaders; that earned him a promotion to the rank of lieutenant-colonel by 1935. Just before World War II broke out, Slim was commandant of the Senior Officers' School at Belgaum, India.

From the Desert to the Jungle

In 1940 Slim was given command of the Tenth Indian Infantry Brigade and was ordered to use his Indian troops in the Sudan to prevent an invasion of Italian troops. A border town called Gallabat had been occupied by the Italians; Slim and his forces were ordered to retake the town. Although the Indians recaptured Gallabat, Slim decided that defense of the area was untenable and pulled his troops back to safer positions, giving up the town. In retrospect, Slim believed he had made a poor military decision. Yet he gained the admiration of others as a leader who could accept blame during bad times but was quick to praise his subordinates during good times.

Soon after, Slim was again wounded when a low-flying aircraft attacked the vehicle in which he was traveling. While recovering in May 1941, he was given command of the Tenth Indian Division in Iraq and Syria where he successfully fought against the Vichy French forces and later advanced through Iran. He described desert fighting to be suitable because you can see your opponent.

By March 1942, General Archibald Wavell, the commander-in-chief in India, sent Slim to Burma to take command of the British-Indian First Burma Corps. The situation in Burma was dismal for allied forces. Because of allied problems in 1942 in Europe and in the Pacific Ocean, low priority was given to the military situation in Burma and India. There was no air cover for the allied troops. Intelligence and communication were poor. Japanese forces from the east were pushing the Burma Corps westward and northward through the jungle toward India. They had also cut supply lines to the Chinese armies in the north. Slim tried to regain the offensive, but his troops had withstood heavy casualties and were exhausted. Therefore, he was forced to lead his troops in an orderly retreat nearly 1,000 miles from Rangoon into India. Thirteen thousand men died during the retreat.

Reinvasion of Burma

After the retreat, Slim commanded the newly formed 15th Indian Corps. He oversaw intensive training to prepare the men for future battles against the Japanese. He restored confidence in his demoralized troops. Slim revised and improved their fighting approach. He gave higher priority to medical attention and made sure drugs were on hand to prevent malaria. In addition, he visited as many units as possible and met as many of his subordinate commanders as possible.

Slim believed that as an officer, he had to set an example for his men. "Officers are there to lead," he was quoted in *Phoenix,* the South East Asia Command magazine. "As officers, you can neither eat, nor drink, nor sleep, nor smoke, nor even sit down until you have personally seen that your men have done these things. If you will do this for them, they will follow you to the end of the world." Slim often paraphrased, as he did in *Phoenix,* the famous line ascribed to Napoleon, "There are no bad soldiers, only bad officers."

The situation in Burma was soon made worse by allied commitments to the Soviet Union. In an agreement with Soviet leader Josef Stalin, England and the United States agreed to conquer Germany first in return for a Soviet declaration of war on Japan. The re-invasion of Burma was not considered critical to the war effort. Landing craft in the Burma theater were transferred to Europe for invasions against the Nazis. Slim, then, was forced to fight the Japanese through the dense jungle rather than by sea.

By October 1943, Slim was commander of the newly established British 14th Army. In 1944, he deliberately let the Japanese cross the frontier into India, thus stretching thin their supply and communication lines. His fully provisioned army waited for the Japanese to arrive then beat the Japanese forces in decisive victories at Imphal and Kohima. As his troops regained the offensive and marched eastward and southward through the jungle. He and Mountbatten developed a plan in which the army was supplied by air drop, thus precluding the need for supply lines. A total of 600,000 tons of supplies was dropped by parachute to Slim's advancing army. Also, Slim's reconquest of Burma was based on a two-pronged attack that confused the Japanese and

caused them to concentrate forces in the wrong locations. His army forced the Japanese out of Burma and inflicted 347,000 casualties. Slim was the only general in World War II to defeat a major Japanese army on the Asian mainland. After retaking Burma until the end of the war, Slim's forces fought clean-up campaigns against small pockets of Japanese resistance.

Beloved Leader

By July 1945, Slim was promoted to full general and then commander-in-chief of all allied land forces in southeast Asia. By 1946, with the war over, he was called back to England to be commandant of the recently reopened Imperial Defence College. He then retired from the army to pursue a private life. But by the end of 1948, he was recalled to the army to be chief of the Imperial General Staff. Two months later, he was promoted to field marshal.

In 1953, Slim was appointed governor-general of Australia, representing the Queen of England and British interests in Australia. He made it a point to meet the people and, thus, he became one of the most popular governor-generals in the history of Australia. The Australian prime minister often commented on the affection the Australians had for Slim.

Occasionally, Slim took his mind off his duties by reading murder-mystery novels. He also wrote mystery serials, as well as poems and short stories, under the pseudonym Anthony Mills. In 1956, he wrote *Defeat into Victory,* considered one of the finest books about World War II.

In 1960, Slim was made a Knight of the Garter by the British monarchy. Eleven universities, including Oxford and Cambridge, conferred honorary degrees on him. He was then appointed Constable of Windsor Castle and left Australia. He held the Windsor Castle position until shortly before his death ten years later, on December 14, 1970. When he died in London, he was given a public funeral with full military honors.

Further Reading

Dictionary of National Biography: 1961-1970, edited by E. T. Williams and C. S. Nicholls, Oxford University Press, 1981.

Keegan, John, and Andrew Wheatcroft, *Who's Who in Military History: From 1453 to the Present Day,* Rutledge, 1996.

Leckie, Robert, *The Story of World War II,* Random House, 1964.

The Oxford Companion to World War II, edited by I.C.B. Dear, Oxford University Press, 1995.

"General Bill Slim, *CBI Info,* http://www.chiinfo.com/billslim.htm (March 13, 1998).

Dean Smith

The winningest basketball coach in college history, Dean Smith (born 1931) retired from the University of North Carolina in 1997 after 36 seasons. His teams won 879 games and had 27 consecutive seasons of at least 20 victories.

Under Dean Smith, the University of North Carolina Tar Heels made 11 appearances in the Final Four of the National Collegiate Athletic Association's Division I college basketball tournament. They won two NCAA titles, in 1982 and 1993. Smith holds many records, including 65 NCAA tournament wins, and 17 regular season titles in the Atlantic Coast Conference.

Beyond his teams' achievements, Smith was known for his innovations, his recruiting prowess, and his loyalty to his players. Smith coached 30 All-Americans, including the man many consider the greatest basketball player who ever lived, Michael Jordan. Many others he coached went on to the National Basketball Association, including 21 first-round NBA draft picks. At least five of his former players became NBA coaches, including NBA Hall of Famer Billy Cunningham. Cunningham told *Time* that Smith "takes as much pride in the doctors and lawyers he coached as he does in the All-Stars." Legendary UCLA coach John Wooden once said, "Dean is the best teacher of basketball that I have observed." When Smith announced his retirement, Jordan commented,"He's a father figure to a lot of players and a lot of people."

The Future Coach

The only son of strict Baptist schoolteachers, Dean Edwards Smith was born February 28, 1931. He grew up in Emporia, Kansas, watching his father coach. Alfred Smith's high school Spartans won the 1934 state championship with the help of the first black player in Kansas high school tournament history. Smith was an intensely competitive yet

sensitive child. In high school he played quarterback in football, catcher in baseball, and point guard in basketball—the positions that demand the greatest intelligence and understanding of each sport.

Despite his desire to succeed, Smith didn't have the talent to make it as a player. He went to the University of Kansas on an academic scholarship. There he majored in math and physical education and was a reserve guard on the basketball team. The team won the 1952 national title, but Smith played little. His coach was Phog Allen, who had been taught by the inventor of the game of basketball, Alexander Naismith. Smith would sit next to Allen on the bench and soak up knowledge. "Everyone understood that he was going to be a coach," said local sportswriter Rich Clarkson.

After graduation, Smith briefly served as an assistant coach at Kansas, then joined the U.S. Air Force in Germany. From 1955 to 1958, Smith was an assistant basketball coach at the U.S. Air Force Academy.

Succeeding A Legend

Smith came to North Carolina as assistant basketball coach in 1958. In 1961, he succeeded the legendary coach Frank McGuire. McGuire had led the Tar Heels to a national championship in 1957, but his aggressive recruiting had put the program in violation of NCAA rules. Smith would polish UNC's image to a fine sheen. In all his seasons, his program never was charged with a single violation.

Smith's only losing season was his first, but it took a while for him to be accepted. In his first five seasons, Smith twice was hung in effigy on campus. "When I was here, Dean Smith was the biggest joke around," said Art Heyman, a player with nearby Duke University. "Everybody wanted him fired."

A liberal politically, Smith joined in protests on campus against segregation. In 1964, he accompanied a local black pastor and a black theology student to a segregated Chapel Hills restaurant Smith and his players often visited. The visit integrated the restaurant. In 1966, Smith recruited the first black player in the ACC, Charlie Scott. "Coach Smith was always there for me," Scott told *Sports Illustrated.* "On one occasion, as we walked off the court following a game at South Carolina, one of their fans called me a 'big, black baboon.' Two assistants had to hold Coach Smith back from going after the guy. It was the first time I had ever seen Coach Smith visibly upset."

Smith combined his outspoken support for liberal causes, including nuclear disarmament and abolition of the death penalty, with a devout Christian faith. He served as director of the Fellowship of Christian Athletes from 1965 to 1970. He ordered his players to go to the church of their choice every Sunday and return with a brochure to prove they had gone.

The Smith Mystique

After his teams won three straight Atlantic Conference championships beginning in 1967, a mystique started to develop around Smith and his "system" of coaching. At the Air Force Academy, he and head coach

Bob Spear had started to develop an offensive delay game. It eventually became a stall strategy known as the "Four Corners." The Four Corners involved stationing a player in each corner of the offensive half-court and passing the ball constantly around the perimeter. The shot clock came to college basketball largely because of the Four Corners.

Smith's teams were known for their passing and for their scrambling trap defenses. He also invented the now-common practice of players huddling at the foul line before a foul shot. And more than any other coach, Smith was responsible for the highly evolved platoon substitution that now characterizes the final minutes of most close games, as coaches shuttle offensive and defensive specialists in and out. "On the sidelines Smith was always several moves ahead of everyone else," wrote Alexander Wolff of *Sports Illustrated.*

Starting in 1967, Smith was six times named Coach of the Year in the ACC. His coaching and recruiting turned North Carolina's program into a juggernaut. But to Smith, winning was not the first priority. "My first goal was to keep my job," he told Wolff. "Then I wanted to win. It was when I got more mature that I said, What's most important is that we play well."

Smith was known for his presence of mind in tense late-game situations. Mitch Kupchak, his center from 1972 to 1976, recalled a game against Duke in which UNC was behind eight points with 17 seconds left. "His calm throughout was amazing," Kupchak told *Sports Illustrated.* "The way he walked us through those 17 seconds, it was as if he said, 'Don't think about this. Just do as I say and we'll win.' There he was in the huddle, looking up at us with a kind of smile." The Tar Heels tied the game and won it in overtime.

Smith was named the nation's top coach in 1977 and 1979. But he didn't win his first national title until 1982, in his seventh trip to the Final Four. It came against Georgetown, when a Hoya player threw the ball to James Worthy of the Tar Heels by mistake. Jordan, then a freshman, got the game-winning jump shot after the team got a pep talk on the sidelines from Smith. Down by a point, Smith told his players: "We're in great shape. I'd rather be in our shoes than theirs. . . . We are going to determine who wins this game." Smith's second title came in 1993, and it was also due to an opponent's blunder, when Chris Webber of Michigan called a time-out when his team had none left. In contrast, the Tar Heels "played with prepossessing calm," noted *Sports Illustrated.*

Legacy of Loyalty

Smith was intensely loyal to his players, visiting them in the hospital and keeping in touch with them after they graduated. Former Charlotte, North Carolina, mayor Richard Vinroot, who played under Smith, said Smith wrote to him weekly after Vinroot graduated and was serving in Vietnam. After Worthy turned pro and was arrested for soliciting a prostitute, Smith called and told him, "We're all human. I know you're a great man. Just deal with it as a man."

"I can't think of a time I've ever heard him blame or degrade one of his players, and in return, his kids are fiercely loyal to him," Duke University coach Mike Krzyzewski told *Sports Illustrated.* "That kind of loyalty doesn't just happen. Things done on a day-to-day basis develop that kind of relationship."

Smith was such a straight arrow that he always wore a tie even in practice. He forbade his players to have facial hair. He and his wife Linnea campaigned to ban alcohol advertising at college sports events. "It's hypocritical for a college conference to have student-athletes tell young people they should say no to drugs when we say yes to beer ads," Smith told Wolff.

Smith always made academics paramount. His players had a 97 percent graduation rate. To the end of his career, he remained firmly opposed to freshman eligibility for high-profile collegiate sports. If freshmen were ineligible, he told Wolff, "colleges would attract young men who are serious about school as well as athletics, because those who want to go pro after one season wouldn't have the patience to wait around." Yet Smith also advocated paying NCAA players, and he encouraged many of his stars to leave college early to turn professional.

Although he was one of the best paid collegiate coaches, Smith criticized coaches' salaries as exorbitant. He insisted that money donated by shoe-company sponsors to the basketball program be spread evenly to all sports programs, men's and women's, at the university. He was also intensely private. Only over his protests was North Carolina's new basketball arena named the Dean E. Smith Center in 1983. He "was the one guy who didn't buy into the myth that had been created around him," said sportswriter S.L. Price.

Smith's players had to talk him out of retiring near the end of the 1996-97 season. Smith didn't want to break University of Kentucky legend Adolph Rupp's record of 876 coaching wins. After he won the game, he congratulated his assistants.

Some critics said Smith should have won more than two titles. "I don't believe that 'winning the big one' says all there is to say about you," Smith told Wolff. "You win big ones to get to the Final Four, or even just to get into the tournament." Smith retired at the start of the 1997-98 season. At 66, he said he could no longer bring the necessary energy to his job. Smith was succeeded by Bill Guthridge, his assistant for 31 years.

"He had a style that no one's ever going to copy," said Krzyzewski. "To be that smart, that psychologically aware, that good with X's and O's—with that system, and to always take the high road—that just isn't going to happen again."

Further Reading

Porter, David L., ed., *Biographical Dictionary of American Sports,* Greenwood Press, 1989.
Sporting News, October 20, 1997.
Sports Illustrated, March 24, 1997; October 20, 1997; December 22, 1997.
Time, October 20, 1997.
U.S. News & World Report, October 27, 1997.

Robert Southey

A contemporary of the great poets Samuel Taylor Coleridge and William Wordsworth, Robert Southey (1774-1843) is one of the best known of the unread poets; that is, his name is better known than the work he produced. While his work leans towards the introspection, skepticism, and symbolism that characterize the period, Southey never fully came to fruition as a Romantic poet.

While Southey may not have been a potential Wordsworth or Coleridge, the talent he did posses was not given the concentration of time and energy poetry demands to mature. Because of Southey's financial and personal commitments to his family, he chose to write articles, pamphlets, tales, and light pieces as well as poetry, all within very constricting time limits: "verse took turn and turn about with history, politics, and reviewing: the four last epics were almost entirely written before breakfast," quips Simmons in his 1948 biography of Southey. This versatility did, however, foster the development of a distinct and admirable prose style.

Comments on His Work

Southey's poetry was first published in 1795 in *Poems; containing The Retrospect, Odes, Sonnets, Elegies, &c. By Robert Lovell and Robert Southey, of Balliol College, Oxford,* which included 21 poems by Southey and 11 by Lovell. His first poem of merit, "Joan of Arc," was published in 1796. The fresh style had a strong appeal to the prevailing Romantic tastes, but to this day is not considered a great work. According to Simmons' bio, Wordsworth once opined that Southey's poetry "does not give anything which impresses the mind strongly and is recollected in solitude." Nonetheless, Southey enjoyed a viable public career as a poet which led to his appointment as Poet Laureate in 1813.

The practice of writing poetry, combined with the time constraints of production, engendered Southey's concise style of prose which has been described as vigorous, direct, unassuming, crisp, and as Simmons quotes one critic, "the style of a man who writes swiftly and voluminously, and who has discovered the true economy of a clear mind and a clean pen." Southey himself is quoted by Simmons as saying, "[t]o write poetry is the best preparation for writing prose. The versemaker gets the habit of weighing the meanings and qualities of words, until he comes to know, as if by intuition, what particular word will best fit into the sentence." Consequently, Southey played a great part in loosening up the English language. At the end of the eighteenth century, the imitators of Burke, Gibbon, and Johnson had twisted the language into elaborate, superfluous styles. Southey's prose offered elegant precision. This fresh voice suited the newly industrialized England, and his work, though sometimes politically challenging, was well received. He gained a respectable reputation in his time and many scholars and critics believe he is certainly worth examining as a contemporary study.

Unfortunately, Southey is often remembered because of his association with Wordsworth and Coleridge or as the ardent young reformer who is corrupted and turns conservative in Byron's "Vision of Judgment." His works are still read but often without knowing who wrote them. *The Story of the Three Bears* is one of his more popular tales. *The Battle of Blenheim* and *The Inchcape Rock* are almost considered mere folklore. His *Life of Nelson* is still is known but not for the vitality of the writing. Other works of Southey include: *Book of the Church,* a popular ecclesiastical history of England published in 1824, *The History of Brazil,* published in three volumes, *A Tale of Paraguay, Lives of the British Admirals,* and many collections of poetry. He is also known for his letters.

Early Life

Robert Southey was born on the 12th of August, 1774 in Bristol, England. Though both his parents had descended from respectable families of the county of Somerset, his father was unsuccessful in business as a linen draper in the city of Bristol. At the age of two, young Southey was sent to live in Bath with his mother's unmarried half-sister, Elizabeth Tyler. Tyler is often characterized as a strong-willed woman who dominated Southey's parents as effectively as she dominated him. Not only strict but also eccentric, his aunt prohibited her young ward from playing outside lest he dirty himself or his clothing. Luckily, he was occasionally afforded the opportunity to escape to his grandmother's farm in Bedminster where he was allowed to play in the garden.

Tyler, who had a great passion for plays and actors, took her nephew first to the theater when he was four and often thereafter. Perhaps the greatest gift Tyler gave to Southey was this early indoctrination to the arts. The Bristol stage was frequently honored by great actors of the day, and they often became visitors at Tyler's home. When in public or receiving guests, Tyler's appearance and manners were those of the well-bred lady. Otherwise, she spent most of her time in the kitchen wearing only rags or bedclothes. She did encourage Southey to read and provided him with the complete set of fashionable children's books published by John Newberry. By the time he was eight, he had even read Shakespeare.

Southey's writing endeavors began as early as the age of nine with a continuation of Ariosto's *Orlando,* written in heroic couplets. Soon after, however, a reading of Bysshe's *Art of Poetry* introduced him to the versatility of blank verse. Continuing his poetic interests, he had by the time he was 15 written three cantos continuing Spencer's *Faerie Queen.*

School and the Conception of Pantisocracy

When Southey was 13, his maternal uncle, the Reverend Herbert Hill, decided to fund the education of his promising nephew. On April 1, 1788, Southey was entered at Westminster, with an eye towards Christ Church College at Oxford, since Hill thought Southey might become a minister. Westminster was then still one of the two leading public schools in England, rivaled only by Eton.

The rivalry included competing satirical newspapers. The publishers of *The Microcosm* from Eton were countered by a group at Westminster with a paper called *The Trifler.* Southey made an attempt to contribute to *The Trifler,* sending in a poem on the death of his infant sister, but this was rejected. In 1792 he and his friends started a second Westminster paper, to emulate *The Trifler.* He didn't actually contribute to their new publication, entitled *The Flagellant,* until its fifth issue, when he wrote an attack on corporal punishment in the school under the pseudonym "Gualbertus." In the article, Southey asserted that "whosoever floggeth, that is, performeth the will of Satan, committeth an abomination; to him therefore [and] to all the consumers of birch as to priests of Lucifer." School officials found the subversive attitude of the article outside the parameters of tolerance as "it advertised to the world that forces of anarchy and irreligion had secured a foothold." Southey was consequently expelled.

In 1793, the Reverend Hill again attempted to provide for Southey's education by entering him at Balliol College, Oxford. A year later, his friend Robert Allen introduced Southey to Coleridge. These young idealists shared political opinions which questioned the ethics of the Church and Christianity, as well as the established social order of England. Together with Burnett, Seward, and Robert Lovell, they conceptualized a plan to start a settlement in America run on egalitarian principles which they coined a "pantisocratic" society. Southey felt that the university system was out of date and merely perpetuated established opinions rather than educating its students. At the end of summer term in 1794, he returned to Bristol, without finishing his degree.

In Bristol, Southey and Coleridge began publishing and holding public lectures to earn money for the impending emigration. The Southey family were close friends to the Fricker family and during this time in Bristol, Southey became engaged to Edith Fricker. Lovell had already married her sister, Mary, and Coleridge married a third sister, Sara. When Southey's aunt heard of his engagement and his plans for a Pantisocracy, she rejected him for the rest of her life. Increased financial obligations and ideological differences eventually led the young group of Pantisocrats to abandon their plans.

Settling Into a Life of Letters and Family

In 1795, the Reverend Hill invited Southey to accompany him to Portugal. His uncle was hoping to distract Southey's interest from Edith Fricker, to give him time away from his angry aunt, and to convince Southey to enter the ministry. Southey accepted the invitation to please his family and to pass time until he had enough money to provide for a wife. However, Southey secretly married Edith the morning he and his uncle began their trip.

While in Portugal, Southey developed a life-long interest in Portuguese and Spanish History. He also developed a contempt for the Roman Catholic Church upon seeing the social inequities and the morals of the ruling class in Lisbon.

And, though he still disliked government, he came to appreciate the benefits of being English when compared to the squalor that he experienced abroad. After six months in Lisbon, he returned to Bristol and to his wife, and then went on to London to study law with the blessing and funding of his uncle, but never finished his studies.

Southey went to Portugal again in 1800 hoping the climate would improve his and Edith's poor health. He took advantage of the time to collect information and begin writing the *History of Portugal.* Upon returning to England in 1801, he obtained an appointment of Private Secretary to the Chancellor of the Exchequer in Ireland, which would divide his time between London and Ireland. He was not satisfied with the position and began to feel the need to settle down: his mother had recently died; Edith was pregnant with their first child; and Coleridge was soliciting advice on his failing marriage. Southey resigned from his new position within a few months and redirected himself towards his family.

The Coleridges had rented an estate named Greta Hall and, in 1803, Southey and Edith joined them. The household also included their landlord, the widowed Mrs. Lovell, the three Coleridge children, and their nurse. Fortunately, *Joan of Arc* was giving Southey something of a literary reputation and he got enough of his writing published that he was able to provide for his large and growing family. By 1810, Southey had fully converted from young revolutionary poet to embrace the established order as an outspoken Tory. He felt that the industrial revolution had made people callously inhumane and he was firmly opposed to children working in factories, which he likened to a form of slavery. Southey was honored, in 1813, with the appointment of Poet Laureate on the recommendation of Sir Walter Scott, who had declined the Laureateship.

Southey spent 30 pleasant years with Edith at Greta Hall, but was greatly distressed when she suffered a nervous breakdown. She went to an asylum, returned home, fell ill, and died in 1837. Two years later, at age 65, Southey married Caroline Anne Bowles, a poet 12 years his junior who enjoyed some renown. Within a month of their marriage, his own mental faculties began to deteriorate. He continued to read and contentedly participate in daily activities, but persistent bouts of confusion prevented him from writing. He failed to recognize his friends and neglected to reply to their letters. In February 1843, Southey suffered an apoplectic seizure and died just over a month later on March 21, 1843. He was buried in Crosswaithe Churchyard, where Edith and the three children who had preceded him had been buried.

Further Reading

Bernhardt-Kabisch, Ernest, *Robert Southey,* Twayne Publishers, 1977.

Carnall, Geoffrey, *Robert Southey,* Longmans, Green & Co., Ltd., 1964.

Cottle, Joseph, *Reminiscences of Samuel Taylor Coleridge and Robert Southey,* Wiley and Putnam, 1847.

Simmons, Jack, *Southey,* Yale University Press, 1948.

Southey, Robert, *The Poetical Works of Robert Southey with a Memoir,* Thomas Y. Crowell & Co., c. 1845

Dawn Steel

When Dawn Steel (1946-1997) was promoted to president of Columbia Pictures, she became the first woman ever to run a major U.S. motion picture studio.

In the foreward to her autobiography, *They Can Kill You, But They Can't Eat You,* Dawn Steel wrote, "My story is far from a Hollywood fantasy. It might sound like one, though, if you don't look deeper: a girl from a struggling, lower-middle-class family grows up, gets through high school, drops out of college when she runs out of money . . . and winds up running a major motion picture studio." Steel would be the first woman to be in charge of such a studio; however, due to cancer, the story of her life did not have the classic happy Hollywood ending.

Early Life

Steel was born August 19, 1946, in the Bronx, New York. Before her birth, her father had changed the Jewish family name from "Spielberg" to "Steel." Her parents raised her in the suburbs of New York in a comfortable setting until her father suffered a nervous breakdown when Steel was nine years old. From that day on her mother became the family provider, and Steel learned her first lessons of male/female equality from her mother.

During her adolescence Steel grew into a perfectionist, trying to win her mother's approval, a trait that would remain with Steel throughout her varied career. She recognized that her mother worked hard, but Steel also sensed her mother was only working a job and not pursuing a career. Steel decided she would have a career. Steel went to college to escape her parents' home. First she attended Boston University, and then transferred to New York University, where she was the only woman in the business school.

Early Employment

In 1968 Steel quit school and took her first full-time job. This first job was as a receptionist for a garment company. A few months later she switched companies, and then became the receptionist for the Stadia Publishing Company, which published sports books. She advanced from receptionist to secretary, and eventually even became a sportswriter. The sports business was where she experienced, first-hand, the inequality between males and females. And as other area newspapers went out of business, freeing up many male sportswriters, Steel knew it was time for a different job.

At this time, a new girlie magazine was starting up. Steel interviewed and was hired by Bob Guccione to work for *Penthouse.* Steel recalled Guccione as someone who "supported women's rights . . . long before it was fashionable to do so." *Penthouse* was a company that consistently promoted women to positions of responsibility, and Steel had an opportunity to try many different roles—from receptionist to editor to interviewer. One of the most important lessons she learned while working at *Penthouse* was the

importance of "taking whatever job you do seriously and doing it better than everyone else." Eventually she was promoted to head of merchandising.

During her *Penthouse* years, Steel met and married her first husband, Ronald Richard Rothstein. Rothstein and Steel formed a business as well as personal partnership, and soon Entrepreneuse Enterprises, Inc. was up and running. In 1976 Entrepreneuse Enterprises introduced the world to designer toilet paper, ripping off Gucci in the process. Gucci sued and the case dragged on for a couple of years before settling out of court.

During this time, Steel's marriage fell apart. But what did not work on the personal level continued to work on the professional level, and in 1977 Steel formed Oh Dawn, Inc. with her ex-husband and started printing books on toilet paper, as well as printing on paper towels and creating novelty soaps. Steel also had a brief relationship with then unknown actor Richard Gere. This proved to be her informal introduction to Hollywood, because just as this relationship was ending, her relationship with Tinsel Town was just beginning.

The Early Days at Paramount

In 1978 Steel accepted a job as director of merchandising at Paramount Pictures. The first movie with which she was involved was *Star Trek: The Motion Picture.* Steel created the first-ever fast food/movie tie in, and had Klingons soon eating McDonalds hamburgers and french fries and drinking Coca-Cola. Her work so impressed her bosses that

Steel was quickly promoted to vice president in the production department. Admittedly, she had no idea what she was to do in that position—at first. But she was soon involved with a film that was to provide her with some credibility—*Flashdance*. This movie ushered in a new era of film and filmmakers, and Steel found herself on top of her field, hailed as one of the newest, brightest, and the best. Her second film—*Footloose*—was also a huge success.

During her early years at Paramount, Steel had a romantic relationship with director Martin Scorsese. This relationship enabled her to see the other side of her profession: the world of film directors and actors. Because Steel had a string of successful movies, she was promoted to Senior Vice President of Production. Her success continued, with such hits as *Top Gun, The Accused* (for which Jodie Foster won an Academy Award), *Fatal Attraction,* and *The Untouchables.*

At the 1984 Crystal Awards (a ceremony honoring women in film), Steel listened to Barbra Streisand's acceptance speech and couldn't help but be inspired to become a woman who helped other women succeed in the film industry. This was the first of two major events that changed her life that year. The second was meeting Chuck Roven, the man who eventually became her second husband.

Late 1984 also saw an exodus of top-ranking executives from Paramount; Ned Tanen was named the new president of Paramount's Motion Picture Division, and Steel was left as the production executive who had the most experience, but she wasn't named president of production until April 1985. The following month she and Roven married. During her tenure as president, Steel earned the nickname "Queen of Mean." She was hardworking and driven, and this bothered many people. Sometimes she had to pass on movies, like *Good Morning Vietnam,* in order for them to be made.

Ouster at Paramount

For some reason, which remained unclear even after her death, Steel's pregnancy in late 1986 led to her ouster from Paramount in early 1987. During her pregnancy, nothing Steel did seemed to please her bosses. Gradually she was no longer invited to meetings, and other employees often served as an intermediary between Steel and the rest of her staff. The ultimate insult was thrown while Steel was in labor with her daughter, Rebecca; an announcement was made that Gary Luccchesi, a new executive, was going to report directly to Tanen. In essence, Steel was no longer the president of production.

Her loss of status at Paramount didn't prevent executives at Columbia Pictures from pursuing Steel as a candidate for president of their motion picture division. Steel was torn about taking the job, but encouragement from her husband and friends, as well as a custom-tailored deal (including a nursery next door to her office), convinced her that this was the chance of a lifetime, the pinnacle of her career. The only glitch was that Paramount refused to let her go unless Columbia paid hundreds of thousands of dollars in reparations, which it did. In 1987 Steel became the first woman to run a major motion picture studio.

President of Columbia Pictures

At Columbia Steel had the daunting task of downsizing a bloated and overgrown division. She also had to convince stars and directors to return to work for Columbia Pictures. Columbia Pictures then ranked eighth out of the nine major studios in the United States. Besides getting sequels like *Ghostbusters II* and *The Karate Kid III* made, Steel supervised the restoration of the David Lean classic *Lawrence of Arabia.* While Steel was lauded for her risk-taking, she viewed such actions as a symbolic of the commitment Columbia Pictures had to quality movies.

Some of Steel's earliest movies at Columbia were *School Daze* and *The Last Emperor.* But for the first few years of her term, the studio was still suffering from decisions and commitments from the earlier administration. All that changed in 1990. Major movies success, in the form of *Casualties of War, Postcards from the Edge, When Harry Met Sally, Awakenings, Look Who's Talking,* and *Flatliners* propelled Columbia to third place in the box office standings. Percentage-wise, they were now only a small fraction from the top. The world—including rival Sony Pictures—took notice.

Life after Columbia Pictures

Before she knew it, Sony purchased Columbia, and in early 1991, Steel found herself out of a job. But not for long; old friends and former colleagues Michael Eisner and Jeffrey Katzenberg convinced her to become an independent producer for Disney. There she produced *Cool Runnings* and *Honey, I Blew Up the Kids.*

In 1993 Steel, husband Chuck Roven, and Bob Cavallo founded Atlas Entertainment, a company that produced films and managed rock stars. Steel also entered into negotiations with Ted Turner to become head of his film studio. He offered; she declined. Instead of running the studio, Atlas Entertainment signed an exclusive four-year deal to produce films for Turner Pictures.

While producing movies, Steel was also an activist. In 1995 she took a leadership role against the industry's decision to drop producers behind both directors and writers when giving credit to a movie. Steel also took an active role in politics, becoming one of the first of many in Hollywood to support Bill Clinton's presidential campaign.

In March of 1996, a malignant tumor was found in Steel's brain. She managed to survive for an additional 21 months, while keeping up a hectic schedule. Steel died December 20, 1997, in Los Angeles, before her final films, *Fallen* and *City of Angels* were even released. She was survived by her husband and daughter, and her loss was felt by an entire industry.

Further Reading

Steel, Dawn, *They Can Kill You, But They Can't Eat You: Lessons from the Front,* Pocket Books, 1993.
New York Times, December 22, 1997, p. B6.
People Weekly, January 12, 1998, p. 81.
Variety, March 7, 1994, p. 18.
Vogue, January 1987, p. 210.

Jimmy Stewart

Jimmy Stewart (1908-1997) was one of Hollywood's most respected and admired stars during his long movie career. He won an Academy Award in 1940 and was considered by many critics to be one of the great leading men from Hollywood's studio era.

In the 81 films made throughout his nearly 50 year career, Jimmy Stewart often played a man of modest means, striving to overcome his situation to reach his dreams. He is probably best remembered for his role in the 1946 sentimental, holiday favorite, *It's a Wonderful Life,* in which he plays the embittered idealist, a decent, small-town citizen, George Bailey.

Growing Up Prosperous and Responsible

James Maitland Stewart was born on May 20, 1908, in Indiana, Pennsylvania, to Alexander Maitland and Elizabeth Ruth Jackson Stewart. He had two younger sisters. According to James Lacayo of *People,* Stewart's mother "had attended college, which was unusual for a woman of her generation," and his father was a "Princeton graduate who had returned home to run the prosperous family hardware store founded in 1853." The Stewarts of Indiana were regarded as a prosperous family by middle America standards and were considered strict parents who, according to James Ansen of *Newsweek* raised their children "in an ethos of service" and sent their sons to Princeton University.

Stewart was a lanky boy—he would grow to six foot three and a half inches tall—and he enjoyed playing the accordion and putting on plays he wrote himself. He attended high school at Mercersburg Academy, a boarding school in Pennsylvania. He played football and was a member of the glee club and the Dramatics Club. He spent his summer vacations working.

In keeping with family tradition, Stewart entered Princeton University in New Jersey in 1928, where he became a member of the Princeton Triangle Club and appeared in their musicals. Although he studied architecture, even before he earned his degree in 1932, Stewart knew he was more interested in acting. After graduation, he headed for the University Players, a theater group in Falmouth, Massachusetts, where he met another soon-to-be-great-film-star, Henry Fonda. They would become lifelong friends even though they had differing views on many subjects. Lacayo noted that Stewart and Fonda "stayed close by agreeing never to discuss politics."

Stewart first stepped on a Broadway stage in October 1932, in the unsuccessful *Carry Nation.* Two months later he had two lines as the chauffeur in *Goodbye Again.* But in 1934, Stewart landed a sizeable role in the story of Walter Reed's battle against yellow fever in *Yellow Jack,* playing the role of Sergeant O'Hara. He received positive reviews for this role, but the play did not do well.

After five more stage appearances, Stewart took a train to Hollywood, where he roomed with Fonda who had set-tled there earlier. An MGM talent scout, Billy Grady, had seen his work and got the studio to cast him in *Murder Man* in 1935. Stewart later said he was awful, but over the next five years he made 24 movies, including Frank Capra's 1938 film *You Can't Take It With You,* which won the Academy Awards for best picture and best director. He then portrayed the idealistic young senator in *Mr. Smith Goes to Washington* (1939) for which Stewart won the New York Film Critics best actor award and an Academy Award nomination. In 1940, he was in *The Philadelphia Story* with Katharine Hepburn and Cary Grant, and won the best actor Academy Award for his performance. His Academy Award was sent home to Indiana to be displayed in the family hardware store.

A Pilot in World War II

Stewart's career was taking off when World War II gave him a new role as a pilot. Having some flying experience, he joined the United States Army and was assigned to the U.S. Army Air Corps in 1941. According to Lacayo, "Stewart was rejected on his first physical for being 10 pounds underweight, an embarrassment that made headlines around the country. . . . Just days after winning the Oscar, Stewart took his second physical. This time he made it, but barely." After some time as an instructor, he was sent to Europe as commander of a bomber squadron in November of 1943. Ansen of *Newsweek* noted, "His war record was distinguished—he flew some 25 missions and returned a highly decorated colonel—but when studios wanted to exploit his real-life heroism in postwar fly boy epics, he refused to play along."

He was awarded the Air Medal and Distinguished Flying Cross and reached the rank of brigadier general in the Air Force Reserve in 1959.

His first movie after the war was *It's a Wonderful Life* in 1946. Although the movie was not a success at the box office, it has since become a holiday classic. Audiences still enjoyed Stewart and related to the depressed, down-on-his-luck George Bailey. Lacayo noted that Stewart's "speaking voice seemed to spring from an ideal American center, both geographic and spiritual, a place of small towns and unhurried people." According to those who knew him, these qualities on screen were part of the real person. From then until his last two films, a television movie with Bette Davis (1983) called *Right of Way* and an animation film entitled *An American Tail: Fievel Goes West* (1991), Stewart's popularity never waned.

A Wonderful Career and Life

In 1949, then Hollywood's most eligible bachelor, Stewart, age 41, married Gloria Hatrick McLean. In a town where marriage and divorce are not considered front page news, the Stewarts managed one of Hollywood's most durable and happy unions. The family included four children, sons Ronald and Michael from his wife's first marriage, and twin girls Judy and Kelly, born in 1951. (Ronald was later killed in battle during the Vietnam War.)

As Stewart aged, he kept many of the screen mannerisms of his youth, but they were displayed in a more mature, confident demeanor that audiences responded to. His long and varied career includes some audience and critic favorites: *Call Northside 777* (1948); *Harvey* (1950), in which he plays a drunk whose friend happens to be a giant, invisible rabbit (Stewart returned once to Broadway for this role in 1947); bandleader Glenn Miller in *The Glenn Miller Story* (1953); pilot Charles Lindbergh in *The Spirit of St. Louis* (1957); the Alfred Hitchcock thriller *Vertigo* (1958); and a number of well-received Westerns, including *Winchester '73* (1950), *Bend of the River* (1952), *The Man From Laramie* (1955), and *The Man Who Shot Liberty Valance* (1962). Some critics did not know how to react to an unshaven Stewart playing a rough and tumble cowboy, but the audiences didn't mind. For his 1959 role as the defense attorney in *Anatomy of a Murder,* Stewart won the New York Film Critics awards as well as honors from the Venice Film Festival.

When Stewart played the quiet, confident American hero, audiences felt he was pretty much playing himself. In 1955, he was a baseball player recalled to the air force in *Strategic Air Command,* opposite June Allyson with whom he played in a number of films. Stewart often liked to work with the same actors or directors. He was also considered to be a good businessman. According to Lacayo, in the 1950s, "he became one of Hollywood's first free agents, moving studio to studio . . . and negotiating contracts that often gave him what was then an usual deal: a percentage of the film's box office receipts instead of a salary." These deals made Stewart a rich man.

In his later years, Stewart worked steadily into the 1970s, even trying his luck with two television series. He never quite lost the boyish charm that had caught the eye of a movie agent back in the 1920s. Graying and still soft spoken, he was always a welcome guest on television late night shows where he delighted audiences with Hollywood stories and sometimes bad poetry. Taking his anecdotes a step further, he had a best selling book, *Jimmy Stewart and His Poems,* which was published in 1989. He also received an Honorary Academy Award in 1985 for, as the Academy noted, "his 50 years of meaningful performances, for his high ideals, both on and off the screen, with the respect and affection of his colleagues."

After a 45 year marriage, Gloria Stewart passed away in 1994. In 1995, Stewart was honored when "The Jimmy Stewart Museum" opened in his hometown. Yet, Stewart was said to be distraught after the loss of his wife. Former co-star Shirley Jones commented to *People* "Gloria's death was a shock he never got over." Stewart died on July 2, 1997, at his home in Beverly Hills, California. As Ansen of *Newsweek* reflected, "It's nice to remember a world when a movie star was also a gentleman." Added Terry Lawson of the *Detroit Free Press,* Stewart's "shy stutter, every-guy charm, and extraordinary range of classic film roles made him one of the most loved and admired of all American actors."

Further Reading

International Directory of Film and Film Makers: Actors and Actresses, St. James Press, 1997.
Detroit Free Press, July 3, 1997.
Entertainment Weekly, July 14, 1997.
London Times, July 4, 1997.
New York Times, July 23, 1997.
Newsweek, July 14, 1997.
People, July 21, 1997.
"James Stewart," *Internet Movie Database,* http://us.imdb.com (May 13, 1998).
The Jimmy Stewart Museum: Homepage, http://www.jimmy.org (May 13, 1998).

Barbra Streisand

For over 30 years, award-winning American performer Barbra Streisand (born 1942) has been performing and singing on the stage, television and in motion pictures, as well as recording popular music.

Barbara Joan Streisand was born on April 24, 1942 in the Williamsburg section of Brooklyn, New York to Emanuel and Diana (Rosen) Streisand. Her father, a high school English teacher, died when Streisand was only 15 months old leaving her mother to raise both her and her older brother, Sheldon. Her mother soon found work as a secretary in the New York public school system and re-married in the late 1940s. Streisand felt rebuffed by her mother and step-father, Lou Kind, a used-car salesman, and attributes many of her personality characteristics to those early experiences. She graduated at age 16 from Erasmus

Hall High School in Brooklyn and moved to Manhattan where she shared an apartment with friends working various jobs hoping to perform on Broadway.

Broadway Debut

On October 21, 1961, Streisand, who had changed the spelling of her first name upon moving to Manhattan, made her off-Broadway debut in *Another Evening with Harry Stoones,* which opened and closed the same night. She then went on to other short-lived off-Broadway productions and became friends with Barry Dennen. Both shared an admiration for the Ziegfield Follies star Fannie Brice, and Streisand, with Dennen's help, crafted a nightclub show around many of Brice's musical numbers. She began performing her act in small nightclubs in Manhattan like the Bon Soir, shaping her act and her voice.

It was while she was performing at the Blue Angel, a showcase for young talent, that she was spotted by a Broadway producer who signed Streisand for the part of Miss Marmelstein in a production of *I Can Get It For You Wholesale.* The production opened in March of 1962 and ran for nine months and produced a very well-received cast album. Streisand appeared on both *I Can Get It For You Wholesale—Original Broadway Cast Recording* as well as *Pins and Needles—25th Anniversary Edition of the Hit Musical Revue* in 1962 and, with the popularity of her stage role, was an almost overnight success.

Buoyed by the popularity of her stage role, Streisand was signed by Columbia records and recorded *The Barbra*

Streisand Album and *The Barbra Streisand Second Album* in 1963. Both albums were very successful, and *The Barbra Streisand Album* won Streisand a Grammy for both album of the year and best female vocal. She followed up with *The Barbra Streisand Third Album* and took the role of Fanny Brice in a production of *Funny Girl* in 1964, winning the role over more experienced stage actors like Anne Bancroft and Mary Martin. This production became one of the most successful stage productions in the history of Broadway and her performance in it would win her first of many Golden Globe Awards. The album *Funny Girl—Original Broadway Cast Recording,* was followed by *People. People* would become one of Streisand's highest-selling albums, and earn her a third Grammy Award.

Television Success

Not content to be successful in only two mediums, Streisand next took aim at television. *My Name Is Barbra* aired in 1965 and its follow-up *Color Me Barbra* followed in 1966. Her third of these one woman television shows, *The Belle of 14th Street,* aired in 1967 and was shown in Europe in addition to North America. In 1968, she performed live to an adoring audience. The performance, *A Happening in Central Park,* was shown on television and was as successful as the three specials that had gone before. She would win a Grammy Award for her performance in *My Name Is Barbra* and two Antoinette Perry Awards.

All of these specials would be re-released as albums and would establish her at the young age of 26 as the largest selling diva of popular standards since Judy Garland. Throughout this period she released *Harold Sings Arlen* and *Je M'appelle Barbra* in 1966. *Simply Streisand* and *A Christmas Album* were released in 1967 and in 1969, she released *What About Today?*

Streisand would appear in eight television specials between 1969 and 1986. *Barbra Streisand . . . and Other Musical Instruments* (1973), *Funny Girl to Funny Lady* (1975), *Barbra Streisand: With One More Look At You* (1977), *Getting in Shape for The Main Event* (1979), *A Film Is Born: The Making of Yentl* (1983), *Putting It Together: The Making of The Broadway Album* (1986), and *One Voice* (1986) were all very popular and endeared Streisand to fans around the world. *Barbra: The Concert* aired in 1994 and 1995 and earned her two more Emmy Awards for Best Individual Performance and Best Variety or Music Special.

Motion Picture Success

This seemingly overnight success continued throughout 1968 as she continued to release albums and perform her concerts. She reprised her role as Fanny Brice for the 1968 film version of *Funny Girl* and in 1969 appeared as Dolly Levi in the motion picture *Hello, Dolly!* These performances would earn her another Golden Globe Award and her performance in *Funny Girl* earned her an Academy Award as the best actress of 1968. *On A Clear Day You Can See Forever* and *The Owl and the Pussycat* were released in 1970 and she would win a Golden Globe Award for these performances as she was voted Best Female World Film Favorite.

Director and Producer

After the success of *Funny Girl,* Streisand began to concentrate more on motion pictures than on live performances. She would appear in *What's Up, Doc?* and *Up the Sandbox* in 1972 before garnering critical acclaim for her work in *The Way We Were* opposite Robert Redford in 1973. She won another Golden Globe Award for this role. Her portrayal could have been a case of art imitating life as she was divorced from her husband Elliot Gould in 1971 after eight years of marriage and one son, Jason. She starred in *For Pete's Sake* and *Funny Lady* before her 1976 movie *A Star Is Born.* The movie and her rendition of the theme song, "Evergreen," earned her a second Academy Award, two Grammy Awards and three Golden Globe Awards. The film was one of the highest grossing of that year despite being panned by critics who believed Streisand was executing too much control as she was listed in the credits as not only the star, executive producer and co-songwriter, but also as the wardrobe consultant and the designer of 'musical concepts.'

Streisand would take yet another leap in her creative life when she decided to direct, produce, and star in *Yentl* in 1983. After *The Main Event* (1979) and *All Night Long* (1981) Streisand was eager to make the story that she had read in 1968 into a movie. Filmed in Eastern Europe, *Yentl* was the story of a female masquerading as a male to overcome traditional orthodox Jewish privileges. The film earned more than $35 million but it would be four years before she appeared in another film.

Streisand's role in *Nuts* (1987), opposite Richard Dreyfuss, is the story of a high-class prostitute who must go through a competency hearing to determine if she is sane enough to stand trial for manslaughter. Most critics disliked the film which Streisand produced, but some called it her best work ever. The more dramatic role prepared her for the tension and emotion that she displayed in her next role. In *The Prince of Tides* (1991) Streisand, opposite Nick Nolte, not only starred, but directed and co-produced the film. The film was nominated for several Academy Awards including the award for best picture. The *New York Times* commented that "Nothing about Barbra Streisand's previous acting or directing is preparation for her expert handling of *The Prince of Tides.*" Streisand was nominated for a Golden Globe Award for directing, but not for an Academy Award, which angered many. She was seemingly unaffected, as she went on to star in *The Mirror Has Two Faces,* opposite Jeff Bridges in 1996. She earned Golden Globe Award nominations for "Best Original Song" and "Best Actress—Comedy or Musical" for this film.

Top of the Charts

Despite performing in motion pictures and on television throughout the 1970s, 1980s and 1990s, Streisand never ceased releasing albums. After *Funny Girl—Original Broadway Cast Recording,* there would be almost 40 Streisand albums released. In 1981, she won a Grammy Award for best pop duo for "Guilty," a duet with Barry Gibb, that became her sixth all-time highest selling single. Over the years she has recorded other duets with performers as diverse as Bryan Adams, Don Johnson, Neil Diamond, Kim Carnes, Johnny Mathis and Michael Crawford.

After receiving a death threat in 1967, Streisand developed stage fright and stopped doing public concerts. She commented to Susan Price of *Ladies Home Journal,* "You don't get over stage fright—you just don't perform." However, new friendships seemed to have a positive impact. In the early 1990s, she began to grow closer to her mother and became friends with Bill and Hillary Clinton. According to Kim Hubbard of *People,* "She forged a warm friendship with Virginia Kelley, President Clinton's mother, and conquered performance fear by taking the stage in Vegas on New Year's Eve '93." Hubbard added that "Kelley's death from breast cancer just days after attending the show forced Streisand to take stock." Streisand did a world tour in 1994, starting in London and ending in New York City. Her shows were some of the highest-grossing concerts of the year.

Streisand became engaged to actor James Brolin in early 1997. They divide their time between homes in Malibu and Beverly Hills, California. She has given concerts to help benefit political candidates and charities that benefit social causes such as AIDS research. Her "Streisand Foundation," was established in 1992 to help advocate women's rights, civil liberties and environmental protection.

She released *Higher Ground* in November of 1997 and it immediately became number one on the Billboard chart. It set a record for the greatest span of time between a performer's first and most recent number one albums at 33 years. The first single released from the album, "Tell Him," a duet with Celine Dion, was immediately a Top 40 hit and was nominated for a Grammy Award. Streisand has recorded 54 albums and has collected an overwhelming collection of 39 gold LP's, 25 platinum LP's and 12 multi-platinum LP's. She was the first person to win an Academy Award, an Emmy Award, a Grammy Award, and an Antoinette Perry Award. She is also the only person to have won an Academy Award for both acting and songwriting.

Further Reading

American Film, January-February 1992.
Chicago Tribune, December 5, 1982.
Ladies Home Journal, February 1992; July 1994.
McCall's, September 1997.
National Review, March 20, 1995.
New Yorker, January 27, 1992.
New York Times, December 22, 1991; December 25, 1991.
People, November 17, 1997; November 24, 1997; December 8, 1997; March 9, 1998.
Washington Post, December 22, 1991.
"Barbra Streisand," *Internet Movie Databank,* http://us.imdb.com (May 11, 1998).

T

Dave Thomas

American businessman Dave Thomas (born 1932) is the founder of the Wendy's Old-Fashioned Hamburgers chain. He is also an advocate for adoption, establishing the Dave Thomas Foundation for Adoption to realize his dream of a home for every child.

Through his successful Wendy's Old-Fashioned Hamburgers television ads, Dave Thomas's lovable, grandfatherly image has made him one of the most recognized faces in the United States. This has gone a long way in promoting the advantages of adoption for his Dave Thomas Foundation for Adoption. His dream of making sure every child has a home and loving family are not just words. He has consistently put his heart and his money into making it easier for all children to realize this dream.

Born on July 2, 1932, to a single mother, R. David "Dave" Thomas was adopted as a six-week-old baby by Rex and Auleva Thomas of Kalamazoo, Michigan. The family unit was short-lived, as his adoptive mother died of rheumatic fever when Thomas was five years old. Travel became a big part of his life as his adoptive father moved from town to town looking for work. Among the few constants in his early life were the summers he spent with his grandmother, Minnie Sinclair, on her small farm in Michigan. He has credited her with providing him with a sense of security and with teaching him the value of an honest day's work.

At an early age, Thomas developed a fascination with restaurants and a love of food. He attributed that to eating out so much as a child and spending time with his grandmother, who worked at an eatery. "I thought if I owned a restaurant," Thomas told Marilyn Achiron of *People,* "I could eat all I wanted for free. What could be better than that?"

His father, who did not participate much in his son's life, remarried three times after his wife died and moved from town to town to find work. By the time Thomas was a teenager, he had lived in a dozen different places. As his company biography noted, Thomas "found himself without roots or a sense of belonging." These feelings deepened when, at thirteen, his grandmother told him he was adopted. "It really hurt that nobody told me before," he recalled to Achiron. "It is a terrible feeling to know my natural mother didn't want me." These long-standing feelings have made it difficult for Thomas's own children to understand why he promotes adoption with such a passion. "Life with my new parents was not easy. . . . Yet without a permanent family of my own, I know I would not be where I am today," he wrote in *Parade* Magazine.

Thomas lied about his age and started in the restaurant business as a busboy at the Hobby House restaurant in Fort Wayne, Indiana, in 1947. The owner, Phil Clauss, was an early mentor to Thomas. Thomas quit school after the tenth grade (he has called this his biggest mistake in life), and began to work full-time. After serving in the U.S. Army for two years, he returned to the Hobby House in 1953 and took a position as a short-order cook. His earnings were $35 a week. It was there he met his future bride, 18-year-old waitress Lorraine Buskirk. They were married seven months later and had five children, Pam, Ken, Molly, Melinda Lou (Wendy), and Lori.

In the 1950s, while working for Clauss, Thomas met his other mentor, Colonel Harland Sanders, founder of Kentucky Fried Chicken (KFC). Sanders impressed him with a

commitment to quality fast food and a talent for salesmanship. In 1962, Clauss asked Thomas to turn around four KFC carryouts that he owned. If Thomas could take over the management of these outlets and make them solvent, Clauss would transfer 45 percent of the ownership of the restaurants to him. Thomas wanted his own restaurant, so he moved his family to Columbus, Ohio.

Thomas took on the challenge and quickly recognized the stores were failing largely because of the intimidating, 100-item menu which was confusing to the customers. He reduced the menu to mostly chicken and introduced the distinctive rotating bucket of chicken sign. In 1968, Thomas sold his share of the franchises back to the Kentucky Fried Chicken Corporation for more than $1.5 million.

After a short stint with the Arthur Treacher's Fish & Chips chain, Thomas was ready to build his own chain. He saw himself as a "hamburger man" and decided that hamburgers would be his specialty. He felt McDonald's and Burger King were not doing hamburgers his way: custom-made with fresh meat and a good choice of toppings. Although friends and family cautioned him the hamburger market was saturated, he opened the first Wendy's Old Fashioned Hamburgers restaurant in downtown Columbus in 1969. The name derived from his daughter, Melinda Lou, whose siblings had difficult pronouncing her name, which came out "Wenda" and eventually became "Wendy."

Thomas envisioned opening a few stores to give his children work during the summer. However, his concept of a restaurant with old-fashioned food and decor, wooden furniture, and carpeted dining rooms was a hit. Thomas turned a profit within six weeks. In 1973 Thomas began selling Wendy's franchises covering entire cities and parts of states, an unprecedented move in the industry. Over 1,000 franchises opened in the first 100 months of the offering, a substantial growth which would continue for twenty years and would make Wendy's the third-largest restaurant chain in the world.

The original menu at Wendy's consisted of some of Thomas's favorite foods, chili, french fries and fresh hamburgers, as well as the Frosty Dairy Dessert. Crisis came in the late 1970s when Thomas's managers suggested introducing a salad bar. Self-doubt plagued Thomas, and when the salad bar proved to be a hit, he wondered if he should be moving in a different direction. "Here's a company I didn't want to screw up," he commented to Linda Killian in *Forbes*. "I see a lot of entrepreneurs start something they can't finish. . . . I think an entrepreneur has limitations. I thought it was the best time to back off and let other people who were smarter than me do things."

In 1982 Thomas gave up his title of chief executive but retained the senior chairmanship, a hands-off executive supervisory position. Although for several years it appeared the corporate ship could sail smoothly without him, he eventually returned to management in a different position. The year 1985 was a great success with the catchy "Where's the beef?" advertising campaign boosting sales to a record $76.2 million, but a downturn was coming. A huge investment in a breakfast program failed as made-to-order omelets and french toast couldn't be made fast enough to meet customer demand. The overall franchise system began showing signs of collapse.

The company reported a $5 million loss in 1986. Thomas hired James Near, a successful franchiser, as the new president. One of Near's conditions for accepting the post was that Thomas come out of retirement and act as the company's spokesperson, ambassador, and unabashed morale booster. It was a rocky road, but Thomas ended up being his own spokesperson. His failure as the company pitchman in 1981 was likely due to the words he was given to say—"Ain't no reason to go anyplace else." His comeback in 1989 was uncomfortable at first, but success came when he found his own voice. Bob Garfield of *Advertising Age* characterized the new spots as "hilarious, pointed, tactically sharp, and beautifully performed." Thomas quickly became one of the most easily recognizable faces in America with over 500 commercials to his credit.

Yet, a hole remained in his personal life. Thomas sought out his birth mother when he was 21. According to Achiron, "his biological mother . . . had died, but he met her family, and didn't feel any particular closeness to them." Without any other leads, he decided not to look for his biological father. His daughter Pam picked up his pursuit in 1988. She found his father's family in Philadelphia and learned Thomas's father, by then dead, had married and had another son. His half brother was a college professor, an MIT graduate, and wanted nothing to do him. "He didn't want his mother to know that his father had a little one-night deal," Thomas told Achiron of *People*. "He might be very, very smart, but he doesn't have much common sense."

The pain of his adoption was still fresh, and although he is quick to acknowledge his own experience was not perfect, he has stated it was far better than growing up in an orphanage. And so, in the late 1980s when the National Council for Adoption asked Thomas for his support, he gave it. In 1990 then President Bush sought his help in publicizing the plight of those who are least likely to be adopted; the handicapped, older children and siblings. In 1990, he established the Wendy's corporate adoption program which helps defray the cost of adoption for employees.

His support is not just for hard-to-place children being adopted, but also for would-be parents seeking to adopt. In 1992, Thomas founded the Dave Thomas Foundation for Adoption. He also tried to reach children waiting to be adopted. "I hope you find a loving home real soon," he wrote in his 1994 book *Well Done! Dave's Secret Recipe for Everyday Success*, "and I can tell you firsthand that, with hard work and values, you can go as far as your greatest dreams."

Dave's Way: A New Approach to Old-fashioned Success (1991) was an autobiographical account of Thomas's creation of the Wendy's fast-food chain and was a top-selling non-fiction book according to the *Chicago Tribune*. His second book, *Well Done! Dave's Secret Recipe for Everyday Success* (1994) was filled with motivational reflections and what he perceives as the skills, attitudes and values shared by successful people. Profits from his two books were donated to national adoption awareness programs and to the Dave Thomas Foundation for Adoption.

In 1993, Thomas rectified what he considered to be his biggest regret. He commented to Achiron, "I had everything to do with not finishing high school. That was a dumb mistake." Thomas earned his G.E.D. and graduated from a Florida high school. According to his company biography, his classmates voted him "Most Likely to Succeed," and he and his wife attended the senior prom, where they were crowned king and queen.

In late 1996, Thomas underwent heart bypass surgery, but he quickly rebounded. In 1997, with 5,000 Wendy's units around the world, Thomas continued to appear in commercials and launched the successful "Eat a Pita!" campaign. However, he still sticks to the basics. He commented to Roberta Maynard of *Nation's Business*, "Even in this computer age, our approach is still one customer at a time."

Further Reading

Thomas, Dave, *Dave's Way: A New Approach to Old-fashioned Success*, 1991.
Thomas, *Well Done! Dave's Secret Recipe for Everyday Success*, HarperCollins/Zondervan, 1994.
Advertising Age, August 6, 1990, p. 3.
Chicago Tribune, October 2, 1991, Business Section, p. 1.
Forbes, August 5, 1991, pp. 106-107.
Grand Rapids Press, December 20, 1996, p. C7.
Nation's World, October 1997, p. 65.
Parade Magazine, December 1, 1996, pp. 8-9.
People, August 2, 1993, pp. 86-87.
Profit, July/August 1992.
Restaurant Business, May 1, 1992, pp. 114-116.
Saturday Evening Post, November/December 1994, pp. 26-28.
"Wendy's International Inc.," http://www.wendys.com (January 5, 1998).

Garfield Todd

To the Western world, Southern Rhodesian prime minister Garfield Todd (born 1908) was seen in the 1960s and 1970s as an enlightened white African hero, who took up the cause of independence and freedom for blacks. In Southern Rhodesia (now called Zimbabwe), he was viewed as a traitor by most whites and even a hypocrite by some blacks he sought to help.

Reginald Stephen Garfield Todd was born to Thomas and Edith Todd on July 13, 1908, in Invercargill, a southern coastal city of the south island of New Zealand. Of Scottish descent, Todd studied at Otago University, the University of the Witwatersrand, and Glen Leith Theological College. He became a Church of Christ minister and worked briefly for Thomas Todd & Sons, a family business. It was the work of the church, which called him.

In southern Africa, a British territory called Rhodesia had existed since the late 19th century. Early white settlers came looking for minerals, mostly gold. Under the British South Africa Company, a government was establish by whites. Prior to this, many factional black tribal groups prevented any one tribe from controlling the region. The new land was named Rhodesia after early settler, Cecil Rhodes. It became one the gems of the old British Empire. The pleasant climate and suitable ranch and farming land attracted more white settlers. The church missionaries, which would eventually include Todd, were not far behind.

The Southern Rhodesian Missionary Conference was founded in 1906 by 15 Christian church bodies. The education of blacks became a priority for the missionaries. That led to the Native Education Ordinance of 1907. Enrollment went from 4,000 blacks in 1907 to more than 40,000 by 1918.

Missionary work and opportunity drew Todd to the African continent in 1934. Prior to leaving New Zealand he married Jean Grace Wilson. He began teaching at the Dadaya Mission School in the Shabani district in the southern portion of the nation. It was here he acquired a huge ranch. Robin Moore, a former American ambassador to Rhodesia, said in his book *Rhodesia* that the ranch was "several thousand acres and would eventually be linked with rail service." Soon Todd was busy raising a family of three daughters.

At Dadaya, some of Todd's early sympathies with blacks were developed. In July 1947 the students staged a protest against alleged racism and poor food. Todd, the superintendent, eventually fired one of the black teachers over the incident. Years later in 1980, Todd criticized the government for its handling of another student strike. The legacy of the missionary schools was vital. The institutions eventually produced most of the black nationalist leaders, who sought to take political control of their country away from the small white minority—never greater than five percent of the total population.

Political Rise and Fall

Todd entered politics in the late 1940s. He was first elected to the Legislative Assembly in the capital city of Salisbury in 1946. He represented Shabani from 1946-1958. He served also as president of the United Rhodesia Party during the same years. In his first seven years in Rhodesia's Parliament, Todd was considered an authority on native affairs. Prime Minister Godfrey Huggins picked Todd to succeed him in 1953.

The years after World War II set a new tone for Rhodesia. The nation's economy brought more white settlers, although never more than an estimated 200,000 of the nation's five to six million people. The defeat of totalitarian regimes in Europe caused many blacks to question when they would attain full citizenship. Although complete freedom did not exist in Rhodesia, the racial climate was believed to be better than in neighboring South Africa, where the strict system of racially segregated apartheid was the law.

Todd heard the concerns of blacks. In his administration, he introduced home-ownership plans for blacks and amended laws that would give black Africans greater access to land ownership. In addition, a commission was appointed to look into the position of trade unions. An electoral act was also passed that allowed more blacks to vote. This caused controversy among many in the white leadership. Todd's administration doubled the number of African pupils taken into the educational system. Some members of his cabinet were displeased when he failed to make adequate provisions for funding of the 500-600 new teachers needed to accommodate the additional students. That dispute, and others, led to the resignation of Todd's five-member cabinet in January 1958. It also ignited a period of turmoil in Rhodesian politics that would eventually spawn a deadly civil war and invoke scorn from the international community.

A.J.A. Peck recounts in his book, *Rhodesia Accuses,* an address made to Parliament by one of Todd's ministers, Sir Patrick Fletcher, on January 11, 1958. He accused Todd of driving a wedge between the black man and the white man by making it appear that he (Todd) was the "champion of the black man against the white." Fletcher maintained that Todd had taken too much of the credit for legislation passed and had not adequately communicated with his cabinet. Some ministers said they were unaware of Todd's decisions until they read the newspapers. Ian Hancock theorized, in *White Liberals, Moderates and Radicals in Rhodesia,* that the ministry may have been trying to avoid a scandal, which allegedly included Todd buying cheap Crown land when he was a lawmaker. Todd attempted to answer Fletcher in Parliament. While he was speaking, Fletcher stood up and told the lawmakers Todd was speaking a "travesty of the truth."

The resignation of his cabinet marked the end of Todd's life as the leader of Southern Rhodesia. He attempted to form a new government, instead of quitting, but was soon voted out of office. Todd attempted to regain power with two other political parties, but failed. With support of the Central Africa Party, Todd sent a letter to Great Britain urging that Rhodesia's constitution be declared invalid and that new democratic measures be enforced with British troops. Todd was forced to resign from the party after other leaders distanced themselves from him. The letter severely damaged his political career.

White Leadership Criticized

Although out of power, Todd continued to crusade for more black participation in government. He criticized the white leadership, particularly Ian Smith, a conservative who served as prime minister from 1964-1978. Smith did not appreciate Todd's sympathies for the blacks. When asked about the possibility of Rhodesia voting for majority rule, Smith said he didn't believe any white person in Rhodesia accepted it, with the exception of Todd and a dozen others. Todd became such an enemy of the whites that *The Rhodesian,* a rival party's publication, said in 1958 that "one white citizen slammed the door in the face of a candidate campaigning for office that had mentioned Todd's name. The candidate knocked again and had to explain he wasn't a Todd ally."

Todd gained international attention after having been confined to his ranch, with his outspoken daughter Judy. Both had supported black causes in the 1970s. Smith wouldn't tolerate such behavior and had him imprisoned in January 1972 for violating the Law and Order (Maintenance) Act. From 1972 to June 1976 Todd was restricted to his ranch. It was then that a civil war erupted with about 30,000 guerrillas fighting against a similar number of government forces. Hancock called Todd's confinement to the ranch ironic, since "hundreds of blacks jammed into jails couldn't draw the same kind of sympathy from the world."

Todd took his case to the international community and found sympathy in the United States. United Nations ambassador, Andrew Young, was willing to listen. Being a black man sensitive to racial matters in own nation, Young was able to persuade President Jimmy Carter to exert pressure on the Smith government to yield to black nationalists. Facing intense economic pressure from most of the world, Smith was reluctantly forced to resign in favor of a black majority government. A transition government was established between 1978 and 1980. The Republic of Zimbabwe came into existence on April 18, 1980. Most of the old colonial names were changed, including the capital city of Salisbury, which became Harare. Todd was elected a senator in the new government, a post he held from 1980-1985.

Todd's Liberal Legacy Questioned

Though Todd was hailed by the West as a savior for blacks, many of the nationalists were skeptical of Todd both during and after the time he held public office. As Robin

Moore stated in *Rhodesia,* Todd would "publicly advocate higher wages for blacks, but paid his own ranch staff the same low wages. Although Todd advocated land ownership for blacks, he adamantly defended his right to own a large tract." The black nationalist leader, Edson Sithole wrote in a *Salisbury Daily News* article that " Todd was selected as prime minister, because of his reputation of knowing the Africans, could deal with them severely without arousing much public criticism." In 1954, Todd had brutally quelled a strike with black workers at the rail junction of Wankie. In *Rhodesia, The Struggle For Freedom,* Leonard T. Kapungu states that Todd settled the strike, "without investigating whether the striking Africans had genuine labor grievances."

Although often criticized during his five decades of public life, not all evaluations of Todd are negative. Dr. Denny Pruett knew Todd for years and said in 1998, "Todd loved the African people and they loved him in return." In the former prime minister's lifetime he had seen Britain and its former empire undergo tremendous change. In the 20th century transformation of Rhodesia into the modern nation of Zimbabwe, Garfield Todd certainly played a major role.

Further Reading

Good, C. Robert, *The International Politics of the Rhodesian Rebellion,* Princeton University Press, 1973.

Hancock, Ian, *White Liberals, Moderates and Radicals in Rhodesia,* St. Martin's Press, 1984.

Kapungu, Leonard T., *Rhodesia, The Struggle For Freedom,* Orbis Books, 1974.

Moore, Robin, *Rhodesia,* Condor, 1977.

Peck, A.J.A., *Rhodesia Accuses,* Three Sisters Books, 1966.

Ranger, Terence, *Peasant Consciousness and Guerilla War in Zimbabwe,* University of California Press, 1985.

Rasmussen, R. Kent, *Historical Dictionary of Rhodesia/Zimbabwe,* Scarecrow Press, 1979.

Shamuyarira, Nathan W., *Crisis in Rhodesia,* Transatlantic Arts, 1966.

Tindall, P.E.N., *A History of Central Africa,* Longman Group, 1968.

Zimbabwe, A Country Study, Foreign Area Studies, The American University, 1982.

Journal of Southern Africa Studies (Great Britain), Volume 18, number 2, 1992.

The Rhodesian, May 30, 1958, p. 5. □

Josef Tosovsky

As governor of the Czech National Bank, Josef Tosovsky (born 1950) served as one of the key figures in the newly privatized Czech economy. In 1997, he was named Prime Minister of the Czech Republic after a scandal forced his predecessor step down.

Widely recognized as one of the premier bankers in Europe, Josef Tosovsky served for several years as Governor of the Czech Republic's National Bank. In late 1997, he was appointed the role of Prime Minister when the previous occupant of that position, Vaclav Klaus, was forced to step down in the midst of a campaign finance scandal. Tosovsky's interim government, which aims to privatize the banking sector, faced a deadline of midsummer 1998, when elections brought in the Socialist Democrats, who do not fully support the reforms Tosovsky favors.

Early Career

Josef Tosovsky was born September 28, 1950, in the Czech city of Nachod. He graduated from the Prague School of Economics with a major in foreign trade in 1973 and began his career in the Czechoslovak State Bank (SBCS), where he held a variety of positions. Two years later, he was married to Bohuska Svetlikova, with whom he had two daughters. During his tenure at the SBCS, he went on study visits to Great Britain in 1977 and France in 1980. Later, in 1984, he took a position as an economist in the London branch of Zivnostenska Banka. It was through these foreign posts that Tosovsky began to develop an appreciation of the power of market-driven economies versus those controlled by the state.

From 1985 until 1989, he worked as an advisor to the SBCS in London, and in 1989, he returned briefly to Zivnostenska Banka, as deputy-director of the London branch. During this period, he became, along with Vaclav

Klaus, Karel Dyba, Ivan Kocarnik, and Dusan Triskaa, a member of a group of liberal economists based first within the SBCS, then in the Academy of Sciences, and others. This group further fueled his belief in free markets, and helped secure his reputation with the opposition forces already surging against the Communist leadership of Czechoslovakia.

Tosovsky Becomes National Bank Governor

In November of 1989, the Communist government under Milos Jakes was abruptly forced out of power in the so-called "Velvet Revolution." A new, democratic government coalesced around the dissident playwright Vaclav Havel, and shortly thereafter, Tosovsky was named Governor of the SBCS, which under his leadership began to assume the functions of a central bank. When Czechoslovakia dissolved in 1993, he was appointed Governor to the SBCS's successor, the Czech National Bank (CNB).

Tosovsky's years with the CNB proved extremely fruitful. He served as a governor of the International Monetary Fund, became a member of the Research Council of the Prague School of Economics, and joined the board of the Center for Economic Research and Graduate Education. He also became a member of the body of advisors to the Rector of Charles University in Prague.

The Czech Republic thrived economically in the first few years after the revolution. With the political stability of a single President and a single Prime Minister for many years, the nation established growth rates far better than Poland and Hungary, both of which cycled through several governments during the same period. State industries were sold off, and under the free market system, performed remarkably well. Until the second half of the 1990s, the Czech Republic was considered by many to be a model for privatization among the former Soviet satellites.

Tosovsky's work in the banking sector of that growing economy did not go unnoticed outside the Czech Republic. In 1993 he was named Central Banker of the Year by *Euromoney* magazine, during the anniversary session of the International Monetary Fund in Washington, D.C. The following year, the European Business Press Federation named him European Manager of the Year. Also in 1994, he became the first economist to receive the Karel Englis Prize from Masaryk University in Brno. Finally, in 1996, he was named European Banker of the Year by an association of European Union journalists called the Group 20.

Czech Financial Crises

Unfortunately, many of the accomplishments of Vaclav Havel's government were based on faulty foundations. For local Czech businesses, there was the problem of inflation. Buoyed by reassurances of a strong, growing economy, wages rose at very generous rates—more generous than could be feasibly sustained. Furthermore, the Czech crown was virtually worthless on the international currency market. As a result, the country was caught in an inflationary spiral, with rates moving regularly into the ten percent range.

For the larger, international businesses, there were bigger worries. When the economy had been initially privatized, the government had naively assumed that a free market would smooth over many potential problems, something Tosovsky had spoken strongly against. In the absence of any meaningful regulation, the nation's large banks had continued their Soviet-era role as a safety net for industry, picking up losses and bad loans. These same banks, however, now held significant percentages of stock in the industries they supported, meaning that debt was merely being shifted around. This was not a problem until these debts began seriously to mount up, due in part to the inescapable inflation. Cash-strapped Czech industry had few sources of income to fall back on.

Banks began to fail. Eleven major banks either closed or were placed under forced administration, and the cost of cleaning up the mess soared. Tosovsky harshly criticized Prime Minister Vaclav Klaus for his failure to regulate the banking sector, and called on the International Monetary Fund to help set up a "hospital bank" which would absorb the bad debts incurred by other banks. Klaus belatedly drew up a plan whereby the largest banks would have most of their assets sold off. At this point, however, ethical issues rose to complicate the situation still further.

Cronyism—the secret brokering of privatization deals with major political contributors—had been a growing problem since the Velvet Revolution. This practice eventually found its way to the highest levels of government, as shown by the discovery in November of 1997 of a secret Swiss bank account belonging to Klaus. The account contained five million dollars in funds contributed to the Civic Democrats—Klaus's party—by investors who were given special favors in the privatization process. The right-center coalition that maintained Klaus's position abandoned him, and even some of his own party members rebelled, forcing him from office.

Tosovsky Becomes Prime Minister

With the bank privatization deal effectively stalled, Klaus's coalition destabilized. With his own party discredited, Vaclav Havel faced a dilemma. A strong supporter of privatization, he knew that Parliamentary elections would most likely take place the following summer, or November at the latest. The Social Democrats, the left wing of Czech politics, would probably sweep into power, and they were very dubious of privatization strategies, especially in the banking sector. Furthermore, Havel himself faced the end of his term in only a couple of months. He had almost died of lung cancer in 1996, and was occasionally stricken with pneumonia. He had already served eight years as President and so had every reason to wish to step down.

In light of the crisis, however, he chose to run again in January of 1998, winning easily. First, though, on December 16, 1997, he selected Tosovsky as the nation's new Prime Minister. Tosovsky, aware of the very short term before him—the Social Democrats would certainly select a Prime Minister from their own ranks if they took the Parliament the following summer—acted as quickly as he could, selecting a broad-based cabinet containing four of those who had rebelled against Klaus. This, of course, denied him the support of Klaus and most of the Civic Democrats in the confidence vote which would take place in January, but it eased tensions with the Social Democrats. This fact, combined with Tosovsky's lack of political affiliation, brought him safely through the vote, which he took as a mandate to complete the privatization projects on the table.

Tosovsky's first piece of legislation backed this agenda. The Banking Act, passed on the first of January, 1998, restricted banks to a maximum 15% holding in any company whose primary business is not finance. It also prevented bank members from sitting on the board of any non-financial company, in order to reduce insider trading.

Since January, the Social Democrats had softened on the privatization issue, saying that they would follow through on the breakup of major banks. Tosovsky had not wasted any time, though. Four banks were slated for sell-offs: Komercni, Ceska Sporitelna, Ceskoslovenska Obchodni, and Investicni a Postovni. The last of these was already in negotiations with a Japanese investment firm to sell 36 percent of their holdings.

Tosovsky was one of the Czech Republic's most popular politicians, due not only to his modesty and strong work ethic, but also because of his determination to avoid political pressures by departing the public stage as soon as his term was up.

Further Reading

Banker, March 1996, p. 6; February 1998, p. 47.
Central European, February, 1998, p. 12.
Economist, January 3, 1998, p. 48.
Euromoney, April 1992, p. 22.
Finance East Europe, October 11, 1996, p. 13.
Wall Street Journal, June 5, 1990, p. A21.
Washington Post, December 18, 1997, p. A30.
"Josef Tosovsky," *Radio Prague,* http://werich.radio.cz/toshovsky.html (March 28, 1998).
"Mr. Tosovsky's Cabinet," http://www.czech.cz/washington/general/tosov.html (March 28, 1998).
"Premier of the Czech Republic," *Czech Info Center,* http://www.muselik.com/czech/premier.html (March 28, 1998).

C. DeLores Tucker

American activist C. DeLores Tucker (born 1927) has risen to national prominence in African American civil rights circles through her tireless activism and political fundraising.

The struggle to end racism and make her world a more equal, multicultural society dates back to the 1940s for C. DeLores Tucker. In the decades since then she has become a respected—and indeed even feared—personality. She counts among her personal friends and associates some equally stellar activists for the black cause, including Coretta Scott King, the Reverend Desmond Tutu, and Colin Powell. Her career in civil rights has spanned the

entire latter half of the twentieth century. In the 1990s, she became a vocal opponent of demeaning images of minorities in rap music and did not shirk from blaming the African Americans she felt were ultimately responsible. Like the other battles she has engaged in, this crusade and her outspokenness earned her enemies. Yet Tucker views the projects to which she commits herself—electing more African Americans to public office, for example, or halting the sale of offensive rap music to minors—as part of a larger goal, "to give our children an alternative environment that will help them shape their character," Tucker told *Washington Post* journalist Judith Weintraub. The organizations which Tucker has founded, led, or become involved on a leadership level include the National Association for the Advancement of Colored People (NAACP), the National Political Congress of Black Women, the Reverend Jesse Jackson's National Rainbow Coalition, the Democratic National Committee, and the Federation of Democratic Women.

Tucker herself grew up in a nurturing, achievement-oriented atmosphere. Born Cynthia DeLores Nottage on October 4, 1927, in Philadelphia, Pennsylvania, she was one of eleven children of the Reverend Whitfield Nottage, a Bahamian immigrant, and his wife, Captilda Gardner Nottage. Tucker was raised in a devout Christian household in Philadelphia where neither dancing nor music were permitted, and the Nottage daughters were forbidden to date before they were twenty-one. Because her father refused to accept a minister's salary for his church pastorships, Tucker's independent-minded mother became an entrepreneur in order to feed and clothe the children. She founded

an employment agency for African Americans who had left the un-industrialized South in search of work, ran a grocery store for a time, then became a landlord. Her daughter would inherit some of those same Philadelphia properties and later faced accusations of being a "slumlord" as she rose to prominence in the civil rights struggle.

Tucker's household and community infused so much support and positive energy into her upbringing that she later said she had been unaware of racism at all until relatively late in adolescence, when she was the only African American in her ninth-grade class. Planning to become a physician, Tucker worked in local hospitals during the summers, and when she graduated from Girls' High in Philadelphia, her father took her to the Bahamas as a treat. On the ship, Tucker realized that minority passengers were given substandard, segregated berths, and refused such accommodations. Instead she spent the night outside on the ship's deck, and shortly afterward was diagnosed with tuberculosis. The serious illness restricted her to a sickbed for an entire year, and her plans for medical school were dashed.

After her recovery, Tucker enrolled at Philadelphia's Temple University. She first became active in the burgeoning postwar civil rights movement when she worked to register black voters during a 1950 mayoral campaign. In July of 1951 she married a friend of her brother, Philadelphia real estate executive William Tucker, and though the two would not have children of their own, they did become foster parents to a number of offspring from their extended families over the years. The real-estate experience Tucker gained first with her mother's holdings and later in business with her husband helped make her a well-known figure in her city. She became the first African American and first female member of Philadelphia Zoning Board, and as the civil rights movement began in earnest in the late 1950s, she discovered more and more outlets into which she could channel her talents. She took part in the major civil-rights actions of the day, participated in the 1965 White House Conference on Civil Rights with Dr. Martin Luther King Jr., and after his 1968 assassination founded the Martin Luther King Jr. Association for Non-Violence. She was a founding member of the National Women's Caucus, and a co-founder of the Black Women's Political Caucus. For a time she also served as vice-president of the Pennsylvania NAACP.

Tucker's full-time involvement in the civil rights movement made her a prime candidate for a secondary career in politics. The only salaried position of her life came in 1971 when Pennsylvania governor Milton J. Shapp appointed her commonwealth secretary, a post equivalent to secretary of state. She became the highest-ranking African American woman in state government in the United States at the time. The responsibilities of her job were serious; her office was charged with regulating the state's businesses, and she also helped implement an affirmative-action program to equalize the state's hiring practices. But in 1977 Tucker came under fire for alleged improprieties—detractors charged her with using her employees to help write speeches for outside public-speaking engagements. She was dismissed by Shapp, but Tucker defended her conduct and countered that it was

her refusal to support Shapp's chosen successor that landed her in trouble; she said the potential governor would likely dismantle the state's affirmative action program once in office. Prominent African Americans such as the Reverend Jesse Jackson also spoke out against what they felt was a politically-motivated firing.

Over the next several years, Tucker herself made several runs for office, but was far more effective as a fundraiser and organizer for other African American political personalities. She was involved in Jackson's presidential campaign in 1984, chaired the Democratic National Committee's Black Caucus for several years after that, founded and led the National Political Congress of Black Women, and served on the national board of trustees of the NAACP. In 1987 she became the first African American run for Pennsylvania's lieutenant governor post; she came in third.

Tucker is usually cited in *Ebony* magazine's list of the "100 Most Influential Black Americans," and her sway galvanized into a full-strength force in the early 1990s when she launched a campaign against offensive rap music. Tucker's words struck a chord with the African American community, and the situation spiraled so far out of control that again, her detractors accused her of a range of misdeeds. The fracas began when Tucker learned that her young grandniece had begun using words she heard in rap songs, and the parents of some of her friends severed their children's contact with the youngster. Tucker began looking into some of the "gangsta" rap popular at the time with teenagers of a variety of backgrounds and was shocked to hear lyrics promoting an array of vices, violence, and a culture of disrespect. She was particularly incensed at the music of Tupac Shakur and Nine Inch Nails, both signed to the Interscope label. Launching a public-relations attack on the record-store chains that profited from such records, she began demonstrating outside retail outlets and was even arrested in Washington, DC, in 1993.

As Tucker explained to *Chicago Tribune* writer Monica Fountain, "these images of black young kids acting like gangstas go all around the world." She objected to such lyrics being sold to minors and asked the Federal Bureau of Investigation to launch an inquiry. Both the NAACP and the Congressional Black Caucus lent support to Tucker's cause. Congressional hearings were held on the subject in 1994, and soon afterward Tucker set her sights on an even larger target, the Time Warner media empire. The company distributed Interscope, whose rap subsidiary, Death Row Records, put out the recordings of some of the most popular gangsta artists. Tucker purchased stock in Time Warner, which allowed her the privilege of attending shareholders' meetings and speaking out. At a May 1995 shareholders' meeting, she stood and asked the executives to read aloud the very lyrics through which their company reaped such profits. They refused. "How long will Time Warner continue to put profit before principle?" she asked at the meeting, according to Fountain's *Chicago Tribune* article. "How long will it continue to turn its back on the thousands of young people who are dying spiritually and physically due to the violence perpetuated in these recordings?"

Tucker also focused her ire at Time Warner chair Gerald Levin. "I told him about the black males—25 percent are either in jail or under some judicial regulation," she declared in another *Chicago Tribune* profile by Sonya Ross. "I said, 'Mr. Levin, how are we going to raise a race of people with no men?'" Tucker has also noted that she has served as surrogate parent to many nieces and nephews, not all of whom went down the right path, and over the years came to realize that cultural forces and images play a large role in shaping self-esteem. Not long after the incident, Time Warner sold its interest in Interscope. Tucker considered it a victory, but Death Row head Marion "Suge" Knight hired investigators and then filed suit against Tucker on behalf of his roster of artists. She was accused of conspiracy and extortion as a result of a meeting with Knight at which two recording artists (who were also National Political Caucus of Black Women members), Melba Moore and Dionne Warwick, were also present. Supposedly the women offered Knight a deal to leave Interscope and sign with a black-owned record company they planned, but Tucker retorted that they had simply asked him to try for more positive messages in his artists' music. He said he would need "distribution" to engineer such a situation, and Moore and Knight agreed then to look into financing for such a possible black-owned enterprise.

Some believed that Knight and the gangsta-rap camp had set Tucker up. A smear campaign had indeed been launched against her, which brought up her 1977 Pennsylvania dismissal as well as the fact that in the 1960s the properties her mother had owned and passed on to Tucker and her husband had deteriorated to substandard conditions. (Tucker recounted in a *Los Angeles Times* interview with Chuck Philips that back then, she and her husband had "rented to displaced women on welfare with six or seven children who couldn't get housing anywhere else. We tried to help them, but the tenants never paid their rent. . . . It got to the point where they had to all be boarded up.")

Still, Tucker refused to back down in her campaign to stop the potentially harmful messages espoused by gangsta rap. "It's important to pay attention to who is dredging up all these charges," Tucker told Philips in the *Los Angeles Times.* "Remember, these are the same people who are out there pimping pornography to your children. Their record and records speak for them." She called for a boycott of a large record chain, and others rallied in support; singer Anita Baker gave a $10,000 check toward her defense fund. Tucker, a lifelong Democrat, also earned support from unlikely corners—former U.S. Secretary of Education William Bennett became an ally. The two often appear at the same speaking engagements against rap lyrics. "She's a daunting figure," Bennett told Weintraub of the *Washington Post.* "Usually I'm the noisy one, but she's ferocious."

Tucker's attack on offensive images of African Americans is by no means her only work, even though she turned seventy in 1997. She is founder and leader of the Bethune-DuBois Fund, which raises and distributes money for voter-registration drives in African American communities and lends political support to its candidates. She was also influential in the reform movement within the NAACP. As a

national executive board member, Tucker spoke out against the financial misdeeds of President William Gibson in 1994, and organized a "Save Our Ship" committee; the board eventually ousted Gibson and advanced Tucker's friend, civil-rights activist Myrlie Evers-Williams (widow of slain 1960s activist Medgar Evers), to the presidency. In her lifetime, Tucker has received over 300 honors, is publisher of *Vital Issues: The Journal of African American Speeches,* and has served as a vice-president of the *Philadelphia Tribune* since 1989. In the interview with Weintraub of the *Washington Post,* Tucker did admit to wondering who might fill her shoes: "I wish other people could do what I'm doing so I could step back and retire."

Further Reading

Smith, Jessie Carney, editor, *Notable Black American Women,* Gale, 1992.
Chicago Tribune, September 15, 1995; November 10, 1996.
Los Angeles Times, March 20, 1996, p. A1.
Washington Post, November 29, 1995, p. C1.

Preston Tucker

Hailed as a visionary by some and a con artist by others, Preston Tucker (1903-1956) was the man behind an innovative, futuristic-looking car that debuted amid great fanfare during the summer of 1948. Within just a couple of years, however, the Tucker Corporation had folded in the wake of suspicions about its founder's business practices.

With the post-war economy booming during the summer of 1948, American consumers were in a buying mood, especially for cars. But the people crowding dealers' showrooms were yearning for something more exciting than the offerings of General Motors, Ford, and Chrysler, whose designs seemed old-fashioned and unimaginative. Into this void stepped Preston Tucker, a brash entrepreneur and master of promotion who insisted that he had just what Americans wanted—"The Car of Tomorrow Today." His namesake automobile boasted a radical new aerodynamic look and a number of innovative safety features. At first, it seemed that Tucker had indeed tapped into the public's growing desire for a sleeker, safer car; his company was flooded with orders in a matter of just a few months. Ultimately, however, his inability to deliver on his promises cost him his business as well as his reputation.

Preston Thomas Tucker was born September 21, 1903, on a peppermint farm in rural Capac, Michigan. He grew up in the suburban Detroit community of Lincoln Park where, even as a child, he was fascinated by anything to do with automobiles. He learned to drive at the age of 11 and quit school two years later to become an office boy for Cadillac. Tucker subsequently worked at a number of other automobile companies, including Ford, Studebaker, Chrys-

ler, and Pierce-Arrow. Although he began his career as a mechanic and test driver, he eventually moved into sales after attending Detroit's Cass Technical High School.

During the 1930s, Tucker dabbled in a number of unsuccessful business ventures, most of them automotive-related. In 1935, for example, he teamed up with famed engine designer Harry A. Miller to build Indianapolis 500 race cars for Ford Motor Company. But none of the ten cars they completed managed to make it across the finish line, prompting Ford to withdraw from the project. Then came World War II, during which time the major automobile manufacturers dedicated their assembly lines to the war effort. From 1942 until 1946, no new models were introduced. Thus, by the mid-1940s, American consumers were desperate for cars. Spying an opportunity to challenge General Motors, Ford, and Chrysler for a share of this eager, fast-growing market, Tucker formed his own automobile manufacturing company, which he named the Tucker Corporation.

Revealed Plans for the "Tucker Torpedo"

As envisioned by Tucker himself, the "Tucker Torpedo" (as the concept vehicle was known) represented quite a departure from the standard fare offered by the Big Three automakers. Long, low, and substantially wider than other large cars then available, with sleek lines reminiscent of a rocket, it had doors that slid up into the roof and six chrome-plated exhaust pipes. Its unique safety features included headlights mounted in fenders that moved with the front wheels to illuminate the road as the car made a turn, a

windshield made of shatterproof glass, seat belts, disc brakes, and a heavily padded dashboard to protect front-seat passengers in the event of a collision. In another unusual twist, the driver's seat was positioned in the middle rather than on the left, with separate passenger seats on either side.

Engineering-wise, too, the Tucker was different. It boasted a gigantic, fuel-injected, six-cylinder engine mounted in the rear that its creator claimed could hit a top speed of 130 mph, maintain a cruising speed of 100 mph, and deliver an astonishing 35 mpg gas mileage. In addition, it sported a revolutionary power delivery system of "hydraulic torque converters" that Tucker said would eliminate the need for a clutch, transmission, drive shaft, and differential.

The American public responded with unbridled enthusiasm to Tucker's "car of tomorrow" and buried him in an avalanche of letters and inquiries. But first he had to secure some factory space in which to make his fantasy a reality. Under the auspices of the War Assets Administration (WAA), the federal government leased him a former B-29 engine plant outside Chicago, Illinois. Because the deal was contingent upon his ability to raise $15 million in capital by March 1, 1947, Tucker then set about lining up potential investors. However, he soon found out that in return for their financial support they expected him to surrender control of his company, a notion he found intolerable.

Struggled to Finance His Dream

Tucker then came up with a rather creative way to finance his dream. Although he had produced nothing more than an idea, he began selling dealer franchises and quickly amassed some $6 million that was to be held in escrow until he delivered the first Tucker. But the scheme prompted an investigation by the Securities and Exchange Commission (SEC), the first of many such probes. Tucker then devised a new strategy that involved issuing $20 million in stock. Before the SEC could rule on his plan, though, the head of the National Housing Agency demanded that the WAA cancel its deal with the Tucker Corporation so that the Lustron Corporation could use the factory to make prefabricated metal houses.

By January 1947, Tucker had won the right to remain in the plant he had leased. In addition, his March 1 capital-raising deadline was extended to July 1. (The SEC's decision on selling stock in the Tucker Corporation was still pending.) But all of the setbacks and squabbles had greatly undermined the public's confidence in the would-be entrepreneur, and the struggle to underwrite the cost of his venture continued.

Meanwhile, efforts to come up with a prototype were under way. Tucker hired noted designer Alex Tremulis to head the project in late 1946, and he and his colleagues managed to fashion a sheet-metal version of the car by hand in less than 100 days, a truly astounding feat. Affectionately known as "The Tin Goose," it went on display in June 1947 as a 1948 model. Many of the revolutionary features Tucker had touted in his original concept vehicle proved unworkable and were revamped or scrapped. Yet it was still an eye-catching car, especially with its distinctive, Cyclops-like third headlight mounted in the center of the grill that moved with the front wheels. The public's response was overwhelming, and the company was flooded with orders. On July 15, the SEC finally cleared the way for Tucker Corporation stock to go on sale.

Targeted for Investigation

By the spring of 1948, Tucker was ready to go into production with his car despite some lingering financial difficulties resulting from insufficient stock sales. In need of some quick cash, he came up with a new fundraising tactic that offered Tucker buyers the opportunity to pre-purchase certain accessories such as seat covers, radios, and custom luggage. But SEC officials took a dim view of his plan given the fact that not a single vehicle had yet rolled off the assembly line. In May 1948, working in conjunction with the Justice Department, they launched a major investigation into Tucker's business practices and the viability of his car. The bad publicity and lawsuits that ensued effectively disrupted production, spooked creditors, and sent the company's stock price plummeting. Finally, in January 1949, the Tucker factory was forced to close and Tucker was ousted from his own organization and replaced by two court-appointed trustees.

In June 1949, Tucker and seven of his associates were indicted on charges of mail fraud, stock irregularities, and conspiracy to defraud. The trial began that October, with government prosecutors using "The Tin Goose" rather than one of the actual production vehicles to try to prove that the Tucker could not be built or perform as promised. But many of the 70-plus witnesses called to testify against the company actually hurt rather than helped the government's case.

Tucker himself hinted darkly that the Big Three automakers and their supporters were behind the attempt to destroy him because of the threat he represented to their domination of the market. Indeed, some evidence suggests that officials of both General Motors and Chrysler actively sought to make it more difficult for Tucker to succeed. Whether they also tried to influence the government to pursue him is less certain. There is no question, however, that Tucker had made some powerful enemies in Washington who repeatedly denounced him as a con artist.

Acquitted on Fraud Charges

The trial dragged on until January 1950. In the end, the jury found Tucker and his associates innocent of all the charges against them. However, Tucker was left bankrupt and with his reputation in tatters; as a result, he was forced to sell his remaining assets, including the 51 vehicles that

had been completed before the plant was shuttered. They would be the only Tuckers ever manufactured.

During the early 1950s, a more subdued but still optimistic Tucker tried one more time to develop and market a new kind of car. Before he could pull together all of the necessary financing, however, he was diagnosed with lung cancer. He succumbed to the disease in 1956 on the day after Christmas.

Tuckers are now prized by car collectors (around 47 are still known to exist), most of whom are active members of the Tucker Automobile Club of America. Meanwhile, the debate continues over Tucker's place in automotive history. His detractors still consider him a fraud who tried to pass off what was basically a lemon as "the car of tomorrow." His fans regard him as a visionary who was brought down by sinister forces with money and power. Others believe the truth lies somewhere in between those two extremes. Even if his ultimate goal was to strike it rich, they argue, he was sincere about his desire to build an exciting, innovative new vehicle that offered a level of comfort, safety, and affordability not available in any other car at the time. What they do fault is his naivete and lack of business sense, which left the Tucker Corporation woefully undercapitalized and in a constant state of financial crisis that doomed it to failure.

Yet as Tucker himself once observed, as quoted in *American History Illustrated,* no matter what the obstacles, it was unthinkable not to try to make his fantasy come true. "A man who has once gotten automobiles into his blood can never give them up," he said. "A man with a dream can't stop trying to realize that dream. . . . It's no disgrace to fail against tough odds if you don't admit you're beaten. And if you don't give up."

Further Reading

Pearson, Charles T., *Preston Tucker: A Biography—The Indomitable Tin Goose* (originally published in hardcover as *The Indomitable Tin Goose: The True Story of Preston Tucker and His Car),* Pocket Books, 1988.

American Film, June 1988, p. 27.

American History Illustrated, July 1980, pp. 18-21; January 1989, pp. 36-41.

Car and Driver, October 1986, pp. 89-93; June 1988, pp. 81-89.

Forbes, September 19, 1988, p. 34.

Harvard Business Review, November-December 1988, pp. 176-177.

People, September 19, 1988, p. 85.

"The 1948 Tucker," *Henry Ford Museum and Greenfield Village,* http://www.hfmgv.org/showroom/1948/tucker.html (March 6, 1998).

"The Tucker Automobile Web Site: 'Keeping the Legend On-line,'" *The Tucker Automobile Club of America,* http://www.tuckerclub.org (April 2, 1998).

Carl Van Vechten

American author and photographer Carl Van Vechten (1880-1964) was a champion of modern music and dance in the early years of the twentieth century, and went on to enjoy critical acclaim for his witty novels that chronicled a charmed set in 1920s New York and Paris. Van Vechten, however, may be best remembered for his interest in the creative output of African-Americans: through his support for its writers and performers, his financial assistance, and enthusiastic, insightful essays for mainstream publications, he served as an unofficial publicist for the cultural movement that came to be known as the Harlem Renaissance.

Carl Van Vechten was born in 1880 in Cedar Rapids, Iowa, into a prosperous and politically liberal family. He was tall and awkward in stature, and gifted with an above-average intelligence. Van Vechten stood out from his Midwestern peers in several ways and would later reflect upon Cedar Rapids and its mores with not a small amount of disdain. At the age of 19 he left Iowa for the more cosmopolitan world of Chicago, where he attended the prestigious University of Chicago. He enjoyed the standard fare of plays, galleries, and concerts that the city offered, but also became fascinated with the city's thriving African-American culture; he sometimes accompanied the housekeeper of his fraternity to chapel services, where Van Vechten—an accomplished musician—played the piano.

From the Tabloids to the *Times*

After graduation in 1903, loathe to return to Cedar Rapids and a post at his uncle's bank, Van Vechten obtained a job at the Chicago *American,* part of the Hearst newspaper chain. After a year, he was fired for writing a particularly barbed gossip column, and eventually moved to New York City in the spring of 1906. In an apartment house on West 39th Street that was also home to the more renowned writer Sinclair Lewis, he continued writing the short stories and essays he had first attempted in college. He also partook of Manhattan's rich cultural offerings.

Early in 1907 Van Vechten convinced the editor of *Broadway Magazine,* Theodore Dreiser, to buy his article on a controversial new musical drama at the Metropolitan Opera House, Richard Strauss's *Salome.* Later that year, having lived on funds borrowed from his father until that point, Van Vechten obtained a permanent job as a staff reporter at the *New York Times.* He was soon made an assistant to their music critic, and covered noteworthy new productions and symphonies premiering on New York's stages.

Paris Years

Van Vechten's passion for opera led him to convince his father to loan him money so that he might experience European opera in its own setting. Furthermore, he planned to marry a friend from Cedar Rapids, Wellesley graduate and fellow cosmopolitan Anna Snyder. The pair were wed in London around 1907 and spent months traveling the Continent and enjoying its cultural treasures, though they were sometimes short on funds. The next year, after returning to New York, they again left the country when Van Vechten was sent to Paris as the *New York Times* correspon-

one of his great loves, and the well-received *In the Garrett,* an erudite collection with essays on Oscar Hammerstein, the Yiddish theater, and the lack of a folk tradition in the American Midwest. His first novel, *Peter Whiffle: His Life and Works,* was published in 1922. The plot revolves around a young man and his adventures in Paris, and was clearly based on his own experiences. "This pseudo-biographical novel," wrote Marvin Shaw in an essay in *Gay & Lesbian Biography,* "depicted the creation of a refined dilettante's temperament and wittily exposed the manners and morals of the author's era of elegant decadence."

The Harlem Renaissance

Van Vechten followed with another novel, *The Blind Bow-Boy,* in 1923, but remained an enthusiastic supporter of the arts. His tastes expanded to include the cultural offerings of Harlem, home to Manhattan's thriving black middle class, and by 1924 he had met the African-American novelist and diplomat James Weldon Johnson. Through this luminary, one of the founders of the National Association for the Advancement of Colored People (NAACP), Van Vechten met many other prominent names in the arts who would play important roles in the cultural movement that came to be known as the Harlem Renaissance. These included novelist Zora Neale Hurston, and poets Countee Cullen and Langston Hughes. It was through Van Vechten's intercession with Knopf on behalf of the latter that the groundbreaking collection of Hughes's verse, *The Weary Blues,* appeared in print in 1926.

Van Vechten became immersed in the Harlem Renaissance and its flowering of African-American culture. He wrote about its blues singers, such as Bessie Smith, in a series of articles for *Vanity Fair* beginning in 1925, and was also a backer for Paul Robeson's staging of African-American spirituals. Yet Van Vechten also led a profligate life—he could be a heavy drinker at times, and though married was known to enjoy the company of others. He would later suffer criticism for his championing of Harlem as a heady, intoxicating playground. It became a fashionable "thrill" for well-heeled white New Yorkers to venture into Harlem's integrated nightclubs to listen to the jazz or blues of performers such as Billie Holiday, or the racy shows of Josephine Baker.

Controversy over Novel

The height of Van Vechten's celebrity came with the publication of his fifth novel, *Nigger Heaven.* The title, shocking by contemporary standards, aroused controversy in 1926 as well. The phrase reflected both Harlem itself at the time, in the African-American vernacular, as well as a term for the top tier of seats in a segregated theater. The novel offered a love-triangle plot, but served more to educate mainstream readers about life in a hidden quarter of America's most cosmopolitan city. Furthermore, it introduced readers to facets of black political and social life heretofore unexplored in literature. Van Vechten biographer Bruce Kellner, in an essay in the *Dictionary of Literary Biography,* termed the novel "a deliberate attempt to educate Van Vechten's already large white reading pub-

dent there, where he wrote on such topics as the Wright Brothers experimental flights in France.

The Van Vechtens divorced around 1912. That same year, he met the actress Fania Marinoff when he was back living in New York and working for the *New York Press* as its drama critic. They were wed in 1914 but Snyder filed charges for back alimony and he spent four months in the Ludlow Street jail; the incident would later appear in one of his novels. His first book, *Music after the Great War,* appeared in 1915 as a result of a publishing contact he had made as a *Times* reporter. The work was a collection of essays on music and ballet, some previously published. It marked him as an influential champion of modern music and dance, both forms then gaining ground in Europe. Van Vechten's first work included essays on Igor Stravinsky and the Russian ballet, among other topics.

Success as an Author

His second book, *Music and Bad Manners,* was also his first for the publishing house Alfred A. Knopf, with whom he would enjoy a long relationship. Over the next few years he continued to write on music and the theater for various publications, and during this time he also became acquainted with some prominent African-Americans, such as the writer and civil-rights personality Walter White. Van Vechten also wrote on seminal African-American works for the stage such as *The Darktown Follies* and *Shuffle Along.*

By 1920, Van Vechten's sixth and seventh titles appeared in print—*Tiger in the House,* about the domestic cat, lic, the novel presents Harlem as a complex society fractured and united by individual and social groups of diverse interests, talents, and values.''

The work was also quite racy, and its author was plagued by charges of sensationalism. The volume sold well, but endured harsh criticism. James Weldon Johnson was virtually its only champion among the black intelligentsia: he reviewed it for *Opportunity*, and opined that Van Vechten ''pays colored people the rare tribute of writing about them as people rather than puppets.'' Others viewed it with far less admiration. In *The Crisis*, W.E.B. Du Bois called it ''neither truthful nor artistic,'' and found fault with its depiction of Harlem solely as a playground for the fatuous and amoral. D. H. Lawrence, in an essay titled ''Literature and Art: *Nigger Heaven*,'' found it ''the usual old bones of hot stuff, warmed up with all the fervour the author can command—which isn't much.'' Nevertheless, it was a commercial success, and enhanced Van Vechten's reputation as a patron of the Harlem Renaissance.

Acclaimed as Photographer

Van Vechten continued to author articles for *Vanity Fair* and other publications, and wrote rather unkindly about his travels in Hollywood in essays which formed the basis for the 1928 novel *Spider Boy: A Scenario for a Moving Picture*. His last work of fiction, *Parties: Scenes from Contemporary New York Life*, was started just a few days after the Wall Street crash of 1929, a calamitous event which served to sober up the heady decade. The volume is the only one of Van Vechten's works ''to stand as a terrible indictment of the period,'' wrote Kellner in *Carl Van Vechten and the Irreverent Decades*. ''The others had laughed at the foibles of the whole drunken generation; this one wept.'' *Parties* was met with derision by critics. Yet Van Vechten had wearied of fiction and essays and began to explore another creative pursuit—portrait photography. By 1932 he had dedicated himself exclusively to this, and his portraits of many luminaries of the day, as well as up-and-coming performers such as Lena Horne, Alvin Ailey, and Harry Belafonte, remain incisive glimpses into the era.

Van Vechten was already in his fifties when he gave up writing, and enjoyed his final years as a philanthropist. He founded the James Weldon Johnson Memorial Collection of Negro Arts and Letters at Yale University, and willed his own archives to it; he also directed that any of posthumous royalties from his books be donated to its endowment fund. Also at Yale he established the Anna Marble Pollock Memorial Library of Books about Cats, dedicated to the wife of playwright Channing Pollock and one of his first friends in New York City. Van Vechten died in his sleep on December 21, 1964, and his ashes were scattered in Central Park's Shakespeare Gardens. Examples of Van Vechten's best photographic work were assembled and published in the 1978 volume *Portraits: The Photography of Carl Van Vechten*, and *''Keep A-Inchin' Along'': Selected Writings of Carl Van Vechten about Black Art and Letters*, a collection of his work about African-American culture, was published in 1979.

Further Reading

Contemporary Literary Criticism, Volume 33, Gale, 1985.
Dictionary of Literary Biography, Volume 51: *Afro-American Writers from the Harlem Renaissance to 1940*, Gale, 1987.
Gay & Lesbian Biography, Gale, 1997.
Kellner, Bruce, *Carl Van Vechten and the Irreverent Decades*, University of Oklahoma Press, 1968.
Lawrence, D.H., *Phoenix: The Posthumous Papers of D.H. Lawrence*, edited by Edward D. McDonald, 1936, reprinted by William Heinemann, 1961.
Lueders, Edward, *Carl Van Vechten*, Twayne, 1965.
Crisis, December, 1926, pp. 81-82.
Opportunity, October, 1926, pp. 316-317, 330.

Sebastien LePrestre de Vauban

Sebastien Vauban (1633-1707) served as France's foremost military engineer under Louis the XIV. A man of humble birth, Vauban's acumen in planning military fortifications and his direction of sieges against France's enemies helped the regime achieve dominance over much of western Europe during the latter part of the seventeenth century.

Sebastien LePrestre de Vauban was born in 1633 in Saint-Leger-de-Foucherest, in France's Morvan region. He was the son of Urbain Vauban and Edmee Corvignolle, and his grandfather, a notary a century before, had been able to buy a partial fief, which ennobled him and his heirs. Unfortunately, the family was too large to amass any real wealth from their title. Vauban was given the name Sebastien after his godfather, who was the local priest; and also educated Vauban, though he reportedly taught himself math and was fascinated by a chance discovery of a book on military fortifications.

Civil Strife in France

In 1651 a famed French royal and officer, Louis II de Bourbon, also known as the Prince de Conde, passed through Saint-Leger-de-Foucherest and Vauban left to join his regiment. The prince was leading an insurrection against the regime of Louis XIV, France's underage king. Through an influential cardinal who held power jointly with the king, many of the princes' rights had been curtailed. Conde waged an all-out war, even allying with France's sworn foe, Spain, and during these battles across France Vauban made a name for himself as a young cadet. He held towns in the Argonne, and more famously helped take Sainte-Menehould by swimming across its river under fire.

In 1653 Vauban was captured by royal forces and taken as a prisoner of war. He then switched sides, as Conde would later do, and helped the crown retake Sainte-Menehould. Vauban served in several capacities, but proved himself most proficient as an engineer in a special officer corps for defense fortifications. Though it was almost

separate from regular military duty, Vauban's post placed him in the middle of fire and he was wounded several times. The princes' rebellion was quelled in 1658, and the years until 1667 marked a relatively peaceful time in French politics. Vauban, now a lead engineer, busied himself with demolishing outmoded fortifications and constructing new ones. He married a woman from his hometown in 1663, but spent little time there. That same year he was rewarded with his own company in the Picardy regiment.

An Integral Royal Advisor

One of Vauban's most noteworthy achievements was his fortification of Dunkirk, a French port on the North Sea that Louis XIV purchased from England in 1662. It was a sandy area with almost no natural geographic defenses. Vauban studied the sea tides, and constructed a series of dams and canals. When a war against the Spanish Netherlands was launched in 1667, Vauban returned to combat and was handsomely rewarded for his successes in taking a number of towns. Louis XIV bestowed upon him a royal pension and made him a lieutenant in the Royal Guards. He also achieved the title as France's Commissary General of Fortifications, and worked closely with the king in determining France's military strategies. There were volumes of correspondence written between the pair, who, wrote Francois Bluche in *Louis XIV,* "urged each other on, oscillating between pragmatism and less objective stances. The result was the corridor running around the realm which is known as the 'military iron curtain.'" Vauban's fortifications of the entire northern border of France were mapped out in exten-

sive blueprints that after his death were part of European military curriculum for the next hundred years; at one point he even suggested to Louis XIV that Paris become a walled enclave.

Peace again reigned in France under Louis XIV from 1668 to 1672, but the Third Dutch War with Holland again, for the next six years, called Vauban's skills into action. Often, the king was alongside his top defense engineer during crucial sieges. For the town of Maastricht Vauban designed a system of zig-zag trenches which ran parallel to the perimeter of defenses and saved French soldiers from enemy artillery fire. Such trenches became quite well-known when used by troops during World War I. Because of the French victory at Maastricht, Vauban was financially compensated with a large sum of money by the king, and with it bought a chateau near where he was born, at Bazoches. He was also elevated to the rank of marechal de camp, equivalent to a brigadier general.

Left French Stamp Upon Europe's Cities

Though officially not at war, Louis XIV and his troops—considered Europe's most formidable military presence of the day—seized a number of important cities. In 1681 the German border city of Strasbourg became the most notable of these, and that same year Vauban began constructing a massive fortress there. He argued in favor of its rather ornate gates, an expenditure for which the king balked—Vauban asserted that they issued the necessary statement of French opulence and might to Strasbourg's German-French populace.

Over the next few years Vauban supervised sieges of key locales, such as the 1684 siege of Luxembourg, for which he invented the cavalier, a tower that allowed French troops to look down and fire upon the besieged town. In 1687 he constructed the fortification at Landau in Bavaria, a structure so masterful in planning that military historians cite it as the apex of Vauban's career. In the War of the Grand Alliance, in which Louis XIV's France battled a trio of formidable powers—the Holy Roman Empire, the Netherlands, and England—Vauban served as a lieutenant general and took the vital town of Phillippsburg on the Rhine. That battle was also notable for Vauban's introduction of ricochet gunfire, in which he ordered cannons to be fired with less gunpowder so they did not immediately sink into the ground but instead hit a number of targets.

In 1693, Vauban was sixty years of age, but was still active in military service as a commanding officer and defense engineer. He led an infantry division in Charleroi that year, traveled to the Atlantic port of Brest to fortify it against the English, and in 1697 was wounded in Ath. Peace came the following year, and his renovation of the Alsace fort at Neuf-Brisach was the last project of his career. His talents were not only restricted to forts and artillery, however. He wrote a number of treatises on matters crucial to France during his day, and undertook important censuses on behalf of Louis XIV from 1678 to 1693.

The Sun King

During Louis XIV's long rule (1643-1715) France grew into a thriving empire and one that reflected the glory of the king and his divine right to the throne. Through a series of measures designed to restrict the power of the nobility and concentrate power in his hands, Louis XIV and his reign virtually epitomized the term "absolute monarchism." As a reflection of his power, he built an impressive new palace at Versailles, and moved his court there in 1682. Art and culture were supposed to reflect the King and his tastes, and his important ministers such as Francois-Michel Louvois (Vauban's immediate superior) and Jean-Baptiste Colbert carried out policies that also reflected the king's firm directives. One of those was to make France as prosperous and self-sufficient as possible, and in some areas, long-standing hostilities that threatened such aims were effectively checked for a time by military victories in which Vauban played a key role.

Not unlike other members of the cadre of advisors close to the King, Vauban saw himself in complete service to the King and was dedicated to the monarch's goals. He was appointed by the king to direct a series of censuses beginning in 1678, and his collected data provided the king with an accurate look at the number of French subjects, their wealth, trade and work, as well as land-use statistics. Vauban authored *General and Simple Method for Counting Peoples,* published in 1686, and his *Projet d'une dixme royale* ("Project for a Royal Tythe, or General Tax") caused a stir in 1707. It did not appear under his own name, for Vauban was well aware of the controversy it would bring. In it, he asserted that France's complicated tax code should be abandoned and a flat tax of ten percent on property and trade be put in place. More significantly, in this book Vauban supported his arguments with a wealth of statistical data he had collected, and thus laid the foundation for the use of statistics to corroborate and forecast economic aims. Louis XIV censored its publication, however, and this devastated Vauban, though it appears they remained friends.

During his lifetime Vauban wrote on a variety of other topics, including pig breeding, canal construction, and even "Leisures" in his collection *Oisivets.* He was considered a kind and personable man, and over his long career was roundly praised for his bravery in battle and regard for the lives of his soldiers. It is said he often passed military accolades due him on to lesser officers. He died March 30, 1707 at the age of 74 and left behind his prolific correspondence with the king, which provided a glimpse into why one of Europe's most influential monarchs relied upon Vauban's wisdom and insight. In a 1673 report back to Louvois and Louis XIV about the haphazardness of France's border with Holland, Vauban, quoted in *The Age of Louis XIV,* remarked that "it should always be our object, either by treaty or by war, not to square the circle but to give our country a square and regular shape. It is a fine thing when one can hold on to one's possessions with one's two hands." The town where Vauban was born, Saint-Leger-de-Foucherest, was later renamed Saint-Leger-Vauban in his honor.

Further Reading

Bluche, Francois, *Louis XIV,* translated by Mark Greengrass, Franklin Watts, 1990.
Gaxotte, Pierre, *The Age of Louis XIV,* translated by Michael Shaw, Macmillan, 1970.

Faye Wattleton

African American activist Faye Wattleton (born 1943) has dedicated her life to preserving and protecting the rights of women, first as an advocate for reproductive self-determination and later as a catalyst for gender equality.

Other than securing the right to vote, one of, if not the most important right women have won in the twentieth century, is the right to obtain a safe and legal abortion. During her fourteen-year tenure as president of the Planned Parenthood Federation of America (PPFA), Wattleton brought the nation's oldest and largest voluntary reproductive health organization to the forefront of the battle to preserve women's right to reproductive self-determination.

As the first African American and the first woman to lead Planned Parenthood since its founder Margaret Sanger, Wattleton expanded the organization's focus on contraception and reproductive education to include a strong advocacy position for abortion rights. This stance placed both Wattleton and Planned Parenthood at the center of heated political crossfire, and at times, violence perpetrated by extremists opposed to the Supreme Court decision in *Roe v. Wade* upholding legal access to abortion. Her no-nonsense eloquence and grace under fire catapulted Wattleton into the national spotlight—amid controversy and pressure—as she dealt with the Moral Majority, the Right to Life movement, and challenges posed by other court decisions on the legality and availability of abortion.

From 1978 to 1992, Wattleton played a major role in defining the national debate over reproductive rights and in shaping family planning policies of governments worldwide. These issues led to broader concerns about women's continuing struggle for equality in addition to the fragility of rights, such as abortion, which, once won, still can be eroded or overturned. In 1995, she established the Center for Gender Equality to promote a national dialogue on the economic, political, and educational aspects of women's lives in addition to health and reproductive rights. Her efforts have been recognized with the Jefferson Award for the Greatest Public Service performed by a Private Citizen (1992), and induction into the National Women's Hall of Fame (1993).

Roots of Conviction

Wattleton grew up as the only child in a family of doers and independent thinkers. Her mother and grandfather were strong-willed evangelical preachers, and her father was a hard-working laborer. Both parents were born and raised in the deep South, and moved to St. Louis, Missouri in search of new opportunities. It was there they met, married, and began family life in the 1940s.

Smart and precocious as a child, Wattleton entered school at the age of four, and immediately advanced to the second grade. She remembers an early childhood filled with family and friends, along with the strong tenets of commitment, love, and hope for each other and God. That foundation gave her the security and strength to cope with an unsettled adolescence. Her mother's reputation as a preacher grew, bringing opportunities that required travel away from home.

For eight years on and off, Wattleton lived with church friends or relatives while her parents traveled for the minis-

try. In Wattleton's autobiography, *Life On The Line,* she said, "Those impermanent 'homes' were governed by strict rules enforced mostly without the love and tolerance of my family. I was left to my own devices, to adapt to every circumstance. It was a lonely, guarded existence."

Awakening of a Mission

College was a time of making dreams come true. Since the age of four, she had talked about becoming a nurse, and when her mother became pastor of a large congregation in Cleveland, Ohio, Wattleton saw in Ohio State University's nursing school the opportunity to pursue that lifelong ambition and be close to her family. The experiential part of her education at Children's Hospital in Columbus had a profound influence on the course her career would take. Caring for children who were victims of disease, abuse, and neglect provided her first understanding of women's needs as they relate to reproductive rights.

She went on to study maternal and infant health care at Columbia University. Again, her clinical rotation made a lasting impression and deepened her commitment to helping women. That year approximately 6,500 women were admitted to Harlem Hospital suffering from complications of incomplete abortion. She shared one particularly vivid case of a pretty teenager in terminal condition with the *Ohio State University College of Nursing Magazine.* She recalled, "Unable to afford the services of an abortionist, the girl and her mother had concocted a solution of Lysol and bleach and injected it into her uterus. The potent mix of chemicals had been absorbed by her blood stream, badly damaging

her kidneys. Her other vital organs were shutting down and there was nothing that could be done." In the 1960s before abortion was legalized, women, particularly poor women, resorted to extraordinary measures to control their own reproductive systems.

In the same article, Wattleton said, "Choosing a career in nursing was perhaps my most important professional decision. Had I not had direct experiences with patients and gained an understanding of what goes on in women's lives, I would not have had the determination and commitment to non-compromise on the gains that women have made with respect to reproductive choice."

Uncompromising Leadership

Following graduate school, she returned to Ohio and worked in public health nursing in Dayton for three years before becoming executive director of that city's Planned Parenthood. Eight years later, she found herself leading the national organization during one of the most tumultuous periods in its history. The debate over reproductive rights became a political power struggle, with many diversions intended to confuse the central issue of whether women should decide what happens inside their bodies, or whether the government should decide. The issues were emotionally charged, and the more Planned Parenthood defended women's rights, the more it became a lightning rod for violence. Personal threats became commonplace not only for Wattleton, but for physicians and the staffs of pro-choice clinics and Planned Parenthood facilities around the country. There were shootings, deaths of doctors and health care workers, bomb threats, and fires. Never one to bow to adversity or equivocate in her beliefs, Wattleton stood her ground in defending reproductive choice.

The hard-won gains of *Roe v. Wade* were challenged legislatively as well; and in 1989, the Supreme Court handed down the *Webster* decision allowing states greater power to restrict abortions. Wattleton's mantra became even stronger as she urged women and the Planned Parenthood Federation to realize that women's rights cannot be taken for granted. She believed greater political activism was incumbent upon the Federation in order to uphold its mission, particularly to disadvantaged women. According to *USA Today,* she also was not pleased that fewer than half of Planned Parenthood affiliates offered abortions. *People* reported internal dissension over its public role in the reproductive rights battles finally led Wattleton to resign from Planned Parenthood in 1992.

Life Goes On

Wattleton took time to reflect about her life—who she was, what she accomplished, and where she wanted to go—which resulted in an autobiography, *Life On The Line.* When asked why publishing her story was so important, she said, "I lived a high profile public life. . . . People know where I stand on the issues . . . but they don't know where my belief system comes from or why I chose to crusade for women's lives." Secure, but not complacent, in her contribution to improving the quality of women's lives, she began exploring ways to parlay her expertise into another venue.

Considered telegenic, as well as glamorous, articulate, and charismatic, she tried to break into the daytime talk show circuit on television. It didn't sell. She approached corporations and foundations to serve on their boards, and was told she was too controversial. Then she started receiving speaking engagements, particularly from colleges, and realized she was still looking for an appropriate venue from which to reach tomorrow's leaders.

The idea of starting a women's policy think tank took hold, and in 1996 the Center for Gender Equality opened its doors. In an interview with the Cleveland *Plain Dealer*, Wattleton said, "I'm deeply disturbed by the backlash against women," referring to the dismantling of affirmative action and welfare, as well as the continuing attacks on reproductive rights. As always, she stresses the link between women's inequality and poverty. In founding the Center, her vision is to provide a national platform and institutional setting for scholars, researchers and strategists to pursue a better, more comprehensive understanding of issues that affect women's lives and prevent them from attaining equal status in society.

The Center's fact sheet speaks directly to Wattleton's belief stating that "sustaining change is often a more subtle and complex challenge than the task of creating change." To this, according to the *Ohio State University College of Nursing Magazine,* she brings the values that have propelled her through life—"respect for others, individual responsibility, unflagging determination, and faith in God." Her memoirs provide a glimpse back, as well as the path ahead, "I have never been able to accept the notion that there are some things I cannot do, some things I cannot change. I have always told myself that it is all just a matter of figuring out *how*."

Further Reading

Wattleton, Faye, *Life On The Line,* Ballantine Books, 1996.
Ms., September 1996, p. 44-53.
Ohio State University College of Nursing Magazine, Volume 7, number 1, 1997.
People, November 25, 1996, p. 31-34.
Plain Dealer, November 4, 1997.
Time, October 7, 1996, p. 99.
Town & Country, October 1996.
USA Today, October 8, 1996.
Center for Gender Equality, fact sheet, 1997.

Julius Caesar Watts Jr.

Julius Caesar Watts (born 1957), a conservative African American politician and former football player, was elected to the U.S. House of Representatives in 1994. His victory represents the first time that a black Republican from a Southern state has won a seat in Congress since Reconstruction.

I n 1994, the American public met a man whom Oklahomans and football fans had known for two decades— J.C. Watts, Jr. That year he was elected to represent Oklahoma's fourth district in the U.S. House of Representatives. The race wasn't even close; he won a three-way competition with 52 percent of the vote. In 1996 he scored another victory in a three-way race, this time winning 58 percent. A decisive win is nice, but not unusual. However, Congressman Watts is an unusual man. He is the first African American Republican from a Southern state to win a seat in Congress since Reconstruction, and the only African American in the Congressional Class of 1994. His victory is all the more remarkable because his constituency is conservative, 93 percent white, and more Democrat than Republican (63 percent are registered Democrats). He is the first African American from either party to deliver an official response to the State of the Union address, which he did following President Clinton's 1996 speech before Congress. As a star quarterback, Watts led the University of Oklahoma football team to consecutive conference championships and Orange Bowl victories. Now, charismatic and well spoken, he has achieved a high profile in the political arena— some have called him the GOP's great black hope for the twenty-first century.

Family Values

Born on November 18, 1957, Watts is the fifth of six children born to hardworking parents from a poor neighborhood in Eufaula, Oklahoma. His family maintains a strong work ethic, commitment to the community, and faith in

God that began generations ago. The strength of his father's guidance belies his sixth grade education. J.C. Jr. often quotes his father to illustrate the source of his conservative values. On the topic of self-reliance, Watts told *Washington Monthly* that his father (who has worked as a policeman, Baptist pastor, and cattle owner) was fond of saying, "the only helping hand you can rely on is at the end of your sleeve." This and other southern adages color the speech of son as well as father.

Keep Your Eye on the Ball

Watts distinguished himself as a high school athlete, and was awarded a football scholarship to the University of Oklahoma. Although he eventually became well known among football fans in Oklahoma, it took time and patience to get there. He related a story about his freshman year as No. 7 on a roster of eight quarterbacks to Mike Tharp for *U.S. News & World Report*, saying that he became so discouraged that he quit and went home. His father's response: "If what you're doing was easy, everybody would be doing it." He went back on to become a football hero at OU, and then played professional ball in the Canadian Football League, where he was named most valuable player in the Grey Cup championship game—Canada's Super Bowl. The advice his father now gives is, "don't lose your common sense."

Watts grew up in a family of conservative Democrats and was himself a registered Democrat. He never considered becoming a Republican until he covered a political debate as a journalism student. Watts found that he agreed with the Republican position and his later experience as a small businessman increased his support for the Republican platform. He observed that Democrats had taken African Americans for granted, not earning their support or rewarding their loyalty. According to Watts' account in *Washington Monthly*, "My uncle [who led the National Association for the Advancement of Colored People in Oklahoma] has probably delivered more black votes for the Democratic Party than any person in the state of Oklahoma, yet it was a Republican who gave him a state job." When Watts sought help from Democrats to start a business project they failed to respond, whereas Republican businessmen did not.

Opportunity Knocks

Oklahoma Republicans were delighted by his interest in their party. "You would have to have been a blind man not to see the potential," says Oklahoma Secretary of State, Tom Cole, whom Watts consulted when he considered joining the Republicans. As he told Amy Waldman for the *Washington Monthly* article, "A good-looking black football star with statewide name recognition and a clean-cut image was a dream come true."

Watts invested in an ill-fated business venture, but also began making a name for himself as a public speaker at civic and Christian events. Already an ordained Baptist minister, he also headed youth activities at a large Baptist church. When he expressed interest in running for public office Democrats turned their backs, but Republicans embraced him. There were many prominent blacks in the Democratic Party, but he was a novelty for the Republicans. Watts succeeded in winning a seat on the powerful state corporation commission, which regulates the telephone, gas, and oil industries. According to the same *Washington Monthly* article, Watts won due to his name recognition, his speaking ability, the incumbent's vulnerable record, and his well-financed campaign—contributions coming largely from Republican business people involved in the industries overseen by the commission. Shortly thereafter he won the race to represent the Fourth Congressional District.

Some people discount Watts as an opportunist out to make a name for himself, but others disagree. Robert Woodson, a black conservative and president of the National Center for Neighborhood Enterprise, has stated, "He already was something. He came here to do something." Even those who question his route to Washington don't believe anything other than conviction brings him to his voting decisions. On most issues he takes a strong stance. He talks about character and family values. He opposes abortion, big government, gun control, and gay rights. He supports a balanced budget, free enterprise, school prayer, and the death penalty—all of which reflect the views of his constituency and make him a Christian Coalition favorite.

Consider the Facts

Since arriving in Washington, Watts has taken an interest in restoring low-income neighborhoods. He is adamant in his view that if Republicans are going to dismantle welfare, it has to be replaced with something constructive. He co-sponsored the American Community Renewal Act, which recommends that enterprise zones be established along with other programs to strengthen civil society and create opportunities in urban areas. As he told *about . . . time,* "The legislation will bring spiritual, moral, and economic reform to communities by encouraging private sector investment and individual savings, offering school choice, and allowing citizens the option to use faith-based programs."

To those who consider him a Republican pawn, he points to his support for issues not commonly addressed by the Republican Party, such as human rights violations in Nigeria. Watts has pointed out that he also supported the budget amendment against the wishes of the Republican leadership. On the subject of race, he is clearly proud of his heritage, and does not distance himself from mainstream African Americans such as Supreme Court Justice, Clarence Thomas. He feels his views mirror those of most average Americans, including African Americans.

Watts expresses ambivalence about affirmative action. He explains, "I don't believe we should pick winners and losers based on skin color or gender. . . . We can lock horns as a group to fight racism and discrimination, but success has to come from the individual." Yet he is not willing to agree that it's a level playing field out there, nor is he willing to politicize the debate, as many Republicans have openly tried to do.

In an interview with *about . . . time* he elaborated, "In this color thing, whether or not we're going to be able to get there, I can't say. But I can say while I've got a voice in the process, that I need to be advocating a system of equity. . . . I think America today is struggling for a definition of what is fair."

The Great Black Hope?

Watts thinks he should be judged by his voting record. He wants to be known as an independent thinker: "In this city, if you don't fit a certain identity, it's tough for people to handle. I didn't come up here with any heartburn or any conviction to be the black Republican or the black Conservative. I came up here to cast a vote on the issues just like any other Republican or Democrat, black or white."

When questioned about his future, Watts will only say that he hopes to make the most of opportunities that come his way. On government and politics, he expresses optimism. Watts thinks people generally trust elected officials, but don't trust the system. He is part of what he hopes is the "new" Republican Party. To that effort Watts brings the athletic charisma of Jack Kemp, the eloquence of a Baptist minister, and a great deal of common sense.

Further Reading

African American Almanac, Gale, 1994.
The Almanac of American Politics, National Journal, 1995.
about . . . time, November-December 1997, p. 18.
New Yorker, February 11, 1997.
U.S. News & World Report, December 26, 1995, p. 90.
Washington Monthly, October 1996, p. 34-40.

Annie Dodge Wauneka

Annie Dodge Wauneka (1910-1997) was a Navajo Nation leader who won the United States Presidential Medal of Freedom for her efforts to improve health care among her people.

A Navajo Nation leader, Annie Dodge Wauneka was the first woman elected to serve on the Navajo Tribal Council. Her efforts to educate her people about the prevention and treatment of disease, especially tuberculosis, saved many Navajo lives. She served as the catalyst to improving Navajo health care in general, bringing the issue to the forefront in the political arena. She was also active in state and federal government, serving as a member of the New Mexico Committee on Aging. In 1963, Wauneka was awarded the United States Presidential Medal of Freedom for her service to the Navajo.

Annie Dodge Wauneka was born on April 10, 1910, in a Navajo hogan near Sawmill, Arizona. She was raised in a non-traditional Navajo setting. Her father, Henry Chee Dodge, was a Navajo rancher and politician. Her mother, K'eehabah, was one of Dodge's three wives. Navajo custom allowed polygamy, and a man's wives were usually related to one another. Navajo society is also matrilineal, so children born to wives who were related were considered full

siblings. Wauneka lived with K'eehabah for only her first year. At that time, Dodge brought Wauneka to live with him, along with her half-siblings. Dodge spoke fluent English and had been an interpreter for the government. He was a tribal council head as well as the owner of a large ranch with all the modern conveniences. For these facts alone, Wauneka's childhood would have been highly unusual for a Navajo. Their home was more like a typical farm house than like the Navajo hogans. They even had servants. Dodge kept his children humble by making them do chores, like sheep herding, so they wouldn't feel superior to the tribe's other children.

Young Wauneka attended a government-run boarding school at Fort Defiance, Arizona, from the age of eight. After that, she went to the Albuquerque, New Mexico, Indian School, which she left after her junior year of high school. The Indian School twice strongly influenced her future. First of all, it was where she met her husband, George Wauneka, whom she married in October of 1929, a year after she left the school. Her marriage was unusual in that it had not been arranged by her parents—she had chosen her husband herself. Second, the influenza outbreak at the school found her assisting nurses—work that made her feel valuable and useful. She had found her calling.

Wauneka's interests eventually expanded to include tribal government as well, no doubt due to her father's influence. Henry Chee Dodge served as the first chair of the Navajo Tribal Council during the time Wauneka was in school. The council was a formal body organized to govern the tribe as a corporation according to the rules of the Indian

Reorganization Act of 1934. Dodge shared his knowledge of Navajo leadership with his daughter, and she took his lessons to heart.

While she was breaking ground in health care and tribal government, Wauneka still held to some traditional female roles—but not entirely. She and her husband, George Wauneka, had six children: Georgia Anne, Henry, Irma, Franklin, Lorencita and Sallie. The children were raised at Klagetoh near Window Rock, Arizona, where their father stayed at home with them, tending the property and the herds. Annie Dodge Wauneka often traveled the reservation as Dodge's aide.

On the reservation, Wauneka witnessed the devastation caused by disease, especially tuberculosis. She knew that conventional Western European, or more colloquially, "white man's medicine," might be the answer. She needed to find a way to bridge the gap between cultures for the good of the Navajo people. First, she tried to explain to the traditional families that they might improve their health by simply changing the way they prepared their food and sanitized their cooking and eating areas. She also attempted to win them over through the medicine men, whom the Navajo respected and trusted. If they could be convinced to try conventional medicine, they might convince the others. Eventually, she decided she could make more changes if she were a part of the tribal government. She ran for, and won, a seat on the Tribal Council in 1951. She was the first Navajo woman ever elected to that office. Wauneka was re-elected to a second term in 1954, and again for a third in 1959. She was also chosen to head the council's Health Committee.

She held the office for three terms, leading a tuberculosis eradication project. One of her biggest contributions to the effort was a dictionary she put together that translated English medical terms into the Navajo language. She thus demystified non-traditional medical practices for the people of the tribe, quelling their fears and superstitions. Wauneka also campaigned for other health care improvements for the Navajo, including better gynecological, obstetric, and pediatric care. She also pushed for regular eye and ear exams and fought alcohol abuse.

In order to better help herself and her people, Wauneka went back to college in the mid-1950s. She graduated from the University of Arizona with a bachelor's degree in public health. In 1959, she was rewarded for her efforts on behalf of the Navajo, winning the Arizona State Public Health Association's Outstanding Worker in Public Health Award.

The next decade saw her helping a larger circle of humanity. She became active on the state level, serving on the New Mexico Committee on Aging, and at the general level, serving as member of the U.S. Surgeon General and the U.S. Public Health Service advisory boards. In 1958, she won the Josephine Hughes Award and the Arizona Press Women's Association Woman of Achievement Award. She was named Outstanding Worker in Public Health of the Arizona Public Health Association the following year, and was honored with the Indian Achievement Award of the Indian Council Fire of Chicago that year as well. Her father had won the latter honor in 1945.

In 1960, Wauneka hosted her own daily radio show on KGAK in Gallup, New Mexico. Broadcast in Navajo, the program had Wauneka covering general interest items along with important health issues. Her community outreach wasn't limited to government and the airwaves, however. She was also active in the Head Start program, combining her belief in education with her commitment to health care, and she participated as a leader in the Girl Scouts.

On December 6, 1963, Wauneka was awarded the Presidential Medal of Freedom for her contributions to health care services. She was the first Native American to win this honor. The citation she received from President Lyndon Johnson read, "First woman elected to the Navajo Tribal Council; by her long crusade for improved health programs, she has helped dramatically to lessen the menace of disease among her people and to improve their way of life."

Wauneka received an honorary doctorate in public health from the University of Arizona in 1976. In 1984, the Navajo council honored her as the legendary mother of the Navajo people. She still served as an advisor to the Navajo Tribal Council into her eighties. On May 9, 1996, her alma mater, the University of Arizona, awarded her a second honorary doctorate, Honorary Degree of Doctor of Laws, which was accepted for her by her grandson, Milton J. Bluehouse, then a student at the university.

Wauneka died in November 1997 at the age of 87. Navajo Tribal President Albert Hale, another one of her grandsons, made note of her many accomplishments and declared, "She made us proud to be Navajo."

Further Reading

Notable Native Americans, Gale, 1995, pp. 453-454.
Great Lives from History, Salem Press, 1995, pp. 1849-1852.
Kulkin, Mary-Ellen, *Her Way: Biographies of Women for Young People,* American Library Association, 1976, pp. 297-298.
Chicago Tribune, November 12, 1997.
Grand Rapids Press, November 11, 1997, p. D9.
Los Angeles Times, November 12, 1997.
Quotes for Learning and Service, http://k2.kirtland.cc.mi.us/~service/quotes.html#w

Wei Jingsheng

Chinese human rights activist Wei Jingsheng (born 1950) has spent most of his adult life either in prison or exile for his participation in protests against his government's policies.

On November 16, 1997, Chinese dissident Wei Jingsheng was released from prison in his country and allowed to fly to the United States. Imprisoned for all but six months since 1979, Wei's crime had not been a physical act but an intellectual one: questioning the policies of his country's Communist government. For his participation in the "Democracy Wall" movement in 1978,

Wei had spent 14 years in prison. When, upon his release in 1993, he had proven himself unwilling to keep quiet about the abridgement of freedoms under China's totalitarian system, he was sentenced to another 14 years. But following talks between United States President Bill Clinton and China's President Jiang Zemin, Wei had been released and flown to Detroit, Michigan, where he received special treatment for medical conditions exacerbated by his long imprisonment. In the next few months, the Nobel Peace Prize nominee would embark on a new career as a free man, an outspoken proponent of human rights. Though he now resided in a country where he was free to speak his mind, it was clear that Wei desired something more: to enjoy that freedom in his homeland, the country for which he had endured nearly 18 years of imprisonment.

In his early days, Wei would hardly have seemed like a future opponent of Communism. His parents were high-ranking officials in the regime established by Mao Zedong, who took power in 1949. The oldest of four, Wei grew up in Beijing, where he was well-acquainted with Mao and his wife, Jiang Qing. Young Wei was steeped in Communist doctrine, learning the precepts not only of his country's leader, but of Mao's intellectual forebears, including Marx, Engels, Lenin, and Stalin. In 1966 Wei was a student at one of China's top-ranking high schools, attached to the People's University in Beijing. That was the year when his country entered a tumultuous series of events called the Great Proletarian Cultural Revolution, which would sweep up Wei and the rest of China.

At the beginning of the Cultural Revolution in August, 1966, Mao called for a reinvigoration of Chinese Communism, and urged young people in the "Red Guards" to direct their energies to the task of rooting out all forces opposed to revolution. In practice this meant enormous bloodshed, with millions of teenagers allowed to wreak violence on the country. One of those teens was Wei, and by the end of 1966 he had graduated from the Red Guards to the elite United Action Committee, a group composed of children of high-ranking party officials. By then, however, the Cultural Revolution had gotten so completely out of hand that even Mao was committed to suppressing the revolutionary fervor he had unleashed. As a result, Wei spent the first months of 1967 in prison, and upon his release became involved in a propaganda movement that included publication of a revolutionary periodical called *Preparation*. The following year saw an increased backlash against the perpetrators of the Cultural Revolution, and Wei fled to Chao County, Anhui Province, in the hinterlands of China.

As he recalled in a 1998 interview with *China News Daily*, Wei's year in the country had a large impact on his political views. Up until that time, Wei had been a fervent believer in Communism, and throughout the upheavals of the Cultural Revolution had remained assured that Mao's system would produce peace and prosperity for the people of China. Now, for the first time removed from the relative luxury of the big city, he glimpsed firsthand the poverty wrought by Mao's forced modernization of agriculture. A subsequent stint in the army (1969-73) further broadened Wei's awareness of conditions in his country, as he realized that most of his fellow soldiers were peasants.

Wei then began to seriously reevaluate the precepts he had accepted without question since childhood. Particularly troublesome was the claim that China under Mao represented a "people's democratic dictatorship." He came to recognize the contradiction in terms inherent in this phrase, as he told the *China News Daily*: "If you want democracy, folks will get together to discuss diverse opinions. If you have dictatorship, nobody can discuss with you. . . . [I]f you still had to listen to [the leader], then what was the point of democracy?"

Events in his personal life contributed further to Wei's questioning of political conditions in China. His mother died in 1976, discredited by the party leadership, and his father suffered in a labor camp. Because his family lost their high position, Wei did not have a variety of career options available to him when he completed his army service in 1973. He became an electrician, and obtained employment at the Beijing Zoo. During this time he met and became engaged to Ping Ni, a Tibetan who had suffered greatly as a result of the Maoist takeover of her country in the 1950s. Her father, formerly a leader in the Communist Party of Tibet, had been in prison since 1961; and her mother committed suicide in 1968. Many years later, while in prison, Wei would write a long letter to Deng Xiaoping (who assumed leadership of China after a power struggle that followed Mao's death) criticizing the Chinese Communist Party for poisoning its people's minds against the Tibetans.

Mao died in 1976, and by 1978, the youth of China had begun to agitate for greater freedom. A focal point for this opposition became the "Democracy Wall," an area near Tienanmen Square in Beijing where students displayed manifestoes called "big-character posters." Particularly noteworthy was a poster by Wei in response to Deng's call for "Four Modernizations": in addition to modernization of areas such as defense and technology, as Deng had outlined, Wei demanded a "Fifth Modernization"—democracy.

He had posted the message, Wei told the *China News Daily* 20 years later, to prove "that not all Chinese were spineless." His poster, written in one night and posted the next day, became particularly popular, and aroused repeated readings and discussions. Wei then wrote his name and address on the poster in the middle of the night, and soon a group of the fiercest agitators for freedom gathered around him. The risks and consequences of such activities, Wei remembered, were quite clear, and he and the others faced them willingly. "In fact," he told Fang Wu in an interview for *China News Digest,* "which country has acquired democracy, freedom, and human rights without hard struggle, and shedding blood and sweat? You could not possibly wait for someone to present you with a democracy. There might have been exceptions with very small countries, but for a major people in the world to achieve democracy, methodical efforts with donations of life, blood, sweat, and pain would be required. Could the Chinese achieve democracy without such donations? Impossible!"

With limited time to act before the inevitable government crackdown, Wei and the small group who joined him proceeded to print and distribute a publication called *Exploration.* As funds were limited, the group took what was considered a highly unusual step: instead of giving away copies of their journal, they sold copies to pay for future issues. Word of the monthly grew, and Wei became so involved in his activities that he had to take an extended leave from his job. A doctor friend wrote him fake medical passes, and when that physician came under scrutiny for it, an elderly doctor stepped in and promised to provide Wei with leave permits.

But Wei knew the end of his freedom was near, and as he told the *China News Daily,* the Chinese withdrawal from the war with Vietnam in March, 1979 signaled the end: "Once the troops were pulled out, I knew it was time to deal with us." He conducted a quick rearguard action, destroying his records. He also met with Ping Ni one last time, and told her that once he was arrested, she would announce that she and Wei had broken off their relationship—thus protecting herself and her family from harm. He was arrested at the end of March, and tried on October 16. Held in various institutions in Beijing, he was routinely denied medical and dental care, and lost a number of his teeth. After five years of imprisonment, he was moved to a labor camp of whose location he was never certain, though it seems to have been in the northwest part of the country. Five more years passed before he was placed in the Nangpu New Life Salt Works in 1989.

Then in 1993, while China was involved in its ultimately unsuccessful bid to host the 2000 Olympics in Beijing, the government announced that Wei would be released a year early. But Wei, physically depleted as he was, refused to accept freedom until the authorities returned to him the large volume of letters he had written over the preceding years but had not been allowed to send. These letters would form the basis for Wei's 1997 publication in the United States, *The Courage to Stand Alone.*

Once he was released from prison on September 14, 1993, Wei returned to his political activities with vigor. Wei's friend and assistant Tong Yi, in her *New York Times* editorial, wrote that Wei met with an American official and told him that "The U.S. should be at least as firm in its position on human rights in China as the Chinese government is." Five days later, both Wei and Tong were arrested. Tong Yi wrote an editorial urging President Clinton in an upcoming meeting with President Jiang, to call for Wei's release. The article was published on September 29, 1997, and six weeks later, on November 16, Wei was released. According to Simon Beck of the *South China Morning Post,* "His release was hailed as a sign of bilateral progress made during the recent Sino-U.S. summit."

On December 5, Columbia University announced that Wei had accepted a position as a visiting scholar in its School of International and Public Affairs, where he would work with Tong Yi.

In a speech at Amnesty International, published in *Index online,* Wei recalled a discussion with a prison guard in which he discovered his purpose in life: "I suddenly realized that my determination to help others was the great cause which had been helping me to withstand physical and mental suffering and helped me maintain my optimism and strength. Once I realized this point, I became aware that I could not shake off my life-long responsibility to other people."

Further Reading

Wei Jingsheng, *The Courage to Stand Alone: Letters from Prison and Other Writings,* edited and translated by Kristina M. Torgeson, Viking Penguin, 1997.

China News Digest, January 15, 1998.

Columbia University Record, December 5, 1997.

New York Times, September 29, 1997.

San Francisco Chronicle, December 23, 1997.

South China Morning Post, November 17, 1997.

"China Rights Forum," *Human Rights in China,* http://www.igc.apc.org/hric (February 22, 1998).

"Further Information on Wei Jingsheng's Release,"*Writers in Prison Committee,* http://www.democracy.org (February 22, 1998).

"A Handful of Pennies" (Amnesty International Address), *Index online,* http://www.oneworld.org (February 22, 1998).

"Interview with Wei Jingsheng," *World News Tonight,* http://www.abcnews.com (February 22, 1998).

"Newsmaker: Wei Jingsheng," *Online Newshour,* http://www.pbs.org (February 22, 1998).

Laura Ingalls Wilder

American author Laura Ingalls Wilder (1867-1957) was the creator of the much-loved children's series of "Little House" books that recounted her life as a young girl on the western frontier during the last half of the nineteenth century.

Laura Ingalls Wilder never set out to become a famous writer when she first began jotting down memories of her girlhood on the newly settled American frontier. Her goal, she later explained, was simply to preserve her pioneer family's stories of adventure and discovery. But the unexpected success of her first published book, *Little House in the Big Woods* (1932), made her stop and realize "what a wonderful childhood I had had," as she remarked in a speech delivered in Detroit in 1937 and excerpted in *Something About the Author.* "How I had seen the whole frontier, the woods, the Indian country of the great plains, the frontier towns, the building of railroads in wild, unsettled country, homesteading and farmers coming in to take possession. I realized that I had seen and lived it all. . . . I wanted children now to understand more about the beginnings of things, to know what is behind the things they see—what it is that made America as they know it. . . ." Wilder's charmingly descriptive tales of that era have captivated several generations of young readers and now rank among the classics of children's literature.

Raised on the American Prairie

Wilder was born Laura Elizabeth Ingalls on February 7, 1867, in Pepin, Wisconsin, the second of four children. She once described her father, Charles Philip Ingalls, as always jolly and inclined to be reckless. Her mother, Caroline Lake Quiner, was thrifty, educated, gentle, and proud, according to her daughter. Her sisters, all of whom would eventually appear in her books, were Mary, Carrie, and Grace. Wilder also had a younger brother, Charles, Jr. (nicknamed Freddie), who died at the age of only nine months.

As a young girl, Wilder moved with her family from place to place across America's heartland. In 1874, the Ingalls family left Wisconsin for Walnut Grove, Minnesota, where they lived at first in a dugout house and watched helplessly as an incredible grasshopper plague destroyed their crops. Two years later, the family moved to Burr Oak, Iowa, where Charles became part-owner of a hotel. By the fall of 1877, however, they had all returned to Walnut Grove. In 1879, the Ingalls family moved again, this time to homestead in the Dakota Territory.

The family finally settled in what would become De Smet, South Dakota, which remained Charles and Caroline's home until they died. Their second winter in De Smet was one of the worst on record. Numerous blizzards prevented trains from delivering any supplies, essentially cutting off the town from December until May. Years later, Wilder wrote about her experiences as a young teenager trying to survive the cold temperatures and lack of food, firewood, and other necessities.

Wilder attended regular school whenever possible. However, because of her family's frequent moves, she was largely self-taught. In 1882, at the age of 15, she received her teaching certificate. For three years, Wilder taught at a small country school a dozen miles from her home in De Smet and boarded with a family who lived nearby. The money she earned was used to help pay for special schooling for her older sister, Mary, who had gone blind in her teens after suffering a stroke.

Married a Farmer

During this same period, Wilder became acquainted with Almanzo (Manly) Wilder, who had settled near De Smet in 1879 with his brother Royal. Almanzo frequently headed out into the country on his sleigh to pick up the young teacher and drop her off at her parents' home for weekend visits. After courting for a little more than two years, they were married on August 25, 1885. Wilder then quit teaching to help her husband farm their homestead. She later wrote about this time in her life in her book *The First Four Years.*

The couple's only child, Rose, was born on December 5, 1886. Although all homesteaders had to endure the hardships and uncertainty of farm life, the Wilders experienced more than their share of tragedy and misfortune. In August 1889, Wilder gave birth to a baby boy who died shortly after, an event that never appeared in any of her books. Her husband then came down with diphtheria, which left him partially paralyzed. Finally, their house, built by Manly himself, burned to the ground.

Homeless and saddled with debts, the Wilders spent a year living with Manly's parents in Spring Valley, Minnesota. In 1890, hoping that a milder climate would improve Manly's health, they moved to Westville, Florida. They returned to De Smet two years later but left due to severe drought in the area. Finally, on July 17, 1894, they began their journey to the place they would call home for the rest of their lives, Mansfield, Missouri. Wilder kept a journal of their experiences as they traveled. When she reached Lamar, Missouri, she sent her account of their travels through South Dakota, Nebraska, and Kansas to the *De Smet News.* This was her first published writing.

Established Rocky Ridge Farm

When the Wilders arrived in Missouri, they bought a plot of land and named it Rocky Ridge Farm. At first the only building was a one-room log cabin with a rock fireplace and no windows. Wilder kept busy raising her daughter and helping her husband, who still had not completely recovered from his illness. She also planted a garden and tended the family's chickens. With money she earned from selling potatoes and eggs, she eventually bought a cow and a pig, too. After several years of hard work and saving every extra penny, the Wilders bought more land (for a total of around 200 acres) as well as more cows, hogs, and chickens. They also started building a new house, a ten-room structure made entirely out of timber and rocks from their own farm.

Wilder was among those progressive farm wives who believed that they were also businesswomen and that their contributions were vital to the family's success. Thus, she began looking into ways to help improve the quality of life for other women in her position. In 1910 she became an Officer of the Missouri Home Development Association. She often spoke at meetings of various farmers' organizations, where she would discuss topics such as her method of raising poultry. In 1911, she published her first article, a piece in the *Missouri Ruralist* entitled "Favors the Small Farm." She subsequently worked as the home editor of the *Missouri Ruralist* and the poultry editor of the *St. Louis Star* and contributed articles to periodicals such as *McCall's* and *Country Gentleman*.

Produced Her First Autobiographical Work

In 1915 Wilder took a trip to San Francisco to visit her daughter, who was a star reporter with the San Francisco *Bulletin*. She wrote back to Manly that she and Rose were planning to visit the Panama-Pacific Exposition and "then I do want to do a little writing with Rose to get the hang of it a little better so I can write something perhaps I can sell," as recorded in the book *West from Home: Letters of Laura Ingalls Wilder to Almanzo*.

By the mid-1920s Wilder and her husband were doing little of their own farming on Rocky Ridge, which allowed her to spend most of her time writing. Around this same time, Rose returned to Missouri, built a new home for her parents on Rocky Ridge, and moved into the old farmhouse. She also began encouraging her mother to write the story of her childhood.

Wilder completed her first autobiographical work in the late 1920s. Entitled *Pioneer Girl,* it was a first-person account of her childhood on the frontier from the time she was 3 until she reached the age of 18. After Rose edited the book, Wilder submitted it to various publishers under the name Laura Ingalls Wilder. But no one was interested in her chronicle, which contained plenty of historical facts about her childhood but little in the way of character development.

Created the "Little House" Books

Refusing to become discouraged, Wilder changed her approach. The "I" in her stories became "Laura," and the focus moved from the story of one little girl to the story of an entire family's experiences on the new frontier. Wilder also decided to direct her writing specifically at children. Although she sometimes streamlined events, created or omitted others entirely (such as the birth and death of her brother), and opted for happier endings, she wrote about real people and things that had actually happened.

Thus, in 1932, at the age of 65, Wilder published the first of her eight "Little House" books, *Little House in the Big Woods*. It told the story of her early childhood years in Wisconsin and was a huge hit with readers. *Farmer Boy,* an account of Manly's childhood in New York state, followed in 1933. Two years later, *Little House on the Prairie* appeared on the shelves. (The popular television series of the late 1970s and early 1980s that was based on Wilder's stories used this title as well.) Five more books followed that took the reader through Wilder's courtship and marriage to Manly—*On the Banks of Plum Creek* (1937), *By the Shores of Silver Lake* (1939), *The Long Winter* (1940), *Little Town on the Prairie* (1941), and *These Happy Golden Years* (1943). New editions of all of the "Little House" books were reissued by Harper in 1953 with the now-familiar illustrations of Garth Williams.

Brought Series to a Close

Wilder was 76 years old when she finished the final book in her "Little House" series. By that time, she and her husband had sold off the majority of their land and virtually all of their livestock, but they still lived on the remaining 70 acres of Rocky Ridge. It was there that Manly died in 1949 at the age of 92.

Although she was quite lonely on the farm without her husband (Rose lived in Connecticut by then), Wilder was heartened by the honors that came her way for the "Little House" books and amazed at the steady outpouring of affection from her many fans. Letters arrived daily from all over the world (on her eighty-fourth birthday, for instance, she received 900 cards), and she did her best to answer all of those that required a response. Her friends and neighbors were a source of comfort, too; they saw to it that groceries were delivered to her door, that her fuel tank was always full, and that everything in her house was in proper working order.

Wilder was 90 when she died at Rocky Ridge Farm on February 10, 1957. After her death, her daughter, Rose Wilder Lane, edited the diary that her mother had written as she and Manly traveled to Missouri, the one that had first appeared in the De Smet newspaper. The resulting book, *On the Way Home: The Diary of a Trip from South Dakota to Mansfield, Missouri, in 1894,* was published in 1962. Several other posthumous works followed, including *The First Four Years* (1971), an unpolished first draft about the early years of her marriage, and *West from Home* (1974), a collection of letters Wilder wrote to her husband during her visit to San Francisco. Through her engaging tales of life on the untamed American frontier, Wilder succeeded beyond her wildest dreams at taking a unique time and place of adventure, hardship, and simple pleasures and making it real to scores of young readers across the world.

Further Reading

Something About the Author, Volume 29, Gale, 1982, pp. 239-249.

Blumberg, Lisa, "Toward the Little House," *American Heritage,* April 1997.

Wilder, Laura Ingalls, *West from Home: Letters of Laura Ingalls Wilder to Almanzo,* edited by R.L. MacBride, Harper, 1974.

Slegg, Jennifer, *My Little House on the Prairie Home Page,* http://www.com/home/jenslegg/index/htm (March 14, 1998).

Maurice Hugh Frederick Wilkins

Although Maurice Wilkins (born 1916) is best known for his role in discovering the "double helix" structure of DNA (deoxyribonucleic acid) molecules—the molecules carrying the genetic information from which all life is formed—he has worked to encourage scientists, lawyers, medical people, and the public to think deeply about the possible cultural, social, and philosophical effects of scientific discoveries.

Maurice Hugh Frederick Wilkins was born on December 15, 1916, in Pongaroa, New Zealand. His parents were Irish, and his father, Edgar Henry Wilkins, was a doctor. When Wilkins was six-years-old, he moved to England to attend King Edward's School in Birmingham. He also attended St. John's College, Cambridge, earning a degree in physics in 1938. In 1940, he received his Ph.D. in physics at Birmingham University, studying phosphorescence as a research assistant to the physicist John T. Randall.

During World War II he applied his knowledge to such problems as the improvement of cathode-ray screens for radar. He then worked with physicist M.L.E. Oliphant on the separation of uranium isotopes for use in atomic bombs, which led to Wilkins' involvement in the Manhattan Project in Berkeley, California, where the hydrogen bomb was invented. "Partly on account of the bomb," he said in the *Saturday Review,* "I lost some interest in physics."

His moral crisis eventually led him to the study of biology. He has credited Erwin Schrodinger's book *What is Life* with sparking his interest in a highly complex molecular structure that could control living processes. His former teachers Randall and Oliphant believed strongly that the field of physics had much to offer biology, and advised him to join a biophysics project begun by Randall at his alma mater, St. John's College, in 1945. In 1946, the project moved to King's College, London, where Wilkins joined the newly formed Medical Research Council Biophysics Research Unit.

While there, he studied the genetic effects of ultrasonics and worked on developing ultraviolet microscopes to study nucleic acids in cells. Although the existence of these acids in cellular nuclei had been acknowledged decades before, recently one of the acids—deoxyribonucleic acid (DNA)—had been recognized as a transmitter of physical characteristics from one generation to the next. Determining the composition of DNA was made more challenging because it varied greatly depending on the type of cell in which it appeared. As Wilkins studied the variations, he realized that any biologist could examine the cells as well as he could. He felt he could contribute better as a physicist by studying DNA in isolation, outside the cell.

Discovering the Double Helix

Using a technique from the field of physics known as the analysis of diachroism patterns, Wilkins placed the DNA specimen under the microscope and then subjected it to two colors of light simultaneously. One color was transmitted directly onto the molecule; the other was reflected. The contrast was intended to reveal the structure of the specimen. However, as Wilkins observed the molecule through the microscope, he observed that each time he lifted the glass rod used to orient the molecule, a small fiber hung from the tip. Wilkins determined that the uniformity of the fibers suggested that the DNA molecules were arranged in a regular pattern. What he could not determine was the pattern.

In what has been called a "moment of truth," Wilkins realized that although the pattern could not be seen in the microscope, the fiber could be studied by X-ray diffraction analysis, in which X-rays are bounced off the object and onto film, leaving a record of the object's shape. With the help of Raymond Gosling and Rosalind Franklin, Wilkins obtained the first evidence of DNA's spiral shape. After studying the patterns from several species of DNA, he could see that in each species the pattern was identical: two long strands coiled around each other in a shape called a double helix.

It was already known that the two strands were made of alternating units of sugar and phosphate, but Wilkins' model did not take into account the other chemicals known to be present in DNA: two large submolecules called adenine and guanine, and two small ones called thymine and cytosine. These four chemicals appeared in DNA in a seemingly random pattern. If the DNA molecule was as regular as Wilkins' model suggested, the irregular presence of these chemicals could not be explained.

The contribution of two biologists, James Watson and Francis Crick, solved the puzzle. They reasoned that the double helix shape of DNA was similar to a spiral staircase, with the chemicals serving as steps on the spiral. When a unit of adenine appeared on one spiral, a unit of thymine appeared on the other; similarly a guanine was linked to a cytosine. Because each step in the staircase consisted of one large and one small unit, all the steps took up the same amount of space. No matter what their arrangement, the regular shape of the double helix would not change.

Nobel Prize Leads to Opportunities and Controversy

As *Science* magazine reported in 1962, this discovery had far-reaching consequences. Now that the structure of DNA was understood, scientists could understand the process of genetic replication, or the method by which the genes of the parent are passed down to its child. "Until about 1950, biochemists had . . . tried to imagine mechanisms by which protein molecules could make replicas of themselves. . . . The double helix of DNA, on the other hand, could be pictured as unwinding into two single chains, each complementary to the other. As unwinding proceeded, each could serve as a template for the replication of another chain, complementary to itself, thereby reproducing both the original chain components of the double helix." With this information, geneticists would be able to make maps of genetic codes, enabling the study of hereditary traits and diseases.

For this achievement, Wilkins, along with Watson and Crick, received the 1962 Nobel Prize in Medicine and Physiology. They had also been recognized in 1960 by the American Public Health Association with the Albert Lasker Award, and Wilkins was made Companion of the British Empire. Wilkins took his position as Nobel Laureate seriously. While he acknowledged that some of the benefits of winning the prize included an "increase in salary and professional status," he told *The American Biology Teacher* that it is "in Alfred Nobel's spirit to accept some responsibility" for larger social issues, outside of his main field of expertise. "Some Laureates feel it's wrong to speak on other topics," he said, adding that this may be "a weak excuse to get out of responsibility."

In addition to his work on ribonucleic acid (RNA), which was discovered to act as a messenger, carrying the genetic code from the nuclear DNA, Wilkins took the opportunities created by the Nobel Prize to speak on such topics as "Science and the World" and "Science and Religion." He joined the British Society for Social Responsibility in Science and became president of that organization in 1969. In 1973 he joined with over 100 other Nobel Laureates to protest the Soviet Union's restrictions on scientist Andrei Sakharov and author Alexander Solzhenitsyn.

In 1975 he participated in a meeting of the Democratic Socialist Organizing Committee, a group formed by American socialists with the aim of advancing their ideas within the existing Democratic Party. While Wilkins did not profess to be a socialist, he joined in the statement of six other Nobel Laureates, saying that "the exploration of alternatives to the prevailing Western economic systems must be placed on the agenda at once." In their greeting to the Organizing Committee, the Laureates stated, "Though we have different attitudes as to what this will mean, the process of discussion and political mobilization must begin now." Following his interests in famine and nuclear disarmament, he became a member of Food and Disarmament International in 1984.

Wilkins also found himself embroiled in controversy over the story of his discovery of the double helix with Watson and Crick. When Watson attempted to publish his book *The Double Helix,* both Crick and Wilkins protested several passages. The book took a very personal approach to the story, describing Crick as egocentric and Wilkins as distracted by his assistant Rosalind Franklin. Although some changes were made, they continued to oppose its publication, and Harvard University Press pulled its support for the book and refused to publish it. Critics complained that the press was "less interested in diversity of viewpoint than bland tranquillity," according to *The New York Times.* In 1987, Wilkins was still critical of his old partners: "They think everything about life and human beings can be explained in terms of atoms and molecules."

Wilkins has remained interested in the implications of his earlier work, especially the possibility of genetic manipulation: "This would be, as people say, playing God. And who would decide what genes you would alter and what the forms of the new genes ought to be?" His concern over the ethical problems raised by genetic research led him to create a course at King's College on the social impact of bioscience.

Further Reading

The American Biology Teacher, March 1989.
Newsweek, October 29, 1962.
New York Times, February 15, 1968; December 2, 1973; January 26, 1975.
Saturday Review, March 2, 1963.
Science, October 26, 1962.
Science Digest, January 1986.
Time, October 26, 1962.
"Maurice Hugh Frederick Wilkins," *The Nobel Foundation,* http://www.nobel.se/index.html (March 20, 1998)

Tiger Woods

American athlete Tiger Woods (born 1975) is the youngest man ever, and the first man of color, to win the Masters Tournament of golf.

On April 13, 1997, Tiger Woods made golfing history when he won the prestigious Masters tournament of golf. The win was a record breaker in many ways. Woods, at age twenty-one, was the youngest person ever to win the Masters Tournament. He beat the competition with a record-breaking score of 270 for seventy-two holes. He secured the win with a twelve-stroke lead, the largest victory margin in the history of the tournament. Woods, a man of ethnic complexity, further distinguished himself as the first non-white to win the Masters, and in doing so he helped to dissolve many stereotypical notions and attitudes regarding minorities in the sport of golf.

Tiger Woods was born Eldrick Woods on December 30, 1975, in Cypress, California. He was the only child of Earl and Kultida Woods. His parents identified their son's talent at an unusually early age. They said that he was playing with a putter before he could walk. The boy was gifted not only with exceptional playing abilities, but he also possessed a passion for the sport itself. Woods first came to notoriety on a syndicated talk show when he beat the famed comedian and avid golfer Bob Hope in a putting contest. The young boy was only three at the time, and he was quickly hailed as a prodigy. Not long after that, when he was five years old, Woods was featured on the popular television magazine *That's Incredible!*

Woods' father has never denied that he devoted his energies to developing his son's talent and to furthering the boy's career as a golfer. During practice sessions, Tiger learned to maintain his composure and to hold his concentration while his father persistently made extremely loud noises and created other distractions. "I was using golf to teach him about life. . . . About how to handle responsibility and pressure," his father explained to Alex Tresniowski of *People.*

All the while, Tiger's mother made sure that her son's rare talent and his budding golf career would not interfere with his childhood or his future happiness. His mother was a native of Thailand and very familiar with the mystical precepts of Buddhism, and she passed this philosophy on to her son.

As Woods' special talents became increasingly evident, his parents stressed personality, kindness, and self-esteem. They impressed upon their son that he was not to throw tantrums or be rude or think of himself as any better than the next person. John McCormick and Sharon Begley of *Newsweek* said of his parents, "[Tiger Woods is] best-known as perhaps the finest young golfer in history. But to his parents, it's more important that Tiger Woods is a fine young man. It took love, rules, respect, confidence and trust to get there."

In many ways Woods grew up as a typical middle-class American boy. He developed a taste for junk food and an affection for playing video games. He also spent a fair share of his time clowning around in front of his father's ever-present video camera. As for playing golf, there is no question that the sport was the focus of his childhood. He spent many hours practicing his swing and playing in youth tournaments. Woods was eight years old when he won his first formal competition. From that point he became virtually unstoppable, amassing trophies and breaking amateur records everywhere. Media accounts of the boy prodigy had reached nearly legendary proportions by 1994, when he entered Stanford University as a freshman on a full golfing scholarship.

During his first year of college, Woods won the U.S. Amateur title and qualified to play in the Masters tournament in Augusta, Georgia, in the spring of 1995. Although he played as an amateur—not for prize money—Woods' reputation preceded him. Biographer John Strege wrote about that first Masters tournament in *Tiger: A Biography of Tiger Woods*, "Golf great Nick Price was there. So were Nick Faldo, John Daly and Fuzzy Zoeller, all of them consigned to relative obscurity on this Monday of Masters week. All eyes were on Woods." By 1996, Woods had won three consecutive U.S. Amateur titles, an unprecedented accomplishment in itself. Woods was only twenty years old, yet there was not much else for him to accomplish as an amateur. He carefully weighed the advantages of finishing college against the prospect of leaving school and entering the sport of professional golf. The temptation to turn professional was enhanced by lucrative offers of endorsement contracts. In August of 1996, Woods decided to quit college in order to play professional golf.

Four months later in December, Woods celebrated his twenty-first birthday. He marked the occasion with a legal name change, from Eldrick to Tiger. Woods had been called Tiger by his father even as a youngster. The nickname stuck, and Woods had always been known to his friends, and to

the press, as Tiger. It soon became evident that he was destined for success. *Sports Illustrated* named him 1996 "Sportsman of the Year," and by January of 1997, he had already won three professional tournaments. He was a media sensation.

In April of 1997, and only eight months into his professional career, Woods played in the prestigious Masters tournament held at Georgia's Augusta National Golf Club. The Masters title is perhaps the most coveted honor in the world of golf. In addition to a hefty prize purse, first-place winners are awarded a green blazer to symbolize their membership among the most elite golfers in the world. Contestants are typically well into their thirties or even their forties by the time they win the Masters Tournament. That year Woods competed against golfing greats, but managed to best the most seasoned competition.

When the tournament was over, Woods had made history as the youngest person ever to win the Masters title. His score was an unprecedented 270 strokes. His victory margin set another record—twelve strokes ahead of the runner-up. This feat was enhanced by the fact that Woods was the first man of color ever to win the title. He accepted all of these honors with grace and humility, and gave tribute to the black golfers who came before him and helped pave the way. He also honored his mother (who is Asian) by reminding the world of his diverse ethnic background; he is African-American, Thai, Chinese, Native American, and Caucasian. He discouraged the press from labeling him exclusively as African American, because it showed complete disregard for his mother's Asian heritage. During an interview for the *Oprah Winfrey Show*, he reiterated an innovative description that he had coined for himself as a child, "I'm a Cablinasian." He was quoted also by John Feinstein of *Newsweek*, concerning the issue of race, "I don't consider myself a Great Black Hope. I'm just a golfer who happens to be black and Asian."

Less than three months passed until July 6, 1997, when Woods won the Western Open. Critics attributed his astounding success to uncanny persistence and an extraordinary desire to win. "He thinks, therefore he wins," reported the *Detroit News*, on the day after the Western Open. Woods seemed unstoppable. Some of the greatest golfers in the world offered sportsmanly tribute to the young hero. His enormous popularity and unprecedented success prompted Frank Deford of *Newsweek* to write, "It's getting so that the only other famous person on the golf circuit is Tiger's caddie . . . suddenly you understand: there is no second-best golfer in the world. . . . It is just Tiger Woods." In less than one year as a professional golfer Woods' career winnings totaled over $1,000,000. In addition to prize money earned, he signed multi-million dollar contracts to endorse a variety of products, from sports equipment to investment funds.

To many observers, Tiger Woods' rise to fame is tied to issues of race and ethnicity as well as to outstanding athletic performance on the golfing course. "Tiger threatened one of the last bastions of white supremacy," wrote Strege in his biography of Woods. Although accusations of racial discrimination had been leveled against the Professional Golf Association (PGA) for many years, little was done. According to Rick Reilly of *Sports Illustrated*, the Augusta National Tournament founder, Clifford Roberts, once remarked, "As long as I'm alive, golfers will be white, and caddies will be black." Policies were slowly changed to ensure that black golfers would be allowed to compete on a par with whites, but the Augusta National Golf Club didn't accept its first African American member until 1990.

Woods, with his easy style, his unpretentious disposition, and his powerful 300-yard drives, successfully commanded the respect and attention of golf's predominantly white culture. "Golf has shied away from [racism] for too long," Woods commented to *Time*. "Some clubs have brought in tokens, but nothing really has changed. I hope what I'm doing can change that." Robert Beck of *Sports Illustrated* called the ethnically diverse golfer, "A one-man Rainbow Coalition." By all reports, he rises graciously to every occasion, handling the media as well as his peers, with tact and aplomb. Joe Stroud of the *Detroit Free Press* commented, "He is a photogenic young man. . . . He is about as remarkable a combination of power and finesse as I've ever seen."

Woods is credited too with popularizing the sport of golf, not only among blacks and other minorities, but among children of all backgrounds. Jennifer Mills of *Cable-TV* explained the depth of the Tiger Woods phenomenon, "He is bringing a whole new set of people to the golf course who have never been here before. . . . Kids of every race are dying to see him. They look up at what he's doing and for the first time feel, 'Hey, maybe I could do that.'" His personal sponsorship of programs for children has been reported for years, and at least one corporate sponsor found that in order to secure an endorsement from Tiger Woods the price would include the added cost of a generous donation to the Tiger Woods Foundation for inner city children. A *Time* review of the twenty-five most influential people of 1997 reported, "Woods doesn't simply take his money and play. He conducts clinics for inner-city kids, and he . . . will create opportunities for youngsters who would otherwise never get a chance."

Further Reading

Strege, John, *Tiger: A Biography of Tiger Woods*, Broadway Books, 1997.
Christian Science Monitor, December 5, 1996.
Detroit Free Press, January 13, 1997; April 14, 1997, p. 1D; April 23, 1997, p. 1D; May 2, 1997, p. 10A; May 7, 1997, p. A1; May 20, 1997; June 11, 1997, p. 3C.
Detroit News, July 7, 1997, 1C.
Newsweek, September 9, 1996, pp. 58-61; December 9, 1996, pp. 52-61; April 28, 1997, pp. 58-62; June 2, 1997, p. 62.
People, April 28, 1997, pp. 89-92; June 16, 1997, pp. 96-102.
Sports Illustrated, December 23, 1996, pp. 29-52; April 21, 1997, pp. 30-46.
Time, April 21, 1997, p. 40.
USA Weekend, May 9-11, 1997, p. 2.
"Unofficial Tiger Woods Web Page," www.geocities.com/Colosseum/2396/tiger.html (January 6, 1998).
"Welcome to Tiger Watch," www.tiger-woods-golf.com/ (January 6, 1998).

Z

Franco Zeffirelli

Franco Zeffirelli (born 1923) is best know for his extravagantly staged operas and films that bring the classics to the masses. His interests also span into the political arena. He was elected to the Italian senate in 1994 and 1996 representing Catania, Sicily.

Franco Zeffirelli has proven himself as a talented director of operas, plays and feature films. He has found the most success in the opera house. Though critics haven't always been in favor of his flamboyant staging, his audiences have been bedazzled by it. In fact, his elaborate set designs have often been thought to upstage the music. Zeffirelli has also brought classics such as *Romeo and Juliet* (1968), *Hamlet* (1990) and *Jane Eyre* (1996) to the silver screen so that the average movie-goer can understand them. While some claim that he oversimplifies the classics, Zeffirelli feels that he popularizes them instead. Even in the world of politics, Zeffirelli has looked out for the common people. William Murray in *Los Angeles Magazine,* noted that Zeffirelli has ''secured jobs, money and other help'' for his constituents in Catania, ''one of the poorest, most Mafia-ridden cities in Sicily.''

A Boy with No Name

Zeffirelli was born on February 12, 1923 in the outskirts of Florence, Italy. He was the result of an affair between Alaide Garosi, a fashion designer, and Ottorino Corsi, a wool and silk dealer. Since both were married, Alaide was unable to use her surname or Corsi's for her child. She came up with ''Zeffiretti'' which are the ''little breezes'' mentioned in Mozart's *Cosi fan tutte* of which she was quite fond. However, it was misspelled in the register and became Zeffirelli. Alaide placed her newborn with a peasant family for two years before bringing him to live with her after the death of her husband. Unfortunately, she succumbed to tuberculosis and a six-year-old Zeffirelli was sent to live with his father's cousin, Lide, whom he called ''Aunt Lide.''

As a child, Zeffirelli's earliest experiences of theater were the traveling actors who visited the peasant village where he spent his summers. He also enjoyed building toy theaters and scenery for his puppets. The first opera he saw was *Die Walkre* which he didn't understand. The music and scenery, though, captivated the young boy. Another early influence was the Catholic Club at his school. The club performed religious and historical plays at various churches. He also went to see movies quite often and knew who all the stars were and the gossip about them.

The War Years

Mussolini marched on Rome the year before Zeffirelli was born and Fascism was all around him. During World War II, Zeffirelli began studying architecture at the University of Florence. By the time most of his friends had been conscripted, he chose to join the partisans in the hills of Italy. After escaping the Italian Fascists and reaching the Allied lines, he ended up as a guide and interpreter for the First Battalion of the Scots Guards. It was with the Scots that his interest in theater was renewed. He helped organize a theatric performance with soldiers in drag. By the time he returned to Florence, Zeffirelli was a different person. He went to live with his father and after seeing Laurence Olivier's *Henry V* he decided to pursue a career in theater.

Count Luchino Visconti

The biggest break of Zeffirelli's career was his acquaintance with Count Luchino Visconti. According to Andrea Lee in *The New Yorker,* meeting Visconti "was the opening of the crucial collaboration of Zeffirelli's life, an artistic and sentimental relationship that would be equaled in intensity only by his passionate friendship with Maria Callas. It also marked an immense step up in the world." He met Visconti while working as a scene-painter and from there his career took off. He spent nearly 9 years with Visconti and worked for his Morelli-Stoppa theatrical company. Lee further noted that "[i]n Visconti, who divided his talents between cinema, opera, and theatre, Zeffirelli had an example of the restless eclecticism that in time became his own trademark." He also adopted Visconti's penchant for detailed research and hands-on demonstrations of how he wanted a scene acted out.

On Stage and Screen

Zeffirelli's career took off in the 1950s as a scene designer for Italian productions of *A Streetcar Named Desire* and *Troilus and Cressida.* From 1958 on, Zeffirelli has demonstrated the flexibility of going from opera to theater to film and back again all over the world. In one decade, he brought out: *Lucia di Lammermoor* (1959) with Joan Sutherland; *Romeo and Juliet* (1960) at the Old Vic; *Othello* (1961) with John Gielgud at Stratford; *Tosca* (1964) at Covent Garden; *Norma* (1964) at the Paris Opera; *Taming of the Shrew*

(1967) with Richard Burton and Elizabeth Taylor; and a film version of *Romeo and Juliet* (1968).

"Opera a la Zeffirelli is the greatest show on earth," claims Murray. His sets tend to be very large in scale and he often has literally crowds of performers on stage at once. He's even been known to use numerous live animals. Bernard Holland in the *New York Times* had this to say about Zeffirelli's productions at the Metropolitan Opera, "The Met—with its huge stage, its magnificent stage equipment and crew, and its pocket of wealthy patrons hungry to gild the status quo—has become for him an irresistible playground and a marriage made in heaven." With regard to a performance of Puccini's *Turandot,* Holland commented that "[s]omewhere in the house that night an opera, and a rich and stageworthy one at that, was going on. It really didn't matter, though. All the glitter and grandiosity descending over it made certain that music wouldn't get in the way of an evening's entertainment."

Zeffirelli's name is linked most often with the operas, *La Traviata, Cavalleria Rusticana,* and *I Pagliacci.* His 1958 staging of *La Traviata* in Dallas, Texas with Maria Callas as Violetta marked Zeffirelli as an up-and-coming international director. Often when Zeffirelli has been asked to direct an opera that he has done before, he will make changes to the time period or the setting. With *I Pagliacci,* he changed the time from 1870 to 1938 in one production and the setting from Calabria to the outskirts of a city like Naples in another. His fondness for opera can be seen in his carefully dictated quote to Murray that, "opera is a river that carries you forward."

Zeffirelli's films have not enjoyed as much critical success as his operas, yet they still appeal to the audiences. His 1977 five-part television miniseries *Jesus of Nazareth* shows the kind of ambitious undertaking Zeffirelli can achieve. This modern classic is broadcast in Italy and around the world every Easter. His film about St. Francis, *Brother Sun and Sister Moon,* was disliked by the critics but has seen cult-like popularity in the Philippines and Brazil due to its religious content.

In an interview with John Tibbetts in *Literature Film Quarterly,* Zeffirelli shed some light on perhaps another reason for the lack of critical acclaim received by his films when he said, "I think culture—especially opera and Shakespeare—must be available to as many people as possible. It irritates me that some people want art to be as 'difficult' as possible, an elitest [sic] kind of thing. I want to give these things back to the people." This can clearly be seen in his treatment of the films he has based on English classic literature such as Shakespeare's *Taming of the Shrew, Romeo and Juliet,* and *Hamlet.*

Zeffirelli's practice of researching the subject to the smallest detail has helped bring these films to the general audience. In *Romeo and Juliet,* he used two very young performers in the lead roles who more closely matched the age of Shakespeare's characters. When criticized about the ages of Glenn Close and Mel Gibson as being unrealistic for a mother and son in *Hamlet,* Zeffirelli responded that it was common at that time for girls to marry at 13 and start having children. He has also done a film version of Charlotte

Bronte's *Jane Eyre*. The book had been a favorite of his since he was ten years old and Mary O'Neal introduced him to it while tutoring him in English. Ian Blair reported in *The Standard-Times* that Zeffirelli said his biggest challenge with the film was "not to impose the eye of an Italian on it."

The Senator

Zeffirelli has been an outspoken rightist for some 40 years. He ran for parliament in Florence in 1983 and lost. He had run as a favor for the Christian Democratic Party which feared the Communist Party might make some gains. Zeffirelli also had an ulterior motive for running. In his autobiography, *Zeffirelli: The Autobiography of Franco Zeffirelli*, he admits, "I genuinely thought I could use the post to realize a long-standing dream: to use my cultural connections and make Florence the European capital for the performing arts ... [and] access to political power was essential for anyone trying to bring this about."

In 1994, Zeffirelli ran for a seat in the Italian senate representing the city of Catania in Sicily. With 63 percent of the vote, he was elected as a candidate for the rightist party, Forza Italia. He ran for re-election and won again in 1996. With regard to his activities as a senator, he told Lee that "he sensibly assigns others to cover areas he is unfamiliar with, and tries to take charge of things with which he has direct experience—culture, historic preservation, education, and the environment, including, in particular, animal rights."

Zeffirelli's political views tend to be on the conservative side. Even though he has not been known to attend mass regularly, he is a staunch supporter of the Vatican. Perhaps the only area in which the Pope and Zeffirelli don't agree is artistic preference. In a Vatican list of 45 films deemed to have worthy religious content, none of Zeffirelli's films are mentioned. Belinda Luscombe reported in *Time* that Zeffirelli felt his films "have brought about many more conversions then all those cited."

Future Plans

Even in his seventies, Zeffirelli is always on the lookout for a new endeavor, be it film or opera. "The more you work, the more you accumulate energy," he told Marion Hart in *Entertainment Weekly*. He has written a script for a film version of *Madame Butterfly* and is looking to cast Cher in the leading role of the film *Tea with Mussolini* which is based on a chapter from his autobiography. With regard to his future, Blair quoted Zeffirelli as saying, "I feel like an airport with all these projects circling around waiting to land. Some get lost in space, others land safely."

Further Reading

Zeffirelli, Franco, *Zeffirelli: The Autobiography of Franco Zeffirelli*, Weidenfeld & Nicolson, 1986.
Entertainment Weekly, April, 26, 1996.
Hartford Courant, February 1, 1998.
Literature Film Quarterly, April-June, 1994.
Los Angeles Magazine, September 1996.
New Perspectives Quarterly, Summer 1994.
New York Times, October 5, 1997.
New Yorker, April 22, 1996.
Time, March 25, 1996.
Victoria, June 1996.
Blair, Ian, "Zeffirelli's 'Eyre' love affair," *The Standard Times*, (April 7, 1996) http://www.s-t.com (March 21, 1998).
"Franco Zeffirelli," http://www.unitel.classicalmusic.com (March 15, 1998).

Helen Zia

A second generation Chinese American who is an activist and journalist, Helen Zia (born 1952) advocated against racism and hate crimes that affected the Asian American community. She also involved herself with gay and lesbian and feminist issues.

In many ways, Helen Zia's activist work has served to strengthen and build coalitions among various Asian American cultural backgrounds. She was a leading voice in protesting and organizing Asian Americans after Vincent Chin, a Chinese American, was killed in 1982 after a racially motivated bar fight. Zia's activism has included fighting hate crimes, organizing for battered Asian American women, and speaking out against ethno-rape, or rape that is motivated by racial bias. Additionally, she has advocated for gay and lesbian rights. Zia also served as a journalist, holding editor positions at *Ms.* magazine and publishing work in a variety of national newspapers and periodicals.

Early Years

"I am not exactly sure when it happened, but somewhere during my childhood I decided I wasn't American," observed Zia in *Essence*. Born in Newark, New Jersey, to parents who immigrated from China, Zia grew up amid the traditions of two very different cultures. "I liked hot dogs, Kool-Aid, apple pie and the two-tone Chevy wagon my dad drove," she has said. However, by the time she was eight, she and her family had encountered racial prejudice because of their perceived "foreignness." Zia concluded, "America didn't want me, and in that case I didn't want to be a part of it." During her teenage years, she very much identified with the black civil rights movement and its leaders.

After receiving her bachelor's degree from Princeton University in 1973, Zia worked briefly for the U.S. Department of State as a public affairs specialist before enrolling in the Tufts University School of Medicine, which she attended until 1975. She then headed to Detroit, where she pursued graduate studies in industrial relations at Wayne State University and was a factory worker for Chrysler Corporation from 1977 until 1979. During this same period, she began her career in journalism, contributing pieces to local and national publications.

Led the Fight for Hate Crime Sentencing in Asian American Case

Zia was one of the co-founders of American Citizens for Justice (ACJ), a group that was formed after a 27-year-old

Asian American man died as the result of racially motivated violence. Vincent Chin was beaten to death in June of 1982 after an altercation in a Detroit bar with two white men. One of the men, an auto-worker who had been laid off, incorrectly assumed that Chin was Japanese. At the time, anti-Japanese sentiment in Detroit was at an all time high, with Japanese auto products being blamed for the ailing U.S. auto industry. Of the events surrounding Chin's assault, Zia commented in *AsianWeek* that "the mood was totally anti-Japanese. People who had Japanese cars were getting their cars shot at, and it didn't matter if they were white. If you were Asian, it was assumed that you were Japanese; there was personal hostility toward us."

The two suspects were initially charged with second degree murder; they eventually pleaded guilty to manslaughter. However, they were given sentences of probation and fines, and the Asian American community perceived these sentences as a slap on the wrist. Asian Americans reacted with outrage at this unjust outcome. Members of ACJ circulated and helped raise funds for legal expenses to challenge the Chin decision. Zia served as the campaign's national spokesperson and was elected president of the group for two terms.

After a long and disheartening legal battle which included an FBI investigation, both men escaped serving any jail time. Later in 1987, a civil suit was filed against one of the men who was ordered to pay $1.5 million to Chin's estate. Despite this less-than-satisfying resolution to the case, Zia and other Asian Americans counted it as a partial victory because it marked the first time they were able to

demonstrate a direct link between anti-Asian prejudice and increasing rates of violence against Asian Americans. However, the money was never collected as the man sold his assets and evaded law officials.

A documentary film, *Who Killed Vincent Chin?*, was later produced that covered the incident and Zia's role in organizing the protest. In the aftermath of the murder, Zia facilitated collaboration between the various Asian American communities and a rallying around a common cause, a condition that had not existed previously. The film was later nominated for an Academy Award.

Zia saw a need for a concerted national effort to address hate crimes against Asian Americans. She claimed that a national organization would streamline dealing with hate crimes as they happened in different parts of the country. A national organization, she said, would lend greater credibility to the fact that hate crimes against Asian Americans were part of a larger trend and not isolated, insignificant events.

Journalism Career

Zia moved into the field of journalism on a full-time basis in 1983 when she joined the staff of *Metropolitan Detroit* magazine as an associate editor. She left in 1985 to become executive editor of *Meetings and Conventions* magazine, part of the Murdoch Magazines/NewsAmerica group located in Secaucus, New Jersey. She remained with the company for the next four years, serving as editorial director of *Travel Weekly* from 1986 to 1987 and then as editor-in-chief of *Meetings and Conventions* magazine from 1987 to 1989.

In 1989, Zia moved to New York to become executive editor of *Ms.* magazine, a post she held until 1992. She then headed to San Francisco, where she was vice president and editor-in-chief of WorldView Systems (an electronic publishing company) through 1994.

Advocated for Asian Political Presence

Zia spoke in favor of a larger role for Asian Americans in U.S. politics and policy setting. In a 1997 National Public Radio interview, she pointed out that Asian Americans had little success in establishing a presence in American politics. This was in part, she claimed, to an emphasis on raising funds rather than what any Asian American individual might have to offer, and the fact that Asian American donations to the Democratic party were being scrutinized under a campaign reform initiative. Speaking for the Asian American community, Zia said that Asian Americans felt singled out first for what they could offer monetarily, then as the sole cause of the campaign scandal.

Protested Racist Journalism

Zia served as the president of the New York Chapter of the Asian American Journalists Association (AAJA), an organization devoted to fighting media stereotyping against Asian Americans. AAJA encouraged members to advance in their field, and publicly protested specific acts of racism, often in the journalistic arena. The organization tracked incidences of racist and stereotypic journalistic reporting. Some of her accomplishments as AAJA president included organizing a community protest against a journalist who made racist and sexist remarks about a Korean-American reporter.

Under Zia's leadership, the AAJA also succeeded in grabbing the attention of the national media during protests which decried the cast choices for the musical *Miss Saigon*, a situation where Caucasians were being cast in Asian roles. As another example, on August 27, 1992, Zia was in Washington, D.C., to deliver the keynote address at the annual convention of the Asian American Journalists Association. The subject of her talk was media coverage of Asian Americans—particularly by other Asian Americans.

Social Activist

In addition to her efforts on behalf of Asian Americans, Zia is also active in the feminist and gay/lesbian movements as well as other social justice causes. All of these interests figure prominently in her speeches, of which she may give up to two dozen or so in the course of a typical year. Zia's activist interests extended beyond protesting racism or stereotypical journalism. She served as a board member of the New York Asian Women's Center, an organization that provided shelter and services for Asian women who had been victims of physical abuse. According to an article in *A. Magazine*, battering of these women was often ignored, since the majority of the battering was instigated by Asian men. Zia organized around other feminist issues as well. She carried out an investigation at the University of Michigan on date rape which incited a demonstration on the grounds and a restructuring of the university's administration.

Continued Work as Journalist

In addition to activist organizing, Zia continued to work as a journalist and published articles in a number of well known periodicals, including *New York Times*, *Essence*, *Washington Post*, *Arizona Republic*, and *Ms*. Zia served as managing editor and contributing editor for *Ms*. She served as executive editor for *Notable Asian Americans* and *Who's Who Among Asian Americans* (both publications of Gale Research). In the late 1990s Zia remained involved in a number of activist fronts; continuing to serve on the boards of Asian groups such as the AAJA and an Asian women's shelter in San Francisco. She continued her involvement in gay and lesbian causes, and family violence prevention.

Further Reading

Daniels, Roger, *Asian America: Chinese and Japanese in the United States Since 1850,* University of Washington Press, 1988.
A. Magazine, April 30, 1992.
AsianWeek, June 19, 1997.
Essence,, May 1993.
Weekend Sunday (NPR),, November 23, 1997.

Paul Zindel

From Pulitzer prize-winning playwright to young adult fiction writer, American author Paul Zindel (born 1936) turned his real-life turbulent teens into fictional stories to show teenagers that their lives and feelings do matter.

Paul Zindel did not choose to become a playwright, a screenwriter or young adult fiction writer. In fact, Zindel told *Teaching PreK-8* interviewer Diane Winarski that he was "wired" to become a writer: "I like storytelling. We all have an active thing that we do that gives us self-esteem, that makes us proud; it's necessary. I have to tell stories because that's the way the wiring went in." However, Zindel also survived a childhood where his tales were born. From his mother's inability to keep a job to his search for his own "Pigman," Zindel has told his stories in ten plays, seven screenplays, and over 20 young adult fiction books. As quoted in *English Journal*, Zindel believes that his writing reflects how he sees the world "as a problem-solving situation, and the solution of those problems through fiction seems to be the adventure that I've chosen for myself."

Early Adventures

Paul Zindel was born on May 15, 1936, in Staten Island, New York. His father, also named Paul, left Zindel, his older sister Betty, and mother, Betty, for a girlfriend when Zindel was just two years old. This event began Zindel's early adventures. After his father left, Zindel's mother started moving from town to town and from job to job. From ship yard worker, to a Lassie-type dog breeder, Betty Zindel always seemed unable to keep any job. Yet, Zindel in his autobiography, *The Pigman and Me*, offered a sort of compliment to his mother, "but what mother lacked in money, she made up for being able to talk a mile a minute." Zindel's mother, however, also constantly threatened suicide. As quoted in *Morning Telegraph*, Zindel described his home as a "house of fear." He coped not only by creating a fantasy life, but also by wishing he was abducted by aliens.

In 1951, when Zindel was 15, his wish to escape from his home was granted—although not by aliens, but by doctors. He was diagnosed with tuberculosis. Since tuberculosis was a highly contagious respiratory disease, he was confined to an adult sanatorium for 18 months. Zindel believed that, as he told *Scholastic Voice* writers, "being the only kid in an adult world has done things to me I don't even know about." However, it was in the sanatorium where Zindel wrote his first play.

After recovering, Zindel graduated from high school and left home once again, this time to attend Wagner College in New York. Zindel did not receive a degree in English, literature, or writing, but in 1958, received his bachelor's degree in chemistry and education. In 1959, he also completed a masters of science degree in chemistry. Zindel, as quoted in the *Dictionary of Literary Biography*, had "a great love . . . of microcosms, of peering at other worlds framed and separate from me." Following college, Zindel found work as a technical writer for a chemical company. After six months, he quit and became a chemistry teacher at Tottenville High School in Staten Island, New York. In his free time, he continued to write plays such as *Dimensions of Peacocks* and *A Dream of Swallows*. In the early 1960s, both plays ran on-stage in New York City. However, years after becoming a successful playwright, Zindel told *Teaching PreK-8* interviewer Diane Winarski that he "finally realized that teaching has a very real connection to show business. You have to learn to perform in front of an audience; . . . you must lead your students to illuminations or epiphanies. You're doing five one-act plays a day! That's a lesson plan."

Success In Two Genres

In the mid-1960s, Zindel wrote *The Effect of Gamma Rays on Man-in-the-Moon Marigolds*. It was chemistry and not any other play that inspired this production. Zindel told *Time* reporters that he remembered "thinking that all carbon atoms on earth had come from the sun. The idea of being linked to the universe by these atoms, which really didn't die, gave me a feeling of meaning." *Gamma Rays* tells the story of Tillie, a teenager who feels smothered by her critical mother and epileptic sister. However, Tillie finds hope for her life when the marigolds she exposed to radiation for a science project, bloom. Zindel won many awards for *Gamma Rays*, including the 1971 Pulitzer Prize in

Drama. Zindel, as stated in the forward to the Bantam Edition, said of this often-awarded play, "I suspect it is autobiographical, because whenever I see a production of it I laugh and cry harder than anyone else in the audience."

After viewing a televised version of *Gamma Rays*, Charlotte Zolotow, an editor at Harper & Row publishers, suggested to Zindel that he write a young adult fiction book. Zindel published *The Pigman* in 1968. *The Pigman* told the story of a betrayed friendship between two high school sophomores, John and Lorraine, and a widower named Mr. Angelo Pignati. After an illness forces Mr. Pignati, the "Pigman," out of his home, he entrusts John and Lorraine with its care and his cherished ceramic pig collection. John and Lorraine betray this trust and the Pigman's friendship, however, by throwing a party where his collection is accidently smashed. With this book, Zindel not only continued collecting awards, including the American Library Association's Best Young Adult Book citation, but also praise. *Horn Book* contributor Diane Farrell declared, "Few books that have been written for young people are as cruelly truthful about the human condition. Fewer still accord the elderly such serious consideration or perceive that what we term senility may be a symbolic return to youthful honesty and idealism."

Over the next two decades, Zindel not only continued writing young adult fiction and plays—although none as highly successful as *Gamma Rays* —but also screenplays. He adapted his own words, such as *Gamma Rays*, as well as those of others, including Patrick Dennis's *Mame* and a children's favorite fairytale, *Alice in Wonderland*. However, it was Zindel's young adult fiction books which became the most popular.

Writing For Teenagers

Throughout the 1970s and 1980s, Zindel continued writing books for teenagers. He commented to *Publishers Weekly*, "teenagers *have* to rebel. It's part of the growing process. In effect . . . I believe I must convince my readers that I am on their side." However, book reviewers Beverly A. Haley and Kenneth L. Donelson, as stated in *Elementary English*, suggested that Zindel not only convinced teenagers that he was on their side, but also presented "questions to his readers, and if they care (and they do), they will search for answers. Their *own* answers." And teenagers, along with Zindel's characters did search for answers—answers to questions about lust, sex, contraception, and abortion in *My Darling, My Hamburger* (1969); about what is true love in *I Never Loved Your Mind* (1970); parental pressure and friendship come under discussion in *Pardon Me, You're Stepping on My Eyeball!* (1976); and truth and the perception of truth in *The Undertaker's Gone Bananas* (1978). A collaboration with his wife, Bonnie Hildebrand whom he had married in 1973, produced *A Star for the Latecomer* in 1980. In that same year, Zindel published a sequel to his most popular book *The Pigman. The Pigman's Legacy* returned readers to Mr. Pignati's house where John and Lorraine have a second chance to do the right thing and help another elderly man, Gus, live out his final days. However, this was not Zindel's final tale about a "Pigman."

In 1991, Zindel wrote about his only year of normalcy as a teenager. In *The Pigman and Me,* he introduced the book by telling readers, "because this is an autobiography I have to really tell the truth." He revealed his nightmares about cockroaches and his wish to be Batman in the volume. He also shared his belief that "in this world it doesn't seem to matter if you know anything as long as you pretend to know it." However, someone changed Zindel's belief—his "Pigman". And a Pigman, Zindel told readers, will come "when you need him most. He'll make you cry, but teach you the greatest secret of life." Zindel's Pigman was Nonno Frankie, the Italian father of his mother's housemate. Zindel claimed in *The Pigman and Me* that Frankie "understood I had a slightly wacko person for a Mom." He also told Zindel silly jokes like, "What is a ghost's favorite food? *Spookghetti.*" Zindel remembered, "[w]hen I think now what it was like for me when I was a teenager, I have to admit that deep inside, my greatest need was to find a meaning to my life. Without meaning I suppose most everybody might as well be dead." Frankie not only helped Zindel with this, but also taught him how to plant a garden and fight. Yet, perhaps the best two pieces of advice Zindel received from Frankie, as quoted in *The Pigman and Me,* were The Rules of School: "when in doubt, a closed mouth gathers no fat! And never get into rock fights with kids who have ugly faces, because they have nothing to lose! And never, *never* play leapfrog with a unicorn!" and "You can go anywhere in your mind. You must *imagine.*"

Zindel's works in the 1990s have stretched his talents even more. In 1993, he published several children's books, including *Fright Party, David and Della,* and *Attack of the Killer.* That same year, he also released *The Fifth-Grade Safari.* Returning to his young adult audience, Zindel published *Loch* in 1994 and *The Doom Stone* the following year.

Over the past 30 years, Zindel has followed his Pigman's advice. From stage and screen plays to young adult fiction books, he has used his imagination and shared his real-life adventures. As he noted in *The Pigman and Me,* "truth *is* stranger than fiction. I think it's often a lot more cruel." However, Zindel has also shown teenagers through his stories that their lives do have worth. As quoted in the New York *Daily News,* worth was something Zindel realized through his writing: "I felt worthless as a kid, and dared to speak and act my true feelings only in fantasy and secret. That's probably what made me a writer."

Further Reading

Contemporary Authors, Volume 31, Gale, 1990.
Contemporary Literary Criticism, Volume 26, Gale, 1983.
Dictionary of Literary Biography, Volume 7: Twentieth-Century American Dramatists Part 2: K-Z, Gale, 1981.
Zindel, Paul, *The Pigman,* Bantam Books, 1968.
Zindel, Paul, *The Effect of Gamma Rays on Man-in-the-Moon Marigolds,* Harper, 1971.
Zindel, Paul, *The Pigman's Legacy,* Bantam Books, 1980.
Zindel, Paul, *The Pigman and Me,* Bantam Books, 1991.
Daily News (New York), March 9, 1978.
Elementary English, October 1974.
English Journal, October 1977.
Horn Book, February 1969, p.61.
Morning Telegraph, July 30, 1970.
Publishers Weekly, December 5, 1977; October 25, 1993, p. 64; October 17, 1994, p. 82; December 4, 1995, p. 63.
Scholastic Voice, April 27, 1970, p. 5.
Teaching PreK-8, November 1994.
Time, May 17, 1971, p. 66.

INDEX

HOW TO USE THE *SUPPLEMENT* INDEX

The *Encyclopedia of World Biography Supplement* Index is designed to serve several purposes. First, it is a cumulative listing of biographies included in the entire encyclopedia (volumes 1-18). Second, it locates information on thousands of specific topics mentioned in volume 18 of the encyclopedia—persons, places, events, organizations, institutions, ideas, titles of works, inventions, and schools, styles, and movements in an art or a field of knowledge. Third, it classifies the subjects of *Supplement* articles according to shared characteristics. Vocational categories are the most numerous—for example, Artists, Authors, Military leaders, Scientists, Statesmen. But there are other groupings, besides the vocational, bringing together disparate people who share a common characteristic.

The structure of the *Supplement* Index is quite simple. The biographical entries are cumulative and often provide enough information to meet immediate reference needs. Thus, people mentioned in the *Supplement* Index are identified and their life dates, when known, are given. Because this is an index to a *biographical* encyclopedia, every reference includes the *name* of the article to which the reader is directed as well as the volume and page numbers. Below are a few points that will make the *Supplement* Index easy to use.

Typography. All main entries are set in boldface type. Entries that are also the titles of articles in *EWB* are set entirely in capitals; other main entries are set in initial capitals and lowercase letters. Where a main entry is followed by a great many references, these are organized by subentries in alphabetical sequence. In certain cases—for example, the names of countries for which there are many references—a special class of subentries, set in small capitals and preceded by boldface dots, is used to mark significant divisions.

Alphabetization. The Index is alphabetized word by word. For example, all entries beginning with *New* as a separate word (*New Jersey, New York*) come before *Newark.* Commas in inverted entries are treated as full

stops (*Berlin; Berlin, congress of; Berlin, University of; Berlin Academy of Sciences*). Other commas are ignored in filing. When file words are identical, persons come first and subsequent entries are alphabetized by their parenthetical qualifiers (such as *book, city, painting*).

Titled persons may be alphabetized by family name or by title. The more familiar form is used—for example, *Disraeli, Benjamin* rather than *Wellesley, Arthur.* Cross-references are provided from alternative forms and spellings of names. Identical names of the same nationality are filed chronologically.

Titles of books, plays, and poems, and of paintings and other works of art beginning with an article are filed on the following word (*Bard, The*). Titles beginning with a preposition are filed on the preposition (*In Autumn*). In subentries, however, prepositions are ignored; thus *influenced by* would precede the subentry *in* literature.

Literary characters are filed on the last name. Acronyms, such as UNESCO, are treated as single words. Abbreviations, such as *Mr., Mrs.,* and *St.,* are alphabetized as though they were spelled out.

Occupational categories are alphabetical by national qualifier. Thus, *Authors, Scottish* comes before *Authors, Spanish,* and the reader interested in Spanish poets will find the subentry *poets* under *Authors, Spanish.*

Cross-references. The term *see* is used in references throughout the *Supplement* Index. The *see* references appear both as main entries and as subentries. They most often direct the reader from an alternative name spelling or form to the main entry listing.

This introduction to the *Supplement* Index is necessarily brief. The reader will soon find, however, that the *Supplement* Index provides ready reference to both highly specific subjects and broad areas of information contained in volume 18 and a cumulative listing of those included in *EWB*.

429

INDEX

A

AALTO, HUGO ALVAR HENRIK (born 1898), Finnish architect, designer, and town planner **1** 1–2

AARON, HENRY LOUIS (Hank; born 1934), American baseball player **1** 2–3

Abarbanel
see Abravanel

ABBA ARIKA (circa 175-circa 247), Babylonian rabbi **1** 3–4

ABBAS I (1571–1629), Safavid shah of Persia 1588–1629 **1** 4–6

ABBAS, FERHAT (born 1899), Algerian statesman **1** 6–7

ABBOTT, BERENICE (1898–1991), American artist and photographer **1** 7–9

ABBOTT, GRACE (1878–1939), American social worker and agency administrator **1** 9–10

ABBOTT, LYMAN (1835–1922), American Congregationalist clergyman, author, and editor **1** 10–11

ABBOUD, EL FERIK IBRAHIM (1900–1983), Sudanese general, prime minister, 1958–1964 **1** 11–12

ABD AL-MALIK (646–705), Umayyad caliph 685–705 **1** 12–13

ABD AL-MUMIN (circa 1094–1163), Almohad caliph 1133–63 **1** 13

ABD AL-RAHMAN I (731–788), Umayyad emir in Spain 756–88 **1** 13–14

ABD AL-RAHMAN III (891–961), Umayyad caliph of Spain **1** 14

ABD EL-KADIR (1807–1883), Algerian political and religious leader **1** 15

ABD EL-KRIM EL-KHATABI, MOHAMED BEN (circa 1882–1963), Moroccan Berber leader **1** 15–16

ABDUH IBN HASAN KHAYR ALLAH, MUHAMMAD (1849–1905), Egyptian nationalist and theologian **1** 16–17

ABDUL-HAMID II (1842–1918), Ottoman sultan 1876–1909 **1** 17–18

'ABDULLAH AL-SALIM AL-SABAH, SHAYKH (1895–1965), Amir of Kuwait (1950–1965) **1** 18–19

ABDULLAH IBN HUSEIN (1882–1951), king of Jordan 1949–1951, of Transjordan 1946–49 **1** 19–20

ABDULLAH IBN YASIN (died 1059), North African founder of the Almoravid movement **1** 20

ABE, KOBO (born Kimifusa Abe; also transliterated as Abe Kobo; 1924–1993), Japanese writer, theater director, photographer **1** 20–22

ABEL, IORWITH WILBER (1908–1987), United States labor organizer **1** 22–23

ABELARD, PETER (1079–1142), French philosopher and theologian **1** 23–25

ABERDEEN, 4TH EARL OF (George Hamilton Gordon; 1784–1860), British statesman, prime minister 1852–55 **1** 25–26

ABERHART, WILLIAM (1878–1943), Canadian statesman and educator **1** 26–27

ABERNATHY, RALPH DAVID (born 1926), United States minister and civil rights leader **1** 27–28

Abolitionists, American
African Americans
Harper, Frances **18** 185–187

ABRAHAMS, ISRAEL (1858–1925), British scholar **1** 29

ABRAMOVITZ, MAX (born 1908), American architect **18** 1–3

ABRAMS, CREIGHTON W. (1914–1974), United States Army commander in World War II and Vietnam **1** 29–31

ABRAVANEL, ISAAC BEN JUDAH (1437–1508), Jewish philosopher and statesman **1** 31

ABU BAKR (circa 573–634), Moslem leader, first caliph of Islam **1** 31–32

ABU MUSA (born Said Musa Maragha circa 1930), a leader of the Palestinian Liberation Organization **1** 32–33

ABU NUWAS (al-Hasan ibn-Hani; circa 756–813), Arab poet **1** 33–34

ABU-L-ALA AL-MAARRI (973–1058), Arab poet and philosopher **1** 32

ABZUG, BELLA STAVISKY (born 1920), lawyer, politician, and congresswoman **1** 34–35

ACHEBE, CHINUA (born 1930), Nigerian novelist **1** 35–37

ACHESON, DEAN GOODERHAM (1893–1971), American statesman **1** 37–38

ACTION, JOHN EMERICH EDWARD DALBERG (1834–1902), English historian and philosopher **1** 38

Activists
Australian
Caldicott, Helen Broinowski **18** 71–73
Chinese
Wei Jingsheng **18** 410–412
Kenyan
Maathai, Wangari Muta **18** 269–271

Activists, American
AIDS
Sarandon, Susan **18** 358–360
Asian American issues
Pran, Dith **18** 328–331

AGA KHAN (title), chief commander of Moslem Nizari Ismailis **1** 74–76

AGASSIZ, JEAN LOUIS RODOLPHE (1807–1873), Swiss-American naturalist and anatomist **1** 76–78

AGEE, JAMES (1909–1955), American poet, journalist, novelist, and screenwriter **1** 78–79

AGESILAUS II (circa 444–360 B.C.), king of Sparta circa 399–360 B.C. **1** 79–80

AGHA MOHAMMAD KHAN (circa 1742–1797), shah of Persia **1** 80–81

AGIS IV (circa 262–241 B.C.), king of Sparta **1** 81–82

AGNELLI, GIOVANNI (born 1920), Italian industrialist **1** 82–83

AGNEW, SPIRO THEODORE (1918–1996), Republican United States vice president under Richard Nixon **1** 83–85

AGNON, SHMUEL YOSEPH (1888–1970), author **1** 85–86

AGOSTINO (1557–1602) **1** 86

AGOSTINO DI DUCCIO (1418–1481?), Italian sculptor **1** 86

Agricola
see Crèvecoeur, St. J.

AGRICOLA, GEORGIUS (1494–1555), German mineralogist and writer **1** 86–87

Agriculture (United States)
unions
Huerta, Dolores **18** 204–207

AGUINALDO, EMILIO (1869–1964), Philippine revolutionary leader **1** 88

Agustin I
see Iturbide, Augustin de

AHAD HAAM (pseudonym of Asher T. Ginsberg, 1856–1927), Russian-born author **1** 88–89

AHERN, BERTIE (Bartholomew Ahern; born 1951), Irish Prime Minister **18** 11–13

AHIDJO, AHMADOU (1924–1989), first president of the Federal Republic of Cameroon **1** 89–90

AIKEN, CONRAD (1889–1973), American poet, essayist, novelist, and critic **1** 90–91

AILEY, ALVIN (1931–1989), African American dancer and choreographer **1** 91–94

AILLY, PIERRE D' (1350–1420), French scholar and cardinal **1** 94

AITKEN, WILLIAM MAXWELL (Lord Beaverbrook; 1879–1964), Canadian businessman and politician **1** 94–96

AKBAR, JALAL-UD-DIN MOHAMMED (1542–1605), Mogul emperor of India 1556–1605 **1** 96

AKHMATOVA, ANNA (pseudonym of Anna A. Gorenko, 1889–1966), Russian poet **1** 96–97

AKIBA BEN JOSEPH (circa 50-circa 135), Palestinian founder of rabbinic Judaism **1** 97–98

AKIHITO (born 1933), 125th emperor of Japan **1** 98–99

ALAMÁN, LUCAS (1792–1853), Mexican statesman **1** 99–100

ALARCÓN, PEDRO ANTONIO DE (1833–1891), Spanish writer and politician **1** 100–101

ALARCÓN Y MENDOZA, JUAN RUIZ DE (1581?-1639), Spanish playwright **1** 101

ALARIC (circa 370–410), Visigothic leader **1** 101–102

ALA-UD-DIN (died 1316), Khalji sultan of Delhi **1** 102–103

ALAUNGPAYA (1715–1760), king of Burma 1752–1760 **1** 103

ALBA, DUKE OF (Fernando Álvarez de Toledo; 1507–1582), Spanish general and statesman **1** 103–104

AL-BANNA, HASSAN (1906–1949), Egyptian religious leader and founder of the Muslim Brotherhood **1** 104–106

ALBEE, EDWARD FRANKLIN, III (born 1928), American playwright **1** 106–108

Albemarle, Dukes of
see Monck, George

ALBÉNIZ, ISAAC (1860–1909), Spanish composer and pianist **1** 108–109

ALBERDI, JUAN BAUTISTA (1810–1884), Argentine political theorist **1** 109–110

ALBERS, JOSEPH (1888–1976), American artist and art and design teacher **1** 110

ALBERT (1819–1861), Prince Consort of Great Britain **1** 110–112

ALBERT I (1875–1934), king of the Belgians 1909–1934 **1** 112

ALBERT II (born 1934), sixth king of the Belgians **1** 112–113

ALBERTI, LEON BATTISTA (1404–1472), Italian writer, humanist, and architect **1** 113–115

ALBERTI, RAFAEL (born 1902), Spanish poet and painter **18** 13–15

ALBERTUS MAGNUS, ST. (circa 1193–1280), German philosopher and theologian **1** 115–116

ALBRIGHT, MADELEINE KORBEL (born 1937), United States secretary of state **1** 116–118

ALBUQUERQUE, AFONSO DE (circa 1460–1515), Portuguese viceroy to India **1** 118–119

ALCIBIADES (circa 450–404 B.C.), Athenian general and politician **1** 119–120

ALCORN, JAMES LUSK (1816–1894), American lawyer and politician **1** 120–121

ALCOTT, AMOS BRONSON (1799–1888), American educator **1** 121

ALCOTT, LOUISA MAY (1832–1888), American author and reformer **1** 122

ALCUIN OF YORK (730?-804), English educator, statesman, and liturgist **1** 122–123

ALDRICH, NELSON WILMARTH (1841–1915), American statesman and financier **1** 123–124

Aldrin, Buzz
see Aldrin, Edwin Eugene, Jr.

ALDRIN, EDWIN EUGENE, JR. (Buzz Aldrin; born 1930), American astronaut **18** 15–17

ALEICHEM, SHOLOM (Sholom Rabinowitz; 1859–1916), writer of literature relating to Russian Jews **1** 124–125

ALEIJADINHO, O (Antônio Francisco Lisbôa; 1738–1814), Brazilian architect and sculptor **1** 125–126

ALEMÁN, MATEO (1547-after 1615), Spanish novelist **1** 126

ALEMÁN VALDÉS, MIGUEL
(1902–1983), Mexican statesman,
president 1946–1952 **1** 126–127

ALEMBERT, JEAN LE ROND D'
(1717–1783), French mathematician
and physicist **1** 127–128

ALESSANDRI PALMA, ARTURO
(1868–1950), Chilean statesman,
president 1920–1925 and 1932–1938
1 128–129

ALESSANDRI RODRIGUEZ, JORGE
(born 1896), Chilean statesman,
president 1958–1964 **1** 129–130

ALEXANDER I (1777–1825), czar of
Russia 1801–1825 **1** 130–132

ALEXANDER II (1818–1881), czar of
Russia 1855–1881 **1** 132–133

ALEXANDER III (1845–1894), emperor
of Russia 1881–1894 **1** 133–134

ALEXANDER VI (Rodrigo Borgia;
1431–1503), pope 1492–1503 **1**
134–135

ALEXANDER, SAMUEL (1859–1938),
British philosopher **1** 141

ALEXANDER OF TUNIS, 1ST EARL
(Harold Rupert Leofric George
Alexander; born 1891), British field
marshal **1** 135–136

ALEXANDER OF YUGOSLAVIA
(1888–1934), king of the Serbs,
Croats, and Slovenes 1921–1929 and
of Yugoslavia, 1929–1934 **1** 136–137

ALEXANDER THE GREAT (356–323
B.C.), king of Macedon **1** 137–141

ALEXIE, SHERMAN (born 1966), Native
American writer, poet, and translator
1 141–142

ALEXIS MIKHAILOVICH ROMANOV
(1629–1676), czar of Russia
1645–1676 **1** 142–143

ALEXIUS I (circa 1048–1118), Byzantine
emperor 1081–1118 **1** 143–144

ALFARO, JOSÉ ELOY (1842–1912),
Ecuadorian revolutionary, president
1895–1901 and 1906–1911 **1**
144–145

ALFIERI, CONTE VITTORIA
(1749–1803), Italian playwright **1**
145–146

ALFONSÍN, RAUL RICARDO (born
1927), politician and president of
Argentina (1983-) **1** 146–148

ALFONSO I (Henriques; 1109?-1185),
king of Portugal 1139–1185 **1** 148

Alfonso I, king of Castile
see Alfonso VI, king of León

ALFONSO III (1210–1279), king of
Portugal 1248–1279 **1** 148–149

ALFONSO VI (1040–1109), king of
León, 1065–1109, and of Castile,
1072–1109 **1** 149

ALFONSO X (1221–1284), king of
Castile and León 1252–1284 **1**
150–151

ALFONSO XIII (1886–1941), king of
Spain 1886–1931 **1** 151

Alfonso the African
see Alfonso V, king of Portugal

Alfonso the Wise
see Alfonso X, king of Castile and
León

ALFRED (849–899), Anglo-Saxon king of
Wessex 871–899 **1** 151–153

Alfred the Great
see Alfred, king of Wessex

ALGER, HORATIO (1832–1899),
American author **1** 153–154

ALGREN, NELSON (Abraham;
1909–1981), American author **1**
154–155

Alhazen
see Hassan ibn al-Haytham

ALI (circa 600–661), fourth caliph of the
Islamic Empire **1** 155–156

ALI, MUHAMMAD (Cassius Clay; born
1942), American boxer **1** 156–158

Ali Shah (died 1885)
see Aga Khan II

ALI, SUNNI (died 1492), king of Gao,
founder of the Songhay empire **1**
158–159

ALIA, RAMIZ (born 1925), president of
Albania (1985-) **1** 159

ALINSKY, SAUL DAVID (1909–1972),
U.S. organizer of neighborhood
citizen reform groups **1** 161–162

ALLAL AL-FASSI, MOHAMED
(1910–1974), Moroccan nationalist
leader **1** 162

ALLEN, ETHAN (1738–1789), American
Revolutionary War soldier **1** 163–164

ALLEN, FLORENCE ELLINWOOD
(1884–1966), American lawyer, judge,
and women's rights activist **1**
164–165

ALLEN, PAULA GUNN (born 1939),
Native American writer, poet, literary
critic; women's rights, environmental,
and antiwar activist **1** 165–167

ALLEN, RICHARD (1760–1831), African
American bishop **1** 168

ALLEN, WOODY (born Allen Stewart
Konigsberg; b. 1935), American actor,
director, filmmaker, author, comedian
1 169–171

ALLENBY, EDMUND HENRY HYNMAN
(1861–1936), English field marshal **1**
171–172

ALLENDE, ISABEL (born 1942), Chilean
novelist, journalist, dramatist **1**
172–174

ALLENDE GOSSENS, SALVADOR
(1908–1973), socialist president of
Chile (1970–1973) **1** 174–176

ALLSTON, WASHINGTON
(1779–1843), American painter **1**
176–177

ALMAGRO, DIEGO DE (circa
1474–1538), Spanish conquistador
and explorer **1** 177–178

ALP ARSLAN (1026/32–1072), Seljuk
sultan of Persia and Iraq **1** 178–179

Alpetragius
see Bitruji, Nur al-Din Abu Ishaq al-

Alphonse the Wise
see Alfonso X, king of Castile

ALTAMIRA Y CREVEA, RAFAEL
(1866–1951), Spanish critic, historian,
and jurist **1** 179

ALTDORFER, ALBRECHT (circa
1480–1538), German painter,
printmaker, and architect **1** 179–180

ALTGELD, JOHN PETER (1847–1902),
American jurist and politician **1**
180–182

ALTHUSSER, LOUIS (1918–1990),
French Communist philosopher **1**
182–183

ALTIZER, THOMAS J. J. (born 1927),
American theologian **1** 183–184

ÁLVAREZ, JUAN (1780–1867), Mexican
soldier and statesman, president 1855
1 184–185

ALVAREZ, JULIA (born 1950), Hispanic
American novelist, poet **1** 185–187

ALVAREZ, LUIS W. (1911–1988),
American physicist **1** 187–189

AMADO, JORGE (born 1912), Brazilian
novelist **1** 189–190

AMBEDKAR, BHIMRAO RAMJI
(1891–1956), Indian social reformer
and politician **1** 190–191

AMBLER, ERIC (born 1909), English
novelist **1** 191–192

AMBROSE, ST. (339–397), Italian bishop
1 192–193

BEATRIX, WILHELMINA VON AMSBERG, QUEEN (born 1938), queen of Netherlands (1980-) **2** 92–93

Beauchamp
see Warwick, Earl of

BEAUMARCHAIS, PIERRE AUGUST CARON DE (1732–1799), French playwright **2** 93–94

BEAUMONT, FRANCIS (1584/1585–1616), English playwright **2** 95

BEAUMONT, WILLIAM (1785–1853), American surgeon **2** 95–96

BEAUREGARD, PIERRE GUSTAVE TOUTANT (1818–1893), Confederate general **2** 96–97

BECARRIA, MARCHESE DI (1738–1794), Italian jurist and economist **2** 97–98

BECHTEL, STEPHEN DAVISON (1900–1989), American construction engineer and business executive **2** 98–99

BECK, LUDWIG AUGUST THEODOR (1880–1944), German general **2** 99–100

BECKER, CARL LOTUS (1873–1945), American historian **2** 100–101

BECKET, ST. THOMAS (1128?-1170), English prelate **2** 101–102

BECKETT, SAMUEL (1906–1989), Irish novelist, playwright, and poet **2** 102–104

BECKMANN, MAX (1884–1950), German painter **2** 104–105

BECKNELL, WILLIAM (circa 1797–1865), American soldier and politician **2** 105–106

BECKWOURTH, JIM (James P. Beckwourth; c. 1800–1866), African American fur trapper and explorer **2** 106–107

BÉCQUER, GUSTAVO ADOLFO DOMINGUEZ (1836–1870), Spanish lyric poet **2** 107–108

BECQUEREL, ANTOINE HENRI (1852–1908), French physicist **2** 108–109

BEDE, ST. (672/673–735), English theologian **2** 109–110

BEDELL SMITH, WALTER (1895–1961), U.S. Army general, ambassador, and CIA director **18** 30–33

BEECHER, CATHARINE (1800–1878), American author and educator **2** 110–112

BEECHER, HENRY WARD (1813–1887), American Congregationalist clergyman **2** 112–113

BEECHER, LYMAN (1775–1863), Presbyterian clergyman **2** 113

BEETHOVEN, LUDWIG VAN (1770–1827), German composer **2** 114–117

BEGAY, HARRISON (born 1917), Native American artist **2** 117–118

BEGIN, MENACHEM (1913–1992), Israel's first non-Socialist prime minister (1977–1983) **2** 118–120

BEHN, APHRA (1640?-1689), British author **18** 33–34

BEHRENS, HILDEGARD (born 1937), German soprano **2** 120–121

BEHRENS, PETER (1868–1940), German architect, painter, and designer **2** 121–122

BEHRING, EMIL ADOLPH VON (1854–1917), German hygienist and physician **2** 122–123

BEHZAD (died circa 1530), Persian painter **2** 123

BEISSEL, JOHANN CONRAD (1690–1768), German-American pietist **2** 123–124

BELASCO, DAVID (1853–1931), American playwright and director-producer **2** 124–125

BELAÚNDE TERRY, FERNANDO (born 1912), president of Peru (1963–1968, 1980–1985) **2** 125–126

BELGRANO, MANUEL (1770–1820), Argentine general and politician **2** 126–127

BELINSKY, GRIGORIEVICH (1811–1848), Russian literary critic **2** 128

BELISARIUS (circa 506–565), Byzantine general **2** 128–129

BELL, ALEXANDER GRAHAM (1847–1922), Scottish-born American inventor **2** 129–131

BELL, ANDREW (1753–1832), Scottish educator **2** 131–132

BELL, DANIEL (Bolotsky; born 1919), American sociologist **2** 132–133

BELL BURNELL, SUSAN JOCELYN (born 1943), English radio astronomer **2** 133–134

BELLAMY, EDWARD (1850–1898), American novelist, propagandist, and reformer **2** 134–135

BELLARMINE, ST. ROBERT (1542–1621), Italian theologian and cardinal **2** 135–136

BELLECOURT, CLYDE (born 1939), Native American activist **2** 136–137

BELLINI, GIOVANNI (circa 1435–1516), Itlalian painter **2** 137–138

BELLINI, VINCENZO (1801–1835), Italian composer **2** 138–139

BELLO, ALHAJI SIR AHMADU (1909–1966), Nigerian politician **2** 139–140

BELLO Y LÓPEZ, ANDRÉS (1781–1865), Venezuelan humanist **2** 140–141

BELLOC, JOSEPH HILAIRE PIERRE (1870–1953), French-born English author and historian **2** 141

BELLOW, SAUL (born 1915), American novelist and Nobel Prize winner **2** 141–143

BELLOWS, GEORGE WESLEY (1882–1925), American painter **2** 143

BELLOWS, HENRY WHITNEY (1814–1882), American Unitarian minister **2** 143–144

BEMBO, PIETRO (1470–1547), Italian humanist, poet, and historian **2** 144–145

BEN AND JERRY ice cream company founders **18** 35–37

BEN BADIS, ABD AL-HAMID (1889–1940), leader of the Islamic Reform Movement in Algeria between the two world wars **2** 147–148

BEN BELLA, AHMED (born 1918), first president of the Algerian Republic **2** 148–149

BEN-GURION, DAVID (born 1886), Russian-born Israeli statesman **2** 160–161

BEN-HAIM, PAUL (Frankenburger; 1897–1984), Israeli composer **2** 161–162

BEN YEHUDA, ELIEZER (1858–1922), Hebrew lexicographer and editor **2** 181–182

BENALCÁZAR, SEBASTIÁN DE (died 1551), Spanish conquistador **2** 145–146

BENAVENTE Y MARTINEZ, JACINTO (1866–1954), Spanish dramatist **2** 146–147

BENCHLEY, ROBERT (1889–1945), American humorist **2** 150–151

BENDA, JULIEN (1867–1956), French cultural critic and novelist **2** 151–152

Bradby, Lucy Barbara
see Hammond, John and Lucy

BRADDOCK, EDWARD (1695–1755), British commander in North America **2** 474–475

BRADFORD, WILLIAM (1590–1657), leader of Plymouth Colony **2** 475–476

BRADFORD, WILLIAM (1663–1752), American printer **2** 476–477

BRADFORD, WILLIAM (1722–1791), American journalist **2** 477

BRADLAUGH, CHARLES (1833–1891), English freethinker and political agitator **2** 478

BRADLEY, ED (born 1941), African American broadcast journalist **2** 478–481

BRADLEY, FRANCIS HERBERT (1846–1924), English philosopher **2** 481–482

BRADLEY, JAMES (1693–1762), English astronomer **2** 482–483

BRADLEY, MARION ZIMMER (born 1930), American author **18** 60–62

BRADLEY, OMAR NELSON (1893–1981), American general **2** 483–484

BRADLEY, TOM (born 1917), first African American mayor of Los Angeles **2** 484–485

BRADMAN, SIR DONALD GEORGE (born 1908), Australian cricketer **2** 485–486

BRADSTREET, ANNE DUDLEY (circa 1612–1672), English-born American poet **2** 486–487

BRADY, MATHEW B. (circa 1823–1896), American photographer **2** 487–488

BRAGG, SIR WILLIAM HENRY (1862–1942), English physicist **2** 488–489

BRAHE, TYCHO (1546–1601), Danish astronomer **2** 489–490

BRAHMS, JOHANNES (1833–1897), German composer **2** 490–492

BRAILLE, LOUIS (1809–1852), French teacher and creator of braille system **2** 492–493

BRAMANTE, DONATO (1444–1514), Italian architect and painter **2** 493–494

BRANCUSI, CONSTANTIN (1876–1957), Romanian sculptor in France **2** 494–496

BRANDEIS, LOUIS DEMBITZ (1856–1941), American jurist **2** 496–497

BRANDO, MARLON (born 1924), American actor **2** 497–499

BRANDT, WILLY (Herbert Frahm Brandt; 1913–1992), German statesman, chancellor of West Germany **2** 499–500

BRANT, JOSEPH (1742–1807), Mohawk Indian chief **2** 500–501

BRANT, MARY (1736–1796), Native American who guided the Iroquois to a British alliance **2** 501–503

BRANT, SEBASTIAN (1457–1521), German author **2** 503–504

BRAQUE, GEORGES (1882–1967), French painter **2** 504–505

BRATTAIN, WALTER H. (1902–1987), American physicist and co-inventor of the transistor **2** 505–507

BRAUDEL, FERNAND (1902–1985), leading exponent of the *Annales* school of history **2** 507–508

BRAUN, FERDINAND (1850–1918), German recipient of the Nobel Prize in Physics for work on wireless telegraphy **2** 508–509

Brazil, Federative Republic of (nation; South America)
1960s
Costa e Silva, Artur da **18** 104–107
economic development
Campos, Roberto **18** 77–79
economic reform
Cardoso, Fernando Henrique **18** 81–83

BRAZZA, PIERRE PAUL FRANÇOIS CAMILLE SAVORGNAN DE (1852–1905), Italian-born French explorer **2** 509–510

BREASTED, JAMES HENRY (1865–1935), American Egyptologist and archeologist **2** 510–511

BRÉBEUF, JEAN DE (1593–1649), French Jesuit missionary **2** 511–512

BRECHT, BERTOLT (1898–1956), German playwright **2** 512–514

BRENNAN, WILLIAM J., JR. (born 1906), United States Supreme Court justice **2** 514–515

BRENTANO, CLEMENS (1778–1842), German poet and novelist **2** 515–516

BRENTANO, FRANZ CLEMENS (1838–1917), German philosopher **2** 516–517

BRESHKOVSKY, CATHERINE (1844–1934), Russian revolutionary **2** 517–519

BRETON, ANDRÉ (1896–1966), French author **2** 519–520

BREUER, MARCEL (1902–1981), Hungarian-born American architect **2** 520–521

Breughel
see Bruegel

BREUIL, HENRI EDOUARD PROSPER (1877–1961), French archeologist **2** 521–522

BREWSTER, KINGMAN, JR. (1919–1988), president of Yale University (1963–1977) **2** 522–523

BREWSTER, WILLIAM (circa 1566–1644), English-born Pilgrim leader **2** 523–524

BREYER, STEPHEN (born 1938), U.S. Supreme Court justice **2** 524–527

BREZHNEV, LEONID ILICH (1906–1982), general secretary of the Communist party of the Union of Soviet Socialist Republics (1964–1982) and president of the Union of Soviet Socialist Republics (1977–1982) **2** 527–528

BRIAN BORU (940?-1014), Irish king **18** 62–64

BRIAND, ARISTIDE (1862–1932), French statesman **2** 528–529

BRICE, FANNY (1891–1951), vaudeville, Broadway, film, and radio singer and comedienne **3** 1–2

BRIDGER, JAMES (1804–1881), American fur trader and scout **3** 2–3

BRIDGES, HARRY A.R. (1901–1990), radical American labor leader **3** 3–5

BRIDGMAN, PERCY WILLIAMS (1882–1961), American physicist **3** 5–6

BRIGHT, JOHN (1811–1889), English politician **3** 6–7

BRIGHT, RICHARD (1789–1858), English physician **3** 7–8

BRIGHTMAN, EDGAR SHEFFIELD (1884–1953), philosopher of religion and exponent of American Personalism **3** 8–9

BRISBANE, ALBERT (1809–1890), American social theorist **3** 9

BRISTOW, BENJAMIN HELM (1832–1896), American lawyer and Federal official **3** 9–10

British Broadcasting Corp.
Davies, Rupert **18** 116–117

BRUTUS, MARCUS JUNIUS (circa 85–42 B.C.), Roman statesman **3** 79–80

BRYAN, WILLIAM JENNINGS (1860–1925), American lawyer and politician **3** 80–82

BRYANT, PAUL ("Bear;" 1919–1983), American college football coach **3** 82–83

BRYANT, WILLIAM CULLEN (1794–1878), American poet and editor **3** 83–85

BRYCE, JAMES (1838–1922), British historian, jurist, and statesman **3** 85

BRZEZINSKI, ZBIGNIEW (1928–1980), assistant to President Carter for national security affairs (1977–1980) **3** 85–87

BUBER, MARTIN (1878–1965), Austrian-born Jewish theologian and philosopher **3** 87–89

Buccleugh
see Monmouth and Buccleugh Duke of

BUCHANAN, JAMES (1791–1868), American statesman, president 1857–1861 **3** 89–90

BUCHANAN, PATRICK JOSEPH (born 1938), commentator, journalist, and presidential candidate **3** 90–91

BUCK, PEARL SYDENSTRICKER (1892–1973), American novelist **3** 91–93

BUCKINGHAM, 1ST DUKE OF (George Villiers; 1592–1628), English courtier and military leader **3** 93–94

BUCKINGHAM, 2D DUKE OF (George Villiers; 1628–1687), English statesman **3** 94–95

BUCKLE, HENRY THOMAS (1821–1862), English historian **3** 95–96

BUCKLEY, WILLIAM F., JR. (born 1925), conservative American author, editor, and political activist **3** 96–97

BUDDHA (circa 560–480 B.C.), Indian founder of Buddhism **3** 97–101

BUDDHADĀSA BHIKKHU (Nguam Phanich; born 1906), founder of Wat Suan Mokkhabalārama in southern Thailand and interpreter of Theravāda Buddhism **3** 101–102

BUDÉ, GUILLAUME (1467–1540), French humanist **3** 102–103

BUECHNER, FREDERICK (born 1926), American novelist and theologian **3** 103–105

BUEL, JESSE (1778–1839), American agriculturalist and journalist **3** 105

BUFFALO BILL (William Frederick Cody; 1846–1917), American scout and publicist **3** 105–106

BUFFETT, WARREN (born 1930), American investment salesman **3** 106–109

BUFFON, COMTE DE (Georges Louis Leclerc; 1707–1788), French naturalist **3** 109–111

BUGEAUD DE LA PICONNERIE, THOMAS ROBERT (1784–1849), Duke of Isly and marshal of France **3** 111

BUKHARI, MUHAMMAD IBN ISMAIL AL- (810–870), Arab scholar and Moslem saint **3** 111–112

BUKHARIN, NIKOLAI IVANOVICH (1858–1938), Russian politician **3** 112–113

BUKOWSKI, CHARLES (1920–1994), American writer and poet **3** 113–115

BULATOVIC, MOMIR (born 1956), president of Montenegro (1990–1992) and of the new Federal Republic of Yugoslavia (1992-) **3** 115–116

BULFINCH, CHARLES (1763–1844), American colonial architect **3** 116–117

BULGAKOV, MIKHAIL AFANASIEVICH (1891–1940), Russian novelist and playwright **3** 117

BULGANIN, NIKOLAI (1885–1975), chairman of the Soviet Council of Ministers (1955–1958) **3** 118–119

BULTMANN, RUDOLF KARL (1884–1976), German theologian **3** 119–120

BUNAU-VARILLA, PHILIPPE JEAN (1859–1940), French engineer and soldier **3** 120–121

BUNCHE, RALPH JOHNSON (1904–1971), African American diplomat **3** 121–122

BUNDY, McGEORGE (born 1919), national security adviser to two presidents **3** 122–124

BUNIN, IVAN ALEKSEEVICH (1870–1953), Russian poet and novelist **3** 124

BUNSEN, ROBERT WILHELM (1811–1899), German chemist and physicist **3** 124–125

BUNSHAFT, GORDON (1909–1990), American architect **3** 125–127

BUÑUEL, LUIS (1900–1983), Spanish film director **3** 127–128

BUNYAN, JOHN (1628–1688), English author and Baptist preacher **3** 128–129

BURBANK, LUTHER (1849–1926), American plant breeder **3** 129–131

BURCHFIELD, CHARLES (1893–1967), American painter **3** 131–132

BURCKHARDT, JACOB CHRISTOPH (1818–1897), Swiss historian **3** 132–133

BURCKHARDT, JOHANN LUDWIG (1784–1817), Swiss-born explorer **3** 133

BURGER, WARREN E. (1907–1986), Chief Justice of the United States Supreme Court (1969–1986) **3** 133–136

BURGESS, ANTHONY (John Anthony Burgess Wilson; 1917–1993), English author **3** 136–137

BURGOYNE, JOHN (1723–1792), British general and statesman **3** 137–138

BURKE, EDMUND (1729–1797), British statesman, political theorist, and philosopher **3** 138–141

BURKE, KENNETH (born 1897), American literary theorist and critic **3** 141–142

BURKE, ROBERT O'HARA (1820–1861), Irish-born Australian policeman and explorer **3** 142–143

BURKE, SELMA (1900–1995), African American sculptor **3** 143–144

BURLINGAME, ANSON (1820–1870), American diplomat **3** 144–145

BURNE-JONES, SIR EDWARD COLEY (1833–1898), English painter and designer **3** 145–146

BURNET, SIR FRANK MACFARLANE (1899–1985), Australian virologist **3** 146–147

BURNET, GILBERT (1643–1715), British bishop and historian **3** 147

BURNETT, FRANCES HODGSON (Frances Eliza Hodgson Burnett; 1849–1924), English-born American author **18** 64–67

BURNEY, FRANCES "FANNY" (1752–1840), English novelist and diarist **3** 147–148

BURNHAM, DANIEL HUDSON (1846–1912), American architect and city planner **3** 148–149

BURNHAM, FORBES (1923–1985), leader of the independence movement in British Guiana and Guyana's first prime minister **3** 149–151

D

DOS PASSOS, RODERIGO
(1896–1970), American novelist 5
69–71

DOS SANTOS, JOSÉ EDUARDO (born
1942), leader of the Popular
Movement for the Liberation of
Angola and president of Angola 5
71–72

DOS SANTOS, MARCELINO (born
1929), Mozambican nationalist
insurgent, statesman, and intellectual
5 72–74

DOSTOEVSKY, FYODOR (1821–1881),
Russian novelist 5 74–77

DOUGLAS, DONALD WILLS
(1892–1981), American aeronautical
engineer 5 77

DOUGLAS, GAVIN (circa 1475–1522),
Scottish poet, prelate, and courtier 5
77–78

DOUGLAS, SIR JAMES (1286?-1330),
Scottish patriot 5 80–82

DOUGLAS, MARY TEW (born 1921),
British anthropologist and social
thinker 5 79–80

DOUGLAS, STEPHEN ARNOLD
(1813–1861), American politician 5
80–82

DOUGLAS, THOMAS CLEMENT
(1904–1986), Canadian clergyman
and politician, premier of
Saskatchewan (1944–1961), and
member of Parliament (1962–1979) 5
82–83

DOUGLAS, WILLIAM ORVILLE
(1898–1980), American jurist 5 83–85

DOUGLASS, FREDERICK (circa
1817–1895), African American leader
and abolitionist 5 85–86

DOVE, ARTHUR GARFIELD
(1880–1946), American painter 5
86–87

DOVE, RITA FRANCES (born 1952),
United States poet laureate 5 87–89

DOW, NEAL (1804–1897), American
temperance reformer 5 89–90

DOWLAND, JOHN (1562–1626), British
composer and lutenist 5 90

DOWNING, ANDREW JACKSON
(1815–1852), American horticulturist
and landscape architect 5 90–91

DOYLE, SIR ARTHUR CONAN
(1859–1930), British author 5 91–92

DRAGO, LUIS MARÍA (1859–1921),
Argentine international jurist and
diplomat 5 92–93

DRAKE, DANIEL (1785–1852),
American physician 5 93–94

DRAKE, SIR FRANCIS (circa
1541–1596), English navigator 5
94–96

DRAPER, JOHN WILLIAM (1811–1882),
Anglo-American scientist and historian
5 96–97

DRAYTON, MICHAEL (1563–1631),
English poet 5 97–98

DREISER, (HERMAN) THEODORE
(1871–1945), American novelist 5
98–100

DREW, CHARLES RICHARD
(1904–1950), African American
surgeon 5 100–101

DREW, DANIEL (1797–1879), American
stock manipulator 5 101–102

DREXEL, KATHERINE (1858–1955),
founded a Catholic order, the Sisters
of the Blessed Sacrament 5 102–103

DREYFUS, ALFRED (1859–1935), French
army officer 5 103–105

DRIESCH, HANS ADOLF EDUARD
(1867–1941), German biologist and
philosopher 5 105

DRUSUS, MARCUS LIVIUS (circa
124–91 B.C.), Roman statesman 5
105–106

DRYDEN, JOHN (1631–1700), English
poet, critic, and dramatist 5 106–107

DRYSDALE, SIR GEORGE RUSSELL
(1912–1981), Australian painter 5
107–109

DUANE, WILLIAM (1760–1835),
American journalist 5 109

DUARTE, JOSÉ NAPOLEÓN
(1926–1990), civilian reformer elected
president of El Salvador in 1984 5
109–111

DUBČEK, ALEXANDER (1921–1992),
Czechoslovak politician 5 112–113

DUBE, JOHN LANGALIBALELE
(1870–1949), South African writer and
Zulu propagandist 5 113

DU BELLAY, JOACHIM (circa
1522–1560), French poet 5 113–114

DUBINSKY, DAVID (1892–1982),
American trade union official 5
114–115

Dublin (city; Ireland)
Guerin, Veronica 18 174–176

DUBNOV, SIMON (1860–1941), Jewish
historian, journalist, and political
activist 5 115–116

**DU BOIS, WILLIAM EDWARD
BURGHARDT** (1868–1963), African
American educator, pan-Africanist,
and protest leader 5 116–118

DU BOIS-REYMOND, EMIL
(1818–1896), German physiologist 5
118–119

DUBOS, RENÉ JULES (1901–1982),
French-born American microbiologist
5 119

DUBUFFET, JEAN PHILLIPE ARTHUR
(born 1901), French painter 5
119–120

DUCCIO DI BUONINSEGNA (1255/
60–1318/19), Italian painter 5
121–122

DUCHAMP, MARCEL (1887–1968),
French painter 5 122–123

DUCHAMP-VILLON, RAYMOND
(1876–1918), French sculptor 5 123

DUDLEY, BARBARA (born 1947),
American director of Greenpeace 5
123–124

DUDLEY, THOMAS (1576–1653),
American colonial governor and
Puritan leader 5 124–125

DUFAY, GUILLAUME (circa
1400–1474), Netherlandish composer
5 125–126

DUFF, ALEXANDER (1806–1878),
Scottish Presbyterian missionary 5
126–127

DUGAN, ALAN (born 1923), American
poet 5 127–128

DUGDALE, RICHARD LOUIS
(1841–1883), English-born American
sociologist 5 128–129

DUHEM, PIERRE MAURICE MARIE
(1861–1916), French physicist,
chemist, and historian of science 5
129

DUKAKIS, MICHAEL (born 1933),
American governor of Massachusetts 5
130–133

DUKE, JAMES BUCHANAN
(1856–1925), American industrialist
and philanthropist 5 133–134

Dukenfield, William Claude
see Fields, W.C.

DULL KNIFE (born Morning Star; c.
1810–1883), Northern Cheyenne
tribal leader 5 135–136

DULLES, JOHN FOSTER (1888–1959),
American statesman and diplomat 5
134–135

DUMAS, ALEXANDRE (1803–1870),
French playwright and novelist 5
136–138

DUMAS, JEAN BAPTISTE ANDRÉ
(1800–1884), French Chemist 5
138–139

G

GENET, EDMOND CHARLES (1763–1834), French diplomat **6** 261–262

GENET, JEAN (1910–1986), French novelist and playwright **6** 262–263

Genetics (biology)
DNA
Wilkins, Maurice **18** 415–416
gene action
Blackburn, Elizabeth H. **18** 43–45

GENGHIS KHAN (1167–1227), Mongol chief, creator of the Mongol empire **6** 263–265

Genoa (Italian city-state)
Doria, Andrea **18** 123–125

GENSCHER, HANS-DIETRICH (born 1927), leader of West Germany's liberal party (the FDP) and foreign minister **6** 265–266

GENTILE DA FABRIANO (Gentile di Niccolò di Giovanni di Massio; circa 1370–1427), Italian painter **6** 266–267

GENTILE, GIOVANNI (1875–1944), Italian philosopher and politician **6** 267

GEOFFREY OF MONMOUTH (circa 1100–1155), English pseudohistorian **6** 268

Geology (science)
petrology
Gold, Thomas **18** 162–164

GEORGE I (1660–1727), king of Great Britain and Ireland 1714–1727 **6** 268–269

GEORGE II (1683–1760), king of Great Britain and Ireland and elector of Hanover 1727–1760 **6** 269–270

GEORGE III (1738–1820), king of Great Britain and Ireland 1760–1820 **6** 270–272

GEORGE IV (1762–1830), king of Great Britain and Ireland 1820–1830 **6** 272–273

GEORGE V (1865–1936), king of Great Britain and Northern Ireland and emperor of India 1910–1936 **6** 273–275

GEORGE VI (1895–1952), king of Great Britain and Northern Ireland 1936–1952 **6** 275

George, David Lloyd
see Lloyd George, David

GEORGE, HENRY (1839–1897), American economist and social reformer **6** 276

GEORGE, JAMES ZACHARIAH (1826–1897), American politician and jurist **6** 276–277

GEORGE, STEFAN (1868–1933), German symbolist poet **6** 277–278

GEPHARDT, RICHARD ANDREW (born 1941), Democratic majority leader in the House of Representatives **6** 278–280

GÉRICAULT, JEAN LOIS ANDRÉ THÉODORE (1791–1824), French painter **6** 280–281

Germanicus, Tiberius Claudius
see Claudius Germanicus, T.

GERONIMO (1829–1909), American Apache Indian warrior **6** 281–282

GERRY, ELBRIDGE (1744–1814), American patriot and statesman **6** 282–283

GERSHOM BEN JUDAH (circa 950–1028), German rabbi, scholar, and poet **6** 283–284

GERSHWIN, GEORGE (1898–1937), American composer **6** 284–285

GERSON, JOHN (1363–1429), French theologian **6** 285–286

GESELL, ARNOLD LUCIUS (1880–1961), American psychologist and pediatrician **6** 286–287

GESNER, KONRAD VON (1516–1565), Swiss naturalist **6** 287

GESUALDO, DON CARLO (Prince of Venosa; circa 1560–1613), Italian composer **6** 287–288

GETTY, JEAN PAUL (1892–1976), billionaire independent oil producer **6** 288–290

GHAZALI, ABU HAMID MUHAMMAD AL- (1058–1111), Arab philosopher and Islamic theologian **6** 290–291

GHIBERTI, LORENZO (circa 1381–1455), Italian sculptor, goldsmith, and painter **6** 291–292

GHIRLANDAIO, DOMENICO (1449–1494), Italian painter **6** 292–293

GHOSE, AUROBINDO (1872–1950), Indian nationalist and philosopher **6** 293–294

GIACOMETTI, ALBERTO (1901–1966), Swiss sculptor and painter **6** 294–295

GIANNINI, A. P. (Amadeo Peter; 1870–1949), Italian-American financier and banker **6** 295–297

GIAP, VO NGUYEN (born 1912), Vietnamese Communist general and statesman **6** 297–299

GIBBON, EDWARD (1737–1794), English historian **6** 299–300

GIBBONS, JAMES (1834–1921), American Roman Catholic cardinal **6** 300–301

GIBBS, JAMES (1682–1754), British architect **6** 301–302

GIBBS, JOSIAH WILLARD (1839–1903), American mathematical physicist **6** 302–303

GIBRAN, KAHLIL (1883–1931), Lebanese writer and artist **6** 303–305

GIBSON, ALTHEA (born 1927), African American tennis player **6** 305–306

GIDDINGS, FRANKLIN HENRY (1855–1931), American sociologist **6** 307–308

GIDE, ANDRÉ (1869–1951), French author **6** 308–309

GIELGUD, JOHN (born 1904), English Shakespearean actor **6** 310–311

GIERKE, OTTO VON (1841–1921), German jurist **6** 311–312

GIGLI, ROMEO (born 1949), Italian designer **6** 312

GILBERT, SIR HUMPHREY (circa 1537–1583), English soldier and colonizer **6** 313

GILBERT, WILLIAM (1544–1603), English physician and physicist **6** 313–314

GILBERT, SIR WILLIAM SCHWENCK (1836–1911), English playwright and poet **6** 314–315

GILBRETH, LILLIAN (born Lillian Evelyn Moller; 1878–1972), American psychologist and industrial management consultant **6** 315–317

GILES, ERNEST (1835–1897), Australian explorer **6** 317–318

GILKEY, LANGDON BROWN (born 1919), American ecumenical Protestant theologian **6** 318–319

GILLESPIE, DIZZY (born John Birks Gillespie; 1917–1993), African American jazz trumpeter, composer, and band leader **6** 320–322

GILLIAM, SAM (born 1933), American artist **6** 322–323

GILMAN, CHARLOTTE ANNA PERKINS (1860–1935), American writer and lecturer **6** 323–325

GILMAN, DANIEL COIT (1831–1908), educator and pioneer in the American university movement **6** 325–326

GILPIN, LAURA (1891–1979), American photographer **6** 326–327

GILSON, ÉTIENNE HENRY (1884–1978), French Catholic philosopher **6** 327–328

GINASTERA, ALBERTO EVARISTO (1916–1983), Argentine composer **6** 328–329

GINGRICH, NEWT (born 1943), Republican congressman from Georgia **6** 329–332

GINSBERG, ALLEN (1926–1997), American poet **6** 332–333

GINSBURG, RUTH BADER (born 1933), second woman appointed to the United States Supreme Court **6** 333–336

GINZBERG, ASHER (Ahad Ha-Am; means ''one of the people;'' 1856–1927), Jewish intellectual leader **6** 336–337

GINZBERG, LOUIS (1873–1953), Lithuanian-American Talmudic scholar **6** 337–338

GINZBURG, NATALIA LEVI (1916–1991), Italian novelist, essayist, playwright, and translator **6** 338–339

GIOLITTI, GIOVANNI (1842–1928), Italian statesman **6** 339–340

GIORGIONE (1477–1510), Italian painter **6** 340–341

GIOTTO (circa 1267–1337), Italian painter, architect, and sculptor **6** 342–345

GIOVANNI DA BOLOGNA (1529–1608), Italian sculptor **6** 345–346

Giovanni da Fiesole, Fra
see Angelica, Fra

GIOVANNI, YOLANDE CORNELIA, JR. (born 1943), African American poet **6** 346–347

GIRARD, STEPHEN (1750–1831), American merchant and philanthropist **6** 347–348

GIRARDON, FRANÇOIS (1628–1715), French sculptor **6** 348–349

GIRAUDOUX, JEAN (1882–1944), French novelist, playwright, and diplomat **6** 349–350

GIRTY, SIMON (1741–1818), American frontiersman **6** 350

GISCARD D'ESTAING, VALÉRY (born 1926), third president of the French Fifth Republic **6** 350–352

GIST, CHRISTOPHER (circa 1706–1759), American frontiersman **6** 352–353

GIULIANI, RUDOLPH WILLIAM (born 1944), mayor of New York City **6** 353–355

GLACKENS, WILLIAM (1870–1938), American painter **6** 355–356

GLADDEN, WASHINGTON (1836–1918), American clergyman **6** 356–357

GLADSTONE, WILLIAM EWART (1809–1898), English statesman **6** 357–360

GLASGOW, ELLEN (1873–1945), American novelist **6** 360–361

GLASHOW, SHELDON LEE (born 1932), American Nobel Prize winner in physics **6** 361–362

GLASS, PHILIP (born 1937), American composer of minimalist music **6** 362–364

GLENDOWER, OWEN (1359?–1415?), Welsh national leader **6** 364–365

GLENN, JOHN HERSCHEL, JR. (born 1921), military test pilot, astronaut, businessman, and United States senator from Ohio **6** 365–367

GLIGOROV, KIRO (born 1917), first president of the Republic of Macedonia **6** 367–369

GLINKA, MIKHAIL IVANOVICH (1804–1857), Russian composer **6** 369–370

GLOUCESTER, DUKE OF (1391–1447), English statesman **6** 370–371

GLUBB, SIR JOHN BAGOT (1897–1986), British commander of the Arab Legion 1939–56 **6** 371–372

GLUCK, CHRISTOPH WILLIBALD (1714–1787), Austrian composer and opera reformer **6** 372–374

GLUCKMAN, MAX (1911–1975), British anthropologist **6** 374–375

Glyndyfrdwy, Lord of Giyndwr and Sycharth
see Glendower, Owen

GOBINEAU, COMTE DE (Joseph Arthur Gobineau; 1816–1882), French diplomat **6** 375–376

GODDARD, ROBERT HUTCHINGS (1882–1945), American pioneer in rocketry **6** 376–377

GÖDEL, KURT (1906–1978), Austrian-American mathematician **6** 377–379

Godfather, The (film)
Coppola, Francis Ford **18** 102–104

GODFREY OF BOUILLON (circa 1060–1100), French lay leader of First Crusade **6** 379

GODKIN, EDWIN LAWRENCE (1831–1902), British-born American journalist **6** 380

GODOLPHIN, SIDNEY (1st Earl of Godolphin; 1645–1712), English statesman **6** 380–381

GODOY Y ÁLVAREZ DE FARIA, MANUEL DE (1767–1851), Spanish statesman **6** 381–382

GODUNOV, BORIS FEODOROVICH (circa 1551–1605), czar of Russia 1598–1605 **6** 382–383

GODWIN, WILLIAM (1756–1836), English political theorist and writer **6** 383–384

GOEBBELS, JOSEPH PAUL (1897–1945), German politician and Nazi propagandist **6** 384–385

GOEPPERT-MAYER, MARIA (1906–1972), American physicist **6** 385–387

GOETHALS, GEORGE WASHINGTON (1858–1928), American Army officer and engineer **6** 387–388

GOETHE, JOHANN WOLFGANG VON (1749–1832), German poet **6** 388–391

GOGOL, NIKOLAI (1809–1852), Russian author **6** 391–393

GOH CHOK TONG (born 1941), leader of the People's Action Party and Singapore's prime minister **6** 393–395

GOIZUETA, ROBERTO (1931–1997), Cuban American businessman and philanthropist **18** 160–162

GÖKALP, MEHMET ZIYA (1875/76–1924), Turkish publicist and sociologist **6** 395–396

GOKHALE, GOPAL KRISHNA (1866–1915), Indian nationalist leader **6** 396

GOLD, THOMAS (born 1920), American astronomer and physicist **18** 162–164

GOLDBERG, ARTHUR JOSEPH (1908–1990), U.S. secretary of labor, ambassador to the United Nations, and activist justice of the U.S. Supreme Court **6** 397–398

GOLDBERG, WHOOPI (born Caryn E. Johnson; born 1949), African American actress **6** 398–402

GOLDEN, HARRY (1902–1981), Jewish-American humorist, writer, and publisher **6** 402–403

GÜNTHER, IGNAZ (1725–1775), German sculptor **7** 41–42

GUSTAVUS I (Gustavus Eriksson; 1496–1560), king of Sweden 1523–1560 **7** 42–43

GUSTAVUS II (Gustavus Adolphus; 1594–1632), king of Sweden 1611–1632 **7** 43–45

GUSTAVUS III (1746–1792), king of Sweden 1771–1792 **7** 45–46

GUSTON, PHILIP (1913–1980), American painter and a key member of the New York School **7** 47–48

GUTENBERG, JOHANN (circa 1398–1468), German inventor and printer **7** 48–49

GUTHRIE, EDWIN RAY (1886–1959), American psychologist **7** 49–50

GUTHRIE, TYRONE (1900–1971), English theater director **7** 50–51

GUTHRIE, WOODROW WILSON ("Woody"; 1912–1967), writer and performer of folk songs **7** 51–52

GUTIÉRRÉZ, GUSTAVO (born 1928), Peruvian who was the father of liberation theology **7** 52–53

GUY DE CHAULIAC (circa 1295–1368), French surgeon **7** 54

Gymnastics
Comaneci, Nadia **18** 98–100

H

HABASH, GEORGE (born 1926), founder of the Arab Nationalists' Movement (1952) and of the Popular Front for the Liberation of Palestine (PFLP; 1967) **7** 55–56

HABER, FRITZ (1868–1934), German chemist **7** 56–58

HABERMAS, JÜRGEN (born 1929), German philosopher and sociologist **7** 58–60

Habitat for Humanity
Fuller, Millard **18** 153–155

HADRIAN (76–138), Roman emperor 117–138 **7** 60–61

HAECKEL, ERNST HEINRICH PHILIPP AUGUST (1834–1919), German biologist and natural philosopher **7** 61–62

HAFIZ, SHAMS AL-DIN (circa 1320–1390), Persian mystical poet and Koranic exegete **7** 63

HAGEN, UTA THYRA (born 1919), American actress **18** 179–180

HAGUE, FRANK (1876–1956), American politician **7** 63–64

HAHN, OTTO (1879–1968), German chemist **7** 64–65

HAIDAR ALI (1721/22–1782), Indian prince, ruler of Mysore 1759–1782 **7** 65–66

HAIG, ALEXANDER M., JR. (born 1924), American military leader, diplomat, secretary of state, and presidential adviser **7** 66–67

HAIG, DOUGLAS (1st Earl Haig; 1861–1928), British field marshal **7** 67–68

HAILE SELASSIE (1892–1975), emperor of Ethiopia **7** 68–70

HAKLUYT, RICHARD (1552/53–1616), English geographer and author **7** 70

HALBERSTAM, DAVID (born 1934), American journalist, author and social historian **18** 180–183

HALDANE, JOHN BURDON SANDERSON (1892–1964), English biologist **7** 70–71

HALE, EDWARD EVERETT (1822–1909), American Unitarian minister and author **7** 71–72

HALE, GEORGE ELLERY (1868–1938), American astronomer **7** 72–74

HALE, SARAH JOSEPHA (née Buell; 1788–1879), American editor **7** 74–75

HALES, STEPHEN (1677–1761), English scientist and clergyman **7** 75

HALÉVY, ÉLIE (1870–1937), French philosopher and historian **7** 76

HALEY, ALEX (1921–1992), African American journalist and author **7** 76–78

HALEY, MARGARET A. (1861–1939), American educator and labor activist **7** 78–79

HALFFTER, CHRISTÓBAL (born 1930), Spanish composer **7** 79–80

HALIBURTON, THOMAS CHANDLER (1796–1865), Canadian judge and author **7** 80

HALIDE EDIP ADIVAR (1884–1964), Turkish woman writer, scholar, and public figure **7** 80–82

HALIFAX, 1ST EARL OF (Edward Frederick Lindley Wood; 1881–1959), English statesman **7** 82–83

HALL, ASAPH (1829–1907), American astronomer **7** 83–84

HALL, DONALD (born 1928), New England memoirist, short story writer, essayist, dramatist, critic, and anthologist as well as poet **7** 84–85

HALL, GRANVILLE STANLEY (1844–1924), American psychologist and educator **7** 85–86

HALLAJ, AL-HUSAYN IBN MANSUR AL (857–922), Persian Moslem mystic and martyr **7** 86–87

HALLAM, LEWIS, SR. AND JR. (Lewis Sr. ca. 1705–55; Lewis Jr. 1740–1808), American actors and theatrical managers **7** 87

HALLER, ALBRECHT VON (1708–1777), Swiss physician **7** 87–88

HALLEY, EDMUND (1656–1742), English astronomer **7** 88–89

HALS, FRANS (1581/85–1666), Dutch painter **7** 89–91

HALSEY, WILLIAM FREDERICK (1882–1959), American admiral **7** 91–92

HAMANN, JOHANN GEORG (1730–1788), German philosopher **7** 92

HAMER, FANNIE LOU (born Townsend; 1917–1977), American civil rights activist **7** 93–94

HAMILCAR BARCA (circa 285–229/228 B.C.), Carthaginian general and statesman **7** 94–95

HAMILTON, ALEXANDER (1755–1804), American statesman **7** 95–98

HAMILTON, ALICE (1869–1970), American physician **7** 98–99

HAMILTON, SIR WILLIAM ROWAN (1805–1865), Irish mathematical physicist **7** 99–100

HAMMARSKJÖLD, DAG (1905–1961), Swedish diplomat **7** 100–101

HAMM-BRÜCHER, HILDEGARD (born 1921), Free Democratic Party's candidate for the German presidency in 1994 **7** 101–103

HAMMER, ARMAND (1898–1990), American entrepreneur and art collector **7** 103–104

HAMMERSTEIN, OSCAR CLENDENNING II (1895–1960), lyricist and librettist of the American theater **7** 104–106

HAMMETT, (SAMUEL) DASHIELL (1894–1961), American author **7** 106–108

HAMMOND, JAMES HENRY (1807–1864), American statesman **7** 108–109

HAMMOND, JOHN LAWRENCE LE BRETON (1872–1952), English historian 7 108–109

HAMMOND, LUCY BARBARA (1873–1961), English historian 7 109

HAMMURABI (1792–1750 B.C.), king of Babylonia 7 109–110

HAMPDEN, JOHN (1594–1643), English statesman 7 110–111

HAMPTON, WADE (circa 1751–1835), American planter 7 111–112

HAMPTON, WADE III (1818–1902), American statesman and Confederate general 7 112

HAMSUN, KNUT (1859–1952), Norwegian novelist 7 113–114

HAN FEI TZU (circa 280–233 B.C.), Chinese statesman and philosopher 7 124–125

HAN WU-TI (157–87 B.C.), Chinese emperor 7 136

HAN YÜ (768–824), Chinese author 7 136–137

HANAFI, HASSAN (born 1935), Egyptian philosopher 7 114

HANCOCK, JOHN (1737–1793), American statesman 7 114–116

HAND, BILLINGS LEARNED (1872–1961), American jurist 7 116

HANDEL, GEORGE FREDERICK (1685–1759), German-born English composer and organist 7 116–119

HANDKE, PETER (born 1942), Austrian playwright, novelist, screenwriter, essayist, and poet 7 119–121

HANDLIN, OSCAR (born 1915), American historian 7 121–122

Handschuchsheim, Ritter von
see Meinong, Alexius

HANDSOME LAKE (a.k.a. Hadawa' Ko; ca. 1735–1815), Seneca spiritual leader 7 122–123

HANDY, WILLIAM CHRISTOPHER (1873–1958), African American songwriter 7 123–124

HANKS, NANCY (1927–1983), called the "mother of a million artists" for her work in building federal financial support for the arts and artists 7 126–127

HANNA, MARCUS ALONZO (1837–1904), American businessman and politician 7 127–128

HANNIBAL BARCA (247–183 B.C.), Carthaginian general 7 128–130

HANSBERRY, LORRAINE VIVIAN (1930–1965), American writer and a major figure on Broadway 7 130–131

HANSEN, ALVIN (1887–1975), American economist 7 131–132

HANSEN, JULIA BUTLER (1907–1988), American politician 7 132–133

HANSON, DUANE (1925–1990), American super-realist sculptor 7 133–135

HANSON, HOWARD (born 1896), American composer and educator 7 135–136

HAPGOOD, NORMAN (1868–1937), American author and editor 7 137–138

HARA, KEI (1856–1921), Japanese statesman and prime minister 1918–1921 7 138

HARAND, IRENE (born Irene Wedl; 1900–1975), Austrian political and human rights activist 7 139–145

HARAWI, ILYAS AL- (Elias Harawi; born 1930), president of Lebanon 7 145–146

HARDENBERG, PRINCE KARL AUGUST VON (1750–1822), Prussian statesman 7 146–147

HARDIE, JAMES KEIR (1856–1915), Scottish politician 7 147–148

HARDING, WARREN GAMALIEL (1865–1923), American statesman, president 1921–1923 7 148–149

HARDY, HARRIET (1905–1993), American pathologist 7 150

HARDY, THOMAS (1840–1928), English novelist, poet, and dramatist 7 150–152

HARE, ROBERT (1781–1858), American chemist 7 152–153

HARGRAVES, EDWARD HAMMOND (1816–1891), Australian publicist 7 153–154

HARING, KEITH (1958–1990), American artist tied to New York graffiti art of the 1980s 7 154–155

HARJO, SUZAN SHOWN (born 1945), Native American activist 18 183–185

HARKNESS, GEORGIA (1891–1974), American Methodist and ecumenical theologian 7 155–156

HARLAN, JOHN MARSHALL (1833–1911), American jurist 7 156–157

HARLAN, JOHN MARSHALL (1899–1971), U.S. Supreme Court justice 7 157–159

Harlem renaissance (American literature)
Van Vechten, Carl 18 400–402

HARLEY, ROBERT (1st Earl of Oxford and Earl Mortimer; 1661–1724), English statesman 7 159–160

HARNACK, ADOLF VON (1851–1930), German theologian 7 160

HARNETT, WILLIAM MICHAEL (1848–1892), American painter 7 160–161

HAROLD I (circa 840–933), king of Norway 860–930 7 161–162

HAROLD II (Harold Godwinson; died 1066), Anglo-Saxon king of England of 1066 7 162

HAROLD III (1015–1066), king of Norway 1047–1066 7 163

HARPER, FRANCES (Frances Ellen Watkins Harper; 1825–1911), African American author, abolitionist and women's rights activist 18 185–187

HARPER, WILLIAM RAINEY (1856–1906), American educator and biblical scholar 7 163–164

HARRIMAN, EDWARD HENRY (1848–1909), American railroad executive 7 164–165

HARRIMAN, PAMELA (1920–1997), American ambassador and patrician 18 187–189

HARRIMAN, W. AVERELL (1891–1986), American industrialist, financier, and diplomat 7 165–166
Harriman, Pamela 18 187–189

HARRINGTON, JAMES (1611–1677), English political theorist 7 166–167

HARRINGTON, MICHAEL (1928–1989), American political activist and educator 7 167–169

HARRIS, ABRAM LINCOLN, JR. (1899–1963), African American economist 7 169–171

HARRIS, BARBARA CLEMENTINE (born 1930), African American activist and Anglican bishop 7 171–172

HARRIS, FRANK (1856–1931), Irish-American author and editor 7 172–173

HARRIS, JOEL CHANDLER (1848–1908), American writer 7 173–174

HARRIS, LADONNA (born 1931), Native American activist 18 189–191

HARRIS, PATRICIA ROBERTS (1924–1985), first African American woman in the U.S. Cabinet 7 174–175

HENZE, HANS WERNER (born 1926), German composer **7** 314

HEPBURN, AUDREY (born Edda Van Heemstra Hepburn-Ruston; 1929–1993), Swiss actress and humanitarian **7** 314–316

HEPBURN, KATHARINE (born 1907), American actress on the stage and on the screen **7** 316–317

HEPPLEWHITE, GEORGE (died 1786), English furniture designer **7** 317–318

HEPWORTH, BARBARA (1903–1975), English sculptor **7** 318–319

HERACLIDES OF PONTUS (circa 388–310 B.C.), Greek philosopher **7** 319–320

HERACLITUS (flourished 500 B.C.), Greek philosopher **7** 320

HERACLIUS (circa 575–641), Byzantine emperor 610–641 **7** 320–321

HERBART, JOHANN FRIEDRICH (1776–1841), German philosopher-psychologist and educator **7** 321–322

HERBERG, WILL (1906–1977), Jewish theologian, social thinker, and biblical exegete **7** 322–323

HERBERT, EDWARD (1st Baron Herbert of Cherbury; 1583–1648), English philosopher, poet, diplomat, and historian **7** 324

HERBERT, GEORGE (1593–1633), English metaphysical poet and Anglican priest **7** 324–326

HERDER, JOHANN GOTTFRIED VON (1744–1803), German philosopher, theologian, and critic **7** 327–328

HERNÁNDEZ, JOSÉ (1834–1886), Argentine poet **7** 328–329

HERNÁNDEZ COLÓN, RAFAEL (born 1936), Puerto Rican governor **7** 329–330

HEROD THE GREAT (circa 73–4 B.C.), king of Judea **7** 333–334

HERODOTUS (circa 484-circa 425 B.C.), Greek historian **7** 330–333

HERON OF ALEXANDRIA (flourished circa 60), Greek engineer, mathematician, and inventor **7** 334–335

HERRERA, JUAN DE (circa 1530–1597), Spanish architect **7** 335

HERRERA LANE, FELIPE (1922–1996), Chilean banker and economist **7** 336

HERRICK, ROBERT (1591–1674), English poet and Anglican parson **7** 336–339

HERRIOT, ÉDOUARD (1872–1957), French statesman and author **7** 339–340

HERSCHEL, SIR JOHN FREDERICK WILLIAM (1792–1871), English astronomer **7** 340–341

HERSCHEL, SIR WILLIAM (1738–1822), German-born English astronomer **7** 341–343

HERSHEY, ALFRED DAY (1908–1997), American microbiologist **7** 343–345

HERSKOVITS, MELVILLE JEAN (1895–1963), American anthropologist **7** 345

HERTZ, HEINRICH RUDOLF (1857–1894), German physicist **7** 346–347

HERTZOG, JAMES BARRY MUNNIK (1866–1942), South African prime minister 1924–39 **7** 347–348

HERUY WÄLDÄ-SELLASÉ (1878–1938), Ethiopian writer and government press director **7** 348–349

HERZBERG, GERHARD (born 1904), German-born Canadian chemist/physicist **7** 349–350

HERZEN, ALEKSANDR IVANOVICH (1812–1870), Russian author and political agitator **7** 351–352

HERZL, THEODOR (1860–1904), Hungarian-born Austrian Zionist author **7** 352–354

HERZOG, CHAIM (1918–1997), president of the state of Israel **7** 354–355

HERZOG, ROMAN (born 1934), president of the German Federal Constitutional Court (1987–1994) and president of Germany **7** 355–357

HESBURGH, THEODORE MARTIN (born 1917), activist American Catholic priest who was president of Notre Dame (1952–1987) **7** 357–358

HESCHEL, ABRAHAM JOSHUA (1907–1972), Polish-American Jewish theologian **7** 358–359

HESELTINE, MICHAEL (born 1933), British Conservative politician **7** 359–361

HESIOD (flourished circa 700 B.C.), Greek poet **7** 361–362

HESS, VICTOR FRANCIS (1883–1964), Austrian-American physicist **7** 362–363

HESS, WALTER RICHARD RUDOLF (1894–1987), deputy reichsführer for Adolf Hitler (1933–1941) **7** 363–365

HESS, WALTER RUDOLF (1881–1973), Swiss neurophysiologist **7** 365

HESSE, EVA (1936–1970), American sculptor **7** 365–367

HESSE, HERMANN (1877–1962), German novelist **7** 367–369

HESSE, MARY B. (born 1924), British philosopher **7** 369–371

HEVESY, GEORGE CHARLES DE (1885–1966), Hungarian chemist **7** 371

HEWITT, ABRAM STEVENS (1822–1903), American politician and manufacturer **7** 371–372

HEYERDAHL, THOR (born 1914), Norwegian explorer, anthropologist and author **18** 194–196

HEYSE, PAUL JOHANN LUDWIG (1830–1914), German author **7** 372–373

HEYWOOD, THOMAS (1573/1574–1641), English playwright **7** 373–374

HICKOK, JAMES BUTLER ("Wild Bill"; 1837–1876), American gunfighter, scout, and spy **7** 374–375

HICKS, EDWARD (1780–1849), American folk painter **7** 375

HIDALGO Y COSTILLA, MIGUEL (1753–1811), Mexican revolutionary priest **7** 375–377

HIDAYAT, SADIQ (1903–1951), Persian author **7** 377–378

Higgins, Margaret
see Sanger, Margaret

HIGGINS, MARGUERITE (1920–1966), American journalist **7** 378–380

HIGGINSON, THOMAS WENTWORTH (1823–1911), American reformer and editor **7** 380

Hildebrand
see Gregory VII, Pope

HILDEBRANDT, JOHANN LUCAS VON (1663–1745), Austrian architect **7** 380–381

HILDRETH, RICHARD (1807–1865), American historian and political theorist **7** 382

HILL, ANITA (born 1956), African American lawyer and professor **7** 382–385

HILL, ARCHIBALD VIVIAN (1886–1977), English physiologist **7** 385–386

HURD, DOUGLAS (born 1930), English Conservative Party politician and foreign secretary **8** 52–55

HURSTON, ZORA NEALE (1903–1960), African American folklorist and novelist **8** 55–56

HUSÁK, GUSTÁV (born 1913), president of the Czechoslovak Socialist Republic (1975–1987) **8** 59–61

HUSAYN, TAHA (1889–1973), Egyptian author, educator, and statesman **8** 61–62

HUSAYNI, AL-HAJJ AMIN AL- (1895–1974), Moslem scholar/leader and mufti of Jerusalem (1922–1948) **8** 62–63

HUSEIN IBN ALI (circa 1854–1931), Arab nationalist, king of Hejaz 1916–1924 **8** 63

HUSSEIN IBN TALAL (born 1935), king of the Hashemite Kingdom of Jordan (1953–80s) **8** 65–67

HUSSERL, EDMUND (1859–1938), German philosopher **8** 67–68

HUTCHINS, ROBERT MAYNARD (1899–1977), American educator **8** 68–69

HUTCHINSON, ANNE MARBURY (1591–1643), English-born American religious leader **8** 69–71

HUTCHINSON, THOMAS (1711–1780), American colonial governor **8** 71–72

HUTTEN, ULRICH VON (1488–1523), German humanist **8** 72–73

HUTTON, JAMES (1726–1797), Scottish geologist **8** 73–74

HUXLEY, ALDOUS LEONARD (1894–1963), English novelist and essayist **8** 74–75

HUXLEY, JULIAN (1887–1975), English biologist and author **8** 75–77

HUXLEY, THOMAS HENRY (1825–1895), English biologist **8** 77–79

HUYGENS, CHRISTIAAN (1629–1695), Dutch mathematician, astronomer, and physicist **8** 79–81

HUYSMANS, JORIS KARL (1848–1907), French novelist **8** 81–82

HYDE, DOUGLAS (1860–1949), Irish author, president 1938–45 **8** 82–83

HYMAN, LIBBIE HENRIETTA (1888–1969), American zoologist **8** 83–84

HYPATIA OF ALEXANDRIA (370–415), Greek mathematician and philosopher **8** 85

I

IACOCCA, LIDO (LEE) ANTHONY (born 1924), American automobile magnate **8** 86–88

IBÁÑEZ DEL CAMPO, CARLOS (1877–1960), Chilean general and president **8** 88

ÍBARRURI GÓMEZ, DOLORES (1895–1989), voice of the Republican cause in the Spanish Civil War **8** 88–90

IBERVILLE, SIEUR D' (Pierre le Moyne; 1661–1706), Canadian soldier, naval captain, and adventurer **8** 90–91

IBN AL-ARABI, MUHYI AL-DIN (1165–1240), Spanish-born Moslem poet, philosopher, and mystic **8** 91

IBN BATTUTA, MUHAMMAD (1304–1368/69), Moslem traveler and author **8** 91–92

IBN GABIROL, SOLOMON BEN JUDAH (circa 1021-circa 1058), Spanish Hebrew poet and philosopher **8** 92

IBN HAZM, ABU MUHAMMAD ALI (994–1064), Spanish-born Arab theologian and jurist **8** 93

IBN KHALDUN, ABD AL-RAHMAN IBN MUHAMMAD (1332–1406), Arab historian, philosopher, and statesman **8** 93–94

IBN SAUD, ABD AL-AZIZ (1880–1953), Arab politician, founder of Saudi Arabia **8** 94–95

IBN TASHUFIN, YUSUF (died 1106), North African Almoravid ruler **8** 95–96

IBN TUFAYL, ABU BAKR MUHAMMAD (circa 1110–1185), Spanish Moslem philosopher and physician **8** 96

IBN TUMART, MUHAMMAD (circa 1080–1130), North African Islamic theologian **8** 96–97

IBRAHIM PASHA (1789–1848), Turkish military and administrative leader **8** 97–98

IBSEN, HENRIK (1828–1906), Norwegian playwright **8** 98–100

ICKES, HAROLD LECLAIRE (1874–1952), American statesman **8** 100–101

ICTINUS (flourished 2nd half of 5th century B.C.), Greek architect **8** 101

IDRIS I (1889–1983), king of Libya 1950–69 **8** 102

IDRISI, MUHAMMAD IBN MUHAMMAD AL- (1100–1165?), Arab geographer **8** 102–103

IGLESIAS, ENRIQUE V. (born 1930), Uruguayan economist, banker, and public official **8** 106–107

IGNATIUS OF ANTIOCH, SAINT (died circa 115), Early Christian bishop and theologian **8** 107–108

IGNATIUS OF LOYOLA, SAINT (1491–1556), Spanish soldier, founder of Jesuits **8** 108–109

IKEDA, DAISAKU (born 1928), Japanese Buddhist writer and religious leader **8** 109–110

IKHNATON (ruled 1379–1362 B.C.), pharaoh of Egypt **8** 110–111

ILIESCU, ION (born 1930), president of Romania (1990-) **8** 111–112

ILLICH, IVAN (born 1926), theologian, educator, and social critic **8** 112–114

IMAM, ALHADJI ABUBAKAR (1911–1981), Nigerian writer and teacher **8** 114–115

IMAOKA, SHINICHIRO (1881–1988), progressive and liberal religious leader in Japan **8** 115

IMHOTEP (ca. 3000 B.C. - ca. 2950 B.C.), Egyptian vizier, architect, priest, astronomer, and magician-physician **8** 116–117

India, Republic of (nation, southern Asia)
• Circa 1600–1947 (BRITISH)
  governors general
    Mountbatten, Louis **18** 297–299
  opponents of British rule
    Mahal, Hazrat **18** 271–273

Indians (North American)
  rights defended
    Bonnin, Gertrude S. **18** 52–54
    Harjo, Suzan Shown **18** 183–185
    Harris, LaDonna **18** 189–191

INGE, WILLIAM RALPH (1860–1954), Church of England clergyman, scholar, social critic, and writer **8** 118–119

INGENHOUSZ, JAN (1730–1799), Dutch physician, chemist, and engineer **8** 119–120

INGERSOLL, ROBERT GREEN (1833–1899), American lawyer and lecturer **8** 120–121

INGRES, JEAN AUGUSTE DOMINIQUE (1780–1867), French painter **8** 121–123

INNESS, GEORGE (1825–1894), American painter **8** 123–124

LAND, EDWIN HERBERT (1909–1991), American physicist, inventor, and manufacturer **9** 183–184

LANDAU, LEV DAVIDOVICH (1908–1968), Soviet theoretical physicist **9** 184–185

LANDINI, FRANCESCO (circa 1335–1397), Italian composer and poet **9** 185–186

LANDOR, WALTER SAVAGE (1775–1864), English poet, essayist and critic **9** 186–187

LANDOWSKI, MARCEL (born 1915), French composer of lyric works **9** 187–188

LANDSTEINER, KARL (1868–1943), Austrian-born American immunologist **9** 188–189

LANE, FITZ HUGH (1804–1865), American marine painter **9** 189

LANFRANC (circa 1010–1089), Italian theologian, archbishop of Canterbury **9** 189–190

LANG, FRITZ (1890–1976), film director **9** 190–192

LANG, JOHN THOMAS (1876–1975), Australian politician **9** 192–193

LANGE, DOROTHEA (1895–1965), American photographer **9** 193–194

LANGLAND, WILLIAM (circa 1330–1400), English poet **9** 194–195

LANGLEY, SAMUEL PIERPONT (1834–1906), American scientist **9** 195–196

LANGMUIR, IRVING (1881–1957), American chemist **9** 196–197

LANGSTON, JOHN MERCER (1829–1897), American educator and diplomat **9** 197

LANIER, JARON (born ca. 1961), American computer engineer **9** 198–199

LANIER, SIDNEY (1842–1881), American poet, critic, and musician **9** 199–200

LANSING, ROBERT (1864–1928), American lawyer and statesman **9** 200

LAO SHÊ (1899–1966), Chinese novelist **9** 200–201

LAO TZU (flourished 6th century B.C.), Chinese philosopher **9** 201–202

LAPLACE, MARQUIS DE (Pierre Simon; 1749–1827), French mathematician **9** 202–204

LARDNER, RINGGOLD WILMER (1885–1933), American author **9** 204–205

LARIONOV, MIKHAIL (1881–1964), Russian artist **9** 205–206

LARKIN, PHILIP (1922–1986), English poet **9** 206–207

LARKIN, THOMAS OLIVER (1802–1858), American merchant and diplomat **9** 208

LARSEN, NELLA (1893–1963), Harlem Renaissance writer **9** 209–210

LARSON, JONATHAN (1961–1996), American playwright, composer, and lyricist **18** 243–145

LAS CASAS, BARTOLOMÉ DE (1474–1566), Spanish Dominican missionary and historian **9** 211–212

LASCH, CHRISTOPHER (1932–1994), American historian and social critic **9** 212–214

LASHLEY, KARL SPENCER (1890–1958), American neuropsychologist **9** 214–215

LASKI, HAROLD J. (1893–1950), English political scientist and Labour party leader **9** 215–216

LASSALLE, FERDINAND (1825–1864), German socialist leader **9** 216

LASSUS, ROLAND DE (1532–1594), Franco-Flemish composer **9** 216–218

LASSWELL, HAROLD DWIGHT (born 1902), American political scientist **9** 218–219

LÁSZLÓ I, KING OF HUNGARY (ca. 1040–1095), king of Hungary and saint **9** 219–221

LATIMER, HUGH (circa 1492–1555), English Protestant bishop, reformer, and martyr **9** 221

LATROBE, BENJAMIN HENRY (1764–1820), English-born American architect **9** 222–224

LAUD, WILLIAM (1573–1645), English archbishop of Canterbury **9** 224–225

LAUDER, ESTEE (née Josephine Esthe Menzer, born ca. 1908), founder of an international cosmetics empire **9** 225–226

Lauenburg, Duke of see Bismarck, Otto Edward Leopold von

LAUREL, SALVADOR H. (Doy; born 1928), member of the Philippine Congress and vice-president **9** 226–227

LAUREN, RALPH (Ralph Lipschitz; born 1939), American fashion designer **9** 228–229

LAURENCE, MARGARET (Jean Margaret Wemyss; 1926–1987), Canadian writer **9** 229–230

LAURENS, HENRI (1885–1954), French sculptor **9** 230–231

LAURENS, HENRY (1724–1792), American merchant and Revolutionary statesman **9** 232

LAURIER, SIR WILFRID (1841–1919), Canadian statesman, prime minister 1896–1911 **9** 232–234

LAURO, ACHILLE (1887–1984), Italian business and political leader **9** 234–235

LAUTARO (circa 1535–1557), Araucanian Indian chieftain in Chile **9** 235

LAVAL, FRANCOIS XAVIER DE (1623–1708), French bishop in Canada **9** 235–236

LAVAL, PIERRE (1883–1945), French politician, chief Vichy minister **9** 237–238

LAVALLEJA, JUAN ANTONIO (1778–1853), Uruguayan independence leader **9** 238–239

LAVIGERIE, CHARLES MARTEL ALLEMAND (1825–1892), French cardinal **9** 240

LAVISSE, ERNEST (1842–1922), French historian **9** 241

LAVOISIER, ANTOINE LAURENT (1743–1794), French chemist **9** 241–244

LAW, JOHN (1671–1729), Scottish monetary theorist and banker **9** 244–245

LAW, WILLIAM (1686–1761), English devotional writer **9** 245–246

LAWRENCE, ABBOTT (1792–1855), American manufacturer and diplomat **9** 246

LAWRENCE, DAVID HERBERT (1885–1930), English novelist, poet, and essayist **9** 247–248

LAWRENCE, ERNEST ORLANDO (1901–1958), American physicist **9** 248–250

LAWRENCE, JACOB (born 1917), African American painter **9** 250–251

LAWRENCE, JAMES (1781–1813), American naval officer **9** 251–252

LYND, HELEN MERRELL (1896–1982), American sociologist and educator **10** 63–64

LYND, ROBERT STAUGHTON (1892–1970), American sociologist **10** 64–65

LYND, STAUGHTON (born 1929), historian and peace militant **10** 65–66

LYNDSAY, SIR DAVID (circa 1485–1555), Scottish poet and courtier **10** 66–67

LYON, MARY (1797–1849), American educator, religious leader, and women's rights advocate **10** 67–69

LYONS, JOSEPH ALOYSIUS (1879–1939), Australian statesman, prime minister 1932–39 **10** 69–70

LYSANDER (died 395 B.C.), Spartan military commander and statesman **10** 70

LYSENKO, TROFIM DENISOVICH (1898–1976), Soviet agronomist and geneticist **10** 71

M

MAATHAI, WANGARI MUTA (born 1940), Kenyan environmental activist **18** 269–271

MABILLON, JEAN (1632–1707), French monk and historian **10** 72

MABINI, APOLINARIO (1864–1903), Filipino political philosopher **10** 72–73

MABUCHI, KAMO (1697–1769), Japanese writer and scholar **10** 73–74

MACAPAGAL, DIOSDADO P. (born 1910), Filipino statesman **10** 74–76

MACARTHUR, DOUGLAS (1880–1964), American general **10** 76–78

MACARTHUR, JOHN (circa 1767–1834), Australian merchant, sheep breeder, and politician **10** 78

MACAULAY, HERBERT (1864–1945), Nigerian politician **10** 78–79

MACAULAY, THOMAS BABINGTON (1st Baron Macaulay of Rothley; 1800–1859), English essayist, historian, and politician **10** 79–80

MACBETH (died 1057), king of Scotland 1040–1057 **10** 81

MACDONALD, DWIGHT (1906–1982), American editor, journalist, essayist, and critic **10** 81–83

MACDONALD, ELEANOR JOSEPHINE (born 1906), American epidemiologist **10** 83–84

MACDONALD, JAMES RAMSAY (1866–1937), British politician **10** 84–85

MACDONALD, SIR JOHN ALEXANDER (1815–1891), Canadian statesman **10** 85–87

MACDOWELL, EDWARD ALEXANDER (1861–1908), American pianist and composer **10** 87–88

MACEO, ANTONIO (1845–1896), Cuban general and patriot **10** 88–90

MACH, ERNST (1838–1916), Austrian physicist **10** 90–91

MACHADO DE ASSIS, JOAQUIM MARIA (1839–1908), Brazilian novelist **10** 91–92

MACHADO Y MORALES, GERARDO (1871–1939), Cuban general and president **10** 92–93

MACHAUT, GUILLAUME DE (circa 1300–1377), French composer and poet **10** 93–94

MACHEL, SAMORA MOISES (1933–1986), socialist revolutionary and first president of Mozambique **10** 94–96

MACHIAVELLI, NICCOLÒ (1469–1527), Italian author and statesman **10** 97–99

MacINTYRE, ALASDAIR CHALMERS (born 1929), Scottish-born philosopher and ethicist **10** 99–100

MACIVER, ROBERT MORRISON (1882–1970), Scottish-American sociologist, political philosopher, and educator **10** 100–101

MACKAY, JOHN WILLIAM (1831–1902), American miner and business leader **10** 101–102

MACKE, AUGUST (1887–1914), Expressionist painter **10** 102–103

MACKENZIE, ALEXANDER (1822–1892), Scottish-born Canadian statesman, prime minister 1873–1878 **10** 104

MACKENZIE, SIR ALEXANDER (circa 1764–1820), Scottish explorer, fur trader, and businessman **10** 103–104

MACKENZIE, WILLIAM LYON (1795–1861), Scottish-born Canadian journalist, politician, and rebel **10** 104–106

MACKILLOP, MARY (1842–1909), first Australian candidate for sainthood in the Roman Catholic Church and foundress of the Sisters of Saint Joseph of the Sacred Heart **10** 106–107

MACKINTOSH, CHARLES RENNIE (1868–1928), Scottish artist, architect, and interior/furniture/textile designer **10** 107–108

MACLEAN, GEORGE (1801–1847), Scottish soldier and agent of British expansion **10** 108–109

MACLEISH, ARCHIBALD (born 1892), American poet, playwright, and public official **10** 109–110

MACLENNAN, HUGH (1907–1990), Canadian novelist, essayist, and academic **10** 110–111

MACMILLAN, DONALD BAXTER (1874–1970), American explorer and scientist **10** 111–112

MACMILLAN, HAROLD (born 1894), British statesman **10** 112–113

MACNEICE, LOUIS (1907–1964), British poet **10** 113–114

MACON, NATHANIEL (1758–1837), American statesman **10** 114–115

MACQUARIE, LACHLAN (1762–1824), British officer, governor of New South Wales 1810–1822 **10** 115–116

MACQUARRIE, JOHN (born 1919), Anglican theologian **10** 116–117

MADERNO, CARLO (1556–1629), Italian architect **10** 117–118

MADERO, FRANCISCO INDALECIO (1873–1913), Mexican politician, president 1911–13 **10** 118–119

MADISON, DOLLY (wife of James Madison, born Dorothea Payne; 1768–1849), American First Lady **10** 119–121

MADISON, JAMES (1751–1836), American statesman, president 1809–1817 **10** 121–123

MADONNA (Madonna Louise Veronica Ciccone, born 1958), American singer and actress **10** 123–125

MAETERLINCK, COUNT MAURICE (1863–1949), Belgian poet, dramatist, and essayist **10** 125–126

MAGELLAN, FERDINAND (1480–1521), Portuguese explorer **10** 126–127

Magicians
Crowley, Aleister **18** 107–109

MAGNASCO, ALESSANDRO (1667–1749), Italian painter **10** 127–128

MAGRITTE, RENÉ (1890–1967), Surrealist painter **10** 128–130

MAGSAYSAY, RAMON (1907–1957), Philippine statesman, president 1953–1957 **10** 130–131

O

POST, CHARLES WILLIAM
(1854–1914), American pioneer in the manufacture and mass-marketing of breakfast cereals **12** 408–409

POST, EMILY PRICE (1873–1960), American authority on etiquette **12** 409–410

POTEMKIN, GRIGORI ALEKSANDROVICH (1739–1791), Russian administrator and field marshal **12** 411–412

POTTER, BEATRIX (Helen Beatrix Potter; 1866–1943), English author and illustrator **18** 326–328

POTTER, DAVID M. (1910–1971), American historian **12** 412

POTTER, DENNIS (1935–1994), British essayist, playwright, screenwriter, and novelist **12** 412–414

POULENC, FRANCIS (1899–1963), French composer **12** 414–415

POUND, EZRA LOOMIS (1885–1972), American poet, editor, and critic **12** 415–417

POUND, ROSCOE (1870–1964), American jurist and botanist **12** 417–418

POUSSIN, NICOLAS (1594–1665), French painter **12** 418–420

POWDERLY, TERENCE VINCENT (1849–1924), American labor leader **12** 420–421

POWELL, ADAM CLAYTON, JR. (1908–1972), African American political leader and Baptist minister **12** 421–422

POWELL, ANTHONY (born 1905), English novelist **12** 422–423

POWELL, COLIN LUTHER (born 1937), African American chairman of the Joint Chiefs of Staff **12** 424–425

POWELL, JOHN WESLEY (1834–1902), American geologist, anthropologist, and explorer **12** 425–426

POWELL, LEWIS F., JR. (born 1907), U.S. Supreme Court justice (1972–1987) **12** 426–428

POWERS, HIRAM (1805–1873), American sculptor **12** 428–429

POWHATAN (circa 1550–1618), Native American tribal chief **12** 429–430

PRADO UGARTECHE, MANUEL (1889–1967), Peruvian statesman **12** 430–431

PRAETORIUS, MICHAEL (circa 1571–1621), German composer and theorist **12** 431–432

PRAN, DITH (born 1942), Cambodian American journalist and activist **18** 328–331

PRANDTAUER, JAKOB (1660–1726), Austrian baroque architect **12** 432

PRASAD, RAJENDRA (1884–1963), Indian nationalist, first president of the Republic **12** 433

PRAXITELES (flourished circa 370–330 B.C.), Greek sculptor **12** 433–434

PREBISCH, RAÚL (1901–1986), Argentine economist active in the United Nations **12** 434–436

PREGL, FRITZ (1869–1930), Austrian physiologist and medical chemist **12** 436–437

PREM TINSULANONDA (born 1920), military leader and prime minister of Thailand (1979–1988) **12** 437

PREMADASA, RANASINGHE (born 1924), president of Sri Lanka (1988-) **12** 437–439

PREMCHAND (1880–1936), Indian novelist and short-story writer **12** 439

PREMINGER, OTTO (1895–1986), Austrian filmmaker and theater producer/director **18** 331–332

PRENDERGAST, MAURICE BRAZIL (1859–1924), American painter **12** 440

PRESCOTT, WILLIAM HICKLING (1796–1859), American historian **12** 440–441

Presidential Medal of Freedom
Wauneka, Annie Dodge **18** 409–410

PRESLEY, ELVIS ARON (1935–1977), American singer and actor **12** 441–442

PRESTES, LUIZ CARLOS (1898–1990), Brazilian revolutionary and Communist leader **12** 442–444

PRETORIUS, ANDRIES (1798–1853), South African politician and general **12** 444–445

PREVIN, ANDRE (Andreas Ludwig Priwin; born 1929), German American composer and conductor **18** 333–334

PRÉVOST, ABBÉ (1697–1763), French novelist, journalist, and cleric **12** 445–446

PRICE, LEONTYNE (Mary Leontyne Price; born 1927), American prima donna soprano **12** 446–447

PRICE, RICHARD (1723–1791), English Nonconformist minister and political philosopher **12** 447–448

PRICHARD, DIANA GARCÍA (born 1949), Hispanic American chemical physicist **12** 448–449

PRIDI PHANOMYONG (1901–1983), Thai political leader **12** 449

PRIEST, IVY MAUDE BAKER (1905–1975), treasurer of the United States (1953–1960) **12** 450–451

PRIESTLEY, J(OHN) B(OYNTON) (1894–1984), English author of novels, essays, plays, and screenplays **12** 451–452

PRIESTLEY, JOSEPH (1733–1804), English clergyman and chemist **12** 452–453

PRIMATICCIO, FRANCESCO (1504–1570), Italian painter, sculptor, and architect **12** 453–454

PRIMO DE RIVERA Y ORBANEJA, MIGUEL (1870–1930), Spanish general, dictator 1923–30 **12** 454–455

PRITCHETT, V(ICTOR) S(AWDON) (born 1900), English short story writer, novelist, literary critic, journalist, travel writer, biographer, and autobiographer **12** 455–457

Pritzker Prize (for architecture)
Ando, Tadao **18** 17–19
Portzamparc, Christian de **18** 324–326

PROCLUS DIADOCHUS (born 410), Byzantine philosopher **12** 457

PROCOPIUS OF CAESAREA (circa 500-circa 565), Byzantine historian **12** 457–458

PROKOFIEV, SERGEI SERGEEVICH (1891–1953), Russian composer **12** 458–460

PROSSER, GABRIEL (circa 1775–1800), Afro-American slave rebel **12** 460–461

PROTAGORAS (circa 484-circa 414 B.C.), Greek philosopher **12** 461

Protestant Episcopal Church (United States)
Schiess, Betty Bone **18** 360–362

PROUDHON, PIERRE JOSEPH (1809–1864), French anarchist political philosopher and journalist **12** 461–463

PROULX, E. ANNIE (born 1935), American author **12** 463–465

PROUST, MARCEL (1871–1922), French novelist **12** 465–467

PROXMIRE, WILLIAM (born 1915), Democratic senator for Wisconsin **12** 467–468

ROBERT, SHAABAN (1909–1962), Tanzanian author who wrote in the Swahili language **14** 128–129

Robert Bruce
see Robert I (king, Scotland)

ROBERTS, FREDERICK SLEIGH (1st Earl Roberts of Kandhar, Pretoria, and Waterford; 1832–1914), British field marshal **13** 195–196

ROBERTSON, SIR DENNIS HOLME (1890–1963), English economist **13** 196

ROBERTSON, MARION G. (Pat Robertson; born 1930), television evangelist who founded the Christian Broadcasting Network and presidential candidate **13** 196–198

ROBESON, PAUL LEROY (1898–1976), American singer, actor, and political activist **13** 198–199

ROBESPIERRE, MAXIMILIEN FRANÇOIS MARIE ISIDORE DE (1758–1794), French Revolutionary leader **13** 199–201

ROBINSON, EDDIE (born 1919), African American college football coach **18** 351–352

ROBINSON, EDWIN ARLINGTON (1869–1935), American poet and playwright **13** 201–202

ROBINSON, FRANK, JR. (born 1935), African American baseball player and manager **13** 202–203

ROBINSON, HARRIET HANSON (1825–1911), American author and suffragist **13** 203–207

ROBINSON, JACK ROOSEVELT (Jackie Robinson; 1919–72), African American baseball player; first African American player in the major leagues **13** 207–208

ROBINSON, JAMES HARVEY (1863–1936), American historian **13** 208

ROBINSON, JOAN VIOLET MAURICE (1903–1983), English economist **13** 209–210

ROBINSON, SIR JOHN BEVERLEY (1791–1863), Canadian political leader and jurist **13** 215–217

ROBINSON, JULIA (1919–1985), American mathematician **13** 210–211

ROBINSON, MARY BOURKE (born 1944), first woman president of Ireland **13** 211–213

ROBINSON, THEODORE (1852–1896), American painter **13** 217

ROCA, JULIO ARGENTINO (1843–1914), Argentine general and president **13** 218

ROCARD, MICHEL (born 1930), French left-wing politician **13** 218–220

ROCHAMBEAU, COMTE DE (Jean Baptiste Donatien de Vimeur, 1725–1807), French general **13** 220–221

ROCHBERG, GEORGE (born 1918), American composer **13** 221–222

ROCHE, KEVIN (born 1922), Irish-American architect **13** 222–224

ROCKEFELLER, DAVID (born 1915), chairman of the Chase Manhattan Bank **13** 224–225

ROCKEFELLER, JOHN DAVISON (1839–1937), American industrialist and philanthropist **13** 226–228

ROCKEFELLER, JOHN D., JR. (1874–1960), American philanthropist and industrial relations expert **13** 225–226

ROCKEFELLER, NELSON ALDRICH (1908–1979), four-term governor of New York and vice-president of the United States **13** 228–230

ROCKINGHAM, 2D MARQUESS OF (Charles Watson-Wentworth; 1730–82), English statesman **13** 230–231

ROCKNE, KNUTE (1888–1931), American football coach **13** 231

Rock-'n'-roll (music)
Bowie, David **18** 58–60

ROCKWELL, NORMAN PERCEVEL (1894–1978), American illustrator **13** 231–233

RODCHENKO, ALEXANDER MIKHAILOVICH (1891–1956), Russian abstract painter, sculptor, photographer, and industrial designer **13** 233–234

RODGERS, RICHARD CHARLES (1902–1972), American composer **13** 234–236

RODIN, AUGUSTE (1840–1917), French sculptor **13** 236–238

RODINO, PETER WALLACE, JR. (born 1909), Democratic U.S. representative from New Jersey **13** 238–239

RODNEY, GEORGE BRYDGES (1st Baron Rodney; 1718–92), British admiral **13** 239–240

RODÓ, JOSÉ ENRIQUE (1872–1917), Uraguayan essayist and literary critic **13** 240–241

ROEBLING, JOHN AUGUSTUS (1806–1869), German-born American engineer **13** 241–242

ROEBLING, WASHINGTON AUGUSTUS (1837–1926), American engineer and manufacturer **13** 243

Roentgen, Wilhelm Conrad
see Röntgen, Wilhelm Conrad

ROETHKE, THEODORE (1908–1963), American poet and teacher **13** 243–244

ROGER II (1095–1154), king of Sicily 1130–54 **13** 244–245

ROGERS, CARL RANSOM (1902–1987), American psychotherapist **13** 245–247

ROGERS, EDITH NOURSE (1881–1960), U.S. congresswoman from Massachusetts **13** 247–248

ROGERS, FRED ("Mr." Rogers; born 1928), American television host **18** 352–354

ROGERS, JOHN (1829–1904), American sculptor **13** 248

ROGERS, RICHARD (born 1933), British architect **13** 248–250

ROGERS, ROBERT (1731–1795), American frontiersman and army officer **13** 250–251

ROGERS, WILL (1879–1935), American actor, humorist, journalist, and performer **13** 251–252

ROH TAE WOO (born 1932), president of the Republic of Korea **13** 253–255

ROHDE, RUTH BRYAN OWEN (1885–1954), U.S. congresswoman **13** 252–253

ROJAS PINILLA, GUSTAVO (1900–1975), Colombian general and politician **13** 255–256

ROLAND, MADAME (Marie-Jeanne Phlipon; 1754–1793), French author and revolutionary **13** 256–259

ROLFE, JOHN (1585–1622), English colonist in Virginia **13** 259–260

ROLLAND, ROMAIN (1866–1944), French writer **13** 260

ROLLE OF HAMPOLE, RICHARD (circa 1290–1349), English prose and verse writer **13** 260–261

ROLLING STONES, THE (formed in 1963), rock and roll band **13** 261–264

ROLLO (Rolf; circa 860–circa 932), Viking adventurer **13** 264–265

RÖLVAAG, OLE EDVART (1876–1931), Norwegian-American writer **13** 265

SCRIPPS, EDWARD WYLLIS (1854–1926), American newspaper publisher **14** 72–73

SCULLIN, JAMES HENRY (1876–1953), Australian politician **14** 73

SEABORG, GLENN THEODORE (born 1912), American chemist and chairman of the Atomic Energy Commission **14** 74–76

SEABURY, SAMUEL (1729–1796), American theologian **14** 76

SEALE, ROBERT GEORGE (Bobby; born 1936), militant activist and a founder of the Black Panther Party **14** 77–78

SEATTLE (c. 1788–1866), Native American tribal chief **14** 80–81

Secession (United States; 1860–61) opponents (South)
Foote, Henry Stuart **18** 144–146

Secret Garden, The (novel)
Burnett, Frances Hodgson **18** 64–67

SEDDON, RICHARD JOHN (1845–1906), New Zealand politician **14** 81–82

SEDGWICK, ADAM (1785–1873), English geologist **14** 82–83

SEEGER, PETE (born 1919), American folksinger and activist **14** 83–84

SEFERIS, GEORGE (Georgios Seferiadis; 1900–71), Greek poet and statesman **14** 84–85

SEGAL, GEORGE (born 1924), American sculptor **14** 85–87

SEGOVIA, ANDRÉS (1893–1987), Spanish guitarist **14** 87–88

SEIBERT, FLORENCE B. (1897–1991), American biochemist **14** 89–90

SEJO (1417–1468), king of Korea 1453–68 **14** 90–91

SEJONG (1397–1450), king of Korea 1418–50 **14** 91–92

SELENA (Selena Quintanilla-Perez; 1971–1995), Hispanic-American singer **18** 365–367

SELEUCUS I (circa 358–281 B.C.), Macedonian general, king of Babylonia and Syria **14** 92–93

SELIGMAN, EDWIN ROBERT ANDERSON (1861–1939), American economist and editor **14** 93–94

SELIM I (circa 1470–1520), Ottoman sultan 1512–20 **14** 94–95

SELIM III (1761–1808), Ottoman sultan 1789–1807 **14** 95–96

SELKIRK, 5TH EARL OF (Thomas Douglas; 1771–1820), Scottish colonizer in Canada **14** 96

SELLARS, WILFRED (1912–1989), American philosopher **14** 96–98

SELLERS, PETER RICHARD HENRY (1925–1980), British comedy genius of theater, radio, television, and movies **14** 98–99

SEMENOV, NIKOLAI NIKOLAEVICH (1896–1986), Russian physicist and physical chemist **14** 101

SEMMELWEIS, IGNAZ PHILIPP (1818–1865), Hungarian physician **14** 101–102

SEMMES, RAPHAEL (1809–1877), American Confederate naval officer **14** 102–103

SEN, RAM CAMUL (1783–1844), Bengali intellectual and entrepreneur **13** 16–17

Senator, Flavius Magnus Aurelius Cassiodorus
see Cassiodorus

SENECA THE YOUNGER, LUCIUS ANNAEUS (circa 4 B.C.-A.D. 65), Roman philosopher **14** 103–105

SENFL, LUDWIG (circa 1486-circa 1543), Swiss-born German composer **14** 105–106

SENGHOR, LÉOPOLD SÉDAR (born 1906), Senegalese poet, philosopher, and statesman **14** 106–107

SENNACHERIB (ruled 705–681 B.C.), king of Assyria **14** 108

SENNETT, MACK (1884–1960), American film producer and director **14** 108–109

Sepoy Mutiny (1857–1858)
Mahal, Hazrat **18** 271–273

SEQUOYAH (circa 1770–1843), American Cherokee Indian scholar **14** 110–111

SERRA, JUNIPERO (Miguel José Serra; 1713–84), Spanish Franciscan missionary, founder of California missions **14** 111–112

SERRANO ELÍAS, JORGE ANTONIO (born 1945), president of Guatemala (1991–1993) **14** 112–113

SERVAN-SCHREIBER, JEAN-JACQUES (born 1924), French journalist and writer on public affairs **14** 113–115

SERVETUS, MICHAEL (circa 1511–53), Spanish religious philosopher **14** 115–116

SESSHU, TOYA (1420–1506), Japanese painter and Zen priest **14** 116–117

SESSIONS, ROGER HUNTINGTON (1896–1985), American composer **14** 117–118

SETON, ELIZABETH ANN BAYLEY (1774–1821), American Catholic leader **14** 118–119

SETON, ERNEST THOMPSON (1860–1946), Canadian author and co-founder of the Boy Scouts of America **14** 119–120

SETTIGNANO, DESIDERIO DA (1428/31–1464), Italian sculptor **4** 509

SEURAT, GEORGES PIERRE (1859–1891), French painter **14** 120–122

SEVERINI, GINO (1883–1966), Italian painter **14** 122

SEVERUS, LUCIUS SEPTIMIUS (146–211), Roman emperor 193–211 **14** 109–110

SEVIER, JOHN (1745–1815), American frontiersman, soldier, and politician **14** 122–123

SEWALL, SAMUEL (1652–1730), American jurist and diarist **14** 123–124

SEWARD, WILLIAM HENRY (1801–1872), American statesman **14** 124–125

SEXTON, ANNE (Anne Gray Harvey; 1928–74), American ''confessional'' poet **14** 125–126

SEYMOUR, HORATIO (1810–1886), American politician **14** 126–127

SEYMOUR, JANE (1509–1537), third wife and queen consort of Henry VIII of England **18** 367–368

SFORZA, LODOVICO (1452–1508), duke of Milan **14** 127–128

SHABAKA (ruled circa 712-circa 696 B.C.), Nubian king, pharaoh of Egypt **14** 130

SHABAZZ, BETTY (1936–1997), African American educator, activist, and health administrator **14** 130–132

SHACKLETON, SIR ERNEST HENRY (1874–1922), British explorer **14** 132–133

SHAFFER, PETER LEVIN (born 1926), English/American playwright **14** 133–135

SHAFTESBURY, 1ST EARL OF (Anthony Ashley Cooper; 1621–83), English statesman **14** 135–136

SHAFTESBURY, 3D EARL OF (Anthony Ashley Cooper; 1671–1713), English moral philosopher **14** 136–137

W